Handbook of Research on Managing Information Systems in Developing Economies

Richard Boateng
University of Ghana, Ghana

A volume in the Advances in Information Quality and Management (AIQM) Book Series

Published in the United States of America by
IGI Global
Business Science Reference (an imprint of IGI Global)
701 E. Chocolate Avenue
Hershey PA, USA 17033
Tel: 717-533-8845
Fax: 717-533-8661
E-mail: cust@igi-global.com
Web site: http://www.igi-global.com

Library of Congress Cataloging-in-Publication Data

Names: Boateng, Richard, 1979- editor.
Title: Handbook of research on managing information systems in developing
    economies / Richard Boateng, editor.
Description: Hershey, PA : Business Science Reference, [2020] | Includes
    bibliographical references and index. | Summary: ""This book focuses on
    the need, development, adoption, usage, and impact of information
    systems among organizations in developing economies"--Provided by
    publisher"-- Provided by publisher.
Identifiers: LCCN 2019042060 (print) | LCCN 2019042061 (ebook) | ISBN
    9781799826101 (hardcover) | ISBN 9781799826118 (ebook)
Subjects: LCSH: Information technology--Developing countries--Management. |
    Management information systems--Developing countries--Management.
Classification: LCC HC59.72.I55 H3325 2020 (print) | LCC HC59.72.I55
    (ebook) | DDC 658.4/038011--dc23
LC record available at https://lccn.loc.gov/2019042060
LC ebook record available at https://lccn.loc.gov/2019042061

This book is published in the IGI Global book series Advances in Information Quality and Management (AIQM) (ISSN: 2331-7701; eISSN: 2331-771X)

British Cataloguing in Publication Data
A Cataloguing in Publication record for this book is available from the British Library.

For electronic access to this publication, please contact: eresources@igi-global.com.

Advances in Information Quality and Management (AIQM) Book Series

Siddhartha Bhattacharyya

RCC Institute of Information Technology, India

ISSN:2331-7701
EISSN:2331-771X

MISSION

Acquiring and managing quality information is essential to an organization's success and profitability. Innovation in information technology provides managers, researchers, and practitioners with the tools and techniques needed to create and adapt new policies, strategies, and solutions for information management.

The **Advances in Information Quality and Management (AIQM) Book Series** provides emerging research principals in knowledge society for the advancement of future technological development. This series aims to increase available research publications and emphasize the global response within the discipline and allow for audiences to benefit from the comprehensive collection of this knowledge.

COVERAGE

- Web Services and Technologies
- Human and Societal Issue
- Electronic Commerce Technologies
- Business Process Management and Modeling
- Supply Chain Management
- Decision Support and Group Decision Support Systems
- IT Innovation and Diffusion
- E-Collaboration
- Emerging Technologies Management
- Knowledge Management

IGI Global is currently accepting manuscripts for publication within this series. To submit a proposal for a volume in this series, please contact our Acquisition Editors at Acquisitions@igi-global.com or visit: http://www.igi-global.com/publish/.

Titles in this Series

For a list of additional titles in this series, please visit:
http://www.igi-global.com/book-series/advances-information-quality-management/73809

Legal and Ethical Issues in Information Management
Peter Mazebe II Mothataesi Sebina (University of Botswana, Botswana) Nathan Mwakoshi Mnjama (University of Botswana, Botswana) Kgomotso Hildegard Moahi (University of Botswana, Botswana) Tachilisa Badala Balule (University of Botswana, Botswana) and Balulwami Grand (University of Botswana, Botswana)
Information Science Reference • © 2020 • 320pp • H/C (ISBN: 9781799824220) • US $195.00 (our price)

Metaheuristic Approaches to Portfolio Optimization
Jhuma Ray (RCC Institute of Information Technology, India) Anirban Mukherjee (RCC Institute of Information Technology, India) Sadhan Kumar Dey (RCC Institute of Information Technology, India) and Goran Klepac (Algebra University College, Croatia)
Business Science Reference • © 2019 • 263pp • H/C (ISBN: 9781522581031) • US $205.00 (our price)

Strategic Management of Business-Critical Information Assets
Denise A.D. Bedford (Georgetown University, USA)
Business Science Reference • © 2019 • 308pp • H/C (ISBN: 9781522584100) • US $205.00 (our price)

Systems Research for Real-World Challenges
Frank Stowell (University of Portsmouth, UK)
Information Science Reference • © 2018 • 398pp • H/C (ISBN: 9781522559962) • US $195.00 (our price)

Ensuring Research Integrity and the Ethical Management of Data
Cees Th. Smit Sibinga (University of Groningen, The Netherlands)
Information Science Reference • © 2018 • 303pp • H/C (ISBN: 9781522527305) • US $275.00 (our price)

Handbook of Research on Global Enterprise Operations and Opportunities
Mehdi Khosrow-Pour, D.B.A. (Information Resources Management Association, USA)
Business Science Reference • © 2017 • 375pp • H/C (ISBN: 9781522522454) • US $245.00 (our price)

Examining Information Retrieval and Image Processing Paradigms in Multidisciplinary Contexts
Joan Lu (University of Huddersfield, UK) and Qiang Xu (University of Huddersfield, UK)
Information Science Reference • © 2017 • 425pp • H/C (ISBN: 9781522518846) • US $245.00 (our price)

Ontologies and Big Data Considerations for Effective Intelligence
Joan Lu (University of Huddersfield, UK) and Qiang Xu (University of Huddersfield, UK)
Information Science Reference • © 2017 • 632pp • H/C (ISBN: 9781522520580) • US $245.00 (our price)

701 East Chocolate Avenue, Hershey, PA 17033, USA
Tel: 717-533-8845 x100 • Fax: 717-533-8661
E-Mail: cust@igi-global.com • www.igi-global.com

Editorial Advisory Board

List of Contributors

Table of Contents

Section 1
Concepts and Theories in Developing and Deploying Information Systems

Acheampong Owusu, Business School, University of Ghana, Ghana
Frederick Edem Broni Jr., Business School, University of Ghana, Ghana

Emmanuel Awuni Kolog, Business School, University of Ghana, Ghana
Acheampong Owusu, Business School, University of Ghana, Ghana
Samuel Nii Odoi Devine, Presbyterian University College, Ghana
Edward Entee, Business School, University of Ghana, Ghana

Section 2
Leveraging New and Emerging Information Systems

Joseph Budu, Department of Information Systems and Innovation, School of Technology,
Ghana Institute of Management and Public Administration, Ghana

Section 3
Information Systems and Socio-Economic Development

Section 4
Future of Information Systems in Developing Economies

Detailed Table of Contents

Section 1
Concepts and Theories in Developing and Deploying Information Systems

Chapter 1
Acheampong Owusu, Business School, University of Ghana, Ghana
Frederick Edem Broni Jr., Business School, University of Ghana, Ghana

The purpose of this chapter is to explore the nature of SISP implementation and also determine the factors that influence as enablers or inhibitors to the implementation and use of SISP in Ghanaian organizations. The methodology adopted was the qualitative method and underpinned by Earl and Lederer and Sethi's approaches to SISP development. The results indicated that many firms have applied Earl's approaches in their SISP implementation. The findings also revealed that factors such as IS alignment, awareness, environmental assessment, budget, and top management involvement are the critical success factors enabling the use of SISP in the organizations studied. Inhibitors to SISP implementation include budget constraint, regulatory requirements, absence of IT/IS steering committee, among others. The study highly recommends that the inhibiting factors are given the necessary attention by the government to enable firms to implement SISP with ease. The originality of this study lies in the dearth of literature about SISP implementation in sub-Saharan economies.

Chapter 2
Emmanuel Awuni Kolog, Business School, University of Ghana, Ghana
Acheampong Owusu, Business School, University of Ghana, Ghana
Samuel Nii Odoi Devine, Presbyterian University College, Ghana
Edward Entee, Business School, University of Ghana, Ghana

Globalizing businesses from developing countries require a thoughtful strategy and adoption of state-of-the-art technologics to meet up with the rapidly changing society. Mobile money payment service is a growing service that provides opportunities for both the formal and informal sectors in Ghana. Despite its importance, fraudsters have capitalized on the vulnerabilities of users to defraud them. In this chapter, the authors have reviewed existing data mining techniques for exploring the detection of mobile payment fraud. With this technique, a hybrid-based machine learning framework for mobile money fraud detection is proposed. With the use of the machine learning technique, an avalanche of fraud-related cases is leveraged, as a corpus, for fraud detection. The implementation of the framework hinges on the formulation of policies and regulations that will guide the adoption and enforcement by Telcos and governmental agencies with oversight responsibilities in the telecommunication space. The authors, therefore, envision the implementation of the proposed framework by practitioners.

Section 2
Leveraging New and Emerging Information Systems

Chapter 3

Joseph Budu, Department of Information Systems and Innovation, School of Technology,
Ghana Institute of Management and Public Administration, Ghana

The purpose of this study is to explore the factors that inform a consumer's behavioural intention to adopt disruptive information technologies. This study uses an inductive reasoning approach to collect qualitative data which is analysed using interpretive analysis guidelines. The outcome of the analysis is the discovery of three new variables, namely, understanding of technology, meta-price value, and perceived need. The knowledge of technology refers to what a consumer knows about disruptive information technology. The meta-price value refers to a consumer's perception of the benefits to be gained from disruptive information technology as compared to those of the disrupted technology. The perceived need refers to a consumer's realisation of the extent to which disruptive information technology is the sole provider for a fundamental requirement. This study is, arguably, the first to propose a different model to explain the adoption of disruptive information technologies.

Chapter 4

Divine Quase Agozie, Cyprus International University, Nicosia, Cyprus
Muesser Nat, Cyprus International University, Nicosia, Cyprus
Sampson Abeeku Edu, Cyprus International University, Nicosia, Cyprus

This chapter examines privacy-focused technology use among Generation Y cohorts and its impact on their intentions and actual use of social commerce. The study employs a partial least squares SEM to evaluate hypothesized relationships stated. Four hundred eighty-seven responses were used for the analysis. Results show that privacy-focused technology use fails to influence behavioural intentions. By inference, knowledge of privacy risks influences the behavioural intentions of Generation Y, but actual use is impacted where the risk is perceived to be beyond control. This empirical analysis provides insights into key behavioural and technical aspects, offering organizations insights into developing effective social commerce strategies.

Chapter 5
Eric Ansong, University of Ghana, Ghana

Firms are in constant competition for dominance and survival. Knowledge of how firms use information systems to improve operational efficiency is limited, especially in developing economies. This chapter, therefore, explored a firm's digital strategic actions for dealing with the competitive forces in the digital economy of a developing country. This chapter adopted a qualitative case study approach. A digital enterprise in a developing economy was selected as a case. Using Porter's five competitive forces model, an analysis of the environment and the strategic actions of the firm was carried out. Findings from this chapter serve as a stepping-stone in expounding the digital strategic actions of firms in dealing with the market forces in the digital economy. This study is, arguably, one of the first to examine the competitive forces and survival strategies of a digital enterprise in the digital economy of a developing country.

Chapter 6
*Ngoc Tuan Chau, University of Economics, The University of Danang, Danang, Vietnam &
RMIT University, Melbourne, Australia*
*Hepu Deng, School of Accounting, Information Systems and Supply Chain, RMIT University,
Melbourne, Australia*

This chapter presents a review of the related literature on organizational mobile commerce (m-commerce) adoption, leading to the development of an integrated model for evaluating the critical determinants of m-commerce adoption in small and medium-sized enterprises (SMEs) in developing countries. Grounded in the innovation diffusion literature and the extension of the technology-organization-environment framework, the model, integrates technological, organizational, environmental, and managerial factors holistically for better understanding m-commerce adoption in a developing context. Eleven hypotheses are proposed and tested using multiple regression with the data collected from a survey with SMEs' managers in Vietnam. The results confirm the significance of factors in the above four dimensions. These findings provide the managers of SMEs with useful insights on how to improve the adoption of m-commerce in SMEs. These are also useful for policymakers in designing policies that promote the wide adoption of m-commerce in SMEs in the context of developing countries.

Chapter 7
Robert Ohene-Bonsu Simmons, University of Ghana, Ghana

The purpose of this chapter is to understand digital innovation in the taxi industrial structure for ridesharing in a developing country. Digital innovations are required in all aspects of an economy including the transportation industry. Drawing on a qualitative interpretive case study methodology, this chapter offers an overview of Uru's digital innovation for ridesharing in the physical taxi industrial structure in a developing country context of Ghana. The findings show that ridesharing provides riders-drivers with better journey activities, which supersedes taxi services in competition. These are electronic booking, riders' and drivers' profiles for security, transparent automatic billing for affordable transportation, and opportunities for drivers to accept a series of riders' requests at proximity. The chapter provides the implications for these findings for research and practice.

Chapter 8

Frederick Edem Broni Jr., Business School, University of Ghana, Ghana
Acheampong Owusu, Business School, University of Ghana, Ghana

Blockchain technology is an emerging innovation, and it is viewed as a better approach to help the necessities of people and institutions in terms of record management. Using the Delphi technique and the PERM model, this chapter seeks to present the perspectives of experts in the field of blockchain on the readiness of the institutions in developing economies to adopt and implement it. The findings suggest that the understanding of the technology, knowledge on how to use it, availability of skilled personnel, availability of technical components, risk, capital, management support, business process, policies and regulations, and government initiatives on technology are key influencing factors assessing the readiness to adopt blockchain in a developing economy. It is expected that these findings will enlighten practitioners on the prospects of the application of blockchain in all sectors. The originality of this study lies in the fact that it is a maiden exploratory study that examines the factors that influence the readiness to adopt and implement blockchain technology in a developing economy.

Chapter 9

Samuel Anim-Yeboah, Business School, University of Ghana, Ghana & Sims Technologies
Ltd., Ghana

New and emerging information systems are significantly transforming organizations through new business models, opportunities, products, and services. This chapter highlights the new and emerging information systems (IS), their usage, and how they drive organizational transformation. The DeLone and McLean Model of IS Success was used as a theoretical lens to discuss existing literature on organizational transformation arising from new and emerging IS. While some organizations succumb to the introduction of the new and emerging IS with its disruptive nature, others tend to manage the changes introduced through new business models, appropriate infrastructure, skills, knowledge, enhanced data security, and effective communication. The chapter contributes to the scholarship and practice of digital transformation of organizations in developing economies.

Chapter 10

Yaa Amponsah Twumasi, Business School, University of Ghana, Ghana
Joshua Ofori-Amanfo, Business School, University of Ghana, Ghana

The chapter seeks to examine how IT enables or constrains counterfeiting and piracy in the fashion and beauty industry in two developing countries. The chapter also highlights the types of IT used in the industry and how IT aids in the ascendance of counterfeiting/piracy. The findings suggest that the escalation of counterfeiting/piracy in the industry is as a result of globalisation and the predominance of technological innovation such as IT, specifically the internet and social media platforms. This chapter contributes to the strategies that the industry in developing countries use in combating counterfeiting/pricy in their business. In academia, arguably, no research has been conducted yet on counterfeiting/piracy in the fashion industry in Ghana and Nigeria, as far as the role of IT is a concern.

Chapter 11
Eunice Yeboah Afeti, Business School, University of Ghana, Ghana
Joshua Ofori Amanfo, Business School, University of Ghana, Ghana

Merchant adoption of mobile payments is facilitating new business models and changing the way merchants run their brick and mortar businesses. Despite the advantages of mobile payment adoption to the merchant, they still hesitate to adopt mobile payments. Thus, the study seeks to explore qualitatively through a case study the enablers and inhibitors to merchant adoption of mobile payments. The study identified that merchants are adopting mobile payments to facilitate new business models, to promote the disintermediation of traditional intermediaries, to offer different possibilities of growing their businesses, and to reduce transaction costs. Even though merchants believe that mobile payments adoption and use improve operational efficiency to their businesses, there are instances of fraud, particularly in the peer-to-peer transfer sector, data breaches, data security, and privacy concerns. Therefore, it is imperative for service providers of mobile payments to enhance technological issues regarding privacy protection that could enhance trust towards mobile payment adoption.

Chapter 12
Obed Kwame Adzaku Penu, Business School, University of Ghana, Ghana

This chapter focuses on riders (consumers) who use the Uber ride-hailing application as a gig platform for accessing transportation services, thereby assigning drivers the task of transporting them from one location to another. Respondents were sampled using a multiple sampling approach comprising convenience, random, and purposive sampling. 20 out of 40 respondents were purposely selected for in-depth interviewing and thematic analysis. The findings suggest that riders found the platform to offer both personal and shared convenience, cost and time saving, as well as trustworthiness. The platform also substituted the means of finding transportation for some of the riders, while for other riders it complemented their means of finding transportation. With these findings, this study contributes to the few scholarly studies that have sought to explore, in detail, user perceptions on gig platforms from a developing economy context and provides stimulating insights on the gig economy and its adoption in developing economies.

Chapter 13
Edward Entee, Univeristy of Ghana, Ghana
Anthony Afful-Dadzie, Business School, University of Ghana, Ghana

Social networking sites such as Facebook have developed massive acceptance as commercial channels among users, and this is commonly known as social commerce. Despite the significance of social media sites for commercial purposes, entrepreneurs struggle with capability development as well as strategies to achieve benefits. To address this gap, this chapter presents a teaching case study that explores how a microentrepreneur used social media as a resource to create social commerce capabilities to achieve benefits. Lessons learnt are proposed in the case, and questions for reflections are proposed whilst a debate topic is also suggested.

Chapter 14
Joshua Ofoeda, University of Professional Studies, Accra, Ghana

Digital platforms continue to contribute to the global economy by enabling new forms of value creation. Whereas the Information Systems literature is dominated by digital platform research, less is said about Application Programming Interfaces (APIs), the engine behind digital platforms. More so, there is a dearth in the literature on how developing economy firms create value through API integration. To address these research gaps, the author conducted a case study on DigMob (Pseudonym), a digital firm that focuses on the sale of indigenous African music to understand how it created value through API integration. Based on Amit and Zott's value creation model, the findings suggest that DigMob's value creation occurs on a broader value network comprising suppliers (e.g., payment service providers) and customers. For instance, DigMob generated value through the API-enabled platform by ensuring that music lovers purchase their preferred songs at competitive prices. DigMob has also been able to increase their revenue and brand image. Similarly, musicians have been able to rake substantial amounts of money through the sales of their music on the platform.

Section 3
Information Systems and Socio-Economic Development

Chapter 15
Ibrahim Osman Adam, University for Development Studies, Ghana

This chapter presents some methodological issues raised in the research process of an interpretive researcher in a maiden doctoral programme in a developing country. The chapter draws on a doctoral research experience which employed an interpretive case study approach as the methodology and a combined lens of activity and agency theories as to the theoretical foundation. The research relied on a single case study in a developing country context. The chapter offers an overview of some practicalities of carrying out a single case study research using an interpretive philosophy by presenting the different viewpoints using semi-structured interviews, documents and participant observation, and analysing the data through hermeneutics. The chapter presents some challenges and how interpretive research methods can be used as a clear methodological strategy, especially in an environment where many researchers are not familiar with this research approach. This reflective account provides lessons for others who wish to go through an interpretive process of researching an information systems phenomenon.

Mansah Preko, Business School, University of Ghana, Ghana
Richard Osei-Boateng, 37 Military Hospital, Ghana & Business School, University of
Ghana, Ghana
Adekunle Ezekiel Durosinmi, Federal Medical Centre, Abeokuta, Nigeria

There is an increasing demand for the healthcare industry in developing economies to reform their existing fragmented paper-based systems to take advantage of the several opportunities that digitalisation brings. However, the existence of specific contextual factors constrains the process of digitalisation in most developing economies. Underpinned by the concepts of installed base and cultivation, this chapter adopts a qualitative multiple-case study approach to examine the contextual factors that influence the development, implementation, and adoption of digital health systems in the Ghanaian and Nigerian contexts. Results of this chapter reveal 13 key challenges and their corresponding mitigating strategies that were adopted in specific instances to facilitate digitalisation in both contexts. A comparison of findings for the two contexts is also discussed.

Harriet Koshie Lamptey, University of Professional Studies, Accra, Ghana

This study is on the rising patronage of mobile data in a developing economy and changes that have ensued from its adoption by a higher education institution. Studies on the growing use of mobiles in higher education exist. This qualitative inquiry advances research on developing economies by providing evidence of transformational effects on a single case. Study participants were administrators who led the adoption process. Primary data was gathered from interviews while local and international reports delivered secondary facts on rising mobile data patronage. Findings indicate that mobile data patronage is influencing its pedagogical use. Adoption has resulted in institutional changes in the form of emerged roles and arrangements. If undisrupted by technological innovations or communal group behavior, the arrangements may gain legitimacy with time. From an institutional theory perspective, mobile technology appears to be playing an agential role on the landscape of the institution. The study cautions institutions to focus on pedagogical aims in their adoption of technology.

Judy Backhouse, United Nations University, Portugal
Hlelo Chauke, University of the Witwatersrand, South Africa

Information and communications technologies (ICTs) promise development gains, yet the complexity and opacity of the relationships between ICT initiative and development effect makes it difficult to identify these development gains or to theorize connections. This case study does both. First, it identifies the connections between the roll-out of free public Wi-Fi by the City of Johannesburg and changes that have resulted in city residents' lives. Second, it uses the choice framework to explain how these changes come about. This qualitative case study conducted interviews with users of the city's free public Wi-Fi service to understand how the service has changed the choices they have, leading to development in the sense of increased capabilities. Benefits identified included easier communications, savings in time and money, social and psychological benefits, as well as increased knowledge, business ideas, access to markets, access to job opportunities, and increased income. This study demonstrates how the linkages can be understood, albeit not in a linear fashion.

Section 4
Future of Information Systems in Developing Economies

Chapter 19

Kingsley Ofosu-Ampong, Business School, University of Ghana, Ghana
Thomas Anning-Dorson, Wits Business School, University of the Witwatersrand, South Africa

Despite advances in information technology, studies suggest that there is little knowledge of how developing countries are applying gamification in agriculture, education, business, health, and other domains. Thus, from a systematic review, this chapter examines the extent of gamification research in the developing country context. In this chapter, 56 articles were reviewed, and the search was done in the Scopus database. This chapter explains the idea of game design elements in information systems and provides real-world examples of gamified systems outcomes from developing countries. The authors conclude with directions for future research to extend our knowledge of gamification and advance the existing methodologies, domains, and theories.

Chapter 20

Sampson Abeeku Edu, Cyprus International University, Cyprus
Divine Q. Agozie, Cyprus International University, Cyprus

Demand for improvement in healthcare management in the areas of quality, cost, and patient care has been on the upsurge because of technology. Incessant application and new technological development to manage healthcare data significantly led to leveraging on the use of big data and analytics (BDA). The application of the capabilities from BDA has provided healthcare institutions with the ability to make critical and timely decisions for patients and data management. Adopting BDA by healthcare institutions hinges on some factors necessitating its application. This study aims to identify and review what influences healthcare institutions towards the use of business intelligence and analytics. With the use of a systematic review of 25 articles, the study identified nine dominant factors driving healthcare institutions to BDA adoption. Factors such as patient management, quality decision making, disease management, data management, and promoting healthcare efficiencies were among the highly ranked factors influencing BDA adoption.

Chapter 21

Kevor Mark-Oliver, Presbyterian University College, Ghana

While information system (IS) curriculum research has enjoyed recent attention from IS scholars, not many reviews exist. Those reviews are either outdated or focused on a particular strand of IS curriculum research which may not be comprehensive. In this chapter, the author presents a systematic review of information systems curriculum research published in information systems journals and selected conference proceedings in the past decade. The results point to many studies on identifying information systems competencies and their implications for curriculum design and delivery. Having observed that many of these issues are discussed at the undergraduate level and predominantly in the USA and UK, this chapter suggests, among others, future research at the graduate level and from other regions.

Chapter 22

Social media (SM) is fundamentally changing the way firms conduct business and, in the process, destroying existing business models (BM). Therefore, businesses need to have a BM adaptable to social commerce (SC), which is commerce utilizing social networking services. This viewpoint for future research has questions on the types of SC BM, the value co-created by these models, and the required resources. The study proposes a framework to explore potential BM associated with social media based on their requirements and evaluate the performance of these BM. On the tenets of the study, this viewpoint argues for the need to develop BM for SC and how value is co-created and the resources underpinning this co-creation.

Chapter 23

Technology addictions (TA) have become a global scourge in recent times, yet in information systems (IS) literature, while a lot of research is being done from developed countries and health-related disciplines, little attention is being paid to this menace by IS scholars from developing countries. To address this issue, this chapter provides a viewpoint on the future research that seeks to investigate from a multidisciplinary and stakeholder perspective what the nature of TA from developing country context is. It will also determine how the socio-technical interaction between human motivations and technology features result in TA, which is novel in IS literature.

Chapter 24

Technological advancements have transformed the way people go about their daily lives. However, this development is not without unintended consequences, as cyber-criminals have also devised ways to gain leverage. The authors conducted a literature review on 106 articles across 40 journals to bring to fore cybercrime studies that have been conducted according to the research themes, methodological approaches, level of analysis, geographical focus, and publication outlets. Themes identified in the review were categorized under an existing typology of cybercrime: cyber-trespass, cyber-deception/ theft, cyber-pornography and obscenity, and cyber-violence. This review suggested two main directions for future research in terms of socio-technical and theoretical approaches with five research questions.

The originality of this review stems from the fact that it is arguably one of the first reviews that have reviewed cybercrime from a holistic perspective.

Chapter 25

Burak Gökalp, Pamukkale University, Turkey
Naci Karkın, Pamukkale University, Turkey
Huseyin Serhan Calhan, Akdeniz University, Turkey

There are many developments affecting societal, cultural, and political relations. The ubiquitous spread of information and communication tools (ICTs) are among these developments. Studies in literature are not indifferent to the impacts brought about in politics by ICTs, particularly by social networking sites (SNSs). During the research, many studies were found that focus on changes and transformations induced by ICTs that unprecedentedly affect interactions and relationships in political life. SNSs, a part of ICTs, have transformative effects on elected and their voters. Though there are many papers that focus on SNSs and political use of SNSs, a void was observed in relevant literature focusing on synthesizing the literature on particular country cases. For this reason, a systematic literature analysis was performed. Findings of this chapter on the political use of SNSs in Turkey indicate that political actors do not fully take advantage of SNSs and their potentialities. The political use of SNSs presents a rhizomatic formation rather than being hierarchical.

Chapter 26

Bryan Acheampong, Business School, University of Ghana, Ghana
Ibrahim Bedi, Business School, University of Ghana, Ghana

While there has been some considerable investment in information systems implementation and usage in the public sector, success has often been limited. Attempts by researchers to address this situation has been diverse and often inconclusive. A publication by the MIS Quarterly journal offers some direction. The study, which focused on information systems development (ISD), highlighted the need to explore how mutual understanding among key stakeholders is created, or the extent to which they have a shared conception of the ISD project, and further how such mutual understanding is changing, develops, or deteriorates over time. On the tenets of the study, this chapter attempts to chart a path for future research in interoperable financial management systems implementation and usage in the public sector. It presents a viewpoint that establishes the need to explore the creation and sustenance of mutual understanding between stakeholders in the implementation and usage of interoperable or integrated financial management systems in the public sector.

Chapter 27

Vonbackustein Klaus Komla, Business School, University of Ghana, Ghana

Digital innovation (DI) drives the digitalisation of goods and services, which also destroys established business models while creating new value chains. This effect is known as disruptive digital innovation (DDI). Beyond transportation and lodging, the effect is also evident in the news media industry. DIs facilitate an ecosystem in which the distinction between service providers and users become blurred – social media is birthing microbloggers as alternatives to incumbent media networks. There are questions on how firms—both incumbent and startups—strategically respond to DDIs and their effects. For the news media in developing countries, the concern is more acute. First, there are fewer established news sources; second, internet and media regulations are often non-existent or nascent stages, so experimentation is easier for DDI-enabled firms and citizen journalists; and third, fake news is not healthy for contexts with a history of political instability or where people have limited avenues to verify news, be it online, radio, or print. The need for this research is now.

Joseph Budu, Department of Information Systems and Innovation, School of Technology,
Ghana Institute of Management and Public Administration, Ghana

Digital platforms bring together different goal-oriented actors to exchange value. This phenomenon has attracted research to understand various aspects of it. These studies show sophisticated technologies are likely to accompany advanced value creation strategies and higher performance gain, and how organizational-level technology usage affects organizational value creation. Nonetheless, we still lack a theoretical and practical understanding of how digital platforms in general, and those for music specifically create value for industry stakeholders. Therefore, the purpose of this chapter is to make a case for future research on digital platform value creation.

Sylvester Tetey Aseidu, Business School, University of Ghana, Ghana
Richard Boateng, Business School, University of Ghana, Ghana

Although innovation adoption has been given much attention in information systems (IS) literature, it has less to account for in user resistance. This chapter contributes to this ongoing debate through a bibliometric review of the user resistance research for the period 1978 to the first quarter of 2019 to provide a coherent overview of the recent research trends and theoretical cornerstones. The authors merged two approaches—co-citation analysis and bibliographic coupling—to (1) create a visualized network of articles that focus on 'user resistance' and (2) to create distinct yet related clusters of articles related thematically. In the findings, they illustrate via the co-citation analysis that user resistance research builds on four main theoretical cornerstones: status quo bias and equity implementation theories, organizational change, social influence and perceived usefulness, power and politics. In conclusion, more research is needed on this theme from a developing economy perspective as IS adoption and usage gains maturity.

Foreword

I am glad to write this forward for a research project that is timely and useful for practitioners, scholars and students in developing economies. The book addresses the issue of rigor and relevance which continue to be a discourse in the IS discipline. Several chapters in this book address concepts and theories to guide the development and deployment of information systems.

Practitioners can apply some of the concepts and implications of findings from the studies in their workplaces. Academics can learn from the studies presented here to contribute to both knowledge and practice in different contexts or similar contexts. Students can also learn from the studies and techniques employed even as they pursue their research agenda.

Some of the papers were through collaborative efforts between industry experts and academics. This collaboration is one of the novel means to build cumulative research with both rigor and relevance in developing economies. The papers are global in nature covering several regions in the world including Africa, Asia, Australia and Europe. The level of analysis was diverse, including individual, private and public institutions, national, societal and global. Emerging digital technologies, services and platforms were studied. Among the diverse dependent variables studied is development which has been reported as eluding IS researchers in the extant ICT for development studies. The research articles demonstrate the application of diverse research methodologies to investigate different IS issues.

Like many other disciplines, the Information systems field finds context to be critical for effective implementation and use of IS. Thus, both academics and practitioners can directly benefit from the context-based implications of the findings presented in the articles included in this book. The specific actions that are promogulated can be applied in the management and practice of information systems in the developing economies where the data was collected or comparable contexts.

One case study research presented here can serve as a useful teaching case study material for institutions of higher learning. This will contribute to addressing lack of pedagogy and adoption of technology instructional material. The papers on literature review and discourse on emerging issues and technologies are useful in building cumulative research and guiding future research in developing economies.

Given the emergence of analytics techniques to address various problems including fraud detection and prevention and healthcare management, the study that developed a hybrid machine learning algorithm to address mobile money fraud is laudable because it reflects a context that is most relevant to developing economies. The study also highlights the fact that socio-technical solutions, including government policies and regulatory frameworks, are needed to realize the full potential of adopting emerging technologies in developing economies. Some studies present insights for small and medium enterprises which are the backbone of most developing economies. Some papers highlight the importance of digital transformation and digital platforms in value creation and fostering innovation.

Researchers in developing countries must continue to build capabilities to write and publish research articles that are rigorous and relevant; this requires continual guidance and guidelines. One paper provides experience in using a less known methodology in the developing economy context. Such guidelines are useful to help future research that seeks to use similar methodology and those who review such works.

Francis Kofi Andoh-Baidoo
University of Texas Rio Grande Valley, USA

Francis Kofi Andoh-Baidoo *is Associate Professor in Information Systems and International Faculty Fellow at the University of Texas Rio Grande Valley, USA. He obtained his PhD in Information Systems from Virginia Commonwealth University. He has an MBA and an MS from University of North Carolina, Greensboro, and a BSc. (Honors) in Materials Engineering from the Kwame Nkrumah University of Science & Technology (KNUST), Ghana. He has published in journals such as Information & Management, Communications of the Association for Information Systems, Information Systems Frontiers, and Database for Advances in Information Systems. He serves on the editorial board of journals such as Information Systems Frontiers and Information Technology for Development. He is an External Examiner for graduate programs in information systems at several universities in Ghana, South Africa, Jamaica and Canada. In 2018, he received an award from the Carnegie African Diaspora Fellowship program to work with KNUST School of Business.*

Foreword

Every aspect of modern age living relies heavily on information systems to strive. Information Systems (IS) are important resources needed to develop other resources. Hence, the development and use of information systems is a modern phenomenon concerned with the use of appropriate information that will lead to better planning, better decision making and better results. In discussing this topic, certain fundamental concepts need to be understood and appreciated. For this simple reason, it is often crucial to highlight the significance of digital technologies and how they impact on the lives of adopters.

The Handbook of Research on Managing Information Systems in Developing Economies provides a distinctive flavour into the theory and practice of managing information systems in developing economies. The book contains chapters carefully selected on the theoretical and practical applications of information systems concepts through a mix of cases, discussions with information systems practitioners and executives, and reviews of contemporary issues and trends in information systems research and practice in developing economies. More precisely, this handbook serves as a reliable source of information about contemporary ways information systems been adopted and are used, especially in developing economy contexts.

The handbook is as comprehensive as possible without reading ambiguities. The definition of concepts and key terms in each chapter explains such aspects of chapters that use specialised terms. The book consists of 29 chapters from across different continents grouped into four sections. Authors of the chapters come from both industry and academia. First, the book reflects on concepts and theories in developing and deploying information systems. Second, it discusses the leveraging new and emerging information systems that are adopted and used in developing economies. Third, it provides insights into information systems and socio-economic development. The fourth and final part touches on the future of information systems in developing economies through numerous research studies that extend IS research ideas.

I, therefore, consider it a great honour to have the opportunity to write the Foreword for Prof Richard Boateng's Edited Book on Managing Information Systems in Developing Economies. At a time when most scholars in the field are not focusing on legacy issues that include documenting knowledge, the editor has taken a giant leap to compile in very succinct and lucid language contents from different world-class and reputable scholars, professionals and focuses on what will assist a broad range of enthusiasts and learners approaching the study and practice of Managing Information Systems in Developing Economies.

I warmly recommend this handbook to institutions; both corporate and academic, public and private sector organisations and various categories of learners approaching the subject of managing information systems from very broad perspectives of business applications, social and enterprise informatics, practice, theories, academics and professionalism. It is my expectation that given editor's scholarship and experience in teaching, researching, collaborations and mentoring early-career faculty and students in the subject matter, the contents presented will provide the needed impetus and zest required to understand how to manage information systems in developing economies and also aid learning and retention as it relates to the focus of the handbook.

Enjoy your reading!

Longe Olumide Babatope
American University of Nigeria, Nigeria

Longe Olumide Babatope *is Professor and Chair of the Department of Information Systems at the American University of Nigeria (AUan) Yola, Nigeria. Prior to joining the services of AUN he was the Dean of the Caleb University Business School and also the Dean of Student Affairs and Deputy Dean of School of Postgraduate Studies at Caleb University, Lagos, Nigeria. A recipient of several national and international awards and recognitions, he is an alumnus Fulbright Scholar, Google Scholar, MacArthur Scholar and an alumnus MIT Scholar. His current research focuses on Management Information Systems Security, social and enterprise informatics (using ubiquitous computing and social theories to aid management decision-making processes). He is also involved in cyber criminality profiling for identifying causation, assisting apprehension and providing treatments for cybercrime cases.*

Preface

OVERVIEW

This book is a contemporary text on the theory and practice of managing information systems in developing economies. It explores theory and applications of information systems concepts through a mix of cases, empirical research and reviews of contemporary issues and trends in information systems research and practice in developing economies.

RELEVANCE AND OBJECTIVE

Though there are quite a number of academic texts, especially teaching texts, which focus on managing information systems, very few tend to feature case examples of management of information systems from a developing economies' perspective. Further, global or international editions of such texts are also particularly focused on the practice of information systems in developed economies. However, there have been several advances or growth in information systems in developing economies, which economies tend to be one of the fastest growing markets for technology adoption, especially considering mobile technologies. As such, the story of theory and practice of information systems in these economies must be told, especially covering their responses to new and emerging technologies/services/information platforms. That is the core objective of this book - it provides real-world experiences and accounts on how entrepreneurs, organisations, and institutions practice information systems, especially using new and emerging technologies, in developing economies. It also seeks to provide review of trends and past research to contribute thematic areas that will shape the future of information systems research and practice.

TARGET AUDIENCE

This book is of direct value to practitioners and professionals who manage information systems in developing economies and who seek to learn from best practices and lessons in contemporary approaches to the management of information systems. Further, it promises direct value to the teaching of management information systems in undergraduate and graduate programs across developing economies. Such comprehensive texts are primarily scarce, and this book tends to address the gap.

STRUCTURE

The book is made up of four section to reflect on the themes of the chapters. Section 1 is made up of two chapters. The chapters explore the adoption, usage and impact of information systems among organisations in developing economies.

Section 2 is made up of 12 chapters. The chapters examine how entrepreneurs, organisations and institutions make specific decisions in leveraging new and emerging digital technologies, services and platforms (e.g., sharing economy and social commerce) to create new products and services.

Section 3 has four chapters. The chapters discuss Information Systems and Socio-Economic Development. They examine how information and communication technologies help to achieve socio-economic development outcomes (particularly in the education, health and public access to technology).

While the final part, Section 4, has 11 chapters. The chapters discuss the future of Information Systems in Developing Economies. The chapters present reviews and viewpoints of contemporary issues and trends in gamification, cybercrime, digital platforms and user resistance to information technology, and how these thematic areas will shape the future of information systems research and practice. Synopsis of the chapters are presented below.

Section 1: Concepts and Theories in Developing and Deploying Information Systems

Chapter 1

This chapter qualitatively explores the nature of Strategic Information Systems Planning (SISP) implementation and the factors that influence as enablers or inhibitors to the implementation and use of SISP in Ghanaian organisations. Findings from the study show that by far firms in Ghana have applied Earl's approaches in their SISP implementation. However, inhibitors to SISP implementation include Budget constraint, Regulatory requirements, Absence of IT/IS Steering Committee, among others. The study highly recommends that the inhibiting factors are given the necessary attention by firms, government and researchers.

Chapter 2

In this chapters, the authors review existing data mining techniques for exploring the detection of mobile payment fraud and propose a hybrid-based machine learning framework for mobile money fraud detection. However, the implementation of the framework hinges on the formulation of policies and regulations that will guide the adoption and enforcement by regulatory stakeholders. This novel approach to mobile payment fraud is an opportunity for new discussions for both practitioners and researchers.

Section 2: Leveraging New and Emerging Information Systems

Chapter 3

In this chapter, the disruptive nature of Uber as platform for ridesharing within a developing economy context is explored. The chapter explores the factors that inform individuals' behavioural intention to adopt disruptive information technologies and identify that consumers' understanding of technology, meta-price value, and perceived need are really what informs their decision to adopt a disruptive technology such as the Uber ride-sharing platform.

Chapter 4

The chapter provides an understanding on Privacy-focused Technology Use among Generation Y's and its Impact on Behavioural Intention and Actual Use of Social Commerce. The results of the study show that Privacy-focused technology use fails to influence behavioural intentions. Hence, knowledge of privacy risks influences the behavioural intentions of Generation Y, but actual use is impacted where the risk is perceived to be beyond control. Thus, the perceptions of the controllability of risk tends to matter to the Generation Y.

Chapter 5

The chapter explores a firm's digital strategic actions for dealing with the competitive forces in the digital economy of a developing country. A qualitative case study approach through a digital enterprise which has been operating in a developing economy for over six years is selected as a case. Findings from this chapter serves as a stepping-stone in expounding the digital strategic actions of firms in dealing with the market forces in the digital economy.

Chapter 6

This chapter presents a review of the related literature on organisational mobile commerce (m-commerce) adoption, leading to the development of an integrated model for evaluating the critical determinants of m-commerce adoption in small and medium-sized enterprises (SMEs) in developing countries. Findings from the study provide managers of SMEs with useful insights on how to improve the adoption of m-commerce in SMEs.

Chapter 7

Using a qualitative interpretive case study, this chapter provides an understanding of digital innovation in the taxi industrial structure for ridesharing in a developing country. The findings show that ridesharing application services provide riders-drivers with better journey activities, which supersedes taxi services in competition. These are electronic booking, riders and drivers' profiles for security, transparent automatic billing for affordable transportation, and opportunities for drivers to accept a series of riders' requests at proximity.

Chapter 8

This chapter, through a Delphi technique and the Perceived E-commerce Readiness Model, presents the perspectives of Blockchain experts on the readiness of the institutions in developing economies to adopt and implement it. The findings suggest that Understanding of the technology, Knowledge on how to use blockchain technology, Availability of skilled personnel, Availability of technical components, Risk,

Capital, Management support, Business process, Policies & Regulations, and Government initiatives on technology are key influencing agents in the readiness to adopt Blockchain in a developing economy.

Chapter 9

Through the DeLone and McLean's success model, this chapter explores the effects of the adoption of new and emerging technologies in organisations. The findings show that while some organisations succumb to the introduction of the new and emerging digital technologies with its disruptive nature, others can conveniently manage the changes introduced through new business models, appropriate infrastructure, skills, knowledge, enhanced data security, and effective communication.

Chapter 10

The chapter discusses how IT enables or constrains counterfeiting and piracy in the fashion and beauty industry in Ghana and Nigeria. The findings point to the escalation of counterfeiting/piracy in the fashion and beauty industry due to globalisation and the predominance of technological innovation, specifically the Internet and social media platforms.

Chapter 11

The chapter qualitatively explores the enablers and inhibitors to merchant adoption of mobile payments. The study identified that merchants are adopting mobile payments to facilitate new business models, promote the disintermediation of traditional intermediaries, to offer different possibilities of growing their businesses and reduce transaction costs.

Chapter 12

This chapter uses a qualitative approach to explore the motivation and outcomes for riders to participate in the gig economy in Ghana. The findings suggest that riders found the platform to be convenient, cost and time saving as well as trustworthy. The platform also substituted the means of finding transportation for some of the riders, whiles for other riders, it complemented their means of finding transportation for themselves and their social and professional networks. Hence, the study denotes that riders are primarily influenced personal perceived benefits and other benefits they can share with others.

Chapter 13

This chapter uses a teaching case to explore how a microentrepreneur uses social media as a resource to create social commerce capabilities to achieve benefits. Lessons learnt are proposed in the case, questions for reflections are proposed at the end whilst a debate topic is suggested.

Chapter 14

The chapter conducts a case study on TelMob (Pseudonym), a digital firm that focuses on the sale of indigenous African music. The findings suggest that TelMob generated value through the API-enabled platform by ensuring that music lovers purchase their preferred songs at competitive prices. TelMob has also been able to increase their revenue and brand image. Similarly, musicians have been able to rake substantial amounts of money through the sales of their music on the platform. The case demonstrates value creation on digital music platforms.

Section 3: Information Systems and Socio-Economic Development

Chapter 15

This chapter presents some methodological issues raised in the research process of an interpretive researcher in a maiden PhD programme in a developing country. The research relied on a single case study in a developing country context and offers an overview of some practicalities of carrying out a single case study research using an interpretive philosophy by presenting the different viewpoints using semi-structured interviews, documents and participant observation and analysing the data through hermeneutics.

Chapter 16

Underpinned by the concepts of installed base and cultivation, this chapter adopts a qualitative multiple-case study approach to examine the contextual factors that influence the development, implementation, and adoption of digital health systems in the Ghanaian and Nigerian contexts. Results of this chapter reveal thirteen key challenges and their corresponding mitigating strategies that were adopted in specific instances to facilitate digitalisation in both contexts. A comparison of findings for the two contexts is also discussed.

Chapter 17

This chapter looks at the rising patronage of mobile data in a developing economy and changes that have ensued from its adoption by a higher education institution. Findings indicate that mobile data patronage is influencing its pedagogical use. Adoption has resulted in institutional changes in the form of emerged roles and arrangements. If undisrupted by technological innovations or communal group behavior, the arrangements may gain legitimacy with time. From an institutional theory perspective, mobile technology appears to be playing an agential role on the landscape of the institution.

Chapter 18

This qualitative case study explores the connections between the roll-out of free public Wi-Fi by the City of Johannesburg and changes that have resulted in city residents' lives. It also uses the Choice Framework to explain how these changes come about. Benefits identified included easier communications, savings in time and money, social and psychological benefits as well as increased knowledge, business ideas, access to markets, access to job opportunities and increased income.

Section 4: Future of Information Systems in Developing Economies

Chapter 19

This chapter systematically examines the extent of gamification research in the developing country context. 56 papers from Scopus were used in the review. This chapter per the authors begins by explicating the idea of game design elements in information systems and provide real-world examples of gamified systems outcomes from developing countries from a variety of research frameworks and disciplinary perspectives and based on available literature we synthesise and provide domains of gamification research. Future research directions are also proposed in this chapter.

Chapter 20

This chapter identifies and reviews what influences healthcare institutions towards the use of Business Intelligence and Analytics. With the use of a systematic review of 25 articles, the study identified nine dominant factors driving healthcare institutions to big data analytics (BDA) adoption. Factors such as patient management, quality decision making, disease management, data management, and promoting healthcare efficiencies were among the highly ranked factors influencing BDA adoption.

Chapter 21

The chapter presents a systematic review of information systems curriculum research published in information systems journals and selected conference proceedings in the past decade. The findings suggest that the studies largely focus on identifying information systems competencies and their implications for curriculum design and delivery. Further, these issues are discussed at the undergraduate level and predominantly in the USA and UK, this paper suggests, future research at the graduate level and from other regions.

Chapter 22

This study reviews studies that have been done on resource and value co-creation in social commerce and proposes a framework to explore potential business models. On the tenets of the study, this viewpoint argues for the need to develop business models for social commerce and how value is co-created and the resources underpinning this co-creation.

Chapter 23

This chapter provides a viewpoint on using a multidisciplinary and stakeholder perspective to investigate the nature of technology addiction in a developing country context. The viewpoint argues on the need to explore how the socio-technical interaction between human motivations and technology features result in TA, which is novel in IS literature.

Chapter 24

This chapter conducts a systematic review of literature on cybercrime. The review suggested two main directions for future research in terms of socio-technical and theoretical approaches with five research questions. The review is arguably one of the first reviews that has reviewed cybercrime from a holistic perspective.

Chapter 25

This chapter performs a systematic review of Political Use of Social Networking and points to the lack of political actors taking full advantage of social network sites (SNS) and their potentialities. The chapter further indicate that political use of SNS presents a rhizomatic formation rather than being hierarchical.

Chapter 26

On the tenets of the mutual understanding and sensemaking, this chapter attempts to chart a path for future research in information systems implementation and usage in the public sector. It presents a viewpoint which establishes the need to explore the creation and sustenance of mutual understanding between stakeholders in the implementation and usage of interoperable or integrated financial management systems in the public sector.

Chapter 27

This chapter makes a case for research on the strategies used by firms – both incumbent and startups to respond to disruptive digital innovations and their effects in the news and media industry. For the news media in developing countries, the concern is more acute - there are fewer established news sources and people have limited avenues to verify news, be it online, radio or print. The need for this research is now.

Chapter 28

Digital platforms bring together different goal-oriented actors to exchange value. This phenomenon has attracted research to understand various aspects of it. In this regard, this chapter explores studies on digital platforms and value creation and proposes pointers for future research.

Chapter 29

This chapters presents a bibliometric review of the user resistance research for the period 1978 to the first quarter of 2019. The findings suggest that the research is oriented around four thematic areas: Status Quo Bias and Equity Implementation Theories; organisational change; Social influence and Perceived Usefulness; Power and Politics. Literature from Africa and other developing economies are largely absent and as IS usage in these regions is gaining maturity, the necessity of this research area cannot be over-emphasised.

CONCLUSION

The chapters presented in this book indicate that information systems practice in developing countries is gaining maturity as most IS implementations (especially at the firm level) are not being done 'loosely' or without a focus, but are guided by some strategic approaches and business models. These chapters also make significant contributions by proposing research frameworks and conceptual models that can be tested and applied in future IS research. Further, the book indicates that for many individuals and firms in developing economies, there is the continuous adoption of new and emerging technologies in order not to be left out of the digital economy.

Further, the adoption and continuous use of these new and emerging technologies are characterised by strategies to mitigate against adoption and user challenges in order to reap considerable benefits from it.

From a socio-economic point of view the book shows that access to internet is a primary concern in both public and educational contexts in developing economies. Future and current strategic initiatives to enhance access should consider these contexts a priority.

The book serves as reference for exploring ongoing research in various aspects of ICTs adoption and implementation in developing economies and it is my hope that these suggested research areas can serve as good foundation for readers' future research in the discipline.

Acknowledgment

The completion of this book would not have been possible without the support of the editorial advisory board and editorial assistants. I, therefore, appreciate the contributions of the members of the editorial team for helping in the review and selection process and providing prompt comments, thereby making the publication of this book possible. I am sincerely grateful to all authors and reviewers for their submissions and contributions as well.

Section 1
Concepts and Theories in Developing and Deploying Information Systems

Chapter 1
Strategic Information Systems Planning (SISP) Implementation and Use in a Developing Economy:
The Case of Ghanaian Organizations

Acheampong Owusu
https://orcid.org/0000-0001-7789-5162
Business School, University of Ghana, Ghana

Frederick Edem Broni Jr.
https://orcid.org/0000-0001-9674-1679
Business School, University of Ghana, Ghana

ABSTRACT

The purpose of this chapter is to explore the nature of SISP implementation and also determine the factors that influence as enablers or inhibitors to the implementation and use of SISP in Ghanaian organizations. The methodology adopted was the qualitative method and underpinned by Earl and Lederer and Sethi's approaches to SISP development. The results indicated that many firms have applied Earl's approaches in their SISP implementation. The findings also revealed that factors such as IS alignment, awareness, environmental assessment, budget, and top management involvement are the critical success factors enabling the use of SISP in the organizations studied. Inhibitors to SISP implementation include budget constraint, regulatory requirements, absence of IT/IS steering committee, among others. The study highly recommends that the inhibiting factors are given the necessary attention by the government to enable firms to implement SISP with ease. The originality of this study lies in the dearth of literature about SISP implementation in sub-Saharan economies.

DOI: 10.4018/978-1-7998-2610-1.ch001

INTRODUCTION

In recent times, technology has advanced which has made it possible for a lot of software tools developed for businesses of varying sizes. Some of the modern tools available include Enterprise Resource Planning (ERP), Customer Relationship Management (CRM), Supply Chain Management (SCM), Business Intelligence (BI), Analytics, Big Data, Artificial Intelligence (AI), Internet of Things (IoT), and Blockchain, among others.

These novel tools are recently needed in modern organizations due to the data explosion. Acquiring data these days by firms is no longer a challenge but getting insights that will aid in management decision making (at the operational, tactical and strategic levels) is the issue. Although these tools and technologies could give organizations a competitive edge and help them remain in business to achieve their mission and vision, yet research (Hoque, Hossin & Khan, 2016) has proven that tools and technologies alone cannot help them remain competitive and prevent folding up. There's the need for policies and strategies to complement Information Systems (IS) Management to ensure compliance with best industry practices, standards, and guidelines which will also help them achieve their goals (Boateng, 2017).

Businesses of all sizes are obliged to navigate a labyrinth of uncertainties and complexities that arises in the business environment. Due to environmental complexities and uncertainties that businesses have to go through, business owners, as well as decision-makers, have to embrace an Information Systems that aligns with their operational strategy in order to gain competitive advantage and grow (Merali et al., 2012; Queiroz, 2018; Zubovic et al., 2014). Information Systems has been viewed as an important resource to successfully drive the business' strategy (Worthen, 2007; Hoque et al., 2016).

Strategic Information Systems Planning (SISP) is a process that supports businesses in attaining their strategic objectives and goals by aligning their business strategy with Information Technology (IT) (Kamariotou & Kitsios, 2017). SISP is intended to support the business goals and objectives using IS as a driving resource (Kamariotou & Kitsios, 2018). By implementing SISP in an organization, businesses tend to enhance customer relationships, cut down costs, develop new products and services, and innovate its operations (Kamariotou & Kitsios, 2015, Ullah & Lai, 2013). Through SISP, businesses are able to fit Information Technology (IT) with their business strategy which supports strategic business objectives and to help them achieve their set goals (Kamariotou & Kitsios, 2015; Kitsios & Kamariotou, 2016). In developing countries, it was confirmed that there should be a hybrid approach as to where SISP will fit best in organizations (Hoque et al., 2016).

As the world is now a global village and firms are competing with products from everywhere, having a SISP in place that can help your firm remain competitive is more than necessary. A survey of the IS literature shows a myriad of papers with examples and case studies from the developed world (Hoque et al., 2016; Kitsios & Kamariotou, 2016; Kamariotou & Kitsios, 2015). However, in the context of developing economies especially sub-Saharan Africa (SSA) countries, for example, Ghana, there is a paucity of research in terms of SISP adoption, implementation, and use. This study will attempt to fill this gap in the literature.

The study, therefore, aims to achieve the following:

1. To explore the nature of SISP implementation in Ghanaian firms
2. To explore the factors that influence as enablers or inhibitors to the adoption, implementation, and use of SISP in Ghanaian firms

The need for this study is originated from the fact that first, many organizations especially lots of private firms have established clearly defined Information Technology (IT) Departments with lots of IT Systems aiding them e.g. the banks and telecoms companies. Yet, little is known with their SISP implementation and use, so it's difficult to tell if the required benefits are being derived from their systems. Secondly, in recent times, Government of Ghana (GoG) is on a mission of digitizing most of its services such as the National Digital Property Addressing System (Ghana Post GPS), paperless port operations (Ports and Harbors), the integrated e-immigration system (Ghana Immigration Service), e-procurement, e-registrar, e-parliament, e-justice, e-cabinet, and smart workplaces among others (http://www.eservices. gov.gh/). Thus, the need for having a SISP framework for its adoption, implementation and use in the country is highly necessary in order not to spend much on these technologies but gain little i.e. ensuring value for money and huge return on investment (ROI).

The rest of the paper is organized as follows: the next section introduces readers to the literature review comprising the concept of SISP and the related studies as well as the theoretical framework. This follows with the methodology section made up of the research approach, the instrument used for data collection, sampling technique adopted, and the analysis performed. The next section introduces readers to the findings and the discussions section. The conclusion section follows with recommendations, limitations, and suggestions for future studies.

LITERATURE REVIEW

This section comprises of the literature survey and synthesis of the chapter. It is made up of the concept of SISP, related studies of SISP and the theoretical framework underpinning the chapter.

The Concept of SISP

SISP has been identified as the main IS/IT strategy underpinning firms to utilize IS/IT to achieve the core objectives and mission of the organization. SISP aims to align the IS/IT strategy of a firm to its business strategy and the resultant effect being IS/IT being used to drive the business to gain a competitive edge but not just seen as a support unit.

Bryson (2011) and Boateng (2017, p.84) defined SISP as "a deliberate focused effort to define and establish fundamental decisions and actions that guide how IT/IS drive or support what an organization is, what it does and why it does". In addition, Lederer and Sethi (1992, p. 25), defined SISP as "the process of creating a long-range plan of computer-based applications to enable an organization to achieve its goals". This definition stems from their earlier definition of SISP as "the process of identifying a portfolio of computer-applications that will assist an organization in executing its business plans and realizing its business goals" (Lederer & Sethi, 1992b, p. 70).

SISP has been identified to have many benefits when effectively implemented and can lead organizations to have a competitive edge. In the literature, some of the identified benefits of SISP include it helping organizations to use IS in "innovative ways to build barriers against new entrants, change the basis of competition, generate new products, build in switching costs, or change the balance of power in supplier relationships" (Porter, 1985). Others are SISP "promotes innovation and creativity. It might employ idea-generating techniques such as brainstorming, value chain analysis, or the customer resource life cycle" (Lederer & Sethi, 1992a; Rackoff, Wiseman, & Ullrich, 1985). Other scholars (Earl, 1990;

Klouwenberg, Koot, & Schaik, 1995; Boateng, 2017) identified the key areas a SISP process should focus on in an organization as "Business-Information systems alignment, leveraging IT for competitive advantage, efficient and effective and responsible management of resources, and developing IT architecture and IT infrastructure". In addition, Boateng (2017, p.84) outlined that when these areas are focused on, SISP becomes relevant to "align IS with business needs; seek competitive advantage from IT; gain top management commitment; forecast IS resource requirements; and establish technology policies".

There are a number of approaches to SISP as discussed by literature (Earl, 1990; Eral, 1989; Klouwenberg et al., 1995; Lederer & Sethi, 1992a). These approaches include formal methods and best practices whilst others are informal (Boateng, 2017, p.66).

Lederer and Sethi (1992a) proposed four popular approaches to carry out SISP as PROplanner, Business Systems Planning (BSP), Method/1, and Information Engineering. In addition, Earl (1993) also identified another set of approaches as Business-led, Method driven, Administrative, Technology-driven, and Organizational.

Common Steps in SISP Implementation

In implementing SISP, Boateng (2017, p.22), Newkirk, Lederer, and Srinivasan (2003), and Al-aboud (2011) outlined the following common steps as follows:

1. Strategic awareness – comprising of the IS planning process by "determining the key planning issues, defining the planning objectives, organizing the planning teams and obtaining the top management commitment"
2. Situation analysis – comprising of analyzing the current environment by "analyzing the current business systems, analyzing the current organizational systems, analyzing the current information systems, analyzing the current external business environment and analyzing the current external IT environment"
3. Strategy conception – comprising of conceiving the strategy alternatives by "identifying major IT objectives, identifying opportunities for improvement, evaluating opportunities for improvement, and identifying high level IT strategies"
4. Strategy formulation - comprising of selecting the strategy by "identifying new business processes, identifying new IT architectures, identifying specific new projects, and identifying priorities for new projects"
5. Strategy implementation – comprising planning the strategy implementation by "justifying IT costs, defining change management approach, defining an action plan, evaluating the action plan and defining follow-up and control procedure".

In addition to these, other scholars such as Rainer, Cegielski, and Prince (2010), Ward and Peppard (2002), Nolan and McFarlan (2005) all proposed different steps to SISP implementation.

Rainer *et al.*'s (2010) Steps in SISP Implementation

According to Rainer et al. (2010), the IT/IS strategic plan begins with the assessment of an Organization's Strategic Plan (Mission and Business Assessment) and its Current IT Architecture (Figure 1). The

Figure 1. Rainer et al.'s (2010) Method. Source: (Rainer et al., 2010; Boateng, 2017, p.93)

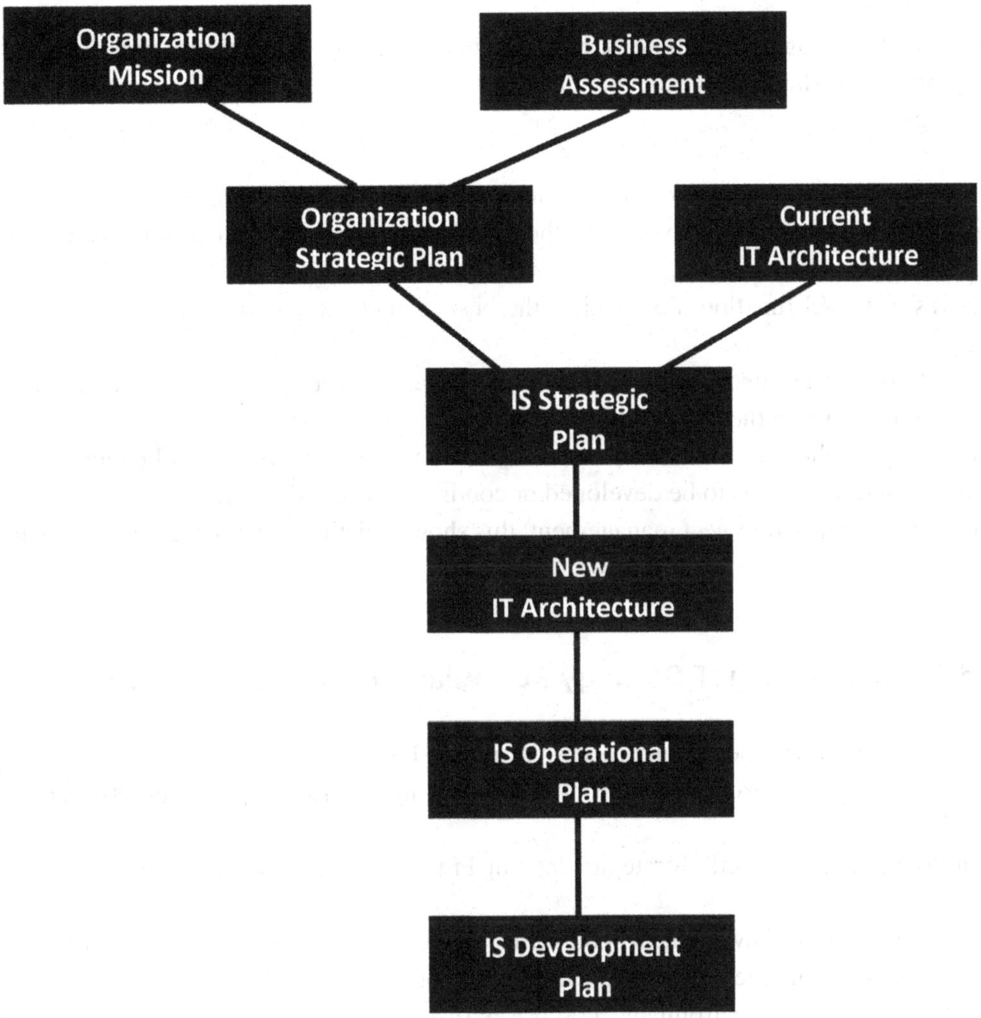

assessment process then informs the IT/IS Strategic Plan. Mentzas (1997) outlined three objectives that the IS/IT Strategic Plan must meet as follows:

a)   Alignment with the strategic plan of the organization
b)   Provision of an Information Technology (IT) architecture which seamlessly networks applications, users, and databases and

c)   Proficiently allocating the Information Systems (IS) development resources among projects that are competing so that these projects can be accomplished within budget, and on time, which will still have the requisite functionality

The next step after an agreed IT strategic plan is to develop the ***IS Operational Plan*** which entails a clear set of projects that the IS department and the functional area manager will accomplish in support of the IT strategic plan.

a)   Mission: consist of the mission of the IS function derived from the IT strategy
b)   IS environment: this shows the outline of the information needs of the functional areas and of the organization as a whole
c)   Objectives of the IS function: this depicts the best current estimate of the aspirations of the IS function
d)   Constraints on the IS function: comprises of the financial, technological, personnel, and other resource restrictions on the IS function
e)   Application portfolio: this is made up of prioritized inventory of current applications and a comprehensive plan of projects to be developed or continued during the current year
f)   Resource allocation and project management: this shows a listing of who is going to do what, how and when

Ward and Peppard (2002) IT Strategy Formulation and Planning Framework

In developing the SISP implementation process, Ward and Peppard (2002) proposed IT Strategy Formulation and Planning framework made up of three building blocks – inputs, outputs, and essential activities as shown in Figure 2.

The inputs to Ward and Peppard's Strategic Planning Framework (Boateng, 2017, p.96) are as follows:

a)   The Internal Business Environment: comprises of the "current business strategy, objectives resources, processes, and the culture and values of the business"
b)   The External Business Environment: comprises of the "economic, industrial, and competitive climate in which the organization operates"
c)   The Internal IT Environment: this comprises of the "current IT perspective in the business, its maturity, business coverage, and contribution to the attainment of the organization's goals (e.g. cost reduction, skills, resources, and the technological infrastructure)"
d)   The External IT Environment: this comprises "technology trends and opportunities and the use of IT by others, especially customers, competitors, and suppliers"

The outputs to Ward and Peppard's Strategic Planning Framework (Boateng, 2017, p.96) are as follows:

a)   IT Management Strategy: this is "the common elements of the strategy that apply throughout the organization, ensuring consistent policies where needed"
b)   Business IS Strategy: this is "how each unit of function will deploy IT in achieving its business objectives"

Figure 2. Ward and Peppard Method. Source: (Ward, 2002; Boateng, 2017, p.95)

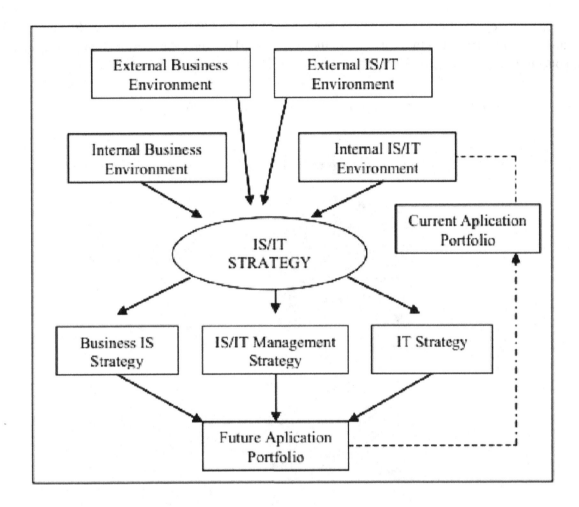

c)   Application Portfolios: this "comprises of applications portfolios to be developed alongside each of the business objectives for the business unit and business models, describing the information architectures of each unit. The portfolio may include how IT will be used at some future date to help the units achieve their objectives"

d)   IT Strategy: this is "the policies and strategies for the management of technology and specialist resources"

The last dimension of the Ward and Peppards Framework (Boateng, 2017, p.96) consists of the core attributes of the framework.

Nolan and Mcfarlan (2005) IT Strategic Grid

In developing steps to SISP implementation, Nolan and McFarlan (2005) proposed the IT Strategic Grid (Figure 3), which "facilitates the evaluation of the relationship between IT strategy and Business strategy and operations" (Boateng, 2017, p.98).

Figure 3. Nolan and Mcfarlan IT Strategic Grid. Source: (Boateng, 2017, p.98)

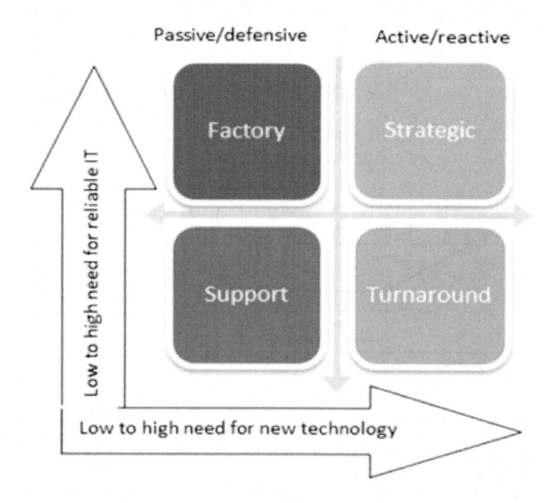

The IT Strategic Grid model analyzes the impacts of IT existent applications and of a future applications portfolio by defining four boxes, each one representing one possible role of IT in the enterprise. The four quadrants described by the model are Support, Factory, Turnaround, and Strategic. The Strategic Grid explains where and how IT investment has been made in firms by classifying IT investment into four categories (Nolan & McFarlan, 2005; McFarlan & McKenny, 1983).

Each of the four quadrants is described below (Boateng, 2017, p.99-100):

- **Strategic**: this quadrant depicts that IT investment is critical for the future success of the business. Features in this quadrant include businesses having High operational impact and high strategic impact. In addition, IT/IS is seen as the backbone of competitive success where new IT/IS applications in development are crucial for future competitive success. Again, IT/IS organizations that have most projects in this quadrant understand that IT/IS can both improve core operations of the firm while simultaneously generating strategic options. The IT/IS budget in this quadrant is very significant. Examples of business in this quadrant are Banks, Retail stores, Airlines.
- **Turnaround**: this quadrant depicts investment in IT/IS applications which may be important to achieving the future success of the business. Features in this quadrant include businesses having a low operational impact but strive to achieve a high strategic impact. This quadrant is about exploiting new technologies to provide strategic opportunities. In addition, IT/IS supports operations but are not dependent on IT/IS absolute. Here, new IT/IS applications are necessary to enable the firm to achieve its strategic objectives. Also, the planned and developed systems may be critical to the firm's survival or growth. The investments in IT/IS in this quadrant should be increasing perhaps rapidly for the survival of the business. Examples of businesses in this quadrant are high fashion, Oil refining among others.
- **Factory**: this quadrant depicts that the investment in IT/IS applications are necessary which the organization currently depends on for success. Features in this quadrant include low operational impact yet strive to achieve a high strategic impact. This quadrant is about exploiting new technologies to provide strategic opportunities. In addition, IT/IS is critical to current operations but is not at the heart of the company's strategic development. IT/IS is enabling critical operations to function smoothly. Here, the future IT/IS applications are not the critical factor for future business success. In this quadrant, the IT/IS budget will always be significant. Examples of businesses in this quadrant are Defense, Government, and Immigration.
- **Support**: this quadrant depicts that the investment in IT/IS applications which are valuable but not critical to the success of the business. Features of businesses in this quadrant include low operational impact yet strive to achieve a high strategic impact. This quadrant is about exploiting new technologies to provide strategic opportunities. In addition, IT/IS supports operations but are not dependent on IT/IS. Also, new IT/IS applications are not necessarily linking to business planning activity rather, IT/IS is used essentially for administrative systems to improve internal efficiency. Again, IT/IS investment is average or below average. Examples are Universities and Consultants.

Boateng (2017, p. 100) asserted that "these classification aid management to see whether IT/IS investments so far have been aligned to business objectives such as to support business growth, competitiveness or new business venture".

In spite of all these approaches to SISP implementation as outlined above, yet in this study, our aim is looking at the approaches proposed by (Lederer & Sethi, 1992a) and (Earl,1989) which are described under the theoretical framework section.

Related Studies

In this section, we outlined the related studies pertaining to SISP implementation in various firms. Table 1 outlined some of the selected studies about SISP adoption, implementation, and use.

From Table 1, theories underpinning SISP implementation varies but it's been mostly conceptual and

Table 1. Related studies of SISP implementation

Research Paper	Theory	Methodology	Context	Perspective/Focus
Hovelja, Rožanec, and Rupnik (2010)	Critical success factors	Survey questionnaire	Slovenia	Development of a new SISP success measurement approach
Zubovic, Pita, and Khan (2014)	Conceptual	Conceptual	Australia	Proposed "a model for investigating the impact of IS collaboration and IS personnel competencies on the SISP process"
Hovelja, Vasilecas, and Rupnik (2013)	Conceptual	Survey questionnaire	Slovenia	Proposed "an extended SISP model which includes influences of environmental stakeholders"
Amrollahi, Ghapanchi, and Talaei-Khoei (2013)	Conceptual	Systematic literature review approach for 12 top rankings IS journals in the past 10 years		Systematic Literature Review on Strategic Information Systems Planning
Kamariotou and Kitsios (2018)	Common steps towards SISP implementation	Survey questionnaire	Greece	"Empirical Evaluation of Strategic Information Systems Planning Phases in SMEs"
Kitsios and Kamariotou (2016)	Conceptual	Conceptual	Greece	Proposed the steps of a framework which combines both the SISP concept and DSS, based on previous models.
Irfan, Putra, Alam, Subiyakto, and Wahana (2017)	Conceptual	Systematic Literature Review (SLR)	Developing countries	System strategic planning among universities in developing countries
Al-aboud (2011)	Conceptual	Review		Best practices and approaches in SISP implementation
Altameem, Aldrees, and Alsaeed (2014)	Conceptual	Conceptual		Overview of SISP including its importance, stages, and success
Musangu and Kekwaletswe (2011)	SISPP	Survey questionnaire	South Africa	"Strategic Information Systems Planning and Environmental Uncertainty"
Harun and Hashim (2017)	Conceptual	Conceptual		A review of the concept of SISP, its definitions, and stages of development
Ali, Mohamad, Talib, and Abdullah (2017)	SISP Process	A qualitative method through face-to-face interviews	Malaysia	SISP Practices in Medium Manufacturing Company in Malaysia
Rangga, Setyohadi, and Santoso (2017)	SISP Process	Collecting primary and secondary data through observation and interview	Indonesia	SISP process in the Ministry of Religious Affairs (e-government)
Pollack (2010)	Conceptual	Conceptual		suggesting a process which will assist in the achievement of the planning success
Alshubaily and Altameem (2017)	Conceptual	Survey questionnaire	Saudi Arabia	"Role of Strategic Information Systems (SIS) in Supporting and Achieving the Competitive Advantages (CA)"

literature review due to the complex nature of the SISP process. Methodology for SISP implementation also varies with most of them being survey questionnaires. In terms of context, most of the studies have been done in the developed economies whilst developing economies are plagued with SISP studies as evident in sub-Saharan African economies. Thus, exploring SISP implementation in Ghanaian firms is apt in order to enrich the IS literature when it comes to SISP in developing economies context.

THEORETICAL FRAMEWORK

This study is underpinned by the Lederer and Sethi (1992a) and Earl (1989) approaches to SISP implementation.

Lederer and Sethi (1992a) proposed four popular approaches to carry out SISP as PROplanner, Business Systems Planning (BSP), Method/1, and Information Engineering. PROplanner was developed by Holland Systems Corp. in Ann Arbor, Michigan and "involves helping planners to analyze the major functional areas within the organization". Business Systems Planning (BSP) was "developed by IBM and it involves top-down planning with bottom-up implementation". Method/1 was developed by Anderson Consulting and "consists of ten phases of work segments that an organization completes creating its strategic plan". Information Engineering developed by Knowledge Ware in Atlanta, "provides techniques for building Enterprise Models, Data Models and Process Models" (Boateng, 2017, p.86-87).

In addition, Earl (1989) also identified another set of approaches as Business-led, Method driven, Administrative, Technology-driven, and Organizational. The Business-led approach involves the "analysis of business plans to identify how and where IT/IS can most effectively enable these plans to be implemented". Method driven approach involves "the use of techniques to identify IS needs by analyzing business processes and objectives". Administrative approach "entails the establishment of an IT capital and expense budget to satisfy approved projects". Technology-driven approach involves "the development of IT architectures as a foundation for expected application needs". The Organizational approach involves "the identification of key themes for IT/IS projects – such as critical success factors for IT/IS projects" (Boateng, 2017, p.88-89).

Factors Influencing Successful Implementation of SISP

One prominent theory that has received a lot of attention in the IS literature for assessing the successful implementation of IS/IT innovations is the Critical Success Factors (CSFs) theory. In brief, the CSF theory was developed by Rockart (1979) and it seeks to identify those key factors that management needs to pay special attention in order to have a successful implementation of IS/IT innovations such as SISP. The CSF has been used to study the successful implementation of diverse IS/IT such as alignment of IS plans with business plans (Teo & Ang, 1999); exploration of Success Factors of Information Systems (Kaur & Aggrawal, 2013); success factors in the implementation of strategic Information Systems (Rishi & Goyal, 2008); brief review of Strategic Information Systems Planning (Al-aboud, 2011); and Strategic Information System Planning Case Study of a Service Delivery Company (Alamri, Almutiri, Ballahmar, & Zafar, 2016).

Lederer and Sethi (1991) classified the thorough list of SISP implementation methodologies problems as output, resource, or planning process. In another study, Lederer and Sethi (1998, p. 454) identified the top nine problems of SISP implementation as follows:

- "Difficult to secure top management commitment
- Post-analysis is necessary after the study
- There is no training plan for IT development
- Success depends on the IT leader
- Difficult to find a team leader who meets the criteria
- Lack of sufficient computer support
- Ignores plan implementation issues
- There is no analysis of IT department strengths and weaknesses
- There is no analysis of the technological environment"

Also, Teo and Ang (2001, p. 461) identified seven key areas for SISP implementation failure as follows:

- "failing to get management support
- not having free communication and commitment
- unable to obtain sufficiently qualified personnel
- distributing the planning responsibility to an individual without sufficient knowledge and experience
- not investing sufficient front-end time
- not having a steering committee and
- not having a clear-cut corporate plan to guide the information systems planning effort"

Again, Samaha and Dahawy (2010) find that the lack of expertise within the organization is the main problem in SISP implementation. Furthermore, unnecessary expenses, and failing to identify the benefits of SISP are the other problems in SISP implementation (Hoque, Hossin, & Khan, 2016).

As there exists a myriad of literature when it comes to the CSF theory, so there are a plethora of factors that have been studied in diverse technologies and in different industry sectors. In the case of SISP success implementation, several factors have been identified as both enablers and inhibitors. These are shown in Table 2:

As shown in Table 2, both the enablers and inhibitors for SISP implementation success factors are diverse and multi-faceted. It differs depending on the focus of the study as well as the context. As there is a dearth of studies when it comes to SISP in the sub-Saharan context, this study aims to add to the study by Ankrah (2016) which was identified in the Ghanaian context. His focus was more on the strategic management of IS implementation in Ghanaian banks (both local and foreign). This study rather goes beyond this and also studied different industries and sectors to complement Ankrah's study.

This study thus seeks to explore the various approaches that were adopted by Ghanaian organizations in their quest to develop, implement and use SISP.

METHODOLOGY

The proposed research used the qualitative approach through interviews as it tends to be more exploratory in nature concerning the phenomenon being investigated.

The instrument used for this study is based on the studies of (Lederer & Sethi, 1992a; Earl, 1989) and modified to suit the context of this study. Interviews were used as the instrument to obtain detailed and

Table 2. Sample related studies on CSFs for SISP implementation

Research Paper	Theory	Method	Context	Findings

Zubovic et al. (2014)	CSFs	Conceptual	Australia	Proposed framework factors include:
				• SISP collaboration competency
				  o Executive collaboration
				  o Internal collaboration
				  o External collaboration
				• SISP personnel competency
				  o SISP Technical knowledge
				  o SISP Business knowledge
				  o SISP Managerial skills
				• SISP Sophistication
				  o Planning comprehensives
				  o Improvement in SISP capabilities
				  o SISP Alignment
				• SISP Contribution
				  o SISP Flexibility
				  o SISP Implementation Effective
				• Use of IT for Competitive Advantage

Yusoff (2015)	CSFs	Secondary data through review of literature	Generic	Success factors identified for SISP implementation are: • stakeholder and management support • the quality business strategic planning • SISP's strategic objectives • strengths of IT infrastructure, • sufficient human resource support and • choosing the right key operational operations

Nezakati, Harati, and Elahi (2014)	Not stated (literature review)	Quantitative survey	Middle East Countries	SISP success is influenced by:
				• Organizational attributes
				  o Change management
				  o Information Systems maturity
				• Interactive organizational attributes
				  o CEO and CIO relationship
				  o Top Management commitment
				• Strategic IT/IS planning dimensions
				  o strategic alignment
				  o environmental assessment

Byrd, Lewis, and Bradley (2006)	Not stated (Literature review)	Quantitative survey method	USA	The findings indicate • "a moderate relationship between the factors of senior IT leadership (the importance of the CIO and the presence of a varied IS advisory committee) and SISP, and • a strong relationship between SISP and three aspects of IS infrastructure (technical integration, application functionality, and data integration)".
Lederer and Sethi (1992b)	Not stated (Literature review)	Quantitative survey method	USA	Problems impeding the success of SISP implementation are: • "The influence of organization problems on hardware, cost, and database problems, and • the influence of the organization, hardware, cost, and database problems on implementation problems. • Cost problems had the largest direct effect on implementation problems."
Hoque et al. (2016)	Not stated (Literature review)	Secondary data through review of literature	Bangladesh	identified key challenges are: • "budget, • healthcare environment and culture, • lack of resources, • lack of motivation for top-level management and • end-user involvement".
Ankrah (2016)	System theory	Quantitative survey method	Ghana	The findings indicate that the most important SISP Success factors are: • "resources, • IS alignment to the business strategy • staff training and staff involvement • organizational and technological changes and • top management involvement"
Rishi and Goyal (2008)	Not stated (Literature review)	Quantitative survey method	India	Successful factors for SIS implementation are: • "Organizational culture • High turnover of professionals • Management involvement • Collaboration • System Standards • Resource Implementation • Resources availability • Market Competition • Organizational Bureaucracy • Organizational Autocracy"

in-depth responses to better understand the phenomenon. The instrument is divided into two sections. The first section seeks to find the background of the respondents and their firms. The second section comprises questions seeking the Nature of SISP implementation in Ghanaian firms as well as the methodology adopted and the success of SISP implementation and use. As the unit of analysis of this study is at the firm level, the target respondents were managers in middle to top management positions who have the technical know-how of their firms.

The purposive sampling method was used to select the qualified executives since not everyone can provide the requisite answers. Respondents were chosen based on their ability to provide accurate responses based on their positions (management) in their firms. In all, 15 respondents were interviewed from six firms cutting across different industries and sectors. The convenience sampling method was also used for respondents who were available and willing to partake in the study.

Data Collection

Primary data collections were done with the developed instrument through face-to-face interviews.

The essential information sources included fifteen (15) respondents, from financial institutions, telecommunication firms, and educational institutions. These sectors were considered based on their size, services rendered and customer base. The respondents were made up of 3 Chief Information Technology Officers (CITOs), 4 bank managers, 3 Information Systems managers, and 5 Business Analysts. The interviews were recorded, transcribed and presented to respondents to make corrections where required.

Analysis and Findings

Table 3 outlines the background and demographics of the respondents.

Table 3. Demographic of respondents

Position of Respondent	Sector	Number Interviewed	Length of Experience
Head of Information Technology IT Officer	Finance	6	5 – 20+ years
Chief IT Officer Deputy Chief IT officer IT Officer	Education	4	5 - 20+ years
IT Manager IT Officer	Telecommunication	5	5 - 17 years

Preliminary results indicated that firms from different sectors in Ghana have adopted and implemented SISP. From the findings, it was revealed that SISP has been adopted and implemented in firms in Ghana and the Earl's approach was very common among the responses obtained from respondents. It was also noted that SISP was the basis of their growth and has helped shape the focus of these firms in a positive direction. Respondents also acknowledged the fact that without SISP, implementation of their IT projects would have failed, therefore, the adoption and use of SISP helped their firm breakdown their IT projects implementation into a long term and short-term plan by prioritizing projects. A respondent said:

The company developed a business strategy with a great focus on IT as the pivot of growth. SISP is used in the implementation of IT projects such as application development and IT infrastructure, development of policies and enhancement to meet industry standards. SISP is used to break down IT implementation projects into long term and short-term plan by prioritizing projects.

Another respondent added:

SISP is how we use technology in fulðlling the strategy of the university this is achieved by having a roadmap that aligns technology to strategy. It takes cognizance of the current state and the desired state and steps to reach the desired state.

Also, in espousing what prompted the use of SISP, respondents explained that when an organization or firm wants to achieve its goals, they need to adopt and implement SISP. Furthermore, SISP activities must take into consideration the firms' tactics/strategies, therefore, some respondents stated that it was necessary to adopt strategies and tactics to fuel the growth of the firm through IT and to do that SISP was used. A respondent stated:

IS/IT strategy is part of the best practice in the industry and the industry evolves. So, it has as a matter of necessity.

Another said:

In view of this, management develops a business strategy with a high focus on IT capability to drive business goals. We had a lot of IT projects to carry out to keep in business and as a matter of fact budget allocation has to be managed adequately to achieve our objectives.

Considering the fact that respondents revealed the factors that influenced their adoption of SISP, it was very clear and evident that elements of Earl's (1990) approach was identified. Therefore, in relation to a business-led approach, respondents indicated that in looking at their operations and business process, they were able to know where and how to improve operations by introducing technology. Others said that by analyzing their business plan they were able to determine where to implement technological plans that will enhance their operation and make them gain a competitive advantage in their industry. A respondent said:

SISP is the basis for our growth since the commencement of the pension business. The company developed a business strategy with a great focus on IT as the pivot of growth...The SISP developed by the IT department was in alignment with the business strategy. Before IT comes out with SISP it conducts meetings with various departments to know departmental needs to know how their needs fit into the broad view of business strategy.

Another respondent added:

As a newly formed company trying to compete in the financial market or pension business, it was necessary to develop a tactics/strategy as to how IT could help the business to grow. In view of this, management develops a business strategy with a high focus on IT capability to drive business goals.

Respondents admitted that they employed techniques or methods in identifying and developing IS strategies for their firms. The method driven approach denotes the procedures or techniques adopted in identifying the IS needs of firms by assessing the goals of the firm (Earl, 1990; Boateng, 2017). In coming out with an effective IS strategy, the business objectives and operations of the firm must be considered. A respondent commented that:

In developing our Information System, we embarked on understanding the value chain of the organiza-tion, collected and analyzed the information needs of the organization, the present state of the systems and establishing the gaps to be addressed in order that the objectives of the core business processes (teaching, Learning, research) can be met in the most effective way and in alignment with the overarch-ing strategy of the Organization.

Another respondent added:

We kept our focus on the requirement of the business strategy, to help the department effort to achieve a common goal to avoid digression. IT strategy help in the allocation of resources for optimal results. IT strategy has helped us to focus on what to be achieved within a specific period.

It is paramount for a firm to align its operations and objectives with the techniques adopted to identify and develop an effective IS strategy for the growth of the firm.

Respondents acknowledged the need for capital to fund the implementation of IT projects in order to meet its objectives and grow the firm. Implementation of IT projects helps the firm to streamline its activities and enhances the operations and processes of the firm, therefore, making provisions in terms of money and other resources are very essential for the successful completion of the IT project. With the Administrative approach, the allocation of funds to finance and satisfy the expenses of IT projects within the firm must be made available. A respondent stated that:

We had a lot of IT projects to carry out to keep in business and as a matter of fact budget allocation has to be managed adequately to achieve our objectives.

However, some respondents confirmed that they faced some financial challenges in the implemen-tation of their IT/IS projects due to the fact that change management in the firm is handled poorly. A respondent argued that:

Problems include the availability of key financial and technical resources to develop and execute the strategy. In addition to this has been the reluctance to do things differently. Change management of at-titudes and processes has been challenging.

Respondents revealed that the implementation of SISP through the technology-driven approach has helped in the effective management of some rolled out enterprise applications that serve the needs of both the firm and their clients. The technology-driven approach ensures the development of technology infrastructures or architectures that supports the needs of applications. Respondents explained that IT systems architectures were put in place to support and manage the services of their applications in use. A respondent revealed that:

The enterprise architecture framework, the information systems strategy plan including the protocols for managing the systems.

Another respondent exclaimed that:

Through SISP the company has been able to implement IT solutions such implementation fund management system, implementation of online members portal, implementation USSD for customers checking the balances and get a mini statement on a pension contribution. Through the successful implementation of strategy, IT was able to implement document management systems as well as customer relationship management systems.

With the adoption of SISP through the organizational approach, respondents admitted that critical success factors for the successful implementation of I/IS projects were looked at. Earl (1989) stated that the organizational approach includes the ability of firms to identify certain themes such as challenges and success factors in implementing IT/IS projects. Respondents said that during their IT/IS project implementation, certain factors were considered and addressed in order to make the project implementation successful. A respondent stated that:

Key success factors include Management and stakeholder awareness and buy-in, general awareness creation, and an overarching corporate business strategy that provides the guidance for alignment as well as effective leadership skills of the IT organization.

Another respondent said:

Key success factors contributing to successful implementation are: executive Committee, comprising Managing Director and Deputy Managing Director were highly committed to the SISP implementations. There is a high level of management support as projects that are carried out by IT were alleviating the pain and stress involved in manual processes.

In terms of the major problems encountered during the SISP implementation, a respondent stated that:

Mainly costs involved in driving IS plans, firming up Technical understanding of Business needs, prioritization of other projects and alignment with the long-term plan of IS, regulatory requirements that must be met before full implementation and operating across regions with integrated systems, other cross border barriers/conditions must be cleared/met are the challenges faced.

Another respondent said:

Budgetary and financial constraints, cultural change and adaptability, lack of top management com-
mitment and their refusal to approve the budget, inadequate human resource, absence of IT/IS steering
committee, change management of attitudes and processes has been challenging

DISCUSSIONS

In this study, a number of objectives have been posed and these objectives were discussed with the conclusions provided to meet the goals mentioned earlier in this review.

In relation to the nature of SISP implementation in Ghanaian firms, it was found that firms from different sectors are aware and have already implemented SISP someway. From the analysis, the findings suggest that SISP implementation and its use is evident in firms from different sectors in Ghana. Some respondents revealed elements of the Earl's (1989) approach in their SISP implementation and identified influencing factors that aided in its use. However, few respondents indicated that their firms have implemented ISO 9000, which is a standard for quality management systems. Even though these firms have not implemented a traditional SISP approach, the ISO 9000 standard also possesses some characteristics of SISP. In relation to the influencing factors (critical success factors), respondents that had ISO 9000 implemented made mention of factors such as IS alignment to the business strategy, budget allocation and top management involvement. These factors can be likened to the influencing factors of SISP.

Nature of SISP Implementation in Ghanaian Firms

To begin, the first objective was to explore the nature of SISP implementation in Ghanaian firms. In exploring the factors that influence as enablers or inhibitors to the adoption, implementation, and use of SISP in Ghanaian firms, this study identified IS alignment to the business strategy, Environmental assessment, Budget, Awareness, Top management involvement as part of the factors that aid in the successful implementation of SISP in firms.

IS Alignment

With IS alignment to the business strategy, we found that the IS/IT strategies must conform and be in line with the business strategy. The business strategy determines how and where IS strategies are deployed and at which stage it's needed. Studies (Earl, 1990; Nezakati et al., 2014; Yusoff, 2015; Ankrah, 2016) confirm that understanding the business will go a long way to plan a better IS strategy for the firm. Environmental assessment is also an important factor in SISP implementation and use. For a firm to successfully implement SISP for its benefit must be able to assess its business environment to determine what is needed. Existing studies (Earl, 1989; Nezakati et al., 2014) confirms that having insights from your competitors will influence a good IS strategy suited for the firm's growth.

Budget

The successful implementation of IS/IT strategies is powered by available funds to finance such projects. Budget allocation plays a very key role in the implementation of SISP in firms. The findings suggest that the allocation of budget helps maintain the flow of IS/IT projects and lack of funds halts such projects affecting the growth of the firm. Studies (Earl, 1989; Hoque et al., 2016) agree that the allocation of funds to finance and satisfy the expenses of IT/IS project implementations will aid in a positive growth of a firm. Awareness of SISP was noted for firms in Ghana.

Awareness

Awareness is very important in the implementation and use of SISP among Ghanaian firms. Understanding the importance and the knowledge of how to use SISP to achieve organizational growth is paramount to these firms. Studies have stated that awareness and proper use of SISP enhance a firm's output and productivity (Zubovic et al., 2014).

Top Management Involvement

Top management involvement influences the SISP implementation process. They are to develop business strategies with a high focus on IT capability to drive business goals. Therefore, if top management does not support the business process in leveraging IS/IT strategies then, organizational growth will not be achieved. Studies (Earl, 1990; Rishi et al., 2008; Nezakati et al., 2014; Yusoff, 2015; Ankrah, 2016) have indicated that management involvement in SISP implementation will lead to the achievement of business goals.

Factors Enabling or Inhibiting SISP Adoption and Implementation in Ghanaian Firms

The second objective of this study was to explore the factors that influence as enablers or inhibitors to the adoption, implementation, and use of SISP in Ghanaian firms. In terms of the inhibiting factors to SISP implementation, the findings identified mainly costs involved in driving IS plans, firming up technical understanding of business needs, lack of top management commitment and their refusal to approve budget, prioritization of other projects and alignment with the long-term plan of IS, regulatory requirements, operating across regions with integrated systems, cultural change and adaptability, inadequate human resource, absence of IT/IS steering committee, and change management of attitudes and processes were identified to be the inhibiting factors to SISP implementation.

Lack of Funds

Whilst this list is not exhaustive as there are several more in various contexts, they are however in line with the findings of (Lederer & Sethi, 1991, 1998; Teo & Ang, 2001). Lack of funds has always been a determinant factor as an inhibitor since without funding, initiating, sustaining and completing most IT projects is not possible (Acheampong & Moyaid, 2016; Owusu, Agbemabiese, Abdurrahman, & Soladoye, 2017; Owusu, Ghanbari-baghestan, & Kalantari, 2017).

Technical Expertise

Technical understanding of business needs in the form of a champion is crucial for the surviving and sustainability of every business and as a result, the lack of an expert who understands these can lead to the right systems not being implemented for the firm's business needs (Owusu et al., 2017a; Acheampong & Moyaid, 2016; Owusu et al., 2017b).

Top Management Support

Top management support is usually inadequate but rather their commitment to a project is a key to the success of it (Owusu et al., 2017a; Acheampong & Moyaid, 2016; Owusu et al., 2017b). Thus, their involvement from the onset till the completion of the project is very crucial and this is not new when it comes to SISP implementation as well.

Regulatory Requirements

Regulatory requirements as an environmental factor is also a key to the success of most IT projects (Owusu et al., 2017a; Acheampong & Moyaid, 2016; Owusu et al., 2017b). Although, this may not be an internal factor, yet lack of proper regulatory framework can inhibit the successful implementation of SISP.

Culture

Cultural change and adaptability to new systems can also be challenging as people by nature are inherently conservative and are not susceptible to change (Aasi et al., 2016). Thus, they prefer doing things in their own way and this can be an inhibitor to SISP implementation.

Lack of Manpower

Another identified inhibitor to SISP is the lack of manpower. This is true as many managers may not know what SISP all is about and why it should be implemented in their organization. Thus, its implementation may not see light as the manager may not see the need (Brown, 2003).

Lack of IT/IS Steering Committee

Lastly, the lack of an IT/IS steering committee can also be an inhibitor to SISP implementation. This is so as the steering committee members decide on the priorities or order of business of an organization and manages the general course of its operations. They are also mandated to steer the affairs of the firm in terms of providing support, guidance, and oversight of the progress of projects. Thus, an absence of such a committee is a great disservice to the successful adoption and implementation of SISP in organizations (Brown, 2003; De Haes & Van Grembergen, 2004).

Table 4 and Figure 4 show a summary of the key findings for the study.

CONCLUSION

This study's objective was to explore the factors that influence as enablers or inhibitors to the adoption, implementation, and use of SISP in Ghanaian firms and in answering this query, we explored the SISP approach that was being used as well as the influencing factors for the adoption and implementation of

Table 4. Summary of key findings

Earl's Approach	Influencing Factor(s)	Findings
Business-led Approach	• IS alignment to the business strategy • Awareness • Environmental assessment • Budget • Top management involvement	A clearly presented business plan/strategy will become a good fit for or align well with an IS strategy implementation
Method driven Approach		In obtaining a successful IS goals in the firm, the best methods must be aligned with the business processes and objectives
Administrative Approach		allocation of funds to finance and satisfy the expenses of IT/IS project implementations will aid in the positive growth of a firm
Technological Approach		The development of a sound IT systems architecture put in place to support and manage the services of their applications will ensure growth by reducing application downtime.
Organizational Approach		Identification and development of key enabling themes help in the successful implementation of IT/IS projects.

Figure 4. Redefined Conceptual Framework (SISP Nature and Adoption in Ghanaian Organizations)

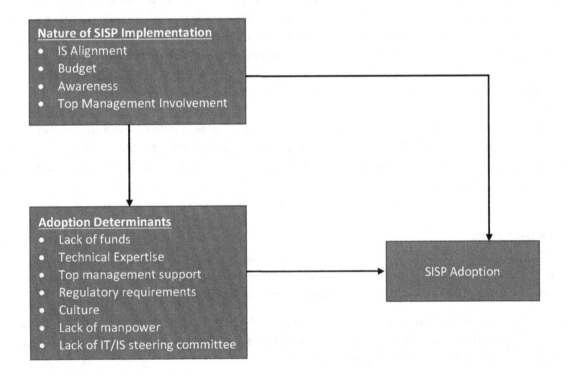

SISP in Ghanaian firms. We noticed that many firms have applied Earl's (1989) approach in their SISP implementation and factors such as IS alignment to the business strategy, Awareness, Environmental assessment, Budget, and Top management involvement were some of the critical success factors enabling the use of SISP. In addition, mainly costs involved in driving IS plans, firming up technical understanding of business needs, lack of top management commitment and their refusal to approve budget, prioritization of other projects and alignment with the long-term plan of IS, regulatory requirements, operating across regions with integrated systems, cultural change and adaptability, inadequate human resource, absence of IT/IS steering committee, and change management of attitudes and processes were identified to be the inhibiting factors to SISP implementation.

Implications

Theoretically, this study has contributed to the body of knowledge by revealing that most implementations of SISP in the Ghanaian context are through the Earl's approach. This is not surprising considering the nature of our organizations and the flexibility of Earl's approaches to SISP implementation compared to the more rigid approaches such as the Lederer and Sethi's. In addition, through the CSFs theory, the study was able to identify the various critical factors that enable organizations in Ghana to implement SISP.

In terms of policy implications, findings from this study are encouraging considering the fact that all the organizations understudied are using SISP in their strategic planning and management. It is therefore recommended to policymakers and government that all the organizations in charge of the new digitization policies being embarked upon such as the Ghana Post GPS, paperless port operations, the integrated e-immigration system, e-procurement, e-registrar, e-parliament, e-justice, e-cabinet, and smart workplaces are all implemented with SISP. In addition, it is highly recommended that the inhibiting factors such as regulatory requirements and operating across regions with integrated systems which are environmental factors are given the necessary attention by the government to enable firms to implement SISP with ease.

Limitations and Suggestions for Future Study

This study used a qualitative approach and interviewed fifteen respondents from four organizations in three industries. Although the results seem encouraging, yet it cannot be generalized for the entire Ghanaian context. Thus, future studies can conduct a quantitative study with many organizations to get the true picture of SISP implementation in Ghana.

REFERENCES

Aasi, P., Rusu, L., & Han, S. (2016). The Influence of Organizational Culture on IT Governance Performance: Case of The IT Department in a Large Swedish Company. doi:10.1109/HICSS.2016.638

Acheampong, O., & Moyaid, S. A. (2016). An integrated model for determining business intelligence systems adoption and post-adoption benefits in banking sector. *Journal of Administrative and Business Studies*, *2*(2), 84–100. doi:10.20474/jabs-2.2.4

Al-aboud, F. N. (2011). Strategic Information Systems Planning : A Brief Review. *International Journal of Computer Science and Network Security*, *11*(5), 179–183.

Alamri, S., Almutiri, N., Ballahmar, H., & Zafar, A. (2016). Strategic information system planning: A case study of a service delivery company. *Iarjset*, *3*(5), 78–84. doi:10.17148/IARJSET.2016.3518

Ali, R. H. R. M., Mohamad, R., Talib, Y. Y. A., & Abdullah, A. (2017). Strategic IS Planning Practices : A Case of Medium Manufacturing Company in Malaysia. In *SHS Web of Conferences* (Vol. 02006, pp. 1–6). 10.1051hsconf/20173402006

Alshubaily, N. F., & Altameem, A. A. (2017). The Role of Strategic Information Systems (SIS) in Supporting and Achieving the Competitive Advantages (CA): An Empirical Study on Saudi Banking Sector. *International Journal of Advanced Computer Science and Applications, 8,* 128–139.

Altameem, A. A., Aldrees, A. I., & Alsaeed, N. A. (2014). Strategic Information Systems Planning (SISP). In *Proceedings of the World Congress on Engineering and Computer Science* (Vol. I, pp. 22–24). San Francisco: WCECS.

Amrollahi, A., Ghapanchi, A. H., & Talaei-Khoei, A. (2013). A Systematic Literature Review on Strategic Information Systems Planning : Insights from the Past Decade. *Pacific Asia Journal of the Association for Information Systems, 5*(2), 39–66. doi:10.17705/1pais.05203

Ankrah, E. (2016). Strategic Issues in Information Systems Planning from the Ghanaian Perspective. *International Review of Management and Marketing, 6*(4), 1055–1065.

Boateng, R. (2017). *Information Technology Policy and Strategy: The Workbook Edition (The Workbook).* Accra: CreateSpace Independent Publishing Platform.

Brown, C. V. (2003). The IT organization of the future. In J. N. Luftman (Ed.), *Competing in the Information Age: Align in the Sand* (pp. 191–207). New York, NY: Oxford University Press; doi:10.1093/0195159535.003.0009

Bryson, J. M. (2011). *Strategic planning for public and nonprofit organizations: A guide to strengthening and sustaining organizational achievement* (Vol. 1). San Francisco, CA: Jossey-Bass.

Byrd, T. A., Lewis, B. R., & Bradley, R. V. (2006). Is Infrastructure : The Influence of Senior it Leadership and Strategic Information Systems Planning IS Infrastructure : The Influence Of Senior It Leadership And Strategic Information Systems Planning. *Journal of Computer Information Systems ISSN, 47*(1), 101–113.

De Haes, S., & Van Grembergen, W. (2004). IT governance and its mechanisms. *Information Systems Control Journal, 1,* 27–33.

Earl, M. J. (1989). *Management strategies for information technology.* Prentice-Hall, Inc.

Earl, M. J. (1990). Approaches To Strategic Information Systems Planning Experience In Twenty-One United Kingdom Companies. In ICIS 1990 Proceedings (pp. 271–277). Academic Press.

Earl, M. J. (1990). Approaches in Information Systems Planning. In R. D. Galliers & D. E. Leidner (Eds.), *Strategic information management: Challenges and strategies in managing information systems* (3rd ed., pp. 181–215). Butterworth-Heinemann.

Earl, M. J. (1993). Experiences in Strategic Information Systems Planning. *Management Information Systems Quarterly, 17*(March), 1–25. doi:10.2307/249507

Harun, H., & Hashim, M. K. (2017). Strategic Information Systems Planning : A Review Of Its Concept, Definitions And Stages Of Development. In *Proceedings of 3rd International Conference on Information Technology and Computer Science Held* (pp. 133–141). Bangkok: Academic Press.

Hoque, R. M., Hossin, E. M., & Khan, W. (2016). Strategic Information Systems Planning (SISP) Practices In Health Care Sectors Of Bangladesh. *European Scientific Journal*, *12*(6), 307–321. doi:10.19044/esj.2016.v12n6p307

Hovelja, T., Rožanec, A., & Rupnik, R. (2010). Measuring The Success Of The Strategic Information Systems Planning. *Management*, *15*(2), 25–46.

Hovelja, T., Vasilecas, O., & Rupnik, R. (2013). A Model Of Influences Of Environmental Stakeholders On Strategic Information Systems Planning Success In And Enterprise. *Technological and Economic Development of Economy*, *19*(3), 465–488. doi:10.3846/20294913.2013.818591

Irfan, M., Putra, S. J., Alam, C. N., Subiyakto, A., & Wahana, A. (2017). Readiness factors for information system strategic planning among universities in developing countries : a systematic review. In *2nd International Conference on Computing and Applied Informatics* (pp. 1–7). IOP Publishing.

Kamariotou, M., & Kitsios, F. (2015). Information Systems Phases and Firm Performance: A conceptual Framework. Paper presented at 1st International Conference on Business Informatics and Modelling.

Kamariotou, M., & Kitsios, F. (2015). Innovating with Strategic Information Systems Strategy. Paper presented at International Conference on Applied Innovation, Arta, Greece.

Kamariotou, M., & Kitsios, F. (2018). An Empirical Evaluation of Strategic Information Systems Planning Phases in SMEs : Determinants of Effectiveness. In Proceedings of 6th International Symposium and 28th National Conference on Operational Research (pp. 67–72). Retrieved from http://eeee2017.uom.gr/HELORS_2017_Book_of_Proceedings.pdf

Kaur, B. P., & Aggrawal, H. (2013). Exploration of Success Factors of Information System. *International Journal of Computer Science Issues*, *10*(1), 226–235.

King, W. R. (1988). How Effective is Your Information Systems Planning? *Long Range Planning*, *21*(5), 103–112. doi:10.1016/0024-6301(88)90111-2

Kitsios, F., & Kamariotou, M. (2016). Decision Support Systems and Business Strategy : A conceptual framework for Strategic Information Systems Planning. 2016 6th International Conference on IT Convergence and Security (ICITCS), 1–5. 10.1109/ICITCS.2016.7740323

Klouwenberg, M. K., Koot, W. J. D., & Van Schaik, J. A. M. (1995). Establishing business strategy with information technology. *Information Management & Computer Security*, *3*(5), 8–20. doi:10.1108/09685229510104945

Lederer, A. L. (2013). The Information Systems Planning Process Meeting the challenges of information systems planning. Strategic Information Management, 216.

Lederer, A. L., & Sethi, V. (1991). Critical dimensions of strategic information systems planning. *Decision Sciences*, *22*(1), 104–119. doi:10.1111/j.1540-5915.1991.tb01265.x

Lederer, A. L., & Sethi, V. (1991). Guidelines for strategic information planning. [PubMed]. *The Journal of Business Strategy*, *12*(6), 38–43. doi:10.1108/eb039454

Lederer, A. L., & Sethi, V. (1992a). Meeting the Challenges of Information Systems Planning. [PubMed]. *Long Range Planning, 25*(2), 69–80. doi:10.1016/0024-6301(92)90194-7

Lederer, A. L., & Sethi, V. (1992b). Root Causes of Strategic Information Systems Planning Implementation Problems. *Journal of Management Information Systems, 9*(1), 25–45. doi:10.1080/07421222.1992.11517946

Lederer, A. L., & Sethi, V. (1998). The Implementation of Strategic Information Systems Planning Methodologies. *Management Information Systems Quarterly, 12*(3), 445–461. doi:10.2307/249212

McFarlan, F. W., & McKenny, J. (1983). *Corporate Information Management: the issues facing senior management*. D OW-Jones-Irein.

Mentzas, G. (1997). Implementing an IS Strategy -A Team Approach. *Long Range Planning, 30*(1), 84–95. doi:10.1016/S0024-6301(96)00099-4

Merali, Y., Papadopoulos, T., & Nadkarni, T. (2012). Information systems strategy: Past, present, future? *The Journal of Strategic Information Systems, 21*(2), 125–153.

Musangu, L. M., & Kekwaletswe, R. M. (2011). Strategic Information Systems Planning And Environmental Uncertainty : *The Case Of South African Small Micro And Medium Enterprises. In IADIS International Conference Information Systems* (pp. 70–78). Academic Press.

Newkirk, H. E., Lederer, A. L., & Srinivasan, C. (2003). Strategic information systems planning : Too little or too much? *The Journal of Strategic Information Systems, 12*(3), 201–228. doi:10.1016/j.jsis.2003.09.001

Nezakati, H., Harati, A., & Elahi, R. (2014). Effective Attributes of Successful Strategic Information Systems Planning for Public Organizations in Middle East - Preliminary Study. *Journal of Applied Statistics, 14*(15), 1701–1710.

Nolan, R., & McFarlan, F. W. (2005). Information technology and the board of directors. [PubMed]. *Harvard Business Review, 83*(10), 96.

Owusu, A., Agbemabiese, G. C., Abdurrahman, D. T., & Soladoye, B. A. (2017). Determinants Of Business Intelligence Systems Adoption In Developing Countries : An Empirical Analysis From Ghanaian Banks. *Journal of Internet Banking and Commerce, 22*(S8), 1–25.

Owusu, A., Ghanbari-baghestan, A., & Kalantari, A. (2017). Investigating the Factors Affecting Business Intelligence Systems Adoption : A Case Study of Private Universities in Malaysia. *International Journal of Technology Diffusion, 8*(2), 1–25. doi:10.4018/IJTD.2017040101

Pollack, T. A. (2010). Strategic Information Systems Planning. In 2010 ASCUE Proceedings (pp. 47–58). Academic Press.

Porter, M. E. (1985). *The Competitive Advantage: Creating and Sustaining Superior Performance*. Free Press.

Premkumar, G., & King, W. R. (1991). Assessing Strategic Information Systems Planning. *Long Range Planning, 24*(5), 41–58. doi:10.1016/0024-6301(91)90251-I

Queiroz, M. (2017). Mixed results in strategic IT alignment research: A synthesis and empirical study. *European Journal of Information Systems*, *26*(1), 21–36.

Rackoff, N., Wiseman, C., & Ullrich, W. A. (1985). Information Systems for Competitive Advantage : Implementation of a Planning Process. *Management Information Systems Quarterly*, *9*(4), 285–294. doi:10.2307/249229

Rainer, R. K., Cegielski, C. G., & Prince, B. (2010). *Introduction to information systems: Supporting and transforming business* (3rd ed.). John Wiley & Sons.

Rangga, A. A., Setyohadi, D. B., & Santoso, A. J. (2017). Strategic Planning of Information System (Case Study: Ministry of Religious Affairs in Southwest Sumba). *International Journal of Computer Engineering and Information Technology*, *9*(7), 143–149.

Rishi, B. J., & Goyal, D. P. (2008). Article information. *Journal of Advances in Management Research*, *5*(1), 46–55.

Rockart, J. F. (1979). Chief executives define their own data needs. [PubMed]. *Harvard Business Review*, *57*(2), 81–93.

Samaha, K., & Dahawy, K. (2010). Information System Strategy Development and Implementation in the Egyptian Small and Medium Construction Enterprises. In E-Strategies for Technological Diffusion and Adoption: National ICT Approaches for Socioeconomic Development (pp. 88–121). IGI Global. doi:10.4018/978-1-60566-388-3.ch005

Synnott, W. R., & Gruber, W. H. (1982). *Information resource management: Opportunities and strategies for the 1980s*. John Wiley & Sons, Inc.

Teo, T. S. H., & Ang, J. S. K. (1999). Critical success factors in the alignment of IS plans with business plans. *International Journal of Information Management*, *19*(2), 173–185. doi:10.1016/S0268-4012(99)00007-9

Teo, T. S. H., & Ang, J. S. K. (2001). An examination of major IS planning problems. *International Journal of Information Management*, *21*(6), 457–470. doi:10.1016/S0268-4012(01)00036-6

Ullah, A., & Lai, R. (2013). A systematic review of business and information technology alignment. *ACM Transactions on Management Information Systems*, *4*(1), 1–30. doi:10.1145/2445560.2445564

Ward, J., & Peppard, J. (2002). *AM Strategic Planning for Information Systems*. Academic Press.

Yusoff. (2015). A Review on Critical Success Factors of SISP Nor Hanani binti Mohd Yusoff. The Journal of Management and Science, 1(2), 1–6.

Zubovic, A., Pita, Z., & Khan, S. (2014). A Framework For Investigating The Impact Of Information Systems Capability On Strategic Information Systems Planning. In *PACIS 2014* (p. 317). Proceedings; Retrieved from http://aisel.aisnet.org/pacis2014

ADDITIONAL READING

Basahel, A. M. (2018). Assessment of Strategic Information Systems Planning (SISP) Techniques From Requirement View. In Global Business Expansion: Concepts, Methodologies, Tools, and Applications (pp. 59-75). IGI Global.

Kamariotou, M., & Kitsios, F. (2019). Strategic information systems planning. In *Advanced Methodologies and Technologies in Business Operations and Management* (pp. 535–546). IGI Global; doi:10.4018/978-1-5225-7362-3.ch039

Kamariotou, M., & Kitsios, F. (2019, May). Information Systems Planning and Business Strategy: Implications for Planning Effectiveness. In Proceedings of the 8th International Symposium & 30th National Conference on Operational Research, Patras, Greece (pp. 16-18).

Kamariotou, M., & Kitsios, F. (2019, June). Information Systems Planning and Success in SMEs: Strategizing for IS. In *International Conference on Business Information Systems* (pp. 397-406). Springer, Cham. doi:10.1007/978-3-030-20485-3_31

Sarif, S. M., Rahman, N. A., Yunus, S. Y. M., & Ab Rahman, N. A. (2018, March). Strategic Information System Planning (SISP) Success: A Case Study. In *International Conference on Kansei Engineering & Emotion Research* (pp. 692-703). Springer, Singapore. doi:10.1007/978-981-10-8612-0_72

KEY TERMS AND DEFINITIONS

Administrative: This approach to SISP implementation entails the establishment of an IT capital and expense budget to satisfy approved projects.

Business Systems Planning (BSP): This approach to SISP implementation involves top-down planning with bottom-up implementation.

Business-Led: This approach to SISP implementation involves analysis of business plans to identify how and where IT/IS can most effectively enable these plans to be implemented.

Information Engineering (IE): This approach to SISP implementation provides techniques for building enterprise models, data models, and process models.

Method/1: This approach to SISP implementation consists of ten phases of work segments that an organization completes in creating its strategic plan.

Method-Driven: This approach to SISP implementation involves the use of techniques to identify IS needs by analyzing business processes and objectives.

Organizational: This approach to SISP implementation involves the identification of key themes for IT/IS projects – such as critical success factors for IT/IS projects.

PROplanner: This approach to SISP implementation involves helping planners to analyze the major functional areas within the organization.

SISP: A process that supports businesses in attaining their strategic objectives and goals by aligning their business strategy with information technology (IT).

Technology-Driven: This approach to SISP implementation involves the development of IT architectures as a foundation for expected application needs.

Chapter 2
Data Avalanche:
Harnessing for Mobile Payment Fraud Detection Using Machine Learning

Emmanuel Awuni Kolog

Business School, University of Ghana, Ghana

Acheampong Owusu

https://orcid.org/0000-0001-7789-5162

Business School, University of Ghana, Ghana

Samuel Nii Odoi Devine

Presbyterian University College, Ghana

Edward Entee

Business School, University of Ghana, Ghana

ABSTRACT

Globalizing businesses from developing countries require a thoughtful strategy and adoption of state-of-the-art technologies to meet up with the rapidly changing society. Mobile money payment service is a growing service that provides opportunities for both the formal and informal sectors in Ghana. Despite its importance, fraudsters have capitalized on the vulnerabilities of users to defraud them. In this chapter, the authors have reviewed existing data mining techniques for exploring the detection of mobile payment fraud. With this technique, a hybrid-based machine learning framework for mobile money fraud detection is proposed. With the use of the machine learning technique, an avalanche of fraud-related cases is leveraged, as a corpus, for fraud detection. The implementation of the framework hinges on the formulation of policies and regulations that will guide the adoption and enforcement by Telcos and governmental agencies with oversight responsibilities in the telecommunication space. The authors, therefore, envision the implementation of the proposed framework by practitioners.

DOI: 10.4018/978-1-7998-2610-1.ch002

INTRODUCTION

Information and communication technologies (ICT) have revolutionized the operations of business enterprises enabling them to embrace more flexible yet efficient approaches to improve customer intimacy. The pervasive impact of ICT can be seen in the developed economies where the transformation has been rapid, with frequent technological innovations to meet societal changes. Conversely, the pace of digital innovations in the developing economies, especially Africa, has been slow over the period (UNCTAD Report, 2018) with many of the businesses relying on the west for technological innovations. This can be attributed to the low level of education on the continent. Nevertheless, the digital revolution has not only brought about efficiency in human activities but has heightened competition in all aspects of business activities. These competitions are not only among businesses wanting to survive but also among individuals competing for superiority. People, for example, are engrossed with technology and inherently desire for the latest and fastest available technologies, such as high-speed mobile phones. The urge for these advances in technological innovations essentially stems from the desire to compete and survive in an increasingly competitive business environment (Obrdovic, 2016). Essentially, while trying to survive in the business ecosystem, the innovative paradigm is geared towards the integration of ICT into automating business processes.

Every serious organization seeks to commit resources into technology innovations in order to survive (Baron & Spulber, 2017). Disruptiveness is the result of many technological breakthroughs. Disruptive innovation is one that generates or drives the formation of new markets and value networks which ultimately leads to the disruption of current markets and the entire value chain from the organizational perspective to their products and related services (Rahman et al., 2018). Presently, to survive and compete favourably through innovative approaches, the paradigm leans towards technology. Accordingly, many companies have invested heavily in ICT infrastructure to stay in business by improving customer intimacy. These businesses must keep challenging the technological status quo at any given time to rapidly create value for customers thereby motivating a disruptive technology. Notably, while the current generation is seamlessly focusing on improving human interactions and communications through technology, there exists the side effect of technology usage. Sadly, as many businesses and individuals are capitalizing on harnessing the potential of the internet to improve their business decisions, others use the internet to commit crimes. In Africa, these crimes, often through social engineering, are committed by fraudsters who take advantage of people's ignorance and greed. In Section 4, these authors have delved into some social engineering strategies that fraudsters use in defrauding mobile money users in Ghana.

Globalizing businesses from developing countries require a thoughtful strategy and adoption of state-of-the-art technologies in order to meet up with a rapidly changing global society. To be competitive in the business environment, a profound understanding of customers' behaviours towards a brand, services and/or products is required. The avalanche of unstructured and structured data, from the web or operational databases, can be harnessed to understand customers' behaviour through data mining with machine learning techniques (Femima & Sudheep (2015). However, many businesses in the developing countries have not capitalized on the potentials of data mining, such as classification, forecasting and clustering, to inform business decisions. This partly informs the reason for this chapter. This situation has been largely attributed to the level of ignorance and lack of knowledge exhibited by corporate managers and related portfolios in the developing country context.

As we are inundated with an avalanche of data, this chapter presents the impact of data mining on business decisions. This chapter is grounded on a review of machine learning approaches with linkage to the developing country context, especially in Africa. Based on the review, the authors have proposed a data mining with a machine learning technique to detect fraud in mobile money activities in Ghana. The technique, also presented as a framework, is to provide real-time detection of fraud through mobile communications. The authors envision that this proposed framework will be adopted by the telecommunication companies to curb the menace on mobile money fraud.

The rest of the sections are presented as follows: Section two presents an overview of existing data mining approaches to business and how these strategies can be leveraged for business decisions. Section three unpacks the definition of data mining with machine learning. The various machine learning techniques are discussed in this section as well. Section four exemplifies the application of machine learning in Mobile Money (MoMo) fraud detection while Section five discusses the study's findings and their implications to policy and academia. Section six concludes the chapter by reflecting on the entire research process.

BACKGROUND

Data Mining Defined

The use of data mining technique to discover knowledge to aid management decisions at all levels (operational, tactical and strategic) of the organizational ladder is a long-established fact. Like many information system (IS) technologies, which comes with different definitions as they are seen as umbrella terms and mean different things to different people, so is data mining. There are several definitions of data mining (DM). Some of the key definitions from both the perspective of academia and industry are discussed in this section.

Gartner (2019) views data mining as a process that focuses on identifying correlations, relevant patterns and trends, meticulously selected from massive datasets resident in some repository. Equally, Hand (1998) also opines that DM is a process of probing data in the quest to ascertain previously unknown associations in the data that are aligned to a user's key interests. In agreement, Weiss and Indurkhya (1998) classify DM as a domain that promotes search of massive volumes of data to discover valuable information. Han and Kanber (2006) posit DM as an interdisciplinary field encompassing computer science and others in order to discover new patterns from some massive dataset. Similarly, Tembhurne, Adhikari and Babu (2019) argue that, as a multifaceted process, DM applies a fusion of approaches from machine learning, statistics and database systems targeted at obtaining information from big data sets.

Others (Ricardo & Barbosa, 2019; Nigania, 2019) situate DM as "nothing but the extraction of data from large databases for some specialized work." These researchers refer to it as knowledge discovery in databases. Westfall (2017) simplify the term DM as the use of statistics and modelling to analyze significant chunks of disparate information and see if they connect in some way. DM is also considered to be a tool of business intelligence (BI) for knowledge discovery (Wang and Wang, 2008). As such, data mining can be carried out in various forms (Ricardo & Barbosa, 2019; Nigania 2019). These include web mining, text mining, video & audio data mining, pictorial data mining, and social networks data mining (Ricardo & Barbosa, 2019; Nigania, 2019). In spite of the myriad of definitions given to data mining by various scholars, they all point to the concept of dealing with big data and using mathematical/ statistical techniques to uncover hidden patterns in data, which can aid in the decision-making process.

Historically, the use of data mining applications in businesses has its origin in the early '90s where highly skilled IT personnel were required due to the technicalities and complexity of the methods and tools involved. However, in recent times, the story is quite different due to the advancement of ICT which has led to the proliferation of data gathering in modern organizations. With the emergence of big data, advanced data mining techniques, often machine learning related, DM has become an imperative tool in any business seeking to remain relevant and gain a competitive edge. Most of the modern data mining tools are highly automated which usually does not require the services of highly skilled IT personnel.

In businesses today, DM applications involve generally a three-step process (Brian & Westfall, 2017). The three-step process involves: *Identifying your data sources*, *Picking the data points from data sources* and *Applying and testing a model that best connects the data points*. As earlier alluded, the applications of DM in today's business is vast and of diverse nature. For example, DM applications are widely used in direct marketing where predictive modelling can enable the analyst to know which of the available channels (print advertising, telemarketing, radio, television advertising, etc.) is best to use in their interaction with customers. Additionally, online scam and other fraudulent activities have heightened the need for using DM techniques to detect. This study seeks to demonstrate the application of data mining to detect fraud in a mobile scam. There is a plethora of evidence in both practice and literature that point to DM applications in the health, education, retail, consumer goods, telecommunication and financial sectors. These applications enable firms to understand consumer research marketing, product, demand and supply analysis, investment trend in stocks and real estates, fault and fraud detection (Peter, 2018).

With the emergence of business intelligence data mining (BIDM), leading corporate houses today are able to stay ahead of their competitors (Ricardo & Barbosa, 2019). Through business intelligence, firms can obtain the latest information and use it for market research, competition analysis, economic forecasting, industry analysis, consumer behaviour analysis, geographical information analysis among others. Thus, BIDM aids firms in decision-making (Ricardo & Barbosa, 2019). Ismail (2017) suggests the integration of DM in businesses to include budgeting and marketing spending in order to optimize budget allocations across marketing drivers. Furthermore, the monitoring of customer behaviour, market changes and trends, setting up of best prices and the categorization of different products based on consumer preferences constitute major returns for DM integration in business operations (Ismail, 2017).

Related Works in Data Mining Applications

Since the inception of the data mining concept in the early 90s, there has been a myriad of literature, from both academia and practitioners, describing the application of DM. As DM is a technology, the literature covers diverse disciplines in business, education, healthcare, crime prevention and detection. Ozyirmidokuza, Uyar and Ozyirmidokuz (2015) studied data mining based on its application to a company's marketing channel with the aim of extracting knowledge to improve the efficiency of its marketing system. Using Cross Industry Standard Process for Data Mining (CRISP-DM) to analyze their survey data, the researchers were able to develop a C5.0 Decision Tree model fit for predicting a company's marketing channel complaints, with a high level of accuracy while extracting decision rules.

The rise of fraud-related cases in electronic commerce prompted Guo and Li (2008) to model the sequence of operations in credit card transaction processing using a confidence-based neural network. Based on the model the researchers were able to propose a framework for detection of fraud-related cases in electronic commerce transactions. With this approach, the researchers introduced receiver operating characteristic analysis technology to ensure the accuracy and effectiveness of fraud detection algorithms.

The fraud detection technique was purely based on the training of a neural network with training data. The model created was made to analyze incoming data to ascertain whether the unseen data is fraud or not. Thus, the technique leans on supervised machine learning where the classification process was applied.

Femima and Sudheep (2015) developed a model, based on an efficient CRM Data mining framework, to predict customer behaviour. Their model enhanced strategies for decision making in the retention of valued customers through the prediction of customer behaviours. They later proposed an efficient CRM data mining framework with two classification models, Naïve Bayes and Neural Networks (NN). After evaluating the two models, NN emerged superior over the Naïve Bayes classifier. Similarly, Daskalaki et. (2003) built a decision support system (DSS) to deal with customer indebtedness for a large telecommunication company. Their model described a process for building a predictive model by employing knowledge discovery and data mining techniques in vast amounts of heterogeneous as well as noisy data and provided a promising proposed model, with a useful tool, in the decision-making process.

Timely and accurate decision making in modern firms is crucial to remain in business and gain competitive advantage. To do this, businesses strive to use modern tools and technologies that can aid management in their operational, tactical and strategic decision-making processes. This is where data mining, business intelligence and analytics come into play. Businesses require *descriptive analytics* to know what is happening to their firms, *diagnostic analytics* to explain why things are going wrong, *predictive analytics* to know how things will be in the future and *prescriptive analytics* to be able to combine different alternatives and gain competitive advantage.

Thelwell (2019), identified areas in business where data mining applications are widely used and matured to aid in management decision making. These include retail where DM and BI are used to segment customers into "Recency, Frequency, Monetary (RFM) groups and target marketing and promotions to those different groups". For instance, a customer who on a regular basis purchases product at a lower price is likely to be rewarded or treated differently than one who performs a onetime or not so frequent purchase but as a comparatively large transaction. As the regular customer receives loyalty offers, upsell or cross-sell offers, the other may be given a win-back offer. In the telecommunication sector, especially in the mobile network operator niche, where a massive set of data is generated daily, DM and BI are best suited for use in predicting the churned rate of customers. In addition to this, the activities of customers can easily be analysed to provide tailor-made services to them. This is carried out by the collation of billing information, customer service interactions and other metrics to allot probability scores to customers, thereby enabling target offers and incentives to be directed at specific customers suspected of desiring to churn.

Moreover, with the insurgence of criminal activities involving theft of customer data and services, particularly identity theft, scam calls and fraudulent payment transactions, DM approaches can be used to effectively arrest the situation. In e-commerce, DM and BI are used extensively through upselling and cross-selling, and other approaches to help customer browsing experience. For instance, like the browsing experience offered by Pinterest and Houzz, Amazon developed a machine learning-powered visual tool that implements a view and likes or dislike product mechanism to enhance the product browsing experience of customers that works with their recommendation system. Through DM techniques, retail companies are able to forecast based on the buying patterns of their customers. Again, apart from the corporate world, data mining and analytics are also used in crime agencies to identify fraudulent tendencies across myriads of data geared towards assisting in investigations and discovering potentially activities from location-based services to counter-terrorism activities (Thelwell, 2019).

Hung, Yen and Wang (2006) applied data mining techniques to manage telecom customers' churn. With empirical evaluation and through different data mining techniques, their findings indicated that both decision tree and neural network techniques can deliver accurate churn prediction models through the analyses of customer demographics and their billing information, contract/service status, call records detail, in addition to service changelogs. Goyal and Vohra (2012) applied data mining in higher education with the aim of proposing the use of data mining techniques to improve the efficiency of higher education institutions. Their conceptual paper delivered the areas that data mining techniques such as clustering, decision tree and association can be applied to higher education processes to assist students in improving their performance, life cycle management, course selection, and in order to measure their retention rate and the grant fund management of the institution.

Lausch, Schmidt, and Tischendorf (2015), in their study, aimed at illustrating the potential of data mining for different research areas by means of sample applications. They observed that most of the conventional data mining methods and techniques are restricted to isolated or "silo" datasets which remain primarily stand-alone and specialized in nature. Thus, highly complex and mostly interdisciplinary questions in environmental research cannot be answered sufficiently using isolated or area-based data mining approaches. They, therefore, proposed the linked open data (LOD) approach as a new possibility in support of complex and inter-disciplinary data mining analysis and explained the LOD using examples from medicine and the environment.

Mishra, Kumar and Gupta (2014) predicted student's performance using data mining techniques. Their aim was to predict the success or failure of students in MCA. Therefore, data of students of colleges affiliated to Guru Gobind Singh Indraprastha University was used to predict their third-semester performance. Their performance prediction model was built based on classification techniques through students' social integration, academic integration, and various emotional skills which have not been considered so far. Two algorithms J48 (Implementation of C4.5) and Random Tree was used.

Iqbal (2018), using data mining techniques and methods, attempted to analyse the role of data mining and its contribution to solving business problems in banking and finance by finding patterns, causalities, and correlations in business information and market prices that are not immediately apparent to managers because of the global market competition and market volatility. The researcher through his conceptual paper highlighted the application of data mining that has definitely a positive impact on risk management, portfolio management, trading, customer profiling and customer care, where data mining techniques can be used in banks and other financial institutions to enhance performance through efficient decision-making.

Correspondingly, Milovic and Milovic (2012) in their study presented a data mining approach to predicting and decision making in health care. Their conceptual paper highlighted areas in healthcare that data can be beneficial and presented patterns that can be used by physicians to determine diagnoses, prognoses and treatments for patients in healthcare organizations. Mosley (2012) research on "Social Media Analytics: Data Mining Applied to Insurance Twitter Posts" presented various techniques and methods through which data mining can be used in social media. The researcher discussed the application of correlation, clustering, and association analyses to social media and demonstrated this by analyzing insurance Twitter posts. His findings indicate the identification of keywords and concepts in social media data and can facilitate the application of relevant information by insurers.

Lee (2013) in his conceptual paper highlighted approaches in which data mining and text mining can be used in business analytics in order to support business competitiveness. His discussion and presentation drew a distinction between data mining, business analytics and business intelligence. He further provided suggestions on how electronic businesses can leverage data mining to enhance their competitiveness. Sharma, Shrivastava and Kumar (2011) presented approaches and methods to extract the useful information on the web and also give the superficial knowledge and comparison about data mining. Their paper discusses issues about the current, past and future of web mining, and introduces online resources for retrieval of information on the web and the discovery of user access patterns from web servers, which improves the data mining drawback. In addition, they also described web mining through cloud computing (cloud mining) and asserted that can be seen as the future of Web Mining.

DATA MINING WITH MACHINE LEARNING

Making sense from data with machine learning is touted as the fastest-growing technique for data analytics. SAS analytics views machine learning as "an application of artificial intelligence (AI) that provides systems with the ability to automatically learn and improve from experience without being explicitly programmed" (Mullakara, 2017). Machine learning focuses on the development of computer programs that can access data and use it to learn for themselves. Machine learning encompasses two learning approaches: Supervised (classification) and unsupervised (Clustering) learning.

Classification

Supervised learning involves the task of learning a function that maps an input to an output based on input-output pairs. Notable supervise machine learning approaches are classification and association rule mining. With machine learning classification, the data to be analysed is tagged with a predefined class or category (corresponding output). This is where the input (x) and output (Y) variables are involved. The input variable is mapped to the output variable, i.e. $Y=f(x)$. Thus, a machine learning algorithm is developed to learn the mapping function from the input to the output. The goal is to approximate the mapping function (model) so well that when you have new input data (x) you can predict the output variables (Y) for that data. Learning stops when the algorithm achieves an acceptable level of performance. Figure 1 shows a pictorial view of a classification process. As indicated in Figure 1, classification involves two different phases: *training and prediction.* In classification, the labelled data has to be partitioned into training and testing data.

Labelling (annotation) of input data can be carried out in three different ways: *manual, automatic and semi-automatic* (Kolog et al., 2018). The *manual labelling* is where experts, usually from a subject domain, are made to analyse the instances of the input data and label them with predefined output class or labels, such as basic emotion categories in emotion classification. With this labelling technique, Kolog *et al.* (2016) investigated the inherent influence that people have on tagging emotional antecedents with plutchnik's basic emotional classes. The researchers found that people's self-emotions and external factors, such as domestic challenges, affect their perception when labelling emotional class (output) to other people's emotional antecedents (input data). The *automatic labelling* involves the use of software applications that are developed, usually from natural language processing, to label input data with a predefined class or category. The *semi-automatic* labelling involves the combination of both the manual and automatic labelling. In all these annotation techniques, the training data should be larger than the testing data. Kappa statistics is expected to be established to define the strength of agreements after labelling.

Figure 1. Classification process

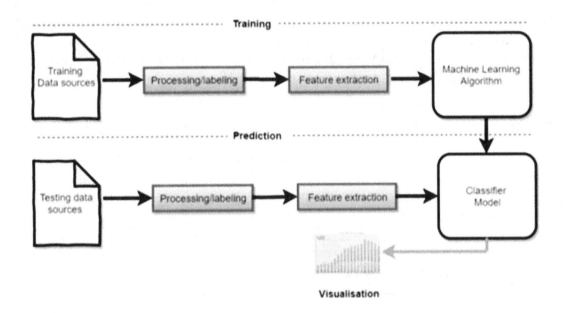

In the training phase, as indicated in Figure 1, the training data is fed into the machine algorithm for learning. Before that, features are extracted from the instances of the training data. The feature extraction techniques play a key role in the quality of the output (results). Several techniques have been used to extract features from training data for a machine learning classifier to learn. Notable feature extraction techniques include the use of Parts-of-Speech-Tagging (POST), term frequency-inverse document frequency (td-idf) among others. The features are fed into a machine learning algorithm aiming to create a model for predicting unseen data. In support vector machine classifier, for instance, the extracted features in the learning process are parsed into numerical data points expressed in high dimensional vector space and eventually separated by a hyperplane. The hyperplanes are decision boundaries that help classify the data points. Irrespective of the feature extraction techniques, extracting features for the classifier involves minimizing or eliminating *stopping words* such as "*is*" and "*the*" in a data. The remaining content after the removal of the stopping words is the *features*. The goal of the training phase is to create a model for classification. After the model is created, the unseen test data by the algorithm is fed into the model for the classification. The unseen data is classified according to the predefined labels or tags. However, the testing data has to go through a similar feature extraction process before the classification. It has been established that the accuracy of the predictive algorithm partly depends on the quality of the data.

The predictive algorithm is expected to be evaluated. The machine learning algorithm can be evaluated using several metrics such as *recall, precision, f-measure*. The proportion of the test data recognized by the learning algorithm during testing is referred to as the *recall,* while the proportion of the recognized data by the learned algorithm is compared with the expected test data and proportion that is accurate relative to the expected test data is the *precision*. The f-measure is the harmonic mean of the recall and the precision. According to Kouch and Landis (1977), the acceptable threshold for the classifier performance is 70% and above. Given a binary classification, equations 1 – 3 are formulas for computing the recall, precision and f-measure, where *TP* is true positing, *FP* is False positives and *FN* is false negatives.

Other evaluation metrics for classifier evaluation include the Receiver Operating Characteristic (ROC) curve, which is a graphical plot that illustrates the diagnostic ability of a binary classifier system as its discrimination threshold is varied (Norris, 2019). The ROC curve is created by plotting the true positive rate against the false positive rate at various threshold settings.

$$Recall = \frac{TP}{TP + FN} \qquad (1)$$

$$Precision = \frac{TP}{TP + FP} \qquad (2)$$

$$F - measure = \frac{2 * (Recall * Precision)}{(Recall + Precision)} \qquad (3)$$

Clustering

Clustering is unsupervised learning. Unlike supervised learning, unsupervised learning is where the input data (x) do not have a corresponding output (Y). The instances of the input data are not tagged or labelled. The goal of unsupervised learning is to identify patterns in the input data by modelling the underlying structure or distribution in the data. The algorithms are left to their own to discover and present the interesting structure, thus natural groupings, in the data (Karthik, 2015). This process is called clustering. In clustering, the pattern is clustered based on the similarities in the data. In business data, clustering can be applied to discover the inherent groupings in the data, such as grouping customers by purchasing behaviour. Clustering is preferred in situations where the data is large. In manual labelling, for instance, it is expensive and time-consuming to get experts to adjudicate and label the data.

Since labelling of input data is not required in clustering, some practitioners rather prefer to use clustering to identify the pattern and used the clustered patterns as labels for the input data. Nevertheless, to use classification or clustering depends on the data and the objectives at hand. In this work, a similar approach has been proposed for fraud detection in Section 4. In a related study, Kolog et al. (2018) used a similar approach to detect social influence and sentiments in text. The researchers developed a technique to cluster their input data with *k-means* algorithm using Euclidean distance for the similarity measure. The clusters (parent, staff and peers) were used as class labels for classification. Among several existing algorithms for clustering, K-means and hierarchical algorithms are the widest and commonly used for discovering patterns in data. Figure 2 shows a typical 3D pictorial view of data points that have been clustered. In clustering, similarity the measure among the data points is key to discover patterns. The similarity measure is the measure of how much alike two data objects or points are. Similarity measure, in a data mining context, is a distance with dimensions representing features of the objects. Euclidean

Figure 2. Typical diagram for datapoints displayed and clustered using k-means algorithm

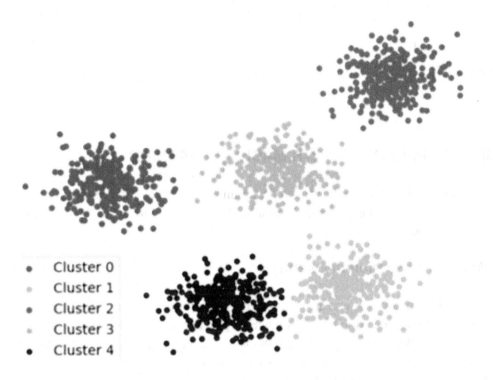

and Cosine similarity measures are the most widely used in clustering. For instance, assuming points **p** = $(p_1, p_2,..., p_n)$ and **q** = $(q_1, q_2,..., q_n)$ in Figure 1, the Euclidean distance between p and q is the length of the line segment connecting them{\displaystyle {\overline {\mathbf {p} \mathbf {q} }}}. The Euclidean distance between the points, using Pythagoras theorem, is computed in the equation (1).

$$d(p,q) = d(q,p) = \sqrt{(q_1 - p_1)^2 + (q_2 - p_2)^2 + ... + (q_n - p_n)^2} \qquad (4)$$

$$= \sqrt{\sum_{i}^{n}(q_i - p_i)^2} \qquad (5)$$

The clustering algorithms are expected to be evaluated to ascertain their efficacy. The commonly used evaluation metric is *Silhouette* index. Silhouette refers to a "method of interpretation and validation of consistency within clusters of data. The technique provides a succinct graphical representation of how well each object has been classified." (Rousseeuw, 1987). The index rates the performance of the clustering algorithm from -1 to +1 where +1 is the highest (strong) while the -1 is the lowest (weak). Silhouette is a measure of cohesion of objects or datapoints in a cluster. The Silhouette index [S(i)] is computed using the mean intra-cluster distance (a) and the mean nearest-cluster distance (b) for each sample. From equation 6, the a(i) is the average dissimilarity of ith object to all other objects in the same cluster while b(i) is the average dissimilarity of ith object with all objects in the closest cluster.

$$S(I) = \frac{(b(i) - a(i))}{(\max\{(a(i), b(i))\}} \qquad (6)$$

DATA MINING APPLICATION WITH MACHINE LEARNING

In this section, we exemplify the application of data mining on mobile money fraud detection in Ghana. A mobile transaction scenario is presented, and a model is deduced to aid in the detection of mobile payment fraud in Ghana.

Mobile Money Transaction in Ghana

Mobile money (MoMo) payment is a growing service that provides opportunities for both the formal and informal sectors in Ghana. Mobile money payment provides secured mobile or online platforms for payment transactions. Despite its importance in mobile money transactions, fraudsters have capitalized on the vulnerabilities of users to defraud them (Chatain et al., 2011). Attempts have been made by the government to tackle the fraudulent in the activities of mobile money space in Ghana. The Minister of communication recently reported that:

The introduction of mobile money has suffered from attempts at defrauding the system by malicious actors. In 2017, one of the telecommunication companies reported that it received about 365 complaints of fraud monthly from its subscribers. The scale of attempts at fraud are staggering as it also indicated that it filtered all the SMS messages that passed through its platforms and blocked more than 400,000 scammed messages on a daily basis, from reaching their recipients. (Ghanaweb, 2018).

With regards to the mobile money payment usage in Ghana, it has been observed that scammers approach their victims from two different angles. The first is by appealing to the emotions or conscience of the intended victim for help. The second is via a claim of familiarity while offering to provide assistance either to win a fictitious prize or guide through a process to understand efficient methods of transferring money from their wallets or managing their MoMo accounts and credentials. With the first approach, the fraudster may report making a mistake in wrongly transferring funds to the account of the intended victim. The fraudster appeals to the emotions and conscience of the victim to revert the funds to the fraudster's account. Another technique that appeals to the emotion of the victim, is to pose as a relative, close acquaintance or associate who requires immediate help for some critical need, such as a medical emergency or being stranded at a place, and therefore seeks urgent assistance. This is often done in a hasty manner via a call in a hysteric tone with claims of having no call credit and therefore borrowing another's phone.

Another claim is that the relation or friend of the victim has asked the fraudster to make the call on their behalf due to their critical condition. With the second approach, the first instance is, the fraudster may claim to be an acquaintance seeking to provide a business opportunity that would require some payment of money. These fraudsters often acquire details of the victims through their social media accounts or via eavesdropping on their conversation when they visit MoMo agents to conduct a transaction. Another instance is the claim that a victim has won a prize and to receive the said price, a small fee has to be paid to obtain it. The remaining defrauding techniques are deployed by posing as an employee of a Telco. The fraudster comes in to provide some assistance to the unsuspecting victim. The claim is either to educate the victim of an efficient and quicker way to transfer money or an intriguing narration of how to easily receive money. Both processes end up with monies being unwillingly transferred from the victim's account. The last of these is where the PIN of the victim is requested for or fraudulently acquired by leading the victim to willingly provide their PIN to a supposed Telco employee, often with the basis that the Telco needs its MoMo subscriber to follow some steps to upgrade or facilitate a transaction which that leads to the transfer of funds and/or acquisition of their PIN.

Scenario: Mobile money and Fraudulent Activities in Ghana

As Ghana makes efforts towards a cash lite and cashless society, the adoption of e-payment methods has become increasingly relevant both in the traditional and non-traditional banking sectors. Mobile money (MoMo) is a service, provided by a telecommunication company, designed to enable one to keep and manage electronic money in an account (wallet) connected to a mobile phone, similar to that of a bank account. According to the Bank of Ghana (BoG), as of the 1st quarter of 2019, the number of active MoMo accounts was 12,725,649. The transaction can be done both locally and internationally. The total number of transactions between the same period was 436,723,487, amounting to GHS 66,356.41 Million (BoG, 2019). The platform is provided by Telecommunication/ Mobile Network Operators (Telcos). Among the Telcos operating in Ghana, MTN has the largest market share. The Telcos operate in collaboration with their banking partners and via accredited agents. These banks act as the providers and keepers of the funds while the agents act as the means by which the service is received. The agent provides means of either sending or receiving money. Internationally, they operate through money transfer services such as Western Union. The main beneficiaries are registered customers, thus subscribers, of the Telcos. All transactions are tied to a mobile number. However, a non-subscriber can send or receive MoMo using a token at any agent or bank. Most banks now in Ghana facilitate MoMo services. On their MoMo platform, several services are provided which may not necessarily be passed through agents. A subscriber can pay utility bills or pay directly for a service or product to a registered MoMo collection service provider or payment point, who may not be an agent. The MoMo service is accessed by dialing a USSD code provided by the Telco. Other services available include financial services such savings, insurance, loans, etc. A subscriber can also retrieve cash from their e-wallet via an agent or bank.

A subscriber may also tie their MoMo account to their bank account. To retrieve MoMo, the subscriber visits an agent or bank. The subscriber then allows cash out to initiate the withdrawal of funds. The agent requests the amount to be withdrawn from subscriber's account that is tied to the mobile number. The subscriber enters a 4-digit PIN and based on the amount requested for, 1% is deducted directly as transaction cost from the subscriber's account. If a transfer is transacted from a bank to a subscriber's wallet, depending on the bank charges, an amount is deducted from their bank account and credited to the e-wallet with no charge being placed on the subscriber. MoMo interoperability is currently being facilities by Ghana e-Payment System.

MoMo transaction has attracted scammers who have been defrauding MoMo subscribers. Several strategies and techniques are employed by fraudsters to defraud patrons of MoMo. These strategies come mainly in the form of text sent as SMS and via telephone calls. The fraudsters contact an unsuspecting victim by posing as an agent, a casualty of a wrong payment/transfer or employee of the Telco providing the Momo service. The SMS messages are often sent using a mobile number from the same Telco the unsuspecting victim receives MoMo services from. For instance, if the intended victim uses MTN, the fraudster will use MTN mobile number to send the SMS message or make the voice call. These fraudulent SMS messages are often riddled with wrong information, poor grammar and spelling mistakes. The calls are presented in two main forms. In the first approach, the fraudster may call claiming the wrong transfer of funds sent by an agent, another subscriber or themselves. The second approach extends the first by now linking with another fraudster who possess as an employee of a Telco. They simulate the call process that registers as a means of obtaining assistance from the Telco. These techniques are focused on socially engineering the victim into agreeing to follow some steps leading to the transfer of money from their account or as a phishing expedition leading to their MoMo transaction Personal Identification Number (PIN) being released to the fraudster.

Machine Learning Application for Fraud detection in Mobile Money Transactions

With the mobile money (MoMo) scenario above, we exemplify the application of data mining with machine learning to detect MoMo fraud. This takes into account the analysis of the various sources of mobile money data, processing of such data into a cleaned data suitable for extracting features and a proposed hybrid machine learning technique for detecting fraud in the data. Figure 3 is the proposed

Figure 3. Proposed framework for detecting fraud in Mobile money transaction

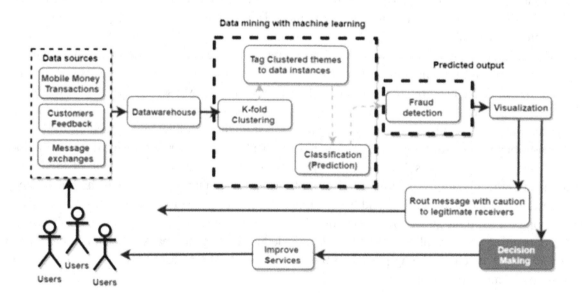

framework for the automated fraud detection system. The subsequent subsections detail the processes in the framework.

Data Source

As indicated in Section 4, data from mobile money transactions can be tracked, archived and analysed to detect fraud cases to minimize or avoid fraudulent activities. Messages and phone calls from one user to the other first goes to the servers of the telecommunication companies before routing to the receivers. While keeping in mind the data protection laws, an automated system for fraud detection could be integrated to detect fraud before routing the message to the receiver. Additionally, as indicated in Figure 6, fraud can also be detected in real-time while there is a communication between a legitimate receiver and the suspected fraudster. Notable sources of data based on the aforementioned scenario are the transaction details, exchange of messages, feedback that customers give either via calls, messages or social media and elicitation of fraud-related cases from users or customers. Figure 4 represents some of the data sources from the mobile money users. In our proposed framework, antecedents of fraud-related cases from customers can be collected, developed into a corpus and the data used to train a machine learning classifier.

Figure 4. Data sources of MoMo

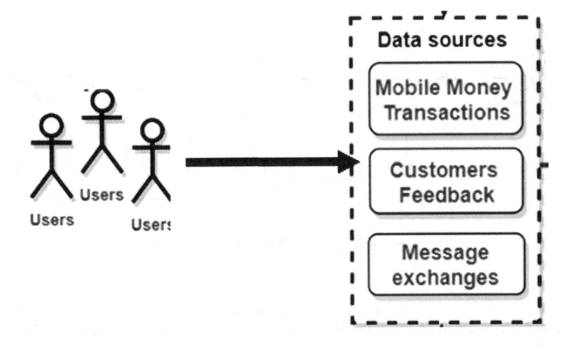

Data Pre-Processing

As indicated in Figure 4, often, these types of data are unstructured which require cleaning and sometimes conversion into structured data for further processing and feature extraction. This process is referred to as *pre-processing*. The processing of the data also entails the extraction of features and morphological analysis before the data is fed to a machine learning classifier to learn. The preprocessed data is expected to be loaded from the operational database or non-relational database to a data warehouse, which is the combination of data from different functional areas, such as marketing and accounting in a firm, or other sources such as social media or the web. The approach to this transition is to use the *extract, transform and load (ETL)*. However, as this study is gear towards data mining, less emphasis is given to the ETL process.

Hybrid-Based Machine Learning Process

The hybrid technique encompasses two-staged processes. The stages involve both supervised and unsupervised learning: *Clustering* and *classification*. Integrating these two learning approaches constitute the hybrid technique. Figure 5 is the two-staged process of machine learning. In our proposed framework, data from the Datawarehouse or collected antecedents of fraud-related cases are cleaned. The data, which

Figure 5. Schematic view of the hybrid process

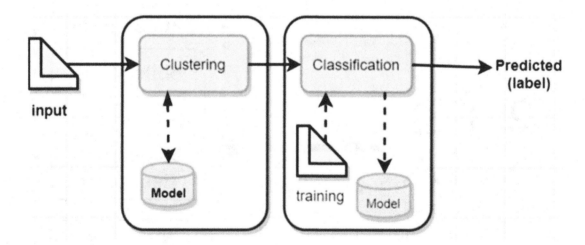

is domain-specific, has no predefined labels or classes. Therefore, the goal of the clustering algorithm is to automatically identify patterns in the data and cluster them based on the similarities of the data (Euclidean distance). Each of the clustered data is used to label the input data allowing further classification. Notable clustering algorithms that can be employed for this task are *k*-means and hierarchical learning algorithms. The labelled input data from the clustered output is pipelined for classification (prediction). Thus, the input data function (f(x)) will be automatically labelled with the clustered themes as outputs (Y). Further, the labelled data will be used to train a classification algorithm or classifier which creates a model for classification. From here, unseen data, such as SMS messages (text messages) between a potential fraudster and legitimate user will then be passed through the model for prediction. Since the goal is to detect mobile money fraud, once the incoming data is detected as fraud, the telecommunication server either retain the fraud message without routing to the users or routing the message with an alert of a potential fraudster. The predicted aggregated output is expected to give a visualization output for decision-makers. Decision-making will be based on the output and some other conditions, such as data protection laws, to make policies that will help reduce or avert mobile money fraud in Ghana.

Real-time Fraud Detection

Figure 6 represents a real-time application of the proposed framework for detecting MoMo fraud in developing countries. In the figure, two people are engaged in a real-time synchronous communication where one is alleged to be a fraudster while the other is a legitimate recipient. The alleged fraudster places a call to the legitimate user for a possible scamming. As has been the case, the call is routed

Figure 6. Detecting fraud in real-time communication using our proposed framework

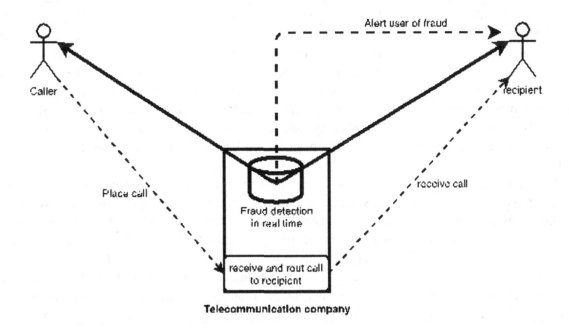

through the telecommunication company's system to the recipient. The proposed data mining tool with training data (training model) from the antecedents of mobile money fraud-related cases is made to listen to the conversation. Based on the content of the conversation, the proposed tool can detect whether the content is a suspected fraudulent activity or not. While the conversation is ongoing, the system alerts the recipient on a potential fraud content with the suspected caller. The process in Figure 6 is expected to be in real-time to alert potential victims of scammers in the mobile money space.

DISCUSSIONS AND IMPLICATIONS

Artificial intelligent applications have been a success in many developed countries such as Finland and Germany and still, efforts are being made to harness its untapped potentials. Conversely, this is not the case in many developing countries where most of the businesses rely on the developed economies for technological innovations. Nowadays, Artificial Intelligence (AI) is touted as the bedrock for future industrial revolution although its potential has and still being harnessed for the greater good of humankind. While business organisations in many parts of the world have capitalized on this potential to motivate competitiveness, African businesses have not done enough to embrace AI to stay glued to the market especially for global competition. Data mining, which forms part of AI, explores historical data to draw patterns or knowledge. Many businesses use data mining to make informed decisions. Petre (2013) observe that data mining has become the cornerstone for business survival. With this observation, the researcher advocated the need for business organisations to apply data mining in order to improve their businesses and gain advantage over their competitors. Failing to use data mining or its related applications to understand the market makes it difficult, especially for born global organizations in Africa to survive.

Often, data mining uses machine learning applications to explore data for business decisions. While we acknowledge the relevance of using machine learning for data mining, there are still efforts being made in the area to improve the efficacy of the machine learning algorithms. This chapter has discussed and shown how machine learning could be employed for data mining with focus on the developing country context. The discussion was holistic from the point of view of explaining both supervised and unsupervised machine learning approaches. By exemplifying data mining in mobile money fraud detection, these authors have shown how this could be implemented. In Figure 6, we have extended our approach by proposing a real-time detection of fraud in mobile money data. The figure indicates that a message or real-time communication between two or more persons can be pipelined through our proposed system for fraud detection. The content of the labelled antecedents of fraud-related cases, which has been used to train a machine learning algorithm, will be made to match with the communication content for possible fraudulent content detection.

The findings from this research have interesting implications for policy and academia. Mobile money fraud has been a subject of concern by the telecommunication companies (Telcos) and the government of Ghana. Over the years, there has been a steady increase in incidents of MoMo related fraud reports in countries across the regions where this mobile payment method has been adopted especially in developing countries (Akomea-Frimpong et al., 2019). The effect is the losses made by stakeholders that have vested interest in the payment method. This encompasses customers (subscribers), Telcos and state agencies that ought to benefit from agreed advantages of the payment method. Calls have been made to both governments and Telcos to put in strategic measures to help counter or curtail the MoMo fraud menace. Ghana's digitalization drive, especially efforts targeted at tackling cybercrime, is crucial due to the huge financial losses over the past three years valued at $200 million experienced by the country (Asiedu-Addo, 2019) which MoMo fraud is included. Telcos have adopted some approaches such a feature termed "allow cash-out" which authorizes a merchant or agent to facilitate the withdrawal of monies from a subscriber's account. Unfortunately, this and other interventions by these Telcos have made little impact as the use of unsophisticated technology is also a key factor (Akomea-Frimpong et al., 2019).

Additionally, the MoMo fraud menace can be viewed as both technological and human. The proposed framework, in this chapter, suggests an approach that seeks to tackle the menace looking at both sides, requiring the active involvement of all stakeholders in the mobile money ecosystem. The adoption and implementation of the framework hinge on the formulation of policies and regulations that will guide the adoption and enforcement by Telcos and governmental agencies with oversight responsibilities in the telecommunication space. To this end, governmental agencies charged with the mandate of licensing and regulating Telecommunication operators must ensure the Telcos introduce novel yet effective approaches to combat the MoMo fraud, identity theft and other related cybercrimes. This can be furthered through the enactment and enforcement of laws related to cybercrime with focus on MoMo fraud. The framework proposed gives a clear approach to curtail the menace which requires stringent and comprehensive legislation that gives limited access to Telcos to implement a middle layer fraud detection system which ensures protection of subscribers and users of MoMo without breaching their privacy. This can be done by enabling Telcos to carefully scrutinize data transmitted in voice or textual form, thus via call or SMS, during transmission to detect possible cases of suspected fraudulent activities. By this policy, the Telcos will be empowered to take proactive steps using a sustainable, progressive technological approach to tackle MoMo fraud through a well-defined law that considers regulatory compliance concerns related to data protection. This will not only provide an easy monitoring system but act as an additional layer of trust to the subscriber and secure the MoMo terrain devoid of fraud. The study has contributed to literature through the explorations of the hybrid-based machine learning-based technique for fraud detection. From our study, the researchers did not find research that has proposed the use of data mining to detect fraud in real-time. The study has reviewed existing approaches for using data mining with machine learning to track mobile money fraudsters in Ghana and developing countries at large.

Artificial intelligence (AI), which subsumes that of a machine learning, has generated tremendous interest for both the academia and the industry. Its application, as elaborated earlier in this chapter, is diverse. It has, for instance, been applied in education to detect learners' behaviour and their academic orientation (Kiruthika & Sivakumar, 2017). Customers' preferences and behaviour (Karthik, 2015) are some aspects by which AI is applied in business. It has been established that AI comes in three stages: *Artificial Narrow Intelligence (ANI), Artificial General Intelligence (AGI)* and *Artificial Super Intelligence (ASI) (*Mullakara, 2017*).* Although, AI evolved several years ago, the ANI applications manifested in two decades ago and has been tremendously applied in diverse disciplines. It has been observed that researchers are advancing AI research which, at present, transitioning from the ANI to AGI. Consequently, "the era of AGI will be characterized by intelligent machines which can tackle any tasks that a human can tackle, be it cognitive or motor skills." (Mullakara, 2017, p1). After this, the researcher has also predicted that ASI will be achieved in the next decade.

CONCLUSION AND FUTURE DIRECTION

While information systems researchers are thriving to unravel the benefit of mobile money inclusion in the financial market, this has inadvertently attracted scammers and other fraudulent activities. Many people are scammed daily prompting a radical action from Ghana's National Communication Authority. The fraudulent situation is dire to the extent that many users have committed suicide or harmed themselves as a result of monies being fictitiously and unwillingly lost. This study has focused on horning the potential of data mining with machine learning, as it forms part of AI, to develop a framework that could be used to aid business decisions. Additionally, this chapter has discussed the various approaches to leverage the avalanche of data for business decisions. With this approach, the study further exemplified the application of machine learning for clustering and classification (hybrid) in mobile money fraud detection in Ghana. The chapter has demonstrated the possibility and the need to apply machine learning to analyse business data in developing countries. Because of this, the authors have given a vivid insight into the relevance of data mining for business survival, especially born global companies. The chapter contributes to literature by proposing a hybrid machine learning technique to track fraud in mobile money transactions in Ghana and Africa at large. To the best of the authors' knowledge, this is the first of its kind in the context of Ghana and Sub-Saharan Africa at large. In future, the authors envision that the proposed framework will be adopted and implemented by the telecommunication companies to reduce mobile money and other related fraudulent activities in the e-payment ecosystem in Ghana and Africa.

REFERENCES

Akomea-Frimpong, I., Andoh, C., Akomea-Frimpong, A., & Dwomoh-Okudzeto, Y. (2019). Control of Fraud on Mobile Money Services in Ghana: an exploratory study. Journal of Money Laundering Control, 300-317.

Apte, C., Liu, B., Pednault, E. P., & Smyth, P. (2002). Business Applications of Data Mining. *Communications of the ACM*, *45*(8), 49–53. doi:10.1145/545151.545178

Aseidu-Addo, S. (2019, November 11). Cyber fraud: Ghanaians lose $200m in 3 years. Retrieved from https://www.graphic.com.gh/business/business-news/ghana-news-momo-fraud-threatens-emerging-payment-technologies.html

Baron, J., & Spulber, D. F. (2017). *The Effect of Technological Change on Firm Survival and Growth-Evidence from Technology Standards*. Chicago: NorthWest University.

Chatain, P., McDowell, J., Cedric, M., Schott, P., & Willebois, E. (2011). *Preventing Money Laundering and Terrorist Financing: A Practical Guide for Bank Supervisors*. Washington, DC: World Bank.

Daskalaki, S., Avouris, N., Goudara, M., & Avouris, N. (2003). Data mining for decision support on customer insolvency in telecommunications business. *European Journal of Operational Research*, *2217*(2), 239–255. doi:10.1016/S0377-2217(02)00532-5

Femina, B. T., & M., S. E. (2015). An Efficient CRM-Data Mining Framework for the Prediction of Customer Behaviour. In Procedia - Procedia Computer Science (pp. Vol. 46, pp. 725–731). Elsevier Masson SAS. . doi:10.1016/j.procs.2015

Gartner. (2019, July 22nd). Data Mining. Retrieved from https://www.gartner.com/it-glossary/data-mining

Ghanaweb. (2019). Retrieved from MoMo fraud: How scammers steal your money: https://www.ghanaweb.com/GhanaHomePage/NewsArchive/Momo-fraud-How-scammers-steal-your-money-791051

Goyal, M., & Vohra, R. (2012). Applications of Data Mining in Higher Education. *International Journal of Computational Science*, *9*(2), 113–120.

Han, J., Kamber, M., & Pei, J. (2011). *Data Mining: Concepts and Techniques*. Elsevier.

Hand, D. (1998). Data Mining : Statistics and More? *The American Statistician*, *52*(2), 112–118.

Hung, S., Yen, D. C., & Wang, H. (2006). Applying data mining to telecom churn management. *Expert Systems with Applications, 31*(3), 515–524. doi:10.1016/j.eswa.2005.09.080

Iqbal, J. (2018). Role of Data Mining in Managerial Decisions. International Journal of Scientific Research in Computer Science. *Engineering and Information Technology, 4*(1), 262–267.

Ismail, N. (2017). The importance of data mining. Retrieved from https://www.information-age.com/importance-data-mining-123469819/

Kiruthika, K., & Sivakumar, S. (2017). Analysis of Students' behaviour and learning using classification of Data mining methods. *International Journal of Computational and Applied Mathematics, 12*(1).

Kolog, E. C.S., M., & T., T. (2018). Using Machine Learning for Sentiment and Social Influence Analysis in Text. In Proceedings of the International Conference on Information Technology & Systems, (pp. 1-14). Ecudor. doi:10.1007/978-3-319-73450-7_43

Kolog, E., Montero, S. C., & Sutinen, E. (2016). Annotation Agreement of Emotions in Text: The Influence of Counselors' Emotional State on their Emotion Perception. In *Proceeding of International Conference on Advanced Learning Technologies (ICALT)* (pp. 357-359). IEEE.

Kolog, E. A., & Montero, C. S. (2018). Towards automated e-counselling system based on counsellors emotion perception. *Education and Information Technologies, 23*(2), 1–23. doi:10.1007/s10639-017-9643-9

Landis, J. R., & Koch, G. G. (1977). The measurement of observer agreement for categorical data. *Biometrics, 33*(1), 159–174. doi:10.2307/2529310 PubMed

Lausch, A., Schmidt, A., & Tischendorf, L. (2015). Data mining and linked open data – New perspectives for data analysis in environmental research. *Ecological Modelling, 295*, 5–17. doi:10.1016/j.ecolmodel.2014.09.018

Lee, P. M. (2013). Use Of Data Mining In Business Analytics To Support Business Competitiveness. *Review of Business Information System, 17*(2), 53–58. doi:10.19030/rbis.v17i2.7843

Milovic, B., & Milovic, M. (2012). Prediction and Decision Making in Health Care using Data Mining. *International Journal of Public Health Science, 1*(2), 69–76. doi:10.11591/ijphs.v1i2.1380

Mishra, T., Kumar, D., & Gupta, S. (2014). Mining Students' Data for Performance Prediction. In *Fourth International Conference on Advanced Computing & Communication Technologies* (pp. 255–262). 10.1109/ACCT.2014.105

Mosley, R. C. Jr. (2012). Social Media Analytics : Data Mining Applied to Insurance Twitter Posts. *Casualty Actuarial Society, 2*, 1–36.

Mullakara, R. (2017). A Perspective on Artificial Intelligence and Machine Learning. IEEE India Infomation, 12(4), 33-36. http://sites.ieee.org/indiacouncil/files/2018/01/p33-p35.pdf

Nigania, J. (2019, July 23rd). Understanding The Term Data Mining And Its Impact On Business. Retrieved from https://www.houseofbots.com/news-detail/4545-1-understanding-the-term-data-mining-and-its-impact-on-business

Noris, J. (2019). *Machine Learning with the Raspberry Pi: Experiments with Data and Computer Vi-SION*. Academic Press.

Obradovic, D. (2016). The role innovation on strategic orientations and competitiveness of enterprises. Ecoforum Journal, 5(1).

Ozyirmidokuza, K. E., Uyar, K., & Ozyirmidokuza, H. M. (2015). *A Data Mining Based Approach to a Firm's Marketing Channel. In 22nd International Economic Conference* (pp. 1–10). Economic Prospects in the Context of Growing Global and Regional Interdep; doi:10.1016/S2212-5671(15)00975-2.

Peter, A. (2018, July 23). Data Mining And Its Relevance To Business. Retrieved from https://analyticstraining.com/data-mining-and-its-relevance-to-business/

Petre, R. (2013). Data mining solutions for the business environment. *Database Systems Journal, 4*(4), 21–29.

Rahman, A., & Airini. (2017). Emerging Technologies with Disruptive Effects: A Review. PERINTIS eJournal, 7(2).

Raman, K. (2015). Machine Learning From Human Preferences And Choices. PhD thesis at Cornell University: https://ecommons.cornell.edu/handle/1813/40961

Report, U. (2018). Technology and Innovation development. Switzerland: *United Nations Conference on Trade and Development*.

Ricardo, & Barbosa. (2019, July 23). Importance Of Data Mining In Today's Business World. Retrieved from https://www.ricardo-barbosa.com/importance-of-data-mining-in-todays-business-world/

Rouse, M. (2018, July 23rd). Disruptive technology. Retrieved from https://whatis.techtarget.com/definition/disruptive-technology

Rousseeuw, P. (1987). Silhouettes: A Graphical Aid to the Interpretation and Validation of Cluster Analysis. *Computational & Applied Mathematics, 20*, 53–65. doi:10.1016/0377-0427(87)90125-7

Sharma, K., Shrivastava, G., & Kumar, V. (2011). Web Mining : *Today and Tomorrow. International Conference on Electronics Computer Technology* (pp. 399–403). IEEE.

Tembhurne, D. S., Adhikari, P. J., & Babu, P. R. (2019). A Review study on Application of Data Mining Techniques in CRM of Pharmaceutical Industry. *IJSRSTInternational Journal of Scientific Research in Science and Technology, 6*(2), 1–7.

Thelwell, R. (2019). 5 real life applications of Data Mining and Business Intelligence. Retrieved from https://www.matillion.com/insights/5-real-life-applications-of-data-mining-and-business-intelligence/

Wang, H., & Wang, S. (2008). A knowledge management approach to data mining process for business intelligence. *Industrial Management & Data Systems, 108*(5), 622–634. doi:10.1108/02635570810876750

Weiss, S. M., & Indurkhya, N. (1998). *Predictive data mining: a practical guide*. Esevier.

Westfall, B. (2019, July 23rd). Can you dig it: what is data mining and how can it help your small business. Retrieved from https://lab.getapp.com/what-is-data-mining-small-business/

Wu, X., Kumar, V., Quinlan, J. R., Ghosh, J., Yang, Q., Motoda, H., & Dan, J. H. (2008). Top 10 algorithms in data mining. *Knowledge and Information Systems*, *14*(1), 1–37. doi:10.1007/s10115-007-0114-2

KEY TERMS AND DEFINITIONS

Classification: This a supervised learning where the input data is tagged with an output data. The goal of classification is to predict the output data based on the input data.

Clustering: Clustering is an unsupervised learning technique where the input is not tagged. Clustering identify patterns in the data based on datapoint similarities.

Data: Data is raw fact that can be processed for information. Examples of data include texts, images, and videos.

Data Avalanche: Is a big data that can computationally be analysed to reveal patterns, trends, and associations.

Data Mining: Data mining is a process that focuses on identifying correlations, relevant patterns, and trends, meticulously selected from massive datasets resident in some repository.

Machine Learning: Machine learning focuses on the development of computer programs that can access data and use it to learn for themselves.

Section 2
Leveraging New and Emerging Information Systems

Chapter 3
Disruptive Technology Adoption in Developing Countries:
The Case of Uber in Ghana

Joseph Budu

(iD) https://orcid.org/0000-0002-0003-5807

Department of Information Systems and Innovation, School of Technology, Ghana Institute of Management and Public Administration, Ghana

ABSTRACT

The purpose of this study is to explore the factors that inform a consumer's behavioural intention to adopt disruptive information technologies. This study uses an inductive reasoning approach to collect qualitative data which is analysed using interpretive analysis guidelines. The outcome of the analysis is the discovery of three new variables, namely, understanding of technology, meta-price value, and perceived need. The knowledge of technology refers to what a consumer knows about disruptive information technology. The meta-price value refers to a consumer's perception of the benefits to be gained from disruptive information technology as compared to those of the disrupted technology. The perceived need refers to a consumer's realisation of the extent to which disruptive information technology is the sole provider for a fundamental requirement. This study is, arguably, the first to propose a different model to explain the adoption of disruptive information technologies.

INTRODUCTION

"Uber has always been controversial. Combine a business plan based on *upending an entrenched industry* with a CEO as aggressive as Travis Kalanick, and conflict is a given" (Lashinsky, 2017). Such is the nature of disruptive information technologies – literally overthrowing traditional business models. Some examples of such technologies are the sharing economy (Henten and Windekilde, 2016; Sovani and Jayawardena, 2017), 5G and internet-of-things (French, 2016), 3D printing (Kothman and Faber, 2016), mobile apps (Tribunella and Tribunella, 2016), ebooks (Frederick, 2016), big data (Schermann *et al.*, 2014), simulation games (Smith, 2007), and internet computing (Carlo, Lyytinen and Rose, 2009).

DOI: 10.4018/978-1-7998-2610-1.ch003

In addition to upsetting existing business models, these information technologies have the potential to challenge existing theories, explanations, and knowledge about them. Despite this potential, academic research is yet to catch up with exploring and providing an understanding of what factors inform individuals' adoption of disruptive information technologies. Unfortunately, trade and industry magazines, and newspapers are at the forefront (see Pines, 2016; Jackson, 2017; Lashinsky, 2017; Steinmetz and Vella, 2017). Academic studies related to disruptive technologies have focused on advanced issues such as value co-creation (Camilleri and Neuhofer, 2017), minimising firm-level risks arising from disruptive technologies (Cheng *et al.*, 2017), how to take advantage of disruptive innovation (Perez, Paulino and CambraFierro, 2017), changes in industrial structures (Henten and Windekilde, 2016), and how to strategically deal with disruptive technologies (Evans, Ralston and Broderick, 2009). While these studies are valuable, they raise several concerns for research concerning the adoption of disruptive information technologies.

First, they are mostly based on issues at the organisational level (e.g. Obal, 2017; Perez, Paulino and CambraFierro, 2017), industry level (e.g. Henten and Windekilde, 2016; Momeni and Rost, 2016; Cheng *et al.*, 2017) or country level (e.g. Bakke and Henry, 2015). Second, they do not speak of what informs individuals' adoption of disruptive technologies. Third, they neither advance nor contribute to the theory of adoption of disruptive technologies. Fourth, they collectively suggest a fixation on developed country contexts (e.g. Zhu, So and Hudson, 2016; Vecchiato, 2017) and innocuous neglect of the adoption of disruptive technologies in developing country contexts. The effects are that we lack knowledge of factors which make individuals adopt or reject disruptive technologies, i.e. a theory of adoption of disruptive technologies; and literature from developing country contexts. This study is a response to these observed gaps. Thus the purpose of this study is to explore the factors that inform individuals' behavioural intention to, and subsequently adopt disruptive information technologies. Qualitative data collected from young people – who are usually early adopters of new information technologies – were analysed using interpretive analysis methods. The outcome of the analysis is the inductive discovery of three variables, *knowledge of technology*, *meta-price value*, and *perceived need*. These new variables are used to propose a model for the adoption of disruptive information technologies.

This paper has six sections. The first presents an overview of the research area, and the gaps identified in existing technology adoption literature, and which warrants this study. The second section discusses existing literature about information technology adoption with an emphasis on uncovering the inherent deficiencies of existing technology adoption theories in explaining or predicting the adoption of disruptive information technologies. The third section presents and justifies the use of induction and interpretivism as a reasoning mode for this study. The fourth section outlays the research methods for this study, followed by the fifth section, which presents the data and findings. The findings are then discussed vis-à-vis UTAUT2 to clarify the paper's theoretical contributions – three new variables that influence behavioural intention to adopt; and a proposed model for the adoption of disruptive information technologies.

LITERATURE REVIEW

As new technologies emerge, understanding their acceptance, adoption and use would remain a trending topic, although it has already been researched extensively. This observation is evidenced by theories and their extensions that either explain or suggest factors influencing technology adoption. Despite their utility, these theories still harbour some inadequacies which yearn for fixing. Prominent amongst these theories are Technology Acceptance Model, Diffusion of Innovation, Theory of Planned Behaviour, and the Unified Theory of Acceptance and Use of Technology. There are several outstanding, thorough reviews of these theories and their use/applications over the years (see Venkatesh *et al.*, 2003; Venkatesh, 2006; Gangwar, Date and Raoot, 2014; Rondan-Cataluña, Arenas-Gaitán and Ramírez-Correa, 2015; Venkatesh, Thong and Xu, 2016). Summarily, these theories have the understood assumption that people accept and use technology because of factors about the technology in question, social conditions, and some personal considerations. Arguably, none of such technology adoption theories identifies or account for peculiarities of disruptive information technologies. For instance, as disruptive technologies are new, and often introduced for niche markets (Schermann *et al.*, 2014), a consumer should know of it before generating any interests or intentions to adopt it.

Ajzen and Fishbein's (1980) Theory of Reasoned Action suggests that a person's use of a technology is determined by his/her intention to carry out a behaviour (referred to as Behavioural Intention), which is also determined by his/her attitude and subjective norms (that is, what his/her associates think of that behaviour). Davis' (1989) Technology Acceptance Model (TAM) also asserts that individuals will accept some technology because of their perception about its usefulness (that is, perceived usefulness), and their perception of easy use of that technology (that is, perceived ease of use). Venkatesh & Davis (2000) expand the antecedents of TAM's perceived usefulness to create TAM2. Venkatesh & Bala (2008) also developed TAM3 by adding more factors which lead to perceived ease of use. Venkatesh, Morris, Davis, & Davis (2003) advances the Unified Theory of Acceptance and Use of Technology (UTAUT), a cumulative theory resulting from a review and synthesis of TRA, TAM, the motivational model, the Theory of Planned Behaviour (TPB), the model of PC utilisation, a model which combines TAM and TPB, the innovation diffusion theory, and the social cognitive theory. Venkatesh, Thong, & Xu (2012) deduces and proves UTAUT2 to explain *consumers'* acceptance and use of technology, by advancing the argument that all previous technology acceptance theories including UTAUT2's predecessor UTAUT is based on technology adoption within organisational contexts. In other words, TAM, TRA, and UTAUT are based on the acceptance of technology within an organisational context which have conditions different from the context of accepting technology outside an organisation (Rondan-Cataluña, Arenas-Gaitán and Ramírez-Correa, 2015).

It must be noted, however, that contextualising technology adoption outside the organisation, but for private consumers open up two new dimensions. First, acceptance becomes volitional, thereby creating prominence for such factors as price; for instance, employees do not bear any costs in accepting workplace technologies (Venkatesh, Thong and Xu, 2012). Second, direct economic motivation significantly affects people's behaviour and characteristics (Bateman and Ludwig, 2003; Goomas and Ludwig, 2007; Garbers and Konradt, 2014), and could facilitate or influence private consumers to accept or use technology (Becker, Clement and Schaedel, 2010). In one instance, some commercial vehicle drivers are offered monthly cash payments to mount and maintain remotely managed electronic screens — which display video advertisements to passengers in their cars — the cost of which the driver bears if there is theft or inexplicable damage. In another instance, a ridesharing application user could compare prices of *regular* transportation services to that offered via the app before making a selection or deciding to use the application. Such instances can reinforce the motivation, and increase the commitment of *technology accepters* (see Govindarajulu and Daily, 2004). Discouragingly, the aforementioned available theories of technology acceptance do not account for such peculiar and noticeable situations.

Further, these theories seem to overlook the peculiarities of disruptive technologies. Generally, disruptive technologies are "technologies that result in a bad product or service performance" (Dhillon, Coss and Hackney, 2001, p. 163). In the notable absence of a definition for disruptive *information* technologies, we could view them as those technologies – for collecting, processing, storing, displaying and transmitting data/information – which result in a bad product or service performance. Drawing on a description of disruptive *information system innovations* (see Lyytinen and Rose, 2003, p. 301), this definition implies that disruptive information technologies do not improve the performance of existing products and services in the same industry as those to which the majority of customers in the market have become accustomed. For instance, Amazon's self-publishing platform could be or is disruptive because, instead of incrementally improving the traditional publishing value chain, it is gradually removing traditional players like publishing houses, and creating new value for authors (see Smith, 2007). Besides, five other properties define disruptive technologies (Christensen, 1997 as cited in Schermann *et al.*, 2014, p. 265); we would use these properties later to evaluate the focal disruptive technology of this paper. The first property is that they perform worse than established technologies according to traditional evaluation criteria. Second, they introduce new rating criteria. Third, they are observed by mainstream users with caution. Fourth, they are initially offered and used by start-ups and persons changing careers or businesses changing their focus. Fifth, they lead to changes in the value creation processes. Based on these properties, we could cite examples of disruptive information technologies or systems like the sharing economy (Henten and Windekilde, 2016; Sovani and Jayawardena, 2017), 5G and internet-of-things (French, 2016), 3D printing (Kothman and Faber, 2016), mobile apps (Tribunella and Tribunella, 2016), ebooks (Frederick, 2016), big data (Schermann *et al.*, 2014), simulation games (Smith, 2007), and internet computing (Lyytinen and Rose, 2003; Carlo, Lyytinen and Rose, 2009).

The effects of disruptive information technologies extend to existing theories, explanations, and knowledge about their adoption. This effect has generated some research focusing on issues such as value co-creation (Camilleri and Neuhofer, 2017), minimising firm-level risks arising from disruptive technologies (Cheng *et al.*, 2017), how to take advantage of disruptive innovation (Perez, Paulino and CambraFierro, 2017), changes in industrial structures (Henten and Windekilde, 2016), and how to strategically dealing with disruptive technologies (Evans, Ralston and Broderick, 2009). Table 1 illustrates the focal issue, conceptual approaches, and contexts of these articles. While these studies are valuable, they have not explored the factors that inform individuals' behavioural intention to, and subsequently, adopt disruptive information technologies.

RESEARCH FRAMEWORK

This study subscribes to induction as a mode of reasoning and arguing for what informs individuals' adoption of disruptive technologies. Induction involves making generalisations about an object using observations of the object's specific instances (Lee and Baskerville, 2003). This reasoning mode is in contrast with deduction in which one needs to postulate an explicit theory or theories that can be tested to generate results which will exhibit a fit between the theory and the observed facts (Ochara, 2013). Due to the criticisms of existing theories as already presented, this study does not postulate theory a priori. This step is similar to a study of academics' adoption of electronic learning in higher education institutions which had no a priori theory (Martins and Nunes, 2016). Figure 1 illustrates the inductive approach used in this study.

Table 1. A survey of existing research about disruptive information technologies (Author's construct)

Issue	Conceptual approach	Paper type/level of research	Technology or Industry/Country	Reference
How to identify candidate application areas for timely adjustment of technology innovation strategies to minimise firm-level risks	SIRS epidemic model	Empirical / industry	RFID technology /	(Cheng *et al.*, 2017)
Co-creation and co-destruction of value in the sharing economy	Service-dominant logic	Empirical	Malta	(Camilleri and Neuhofer, 2017)
Taking advantage of disruptive innovation through value networks	Capabilities approach	Empirical	Space / France	(Perez, Paulino and CambraFierro, 2017)
Changes industrial structures concerning the sharing economy	Transaction cost theory	Conceptual	Not applicable	(Henten and Windekilde, 2016)
How intrinsically motivated competence and autonomy in concert with personal innovativeness in IT motivate individuals to try new information technologies.	Self-determination theory		General Software / USA (apparently)	(Bakke and Henry, 2015)
Improving the negative consequences of the sharing economy	None	Conceptual	N/A	(Malhotra and Alstyne, 2014)
Strategically thinking about disruptive technologies	None	Somewhat empirical	Biogeron-technology / USA	(Evans, Ralston and Broderick, 2009)
The need for a formal problem representation structure for the analysis of information technology development trends	Design science	Individual	Music and wireless networking technology / USA (apparently)	(Adomavicius *et al.*, 2008)
How to manage peer-to-peer conflicts in disruptive technology innovations	Theories of conflict, coordination, and learning	Empirical / Organisational	Software / USA	(Sherif, Zmud and Browne, 2006)
User responses to major IT events	Coping theory	Empirical	North America	(Beaudry and Pinsonneault, 2005)
Pre-adoption antecedents of disruptive technology continuous adoption intentions	Literature-based conceptual model	Empirical / firm-level	Cloud computing	(Obal, 2017)
The need to identify potentially disruptive technologies	Patent-development paths, k-core analysis, topic modelling	Empirical / industry	Photovoltaic industry	(Momeni and Rost, 2016)
Incumbent firms' inability to identify new markets in the face of disruptive technologies	New conceptual framework	Empirical / industry	Operating systems	(Vecchiato, 2017)
Why consumers adopt ridesharing applications	Social cognitive theory	Empirical/individual	Ridesharing application / USA	(Zhu, So and Hudson, 2016)
Why individual consumers do not adopt ridesharing applications	UTAUT2-based framework	Empirical/individual	Ridesharing application / Ghana	This paper

First, the study reviewed existing knowledge from prior research to guide what to look out for when making real-life observations; this was done under the literature review section. The real-life observations that define a resulting set of theoretical contributions and generalisations would be presented in the Results section. After that, we would draw a general conclusion which describes the relationships shared by the real-life observations to inform future predictions for other instances (Rasmussen and Eliasmith, 2011).

The choice of induction not arbitrary, but justified for several reasons. First, there is a contemporary shift from making deductions from theory-led assumptions to concluding based on actual beliefs (Evans and Over, 2013). This shift may be because of a growing realisation that a priori theories even though useful in explaining some situation, place the researcher in a tight corner from which to work with little room for serendipity. She is forced to either prove or disprove a particular theory. Second, there is a

Figure 1. [The Inductive Approach to Reasoning (Kovacs and Spens, 2005, p. 139)]

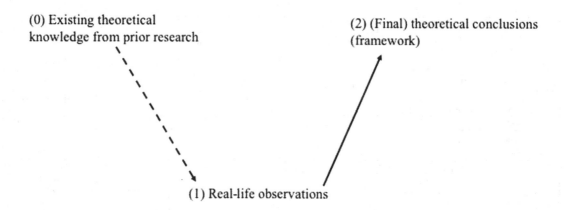

growing interest in studying the influence of context in the information systems area (see Wiredu 2007; Durkin et al. 2015; Avgerou 2008). For instance, previous research has reported how the contextual processes of implementing an information system can have an impact on the implementing organisation (Avgerou, 2001). If the context is this important, then there is a need to make observations first before drawing generalisations, instead of drawing a priori generalisations before testing. Induction affords us to make the observations first before drawing such general conclusions. One may raise the argument that deduction can also be used to test for contextual differences. However, this essay raises a counterargument that if contextual differences are drawn from theory, there is still a high likelihood of overlooking some pertinent issues which may not be available in a priori selected theory. Hence, the researcher will be forced to conform to the theory's conceptualisation of a context be it accurate or not. Therefore, choosing induction is more suitable, considering that this approach affords him first to observe empirically and then make generalisations – be it far-reaching, immediate, or approximate (Achinstein, 2010).

Research Methods

This study is interpretive. Induction is a defining characteristic of interpretivism. We used interpretivism to help understand the thought and action in a social context. This paradigm was useful in producing deep insights into an information systems phenomenon such as the adoption of disruptive technologies (Klein and Myers, 1999, p. 67). The primary methodological requirements involved in conducting an interpretive study include "...the details of the research sites chosen, the reasons for this choice, the number of people who were interviewed, what hierarchical or professional positions they occupied, what other data sources were used, and over what period the research was conducted" (Walsham, 1995).

Research Site

The research site chosen for this study is a public university situated in a capital city [actual name withheld for review purposes]. This site was selected because Uber is operational therein, and much patronized by the students there. Further, many of the students fall in the younger generation who are perceived to be leading the way in adopting and using new technologies (Liu *et al.*, 2015, p. 487; French, 2016; Zhu, So and Hudson, 2016). The author is a member of faculty in the said institution where he teaches undergraduate and postgraduate diploma courses in information technology, management information systems, and computer science. The authors use Google Classroom to engage with course participants during and after a class.

Data Collection

Data was solicited from students in four different classes. The first is a combination of third-year BSc. Computer Science and BSc Information Communication Technology (ICT) students; the second is a second-year BSc. Management Information Systems class; the third is a fourth-year BSc ICT class; and the fourth is a mix of third-year BSc ICT and 4th year BSc Computer Science students. The total number of students in the course and the final number of respondents are captured in Table 2. Most of the students in these classes are either Gen Y (born between 1981 and 1989) or Gen I (born after 1990) (see French, 2016, p. 846 for a detailed description of these generations). Gen *Yers* multitask, are goal-oriented and focus on efficiency. They communicated with memos and email, prefer a balance between work and home, prefer individuality, and obtain news from gossip and Internet. *Gen Iers*, like Internet search, are resourceful, and immediate. They also like texting and social networking and prefer meaningful integrated work. They want exposure and obtain news from the Internet and social media. Therefore, these respondents are most likely to be familiar with disruptive technologies, more so ride-sharing applications like Uber.

Interview questions were posted as a non-scoring quiz in the Google Classroom pages for all the classes with a one-week submission deadline (see Figure 2). Students immediately received email notifications through their official student email addresses. Students could still submit their responses after the deadline. After two weeks, there were twenty-nine (29) responses across the class pages.

The questions posted were

Have you ever used Uber? (adopter identification)
If no, why haven't you? (Laggard identification)
What is keeping you? (Laggard identification)
What will make you use it soon? (Influencing factor)

Some of the responses had to be edited to correct grammatical and spelling errors. For instance, one respondent wrote an answer to the first question that

Yes, I have used it twice...it's convenience and cheaper.

The edited form "Yes, I have used it twice...it's convenient and cheaper", was instead presented to enhance ease of reading.

Table 2. Distribution of Respondents

Class group	Total number of students	Number of respondents	Average age
3rd year BSc ICT and BSc Computer Science class (Day and Evening)	64	13	26
2nd Year BSc MIS class (Systems Thinking & Practice)	27	8	25
4th year BSc ICT class	21	3	24
3rd year BSc ICT and 4th year BSc Computer Science class	58	5	22
Total	170	29	N/A

Data Analysis

This paper followed an interpretive approach to data analysis (Walsham, 2006, p. 325). First, even though this study did not choose an explicit theory, it was guided by the constructs in the UTAUT2 (Venkatesh, Thong and Xu, 2012). This lens helped to develop a data-theory link in viewing the data to identify *existing* and *novel* factors influencing respondents in their adoption of a disruptive information technology platform like Uber. The responses collected from Google Classroom were grouped and coded to arrive at factors influencing the adoption of Uber. These factors were then compared to those in the UTAUT to derive similarities and differences between the two sets. Any identified difference hinted on the earlier assertion that previous theory had overlooked certain factors that could be important in understanding the adoption of disruptive technologies.

Figure 2. [Posting of Interview Questions on Google Classroom]

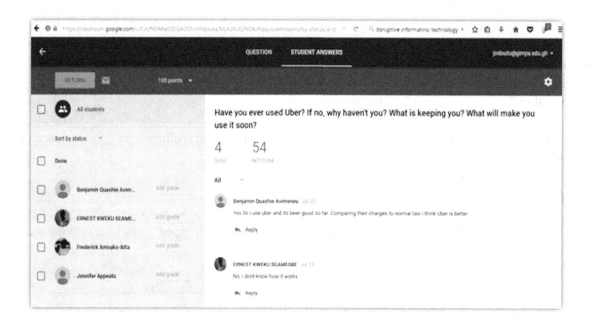

Findings

Uber in Ghana

Uber develops and markets a computer application that serves as an alternative service to standard taxi cabs by allowing users to electronically hail drivers contracted by Uber (Goode, 2011). Uber claims to be a marketplace where Uber's drivers as independent agents meet Uber's customers. It is a technology platform that enables its mobile application users or web sites to arrange and schedule transportation or logistics services with third-party providers of such services, including independent third-party transportation providers and third-party logistics providers under agreement with Uber or certain Uber affiliates. It operates in over seventy (70) cities across the world. In Africa, Ghana is one of the fastest- and third-fastest- growing car markets in the world, helping Uber amass more than 60,000 drivers in Africa (Jackson, 2017). Increasing connectivity and mobile penetration in the country also suggest a substantial future customer base. Uber was selected as the case of disruptive information technology for this study because it has such characteristics as evaluated in Table 3.

Adopter Identification

The first question "Have you ever used Uber?" was aimed at identifying Uber adopters and non-adopters. A majority of the respondents said they had ever used Uber. Out of the twenty-nine (29) respondents, nineteen (19) said they had used it before – these we refer to as *adopters*, while ten (10) said they had never used, i.e. *non-adopters*. Some of the responses suggest continuous and frequent use of the application. They wrote that

Yes, I have. Use it often ~ Male, 32

Yes, I have used Uber on several occasions ~ Female, 22

Yes, I have used Uber so many times. ~ Male, 21

Even though the question did not seek reasons from adopters, some gave reasons and evaluations of the ridesharing application. It seems that lower prices, convenience and transparency are paramount amongst the reasons proffered. Four adopters mentioned that;

Yes Sir, I use Uber, and it's been good so far. Comparing their charges to normal taxi, I think Uber is better. ~ Male, 22

I have used Uber, and I love using it. It's so convenient and hustle-free. No bargaining power needed. Everything is nice and fair ~ Male, 26

Yes, I have used it twice...it's convenient and cheaper ~ Male, 35

Yes, I have. Great service, convenient and fairly cheaper than traditional taxing service. ~ Male, 26

Table 3. An evaluation of Uber as a disruptive information technology (adapted from Schermann et al., 2014)

Properties of disruptive technologies	Evaluation of Uber as disruptive
The technology performs worse than established technologies according to traditional evaluation criteria	"Uber seems to be losing battles, whether in court, in the public's perception, over the loyalty of riders and drivers, even among its own rapidly departing executive team" (Lashinsky, 2017)
The technology introduces new rating criteria	Uber drivers and vehicles need to meet specific requirements (Uber, 2017).
Mainstream users are observing the technology with caution.	There are several lawsuits against Uber, especially in the USA. Uber also faced online protests using the #deleteUber hashtag (see Jackson, 2017)
Initially, the technology will be offered and used by start-ups and persons changing careers or businesses changing their focus.	Uber is being patronised mostly by the youth – *Gen Yers* and *Gen Iers*
The technology leads to changes in the value creation process	Uber is removing the need for taxi drivers to belong to unions. Owners of private vehicles can now generate rent from passengers.

Yes, I have used Uber. What made me use it was the fact that the fare was relatively cheaper than the average taxi. Every driver had a profile, and every trip was recorded, so it was a safer option in case you had to get home late at night. ~ Male, 23

Some of those who had never used it posted responses such as

No, I have not used Uber ~ Female, 25

I have not picked it before. ~ Male, 24

No, please. ~ Female, 23

Identification of Non-Adopters

The second question "If no, why haven't you?" was to find out factors influencing non-adopters or Uber. The first factor derived from the responses is ignorance; the respondent either did not know of the application's existence, or she had never considered using it. Three respondents said that:

No, I don't know how it works ~ Male, 24

I think it's probably because I have never thought about it. Male, 25

No, hasn't occurred to me to use it ~ Male, 23

Another factor for non-adoption could be the transaction cost. It is unclear how users know of Uber's fares so that they could compare with *average* taxi fares. Therefore, what the respondents said about the fares seem to be speculative.

The reason is that I won't have any bargaining power with that, unlike normal Taxi ~ Male, 24

I prefer the bus because it's cheaper. ~ Male, 23

Interestingly, some respondents do not see the need to use the service. Here, we see a third factor, apathy. One female third-year student said she had not used it simply because she is "not interested". Another wrote that

I... have no special reason for not using it ~ Male, 26

It must be noted that within the city, there are several public buses (locally called *trotros*) whose fares are about twice cheaper than regular taxi fares. It may thus be *unnecessary* to use Uber unless there was something *special*; using the trotro is still ridesharing. Besides, some would not like to wait for an Uber to arrive when they could easily hail a taxi, and negotiate the fare. Someone gave a related reason he has not used Uber;

...because I find taxi faster and efficient unlike Uber where you have to wait minutes before it arrives ~ Male, 28

Influencing Factors

To further explore what factors inform non-adoption, the third question "What is keeping you?" was asked. The responses to this question bothered on perceived high costs, efficiency, and untimeliness. While some believed that an Uber ride would be more expensive, others thought that it was the wrong time to use the application. The following are the responses;

...I am also thinking it's going to be more expensive to me ~ Male, 25

because I find taxi faster and more efficient unlike Uber where you have to wait minutes before it arrives ~Male, 26

It's not useful to me now ~ Male, 25

There has not been any emergency case that I am pressurized.

One response somewhat confirms an earlier factor of apathy towards adopting the application.

Nothing is keeping me from using it.

The final question as to find out what factors the non-adopters would consider in deciding to change their minds about using the application? They were asked the question "What will make you use it soon?" Again, the responses related to need, inquisitiveness, efficiency, and marketing. The responses are presented below.

When stranded in a remote area ~Female, 25

I'll use Uber only when I urgently need to get to a destination. ~ Male, 26

If they are able to convince me well enough as to how they are preferable, then I might use it. ~ Male, 26

I'd probably use it soon just because I would want to know how they also operate. Male, 24

If Uber becomes faster and efficient ~ Male 26

I think am always on time and does not need that service. ~ Female, 24

ANALYSIS AND DISCUSSION

The purpose of this study is to explore the factors that inform individuals' adoption of disruptive information technologies. The findings presented suggest different factors that individuals consider in adopting disruptive technologies. While some of these factors could be accounted for by existing theories of technology adoption, others could not. UTAUT2, which this study adopted as a lens to explain its findings, has eight factors influencing the adoption of information technology (Table 4 enumerates the factors in the other theories). *Performance expectancy* is the degree to which technology will provide benefits to a consumer in performing an activity; *effort expectancy* is the degree of ease a consumer associates with the use of technology. *Social influence* is the extent to which consumers perceive that important others like family, believe they should use a technology; *facilitating conditions* refer to consumers' perceptions of the resources and support available to use technology. *Hedonic motivation* is the fun or pleasure derived from using a technology; *experience* is the passage of time from the initial use of technology by an individual. *Habit* is the extent to which people tend to perform behaviours because of learning; *price value* is a consumer's cognitive trade-off between the perceived benefits of technology and the cost for using them (definitions gathered from Venkatesh, Thong and Xu, 2012). The above factors account for some of the factors found in this study. For instance, price value accounts for the finding that adopters of a disruptive technology compared the cost of using it with the cost of using the disrupted technology. However, one ontological difference is that consumers go beyond comparing the technology's benefits with the cost of using it – or calculating a technology's price value – to comparing the price value of *disruptive* technology to that of the *disrupted* technology. In effect, the *meta*-price value of technology influences a consumer's behavioural intention to adopt it. Benefits such as convenience and efficiency could be accounted for as part of 'calculating' the meta-price.

Instructively, factors for non-adoption could provide some understanding of the issue of adopting disruptive technologies. This study discovered factors such as ignorance, transaction cost, and apathy influencing non-adoption. While transaction cost is accounted for by *meta*-price value as earlier explained, ignorance is not. Knowledge of technology should be considered essential to the adoption of disruptive information technologies most of which are new and do not enjoy mass-scale publicity and adoption yet; they are initially offered to a niche market of customers (Christensen, 1997). For these early adopters (see Rogers, 1995), the technology provider provides some education (Henten and Windekilde, 2016). Therefore, we could say that the *extent of knowledge* of disruptive information technology influences a consumer's behavioural intention to adopt it. *Knowledge* herein referring to the stage "when an individual is exposed and gives attention to a new idea and how it works" (Rogers, 1995) is even more critical because it could inform the calculation of the meta-price value. Also, when one does not know about technology, it is quite easy to exhibit disinterest or apathy towards it – a factor which is expressed in this study.

The influencing factors found in this study relate to cost, efficiency, and untimeliness. We also see that respondents mentioned the need, inquisitiveness, efficiency, and marketing as conditions to adopting the case disruptive technology. As already discussed, meta-price value accounts for the cost factor; while efficiency and need for timeliness are accounted for by UTAUT2's performance expectancy variable. Need as an influencing factor is two-edged. On the one hand, a consumer's perception of *the need* for technology is a result of *knowing* it. However, the consumer's move from the knowledge stage to the persuasion stage (see the innovation-decision process in Rogers, 1995) is premised on the customer's realization of that technology's utility.

On the other hand, a need may be genuinely absent when a disruptive technology does not exist yet. However, changes – mostly radical – to the existing value chain creates a new need which could only be fulfilled by the latest *disruptive* technology. This new need and its fulfilling attendant technology must be communicated or *marketed* to generate knowledge of it to its intended market. A potential argument that arises here is whether TAM's perceived usefulness or UTAUT's performance expectancy does not account for need as advanced in this study. A response would be that perceived usefulness is an extrinsic motivation that emphasises on the outcome albeit in a work environment (Davis, Bagozzi and Warshaw, 1992), while the need is a natural outcome of a fundamental mechanism of determining whether one has used for technology or not. Furthermore, need is purely voluntary, whereas perceived usefulness is somewhat compulsory for work and its attendant technologies are directed by an organisation, not by the using individual.

In summary, the behavioural intention to adopt disruptive information technology is affected by three main variables; the *meta*-price value of the technology influences; the *extent of knowledge* of the technology; and the *perceived need* for the technology. This new need and its fulfilling attendant technology must be communicated or *marketed* to create an understanding of it to its intended market. The derivation of these three new variables from the analysis is the first of this paper's two contributions. Their novelty is further illustrated in Table 4, which shows all the factors in existing technology adoption theories.

The second contribution is the fusion of the three new constructs with those of the UTAUT2, which was used as a lens to analyse this study's data. The observable outcome of the fusion is a proposed disruptive information technology adoption framework, as shown in Figure 3.

CONCLUSION AND FUTURE RESEARCH POINTERS

This study purposed to explore the factors that inform individuals' behavioural intention and adoption of disruptive technologies. This purpose was based on the observed lack of research on the factors affecting individuals' adoption of disruptive technologies. Previous research had focused on organisational level, industry level or country level issues concerning disruptive technologies. Consequently, previous studies neither advanced nor contributed to the theory of adoption of disruptive technologies. Moreover, they were fixated on developed country contexts and neglected the adoption of disruptive technologies in developing country contexts. By analysing qualitative data inductively, this study concludes that people adopt disruptive technology when they first know about it through the technology provider's education. This knowledge leads people to compare the cost of using disruptive technology with that

Table 4. Factors in the various technology adoption models

Theory	Source	Factors influencing Technology Adoption
Theory of Reasoned Action	Ajzen and Fishbein (1980)	Behavioural Intention; Attitude; Normative beliefs and motivation to comply; subjective norms
Technology Acceptance Model (TAM)	Davis' (1989)	External variables; perceived usefulness; perceived ease of use; attitude; behavioural intention to use
TAM2	Venkatesh & Davis (2000)	External variables perceived usefulness; perceived ease of use; behavioural intention to use
TAM3	Venkatesh & Bala (2008)	Subjective norm; image; job relevance; output quality; result demonstrability; anchors [computer self-efficacy, perceptions of external control, computer anxiety, computer playfulness], adjustment [perceived enjoyment, objective usability], experience, voluntariness, perceived usefulness, perceived ease of use, intention to use
Unified Theory of Acceptance and Use of Technology (UTAUT)	Venkatesh, Morris, Davis, & Davis (2003)	Performance expectancy, effort expectancy, social influence, facilitating conditions, behavioural intention
UTAUT2	Venkatesh, Thong, & Xu (2012)	Performance expectancy, effort expectancy, social influence, facilitating conditions, hedonic motivations, price value, habit, behavioural intention
Disruptive information technology adoption model	This paper	Meta-price value, knowledge of the technology, perceived need

of using disrupted technology. At the same time, adopters evaluate their need for disruptive technology after they come to know of it. They form an intention to adopt, and adopt the disruptive technology if they perceive a lower cost of, and a need to use a disruptive technology.

The three independent variables discovered and discussed in this study disrupt those in existing technology adoption theories. As such, they need further conceptualisation, development, and testing. Therefore, we encourage future studies, especially on disruptive technology adoption, to use this paper's framework as a guiding lens or as a research model for further testing in the study of other disruptive technologies apart from ridesharing applications. Furthermore, other future studies can develop a scale and measurement instrument for these variables to facilitate quantitative hypothesis development, data collection and analysis. Also, future studies may consider a quantitative survey strategy to explore the factors identified in this study. A quantitative study, especially using structural equation modelling, would help identify the strength of the relationships between the variables. Such a study will also enhance the generalisability of the findings.

REFERENCES

8.

Figure 3. [Disruptive Information Technology Adoption Model]

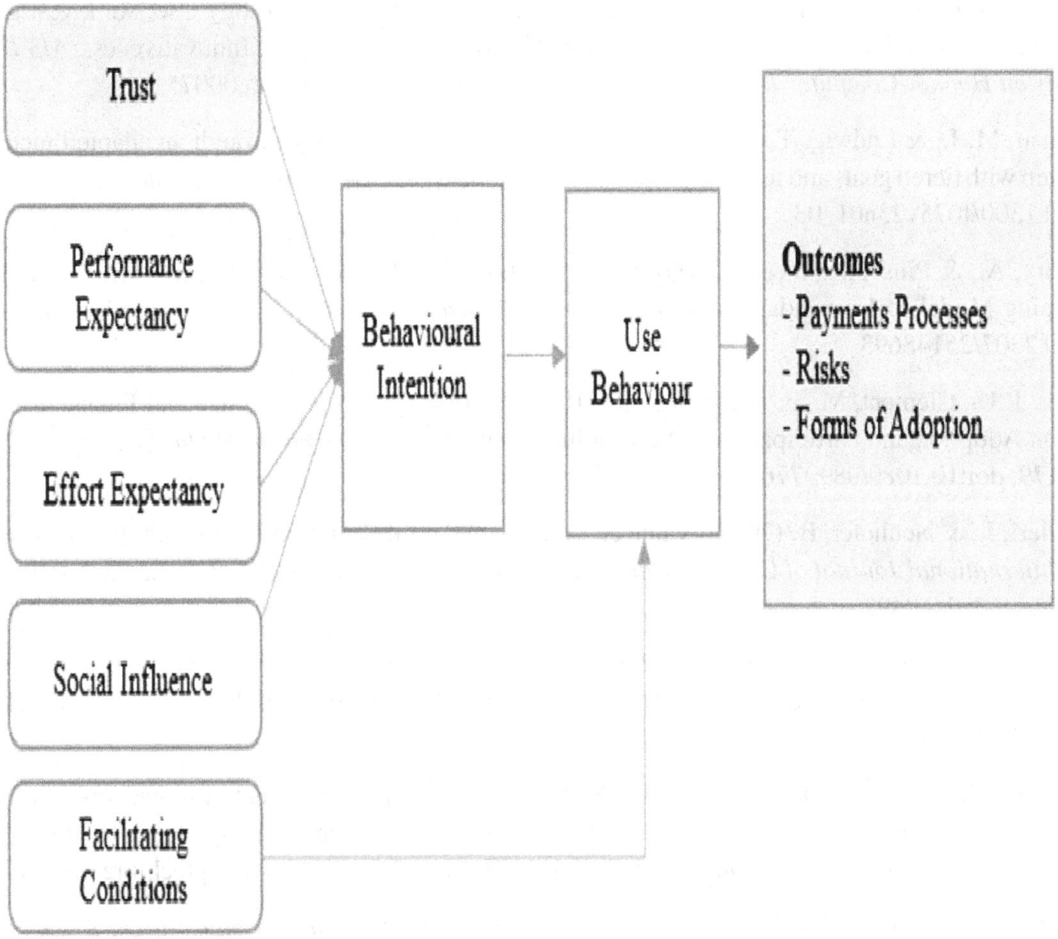

Achinstein, P. (2010). The War on Induction : Whewell Takes On Newton and Mill (Norton Takes On Everyone). *Philosophy of Science*, *77*(December), 728–739. doi:10.1086/656540

Adomavicius, G., Bockstedt, Gupta, & Kauffman. (2008). Making Sense of Technology Trends in the Information Technology Landscape : A Design Science Approach. *Management Information Systems Quarterly*, *32*(4), 779–809. doi:10.2307/25148872

Ajzen, I., & Fishbein, M. (1980). *Understanding attitudes and predicting social behaviour*. Englewood Cliffs, NJ: Prentice-Hall.

Avgerou, C. (2001). The significance of context in information systems and organizational change. *Information Systems Journal*, *11*(1), 43–63. doi:10.1046/j.1365-2575.2001.00095.x

Avgerou, C. (2008). Information systems in developing countries : A critical research review. *Journal of Information Technology*, *23*(3), 133–146. doi:10.1057/palgrave.jit.2000136

Bakke, S., & Henry, R. M. (2015). Unraveling the Mystery of New Technology Use: An Investigation into the Interplay of Desire for Control, Computer Self-efficacy, and Personal Innovativeness. *AIS Transactions on Human-Computer Interaction*, *7*(4), 270–293. doi:10.17705/1thci.00075

Bateman, M. J., & Ludwig, T. D. (2003). Managing distribution quality through an adapted incentive program with tiered goals and feedback. *Journal of Organizational Behavior Management*, *23*(1), 33–55. doi:10.1300/J075v23n01_03

Beaudry, A., & Pinsonneault, A. (2005). Understanding User Responses to Information Technology: A Coping Model of User Adaptation. *Management Information Systems Quarterly*, *29*(3), 493–524. doi:10.2307/25148693

Becker, J. U., Clement, M., & Schaedel, U. (2010). The Impact of Network Size and Financial Incentives on Adoption and Participation in New Online Communities. *Journal of Media Economics*, *23*(3), 165–179. doi:10.1080/08997764.2010.502515

Camilleri, J., & Neuhofer, B. (2017). Value co-creation and co-destruction in the Airbnb sharing economy. *International Journal of Contemporary Hospitality Management*, *29*(9), 2322–2340. doi:10.1108/IJCHM-09-2016-0492

Carlo, J. L., Lyytinen, K., & Rose, G. M. (2009). Internet computing as a disruptive information technology innovation: The role of strong order effects. *Information Systems Journal*, 1–36. doi:10.1111/j.1365-2575.2009.00345.x

Cheng, Y., Huang, L., Ramlogan, R., & Li, X. (2017). Forecasting of potential impacts of disruptive technology in promising technological areas: Elaborating the SIRS epidemic model in RFID technology. *Technological Forecasting and Social Change*, *117*, 170–183. doi:10.1016/j.techfore.2016.12.003

Christensen, C. (1997). *The innovator's dilemma: when new technologies cause great firms to fail*. Boston, MA: Harvard Business Review.

Davis, F. D. (1989). Perceived usefulness, perceived ease of use, and user acceptance of information technology. *Management Information Systems Quarterly*, *13*(3), 319–340. doi:10.2307/249008

Davis, F. D., Bagozzi, R. P., & Warshaw, P. R. (1992). Extrinsic and intrinsic motivation to use computers in the workplace. *Journal of Applied Social Psychology*, *22*(14), 1111–1132. doi:10.1111/j.1559-1816.1992.tb00945.x

Dhillon, G., Coss, D., & Hackney, R. (2001). Interpreting the role of disruptive technologies in e-businesses. *Logistics Information Management*, *14*(1/2), 163–171. doi:10.1108/09576050110363167

Durkin, M., Mulholland, G., & Mccartan, A. (2015). A socio-technical perspective on social media adoption : A case from retail banking. *International Journal of Bank Marketing*, *33*(7), 944–962. doi:10.1108/IJBM-01-2015-0014

Evans, J. S. B. T., & Over, D. E. (2013). Reasoning to and from belief : Deduction and induction are still distinct. *Thinking & Reasoning*, *19*(3), 267–283. doi:10.1080/13546783.2012.745450

Evans, N., Ralston, B., & Broderick, A. (2009). Strategic thinking about disruptive technologies. *Strategy and Leadership*, *37*(1), 23–30. doi:10.1108/10878570910926034

Frederick, D. E. (2016). Ebooks as a disruptive technology. Managing Ebook Metadata in Academic Libraries, 11–24. doi:10.1016/B978-0-08-100151-6.00002-0

French, A. M. (2016). The Digital Revolution: Internet of Things, 5G, and Beyond. *Communications of AIS*, *38*(May), 840–850.

Gangwar, H., Date, H., & Raoot, A. D. (2014). Review on IT adoption : Insights from recent technologies. *Journal of Enterprise Information Management*, *27*(4), 488–502. doi:10.1108/JEIM-08-2012-0047

Garbers, Y., & Konradt, U. (2014). The effect of financial incentives on performance : A quantitative review of individual and team-based financial incentives. *Journal of Occupational and Organizational Psychology*, *87*(1), 102–137. doi:10.1111/joop.12039

Goode, L. (2011) *Worth It? An App to Get a Cab, Wall Street Journal (Blog)*. Available at: http://blogs.wsj.com/digits/2011/06/17/worth-it-an-app-to-get-a-cab/.

Goomas, D. T., & Ludwig, T. D. (2007). Enhancing incentive programs with proximal goals and immediate feedback. *Journal of Organizational Behavior Management*, *27*(1), 33–68. doi:10.1300/J075v27n01_02

Govindarajulu, N., & Daily, B. F. (2004). Motivating employees for environmental improvement Motivating employees for environmental improvement. *Industrial Management & Data Systems*, *104*(4), 364–372. doi:10.1108/02635570410530775

Henten, A. H., & Windekilde, I. M. (2016). Transaction costs and the sharing economy. *Info*, *18*(1), 1–15. doi:10.1108/info-09-2015-0044

Jackson, T. (2017, May). Uber's Africa Push Hits Roadblocks. Fortune, 14.

Klein, H. K., & Myers, M. D. (1999). A set of principles for conducting and evaluating interpretive field studies. *Management Information Systems Quarterly*, *23*(1), 67–94. doi:10.2307/249410

Kothman, I., & Faber, N. (2016). How 3D printing technology changes the rules of the game: Insights from the construction sector. *Journal of Manufacturing Technology Management*, *27*(7), 932–943. doi:10.1108/JMTM-01-2016-0010

Kovacs, G., & Spens, K. M. (2005). Abductive reasoning in logistics. *International Journal of Physical Distribution & Logistics Management*, *35*(2), 132–144. doi:10.1108/09600030510590318

Lashinsky, A. (2017) *What could take down Uber, Fortune.com*. Available at: http://fortune.com/2017/05/18/uber-travis-kalanick-woes/

Lee, A. S., & Baskerville, R. L. (2003). Generalizing Generalizability in Information Systems Research. *Information Systems Research*, *14*(3), 221–243. doi:10.1287/isre.14.3.221.16560

Liu, F., Zhao, X., Chau, P. Y. K., & Tang, Q. (2015). Roles of perceived value and individual differences in the acceptance of mobile coupon applications. *Internet Research*, *25*(3), 471–495. doi:10.1108/IntR-02-2014-0053

Lyytinen, K., & Rose, G. M. (2003). The Disruptive nature of Information Technology innovations: The case of Internet computing in systems development in organisations. *Management Information Systems Quarterly, 27*(4), 557–596. doi:10.2307/30036549

Malhotra, A., & Van Alstyne, M. (2014). The dark side of the sharing economy... and how to lighten it. *Communications of the ACM, 57*(11), 24–28. doi:10.1145/2668893

Martins, J. T., & Nunes, M. B. (2016). 'Academics' e-learning adoption in higher education institutions : A matter of trust adoption'. *The Learning Organization, 23*(5), 299–331. doi:10.1108/TLO-05-2015-0034

Momeni, A., & Rost, K. (2016). Identification and monitoring of possible disruptive technologies by patent-development paths and topic modelling. *Technological Forecasting and Social Change, 104*, 16–29. doi:10.1016/j.techfore.2015.12.003

Obal, M. (2017). What drives post-adoption usage? Investigating the negative and positive antecedents of disruptive technology adoption intentions. *Industrial Marketing Management, 63*, 42–52. doi:10.1016/j.indmarman.2017.01.003

Ochara, N. M. (2013). Linking Reasoning to Theoretical Argument in Information Systems Research. *Proceedings of the Nineteenth Americas Conference on Information Systems*, 1–11.

Perez, L., & Paulino, V. D. S. (2017). Taking advantage of disruptive innovation through changes in value networks : Insights. *Supply Chain Management, 22*(2), 97–106. doi:10.1108/SCM-01-2017-0017

Pines, E. (2016, Dec.). Uber's bold move. *Forbes*, 58–74.

Rasmussen, D., & Eliasmith, C. (2011). A Neural Model of Rule Generation in Inductive Reasoning. *Topics in Cognitive Science, 3*(1), 140–153. doi:10.1111/j.1756-8765.2010.01127.x PMID:25164178

Rogers, E. M. (1995). *Diffusion of Innovations*. New York, NY: The Free Press.

Rondan-Cataluña, J. F., Arenas-Gaitán, J., & Ramírez-Correa, P. (2015). A comparison of the different versions of popular technology acceptance models A non-linear perspective. *Kybernetes, 44*(5), 788–805. doi:10.1108/K-09-2014-0184

Schermann, M., Hemsen, H., Buchmüller, C., Bitter, T., Krcmar, H., Markl, V., & Hoeren, T. (2014). Big data: An interdisciplinary opportunity for information systems research. *Business & Information Systems Engineering, 5*(5), 261–266. doi:10.100712599-014-0345-1

Sherif, K., Zmud, R. W., & Browne, G. J. (2006). Managing Peer-to-Peer Conflicts in Disruptive Information Technology Innovations: The Case of Software Reuse. *Management Information Systems Quarterly, 30*(2), 339–356. doi:10.2307/25148734

Smith, R. (2007). The disruptive potential of game technologies. *Research Technology Management, 50*(2), 57–64. doi:10.1080/08956308.2007.11657431

Sovani, A., & Jayawardena, C. (2017). How should Canadian tourism embrace the disruption caused by the sharing economy? *Worldwide Hospitality and Tourism Themes, 5*. doi:10.1108/WHATT-05-2017-0023

Steinmetz, K., & Vella, M. (2017, June). Chaos at the world's most valuable venture-backed company is forcing to question its values. *Time*, 23–28.

Tribunella, T., & Tribunella, H. (2016, May). Twenty questions on the Sharing economy and mobile accounting apps. *The CPA Journal*.

Uber. (2017). *Driver requirements: how to drive with Uber, Uber website.* Available at: https://www. uber.com/en-GH/drive/requirements/

Vecchiato, R. (2017). Disruptive innovation, managerial cognition, and technology competition outcomes. *Technological Forecasting and Social Change, 116*, 116–12. doi:10.1016/j.techfore.2016.10.068

Venkatesh, V. (2006). Where To Go From Here? Thoughts on Future Directions for Research on Individual-Level Technology Adoption with a Focus on Decision Making. *Decision Sciences, 37*(4), 497–519. doi:10.1111/j.1540-5414.2006.00136.x

Venkatesh, V., & Bala, H. (2008). Technology acceptance model 3 and a research agenda on interventions. *Decision Sciences, 39*(2), 273–315. doi:10.1111/j.1540-5915.2008.00192.x

Venkatesh, V., & Davis, F. D. (2000). A theoretical extension of the technology acceptance model: Four longitudinal field studies. *Management Science, 46*(2), 186–204. doi:10.1287/mnsc.46.2.186.11926

Venkatesh, V., Morris, M. G., Davis, G. B., & Davis, F. D. (2003). User acceptance of information technology: Toward a unified view. *Management Information Systems Quarterly, 27*(3), 425–478. doi:10.2307/30036540

Venkatesh, V., Thong, J. Y. L., & Xu, X. (2012). Consumer Acceptance and Use of Information Technology: Extending the Unified Theory of Acceptance and Use of Technology. *Management Information Systems Quarterly, 36*(1), 157–178. doi:10.2307/41410412

Venkatesh, V., Thong, J. Y. L., & Xu, X. (2016). Unified Theory of Acceptance and Use of Technology: A synthesis and the road ahead. *Journal of the Association for Information Systems, 17*(5), 328–376. doi:10.17705/1jais.00428

Walsham, G. (1995). Interpretive case studies in IS research : Nature and method. *European Journal of Information Systems, 4*(2), 74–81. doi:10.1057/ejis.1995.9

Walsham, G. (2006). Doing interpretive research. *European Journal of Information Systems, 15*(3), 320–330. doi:10.1057/palgrave.ejis.3000589

Wiredu, G. O. (2007). User appropriation of mobile technologies: Motives, conditions and design properties. *Information and Organization, 17*(2), 110–129. doi:10.1016/j.infoandorg.2007.03.002

Zhu, G., So, K. K. F., & Hudson, S. (2016). Inside the sharing economy: Understanding consumer motivations behind the adoption of mobile applications. *International Journal of Contemporary Hospitality Management, 9*, 1–56. doi:10.1108/ IJCHM-09-2016-0496

Chapter 4
Understanding Privacy–Focused Technology Use Among Generation Y:
Its Impact on Behavioural Intention and Actual Use of Social Commerce

Divine Quase Agozie
Cyprus International University, Nicosia, Cyprus

Muesser Nat
 https://orcid.org/0000-0002-1539-3586
Cyprus International University, Nicosia, Cyprus

Sampson Abeeku Edu
Cyprus International University, Nicosia, Cyprus

ABSTRACT

This chapter examines privacy-focused technology use among Generation Y cohorts and its impact on their intentions and actual use of social commerce. The study employs a partial least squares SEM to evaluate hypothesized relationships stated. Four hundred eighty-seven responses were used for the analysis. Results show that privacy-focused technology use fails to influence behavioural intentions. By inference, knowledge of privacy risks influences the behavioural intentions of Generation Y, but actual use is impacted where the risk is perceived to be beyond control. This empirical analysis provides insights into key behavioural and technical aspects, offering organizations insights into developing effective social commerce strategies.

DOI: 10.4018/978-1-7998-2610-1.ch004

INTRODUCTION

The desire for social interaction is not an entirely new human sensation, as humans have always sought to interact with others (Duffett, 2017). Technologies as social media offer innovative avenues that facilitate social interactions between people with shared interests (Yablonski, 2016). The myriad of benefits accrued to social media has increased the dependence of people on them (Harrigan, Evers, Miles, & Daly, 2017), thus igniting significant behavioural changes across domains (Barreda, Bilgihan, Nusair, & Okumus, 2015). For example, organizations have drifted from traditional commerce models to social networking channels to stimulate awareness and customer engagement (Duffett, 2017). Rather than printing adverts in magazines, and expecting to spark public interest, social media channels, favour businesses to target customers at the point of expressed interest (Kim & Kim, 2018).

Social networking sites (SNS) have made the digital space a viable commerce destination (Nisar & Whitehead, 2016) however, they have also made it content and media dystopia never imagined (Zhang & Lin, 2018). Concerns over illicit access to user data and obscure surveillance of user activity by unknown agencies on social media have risen significantly (Rainie, 2018). Besides, the growing occurrence of data breaches on social media sites has also reduced trust levels among users (Rainie, 2018). These concerns generally depict the dystopia referenced earlier and have sparked behavioural changes among users (Stouthuysen, Teunis, Reusen, & Slabbinck, 2018). For instance, Pew Research (2018) reports about 30% of the adult population in the USA taking steps to hide their social media information, and another 22% altering their online behaviour to remain anonymous. Carr, Barnidge, Lee and Tsang (2014) support the fact that behavioural changes emanating from security-related issues online bother on the lack of trust, as also alluded by Rainie (2018).

Scholars maintain that trust is at the core of all social interactions, and that lower trust levels increase the susceptibility of people to agenda setting (Carr, Barnidge, Lee, & Tsang, 2014), whereas mistrust reduces self-efficacy leading to withdrawal (Fabian and Wolfgang, 2018). Where users perceive negative trust or risks, they may disengage due to lack of motivation (Choi, Park, & Jung, 2018). Thus, negative trust implications generate undesirable reactions towards social media and its other uses social media like social commerce. Particularly because social commerce activities rely on the transfer of trust from SNS to redirect traffic onto the actual commerce sites (Hajli, et al., 2017), the increasing vertical privacy concerns and falling trust levels could affect social commerce engagements (Susanne & Menno, 2017).

Further, there has been a rapid growth in popularity of privacy-focused innovations offering personalized privacy and security control (Rainie, 2018). For example, browsers as Mozilla Firefox offer default private browsing, anti-ad-blockers, and cookie removers. Besides privacy and security protection, these innovations present a potential disruption to the online commerce ecosystem (Rainie, 2018). The objective PFTs is to offer user-side privacy solutions (Rainie, 2018), but this objective as opposed to the operations of many online organizations. Service providers like commerce businesses thrive on user data to improve services, promote sales, maintenance and improve user satisfaction. The opposing dimension of these objectives is also likely to generate mixed reactions from online vendors towards the use of PFTs on their platforms. Some scholars are of the view that users perceive PFTs as better alternatives to platform assurances (Rainie, 2018). However, there is no clarity on the influence of PFTs on usage dimensions, particularly in the social commerce domain. Widjaja et al., (2019) revealed that the use of such innovations reduces user considerations to privacy consequences, suggesting PFTs boost technology-based trust. Contrary, Kwon and Johnson, (2015) found privacy innovations to increase fatigue online. Hargittai & Marwick, (2016) asserts that because privacy technologies are also susceptible to some privacy risks, it reduces user confidence. These differing viewpoints and others present the lack of consensus on the influence of PFTs identified early on.

Widjaja, et al., (2019) asserts that usage patterns of technology among different age cohorts is relevant to identify unique elements relevant to that cohort. Thus far, the role of age, often assessed in most information systems studies, is found to be vital to usage patterns (Pinto & Yagnik, 2016). However, scholars have yet to examine its role in the use of PFTs for privacy protection. For instance, the determinants of PFTs among different generational cohorts, (Pinto & Yagnik, 2016). Duffett (2017), conceives that there is little evidence on the assessments of PFTs use in social commerce among generation Y cohorts. Generation Y's are the most technology savvy cohort (Schroer, 2014), and spend about $200 million annually on e-commerce transactions (GAIA Insights, 2018). This evidence and many others exert the significance of Generation Y cohorts. In pursuance of this gap, this study explores two main objectives. First, it examines the use of PFTs among generation Y cohorts, by elucidating the antecedents of PFT use among this generational cohort. Next, it examines the role of PFTs in the intentions and actual use decisions of generation Y's.

BACKGROUND

Social Media and the Privacy Paradox

The semantic web carries with it numerous opportunities. Among these are big data affordances, the ubiquity of communication and endless social networking (Susanne & Menno, 2017). These opportunities have effectively integrated humans and these technologies. Simultaneously, the increasing popularity of technologies as social media have increased information privacy risks (Smith & Kollars, 2015). Technology acceptance studies, establish that users' decision to use technology is informed mostly by popularity, cost and usability of a technology (Smith & Kollars, 2015), and not often based on technical factors. By implication, security and privacy issues have minimal considerations among individual users. Concerns over data and privacy breaches have risen (Susanne & Menno, 2017), yet studies show users consider less, these concepts when accepting or using technology. Smith and Kollars, (2015) argues that privacy concerns and actual privacy behaviour of people are often mismatched. This is known as the privacy paradox (Smith, Diney, & Xu, 2011). Thus, users express privacy concerns, yet commit little effort to protect their privacy (Kim, Park, Park, & Ahn, 2019).

The increasing perception of risk depicts a superior knowledge of privacy protection and strategies (Oomen & Leenes, 2008). In theory, the concerns of users do not match their actual protective behaviour exhibited online (Lee, Son, & Kim, 2016; Sundar, Kang, Wu, Go, & Zhang, 2013). Choi et al., (2018) attributes this behaviour partly to fatigue from frequent privacy issues. Fatigued people commit less effort to decision making. For instance, despite online privacy risks, users still share personal information in exchange for retail value. Similar behaviour is shown on social media (Kind, 2015; Sundar et al., 2013). Regulating the flow of information on SNS has been reduced to some inherent protection strategies, like restricting profile and post access, private messaging instead of posting open content (Young & Quan-Haase, 2013). Privacy literacy among users is highlighted as an antecedent to this fatigued disposition of users (Choi et al., 2018), as there is scant, information published on privacy risk perception levels among different user categories. Behavioural studies on privacy-related threats on online have mainly considered adult populations (Kokolakis, 2017), and there is little evidence of consensus on a unified model for explaining actual usage behaviour of people regarding information disclosure (Kokolakis, 2017).

Privacy Innovations and Online Trust

There is profound evidence of the positive influence and role of technological innovations on ensuring trust for online platforms. Among the various trust constructs, many scholars have paid attention to technology-based trust. Technology-based trust, for instance, relative to online commerce, refers to the trust in mechanisms and, or technologies used by vendors in the online commerce ecosystem, e.g. online payment systems, database systems, servers etc. (Abayad, 2017). Functionality, reliability and effectiveness form the basis of technology-based trust (Abayad, 2017). The assurance, that these technologies will perform the intended task they are designed for is enough to form trust from users (Yu & Asgarkhani, 2015). For users to engage safely and securely, they must trust these platforms and technologies in the digital commerce ecosystem. However, engagements with third-party developers pose concerns to technology-based trust (Yu & Asgarkhani, 2015). Wingreen and Baglione, (2005) asserts that technology-based trust is tied to the existence of third-party structures that are independent of a system. Thus far, to build trust for digital commerce systems, mechanisms that handle activities of third-party involvements must be designed to prioritize the security interests of clients and not subjected to any form of manipulations (Stouthuysen, et al., 2018). The difficulty in achieving this objective generally threatens trust for online commerce.

Emerging privacy innovations offer personalized privacy control (Stouthuysen, et al., 2018), and attempt to influence technology-based trust online (Chen and Chen, 2015) because most online platforms have failed at this need. Scholars establish that users now perceive PFTs as an alternative for online structural assurance (Hargittai & Marwick, 2016). Despite the protection offered by PFTs, studies also suggest several challenges of information privacy risk persist (Rainie, 2018). For instance, PFTs may not sufficiently offer protection on sites that request an alteration to privacy settings to access site utilities. This is attributed to the fact that the objective of PFTs opposes the data operations of online organizations. Online organizations make extensive use of consumer data, for direct marketing, personalized services, platform maintenance, and performance evaluations (Duffet, 2017). As such, any mechanism that seeks to curb their access to user data poses a threat to their operations.

As such, these emerging privacy innovations introduce new dimensions for rebuilding online trust (Rainie, 2018). Users adopt these technologies with the belief that they are ensuring personal safety online, rather than depending on platform provided mechanisms (Stouthuysen, et al., 2018)

Unified Theory of Acceptance and Use of Technology *and* Generation Y's use of Technology

Technology acceptance has been extensively researched in the IS discipline (Zhang & Lin, 2018). Various theoretical models have emerged from this discourse, explaining usage intentions and behaviour (see, Technology Acceptance Model TAM, Theory of Reasoned Action TRA, etc.). These theories have offered varying approaches to understanding technology acceptance and use based on technology attributes, and contextual factors (El-Masri & Tarhini, 2017). A composite assessment of all the other theories led to the conceptualization of the Unified Theory of Acceptance and Use of Technology (UTAUT) (Venkatesh, Morris, & Davis, 2003). The theory has since seen extensive usage for studying behavioural intention and usage behaviour. In their observation, Venkatesh, et al., found most researchers were faced with a multiplicity of theories, and many arbitrarily picked constructs. Hence, the UTAUT theory fuses the suggestions put forward by the different models of technology acceptance.

Originally, there are four main constructs in the UTAUT framework, categorized into technology attributes (performance expectancy, and effort expectancy) and contextual factors (facilitating factors, and social influence) (Hanitzsch, Van-Dalen, & Steindl, 2017). Although the UTAUT model possesses the good predictive ability, some authors have raised some valid criticisms. Firstly, the model misses out on "individual" engaging elements of a behaviour (Dwivedi, Rana, Jeyaraj, Clement & Williams, 2017). The individual engaging elements are personal characteristics that describe the disposition of a user (Dwivedi et al., 2017). This is highlighted in prior studies that have introduced characteristics like attitude, computer efficacy, personal innovativeness etc. (Chong, 2013; Vekantesh, et al., 2011). Moreover, aside Dwivedi et al., (2017), Vekantesh, et al., (2012) themselves have questioned that the usefulness of the moderators introduced into the original model in some contexts. As such, few studies have employed the full complements of the UTAUT model with the moderators (Banyopadhyay & Barnes, 2012; Zhang, Guo, Lu, & Liu, 2017).

This study relies on an extended UTAUT model as its theoretical foundation of an integrated model. It excludes the moderators from the original UTAUT model, and integrates 'privacy concern' and 'privacy-focused technology use'. Prior studies have empirically used the individual engaging element to mediate the path along with performance and effort expectancy (Kim et al., 2010; Aboelmaged, 2010). Whereas, in many studies, the individual engaging element is constructed as an attitude element, mediating performance expectancy, effort expectancy and behavioural intention (Rana et al., 2017, Koh, Prybutok, Ryan, & Wu, 2010; Alshare and Lane, 2011). For these reasons, we note that the current study's variables, do not fully replicate the extended UTAUT conceptualization. Some new variables have been introduced into the framework. The inclusion of the individual engaging element aligns with Ajzen and Fishein's (1980) TRA, TPB (Ajzen, 1991), and DTPB (Taylor and Todd, 1995b). For instance, the inclusion of privacy-focused technology use (PFTU) and privacy concern as engaging elements is unique to this study and founded on sound theoretical precedence.

Further, the age of the user is highlighted as a vital element or factor that influences technology adoption. Venkatesh et al., (2003) showed the significance of age in the UTAUT framework. Studies reveal that the generation Y cohort is unique, as they are considered the most willing generational cohort to adopt new technologies (Goi & Ng, 2011). In addition, people within this age category patronize and consume more online services, thus they are found to engage more online than the other cohorts do (Freestone and Mitchell, 2004). Recent evidence indicates they are most capable of selecting suitable technology and learn how to use them effectively (Boonsiritomachai & Pitchayadejanant, 2017). By inference, generation Y's will find it easier to use PFTs compared to the generations. Therefore, PFT uses best suits their online behaviour, as they provide convenience and online protection.

RESEARCH MODEL AND HYPOTHESES

Performance Expectancy (PE)

Users will often adopt and use one system that they find useful (Alain, Lacka, Li, & Chan, 2018) Thus, they believe that using the system can support their immediate goals and help them perform more with

Figure 1. Research framework (Source: Adapted from Venkatesh et al., 2003 and Dwivedi et al., 2017]

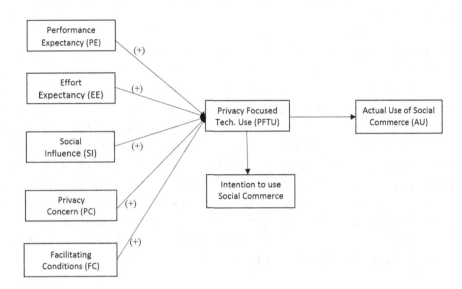

less effort (Venkatesh et al., 2003). PE is influential for explaining usage decisions of people relative to the current digital dystopia. Particularly, in order to adopt online technology, PE plays a vital role in helping users decide to or not adopt the technology. (Tarhini et al., 2016; Alain, et al., 2018). According to many scholars, PE consistently influences intentions to use a technology (Tarhini, et al., 2016). For instance, Liew, Kang, Yoo, and You, (2013) studied factors influencing mobile technology acceptance and found PE highly influential to behavioural intentions. Also, Goswami and Dutta (2016) examined e-commerce adoption by women entrepreneurs and showed PE strongly influences women entrepreneur's decision to accept e-commerce. Further, Lakhal, Khechine, and Pascot, (2013) also showed Pes positive role in the acceptance of webinar technology. Similarly, PE can influence young people's usage of privacy-focused technologies. Therefore, the study assumes that;

H1: Performance expectancy influences PFTU, among generation Y.

Effort Expectancy (EE)

Effort expectancy according to Venkatesh, et al., (2003, pp.450) "describes the degree of ease associated with the use of a system". In essence, where users find a technology or service easy to use, they are likely to adopt it. EE has played a positive mediating influence on user acceptance. Users who perceive the use of privacy-focused technologies to be easy will have positive inclinations towards it (Tarhini, El-Masri, Ali, & Serrano, 2016a). Li and Ho (2015) showed EE influences intentions to adopt online commerce. The role of EE is rather inconspicuous and not limited only to the E-commerce domain. For example, Tan (2013) showed that EE influences student's use of e-learning websites, and Pappas, Giannakos, and Mikalef (2017), also evaluated students' acceptance of game-based technologies online, and showed that effort expectancy increasingly influences the use of social networking sites as YouTube for information search. In this study, it is believed that EE influences user intentions to use PFTs. It hypothesizes that:

H2: Effort expectancy positively influences privacy-focused technology use, for social commerce by Y generation.

Social Influence (SI)

Venkatesh, et al., (2003) conceived that social influence describes the degree to which individuals perceive their important associations believe they should use a technology (pp. 451). This means that, if generation Y users are happy with PFTU, they are likely to recommend and share this experience with others (Gitau & Nzuki, 2014). Alain et al., (2018) also conceive that social influence exerts a positive influence on users' decisions to use m-commerce. Scholars have generally established that considering social influence as a factor for technology use is important (Gitau & Nzuki, 2014, Prassary et al., 2015) although some studies have shown otherwise. For instance (Alkhunaizan, A. & Love 2012; Li & Ho, 2015) showed social influence plays no relevant or significant role in facilitating intentions to use m-commerce. In the current study, it is believed that social influence is relevant to the use of privacy-focused technologies. Therefore, it hypothesizes that:

H3: Social influence exerts a positive influence on PFTU among generation Ys.

Privacy Concern (PC)

Privacy concern decreases the willingness of users to disclose personal information online, as well as changing their willingness to use online systems (Wu & Zhang, 2014). Privacy concerns of users do not only affect the use of technology, but they could also affect the validity and completeness of user information for databases. Schermer, et al., (2014), reports that increasing privacy concerns negatively affects online behaviour. For instance, privacy concerns among users may lead to inaccurate targeting, wasted efforts and frustrated mobile users. Privacy concerns also influence trust for online systems, especially in the case of less technically inclined users (Zhang, et al., 2014). Scholars posit that these people are found making little actual efforts toward achieving privacy. Choi, et al., (2018) attributes this behaviour to online fatigue and indicates that people experiencing fatigue tend to minimize decision-making efforts, thus by choosing the easier option available. Choi et al., (2018) hypothesized that privacy fatigue increases with a user's intention to disengage from personal information disclosure online, and found evidence supporting this claim. It is thus, hypothesized that:

H4: Privacy concerns increases PFTU for social commerce use among generation Y's.

Facilitating Conditions (FC)

Facilitating conditions describe, "the degree to which individuals believe that appropriate technical and societal structures exist to support their use of technology" (Venkatesh et al., 2003, pp. 450). Some extant works have identified facilitating conditions to have a positive influence on behavioural intentions. Particularly, Sumak & Sorgo (2016) found facilitating conditions to have a significant effect on behavioural intentions of using interactive whiteboards. Likewise, Bhimasta & Suprato (2016) also stressed the same positive association between facilitating conditions and students' usage intentions of mobile technologies. This study operationalizes facilitating conditions, as the belief that online organizations and content providers have made adequate mechanisms and support to facilitate the use of PFTs. These mechanisms include adequate information on how to install and effectively use technology. Thus far, we hypothesize that,

H5: facilitating conditions positively increases the use of PFTs by generation Y.

Privacy-Focused Technology Use (PFTU)

The prominence of online privacy and surveillance threats has sparked the need for increased protective behaviour among users online (Wells, 2015), likewise the risks associated with having a poor online presence (Kind, 2015). Poor online presence presents high chances of susceptibility to online threats. Already, the challenge of the lack of an effective means of ensuring online privacy amplifies the need for online protection (Chretien & Tuck, 2015).

Privacy innovations in the digital ecosystem have come to ensure personalized user privacy (Rainie, 2018). They are equipped with unique abilities to ensure protection privacy through controlling unsolicited data access by online organizations. Smith & Kollars, (2015), conceived that the increasing threat to privacy on platforms, as social media and some commerce platforms increases the popularity of privacy innovations. As such, the responsibility of privacy assurance has become an individual affair, thus, the need for privacy assurance being met by users with PFTS (Rainie, 2018). Thus far, we hypothesize that,

H6: Privacy-focused technology positively influences intentions to use social commerce
H7: Privacy-focused technology use mainly influences actual use of social commerce by generation Ys

METHOD

In line with the study objectives to the study examines the influence of privacy-focused technology use on social commerce usage intention and actual use among generation Y. The population of the study covered young people within the ages of 19 and 34 defined as the generation Y's in Cyprus. Respondents were sampled from one of the biggest higher educational institutions in the region. This setting offers a combination of actual users and prospective users of social commerce, as well as respondents with different cultural, economic and educational backgrounds. The study employs an online survey questionnaire to obtain the appropriate responses from subjects. In all, 487 responses collected over three weeks and used for the analysis.

The measurement items adapted for the study were originally drawn from Venkatesh et al., (2003), Rana et al., (2017), and Dwivedi, et al., (2017). To note, Performance Expectancy PE, Effort Expectancy EE, Social Influence SI, Facilitating condition FC and behavioural intention (BI) were originally proposed by Venkatesh, et al., (2003). However, to better contextualize the study in the current context, we integrate privacy concern PC and privacy-focused technology use PFTU into the existing model. These items have been extensively used and validated in several IS/IT studies (Alalwan et al., 2018). Items for Privacy concern were adapted and modified from Jalayer et al., (2018), and privacy-focused technology use from Rainie, (2018).

The study relies on a 7-point Likert scale, ranging from strongly disagree (1) to strongly agree (7). Demographic information on variables as age, gender, and social commerce experience, were assessed

Table 1. Respondents' demographic profile

Attributes	Categories	Count	Percent (%)
Gender	Male	255	52.43
	Female	232	47.57
Age Ranges	19 – 24	91	18.51
	25 – 29	349	71.84
	30 – 34	47	9.65
Social commerce usage experience	Never	112	22.99
	Once yearly	145	29.78
	Several times yearly	40	8.21
	Once monthly	117	24.02
	Several times weekly	45	9.25
	Several times daily	28	5.75

using closed-ended items in the questionnaire. A six-point scale adapted from Venkatesh, et al., (2012) was used to assess social commerce usage experience.

RESULTS

Measurement Model Evaluation

Assessment of the constructs' convergent and discriminant validity included the item loadings, Average Variances Extracted (AVE), and the Composite Reliabilities (CR). The model exhibited a good fit with the data, thus; $x^2=1152.17$ with 413 *df, x^2/df* = 2.79, p = 0.002; Non-Normed Fit Index (NNFI) = 0.962; Comparative Fit Index (CFI) = 0.95; Standard Root Mean Square Residual (SRMSR) = 0.04; Root Mean Square Error of Approximation (RMSEA) = 0.05. Generally, the CFI, NNFI values are expected to be > 0.90, RMSEA, and SRMR < 0.08 (Alalwan, et al., 2018) to indicate a good model fit. Overall, the model showed an adequate fit to data.

Construct Reliability

Construct reliability is assessed via internal consistency, however, Cronbach's alpha, AVE, and CR for each construct were determined. Depicted in Table 2, the Cronbach's alpha values for all constructs were above the threshold of 0.70 (Wu and Chen, 2017; Hair et al., 2010). The least exhibited alpha coefficient was 0.808 for Privacy concern and the highest of 0.896 for Behavioural intention. The skewness and kurtosis indices presented also shows adequate normality. Lei and Lomax (2005), suggests a less than an absolute value of |2.3| for both skewness and kurtosis indices to ensure adequate data normality.

Further, on reliability assessment, Average Variances Extracted (AVE) and the composite reliability (CR) for each construct are shown in Table 3. AVE values are to be above 0.50, while CR values are also expected to be greater than 0.70 (Hair et al., 2010). All latent constructs reflect adequate composite

Table 2. Summary of descriptive statistics of measurement Items

Construct	Item	Descriptions	Kurtosis	Skewness	Cronbach Alpha
Performance Expectancy (PE)	PE1	I find social commerce sites equally useful as e-commerce sites (e.g. Amazon, AliExpress)	-0.84	-0.36	0.844
	PE2	Using social commerce sites increases my chances of accessing specific products I want faster	-0.39	-0.34	
	PE3	Using social commerce sites increases my productivity in doing digital commerce	-0.69	-0.21	
Effort Expectancy (EE)	EE1	I find using social commerce sites easy and making me more skilful at digital commerce	-0.73	0.05	0.883
	EE2	My interaction with social commerce sites is clear and understandable	-0.45	-0.46	
	EE3	Learning to use social commerce sites is easy for me	-0.35	-0.47	
Social Influence (SI)	SI1	People around me think it's okay to do commerce transactions via Social Media	-0.77	-0.37	0.867
	SI2	Important people to me also find the use of Social media for commerce useful	-0.77	-0.36	
	SI3	Some of our school-related information is communicated via social media	-0.68	-0.24	
Privacy Concern (PC)	PC1	Using social commerce puts my privacy at risk	-0.99	-0.17	0.808
	PC2	Businesses or third parties will collect my information if I use social commerce	-0.74	-0.07	
	PC3	Using social commerce exposes me to an overall internet risk (phishing, pharming, hacking etc.)	-1.11	-0.123	
Privacy Focused Technology use (PFTU)	PFI1	Privacy-focused technologies guarantee my privacy compared to the platform provided privacy mechanisms	-0.40	-0.42	0.873
	PFI2	My data logs and systems are protected from unknown privacy threats (as third party cookies, tracking scripts etc.).	-0.45	-0.44	
	PFI3	I expect no adverse privacy consequences in using privacy-focused technologies on social commerce sites	0.07	-0.62	
Facilitating Conditions (FC)		I have resources necessary to use social commerce	-0.96	-0.76	0.859
		I know necessary to use social commerce	-0.67	0.45	
		I can get help from people when having difficulties using social commerce	-0.62	-0.12	
Behavioural Intention (BI)	SA1	I intend using social commerce sites in the future	-0.76	0.07	0.896
	SA2	I will always try to use social commerce sites in my daily interactions on social media	-0.52	-0.06	
	SA3	I predict I will use social commerce often in the future	-0.62	-0.01	
Actual Use (AU)	BIT1	I use social commerce sites to compare prices	-0.596	-0.327	0.873
	BIT2	I use social commerce sites to purchase items	-0.537	-0.375	
	BIT3	I use social commerce sites to check product reviews	-0.477	-0.07	

reliability of least 0.85. As a measure of validity, an assessment of item factor loadings for each construct is also presented in Table 3. Loading above 0.70 are considered adequate. All factor loadings were significant ($p < 0.005$), and above 0.70.

Table 3. Construct reliability

Constructs	Items	Loadings	AVE	CR
Performance Expectancy (PE)	PE1	.846	.855	.85
	PE2	.752		
	PE3	.744		
Effort Expectancy (EE)	EE1	.829	.897	.86
	EE2	.791		
	EE3	.845		
Social Influence (SI)	SI1	.842	.752	.90
	SI2	.918		
	SI3	.886		
Privacy Condition (PC)	PC1	.734	.845	.86
	PC2	.830		
	PC3	.815		
Privacy Focused Technology Use (PFTU)	PFI1	.828	.831	.89
	PFI2	.794		
	PFI3	.804		
Behavioural Intention (BI)	BI1	.808	.769	.88
	BI2	.887		
	BI3	.832		
Actual Use (AU)	AU1	.799	.811	.85
	AU2	.920		
	AU3	.840		
Facilitating Conditions (FC)	FC1	.834	.761	.91
	FC2	.930		
	FC3	.851		

Discriminant Validity

As shown in Table 4, the Heterotrait-Monotrait (HTMT) criteria for determining discriminant validity is used to determine discriminant validity. Criticisms of the low sensitivity of the traditional Fornell-Larcker criterion informed the HTMT criterion in the SEM community in recent times (Henseler & Chin, 2010). The HTMT compares the construct HTMT-ratio to a defined threshold. Where HTMT values fall below the threshold value, it is concluded that there is discriminant validity. A few authors have proposed criteria for the threshold level of the HTMT. For instance, Kline, (2011); Clark and Watson,

Table 4. Discriminant Validity using HTMT Criterion

	EE	FC	PC	PE	PDF	BI	SI	AU
EE								
FC	0.773							
PC	0.676	0.457						
PE	0.234	0.132	0.131					
PFTU	0.644	0.772	0.509	0.224				
BI	0.746	0.659	0.629	0.141	0.627			
SI	0.692	0.574	0.739	0.115	0.594	0.618		
AU	0.197	0.138	0.357	0.368	0.494	0.511	0.112	

(1995) suggest >= 0.85 criteria, whereas others like (Gold et al, 2001; Teo et al., 2008) have also stated >= 0.90. Irrespective, the study's results exhibited enough discriminant validity in both instances.

Evaluation of Structural Model and Hypotheses

Shown in Table 5, results show a significant Chi-square statistic, with similar fit indices of the structural model, CMIN = 2.79, CFI =0.95, RMSEA = 0.063, NNFI = 0.962, and SRMSR = 0.054. Thus, the structural model shows an adequate fit.

Table 5. Fit indices of the structural model

Fit indices	Statistic	Structural Model
CMin/df	<= 3.00	2.79
CFI	>= 0.90	0.95
NNFI	>= 0.90	0.962
SRMSR	<= 0.90	0.054
RMSEA	<= 0.08	0.063

All determinants considered except 'facilitating conditions' were significant as antecedents of privacy-focused technology use. Performance expectancy (β= 0.419, t-stats 3.294, p < .001) and effort expectancy (β= 0.383, t-stats, 2.971, p<.003) indicating statistically significant relationships. In that, Generation Ys perceive the use of PFTs to enhance their performance or abilities to use social commerce safely and perceive low effort expectations regarding their use. Social influence also showed a significant influence on privacy-focused technology use (β= 0.318, t-stats 2.766, p < .006). By implication, the opinions of close associates of the study's subjects influence their decision to use PFTs. Similarly, privacy concerns ultimately increase the use of PFTs among generation Y's (β= 0.398, t-stats, 3.945, p<.000). However, facilitating conditions played no significant role in respondent's decision to use PFTs (β= 0.045, t-stats 0.403, p < .687).

Figure 2. Structural model evaluation

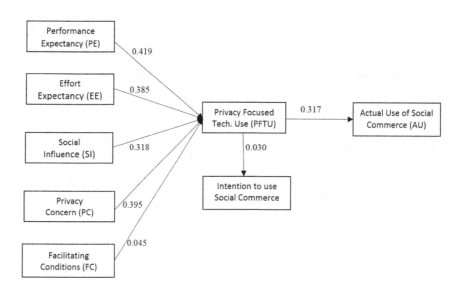

DISCUSSION

The measurement and structural models both exhibit good fits and predictive ability. Statistical indices evaluated were all within acceptable thresholds to support the conclusions drawn from the study. All eight constructs (PE, EE, SI, PC, FC, PFTU, BI and AU) showed sufficient reliability and validity to support any generalizations from the study. The study relies on the UTAUT framework to study the PFTU phenomenon among generation Y's. Originally, the UTAUT constructs predicted about 58% of the variance in behavioural intention. The current study's R^2 coefficient for the behavioural intention was higher, thus 69.6%. By inference, the study's model better predicts behavioural intention with the inclusion of the new constructs (privacy concern and PFTU.

PE shows to be a crucial determinant of generations Y's acceptance and use of privacy-focused technologies. Thus, hypothesis 1, assesses users' perception of how PFTs improves their safety while

Table 6. Summarized Structural Modelling results

	Hypotheses	Path Coefficient	T-statistic	P-value	Conclusion
H1	PE –> PFTU	0.419	3.294	0.001**	Significant
H2	EE –> PFTU	0.383	2.971	0.003**	Significant
H3	SI –> PFTU	0.318	2.766	0.006	Significant
H4	PC –> PFTU	0.398	3.945	0.000**	Significant
H5	FC –> PFTU	0.045	0.403	0.687	Not Significant
H6	PFTU –> AU	0.317	2.888	0.004**	Significant
H7	PFTU –> BI	0.030	0.305	0.760	Not Significant

Note: *Significant at .005 level

using social commerce. Results show a positive influence. Practically, PFTs enhances user's confidence online, and this confidence translates into self-efficacy (Martins et al., 2014). Giving that, generation Y's are more technology savvy and more willing to acquire information about new phenomena compared to other generational cohorts, the desire to use social commerce sites with reduced information risks is essential to them. Dienlin and Trepte (2015) supports this assertion by indicating, privacy literacy and digital education increases user's privacy consciousness. This backs the finding that PFTU enhances their safety effectiveness online.

Effort expectancy also emerged a significant factor contributing to PFT use. Generation Y's are able to learn how to use new technologies faster (Boonsiritomachai & Pitchayadejanant, 2017). Thus far, this ability to learn fast potentially underlies the perception that the use of PFTs to protect against privacy threats on social commerce sites is easy. These users will adopt PFTs online if they believe it makes browsing online safe or easy to use effectively. For instance, privacy settings on many online platforms have proven to be difficult to understand or manipulate for effective use. Thus, users find them difficult to use compared to the ease and flexibility offered by privacy protection software or applications. Hence, the ease of convenience of this experience drives users to use PFTs more often.

Further, social influence maintains its significance on intentions to use technology. Subsequently, generation Y's are motivated to use PFTs when they perceive it to be important to their peers and people found to be relevant to them. Everyone is susceptible to some influence at some point by people around them (Malaquias & Hwang, 2016). This influence is most apparent among young adults and adolescents (Piper, et al., 1987). Further, generation Y's, are known for the ability to adopt new technologies and search for information faster, are most likely to easily join in the use of new technological trends. A broad societal appeal for a type of technology is enough social appeal or influence to entice these users. For example, the Uber mobile technology offers a 5% off a ride for users when they invite friends for their first ride in an Uber cab. Undoubtedly, this concept effectively promotes the adoption of technology as people tend to be easily influenced by their networks. This influence of SI is also useful for the nature of social commerce as well. Many generations Y's are on multiple social media, and chances of friends and other social networks making recommendations, about a new phenomenon is high, or social networks advertising the need to use technologies like PFTs online (Kelly et al., 2013). Hence, a little word of mouth online will influence other cohorts to adopt and use them.

The study results confirm privacy concern as the most significant influencer of PFTU. Prior studies reveal that users express much concern about online privacy threats, and the increasing digital and privacy literacy makes this phenomenon more prevalent (Dienlin & Trepte, 2015). This finding goes on to explain the impact PFTU establishes with the actual use of social commerce sites. This result depicts Dienlin and Trepte's, assertion that sufficient knowledge of privacy threats, increases awareness behaviour. Users, who are motivated to form an effective privacy protection behaviour, do so because they are able to perceive the consequences. In this study, this assertion is supported by the significant influence of privacy concerns on PFT use. Thus far, the more information a user gains on privacy issues the more knowledgeable they become on how to protect privacy.

In assessing the role of PFTU on behavioural intentions and actual use, PFTU fails to influence behavioural intentions but significantly influences actual use. The finding also supports the belief that users consider privacy innovations to be useful alternatives for ensuring privacy protection online. Thus far, it concludes that privacy-focused technology use increases the actual use of social commerce.

CONCLUSION

Contributions to Theory

The current study contributes to the social commerce discourse by extending knowledge on its usage and providing empirical evidence for academic purposes. Specifically, the study relies on the UTAUT framework, to explain behavioural intentions and actual use within an organizational broad context. Theoretically, the UTAUT theory is developed to examine the adoption and use of technologies from users' perspective (Venkatesh, et al., 2012), hence, it is an appropriate theory to build a new model for new phenomena. Thus far, this study contributes to theory, by extending the validity of the UTAUT framework.

Although the UTAUT model provides precision on understanding peoples' usage behaviour toward a technology, proposing a model capable of interpreting actual user behaviour in a sensitive context as privacy assurance requires the integration of relevant factors and modified relationships. The model in this study, introduced new factors and relationships, as privacy concern and privacy-focused technology use. Thus, extending the UTAUT model to examine new causal relationships and factors in a different context from the original. Particularly, it provides empirical evidence on the role of privacy-focused technology use in determining behavioural intentions and actual usage of social commerce. This further represents a worthwhile direction for future technology adoption and privacy-related studies in other domains as M-commerce, and other online booking fields.

Practical Implications

The full potential of social commerce is undermined unless a wide and sustained usage by customers is achieved (Simintiras, et al., 2014). Conversely, this empirical analysis provides insights into key behavioural and usage aspects that offer organizational insights into developing effective social commerce strategies. For example, given the evidence of privacy-focused technologies' significant influence on actual usage decisions, it is inferred that respondents perceive a lack of effective privacy assurances of online commerce sites. Since trust for online platforms partly bothers on structural assurances (Wingreen, Mazey, Baglione & Storholm, 2018), is significant to enhance technology-based trust. Thus, online vendors and firms, by reinventing structural assurances on commerce platforms are also reinstating trust among users. Pew Research (2018) reveals a significant drop in trust levels among users for social media and commerce sites. Unfortunately, these two settings are interdependent to thrive. Therefore, recapturing trust among users for these technologies goes a long way to contribute to the needed sustained user engagements needed. Further, demographic responses from the study reveal significant usage experience of subjects (see Table 1). This is an indication of a high willingness of these users to become actual users of social commerce. In this respect, intensified public and personalized campaigns to rebuild structural assurance trust, and privacy assurances for effective social commerce use among generation Y's. Chen & Zahedi, (2016), also suggests official social media platforms are a viable and economical means of undertaking such persuasive campaigns. Social commerce organizations can utilize social media channels for marketing communication to sensitive this campaign among this generational cohort and others to use social commerce.

Moreover, the significance of PFTU on actual use explains users' willingness to employ PFTs to access online platforms, as social commerce sites. The prominence of this phenomenon is likely to result in a grave challenge for social commerce. Online organizations rely on user data to improve their service offerings, optimize operations and run direct marketing sales campaigns as well. However, PFTs seek to curb unsolicited access to user data by the online organization. In essence, these opposing objectives can potentially start usage challenges between users and vendors. Among the numerous possible consequences, privacy fatigue (Choi et al., 2018), is prominently highlighted. Studies establish that fatigue is characterized by withdrawal and disengagement symptoms (Choi, et al., 2018; Demerouti et al., 2010). Online organizations and social commerce sites risk user disengagements if such usage and data collection trade-off persists.

FUTURE RESEARCH DIRECTIONS

The study considered only generation Y cohorts in the Cyprus region, without to study the influence of PFTs on user intentions and actual use. However, we believe other generational cohorts are prospective users of PFTs. As such, it will be valuable to consider the opinions of other cohorts. Further, age has been found to play significant roles in technology adoption and use in the information systems literature. As such, controlling for the effects of different age groups, and demographic characteristics as gender could also prove valuable to revealing latent information embedded in the phenomenon under study. For example, gender differences in attitudes or intentions to use PFTs online. Future studies can consider expanding the current work by addressing these limitations.

Conflict of Interests

Authors declare that we have no competing interests.

REFERENCES

Aboelmaged, M. G. (2010). Predicting e-procurement adoption in a developing country: An empirical integration of technology acceptance model and theory of planned behaviour. *Industrial Management & Data Systems, 110*(3), 392–414. doi:10.1108/02635571011030042

Agag, G. M., & El-Masry, A. A. (2016). Why do consumers trust online travel websites? Drivers and outcomes of consumer trust toward online travel websites. *Journal of Travel Research.* doi:10.1177/0047287516643185

Ajzen, I. (1991). The theory of planned behaviour. *Organizational Behavior and Human Decision Processes, 50*(2), 179–211. doi:10.1016/0749-5978(91)90020-T

Ajzen, I., & Fishbein, M. M. (1980). *Understanding attitudes and predicting social behaviour.* Prentice-Hall.

Al-Gahtani, S. S. (2016). Empirical investigation of e-learning acceptance and assimilation: A structural equation model. Applied Computing and Informatics, 12(1), 27–50. doi:10.1016/j.aci.2014.09.001

Alain, Y. C., Lacka, E., Li, B., & Chan, H. K. (2018). The role of social media in enhancing Guanxi and perceived effectiveness of e-commerce institutional mechanism in the online marketplace. *Information & Management*, *55*(5), 621–632. doi:10.1016/j.im.2018.01.003

Alarcón-Del-Amo, M. D. C., Lorenzo-Romero, C., & Gómez-Borja, M.-A. (2012). Analysis of acceptance of social networking sites. *African Journal of Business Management*, *6*(29), 8609–8619. doi:10.5897/AJBM11.2664

Algharabat, R., Alalwan, A. A., Rana, N. P., & Dwivedi, Y. K. (2017). Three-dimensional product presentation quality antecedents and their consequences for online retailers: The moderating role of virtual product experience. *Journal of Retailing and Consumer Services*, *36*, 203–217. doi:10.1016/j.jretconser.2017.02.007

Alkhunaizan, A., & Love, S. (2012). Predicting consumer decisions to adopt mobile commerce in Saudi Arabia. *Proceedings from 19th Americas Conference on Information Systems*, 1 – 9

Alshare, K. A., & Lane, P. L. (2011). Predicting student-perceived learning outcomes and satisfaction in ERP courses: An empirical investigation. *Communications of the Association for Information Systems*, *28*(1), 571–584.

Alwan, A. A., Dwivedi, Y. K., Nripendra, P. R., & Algharabat, R. (2018). Examining factors influencing Jordanian customers' intentions and adoption of internet banking: Extending UTAUT2 with risk. *Journal of Retailing and Consumer Services*, *40*, 125–138. doi:10.1016/j.jretconser.2017.08.026

Alwan, A. A., Dwivedi, Y. K., Rana, N. P., Lal, B., & Williams, M. D. (2015). Consumer adoption of Internet banking in Jordan: Examining the role of hedonic motivation, habit, self-efficacy and trust. *Journal of Financial Services Marketing*, *20*(2), 145–157. doi:10.1057/fsm.2015.5

Arpaci, I. (2015). A comparative study of the effects of cultural differences on the adoption of mobile learning. *British Journal of Educational Technology*, *46*(4), 699–712. doi:10.1111/bjet.12160

Bandyopadhyay, K., & Barnes, C. (2012). An analysis of factors affecting user acceptance of ERP Systems in the United States. *International Journal of Human Capital and Information Technology Professionals*, *3*(1), 1–14. doi:10.4018/jhcitp.2012010101

Barreda, A. A., Bilgihan, A., Nusair, K., & Okumus, F. (2015). Generating brand awareness in Online Social Networks. *Computers in Human Behavior*, *50*, 600–609. doi:10.1016/j.chb.2015.03.023

Boonsiritomachai, W., & Pitchayadejanant, K. (2017). Determinants affecting mobile banking adoption by generation Y based on the Unified Theory of Acceptance and Use of Technology Model modified by the Technology AcceptanceModel concept. Kasetsart Journal of Social Sciences. doi:10.1016/j.kjss.2017.10.005

Buying, M. (2016). Facebook and Twitter will take 33per cent share of US digital display market by 2017. http://www.emarketer.com/Article/Facebook-Twitter

Carr, D. J., Barnidge, M., Lee, B. G., & Tsang, S. J. (2014). Cynics and sceptics: Evaluating the credibility of mainstream and citizen journalism. *Journalism & Mass Communication Quarterly*, *91*(3), 452–470. doi:10.1177/1077699014538828

Chen, Y., & Zahedi, F. M. (2016). Individuals' internet security perception and behaviour: Polycontextual contrast between the United States and China. *Management Information Systems Quarterly*, *40*(1), 205–222. doi:10.25300/MISQ/2016/40.1.09

Cheung, R., & Vogel, D. (2013). Predicting user acceptance of collaborative technologies: An extension of the technology acceptance model for e-learning. *Computers & Education*, *63*(2), 160–175. doi:10.1016/j.compedu.2012.12.003

Choi, H., Park, J., & Jung, Y. (2018). The role of privacy fatigue in online privacy behaviour. *Computers in Human Behavior*, *81*, 42–51. doi:10.1016/j.chb.2017.12.001

Chong, A. Y. L. (2013). Predicting m-commerce adoption determinants: A neural network approach. *Expert Systems with Applications*, *40*(2), 523–530. doi:10.1016/j.eswa.2012.07.068

Chu, T. H., & Chen, Y. Y. (2016). With good, we become good: Understanding e-learning adoption by the theory of planned behaviour and group influences. *Computers & Education*, *92*(1), 37–52. doi:10.1016/j.compedu.2015.09.013

Coleman, S. (2012). Believing the news: From sinking trust to atrophied efficacy. *European Journal of Communication*, *27*(1), 35–45. doi:10.1177/0267323112438806

Demorouti, E., Mostert, K., & Bakker, A. B. (2010). Burnout and work engagement: A thorough investigation of the independency of both constructs. *Journal of Occupational Health Psychology*, *15*(3), 209–222. doi:10.1037/a0019408 PubMed

Dienlin, T., & Trepte, S. (2015). Is the privacy paradox a relic of the past? An in-depth analysis of privacy attitudes and privacy behaviours. *European Journal of Social Psychology*, *45*(3), 285–297. doi:10.1002/ejsp.2049

Duffett, R. G. (2015c). The influence of Facebook advertising on cognitive attitudes amid Generation Y. *Electronic Commerce Research*, *15*(2), 243–267. doi:10.1007/s10660-015-9177-4

Duffett, R. G. (2017). Influence of social media marketing communications on young consumers' attitudes. *Young Consumers*, *18*(1), 19–39. doi:10.1108/YC-07-2016-00622

Dwivedi, Y. K., Rana, N. P., Jeyaraj, A., Clement, M., & Williams, M. D. (2017). Re-examining the Unified Theory of Acceptance and Use of Technology (UTAUT): Towards a Revised Theoretical Model. doi:10.100710796-017-9774-y

Fabian, P., & Wolfgang, S. (2018). How to measure generalized trust in news media? An adaptation and test of scales. *Communication Methods and Measures*. doi:10.1080/19312458.2018.1506021

Fletcher, R., & Park, S. (2017). The impact of trust in the news media on online news consumption and participation. Digital Journalism, 1–19. Doi:10.1080/21670811.2017.1279979

Gallup. (2016). Americans' trust in mass media sinks to new low. Retrieved from http://www.gallup.com/poll/195542/Americans-trust-mass-media-sinks-new-low.aspx

Gitau, L., & Nzuki, D. (2014). Analysis of Determinants of M-commerce Adoption by Online consumers. *Journal of Theoretical and Applied E-commerce Research*, *4*, 88–94.

Goswami, A., & Dutta, D. (2016). E-Commerce Adoption by Women Entrepreneurs in India: An Application of the UTAUT Model. 8TH IEEE International Conference on Control System, Computing and Engineering. DOI:10.5296/ber.v6i2.10560

Hajli, N., Sims, J., Zadeh, A. H., & Richard, M. O. (2017). A social commerce investigation of the role of trust in a social networking site on purchase intentions. *Journal of Business Research, 71*, 133–141. doi:10.1016/j.jbusres.2016.10.004

Han, L., Xin, R. L., & Zhang, H. X. (2017). Resolving the privacy paradox: Toward a cognitive appraisal and emotion approach to online privacy behaviours. Information & Management Journal, 54(8), 1012–1022. doi:10.1016/j.im.2017.02.005

Hanitzsch, T., Van-Dalen, A., & Steindl, N. (2017). Caught in the nexus: A comparative and longitudinal analysis of public trust in the press. *The International Journal of Press/Politics, 20*(2), 1–21. doi:10.1177/1940161217740695

Harrigan, P., Evers, U., Miles, M., & Daly, T. (2017). Customer engagement with tourism social media brands. *Tourism Management, 59*, 597–609. doi:10.1016/j.tourman.2016.09.015

Henseler, J., & Chin, W. W. (2010). A comparison of approaches for the analysis of interaction effects between latent variables using partial least squares path modeling. *Structural Equation Modeling, 17*(1), 82–109. doi:10.1080/10705510903439003

Highfield, T., Harrington, S., & Bruns, A. (2013). Twitter, as a technology for audience and fandom. *Information Communication and Society, 16*(3), 16–33. doi:10.1080/1369118X.2012.756053

Hofstede, G. (1980). *Culture's consequences: Comparing values, behaviours, institutions and organizations across nations*. Thousand Oaks, CA: Sage Publications.

Johnson, T. J., & Kaye, B. K. (2015). Reasons to believe: Influence of credibility on motivations for using social networks. *Computers in Human Behavior, 50*, 544–555. doi:10.1016/j.chb.2015.04.002

Joinson, A. N., Reips, U. D., Buchanan, T., & Paine Schofield, C. B. (2010). Privacy, trust, and self-disclosure online. *Human-Computer Interaction, 25*(1), 1–24. doi:10.1080/07370020903586662

Kapoor, K. K., Tamilmani, K., Rana, N. P., Patil, P., Dwivedi, Y. K., & Nerur, S. (2018). Advances in social media research: Past, present and future. *Information Systems Frontiers, 20*(3).

Kelley, P. G., Cranor, L. F., & Sadeh, N. (2013). Privacy as part of the app decision-making process. *CHI, 2013*, 1–11.

Kim, D., Park, K., Park, Y., & Ahn, J. H. (2019). Willingness to provide personal information: Perspective of privacy calculus in IoT services. *Computers in Human Behavior, 92*, 273–281. doi:10.1016/j.chb.2018.11.022

Kim, G. S., Park, S. B., & Oh, J. (2008). An examination of factors influencing consumer adoption of short message service (SMS). *Psychology and Marketing, 25*(8), 769–786. doi:10.1002/mar.20238

Kim, T. T., Suh, Y. K., Lee, G., & Choi, B. G. (2010). Modelling roles of task-technology fit and self-efficacy in hotel employees' usage behaviour of hotel information systems. *International Journal of Tourism Research, 12*(6), 709–725. doi:10.1002/jtr.787

Kind, T. (2015). Professional guidelines for social media use a starting point. *AMA Journal of Ethics, 17*(5), 441–447. doi:10.1001/journalofethics.2015.17.5.nlit1-1505 PubMed

Kline, R. B. (2011). *Principles and practice of structural equation modelling.* New York, NY: The Guilford Press.

Koh, C. E., Prybutok, V. R., Ryan, S. D., & Wu, Y. A. (2010). A model for mandatory use of software technologies: An integrative approach by applying multiple levels of abstraction of informing science. Informing Science. *The International Journal of an Emerging Trans Discipline, 13,* 177–203.

Kokolakis, S. (2017). Privacy attitudes and privacy behaviour: A review of current research on the privacy paradox phenomenon. *Computers & Security, 64,* 122–134. doi:10.1016/j.cose.2015.07.002

Kurnia, S., Smith, S. P., & Lee, H. (2014). Consumer's perception of mobile internet in Australia. *E-Business Review, 5*(1), 19–32.

Lakhal, S., & Khechine, H. (2017). Relating personality (Big Five) to the core constructs of the unified theory of acceptance and use of technology. *Journal of Computers in Education, 4*(3), 251–282. doi:10.1007/s40692-017-0086-5

Lakhal, S., Khechine, H., & Pascot, D. (2013). Student behavioural intention to use desktop video conferencing in a distance course: Integration of autonomy to the UTAUT model. *Journal of Computing in Higher Education, 25*(2), 93–121. doi:10.1007/s12528-013-9069-3

Lamberton, C., & Stephen, A. T. (2016). A Thematic Exploration of Digital, Social Media, and Mobile Marketing: Research Evolution from 2000 to 2015 and an Agenda for Future Inquiry. *Journal of Marketing, 80*(6), 146–172. doi:10.1509/jm.15.0415

Lee, A. R., Son, S. M., & Kim, K. K. (2016). Information and communication technology overload and social networking service fatigue: A stress perspective. *Computers in Human Behavior, 55,* 51–61. doi:10.1016/j.chb.2015.08.011

Lee, Y. H., Hsiao, C., & Purnomo, S. H. (2014). An empirical examination of individual and system characteristics on enhancing e-learning acceptance. *Australasian Journal of Educational Technology, 30*(5), 561–579. doi:10.14742/ajet.381

Li, T. Y., & Ho, B. C. T. (2015). Factors influencing the Technology Adoption of Mobile Commerce in Taiwan by Using the Revised UTAUT Model. *The Asian Conference on Psychology and Behavioural Sciences,* 1-17.

Liew, B. T., Kang, M., Yoo, E., & You, J. (2013). Investigating the determinants of mobile learning acceptance in Korea. In J. Herrington, A. Couros, & V. Irvine (Eds.), Proceedings of EdMedia 2013 – world conference on educational media and technology (pp. 1424 – 1430). Academic Press.

Lin, C. S., Tzeng, G. H., Chin, Y. C., & Chang, C. C. (2010). Recommendation sources on the intention to use e-books in academic digital libraries. *The Electronic Library*, *28*(6), 844–857. doi:10.1108/02640471011093534

Lin, H. M., Chen, W. J., & Nien, S. F. (2014a). The study of achievement and motivation by e-learning: A case study. *International Journal of Information and Education Technology (IJIET)*, *4*(5), 421–425. doi:10.7763/IJIET.2014.V4.442

Mayer, R. C., Davis, J. H., & Schoorman, D. F. (1995). An integrative model of organizational trust. *Academy of Management Review*, *20*(3), 709–734. doi:10.5465/amr.1995.9508080335

Merhi, M. I. (2015). Factors influencing higher education students to adopt podcast: An empirical study. *Computers & Education*, *83*(2), 32–43. doi:10.1016/j.compedu.2014.12.014

Metzger, M. J., & Flanagin, A. J. (2017). Psychological approaches to credibility assessment online. In S. S. Sundar (Ed.), *The handbook of the psychology of communication technology* (pp. 445–466). Chichester, UK: Wiley.

Nisar, T. M., & Whitehead, C. (2016). *Brand interactions and social media: Enhancing user loyalty through social networking sites*. Computers in Human Behaviour.

Oomen, I., & Leenes, I. (2008). Privacy risk perceptions and privacy protection strategies. In E. de Leeuw, S. Fischer-Hübner, J. Tseng, & J. Borking (Eds.), *Policies and Research in Identity Management* (pp. 121–138). Boston: Springer Verlag; doi:10.1007/978-0-387-77996-6_10.

Pappas, I. O., Giannakos, M. N., & Mikalef, P. (2017). Investigating students' use and adoption of with-video assignments: Lessons learnt for video-based open educational resources. *Journal of Computing in Higher Education*, *29*(1), 160–177. doi:10.1007/s12528-017-9132-6

Park, Y., Ju, J., & Ahn, J. H. (2015). Are People really concerned about their privacy? Privacy paradox in a mobile environment. *The Fifteenth International Conference on Electronic Business*, 123-128.

Pinto, M. B., & Yagnik, A. (2016). Fit for Life : A content analysis of fitness tracker brands use of Facebook in social media marketing. *Journal of Brand Management*, *24*(1), 49–67. doi:10.1057/s41262-016-0014-4

Pötzsch, S. (2009). Privacy awareness: a means to solve the privacy paradox? In The Future of Identity in the Information Society. Springer-Verlag. doi:10.1007/978-3-642-03315-5_17

Prasarry, Y. V., Astuti, E. S., & Suyadi, I. (2015). Factor Affecting the Adoption of Mobile Commerce (A study on SMEs in Malang). *European Journal of Business and Management*, ▪▪▪, 30–35.

Rainie, L. (2018). Americans' complicated feelings about social media in an era of privacy concerns (White paper). Fact Tank News.

Rana, N. P., Dwivedi, Y. K., Lal, B., Williams, M. D., & Clement, M. (2017). Citizens' adoption of an electronic government system: Towards a Unified View. *Information Systems Frontiers*, *19*(3), 549–568. doi:10.1007/s10796-015-9613-y

Rauniar, R., Rawski, G., Yang, J., & Johnson, B. (2014). Technology acceptance model (TAM) and social media usage: An empirical study on Facebook. *Journal of Enterprise Information Management, 27*(1), 6–30. doi:10.1108/JEIM-04-2012-0011

Schermer, B. W., Custer, B., & van der Hof, S. (2014). The crisis of content: How stronger legal protection may lead to weaker consent in data protection. *Ethics and Information Technology, 16*(2), 171–182.

Shklovski, I., Mainwaring, S. D., Skúladóttir, H. H., & Borgthorsson, H. (2014). Leakiness and creepiness in-app space: Perceptions of privacy and mobile app use. CHI 2014, 2347-2356. doi:10.1145/2556288.2557421

Simmel, G. (2009). *Sociology: Inquiries into the construction of social forms.* Leiden: Brill; doi:10.1163/ej.9789004173217.i-698.

Smith, E. J., & Kollars, N. A. (2015). QR panopticism: User behaviour triangulation and barcode-scanning applications. Inf. Secure. J. Global Perspect, 24(4–6), 157–163. doi:10.1080/19393555.2015.1085113

Smith, H. J., Dinev, T., & Xu, H. (2011). Information privacy research: An interdisciplinary review. *Management Information Systems Quarterly, 35*(4), 989–1015. doi:10.2307/41409970

Stouthuysen, K., Teunis, I., Reusen, E., & Slabbinck, H. (2018). Initial trust and intentions to buy: The effect of vendor-specific guarantees, customer reviews and the role of online shopping experience. *Electronic Commerce Research and Applications, 27*, 23–38. doi:10.1016/j.elerap.2017.11.002

Sundar, S. S., Kang, H., Wu, M., Go, E., & Zhang, B. (2013). Unlocking the privacy paradox: Do cognitive heuristics hold the key? Proceedings of CHI'13 Extended Abstracts on Human Factors in Computing Systems, 811–816. doi:10.1145/2468356.2468501

Susanne, B., & Menno, D. T. (2017). The privacy paradox – Investigating discrepancies between expressed privacy concerns and actual online behaviour – A systematic literature review. *Telematics and Informatics, 34*(7), 1038–1058. doi:10.1016/j.tele.2017.04.013

Tan, P. J. B. (2013). Applying the UTAUT to understand factors affecting the use of English E-Learning websites in Taiwan. *SAGE Open, 3*(4), 1–12. doi:10.1177/2158244013503837

Tarhini, A., El-Masri, M., Ali, M., & Serrano, A. (2016a). Extending the UTAUT model to understand the customers' acceptance and use of internet banking in Lebanon: A structural equation modelling approach. *Information Technology & People, 29*(4), 783–801. doi:10.1108/ITP-02-2014-0034

Tarhini, A., Hone, K., Liu, X., & Tarhini, T. (2016b). Examining the moderating effect of individual-level cultural values on users' acceptance of E-learning in developing countries: A structural equation modelling of an extended technology acceptance model. *Interactive Learning Environments.* doi:10.10 80/10494820.2015.1122635

Taylor, S., & Todd, P. A. (1995b). Understanding information technology usage: A test of competing models. *Information Systems Research, 6*(4), 144–176. doi:10.1287/isre.6.2.144

Tsfati, Y., & Ariely, G. (2014). Individual and contextual correlates of trust in media across 44 countries. *Communication Research, 41*(6), 760–782. doi:10.1177/0093650213485972

Venkatesh, V., Morris, M. G., Davis, G. B., & Davis, F. D. (2003). User acceptance of information technology: Toward a unified view. *Management Information Systems Quarterly*, *27*(3), 425–478. doi:10.2307/30036540

Venkatesh, V., Thong, J., & Xu, X. (2012). Consumer acceptance and use of information technology: Extending the unified theory of acceptance and use of technology. *Management Information Systems Quarterly*, *36*(1), 157–178. doi:10.2307/41410412

Venkatesh, V., & Zhang, X. (2010). Unified theory of acceptance and use of technology: uS vs. China. *Journal of Global Information Technology Management*, *13*(1), 5–27. doi:10.1080/1097198X.2010.10856507

Widjajaa, A. E. Jengchung V. C., Sukococ, B. M., & Quang-An, H. (2019). Understanding users' willingness to put their personal information on the personal cloud-based storage applications: An empirical study. Computers in Human Behavior Journal, 167-185.

Wingreen, S. C., Mazey, N. C. H. L., Baglione, S. L., & Storholm, G. R. (2018). Transfer of electronic commerce trust between physical and virtual environments: Experimental effects of structural assurance and situational normality. *Electronic Commerce Research.* doi:10.100710660-018-9305

Wu, B., & Zhang, C. (2014). Empirical study on continuance intentions towards E-learning 2.0 systems. *Behaviour & Information Technology*, *33*(10), 1027–1038. doi:10.1080/0144929X.2014.934291

Yablonski, S.A. (2016). Multi-sided search platforms: global and local. Doi:10.1504/IJTMKT.2016.077394

Yale, R. N., Jensen, J. D., Carcioppolo, N., Sun, Y., & Liu, M. (2015). Examining first- and second-order factor structures for news credibility. *Communication Methods and Measures*, *9*(3), 152–169. doi:10.1080/19312458.2015.1061652

Young, A. L., & Quan-Haase, A. (2013). Privacy protection strategies on Facebook. *Information Communication and Society*, *16*(4), 479–500. doi:10.1080/1369118X.2013.777757

Zafeiropoulou, A. M., Millard, D. E., Webber, C., & O'Hara, K. (2013). Unpicking the privacy paradox: Can structuration theory helps to explain location-based privacy decisions? WebSci '13 Proceedings of the 5th Annual ACM Web Science Conference, 463–472.

Zhang, B., Wu, M., Kang, H., Go, E., & Sundar, S. S. (2014). Effects of security warnings and instant gratification cues on attitudes toward mobile websites. *Telematics and Informatics*, *34*, 1038–1058. doi:10.1145/2556288.2557347

Zhang, M., Guo, L., Hu, M., & Liu, W. (2017). Influence of customer engagement with company social networks on stickiness : Mediating effect of customer value creation. *International Journal of Information Management*, *37*(3), 229–240. doi:10.1016/j.ijinfomgt.2016.04.010

Zhang, Y., & Lin, Z. (2018). Predicting the helpfulness of online product reviews: A multilingual approach. *Electronic Commerce Research and Applications*, *27*, 1–10. doi:10.1016/j.elerap.2017.10.008

Chapter 5

Survival Strategies in the Digital Economy of a Developing Country:
The Case of a Digital Enterprise

Eric Ansong
https://orcid.org/0000-0002-0262-3485
University of Ghana, Ghana

ABSTRACT

Firms are in constant competition for dominance and survival. Knowledge of how firms use information systems to improve operational efficiency is limited, especially in developing economies. This chapter, therefore, explored a firm's digital strategic actions for dealing with the competitive forces in the digital economy of a developing country. This chapter adopted a qualitative case study approach. A digital enterprise in a developing economy was selected as a case. Using Porter's five competitive forces model, an analysis of the environment and the strategic actions of the firm was carried out. Findings from this chapter serve as a stepping-stone in expounding the digital strategic actions of firms in dealing with the market forces in the digital economy. This study is, arguably, one of the first to examine the competitive forces and survival strategies of a digital enterprise in the digital economy of a developing country.

INTRODUCTION

The digital economy includes that sector of the economic output solely or primarily derived from business models with digital technologies based on digital goods and services (Bukht & Heeks, 2017). The digital economy is, therefore, an emerging phenomenon which has had a very significant impact on the annual growth rate of countries (World Economic Forum, 2015). Even though economics and politics have been the driving forces behind the development of nations, the role of innovations in digital technologies cannot be downplayed (Heeks, 2017). For instance, transformations in the economies of countries in the 1990s were mainly attributed to the internet evolution. This evolution continued into the 2000s and the

DOI: 10.4018/978-1-7998-2610-1.ch005

2010s with the introduction of Information and Communication Technologies (ICTs) which has been the bedrock of economic transformations. These ICTs include but not limited to electronic devices with connected embedded sensors (the internet of things); and new digital models such as digital platforms, cloud computing and digital services. Others include new sophisticated end-user devices and gadgets such as smartphones, laptops, netbooks, 3D printers, among others. Also, there has been an increase in the usage of data through the application of concepts such as big data analytics and algorithms for decision making (Organisation for Economic Co-operation and Development, 2015).

These new technologies have given rise to the concept of digital affordances which Heeks (2017) refers to as "potential actions an individual or organisation with a purpose can undertake with a digital system within the context of the environment within which they function." These actions may include datafication, digitisation, virtualisation and generativity (Heeks, 2016). Virtualisation refers to the act of physically disembedding processes. Generativity also applies to the recombination and reprogramming of electronic devices and data, which leads to a function which was not the initially planned purpose for the device or data. Digitisation is also the transformation of every unit in the value chain of information from the analogue mode into the digital mode. Another modern term introduced by Victor Mayer-Schöenberger and Kenneth Neil Cukier in 2013 is Datafication (Strauß, 2015). Mai (2016) assert that datafication deals with the conversion of personal human life information into a digital form which is of value to businesses. The impact of datafication extends to Human Resources data which helps to identify potential employees and their specific characteristics such as risk-taking profile and personality obtained from the usage of social media, personal phone usage and apps. This technique has been predicted to replace the traditional personality tests associated with recruitments and also in customer relationship management (Moore, 2017).

The foregoing arguments show that the impact of these digital technologies on existing economies have been disruptive. Thus, it has reshaped the behaviour and purchase patterns of consumers, business models and processes and even in human interactions (Dahlman, Mealy, & Wermelinger, 2016). Instances of these transformations can be seen in almost all the sectors of the economy of countries. For example, in the transportation industry, "Uber" which is one of the world's largest taxi firms rides on the back of the digital technologies. In social media, Facebook, which is also the world's largest social media company thrives on digital technologies. In marketing, Alibaba and Amazon also dominate. In the hospitality industry, Airbnb, which is also the world's largest hotelier depends on digital business technologies.

On the other hand, digital enterprises such as Nokia and Dell are struggling to identify the appropriate digital business strategy to implement (Keen & Williams, 2013; Weill & Woerner, 2015). Businesses in the digital economy face a major challenge which is related to their ability to manufacture products and services that benefit from the available digital resources while integrating well with other platforms and environments (Bharadwaj, El Sawy, Pavlou, & Venkatraman, 2013; El Sawy & Pereira, 2013). Thus, these digital enterprises are expected to develop specific strategies around digital technologies to survive and grow.

However, research into the survival strategies of these digital enterprises has been in the nascent stages, especially in the context of developing economies with little to no formalised structures in the digital landscape. For instance, Ansong and Boateng (2019) explored the business models and strategies of digital enterprises to understand the nature of their operations, as well as their survival tactics in a developing economy. It was discovered that digital enterprises leveraged on accessible and low-cost social networking services to remain competitive and grow. This current study, therefore, responds to the recommendation for further studies to be conducted to explore the nature of competition and the survival strategies of digital enterprises by expounding their digital strategic actions in dealing with the market forces in the digital economy of a developing country. This exposition, thus, contributes to the literature on digital business strategy of digital enterprises from a developing economy perspective. Again, the findings of the chapter contribute to informing business managers and policymakers on the nature of digital business strategic actions to undertake to deal with the competitive forces within the digital economy. This study is arguably one of the first to examine the competitive forces and survival strategies of a digital enterprise in the digital economy of a developing country.

The remainder of the chapter is divided into five sections. The next section reviews the literature on digital business strategy, including a review of frameworks and theories on strategy aimed at developing a framework for the study. The third section presents a discussion of the methodology for conducting the study. The analysis and discussion of findings are shown in the fourth section. The study concludes in the fifth section with the summary, conclusion and recommendations for further studies on digital business strategy.

LITERATURE REVIEW

The internet and digital technologies such as cloud computing, virtual reality, the Internet of Things and mobile devices have become indispensable in the operations of businesses in modern times. These new digital technologies have led to the proliferation of digital ventures, also referred to as digital enterprises. These are blossoming enterprises or new organizations established in an uncertain and volatile environment with the intent of bringing new opportunities to the marketplace. Again, these enterprises, which basically operate in the digital economy, tend to have business models which are dependent on digital technologies (Veit et al., 2014). Thus, the nature of their operations, revenues and survival are influenced by digital technologies. These digital enterprises use digital technology as a competitive advantage in their internal and external activities (Rouse, 2011).

Strategy in the Digital Economy

Regardless of the industry or sector, the critical force in the operation of businesses, in general, has been competition (Indiatsy, Mwangi, Mandere, Bichanga, & George, 2014). Enterprises are expected to develop strategies to remain in the competition and survive. Strategy in business consists of a set of decisions such as; the choice of an industry within which to operate; investments in resources; tactics for pricing; and the configuration of the firm (Williamson, 1991). Other decisions may consist of managing the business' trade-offs between efficiency – cost reduction – and also effectiveness – value creation and capture (Drnevich & Croson, 2013). Even though these high-level decisions might seem easy, they require thorough analysis. Thus, several factors must be taken into consideration before effective decisions can be taken. These decisions, therefore, make strategy in businesses very crucial which is not different from other endeavours. Failure of the strategy may even result in the closure of the enterprise.

The digital economy has redefined business strategy into a term referred to as "Digital Business Strategy." This new phenomenon started with Information Technology (IT) strategy which was viewed as a functional–level strategy and hence a subset of the entire business strategy (Bharadwaj et al., 2013; Henderson & Venkatraman, 1993). Thus, the IT strategy was headed by an IT manager whose activities were guided by the overall business strategy of the firm. This subordinate role of the IT strategy is highlighted in extant Information Systems research (Chan & Reich, 2007; Sledgianowski, Luftman, & Reilly, 2006). Chan and Reich (2007) who studied IT alignment in businesses, for instance, outlined the dominating role of the business strategy over the IT strategy and hence asserting that the IT strategy must be aligned to the Business strategy. Mata et al. (1995) also argue that the role of the IT strategy has been to help the business to avoid a disadvantageous position. Again, Miller (2003) and Zott (2003) see the IT strategy as a means to improving the company to increase their competitive advantage.

The last decade has seen a significant transformation in the operations of businesses due to the new functionalities introduced by ICT and other technologies (Bharadwaj et al., 2013). That is, the firms in the post-dotcom decade have taken advantage of the numerous potentials of ICTs – global connectivity through mobile web and the internet, lower prices and high performance of computing. These technologies are reshaping the way businesses operate. Thus, the strategic actions of companies are being transformed by digital technologies. Such transformations include telecommuting where work can be done across borders, time and distance (Ansong & Boateng, 2017). Besides, social relations existing between and in both the enterprise space and consumers have been transformed through social networking and social media (Susarla, Oh, & Tan, 2012). Again, products and services have become entangled in the digital technologies which have made it difficult to disassociate these digital products (goods and services delivered over digital networks) from their underlying Information Technology infrastructure (Orlikowski, 2009). This situation has resulted in the development of entirely new strategic actions of businesses as postulated by Burgelman and Grove (2007). In addition, the turbulence and disruptions caused by digital platforms have caused an emerging new wave of strategy formulation (Pavlou & El Sawy, 2010), which is referred to as the Digital business strategy.

Digital business strategy involves a new situation where businesses are required to re-analyse and rethink about the business roles of IT strategy not just as a functional-level strategy but a fusion between the business strategy and the IT strategy. Digital business strategy is, therefore, a multidimensional concept comprising of coordination, flexibility, governance and competence (Bharadwaj et al., 2013). Thus, a comprehensive digital business strategy must focus on these four major business dimensions.

The Digital Economy of Developing Countries

Most developed economies are increasingly leveraging on ICT in small business enterprises for socio-economic development. For instance, in France alone, as early as 2001, 84,535 new firms had been created in the field of Information Communication Technology, which led to the creation of 160, 000 jobs. Politicians, experts and statesmen have asserted that the digital economy presents a new paradigm shift for countries. Thus, providing employment opportunities. This phenomenon is not different from the developing countries. In Ghana, for instance, it has been projected that the digital economy will contribute to 10.2% of Ghana's GDP in the next five years (Blay, 2019).

In probing the nature of the online presence of digital enterprises, Ansong and Boateng (2019) discovered that e-commerce was dominant with a few firms operating service-oriented websites. Almost all digital enterprises in the digital economy of developing countries leveraged on social networking services in their business operations and as an avenue to engage their target customers. Due to the online nature of these new businesses, social networking sites such as Facebook, Twitter, Instagram, LinkedIn and others present an immense opportunity for them to promote their brand, understand customer preference and offer personalized services. However, Facebook was the predominant channel for business promotion in Ghana. The other technologies employed were cloud computing and Big Data analytics technologies. The cloud with its cost-effective, flexible and scalable structures give these firms access to infrastructure and software that shapes their growth and development. Big Data, on the other hand, is substantially under-explored, perhaps due to the limited computational capacity of the digital firms.

Frameworks for Analysing Digital Business Strategy

A number of issues were realized from the review of digital business strategy literature. The review focused on the four major dimensions of digital business strategy – coordination, flexibility, governance and competence. In addition, frameworks for analysing the dimensions of the digital business strategy were reviewed. Some of these theories include Structure-Conduct–Performance theory, Knowledge-Based, View I/O Economics theory, Transaction Cost Economics theory, Resource-Based View, Agency Theory, Real Options theory and Dynamic capabilities theory. These theories and their applications in digital business strategy research are discussed in this subsection.

The Agency Theory: The Agency theory relates to understanding the application of division of labour which is necessitated by the problems involved in cooperating parties with different goals. Thus, the focus of the agency theory is on the relationship between parties where one party (the principal(s)) engages another person (the agent) to undertake some task on their behalf (Jensen & Meckling, 1976). The theory postulates that the cooperating parties (principal and agent) are individuals with rational economic-maximizing interests. The agent, in most cases, take decisions which are not in the interest of the principal, which is due to the separation of ownership and control. These decisions, therefore, result in costs – agency cost – in guiding the behaviour of the agent. For instance, the principal incurs costs in monitoring and controlling the behaviour of the agent – monitoring costs. The agent also incurs costs in demonstrating compliance with the principal's guidelines – bonding costs.

The role of the Agency theory is to review the governance dimension of strategy which deals with the ability of the digital enterprise to allocate resources to create and capture value efficiently. For instance, Liu, Kauffman and Ma (2015) researched on understanding how the mobile payment system has evolved, especially in terms of the regulatory forces' role in promoting or delaying innovation in businesses. The findings suggested that patterns in innovations are industry-specific which influence cooperation, competition and regulation within enterprises.

Dynamic Capabilities Theory: Dynamic Capabilities theory conceptualises those features of the enterprise which are presumed to consist of both managerial and organizational processes. The processes allow the enterprise to identify its needs or opportunities for change in most dynamic environments (Helfat et al., 2007). These Dynamic Capabilities may be referred to as a process (Ambrosini & Bowman, 2009), or as consisting of a set of processes (Teece, Pisano, & Shuen, 1997). Again, these capabilities are by implication very dynamic hence operate within time and space. It is argued that Dynamic Capability arises out of three learning processes which are generic. These learning processes include; accumulation of experience; articulation of knowledge; and codification of knowledge (Zollo & Winter, 2002). In another breadth, the dynamic capability may be seen to be processes which are identifiable and specific that reconfigure or integrate resources which may include product development and alliancing (Eisenhardt & Martin, 2000).

Dynamic Capabilities theory, therefore, focuses on the flexibility dimension of digital business strategy, which is the ability of the digital enterprise to be agile and adapt to changing conditions in the industry. Sia, Soh and Weill (2013), for instance, studied how a bank in Asia responded to the digital disruptions and opportunities through the adoption of digital business strategy. Thus, the study focused on how the firm developed some capabilities to survive in the agile Digital economy. It was therefore discovered that the managers of the firm must cultivate leadership for digital transformation.

The Resource-Based View Theory: The ability of the management of the firm to effectively combine the set of specific resources to exploit market opportunities and remain competitive is the focus of the Resource-Based View (RBV) of a firm (Penrose, 1959). Also, it has been asserted by Grant (1999) that resources of the firm are the most fundamental unit of analysis in the firm's processes. The Resource-Based View theory, therefore, argues that enterprises possess a collection of resources which may lead to enhancing their advantage competitively (Barney, 2001). It is worth noting that the attainment of the competitive advantage is primarily dependent on characteristics of the resources in question. These may include being unique and difficult for others to imitate; appropriate; durable; non-substitutable; rare; imperfectly mobile or immobile; and have value in the environment of the firm (Birkinshaw & Goddard, 2009). Nevo and Wade (2010), for instance, conducted a study on identifying a firm's IT assets which play strategic roles for competitive advantage. They discovered that these IT assets could only be used to achieve strategic advantages when organisational resources are combined with them, leading to the creation of IT-enabled resources.

The Resource-Based View theory focuses on the competence dimension of digital business strategy, which is the ability of the enterprise to exploit resources to create and capture value. In other words, the competence dimension explores how the enterprise is able to manage its resources to remain profitable and competitive.

Structure-Conduct-Performance Framework: The basic tenets of the Structure-Conduct-Performance framework is that the behaviour of sellers and buyers which is a function of the structure of the industry determines the industry's economic performance (Bain, 1956). Economic performance is viewed according to the effective utilization of resources to produce the highest returns. Conduct in the Structure-Conduct-Performance framework includes all the activities of the participants in the industry. These participants include sellers and buyers. The activities of sellers may involve; capacity installation and utilization; influencing policies on promotions and pricing; conducting market surveys and development; and finally, creating cooperation or competition between firms. The determinant of the conduct is the industry structure which according to Scherer (1980) includes issues such as; the technology; the number and size of the buyers and sellers; the level of barriers to entry; the degree of product differentiation; and the extent of vertical integration. Other elements within the industry structure include product differentiation, the concentration of buyer or seller, and the elasticity of demand for products and services. Barriers to entry has been one of the significant issues which affect the structure of the industry. For instance, Uotila, Keil and Maula (2017) modelled how technology suppliers developed standards in the Digital economy. It was discovered that the coordination among the suppliers facilitated the convergence of standards which in some cases may be inferior to other alternative or undiscovered standards or solutions. It was also discovered that powerful or influential consortia mostly coordinate the selection of the standards which mostly lead to technological lock-ins where suppliers commit to inferior solutions and are not able to subsequently reverse their commitments.

The Structure-Conduct-Performance framework focuses on the coordination dimension of digital business strategy where profitability is achieved when the firm is able to restrain competition and restrict the entry of new firms into the industry. For instance, Choi et al. (2017) examined how a consortium of digital enterprises could enhance group cohesiveness. The findings of the study indicated that group effectiveness in a consortium could be improved through the active involvement of the IT users and vendors.

Porter's 5 Competitive Forces Model

Generally, Porter's Five Forces model deals with a continuous process of scanning and monitoring the environment of businesses. It also involves obtaining competitive intelligence on the present and potential rivals of enterprises (Porter, 2008). Thus, the survival of the enterprise is influenced by some competitive forces which are either within (internal) or outside (external) of the firm (Liang, Saraf, Hu, & Xue, 2007). The firm, therefore, must strategize to survive this competition. Michael Porter's (2008) model has become a handy tool for analysing the various competitive forces that exist within the industry. The Five Forces Model includes analysis of; the bargaining power of suppliers; the threat of entrants or potential competitors; the threat of substitute products or services; the bargaining power of buyers or potential customers; and the intensity of rivalry among existing competitors. Figure 1 shows the five competitive forces model.

Figure 1. Porter's five competitive forces model

Information Systems scholars and practitioners at both the international and local levels highly value and use Porter's Five competitive forces model (Indiatsy et al., 2014). This is because the model provides a better understanding of the industry environment; a comparison of rivals for business obstructions, advantages and disadvantages in technology, production and quality (Rachapila & Jansirisak, 2013). Thus, this evaluation helps to determine the continuation, termination or development of the business.

This study, therefore, adopts this model to identify the various competitive forces a digital enterprise in a developing economy face in the quest to identifying the digital strategic actions to be taken for survival.

RESEARCH METHODOLOGY

This study was conducted using the qualitative research approach. A qualitative research approach emphasizes the qualities of entities, processes and meanings that are not experimentally examined or measured in terms of quantity, amount, intensity or frequency (Denzin & Lincoln, 2008; Lincoln & Denzin, 2000). Creswell (2014) explains that in a qualitative research approach, the researcher collects open-ended, emerging data from which themes are developed. In other words, the researcher relies on the perspectives and experiences of a small number of persons associated with the phenomenon in understanding and forming judgments about it.

Case study research is an increasingly popular approach among qualitative researchers (Thomas, 2011). Case study research is carried out by investigating and analyzing a single or collective case, intended to capture the complexity of the object of study (Stake, 1995). Qualitative case study research, as described by Stake (1995), draws together "naturalistic, holistic, ethnographic, phenomenological, and biographic research methods." Case study research has a level of flexibility that is not readily offered by other qualitative approaches such as grounded theory or phenomenology. The researcher may present the genesis of ideas, explore what happened and why, give an account of the human side of the project, its dynamism and investigate a particular phenomenon, present outcomes in their complexity without being subjected to the confines inherent in most other evaluation methods. The freedom to collect multiple kinds of information makes the case study method useful for exploring ideas and constructing theories about project dynamics. This study, therefore, adopted the case study method.

This study was centred on a digital enterprise known as Jumla Ghana Limited (a pseudonym) (hereinafter referred to as Jumla) as the case. Jumla fulfilled the criteria to be considered as a digital enterprise. In addition, the focus of the study also called for a digital enterprise which has gained a considerable reputation in the digital economy of Ghana. This digital enterprise has been in operation in Ghana since 2014.

Two main data sources were used in this study: primary data and secondary data. In this study, primary data was gathered mainly through open-ended interviews. This is to ensure a guided interaction, where respondents are allowed to speak extensively on a topic without straying from the relevant context. In-depth interviews were conducted with three representatives of the digital enterprise; the Operations officer, Sales manager and IT officer. These officials of the digital enterprise were selected due to their positions as strategic leaders who formulate or implement the major strategic decisions of the digital enterprise. Duration for each interview section was One hour. During the discussions, the respondents were encouraged to relate experiences and attitudes relevant to the study. The research technique also involved structured and unstructured interviews. The data was collected in textual form as field notes and tape-recorded interviews.

Secondary data used in this study were obtained from publicly available documents such as reports, newsletters, journal articles, news bulletins, documentaries, and other web resources. Collecting Secondary data does not only save time but also provides baseline data with which Primary data is compared. The analysis was done by drawing themes from the tape-recorded interviews, which were transcribed verbatim without paraphrasing.

CASE STORY

Profile of Jumla

Jumla is an online shopping destination where customers browse and shop for an assortment of products – computers, laptop, tablets, mobile devices, among others. These items are delivered at the doorsteps of the buyers. Jumla's value proposition is to provide customers with the widest selection of new and branded products at best prices combined with the ease of not having to visit a shop physically. Jumla's vision is to become the "Amazon of Africa." The product range is already quite impressive with over 10,000 stock-keeping units (SKU) online since their launch in Ghana on August 2014, and it covers categories such as phones, computers, home appliances, fashion and many more. However, it is still a long way to go compared to its Nigerian counterpart, which has roughly over 140,000 SKU's or its US idol Amazon (4.1 billion SKUs live).

Jumla has been a registered company in Ghana since August 2014. The firm operates officially under the name "Jumla Ghana." It belongs to a group which is a holding of eight different online start-ups operating in Africa. Even though these start-ups belong to the same group, they are distinct and autonomous acting entities. Jumla offers free return and refund within seven days after purchase. It also has various payment options such as cash-on-delivery, mobile money or bank transfer.

Jumla has a mixed business model of online retail and online marketplace. Jumla directly procures some of its products from manufacturers and suppliers. In this case, Jumla acts as a retailer as the company resells the products. However, since Jumla's goal is to offer a great variety of products, it allows suppliers/brand distributors to sell their products via the Jumla online platform. This constitutes the marketplace section of the business model. For each sale going through Jumla online marketplace, it receives a commission of between 6 – 15%. It is imperative to note that this is by no means visible to customers. Thus, customers do not know whether the product comes directly from Jumla retail or the marketplace. This is a smart strategy as the Operations officers indicated;

This is really a smart strategy as the combination of the two business models allow us to offer a vast product range. This adds value to customers as the variety for them is much bigger than in a physical shop.

It must also be noted that products sold through the retail section are physically stocked in Jumla's warehouse under a consignment agreement with the suppliers. The consignment enables Jumla to pay the supplier only when a customer buys the product. In case the product is not sold, Jumla returns the product to the supplier.

On the other hand, products sold at the marketplace are not physically stocked in Jumla's warehouse but remain at the supplier's warehouse. Once an order is placed, the product will be picked up by the delivery fleet.

Jumla operates in a very agile and dynamic environment where prices and product availability change daily. Employees are therefore trained to be in constant communication with vendors on a daily basis to update the website and the internal systems with new prices and product availability statuses. Customers are also notified continuously of all changes to their order.

Evaluation of Jumla's Competitive Environment

The Porter's Five forces model assumes that five important forces determine competitive power in a business situation. The competitive environment of Jumla is analysed based on these five forces in this section.

Power of Suppliers

In general, the power of suppliers is high if the company works with a small number of suppliers. This gives the supplier a higher bargaining power which often results in unfavourable deals for the company (e.g. lower margins). As Jumla procures its products from various sources (e.g. brands, distributors, physical shops, among others), their suppliers' bargaining power should be quite low. In addition, Jumla has the advantage of providing suppliers with higher traffic. With already multiple thousand visitors on their website and mobile application per day, Jumla can offer their suppliers a lot of value. Jumla is also involved in a number of co-branding initiatives. An example of co-branding at Jumla was the launch of the Infinix Hot 2 phone in 2015. This phone was exclusively available for purchase on Jumla which in turn offered visibility for the product through their ads, newsletters and other platforms.

Power of Customers

The power of customers is determined depending on how easy it is for buyers to drive prices down. Again, this is driven by; the number of buyers; the importance of each individual buyer to the business; and the cost to the customer involved in switching from the products and services to competitors. It was observed that the customers of Jumla had higher bargaining power. This can be explained by the fact that customers could freely choose whether to buy from other online shopping options such as Tonaton, Zoobashop, Superprice among others or buy offline through brick and mortar businesses or street vendors. Also buying once at Jumla does not come along with any duty to buy from Jumla again. In other words, there are no switching costs for Jumla customers. This assertion is corroborated by one of Jumla's IT managers who indicated that;

For instance, if they see a product cheaper at another place, they most likely will decide to purchase it instead of Jumla.

Competitive Rivalry

Generally, the level of competitive rivalry is determined by the number and capability of competitors. If a company has many competitors that are capable of offering equally attractive products and services, the company is likely to have some power. In Ghana, direct competitors to Jumla are Tisu, Ahonya, Superprice, Zoobashop and others, as they also engage in online retailing of new and branded products. Jumla is therefore confronted with intense rivalry. Note here that digital enterprises such as OLX, Kaymu or Tonaton were not considered to be direct rivals to Jumla. This is because these enterprises do not engage in direct retailing; thus, they are purely online marketplaces that allow sellers to advertise their products with little or no intervention directly.

Threat of Substitute Products and Services

The threat of substitution is high if customers can easily find a different way of satisfying their needs. Customers might decide to buy non-branded or used products instead of buying new and branded products from Jumla. For these alternatives, Tonaton and Kaymu are actively growing online marketplaces offering similar products and services. This may speak for the high threat from substitutes. However, Jumla's provision of high-quality products at very attractive prices separates them enough from the substitutes. Thus, it can be concluded that the threat from substitutes for Jumla is medium.

Threat of New Entrants

The threat of new entrants depends on how much time and money are involved in entering the industry or market to compete effectively. Furthermore, the more barriers for entries (patients, legislation, etc.) exist, the lower is the chance of new entrants. Besides, the more companies already operating in the market, the lower the threat of new market entrants. Considering the promising nature of budding Ghana's digital economy, a lot of foreign companies could be keen to enter later. One of such international firms which might be interested in joining the Ghanaian market is Amazon.

ANALYSIS OF JUMLA'S DIGITAL BUSINESS STRATEGY FOR SURVIVAL

The previous section focused on the various forces that influenced the survival of Jumla. The survival strategies of Jumla are, therefore presented in this section. These strategies are discussed based on the four major dimensions of digital business strategy, which include Governance, Competence, Coordination and Flexibility.

Governance Dimension of Jumla's Digital Business Strategy

The focus of the governance dimension of digital business strategy is the ability of the digital enterprise to allocate resources to create and capture value efficiently. For instance, Aubert et al. (2017) investigated the factors that determine the completeness of contracts when outsourcing IT projects. They discovered that the managers of firms must ensure there is a complete contract spelling out all instructions on the execution of outsourced IT projects.

Guided by the Agency theory, Jumla's strategy was analysed. It was revealed that Jumla started operations in Ghana with three employees. This number of highly motivated staff has now increased to 80 young entrepreneurial Ghanaians, including an 8-man strong customer service team who are available six days a week. The operations officer has a dashboard which provides a constant update of activities. In terms of governance, Jumla's staff are supervised continuously to provide up-to-date information to their customers. The team maintains excellent communication with suppliers (vendors as they are referred to by Jumla) as it is necessary for delivering up-to-date stock information to customers. If Jumla fails to do so, they may lose customers who primarily require per minute information concerning the status of their orders. This finding is corroborated by Pereira and Pereira (2011) who discovered that having more information shared between the agent who is the Management of Jumla and Principal – vendors and other parties – lead to a higher commitment which improves productivity.

Another governance issue worth noting is the management of the online shop (both webpage and mobile application). Besides content management – which concentrates on displaying products with beautiful pictures and a good description – Jumla ensures the online shop is easy to navigate. This discussion leads to a suggestive finding that;

Finding One; *multinational digital enterprises tend to depend on a governance strategy which is more encompassing and useful. This can be attributed to their prior operations in other digital economies which gives them an avenue to replicate their successful strategies in their new markets through effective governance of their resources.*

Coordination Dimension of Jumla's Digital Business Strategy

Coordination dimension of digital business strategy looks beyond the boundaries of the enterprise into the industry and how the firm is able to collaborate with competitors and other stakeholders to achieve profitability. Guided by the Structure-Conduct-Performance framework, it was discovered that Jumla was one of the only e-commerce enterprises in Ghana to physically store vendor products in its warehouse under the consignment business model. This allows for faster delivery and increases Jumla's control of operations. It was also discovered that Jumla had access to robust and first-class information systems and rich research data on e-commerce in emerging markets via their parent organisation. The parent organisation of Jumla has commissioned market research projects on customer behaviour and trends in e-commerce in Africa, Asia and Latin America. Another survival strategy is Jumla's access to international vendors. Jumla can leverage its connections with other subsidiary e-commerce enterprises within Africa to market and introduce new vendors into its product line.

In terms of coordination, another strategy is the simple three-step process for firms to register to become partners and trade on the Jumla platform. The first step which can be done within five minutes involves; filling a registration form; and submitting the required documents which include Business Registration and Bank Account details. The second step involves becoming an e-commerce expert by completing a dedicated new seller training online. The third step also entails activating the seller centre account to manage the online shop by listing products to sell; uploading bestselling products; and selling.

In addition to direct bank transfers, Jumla has also entered into a partnership with mobile money services which allows customers to make direct payments from their mobile money wallets for items purchased. These observations are similar to the findings of Mohammed, Ismail and Muhammad (2015) who asserted that developments in the digital economy such as the payment platforms are significant causes of structural changes in the market which businesses are entreated to capitalise on for development. This leads to the finding that;

Finding two; *the availability of online payment platforms serves as a significant catalyst for the developments or growth in the digital economy*

Competence Dimension of Jumla's Digital Business Strategy

Competence dimension of digital business strategy focuses on the ability of the enterprise to exploit resources to create and capture value. In other words, the resources available to the firm and how they support in achieving competitive advantage. According to Barney (2001), a company's performance or success can largely be explained by how heterogeneous, and immobile its resources are. Resources can be distinguished into assets – anything tangible and intangible a company uses in its processes – and capabilities – the repeatable patterns of actions to make use of assets (Nevo & Wade, 2010). The Resource-Based theory, which was used to review the competence dimension postulates that thriving companies manage to obtain a competitive advantage by holding valuable, rare, only imperfectly imitable and strategically non-substitutable assets and capabilities.

Jumla's assets are basically digital in nature. Jumla uses a high number of electronic devices such as laptops, tablets, phones, among others to manage its online shop. The fax machines and printers are only randomly used as most of the communication is done online. Just as the devices are essential themselves, so also are the various software and information tools running on them. Most of these systems are cloud-based to facilitate usage from different physical locations. Jumla also has a number of physical assets such as warehouse, office space, delivery fleet, among others. Out of these, the probably most heterogeneous and hence valuable asset is the delivery fleet which enables Jumla to avoid the often unreliable and expensive logistical services offered on the market in the developing country. This finding is corroborated by Zhou, Zhang, Chen and Han (2017) who assert that incumbent digital enterprises must be willing to integrate their digital resources with more advanced information technologies in order to achieve profitability.

These technological and physical assets would indeed have been worthless without the workforce of Jumla. Jumla strives to recruit only the most motivated and talented workforce in the country. Something that gives Jumla an edge over its competitors, for instance, is the financial and organisational assets available to them. Jumla's counterpart in Nigeria was launched in 2012. Thus, experiences from the Nigerian environment serve as lessons for the Ghanaian counterparts. This goes in line with Jumla's reputational asset, which is its brand. Thus, reputation serves as an essential market signal for every firm (Wiles, Jain, Mishra, & Lindsey, 2010). A number of Ghanaian customers might have already heard of the Nigerian brand and thus be moved to shop on the Ghanaian platform. A suggestive finding from this discussion is thus made;

Finding three: *Even though there is an increasingly vital role of digital technologies in contemporary business operations, the strong connection between the actions taken in relation to the resources of the firm and competitive advantage cannot be overemphasized.*

Flexibility Dimension of Jumla's Digital Business Strategy

In terms of flexibility, the output of the digital business strategy is the digital enterprise being agile and adapting to changing conditions in the industry. Dynamic Capabilities theory conceptualises those features of the enterprise which are presumed to consist of both managerial and organizational processes. These processes allow the enterprise to identify its needs or opportunities for change in most dynamic environments (Helfat et al., 2007). These Dynamic Capabilities may be referred to as a process (Ambrosini & Bowman, 2009), or as consisting of a set of processes (Helfat et al., 2007). Again, these capabilities are by implication very dynamic hence operate within time and space.

Over the years, Jumla has been able to overcome competition by being flexible and dynamic in the digital economy of Ghana. Extant research (e.g. Chen et al., 2014; Queiroz, Tallon, Sharma, & Coltman, 2018; Roberts & Grover, 2012) have argued that firms which continuously monitor, and sense market opportunities and threats are able to respond quickly. In the case of Jumla, continuous monitoring of the operating environment is carried out. Thus, Jumla dedicates a significant part of its human resources to finding brands and distributors in Ghana. It has even launched the JForce initiative that empowers and enriches budding entrepreneurs with the full support of an established brand. Customers become sales consultants for Jumla where they earn money through commissions by selling items supplied by Jumla. Besides, these sales consultants earn money by recruiting new sales consultants for Jumla.

Finding four: *Digital enterprises are expected to continuously anticipate and prepare to adapt to changes which are a significant feature of the digital economy.*

CONCLUSIONS AND RECOMMENDATIONS

This chapter sought to analyse the digital business strategy of a Ghanaian digital enterprise. The literature review highlighted that the digital economy had redefined business strategy into a term now referred to as "Digital Business Strategy." Thus, initially, Information Technology (IT) strategy was viewed as a functional–level strategy and a subset of the entire business strategy (Bharadwaj et al., 2013; Henderson & Venkatraman, 1993). The IT strategy was headed by an IT manager whose activities were guided by the overall business strategy of the firm. The last decade, on the other hand, has seen a significant transformation in the operations of businesses due to the new functionalities introduced by ICT and other technologies (Bharadwaj et al., 2013). Thus, the strategic actions of companies are being transformed by digital technologies. An example of such transformation includes telecommuting where work can be done across borders, time and distance (Ansong & Boateng, 2017). Another transformation is in the nature of interactions between enterprises and customers which is now mediated through social networking and social media (Susarla, Oh & Tan, 2012). In addition, products and services have become entangled in digital technologies leading to the proliferation of digital products and digital markets (goods and services delivered over digital networks) (Orlikowski, 2009). This situation has resulted in the development of entirely new strategic actions of businesses (Burgelman & Grove, 2007). This is what is referred to as digital business strategy, which is the fusion between the business strategy and the IT strategy (Bharadwaj et al., 2013).

In this study, it was argued that digital business strategy is a multidimensional concept comprising of coordination, flexibility, governance and competence (Bharadwaj et al., 2013). Thus, a comprehensive digital business strategy must focus on these four dimensions. Based on this postulation, there was a review of the competitive digital environment of Jumla Ghana Limited (a digital enterprise), which is the case for this study. Guided by Porter's five competitive forces model, it was discovered that the bargaining power of Jumla's customers was very high. This was because the online media provides customers with the opportunity to compare prices of products of other online shops. Figure 2 summarizes the major competitive forces that influence Jumla's survival.

The intensities of the forces were also determined. From the Figure 1, it was discovered that there was a high intensity of the rivalry between the digital enterprises in the Ghanaian digital economy.

Similarly, the bargaining power of customers was also high. On the other hand, threat from market entrants and the bargaining power of suppliers were both low. Whiles, the threat of substitute products and services was medium.

Figure 2. The major competitive forces that influence Jumla's survival

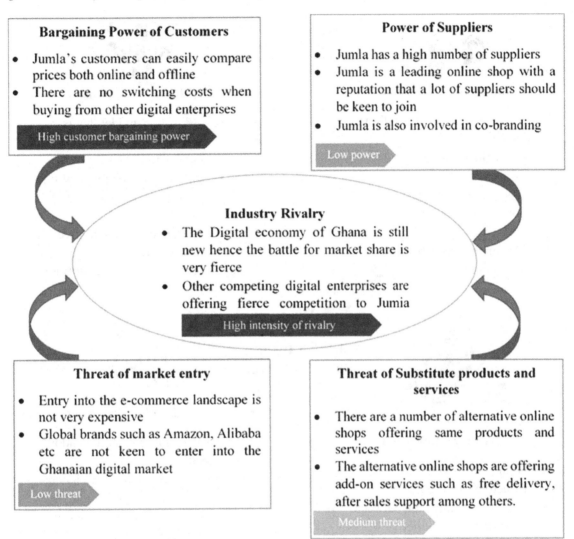

Digital Business Strategy to Overcome Competition

The knowledge of the various competitive forces existing in the digital economy allowed for probing further to identify the strategic actions undertaken by Jumla to remain competitive and survive. As indicated earlier, a comprehensive digital business strategy has four major dimensions. These are Governance, Competence, Flexibility and Coordination. Based on these four dimensions, the survival strategies of the digital enterprise were reviewed. Figure 3 provides a summary of the digital business strategy of Jumla.

Figure 3. Jumla's dimensions of digital business strategy

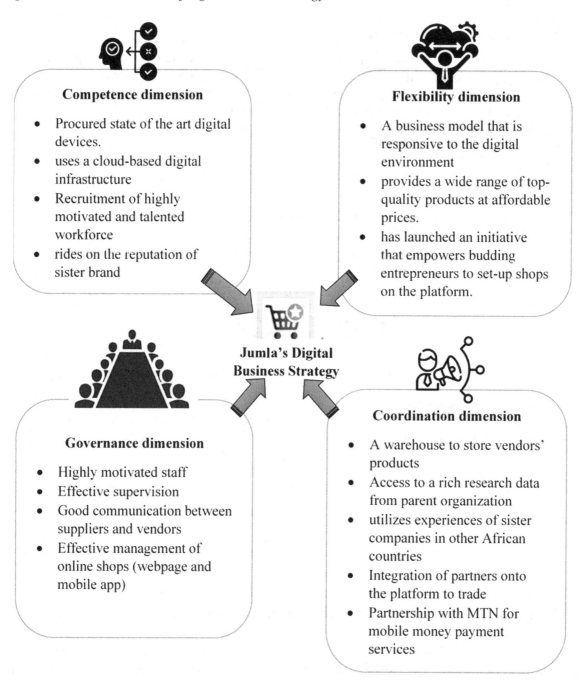

Recommendations

The study contributes to knowledge by providing a review of the competitive digital environment of a Ghanaian digital enterprise and the strategic actions for overcoming these forces and surviving. This knowledge is arguably, the first in the context of a developing economy and hence provides a steppingstone for future studies to explore the levels of significance of the various dimensions of the digital business strategy at the various stages of growth of the enterprise.

The case story presented in this chapter provides the success story of how a digital enterprise is surviving in a very competitive and unstructured digital economy of a developing country. This is meant to draw to the attention of current and hopeful entrepreneurs that there is fierce competition in the digital economy as well as opportunities.

In terms of policy, it is important for the government to realize that there is an increasing rise in digital enterprises in the developing economies; thus, these enterprises are creating jobs and providing business solutions locally that would hitherto be sought from developed economies. There is, therefore, the need for some legal foundations that will cushion these enterprises from the fierce competitions that stagnate their growth. Also, infrastructure and financial support should be given to these enterprises to enable them to develop and employ much more people. Finally, more accelerator and incubator programs should be run to give exposure to the innovative ideas of the indigenes of developing countries to take the opportunities available in the digital economy instead of waiting for foreign investments as the case presented was a foreign-owned company.

REFERENCES

Ambrosini, V., & Bowman, C. (2009). What are dynamic capabilities and are they a useful construct in strategic management? *International Journal of Management Reviews*, *11*(1), 29–49. doi:10.1111/j.1468-2370.2008.00251.x

Ansong, E., & Boateng, R. (2017). Organisational adoption of telecommuting: Evidence from a developing country. *The Electronic Journal on Information Systems in Developing Countries*, *12008*. doi:10.1002/isd2.12008

Ansong, E., & Boateng, R. (2019). Surviving in the digital era–business models of digital enterprises in a developing economy. Digital Policy. *Regulation & Governance*, *21*(2), 164–178. doi:10.1108/DPRG-08-2018-0046

Aubert, B. A., Houde, J. F., Rivard, S., & Patry, M. (2017). Determinants of contract completeness for information technology outsourcing. *Information Technology Management*, *18*(4), 277–292. doi:10.1007/s10799-016-0265-5

Bain, J. S. (1956). Barriers to new competition (Vol. 3). Harvard University Press. doi:10.4159/harvard.9780674188037

Barney, J. (2001). Is the resource-based "view" a useful perspective for strategic management research? Yes. *Academy of Management Review*, *26*(1), 41–56.

Bharadwaj, A., El Sawy, O. A., Pavlou, P. A., & Venkatraman, N. V. (2013). Digital business strategy: Toward a next generation of insights. *Management Information Systems Quarterly*, *37*(2), 471–482. doi:10.25300/MISQ/2013/37:2.3

Birkinshaw, J., & Goddard, J. (2009). The management spectrum. *Business Strategy Review*, *20*(4), 30–35. doi:10.1111/j.1467-8616.2009.00627.x

Blay, A. (2019). Creating jobs using the digital economy. Retrieved July 28, 2019, from http://www.ghanaweb.com/GhanaHomePage/NewsArchive/Creating-jobs-using-the-digital-economy-448958

Bukht, R., & Heeks, R. (2017). Defining, Conceptualising and Measuring the Digital Economy (No. 68). Retrieved from http://www.gdi.manchester.ac.uk/research/publications/working-papers/di/

Burgelman, R. A., & Grove, A. (2007). Cross-Boundary Disruptors: Powerful Inter-Industry Entrepreneurial Change Agents. *Strategic Entrepreneurship Journal*, *1*(3–4), 315–327. doi:10.1002/sej.27

Chan, Y. E., & Reich, B. H. (2007). IT Alignment: What Have We Learned? *Journal of Information Technology*, *22*(4), 297–315. doi:10.1057/palgrave.jit.2000109

Chen, Y., Wang, Y., Nevo, S., Jin, J., Wang, L., & Chow, W. S. (2014). IT capability and organizational performance: The roles of business process agility and environmental factors. *European Journal of Information Systems*, *23*(3), 326–342. doi:10.1057/ejis.2013.4

Choi, B., Raghu, T. S., Vinzé, A., & Dooley, K. J. (2017). Effectiveness of standards consortia: Social network perspectives. *Information Systems Frontiers*, ▪▪▪, 1–12.

Creswell, J. W. (2014). Research Design: Qualitative, Quantitative, and Mixed Methods Approaches. Retrieved from https://books.google.com.gh/books?id=PViMtOnJ1LcC

Dahlman, C., Mealy, S., & Wermelinger, M. (2016). *Harnessing the Digital Economy for Developing Countries*. Paris: OECD.

Denzin, N. K., & Lincoln, Y. S. (2008). *The landscape of qualitative research*. Los Angeles, CA: SAGE Publications.

Drnevich, P. L., & Croson, D. C. (2013). Information Technology and business-level strategy: Toward an integrated theoretical perspective. *Management Information Systems Quarterly*, *37*(2), 483–509. doi:10.25300/MISQ/2013/37.2.08

Eisenhardt, K., & Martin, J. (2000). Dynamic capabilities: What are they? *Strategic Management Journal*, *21*(10–11), 1105–1121. doi:10.1002/1097-0266(200010/11)21:10/11<1105::AID-SMJ133>3.0.CO;2-E

El Sawy, O. A., & Pereira, F. (2013). Digital business models: review and synthesis. In *Business Modelling in the Dynamic Digital Space* (pp. 13–20). Springer; doi:10.1007/978-3-642-31765-1_2.

Grant, R. M. (1999). The resource-based theory of competitive advantage: implications for strategy formulation. In *Knowledge and strategy* (pp. 3–23). Elsevier; doi:10.1016/B978-0-7506-7088-3.50004-8.

Heeks, R. (2016). Examining "Digital Development" (No. 64). Retrieved from http://www.gdi.manchester.ac.uk/research/publications/di/

Heeks, R. (2017). *Information and Communication Technology for Development*. Abingdon, UK: Routledge; doi:10.4324/9781315652603.

Helfat, C. E., Finkelstein, S., Mitchell, W., Peteraf, M., Singh, H., Teece, D. J., & Winter, S. G. (2007). *Dynamic Capabilities- Understanding Strategic Change in Organizations*. Oxford: Blackwell Publishing.

Henderson, J. C., & Venkatraman, N. (1993). Strategic Alignment: Leveraging Information Technology for Transforming Organizations. *IBM Systems Journal, 32*(1), 4–16. doi:10.1147/sj.382.0472

Indiatsy, C. M., Mwangi, M. S., Mandere, E. N., Bichanga, J. M., & George, G. E. (2014). The application of Porter's five forces model on organization performance: A case of cooperative bank of Kenya Ltd. *European Journal of Business and Management, 6*(16), 75–85.

Jensen, M. C., & Meckling, W. H. (1976). Theory of the firm: Managerial behavior, agency costs and ownership structure. *Journal of Financial Economics, 3*(4), 305–360. doi:10.1016/0304-405X(76)90026-X

Keen, P., & Williams, R. (2013). Value architectures for digital business: Beyond the business model. *Management Information Systems Quarterly, 37*(2), 643–648.

Liang, H., Saraf, N., Hu, Q., & Xue, Y. (2007). Assimilation of enterprise systems: The effect of institutional pressures and the mediating role of top management. *Management Information Systems Quarterly, 31*(1), 59–87. doi:10.2307/25148781

Lincoln, Y. S., & Denzin, N. K. (2000). *The handbook of qualitative research*. Los Angeles, CA: SAGE Publications.

Liu, J., Kauffman, R. J., & Ma, D. (2015). Competition, cooperation, and regulation: Understanding the evolution of the mobile payments technology ecosystem. *Electronic Commerce Research and Applications, 14*(5), 372–391. doi:10.1016/j.elerap.2015.03.003

Mai, J. E. (2016). No TitleBig data privacy: The datafication of personal information. *The Information Society, 32*(3), 192–199. doi:10.1080/01972243.2016.1153010

Mata, F., Fuerst, W., & Barney, J. (1995). Information Technology and Sustained Competitive Advantage: A Resource- Based Analysis. *Management Information Systems Quarterly, 19*(4), 487–505. doi:10.2307/249630

Miller, D. (2003). An Asymmetry-Based View of Advantage: Towards an Attainable Sustainability. *Strategic Management Journal, 24*(10), 961–976. doi:10.1002/smj.316

Mohammed, N., Ismail, A. G., & Muhammad, J. (2015). Evidence on market concentration in Malaysian dual banking system. *Procedia: Social and Behavioral Sciences, 172*, 169–176. doi:10.1016/j.sbspro.2015.01.351

Moore, M. (2017). *Turning Personality Into Data. The Chemistry of Conversation*. Mattersight.

Nevo, S., & Wade, M. R. (2010). The formation and value of IT-enabled resources: Antecedents and consequences of synergistic relationships. *Management Information Systems Quarterly, 34*(1), 163–183. doi:10.2307/20721419

Organisation for Economic Co-operation and Development. (2015). OECD Digital Economy Outlook. Retrieved from http://www.oecd.org/sti/oecd-digital-economy-outlook-2015-9789264232440-en.html

Orlikowski, W. (2009). The Sociomateriality of Organisational Life: Considering Technology in Management Research. *Cambridge Journal of Economics*, *34*(1), 125–141. doi:10.1093/cje/bep058

Pavlou, P. A., & El Sawy, O. A. (2010). The 'Third Hand': IT-Enabled Competitive Advantage in Turbulence through Improvisational Capabilities. *Information Systems Research*, *21*(3), 443–471. doi:10.1287/isre.1100.0280

Penrose, E. G. (1959). *The Theory of the Growth of the Firm*. New York: Wiley.

Pereira, G. M. de C., & Pereira, S. C. F. (2011). A quantitative analysis applying Agency theory to Purchasing Department. POMS 23rd Annual Conference, 25–85.

Porter, M. E. (2008). *Competitive strategy: Techniques for analyzing industries and competitors*. Simon and Schuster.

Queiroz, M., Tallon, P. P., Sharma, R., & Coltman, T. (2018). The role of IT application orchestration capability in improving agility and performance. *The Journal of Strategic Information Systems*, *27*(1), 4–21. doi:10.1016/j.jsis.2017.10.002

Rachapila, T., & Jansirisak, S. (2013). Using Porter's Five Forces Model for analysing the competitive environment of Thailand's sweet corn industry. *International Journal of Business and Social Research*, *3*(3), 174–184.

Roberts, N., & Grover, V. (2012). Leveraging information technology infrastructure to facilitate a firm's customer agility and competitive activity: An empirical investigation. *Journal of Management Information Systems*, *28*(4), 231–270. doi:10.2753/MIS0742-1222280409

Rouse, M. (2011). Digital Enterprise. Retrieved May 3, 2018, from https://searchcio.techtarget.com/definition/Digital-enterprise

Scherer, F. M. (1980). *Industrial market structure and economic performance*. Boston: Houghton Mifflin.

Sia, S. K., Soh, C., & Weill, P. (2013). How DBS Bank Pursued a Digital Business Strategy. *Management Information Systems Quarterly*, *27*(2), 471–662.

Sledgianowski, D., Luftman, J., & Reilly, R. R. (2006). Development and Validation of an Instrument to Measure Maturity of IT Business Strategic Alignment Mechanisms. Information Resources Management, 13(6), 18–33. doi:10.4018/irmj.2006070102

Stake, R. E. (1995). *The art of case study research*. Los Angeles, CA: SAGE Publications.

Strauß, S. (2015). Datafication and the Seductive Power of Uncertainty—A Critical Exploration of Big Data Enthusiasm. Information-an International Interdisciplinary Journal, 6(4), 836–847. Retrieved from http://mdpi.com/2078-2489/6/4/836

Susarla, A., Oh, J.-H., & Tan, Y. (2012). Social Networks and the Diffusion of User-Generated Content: Evidence from YouTube. *Information Systems Research*, *23*(1), 123–141. doi:10.1287/isre.1100.0339

Teece, D., Pisano, G., & Shuen, A. (1997). Dynamic Capabilities and Strategic Management. *Strategic Management Journal*, *18*(7), 509–533. doi:10.1002/(SICI)1097-0266(199708)18:7<509::AID-SMJ882>3.0.CO;2-Z

Thomas, G. (2011). A typology for the case study in social science following a review of definition, discourse, and structure. *Qualitative Inquiry*, *17*(6), 511–521. doi:10.1177/1077800411409884

Uotila, J., Keil, T., & Maula, M. (2017). Supply-side network effects and the development of information technology standards. *Management Information Systems Quarterly*, *41*(4), 1207–1226. doi:10.25300/MISQ/2017/41.4.09

Veit, D., Clemons, E., Benlian, A., Buxmann, P., Hess, T., Kundisch, D., & Spann, M. (2014). Business models. *Business & Information Systems Engineering*, *6*(1), 45–53. doi:10.1007/s12599-013-0308-y

Weill, P., & Woerner, S. (2015). Thriving in an increasingly digital ecosystem. *MIT Sloan Management Review*, *56*(4), 27–34.

Wiles, M. A., Jain, S. P., Mishra, S., & Lindsey, C. (2010). Stock market response to regulatory reports of deceptive advertising: The moderating effect of omission bias and firm reputation. *Marketing Science*, *29*(5), 828–845. doi:10.1287/mksc.1100.0562

Williamson, O. E. (1991). Strategizing, Economizing, and Economic Organization. Strategic Management Journal, 12(Winter Special Issue), 75–94.

World Economic Forum. (2015). The Global Competitiveness Report 2015. Retrieved August 4, 2018, from The Global Competitive Report website: http://www.weforum.org/reports/global-competitiveness-report-2015

Zhou, N., Zhang, S., Chen, J. E., & Han, X. (2017). The role of information technologies (ITs) in firms' resource orchestration process: A case analysis of China's "Huangshan 168.". *International Journal of Information Management*, *37*(6), 713–715. doi:10.1016/j.ijinfomgt.2017.05.002

Zollo, M., & Winter, S. G. (2002). Deliberate learning and the evolution of dynamic capabilities. *Organization Science*, *13*(3), 339–351. doi:10.1287/orsc.13.3.339.2780

114

Chapter 6
Evaluating the Critical Determinants for Mobile Commerce Adoption in SMEs in Developing Countries:
A Case Study of Vietnam

Ngoc Tuan Chau

(iD) https://orcid.org/0000-0001-5023-0013

University of Economics, The University of Danang, Danang, Vietnam & RMIT University, Melbourne, Australia

Hepu Deng

School of Accounting, Information Systems and Supply Chain, RMIT University, Melbourne, Australia

ABSTRACT

This chapter presents a review of the related literature on organizational mobile commerce (m-commerce) adoption, leading to the development of an integrated model for evaluating the critical determinants of m-commerce adoption in small and medium-sized enterprises (SMEs) in developing countries. Grounded in the innovation diffusion literature and the extension of the technology-organization-environment framework, the model, integrates technological, organizational, environmental, and managerial factors holistically for better understanding m-commerce adoption in a developing context. Eleven hypotheses are proposed and tested using multiple regression with the data collected from a survey with SMEs' managers in Vietnam. The results confirm the significance of factors in the above four dimensions. These findings provide the managers of SMEs with useful insights on how to improve the adoption of m-commerce in SMEs. These are also useful for policymakers in designing policies that promote the wide adoption of m-commerce in SMEs in the context of developing countries.

DOI: 10.4018/978-1-7998-2610-1.ch006

INTRODUCTION

Mobile commerce (m-commerce) is related to the transactions involving the transfer of the ownership of goods and services with the help of mobile devices (Khalifa, Cheng & Shen, 2012; Njenga, Litondo & Omwansa, 2016). It is an extension of electronic commerce (e-commerce) from wired to wireless devices as well as from fixed locations to anywhere and anytime transactions (Coursaris, Hassanein & Head, 2008). In this chapter, m-commerce is simply about buying and selling of goods and services through wireless handheld devices such as cellular phones and personal digital assistants (Zhiping, 2009; Njenga et al., 2016; Chau & Deng, 2018a).

M-commerce is becoming increasingly popular due to a variety of benefits that it can provide businesses including improving productivity, increasing customer satisfaction, and lowering operational cost (Chau & Deng, 2018b; Duan, Deng & Luo, 2019). It is becoming a cost-effective way for businesses, especially small and medium-sized enterprises (SMEs) to promote their products and services online (Alfahl, Houghton & Sanzogni, 2017). Consequently, there is a significant increase in revenue in m-commerce in the global market from $1.357 trillion in 2017 to $1.804 trillion in 2018, and such revenue is predicted to surpass $2.321 trillion for 2019 (eMarketer, 2018).

Our literature review on organizational m-commerce adoption reveals that there is a huge difference in the adoption of m-commerce between developing countries and developed countries (Chau & Deng, 2018a). While m-commerce has had a high level of adoption in developed countries, it has not been popularly adopted in developing countries (Nafea & Younas, 2014). In Vietnam, for example, a national e-commerce survey in 2018 indicates that only 11% of enterprises in which 90% of them are SMEs conduct their business transactions via e-commerce applications. There are, however, only 13% of these enterprises adopt m-commerce (Vietnam eCommerce and Digital Economy Agency, 2018). The difference in the adoption of m-commerce between developed countries and developing countries is also reflected in the total sales achieved respectively in different countries. For example, the business-to-customer e-commerce sales (including m-commerce sales) in the United State and Australia were recorded at around $421.1 billion and $10.6 billion respectively in 2017. This is in direct contrast to those sales in Thailand and Philippines at $3 billion and $1.2 billion respectively, and only at $6.2 billion in Vietnam in the same year (Vietnam eCommerce and Digital Economy Agency, 2018).

SMEs are a distinct group of organizations with their specific characteristics (Duan, Deng & Corbitt, 2012). These characteristics make them more flexible in adopting technological innovations. The flattened structure of SMEs, in particular, enables much fast decision making in the adoption of a specific technology. There are, however, several critical factors including the lack of ICT skills (Huy, Rowe, Truex & Huynh, 2012), the lack of financial resources (Hamdan, Yahaya, Deraman & Jusoh, 2016), small management team, strong owner influence, centralized power and control, multifunctional management, lack of control over business environment, limited market share, low employee turnover, reluctance to take risk (Seyal & Rahman, 2003), and the dependence on business partners (Stockdale & Standing, 2004) that often pose numerous challenges in their adoption of technological innovations. Although the adoption of such technological innovations can effectively develop their business, the financial, technological, and human resources constraints cause SMEs to lag behind large enterprises in this regard (Alqatan, Noor, Man & Mohemad, 2017).

Despite the numerous benefits of m-commerce, it has not been fully utilized by SMEs in many developing countries (Nafea & Younas, 2014). This is due to the insufficiency of ICT infrastructure and the limitation of financial resources. The low computer literacy, the high cost of ICT equipment, and the lack of sufficient laws and regulations for regulating these developing markets have also made the development of m-commerce difficult (Alrousan & Jones, 2016). Furthermore, the presence of different cultures and business philosophies in developing countries limits the applicability and transferability of the successful m-commerce models commonly used in developed countries (Molla & Licker, 2005). To accelerate the development of m-commerce in developing countries, there is a need for not only establishing the physical ICT infrastructure but also evaluating the critical determinants of m-commerce adoption in SMEs concerning the specific characteristics of developing countries.

LITERATURE REVIEW

Definition of M-Commerce

There are various definitions of m-commerce. Most previous studies consider m-commerce as the extension of e-commerce from wired to wireless devices and telecommunications, and from fixed locations to anywhere and anytime of transactions (Tsai & Gururajan, 2007). Therefore, m-commerce is described as any transaction involving the transfer of ownership of goods and services with the help of mobile devices (Khalifa et al., 2012; Njenga, Litondo & Omwansa, 2016). A transaction-focused perspective describes m-commerce as a business transaction with an economic value using a mobile terminal (Sadeh, 2003; Clarke III, 2008). This chapter focuses on the business-to-customer m-commerce. As a result, a service-focused perspective is adopted, in which m-commerce is simply about buying and selling of goods and services through wireless handheld devices such as cellular phones and personal digital assistants (Zhiping, 2009; Njenga et al., 2016).

M-commerce enables the accomplishment of commercial transactions at any time and any location through wireless connections (Harry, Vos & Haaker, 2008). It possesses unique characteristics regarding internet access devices, communication modes and protocols, enabling technologies, and development languages (Coursaris et al., 2008). Particularly, m-commerce has many unique characteristics such as ubiquity, flexibility, and personalization (Hong, 2015). Hence, m-commerce has been attracting attention from businesses not only for promoting their products and services but also for enhancing their international competitive advantages (Njenga et al., 2016; Alfahl et al., 2017).

Small and Medium-Sized Enterprises in Vietnam and Mobile Commerce Adoption

SMEs can be defined differently across countries and sectors concerning the number of employees, the turnover, and the ownership structure (Ayyagari, Beck & Kunt, 2007). The most commonly used measure is the level of employment due to its easy availability and reliability in data collection. The European Union, for example, defines an SME as a business with less than 250 employees (European Commission, 2018). Asia Pacific Economic Cooperation defines SMEs as businesses with less than 100 employees (Asia-Pacific Economic Cooperation, 2018). In Vietnam, an SME is an independent business with the average number of permanent workers not exceeding 300 (Business Insides, 2011).

SMEs play a strategic role in the economies of their countries. They have a significant contribution to economic growth, social structure, employment, as well as local and regional development. Therefore, most governments regard SMEs as a major driver of the economy and a source of employment opportunities (MacGregor, Bunker & Kartiwi, 2010). In Vietnam, SMEs perform a critical role in the economy. Particularly, they represent 98% of the total number of enterprises in Vietnam, employing more than 50% of labor forces and contributing more than 48% to national gross domestic product (General Statistics Office of Vietnam, 2019b). These show that the success of SMEs is very important to the economic growth in Vietnam. In this regard, how to effectively improve the productivity of Vietnamese SMEs by adopting the latest technologies becomes strategically significant.

The contribution of SMEs to the Vietnamese economy is increasing over time. There is around 8.96% increase of the active SMEs each year in Vietnam (General Statistics Office of Vietnam, 2017), leading to the fierce challenge for the survival of SMEs in the competitive market. This is exemplified by the high exit rate of SMEs in the Vietnam economy. Particularly, there are 16.314 enterprises completing dissolution procedures in 2018, increasing by 34% in comparison with the year 2017, in which 91.2% of these enterprises are SMEs (General Statistics Office of Vietnam, 2019a). As a result, how to actively respond to the changing economy and successfully adopt the latest technologies for promoting competitive advantages is crucial for Vietnamese SMEs.

Vietnam is a developing country with a population of approximately 95 million (Statista, 2019b). There are 32.3 million smartphone users (approximately 34% of the population) (2019a). This shows that Vietnam has a potential market for m-commerce. Moreover, m-commerce is a powerful technology in cutting costs, improving efficiency, and enhancing trade links in Vietnamese SMEs (Chau & Deng, 2018a). As a result, both the Vietnam E-commerce Association and the Vietnamese Government act actively in assisting SMEs with expanding and growing their businesses through the development of a series of policies and programs for improving the economic environment. Such initiatives have created a sound environment for supporting Vietnamese SMEs financially and promoting the adoption of the latest technologies for developing their respective businesses. There are, however, about 20% of SMEs have built websites for promoting their business online. Furthermore, about 70% of these websites are difficult to access by mobile devices (VECITA, 2017). This shows that the adoption of m-commerce in Vietnamese enterprises is still quite low. Therefore, the benefits of m-commerce have not been fully utilized in Vietnamese SMEs.

Despite the investment and encouragement from the government, the adoption of m-commerce in SMEs does still not match with an extremely potential market in Vietnam. This is due to Vietnamese SMEs commonly sharing the same barriers to the adoption of technologies as SMEs in other developing countries. They are lack of ICT skills (Huy et al., 2012), lack of financial resources (Hamdan et al., 2016), and high dependence on business partners (Stockdale & Standing, 2004). Additionally, Vietnamese SMEs also face some other challenges in adopting m-commerce. Particularly, in addition to the lack of awareness of m-commerce benefits, there is a business perception that the adoption of m-commerce is costly. There is also a lack of opportunities to access investment funds and internal technical expertise. Finally, the habit of using cash and the concerns about security issues are also the main barriers to the adoption of internet commerce in general and m-commerce in particular (VCCI, 2016). As a result, these issues faced by SMEs need to be properly addressed while investigating the critical determinants for the adoption of m-commerce.

Related Works in Organizational Mobile Commerce Adoption

The lack of research in evaluating the critical determinants for m-commerce adoption in organizations has attracted much attention in the existing literature (Chau & Deng, 2018a). An analysis of related empirical studies on m-commerce adoption in organizations reveals that there is a concentration on the testing and validation of specific conceptual frameworks for better understanding the adoption of m-commerce in organizations. This often leads to the identification and evaluation of numerous critical determinants for organizational m-commerce adoption under perspectives of different technology adoption theories such as theory of reasoned action (TRA) (Fishbein & Ajzen, 1975), theory of planned behavior (TPB) (Ajzen, 1991), technology acceptance model (TAM) (Davis, 1989), diffusion of innovation theory (DOI) (Rogers, 2010), and technology-organization-environment framework (TOE) (Tornatzky & Fleischer, 1990).

The use of TAM for better understanding the adoption of m-commerce in organizations assumes that the intention of an organization in adopting m-commerce is influenced by the perceived usefulness and the perceived ease of use (Davis, 1989). Such a theory has been widely applied with specific extensions in various contexts for exploring the adoption of m-commerce in organizations. Shih, Chen, Wu, Huang & Shiu (2010), for example, apply TAM and find that perceived usefulness, perceived ease of use, and tool experience are critical for the adoption of m-commerce. Mashagba, Mashagba & Nassar (2013) revise TAM and confirm that perceived usefulness, perceived ease of use, IT trust, level of e-commerce adoption, security, and IT infrastructure significantly impact the adoption of m-commerce. Pipitwanichakarn & Wongtada (2019) extend TAM and indicate that perceived usefulness, perceived ease of use, trust, and entrepreneurial orientation are the critical determinants for the adoption of m-commerce.

The adoption of TOE for exploring the m-commerce adoption in organizations suggests three main aspects of an organization that influence the adoption of m-commerce, namely technology, organization and environment (Tornatzky & Fleischer, 1990). Martin & Jimenez (2015), for example, adopt TOE and identify various critical determinants including motivation, perceived benefits, managers' and employees' support, impediments to implement, perceived customer value, competitive pressure, and the propensity to innovation and ICT. Lu, Hu, Huang & Tzeng (2015) employ TOE and confirm nine critical determinants including data security, network reliability, technology complexity, top management emphasis, employees' IS knowledge, firm size, competitive pressure, partner support, and regulatory support. Rana, Barnard, Baabdullah, Rees & Roderick (2019) adopt TOE and find that perceived cost, perceived risk, inconvenience of use, compatibility issues, privacy and security issues, lack of technology knowledge, forced changes to business strategy, unawareness of benefits, lack of customer trust and confidence, and lack of external pressure are the critical determinants for the adoption of m-commerce.

An integration of several theories is commonly used for better investigating the critical determinants for m-commerce adoption in organizations. Otieno & Kahonge (2014), for example, integrate TOE with DOI and identify eleven critical determinants including benefits, friendliness, security, managerial support, organizational size, organizational readiness, firm scope, mimetic pressure, coercive pressure, normative pressure, and intensity of competition. Picoto, Belanger & Palma-dos-Reis (2014) combine TOE with DOI and RBT and indicate that relative advantage, technology competence, technology integration, managerial obstacles, competitive pressure, partner pressure, and mobile environment significantly affect mobile business adoption. Alfahl et al. (2017) integrate TOE with TAM, DOI, TRA, and TPB, and confirm that relative advantages, perceived usefulness, perceived ease of use, complexity, compatibility, and job-fit, policy and legal environment, organizational policy, ICT infrastructure, organizational culture, top management support, subjective norms, social factors, security, and trust are the critical determinants for the adoption of m-commerce.

Several studies are combining TAM with other theories for investigating the adoption of m-commerce in organizations. Grandhi & Wibowo (2016), for example, integrate TAM with DOI and find that organization strategy, perceived business benefits, inhibitors, and interface design features are critical for the adoption of m-commerce. Amegbe, Hanu & Nuwasiima (2017) combine TAM and DOI and confirm that perceived trust, perceived risk, technology failure, perceived usefulness, perceived cost-effectiveness, convenience, and perceived ease of use are the critical determinants for m-commerce adoption. Sun & Chi (2018) integrate TAM with TRA and DOI and identify seven critical determinants including perceived usefulness, perceived ease of use, subjective norm, observability, compatibility, past non-store shopping experience, and personal innovativeness trait.

The above analysis of empirical studies on organizational m-commerce adoption shows that there are various critical determinants of m-commerce adoption in organizations under various circumstances. Such determinants can be categorized into three main dimensions, namely technological dimension, organizational dimension, and environmental dimension. Table 1 presents a summary of the findings of such studies in the literature. These findings, however, cannot be fully applied for explaining m-commerce adoption in SMEs in developing countries. This is due to (a) the lack of consideration of the unique characteristics of SMEs in the adoption of m-commerce and (b) the lack of empirical results for m-commerce adoption in SMEs in the context of developing countries. As a result, an evaluation of the critical determinants for m-commerce adoption in SMEs in developing countries is significant for the improvement of such adoption in SMEs.

THEORETICAL BACKGOUND

There are several theories for investigating the adoption of technology from individual and organizational perspectives. This chapter aims to identify the critical determinants for m-commerce adoption in SMEs. Consequently, this section reviews and discusses the two prominent theories for investigating the adoption of technology in organizations: the diffusion of innovation theory and the technology-organization-environment framework.

Diffusion of Innovation Theory

DOI is a process-based framework for explaining how, why, and at what rate technology is adopted in an organization. It describes the patterns of adoption, illustrates the process, and assists in understanding whether and how innovation will be successful (Rogers, 2010). DOI identifies the factors which facilitate the adoption of technology from assessing the rate of diffusion of a technology (Seyal, Rahman & Mohammad, 2007). With the use of this theory, five attributes of innovation that influence the adoption of innovation including relative advantage, compatibility, complexity, trialability, and observability can be identified.

DOI is the most influential theory in innovation adoption studies as it proposes a comprehensive framework for understanding the technology adoption process in organizations (Duan et al., 2012). It also proposes the fundamental determinants for investigating the adoption of technology by individuals and organizations. As a result, DOI theory, particular the attributes of innovation, are widely used as the theoretical basis in various empirical studies for identifying the critical determinants for technology adoption in SMEs (Zhu, Kraemer & Xu, 2006; Seyal et al., 2007; Alam, Khatibi, Ahmad & Ismail, 2008).

DOI has received substantial criticism in its application at an organizational level (Chau & Tam, 1997). First, it cannot address the full implementation process of technology. Second, it does not provide a lens for examining the nature of relationships between the organization and individual decision-making,

Table 1. An overview of studies on m-commerce adoption in organizations

Dimensions	Critical Determinants	Literature sources
Technology	Relative advantage	Jain, Le, Lin & Cheng (2011); Picoto et al. (2014); Alfahl et al. (2017).
	Compatibility, technology integration	Picoto et al. (2014); Alfahl et al. (2017); Sun & Chi (2018); Rana et al. (2019).
	Complexity, inconvenience of use	Jain et al. (2011); Lu et al. (2015); Alfahl et al. (2017); Rana et al. (2019).
	Perceived usefulness	Shih et al. (2010); Mashagba et al. (2013); Alfahl et al. (2017); Amegbe et al. (2017); Sun & Chi (2018); Pipitwanichakarn & Wongtada (2019).
	Perceived ease of use, friendliness, convenience	Shih et al. (2010); Mashagba et al. (2013); Otieno & Kahonge (2014); Alfahl et al. (2017); Amegbe et al. (2017); Sun & Chi (2018); Pipitwanichakarn & Wongtada (2019).
	Perceived costs	Amegbe et al. (2017); Rana et al. (2019).
	Trust	Mashagba et al. (2013); Alfahl et al. (2017); Amegbe et al. (2017); Pipitwanichakarn & Wongtada (2019); Rana et al. (2019).
	Security	Mashagba et al. (2013); Otieno & Kahonge (2014); Lu et al. (2015); Alfahl et al. (2017); Rana et al. (2019).
	Perceived benefits, unawareness of benefits	Otieno & Kahonge (2014); Martin & Jimenez (2015); Grandhi & Wibowo (2016); Rana et al. (2019).
Organization	Organizational innovativeness	Martin & Jimenez (2015); Sun & Chi (2018).
	Business strategy	Rana et al. (2019).
	Organizational readiness	Jain et al. (2011); Otieno & Kahonge (2014).
	Top management support	Picoto et al. (2014); Otieno & Kahonge (2014); Lu et al. (2015); Martin & Jimenez (2015); Alfahl et al. (2017).
	Employees' IT knowledge	Jain et al. (2011); Lu et al. (2015); Rana et al. (2019).
	Technology competence	Shih et al. (2010); Martin, Catalan & Jeronimo (2012); Picoto et al. (2014).
Environment	Competitive pressures	Picoto et al. (2014); Otieno & Kahonge (2014); Lu et al. (2015); Martin & Jimenez (2015).
	Support from technology vendors	Jain et al. (2011).
	Customer pressures, perceived customer value	Martin et al. (2012); Picoto et al. (2014); Otieno & Kahonge (2014); Lu et al. (2015); Martin & Jimenez (2015).
	External pressures	Rana et al. (2019).
	Government support and regulation	Otieno & Kahonge (2014); Lu et al. (2015); Alfahl et al. (2017).
	ICT infrastructure	Jain et al. (2011); Mashagba et al. (2013); Alfahl et al. (2017).

and the complex social contexts in which organizations make decisions (Parker & Castleman, 2009). Third, it tends to ignore the influence of the organizational and environmental factors on the adoption of technology (Lee & Cheung, 2004). Considering that m-commerce is a complex technology, the adoption of such a technology may be influenced by the organizational factors and the external environment in which SMEs are embedded in (Alrousan & Jones, 2016). As a result, the classical assimilation variables by the DOI are unlikely to be strong predictors of such adoption; therefore, a proper consideration of organizational and environmental factors for the adoption of m-commerce in SMEs is highly desirable for better outcomes (Perez, Martinez, Carnicer & Jimenez, 2004).

Figure 1. Stages in the innovation-decision process

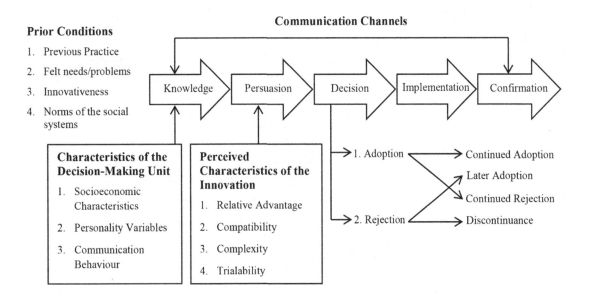

Technology-Organization-Environment Framework

TOE is an organizational-level theory that describes how the organizational context influences the adoption of technological innovations (Baker, 2012). It consists of three contexts for identifying the factors influencing the process by which an organization adopts technological innovations including the technological context, the organizational context, and the environmental context. The technological context is related to the characteristics of the available technologies, whether external or internal to the organization. The organizational context is related to the characteristics of an organization and internal resources available to an organization that encourages or discourages the adoption of technological innovations. The environmental context refers to the environment surrounding the organization and its dealings with trading partners, competitors, and government (Tornatzky & Fleischer, 1990). These contexts make a useful analytical framework for studying the adoption of various technological innovations in organizations (Chuang, Nakatani, Chen & Huang, 2007). TOE becomes a solid theoretical basis for identifying the critical determinants for the adoption of technology in organizations. Hence, it is widely used in a variety of technological innovations adoption studies (Lin, 2014; Hsu & Lin, 2016).

TOE is becoming a comprehensive theoretical lens for understanding the adoption of various technological innovations in organizations. It, however, does not identify in depth the managerial factors where SMEs' managers are considered the most critical decision-makers in adopting new technologies (Hashim, 2007). As a result, it is suggested to be expanding by adding the fourth context which describes the managerial factors (Bao & Sun, 2010). TOE is also a flexible framework that can be extended to accept more categories and factors that help to identify the critical determinants for technology adoption in organizations (Zhu et al., 2006). Additionally, it introduces a broader scope and provides links between the three contextual elements. Consequently, it provides the potential for including broader aspects associated with cultural differences and industry type (Oliveira & Martins, 2011).

Figure 2. TOE framework

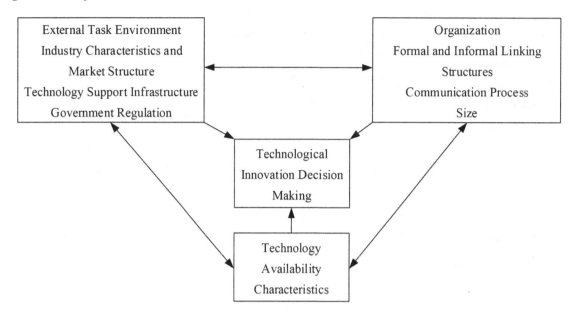

A CONCEPTUAL FRAMEWORK

This section presents a conceptual framework for investigating the critical determinants for m-commerce adoption in Vietnamese SMEs. Such a framework is grounded from the combination of DOI theory and TOE framework. M-commerce adoption in organizations is a complex process with various factors involved. For that reason, the use of multiple theories for investigating the adoption of m-commerce in organizations would provide more comprehensive explanations of such adoption (Wymer & Regan, 2005). Additionally, a review of the literature shows that DOI and TOE are commonly used for understanding technology adoption in organizations (Zhu et al., 2006). Furthermore, m-commerce is commonly considered as a type of technological innovation in organizations. The decision to adopt such innovation in organizations is therefore certainly influenced by not only the characteristics of the m-commerce technology itself but also other factors related to the internal organization and external business environment. As a result, DOI and TOE are the most suitable theories for investigating the critical determinants for m-commerce adoption in SMEs.

Integrating DOI and TOE provides a solid theoretical foundation for a better understanding of the adoption of m-commerce in Vietnamese SMEs (Chau & Deng, 2018b). The use of DOI, for example, can focus more on technology characteristics in considering the adoption of a specific technology. It tends to ignore the influence of organizational and environmental factors (Lee & Cheung, 2004). The adoption of TOE presents a useful model for investigating the technology adoption from several perspectives in SMEs (Huy et al., 2012). TOE, however, does not sufficiently identify the managerial factors which are critical for the technology adoption in SMEs. This shows that using both theories provides a robust explanation in technology adoption in SMEs in developing countries (Oliveira & Martins, 2010).

Figure 3 presents a conceptual framework for investigating the critical determinants for m-commerce adoption in Vietnamese SMEs. The perceived cost and the perceived security are included for extending DOI, and the managerial context is added for extending TOE to have a more robust explanation of m-

Figure 3. A conceptual framework

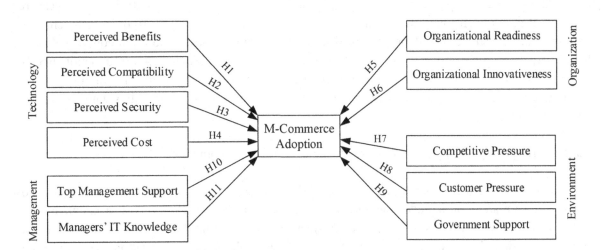

commerce adoption in SMEs. The proposed framework conceptualizes that factors affecting the adoption of m-commerce in SMEs can be categorized into four main contexts including the technological context, the organizational context, the environmental context, and the managerial context.

Technological Context

The technological context is related to the characteristics of technologies in SMEs (Rogers, 2010). A review of the related literature shows that among five characteristics of the technology, perceived benefits, and perceived compatibility are the most important factors affecting m-commerce adoption in organizations. Furthermore, the cost of adoption is also a big concern for SMEs, especially SMEs in developing countries (Chau & Deng, 2018b). In Vietnam, the slow adoption of technologies by SMEs has attributed to the lack of awareness of the benefits and a business perception that technology adoption is costly. Such a slow adoption is also attributed to the concerns about security (VCCI, 2016). As a result, perceived cost and perceived security are included in the technological context to investigate m-commerce adoption in Vietnamese SMEs. These lead to the determination of four technological determinants in the conceptual framework: perceived benefits, perceived compatibility, perceived cost, and perceived security.

Perceived benefits of m-commerce adoption are a set of anticipated advantages that can be gained by an organization when m-commerce has been accepted (Duan et al., 2019). In the technology adoption context, perceived benefits are reflected in two dimensions including the degree to which the new technology is expected to bring better business performance and the extent to which business activities are covered when the new technology is adopted (Jeon, Han & Lee, 2006). Perceived benefits are the key determinant for the adoption of various technological innovation in SMEs (Ifinedo, 2011; Otieno & Kahonge, 2014). The higher the perceived benefits of innovations, the greater the intention to adopt such innovations (Chwelos, Benbasat & Dexter, 2001). This leads to the following hypothesis:

H1: Perceived benefits positively affect the adoption of m-commerce

Perceived compatibility of m-commerce is the degree to which m-commerce is consistent with existing values, needs and past experiences of the potential adopter (Rogers, 2010). It can be measured by the fit of m-commerce with the organizations' customers and suppliers, the fit of m-commerce with the organizational structure and the perceived suitability of the business to adopt m-commerce (Salah, 2013). Perceived compatibility is one of the most critical determinants for technology adoption in SMEs (Kurnia, Karnali & Rahim 2015; Alfahl et al., 2017). A higher level of perceived compatibility is associated with an increased intention to adopt the technology in businesses (Alam, Ali & Jani, 2011). This leads to the following hypothesis:

H2: Perceived compatibility positively affects the adoption of m-commerce

Perceived cost of m-commerce adoption is the relative cost to the benefits of m-commerce. The cost of m-commerce adoption includes the cost of m-commerce technologies, the cost of maintenance of these technologies and the cost of training employees to use such technologies. Perceived cost has been found as a critical determinant for the adoption of various technological innovations in organizations (Tan, Chong, Lin & Eze, 2009; Amegbe et al., 2017). The higher the perceived adoption cost of the technology, the slower the pace of its adoption. This leads to the following hypothesis:

H3: Perceived cost negatively affects the adoption of m-commerce

Perceived security in m-commerce is the awareness of an organization about the security of m-commerce technologies. Security is the main concern hindering the adoption of technologies in SMEs in developing countries (Tan et al., 2009). It is a critical determinant for the adoption of various technological innovations in organizations (Lu et al., 2015; Rana et al., 2019). M-commerce transactions are mainly conducted via the internet using mobile devices. As a result, the higher level of perceived security certainly increases the intention to adopt m-commerce in SMEs. This leads to the following hypothesis:

H4: Perceived security positively affects the adoption of m-commerce

Organizational Context

The organizational context presents the internal factors to an organization that affects the adoption of new technologies (Lippert & Govindarajulu, 2006). The reviewed literature on organizational m-commerce adoption shows that organizational readiness is the most important determinant for such adoption (Chau & Deng, 2018b). Additionally, the innovativeness ability of an organization acts as the prerequisite and facilitator of the successful adoption of technological innovations (Wamba & Carter, 2013). As a result, organizational innovativeness is included in the organizational context for examining the adoption of m-commerce in SMEs. This leads to the determination of two organizational determinants in the conceptual model: organizational readiness and organizational innovativeness.

Organizational readiness is about the availability of the technological, financial, and human resources in the organization for adopting technological innovations. It is a critical determinant of technology adoption in organizations, especially in SMEs (Alam et al., 2011; Huy et al., 2012). The higher level of organizational readiness is a predictor of successful technology adoption in organizations (Jain et al., 2011; Otieno & Kahonge, 2014; Kurnia et al., 2015). This leads to the following hypothesis:

H5: Organizational readiness positively affects the adoption of m-commerce

Organizational innovativeness is about the intentional introduction and application of new ideas, processes, products or procedures to the relevant unit of the organization (Siamagka, Christodoulides, Michaelidou & Valvi, 2015). It is essential for organizations to gain competitive advantages. Organizational innovativeness is a significant predictor of technology adoption in organizations (Wamba & Carter, 2013; Martin & Jimenez, 2015; Sun & Chi, 2018). The adoption of new technologies is dependent upon an innovative climate within an organization (Siamagka et al., 2015). As a result, the more innovative of an organization, the more likely they will adopt innovations for their business. This leads to the following hypothesis:

H6: Organizational innovativeness positively affects the adoption of m-commerce

Environmental Context

The environmental context is the environment surrounding the organization concerning the business, competitors, government support, suppliers, and customers (Baker, 2012). The literature review on organizational m-commerce adoption has identified the three most important environmental factors, including competitive pressures, trading partner pressures, and government support (Chau & Deng, 2018b). This chapter concentrates on business-to-customer m-commerce. Therefore, the key trading partner is the customers. This leads to the determination of three environmental determinants in the conceptual model: competitive pressures, customer pressures, and government support.

Competitive pressures refer to the degree that an organization is affected by its competitors in the market (Porter & Millar, 1985). Competitive threats from the external environment are the major factor affecting the adoption of technological innovations in organizations, especially in SMEs (Awa, Ukoha & Emecheta, 2016). By adopting technological innovations, organizations can be able to alter rules of competition, affect the industry structure and leverage new ways to outperform rivals, and so changing the competitive environment (Porter & Millar, 1985). The relationship between competitive pressures and technological innovations adoption in organizations can be extended to m-commerce, which is a useful way of enhancing international competitive advantage for SMEs. This leads to the following hypothesis:

H7: Competitive pressures positively affect the adoption of m-commerce

Customer pressures are about the requirements and expectations from customers leading to the adoption of an innovation by an organization. When an organization's dominant customers have adopted a technological innovation, the organization may adopt such innovation to show its fitness as a business partner (Al-Bakri & Katsioloudes, 2015). Customer pressures are found as a facilitator for innovation adoption in SMEs (Otieno & Kahonge, 2014; Lu et al., 2015; Rahayu & Day, 2015). The greater the pressures from customers perceived by SMEs, the more likely they are to adopt technological innovations (Duan et al., 2012). This leads to the following hypothesis:

H8: Customer pressures positively affect the adoption of m-commerce

Government support is about the availability of government policies and initiatives to promote the adoption of new technologies in organizations. It is commonly manifested in three different aspects, including policies and legislation, funding and ICT infrastructure (Saprikis & Vlachopoulou, 2012). Governmental incentives in the form of economic, financial and technological support lower the barriers of the technology adoption in SMEs (Alrousan & Jones, 2016). The support from the government is a critical factor affecting the adoption of various technological innovations in SMEs (Alfahl et al., 2017; Miao & Tran, 2018). This leads to the following hypothesis:

H9: Government support positively affects the adoption of m-commerce

Managerial Context

The managerial context includes factors relating to employee members who play important roles in deciding to adopt new technologies in their organization. In the context of SMEs, both operational and strategic decisions are commonly taken by a single person (Ghobakhloo & Tang, 2013). As a result, the attitudes, skills, and ICT background of SMEs' managers play as a driving force for the adoption of new technologies. Consequently, the support from top management and the IT knowledge of managers are considered in the managerial context for investigating the adoption of m-commerce in Vietnamese SMEs.

Top management support refers to the involvement, enthusiasm, motivation, and encouragement provided by the board of management toward the adoption of technological innovations (Ramdani, Kawalek & Lorenzo, 2009). Top management support is an important factor for the adoption of technological innovations in SMEs as the decision-making process is mostly centralized in a few persons. Such persons can provide a vision, support and a commitment to creating a positive environment for new technologies adoption (Al-Alawi & Al-Ali, 2015). Top management support is the most important factor in technology adoption in organizations, especially in SMEs (Lu et al., 2015; Alfahl et al., 2017). This leads to the following hypothesis:

H10: Top management support positively affects the adoption of m-commerce

Managers' IT knowledge is about IT knowledge and skills of decision-makers that can influence the adoption of technological innovations in organizations. The ability of the managers in IT knowledge and skills increases the opportunity for IT adoption in SMEs (Apulu & Latham, 2011). A manager who is knowledgeable in innovation will be able to champion the adoption of such an innovation (Hussin & Noor, 2005). Managers' IT knowledge is a critical determinant for the adoption of various technological innovation in SMEs (Huy et al., 2012; Alrousan & Jones, 2016). This leads to the following hypothesis:

H11: Managers' IT knowledge positively affects the adoption of m-commerce

RESEARCH METHODOLOGY

The approach for data collection conforms to the quantitative technique using a survey. This study uses multiple items to measure each research variables, with variables previously verified by experts serving as a reference for the questionnaire design. A five-point Likert-type scale is adopted in which the value "1" represents "strongly disagree", and the value "5" represents "strongly agree".

Before distributing the questionnaire, a pre-test for improving the clarity, question-wording, and validity of individual questions was conducted. Three professors and five doctoral students in business information systems were invited to analyze the content and wording of the question. A minor modification was made based on the suggestion of such experts. As the survey is conducted in Vietnam, the questionnaire is translated into Vietnamese using a parallel translation technique to ensure an accurately-worded translation. A pilot test with thirty-two Vietnamese SMEs' managers was then conducted to increase the validity and reliability of the questionnaire before it was administered to the participants. Based on the feedback of these managers, the final version of the questionnaire was used for the main study. A total of eleven independent variables and one dependent variable with 44 items were used in the final questionnaire. Table 2 presents a summary of these measurement items.

The self-administered survey was conducted in Vietnam between April 2018 and August 2018. The target population was managers of SMEs in Vietnam. The sampling frame is obtained from the Vietnam Association of SMEs (VINASME) website using the probability sampling method. The sample unit was the managers of selected SMEs. A total of 700 SMEs were randomly selected from the list of members of the VINASME. With the help of the VINASMEs in delivering the survey, a mail package that includes a printed version of the questionnaire and the invitation letter along with a postage-paid return envelope was delivered to the managers of selected SMEs. A total of 388 responses are received. A data examination process is conducted for addressing missing values, outliers, and normality, leading to the removal of thirty-four responses. As a result, 354 usable responses were retained and used for the empirical analysis.

DATA ANALYSIS AND RESULTS

To evaluate the critical determinants for m-commerce adoption in Vietnamese SMEs, an investigation of the relationships between independent variables and the dependent variable was conducted through multiple regression analysis with the use of IBM SPSS version 25. Before conducting such an analysis, tests concerning reliability, normality, homoscedasticity, linearity, and multicollinearity were carried out. The results of these tests are presented in this section.

Characteristics of the Sampled SMEs

The cleaned data were examined for identifying sample characteristics before conducting the main data analysis. This involves an analysis of the demographic information of the respondent. Respondents are general and department managers of the selected SMEs. Table 3 presents the profile of such sample SMEs. The majority of SMEs were from trading and services sectors, accounting for 30.5% and 29.6% respectively, followed by SMEs in construction (13.3%). There were 10.5% of SMEs in manufacturing and 9.3% of SMEs in transportation. The rest were SMEs from other sectors such as finance & insurance, ICT and healthcare. Most SMEs have been running their business for less than five years (41.5%), 39.3% between 5 to 10 years, 13.3% between 11 to 15 years, and 5.9% for more than 15 years. 37.3% of SMEs have less than 10 employees, 57.9% have 10 to 200 employees, and 4.8% have 201 to 300 employees. These results indicate that the survey data were a representative sample for the population.

Table 2. A summary of measurement items used in the questionnaire design

Variables		Items and References
Perceived benefits	BENE1	Operating cost-saving (Zhu et al., 2006)
	BENE2	Simplification of the operating procedures (Zhu et al., 2006)
	BENE3	Increase in market share (Scupola, 2009)
	BENE4	Growth of revenue (Zhu et al., 2006)
	BENE5	Creation of marketing channels (Scupola, 2009)
	BENE6	Improvement of the organizational image (Zhu et al., 2006)
	BENE7	Improvement in competitiveness (Teo et al., 2009)
	BENE8	Enhancement of customer services (Scupola, 2009)
Perceived compatibility	CMPA1	Alignment with ICT infrastructure (Zhu et al., 2006)
	CMPA2	Integration with current business processes (Zhu et al., 2006)
	CMPA3	The adaptability of existing distribution channels (Zhu et al., 2006)
	CMPA4	Consistency with the organizational culture (Ghobakhloo et al., 2011)
	CMPA5	Suitability with customers' ways of business (Ghobakhloo et al., 2011)
	CMPA6	Richness of experience in adopting an innovation (Ghobakhloo et al., 2011)
Perceived security	SECU1	Awareness of the security of m-commerce (Alam et al., 2011)
	SECU2	Availability of industrial security standards (Alam et al., 2011)
	SECU3	Availability of laws and regulations (Alam et al., 2011)
Perceived cost	CSTS1	Infrastructure cost requirements (Al-Qirim, 2006)
	CSTS2	Training cost requirements (Al-Qirim, 2006)
	CSTS3	Maintenance cost requirements (Al-Qirim, 2006)
Organizational readiness	READ1	Financial readiness (Alam et al., 2011)
	READ2	Technological readiness (Alam et al., 2011)
	READ3	Human resource readiness (Alam et al., 2011)
Organizational innovativeness	INNO1	Innovativeness ability (Wamba & Carter, 2013)
	INNO2	Ability to adopt new management approaches (Wamba & Carter, 2013)
	INNO3	Ability to improve business processes continuously (Wamba & Carter, 2013)
Competitive pressures	CMPE1	Similar products/services of competitors (Thong & Yap, 1995)
	CMPE2	Similar products/services of new entrants (Thong & Yap, 1995)
	CMPE3	Substitute products/services (Thong & Yap, 1995)
Customer pressures	CUST1	Requirement for adopting m-commerce (Teo et al., 2009)
	CUST2	The expectation for adopting m-commerce (Teo et al., 2009)
	CUST3	Maintain relationships with customers (Teo et al., 2009)
Government support	GOVE1	Legal considerations for m-commerce (Huy et al., 2012)
	GOVE2	Financial support (Huy et al., 2012)
	GOVE3	Training and education programs (Huy et al., 2012)
Top management support	TMSP1	Awareness of the benefits of m-commerce (Seyal & Rahim, 2006)
	TMSP2	Allocation of necessary resources (Seyal & Rahim, 2006)
	TMSP3	Championship of management for m-commerce (Seyal & Rahim, 2006)
Managers' IT knowledge	TMIT1	Understanding of m-commerce (Huy et al., 2012)
	TMIT2	Proficiency in using IT (Huy et al., 2012)
	TMIT3	Competence about the new technology (Huy et al., 2012)
Adoption	ADPT1	Have an intention for adoption (Davis, 1989)
	ADPT2	Have a certain plan for adoption (Davis, 1989)
	ADPT3	Have a strong commitment to adoption (Davis, 1989)

Reliability Test

Reliability measures the degree to which items are free from random errors. A variable can be said to demonstrate acceptable reliability if the scores from individual items correspond highly with each other (Straub, Boudreau & Gefen, 2004). Cronbach's alpha (α) coefficient is the most widely used measure for assessing the reliability of the measurement instrument (Hair, Black, Babin, Anderson & Tatham, 2010).

Table 3. The profile of sample SMEs

Category	Description	Frequency	%	Category	Description	Frequency	%
Location of SMEs	North Vietnam	80	22.6%	Duration of business	<5 years	147	41.5%
	Central & Highland	173	48.9%		5-10 years	139	39.3%
	South Vietnam	101	28.5%		11-15 years	47	13.3%
Industry	Services	105	29.6%		>15 years	21	5.9%
	Trading	108	30.5%	Size (No. of employees)	<10	132	37.3%
	Construction	47	13.3%		10-50	143	40.4%
	Manufacturing	37	10.5%		51-100	44	12.4%
	Transportation	33	9.3%		101-200	18	5.1%
	Finance & Insurance	13	3.7%		201-300	17	4.8%
	ICT	7	2.0%	Adoption	Adopter	95	26.8%
	Healthcare	4	1.1%		Non-adopter	259	73.2%

The value of the α coefficient ranges from 0 (completely unreliable) to 1.0 (perfectly reliable). Hair et al. (2010) suggest that the α coefficient of 0.5 to 0.6 is considered acceptable for exploratory research, but the value of 0.7 or above is highly acceptable. Twelve variables in the measurement instrument were estimated for reliability by calculating α coefficients. The results are presented in Table 4. These results show that the average of α coefficients of all variables ranges from 0.827 for the perceived cost to 0.929 for m-commerce adoption intention, confirming that all variables in the measurement instrument are considered to be satisfactory for the reliability of a multi-item scale.

Normality Test

Normality refers to the shape of the distribution and characteristics of its statistics for a single individual metric item that approximates the normal distribution (Hair et al., 2010). The normality assessment can be done both graphically and statistically. Graphically, the deviance form of normality is assessed through a visual check of the histogram or normality plots. Statistically, normality is empirically tested through the distribution's shape using skewness and kurtosis measures for each item. In this chapter, the statistical method, particularly the skewness and kurtosis measures, is adopted for examining the normality of all items. Table 5 presents the results of this test. Such results indicate that all items normally distributed with the skewness values range between -0.951 and -0.138 and the kurtosis values range between -0.305 and 1.915 that belong to the critical value ranges of +/-2.58 and +/-1.96 respectively (Hair et al., 2010).

Homoscedasticity Test

Homoscedasticity concerns about the assumption that the dependent variable exhibit equal levels of variance across the range of predictor variables (Hair et al., 2010). It describes a situation in which the error term is the same across all values of independent variables. The violation of homoscedasticity creates serious bias in the standard errors. This leads to incorrect conclusions about the significance of the regression coefficients. Homoscedasticity can be evaluated either by graphical or statistical methods.

Table 4. Reliability test results

Variables	No. Items	Item	Mean	Std. Deviation	α
Perceived benefits	8	BENE1	3.707	0.794	0.879
		BENE2	3.663	0.846	
		BENE3	3.754	0.814	
		BENE4	3.864	0.796	
		BENE5	4.102	0.686	
		BENE6	4.085	0.664	
		BENE7	4.034	0.713	
		BENE8	4.127	0.619	
Perceived compatibility	6	CMPA1	3.766	0.729	0.873
		CMPA2	3.703	0.752	
		CMPA3	3.760	0.787	
		CMPA4	3.722	0.787	
		CMPA5	3.924	0.739	
		CMPA6	3.811	0.765	
Perceived security	3	SECU1	3.873	0.766	0.839
		SECU2	3.788	0.766	
		SECU3	3.799	0.735	
Perceived cost	3	CSTS1	3.944	0.724	0.827
		CSTS2	3.802	0.783	
		CSTS3	3.819	0.727	
Organizational readiness	3	READ1	2.125	0.735	0.850
		READ2	2.057	0.700	
		READ3	2.105	0.684	
Organizational innovativeness	3	INNO1	3.989	0.686	0.841
		INNO2	3.944	0.739	
		INNO3	3.952	0.726	
Competitive pressures	3	CMPE1	3.941	0.793	0.868
		CMPE2	3.844	0.849	
		CMPE3	3.782	0.815	
Customer pressures	3	CUST1	3.972	0.827	0.895
		CUST2	3.946	0.842	
		CUST3	4.051	0.784	
Government support	3	GOVE1	2.138	0.764	0.907
		GOVE2	2.192	0.805	
		GOVE3	2.153	0.771	
Top management support	3	TMSP1	4.130	0.648	0.846
		TMSP2	4.003	0.700	
		TMSP3	4.144	0.629	
Managers' IT knowledge	3	TMIT1	4.172	0.635	0.865
		TMIT2	4.065	0.744	
		TMIT3	4.071	0.684	
Adoption	3	ADPT1	3.686	0.811	0.929
		ADPT2	3.579	0.865	
		ADPT3	3.376	0.883	

Graphically, homoscedasticity can be checked through a scatterplot between a dependent variable and an independent variable. Statistically, homoscedasticity can be examined using Levene's test. Particularly, the assumption of homoscedasticity is confirmed when Levene's test is insignificant with the *p*-value greater than 0.05. There is a close link between homoscedasticity and normality of variables. This means that the relationship between variables is homoscedastic when the assumption of normality is satisfied.

Table 5. Normality test results

Item	Skew	Kurt	Item	Skew	Kurt	Item	Skew	Kurt	Item	Skew	Kurt
BENE1	-0.411	-0.138	CMPA4	-0.480	0.150	READ3	-0.558	1.080	GOVE2	-0.718	0.795
BENE2	-0.421	-0.357	CMPA5	-0.513	0.312	INNO1	-0.569	0.819	GOVE3	-0.701	0.889
BENE3	-0.410	-0.204	CMPA6	-0.468	0.100	INNO2	-0.460	0.175	TMSP1	-0.698	1.980
BENE4	-0.531	0.066	SECU1	-0.502	0.154	INNO3	-0.596	0.838	TMSP2	-0.502	0.498
BENE5	-0.662	1.000	SECU2	-0.378	-0.048	CMPE1	-0.615	0.573	TMSP3	-0.602	1.905
BENE6	-0.622	1.149	SECU3	-0.354	0.041	CMPE2	-0.534	0.092	TMIT1	-0.361	0.258
BENE7	-0.615	0.685	CSTS1	-0.636	0.960	CMPE3	-0.591	0.362	TMIT2	-0.686	0.599
BENE8	-0.376	0.736	CSTS2	-0.672	0.519	CUST1	-1.003	1.487	TMIT3	-0.677	1.124
CMPA1	-0.313	-0.002	CSTS3	-0.377	0.366	CUST2	-0.644	0.156	ADPT1	-0.329	-0.300
CMPA2	-0.133	-0.301	READ1	-0.662	0.894	CUST3	-0.764	0.913	ADPT2	-0.312	-0.190
CMPA3	-0.214	-0.358	READ2	-0.669	1.256	GOVE1	-0.641	1.040	ADPT3	-0.065	-0.231

In this study, the test for normality of all items in the above section is confirmed to be satisfied. As a result, it can also be confirmed the presence of homoscedasticity.

Linearity Test

Linearity refers to the assumption that the relationship between the independent and dependent variables is linear (Tabachnick & Fidell, 2013). Linearity can be checked by examining the scatterplot between a dependent variable and an independent variable. The linearity exists when a straight line can be drawn from the dispersion of the standardized residuals against the predicted values. In this chapter, linearity is checked by examining eleven scatterplots generated from multiple regression between eleven independent variables and m-commerce adoption intention. These scatterplots show that all standardized residuals have straight-line relationships with the predicted values. As a result, the assumption of linearity in this study is confirmed.

Multicollinearity Test

Multicollinearity depicts the relationship between two or more independent variables. Multicollinearity exists when there are high correlations between a single independent variable and a set of other independent variables. Multicollinearity can be detected by checking the correlation matrix or examining the values of tolerance and variance inflation factor (VIF) as part of the multiple regression analysis. When computing a matrix of Pearson's bivariate correlations between all independent variables, correlation coefficients should be less than 0.8. Otherwise, the tolerance values smaller than 0.1 and the VIF values higher than 10 indicate that multicollinearity is a problem. This chapter adopts these measures for checking the multicollinearity between the proposed independent variables. Pearson's bivariate correlations, the tolerance values, and the VIF values are presented in Table 6 and Table 7. These results show that all correlation coefficients between independent variables are less than 0.8. The tolerance values of these independent variables range from 0.388 to 0.674 which are greater than 0.1. The VIF

Table 6. Pearson's bivariate correlations matrix

	(1)	(2)	(3)	(4)	(5)	(6)	(7)	(8)	(9)	(10)	(11)
(1) BENE	1	.662*	.533*	.472*	-.485*	.525*	.535*	.415*	-.216*	.426*	.434*
(2) CMPA	.662*	1	.646*	.573*	-.472*	.531*	.571*	.460*	-.340*	.457*	.449*
(3) SECU	.533*	.646*	1	.562*	-.432*	.594*	.520*	.470*	-.471*	.484*	.450*
(4) CSTS	.472*	.573*	.562*	1	-.540*	.390*	.401*	.381*	-.419*	.458*	.316*
(5) READ	-.485*	-.472*	-.432*	-.540*	1	-.507*	-.466*	-.420*	.363*	-.411*	-.308*
(6) INNO	.525*	.531*	.594*	.390*	-.507*	1	.519*	.435*	-.406*	.503*	.465*
(7) CMPE	.535*	.571*	.520*	.401*	-.466*	.519*	1	.519*	-.293*	.500*	.390*
(8) CUST	.415*	.460*	.470*	.381*	-.420*	.435*	.519*	1	-.239*	.496*	.349*
(9) GOVE	-.216*	-.340*	-.471*	-.419*	.363*	-.406*	-.293*	-.239*	1	-.376*	-.337*
(10) TMSP	.426*	.457*	.484*	.458*	-.411*	.503*	.500*	.496*	-.376*	1	.540*
(11) TMIT	.434*	.449*	.450*	.316*	-.308*	.465*	.390*	.349*	-.337*	.540*	1
*. Correlation is significant at the 0.01 level (2-tailed).											

values range from 1.484 to 2.575 which are less than 10. These indicate no multicollinearity among the independent variables.

Hypotheses Testing

Multiple regression analysis is conducted to test the proposed hypotheses. The results of such an analysis are presented in Table 7. These results show that seven of the eleven independent variables: perceived benefits, perceived security, organizational readiness, organizational innovativeness, customer pressures, government support, and managers' IT knowledge are significantly contributing towards the multiple regression equation. These results support hypotheses H1, H3, H5, H6, H8, H9, and H11. The model has a high and significant F ratio, indicating its overall good fit. Furthermore, the results indicate that there are 45.4% ($R^2 = 0.454$) of the variance is shared by the independent variables, confirming that the model is effective in predicting the adoption of m-commerce in Vietnamese SMEs.

DISCUSSION

The chapter reveals two critical technological determinants: perceived benefits and perceived security. This indicates that managers of SMEs perceiving m-commerce to be more useful are more likely to adopt m-commerce. This is consistent with the studies of Kurnia et al. (2015), Ilin et al. (2017) and Alfahl et al. (2017). The results are also consistent with the notion that m-commerce is a complex innovation whose successful adoption is closely related to the high level of security (Mashagba et al., 2013; Amegbe et al., 2017). The chapter also indicates the insignificance of perceived compatibility and perceived cost for the adoption of m-commerce. This is in contrast to the studies of Alfahl et al. (2017) and Rana et al. (2019) that indicate the positive relationship between perceived compatibility and the adoption of m-commerce. However, it is consistent with the studies of Mahroeian (2012) and Rahayu & Day (2015)

Table 7. Multiple regression analysis results

Constructs	Mean	Beta	Significance	Tolerance	VIF	Remarks
Perceived Benefits	3.917	0.131	0.026	0.464	2.156	Supported
Perceived Compatibility	3.781	0.084	0.194	0.388	2.575	Not supported
Perceived Security	3.820	0.265	0.000	0.415	2.411	Supported
Perceived Cost	3.855	-0.012	0.837	0.499	2.002	Not supported
Organizational Readiness	2.095	0.128	0.017	0.555	1.802	Supported
Organizational Innovativeness	3.961	0.151	0.009	0.485	2.064	Supported
Competitive Pressure	3.856	0.055	0.327	0.516	1.939	Not supported
Customer Pressure	3.990	0.192	0.000	0.611	1.637	Supported
Government Support	2.161	0.173	0.000	0.674	1.484	Supported
Top Management Support	4.092	0.064	0.247	0.517	1.933	Not supported
Managers' IT Knowledge	4.103	0.121	0.018	0.613	1.631	Supported
Dependent Variable: Adoption Intention						
Model summary characteristics						
R^2	0.454	df		11		
Adjusted R^2	0.437	F		25.889***		
*Notes: Level of significance of F: *** p < 0.001*						

that confirm the insignificance of perceived compatibility for the adoption of e-commerce. Also, the insignificance of perceived cost is inconsistent with the findings of Rana et al. (2019), but it is consistent with the studies of Alam et al. (2011) and Rahayu & Day (2015).

The chapter reveals two critical organizational determinants: organizational readiness and organizational innovativeness. The significance of organizational readiness for m-commerce adoption is consistent with the studies of Otieno & Kahonge (2014) and Lim et al. (2016). This means that increasing resources readiness for SMEs enhances their intention to adopt m-commerce. The significance of organizational innovativeness for the adoption of m-commerce has been confirmed in the studies of Martin & Jimenez (2015) and Njenga et al. (2016). This implies that innovation-oriented organizations are more likely to adopt m-commerce.

The chapter reveals two critical environmental determinants: customer pressures and government support. The significance of customer pressures implies that the adoption of m-commerce is not only the result of a rational assessment of the implication of m-commerce but also a response to satisfy external pressures, especially the pressures from customers. This finding is consistent with the studies of Otieno & Kahonge (2014) and Li & Wang (2018). The findings also suggest that the support from the government in terms of legal consideration, financial and training for m-commerce increases the likelihood of SMEs to adopt m-commerce. This is consistent with the studies of Alfahl et al. (2017) and Li & Wang (2018). The chapter also reveals the insignificance of competitive pressures for the adoption of m-commerce. This is in contrast with the studies of Picoto et al. (2014) and Martin & Jimenez (2015). However, it is consistent with the study of Martin et al. (2012) that find competitive pressures are not significant for the adoption of m-commerce in organizations in Spain.

The chapter also reveals a significant association between managers' IT knowledge and m-commerce adoption. This suggests that SMEs need knowledgeable managers for the successful adoption of m-commerce. This finding is consistent with the studies of Ghobakhloo & Tang (2013) and Rahayu & Day (2015) that confirm the positive association between managers' IT knowledge and the adoption of e-commerce in SMEs. The chapter also shows the insignificance of top management support for the adoption of m-commerce. This is inconsistent with the studies of Otieno & Kahonge (2014) and Li & Wang (2018) that confirm the positive relationship between top management support and m-commerce adoption. This finding, however, is consistent with the study of Salwani, Marthandan, Norzaidi & Chong (2009) that find top management support is insignificant for the adoption of e-commerce in Malaysian SMEs.

CONCLUSION

M-commerce has significantly transformed how SMEs conduct their businesses. It allows SMEs to gain numerous benefits and to improve their competitive advantage. However, the adoption of m-commerce in SMEs, especially SMEs in developing countries is still quite low. The literature review on organizational m-commerce adoption indicates a huge difference in the adoption of m-commerce between developed and developing countries. This shows that an evaluation of the critical determinants for m-commerce adoption in SMEs in developing countries is significant for the successful adoption of m-commerce.

The descriptive analysis of the sample SMEs in Table 3 reveals that there is only 26.8% of the surveyed SMEs have adopted m-commerce, whereas the majority of SMEs are the non-adopters of m-commerce (73.2%). This is therefore evident that Vietnamese SMEs have not fully utilized m-commerce. It is probably due to several technological, organizational, environmental, and managerial constraints, experienced by SMEs across the world. The linear regression further investigates which factors best-predicted m-commerce adoption intention, leading to the identification of seven critical determinants including perceived benefits, perceived security, organizational readiness, organizational innovativeness, customer pressures, government support, and managers' IT knowledge.

This study has several theoretical and practical contributions. Theoretically, the study develops an integrated model for a better understanding of m-commerce adoption in SMEs, which expands the body of knowledge in m-commerce in developing countries. The study extends the DOI theory and TOE framework for investigating the adoption of m-commerce in SMEs in developing countries. This is an important contribution to the existing literature in organizational m-commerce adoption. Practically, the findings of this study enhance practitioners' understanding of the critical determinants for the adoption of m-commerce. Particularly, the results imply that the greater perception of the benefits and the high level of confidence and awareness of m-commerce security, reflect the relative increases in m-commerce adoption in SMEs. Additionally, SMEs that intend to adopt m-commerce need to prepare themselves regarding financial readiness, technological readiness, and human resource readiness. The empirical results also imply that innovation-oriented SMEs are more likely to adopt m-commerce than non-innovative ones. This is due to innovative SMEs tending to be early innovation adopters because of their close attention to emerging technologies and business practices in the external market (Wang & Cheung, 2004). In another aspect, increasing external pressures from customers and support from the government tend to stimulate the adoption of m-commerce in SMEs. Finally, the empirical results imply that an SME which has more IT/m-commerce knowledgeable managers will have a higher probability of successfully adopting m-commerce. These findings provide useful insights for SMEs' managers and policy-makers in formulating specific strategies and policies to promote the development of m-commerce in SMEs in Vietnam and other developing countries.

This chapter attempts to develop a conceptual model that allows evaluating the critical determinants for m-commerce adoption in SMEs in the context of developing countries. It also conducts a preliminary quantitative study for testing proposed hypotheses using multiple regression with the data collected through a survey with managers of SMEs in Vietnam. A way forward would require advanced techniques for testing and validating the model in a longer more complex study. We suggest that authors wishing to conduct a comparison study on the critical determinants for m-commerce adoption in SMEs between adopters and non-adopters in the future to have appropriate suggestions for SMEs' managers as well as policy-makers in their formulation of specific strategies and policies to facilitate the diffusion of m-commerce in SMEs in developing countries.

REFERENCES

Ajzen, I. (1991). The theory of planned behaviour. *Organizational Behavior and Human Decision Processes*, *50*(2), 179–211. doi:10.1016/0749-5978(91)90020-T

Al-Alawi, A. I., & Al-Ali, F. M. (2015). Factors affecting e-commerce adoption in SMEs in the GCC: An empirical study of Kuwait. *Research Journal of Information Technology*, *7*(1), 1–21. doi:10.3923/rjit.2015.1.21

Al-Bakri, A. A., & Katsioloudes, M. I. (2015). The factors affecting e-commerce adoption by Jordanian SMEs. *Management Research Review*, *38*(7), 726–749. doi:10.1108/MRR-12-2013-0291

Alam, S. S., Ali, M. Y., & Jani, M. F. M. (2011). An empirical study of factors affecting electronic commerce adoption among SMEs in Malaysia. *Journal of Business Economics and Management*, *12*(2), 375–399. doi:10.3846/16111699.2011.576749

Alam, S. S., Khatibi, A., Ahmad, M. I. S., & Ismail, H. B. (2008). Factors affecting e-commerce adoption in the electronic manufacturing companies in Malaysia. *International Journal of Commerce and Management*, *17*(1/2), 125–139. doi:10.1108/10569210710776503

Alfahl, H., Houghton, L., & Sanzogni, L. (2017). Mobile Commerce Adoption in Saudi Organizations: A Qualitative Study. *International Journal of Enterprise Information Systems*, *13*(4), 31–57. doi:10.4018/IJEIS.2017100103

Alqatan, S., Noor, N. M. M., Man, M., & Mohemad, R. (2017). A theoretical discussion of factors affecting the acceptance of m-commerce among SMTEs by integrating TTF with TAM. *International Journal of Business Information Systems*, *26*(1), 66–111. doi:10.1504/IJBIS.2017.086057

Alrousan, M. K., & Jones, E. (2016). A conceptual model of factors affecting e-commerce adoption by SME owner/managers in Jordan. *International Journal of Business Information Systems*, *21*(3), 269–308. doi:10.1504/IJBIS.2016.074762

Amegbe, H., Hanu, C., & Nuwasiima, A. (2017). Small-scale individual entrepreneurs and the usage of mobile money and mobile commerce in facilitating business growth in Ghana. *Management Science Letters*, *7*(8), 373–384. doi:10.5267/j.msl.2017.5.004

Apulu, I., & Latham, A. (2011). Drivers for information and communication technology adoption: A case study of Nigerian small and medium-sized enterprises. *International Journal of Business and Management*, *6*(5), 51–60. doi:10.5539/ijbm.v6n5p51

Asia-Pacific Economic Cooperation. (2018). *Small and Medium Enterprises Working Group*. Retrieved from https://www.apec.org/Groups/SOM-Steering-Committee-on-Economic-and-Technical-Cooperation/Working-Groups/Small-and-Medium-Enterprises

Awa, H. O., Ukoha, O., & Emecheta, B. C. (2016). Using TOE theoretical framework to study the adoption of ERP solution. *Cogent Business & Management*, *3*(1), 1–23. doi:10.1080/23311975.2016.1196571

Ayyagari, M., Beck, T., & Kunt, A. D. (2007). Small and medium enterprises across the globe. *Small Business Economics*, *29*(4), 415–434. doi:10.100711187-006-9002-5

Baker, J. (2012). The technology–organization–environment framework. In *Information Systems Theory* (pp. 231–245). New York: Springer. doi:10.1007/978-1-4419-6108-2_12

Bao, J., & Sun, X. (2010). *A conceptual model of factors affecting e-Commerce adoption by SMEs in China*. Paper presented at the Fourth International Conference on Management of e-Commerce and e-Government, Chengdu, Sichuan, China. 10.1109/ICMeCG.2010.43

Business Insides. (2011). *The Development of Small and Medium Enterprise in Vietnam*. Retrieved from http://businessinsides.com/development-vietnam-small-medium-enterprises.html

Chau, N. T., & Deng, H. (2018a). Critical Determinants for Mobile Commerce Adoption in Vietnamese SMEs: A Conceptual Framework. *Procedia Computer Science*, *138*, 433–440. doi:10.1016/j.procs.2018.10.061

Chau, N. T., & Deng, H. (2018b). *Critical Determinants for Mobile Commerce Adoption in Vietnamese SMEs: A Preliminary Study*. Paper presented at the 29th Australasian Conference on Information Systems, Sydney, Australia. 10.5130/acis2018.am

Chau, P. Y., & Tam, K. Y. (1997). Factors affecting the adoption of open systems: An exploratory study. *Management Information Systems Quarterly*, *21*(1), 1–24. doi:10.2307/249740

Chuang, T. T., Nakatani, K., Chen, J. C. H., & Huang, I. L. (2007). Examining the impact of organizational and owner's characteristics on the extent of e-commerce adoption in SMEs. *International Journal of Business and Systems Research*, *1*(1), 61–80. doi:10.1504/IJBSR.2007.014770

Chwelos, P., Benbasat, I., & Dexter, A. S. (2001). Empirical test of an EDI adoption model. *Information Systems Research*, *12*(3), 304–321. doi:10.1287/isre.12.3.304.9708

Clarke, I. III. (2008). Emerging value propositions for m-commerce. *The Journal of Business Strategy*, *25*(2), 41–57.

Coursaris, C., Hassanein, K., & Head, M. (2008). Mobile Technologies and the Value Chain: Participants, activities and value creation. *International Journal of Business Science and Applied Management, 3*(3), 14–30.

Davis, F. D. (1989). Perceived usefulness, perceived ease of use, and user acceptance of information technology. *Management Information Systems Quarterly, 13*(3), 319–340. doi:10.2307/249008

Duan, X., Deng, H., & Corbitt, B. (2012). Evaluating the critical determinants for adopting e-market in Australian small and medium-sized enterprises. *Management Research Review, 35*(3), 289–308. doi:10.1108/01409171211210172

Duan, X., Deng, H., & Luo, F. (2019). An integrated approach for identifying the efficiency-oriented drivers of electronic markets in electronic business. *Journal of Enterprise Information Management, 32*(1), 60–74. doi:10.1108/JEIM-05-2018-0090

Dyer, J. H., & Singh, H. (1998). The relational view: Cooperative strategy and sources of inter-organizational competitive advantage. *Academy of Management Review, 23*(4), 660–679. doi:10.5465/amr.1998.1255632

eMarketer. (2018). *Worldwide Retail and Ecommerce Sales: eMarketer's Updated Forecast and New M-commerce Estimates for 2016-2021*. Retrieved from https://www.emarketer.com/Report/Worldwide-Retail-Ecommerce-Sales-eMarketers-Updated-Forecast-New-Mcommerce-Estimates-20162021/2002182

European Commission. (2018). *User guide to the SME definition*. Retrieved from http://ec.europa.eu/regional_policy/sources/conferences/state-aid/sme/smedefinitionguide_en.pdf

Fishbein, M., & Ajzen, I. (1975). *Belief, attitude, intention, and behavior: An introduction to theory and research*. Addison-Wesley.

General Statistics Office of Vietnam. (2017). *Small and medium enterprises are getting smaller*. Retrieved from gso.gov.vn

General Statistics Office of Vietnam. (2019a). *The Socio-Economic Situation in 2018*. Retrieved from https://www.gso.gov.vn/default.aspx?tabid=621&ItemID=19037

General Statistics Office of Vietnam. (2019b). *Statistical Yearbook of Vietnam 2018*. Retrieved from https://www.gso.gov.vn/default_en.aspx?tabid=515&idmid=5&ItemID=19299

Ghobakhloo, M., & Tang, S. H. (2013). The role of owner/manager in adoption of electronic commerce in small businesses: The case of developing countries. *Journal of Small Business and Enterprise Development, 20*(4), 754–787. doi:10.1108/JSBED-12-2011-0037

Grandhi, S., & Wibowo, S. (2016). Mobile Commerce Adoption in North American Organizations: An Empirical Study of Organizational Factors. *Communications of the IBIMA, 2016*, 1–17. doi:10.5171/2016.682007

Hair, J. F., Black, W. C., Babin, B. J., Anderson, R. E., & Tatham, R. L. (2010). *Multivariate data analysis* (7th ed.). Upper Saddle River, NJ: Pearson Prentice Hall.

Hamdan, A. R., Yahaya, J. H., Deraman, A., & Jusoh, Y. Y. (2016). The success factors and barriers of information technology implementation in small and medium enterprises: An empirical study in Malaysia. *International Journal of Business Information Systems*, *21*(4), 477–494. doi:10.1504/IJBIS.2016.075257

Harry, B., Vos, H. D., & Haaker, T. (2008). Mobile service innovation and business models. Springer.

Hashim, J. (2007). Information and communication technology adoption among SME owner in Malaysia. *International Journal of Business and Information*, *2*(2), 221–240.

Hong, H. G. (2015). Success Factors of Mobile-Commerce System. *Indian Journal of Science and Technology*, *8*(7), 630–637. doi:10.17485/ijst/2015/v8iS7/70451

Hsu, C. L., & Lin, J. C. C. (2016). Factors affecting the adoption of cloud services in enterprises. *Information Systems and e-Business Management*, *14*(4), 791–822. doi:10.100710257-015-0300-9

Hussin, H., & Noor, R. M. (2005). *Innovating business through e-commerce: Exploring the willingness of Malaysian SMEs.* Paper presented at the Second International Conference on Innovation in IT, Dubai, UAE.

Huy, L. V., Rowe, F., Truex, D., & Huynh, M. Q. (2012). An empirical study of determinants of e-commerce adoption in SMEs in Vietnam: An economy in transition. *Journal of Global Information Management*, *20*(3), 23–54. doi:10.4018/jgim.2012070102

Ifinedo, P. (2011). Internet/e-business technologies acceptance in Canada's SMEs: An exploratory investigation. *Internet Research*, *21*(3), 255–281. doi:10.1108/10662241111139309

Ilin, V., Ivetic, J., & Simic, D. (2017). Understanding the determinants of e-business adoption in ERP-enabled firms and non-ERP-enabled firms: A case study of the Western Balkan Peninsula. *Technological Forecasting and Social Change*, *125*, 206–223. doi:10.1016/j.techfore.2017.07.025

Jain, M., Le, A. N. H., Lin, J. Y. C., & Cheng, J. M. S. (2011). Exploring the factors favoring m-commerce adoption among Indian MSMEs: A TOE perspective. *Tunghai Management Review*, *13*(1), 147–188.

Jeon, B. N., Han, K. S., & Lee, M. J. (2006). Determining factors for the adoption of e-business: The case of SMEs in Korea. *Applied Economics*, *38*(16), 1905–1916. doi:10.1080/00036840500427262

Khalifa, M., Cheng, S. K. N., & Shen, K. N. (2012). Adoption of mobile commerce: A confidence model. *Journal of Computer Information Systems*, *53*(1), 14–22.

Kurnia, S., Karnali, R. J., & Rahim, M. M. (2015). A qualitative study of business-to-business electronic commerce adoption within the Indonesian grocery industry: A multi-theory perspective. *Information & Management*, *52*(4), 518–536. doi:10.1016/j.im.2015.03.003

Lee, M. K. O., & Cheung, C. M. K. (2004). Internet retailing adoption by small-to-medium sized enterprises: A multiple-case study. *Information Systems Frontiers*, *6*(4), 385–397. doi:10.1023/B:ISFI.0000046379.58029.54

Li, L., & Wang, X. (2018). M-Commerce Adoption in SMEs of China: The Effect of Institutional Pressures and the Mediating Role of Top Management. *Journal of Electronic Commerce in Organizations*, *16*(2), 48–63. doi:10.4018/JECO.2018040103

Lim, S. C., Baharudin, A. S., & Low, R. Q. (2016). E-commerce adoption in Peninsular Malaysia: Perceived strategic value as moderator in the relationship between perceived barriers, organizational readiness and competitor pressure. *Journal of Theoretical & Applied Information Technology, 91*(2), 228–237.

Lin, H. F. (2014). Understanding the determinants of electronic supply chain management system adoption: Using the technology–organization–environment framework. *Technological Forecasting and Social Change, 86*, 80–92. doi:10.1016/j.techfore.2013.09.001

Lippert, S. K., & Govindarajulu, C. (2006). Technological, organizational, and environmental antecedents to web services adoption. *Communications of the IIMA, 6*(1), 146–160.

Lu, M. T., Hu, S. K., Huang, L. H., & Tzeng, G. H. (2015). Evaluating the implementation of business-to-business m-commerce by SMEs based on a new hybrid MADM model. *Management Decision, 53*(2), 290–317. doi:10.1108/MD-01-2014-0012

MacGregor, R. C., Bunker, D., & Kartiwi, M. (2010). The perception of barriers to e-commerce adoption by SMEs: A comparison of three countries. In *Global perspectives on small and medium enterprises and strategic information systems: International approaches* (pp. 145–168). Hershey, PA: IGI Global. doi:10.4018/978-1-61520-627-8.ch008

Mahroeian, H. (2012). A study on the effect of different factors on e-Commerce adoption among SMEs of Malaysia. *Management Science Letters, 2*(7), 2679–2688. doi:10.5267/j.msl.2012.08.021

Martin, S. S., Catalan, B. L., & Jeronimo, M. A. R. (2012). Factors determining firms' perceived performance of mobile commerce. *Industrial Management & Data Systems, 112*(6), 946–963. doi:10.1108/02635571211238536

Martin, S. S., & Jimenez, N. (2015). A Typology of Firms Regarding M-Commerce Adoption. *International Journal of Information System Modeling and Design, 6*(4), 42–56. doi:10.4018/IJISMD.2015100103

Mashagba, F. F. A., Mashagba, E. F. A., & Nassar, M. O. (2013). Exploring Technological Factors Affecting the Adoption of M-Commerce in Jordan. *Australian Journal of Basic and Applied Sciences, 7*(6), 395–400.

Miao, J. J., & Tran, Q. D. (2018). Study on E-Commerce Adoption in SMEs Under the Institutional Perspective: The Case of Saudi Arabia. *International Journal of E-Adoption, 10*(1), 53–72. doi:10.4018/IJEA.2018010104

Molla, A., & Licker, P. S. (2005). eCommerce adoption in developing countries: A model and instrument. *Information & Management, 42*(6), 877–899. doi:10.1016/j.im.2004.09.002

Nafea, I., & Younas, M. (2014). *Improving the performance and reliability of mobile commerce in developing countries.* Paper presented at the International Conference on Mobile Web and Information Systems, Barcelona, Spain. 10.1007/978-3-319-10359-4_9

Njenga, A. K., Litondo, K., & Omwansa, T. (2016). A Theoretical Review of Mobile Commerce Success Determinants. *Journal of Information Engineering and Applications, 6*(5), 13–23.

Oliveira, T., & Martins, M. F. (2010). Understanding e-business adoption across industries in European countries. *Industrial Management & Data Systems, 110*(9), 1337–1354. doi:10.1108/02635571011087428

Oliveira, T., & Martins, M. F. (2011). Literature review of information technology adoption models at firm level. *The Electronic Journal Information Systems Evaluation*, *14*(1), 110–121.

Otieno, E. O., & Kahonge, A. M. (2014). Adoption of Mobile Payments in Kenyan Businesses: A Case Study of Small and Medium Enterprises in Kenya. *International Journal of Computers and Applications*, *107*(7), 5–12. doi:10.5120/18761-0041

Parker, C. M., & Castleman, T. (2009). Small firm e-business adoption: A critical analysis of theory. *Journal of Enterprise Information Management*, *22*(1/2), 167–182. doi:10.1108/17410390910932812

Perez, M. P., Martnez, S. A., Carnicer, P. L., & Jimenez, M. J. V. (2004). A technology acceptance model of innovation adoption: The case of teleworking. *European Journal of Innovation Management*, *7*(4), 280–291. doi:10.1108/14601060410565038

Picoto, W. N., Belanger, F., & Palma-dos-Reis, A. (2014). An organizational perspective on m-business: Usage factors and value determination. *European Journal of Information Systems*, *23*(5), 571–592. doi:10.1057/ejis.2014.15

Pipitwanichakarn, T., & Wongtada, N. (2019). Mobile commerce adoption among the bottom of the pyramid: A case of street vendors in Thailand. *Journal of Science and Technology Policy Management*, *10*(1), 193–213. doi:10.1108/JSTPM-12-2017-0074

Porter, M. E., & Millar, V. E. (1985). How information gives you competitive advantage. *Harvard Business Review*, *63*(4), 149–174.

Rahayu, R., & Day, J. (2015). Determinant factors of e-commerce adoption by SMEs in developing country: Evidence from Indonesia. *Procedia: Social and Behavioral Sciences*, *195*, 142–150. doi:10.1016/j.sbspro.2015.06.423

Ramdani, B., Kawalek, P., & Lorenzo, O. (2009). Predicting SMEs' adoption of enterprise systems. *Journal of Enterprise Information Management*, *22*(1), 10–24. doi:10.1108/17410390910922796

Rana, N. P., Barnard, D. J., Baabdullah, A. M., Rees, D., & Roderick, S. (2019). Exploring barriers of m-commerce adoption in SMEs in the UK: Developing a framework using ISM. *International Journal of Information Management*, *44*, 141–153. doi:10.1016/j.ijinfomgt.2018.10.009

Rogers, E. M. (2010). *Diffusion of Innovations*. New York: Simon and Schuster.

Sadeh, N. (2003). *M-commerce: Technologies, services, and business models*. John Wiley & Sons.

Salah, K. (2013). *E-commerce and small and medium enterprises in least developed countries: The case of Tanzania (PhD)*. University of Cape Town.

Salwani, I. M., Marthandan, G., Norzaidi, M. D., & Chong, S. C. (2009). E-commerce usage and business performance in the Malaysian tourism sector: Empirical analysis. *Information Management & Computer Security*, *17*(2), 166–185. doi:10.1108/09685220910964027

Saprikis, V., & Vlachopoulou, M. (2012). Determinants of suppliers' level of use of B2B e-marketplaces. *Industrial Management & Data Systems*, *112*(4), 619–643. doi:10.1108/02635571211225512

Seyal, A. H., & Rahman, M. N. A. (2003). A preliminary investigation of e-commerce adoption in small & medium enterprises in Brunei. *Journal of Global Information Technology Management*, *6*(2), 6–26. doi:10.1080/1097198X.2003.10856347

Seyal, A. H., Rahman, M. N. A., & Mohammad, H. A. Y. (2007). A quantitative analysis of factors contributing electronic data interchange adoption among Bruneian SMEs: A pilot study. *Business Process Management Journal*, *13*(5), 728–746. doi:10.1108/14637150710823183

Seyal, A. H., Rahman, M. N. A., & Mohammad, H. A. Y. H. A. (2007). A quantitative analysis of factors contributing electronic data interchange adoption among Bruneian SMEs: A pilot study. *Business Process Management Journal*, *13*(5), 728–746. doi:10.1108/14637150710823183

Shih, Y. Y., Chen, C. Y., Wu, C. H., Huang, T., & Shiu, S. H. (2010). *Adopted intention of mobile commerce from TAM perspective: An empirical study of real estate industry*. Paper presented at the Portland International Center for Management of Engineering and Technology Conference, Phuket, Thailand.

Siamagka, N. T., Christodoulides, G., Michaelidou, N., & Valvi, A. (2015). Determinants of social media adoption by B2B organizations. *Industrial Marketing Management*, *51*, 89–99. doi:10.1016/j.indmarman.2015.05.005

Statista. (2019a). *Smartphone penetration rate as share of the population in Vietnam from 2017 to 2023*. Retrieved from https://www.statista.com/statistics/625458/smartphone-user-penetration-in-vietnam/

Statista. (2019b). *Vietnam - Statistics & Facts*. Retrieved from https://www.statista.com/topics/4598/vietnam/

Stockdale, R., & Standing, C. (2004). Benefits and barriers of electronic marketplace participation: An SME perspective. *Journal of Enterprise Information Management*, *17*(4), 301–311. doi:10.1108/17410390410548715

Straub, D., Boudreau, M. C., & Gefen, D. (2004). Validation guidelines for IS positivist research. *Communications of the Association for Information Systems*, *13*(1), 379–427.

Sun, J., & Chi, T. (2018). Key factors influencing the adoption of apparel mobile commerce: An empirical study of Chinese consumers. *Journal of the Textile Institute*, *109*(6), 785–797. doi:10.1080/00405000.2017.1371828

Tabachnick, B. G., & Fidell, L. S. (2013). *Using multivariate statistics*. Boston: Allyn and Bacon.

Tan, K. S., Chong, S. C., Lin, B., & Eze, U. C. (2009). Internet-based ICT adoption: Evidence from Malaysian SMEs. *Industrial Management & Data Systems*, *109*(2), 224–244. doi:10.1108/02635570910930118

Tornatzky, L. G., & Fleischer, M. (1990). *The Processes of Technological Innovation*. Lexington, MA: Lexington Books.

Tsai, H. S., & Gururajan, R. (2007). Motivations and challenges for M-business transformation: A multiple-case study. *Journal of Theoretical and Applied Electronic Commerce Research*, *2*(2), 19–33.

VCCI. (2016). *Digital technologies: Opportunities for Vietnamese SMEs*. Retrieved from http://www.nhandan.com.vn/hangthang/van-hoa/item/29999102-co-hoi-cho-cac-doanh-nghiep-nho-va-vua-viet-nam.html

VECITA. (2017). *Only 20% of small and medium-sized enterprises have been ready for electronic commerce*. Retrieved from https://tintuc.inet.vn/chi-20-doanh-nghiep-vua-va-nho-tiep-can-thuong-mai-dien-tu.html

Vietnam eCommerce and Digital Economy Agency. (2018). *Vietnam E-commerce White Paper 2018*. Retrieved from http://www.idea.gov.vn/?page=document

Wamba, S. F., & Carter, L. (2013). *Twitter adoption and use by SMEs: An empirical study*. Paper presented at the 46th Hawaii International Conference on System Sciences. 10.1109/HICSS.2013.577

Wang, S., & Cheung, W. (2004). E-business adoption by travel agencies: Prime candidates for mobile e-business. *International Journal of Electronic Commerce*, *8*(3), 43–63. doi:10.1080/10864415.2004.11044298

Wymer, S. A., & Regan, E. A. (2005). Factors influencing e-commerce adoption and use by small and medium businesses. *Electronic Markets*, *15*(4), 438–453. doi:10.1080/10196780500303151

Zhiping, W. (2009). *Chinese customer's attitude and adopt intention on mobile commerce*. Paper presented at the 6th International Conference on Service Systems and Service Management, Xiamen, China. 10.1109/ICSSSM.2009.5174977

Zhu, K., Dong, S., Xu, S. X., & Kraemer, K. L. (2006). Innovation diffusion in global contexts: Determinants of post-adoption digital transformation of European companies. *European Journal of Information Systems*, *15*(6), 601–616. doi:10.1057/palgrave.ejis.3000650

Zhu, K., Kraemer, K. L., & Xu, S. (2006). The process of innovation assimilation by firms in different countries: A technology diffusion perspective on e-business. *Management Science*, *52*(10), 1557–1576. doi:10.1287/mnsc.1050.0487

Chapter 7
Digital Innovation and Ridesharing in a Developing Country:
The Case of Uru

Robert Ohene-Bonsu Simmons
University of Ghana, Ghana

ABSTRACT

The purpose of this chapter is to understand digital innovation in the taxi industrial structure for ridesharing in a developing country. Digital innovations are required in all aspects of an economy including the transportation industry. Drawing on a qualitative interpretive case study methodology, this chapter offers an overview of Uru's digital innovation for ridesharing in the physical taxi industrial structure in a developing country context of Ghana. The findings show that ridesharing provides riders-drivers with better journey activities, which supersedes taxi services in competition. These are electronic booking, riders' and drivers' profiles for security, transparent automatic billing for affordable transportation, and opportunities for drivers to accept a series of riders' requests at proximity. The chapter provides the implications for these findings for research and practice.

INTRODUCTION

Understanding of how emerging information systems (IS) in the transportation industry can create service change is crucial. In recent years, IS has become more advanced and diversified and the transportation industry is not exempted (Garcia-murillo, Macinnes, & Bauer, 2018). The strategy which underpins this process is referred to as digital innovation. Digital innovation is prevalent in both developed and developing economies and it is cost-effectively transforming every aspect of life (Greenwood & Wattal, 2017). Digital innovation is defined as an opportunity to combine existing physical industrial structure and digital technology to create new products, markets, and services. It enables innovators to combine

DOI: 10.4018/978-1-7998-2610-1.ch007

existing mainstream products, markets, and services with digital technology to develop new forms of products, services, and markets.

Car ridesharing (ridesharing) is an example of digital innovation in the transportation industry, which involves digital arrangement that enables a rider (traveller or commuter) to travel in a physical private car (ride) driven by a potential driver from a ridesharing company for a fee. Such IS or transportation information system has partially helped to minimize both riders-drivers' challenges. As digital platforms for ridesharing continue to advance, ridesharing, however, is all about arrangement via mobile application (app) that provides on-demand ride service for riders in the taxi industry. For example, Uru ridesharing uses digital technologies to connect remote riders-drivers with an efficient matching between them for journey activities (e.g., Simmons, Effah, & Boateng, 2019). Essentially ridesharing is a digital and a physical (digital-physical). Digital-physical is a digital innovation in the physical taxi industrial structure paradigm, which has emerged to address the challenges of riders-drivers in taxi services.

Ridesharing creates competition and opposition in the transportation industry, especially among the taxi operators (Simmons, 2018). Among the challenges that riders face are shortage of services available during the raining season and peak hours in the morning and evening, and relatively high charges compared those of taxi operators (e.g., Zhou, Dou, Jia, Hu, & Xu, 2016). Ridesharing provides relief to riders who might have faced the challenges using taxi services. Nevertheless, some studies have found that ridesharing has also its challenges (e.g., Billhardt, Fernández, Ossowski, Palanca, & Bajo, 2019; Greenwood & Wattal, 2017). Thus, there is little emphasise on ridesharing in a developing country. It is, therefore, necessary to do further study to better understand the true nature and scope of the relief and challenges of ridesharing in a case study, focusing on Uru Company in Ghana. The objective of this chapter is to understand how digital innovation for ridesharing in taxi industry provides riders-drivers with better journey activities in a developing country context of Ghana. The chapter provides a conceptual framework of digital platform to explain the workflow of Uru ridesharing.

BACKGROUND

Digital Innovation

Digital innovation is pervasive, core to digital economy, and not limited to any specific industry. Digital innovation is an ideal for creating a new or renewing product, service, or market via the synergy of information and communication technology (ICT) and existing business model, social, and organisational (Lokuge, Sedera, Grover, & Xu, 2019). Innovation, however, as an idea, practice, behavior, is primarily market driven, or an artifact that is perceived as being new to create new products, administrations, and services by people with interest and knowledge (Alter, 2006). Therefore, innovation is required in every aspect of service to meet the users' needs such as riders-drivers based on the rapid emerging digital technology changes. Digital innovation refers to a new digital technology that has lower cost and advanced performance measured by traditional criteria, and higher ancillary performance (Christensen, 1997; 2006) for companies to effectively and rapidly deliver new services. Digital technologies, however, are collective terms of ICT such as mobile works (Chatterjee, Sarker, & Siponen, 2017); Internet of things, mobile devices, and social media (Lokuge et al., 2019); mobile apps (Mounce & Nelson, 2019); digital platforms (Tan et al., 2017); and digital stores and mobile networks (Junglas & Watson, 2006). The outcome, however, provides the innovative company to effectively and rapidly deliver new service for effective digital communication and users engagement tools (e.g., Kim & Hyun, 2018). Therefore, displacing established competitors in the markets, products, or services.

Ridesharing

Ridesharing is a synergy of digital technology and traditional taxi industrial structure. Innovation in digital technology has transformed the travel activities, especially in the taxi services (Simmons, 2018). Ridesharing broadly refers to an act of sharing a vehicle via digital platform with rider(s) to travel from location to destination (Greenwood & Wattal, 2017; Rogers, 2016; Teubner & Flath, 2015). Some authors defined ridesharing as a model of renting vehicles for short periods of time, where the payment is made according to the time and distance effectively travelled (Almeida, Silva, & Leite, 2017). Additionally, the ridesharing refers to as carsharing (Almeida, Silva, & Leite, 2017; Mounce & Nelson, 2019); car-pooling (Cetin & Deakin, 2019); parataxis, ridesourcing (Rayle et al., 2014; Rayle et al. 2016); vanpooling (Schreffler, 2018); ride-hailing service (Tan, Tan, Lu, & Land, 2017; Young & Farber, 2019); transportation network companies (Gurumurthy & Kockelman, 2018), real-time ridesharing (Ge, Jabbari, Mackenzie, & Tao, 2017); ride-sharing (Elbanna & Newman, 2016; Gecchelin & Webb, 2019); E-hailing (Tan et al., 2017; Wyman, 2017); and on-demand rides (Chen, 2017; Lee et al., 2019). Therefore, the definitions are vague from different authors as digital platforms for ridesharing continue to advance. This innovation in the taxi industrial structure, however, thrives on ICT (Wyman, 2017) to provide multi-sided digital platforms for riders-drivers. However, in the view of multi-sided digital platforms, some authors for instance (Tan et al., 2017; Teubner & Flath, 2015) maintain that they provide quality services for riders better than the taxi services.

Taxi Services

Taxi services contribute to cities transportation systems (Li & Hou, 2019; Li & Szeto, 2019). A taxi, also known as a taxicab or a cab is defined as a means of conveying a rider or a maximum of four riders based on their pick and drop locations by a driver with a ride (Billhardt et al. 2019). Several authors describe taxi sector as "taxi industry" (e.g., Tan et al., 2017), which provides an open environment to "individualise and tailor-made transportation services" such as ridesharing companies to meet riders-drivers' needs (Li & Hou, 2019). Salanovaa et al. (2011) maintain that the demand for urban trips is rapidly growing based on periodic increased in cities population, therefore, there is a need for effective cost transportation management system to handle urban population growth. Taxi services are more convenient due to their speediness services ibid to enhance public transit accessibility in cities (Abe, 2019). However, they lack central management which generates problems such as independent drivers (Salanovaa et al., 2011), unfair charges (Li & Hou, 2019), congestion (Cetin & Deakin, 2019), and traffic jams (Alonso, Barreda, Olio, & Ibeas, 2018). Therefore, to address the highlighted taxi services issues, Alonso et al. (2018) suggest that in order to maintain sustainable mobility, taxis alone are not the best way in the cities to travel around with.

The elements of taxi services infrastructure are rides, taxi companies or taxi associations, drivers, and riders (Billhardt et al. 2019; Tan et al. 2017). The infrastructure is a physical, unlike the ridesharing with digital-physical. The process for the taxi services consists of seven stages. Namely: (1) stand on the roadside (Greenwood & Wattal, 2017), (2) hail with hand or any other means in order to stop a taxi (Tan et al. 2017), (3) negotiate for the charge (Cetin & Deakin, 2019), (4) pick-up from a required location (Billhardt et al., 2019), (5) directions, (6) payment, and (7) drop-off at the destination (Wyman, 2017). Notable, some authors observe that travelling with taxis, especially the hailing period takes a longer and time consuming than the electronic hailing systems (Wyman, 2017; Young & Farber, 2019; Zhou et al., 2016).

METHODOLOGY

This study was based on an interpretivist research philosophy (Walsham, 2006). The ontology in the study referred to the understanding of digital innovation in taxi industrial structure for ridesharing in Ghana. Epistemologically, the author believed that the research issue can be best understood from the lived experiences actors. Concerning methodology, the study used an interpretive case study approach to develop an in-depth understanding of Uru ridesharing innovation in taxi industrial structure in Ghana. There were nine different ridesharing companies in Ghana as at June 2019, namely, Uber, Uru, Dropping, Yenko Taxi, Taxify (Bolt), Enshika, Fameko Taxi, Yango, and Pokicab, and all were located in Accra, the capital city of Ghana. However, Uru was selected as a case study via case selection techniques (Ponelis, 2015) and how interesting the case was (Baškarada, 2014). Case studies are often conducted in IS research in order to gain a rich understanding of a phenomenon (Ponelis, 2015).

Data Collection and Data Analysis

In interpretive paradigm, data collection and data analysis can be concurrent (Myers, 2009) and these informed the author to ask further questions that needed clarifications from the respondents. Various sources were used for data collection, namely, interviews, ICT artifacts observations, printed, and online information (Walsham, 2006) in order to obtain rich insights into the phenomenon. Field data were gathered between October 2017 and January 2019 via observations, telephone, and face-to-face semi-structured interviews. Interviews are the main primary data source in interpretive research (Cousins & Robey, 2015; Myers, 2013) and these always support a researcher to access the interpretations of participants (Green et al., 2007). Snowballing was used to identify relevant documents (Boell & Cecez-Kecmanovic, 2014) from the year 2011 to 2019 and for potential case selection (Ponelis, 2015) as well as the respondents. The study collected data from IS professionals (operations manager, administrator, and assistant administrator), riders, and drivers through an interpretive epistemology by ensuring that reality is socially constructed (Walsham, 2006). The participants selected for the interview were thirty-five through a purposive sample (Yanchar, South, Williams, Allen, & Wilson, 2010). The breakdown of the participants is as follows: IS professional (3), riders (17), and drivers (15).

The interview was achieved via face-to-face and technically-enabled conversations. Green et al. (2007) maintain that the researcher must always immerse in the data collection in order to provide analysis beyond the interview transcript. The data collected were based on field notes and audio recording with permission from the interviewees. The author coded and analyzed the interview transcripts (Walsham, 1995b) to contextualize the Uru ridesharing. Finally, follow-up interviews via telephone, WhatsApp, and e-mail were used to clarify essential points.

CASE DESCRIPTION

Uru technologies LLC (Uru) is a mobile app digitally-enabled online transportation services company that connects riders-drivers at the touch of a button together on a screen. Even though Uru ridesharing is not the first in Ghana, it was officially launched in Ghana for nationwide service on 21ˢᵗ April 2017 and as at now, it also operates in Kenya and Nigeria all in Africa. The company has different online transportation services, namely, taxi, charter services, business cars, and special travel cars. However, the concentration is on Uru taxi service which disrupts the taxi services in Ghana. The company's operation is backed by ICT related fields such as computing devices, google maps, and advanced global payment security encryptions for online transportation services between riders-drivers. The company operates with two ridesharing mobile apps, namely, Uru app and Uru Driver app. The Uru app is available for riders with compatible computing devices such as smartphones and iPads. The Uru Driver app, on the other hand, is extremely made for drivers with compatible computing devices who are fully–licensed and commercially-insured their rides. The core function of the company is to match riders with Uru app and drivers with Uru Driver app via compatible computing devices for journey activities. That is, a smart booking app made with the aim of forming enjoyable rides in which riders-drivers are fully connected by modern automotive technology.

The company offers the cheapest and most convenient means of online taxi giving both riders-drivers a transparent dashboard that can easily be modified to fit riders' specifications during trips. Uru connects riders-drivers on its ridesharing platform with an opportunity to take charge of their own careers and in doing so, have control over their own time and money via their apps. The outcome of Uru digitally-enabled online transportation service is disrupting the taxi services in competition. Thus, most taxi riders-drivers are migrating into the Uru system. The company is, therefore, described as a disruptive digitally-enabled online transportation service in Ghana because of its superb performance against taxi services. In addition, Uru ridesharing is attracting most digital technology enthusiasts in Ghana for affordable, secure, and fast travelling by disrupting taxi services, especially among young people who are more digital technologically knowledgeable. The operations manager of the company explained their digitally-enabled nature in the taxi industry as:

Our service is just a digital innovation in the taxi industrial structure. As a result, there is no Uru without ICT and its related fields. The outcome, however, is disrupting the taxi services in Ghana because of our digitally-enabled functions. Most riders-drivers consider our service as superb and convenience than the taxi services. On the other hand, taxi drivers have complained that our service in the taxi business is making them unpopular.

One of the riders expressed her view on how digitally-enabled Uru ridesharing is disrupting the taxi services in Ghana:

Our generation has more advantages than prior generations. This digital age has improved all my travel activities, especially in the cities. My mobile phone with Uru and other ridesharing apps provide me with swift, efficient, and economical ways to travel in the cities, unlike taxis. Thus, all the challenges in the taxi services have been solved by Uru and other ridesharing operators. I have stopped using taxis and now enjoying Uru ridesharing.

Another rider described how Uru ridesharing has solved his challenges for hailing a taxi as:

I have stopped using taxi services in the cities because sometimes, I have to spend about an hour before getting my match. The Uru app on my phone provides me opportunities to book a ride online at my convenient time with quick service and security for post journey issues.

One of the drivers expressed his understanding of how Uru ridesharing is disrupting the taxi services in Ghana as:

Today, I have stopped the taxi business, which involves tedious processes for getting a match. The Uru app on my phone provides me opportunities to accept a series of riders' requests at proximity, unlike taxi services.

Conceptualise Framework: Digital Platform for Uru Ridesharing

Digital platforms stimulated by rapid development of mobile apps such as ridesharing apps in this digital age have radically restructured and ever increasing services in the taxi industry. Notable, the intensive use of ICT in business organisations has created the concept of a digital platform. In a digital platform, the Internet is the backbone and any piece of information required to support key business decisions is available at anytime and anywhere in the organisation. Digital platform for Uru ridesharing has significantly experienced growth between riders-drivers for journey activities. The main objective of ridesharing is to increase vehicle utilization via digital platforms by providing riders with convenience, reliability, affordability, and on-demand transport service. Thus, to reduce the challenges for matching riders-drivers for trip activities through information sharing. The platform connects riders-driver with ridesharing apps via a centralised and automated matching and pricing system, which occurs within geolocation of the company. Figure 1 below shows a conceptual framework of Uru ridesharing platform with real-time journey transactions between riders and drivers. The framework shows that the workflow on Uru ridesharing platform involves seven stages for rider-driver journey activities. Although, the entire ridesharing activities are digital-physical. The physical component involves opening and closing doors, driving of the ride, and paying cash manually. The digital component, on the other hand, involves the real-time sharing of information via the Uru ridesharing platform from riders' requests to payment & drop-off. For example, a rider uses his/her riders' app to request a ride by inputting and sending a request to the Uru ridesharing platform, which contains information on the rider's source and destination addresses. The Uru ridesharing platform instantaneously computes a proposed fare based on the available rides within the geolocations of the rider's source location for confirmation of booking.

However, if a driver rejects the rider's request, the ridesharing platform automatically reassigns another driver before the rider's request is approved. Once the request is approved, then the platform automatically provides the driver with the rider's source address, name, and picture without the destination address. In addition, the rider also receives the driver's profile such as name, picture, and the ride details including estimated time of arrival. The Uru ridesharing platform provides them access to exchange information until the end of the journey for payment & drop-off. The fare, however, is dynamic based on the peak period, interrupted activities, and distance covered in kilometer. At the end of the trip, the platform provides riders-drivers an option to rate their experiences during the journey.

Figure 1. Workflows on Uru ridesharing platform between a rider and a driver

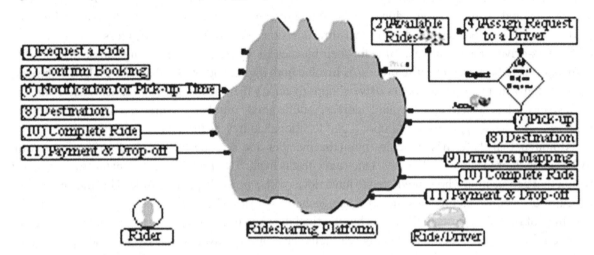

Uru Business Model

This section provides three stages of Uru business model that supports riders-drivers journey activities.

Step 1: Data Collection for a Ride Request

Data collection is the process that underpins registration for riders-drivers with compatible mobile devices before they can be part of Uru platform. Interestingly, riders' data collection for registration can be done at anywhere once Uru riders' app is downloaded and installed via Internet. The requirements for registration include riders' name, e-mail, cellphone number, and profile picture. Riders' data are stored permanently on Uru system upon confirmation of the registration via text message or/and e-mail, which can be used at anytime once the app is loaded without going through the registration process again. After installation and registration, the app automatically opens for rides request or log-in later with just a tap of a button. Upon log-in, riders' app fetches configuration location address for identification so that drivers may know where to pick riders'. Uru app is inbuilt with google maps and global positioning system (GPS), which provides riders location address anytime the app is connected to book a ride online instantly (book now) or schedule it for some time later (book later). Thus, locational address is temporal and must always be active before riders can book rides. However, the drivers' app registration is done only at the Uru office with terms and conditions. Requirements for drivers' registration are valid license, drivers and vehicles license authority (DVLA) certificate, and valid commercial insurance of rides for security reasons.

Step 2: Matching Riders to Drivers

This stage of Uru business model can be compared to taxi stations, which is managed by taxi operators and approved by drivers based on riders' requests. Matching means dispatching riders' requests to available rides within geolocation for approval by drivers on Uru platform. The matching process involves riders waiting for Uru to broadcast or dispatch requests according to riders' locational address; drivers within that proximity or redirecting drivers to unavailable rides at certain locations; drivers' approval; and pick-up and set destination, which comes with a dynamic charge. Apart from the physical driving by drivers, all the processes are done in real-time decisions via Uru platform with less waiting time, as both riders-drivers are sensitive in time for their businesses. Therefore, ridesharing can be described as digital-physical because the entire processes involve both digital and physical activities. Uru is the central dispatcher that works with riders-drivers' apps to certify their needs. Riders' requests automatically retrieve basic data such as name, e-mail address, mobile phone number, picture, and location addresses. Both riders-drivers' apps provide temporal and locational addresses for data collection.

Although, Uru platform is the central point that matches riders' requests to available drivers in proximity based on their locational addresses. Once a request is made, Uru immediately dispatches a free driver within that geolocation who is predicted to have riders with a possible pick-up time. This matching stage is veil to drivers, which prevents them to take decisions on riders' destinations. Though, Uru does the matching of riders' requests with drivers but the final decision relies on drivers to accept or reject. If the assigned driver rejects, then Uru quickly reassigns the request to available drivers for acceptance then prompt riders with notification. The matching requires prediction time of locational addresses between approved drivers-riders for a pick-up. This also includes pick-up time, details of riders, drivers, and rides to identify themselves as both of them are always strangers in the ride. All these actions are facilitated by data-driven from riders-drivers on Uru ridesharing platform.

The matching provides drivers with openness for a series of services by dispatching drivers to incoming riders' requests. This stage enables Uru to provide riders-drivers with significant benefits such as less waiting time, accessibility, and efficiency for travelling within cities. However, if there is no ride available for riders' requests, Uru then automatically redirects rides into those areas and match them accordingly. This issue makes riders wait until they get their match.

Step 3: Pick-Up and Drop-Off

This stage involves activities for pick-up, on-trip, payment, and drop-off. Pick-up involves arrival of rides at riders' locations via estimated time of arrival on their apps. At the arrival, drivers normally send messages or calls to notify riders to come for pick-up. The available information about riders, rides, and drivers enable them to easily locate each other for a pick-up. This stage also involves physical opening and closing of doors. Interaction between riders-drivers starts once the pick-up takes off, which enables drivers to know the destination addresses for necessary action. Uru ridesharing platform provides a transparent dashboard for drivers to set pick-up and destination addresses according to the riders' data, which comes with automatic (dynamic) billing according to travel time estimate between the two addresses. The dashboard enables drivers to set meter reading when ready with riders' pick-up, which can be tracked through riders' apps as well. The dashboard with travel time prediction provides route options for drivers to match and predict travel time between the two set addresses. Drivers then opt for the fastest route with real-time traffic information from GPS for speed prediction and drive after the system has computed for the travel time predictions. Consequently, drivers have no option to reject the offer during the pick-up conversations for a destination, which can be done by taxi drivers when they are not interested in the riders offer. The ultimate goal for drivers on Uru platform is to match and predict expected travel time based on pick-up location address, destination address, and trip start time.

The on-trip involves mapping technologies such as google maps for directions, which provide location updates for riders-drivers for flexible routing. However, the actual driving is physical which involves human power. The mapping technology guides drivers on the Uru ridesharing platform with automatic directions without any directional support from riders or anyone. Thus, the platform provides drivers a route choice with convenience and efficient for riding riders as a strategy to address transport challenges such as traffic jams, carbon, and road accidents in the fast-growing cities. Figure 2 below shows how this trend in the transport industry is shaping the relationship between riders and rides in cities.

Uru riders' payment is in the form of physical cash based on dynamic journey charges. Though, the company has made provision for digital payment via mobile money and electronic cards on riders' stored cards. Uru leverages data to obtain charges for payment based on the distance covered in kilometers and demand predictions of the rider's sessions. These involve start time, rate per kilometer, rate per minute, wait time charges, and distance covered as shown in Figure 3 below.

The charges start immediately riders take a seat in rides with pick-up time and trip completion associated with traffics and any interruption by riders. However, there is a minimum fixed price within a specific distance, which does not compute any additional condition for payment. Interestingly, this payment section of ridesharing is transparent and manageable, and it is gaining more popularity than taxi services in the transport industry. Thus, the price estimation changes if initial surcharges differ from destination-based journey interruptions. However, the company describes drivers as independent contractors and takes a commission on payment automatically on riders' trips. The payment system is real-time and synchronises charges on riders and drivers' apps for physical payment without any negotiation, irrespective of the journey condition, unlike taxi services.

Drop-off is the final section which comes with an option for rating each other after the payment. The system automatically displays messages on drivers' app for a reminder as collect cash from riders' at drop-off and destination addresses as shown in Figure 4 below. On the other side, riders' app also displays final fare for payment, rate driver, and drop-off.

The rating enables riders to know the status of drivers' performances for riding. Though, drop-off is the final section to separate riders-drivers, but the system keeps track of digital relationship for any post riding complaints.

SOLUTIONS AND RECOMMENDATIONS

Ridesharing is a partial digital transformation in the taxi industry. Although, taxi services provide riders' needs, especially those who would not be able to access private vehicles. Essentially, taxis have some challenges that affect the quality of riders' lives such as insecurity, difficult to get a ride during peak periods, and unfair charges. Furthermore, taxi services are insufficient to cover the entire range of the population in an effective way, especially those located in the cities. The introduction of Uru ridesharing in the taxi industry has resolved some of the taxis issues with electronic booking, security, and affordable transportation. The electronic booking provides riders a convenience approach to book rides at any location where Internet is available, unlike taxis where riders have to be at the roadside before getting a ride. Concerning security by Uru ridesharing, although, riders-drivers are always strangers in a ride but the system provides their profiles to keep track of every transaction on pre and post journey. Uru ridesharing provides automatic billing, which most riders who have migrated from taxi services into Uru describe it as affordable and transparent. The chapter, therefore, recommends taxi operators and drivers to take advantage of digitally-enabled transport services to enhance their services in order to avoid digital disruption by ridesharing operators.

Figure 2. Digital mapping for directions

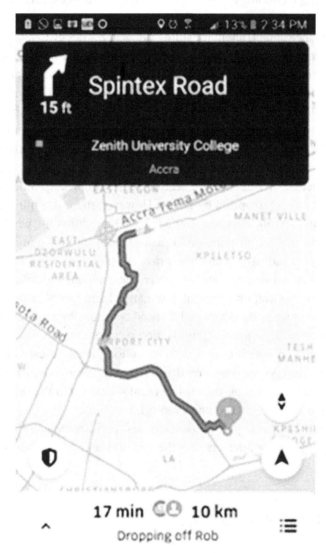

FUTURE RESEARCH DIRECTIONS

The chapter focused on Uru, a ridesharing company in a developing country context of Ghana. In recent times, innovation is no longer associated with new product development because the digital era has changed the status of innovation. Despite these findings, there is a need for further studies to understand how other ridesharing companies compete with taxi services in or outside Ghana. There is a need also to understand how emerging digital-physical affords riders-drivers' interactions in the transport services. Furthermore, future research can focus on the nature of digital innovation in other services.

Figure 3. Payment with a price estimation

CONCLUSION

The chapter explored digital innovation for Uru ridesharing in physical taxi industrial structure and trends in IS research in a developing country context of Ghana. Areas covered include literature on digital innovation, ridesharing, and taxi services; case description of Uru (the case study); a conceptual framework for ridesharing platform workflow between riders-drivers; and Uru business model for ridesharing. The chapter highlighted services challenges from taxis and how such challenges have been resolved by Uru ridesharing. Thus, disruptive digitally-enabled transport services, which is creating service change in the taxi industry by attracting most riders-drivers who are ICT-oriented from taxi services in Ghana. The findings offer insight into ridesharing innovation in a developing country and how it has resolved

Figure 4. Destination drop-off

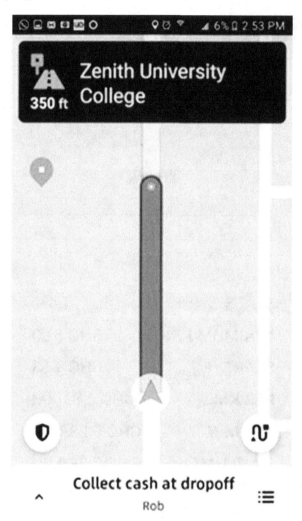

riders-drivers' challenges in the taxi industry. These include electronic booking, which enables riders to hail taxi at any location; security, which provides records for journey activities as both riders-drivers are always strangers in the ride; affordable transportation; and opportunities for drivers to accept a series of riders' requests at proximity.

The study is suitable for the taxi industry to understand the service change by ridesharing operators, especially taxi operators, drivers, and riders. The study is also appropriate for transport regulatory bodies in Ghana such as ridesharing operators, Commercial Taxi Drivers Association of the Ghana Private Road Transport Union (GPRTU), Police, and the Ministry of Transport. The study could be used at both undergraduate and graduate levels for IS and transportation systems disciplines as well as any developing country with the same settings. However, this is not limited to only IS and transportation systems, other disciplines can adapt it for their purpose. The chapter contributes to the existing literature on digital innovation for ridesharing. Finally, it forms the basis for future debate on the phenomenon.

REFERENCES

Abe, R. (2019). Introducing autonomous buses and taxis : Quantifying the potential benefits in Japanese transportation systems. *Transportation Research Part A, Policy and Practice, 126*(1), 94–113. doi:10.1016/j.tra.2019.06.003

Almeida, F., Silva, P., & Leite, J. (2017). Proposal of a carsharing system to improve urban mobility. *Theoretical and Empirical Researches in Urban Management, 12*(3), 32–44.

Alonso, B., Barreda, R., Olio, L., & Ibeas, A. (2018). Modelling user perception of taxi service quality. *Transport Policy, 63*(1), 157–164. doi:10.1016/j.tranpol.2017.12.011

Alter, S. (2006). Work Systems and IT Artifacts - Does the Definition Matter? *Communications of the Association for Information Systems, 17*(14), 299–313.

Baškarada, S. (2014). Qualitative Case Study Guidelines. *Qualitative Report, 19*(24), 1–18.

Billhardt, H., Fernández, A., Ossowski, S., Palanca, J., & Bajo, J. (2019). Taxi dispatching strategies with compensations. *Expert Systems with Applications, 122*(1), 173–182. doi:10.1016/j.eswa.2019.01.001

Boell, S. K., & Cecez-Kecmanovic, D. (2014). A Hermeneutic Approach for Conducting Literature Reviews and Literature Searches. *Communications of the Association for Information Systems, 34*(12), 257–286.

Cetin, T., & Deakin, E. (2019). Regulation of taxis and the rise of ridesharing. *Transport Policy, 76*(1), 149–158. doi:10.1016/j.tranpol.2017.09.002

Chatterjee, S., Sarker, S., & Siponen, M. (2017). How Do Mobile ICTs Enable Organizational Fluidity : Toward a Theoretical Framework. *Information & Management, 54*(1), 1–13. doi:10.1016/j.im.2016.03.007

Chen, C. (2017). Modelling Passengers ' Reaction to Dynamic Prices in Ride-on-demand Services : A Search for the Best Fare. In *Proceedings of the ACM on Interactive, Mobile, Wearable and Ubiquitous Technologies* (Vol. 1, pp. 1–23). ACM.

Christensen, C. M. (1997). The Innovator's Dilemma: When New Technologies Cause Great Firms to Fail. Boston, MA: Harvard Business School Press.

Christensen, C. M. (2006). The ongoing process of building a theory of disruption. *Journal of Product Innovation Management, 23*(1), 39–55. doi:10.1111/j.1540-5885.2005.00180.x

Cousins, K., & Robey, D. (2015). Managing work-life boundaries with mobile technologies: An interpretive study of mobile work practices. *Information Technology & People, 28*(1), 34–71. doi:10.1108/ITP-08-2013-0155

Elbanna, A., & Newman, M. (2016). Disrupt the Disruptor : Rethinking 'Disruption' in Digital Innovation. In *10th Mediterranean Conference on Information Systems* (p. pp.58-71). Paphos, Cyprus: Academic Press.

Garcia-murillo, M., Macinnes, I., & Bauer, J. M. (2018). Techno-unemployment : A framework for assessing the effects of information and communication technologies on work. *Telematics and Informatics*, *35*(1), 1863–1876. doi:10.1016/j.tele.2018.05.013

Ge, Y., Jabbari, P., Mackenzie, D., & Tao, J. (2017). Effects of a Public Real-Time Multi-Modal Transportation Information Display on Travel Behavior and Attitudes. *Journal of Public Transportation*, *20*(2), 40–65. doi:10.5038/2375-0901.20.2.3

Gecchelin, T., & Webb, J. (2019). Modular dynamic ride-sharing transport systems. *Economic Analysis and Policy*, *61*(1), 111–117. doi:10.1016/j.eap.2018.12.003

Green, J., Willis, K., Hughes, E., Small, R., Welch, N., Gibbs, L., & Daly, J. (2007). Generating best evidence from qualitative research: The role of data analysis. *Australian and New Zealand Journal of Public Health*, *31*(6), 545–550. doi:10.1111/j.1753-6405.2007.00141.x PMID:18081575

Greenwood, B. N., & Wattal, S. (2017). Show Me the Way to Go Home: An Empirical Investigation of Ride-Sharing and Alcohol Related Motor Vehicle Fatalities. *Management Information Systems Quarterly*, *41*(1), 163–187. doi:10.25300/MISQ/2017/41.1.08

Gurumurthy, K. M., & Kockelman, K. M. (2018). Analyzing the dynamic ride-sharing potential for shared autonomous vehicle fleets using cellphone data from Orlando, Florida. *Computers, Environment and Urban Systems*, *71*(1), 177–185. doi:10.1016/j.compenvurbsys.2018.05.008

Junglas, I., & Watson, R. T. (2006). The U-Constructs : Four Information Drives. *Communications of the Association for Information Systems*, *17*(26), 569–592.

Kim, S., & Hyun, T. (2018). Examining the antecedents and consequences of mobile app engagement. *Telematics and Informatics*, *35*(1), 148–158. doi:10.1016/j.tele.2017.10.008

Lee, S., Lee, B., & Kim, H. (2019). Decisional factors leading to the reuse of an on-demand ride service. *Information & Management*, *56*(4), 493–506. doi:10.1016/j.im.2018.09.010

Li, B., & Szeto, W. Y. (2019). Taxi service area design : Formulation and analysis. *Transportation Research Part E, Logistics and Transportation Review*, *125*(1), 308–333. doi:10.1016/j.tre.2019.03.004

Li, J., & Hou, L. (2019). A reflection on the taxi reform in China: Innovation vs. Tradition. *Computer Law & Security Review*, *35*(1), 251–262. doi:10.1016/j.clsr.2019.02.005

Lokuge, S., Sedera, D., Grover, V., & Xu, D. (2019). Organizational readiness for digital innovation : Development and empirical calibration of a construct. *Information & Management Journal*, *56*(3), 445–461. doi:10.1016/j.im.2018.09.001

Mounce, R., & Nelson, J. D. (2019). On the potential for one-way electric vehicle car-sharing in future mobility systems. *Transportation Research Part A, Policy and Practice*, *120*(1), 17–30. doi:10.1016/j.tra.2018.12.003

Myers, M. (2009). Qualitative research in business and management. *Sage (Atlanta, Ga.)*.

Myers, M. D. (2013). *Qualitative Research in Business & Management* (N. S. Kirsty Smy, Ed.). 2nd ed.). Sage Publications.

Ponelis, S. R. (2015). Using interpretive qualitative case studies for exploratory research in doctoral studies: A case of Information Systems research in small and medium enterprises. *International Journal of Doctoral Studies*, *10*(1), 535–550. doi:10.28945/2339

Rayle, L., Shaheen, S., Chan, N., Dai, D., & Cervero, R. (2014). App-Based, On-Demand Ride Services: Comparing Taxi and Ridesourcing Trips and User Characteristics in San Francisco. University of California Transportation Center.

Rogers, B. (2016). The Social Costs of Uber. *University of Chicago Law Review Dialogue*, *82*(85), 85–102.

Salanovaa, J. M., Estrada, M., Aifadopoulou, G., & Mitsakis, E. (2011). A review of the modeling of taxi services. *Procedia: Social and Behavioral Sciences*, *20*(1), 150–161. doi:10.1016/j.sbspro.2011.08.020

Schreffler, E. N. (2018). Better Integrating Travel Choices into Future Urban Mobility Systems : The Day the Highways Stood Still. *Journal of Public Transportation*, *21*(1), 82–91. doi:10.5038/2375-0901.21.1.9

Simmons, R. O. (2018). Disruptive Digital Technology Services: The Case of Uber Car Ridesharing in Ghana. In *Twenty-fourth Americas Conference on Information Systems, AMCIS 16-18 August*. New Orleans, LA: AIS.

Simmons, R., Effah, J., & Boateng, R. (2019). Digital Innovation and Taxi Services : The Case of Uru in Ghana. In *Twenty-fifth Americas Conference on Information Systems* (pp. 1–10). Cancun: AIS.

Tan, F. C., Tan, B., Lu, A., & Land, L. (2017). Delivering Disruption in an Emergent Access Economy : A Case Study of an E-hailing Platform. *Communications of the Association for Information Systems*, *41*(22), 497–516. doi:10.17705/1CAIS.04122

Teubner, T., & Flath, C. M. (2015). The Economics of Multi-Hop Ride Sharing Creating New Mobility Networks Through IS. *Business & Information Systems Engineering*, *57*(5), 311–324. doi:10.100712599-015-0396-y

Walsham, G. (1995). The emergence of interpretivism in IS research. *Information Systems Research*, *6*(4), 376–394. doi:10.1287/isre.6.4.376

Walsham, G. (2006). Doing interpretive research. *European Journal of Information Systems*, *15*(3), 320–330. doi:10.1057/palgrave.ejis.3000589

Wang, X., Ardakani, H. M., & Schneider, H. (2017). Does Ride Sharing have Social Benefits? In *Twenty-third Americas Conference on Information Systems* (pp. 1–8). Boston: Academic Press.

Wyman, K. M. (2017). Taxi Regulation in the Age of Uber. *New York University Journal of Legislation and Public Policy*, *20*(1), 2–51.

Yanchar, S. C., South, Æ. J. B., Williams, Æ. D. D., Allen, S., & Wilson, Æ. B. G. (2010). Struggling with theory? A qualitative investigation of conceptual tool use in instructional design. *Educational Technology Research and Development*, *58*(1), 39–60. doi:10.100711423-009-9129-6

Young, M., & Farber, S. (2019). The who, why, and when of Uber and other ride-hailing trips : An examination of a large sample household travel survey. *Transportation Research Part A, Policy and Practice*, *119*(1), 383–392. doi:10.1016/j.tra.2018.11.018

Zhou, Z., Dou, W., Jia, G., Hu, C., Xu, X., Wu, X., & Pan, J. (2016). A method for real-time trajectory monitoring to improve taxi service using GPS big data. *Information & Management, 53*(8), 964–977. doi:10.1016/j.im.2016.04.004

ADDITIONAL READING

Cherry, M. A. (2017). Are Uber and Transportation Network Companies the Future of Transportation (Law) and Employment (Law)? *Texas A&M Law Review, 4*(2), 173–195.

Cramer, J., & Krueger, A. B. (2016). Disruptive Change in the Taxi Business: The Case of Uber. *The American Economic Review, 106*(5), 177–182. doi:10.1257/aer.p20161002

Kane, M., & Whitehead, J. (2017). How to ride transport disruption –a sustainable framework for future urban mobility. *Australian Plants, 54*(3), 177–185. doi:10.1080/07293682.2018.1424002

Liyanage, S., Dia, H., Abduljabbar, R., & Bagloee, S. A. (2019). Flexible Mobility On-Demand : An Environmental Scan. *Sustainability, 11*(1262), 1–39.

Sun, H., & Mcintosh, S. (2016). Big Data Mobile Services for New York City Taxi Riders and Drivers. In *IEEE International Conference on Mobile Services* (pp. 57–64). IEEE. 10.1109/MobServ.2016.19

Wang, Y., Zheng, B., & Lim, E. (2018). Understanding the effects of taxi ride-sharing : A case study of Singapore. *Computers, Environment and Urban Systems, 69*(1), 124–132. doi:10.1016/j.compenvurbsys.2018.01.006

Wyman, K. M. (2017). Taxi Regulation in the Age of Uber. *New York University Journal of Legislation and Public Policy, 20*(1), 2–51.

Yu, B., Ma, Y., Xue, M., Tang, B., Wang, B., Yan, J., & Wei, Y.-M. (2017). Environmental benefits from ridesharing : A case of Beijing. *Applied Energy, 191*(1), 141–152. doi:10.1016/j.apenergy.2017.01.052

KEY TERMS AND DEFINITIONS

Digital Innovation: Digital innovation is an ideal for creating new product, service, or market via synergy of emerging ICT and existing systems.

Digital Platform: Interactions on digital environments such as laptops, iPhones, iPads, credit cards, social media, and mobile applications that allows resource providers and resource users to perform electronic transactions.

Digital-Physical: A digital innovation in a physical industrial structure such as taxi industrial structure (ridesharing) and port (digital port).

Disruptive Technology: Innovations in digital technologies, which have potentials to disrupt existing systems in competitions.

Driver App: Ridesharing mobile application installed on computing devices such as smartphones that supports drivers to connect on ridesharing platform.

Rider: A traveller or commuter without a vehicle who arranges and travels with a private vehicle for a fee.

Rider App: Ridesharing mobile application installed on computing devices such as iPhones that supports riders to connect on ridesharing platform.

Ridesharing: Digital arrangements between riders-drivers for travel transactions via ridesharing platform.

Chapter 8
Blockchain Readiness:
Expert Perspectives From a Developing Economy

Frederick Edem Broni Jr.
https://orcid.org/0000-0001-9674-1679
Business School, University of Ghana, Ghana

Acheampong Owusu
https://orcid.org/0000-0001-7789-5162
Business School, University of Ghana, Ghana

ABSTRACT

Blockchain technology is an emerging innovation, and it is viewed as a better approach to help the necessities of people and institutions in terms of record management. Using the Delphi technique and the PERM model, this chapter seeks to present the perspectives of experts in the field of blockchain on the readiness of the institutions in developing economies to adopt and implement it. The findings suggest that the understanding of the technology, knowledge on how to use it, availability of skilled personnel, availability of technical components, risk, capital, management support, business process, policies and regulations, and government initiatives on technology are key influencing factors assessing the readiness to adopt blockchain in a developing economy. It is expected that these findings will enlighten practitioners on the prospects of the application of blockchain in all sectors. The originality of this study lies in the fact that it is a maiden exploratory study that examines the factors that influence the readiness to adopt and implement blockchain technology in a developing economy.

INTRODUCTION

Due to the advancing nature of information Communication technology (ICT) and the internet, this phenomenon of generating fake certificates has worsened over the years. There are problems with counterfeit documents and records, as well as authentication and verification issues by institutions. However, these issues of authentication and verification of certificates can be tackled with the use of Blockchain

DOI: 10.4018/978-1-7998-2610-1.ch008

technology. Blockchain technology is an emerging technology that enhances reliability and ensures data integrity in records. Subsequently, blockchain innovation appears perfect to irradiate numerous of the issues mentioned above of fake paper documents.

The blockchain technology provides a better way of authenticating and verifying records and results from issuing authorities, allowing others to trust to prevail in a system (Yumna, Khan, Ikram, & Ilyas, 2019). Blockchain ensures better record verification in many fields (Grech & Camilleri, 2017; Rooksby & Dimitrov, 2017). Evidence of this technology is found mostly in fintech and supply chain platforms as well as record maintenance platforms (Sharples & Domingue, 2016; Chen, Xu, Lu & Chen, 2018). However, the scope of blockchain goes beyond the earlier mentioned platforms and can be incorporated into the applications and services in other sectors to verify and authenticate records and results across stakeholders (Yli-Huumo, Ko, Choi, Park, & Smolander, 2016; Lemieux, 2016).

This study employs a theory-based understanding of the readiness factors of Blockchain adoption in institutions in other sectors since there is arguably little or no research on Blockchain in a developing economy's perspective using a theory. Hence this study.

This study is exploratory, and it is aimed at obtaining preliminary insights from Blockchain experts on how technology can benefit the other industries. Blockchain is now gaining recognition in developing economies, and there is a need for research to investigate its potential and how it will benefits firms in emerging economies.

The purpose of this study is to explore the influencing readiness factors of institutions in the adoption of Blockchain technology in Ghana.

These objectives will be addressed in this study:

1. To explore the awareness of Blockchain in institutions in Ghana.
2. To explore the readiness factors of institutions in the adoption of blockchain technology.

From the objectives, these are the questions of this study:

1. What is the nature of awareness of Blockchain in institutions in Ghana?
2. What are the readiness factors that influence the adoption of Blockchain in institutions in Ghana?

This question will help us better analyze the factors that influence the readiness of institutions to adopt and implement blockchain.

The importance of this study can be towed along the lines of research, policy, and practice; therefore, it will help contribute to knowledge in the Blockchain field.

This study is to explore the factors that influence the readiness of institutions to adopt and implement blockchain. The Chapter is organized into five sections. The first section is the introduction to the chapter. The second section presents an overview of Blockchain, advantages, and disadvantages of Blockchain, applications of Blockchain, related work on Blockchain, and the research framework as well as the research methods used in the chapter. The third section deals with the findings, analysis, and discussion. The fourth section presents future studies directions. The last part deals with the precis of the study, implications (and suggestions) to investigate, practice, and policy.

BACKGROUND

Fundamentally, Van Alstyne (2014) defined blockchain as a chronologically distributed database where transaction history is stored on a block and shared in a chain in a public ledger. Blockchain functions under the concepts of distributed computing and encryption, which has been around for a while now and has been in operation in their domain (operated separately) (Jamsrandorj, 2017). For Blockchain to function, Nakamoto (2008) fused these two concepts of encryption and distributed computing. This development of Blockchain was necessary due to the inherent weakness of the trust-based model, which were third party firms that verify and authenticate the transaction before getting the recipient (Nakamoto, 2008). These third-party intermediaries such as financial institutions and payment gateways act as middlemen during an operation to facilitate the process on behalf of clients, which can sometimes be chaotic (Gupta, 2017). Therefore, Nakamoto (2008) proposed an electronic system based on cryptographic proof to all transactions to be made directly to peers, enhancing transparency, cutting down transaction costs, minimizing delay and uncertainties, and enhancing trust.

Advantages and Disadvantages of Blockchain Technology

Blockchain has various merits and hindrances that will impact on the adoption. Some benefits are Peer-to-peer exchanges- where exchanges are without third parties, no centralized control, no limits - which makes it conceivable to send exchanges crosswise over nations, low costs, transparency, anonymity, and so on (Ivaschenko, 2016). The drawbacks of Blockchain are that; it is precarious, can support money laundry, and utilized for other unlawful exercises like funding of illegal activities (Ivaschenko, 2016).

Applications of Blockchain

Blockchain usage is gaining recognition around the world, and with it being beneficial in many sectors, individuals and firms are adopting it for use, with it being evident in the financial sector. Its application in other sectors is still in its infancy; however, some institutions have begun experimenting with the technology (Collins, 2017). In the port logistics environment, blockchain has been considered a better option in dealing with trusted digital records by various stakeholders (Francisconi, 2017). Blockchain has served as the underlying driver of cryptocurrencies, such as Bitcoin, which has transformed the way money is transferred from one person to another (Nakamoto, 2008). Again, Blockchain is also very capable when it comes to asset management. Lemieux (2016) suggested that technology can be used for information integrity, to protect assets, and enhance trust and transparency.

Selected studies on Blockchain in diverse issues and contexts are being presented in Table 1.

Concerning the literature presented in Table 1, most studies focused on Blockchain implementation in developed economies, with cases and issues on the application of Blockchain mostly centered around cryptocurrencies. In Africa, Rejeb (2018) looked at the potential of Blockchain technology in the Tilapia supply chain, where the study analyzed the tilapia supply chain in Ghana and highlighted the role of blockchain in ensuring transparency and food safety in building a secure network of tilapia distributors, producers, and consumers. Azogu, Norta, Papper, Longo, and Draheim (2019) also proposed a framework to tackle issues of privacy, record keeping, and information sharing in the Nigerian health sector concerning blockchain adoption yet; these studies were silent on the readiness factors of institutions to adopt blockchain.

Table 1. Related works on Blockchain

Author	Focus	Theory	Findings	Gaps
Reijers et al. (2016)	to examine the way Blockchain technologies can bring about and justify new models of governance	Social contract theory		the analysis was based on a technology that is still in its development phase, which means that empirical support for much of our discussions is lacking or in its infancy, therefore the need for more literature in developing countries
Yli-Huumo et al. (2016)	to understand the current research topics, challenges and future directions regarding Blockchain technology from the technical perspective	Conceptual	The results show that focus in over 80% of the papers is on the Bitcoin system and less than "20% deals with other Blockchain applications including e.g., smart contracts and licensing"	Conclude that most literature is still focused on BitCoin implementations and the technical challenges of implementing Blockchain technology. They call for research on "the possibilities of using Blockchain in other (than BitCoin and Cryptocurrency) environments."
Mejier (2017)	used a Grounded Theory approach to map the ongoing Blockchain discussion, which leads to our empirical core category that explains the core of the Blockchain discussions	Grounded Theory	A Blockchain enables the creation of organizations entirely based on Blockchain technology. In these organizations, all corporate actions are decided upon by the shareholders directly, which creates a decentralized corporate decision-making process for organizations on the Blockchain.	Further development of this conceptualization of trust and control is needed to structure the ongoing Blockchain discussions in both scientific literature and practice.
Lemieux (2016)	To explore the value of Blockchain technology as a solution to creating and preserving trustworthy digital records, presenting some of the limitations, risks, and opportunities of the approach	a "general evaluative framework for a risk-based assessment."	The results of the "analysis suggests that Blockchain technology can be used to address issues associated with information integrity" in the present and near term, assuming proper security architecture and infrastructure management controls. It does not, however, guarantee the reliability of the information in the first place, and would have several limitations as a long-term solution for maintaining trustworthy digital records	The need for the development of Trusted Digital Repositories on Blockchain to foster recordkeeping and preservation of original records
Connolly and Kick (2015)	describes "a study to understand what differentiates organization adopters of Bitcoin from non-adopters by comparing their IT-readiness, innovativeness and social media presence."	Conceptual	that to bound the study, we chose to focus on the most logical organization characteristics because other factors may influence Bitcoin adoption, which their study did not look at.	This "research serves as a basis for future research on Bitcoins and Bitcoin adoption by highlighting some important hurdles to its adoption as an innovation, in the hope that such endeavors move us ever closer to the vision of a true people's currency."
Francisconi (2017)	To identify the impact of the technology on port logistics, some process KPIs were defined as an evaluation framework	Conceptual	Identified four Blockchain business cases and evaluated their relative impact on port logistics. Subsequently, these business cases were used as stress factors for the stress-test analysis to provide a recommendation for Portbase on how to adapt its business model. This led to the identification of new potential roles for Portbase as an intermediary in port logistics	"lack in-process visibility a technological issue that can be solved with a Blockchain implementation, or is it an intrinsic feature of the supply chain that requires a mind-shift? Second, is Blockchain going to disintermediate the whole supply chain, or it generates new intermediaries?"
Nakamoto (2008)	A solution to the double-spending problem using a peer-to-peer network	Conceptual	we "proposed a peer-to-peer network using proof-of-work to record a public history of transactions that quickly becomes computationally impractical for an attacker to change if honest nodes control a majority of Central Processing Unit (CPU) power."	
Rejeb (2018)	examines the major issues and problems in Tilapia supply chain and logistics in Ghana, and it suggests the intervention of the new and disruptive technology of blockchain	Conceptual	it highlights the role of blockchain in ensuring food safety and in rebuilding a secure network of Tilapia distribution between producers and customers.	
Azogu, Norta, Papper, Longo and Draheim (2019)	proposed a scalable framework that supports the adoption of blockchain technology in addressing the issues of privacy, information sharing, and record-keeping in the health sector.	Conceptual Framework	Found out that blockchain enhances transparency and trust thereby ensuring easy access of uncompromised patient records, which aids in the making of healthcare decisions	Current approaches adopted in many hospitals face challenges of missing files, or records, lack of information sharing between healthcare providers, insecure records, and also inaccessibility of patients' health information for healthcare providers that are needed to make informed health decisions.

Furthermore, a theoretical understanding of Blockchain adoption in firms in developing economies was arguably non-existent. Therefore, this study fills these gaps identified in the studies reviewed with the emphasis on Blockchain adoption in a developing economy through a theory-based understanding, to explore the external readiness factors of institutions in the adoption of Blockchain in Ghana. This will add up to, and enrich the scarce Information systems literature of Blockchain in developing economies.

RESEARCH FRAMEWORK

The Perceived E-Readiness Model (PERM) Model by Molla and Licker (2005a) is defined as "an organization's assessment of the e-commerce, managerial, organizational, and external situations in making decisions about adopting e-commerce." It consists of two (2) essential constructs, which are Perceived Organizational E-Readiness (POER) and Perceived External E-Readiness (PEER), which also embraces four (4) contextual issues (organizational, environmental, managerial and innovation) relating to adoption (Molla & Licker, 2005a). It captures innovativeness, technical knowledge, strategic insight, and expertise, which aids or influences the readiness to adopt the technology within an organization (Boateng, Heeks & Molla, 2011).

In a quest to analyze the external readiness factors that influence the adoption of Blockchain by firms in Ghana, this study adopts the Perceived External E-Readiness variables from the PERM Model. Perceived External E-Readiness denotes domineering environmental factors such as the assessment level and evaluation of governmental support and other agency support as well as market forces readiness that affects the behavior towards the technology (Molla & Licker, 2005b). The PERM is arguably the only model that incorporates a broad approach to better understand and evaluate the influencers on the readiness of Blockchain adoption and implementation in developing economies (Boateng et al., 2011). This study carefully and critically discusses issues that influence the adoption and implementation of Blockchain in Ghanaian institutions.

Blockchain External E-Readiness (BEER) was defined as the level to which the government readiness, market forces readiness, technological readiness, and educational readiness are ready and willing to offer help in the implementation of the Blockchain technology.

Government Readiness analyses how a nation and institutions within it are prepared to support, facilitate, and regulate the use of Blockchain. Government support will have a very positive impact on how institutions adopt and implement Blockchain technology in the country. The government's readiness to instill confidence by laying down policies and other technological initiatives tends to standardize the environment of industries hence, lead to the adoption and implementation of Blockchain (Dutta, Lanvin, & Paua, 2004; Oxley & Yeung, 2001). Studies have argued that policies and governmental initiatives will affect the readiness of institutions to adopt and implement Blockchain technology (Kuan & Chau, 2001; Oxley & Yeung, 2001).

Proposition 1: Government readiness may influence the initial adoption and implementation of blockchain.

Market Forces readiness which looks at the related partners and customers in utilizing the Blockchain applications to offer and render solutions and services, and how it is incorporated into other systems Institutions are happy to embrace and utilize Blockchain when they regard market forces available, because of the frightfulness of competition or expanding innovative patterns. Molla and Licker (2005) expressed that there is a considerable impact on the status to adopt and execute Blockchain. Humphrey, Mansell,

Pare, and Schmitz (2003) discovered that pressure, for example, innovative advances and rivalry in the market, will help in the adoption of an innovation that will prompt its usage.

Proposition 2: Market force readiness may have an impact on the initial adoption and implementation of blockchain.

Technological Readiness which analyzes how the institution is prepared and willing to put resources into Information Technology (IT) assets to engage the usage of Blockchain technology. An institution putting resources into programming and equipment assets to control the Blockchain will help in the adoption and usage of the technology.

Proposition 3: Technological readiness may impact the initial adoption and implementation of blockchain.

Educational readiness to look at the learning expected to create Blockchain applications. Institutions will adopt and implement Blockchain if some firms or institutes give preparation on the most proficient method to build and utilize it in their organizations. Training in Blockchain is essential since, without legitimate information of how it functions, it will be the limitation in the implementation of the Blockchain innovation (Ruhizan, Bekri, and Faizal, 2014). Getting quality information from learning through training and assessing the new knowledge gotten can tremendously impact the utilization of technology (Ruhizan et al., 2014).

Proposition 4: Educational readiness may impact the initial adoption and implementation of blockchain.

Research Method

This study employed a qualitative study through interviews. In getting a detailed comprehension of the impression of respondents, this research utilizes interviews. The approach for data collection was expected to consider the data accumulated, while preferably conceding to views. In the accomplishments of these objectives, the Delphi strategy (Whitman, 1990) was considered necessary for this study. The Delphi strategy came to fruition during the 1950s, and RAND Corporation created it. It was a procedure for tackling complex issues that rely upon inputs that are iterative to accomplish consensus building. An adapted Delphi strategy through rounds (2 rounds) of meetings was ideal for achieving the objectives for this study.

The researcher chose the experts who have in any event worked with the Blockchain technology for a minimum of 2 years through purposive sampling. This sampling procedure was utilized because of the set number of people and institutions effectively engaged with Blockchain. Eighteen (18) experts were examined purposively from the Blockchain communities, Blockchain startup firms, and some institutions belonging to the government. These are people or firms that are effectively utilizing Blockchain, enlightening the public about blockchain (through boot camps, hackathons, meetups, roundtable discussions, conferences, and so on.) and considering embracing the technology.

The outcomes from the interviews were gathered, transcribed, and presented dependent on the external variables of the BEER construct of the PERM model. This made for a more straightforward relationship, and drawing of insights and recommendations in light of the similarities and differences between the responses from the experts on the readiness factors to adopt and implement Blockchain.

Achieving consensus in Delphi studies is usually between 55% to 100%; moreover, 70% is considered as the standard acceptable point (Vernon, 2009). The impacting factors recognized from the findings through the interviews in the first round were tried in the second round before they were accepted or dismissed. A factor index to quantify reactions was assigned in the order of 2 to agree, one neutral, and 0 disagree. The scores derived were multiplied by the frequency, which was added to get the factor index by utilizing the equation $\Sigma[(f)+(f)+(f)]$ (Doe, van de Wetering, Honyenuga, Versendaal & Boateng, 2018). Influencing factors that accomplish a score of 25 (0.6944) or above were maintained and dismissed if the score was less, as shown in Figure 1.

Findings, Analysis and Discussion

This section feeds from the groups of critical realism to analyze the data obtained through the perspective of the research framework, which decides the nature of Blockchain, what it is being utilized for, and the factors that impact its readiness to adopt the technology.

Figure 1. factor index quantify reactions

Legend: *Agree (A), Neutral (N), Disagree (D), Item Content Validity Index (X) for item score in round one, Item Content Validity Index (X[1]) for item score in round one, responses from Developers (D), responses from Bitcoin Traders (T), responses from CTOs & Consultants (C), responses from Blockchain Society members (B) and responses from academia (L); X and X[1] are calculated by $\Sigma[(f(A))+(f(N))+(f(D))]$, where f is frequency.*

Blockchain External E-Readiness	External Factor(s)	A=2	N=1	D=0	X	A=2	N=1	D=0	X[1]	X	X[ll]	
Governmental Readiness	Policies & Regulations, Government initiative on technology	DDDD T CC BBB LL	DDD B	TT	28	DDDDDD TT CC BBB LL	D T	B	32	0.77	0.88	Accept
Technological Readiness	Affordability of IT resources, Availability of IT resources, Accessibility of IT resources	TTT BBBB DDDDDDD CC LL			36	TTT BBBB DDDDDDD CC LL			36	1.00	1.00	Accept
Market Readiness	Efficiency of technology, Extent of usage	DDDDDDD CC LL BBBB TTT			36	DDDDDDD CC LL BBBB TTT			36	1.00	1.00	Accept
Educational Readiness	Availability of Learning Platforms, Accessibility to relevant courses	LL CC BBB T DDDDDDD	TT B		33	LL CC BBBB TTT DDDDDDD			36	0.916	1.00	Accept

Selection of Respondents

Table 2 outlines the profile of the respondents interviewed for the study. In all, developers of blockchain were the highest represented by seven respondents. This was followed by the blockchain community members comprising of 4 respondents. Bitcoin traders with three respondents follow.

Nature of Blockchain

In analyzing the nature of Blockchain in Ghana summarized in Table 3, it was found that Blockchain was utilized for both crypto and non-crypto purposes. Crypto, as in its advantages, are money related and can be utilized for exchange and to satisfy budgetary commitments, for example, purchasing and

Table 2. Respondents Selection Criterion

Type of Respondent	Number Interviewed	Length of Experience
Developers	2	12-18 Months
	2	18-24 Months
		24-36 Months
	3	36-48 Months
	Total: 7	
Bitcoin Traders	1	12-18 Months
	1	18-24 Months
	1	24-36 Months
	Total: 3	36-48 Months
CTO & Tech-consultants	1	12-18 Months
	1	18-24 Months
	Total: 2	24-36 Months
		36-48 Months
Blockchain Community members	1	12-18 Months
	1	18-24 Months
	2	24-36 Months
	Total: 4	36-48 Months
Lecturers, Facilitators & Instructors		12-18 Months
	2	18-24 Months
	Total: 2	24-36 Months
		36-48 Months

accepting installments on the web. For instance, utilizing cryptographic money, for example, Bitcoin to exchange merchandise and enterprises just as investments. Non-crypto uses of blockchain was likewise found whereby, it was utilized for supply chain and record-keeping purposes. This was clear with three firms in Ghana utilizing the innovation. To start with, BenBen and BitLand utilized blockchain for tracking land enlistment and proprietorship in the nation lastly, AgriXchain likewise utilized the blockchain to associate all partners, to encourage purchasing and selling of homestead produce.

A respondent indicated that:

Bitcoin is the most Blockchain technology used in Ghana because it helps in financial exchanges across borders, and due to its effectiveness and transparency, there is trust, and people feel comfortable using it to trade.

Another also said:

Being a Bitcoin trader, I invest in bitcoin to store value. I buy the coins, and when the price increases, I make a higher return.

The findings also suggest that people and firms are experimenting with blockchain technology. A large portion of them are extremely intrigued by it and need to profit by it. More know about this innovation and recognize what it is about notwithstanding, few have just begun testing as well as, embraced and executed it into their business. Others are likewise learning and picking up information about blockchain through going to meetings, workshops, and online courses.

A respondent stated that:

AgriXchain is a platform used in the Agriculture sector. The world is changing, and as it changes, it comes with new technology and innovations that make working easy, more reliable, and effective. The traditional way of contract enforcement with its relative performance has changed. Africa agri-businesses need a system that is effective, efficient, and productive without much bureaucracy where actors in the agri-supply chain facilitate trade among themselves, share information, and ensure good standards of produce required.

Another also indicated that:

Benben is also another local-based Blockchain platform that individuals use to acquire lands in the country. It has helped solve the problem of the land search, validation, and ownership. Users can access BenBen's interactive maps to search for land information before buying or selling.

In answering the second research question, analysis and discussion of the findings were done with the Blockchain External E-Readiness factors.

Government Readiness

Concerning the second objective of this study, which is to find the external factors that influence the readiness of institutions to adopt and implement Blockchain, from the findings, it was found that policies on the most proficient method to utilize blockchain are non-existent in Ghana. Regulatory bodies have not set up any policy or legal framework to fill in as a rule on the utilization of the innovation. Be that as it may, the Bank of Ghana (BoG) is checking advancements relating to Blockchain and will, along these lines, help in its selection through policies and guidelines in the financial industry. For example, The BoG has revised its payments system act, referred to as the payment systems and services bill, to safeguard online or digital transactions, which will include guidelines for transacting with cryptocurrencies. The government trying to reduce the land registration issues, marked an MOU with IBM to implement a Blockchain technology to be utilized by the Lands commission to capture land records.

Table 3. Nature of Blockchain in Ghana

Type	Platform	Purpose	Why Used?
Bitcoin	Web & Mobile	Used for transactions online	• Faster transaction • Price value • Lower transactional cost • Trust • Anonymity and security
BenBen	Web & Mobile	allows users to manage their land records and perform land transactions.	• Transparency • Data integrity • Security
BitLand	Web	allow individuals and organizations to survey land and record deeds onto the Bitshares Blockchain	• Security • Integrity
AgriXchain	Web	allows farmers to get all the inputs, tools, technology, and all other services they need to produce to meet standards even on credit.	• Transparency • Easy tracking of goods • integrity
Ethereum.org	Web	Platform to develop Blockchain applications and services	• Ease of use • Security • Perceived Usefulness

This is to help eliminate the irregularities relating to land-related issues. This shows the state is making significant strides to receive the Blockchain technology to help in transparency and increase trust in the land procurement process.

Moreover, firms engaged with the land registration and real estate will utilize the Blockchain to render benefits in this manner, adopting the technology into their business operations. A respondent stated that:

To maximize its potential benefits, it is necessary to identify the inherent risks and institute mitigating measures to contain the risks. Also, clarity has to be established for terminologies, technical standards, and approaches in its implementation. Governance and standardization issues are also necessary to foster end-to-end security and interoperability among different systems. The Bank of Ghana is, therefore, monitoring developments in the Blockchain Technology space and will facilitate its adoption in the financial sector.

Another respondent said:

IBM will work directly with the Ministry of Lands and Natural Resources to develop plans to take this initiative forward. A secondary aspect of the project is to enhance port logistics and processes. Smart contracts could be used to improve customs and logistics in the ports of the country. This decision by the government will greatly allow for more security and transparency in the industry at the same time that it would be able to reduce frauds in the system and amplify the access to investment and capital in the country.

Studies have confirmed (Dutta, Lanvin, & Paua, 2004; Oxley & Yeung, 2001) that the government's preparation impacts the readiness to adopt and execution of innovation. However, a study by Molla and Licker (2005) repudiates this finding expressing that the government's preparation had no considerable influence on the availability to receive and execute innovation. Studies (Kuan & Chau, 2001) demonstrate that polices and guidelines executed to control the utilization of innovation, positively influence the readiness to adopt and usage of the innovation. Concerning BEER, Government Readiness influences the initial adoption of Blockchain.

Technological Readiness

With technological readiness, this study recognized issues, for example, accessibility, availability, and affordability. From the findings, this research found that assets, for example, cloud platform services and powerful IT components, can help in the fruitful utilization of Blockchain technology. The availability of the assets and having the option to manage the cost of such assets are significant for the adoption of Blockchain. A development machine for the building of Blockchain applications and services ought to be of high specifications. A Machine, for example, with an i7 processor, 1 Terabyte Hard Disk Drive (HDD), and an 8-16 gigabyte RAM is a decent machine for the development of which is accessible and effectively available in different electronic shops in the nation.

Furthermore, services, for example, internet providers and cloud platforms, are exceptionally fundamental to empower online abilities for the development and running of Blockchain applications. For internet providers, different Internet Service Providers (ISPs) are accessible and effectively available in the country. ISPs, for example, Surfline, Vodafone, MTN, Telesol, Busy, Blu, and so forth, are accessible with different branches everywhere throughout the country. Services of these ISPs are effectively affordable and accessible since their network coverage covers most places in the country. A respondent commented that:

you will need access to cloud services, and you will also need some good development machines. So, what will happen is you get machines on the cloud, and you get companies like Microsoft and IBM that offer Blockchain-as-a-Service (Baas). So, once you have these, you can start experimenting with the technology.

Another respondent revealed that:

When you are developing Blockchain you need two things, development machines like an i7 processor, 1 TB HDD, and an 8-16 GB, then you would have to install what they call a test net or a testing Blockchain, and then you have the actual one which you might like to host on a cloud because if you host it locally, you would need a lot of storage and network expenses.

Technological readiness influences the readiness of institutions to adopt and implement Blockchain. This is affirmed by studies (Molla & Licker, 2005; Boateng et al., 2011), expressing that a firms' technology position will go far to influence the readiness of firms to adopt a technology.

Concerning BEER, Technological Readiness influences the initial adoption of Blockchain.

Market Forces Readiness

With Market readiness, this research identified two issues from the findings acquired, which will be talked about in connection to this variable. These issues are the incorporation of blockchain into the firm's business process and the level of difficulty using utilizing blockchain. These issues, contingent upon the industry they operate in, would impact their readiness to adopt and implement blockchain to fit business needs. Considering the degree of difficulty in utilizing blockchain, the technology was found to be anything but difficult to utilize. Most firms that have incorporated the innovation into their business model intending to utilize it (blockchain) to tackle issues that exist in their industries and these institutions usually are tech startups. These firms offer their software solutions to take care of the industry-related issues, which is supported by the blockchain innovation. A respondent said:

Land records are stored in a centralized database with no additional benefits other than being a paper registry. It is virtually impossible to collateralize property rights in Ghana because the paper registry system is unenforceable in court.

Another stated that:

IBM and the Ghanaian government have signed an MOU to replace the existing centralized and paper-based land registry process with an entirely new Blockchain-based land administration system.

Another commented that:

BenBen is a team of motivated engineers and innovators dedicated to improving Government Technology in Ghana. We focus on Land & Property Management as we aim to create reliable land information and transaction system.... Bitland uses Blockchain to register local land. Bitland cooperates with local authorities to help record property rights in a decentralized, immutable format.

Blockchain technology, having features like Storing of digital duplicates of verified land title, land Registry tracking ownership, and archiving the procedure for land records, can get rid of these mediators and ensure trust and transparency in the system. Market readiness majorly influences the readiness of firms to adopt Blockchain. This is argued by Molla and Licker (2005), expressing that there is a critical influence on the readiness to adopt and implement Blockchain. Once more, Humphrey, Mansell, Pare and Schmitz (2003) discovered that pressures, for example, technological advances will help in the adoption of an innovation that will prompt its usage.

Concerning BEER, Market Readiness influences the initial adoption of Blockchain.

Educational Readiness

Concerning education, this research analyzes two issues being: the required courses needed to be knowledgeable to develop blockchain applications and where one can access these courses/computer programs.

Concerning the courses expected to help acquire skills in building Blockchain applications, the current research found that one ought to be educated in programming, for example, Solidarity, C++, Python, and so on. A few projects and boot camps are organized to become a Blockchain engineer, and these are Ethereum Developer Masterclass - Build Real-World Projects, Become a Blockchain Developer with Ethereum and Solidity, Blockchain for Business, IBM Blockchain Foundation for Developers, and so forth. These courses are organized to help people with no IT foundation progress toward becoming Blockchain developers toward the finish of the course. This likewise helps by furnishing the ordinary individual with blockchain development abilities to have the option to create Blockchain applications. In any case, there are courses accessible for non-technical people who need to comprehend the operations of Blockchain. A respondent said:

the end goal is to develop blockchain-related applications, any programming language, and some platforms. There is a platform called ethereum.org, and it uses a programming language called solidity, and these are some of the things you need to know... you need to be competent in one programming language and once you are competent with one, you can pick the basis of any Blockchain-related development tool easily.

Also, in connection to where to get to these courses, there are online platforms. Online platforms are incredible in acquiring information. Blockchain courses can be accessed everywhere throughout the web, either paid or free. E-learning Platforms, for example, Coursera, Udemy, Edx, BlockGeeks, Youtube, and so on, are few worth mentioning. This approach is most basic because these platforms permit self-managed learning where an individual can feel free and gain understanding dependent on the person's capacities. Likewise, there are brick and mortar schools like the Knowledge Academy, unichrone, and Entirety Technologies who offer physical training based on people who need to acquire Blockchain advancement abilities. A respondent revealed that:

others have also developed themselves through online educational platforms such as Lynda, IBM, and Coursera. Through these platforms, individuals have acquired programming skills to help them take advantage of Blockchain.

Another said:

You have developers like me, teaching the technical side, and some more business-minded people teaching the business skills and general awareness of its potential benefits.

Educational readiness supposedly has influenced the readiness to adopt Blockchain as in, after the skills have been gained, it tends to be diverted in the development of Blockchain solutions. This is affirmed by Ruhizan et al. (2014), expressing that without adequate information of the technology, it will be a constraint in the adoption of the Blockchain. Procuring quality information derived from learning through education and assessing the new information obtained can exceedingly influencing the utilization of technology.

Concerning BEER, Educational Readiness influences the initial adoption of Blockchain.

Table 4 outlines the summary of the findings of the study.

Below is a summary of the external influencing factors from the analysis and discussions. It displays the external influencing factors that influence the readiness of institutions to adopt Blockchain technology.

FUTURE RESEARCH DIRECTIONS

It is recommended that further research can receive the quantitative methodology from having a more prominent example size of firms just as people or both to generalize concerning Blockchain adoption.

Table 4. Summary of findings

Construct	Variables	Influencing Factors	Lessons Obtained
Blockchain External E-Readiness	Governmental Readiness	• Policies & Regulations • Government initiative on technology	The implementation of regulations and policies are necessary to successfully guide the readiness to adopt and proper implementation of Blockchain. The move on the part of the Government to implement Blockchain in its Land registry institution will boost the confidence of firms and positively influence the readiness to the adoption of the technology by other firms.
	Technological Readiness	• Affordability of IT resources • Availability of IT resources • Accessibility of IT resources	Technological readiness addresses the adoption and implementation of Blockchain due to the level of affordability, availability, and accessibility of IT resources.
	Market Readiness	• Efficiency of technology • Extent of usage	Firms are ready to adopt Blockchain due to its features, which are essential in their industry to provide services.
	Educational Readiness	• Availability of Learning Platforms • Accessibility to relevant courses	The necessary learning materials to aid in the skills acquisition are available to equip firms to adopt Blockchain

CONCLUSION

The objective of this study was to analyze the status factors that impact the readiness to adopt and implement Blockchain in firms and likewise to build up a theory-based understanding of Blockchain technology readiness in developing economies. This study uses a conceptual framework that develops the Perceived E-Readiness Model; hence, may inform future research on the readiness to adopt the Blockchain technology and other technologies alike. It was clear that Blockchain was being used actively by some institutions, and others are also in line to leverage its benefits. The variables analyzed, also revealed that government readiness, market forces readiness, technological readiness, and educational readiness heavily influence these institutions in Ghana on their readiness to adopt and implement Blockchain technology.

This study reacts to the gap of limited research work done in the field of Blockchain in developing economies by utilizing the external elements of PERM. For practitioners, this study fills in as a guideline for firms that are anticipating the adoption and implementation of Blockchain innovation. For policy, the findings give away of how regulators can present an assessment party in a Blockchain business network to track appropriate tax documenting by the business parties in the Blockchain network. Also, the findings provide a change in the educational curriculum to suit Blockchain training.

REFERENCES

Azogu, I., Norta, A., Papper, I., Longo, J., & Draheim, D. (2019). A Framework for the Adoption of Blockchain Technology in Healthcare Information Management Systems: A Case Study of Nigeria. In *Proceedings of the 12th International Conference on Theory and Practice of Electronic Governance* (pp. 310-316). ACM. 10.1145/3326365.3326405

Boateng, R., Heeks, R., Molla, A., & Hinson, R. (2011). Advancing E-Commerce Beyond Readiness in a Developing Country. *Journal of Electronic Commerce in Organizations*, *9*(1), 1–16. doi:10.4018/jeco.2011010101

Boateng, R., Molla, A., & Heeks, R. (2009). E-commerce in Developing Economies: A Review of Theoretical Frameworks and Approaches. In K. Rouibah, O. Khalil, & H. Ella (Eds.), *Emerging Markets, and E-commerce in Developing Economies*. Hershey, PA: IGI Publishing. doi:10.4018/978-1-60566-100-1.ch001

Buterin, V. (2015). *On Public and Private Blockchains*. Retrieved from https://blog.ethereum.org/2015/08/07/on-public-and-private-Blockchains/

Chen, G., Xu, B., Lu, M., & Chen, N. S. (2018). Exploring blockchain technology and its potential applications for education. *Smart Learning Environments*, *5*(1), 1. doi:10.118640561-017-0050-x

Collins, A. (2017). *Four reasons to question the hype around Blockchain*. https://www. weforum. org/agenda/2017/07/four-reasons-to-question-the-hype-around-blockchain

Connolly, A., & Kick, A. (2015). *What Differentiates Early Organization Adopters of Bitcoin From Non-Adopters?* Academic Press.

Doe, J., van de Wetering, R., Honyenuga, B., Versendaal, J., & Boateng, R. (2018). *Delphi Panel Discussion of F-TAM: Industry Experts and Academic Perspectives*. Academic Press.

Duranti, L., & Rogers, C. (2012). Trust in digital records: An increasingly cloudy legal area. *Computer Law & Security Report*, *28*(5), 522–531. doi:10.1016/j.clsr.2012.07.009

Francisconi, M. (2017). *An explorative study on blockchain technology in application to port logistics*. Academic Press.

Gräther, W., Kolvenbach, S., Ruland, R., Schütte, J., Torres, C., & Wendland, F. (2018). Blockchain for Education: Lifelong Learning Passport. In W. Prinz & P. Hoschka (Eds.), *Proceedings of the 1st ERCIM Blockchain Workshop 2018, Reports of the European Society for Socially Embedded Technologies*. Doi:10.18420/blockchain2018_07

Grech, A., & Camilleri, A. F. (2017). *Blockchain in education*. Academic Press.

Gupta, V. (2017). A brief history of blockchain. *Harvard Business Review*, 28.

Harpool, R. (2017). *Perceptions of Distributed Ledger Technology by Financial Professionals With Fiduciary Responsibilities at Select institutions of Higher Education.* ProQuest LLC.

Hileman, G. (2016). *State of Blockchain Q1 2016: Blockchain Funding Overtakes Bitcoin – CoinDesk.* Retrieved from https://www.coindesk.com/state-of-Blockchain-q1-2016/

Hollenstein, H. (2002). *Determinants of the adoption of information and communication technologies (ICT): An empirical analysis based on firm-level data for the Swiss business sector.* KOF Working Papers, No. 60. ETH Zurich, KOF Swiss Economic Institute.

Jamsrandorj, U. (2017). *Decentralized access control using blockchain* (Master's thesis, University of Saskatchewan, Saskatoon). Retrieved from https://ecommons.usask.ca/bitstream/handle/10388/8087/JAMSRANDORJ-THESIS 2017.pdf?sequence=1

Khudnev, E. (2017). *Blockchain: Foundational technology to change the world* (Master's thesis, Lapland University of Applied Sciences). Retrieved from https://www.theseus.fi/bitstream/handle/10024/138043/Evgenii_Khudnev_Thesis.pdf?sequence=1

Kuan, K. K. Y., & Chau, P. Y. K. (2001). A Perception-based Model for EDI Adoption in Small Business Using a Technology-Organization-environment Framework. *Information & Management, 38*(8), 507–512. doi:10.1016/S0378-7206(01)00073-8

Kuhn, T. S. (1962). The structure of scientific revolutions. *Journal of the History of the Behavioral Sciences, 2,* 274–276.

Lemieux, V. L. (2016). Trusting records: Is Blockchain technology the answer? *Records Management Journal, 26*(2), 110–139. doi:10.1108/RMJ-12-2015-0042

Meijer, D.B. (2017). *Consequences of the implementation of blockchain technology.* Academic Press.

Molla, A., & Licker, P. S. (2005a). e-Commerce Adoption in Developing economies: A Model and Instrument. *Information & Management, 42*(6), 877–899. doi:10.1016/j.im.2004.09.002

Molla, A., & Licker, P. S. (2014). Perceived E-Readiness Factors in E-Commerce Adoption. *An Empirical Investigation in a Developing Country Perceived E-Readiness Factors in E-Commerce Adoption : An Empirical Investigation in a, 4415.* doi:10.1080/10864415.2005.11043963

Mulligan, C. (2017). *Blockchain and Digital Transformation.* Retrieved from Imperial College London website: https://www.imperial.ac.uk/media/imperial-college/research-and-innovation/thinkspace/public/1000_Catherine-Mulligan.pdf

Nakamoto, S. (2008). *Bitcoin: A Peer-to-Peer Electronic Cash System.* Academic Press.

Reijers, W., & Coeckelbergh, M. (2016). The Blockchain as a Narrative Technology: Investigating the Social Ontology and Normative Configurations of Cryptocurrencies. *Philosophy & Technology,* 1–28.

Rejeb, A. (2018). Blockchain Potential in Tilapia Supply Chain in Ghana. *Acta Technica Jaurinensis, 11*(2), 104–118. doi:10.14513/actatechjaur.v11.n2.462

Rooksby, J., & Dimitrov, K. (2017). Trustless education? A blockchain system for university grades. In *New Value Transactions*. Understanding and Designing for Distributed Autonomous Organisations, Workshop at DIS.

Sharples, M., & Domingue, J. (2016, September). The blockchain and kudos: A distributed system for educational record, reputation, and reward. In *European Conference on Technology Enhanced Learning* (pp. 490-496). Springer. 10.1007/978-3-319-45153-4_48

Turk, Ž., & Klinc, R. (2017). Potentials of blockchain technology for construction management. *Procedia Engineering, 196*, 638–645. doi:10.1016/j.proeng.2017.08.052

Underwood, S. (2016). Blockchain Beyond Bitcoin. *Communications of the ACM, 59*(11), 15–17. doi:10.1145/2994581

Vernon, W. (2009). The Delphi technique: A review. *International Journal of Therapy and Rehabilitation, 16*(2), 69–76. doi:10.12968/ijtr.2009.16.2.38892

Wardlow, G. (1989). Alternative Modes of Inquiry for Agricultural Education. *Journal of Agricultural Education, 30*(4), 2–7. doi:10.5032/jae.1989.04002

Whitman, N.I. (1990). The committee meeting alternative: Using the Delphi technique. *Journal of Advanced Nursing, 20*(7-8), 30-36.

Yli-Huumo, J., Ko, D., Choi, S., Park, S., & Smolander, K. (2016). Where is current research on blockchain technology?—A systematic review. *PLoS One, 11*(10), e0163477. doi:10.1371/journal.pone.0163477 PMID:27695049

Yumna, H., Khan, M. M., Ikram, M., & Ilyas, S. (2019, April). Use of Blockchain in Education: A Systematic Literature Review. In *Asian Conference on Intelligent Information and Database Systems* (pp. 191-202). Springer. 10.1007/978-3-030-14802-7_17

ADDITIONAL READING

Chen, S., Yan, J., Tan, B., Liu, X., & Li, Y. (2019). Processes and challenges for the adoption of blockchain technology in food supply chains: A thematic analysis. iConference 2019 Proceedings.

Chod, J., Trichakis, N., Tsoukalas, G., Aspegren, H., & Weber, M. (2019). On the financing benefits of supply chain transparency and blockchain adoption. *Management Science*.

Hughes, L., Dwivedi, Y. K., Misra, S. K., Rana, N. P., Raghavan, V., & Akella, V. (2019). Blockchain research, practice, and policy: Applications, benefits, limitations, emerging research themes, and research agenda. *International Journal of Information Management, 49*, 114–129. doi:10.1016/j.ijinfomgt.2019.02.005

Queiroz, M. M., & Wamba, S. F. (2019). Blockchain adoption challenges in supply chain: An empirical investigation of the main drivers in India and the USA. *International Journal of Information Management, 46*, 70–82. doi:10.1016/j.ijinfomgt.2018.11.021

Wüst, K., & Gervais, A. (2018, June). Do you need a Blockchain? In *2018 Crypto Valley Conference on Blockchain Technology (CVCBT)* (pp. 45-54). IEEE. 10.1109/CVCBT.2018.00011

KEY TERMS AND DEFINITIONS

Bitcoin: A computerized and worldwide form of money. It enables individuals to send or receive cash over the web, even to somebody they don't know or don't trust.

Blockchain: A public ledger of unchangeable transactions of records in a block, linked in a chain that is distributed over a public network of nodes (computers) visible to everyone on the network.

Cryptocurrency: A virtual cash intended to fill in as a model of trade.

Cryptography: A strategy for encoding data in a specific way with the goal that those for whom it is planned can peruse and process it.

Payment Gateway: An online service that facilitates cashless transactions.

Peer-to-Peer: A distributed service whereby one person communicates with another, without intermediation by an outsider.

Proof-of-Work: An algorithm used to affirm transactions and produce new blocks to the chain.

Chapter 9

Organizational Transformation in Developing Economies by New and Emerging Information Systems:
The Usage, Transformations, Impacts, Benefits, and Management

Samuel Anim-Yeboah

ⓘD https://orcid.org/0000-0002-1627-7536

Business School, University of Ghana, Ghana & Sims Technologies Ltd., Ghana

ABSTRACT

New and emerging information systems are significantly transforming organizations through new business models, opportunities, products, and services. This chapter highlights the new and emerging information systems (IS), their usage, and how they drive organizational transformation. The DeLone and McLean Model of IS Success was used as a theoretical lens to discuss existing literature on organizational transformation arising from new and emerging IS. While some organizations succumb to the introduction of the new and emerging IS with its disruptive nature, others tend to manage the changes introduced through new business models, appropriate infrastructure, skills, knowledge, enhanced data security, and effective communication. The chapter contributes to the scholarship and practice of digital transformation of organizations in developing economies.

INTRODUCTION

Organizations are significantly transformed by the unceasing use of Information Systems (IS). The development and continued innovations in the field of IS have disrupted, almost wholly, how an organization's activities are being conducted. In the recent past, many organizations that were operating with manual

DOI: 10.4018/978-1-7998-2610-1.ch009

systems have embarked on a partial or complete migration to digital information systems through what is termed as digital migration or digital transformation. Digital migration has enabled organizations to improve their competitiveness since the dynamics in the markets have increasingly changed over time, forcing organizations to improve their operating techniques or else face extinction.

Individuals and organizations are challenged with new and emerging technologies as they are rapidly being introduced to the current computer and digital era, which is transforming people's lives and thinking and also changing organizations (Pettenati & Cigognini, 2018). The decision to migrate to digital space by organizations that were previously operating with manual systems would be a very uninviting risk. This is because digitalization could block all the customers that are not knowledgeable about the use of the technology. Meanwhile, organizations that migrate to the use of new and emerging technologies improve their efficiency, irrespective of the industry type. Hence, their respective consumers have increased with the introduction of such technologies in the market.

With hastened globalization and inevitable market changes, organizations that were established before the introduction of innovative IS have had to improve their systems. This is done in order to be at the same level as the new ones and offer significant market competitiveness to new brands that are being introduced in the market (Archibugi & Michie, 1997). The digital migration is necessitated by the fact that in recent times Information Technology (IT) is at the center of how business is done and how the business model itself evolves. Additionally, organizations cannot shun away from the digitization processes unless the organizations are no longer interested in making substantive profits. The organizational transformations due to new and emerging information systems have led to the significant growth of developing economies as a result of the emergence of entirely new business fields when such technologies are embraced. This outcome has widened the capabilities of organizations, whereby new operations are introduced to meet changing demands from consumers. Notably, the transformations have also been necessitated by the inevitable need to endure market dynamics. Most organizations integrate IS in their operational systems to improve service delivery to their consumers. Apart from the improvement of the previous operations and services of existing organizations, new organizations altogether have also emerged in developing economies. With increased employment opportunities being created by these new and emerging IS, the developing economies have increased their development potential.

It is also important to mention that organizations must develop measures to ensure seamless transformation when new and emerging IS are introduced. The significance of managing the transformation is to ensure that the workers become conversant with the new ways of operating and that there is no misuse of these technologies, which have the potential of denting the organization's position in the market. Therefore, management of such emerging technologies like social media platforms is essential because once incorrect or malicious information is relayed through such platforms, it is almost impossible to retract it when it has already reached millions of users. The new and emerging IS have led to positive organizational transformations that have increased competitiveness, output quality, and efficiency.

This chapter seeks to elucidate the new and emerging information systems and their usage, expound on how they drive organizational transformation, emphasize on the impact and benefits of the digital transformation, and also show how the transformations can be managed, in the developing countries context. An attempt is made to achieve the purpose by answering the questions: What are the new and emergent information systems and their applications? How do digital technologies drive organizational transformation? What are the impacts and consequences of digital transformation? How should organizations manage the effects of the transformations? The chapter, therefore, highlights some of the most typical new and emerging IS and gives a detailed description of how these technologies have caused vivid transformations and impacted organizations in different sectors of developing economies. The impacts, benefits, and consequences of the transformation, as well as the management of the effects, are further discussed.

THEORETICAL FRAMEWORK AND METHODOLOGICAL APPROACHES

Theoretical Framework

The study is underpinned by the Updated DeLone and McLean Model of Information Systems Success, which is a popular framework and model for measuring the complex dependent variable in IS research. The Model of Information Systems Success was initially proposed by William H. DeLone and Ephraim R. McLean in 1992 based on a review and integration of 180 research studies (DeLone & McLean, 1992). It was revised a decade later, following feedback and critiques from other scholars to what is now known as the Updated DeLone and McLean Model of Information Systems Success (D & M IS Success Model) (DeLone & McLean, 2003).

The D & M IS Success Model is appropriate for studying the impact and management of new and emergent IS. This is because it provides a comprehensive understanding of IS success, by identifying, describing, and explaining the relationships among the most critical dimensions of success, along which IS are usually evaluated (DeLone & McLean, 2003). The updated D & M IS Success Model categorizes IS success into seven (7) dimensions, which are: information quality, system quality, service quality, intention to use, use, user satisfaction, and net benefits. These are grouped as quality dimensions, use dimensions, and net benefits. A diagrammatical representation of the updated D & M IS Success Model is presented in Figure 1.

The quality dimensions of IS (information quality, system quality and service quality) affect the Use dimensions of IS (intention to use, the use and the user satisfaction) which further determine the impacts and benefits of IS, hence reflecting the success of IS introduction (DeLone & McLean, 2003). Positive experience with using an IS will lead to increased user satisfaction and then positive net benefits. However, if there are negative experiences, user satisfaction will reduce, and there will be discontinuation of the use of the IS. For a successful new and emerging IS, the IS quality dimension (information quality, system quality, and service quality) are expected to be positive to enhance user satisfaction and intention to use the IS. The user satisfaction and intention to use the IS, in turn, impact the extent to which the system yield benefits for the user and subsequently, the organization at large.

This comprehensive and dynamic relationship of IS success dimensions by the D & M IS Success Model is critical to understanding the value and efficacy of IS management actions and IS investments by organizations. Thus, in evaluating the impact, benefits, and management of the new and emergent IS on organization, the D&M IS Success Model provides a useful framework for conceptualizing and operationalizing IS success. The application of The D & M IS Success Model in this study provided a framework for identifying, synthesizing and reporting the success, impact, benefits, and management of new and emerging IS on organizational transformation with a focus on developing countries.

Figure 1. The Updated D&M IS Success Model
Source: DeLone and McLean (2003)

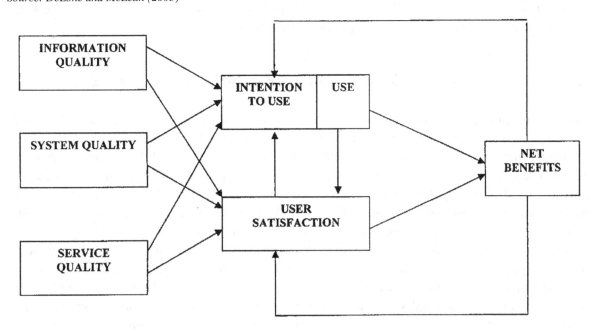

Methodological Approach

This chapter was developed using a narrative review approach to elucidate, highlight, discuss, and sum-marize existing literature on the subject of organizational transformation arising from new and emerging IS. The chapter thus relied entirely on secondary information from publications, reports, and anecdotal findings on how new and emerging information systems result in organizational transformation, the benefits and consequences of the transformation, and how the transformations are managed within the context of developing countries. The development of the chapter followed the six (6) generic steps for conducting review outlined by Templier and Paré (2015) viz: "formulating the research question(s) and objective(s); searching the extant literature; screening for inclusion; assessing the quality of primary studies; extracting data, and analyzing data." The search and review also considered the Paré and Kitsiou (2017) three approaches to searching the literature for review papers viz. exhaustive, representative coverage, and analysis of documents central to the particular topic.

In this chapter, the literature search involved the review of prior works that have been central or pivotal to organizational transformation through new and emerging information technologies, emphasizing the usage, transformations, impacts, benefits, and the management of the transformation. Thus, the search was not intended to examine all studies done on the topic but the identification of critical studies that are pivotal to understanding the process of organizational change due to new and emerging information technologies, especially within developing countries context. In screening the articles for inclusion, three independent reviewers were used, in line with each reviewer being given a set of predetermined rules for including or excluding certain studies based on Liberati et al. (2009) recommendation. The selected studies were also assessed for their scientific quality by appraising the vigor of the research design and methods. After evaluating the quality of the primary studies, data extraction was done by eliciting the information in each article that addresses the objectives of the study and the themes outlined for the literature review. Analysis and synthesis of the data were done by collating, organizing, and comparing the evidence extracted from the included studies on each theme.

NEW AND EMERGING INFORMATION SYSTEMS AND THEIR USAGE

There are numerous new and emerging information systems and digital technologies around the world. The adoption of such technologies in organizational practices depends on their value and alignment to the organizations' goals, missions, and objectives. The value and alignment of the systems to organizations also depend on the quality of the systems or technologies themselves, the quality of information churned out and the quality of the service experienced by the organizations. These, in turn, influence the intention to use the technologies, the usage of the technologies, the nature and extent of user satisfaction, and eventually, the impact and net benefits (DeLone & McLean, 2003).

Some of the most common new and emerging technologies include internet, cloud computing, mobile computing, Internet of Things, social media, social commerce, artificial intelligence, robotics, big data analytics, 3-D printing, blockchain, and smart devices. Others include user-generated content, fake news networks, social media journalism, video search, video content, virtual/augmented reality, and pre-cognitive technologies, and Data Security technologies among several others (Yaeger, Martini, Rasouli, & Costa, 2019). The system, information and service qualities of some of these technologies, their usage and user satisfaction, impacts, and benefits would be discussed further.

Internet

The Internet as digital technology is made up of a global system of interconnected networks of computers that use the Internet protocol suite (TCP/IP) of Transmission Control Protocol (TCP) and the Internet Protocol (IP) to link devices worldwide (Dutton, 2013; Leiner et al., 2009). The internet comprises a network of networks that consists of public, private, business, academic and government networks, and of local to global scope, linked by a broad array of electronic, wireless, and optical networking technologies. The invention of the internet significantly caused the rapid technological growth that has since been experienced in the world all over, particularly in terms of social and commercial communication (Yılmaz, Sirel & Esen, 2019). Through the internet, several technologies and operations have been enabled, such as cloud computing, social commerce, e-commerce, social media journalism, data mining, fake news networks, among others.

Most importantly, the internet has impacted the lives of people as a result of the access to information that has significantly improved in the last two or three decades. In Africa, the impact is indeed significant, considering the number of smartphone ownership and membership in social media sites. Internet connectivity and penetration over the last five years has increased fundamentally. The world's average internet penetration is 56.1%, while Africa's penetration rate is 35.9%, with 60.2% being for the rest of the world (Internet World Stats, 2019). Although the African rates seem relatively lower compared to the rest of the world, it is such a significant improvement compared to the growth rate and future projections.

The significance of internet connectivity in business and government organizations is indeed immense. In many business organizations, most of the functions rely on internet connectivity. The internet-enabled e-procurement system, for example, reduces the cost of production and increases the net benefit of businesses. Further, through internet connectivity, business communication becomes instant, reducing the time for most business activities.

The internet has also enhanced the global integration of Africa into the rest of the world. Through globalization and international trade, many companies have established offshore subsidiaries, all of which are effectively managed by constant communication, which is enabled by the internet. Board and management meetings can occur instantly through video conferences without the necessity of the physical presence of every member. Public organizations in Africa are also using the internet to enhance service delivery to their citizens. In some developing countries, application and renewal of driving license and passport are no longer done manually. In Kenya, for example, there is an online platform called e-citizen, which enables the citizens to access several government services through the internet (Ondego & Moturi, 2016). Many corporate employees and workers in government institutions, as well as non-employed citizens, have been able to access and enhance their education through the internet, as several universities in both developed and developing countries offer online courses for students.

Cloud Computing

Cloud computing is one of the new and emerging IS that provides on-demand availability of computer system resources, which include data storage and computing power without direct active management by the user or organization (Avram, 2014). The term "cloud" is used to describe data centers over the internet that are available anytime and anywhere to many different users in an organization ("enterprise cloud") or open to the general public ("public cloud") (Avram, 2014; Trivedi, 2013; Wang, He, & Wang, 2012). Cloud computing is one of the fastest-growing IS in recent years following an increase in hardware virtualization inspired by high-capacity network availability, low-cost computers, and storage devices (Knorr & Gruman, 2008). One primary reason for the increased usage of cloud technologies is that it allows users to benefit from all of the available technologies in the cloud, even with little or in-depth knowledge or expertise with each one of the technologies. Thus, even in places, especially in developing countries where technology infrastructure and expertise are seldom available, people nevertheless can reap the full benefits of IS technologies in the cloud.

In both developed and developing countries, the use of cloud services has allowed many organizations to cut down costs and focus more on their core business without been impeded by IT obstacles (Jones, Irani, Sivarajah, & Love, 2017). However, for organizations to reap the full benefit from cloud servers, organizational changes are inevitable (Jones et al., 2017; Dimitrov & Osman, 2012).). The usage of cloud service results in organizational transformation leading to changes in roles and responsibilities of staff with less technical roles required in the organization. In contrast, new roles such as technical engineers for Platform as a Service (PaaS) and functional managers for Software as a Service (SaaS), services emerge. Dependence on cloud service has an impact on skills required of both IT and business personnel with the gradual decrease in technically skilled employees and the focus of business shifting from technical knowledge to service orchestration (Zhu, 2017).

According to Muhammed, Zaharaddeen, Rumana, and Turaki (2015), cloud computing is suited for developing countries, especially those in Africa as a result of the lack of high technology infrastructures, less availability of IT competencies and ease of implementation. Other threats, however, include the need for immediate access to the latest innovations and the possibility for an organization to do away with substantial investment in infrastructure. Reliance on cloud servers by firms requires improvement in employees' existing skills or completely reskilling of employees whose job descriptions change because of the introduction of cloud computing services (Zhu, 2017). For many such firms, the usage of cloud computing services results in changes in the organizational structure or organogram, sizes, culture, values, and vision, among others (Jones et al., 2017). The resulting outcome of this organizational transformation propelled by cloud computing services among many firms in Africa is that enterprise IT budgets are shrunk or reallocated to more strategic projects. Also, enterprise IT staffs are reduced or reskilled to meet new requirements, or hardware distribution are changed radically to meet the requirements of new IT hardware buying points (Abubakar, Bass, & Allison, 2014; Adam & Musah, 2015: Gillwald, Moyo, Odufuwa, Frempong, & Kamoun. 2014).

Mobile Apps

Mobile apps or mobile applications constitute new and emerging technologies that are playing significant roles in developing economies. Mobile apps are computer programs or application software that is designed in such a way that they can run on mobile devices such as smartphones and tablet among others (Baktha, 2017; Feigin, 2008; Islam, Islam, & Mazumder, 2010; Sturm et al., 2018). Mobile applications were originally intended to be informational and productivity assistant applications, supporting email, calendar, and contact databases. However, high demands have resulted in many diverse usages, including mobile games, factory automation, GPS and location-based services, sales, and purchasing platforms, among others (Inukollu, Keshamoni, Kang, & Inukollu, 2014). Commercial usage of mobile apps has resulted in many companies using mobile apps to ensure quick and easy delivery of their products and services, thereby impacting their profitability (Baktha, 2017). Mobiles apps have been used in various sectors such as hospitality, finance, healthcare, and transportation, among others.

The mobile apps integrated with maps, GPS, and communication features have made it easy for riders as well as drivers to communicate and schedule trips, with convenience and efficiency. Pickups and the entire trip are monitored by the passenger, driver, and the host company. Payment can be made directly with cash or electronically with a credit card or mobile money. A typical example is the UBER taxi mobile app service, which though originated in a developed country but has now become very popular in several developing countries (Henama, & Sifolo, 2017; Smith, 2016). CURB is another travel company that uses a mobile app to enhance its transportation system. Other companies that are international and also popular in developing countries include BOLT (formerly Taxify), Easy Taxi, and Tranzit. Several other local companies in several developing countries have also come up with the taxi service via mobile apps, including Afro Cab in Nigeria (Adewumi, Odunjo, & Misra, 2015). Capitalizing on the increased use of smartphones and mobile apps, the emergence of such service providers have changed the scope of doing taxi business worldwide. The traditional taxi business has been entirely disrupted by the introduction of digital taxi services in major cities across the world. New disruptive technology and business model has, therefore evolved, which has been of immense benefit to developing countries, offering convenience (Kavadias, Ladas, & Loch, 2016; Nagy, Schuessler, & Dubinsky, 2016). Consumers have increasingly embraced the new technology due to its efficiency and quality outcomes while creating employment and income opportunities for drivers and car owners in developing countries (Alkhalisi, 2019).

Social Media

Social media arguably is the most popular and dynamic technology that has emerged in the last two to three decades. Obar and Wildman (2015) defined social media as a computer-mediated technology that provides interactive platform use in the sharing and creation of information, ideas, interests, opinions, among others, through networks of virtual communities. Social media uses interactive web 2.0 Internet-based applications and relies on user-generated content in forms of text, videos, photos, among others (Kaplan, & Haenlein, 2010). The most distinctive features of social media are that it creates a platform that enables users to connect with other users, groups, and organizations, therefore, leading to the development of several online social networks (Obar & Wildman, 2015). The social network creation that is facilitated by social media is its lifeblood. Social media users access social media services through web-based technologies using desktop or laptop computers or smartphones or tablets or downloaded mobile apps that offer social media functionality. The global expansion of internet access and access to mobile devices such as smartphones have revolutionized and greatly enhanced access to social media services in recent years (Ortutay, 2012).

There is no doubt that social media influences the economy and the way businesses operate. Social media has been used as engagement as well as a communication platform for both consumers and suppliers (Azemi & Ozuem, 2015). Research shows that, since the invention of social media, most people spend a lot of their time online. This is the result of the rise in the production of smartphones as mobile companies such as Samsung, Huawei, and Apple are releasing smartphones every year (Azemi & Ozuem, 2015). In developing countries, social media platforms such as Twitter and Facebook are gaining increasing attention and usage over the years (Bolton et al., 2013). This shows how fast social media is growing, and companies have taken advantage of this trend and have used such platforms to advertise their products (Siamagka, Christodoulides, Michaelidou, & Valvi, 2015). This has made it easy to attract new consumers, and therefore, the economy is easily fueled, and brands have expanded with the use of social media (Moncrief, Marshall, & Rudd, 2015).

Hospitality companies have much embraced social media to advertise their business. Before the invention of social media, hotels, and other hospitality companies depended on brands and reviews from loyal guests to advertise their services. However, social media has changed this as consumers can help create a reputation in any given company (Van Doorn et al., 2017). This is because consumers can express the experience, whether enjoyment or frustration on social media, which makes it difficult for these companies to avoid social media. Furthermore, hospitality companies in developing countries find social media a cost-effective platform of engagement compared to having their websites and e-commerce platforms. Hence hospitality businesses are using popular social media platforms like Facebook, Instagram, and Twitter to advertise their products (Dwivedi, Yadav, & Venkatesh, 2011).

These social media platforms are giving businesses in many sectors a great exposure to consumers and attracting new customers. Furthermore, most companies have shifted their focus to social media influencers to help them advertise. This method of advertisement is cheaper than celebrity endorsement and an easy way to sway the way consumers behave. Moreover, influencers can engage in conversation with consumers, and therefore, consumers find it easy to trust them than celebrities.

It is essential to emphasize the use of social media as a fundamental trend. In the African context, social media makes up for the low usage of big data analytics and is mainly used by small and medium-sized enterprises as it enhances the interaction between targeted clients and marketers. In a study which examined the impact of social media on performance; and the related drivers for successful implementation, in Ghana, Odoom, Anning-Dorson and Acheampong (2017), showed that many SMEs were using the online platform, particularly Facebook, Instagram and Twitter to market their products. However, the strategy used varied depending on the nature of the brand. For SMEs who deal with physical products, the social media sites were used mostly for advertisement. In contrast, service-based SMEs, the social sites were mainly used for interaction with customers to enhance performance. Similar findings were also reported by Awiagah, Kang, and Lim (2016), who found that most organizations, both government and private, use social media for various purposes.

Social Commerce

Social commerce is one of the most fundamental marketing tools used by most companies today, both in developed and developing countries. Social commerce can be regarded as a part or subset of the general electronic commerce, except for the purchase options since, in most cases, it does not cover the same (Hajli, 2015). Social commerce is one of the latest trends in e-commerce created using social media to allow customers to interact on the Internet. The recent improvements in ICTs and the advent of Web 2.0 technologies, together with the popularity of social networking sites and social media, have seen the development of new social platforms (Hajli, 2015). Primarily, it enables companies to use their customers' social behavior as a way of engaging them with their brand (Baethge, Klier, & Klier, 2016; Han & Trimi, 2017).

Social commerce often contains interactive media segments where the customers can talk about a particular brand. Sometimes, a company may use celebrity endorsement to create reviews about a specific brand, with the hope that his or her followers are likely to be interested in the product or service. Other than strategies such as celebrity endorsements, social commerce also allows personal review by clients who have had experience with a given brand. From such reviews, other customers intending to use the brand can also make their decision for or against the same.

In Africa, social commerce has indeed had a significant impact on organizational performance, mainly as a result of the high number of smartphone owners and access to the internet as well. As of 2017, the number of mobile phone subscribers had reached 44% of the total African population compared to 25% when the decade started (Pitchford, Chigeda, & Hubber, 2019). Currently, Ghana is considered one of the countries in the world with the most significant mobile penetration at a rate of 119%; and the rate is expected to reach 130% by 2020. This implies the importance of Ghana in Africa concerning technological growth with such significant mobile penetration and usage (Tamakloe, 2018).

Internet of Things

The internet of things (IoT) means the internet connectivity of various technological devices, mechanical and digital machines, objects, animals or people, and any other gadget that is designed and enabled to connect to the internet (Hendricks, 2015). Internet of things entails platforms that link multiple sensors and data devices to generate a complete vision of the behavior of an organization, a system, a business operation, or a phenomenon (Katz, 2017). The Internet of things provides a system that enables the transfer of data without human-to-human or human-to-computer interaction. As one of the new and emerging IS technologies, the Internet of things has been applied in developing countries with an attempt to boost their economy (Miazi, Erasmus, Razzaque, Zennaro, & Bagula, 2016; Weinman, 2016).

According to Dang, Piran, Han, Min, & Moon (2019) Internet of things involves the connection of ordinary or physical devices to computer devices, so they can communicate and be monitored. One common application is precision agriculture (which controls fertilizer application, monitors rain, and determines the most appropriate harvest). Another application is smart cities (which allow the control of traffic flows or manage energy use in public places), and telemedicine (which monitor hospital patients health) (Katz, 2017). Ahmed (2019) has noted that the Internet of things has brought a transformation in the way developing countries distribute their products such as water, aid, food as well as energy.

There are three domains in which developing economies are putting the internet of things into practice, which are social, financial, and environmental (Bonilla, Silva, Terra da Silva, Franco Gonçalves, & Sacomano, 2018). There are various ways in which the internet of things is improving development work, such as health, farming, disaster management, as well as wildlife management. For example, India uses a 'nexleaf' to monitor vaccines' temperature before they are transported to rural clinics (Goodier, 2016). This device is connected to a computer and transfer the temperature information via GPRS and gives a warning in case the temperatures are not favorable. Commonsense net or remote sensor is used in most developing countries for farming. Countries such as India use this device to measure humidity, the moisture content in the soil as well as other conditions that may lead to crop failures (Mital, Chang, Choudhary, Papa, & Pani, 2018). The sensor is connected to the computer, and data collected can readily be displayed on the project's website. For disaster management, devices such as kinetic sensors have been developed to quickly warn people against a tsunami (Goodier, 2016). The sensors measure how the water and the waves in the ocean flow. In case of a potential tsunami, the sensor transmits information to a floating disk on the ocean, which then transfers data to a computer. Therefore, such devices can help manage disasters in areas around oceans and seas in developing countries (Goodier, 2016). IoT is designed to improve efficiency as well as effectiveness during the work process.

Artificial Intelligence

Artificial Intelligence (AI) is described as the simulation of human intelligence processes by machines, especially computer systems (Bowser, Sloan, Michelucci, & Pauwels, 2017; Kok, Boers, Kosters, Van der Putten, & Poel, 2009; Miailhe & Hodes, 2017). These processes include learning (which is the acquisition of information and rules for using the data), reasoning (which involves using rules to reach approximate or definite conclusions), and self-correction. Specific applications of AI include expert systems, speech recognition, machine vision, and machine learning. These are systems and machines that resemble humans in most of their works (Burns & Laskowski, 2018). They are designed to complete tasks in a much easier and faster way (Russell & Norvig, 2016). The machines have the ability to recognize voice and sound, solve problems, forecast and plan, as well as learning and imitating. Most business companies have embraced the use of artificial intelligence in their business to improve consistency in their work as well as efficiency, to ensure economic sustainability and stability.

Google has been involved in the development of artificial intelligence, and its first artificial intelligence lab in Africa has been opened in Ghana. The Internet technology giant aims to offer researchers with the needed tools to build products that can solve Africa's problems in every field, principally in health and agriculture. Most of the AI experts and hubs are based in developed countries, mainly North America, Europe, and Asia regions, but this is set to change, given that the developing world offers a lower cost of human resources. This representation in Africa will unearth AI researchers, engineers, and talent, which would help provide a solution to the continent's specific problems and offer opportunities to use AI to improve the lives of Africans (Kiunguyu, 2019).

Artificial intelligence is also being used to predict forest fire outbreak in some developing countries (Sakr, Elhajj & Mitri, 2011). Additionally, Artificial intelligence makes it easy to complete within a short time; those works that are frequently repeated, such as X-rays. Radiology and cardiology are fields in healthcare that have been improved with the use of AI due to the overwhelming amount of data (Russell & Norvig, 2016). Apart from data recording, AI plays other roles such as the detection of diseases at their early stages, the creation of drugs and prescription treatment. These help in cost reduction and hence make a positive impact on the economy and considerable potential for developing countries.

Big Data Analytics

Big data analytics is defined as the capability of processing massive data-sets to identify patterns of relationships (correlation, causality) among data to be used in detecting market trends, consumer behavior and preferences (Katz, 2017). Big data analytics is reported by many researchers as the next significant technological innovation that is set to change the world, regarding business (Kayser, Nehrke, & Zubovic, 2018; Lehrer, Wieneke, vom Brocke, Jung, & Seidel, 2018; Mikalef, Pappas, Krogstie, & Giannakos, 2018). Data sometimes exists in disarray with no specific patterns, and as such, making sense or rational decisions based on the same is often tricky. Big data analytics provides a solution to the problem. Big data provides the technical capability of analyzing the big or numerous but disarrayed data into specific patterns and correlations that makes sense and helps in decision making, especially for business organizations.

The growth rate of big data analytics utilization by both private and government organizations in developing countries remains relatively low. The growth rate in specific countries in the Middle East, including Saudi Arabia, United Arab Emirates, Qatar, and Oman, is relatively higher compared to Africa (UNDP, 2017). Big data analytics is also of crucial importance to organizations. However, its implementation in Africa is still minimal except in South Africa, Egypt, and few companies operating in West Africa, including Ghana (Luna, Mayan, García, Almerares, & Househ, 2014; Umezurike & Olusola, 2017).

Meanwhile, several companies operate in developing countries, which offer prospects for growth in big data analytics. Ghana is targeted as one of the fastest-growing economies in Sub-Saharan Africa, and the opportunities for digital growth are immense, as evidenced by IBM's 'Digital Nation Africa,' a program that seeks to educate more millennial generations in technological advancement including data analytics (UNDP, 2017). Ghana is one of the countries where the project is currently being piloted.

As mentioned earlier, digital technology is critical, especially for a commercial organization. Marketing, for example, relies heavily on big data analytics. Erevelles, Fukawa, and Swayne (2016) examined the impact of big data analytics on marketing and related companies' financial performance. The study compared the annual net profits of 100 companies, half of which rely on big data analysis to make management decisions, while the other half used conventional marketing research strategies. The results showed a significant difference in average profit earnings on firms that used big data analytics compared to those that did not. Using this technology in making marketing decisions is just one of the practical uses. Big data can be used in various organizational settings, including government organizations. For example, big data analytics can be used by government security agencies to generate critical information about security activities and make positive decisions from the same. Unfortunately, the extent of implementation of big data analytics is indeed limited in Africa. As a result, studies that can report their effect on organizational performance, and how organizations respond to the changes are few.

3-D Printing

3D printing, also called additive manufacturing, involves the process of building three-dimensional items from a computer-aided design (CAD) model. This is achieved by successively adding material layer by layer (Hamzah, Keattch, Covill, & Patel, 2018; Taufik & Jain, 2013). 3D printing is a technology that allows the creation of objects using the successive printing of adhesive materials such as polymers (Katz, 2017). 3-D is one of the new technological advancements that will be of great use when fully operationalized. The 3-D Printing mechanisms enable the use of computers to join materials to form 3-D objects. The use of 3-D Printing has improved additive manufacturing that was invented in the 1980s by ensuring that many objects, even those with complicated shapes and geometries, are being manufactured using 3-D Printing technologies (Jensen-Haxel, 2015; Ventola, 2014). The technology ensures that the cost of producing materials becomes cheaper as compared to the initial cost incurred for the processes of additive manufacturing (Jiménez, Romero, Domínguez, Espinosa, & Domínguez, 2019; Thomas, 2016; Thomas & Gilbert, 2014). For that reason, the growth being experienced in the 3-D Printing technology is immense, and shortly, most of the materials manufactured in industries will be a result of this technology (Vasquez, 2015).

The cost-effectiveness and ease of printing make 3-D Printing an attractive option for developing countries (Birtchnell & Hoyle, 2014; Ibrahim et al., 2015). Homes have been constructed using this technology, and a house which measured 400 Square foot was built in just 24 hours from the start to completion (Marr, 2018). In China, a 2-story building was entirely built using concrete and 3-D Printing technology in just 45 days (Marr, 2018). 3-D Printing could also be used to produce prosthetic limbs, bones, and organs. In India, a team of surgeons from Medanta -The Medicity, Gurugram, replaced the damaged vertebrae with 3-D printed titanium vertebrae to bridge the gap between the first and fourth cervical vertebrae. This helped the patient to walk again just four days after the complex surgery as done, which is contrary to the traditional methods which would have taken months before the patient could walk again (Medanta, 2018). In China and the USA, for example, 3-D bicycle printing has been in progress, and companies such as Arevo Company have been providing the necessary software that is required in the processes of printing such bicycles (Antonova, 2015).

The manufacturing of such products has been entirely done through IS, which reduces labor costs and increases efficiency (Attaran, 2017). This shows that 3-D printing technology could be tapped into making resourceful things and saving on the cost as well as time. It clear that 3-D printing can transform various sectors, including construction, manufacturing, transport, and health. Although the market for complete 3-D printed materials has not grown significantly in the developing economies, it is expected to increase as soon as it is embraced for mainstream manufacturing (Attaran, 2017). Although 3-D printing is an expensive technology to adopt, the developing world could still shift to it for some specific commodities, due to the higher quality and enhanced efficiency. 3D printing is commonly used in product design like medicinal prosthetics, architectural models, and textile design, as well as the development of spare parts in consumer electronics and industrial products.

ORGANIZATIONAL DIGITAL TRANSFORMATION IN DEVELOPING COUNTRIES

Technology has been identified as a critical internal dimension aiding organizational transformation globally. The role of new information and communication technologies has been widely recognized because of their rapid development and diffusion, resulting in triggering business transformation considerations within many organizations in both developed and developing nations (Morgan & Page, 2008). Most often, organizational transformation as a result of digital technology adoptions happens through small but incremental changes rather than a one-time significant change (Goerzig & Bauernhansl, 2018).

The concept of organizational transformation as a result of information technology adoption occurs when there is a fundamental change in the organizational logic, which results in or is caused by significant shifts in behaviors (McKeown & Philip 2003). Ismail, Khater, and Zaki (2017), categorized the processes of organizational transformation into four viz: adapting stage, evolving stage, envisioning stage, renewing stage. The adapting stage is where selected activities are automated, whereas the evolving stage is where ICT alignment is created. The envisioning stage, where the business network process is redesigned while the renewing stage, where the business scope is reframed. The length of time organizations spend at each of these stages differs based on the digital maturity of the organization, the nation, and the developmental context, among others.

The types of organizational transformation, according to Ismail et al. (2017), are four viz. re-engineering, restructuring, renewing, and regeneration. Re-engineering involves improving overall organizational efficiency while only partially addressing the better engagement of the workforce. The restructuring is about improving efficiency without necessarily enhancing the organizational ability to achieve its long-term goals. Renewing is also about gaining improved efficiency, effectiveness, and innovativeness through employee empowerment without a clear focus on the desired results. Regeneration involves improving existing processes and fundamentally revisiting the direction and portfolio of available opportunities. Regardless of the organization, tension is created among old competencies, present, and future challenges, in terms of norms and behaviors. According to Galliers and Leidner (2014), information systems or technology-induced organizational transformation result in changes in the entire organization. Further, top managers change their worldview of the organization and also improve their deeply embedded values and beliefs, which require a new set of skills to be built at all levels. The final process of organizational changes, according to Galliers and Leidner (2014), involves changes in management processes, including performance evaluations, rewards, career management, product development, and logistics.

Due to globalization and internationalization of business and trade, technological development and innovations are easily spread from one country to the other with almost no significant restrictions. Against this backdrop, digital technologies development and usage have been assumed to have common grounds across different geographies and developmental contexts regardless of socioeconomic, cultural, and political hindrances (Heeks, 2002). The preponderance of empirical studies in recent years shows that several factors have resulted in considerable differences in the need and nature of organizational transformation. These factors include the availability of infrastructure, sociodemographic traits, users' requirements, and business dynamics as well as national regulations. This results from different levels of adoption and usage of digital technologies in developing countries when compared with developed countries (Rachinger, Rauter, Müller, Vorraber, & Schirgi, 2018). An important factor for most of the difference in nature and extent of digital transformation, according to Parviainen, Tihinen, Kääriäinen, and Teppola (2017), is the nature of the industry and most importantly the digital maturity of the country.

Meanwhile, there is a significant variation in sociodemographic traits between nations in the developing world and that of the developed world, and these traits result in a difference in user requirements and demands for digital technology and solutions (González, Schlautmann, Casahuga & Romero, 2017). The significant difference between developing countries and that of developed countries that significantly contribute to variation in digital transformation is that in developing countries, there is less access to digital electronics, which are considered luxury goods (Acılar, 2011). There are also the issues of low trust in digital transactions and lower internet penetration in developing countries as compare with their developed countries counterparts (Gonzalez et al., 2017; Mahadevan & Venkatesh (2000).

Gonzalez et al. (2017) have indicated that the major hindrance to digital technology adoption and the level of organization transformation witnessed in developing countries include low internet access and connectivity, as well as voice-driven mobile service usage instead of data. Other hindrances include millennials' low access to and contact with technology and low access to banking and electronic payment services. Ciuriak and Ptashkina (2019) also indicated that many developing countries are now only starting to catch-up in making foundational and infrastructure investments that can accelerate the pace of digital technology adoption. Beyond the unmet infrastructure requirement, there are skills requirements for successful digital technology adoption and the nature of organizational changes inspired by developing countries.

Another aspect of digital technology adoption and the changes it brings to organizations in developing countries is the issue of intellectual property rights and royalties (Ciuriak & Ptashkina, 2019). Due to the lack of infrastructure and limited intellectual property rights over digital technologies, many organizations in developing countries rely on third-party platforms. This makes many organizations primarily rent payers and not rent earners in the global digital technology market (Baker, 2013). Notwithstanding these challenges, information system technology adoption in developing countries is increasing, and significant transformation of organizations is also witnessed.

IMPACT AND BENEFITS OF THE ORGANIZATIONAL DIGITAL TRANSFORMATION

Organizational changes or transformation as a result of digital transformation is uncomfortable because of the destructive nature of such changes, but the benefits are numerous as well. Technology and organizational change go hand in hand; therefore, for companies to enjoy the benefits of technological advances, they must have a positive quality experience, user satisfaction, and also be willing to adjust their business models and their culture in line with the conditions for a digital revolution.

A significant benefit derived from the digital transformation of organizations is that it enhances the interaction between employees and customers in a way that improves service delivery and customer loyalty (Ismail et al., 2017). The overriding observations from most of the studies of the review are that organizations change as a result of digital transformation with improved communications and nature of interactions that employees have with customers which in eventually enhance service delivery (Foerster-Metz, Marquardt, Golowko, Kompalla, & Hell, 2018; Ismail et al., 2017; Leclercq-Vandelanoitte & Plé, 2016).

At a strategic level, the digital transformation of organizations has also been noted to have resulted in improvement in management decisions by enabling organizations to have access to their big data and information from the Internet of Things (Nylén & Holmström, 2015). Effective decision making requires quick access to adequate and accurate data or information and flexibility of operational activities. According to Kane, Palmer, Phillips, Kiron, & Buckley (2015), companies often disseminate new digital technologies for improved decision-making when transforming operations and organizations. The above position is supported by Kaufman and Horton (2015) and Kohli and Johnson (2011).

Most often, the newly shaped organizational culture resulting from digital transformation creates a more flexible and employee-friendly work environment and enhance knowledge sharing as a result of virtualized offices, for instance (Westerman, Bonnet, & McAfee, 2014; Webb 2013). These conditions, Westerman et al. (2014) consider critical for improving decision making and the implementation of such decisions. Perhaps, the most reported benefits of the digital transformation of firms or organizations are that it improves efficiency, profitability, and productivity (Kane et al., 2015). Automation of task results in the use of fewer resources, quick results at a lower cost, and reduction in employee numbers, which free expenses on labor, which can then be reinvested to earn more income.

Through digitization, many economic sectors have experienced significant growth as a result of the reduced cost of production, transactions, and even distribution. Indeed, digital technology has impacted both the private and public organizations at large. Digital technology has had a significant impact in various sectors, including education, finance, agriculture, government, communication, and many others. As such, studies that have explored the impact or importance of digital technology have primarily categorized the effects on specific sectors. Several studies have been conducted in the context of Africa and developing countries in general, although there are significant variations in the researchers' focus area. From the studies that have been reviewed herein, digital technology – new and emerging already have affected developing countries in various positive ways. Also, the review indicates that the impact of technology is, however, varied among countries and regions. Generally, efficiency in service delivery is the critical determinant of how digital technology has been able to impact various organizations and sectors, both private and government.

All these beneficial impacts by digital technologies, confirms how systems, information and service quality could impact on intention to use, use and user satisfaction, which result in net benefits for the organizations and sectors, as explained by the D & M IS success model.

Despite several benefits, there are other negative consequences that information system technology-induced changes have brought. According to Brynjolfsson and McAfee (2011), though the digital transformation of organizations creates new employment, yet it also results in many employees being displaced with automation, leading to a reduction in workforce. According to Aral and Weill (2007), major IT-induced, organizational changes compel firms into not only developing or acquiring IT infrastructure but also IT human resource as well. Technology induced transformation of the organization requires firms to cultivate new organizational capabilities that match the demands of the technology they intend to adopt (Singh et al., 2011). Thus, one consequence of technology-induced transformation includes significant changes in the technical and managerial capabilities of the firms, which may require both short term and long-term capital investment.

Firms in developing countries have unique sociodemographic traits, levels of digital maturity, political context, institutional context, and, more importantly, developmental context, which present conditions for other consequences of technology-induced organizational transformation. In developing countries, there are challenges with regards to technology, governance, and international cooperation issues, which affect the operations of firms that have been extensively transformed and hugely dependent on technology (Cepal, 2018). Existing studies such as that of Parida, Sjödin, and Reim (2019) have pointed that digital technologies adoptions in many developing countries do not follow clear systematic processes that enable individuals and organizations to exploit the synergistic structure of digital technologies. This phenomenon leads to a system of incomplete and partial digital transformation where firms are unable to harness the benefits of these technologies, which bolster the need for the transformation to be managed effectively.

MANAGING THE ORGANIZATIONAL DIGITAL TRANSFORMATION

Technological change in any organizational setting often causes significant changes in the regular routines of conducting business and government activities. Further, although individuals may not entirely initiate such changes, the effective implementation of such policies requires significant corporation from the members within the organization. Many studies indeed have reported on the difficulties and challenges of managing change (Hayes, 2018; Tidd & Bessant, 2018). Employees within an organization have different skills, academic qualifications, experience, and even relationships with other workers.

Further, the organizational culture that exists within a given institution plays a significant role in determining how change is perceived and implemented. The new and emerging digital technologies are indeed fundamental to the success of individual and collective organizations of a given country. It is, therefore, prudent that organizations find ways of dealing with challenges that often affect the implementation of digital technologies (Kotabe & Kothari, 2016). In determining how organizations manage the transformation brought about by digital technology, it is prudent to admit that implementing the technology is challenging and that certain factors are critical determinants of the same.

Despite the importance of e-commerce as a modern strategy of promoting the relationship between business-to-customers, and business-to-business, Awiagah et al. (2016) reported that several challenges; often organizational, continue to remain as challenges and indicated that government and managerial support were the most significant determinants of the same for government and private organizations respectively. Nkohkwo and Islam (2013) revealed that several factors were responsible for the e-commerce challenges facing African organizations. These factors were financial, infrastructural, organizational, political, human, and socio-economic. Specifically, the study revealed that human resources, internet access, legal framework, infrastructure, and digital divide were contributing to the challenges. Similar results by Mutula and Mostert (2010) show that critical factors that make the implementation of digital technologies more challenging in Africa include alleviation of poverty, ICT infrastructures, legal frameworks, and enabling policies.

The new and emerging technologies, coupled with digital migration, is a change that can disrupt an organization's way of doing things. It is enough to argue that, indeed, new and emerging technology has fundamentally changed Africa in a very positive way. Despite the positive effect, the implementations of some of these technologies often come with challenges in which organizations must find ways of navigating around. Organizations use various techniques to manage the impact of these technologies, and the following section discusses the appropriate strategies and how organizations manage the transitional challenge.

Appropriate Infrastructure

Infrastructural challenges are indeed critical in implementing digital technology. To manage the infrastructural challenges, organizations need to have adequate planning. Private or corporate organizations are often resourced compared to public institutions. As such, corporations can plan for the infrastructures before they are implemented. For public organizations, overcoming the infrastructural challenge depends on the importance of the government organization or department that is in question. The government allocates resources according to the multiplier effect of the department in question.

Establishing the appropriate infrastructure is essential in ensuring that the transition goes on smoothly. In Africa, most of the government projects are characteristically implemented using the top-bottom approach (Griffiths, 2016). If such is the case, then the national government or the relevant authority is often responsible for financing the infrastructure. On the other hand, if the proposal for the technology project is through a bottom-top approach, organizations may often have to plan and budget in advance to secure resources during a given financial year.

Partnerships

Undoubtedly, budgets and expenditure on digital transformation infrastructure for many companies is enormous and increasing (Ciuriak & Ptashkina, 2019; Hill, 2019). These investments are aimed at improving profitability, business growth, and transformation. Digital transformation path for companies differ, but most share one or two features in common (Nsengimana, 2017). Successful partnerships with innovative technology specialists who help digitalize key business processes and embrace the ambiguity of digital transformation are essential for a successful digital transformation agenda. Managing digital transformation requires securing and managing profitable partnerships and sustaining them. In developing countries where resources are limited, digital transformation mostly involves collaboration with digital technology infrastructure and service providers, rather than acquiring or building the structures themselves (Nsengimana, 2017).

Autonomous government institutions such as parastatals have the mandate to seek other development partners to help with the implementation projects. Alternatively, in cases where the government budget or priority is not immediately for the technological project, it can partner with big corporations and other development partners to co-fund and support the transformation. Currently, Ghana is partnering with IBM for the Digital Nation Africa program. IBM has also partnered with Kenya to establish a technology center in Nairobi, and more other African countries are also having the Digital Nation Africa pilot program (UNDP, 2017). It is important to note herein that infrastructural and financial challenges occur together, and hence, they are often solved together.

Leadership Style and Organizational Culture

Managers, therefore, have a critical role within organizations of ensuring that the change and transformation process is smooth and effective. Often, organizational culture plays a crucial role in enhancing organizational changes (Krantz, 2001). Kaaria and Njuguna (2019) researched to determine the impact of leadership style and organizational culture on the implementation of an Electronic Reporting System (ERS) in Kenya, among government and private organizations. The results showed that a positive organizational culture was positively related to the implementation of the ERS system, its adoption, and its use by the targeted employees. The results further showed that the leadership style was yet a critical factor. Transformational leadership was reported to be positively correlated with organizational culture and hence, organizational performance (Karimi, 2017; Sedmak, 2016).

Effective Communication

Another essential technique commonly and effectively used to manage the transition brought about by digital technology is communication. According to Keyton (2017), effective communication in an organizational setting is different from the regular passing of messages across the firm. Hence, effective communication involves the persuasion of employees to commit their efforts to attain the overall goals and objectives of the organization. An employee who is committed to the goals, objectives, mission, and vision of a company is more likely to be loyal to the organizations' practices (Keyton, 2017). The management must, therefore, identify the best communication and engagement strategies (Ott & Theunissen, 2015).

Notices, for example, are useful when there is the need to convey a short, concise, and urgent message which is supposed to reach everyone or targeting large groups within the organization. On the other hand, they may not be effective in communicating more profound messages that seek to elicit the commitment of the employees to the ideals of the organization. In the latter case, an email or personal communication strategy would be useful than group communication. The choice of language and tone is also essential in ensuring that the message is not distorted in any way (Petronio, 2015).

New Business Models

New business models have been delivered with the introduction of new and emerging IS to manage the impact (Schiavi & Behr, 2018). This is to say that the businesses have changed their models of operations to blend with new technology, to produce output that is technologically developed and meets the demands of the current digitized market environment. However, although all the business organizations, wherever they are, face some of these disruptive IS that create new business models and ideas, many problems are associated with the new and emerging technologies (Schiavi & Behr, 2018).

Significantly, the new technologies are expanding the organization's boundaries creating room for innovations that helps to expand the organization's operations by creating new businesses. However, whenever a new technology is embraced, the organizations must realign their business operations, their services, and product, the skills of the workers, among other things, so that they can operate within the guidelines of the new technology (Schiavi & Behr, 2018). Such an exercise is costly, and in some cases, the organizations might not realize the essence of technological transformation, mainly when other competitors have also geared up the same measures. This means that the competition will remain high as the technological transformation has promoted no new uniqueness.

Skills and Knowledge Upgrade

Another critical challenge of implementing emerging digital technology is knowledge of ICT, particularly in an organizational setting. Due to specialization within the organization, the implementation of such a comprehensive program may require the skills and knowledge set of specific people. It is, therefore, essential to determine in advance the right personnel to lead the implementation program. A critical factor in managing change and transformation in an organization is training (Carlsson & Wadensten, 2018). Without adequate training, the implementation of the technical program is likely to fail. Training is not only necessary for educating the employees on how to use technology. It is also an essential tool for transforming the employees' attitudes towards the program. Like training, studies also indicate that instilling a positive attitude to the employees may have positive results in change implementation and transformation.

This is one of the best options that many organizations take to manage the changes as a result of the introduction of new and emerging technologies. When technology is embraced to enhance communications, such as online booking through apps and other computer software, workers are provided with training so that they can understand the new systems. Based on the Net-Aware theories, the training of workers to upgrade their skills so that they can effectively use these technologies is a way of ensuring that the organizations retain their employees even after new systems have been introduced.

Employee Layoffs

This is another possible management technique that transformed organizations are embracing. In today's highly competitive world, reduction in workforce is a common phenomenon associated with corporate reorganization in response to the dynamic environment, such as recess or advancement in technology (Beheshti & Bures, 2000; Boone, 2000; Razzaq, Ayub, Arzu, & Aslam, 2013; Schiro & Baker, 2013). For instance, when robots and other technologies are embraced, such as mobile apps for bookings of the transport services and hotel rooms, the organizations replace the work that was being conducted manually with these machines (West, 2015). The net effect of this is that some workers are either re-deployed to other sectors that require human resources or dismissed until there are more opportunities for such workers; then they can be re-hired. The organizations then reduce their wage bill by downsizing their workers, but at the same time, they improve their standards of operating as well as the results of their operations.

Job loss or employee lay off as a consequence of digital transformation is increasing and widely reported. The McKinsey Global Institute in 2017 said that from the analysis of about 800 occupations in 46 countries, it was estimated that between 400 million and 800 million jobs could be lost due to robotic automation by 2030 (Manyika et al., 2017). In Indonesia, Tehubijuluw (2017) observed that digital transformation reduces the number of employees in the banking industry as more and more manual financial transactions become automated to achieve efficiency, reduce process errors, enhance productivity and delight the customers. The advantage of increased efficiency, productivity, and competitive advantage have driven most technology-induced employee layoff and general downsizing of modern companies. Firms undergoing a digital transformation must know how to handle job losses and the concomitant downsizing of the firm that may be required, as they increase efficiency by automation and technology adoption.

Enhanced Data Security

One of the inevitable outcomes of digital transformation and an area of great concern is cybercrimes and data security issues (Spremić & Šimunic, 2018; Nsengimana, 2017; Williams & Woodward, 2015). The evolution of digital transformation has raised concerns about cybercrime and risk perception among users of digital technologies and innovations. In recent years, cybercrimes have been industrialized, resulting in a compelling impact on organizational security, business transformation, and growth (Connolly & Wall, 2019). Therefore, in managing digital transformation, businesses are confronted with the risk of cybercrimes and online attacks that may have an impact on the organization economically or impugn the integrity of the firm. According to Spremić and Šimunic (2018), online data attacks have been on the rise, with many cyber attackers hacking into systems and introducing malware to solicit bribes or maliciously destroy various information activities. In this digital age, cybercrime is considered the greatest threat to every company and business world over (Aldrich, 2018). It is predicted to cost the world $6 trillion annually by 2021, up from $3 trillion in 2015 (Cybersecurity Ventures, 2019). Against this backdrop, managing digital transformation require that data security and online transactions are safe.

The first practices in managing cybercrime threats associated with digital transformation are to enhance data security by applying techniques that ensure that data stored in the computer systems are safe

(Galinec, Možnik, & Guberina, 2017). Many companies in response to cybercrimes have embarked on a rigorous data protection and management systems whereby most of the IS are aligned with the security and standards guidelines provided for by international bodies such as the International Organization for Standardization ISO. The use of sophisticated security features to keep unauthorized people at bay from the organizations' information is an inevitable adventure. The use of antivirus and internet security software has been on the rise with the organizations realizing the dangers that could arise when their stored data is damaged, and they do not have a manual backup for such information (Rao & Nayak, 2014).). These actions, among many other online security measures, are emerging in response to many cybercrimes and related activities as companies proceed on the digital transformation drive.

FUTURE RESEARCH DIRECTIONS

Although there has been an improvement in understanding the usefulness of various new and emerging information system technologies in transforming organizations, there is still a lack of data in the developed country's contexts that focus on the impact of the technologies and the management of the organizational transformations. There is, therefore, the need for further research on the digital transformation of organizations due to the new and emerging technologies in the developing country context.

There is also the need to develop indicators for IS technology success for organizations, especially in developing countries, and established the reciprocal relationship between the organizational context of transformation and IS technology dependence.

The impact of IS technology on organizational transformation has been widely studied but almost in isolation of psychosocial dimensions of the organizational changes informed by IS technologies. As noted by Coovert and Thompson (2013), the critical issue for IS research now is not to consider IS technology itself and its impact as the DeLone and McLean Model of Information Systems Success demonstrate. On the contrary, IS research should focus on how to create and use psycho-social theories and research to deepen our understanding of how to manage the impact and implementation of the emerging and new IS technology developments. IS research should go far beyond the fundamental effort to align technology and the work done in organizations.

CONCLUSION

In conclusion, this chapter has highlighted the nature, importance, and use of some of the most prevalent new and emerging IS, including Mobile Apps, Artificial Intelligence, Social Media, Social Commerce, Internet, Internet of Things, Big Data Analytics, 3-D Printing, among others. The chapter also gives a detailed description of how these technologies have caused a vivid transformation of organizations and how some sectors have been impacted by the new and new and emerging technologies, including finance, agriculture, government, transport, and health organizations, among others in developing economies.

These emerging and new technologies have had a profound impact on the economic, social, and environmental aspects of developing economies and particularly the African continent. The internet, for example, has significantly enhanced business transactions and consequently reducing the cost of doing business. It has also provided a new dimension to education, and as such, more people can now access education even from overseas. The smartphones are continuously used to develop mobile phone applications that are used to support various commercial, social, and educational purposes.

Despite the numerous benefits, the management of the organizational transformations and related effects due to these digital technologies has often been challenging. Nevertheless, the management of some organizations are responding to such challenges through new business models, adequate planning, solicitation of sufficient infrastructural and financial resources, training of the relevant personal, enhanced data security, and communicating effectively.

This chapter contributes to the burgeoning field of scholarship in digital transformation through a review of new and emergent digital technologies that are transforming organizations in emerging economies. The chapter also contributes to practice by helping managers identify how digital technologies drive organizational transformation and how the effects and impacts of the transformation can be managed. Organizations in developing economies would certainly benefit hugely from emerging and new digital technologies. However, more planning and research need to be considered in determining the best ways of prioritizing and selecting the technologies to manage limited resources.

REFERENCES

Abubakar, A. D., Bass, J. M., & Allison, I. (2014). Cloud computing: Adoption issues for sub-Saharan African SMEs. *The Electronic Journal on Information Systems in Developing Countries*, 62(1), 1–17. doi:10.1002/j.1681-4835.2014.tb00439.x

Acılar, A. (2011). Exploring the aspects of digital divide in a developing country. *Issues in Informing Science and Information Technology*, 8, 231–244. doi:10.28945/1415

Adam, I. O., & Musah, A. (2015). Small and medium enterprises (SMEs) in the cloud in developing countries: A synthesis of the literature and future research directions. *Journal of Management and Sustainability*, 5(1), 115. doi:10.5539/jms.v5n1p115

Adewumi, A., Odunjo, V., & Misra, S. (2015). Developing a mobile application for a taxi service company in Nigeria. In *2015 International Conference on Computing, Communication and Security (ICCCS)* (pp. 1-5). IEEE. 10.1109/CCCS.2015.7374204

Ahmed, A. A. G. E. (2019). Benefits and Challenges of Internet of Things for Telecommunication Networks. In Telecommunication Networks-Trends and Developments. IntechOpen.

Aldrich, R. S. (2018). *Resilience (Library Futures Series, Book 2)* (Vol. 2). American Library Association.

Alkhalisi, Z. (2019). Uber is buying its Middle East rival Careem for $3.1 billion. *CNN Business*. Retrieved from https://edition.cnn.com/2019/03/26/tech/uber-careem-acquisition/index.html

Antonova, A. (2015). Emerging technologies and organizational transformation. In Technology, Innovation, and Enterprise Transformation (pp. 20-34). IGI Global. doi:10.4018/978-1-4666-6473-9.ch002

Aral, S., & Weill, P. (2007). IT assets, organizational capabilities, and firm performance: How resource allocations and organizational differences explain performance variation. *Organization Science*, 18(5), 763–780. doi:10.1287/orsc.1070.0306

Archibugi, D., & Michie, J. (1997). Technological globalization and national systems of innovation: an introduction. *Technology, globalization and economic performance*, 1-23.

Attaran, M. (2017). The rise of 3-D printing: The advantages of additive manufacturing over traditional manufacturing. *Business Horizons*, *60*(5), 677–688. doi:10.1016/j.bushor.2017.05.011

Avram, M. G. (2014). Advantages and challenges of adopting cloud computing from an enterprise perspective. *Procedia Technology*, *12*, 529–534. doi:10.1016/j.protcy.2013.12.525

Awiagah, R., Kang, J., & Lim, J. I. (2016). Factors affecting e-commerce adoption among SMEs in Ghana. *Information Development*, *32*(4), 815–836. doi:10.1177/0266666915571427

Azemi, Y., & Ozuem, W. (2015). Social media and SMEs in transition countries. In *Computer-mediated marketing strategies: Social media and online brand communities* (pp. 114–133). IGI Global. doi:10.4018/978-1-4666-6595-8.ch005

Baethge, C., Klier, J., & Klier, M. (2016). Social commerce—State-of-the-art and future research directions. *Electronic Markets*, *26*(3), 269–290. doi:10.100712525-016-0225-2

Baker, A. (2013). The gradual transformation? The incremental dynamics of macroprudential regulation. *Regulation & Governance*, *7*(4), 417–434. doi:10.1111/rego.12022

Baktha, K. (2017). Mobile Application Development: All the Steps and Guidelines for Successful Creation of Mobile App: Case Study. *International Journal of Computer Science and Mobile Computing*, *6*(9), 15–20.

Beheshti, H. M., & Bures, A. L. (2000). Information technology's critical role in corporate downsizing. *Industrial Management & Data Systems*, *100*(1), 31–35. doi:10.1108/02635570010310575

Birtchnell, T., & Hoyle, W. (2014). *3D printing for development in the global south: The 3D4D challenge*. Springer. doi:10.1057/9781137365668

Bolton, R. N., Parasuraman, A., Hoefnagels, A., Migchels, N., Kabadayi, S., Gruber, T., ... Solnet, D. (2013). Understanding Generation Y and their use of social media: A review and research agenda. *Journal of Service Management*, *24*(3), 245–267. doi:10.1108/09564231311326987

Bonilla, S., Silva, H., Terra da Silva, M., Franco Gonçalves, R., & Sacomano, J. (2018). Industry 4.0 and sustainability implications: A scenario-based analysis of the impacts and challenges. *Sustainability*, *10*(10), 3740. doi:10.3390u10103740

Boone, J. (2000). Technological progress, downsizing and unemployment. *Economic Journal (London)*, *110*(465), 581–600. doi:10.1111/1468-0297.00555

Bowser, A., Sloan, M., Michelucci, P., & Pauwels, E. (2017). *Artificial Intelligence: A Policy-Oriented Introduction*. Academic Press.

Brynjolfsson, E., & McAfee, A. (2011). *Race against the machine: How the digital revolution is accelerating innovation, driving productivity, and irreversibly transforming employment and the economy*. Brynjolfsson and McAfee.

Burns, E., & Laskowski, N. (2018). *A machine learning and AI guide for enterprises in the cloud*. Retrieved from https://searchenterpriseai.techtarget.com/definition/AI-Artificial-Intelligence

Carlsson, Õ. U., & Wadensten, B. (2018). Professional practice-related training and organizational readiness for change facilitate implementation of projects on the national core value system in care of older people. *Nursing Open*, *5*(4), 593–600. doi:10.1002/nop2.185 PMID:30338105

Cepal, N. (2018). *Emerging challenges and shifting paradigms: New perspectives on international cooperation for development*. Academic Press.

Ciuriak, D., & Ptashkina, M. (2019). *Leveraging the Digital Transformation for Development: A Global South Strategy for the Data-Driven Economy. Policy Brief*. Centre for International Governance Innovation.

Connolly, L. Y., & Wall, D. S. (2019). The rise of crypto-ransomware in a changing cybercrime landscape: Taxonomising countermeasures. *Computers & Security*, *87*, 101568. doi:10.1016/j.cose.2019.101568

Coovert, M. D., & Thompson, L. F. (2013). Toward a synergistic relationship between psychology and technology. In *The psychology of workplace technology* (pp. 25–42). Routledge. doi:10.4324/9780203735565

Cybersecurity Ventures. (2019). *Cyberattacks are the fastest growing crime and predicted to cost the world $6 trillion annually by 202*. Available at: https://www.prnewswire.com/news-releases/cyberattacks-are-the-fastest-growing-crime-and-predicted-to-cost-the-world-6-trillion-annually-by-2021-300765090.html

Dang, L. M., Piran, M., Han, D., Min, K., & Moon, H. (2019). A Survey on Internet of Things and Cloud Computing for Healthcare. *Electronics (Basel)*, *8*(7), 768. doi:10.3390/electronics8070768

DeLone, W. H., & McLean, E. R. (1992). Information systems success: The quest for the dependent variable. *Information Systems Research*, *3*(1), 60–95. doi:10.1287/isre.3.1.60

DeLone, W. H., & McLean, E. R. (2003). The DeLone and McLean Model of Information Systems Success: A Ten-Year Update. *Journal of Management Information Systems*, *19*(4), 9–30. doi:10.1080/07421222.2003.11045748

Dimitrov, M., & Osman, I. (2012). *The Impact of Cloud Computing on Organizations in Regard to Cost and Security* (Unpublished Master's Thesis). Umea University, Umea, Sweden.

Dutton, W. H. (2013). *Internet studies: The foundations of a transformative field*. Oxford University Press. doi:10.1093/oxfordhb/9780199589074.013.0001

Dwivedi, M., Yadav, A., & Venkatesh, U. (2011). Use of social media by national tourism organizations: A preliminary analysis. *Information Technology & Tourism*, *13*(2), 93–103. doi:10.3727/109830512X13258778487353

Erevelles, S., Fukawa, N., & Swayne, L. (2016). Big Data consumer analytics and the transformation of marketing. *Journal of Business Research*, *69*(2), 897–904. doi:10.1016/j.jbusres.2015.07.001

Feigin, B. (2008). *Mobile Application Development*. A presentation for Android Mobile Development.

Foerster-Metz, U. S., Marquardt, K., Golowko, N., Kompalla, A., & Hell, C. (2018). Digital Transformation and its Implications on Organizational Behavior. *Journal of EU Research in Business*.

Galinec, D., Možnik, D., & Guberina, B. (2017). Cybersecurity and cyber defense: national level strategic approach. *Automatika: časopis za automatiku, mjerenje, elektroniku, računarstvo i komunikacije, 58*(3), 273-286.

Galliers, R. D., & Leidner, D. E. (2014). *Strategic information management: challenges and strategies in managing information systems*. Routledge. doi:10.4324/9781315880884

Gillwald, A., Moyo, M., Odufuwa, F., Frempong, G., & Kamoun, F. (2014). *The cloud over Africa*. Cape Town, South Africa: Research ICT Africa.

Goerzig, D., & Bauernhansl, T. (2018). Enterprise architectures for the digital transformation in small and medium-sized enterprises. *Procedia CIRP, 67*, 540–545. doi:10.1016/j.procir.2017.12.257

Golshan, B. (2018). *Digital Capability and Business Model Reconfiguration: a co-evolutionary perspective* (Doctoral dissertation). Linnaeus University Press.

Gonzalez, A., Schlautmann, A., Casahuga, G., & Romero, M. (2017) Digital transformation in developing countries. *Public services, Technology & innovation management, Arthur D Little*. Retrieved from https://www.adlittle.se/sites/default/files/viewpoints/adl_digital_in_emerging_markets.pdf

Goodier, R. (2016). Sensors ring the changes. *Appropriate Technology, 43*(3), 50.

Griffiths, P. (2016). Bolstering Urbanization Efforts: Africa's Approach to the New Urban Agenda. Academic Press.

Hajli, N. (2015). Social commerce constructs and consumer's intention to buy. *International Journal of Information Management, 35*(2), 183–191. doi:10.1016/j.ijinfomgt.2014.12.005

Hamzah, H. H. B., Keattch, O., Covill, D., & Patel, B. A. (2018). The effects of printing orientation on the electrochemical behaviour of 3D printed acrylonitrile butadiene styrene (ABS)/carbon black electrodes. *Scientific Reports, 8*(1), 9135. doi:10.103841598-018-27188-5 PMID:29904165

Han, H., & Trimi, S. (2017). Social commerce design: A framework and application. *Journal of Theoretical and Applied Electronic Commerce Research, 12*(3), 50–68. doi:10.4067/S0718-18762017000300005

Hayes, J. (2018). *The theory and practice of change management*. Palgrave. doi:10.1057/978-1-352-00132-7

Heeks, R. (2002). i-development, not e-development: Special issue on ICTs and development. Journal of International Development. *The Journal of the Development Studies Association, 14*(1), 1–11.

Henama, U. S., & Sifolo, P. P. S. (2017). Uber: The South Africa experience. *African Journal of Hospitality, Tourism and Leisure, 6*(2), 1–10.

Hendricks, D. (2015). The Trouble with the Internet of Things. London Datastore. *Greater London Authority*. Retrieved from https://data.london.gov.uk/blog/the-trouble-with-the-internet-of-things/

Hill, C. (2019). *The Future of British Foreign Policy: Security and Diplomacy in a World After Brexit*. John Wiley & Sons.

Ibrahim, A. M., Jose, R. R., Rabie, A. N., Gerstle, T. L., Lee, B. T., & Lin, S. J. (2015). Three-dimensional printing in developing countries. *Plastic and Reconstructive Surgery. Global Open*, *3*(7), e443. doi:10.1097/GOX.0000000000000298 PMID:26301132

Internet World State. (2019). *Internet penetration in Africa March 31, 2019*. Retrieved July 3, 2019, from, https://www.internetworldstats.com/stats1.htm

Inukollu, V. N., Keshamoni, D. D., Kang, T., & Inukollu, M. (2014). *Factors influencing quality of mobile apps: Role of mobile app development life cycle*. arXiv preprint arXiv:1410.4537

Islam, R., Islam, R., & Mazumder, T. (2010). Mobile application and its global impact. *IACSIT International Journal of Engineering and Technology*, *10*(6), 72–78.

Ismail, M. H., Khater, M., & Zaki, M. (2017). *Digital Business Transformation and Strategy: What Do We Know So Far*. Cambridge Service Alliance.

Jensen-Haxel, P. (2015). A New Framework for a Novel Lattice: 3D Printers, DNA Fabricators, and the Perils in Regulating the Raw Materials of the Next Era of Revolution, Renaissance, and Research. *Wake Forest JL & Poly*, *5*, 231.

Jiménez, M., Romero, L., Domínguez, I. A., Espinosa, M. D. M., & Domínguez, M. (2019). Additive Manufacturing Technologies: An Overview about 3D Printing Methods and Future Prospects. *Complexity*.

Jones, S., Irani, Z., Sivarajah, U., & Love, P. E. (2017). Risks and rewards of cloud computing in the UK public sector: A reflection on three Organizational case studies. *Information Systems Frontiers*, 1–24.

Kaaria, S. K., & Njuguna, R. (2019). Organizational Attributes and Implementation of Enterprise Resource Planning: A Case of Kenya Medical Research Institute, Kilifi County. *International Journal of Current Aspects*, *3*(II), 231–242. doi:10.35942/ijcab.v3iII.20

Kane, G. C., Palmer, D., Phillips, A. N., Kiron, D., & Buckley, N. (2015). Strategy, not technology, drives digital transformation. *MIT Sloan Management Review and Deloitte University Press*, *14*, 1–25.

Karimi, J. (2017). *Effects of Enterprise Resource Planning Implementation on Organizational Performance in the Transport Industry in Kenya* (Doctoral dissertation). United States International University-Africa.

Katz, R. (2017). Social and economic impact of digital transformation on the economy. *International Telecommunication Union (ITU)*. Retrieved from https://www.itu.int/en/ITU-D/Conferences/GSR/Documents/GSR2017/Soc_Eco_impact_Digital_transformation_finalGSR.pdf

Kaufman, I., & Horton, C. (2015, Dec.). Digital transformation: leveraging digital technology with core values to achieve sustainable business goals. *Eur. Financ. Rev.*, 63-67.

Kavadias, S., Ladas, K., & Loch, C. (2016). The transformative business model. *Harvard Business Review*, *94*(10), 91–98.

Kayser, V., Nehrke, B., & Zubovic, D. (2018). Data science as an innovation challenge: from big data to value proposition. *Technology Innovation Management Review, 8*(3).

Keyton, J. (2017). Communication in organizations. *Annual Review of Organizational Psychology and Organizational Behavior*, *4*(1), 501–526. doi:10.1146/annurev-orgpsych-032516-113341

Kiunguyu, K. (2019). Ghana: Google Opens Its First Artificial Intelligence Lab on the Continent. *All Africa*. Retrieved from https://allafrica.com/stories/201904180055.html

Knorr, E., & Gruman, G. (2008). What cloud computing really means. *InfoWorld*, *7*, 20–20.

Kohli, R., & Johnson, S. (2011). Digital Transformation in Latecomer Industries: CIO and CEO Leadership Lessons from Encana Oil & Gas (USA) Inc. *MIS Quarterly Executive*, *10*(4).

Kok, J. N., Boers, E. J., Kosters, W. A., Van der Putten, P., & Poel, M. (2009). Artificial intelligence: Definition, trends, techniques, and cases. *Artificial Intelligence*, *1*.

Kotabe, M., & Kothari, T. (2016). Emerging market multinational companies' evolutionary paths to building a competitive advantage from emerging markets to developed countries. *Journal of World Business*, *51*(5), 729–743. doi:10.1016/j.jwb.2016.07.010

Krantz, J. (2001). Dilemmas of organizational change: A systems psychodynamic perspective. *The systems psychodynamics of organizations: Integrating the group relations approach, psychoanalytic, and open systems perspectives*, 133-156.

Leclercq-Vandelanoitte, A., & Plé, L. (2016). *How do Customers-Employees interactions influence Organizational Change? A Theoretical Framework*. Retrieved from https://pdfs.semanticscholar.org/b0 1b/79404a40663ac7a9ab626b933b5c8b56a7ad.pdf

Lehrer, C., Wieneke, A., vom Brocke, J., Jung, R., & Seidel, S. (2018). How big data analytics enables service innovation: Materiality, affordance, and the individualization of service. *Journal of Management Information Systems*, *35*(2), 424–460. doi:10.1080/07421222.2018.1451953

Leiner, B. M., Cerf, V. G., Clark, D. D., Kahn, R. E., Kleinrock, L., Lynch, D. C., ... Wolff, S. (2009). A brief history of the Internet. *Computer Communication Review*, *39*(5), 22–31. doi:10.1145/1629607.1629613

Liberati, A., Altman, D. G., Tetzlaff, J., Mulrow, C., Gøtzsche, P. C., Ioannidis, J. P., ... Moher, D. (2009). The PRISMA statement for reporting systematic reviews and meta-analyses of studies that evaluate health care interventions: Explanation and elaboration. *PLoS Medicine*, *6*(7), e1000100. doi:10.1371/journal.pmed.1000100 PMID:19621070

Luna, D. R., Mayan, J. C., García, M. J., Almerares, A. A., & Househ, M. (2014). Challenges and potential solutions for big data implementations in developing countries. *Yearbook of Medical Informatics*, *23*(01), 36–41. doi:10.15265/IY-2014-0012 PMID:25123719

Mahadevan, B., & Venkatesh, N. S. (2000, November). Building On-line Trust for Business to Business E-Commerce. *IT Asia Millennium Conference*.

Manyika, J., Lund, S., Chui, M., Bughin, J., Woetzel, J., Batra, P., & Sanghvi, S. (2017). *Jobs lost; jobs gained: Workforce transitions in a time of automation*. McKinsey Global Institute.

Marr, B. (2018). 7 Amazing Real-World Examples Of 3D Printing In 2018. *Forbes*. Retrieved from https://www.forbes.com/sites/bernardmarr/2018/08/22/7-amazing-real-world-examples-of-3d-printing-in-2018/#73d2cca06585

McKeown, I., & Philip, G. (2003). Business transformation, information technology and competitive strategies: Learning to fly. *International Journal of Information Management, 23*(1), 3–24. doi:10.1016/S0268-4012(02)00065-8

Medanta. (2018). *Life-Saving Creativity- 3D Printed Titanium Spine.* Retrieved from https://www.medanta.org/life-saving-creativity-3d-printed-titanium-spine/

Miailhe, N., & Hodes, C. (2017). The Third Age of Artificial Intelligence. *Field Actions Science Reports. The Journal of Field Actions*, (17), 6-11.

Miazi, M. N. S., Erasmus, Z., Razzaque, M. A., Zennaro, M., & Bagula, A. (2016). Enabling the Internet of Things in developing countries: Opportunities and challenges. In *2016 5th International Conference on Informatics, Electronics and Vision (ICIEV)* (pp. 564-569). IEEE.

Mikalef, P., Pappas, I. O., Krogstie, J., & Giannakos, M. (2018). Big data analytics capabilities: A systematic literature review and research agenda. *Information Systems and e-Business Management, 16*(3), 547–578. doi:10.100710257-017-0362-y

Mital, M., Chang, V., Choudhary, P., Papa, A., & Pani, A. K. (2018). Adoption of Internet of Things in India: A test of competing models using a structured equation modeling approach. *Technological Forecasting and Social Change, 136*, 339–346. doi:10.1016/j.techfore.2017.03.001

Moncrief, W. C., Marshall, G. W., & Rudd, J. M. (2015). Social media and related technology: Drivers of change in managing the contemporary sales force. *Business Horizons, 58*(1), 45–55. doi:10.1016/j.bushor.2014.09.009

Morgan, R. E., & Page, K. (2008). Managing business transformation to deliver strategic agility. *Strategic Change, 17*(5-6), 155–168. doi:10.1002/jsc.823

Muhammed, K., Zaharaddeen, I., Rumana, K., & Turaki, A. M. (2015). Cloud computing adoption in Nigeria: Challenges and benefits. *International Journal of Scientific and Research Publications, 5*(7), 2250–3153.

Mutula, S. M., & Mostert, J. (2010). Challenges and opportunities of e-government in South Africa. *The Electronic Library, 28*(1), 38–53. doi:10.1108/02640471011023360

Nagy, D., Schuessler, J., & Dubinsky, A. (2016). Defining and identifying disruptive innovations. *Industrial Marketing Management, 57*, 119–126. doi:10.1016/j.indmarman.2015.11.017

Nkohkwo, Q. N. A., & Islam, M. S. (2013). Challenges to the Successful Implementation of e-Government Initiatives in Sub-Saharan Africa: A Literature Review. Electronic. *Journal of E-Government, 11*(1).

Nsengimana, J. P. (2017). Reflections upon periclitations in privacy: Perspectives from Rwanda's digital transformation. *Health and Technology, 7*(4), 377–388. doi:10.100712553-017-0196-0

Nylén, D., & Holmström, J. (2015). Digital innovation strategy: A framework for diagnosing and improving digital product and service innovation. *Business Horizons, 58*(1), 57–67. doi:10.1016/j.bushor.2014.09.001

Obar, J. A., & Wildman, S. S. (2015). Social media definition and the governance challenge: An introduction to the special issue. *Telecommunications Policy, 39*(9), 745–750. doi:10.1016/j.telpol.2015.07.014

Odoom, R., Anning-Dorson, T., & Acheampong, G. (2017). Antecedents of social media usage and performance benefits in small and medium-sized enterprises (SMEs). *Journal of Enterprise Information Management, 30*(3), 383–399. doi:10.1108/JEIM-04-2016-0088

Ondego, B., & Moturi, C. (2016). Evaluation of the Implementation of the e-Citizen in Kenya. *Evaluation, 10*(4).

Ortutay, B. (2012). *Beyond Facebook: A look at social network history.* Academic Press.

Ott, L., & Theunissen, P. (2015). Reputations at risk: Engagement during social media crises. *Public Relations Review, 41*(1), 97–102. doi:10.1016/j.pubrev.2014.10.015

Ozili, P. K. (2018). Impact of digital finance on financial inclusion and stability. *Borsa Istanbul Review, 18*(4), 329–340. doi:10.1016/j.bir.2017.12.003

Paré, G., & Kitsiou, S. (2017). Methods for Literature Reviews. In *Handbook of eHealth Evaluation: An Evidence-based Approach.* University of Victoria.

Parida, V., Sjödin, D., & Reim, W. (2019). *Reviewing literature on digitalization, business model innovation, and sustainable industry: Past achievements and future promises.* Academic Press.

Parviainen, P., Tihinen, M., Kääriäinen, J., & Teppola, S. (2017). Tackling the digitalization challenge: How to benefit from digitalization in practice. *International Journal of Information Systems and Project Management, 5*(1), 63-77.

Petronio, S. (2015). Communication privacy management theory. *The international encyclopedia of interpersonal communication*, 1-9.

Pettenati, M. C., & Cigognini, M. E. (2007). Social networking theories and tools to support connectivist learning activities. *International Journal of Web-Based Learning and Teaching Technologies, 2*(3), 42–60. doi:10.4018/jwltt.2007070103

Pitchford, N. J., Chigeda, A., & Hubber, P. J. (2019). Interactive apps prevent gender discrepancies in early grade mathematics in a low-income country in Sub-Sahara Africa. *Developmental Science*, 12864. doi:10.1111/desc.12864 PMID:31120168

Rachinger, M., Rauter, R., Müller, C., Vorraber, W., & Schirgi, E. (2018). Digitalization and its influence on business model innovation. *Journal of Manufacturing Technology Management.*

Rao, U. H., & Nayak, U. (2014). *Malicious software and anti-virus software. In The InfoSec Handbook* (pp. 141–161). Berkeley, CA: Apress.

Razzaq, A., Ayub, A., Arzu, F., & Aslam, M. S. (2013). The nexus between technological learning, downsizing, employee commitment, and organizational performance. *Business Management Dynamics, 2*(10), 74.

Russell, S. J., & Norvig, P. (2016). *Artificial intelligence: a modern approach.* Malaysia: Pearson Education Limited.

Sakr, G. E., Elhajj, I. H., & Mitri, G. (2011). Efficient forest fire occurrence prediction for developing countries using two weather parameters. *Engineering Applications of Artificial Intelligence*, *24*(5), 888–894. doi:10.1016/j.engappai.2011.02.017

Schiavi, G. S., & Behr, A. (2018). Emerging technologies and new business models: A review of disruptive business models. *Innovation & Management Review*, *15*(4), 338–355. doi:10.1108/INMR-03-2018-0013

Schiro, J. B., & Baker, R. L. (2009). Downsizing and organizational change survivors and victims: Mental health issues. *International Journal of Applied Management and Technology*, *7*(1), 3.

Sedmak, A. (2016). The Innovator's Dilemma: When New Technologies Cause Great Firms to Fail. *Defense AR Journal*, *23*(4), 414.

Siamagka, N. T., Christodoulides, G., Michaelidou, N., & Valvi, A. (2015). Determinants of social media adoption by B2B organizations. *Industrial Marketing Management*, *51*, 89–99. doi:10.1016/j.indmarman.2015.05.005

Smith, J. W. (2016). The Uber-all economy of the future. *Independent Review*, *20*(3), 383–390.

Spremić, M., & Šimunic, A. (2018). Cyber Security Challenges in Digital Economy. In *Proceedings of the World Congress on Engineering* (*Vol. 1*). Academic Press.

Sturm, U., Gold, M., Luna, S., Schade, S., Ceccaroni, L., Kyba, C. C. M., . . . Piera, J. (2018). *Defining principles for mobile apps and platforms development in citizen science*. Retrieved from https://nhm.openrepository.com/bitstream/handle/10141/622315/Defining+principles+for+mobile+apps+and+platformsdevelopment+in+citizen+science.pdf?sequence=1

Taufik, M., & Jain, P. K. (2013). Role of build orientation in layered manufacturing: A review. *International Journal of Manufacturing Technology and Management*, *27*(1-3), 47–73. doi:10.1504/IJMTM.2013.058637

Tehubijuluw, F. K. (2017). The Digital Technology and the Threat of Downsizing into Indonesia's Banking Industry Performance. *International Journal of Trade, Economics and Finance, 8*(4).

Templier, M., & Paré, G. (2015). A framework for guiding and evaluating literature reviews. *Communications of the Association for Information Systems*, *37*(1), 6.

Thomas, D. (2016). Costs, benefits, and adoption of additive manufacturing: A supply chain perspective. *International Journal of Advanced Manufacturing Technology*, *85*(5-8), 1857–1876. doi:10.100700170-015-7973-6 PMID:28747809

Thomas, D. S., & Gilbert, S. W. (2014). Costs and cost-effectiveness of additive manufacturing. *NIST Special Publication*, *1176*, 12.

Tidd, J., & Bessant, J. R. (2018). *Managing innovation: integrating technological, market and organizational change*. John Wiley & Sons.

Trivedi, H. (2013). *Cloud computing adoption model for governments and large enterprises* (Doctoral dissertation, Massachusetts Institute of Technology). Retrieved from https://dspace.mit.edu/bitstream/handle/1721.1/80675/857768311-MIT.pdf?sequence=2&isAllowed=y

Umezurike, S. A. & Olusola, O. (2017). South Africa's 'Africa Renaissance' Project: Between Rhetoric and Practice. *The Scientific Journal for Theory and Practice of Socio-Economic Development 2016, 5*(10), 263-278

UNDP. (2017). *IBM launches "digital"- nation Africa": invests $70 to bring digital skills to Africa with Free, Watson-powered skills platform for 25 million people.* United Nations Development Program. Retrieved from, http://www.za.undp.org/content/south_africa/en/home/presscenter/pressreleases/2017/02/08/ibm-launches-digital-nation-africa-invests-70-million-to-bring-digital-skills-to-africa-with-free-watson-powered-skills-platform-for-25-million-people.html

Van Doorn, J., Mende, M., Noble, S. M., Hulland, J., Ostrom, A. L., Grewal, D., & Petersen, J. A. (2017). Domo arigato Mr Roboto: Emergence of automated social presence in organizational frontlines and customers' service experiences. *Journal of Service Research, 20*(1), 43–58. doi:10.1177/1094670516679272

Vasquez, M. (2015). Embracing 3D Printing. *Mechanical Engineering Magazine Select Articles, 137*(08), 42–45.

Ventola, C. L. (2014). Medical applications for 3D printing: Current and projected uses. *P&T, 39*(10), 704. PMID:25336867

Wang, H., He, W., & Wang, F. K. (2012). Enterprise cloud service architectures. *Information Technology Management, 13*(4), 445–454. doi:10.100710799-012-0139-4

Webb, N. (2013). Vodafone puts mobility at the heart of business strategy: Transformation improves performance of employees and organization as a whole. *Human Resource Management International Digest, 21*(1), 5–8. doi:10.1108/09670731311296410

Weinman, J. (2016). The Internet of Things for Developing Economies. *CIO.* Available at: https://www.cio.com/article/3027989/the-internet-of-things-for-developing-economies.html

West, D. M. (2015). *What happens if robots take the jobs? The impact of emerging technologies on employment and public policy.* Washington, DC: Centre for Technology Innovation at Brookings.

Westerman, G., Bonnet, D., & McAfee, A. (2014). The nine elements of digital transformation. *MIT Sloan Management Review, 55*(3), 1–6.

Williams, P. A., & Woodward, A. J. (2015). Cybersecurity vulnerabilities in medical devices: A complex environment and multifaceted problem. *Medical Devices (Auckland, N.Z.), 8,* 305. doi:10.2147/MDER.S50048 PMID:26229513

Yaeger, K., Martini, M., Rasouli, J., & Costa, A. (2019). Emerging Blockchain Technology Solutions for Modern Healthcare Infrastructure. *Journal of Scientific Innovation in Medicine, 2*(1), 1. doi:10.29024/jsim.7

Yılmaz, H. E., Sirel, A., & Esen, M. F. (2019). The Impact of Internet of Things Self-Security on Daily Business and Business Continuity. In *Handbook of Research on Cloud Computing and Big Data Applications in IoT* (pp. 481–498). IGI Global. doi:10.4018/978-1-5225-8407-0.ch021

Zhu, Y. (2017). *Cloud computing: current and future impact on organizations* (Unpublished Master's Thesis). Western Oregon University.

ADDITIONAL READING

Canessa-Terrazas, E. C., Morales-Flores, F. J., & Maldifassi-Pohlhammer, J. O. (2017). The impact of IT-enhanced organizational learning on performance: Evidence from Chile. *Revista Facultad de Ingenieria Universidad de Antioquia (Medellín)*, (82): 60–67. doi:10.17533/udea.redin.n82a08

Cortellazzo, L., Bruni, E., & Zampieri, R. (2019). The role of leadership in a digitalized world: A review. *Frontiers in Psychology*, *10*, 1938. doi:10.3389/fpsyg.2019.01938 PMID:31507494

Crespi, G., Criscuolo, C., & Haskel, J. (2007). Information technology, organisational change and productivity. Centre for Economic Performance, CEP Discussion Paper No 783 March 2007

Dhurkari, R. K. (2017). Information Technology and Organizational Change: Review of Theories and Application to a Case of Indian Railways. *Management and Labour Studies*, *42*(2), 135–151. doi:10.1177/0258042X17716599

Jones, M., & Orlikowski, W. J. (2007). Information technology and the dynamics of organizational change. In The Oxford handbook of information and communication technologies.

Šehanović, J., & Etinger, D. (2003, January). Impact of information technologies on elements of organisational culture. In *22nd International Scientific Conference on Development of Organizational Sciences*.

Sibanda, M., & Ramrathan, D. (2017). Influence of information technology on organization strategy. *Foundations of Management*, *9*(1), 191–202. doi:10.1515/fman-2017-0015

Zand, F., Van Beers, C., & Van Leeuwen, G. (2011). Information technology, organizational change and firm productivity: A panel study of complementarity effects and clustering patterns in Manufacturing and Services.

Chapter 10
Counterfeiting and Piracy:
The Role of IT – The Case of the Ghanaian and Nigerian Fashion and Beauty Industry

Yaa Amponsah Twumasi
Business School, University of Ghana, Ghana

Joshua Ofori-Amanfo
https://orcid.org/0000-0002-7114-527X
Business School, University of Ghana, Ghana

ABSTRACT

The chapter seeks to examine how IT enables or constrains counterfeiting and piracy in the fashion and beauty industry in two developing countries. The chapter also highlights the types of IT used in the industry and how IT aids in the ascendance of counterfeiting/piracy. The findings suggest that the escalation of counterfeiting/piracy in the industry is as a result of globalisation and the predominance of technological innovation such as IT, specifically the internet and social media platforms. This chapter contributes to the strategies that the industry in developing countries use in combating counterfeiting/ pricy in their business. In academia, arguably, no research has been conducted yet on counterfeiting/ piracy in the fashion industry in Ghana and Nigeria, as far as the role of IT is a concern.

INTRODUCTION

Counterfeiting notably, industrial product counterfeit is one of the fasters growing segments in the world today despite its resistance by many parties. This segment exists and continues to increase due to the enormous demand for the imitation of reputable and well-known brands, at a fraction of the cost of the original product. It is so because counterfeiters do not incur any research and development cost (Stroppa, di Stefano & Parrella, 2016; Ong, Chiang & Pung, 2015: Hamelin, Nwankwo & El Hadouchi, 2013). Not only but destroying many industries, bringing about employee redundancy, robbing governments of tax revenues and killing economies, funding terrorism and organised crime, as well as posing a danger to the well-being of society (Kennedy, Wilson & Labrecque, 2017; Quoquab, Pahlevan, Mohammad

DOI: 10.4018/978-1-7998-2610-1.ch010

& Thurasamy 2017; Guin, DiMase & Tehranipoor, 2014). One has to consider a whole industry on its right when talking about counterfeiting and piracy. Even though counterfeiting is unlawful, it is a keen competitor for legitimate businesses and interestingly protecting their market share.

In the same way, piracy of authentic products has led to millions of business losing their market share (Arli, Tjiptono & Porto, 2015; Hamelin et al., 2013; Harvey, 1987). For instance, a study by Chaudhry and Zimmerman (2013) put forward that, over the past two decades, the growth rate of counterfeiting and piracy has exceeded 10,000% worldwide. They are causing lots of harm to most businesses, economies, and individual consumers.

Most researchers on product counterfeit and piracy have made it clear that the escalation of counterfeiting and piracy is as a result of globalisation and the predominance of technological innovation such as Information Technology (IT) and in particular the Internet and mobile devices.

On the other hand, the internet and mobile devices also help in the promotion of globalisation in trade and give both business and individual consumers easy access to shop and pay online globally (Li & Yi, 2017; Quoquab et al., 2017; Inamdar, 2015). These technological innovations are also used to manage the process and communicate information as well as an essential representation of this modern era (Laurell, 2016; Meraviglia, 2015; Asongu, 2013). As has been mentioned, these technological innovations play dual or double-edged roles in most businesses. The fashion and beauty industry (F&B industry) is one of such industries that have seen the dual effect of these technological innovations (Herstein, Drori, Berger & Barnes, 2015; Meraviglia, 2015; Fernandes, 2013; Kim & Karpova, 2010).

LITERATURE REVIEW

Counterfeiting and Piracy

There is an ongoing debate on whether counterfeiting and piracy are the same or can be used in the same manner or interchangeably. Kim, Ko & Koh. (2016), and Lai and Zaichkowsky (1999) are with the opinion that counterfeiting and piracy are the same indicating that, in, either way, there has been a deliberate imitation of genuine goods. On the other hand, Li and Yi (2017); Quoquab et al., (2017); Meraviglia (2015); Fernandes (2013) and Kim and Karpova (2010) are with the view that counterfeiting and piracy have a different meaning.

Counterfeiting

Notwithstanding these arguments, Hoe, Hogg, and Hart (2003) suggested that before deliberating on the studies of counterfeiting, it is necessary to have a clear understanding of what counterfeiting is as well as its confines. They gave their definition of counterfeiting as the deliberate endeavours to mislead consumers by copying and marketing goods bearing well-known trademarks, generally with its packaging and product configuration, for it to look like that of the reputable manufacturer when they are, in fact, inferior copies. Similarly, Abid and Abbasi (2014) define counterfeiting, as the reproduction of genuine products that exist with remarkable brand value and have a good market share - emphasising that counterfeiting comprises packaging, labelling, and trademarks of the original brands, which are copied in a way that looks like the original product to consumers.

Additionally, the term counterfeiting has been defined as products that have undistinguishable characteristics as that of the registered ones, made purposely to misinform consumers into accepting that they are genuine products (Turkyilmaz &Uslu, 2014; Phau & Teah, 2009).

Further, the term counterfeiting can be argued as an infringement of the licit rights of an owner of intellectual property (IP), though referring only to specific cases of trademark infringement. Nonetheless, in practice, the term is permissible to encompass any product that in appearance is closely imitated of a product of another as to mislead a consumer (Magazzino & Michela, 2014).

In 2014, the World Trade Organisation (WTO) defined counterfeiting as an "unauthorised representation of a registered trademark carried on goods identical to or similar to goods for which the trademark is registered; the intention is to deceive the purchaser into believing that he/she is buying the original goods".

Based on the confines of counterfeiting, counterfeiting has been categorised into deceptive and non-deceptive (Li & Yi 2017; Cho, Fang & Tayur, 2015; Yao, 2015).

Deceptive Counterfeiting

Deceptive counterfeiting according to Hoe et al. (2003) is the reproduction of products that are identically packaged, including trademarks and labelling, clichéd to give the impression to a consumer that it is a genuine artefact. In this circumstance, the consumer is a victim of deception, meaning the consumer is unknowingly purchasing a counterfeit product. Besides this, deceptive counterfeiting is an imitation a consumer believes to be authentic at the time of purchase, and it is usually sold at the same price as or close to that of its branded (authentic) product to deceive consumers (Yao, 2015; Hamelin, Nwankwo & El Hadouchi, 2013). Deceptive counterfeiting comes about when the consumer is convinced in believing that the product being purchased is a product of company "A" while the product is from company "B" instead (Li & Yi, 2017; Bian & Veloutsou, 2017; Cho, Fang & Tayur, 2015; Abid & Abbasi, 2014).

Non-Deceptive Counterfeiting

Non-deceptive counterfeiting is the imitation a consumer can distinguish from the brand-name product at the time of purchase, which means that consumers are fully aware that they are buying non-genuine brands. This type of imitation products tends to be sold at a substantial discount through an unauthorised sales channel. Non-deceptive counterfeiting comes about when consumers know or strongly believe that the product or service being purchased is not the original product after close examination and inference, but go ahead and purchase the counterfeit or pirated product or service nonetheless (Bian & Veloutsou 2017; Li & Yi 2017; Yao 2015; Abid & Abbasi, 2014).

For instance, in the Chinese footwear industry, the counterfeiters use cheap materials to produce shoes, and they charged a small fraction of the authentic product's price to attract customers, and in this case, the consumers could quickly tell that the shoes being sold are not genuine products yet the go-ahead to purchase (Cho, Fang & Tayur, 2015).

BACKGROUND

The F&B industry presently is one of the most creative and vibrant industries that is stimulating several economies in the world (Bhatia, 2018; Laurell, 2016; Łopaciuk & Łoboda, 2013). According to the Joint

Economic Committee of the United States Congress, the industry worldwide makes more than $1.2 trillion whiles the United States alone consumes over $250 billion yearly on fashion. The industry is viewed as an organisation that produces a model of communication in terms of personal care and clothing. The industry is diverse, extending from major international wholesalers and retailers to big design houses as well as individual design shops. The foundation of the F&B industry can be traced to the fields of ideology, sociology and history. Additionally, the industry employs people from different occupational backgrounds: including fashion designers, project managers, directors, lawyers, accountants, copywriters, computer programmers and many more (Zhang, Kang, Jiang & Bian, 2018; Laurell, 2016; Petrenkoa, 2015; Meraviglia, 2015; Hoecht & Trott, 2014; Łopaciuk & Łoboda, 2013; Mohr, 2013).

More importantly, fashion can be seen as a way people express themselves and a momentary recurring phenomenon that consumers adopt for a specific circumstance and period. Fashion can also be referred to as a style of cosmetic, clothes or accessories that are trendy and worn by numerous individuals at a point in time. Additional, fashion usually interplays with consumption, art, politics and economics, creating a unique blend of the hoary and novel (Ciarniene & Vienazindiene, 2014; Delbufalo, 2015; Laurell, 2016). Fashion is persistently evolving, and its phenomenon today has become a cultural factor of vital importance to people of diverse culture, social class and background, as there is something for everybody.

In Africa, especially in Ghana and Nigeria, the F&B industry has become more popular, within and outside their shores. Most designers from both countries have made it in the fashion industry they have also had the opportunity to showcase their work on international runways as a means of promoting the Ghanaian and Nigerian culture (Bada, 2013; Sarpong, Howard and Osei-Ntiri, 2011; Oppenheimer, Spicer, Trejos, Zille, Benjamin, Cavallo & Leo, 2011). The African fashion history is one of a perpetual interchanging, assumption and a challenging journey through ill documentation with diverse influences coming into play across time and place. From the perspective of Jennings and Ude, (2011), the aesthetics of Africa have travailed through empires, slavery, conflicts, migration, urbanisation as well as globalisation until this present time. Emphasising that, "Africa is fashion's new frontier" showing the world how African fashion is done". However, this industry is facing a fearsome competitor that, so far as counterfeiting and piracy is a concern, therefore if proper precautions are not taken, the future of the F&B industry can be jeopardy (Li & Yi, 2017; Ong et al., 2015).

Although, fashion has become popular in developing countries especially in Ghana and Nigeria and in Africa as whole much research has not been done in this area of study (Bada, 2013; Sarpong et al., 2011; Oppenheimer et al., 2011). Above all, counterfeiting and piracy are increasingly exceedingly in the F&B industry; however, most studies on fashion only deliberate on consumers' intentions to purchase, consumers' attitudes and the legal protection of counterfeiting and piracy (Bhatia 2018; Koay 2018; Kim et al., 2016; Fernandes 2013). However, these studies did not specify how IT enables or constrain counterfeiting and piracy in the F&B industry, especially in developing countries. Additionally, these studies did not also clarify the types of IT use in curbing counterfeiting and piracy in the industry.

Therefore, this chapter discusses how IT enables or constrains counterfeiting and piracy in the F&B industry in developing countries (Ghana and Nigeria). It also highlights some of the types of IT used in the industry and especially how IT aid in the ascendance of counterfeiting and piracy, its influence and the strategies that some stakeholders in the industry use in constraining counterfeiting and piracy, as well as its impact on stakeholders.

The Lemon Market Theory (LMT)

The LMT is the theory underpinning this book chapter. The theory proposed that "there can be an incentive for sellers who market poor quality goods, resulting in a reduction of the average quality, leading to a death spiral, which eventually brings about a complete market deterioration" (Akerlof,1970). The level of analysis for the LMT is a market (external or internal) where there is transacting between two parties. These parties can be either individuals or organisations. Besides, the basic construct for the theory is information asymmetry with other constructs like *trust, reputation, moral hazard, adverse selection, opportunistic behaviour and perceived quality* (Devos, Van Landeghem, & Deschoolmeester, 2012). The phenomenon of a "lemon" market comes about where there is lack of information asymmetry between buyers and sellers in the market, and in general, the quality of goods and services offered is reflected by the entire group of sellers, rather than by individual sellers. (Bond, 1982; Afzal, Roland & Al-Squri 2009; Christozov, Chukova & Mateev, 2009).

According to, Dewan and Hsu (2004); Lee et al. (201) and Pavlou and Gefen, (2004) a lemon market essential can be seen as a dynamic process encompassing positive and negative feedback coming from closed transactions. Where, because of *information asymmetry* (lack information) seller take *opportunistic behaviour* (advantage) of buyers and offer them poor/counterfeit product or services (*perceived quality*). Where a *moral hazard* is an outcome or the danger a counterfeit product poses on the buyer or consumer. Buyers, therefore, lose *trust* in the sellers and the product or service offered them spoiling seller's reputation then bringing a death spiral.

METHODOLOGY

The data for this book chapter was directed at some of the manufacturers and importers of fashion and beauty products in Ghana and Nigeria, precisely, those from Accra and Lagos.

The data collection was conducted between the 22nd and 26th of February, 2019, through an interview guide and a face-to-face interview.

The responses were audio-recorded (Saunders, Lewis & Thornhill 2009; Yin, 1994). The interviews and the other discussions took around an hour and 20 minutes at the respondents' offices. All interviews were later transcribed manually, and notes adequately arranged to make sense of the data. A thematic approach was used as a guide for the data analysis, as well as pattern-matching in analysing the case studies, to help establish the findings that support the research questions (Braun & Clarke 2014; Yin 1994).

ENCOUNTERS

The F&B industry in Ghana and Nigeria, according to the five (5) companies interviewed are faced with several challenges in their line of business. Still, counterfeiting and piracy seem to be the foremost concern for both countries. Fibees Ltd. designs and sells women and men's clothing and exports some of the company's clothing to other African countries as well as to Europe and the United States of America (USA). Beaters Beauty is one of the leading make-up, and skincare manufacturers in West Africa while Colonic Hair & Make-up and Mariachi Cosmetics imports beauty products, for instance, body creams, make-up, hair products, hairbrushes, and other beauty care products, from Italy and the USA. Whereas

Ife Hair, produces hair relaxes, hair shampoos and conditioners, damaged hair treatments and other hair products.

From the perspective of the respondents, the challenges they encounter in their line of business are the infiltration of cheaper fashion and beauty products from both the local and foreign markets, particularly China. More importantly, the respondents of the interviewed companies also complained desperately that the domestic market has also imitated the F&B industry's products. While other similar products from neighbouring African countries also compete with them in the same market. The F&B industry is said to be the world's largest manufacturer of counterfeit and pirated products, and it is a serious threat to the industry (Pan, 2015; Meraviglia, 2015; Inamdar, 2015; Kim & Johnson, 2014; Fernandes, 2013). The F&B industry in Ghana and Nigeria have also not been spared so far as piracy and counterfeiting is a concern. The industry seems to be affected so much by counterfeiting and piracy.

Colonic Hair & Make-up and Mariachi Cosmetics importers of beauty products bitterly complained that some of the products they import from the United Arab Emirates, and Italy are at times pirated products, but they could not detect even though they are experts in their line of business. Their respondents asserted that,

It is continually becoming very challenging for us in this business, as most of our products have been imitated. Interestingly, these imitated products are so close in resemblance to the original products that, it is difficult to differentiate between them. Even though, as experts in cosmetology, we are most times deceived by the counterfeit and pirated products. Sadly, sometimes, our trusted sources of supply are also deceived. As some of the ingredients they purchase for their production is not authenticated because of counterfeiting and piracy, therefore, producing substandard beauty products.

Beaters Beauty a make-up and skincare manufactures in Accra (the largest city in Ghana) attested to the fact that the rate of counterfeiting and piracy in the F&B industry is very alarming. Also, if care is not taken, most companies will collapse, and the welfare of society will also be at risk. From the perspective of their respondent Beaters Beauty has come across lots of challenges of late as most of the products (ingredients) they purchase for their production are at times, not authentic products; therefore, the company losing so much money.

*I remembered early last year (2018), we purchase some **Isopropyl myristate** (it is an emollient that helps strengthen the natural skin moisture and also helps the skin to stay hydrated) from our reliable source of supply for the production of our beauty creams. Unfortunately, we realise that all the **Isopropyl myristate** were imitation after mixing with other products, Beaters Beauty lost over $50,000 (Fifty Thousand US Dollars) crippling the company.*

The respondent iterated that,

We were very fortunate to have found out this disaster at the production level; it would have been deadly if the finished product has gone to the market. The finished products could have caused severe health problems to those who would have come into contact with the product. Imitated skincare products can cause permanent or major skin damage to its users. Most times, imitated skincare products can cause eyesight problems that can lead to blindness, and in some cases, death. Besides, this problem could have caused a slander to Beaters Beauty image and the company might have been closed done by the regulation authorities.

According to the respondent from Colonic Hair & Make-up, *"lots of fake products are on our market, making it very difficult to identify the original products. In the hair business, fake products are so much that, one cannot believe it. I can tell you emphatically that on our market, the original hair weaves and wigs are less than 30%, which makes about 70% of the hair weaves and wigs on our market imitations. The most serious problem here is with the beauty and make-up products, these products are a kind of medication, and if imitated can be very dangerous to the consumers' health."*

But people do buy them, some of them knowing very well that what they are buying is an imitated product, but they do not mind. On the other hand, most people, unfortunately, do not know that what they are buying is an imitated product.

Similarly, the respondent from Ife Hair, ascertain that, as a result of counterfeiting and piracy, their company incurred so much debit when a product that they use in the production of their hair products was an authentic product.

The respondent stated that *"At times some of our (Ife Hair) products stay on the shelves for a long time, because of the fake hair products on the market which are quite cheaper."*

Fibees Ltd, a designer of men and women clothing, also has its challenges as far as counterfeiting and piracy are a concern. According to, their Public Relation Manager (PR), most of their clothing designs are copied by the local fashion shops, others also steal their designs, and make imitations in China and bring them back to the country and sell at a lower price. On the contrary, the respondent stated that they (Fibees Ltd.) could not sell their products at much lower prices because their cost of production is very high. They also have to pay so many employees who are part of their production team: including research team, graphic designers, social media team, salaries, fashion designer, outlets, retail shops, utility bills and so many others.

The respondent (the PR Manager) reiterated that the F&B industry's biggest challenge has always been with counterfeiting and piracy. For instance, the prominent designer house's product has always been copied by the small fashion shops and kiosk around the cities and villages and also sold at a fraction of our cost of production. This behaviour was seen as a petty crime because Fibees Ltd. was still making a profit. However, since the Chinese came to our market with their counterfeit and pirated products, the F&B industry in our part of the world is at the verge of collapsing. Because these imitated products come on an enormous scale, making it very difficult for us to sell our products for the reason that they are on highly-priced compared to imitated ones.

Because these small fashion shops do not have much money, their representatives come around our showrooms, pretending to buy and then be taking snapshots of our products. They go back to their shops and use different fabrics to make similar ones for their customer. Our business was not affected because our target market is different from theirs. On the contrary, the Chinese come to our showrooms and buy some of our clothing and other products that we sell, take them to China and make practically the same products. These imitated products are brought to the market and sold cheaper because these who manufacture them do not incur any research cost or government taxes. Thereby take our market share and leaving us in total debt.

In addition, the PR Manager emphasised that *"the most painful thing is that most consumers know that what they are buying is an imitation yet they go ahead and buy"*.

Also, the Marketing Manager of Fibees Ltd. said that these counterfeit and pirated products are causing so much health problems to their consumers, as well as the firm, is losing so much revenue.

If care is not taken one can sell a fake product to a customer, and you will never know unless the customer comes back to complain, if they don't it means you have lost a potential customer and this is bringing down our sales.

The PR Manager continued by saying that *"the most painful thing is that most consumers know that what they are buying is an imitation yet they go ahead and buy"*.

Similarly, Ife Hair is also suffering from the challenges that come about as a result of counterfeiting and piracy. According to the firm's Managing Director, its foremost problem is piracy.

The Managing Director stated emphatically that, *"Imitated products can be very detrimental to the health of the people who use them and can also gradually collapse the business of those doing genuine business"*. Moreover, the Managing Director thinks, *"the authorities are not doing much in the prevention of counterfeiting and piracy as other nations are doing"*.

One might assume, therefore, that counterfeit goods have a unique appeal only for consumers with lower incomes; however, many empirical studies have shown that a significant number of high-income consumers also, buy non-authentic goods. Surprisingly, the consumption of fake luxury goods have been repeatedly found to be viewed as "fun" and harmless by the consumer especially with inedible products (Tang, Tian & Zaichkowsky, 2014)

Research has also shown that in the F&B industry, IT plays an important role as far as counterfeiting and piracy is a concern.

THE ROLE OF IT IN F&B INDUSTRY

In the F&B industry, technological innovations such as IT, specifically the Internet, tablets and mobile devices as well as other social media platforms (e.g. Instagram, Facebook, Pinterest and Twitter) play dual roles in the industry (Zhang et al., 2018; Herstein et al., 2015; Meraviglia, 2015; Fernandes, 2013; Kim & Karpova, 2010). Foremost, IT is a means to manage, process, or communicate information as well as an essential representation of in the F&B industry in this modern era. For instance, promoting globalisation in trade (e-business and e-commerce) and shopping online, as well as giving both business and individual consumers easy access to shop and pay online worldwide. (Laurell, 2016; Inamdar, 2015). Subsequently, from the perspective of Kennedy, Wilson and Labrecque (2017), the predominance of IT has also brought about the proliferation of counterfeit and pirated goods. On the other hand, the Internet and mobile devices also give counterfeiters easy access to the industry's products online, which is a threat to the F&B industry.

From the findings of the study, all the companies interviewed attested to the fact that the Internet and mobile devices especially, social media platforms, have given their companies a broader consumer reach. Nonetheless, this same IT has exposed their business and products to criminals who are trying to ripe their business off their market share. To affirm this Fibees Ltd.'s respondent stated that,

To give our customers easy access to our products wherever they may be, and also, for them to see and make a choice, we put our products online. Also, to make payments easy for our consumers globally, Fibees Ltd., use online payment methods like Authorize.Net, PayPal, and Google Checkout in conducting our business. Doing business online promotes Fibees Ltd. business. In contrast, because most of our products are online, it is easy for counterfeiters to copy our designs.

In like manner, the respondent from Beaters Beauty attested to the fact that these technological innovations have their positive as well as adverse effects on their business.

The internet has helped this business as far as sales are a concern; we now have customers both individuals and companies from neighbouring countries ordering make-up and other beauty products from us. Business is easier done online; however; it gives unscrupulous people in the fashion business the opportunity to imitate our products. Moreover, selling them very cheap on the market spoiling the reputation of this business because it is not everyone who can detect fake products.

According to, the respondents from Colonic Hair & Make-up and Mariachi Cosmetics, as importers of beauty care products their companies do not usually place their products online it is done by the manufactures. However, some of the imported beauty care products have been imitated because there are online. Mariachi Cosmetics respondents said that,

Because our beauty care products come from well-established companies like MAC Cosmetics, Maybelline New York, and L'Oréal, these products are already online. Therefore, the only thing we do is to put what we have on our social media platforms for our customers to know what we have in stock. By doing so, we pull many customers to buy in our shops and on the social media platform as well. Our main problem with this business is counterfeiting, is very common in our line of business. Most consumers come around with complains of buying fake Mac or Maybelline products online, but at a closer look at what they brought, we can realise that it not some of our products. In our part of the world, most consumers are not able to afford the original products, as they are a bit expensive; therefore, they opt to buy imitated products. Surprisingly, some of the consumers who can afford the original products at times buy imitation beauty products knowingly, some also buy these imitation products unknowing meaning they have been ripped off.

Similarly, the respondent from Ife Hair also complained about their products being imitated because they are online. However, many people get to know their products because of their online presence.

Controlling Measures in the F&B industry (Anti-Piracy/ Counterfeiting Technologies)

Anti-counterfeiting technologies, according to Li, (2013), Ting and Ip (2015), are used in the identification of authentic products from imitated ones. However, a study conducted by Hoecht and Trott (2014) discussed some of the strategies that firms must use in the fight against counterfeiting and piracy but did not discuss the technological innovations (anti-piracy/counterfeiting technologies) that should be used.

From the findings of this study showed that some of the companies in the F&B industry had devised their anti-counterfeiting technology to help in the detection of excessive counterfeiting and piracy in the industry. According to Meraviglia (2015) and Kim and Johnson (2014), the F&B industry is one of the leading producers of counterfeit and pirated products in the world; therefore, it needs to be protected.

From the perspective of some of the interviewed companies, the anti-piracy/counterfeiting technologies used in the F&B industry in Ghana and Nigeria only help in the protection of some of the industry's products from being imitated. However, these anti-piracy/counterfeiting technologies, according to the respondents, has not been able to stop the damage that counterfeiting and piracy are causing the industry.

The respondent from Ife Hairs attested to the fact that the anti-piracy/counterfeiting technologies that Ife Hair is using "does not stop counterfeiters from imitating their hair products however it has made it easier for us (Ife Hairs) to monitor our product on the market, and it has also made it difficult for others to imitate our products".

According to, Fibees Ltd. respondent, the company, has tried different types of anti-piracy/counterfeiting technologies such as bar code technology and another anti-piracy/counterfeiting technologies improvised by their company.

When we realised that the bar code technology was not very effective in our line of business, we then made a specially "Adinkra" (a traditional symbol that commonly depicts the West African culture) doll heads which are carved out of silver and brass with the firm's initials and manufacturers' codes to use as buttons for our clothing line. This improvised anti-counterfeiting/piracy technology is helping our customers to differentiate our products from that of the imitated ones.

Whiles the respondent from Beaters Beauty thinks that the anti-counterfeiting technologies that they are using are helpful but have not eased the counterfeiting and piracy going on in the F&B industry. Beaters Beauty has also tried different types of anti-piracy/counterfeiting technologies which include: barcode, colour codes and protective packaging technologies.

In this business, not much can be done so far as counterfeiting and piracy are a concern. Nonetheless, we have introduced different types of anti-piracy/counterfeiting technologies in preventing others from imitating our products. We have use colour codes, packaging protective technology, as well as barcode technology to differentiate our products. Unfortunately, in our part of the world, most of the customers do not even watch when buying a product. It only helps us when we go on our routine check on the market.

According to, Colonic Hair & Make-up respondent, their company do not produce their products; therefore, there is little or nothing that can be done as far as counterfeiting and piracy are a concern. *"We just look for a reliable source and buy from".*

Effects of Counterfeiting and Piracy

The findings of this study revealed that counterfeiting and piracy have a very negative effect on the F&B industry as it is putting the industry under a severe threat globally (Li & Yi, 2017; Arli et al., 2015; Meraviglia, 2015).

The respondent of Colonic Hair & Make-up said that, because of counterfeiting and piracy, their company has been losing potential customers, which are gradually collapsing their business. This problem has come about because most counterfeit and pirated products on the market are quite cheaper compared to that of Colonic Hair & Make-up. Therefore, Colonic Hair & Make-up is not able to make good sales.

The company is not able to meet its target sale making it difficult for them to pay their salaries, rents and bank loans and even their taxes. According to, the respondent because of the imitated products on the market, the company's personnel have to go round customer's shop to convince them to buy their products. On the negative side, this brings much stress on management and employees of Colonic Hair & Make-up; therefore, management at times has to forfeit their salaries, making it difficult for them in fulfilling their obligations.

Likewise, Mariachi Cosmetics is also struggling with the payments of staff salaries and banks loans, therefore, laying off some of their workers.

Ife Hair respondent complained bitterly as well that, *"Because there are a whole lot of imitation products on the market, these fake products have taken a greater part of our market share making it very difficult for our products to sell. Some of Ife's product line is not selling, as customers think they are expensive, and can get a cheaper alternative elsewhere even though it might be an imitation".*

The respondent from Colonic Hair & Make-up said that *"Since most of the products on the market are fake, they are quite cheap compared to ours, meaning it is very challenging for us to make adequate sales. As a result, the firm is finding it very difficult to pay salaries, rents, bank loans and even government taxes; this brings so much stress on management".*

OTHER FINDINGS

Some researchers including, Laurell (2016); Inamdar (2015); Meraviglia (2015) and Sarpong, Howard and Osei-Ntiri (2011) postulated that the increase in globalisation in trading and shopping online has changed how the F&B industry operates immensely making it very convenient to access, shop and pay online for virtually every product or service worldwide. According to Li and Yi (2017), the development of technologies, specifically the internet, has enabled the distribution of products. However, the ascendance of counterfeiting and piracy rescinding livelihoods, businesses and their products as well as reducing revenue according to Herstein et al. (2015) and Guin, et al. (2014) is due to the predominance of technological innovations, especially IT. According to Li and Yi (2017); Stroppa et al. (2016) the commonly recognised factor for the increase in piracy is as a result of the development of technologies that enable the unlawful distribution of exclusive rights products, especially the internet. Important to realise, both legal and illegal commodities can be accessed online by users from anywhere around the globe (Broséus et al., 2017).

Enables

The finding of this study revealed that in the F&B industry most of the manufacturers of fashion and beauty products put their products online for consumer's easy accessibility, especially for their customers outside the country of origin. Also, the products online make it easier for consumers to select the ones they want and to read about the products. Some consumers also bring a snapshot of what they have seen online to the manufacturer's showrooms, outlets as well as shops to make it easy for consumers to purchase what they want. Similarly, with the help of IT, payments of goods purchased, online can be paid through online payment methods such as *Authorize.Net, PayPal, and Google Checkout*. The findings of the study also shown that some people in a similar business copy the designs of the F&B industry then takes them to China, make imitations, and bring them to the local markets at a lower price. Another critical point is that the Internet and mobile devices aid in the promotion of the F&B industry's products as well as encouraging counterfeiting and piracy.

Constrain

Besides the findings shown that there is another technological innovation (anti-counterfeiting and piracy) use in the constraining of counterfeiting and piracy in the F&B industry. Nonetheless, the type of anti-counterfeiting and piracy technologies used depends on the kind of firm in the industry. For instance, those into clothing uses specially made *'Adinkra' doll heads carved out of silver and brass with the firm's initials* and manufactured code as an anti-counterfeiting/piracy technology. These findings are not different from a study by Hoecht and Trott (2014), which discussed the strategies that firms should use to fight against counterfeiting and piracy but not the type of anti-piracy/counterfeiting and technologies. Others in the industry such as the manufacturers of hair products use technologies such as *bar code technology, colour codes and packaging protective Technology*. In the same manner, some existing literature on counterfeiting and piracy in the F&B industry did not suggest any particular anti-counterfeiting and piracy technologies that should be used in the industry instead they discussed the damage that counterfeiting and piracy is causing the sector (Kim & Johnson, 2014; Meraviglia, 2015; Inamdar, 2015). Meaning, there is not a single or specified anti-counterfeiting/piracy technology for the F&B industry, rather any anti-counterfeiting and piracy technology that can detect counterfeiting and piracy products are acceptable (Herstein et al., 2015 Hoecht & Trott, 2014; Li, 2013). The findings also ascertained that even though there are several anti-counterfeiting and piracy technologies on the market, counterfeiting and piracy is still in ascendance (Li, 2013).

THE IMPACT OF COUNTERFEITING AND PIRACY

Even though the F&B industry presently, is one of the most creative and vibrant industries that is stimulating several economies in the world (Laurell, 2016; Łopaciuk & Łoboda, 2013). However, the F&B industry is seen as the world's biggest manufacturer of counterfeiting and piracy products (Li & Yi, 2017; Meraviglia, 2015; Kim & Johnson, 2014). Counterfeiting and piracy from the perspective of Ong et al. (2015) have now become prominent and an excessive threat to the F&B industry in the competitive market. It is now a concern to governments because of the negative impact that they have on economic growth, employment and modernisation as well as posing a danger to the well-being of society (Quoquab et al., 2017; Arli et al., 2015; Magazzino & Michela, 2014). From the findings, counterfeiting and piracy are a significant threat to the Ghanaian and Nigerian F&B industry.

According to Magazzino and Michela (2014) counterfeiting impact legitimate businesses negatively, causing loss of brand trust and value, loss of sales and lower profits. However, in an interconnected economy, governments and consumers also suffer. Governments realise lower tax revenues and higher spending on welfare, health services and crime prevention. Consumers receive poorer-quality products that are unregulated and unsafe.

Impact on Stakeholders

The findings, therefore, revealed that the F&B industry is suffering from the negative effect of piracy and counterfeiting. Because some people in similar industries copy, the industry's designs send them to China and make imitations (counterfeiting and pricy) then later bringing them to the local markets. At times, these imitated products even get to the market before the original ones and are most times far cheaper than the original products.

The findings asserted that counterfeiting and piracy has a negative effect, on both individuals and the industry as a whole. Some of the effects counterfeiting and piracy poses to the F&B industry includes the loose of potential customers, which in effect slows down the sales and demand for the industry's products as well as difficulty in paying salaries, bank loans and rents which leads to the closing of some firms of the industry. Since there is also a lack of information; buyers find it challenging to identify the original products.

The research findings were pointing to the fact that, because some of the firms in the F&B industry do not manufacture their products, these firms, at times, purchase counterfeit or pirated products unknowingly. Consequently, they are selling counterfeit and pirated product to their customers. Resulting in the loose of customers and causing several health problems to consumers. The findings also made known that most consumers do not know the difference between counterfeit and authentic products; therefore, buying whatever is available. While some consumers know very well that what they are buying is a counterfeit product, nonetheless they go ahead to buy because of its price.

In line with literature, a study by Yao (2015), Li and Yi (2017) indicated that there are two types of counterfeiting deceptive and non-deceptive, deceptive counterfeiting is when buyers/consumers are convened that they are buying a product of company "A" while the product is from company "B" instead. Whereas non-deceptive counterfeiting, come about when consumers know or strongly believe that the product they are purchasing is not the original product after close examination and inferring. Nevertheless, they go ahead to buy that product.

The findings of this study revealed that because of the counterfeit and pirated products on the market, the F&B industry is drastically losing its market share and not being able to pay its taxes; as a result, government losing tax and revenue. This assertion is also in support of the finding form literature, which posit that counterfeiting and piracy are destroying many industries and concern to governments because of the negative impact they have on economic growth, employment and posing a danger to the well-being of society (Quoquab et al., 2017; Arli, 2015; Meraviglia, 2015; Guin et al., 2014; Magazzino & Michela, 2014).

CONCLUSION AND IMPLICATION

Counterfeiting and piracy are now a dominant factor destroying economies, business and the well-being of society. Over the past two decades, counterfeiting and piracy have grown over 10,000 per cent, and its estimated cost is around USD600 billion a year, and predominate in the F&B industry even though it is illegal. According to most literature, the ascendance of counterfeiting and piracy is due to the pervasiveness of technological innovations, especially IT. Our aim for this chapter is to explore how IT enables or constrains counterfeiting and piracy in the F&B industry in developing countries (Ghana and Nigeria). The study highlighted some of the types of IT used in the industry and especially how IT aid in the ascendance of counterfeiting and piracy, its influence and the strategies that stakeholders in the industry use in constraining counterfeiting and piracy as well as its impact on stakeholders.

Base on the findings of this study, it was ascertained that counterfeiting and piracy have very harmful effects on both individuals and the industry as a whole. The F&B industry is losing potential customers because of counterfeit and pirated products on the market, which in effect slows down the sales and demand for the industry's products — making it very difficult for the F&B industry to pay salaries, rents and bank loans as well as leading to the closing of most firms in the industry. The analysis of the findings also asserted that counterfeiting and piracy are having an undesirable effect on the entire Ghanaian, and the Nigerian economy as some of the industries in the country is suffering from product imitation and inevitably restraining the payment of taxes. Additionally, the findings revealed that counterfeiting and piracy are rescinding livelihoods, businesses and their products as well as reducing revenue, due to the prevalence of technological innovations. Several anti-counterfeiting/piracy technologies on the market can be used in the fight against counterfeiting and piracy.

Nonetheless, the F&B industry does not have any specific anti-counterfeiting and piracy technologies that the industry uses. Therefore, this chapter is contributing to the strategies that some of the F&B industry in developing countries use in combating counterfeiting and pricy in their line of business.

In academic terms, no advanced research has been conducted yet on counterfeiting and piracy in the F&B industry in Ghana and Nigeria as far as the role of information technology is a concern.

LIMITATIONS AND FUTURE RESEARCH DIRECTIONS

In this study, we considered some of the firms in the subsector of the F&B industry in Ghana and Nigeria. The study covered only the hair products, cosmetics and clothing subsector of the F&B industry and from the manufacturers and imports perspective. The study also touched on the impact of counterfeiting and piracy on the F&B industry and the role IT plays in the industry. Future research can concentrate on the effect of piracy and counterfeiting on the consumers in the F&B industry in Ghana and Nigeria as this research did not take an in-depth invitation in that area as well as their reasons for purchasing counterfeiting and piracy products of the F&B industry.

Relating to practice, the study provides an insight into the negative effect of piracy and counterfeiting on society, hence using some of the subsectors of the F&B industry as a case for the study. This study can also serve as a guideline for other sectors of the Ghanaian and the Nigerian economy, which wants to investigate the impact of counterfeiting and piracy on their line of business.

Concerning policy, this study provides guidelines for discussions on the national policy concerning counterfeiting and piracy and its' negative effect on consumers' health as well as national revenue.

REFERENCES

Abid, M., & Abbasi, M. (2014). *Antecedents and Outcomes of Consumer Buying Attitude: The Case of Pakistani Counterfeit Market*. Academic Press.

Afzal, W., Roland, D., & Al-Squri, M. N. (2009). Information asymmetry and product valuation: An exploratory study. *Journal of Information Science, 35*(2), 192–203. doi:10.1177/0165551508097091

Andrés, A. R., & Asongu, S. A. (2013). Fighting Software Piracy: Which Governance Tools Matter in Africa? *Journal of Business Ethics, 118*(3), 667–682. doi:10.100710551-013-1620-7

Arli, D., Tjiptono, F., & Porto, R. (2015). The impact of moral equity, relativism and attitude on individuals' digital piracy behaviour in a developing country. *Marketing Intelligence & Planning, 33*(3), 348–365. doi:10.1108/MIP-09-2013-0149

Asongu, S. A. (2013). Harmonizing IPRs on software piracy: Empirics of trajectories in Africa. *Journal of Business Ethics, 118*(1), 45–60. doi:10.100710551-012-1552-7

Bada, O. (2013). *The Emerging Role of Fashion Tourism and The Need for A Development Strategy in Lagos, Nigeria.* Case Study: Lagos Fashion and Design Week.

Bhatia, V. (2018). Examining consumers' attitude towards the purchase of counterfeit fashion products. *Journal of Indian Business Research, 10*(2), 193–207. doi:10.1108/JIBR-10-2017-0177

Bian, X., & Veloutsou, C. (2017). Consumers' attitudes regarding non-deceptive counterfeit brands in the UK and China. In Advances in Chinese Brand Management (pp. 331-350). Palgrave Macmillan.

Bond, E. W. (1982). A direct test of the" lemons" model: The market for used pickup trucks. *The American Economic Review, 72*(4), 836–840.

Braun, V., Clarke, V., & Terry, G. (2014). Thematic analysis. Qual Res Clin Health Psychol, (24), 95-114.

Broséus, J., Rhumorbarbe, D., Morelato, M., Staehli, L., & Rossy, Q. (2017). A geographical analysis of trafficking on a popular darknet market. *Forensic Science International, 277*, 88–102. doi:10.1016/j.forsciint.2017.05.021 PMID:28624673

Chaudhry, P., & Zimmerman, A. (2013). The global growth of counterfeiting trade. In *Protecting Your Intellectual Rights*. New York, NY: Springer. doi:10.1007/978-1-4614-5568-4_2

Cho, S. H., Fang, X., & Tayur, S. (2015). Combating Strategic Counterfeiters in Licit and Illicit Supply Chains. *Manufacturing & Service Operations Management: M & SOM, 17*(3), 273–289. doi:10.1287/msom.2015.0524

Christozov, D., Chukova, S., & Mateev, P. (2009). On two types of warranties: Warranty of malfunctioning and warranty of misinforming. *Asia-Pacific Journal of Operational Research, 36*(3), 399–420. doi:10.1142/S0217595909002274

Čiarnienė, R., & Vienažindienė, M. (2014). Management of the contemporary fashion industry: Characteristics and challenges. *Procedia: Social and Behavioral Sciences, 156*, 63–68. doi:10.1016/j.sbspro.2014.11.120

Delbufalo, E. (2015). The influence of supply network structure on firm's multiple innovation capabilities: A longitudinal study in the fashion industry. *Management Decision, 53*(10), 2457–2476. doi:10.1108/MD-07-2014-0431

Devos, J., Van Landeghem, H., & Deschoolmeester, D. (2012). The theory of the lemon markets in IS research. *Information Systems Theory*, 213-229.

Dewan, S., & Hsu, V. (2004). Adverse selection in electronic markets: Evidence from online stamp auctions. *The Journal of Industrial Economics, 52*(4), 497–516. doi:10.1111/j.0022-1821.2004.00237.x

Fernandes, C. (2013). Analysis of counterfeit fashion purchase behaviour in UAE, Journal of Fashion Marketing and Management. *International Journal (Toronto, Ont.), 17*(1), 85–97.

Guin, U., DiMase, D., & Tehranipoor, M. (2014). Counterfeit integrated circuits: Detection, avoidance, and the challenges ahead. *Journal of Electronic Testing, 30*(1), 9–23. doi:10.100710836-013-5430-8

Hamelin, N., Nwankwo, S., & El Hadouchi, R. (2013). 'Faking brands': Consumer responses to counterfeiting. *Journal of Consumer Behaviour, 12*(3), 159–170. doi:10.1002/cb.1406

Harvey, M. G. (1987). Industrial product counterfeiting: Problems and proposed solutions. *Journal of Business and Industrial Marketing, 2*(4), 5–13. doi:10.1108/eb006038

Harvey, M. G. (1987). Industrial Product Counterfeiting: Problems and Proposed Solutions. *Journal of Business and Industrial Marketing, 2*(4), 5–13. doi:10.1108/eb006038

Herstein, R., Drori, N., Berger, R., & Barnes, B. R. (2015). Anti-counterfeiting strategies and their influence on attitudes of different counterfeit consumer types. *Psychology and Marketing, 32*(8), 842–859. doi:10.1002/mar.20822

Hoe, L., Hogg, G., & Hart, S. (2003). Faking it: Counterfeiting and consumer contradictions. *European Advances in Consumer Behaviour, 6*, 60–67.

Hoecht, A., & Trott, P. (2014). How should firms deal with counterfeiting? A review of the success conditions of anti-counterfeiting strategies. *International Journal of Emerging Markets, 9*(1), 98–119. doi:10.1108/IJOEM-02-2011-0014

Inamdar, P. (2015). "PVO"-a solution to brand piracy. *The Business & Management Review, 5*(4), 62.

Jennings, H., & Ude, I. (2011). *New African Fashion*. New York: Prestel.

Kennedy, J. P., Wilson, J., & Labrecque, R. (2017). Towards a more proactive approach to brand protection: Development of the Organisational Risk Assessment for Product Counterfeiting (ORAPC). *Global Crime, 18*(4), 329–352. doi:10.1080/17440572.2017.1313733

Kim, C., Ko, E., & Koh, J. (2016). Consumer attitudes and purchase intentions toward fashion counterfeits: Moderating the effects of types of counterfeit goods and consumer characteristics. *Journal of Global Fashion Marketing, 7*(1), 15–29. doi:10.1080/20932685.2015.1105109

Kim, H., & Karpova, E. (2010). Consumer attitudes toward fashion counterfeits: Application of the theory of planned behaviour. *Clothing & Textiles Research Journal, 28*(2), 79–94. doi:10.1177/0887302X09332513

Kim, J. E., & Johnson, K. P. (2014). Shame or pride? The moderating role of self-construal on moral judgments concerning fashion counterfeits. *European Journal of Marketing, 48*(7/8), 1431–1450. doi:10.1108/EJM-02-2013-0110

Lai, K. K. Y., & Zaichkowsky, J. L. (1999). Brand imitation: Do the Chinese have different views? *Asia Pacific Journal of Management, 16*(2), 179–192. doi:10.1023/A:1015482707900

Laurell, C. (2016). Fashion spheres – from a systemic to a stereological perspective of fashion. *Journal of Fashion Marketing and Management: An International Journal*, 20(4), 520–530. doi:10.1108/JFMM-04-2016-0033

Li, F., & Yi, Z. (2017). Counterfeiting and piracy in supply chain management: Theoretical studies. *Journal of Business and Industrial Marketing*, 32(1), 98–10. doi:10.1108/JBIM-09-2015-0171

Li, L. (2013). Technology designed to combat fakes in the global supply chain. *Business Horizons*, 56(2), 167–177. doi:10.1016/j.bushor.2012.11.010

Łopaciuk, A., & Łoboda, M. (2013). Global beauty industry trend in the 21st century. *Management, knowledge and learning international conference,* 19-21.

Magazzino, C., & Michela, M. (2014). Counterfeiting in Italian regions: An empirical analysis based on new data. *Journal of Financial Crime*, 21(4), 400–410. doi:10.1108/JFC-01-2014-0001

Meraviglia, L. (2015). Counterfeiting, fashion and the civil society. *Journal of Fashion Marketing and Management*, 19(3), 230–248. doi:10.1108/JFMM-06-2013-0084

Mohr, I. (2013). The impact of social media on the fashion industry. *Journal of Applied Business and Economics.*, 15(2), 17–22.

Ong, D. L. T., Chiang, T. T. S., & Pung, A. X. Y. (2015). To Buy or To Lie: Determinants of Purchase Intention of Counterfeit Fashion in Malaysia. *International Conference on Marketing and Business Development Journal*, (1), 49-56.

Oppenheimer, J., Spicer, M., Trejos, A., Zille, P., Benjamin, J., Cavallo, D., & Leo, B. (2011). Putting young Africans to work: Addressing Africa's youth unemployment crisis. *The Brenthurst Foundation, Discussion Paper*, 8.

Pan, Y. (2015). How to counteract negative effect of adverse selection in Chinese e-commerce market? *Comparative analysis on credit scoring system and guarantee system of TAOBAO.*

Pavlou, P. A., & Dimoka, A. (2006). The nature and role of feedback text comments in online marketplaces: Implications for trust building, price premiums, and seller differentiation. *Information Systems Research*, 17(4), 392–414. doi:10.1287/isre.1060.0106

Petrenkoa, V. V. (2015). Fashion: The Game of Social Meaning as the Cynical Strategy of Consumption. *Procedia: Social and Behavioral Sciences*, 200, 506–513.

Phau, I., & Teah, M. (2009). Devil wears (counterfeit) Prada: A study of antecedents and outcomes of attitudes towards counterfeits of luxury brands. *Journal of Consumer Marketing*, 26(1), 15–27. doi:10.1108/07363760910927019

Quoquab, F., Pahlevan, S., Mohammad, J., & Thurasamy, R. (2017). Factors affecting consumers' intention to purchase counterfeit product: Empirical study in the Malaysian market. *Asia Pacific Journal of Marketing and Logistics*, 29(4), 837–853. doi:10.1108/APJML-09-2016-0169

Sarpong, G. D., Howard, E. K., & Osei-Ntiri, K. (2011). Globalization of the fashion industry and its effects on Ghanaian independent fashion designers. *Journal of Science and Technology*, 31(3), 97–106.

Saunders, M., Lewis, P., & Thornhill, A. (2009). *Research methods for business students*. Pearson education.

Stroppa, A., di Stefano, D., & Parrella, B. (2016). *Social media and luxury goods counterfeit: a growing concern for government, industry and consumers worldwide*. Academic Press.

Tang, F., Tian, V. I., & Zaichkowsky, J. (2014). Understanding counterfeit consumption. *Asia Pacific Journal of Marketing and Logistics*, 26(1), 4–20. doi:10.1108/APJML-11-2012-0121

Ting, S. L., & Ip, W. H. (2015). Combating the counterfeits with web portal technology. *Enterprise Information Systems*, 9(7), 661–680. doi:10.1080/17517575.2012.755713

Turkyilmaz, C. A., & Uslu, A. (2014). The role of individual characteristics on consumers counterfeit purchasing intentions: Research in fashion industry. *Journal of Management Marketing and Logistics*, 1(3), 259–275.

Wilson, B. J., & Zillante, A. (2010). More information, more ripoffs: Experiments with public and private information in markets with asymmetric information. *Review of Industrial Organization*, 36(1), 1–16. doi:10.100711151-010-9240-1

Yao, J. T. (2015). The impact of counterfeit-purchase penalties on anti-counterfeiting under deceptive counterfeiting. *Journal of Economics and Business*, 80, 51–61. doi:10.1016/j.jeconbus.2015.04.002

Yin, R. K. (1994). Discovering the future of the case study. Method in evaluation research. *Evaluation Practice*, 15(3), 283–290. doi:10.1016/0886-1633(94)90023-X

Zhang, W., Kang, L., Jiang, Q., & Bian, Y. (2018). More than the Tone: The Impact of Social Media Opinions on Innovation Investments. In *The 26th European Conference on Information Systems (ECIS) 2018. European Conference on Information Systems*.

KEY TERMS AND DEFINITIONS

Adinkra: A traditional symbol that usually depicts the culture of West Africans.

Anti-Counterfeiting Technologies: A system used in the combating of fake products.

Cosmetics: They are products used to enhance the body.

Isopropyl Myristate: It is a soothing chemical added to beauty products, which help the skin from losing its natural moisture.

Make-Up: An example of cosmetics such as eyeliner, mascara or lipstick used to enhance the body, especially the face.

PayPal: A company that facilitate the payment of online transactions.

Unscrupulous People: Dishonest people who can do anything for money.

Chapter 11
Enablers and Inhibitors of Merchant Adoption of Mobile Payments:
A Developing Country Perspective

Eunice Yeboah Afeti

Business School, University of Ghana, Ghana

Joshua Ofori Amanfo

ⓘ https://orcid.org/0000-0002-7114-527X

Business School, University of Ghana, Ghana

ABSTRACT

Merchant adoption of mobile payments is facilitating new business models and changing the way merchants run their brick and mortar businesses. Despite the advantages of mobile payment adoption to the merchant, they still hesitate to adopt mobile payments. Thus, the study seeks to explore qualitatively through a case study the enablers and inhibitors to merchant adoption of mobile payments. The study identified that merchants are adopting mobile payments to facilitate new business models, to promote the disintermediation of traditional intermediaries, to offer different possibilities of growing their businesses, and to reduce transaction costs. Even though merchants believe that mobile payments adoption and use improve operational efficiency to their businesses, there are instances of fraud, particularly in the peer-to-peer transfer sector, data breaches, data security, and privacy concerns. Therefore, it is imperative for service providers of mobile payments to enhance technological issues regarding privacy protection that could enhance trust towards mobile payment adoption.

DOI: 10.4018/978-1-7998-2610-1.ch011

INTRODUCTION

The liberalisation of ICT in developing countries in the past decade has brought a considerable transformation to the macro and micro-economic landscape of developing countries. Through the provision of technical support, interactive network, and service to underserved sectors such as health and finance (Asongu, Nwachukwu, & Orim, 2018; Murphy & Carmody, 2017). More so, mobile phones are receiving attention globally; as a result, developing economies have gradually seen an expansion in mobile phones used to facilitate different services. Prominent among these services is using the mobile phone in payment transactions known as mobile payment (Dahlberg, Guo, & Ondrus, 2015; Iman, 2018). The mobile payment revolution has been transforming households and businesses by providing a business solution to small and medium-sized businesses as well as mobile phone-related financial services to the underserved population in developing countries (Asongu et al., 2018). Also, the deployment of mobile payments is an avenue to helps developing economies leapfrog poor non-existing payment infrastructure, which is seen as a burden to economic growth in these countries. This lack of quality means of payment is an opportunity to open a high window of m-payments for future use in developing countries (Asongu & Boateng, 2018). Mothobi and Grzybowski (2017) report that the availability and access to mobile payment dramatically improve the standard of living, and provide potential mechanisms to steer economic benefits to consumers and producers in developing countries. For instance, it can increase market efficiency by improving and facilitating services which in general are not available to low-income households, such as mobile phone-based financial services (Aker & Mbiti, 2010).

This innovation has been swiftly accepted in developing countries by leading the way as a critical driver of economic growth and better financial access to reduce economic vulnerability and increase investment in human capital (Asongu & Boateng, 2018; Humbani & Wiese, 2018). Different authors have outlined the importance of mobile payment as creating distinct value to both merchants and consumers and is considered as one most essential success driver of mobile commerce (Liébana-Cabanillas, De Luna, & Montoro-Ríos, 2015; Asongu & Boateng, 2018). Arguably this innovation suggests a significant advantage for merchants. However, aligning the high penetration of mobile phones and the low level of mobile payment adoption by merchants continues to challenge mobile payment researchers and practitioners globally. This seems to defeat the usefulness of mobile payments, and yet it has not been explored (Dahlberg et al., 2015; Slade, Dwivedi, Piercy, & Williams, 2015). Therefore, the reason for non-adoption by merchants is not firmly established. This suggests the need for mobile payment providers to understand the enablers and inhibitors of merchant adoption and use of mobile payments to design strategies and develop their marketing tools to suit the needs of merchants.

Nevertheless, the literature on mobile payments has explored and conceptualized the benefits and challenges of mobile payment, technical dimensions that affect consumer intentions to adopt mobile payments (Jin, Zheng, Jin, & Li, 2017; Liébana-cabanillas & Lara-rubio, 2017; Madan & Yadav, 2016; Miao & Jayakar, 2016). These studies are often silent on merchants 'adoption and perceptions about the maturity of mobile payment technology as a means of payment transactions and, the preparedness of merchants to adopt mobile payment to their benefit (Cabanillas et al., 2017; Mallat, Rossi, Tuunainen & Oorni, 2006; Pousttchi, 2008). Secondly, mobile payment failures have a secure connection to the lack of critical mass of users as well as having limited adoption of merchants and non-involvement of merchants (Dahlberg et al., 2015). Nevertheless, existing studies on mobile payment fail to provide a comprehensive explanation of the merchant's role in the growth and development of mobile payment ecosystem, and the resources needed to develop and establish a sustainable two-sided market that generates critical mass for mobile payment adoption (Guo & Bouwman, 2015). More importantly, context-specific issues, varying cultural and market restrictions such as economic, technology, and social dynamics do not allow successful business models to be imported directly to another cultural context. Therefore, examining the merchant's mobile payment adoption in the developing country context where minimal research has been conducted, is also essential.

This chapter will depend on the explanatory power of Diffusion Innovation Theory and Perceived Technology Security to explore factors that could impact the adoption of mobile payment by merchants. Therefore, the purpose of this study is to explore the enablers and inhibitors of merchant adoption of mobile payment from a developing country perspective. The chapter will seek to respond to the questions: what are the enablers of merchant adoption of mobile payments in Ghana and what are the inhibitors of merchant adoption in Ghana. The study will adopt a qualitative method to explore the subject under study. The remainder of this chapter is organised as follows: The next section reviews the literature on mobile payments and briefly discusses the theoretical underpinnings. The third section presents the conceptual framework guiding the study; the section that follows details the methodology employed for the study. Subsequently, the findings are analysed, and discussions of the findings presented. Finally, the chapter concludes with specific contributions and directions for future research.

LITERATURE REVIEW

Mobile Payments Conceptualisation

Mobile payment is regarded conceptually, as a novel form of value transfer, comparable to other payments; nevertheless, the distinction is the use of mobile devices as a medium. Mobile payments as a concept has been defined from different perspective in the literature. Different researchers like (Liu, Kauffman & Ma 2015; Dahlberg, 2015; de Reuver et al., 2014; Au & Kauffman, 2008; Dahlberg et al., 2008 ; Dewan & Chen, 2005) have explained mobile payments from the technical angle thus considering mobile payments as making payment with the assistance of technology through a mobile device. However, a researcher like Zhong 2009 views mobile payment as having strategic, participatory and operational functions. Also, Upadhyay and Chattopadhyay (2015) and Mallat (2007) looked at mobile payments (M-payment) as an m-commerce sub-set, which offers a technique for conducting practical and innovative micropayment to facilitate mobile commerce transactions through non-banking channels. In this paper, mobile payment is defined as an exchange of value with the assistance of mobile devices (mobile phones, smartphone Personal Digital Assistant or any wireless device) to securely complete a transaction over a mobile network or via various wireless technologies within the mobile payment's ecosystem. Mobile payment technology has been categorised mainly into two by the literature; remote payments and proximity payments (Agarwal, Khapra, Menezes, & Uchat, 2007). Mobile payment via SMS, direct billing, entering bank account number on a mobile website, registering on merchant's website such as Amazon and using an electronic wallet are classified as remote payment. On the other hand, the scenario where the user can integrate mobile phones or mobile device contactless facilitated by Near Field, Communication (NFC) where the user can make payment as the individual passes the mobile next to the receiving terminal is known as proximity payments, this is common in the public transport industry (Tylor, 2016; Zhao & Kurnia,2014). Mobile payment can further be differentiated based on the transaction; into peer to peer payments, consumer to business payments and business to business payments. Further, the providers of mobile payments can also be analysed from three perspectives, that is mobile network operator-centric, financial institution and the third-party operators (Zhao & Kurnia, 2014).

Prior Research on Mobile Payment

Mobile payment adoption has received much attention in the literature; the reason is that researchers have bemoaned the lack of widespread adoption of mobile payment against the prediction and hype of mobile payment usage (Williams, Roderick, Davies & Clements, 2017). For example, in North America, 52% of the population know about mobile payments, but only 18% are patronising mobile payments on a routine basis (Silbert, 2015). In comparison to similar areas of research such as e-commerce, internet banking or mobile banking, where research has been extensively conducted, mobile payment is a relatively new area of research and underexplored. As such, some researchers view mobile payment research to be in its developing stages (Slade et al., 2013). Despite mobile payment research being in its infancy, the technology supporting mobile payment systems has grown dramatically, due to the diffusion of mobile phones and smart devices. Even though, the number of studies increased in the last couple of years very few analyzed the adoption of mobile payments from the merchant perspective (Leong et al., 2013; Slade, Williams, Dwivedi, & Piercy, 2016; Tan, Ooi, Chong, & Hew, 2014). Hence mobile payment research conducted from the perspective of the merchant is not fully matured (Li, 2018).

In Ghana, research focusing on merchant adoption is scarce, irrespective of the potential benefits of mobile payment adoption to the merchant. In Ghana, literature has fairly covered mobile payment use and adoption, among the studies are; Preliminary insights into m-commerce adoption in Ghana (Boadi et al., 2007); Determinants of mobile banking adoption in the Ghanaian banking industry: a case of access bank Ghana limited (Cudjoe et al., 2015); Adoption of mobile money transfer technology using the structural equation modelling approach (Tobbin & Kuwornu, 2011). It is abundantly evident from the review that there is not much work done on merchant adoption of mobile payment in the Ghanaian context. It is not surprising because the nonexistence of research from, the merchant perspective seems to be a universal phenomenon (de Albuquerque et al., 2016).

Nonetheless, a limited number of studies have investigated adoption from, the merchant's perspective. For instance, Teo, Fraunholz, and Unnithan (2005) investigated inhibitors and facilitators of mobile payment adoption by businesses in Australia. Their finding was that some firms were not willing to trial with mobile payment before mass adoption. Again, the businesses were not comfortable with restricted participation of users based on monopoly from solution-providers. Furthermore, Mallat and Tuunainen (2008) explored qualitatively in Finland the determinants of merchant adoption intention. The findings established that a lack of standardisation and critical mass, as well as the complexity of mobile payment systems, were the main barriers to merchant adoption. Aditionally, Lai and Chuah (2010) interviewed industry experts in an attempt to explore the merchant adoption of mobile payment. Inadvertently, finding from consumer adoption research on mobile payment has espoused factors like compatibility (e.g., Lu et al., 2011; Mallat et al., 2009) and trust (e.g., Chandra et al., 2010; Zhou, 2013) as positive drivers of mobile payment adoption. Also, Iacovou, Benbasat and Dexter (1995) identified organisational readiness, external pressure toward adoption and perceived benefits, as the first features that could impact firms to adopt innovation. Existing studies on electronic payments are of the view that the comparative advantages of electronic payment systems include convenience, costs savings, enhanced inventory management, speed and efficiency at checkout counters, more accessible and faster collection of funds, and reduction in the processes of paper-based payments, such as cash and cheques.

Despite the advantages of mobile payments, merchant adoption research indicates that significant resistance to adoption can be attributed to the fact that merchants do not think it is safe to use mobile payments due to the security vulnerabilities. More so, Kazan and Damsgaard (2016) argue that the non-adoption of mobile payment by merchants can be attributed to a lack of highly compatible and accessible infrastructure that is compatible with their existing payment infrastructure. Additionally, more inherent challenges to the adoption of electronic payments comprise the need for substantial investment in financial operation, the immaturity of mobile technology and possible non-usage by customers as an alternative for payment (Liébana-Cabanillas et al., 2014). Wang and Cheung (2004) explored twelve travel agency CEOs understanding and acceptance of mobile business in Taiwan. The findings reveal that even though all the CEOs anticipated a long-term diffusion of mobile commerce, they revealed that the applicability and usage of mobile commerce are low. This is because, there is fewer competitive pressure, lack of customer need for the service, limited performance and possible incompatibility of current mobile technologies in the purchase process of complex travel services. Again, factors like perceived financial cost and perceived risk have been identified as barriers to adoption in most consumer-centric research on mobile payment (Liébana-Cabanillas et al., 2014; Lu et al., 2011; Slade et al., 2015). The above-stated factors may likely influence merchant adoption of mobile payment.

THEORETICAL BACKGROUND

Diffusion of Innovation (DOI)

As confirmed by Grewal et al. (2017), the extent of merchant adoption and acceptance of mobile payment is slow and has not increased as expected. Various instances of merchants not using the mobile payment system installed in their businesses have also been reported by previous studies (Mallat, 2007). This brings to light the gap in identifying merchants' expectation from technology and factors contributing to enabling technology acceptance and usage (Duarte et al., 2018). Issues of intention and acceptance of mobile payment technology have been researched over the year by several authors (Liébana-Cabanillas et al., 2018; Li, 2018; Liébana Cabanillas et al., 2016; Mallat & Tuunainen, 2008). Different models and conceptual framework which includes The Technology Acceptance Model (TAM), Innovation Diffusion Theory (DOI), Theory of Planned Behavior, Unified Theory of Acceptance and Use of Technology (UTAUT2) and social cognitive theory have been adopted to study the factors they may influence technology adoption (Dahlberg et al., 2008; Ondrus et al., 2009; Venkatesh et al., 2012). Because In the field of Information technology, research in IS innovation adoption has mainly focused on establishing the factors that affect the adoption of different technologies. (Hayashi, 2012; Singh, 2016; Abhishek & Hemch, 2016; Singh & Srivastava, 2018).

More importantly, IT innovation adoption is extensive and has been studied from a different perspective; among them are technology features individual adopters, organization and environment (Rogers 1995; Premkumar, 2003; Goodhue & Thompson, 1995). According to Cooper and Zmud (1990), it is appropriate for stages of IT innovation to be examined when analyzing the diffusion of IT innovation in an organization. The DOI framework is a process-based model that can explain how technology adoption diffuses in an organisation. The theory determines the extent to which innovation will be successful and the factors that enhance the adoption of technology and the extent of diffusion in an organisation. The theory espoused five attributes of innovation that influence the adoption of innovation. (1) relative advantage, the extent to which innovation can bring returns to an organization; (2) compatibility, the extent to which innovation is compatible with existing business processes, practices and value systems; (3) complexity, relates to how difficult it is to use an innovation ; (4) observability, refers to the extent to which the outcomes of innovation are evident to others; and (5) trialability, the degree to which innovation may be experimented with. Tornatzky and Klein (1982) in meta-analysis established that relative advantage, compatibility, and costs were found to be the most frequently identified factors for innovation diffusion among organizations. The literature shows that the DOI theory has a solid theoretical foundation and consistent empirical support (e.g. Premkumar et al., 1994; Beatty et al., 2001; Zhu et al., 2006). It is an essential theory for studying a diversity of information systems (IS) innovations (Moore & Benbasat, 1991; Lai & Chuah, 2010). With its comprehensive framework, DOI is one of the most robust innovation adoption theory to understand the technology adoption process in an organisation. Besides, the theory's fundamental constructs are suitable for the investigation of individual and organisational level adoption. As a result the DOI is often used as the therotical foundation for varying studies in identifying the factors for the adoption of technology.

Relative Advantage

The relative, advantage in the organizational context and from an information system point of view relates to performance attributes such as an increase in performance, efficiency and convenience (Davis, 1989; Moore & Benbasat, 1991). Existing studies from mobile payment and mobile commerce context argue that the attributes of ubiquity and independence of time and location has a significant impact on relative advantage and merchant ability to provide service irrespective of location and time (Carlsson et al., 2006; Constantiou et al., 2006; Jarvenpaa & Lang, 2005). Mobile payment technologies deliver ubiquitous payment possibilities, timely access to financial assets and cash payments alternative to merchants. Thus, merchants can perform their transactions remotely without the need to move from one location to the other (Mallat et al., 2009). Therefore, in comparing traditional payment with mobile payment relative advantage include the possibility of time location independent payment.

Compatibility

Deals with the extent to which an innovation meets the expectations, the experiences and needs values of the adopter of the technology (Rogers, 1995). Technology compatibility is usually evaluated in IS adoption research from the individual task and work (Moore & Benbasat, 1991; Taylor & Todd, 1995). In the task of payment, the ability of a merchant to integrate them into their routine is an essential feature of compatibility. Several studies have found compatibility as a critical predictor of mobile payment adoption (Teo & Pok, 2003; Wu & Wang, 2005). Merchant transactions and mobile payments compatibility are likely to impact the adoption.

Complexity

In the diffusion of innovations theory, complexity is determined as the "degree to which an innovation is perceived as challenging to understand and use" (Rogers, 1995, p. 16). Challenges regarding usability and complexity are contributory factors to the minimal adoption of several technologically related payment systems, among them are smart cards and mobile banking (Laukkanen & Lauronen,

2005). On the other hand, studies have shown that ease of use and convenience positively influence a merchant's willingness to adopt mobile technologies and services (Jarvenpaa et al., 2005; Teo & Pok, 2003). Mobile payments are commonly expected to increase merchant's convenience by reducing the need for coins and cash in small transactions and increasing the availability of payment possibilities (Mallat et al., 2009). Limitations in mobile device features, however, diminish the usability of mobile technologies (Siau et al., 2004).

Trialability

Trialability denotes the ability to test new technology before adoption. When Potential adopters are given an opportunity to try and experiment with innovation, they become more comfortable with it and can influence the potential adopter to adopt the innovation (Agarwal & Prasad, 1998; Rogers, 1995). Also, a researcher like Tan & Teo (2000) argue that if a potential adopter is allowed the opportunity to try the innovation it will reduce the uncertainties surrounding the innovation, and can influence the individual to adoption.

Observability

Observability aspect talks about the visibility of innovation to members in the social system and the advantages that can be visibly observed and be communicated Observability of an innovation describes the extent to which innovation is visible to the members of a social system, and the benefits can be easily observed and communicated Rogers (1995). Moore and Benbasat (1991) simplified the original construct by redefining observability into two constructs: visibility and result demonstrability. In the context of mobile payment, observability is defined as the ability to make payment at any time and from any location without any delay or queue, and seeing the effect of mobile payment transactions immediately, and conveying the accessibility benefits to others. Through such exposure, merchant gains knowledge about mobile payment and its benefits, thereby facilitating adoption.

Perceived Technology Security

Perceived technology security takes into consideration the feelings of uncertainties inherent in technology usage (Cheng et al., 2006). These Information security concerns are measured by the perception of the buyer, on how sellers unwilling and unable to secure information on individuals' transactions. This makes the buyer uncertain and is seen as a barrier to e-commerce adoption and a significant barrier to broad adoption and use of mobile payment (Chang et al., 2014). Previous studies have pointed out that apprehensions about security, where financial information is managed constitute a barrier to the intention of adopting the technologies (Cheng et al., 2006; Pavlou, Liang & Xue, 2007; Salisbury et al., 2001).

Conceptual Model

The conceptual model guiding the study is adopted from the diffusion innovation theory by Rogers (1995) and literature from perceived technology security. The combination of DOI theory and the perceived technology security will enable a comprehensive appreciation of mobile payment phenomenon and merchant intention to adopt. Acceptance of new technology by users can be quite complicated and requires more than a single model hence, the two theories (Shen, Huang, Chu, & Hsu, 2010). Also, a more integrative approach will provide complete evidence of the issues underpinning the relationship as well as a unique insight that cannot be obtained with a single theory (Jackson, Yi, & Park, 2013). DOI constructs were included in the research model to determine their influence on the adoption of mobile payment by merchants. More so, innovation factors are essential factors to consider in mobile payment adoption because mobile payment is a disruptive technology. As such, innovation factors play a significant role in the behavioural intention leading to its adoption. Earlier studies on information technology innovation have confirmed the suitability of diffusion innovation theory in predicting the adoption of different technologies (Zhu, Dong, Xu & Kraemer, 2006).

Arguably, mobile payment involves financial information that is personal and sensitive; security concerns can become a barrier to technology adoption (Duane, O'Reilly, & Andreev, 2014). The minimisation of the security concerns of the use of technology is an essential element to enable the merchant to feel secure in conducting financial transactions with mobile payments (Oliveira, Thomas, Baptista, & Campos, 2016). There is likely to be a positive influence in the behaviour of the merchant to adopt the mobile payment technology when the merchant perceives security around technology use. This informed the inclusion of Perceived Technology Security in the research model. However, extent review of IS innovation research indicates specifically that relative advantage, ease of use and compatibility are the three most consistent innovation characteristics that determine adoption. More so, studies on innovation diffusion demonstrate that innovation is a critical element, but individual innovativeness is also a vital variable in predicting the outcomes of technology adoption.

RESEARCH METHODOLOGY

The qualitative research aimed to acquire detailed information about merchant perceptions on enablers and inhibitors of mobile payment adoption. The study is an exploratory study to help bring a deeper understanding of the issues under study (Saunders et al., 2012; Denzin & Lincoln, 2005; Myers, 1999). As such, the study utilizes; a case study approach to investigate the determinant of the merchant intention to adopt mobile payment, a case study was considered appropriate for this research based on Yin's (2009) assertion of a case study where the "why and the how "questions are asked. Also, case studies are helpful in situations where there is not much theory to explain issues adequately, and the researcher does not have much control over the issues under investigation. Also, the case study allows an in-depth contextual understanding of the phenomenon under investigation. (Cavaye, 1996; Yin, 1994; Eisenhardt, 1989). Merchant adoption of mobile payments is a new phenomenon that needs an in-depth understanding from the perspective of the merchants in a resource-constrained environment to better appreciate merchant perceptions on enablers and inhibitors of mobile payment adoption in Ghana. The study will follow a descriptive case study approach to enables theory to guide the data collection process (Yin, 2009). Given this, The Diffusion Innovation Theory and Perceived Technology Security are reviewed as the theory underpinning the case study design. This approach was used due to its flexibility in allowing for multiple sources of data gathering. In this study, the author used face to face interviews as a data collection method. The interview guide consisted of both open and close-ended. The questions were such that it satisfies the objectives of the study. The interview guide was reviewed to conform to the objectives of the research went through a process of review to ensure that the questions were adequate and conform to the objective of the study.

Figure 1. Conceptual framework for merchant adoption of mobile payment

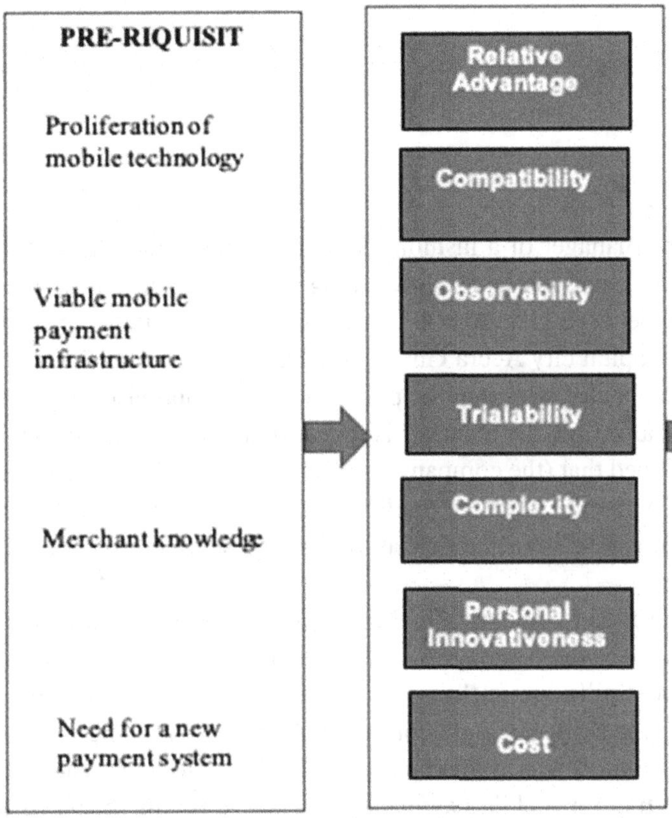

The study interviewed a small-scale cottage industry that is into the production of fruit juices for local restaurants and eateries and a small clothing retail company that is benefiting from mobile payments. These companies were strategically selected because they have adopted mobile payments innovation and thus have firsthand experience and an in-depth view on the topic, and therefore can provide insightful comments about the enablers and inhibitors of mobile payments adoption. Data was collected for this research work from April 28th, 2019 to June 17th, 2019, the field data collected were appropriately organised to ensure no data is lost and also to make sense of the data. Afterwards, the author listened to the recorded interviews to be familiar with the data and also to engage the data. Further, each interview was transcribed and typed in Microsoft word. Also, notes taken on the field were arranged correctly to make logical sense and meaning. As emphasised by Boateng (2016) a researcher is advised to take notes and read through the notes, this will help in categorising each respondent's response according to how relevant each response is to the research questions. Based on this understanding, the scripts were read many times for a general understanding of the responses and to understand its contributions to the research and the research objectives. Thematic approach, as illustrated by Braun and Clarke (2006), was used as a guide for the data analysis. The data was initially summarised, edited for accuracy and segmented; this was to help the author to present issues and conversation rather than actual words used in the conversation. The second stage in the analysis grouped the summaries into a smaller number of categories, themes and constructs to help create a more meaningful construct. The case study was analysed using a pattern- matching as described by Yin (1994) to help establish the findings that support the research questions. As a result, the key constructs in the data were extracted based on the research framework.

DATA ANALYSIS

Case A

The interview was conducted with the manager of a fashion retail shop who is also the owner of the business. The manager has tertiary education and has been working as the manager of the shop since 2010. The shop turnover is estimated between GHS30,000 to 50,000 (Thirty thousand cedi and Fifty thousand) annually in a suburb of the capital city Accra Ghana. She has two shop attendants with secondary school education who act like the customer contact point in the shop and also responsible for the day to day sales at the shop at the same time the manager is responsible for the more strategic issue of the business. The respondent mentioned that (the company) is officially registered as a business with a particular SIM and code on the MTN mobile payment platform. The manager attributed this choice to the service provider's critical mass, and full reachability as well as the service providers ability to transfer money across borders.

Further, she intimated that her motivation for adopting mobile payment is also based on the fact that, the particular merchant SIM is registered to the business, so all payments are made in the name of the business which according to her reduces pilfering in the shops and helps with tracking of income no matter the location. Before registering the company and adopting mobile payments, she was using her mobile account as compliments for customers who wanted to pay via mobile. However, she discovered that a lot more customers were requesting for mobile payments. That was when the business realised that mobile payments could be the game-changer for the business and benefit their customers through faster service. Also, her wholesale partner encouraged her to register the company for an official company mobile payment account. She registered with MTN the most prominent mobile network operator in Ghana as her service provider, and she was set up officially with a code, a display sign to reinforce to customers that the shop accepts mobile payment.

Mobile payments give the merchant the opportunity and affordances to facilitate efficient business transactions and an innovative business solution, which serves as a vehicle to uniquely position the merchant to provide value-added services for their customers (Yu & Ibtasam, 2018). The fashion shop manager mentioned that the fashion business is very dynamic and to remain profitable and competitive, there is a need for an innovative business model. According to her; The affordance of mobile payment enables the company to buy clothes online and pays online via a mobile payment through MTN. Even though the company has two brick and mortar shop, the strategy is not to stock most of the items physically in the shop but download the clothes online and display the various items in the client WhatsApp page on the company mobile phone status for her customers to make a choice. She orders the clothes online, and pay through mobile payment. The items are delivered to her within two weeks of ordering then she distributes to the clients via delivery according to the client's order, and they also pay her via mobile money.

I do not have to go to China or go to Accra Central, the capital city of Ghana to sort among large bails of clothes. I use, the KIKU app to shop online, and order the items my clients have selected from the list posted on their various WhatsApp pages and pay with MTN Momo. In two weeks, I have my orders delivered to me, and I also deliver to my customers who have the option of paying by cash on delivery or mobile money directly into my company mobile payment account.

Merchant use of mobile payments provides leverage for convenient business transactions with value-added services for competitive advantage in their business environment. The improvement in mobile payment solutions, which includes a multicurrency wallet is facilitating payment worldwide. It is a significant potential that companies can leverage to serve their customers in developing countries. The adoption of mobile payment with its multicurrency features is helping the small retail business to make payments to their business partners payments to suppliers, receiving payments from the customers, paying utility bills, and paying salaries of employees, simply and cheaply across borders without incurring exorbitant currency exchange fees. It also provides small businesses with faster and less expensive transactions than those completed in traditional settings, which reduce the transaction cost and time for the respective parties.

As intimated by the shop manager: "My official registration with the service provider enables me to use my mobile money account to buy clothes online without hassle which was not possible before I adopted mobile payment" as soon as I, place the order, I can pay via the mobile payment without changing my cedis into dollars. The beauty is that with the app, the prices are quoted in cedis, and I pay without foreign exchange issues".

The respondent also emphasised that the use of mobile payment has simplified international trade and has reduced intermediaries in trade and have reduced the cost of doing business.

As stated by the shop owner: Mobile payment and the internet with the App, I can buy online and pay. Before, I was buying in bulk from an importer locally, but now I buy myself online no matter the quantity they are willing to deliver. Which has simplified doing business and I make a profit than before because the prices online are competitive for example a nightdress delivered to me at the shop cost 18ghc at the same time, my distributor was selling to me at 25gh with such a price I can sell more at lower prices to my customers.

Nevertheless, the retail manager at the shop hinted that she believes many merchants have not yet adopted mobile payment simply because they do not know the benefit it provides. The merchants do not have enough information about the service.

I am not sure most of the small-scale businesses understand the benefit of using mobile payment.

Also, there was the issue of transaction fees charged and the cap on the daily amount that individuals or businesses can transfer in one goal. They also assume that the service is not easy to use and the issue of education and confidence to use the technology also came up as one of the factors that inhibit merchant adoption of mobile payment.

Case B

The company is a cottage fruit processing business, a startup that was established in 2016. The factory employs ten factory operatives and a general manager, who is also the owner. The business, according to the owner-manager uses the personal customer SIM of the manager to do transactions on behalf of the company but not an official unique SIM design for merchants from the service provider the individual consumer SIM is hooked onto the MTN payment platform. According to the general manager, the company adopted mobile payments because the business is virtually run by one person hence, for the sake of convenience and efficiency mobile payment was going to play a vital role in payment transactions. Besides a lot of consumers and smaller businesses like theirs were using mobile payment, especially MTN mobile money; hence, it was not out of place for my business to adopt mobile payment. As stated by the manager

Using mobile payments makes business sense because a lot of small businesses are also using it and is also convenient.

According to the general manager of the fruit juice processing company, the orders are sold on 14 days credit to restaurants, eateries and retail shops. The sourcing of raw materials for processing are from out-growers in the sounding villages directly by the company. Sometimes, raw materials are sourced from micro traders who retail the raw materials in the local market. However, the packaging materials are supplied by small scale labelling manufacturing companies who deliver directly to the company. Before, adopting mobile payment for the business, most of the transactions were done in cash and were mostly face to face, which was very stressful and time-wasting. For example, I was personally going around manually to collect credit sales. The manager believes that the adoption of mobile payment in their business is instrumental, because it enables the company to initiate a payment from the system and able to receive it. It helps to accomplish a lot, sending money from one point to the other we no longer travel to suppliers to pay, I can initiate payments at every location.

This is helping the business focus on activities that add more value and generate more significant revenues while saving time and money in the collection of payment; customers do not reschedule payment once there is electronic money, they can pay instantly.

According to the general manager, as a startup business, they have limited resources; the use of mobile payment has helped simplify the payment process and make transactions efficient. This is because the business can receive payments, move money cheaply to pay for transactions in their value chain without going to the bank or moving from one client to the order.

I do not go to villages as often as I use to do, I have built relationships and trust with my supplier over the years, and they supply me with raw materials, and I pay with mobile payment.

From the assertion, mobile payment as an innovative payment solution has led to the reduction of cost for the company, which has the potential of increasing the profit of the organisations. The manager interviewed was of the view the service providers in the country, are reputable; however, they believe that customers, especially businesses, could be at risk with their information that is with the service provider; thinking that they can release the customer information to a third party.

Because most of the time, an individual can receive information from third parties, you have not subscribed to their services, and you wonder if your personal information is in wrong hands. This makes merchants unsure of the security of their information with the service provider, which she thinks could be detrimental to the business when given to a competitor.

According to the respondent, using mobile payment as a business comes with a considerable risk because mobile payment operates in a wireless environment, people can steal information from the provider. Also, there are criminal activities in the cyberspace. Criminals can access customers' mobile accounts fraudulently and to defraud an unsuspecting business individual. They can hack into individual accounts and wipe the accounts of unsuspecting customers. Most of the time merchants, are unable to retrieve their money back. Further, the respondent intimated that the telecom companies lack experience in financial regulations and do not have expertise and experience in financial service delivery. Hence, their expansion into financial services can poses business risk to businesses who adopt mobile payment. As responded by the manager;

With mobile payment, you are not sure where to seek reimbursement when your money 'gets lost' in the virtual payment network between agent and service provider. However, with the banks, you can always go to the bank to address theft issues, so I think banks must take the lead in developing mobile payment while telecom operators provide technological support.

The manager also stated that one of the challenges with mobile payment adoption for businesses is the inability of mobile payment to deal with large sums of money. There is a daily quota a business can transact depending on the business documentation and the regulatory guidelines. This, according to the respondent, can inhibit large organisations, from adopting mobile payment.

One other challenge that came up with mobile payment adoption is the lack of technical skills and English language skills. For example, most of the local farmers and the market traders are not literate .They cannot read and write, as such are not confident to appreciate the transactions, so they do not adopt mobile payment for lack of confidence and literacy to carry the payment instruction through, which serves as an inhibitor for the adoption of mobile payments, especially for rural small scale merchant.

Sometimes the farmers I deal with are not willing to accept mobile payment because they do not trust the system.

According to the respondent: Notwithstanding these concerns, mobile payment is very efficient and does not require much to understand and operate as a merchant. It is vital that the nation develops regulations for it and increases the security measures around mobile payment and guard against the charging of double fees.

It is a very excellent system that needs to be developed to make our country cash "lite".

FINDINGS

Enablers

Business managers are adopting mobile payment for businesses to facilitate new business models within an organisation, by offering different possibilities for the growth of businesses. It is evident from the case that the adoption of mobile payment is helping small businesses to creatively develop an innovative business model which ultimately enhances profitability and substantial operational efficiency (see Boateng,2011). Further, the use of mobile payment can create access to a different segment of the market, which was not reachable before which help create different customer segments for business to create value. Instead of moving physical objects or tokens, such as paper money, checks, or notes, mobile payment has transformed the nature of payment among businesses by allowing the value to be transfer electronically through a mobile phone across borders. The finding is similar to the finding of Liébana-Cabanillas et al. (2018) who established that Payments made through mobile phones are one aspect leading to essential changes in international trading due to the accessibility that the technology provides. Innovatively, from the analysis, it is evident that businesses adopt mobile payment to enhances key partnerships by firming buyer-supplier relationships, which ensure reliable supplies. The adoption of mobile payment by merchants can increase market efficiency by improving access to supply, and to help reduce search costs, which can improve the management of supplies and increase the productive efficiency of firms. Arguably, this peer-to-peer partnerships between businesses, are strengthening and extending supply chains (see Mothobi & Grzybowski, 2017).

More importantly, from the analysis, the adoption of mobile payment by businesses is altering the "status quo" by reducing transaction costs and promoting the disintermediation of traditional intermediaries (e.g., banks, currency exchanges). It is also reducing processing costs through instant authentication and confirmation of the payments. This affords businesses a secure, faster and less expensive payment transactions without merchants experiencing delays sending money abroad without exorbitant exchange fees. The authentication and authorisation, making a payment, initiating accounting and confirming the completed transaction, are done in real-time through the mobile phone. This has potentially reduced the time and cost associated with physical transmission, especially across distance. This finding is in line with previous research; Boateng (2011) identified the impact of mobile payment as a reduction in operational costs, it also enhances shorter settlement time, reduction of risk, new revenue opportunities, and a reduction in the costs of capital (Kabanda & Brown, 2017). More importantly, the use of mobile payment has enabled partnership and startups, such as delivery companies and technology startups that develop application programming interfaces (APIs) and software development kits (SDKs) which maintain the transactional algorithms to enable retailers to quickly and easily accept mobile payment at point of sale without requiring the installation of additional terminal hardware. The MTN mobile payment platform does not require an additional point of sales device for the businesses that adopt mobile payment (see De Kerviler, Demoulin & Zidda, 2016).

Inhibitors

From the findings, one of the limiting factors that affect a manager's considerations for mobile payment adoption includes data breaches and data security as well as privacy concerns. This is seen as significant issues that could affect merchant adoption of mobile payment. Merchants believe that although mobile payments improve operations, there are instances of fraud, particularly in the peer to peer transfer sector. Fraudsters can assess merchant account to defraud them and abscond with tens of millions of cedi. This is the respondent said it is a significant hindrance to merchant adoption. The merchant believes that mobile transaction is almost like a web-based transaction, so it needs to be secured to protect sensitive information. This finding is similar to the finding by other researchers like Musa et al. (2015) and De Kerviler et al. (2016) argued that security and privacy are significant factors influencing mobile technology-related financial transactions. Privacy is critical in adopting location-based services for m-commerce. (Wang et al., 2016; Jin et al., 2017), also argue that one of the vital inhibitors that can influence merchant decision to adopt mobile payment technologies for financial transactions is security issues.

Furthermore, the findings demonstrate that lack of technology skills and English language skills demotivate small scale merchants who are not educated to adopt mobile payment. This is because they perceive the use of technology as severe, and usually, develop a negative impression of mobile payment. The finding established that the merchants expressed interest in the technology but the lack of knowledge and the perception that the technology is sophisticated makes them uncomfortable to use the mobile payment for their transactions. This plays a significant role in inhibiting merchants from using mobile technology for financial transactions, especially among the less educated merchants (see Dauda & Lee, 2015; Musa et al., 2015). This finding also agrees with existing research (Liebana-Cabanillas et al., 2015; Yoon & Kim, 2013; Slade et al., 2013; Liu et al., 2015) who stated that limited knowledge of mobile and Internet usage might prevent users from using mobile payment transactions.

The challenge of gaining the trust of merchants is one of the significant challenges confronting mobile payment adoption by merchants in small scale businesses in Ghana. There are linkages among technological skills, the complexity of the technology, which also leads to privacy concerns, and security, concerns for the merchant. In Ghana, for example, the regulatory framework on mobile payments is not very well developed and firmed up most merchants do not understand where to address an issue regarding fraud and security related issues. This confirms the suggestion by Mallat (2007) that users' perception of 'lack of security' and 'trust in payment systems' are among the vital problematic issues to e-commerce/m-commerce transactions. Finally, from the analysis, the merchants complained about the cost, especially about the charges involved in using mobile payment, especially when it has to do with bulk payment, which does not encourage merchants to transfer large sums of money using mobile payment. Hence mobile payment is unable to replace traditional payment but as a complement to traditional payment (see Van der Boor et al., 2014).

Other Findings

From the analysis, it is clear that the benefit of mobile payment adoption by merchant depends on the target market, because most educated people have adopted mobile payment and are using in paying for goods and services directly from their wallet making all kinds of transactions using their mobile payment. In contrast, in the village, most farmers who are paid via mobile payment do not spend from their wallet but rather cash the money and transact in cash, which may be attributed to education and technology savviness. There is evidence in the analysis that managers are adopting mobile payment because of the growth of technology and especially the advancement of mobile technologies and the reduction of the barriers (see de Luna et al., 2019). Managers believe that mobile payment is likely to become the means of payment in the future and businesses do not want to be left out. This finding is confirmed by a study conducted by Accenture Consulting (2015), where consumers anticipate a reduction in traditional payment to the advantage of digital payments. Business managers are anticipating future critical mass where mobile payment is regarded as the next big thing in payments. Especially in developing countries where there is lack of quality infrastructure for payments (see Bourreau & Verdier, 2010).

CONCLUSION

From the studies, it is imperative for service providers of mobile payments to enhance technological issues, especially with regards to privacy protection which, in turn, could enhance users' experience and trust towards mobile payment adoption. This is because of the lack of trust and risk issues are regarded as critical limiting factors to the adoption of mobile payments by both merchants interviewed (see Ramadan & Aita, 2018). Despite the challenges expressed by managers in adopting mobile payment. It is reassuring to see a growing interest by companies to explore opportunities with mobile payment technology. Managers are well advised to continuously monitor mobile payment technologies to assess their impact and consider the strategic importance of mobile payment for their business. If they do not do so, they will lose their competitive edge to those managers of firms, whether new or old, who understand the mobile payment and who are ready to innovate their business models. This is because the merchant adoption of mobile payment is advancing rapidly toward greater acceptance. Smart executives and managers should understand how the technology fits in their business and how it can help improve operations to capture its advantages ahead of its competitors. One significant contribution of this study lies in the development of a conceptual framework for merchant adoption of mobile payment with, a particular focus on small and medium size merchants in developing countries. A relatively unexplored area of study after a decade of mobile payment research.

The study does not only contribute to mobile payment adoption analysis from the supply side of the market, but also, incorporate additional merchant adoption enablers and inhibitors that merit attention in mobile payment application. Additionally, the study offers various practical insight from developing country perspective, which will serve as a guide for future studies in merchant adoption. The study of merchant perceptions of mobile payments adoption will enable practitioners, especially mobile service providers, to understand merchants' perspective on mobile payment, which will be a foundation for the delivery of appropriate service to their clients. Despite these contributions, the study has a limitation in that it considers a limited number of cases. However, the purpose of selecting the cases was to enhance the external validity of the case strategically and not to address statistical considerations. As an initial step in understanding merchant adoption issues from a developing country perspective, this finding has thrown light on how future studies could be conducted.

REFERENCES

Abhishek, & Hemchand, S. (2016). Adoption of sensor-based communication for mobile marketing in India. Journal of Indian Business Research, 8(1), 65-76.

Abrahão, R., Moriguchi, S. N., & Andrade, D. F. (2016). Intention of adoption of mobile payment: An analysis in the light of the Unified Theory of Acceptance and Use of Technology (UTAUT). RAI Revista de Administração e Inovação, 13(3), 221–230. doi:10.1016/j.rai.2016.06.003

Accenture Consulting. (2015). North America consumer digital payments survey. Retrieved from https://www.accenture.com/t20151021T165757__w__/us-en/_acnmedia/Accenture/next-gen/na-payment-survey/pdfs/Accenture-Digital-Payments-Survey-North-America-Accenture-Executive-Summary.pdf

Agarwal, R., & Prasad, J. (1998). A conceptual and operational definition of personal innovativeness in the domain of information technology. *Information Systems Research, 9*(2), 204–215. doi:10.1287/isre.9.2.204

Agarwal, S., Khapra, M., Menezes, B., & Uchat, N. (2007). *Security issues in mobile payment systems.* Indian Institute of Technology Bombay India.

Aker, J. C., & Mbiti, I. M. (2010). Mobile phones and economic development in Africa. *The Journal of Economic Perspectives, 24*(3), 207–232. doi:10.1257/jep.24.3.207

Asongu, S., & Boateng, A. (2018). Introduction to Special Issue : Mobile Technologies and Inclusive Development in Africa Introduction to Special Issue : Mobile Technologies and. *Journal of African Business, 19*(3), 297–301. doi:10.1080/15228916.2018.1481307

Asongu, S., & Boateng, A. (2018). *Introduction to special issue: mobile technologies and inclusive development in Africa.* Academic Press.

Asongu, S. A., Nwachukwu, J. C., & Orim, S. M. I. (2018). Mobile phones, institutional quality and entrepreneurship in Sub-Saharan Africa. *Technological Forecasting and Social Change, 131*, 183–203. doi:10.1016/j.techfore.2017.08.007

Au, Y. A., & Kauffman, R. J. (2008). The economics of mobile payments: Understanding stakeholder issues for an emerging financial technology application. *Electronic Commerce Research and Applications, 7*(2), 141–164. doi:10.1016/j.elerap.2006.12.004

Beatty, R. C., Shim, J. P., & Jones, M. C. (2001). Factors influencing corporate web site adoption: A time-based assessment. *Information & Management, 38*(6), 337–354. doi:10.1016/S0378-7206(00)00064-1

Boadi, R. A., Boateng, R., Hinson, R., & Opoku, R. A. (2007). Preliminary insights into m-commerce adoption in Ghana. *Information Development, 23*(4), 253–265. doi:10.1177/0266666907084761

Boateng, R. (2011). Mobile phones and micro-trading activities–conceptualizing the link. *Info, 13*(5), 48–62.

Boateng, R. (2016). *Research made easy.* CreateSpace Independent Publishing Platform.

Bourreau, M., & Verdier, M. (2010). *Cooperation for innovation in payment systems: The case of mobile payments.* Academic Press.

Braun, V., & Clarke, V. (2006). Using thematic analysis in psychology. *Qualitative Research in Psychology, 3*(2), 77–101. doi:10.1191/1478088706qp063oa

Carlsson, C., Carlsson, J., Hyvonen, K., Puhakainen, J., & Walden, P. (2006, January). Adoption of mobile devices/services-searching for answers with the UTAUT. In Proceedings of the 39th annual Hawaii international conference on system sciences (HICSS'06) (Vol. 6, pp. 132a-132a). IEEE. doi:10.1109/HICSS.2006.38

Cavaye, A. L. (1996). Case study research: A multi-faceted research approach for IS. *Information Systems Journal*, *6*(3), 227–242. doi:10.1111/j.1365-2575.1996.tb00015.x

Chandra, S., Srivastava, S. C., & Theng, Y. L. (2010). Evaluating the role of trust in consumer adoption of mobile payment systems: An empirical analysis. CAIS, 27(29), 27.

Cheng, T. E., Lam, D. Y., & Yeung, A. C. (2006). Adoption of internet banking: An empirical study in Hong Kong. *Decision Support Systems*, *42*(3), 1558–1572. doi:10.1016/j.dss.2006.01.002

Constantiou, I. D., Damsgaard, J., & Knutsen, L. (2006). Exploring perceptions and use of mobile services: User differences in an advancing market. *International Journal of Mobile Communications*, *4*(3), 231–247. doi:10.1504/IJMC.2006.008940

Cooper, R. B., & Zmud, R. W. (1990). Information technology implementation research: A technological diffusion approach. *Management Science*, *36*(2), 123–139. doi:10.1287/mnsc.36.2.123

Cudjoe, A. G., Anim, P. A., & Nyanyofio, J. G. N. T. (2015). Determinants of mobile banking adoption in the Ghanaian banking industry: A case of access bank Ghana limited. *Journal of Computer and Communications*, *3*(02), 1–19. doi:10.4236/jcc.2015.32001

Dahlberg, T., Guo, J., & Ondrus, J. (2015). A critical review of mobile payment research. *Electronic Commerce Research and Applications*, *14*(5), 265–284. doi:10.1016/j.elerap.2015.07.006

Dahlberg, T., Mallat, N., Ondrus, J., & Zmijewska, A. (2008). Past, present and future of mobile payments research: A literature review. *Electronic Commerce Research and Applications*, *7*(2), 165–181. doi:10.1016/j.elerap.2007.02.001

Dauda, S. Y., & Lee, J. (2015). Technology adoption: A conjoint analysis of consumers' preference on future online banking services. *Information Systems*, *53*, 1–15. doi:10.1016/j.is.2015.04.006

Davis, F. D. (1989). Perceived usefulness, perceived ease of use, and user acceptance of information technology. *Management Information Systems Quarterly*, *13*(3), 319–340. doi:10.2307/249008

de Albuquerque, J. P., Diniz, E. H., & Cernev, A. K. (2016). Mobile payments: A scoping study of the literature and issues for future research. *Information Development*, *32*(3), 527–553. doi:10.1177/0266666914557338

De Kerviler, G., Demoulin, N. T., & Zidda, P. (2016). Adoption of in-store mobile payment: Are perceived risk and convenience the only drivers. *Journal of Retailing and Consumer Services*, *31*, 334–344. doi:10.1016/j.jretconser.2016.04.011

de Luna, I. R., Liébana-Cabanillas, F., Sánchez-Fernández, J., & Muñoz-Leiva, F. (2019). Mobile payment is not all the same: The adoption of mobile payment systems depending on the technology applied. *Technological Forecasting and Social Change*, *146*, 931–944. doi:10.1016/j.techfore.2018.09.018

de Reuver, M., Verschuur, E., Nikayin, F., Cerpa, N., & Bouwman, H. (2015). Collective action for mobile payment platforms: A case study on collaboration issues between banks and telecom operators. *Electronic Commerce Research and Applications*, *14*(5), 331–344. doi:10.1016/j.elerap.2014.08.004

Denzin, N. K., & Lincoln, Y. S. (2005). Introduction: The discipline and practice of qualitative research. In N. K. Denzin & S. Lincoln (Eds.), *The Sage handbook of qualitative research* (pp. 1–32). Thousand Oaks, CA: Sage.

Dewan, S. G., & Chen, L. D. (2005). Mobile payment adoption in the US: A cross-industry, cross platform solution. *Journal of Information Privacy and Security, 1*(2), 4–28. doi:10.1080/15536548.2005.10855765

Duane, A., O'Reilly, P., & Andreev, P. (2014). Realising M-Payments: Modelling consumers' willingness to M-pay using Smart Phones. *Behaviour & Information Technology, 33*(4), 318–334. doi:10.1080/0144929X.2012.745608

Duarte, P., Silva, S. C., & Ferreira, M. B. (2018). How convenient is it? Delivering online shopping convenience to enhance customer satisfaction and encourage e-WOM. *Journal of Retailing and Consumer Services, 44*, 161–169. doi:10.1016/j.jretconser.2018.06.007

Eisenhardt, K. M. (1989). Building theories from case study research. *Academy of Management Review, 14*(4), 532–550. doi:10.5465/amr.1989.4308385

Goodhue, D. L., & Thompson, R. L. (1995). Task-technology fit and individual performance. *Management Information Systems Quarterly, 19*(2), 213–236. doi:10.2307/249689

Grewal, D., Roggeveen, A. L., & Nordfält, J. (2017). The future of retailing. *Journal of Retailing, 93*(1), 1–6. doi:10.1016/j.jretai.2016.12.008

Guo, J., Nikou, S., & Bouwman, H. (2015). Business model for mobile payment in China. *International Journal of Systems and Service-Oriented Engineering, 5*(2), 20–43. doi:10.4018/IJSSOE.2015040102

Hamka, F., Bouwman, H., De Reuver, M., & Kroesen, M. (2014). Mobile customer segmentation based on smartphone measurement. *Telematics and Informatics, 31*(2), 220–227. doi:10.1016/j.tele.2013.08.006

Hayashi, F. (2012). Mobile payments: What's in it for consumers. Economic Review-Federal Reserve Bank of Kansas City, 35.

Humbani, M., & Wiese, M. (2018). A cashless society for all: Determining consumers' readiness to adopt mobile payment services. *Journal of African Business, 19*(3), 409–429. doi:10.1080/15228916.2017.1396792

Iacovou, C. L., Benbasat, I., & Dexter, A. S. (1995). Electronic data interchange and small organizations: Adoption and impact of technology. *Management Information Systems Quarterly, 19*(4), 465–485. doi:10.2307/249629

Iman, N. (2018). Is mobile payment still relevant in the fintech era. *Electronic Commerce Research and Applications, 30*, 72–82. doi:10.1016/j.elerap.2018.05.009

Jackson, J. D., Mun, Y. Y., & Park, J. S. (2013). An empirical test of three mediation models for the relationship between personal innovativeness and user acceptance of technology. *Information & Management, 50*(4), 154–161. doi:10.1016/j.im.2013.02.006

Jarvenpaa, S. L., & Lang, K. R. (2005). Managing the paradoxes of mobile technology. *Information Systems Management, 22*(4), 7–23. doi:10.1201/1078.10580530/45520.22.4.20050901/90026.2

Jin, H., Park, S. T., & Li, G. (2015). Factors influencing customer participation in mobile SNS: Focusing on Wechat in China. *Indian Journal of Science and Technology*, 8(26), 1–8. doi:10.17485/ijst/2015/v8i26/80714

Jin, X., Zheng, H., Jin, R., & Li, Y. (2017). Understanding Consumers' trust in third-party Online Payment. In PACIS (p. 175). Academic Press.

Kabanda, S., & Brown, I. (2017). A structuration analysis of Small and Medium Enterprise (SME) adoption of E-Commerce: The case of Tanzania. *Telematics and Informatics*, 34(4), 118–132. doi:10.1016/j.tele.2017.01.002

Kazan, E., & Damsgaard, J. (2016). Towards a Market Entry Framework for Digital Payment Platforms. CAIS, 38, 37.

Lai, P. M., & Chuah, K. B. (2010, October). Developing an analytical framework for mobile payments adoption in retailing: A supply-side perspective. In 2010 Fourth International Conference on Management of e-Commerce and e-Government (ICMeCG) (pp. 356–361). IEEE doi:10.1109/ICMeCG.2010.79

Laukkanen, T., & Lauronen, J. (2005). Consumer value creation in mobile banking services. *International Journal of Mobile Communications*, 3(4), 325–338. doi:10.1504/IJMC.2005.007021

Lee, Y. H., Hsieh, Y. C., & Hsu, C. N. (2011). Adding innovation diffusion theory to the technology acceptance model: Supporting employees' intentions to use e-learning systems. *Journal of Educational Technology & Society*, 14(4), 124–137.

Leong, L. Y., Hew, T. S., Tan, G. W. H., & Ooi, K. B. (2013). Predicting the determinants of the NFC-enabled mobile credit card acceptance: A neural networks approach. *Expert Systems with Applications*, 40(14), 5604–5620. doi:10.1016/j.eswa.2013.04.018

Li, Y. (2018). *The Strategic Decision on Mobile Payment: A Study on Merchants Adoption*. Academic Press.

Liébana-Cabanillas, F., Marinkovic, V., de Luna, I. R., & Kalinic, Z. (2018). Predicting the determinants of mobile payment acceptance: A hybrid SEM-neural network approach. *Technological Forecasting and Social Change*, 129, 117–130. doi:10.1016/j.techfore.2017.12.015

Liébana-Cabanillas, F., Ramos de Luna, I., & Montoro-Ríos, F. (2017). Intention to use new mobile payment systems: A comparative analysis of SMS and NFC payments. *Economic Research Journal*, 30(1), 892–910.

Liébana-Cabanillas, F., Ramos de Luna, I., & Montoro-Ríos, F. J. (2015). User behaviour in QR mobile payment system: The QR Payment Acceptance Model. *Technology Analysis and Strategic Management*, 27(9), 1031–1049. doi:10.1080/09537325.2015.1047757

Liébana-Cabanillas, F., Sánchez-Fernández, J., & Muñoz-Leiva, F. (2014). Antecedents of the adoption of the new mobile payment systems: The moderating effect of age. *Computers in Human Behavior*, 35, 464–478. doi:10.1016/j.chb.2014.03.022

Liu, J., Kauffman, R. J., & Ma, D. (2015). Competition, cooperation, and regulation: Understanding the evolution of the mobile payments technology ecosystem. *Electronic Commerce Research and Applications*, *14*(5), 372–391.

Lu, Y., Yang, S., Chau, P. Y., & Cao, Y. (2011). Dynamics between the trust transfer process and intention to use mobile payment services: A cross-environment perspective. *Information & Management*, *48*(8), 393–403.

Madan, K., & Yadav, R. (2016). Behavioural intention to adopt mobile wallet: A developing country perspective. *Journal of Indian Business Research*, *8*(3), 227–244. doi:10.1108/JIBR-10-2015-0112

Mallat, N. (2007). Exploring consumer adoption of mobile payments - A qualitative study. *The Journal of Strategic Information Systems*, *16*(4), 413–432. doi:10.1016/j.jsis.2007.08.001

Mallat, N., Rossi, M., Tuunainen, V. K., & Oorni, A. (2006, January). The impact of use situation and mobility on the acceptance of mobile ticketing services. In Proceedings of the 39th Annual Hawaii International Conference on System Sciences (HICSS'06) (Vol. 2, pp. 42b-42b). IEEE. doi:10.1109/HICSS.2006.472

Mallat, N., Rossi, M., Tuunainen, V. K., & Öörni, A. (2009). The impact of use context on mobile services acceptance: The case of mobile ticketing. *Information & Management*, *46*(3), 190–195. doi:10.1016/j.im.2008.11.008

Mallat, N., & Tuunainen, V. K. (2008). Exploring merchant adoption of mobile payment systems: An empirical study. e-Service Journal, 6(2), 24–57. doi:10.2979/esj.2008.6.2.24

Miao, M., & Jayakar, K. (2016). Mobile payments in Japan, South Korea and China: Cross-border convergence or divergence of business models? *Telecommunications Policy*, *40*(2-3), 182–196. doi:10.1016/j.telpol.2015.11.011

Moore, G. C., & Benbasat, I. (1991). Development of an instrument to measure the perceptions of adopting an information technology innovation. *Information Systems Research*, *2*(3), 192–222. doi:10.1287/isre.2.3.192

Mothobi, O., & Grzybowski, L. (2017). Infrastructure deficiencies and adoption of mobile money in Sub-Saharan Africa. *Information Economics and Policy*, *40*, 71–79. doi:10.1016/j.infoecopol.2017.05.003

Murphy, J. T., & Carmody, P. (2017). Africa's information revolution : Technical regimes and production networks in South Africa and Tanzania. *Journal of Economic Geography*, *17*, 265–266. doi:10.1093/jeg/lbw038

Musa, A., Khan, H. U., & AlShare, K. A. (2015). Factors influence consumers' adoption of mobile payment devices in Qatar. *International Journal of Mobile Communications*, *13*(6), 670–689. doi:10.1504/IJMC.2015.072100

Myers, M. D. (1999). Investigating information systems with ethnographic research. *Communications of the Association for Information Systems*, *2*(1), 23.

Nikou, S., Bouwman, H., & de Reuver, M. (2014). A Consumer Perspective on Mobile Service Platforms: A Conjoint Analysis Approach. CAIS, 34, 82.

Oliveira, T., Thomas, M., Baptista, G., & Campos, F. (2016). Mobile payment: Understanding the determinants of customer adoption and intention to recommend the technology. *Computers in Human Behavior, 61*, 404–414. doi:10.1016/j.chb.2016.03.030

Ondrus, J., & Pigneur, Y. (2009). Near field communication: An assessment for future payment systems. *Information Systems and e-Business Management, 7*(3), 347–361. doi:10.1007/s10257-008-0093-1

Pavlou, P. A., Liang, H., & Xue, Y. (2007). Understanding and mitigating uncertainty in online exchange relationships: A principal-agent perspective. *Management Information Systems Quarterly, 31*(1), 105–136. doi:10.2307/25148783

Pousttchi, K. (2008). A modeling approach and reference models for the analysis of mobile payment use cases. *Electronic Commerce Research and Applications, 7*(2), 182–201. doi:10.1016/j.elerap.2007.07.001

Premkumar, G. (2003). A meta-analysis of research on information technology implementation in small business. *Journal of Organizational Computing and Electronic Commerce, 13*(2), 91–121. doi:10.1207/S15327744JOCE1302_2

Premkumar, G., Ramamurthy, K., & Nilakanta, S. (1994). Implementation of electronic data interchange: An innovation diffusion perspective. *Journal of Management Information Systems, 11*(2), 157–186. doi:10.1080/07421222.1994.11518044

Ramadan, R., & Aita, J. (2018). A model of mobile payment usage among Arab consumers. *International Journal of Bank Marketing, 36*(7), 1213–1234. doi:10.1108/IJBM-05-2017-0080

Ramos-de-Luna, I., Montoro-Ríos, F., & Liébana-Cabanillas, F. (2016). Determinants of the intention to use NFC technology as a payment system: An acceptance model approach. *Information Systems and e-Business Management, 14*(2), 293–314. doi:10.1007/s10257-015-0284-5

Rogers, E. M. (1995). Lessons for guidelines from the diffusion of innovations. *Joint Commission Journal on Quality and Patient Safety, 21*(7), 324–328. PubMed

Salisbury, W., Pearson, R., Pearson, A., & Miller, D. (2001). Identifying barriers that keep shoppers off the world wide web: Developing a scale of perceived web security. *Industrial Management & Data Systems, 101*(4), 165–176.

Saunders, M., Lewis, P., & Thornhill, A. (2012). *Research methods for business students* (6th ed.). Pearson Education Limited.

Shen, Y. C., Huang, C. Y., Chu, C. H., & Hsu, C. T. (2010). A benefit–cost perspective of the consumer adoption of the mobile banking system. *Behaviour & Information Technology, 29*(5), 497–511. doi:10.1080/01449290903490658

Siau, K., Sheng, H., Nah, F., & Davis, S. (2004). A qualitative investigation on consumer trust in mobile commerce. *International Journal of Electronic Business, 2*(3), 283–300. doi:10.1504/IJEB.2004.005143

Silbert, S. (2015). *How mobile payments will grow in 2016.* Academic Press.

Singh, A. (2016). The future of mobile wallets in India. The Hindu Business Line, 10.

Singh, S., & Srivastava, S. (2018). Moderating effect of product type on online shopping behaviour and purchase intention: An Indian perspective. Cogent Arts & Humanities, 5(1), 1495043. doi:10.1080/23 311983.2018.1495043

Slade, E., Dwivedi, Y., Williams, M., & Piercy, N. (2016). An empirical investigation of remote mobile payment adoption. In *Let's Get Engaged! Crossing the Threshold of Marketing's Engagement Era* (pp. 441–442). Cham: Springer; doi:10.1007/978-3-319-11815-4_122.

Slade, E. L., Dwivedi, Y. K., Piercy, N. C., & Williams, M. D. (2015). Modeling consumers' adoption intentions of remote mobile payments in the United Kingdom: Extending UTAUT with innovativeness, risk, and trust. *Psychology and Marketing, 32*(8), 860–873. doi:10.1002/mar.20823

Slade, E. L., Williams, M. D., & Dwivedi, Y. K. (2013). Mobile payment adoption: Classification and review of the extant literature. *The Marketing Review, 13*(2), 167–190. doi:10.1362/14693471 3X13699019904687

Tan, G. W. H., Ooi, K. B., Chong, S. C., & Hew, T. S. (2014). NFC mobile credit card: The next frontier of mobile payment? *Telematics and Informatics, 31*(2), 292–307. doi:10.1016/j.tele.2013.06.002

Tan, M., & Teo, T. S. (2000). Factors influencing the adoption of Internet banking. *Journal of the Association for Information Systems, 1*(1), 5. doi:10.17705/1jais.00005

Taylor, E. (2016). Mobile payment technologies in retail: A review of potential benefits and risks. *International Journal of Retail & Distribution Management, 44*(2), 159–177. doi:10.1108/IJRDM-05-2015-0065

Taylor, S., & Todd, P. A. (1995). Understanding information technology usage: A test of competing models. *Information Systems Research, 6*(2), 144–176. doi:10.1287/isre.6.2.144

Teo, E., Fraunholz, B., & Unnithan, C. (2005, July). Inhibitors and facilitators for mobile payment adoption in Australia: A preliminary study. In ICMB 2005. International Conference on Mobile Business, 2005 (pp. 663–666). IEEE. doi:10.1109/ICMB.2005.47

Teo, T. S., & Pok, S. H. (2003). Adoption of WAP-enabled mobile phones among Internet users. *Omega, 31*(6), 483–498. doi:10.1016/j.omega.2003.08.005

Tobbin, P., & Kuwornu, J. K. (2011). Adoption of mobile money transfer technology: Structural equation modeling approach. *European Journal of Business and Management, 3*(7), 59–77.

Tornatzky, L. G., & Klein, K. J. (1982). Innovation characteristics and innovation adoption-implementation: A meta-analysis of findings. *IEEE Transactions on Engineering Management, EM-29*(1), 28–45. doi:10.1109/TEM.1982.6447463

Upadhyay, P., & Chattopadhyay, M. (2015). Examining mobile based payment services adoption issues. *Journal of Enterprise Information Management, 28*(4), 490–507. doi:10.1108/JEIM-04-2014-0046

Van der Boor, P., Oliveira, P., & Veloso, F. (2014). Users as innovators in developing countries: The global sources of innovation and diffusion in mobile banking services. *Research Policy, 43*(9), 1594–1607. doi:10.1016/j.respol.2014.05.003

Venkatesh, V., Thong, J. Y., & Xu, X. (2012). Consumer acceptance and use of information technology: Extending the unified theory of acceptance and use of technology. *Management Information Systems Quarterly, 36*(1), 157–178. doi:10.2307/41410412

Wang, S., & Cheung, W. (2004). E-business adoption by travel agencies: Prime candidates for mobile e-business. *International Journal of Electronic Commerce, 8*(3), 43–63. doi:10.1080/10864415.2004.11044298

Wang, Y. S., Li, H. T., Li, C. R., & Zhang, D. Z. (2016). Factors affecting hotels' adoption of mobile reservation systems: A technology-organization-environment framework. *Tourism Management, 53*, 163–172. doi:10.1016/j.tourman.2015.09.021

Williams, M. D., Roderick, S., Davies, G. H., & Clement, M. (2017). *Risk, trust, and compatibility as antecedents of mobile payment adoption.* Academic Press.

Wu, J. H., & Wang, S. C. (2005). What drives mobile commerce: An empirical evaluation of the revised technology acceptance model. *Information & Management, 42*(5), 719–729. doi:10.1016/j.im.2004.07.001

Yin, R. K. (1994). Discovering the future of the case study: Method in evaluation research. *Evaluation Practice, 15*(3), 283–290. doi:10.1016/0886-1633(94)90023-X

Yin, R. K. (2009). *Case study research, design and methods* (3rd ed.). Newbury Park, CA: Sage.

Yoon, C., & Kim, H. (2013). Understanding computer security behavioral intention in the workplace: An empirical study of Korean firms. *Information Technology & People, 26*(4), 401–419. doi:10.1108/ITP-12-2012-0147

Yu, S., & Ibtasam, S. (2018, June). A qualitative exploration of Mobile money in Ghana. In *Proceedings of the 1st ACM SIGCAS Conference on Computing and Sustainable Societies* (p. 21). ACM; doi:10.1145/3209811.3209863.

Zhao, Y., & Kurnia, S. (2014). *Exploring Mobile Payment Adoption in China.* PACIS.

Zhong, J. (2009). *A comparison of mobile payment procedures in Finnish and Chinese markets.* BLED.

Zhou, T. (2013). An empirical examination of continuance intention of mobile payment services. *Decision Support Systems, 54*(2), 1085–1091. doi:10.1016/j.dss.2012.10.034

Zhu, K., Dong, S., Xu, S. X., & Kraemer, K. L. (2006). Innovation diffusion in global contexts: Determinants of post-adoption digital transformation of European companies. *European Journal of Information Systems, 15*(6), 601–616. doi:10.1057/palgrave.ejis.3000650

Chapter 12
Riders' Participation in the Ride–Hailing Sector of the Gig Economy

Obed Kwame Adzaku Penu

https://orcid.org/0000-0002-8237-4588

Business School, University of Ghana, Ghana

ABSTRACT

This chapter focuses on riders (consumers) who use the Uber ride-hailing application as a gig platform for accessing transportation services, thereby assigning drivers the task of transporting them from one location to another. Respondents were sampled using a multiple sampling approach comprising convenience, random, and purposive sampling. 20 out of 40 respondents were purposely selected for in-depth interviewing and thematic analysis. The findings suggest that riders found the platform to offer both personal and shared convenience, cost and time saving, as well as trustworthiness. The platform also substituted the means of finding transportation for some of the riders, while for other riders it complemented their means of finding transportation. With these findings, this study contributes to the few scholarly studies that have sought to explore, in detail, user perceptions on gig platforms from a developing economy context and provides stimulating insights on the gig economy and its adoption in developing economies.

INTRODUCTION

On-the-demand jobs are emerging and growing rapidly in developing countries (O'Sullivan & Shiffrin, 2003). More recently, the advancement in technology otherwise seen as the 'digital revolution' using digital platforms has influenced the way job seekers and employers negotiate for work in what is now known as the 'gig' economy (Brinkley, 2016). The term "gig(s)" was initially used in the 1920s in the music industry to refer to 'one-time' music performance (Zumbrun & Sussman, 2016). However, it is now actively used in the employment and labour sector in reference to technology-facilitated short-term consultative tasks that are performed on a project-by-project basis (Cutter, Litan, & Stangler, 2016; Kes-

DOI: 10.4018/978-1-7998-2610-1.ch012

sler, 2014; Manyika, Lund, Robinson, Valentino, & Dobbs, 2015). Instead of signing long-term contracts, workers are independent and self-employed, engaging with firms only on a temporary or short-term basis. This implies that the new generation of gig work is not distinguished by the type of work or skill set but rather by the nature of the underlying work relationship (Friedman, 2014). The gig economy is seen to be making inroads in a number of sectors. These include (i) the field of computer and information technology (where jobs are done in web and software development, computer programming and graphic designing), (ii) media and communications (where technical writers, interpreters, translators, musicians, and photographers are hired) and (iii) the transportation and dispatch sector (where there are services such as Uber, Deliveroo and Foodora) (Torpey & Hogan, 2016).

On the part of employers, the gig economy aided by digital platforms present an opportunity to access a broader number of prospective job seekers, to speed up the hiring process and more importantly to reduce the cost of hiring workers (Broughton, Gloster, Marvell, Green, Langley & Martin, 2018). These ever-evolving benefits in employing and working gigs supported by technology (online platforms) have become vastly widespread, and many persons seeking to employ or to be employed are taking advantage of this opportunity to hire and be hired respectively. As with all peer-to-peer platforms of which the gig economy is included, there are generally three actors in the ecosystem; The (1) riders (consumers), (2) drivers (service providers) and (3) market aggregator (the digital platform) (Brinkley, 2016). However, this chapter focuses on only one of the actors; riders (consumers) on the Uber platform.

In this regard, this chapter by way of purpose seeks to explore, qualitatively, riders' perceptions of their use of the Uber ride-hailing application as a gig economy platform for accessing transportation in Ghana. Specifically, the chapter addresses the following questions:

1. What is the perception of riders on the nature of the ride-hailing sector of the gig economy in Ghana?; indicating the forms of digital technologies used by riders as well as riders' characteristics and;
2. What are riders' perceptions of the motivations and outcomes of participating in the ride-haling sector of the gig economy in Ghana?

The next section of this chapter provides a background on how the gig economy has been defined. Following this section is a section that discusses how digital platforms aid the gig economy and also touches on the various ways the gig economy has been categorised. Next is a discussion of the benefits and challenges of the gig economy. Following this section is a presentation of the research problem, followed by a section that presents the analytical framework employed in this research. Then is the section which presents the methods employed for data collection and analysis. Next is a presentation of the findings and analysis of the research and then a discussion of the findings. Next is a presentation of the implications and recommendations for future research and finally, a conclusion of the chapter.

BACKGROUND

Defining the Gig Economy

The concept of Online labour is fast becoming an economic phenomenon and thus, will shape how work is done in the future for both developed and developing countries (Heeks, 2017). In the basic form of the gig economy, gig workers enter into formal agreements with on-the-demand companies to render services to them(Brinkley 2016; Baranowski, 2018). Clients or employers, on the other hand, request a service or a task to be done for them using online platforms through the internet which enables them to specify jobs or to find gig workers to provide them the service. The providers of the service (known as gig workers) having been engaged based 'on the demand' of the service by the client receive payment for the job after its completion (Donovan, Bradley & Shimabukuru, 2016). *Table 1* provides some definitions given to the gig economy.

Table 1. Some Definitions of the Gig Economy

Author(s)	Definition
Donovan, Bradley & Shimabukuru (2016)	A matchmaking process where providers are matched with clients on a gig (or job) basis in support of on-demand commerce.
Brinkley (2016)	A form of work engagement by direct connection between individual providers and customers and clients through a digital platform in order to have some task undertaken and delivered.
Manyika *et al.* (2015)	A digital market space for temporary work engagements.
Baranowski (2018)	An emerging employment business model which is different from the traditional forms of employment. Workers accept jobs on a short-term basis from those who demand their services.
Broughton *et al.* (2018)	Receiving payment for a short-term job between individuals or companies via digital platforms through a matchmaking process.
Stewart & Stanford (2017)	The type of work that is performed and coordinated through faceless online platforms and compensated through digital transfers.
Burtch, Carnahan & Greenwood (2018)	New models of platform-enabled, peer-to-peer businesses that are collectively referred to as the collaborative or sharing economy.
Graham, Hjorth & Lehdonvirta (2017)	Work that is digitally mediated to allow business processes to be outsourced without the mediation of formal Business Process Outsourcing (BPO) organisations (and their associated overheads).
De Stefano (2015)	Work that is executed online and allows platform, clients, and workers to operate from different geographical regions. It also represents a platform that matches online supply and demand of tasks that are later executed locally.
Kässi & Lehdonvirta (2018)	A labour market that is characterised by supplemented or substituted temporary jobs mediated by online platforms. Instead of hiring a standard employee or contracting with conventional outsourcing, online platforms are used to find, hire, supervise, and pay workers on a project, piece-rate, or hourly basis.

DIGITAL PLATFORMS AND THE GIG ECONOMY

Digital platforms can broadly be defined as "digital infrastructures that enable two or more groups to interact" (Srnicek, 2017, p. 43). Digital platforms are digital frameworks that "serve to organise and structure economic and social activity" (Kenney & Zysman, 2016, p. 65) and are built upon a complex combination of algorithms, software, hardware, networks, and cloud computing. Some digital platforms provide users with the tools to create their own products or marketplaces (Srnicek, 2017) and mediate interactions between different groups of users including producers, consumers, suppliers, service providers, and advertisers.

The Gig Economy in Africa: An Overview

The rapid change in internet connectivity has generated a lot of hope and excitement for the potentials of an emergent knowledge economy in region of Africa (Graham, Ojanperä, Anwar & Friederici, 2017). In some African countries, there have been attempts by governments to establish fully-fledged gig economies that will ensure the reduction of unemployment. Kenya, for example, has the highest rate of youth joblessness in East Africa and according to the World Bank, about 17 percent of young people who are eligible for work in Kenya lack jobs. Interventions by the government, however, places an estimated 40,000 Kenyans in secured online work to perform tasks such as transcription services to software development on sites like Amazon's MTURK and the Kenyan-owned KuHustle platform. These effort to reduce employment is dubbed "Ajira" and has full support from the Kenyan government (Miriri, 2017). Similarly, in the Federal Republic of Nigeria, its Ministry responsible for Communication has launched a Microwork for Job Creation initiative called "Naijacloud" in a bid to reduce unemployment. Through the initiative, the government seeks to create wealth through Microwork. The initiative has backing from the World Bank and the Rockefeller Foundation where individuals are given access to five of the major global online platforms and microwork intermediaries such Samasource, CrowdFlower, Mobile Works, oDesk and Elance (Graham, Hjorth & Lehdonvirta, 2017).

The Categorisation of the Gig Economy

Australia's Productivity Commission (2016) identifies three broad task-oriented categories of the gig economy: (i) matching platforms (which connect workers and end-users, or buyers and sellers); (ii) platforms which allow analysis and sorting (for example, by providing referrals and reviews); and (iii) platforms which allow value to be added directly to a product (by facilitating the performance of incremental online work). Another common distinction is made between 'labour platforms' (which organise the execution of productive tasks) and 'capital platforms'(which facilitate the sale or rent of assets) (Farrell & Greig, 2016). Among labour platforms, there is a distinction between two major categories (De Stefano, 2015; Cardon & Casilli, 2015). The first is 'Crowd work' systems, involving bidding for and completing work through open websites; these platforms usually include jobs that can be completed and delivered online. The role of such crowd work platforms is typically limited to matching workers with the end patrons of their services. The second is 'Work-on-demand' systems, involving more traditional, physical or 'real world' tasks and jobs. These jobs are organized through online platforms managed by companies that may retain control over important aspects of the work (including setting prices and standards and selecting and managing the workforce). These systems have essential differences. For example, the means of payment is usually decentralised in crowd work systems but centralised in work-on-demand systems.

The implications of these different platforms for workers and labour regulation are also quite different: work-on-demand intermediaries generally take on more responsibility associated with the selection, supervision, and discipline of gig workers than is the case with crowdsourcing platforms, hence may ultimately be found to possess more of the expected characteristics of an 'employer' than those who facilitate crowd work (De Stefano, 2015).

Benefits and Challenges of the Gig Economy

Benefits of the Gig Economy

Job seekers perceive the benefits of working gigs to being better than that for alternative employment (Heeks, 2017). Some studies have highlighted some specific positive impacts of the gig economy. First, gigs offer flexible and reduced time and cost in finding and providing employment (Heeks, 2017). The digital nature of the gig economy provides flexible cost and time in having to travel long distances to work as compared to local market employment (Fidler, 2016). Employers, in turn, are not obliged to provide working space and having to meet all the regulatory requirements such as worker insurance and welfare package as compared to traditional forms of employment or work engagements. Work in the gig economy can be undertaken under flexible work conditions in terms of timing and location, much more than most of the work available in developing countries (D'Cruz & Noronha, 2016). Locational flexibility has included the ability to work from home, even when the 'home' is a relatively remote village provided there is the accessibility to the required tools (Crosby & Rina, 2017) and according to Agrawal *et al.* (2013) flexibility is identified by workers as the foremost benefit of online labour. Second, the gig economy offers broader access to employment opportunities (D'Cruz & Noronha, 2016; Agrawal *et al.,* 2013).

For employers, the absence of gig platforms would mean that jobs would either be done by in-house experts or not done at all, thereby limiting access to employment by others across different geographical regions who can deliver on the service (Agrawal *et al.,* 2013). Being able to outsource jobs via online platforms provides new employment opportunities for people living in different parts of the globe (D'Cruz & Noronha, 2016) and in the case of unemployed job seekers living in developing countries, gigs provide them with a temporary livelihood that they hitherto could not have accessed (Berg, 2016). Also worth noting in this benefit is the provision of an all-inclusive labour market which is different from the traditional labour market, especially in developing countries where specific group of workers such as those without formal education, parenting job seekers as well as people with disabilities or health problems are able to find jobs to do (De Stefano, 2015; Graham *et al.,* 2017). Third, the gig economy presents an opportunity for talents to be identified and skills to be developed. Gigs empower job seekers, including high school students, to seek a mid-career change with better information about educational investment and training. Gig platforms, for example, make it easier for highly talented individuals to find one another, offering new possibilities for collaboration and innovation (Manyika *et. al.,* 2015) and an opportunity "to renew existing skills through practice, to discover and utilise skills and to develop specialist skills" (Barnes *et al.,* 2015, p.28). This point of view is further supported by Malik *et al.* (2017) that working gigs enables people to acquire new knowledge in order to develop their skills.

Challenges of the Gig Economy

In as much as working gigs is beneficial, it also presents some level of disruption (Heeks 2017). Online labour platforms disrupt clients, competitors, workers, and "the social state and its welfare systems" (Schmidt, 2017, p.9). First, working gigs present issues of low remuneration, which is usually below the minimum wage as a primary concern for the worker. Workers are inadequately paid due to weak regulatory and policy in monitoring gig employment earnings (Martin *et al.,* 2016; Berg, 2016). Second, the work process of the gig economy is also of the most significant concern (Heeks, 2017).

For the type of gigs where there is little or no interaction between the worker and the employer, there is the lack of broader information about who the employers are and what the purpose of the task is (Bergvall-Kareborn & Howcroft, 2014; Brawley & Pury, 2016) a challenge that is mostly present in 'crowd work' platforms where there is little or no physical interaction with the tasker and the person who has been assigned the task (De Stefano, 2015). Additionally, with regards to the work process, there is worker complains about the unclear nature of procedures which may lead to rejection of work, suspension from the platform or account termination (Martin *et al.,* 2016). These information and interactions issues lead to job dissatisfaction and job stress in executing gigs (D'Cruz & Noronha, 2016; Graham *et al.,* 2017).

MAIN FOCUS OF THE CHAPTER

Research Problem

The gig economy has arguably generated a lot of interest for information systems researchers. Of such interests are an understanding of the nature of the gig economy and the motivation for joining it. The gig economy through the use of internet-enabled platforms facilitates the exchange of information between employers and workers, thereby creating opportunities for all involved (Barnes, Green & de Hoyos, 2015). Yet, the gig economy remains elusive and poorly understood (Behrendt & Nguyen, 2018), and the understanding and use of these platforms are still in their infant stages, with little known about them within the developing economy context (Drahokoupil & Fabo, 2016). Also, most of the studies done on the gig economy have focused on worker perspectives (e.g. Dokko, Mumford & Schanzenbach, 2015; Berg, 2015; Barnes, Green, & de Hoyos, 2015) with not many studies on consumers who sign up to the platforms to find worker to undertake a task for them. Further, there is a need to explore the role of software and digital technologies in shaping power and information differentials in the gig economy (Lee *et al.,* 2015). Additionally, few studies have sought to use theories to explain the study of the gig economy (e,g. Alamyar, 2017; Green & de Hoyos, 2015; Barrenechea, 2016). This points to the lack of theoretical underpinnings on the conduct of the studies regarding the gig economy (Dokko, Mumford & Schanzenbach, 2015; Graham, Hjorth & Lehdonvirta, 2017). It is within these identified gaps that further research is needed and which serves as the main foundation of this chapter.

Analytical Framework

For this research, the author develops and applies a unique conceptualisation of the Unified Theory of Acceptance and Use of Technology framework, as shown in *Figure 1*. The Unified Theory of Acceptance and Use of Technology (UTAUT) was developed by Venkatesh *et al.* (2003) to predict user adoption of information technology (Alwahaishi & Snásel, 2013). It is one of the generally used research frameworks for assessing the acceptance of technology by explaining the intention of users to use an information system and the usage behaviour thereafter (Alshehri, Drew, Alhussain & Alghamdi, 2012). According to the UTAUT model, the degree to which technology or innovation is adopted is dependent heavily on some factors such as Performance expectancy, Effort Expectancy, Social Influence, and Facilitating conditions.

Figure 1. A conceptual framework based on the Unified Theory of Acceptance and Use of Technology (UTAUT) Framework (Author, 2019)

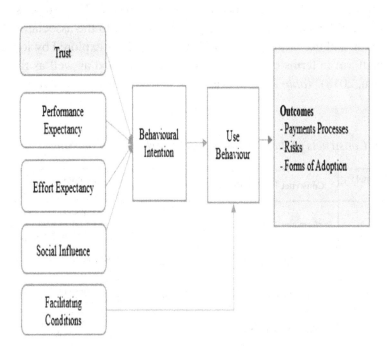

The term Performance expectancy (PE) is conceptualised in this study as riders' adoption of the platform to search for transportation services based on how they perceive the platform to be useful and beneficial (Venkatesh *et al.,*2003; Kumar, Maheshwari & Kumar, 2002). Further, Effort expectancy is explored by looking at the perceptions of the ease of use of the platform as well as the ease of learning how to use the platform. Effort expectancy considers factors such as Perceived Ease of Use (PEU), which is from the Technology Acceptance Model / Technology Acceptance Model 2 and defines the level of effort that is needed to use the system by the riders. The construct of Social Influence will be explored by looking at how the perception of peers and other influencing persons or organisations affect the user's use of the platform. Facilitating conditions is examined by looking at the perception users of the platform have about having the resources to use the platform as well as the knowledge and the necessary support to use the platform. Also, a factor called "Trust" proposed by Alzahrani and Goodwin, (2012) and Lubrin *et al.* (2006) to be explored as part of the UTAUT model was added. Lubrin, *et al.* (2006) argue that the extension of the UTAUT to include trust is in line with prior studies that suggest that the traditional models on technology adoption lack the issue of trust.

It is noted that the UTAUT model has been applied in a number of studies explaining technology use already (Venkatesh *et al.,* 2003), and its application in research continues to thrive (Venkatesh *et al.,* 2012). Yet, research done with the UTAUT model had mostly been applied "as is", with other theories, or been extended to study different types of technologies in both organizational and non-organizational contexts.

In this regard, Venkatesh, Thong and Xu (2016) propose the exploration of new outcome mechanisms as an extension to the UTAUT model. "New outcome mechanisms refer to the new consequences of behavioural intention and technology use added to the original UTAUT" (Venkatesh et *al.,* 2016.p.8).

Hence, the construct of Outcomes in this study is in reference to the associated developments that arise out of the adoption and use of the platform. Outcomes will be explored by looking at the perceptions of using the platform in terms of payment process and method as well as the risks of using the platform (Fuad & Hsu, 2018). *Table 2* summarises the constructs of the analytical framework as used in this chapter.

Table 2. Summary of Constructs of the Analytical framework used in the Study

Constructs of the Original Framework	Construct Used in this study	Status	Reason/Source for Using or Dropping the construct
Performance Expectancy	Performance Expectancy	Used	Venkatesh *et al.* (2003); Thomas, Singh, & Gaffar (2013,p.73); Kumar, Maheshwari, & Kumar (2002); (Davis *et al.,* (1989)
Effort Expectancy	Effort Expectancy	Used	Venkatesh *et al.* (2003); Thomas, Singh, & Gaffar (2013)
Social Influence	Social Influence	Used	Venkatesh *et al.* (2003); Thomas, Singh, & Gaffar (2013)
Facilitating Conditions	Facilitating Conditions	Used	Venkatesh *et al.* (2003); Thomas, Singh, & Gaffar (2013)
Behavioural intention	Behavioural intention	Used	Venkatesh *et al.* (2003); Thomas, Singh, & Gaffar (2013)
Use behaviour of the adopter	Use behaviour	Used	Venkatesh *et al.* (2003): Thomas, Singh, & Gaffar (2013)
Moderating Variables			
Gender		Dropped	(Rilling, 2015)
Age		Dropped	(Rilling, 2015)
Experience		Dropped	(Rilling, 2015)
Voluntariness		Dropped	(Rilling, 2015)
Additional Constructs			
	Trust	Used	Alzahrani & Goodwin (2012); Lubrin *et al.* (2006)
	Outcomes	Used	Venkatesh, Thong & Xu (2016); Fuad & Hsu (2018).

METHOD

Drawing on the Unified Theory of Acceptance and Use of Technology(UTAUT), the author conducted interviews with riders who use the Uber ride-hailing application. The application enables persons looking for transportation services to find a taxi, and by doing so assign drivers the task of driving them from one location to the other facilitated by technology (Cutter, Litan & Stangler, 2016). Given that there are little empirical researches on the gig economy (especially in a developing economy context), the study was designed as an inductive exploration. Qualitative data was collected using semi-structured interviews based on a conceptualisation of the UTAUT model, as shown in *Figure 1*. Respondents' participation was voluntary, through verbal consent and without any form of inducement. Respondents were also made aware that they were at liberty to pull out of the study if they so wished at any point in time without any form of charges pressed against them. Their anonymity to the responses they provided was also highly upheld.

Sampling and Data Collection

In order to get respondents for the study, the researcher contacted the Uber secretariat in Accra for assistance. However, this was not as successful as the Uber secretariat was not willing to disclose any information on riders 'and drivers' due to issues of confidentiality and non-discloser agreements in using the platform. Unable to get this assistance, the researcher resorted to identify sites in Accra where riders could be engaged or contacted to participate in this study.

A set of criteria can be used in selecting respondents for a study (Slavin, 1986). Therefore, in this study, the criteria included: convenience sampling, random sampling, and purposive sampling. The convenience sample comprised of 4 locations in Accra, Ghana, where riders were usually located and could easily be accessed. The factors that were taken into consideration were geographical proximity and timely collection of data. The locations are; (1) University of Ghana, Legon Campus; (2) University of Professional Studies, Legon (3) A & C Mall, located at East Legon and (4) Accra Mall also located near Legon. Following the convenience sampling of the sites, 40 riders were then randomly selected from the 4 locations to be interviewed. From the riders that were randomly selected, 20 were purposively sampled based on the duration that they had been actively using the platform and the total number of trips they had made, after which their responses were analysed. The average length for an interview with a respondent lasted about 45 minutes.

Data Analysis

Data collected for this study were manually analysed using thematic analysis techniques. Thematic analysis is used to classify data and present it in the form of themes or patterns that relate to the data (Alhojailan, 2012). As such, by using thematic analysis, responses received were sorted into various categories, and the author was able to read and analyse the data from a broader sense towards discovering patterns and developing themes. This made it easier to identify similarities and differences in responses. Before analysing the data, responses were transcribed and carefully read over and over to take note of critical views expressed by respondents and to reflect on the essential items in the research questions.

Findings

Overall, the riders who participated in the study provided detailed responses to the interview questions that were posed to them. The questions posed to respondents dwelled on the nature of the platform (perception about the platform, how to access it and riders' characteristics), motivation for joining and platform and the outcomes of joining the platform. The findings of the study are presented in themes from the analysis being described and appropriate responses provided. A summary of lessons drawn from findings on the motivation and outcomes are presented in *Table 3* of this chapter.

Nature of the Platform

The essence of this theme was to capture the overall perception with regards to how riders generally see the platform. The theme of nature touched on issues such as the type of platform it is, and technologies for accessing the platform. The theme also looked at the characteristics of respondents who had signed up to the platform. The general perception of riders with regards to the platform in terms of the type of platform it is and technologies for accessing the platform was undivided.

Type of Platform and how it is Accessed

Generally, all the riders regarded the nature of the platform as a 'mobile application', which is 'installed on smartphones and iPhones' and used 'on-the-demand'. For example, some riders said:

I know the platform to be mobile-based so it's a mobile application. I have the application installed on my smartphone.

Another also said

Uber is a mobile-based application and makes the hiring of taxi service an on-the- demand service. I use my phone to access it. My phone is an iPhone.

In summary, the findings identified that riders found the platform to be a mobile application that was installed on the smartphones of riders. Additionally, riders use the platform 'on-the-demand (used as and when they need the service).

Characteristics of the Platform's Riders

The level of education and working life forms an essential factor for participating in the gig economy. The findings reveal that riders on the platform have some considerable level of education and could be considered as part of the working class. They either run businesses or consultancy services of their own or work in the formal sector. Below are some of the responses of riders when they were asked about their backgrounds.
For example, one respondent said;

I hold a first degree in Information technology, and I work as an IT systems administrator, but I also run on the side a private Information Technology consultancy services.

Another respondent said:

I am a businessman. I trade in IT devices like phones and laptops. I have an ACCA.

Another respondent also said;

I have a Bachelor of Arts degree in Psychology from the University of Ghana, and I'm currently working as an office administrator at a physiotherapy clinic in Accra.

Hence, with regards to the characteristics of riders, the findings identified an appreciable level of education with the least educated person being a Post-Senior High School professional certificate holder. Also, riders were either formally employed, were in school or were involved in 'on-the-side' private work engagements.

The Motivation for Using the Platform

This theme captures riders' perceptions concerning what motivates them to sign onto the platform. The motivation helps to capture Performance expectancy, Effort Expectancy, Social influence, Facilitating conditions, Trust, Behavioural intention and Use behaviour of riders on the platform.

Motivation by Performance Expectancy

With regards to Performance expectancy, the riders' perceptions were the usefulness of the platform in terms of cost in using the platform, the convenience that it provides and time it saves them in moving from one location to another. For example, a rider in relation to Performance expectancy of the platform said;

It's very convenient for me, especially when I can order a ride at my own comfort. The cost of using an Uber is also cheaper as compared to the traditional taxis.

Another said:

The fare is much cheaper as compared to traditional taxis because it's the application that determines the fare and also it's convenient and saves time. I don't have to struggle to walk to look for a taxi, and I can just order it to where I am.

A respondent said:

I can schedule my day well knowing that I have Uber at my disposal and so I don't have to worry about transportation.

Another respondent said:

I get to my destination on time because there is no long bargaining like one would do with the other taxis.

Hence the extent of usefulness and benefits obtained includes cheaper cost is as a result of the platform determining what the riders should pay as fare for a ride. There is no room for time-consuming bargaining, and it is also convenient to order an Uber.

Motivation by Effort Expectancy

With regards to Effort expectancy which is in reference to the level to which riders perceive the platform as easy to use, the responses were as follows;

A respondent said;

I think it's easy to understand. First of all, when I heard the concept of how Uber works, right away, I had an idea what it does and how it will work even though the technicalities behind it were quite intriguing. But generally, I understand how the platform works. Learning to use the application is easy. There are even times when I've had to teach people to use the application, and they have been able to use it afterwards.

Another in a response also said:

The platform is straightforward to use, and this is so because of my IT savvy background, and so I can confidently say I understand how the platform works. It's straightforward, as easy as ABC. For example, my mum is not technology savvy, but I was able to use a few minutes to teach her how to request a ride, so the learning process is straightforward.

Another respondent, a female said:

I understand how features of the application work. It was very easy for me. In the beginning, I didn't know how to read the map on the application when requesting a taxi, but then my husband showed me, and since then I've been able to read the map to know my current location and my destination in requesting for a ride.

Motivations by Social Influence

On the aspect of Social influence, majority of riders were of the view that their decision to use the platform is in one way or the other influenced by the organisations they work for or with individuals they interact with directly or indirectly. For example, one respondent said;

I happen to work with an organisation where whenever you go for an errand without the company vehicle and need to pick a taxi there was always an argument with the finance people about the fare that you'd come and report so that you can be reimbursed. And so when Uber came, it became the norm that whenever we had to go out on an official assignment without the company vehicle, we had to use Uber because with Uber you can come and show proof of the fare. And so in this regard, I think the organisation had an influence.

Another also said:

Where I work, we use Uber a lot. Usually when you need to go somewhere but the company driver isn't available you have to use the application to request for a Uber because with that one there is receipt evidence to show how much the fare is. If you don't come with an Uber evidence, you won't get the refund on the fare.

Others who were influenced by engagement with others said:

I happen to teach some kids, and their parents are well to do persons in society, so they influence me. Most often, after I have taught the kids and I'm leaving they give me money to order an Uber.

Another also said;

On a normal day, I wouldn't order an Uber, but when I'm going out on a date with my girlfriend I order one so that we ride her.

These responses indicate that riders are generally socially influenced by the organisations they work for or the people with whom they engage or associate themselves with.

Motivation by Facilitating Conditions

With regards to Facilitating conditions, which has to do with knowledge on how to use the platform, the availability of support structures, or resource to use a technology, riders gave the following responses;

You need a smartphone that has Global Positioning Systems and internet access, and I have all of these.

Another said;

Even the next person around you may be able to assist you because most people use it. I also think the platform itself also has features where you can ask for assistance, but I still think they need to work on their support system and structures.

Another said:

You need to know how to use a phone, and how to know whether your Global Positioning System is on or not and you also need to be able to read the location on the map that the application shows you when you are requesting a car.

Another respondent said:

There is even a section on the application called Frequently Asked Questions(FAQs) where you can refer to find answers to some issues that have already happened and have been answered.

Hence from the responses, it is indicative that having the resources and tools such as a smartphone to install the application on, backed by internet access and the knowledge to use the platform contributes immensely to its adoption. Again, the availability of support features on the application as a means to ask for help and support through the application also contributes to riders' use of the platform.

Motivation by Trust

With regards to Trust which has to do with how riders perceive the platform to perform its key operation of aiding them to find a ride and to perform the financial transactions of the service such as generating fares, the responses were;

I trust the application because the application is able to get me a ride, and I'm even able to check the background of the driver.

Another said:

The fares charged are also something that I trust because it's the application that determines how much the driver should take, so I usually don't complain about the fare like it's done in normal taxis.

Another respondent said:

In terms of payment, yes, but with the drivers no. I have had an experience where the driver showed me a fare that was different from the one I had on my phone, so it even generated an argument between us; apparently, he had screenshotted someone's fare from an earlier trip and was showing that to me as my fare.

Another respondent said;

Yes, I do. I do trust the platform, but it's the drivers don't trust. Some of them show you a different price on their phone.

Hence, riders have trust in the platform as a system but not necessarily the drivers who are the interface between the platform and riders in terms of the delivery of the service. In essence, riders trust the platform to operate properly and to perform transactions faithfully, but they, however, do not trust the drivers to do the same.

Motivation by Behavioural Intention

Behavioural intention of riders concerns their intention to continue to use the application. For example, a respondent said;

I' will use it for as long as the application remains useful to me. I can't predict, but as long as the application remains useful to me. Maybe I will use it for 1 or 2 years more, by then I'd have bought a car, even with that I think I will park my car and still use the application if I still find it useful.

Another said:

Yes, I don't have a car and the traditional taxis are not really favourable so I'll use it for long. Maybe until I buy my own car that I can use to do my own rounds, but even that if I see that taking Uber will work for me I can park my car and use the Uber.

Another respondent said:

I can't tell how long I'll use it but even if I stop using it I'm sure I'll still have it on my phone, even when I have my own car so that days that my car isn't available I can still use the application.

However, there were other riders whose behavioural intention towards the use of the application was as a result of the emergence of a competitor who could provide them with better service delivery. A respondent for example stated that:

It depends, until some better competitor comes up I think I'll continue to use it. I can't predict how long I'd use it but it depends on how soon the competitor comes. For now I know there is another competitor but their services is still not up to the standard of Uber.

Another respondent said:

I can't tell, maybe when there is a lot more competition in the business. When a better competitor arrives, that can challenge them.

Hence, riders' behavioural intention to use the platform depended on how useful the platform remains to them and the availability of a competitor that would offer a better service delivery than the platform under study. For now, riders find the platform to be useful and very competitive in the midst of similar platforms that were also rendering taxi services.

Motivation by Use Behaviour

Regarding the actual use behaviour of the platform by the riders, the following were some of the responses;

Basically, I make sure my location feature my phone is on and I have internet bundle. Then I open the Uber application and then I type in where I want to go. The application shows me the available drivers near me and I then select the type of ride I want, where I want the regular Uber or the Uber Select and then I proceed to confirm it. The driver arrives and I board but before we set off the driver uses the application on his phone to start the journey because he also has a driver's version of the application on his phone that is able to view and process riders' requests. When I get to my destination, the driver stops the journey on his application and then tells me the cost of the journey, but then I also have a copy of the price on my application for confirmation. I then make payment and get off the taxi. But after the journey the application tells me to rate the driver based on my experience during the journey.

Another said:

I go into the application and input the location where I want to go, because it's a location based service. Because the application is location based I need to make sure the location featured on my phone is on and also make sure I have internet. I then would have to enter my destination and confirm it by entering where I want the driver to pick me up. When the driver picks me up and I get to my destination the driver ends the trip and the price is calculated by the application then I make payment. After paying, I then rate the driver.

Hence, the use of behaviour of the platform for riders was identified to be in three stages. The Pre-request where riders look for a ride, the Request confirmation stage where riders confirm a ride and finally the Post-request stage where riders perform an evaluation of the service provided them by the driver.

Perceived Outcomes

This theme captures the outcomes of the platform perceived by the riders from using the platform. The perceived outcomes explored were complementary or substitutive. Additionally, outcomes such as risks involved in using the platform as well as how payment of fares are made after the service are delivered were explored. With regards to the complementary outcome, some of the riders indicated that they used the platform as an alternate means of requesting for taxi service because they sometimes resorted to other means of requesting transport especially taxi services.

Outcomes on How the Platform Has Been Adopted

Whiles others indicated that using the platform substituted their existing means of finding taxi services; some riders said the platform complemented their means of finding transportation, specifically regarding taxi services.

Respondents who found the platform to be complementary said:

It is not the only means of requesting a taxi service for me. I don't always use the application when I need a taxi, but when I'm at work and need to go on errands for the office I use it.

Another said:

No, it's not the only means, sometimes I use the traditional taxis. Even yesterday I used a traditional taxi.

Respondents who however found the use of the platform to substitute their means of taxi transportation said:

When I am looking for a taxi I use Uber. I even think Uber has taken a large portion of my expenses when it comes to transportation. I don't even remember the last time I took a traditional taxi.

Another said:

I think for me Uber is my main means of transport, except for days when due to pressure on the request there is none available to pick me up on time so then I resort to other means of transport.

Hence, riders used the platform in two different forms. Some riders found it to be a complementary means of finding transportation whiles others found it to substitute their means of finding transportation.

Payment Outcomes

With regards to how riders make payments for the services rendered to them. Some of the riders had this to say regarding how they make payments;

There is the option of using credit card payment and to pay by cash, but I prefer to pay by cash. I've always used cash...and sometimes too I pay using mobile money.

Another said:

I mostly pay my fare using cash.

Another said;

I pay by cash or mobile money.

Another respondent said:

On the Uber application, there is a credit card or cash payment but I mostly pay by cash...and sometimes too I pay using mobile money but not all the drivers accept mobile money.

Hence, riders generally know about the payment options of cash or credit card available on the platform. However, the main means of payment for the taxi services rendered to them was by cash even though they were aware they could pay by electronic means using a credit card.

Additionally, riders used "Mobile Money" which is another electronic form of payment, to make payment for their fares even though that option is not supported by the platform.

Outcomes on Risks

On the aspect of risks involved in seeking for ride-hailing using the platform, some of respondents said:

One of the risks is when your fare goes up because you are caught up in traffic. As compared to the traditional taxis, when the driver charges you even if you spend hours in traffic that fare doesn't change. But with Uber the more time you spend in traffic the higher your fare.

Another said:

Your fare can go up when you delay in traffic.

Another said:

Table 3. Summary of Lessons drawn from Findings on Motivation and Outcomes

Framework Construct	Factors	Lessons Learnt
Performance Expectancy	Cost	The cost of moving from one location to the other could be significantly reduced with the adoption of the application as it is cheaper to use in finding transportation. This cost savings is both personal and shared especially for riders who ride with others when they make a request.
Performance Expectancy	Convenient and time-saving	The application provides riders with the convenience to request for taxi rides and eliminates the need to physically look for taxi transportation and to bargain on fares and charges. This convenience and time-saving is both personal and shared especially for riders who ride with others when they make a request.
Effort Expectancy	Understanding of the Platform	Riders generally understood the functions and features of the platform.
Effort Expectancy	Ease of Use	The ease with which most riders found the platform was because they understood how it works
Effort Expectancy	Ease of Learning	Learning to use platforms came to riders naturally and for others, they learned along the way and so they found the platform to be easy to use.
Social Influence	Organisational Influence	Riders were influenced by the organisations they work for to use the platform because the organizations found the platform to provide better accountability.
Social Influence	Association with other individuals	For some riders, the influence to use the platform comes from engaging or associating with other individuals as a result of the image they want to present to such individuals.
Facilitating Conditions	Knowledge in using the platform	Knowing how to use the platform contributes immensely to its adoption
Facilitating Conditions	Availability of needed resource	Having the resources and tools such as a smartphone to install the application on backed by internet access contributes to the adoption of the platform
Trust	Operational Trust	Riders trust the platform to aid them to request and find a ride.
Trust	Fares and Payment Trust	Riders trust the platform and to generate fares and perform payment transactions faithfully.
Behavioural intention	Competitiveness of the Platform	The availability of a competitor that would offer a better service delivery than the platform understudy could influence the behavioural intention of riders to use the platform.
Behavioural intention	Continuous Usefulness of the Platform	The continuous use of the platform in aiding riders to find transport will influence their decision to use it.
Use Behaviour	Pre-request	The Use behaviour stage where riders look for a ride.
Use Behaviour	Request confirmation	The Use behaviour stage where riders use the application to confirm a ride.
Use Behaviour	Post-request	The use behaviour stage where riders perform an evaluation of the service provided them by the driver.
Outcomes	Complementing	Some consumers found the platform to complement their request or taxi services as they didn't always use the application but sometimes resorted to using traditional taxis.
Outcomes	Substituting	Other consumers used the platform always when they need to get a taxi and so to them the platform has substituted the traditional means of finding a taxi
Outcomes	Payment Process	Payment options available on the platform is by cash or electronic card. However, riders usually paid by cash. Additionally, riders sometimes make payments using Mobile Money even though the platform does not support that mode of payment.
Outcomes	Risks	Delays in getting to one's destination lead to a rise in fare, especially during traffic hold-ups and intentional driver delays. Additional risks have to do with data confidentially, especially with regards to riders' contact details.

Because with Uber it's the application that determines the fare and it's based on the time you spend in getting to your destination the fare usually goes up when you are not lucky to land yourself in traffic.

Another respondent also said:

Some of the drivers can take your contact details and stalk you. I remember there was a time where a driver called me and wanted to ask me out.

Hence, riders found the risks in using the platform to be escalations in fare charges as a result of delays during traffic hold-ups and deliberate delays by drivers on the road. Additionally, the lack of data confidentially especially with regards to consumer contact details was also identified.

DISCUSSION

This section examines the afore-mentioned riders' perceptions in relation to the literature. In this section, the findings are discussed in accordance with the questions indicated in the introductory part of this chapter.

Nature of the Platform

Type of Platform and how it is Accessed

Findings from the study suggest that riders' perceptions about the platform are consistent with the characteristics that make it a gig platform. Overall, most of the respondents regarded the platform as a 'mobile application' which is 'installed on smartphones' and used 'on-the-demand'. These findings are consistent with assertions by Cardon and Casilli, (2015) as well as Smith and Leberstein, (2015) that "work on-demand" jobs are acquired via mobile applications but are executed through traditional working activities such as transportation, running errands as well as cleaning services.

Characteristics of Riders

Regarding rider characteristics, the findings identified an appreciable level of education among riders with the least educated person being a Post-Senior High School professional certificate holder. This assertion is against the backdrop that in a developing economy like Ghana, the minimum level of education where a person is considered literate is when the person has acquired a Basic Education Certificate (Junior High School graduate) ("Basic Education Division", 2018). Also, riders were either formally employed, were pursuing further studies at the University or were involved in 'on-the-side' private work engagements. This appreciable level of education by riders may translate into higher rates of the adoption of this innovative means of living through the Uber ride-hailing platform, which may improve the overall productivity of riders.

The Motivation for Using the Platform

Riders' motivation to use the platform touched on factors of Performance expectancy, Effort Expectancy, Social influence, Facilitating conditions, Trust, Behavioural intention and Use Behaviour of the platform.

Regarding Performance expectancy, the cost of moving from one location to the other is significantly reduced with the adoption of the Uber application as it is cheaper to use as a means of taxi transportation. Using Uber also provides riders with the convenience needed to look for taxi transportation. For instance, the rider does not need to bargain fares with a driver or personally spend time looking for a taxi because with Uber the request for a ride comes right to your doorstep as long as the application can locate your doorstep. This is in line with gig economy research by Sørensen and Shklovski (2011) that technology plays a role in providing broader access to more people by removing barriers such as difficulties in scheduling, distance, and time differences.

Regarding Effort expectancy, riders indicated it is indicative that users had an understanding of the platform, which makes it easy for them to use the platform. This confirms the stance of Tarhini, El-Masri, Ali and Serrano (2016) in their study in relation to the adoption of internet banking that the decision to by users to adopt internet banking technology is when they find it easy to use and do not require much effort then they are more likely to adopt it. A similar confirmation is made by Martins, Oliveira, and Popovič, (2014) that Effort expectancy was significant in positively influencing users' behavioural intention to use an innovation like internet banking. In view of these findings, the features and the functions of the ride-hailing platform are easier to use by the riders and as such so as to encourages them to use it to seek transportation services.

Riders were also under the social influence of two categories of people, which are; organisations they work for and also the people they associate themselves with such as family and friends. Regarding how organisations influenced riders, the organisations' riders work for find the Uber platform to offer a much better way to make their staff accountable in terms of cost of transportation when they have to use a taxi to go on errands for the organisation. This so because they make it mandatory for their staff to use the Uber mobile application. With regards to those who riders associate themselves with, it was indicative that such influence comes from family and friends as well as other persons who they had to engage with and needed to portray a particular image to such people. Similarly to these findings, much of the empirical research in information systems found social influence to be an important antecedent to users' behavioural intention to adopt a technology (Venkatesh & Zhang, 2010). Further, users may be motivated to use an information system if important others influence their attitude and behaviour to use it (Taiwo, Mahmood & Downe, 2012). These social influencing factors identified indicates that social ties influence Behavioural intention of riders who have subscribed to ride-hailing application.

With regard to facilitating conditions, riders also readily had the resources to access the platform. Additionally, the platform has inbuilt support systems where users can readily send their complaints and grievances in order to have them addressed. Additionally, the knowledge is using the system was something that riders had which made it possible for them to use the platform. This is consistent with the view of Hamzat, and Mabawonku, (2018) in a user technology adoption study where they identify facilitating conditions such as skills in using the technology, infrastructure and the availability of resources that can significantly contribute to the use of digital library among lecturers who teach engineering. This is indicative that the support features that riders have in their use of the platform keep them using it.

With regards to trust, it is indicative that riders have some substantial level of trust in knowing that the platform is fair in its operations in terms of matchmaking and facilitating the request process. It was however identified that this level of trust was for the platform and not the drivers as riders had trust in the platform to perform its key operation of aiding them to find a ride but did not trust the drivers.

Riders also trusted the transitional aspect of the system such as generating fare pricing since it was a computerized system and not human-generated which was based on human judgment or discretion and as such trust of the platform was influential in their adoption of the platform. This is related to the assertion by Alzahrani and Goodwin (2012) that the use of technology by two parties especially one that is transactional in nature requires data, personal and sensitive information such as credit card details to be sent across the online platform in other to complete transactions.

Behavioural intention to use the application for riders was found to be aligned to the usefulness with which they found the platform. For most riders, they had no predictive time with which they see themselves using the platform but will continue to use the application as long as it remains useful to them. Additionally, riders intended to use the platform as long as it remains competitive. This is coherent with the assertion by Kumar, Maheshwari, and Kumar, (2002) that the quality of services and provision of quality services of information systems will influence users' intention to adopt a technology.

Riders' Use behaviour of the platform is in three (3) stages. These are the Pre-request, Request confirmation and the Post-request stages. At the Pre-request stage is where riders look for a ride, the Request confirmation stage is where riders confirm a ride and finally, the Post-request stage is where riders perform an evaluation of the service provided them by the driver. These findings are not far from an existing study on technology adoption that was done by Boateng (2011) on Mobile phones as a digital tool for e-commerce trade where he identified mobile phones to be used by market women in three phases; pre-trade activities, during trade activities and post-trade activities. This is indicative that the users through the pre-trade are able to get some preliminary details on the ride; such as cost; can bring the ride to their doorsteps at the confirmation stage and can review their rides at the post-confirmation stage.

Outcomes of the Platform Usage

Regarding the outcomes, as asserted by Venkatesh, Thong, and Xu, (2016), the adoption of technology generates some outcomes for users, and in this study, some outcomes were accordingly identified. Most riders in paying for their fares after a service is usually through cash payments even though they were aware of an electronic form of payment which is by credit or debit card. The findings also discovered that there were some riders who make payment using another electronic mode called "Mobile Money", even though the Uber platform does not support Mobile Money as a mode of payment. This can be seen to fall line with the assertion made by Stewart and Stanford (2017) that on gig platforms, when work is performed, one of the ways workers are remunerated is through digital transfers.

Regarding risks, riders identified issues such as delays in getting to one's destination since the fare is calculated based on the time and distance spent on the journey. The application calculates the fare per minute spent on the trip and so delays such as traffic hold-ups can cause the fare to shoot up. Additionally, some riders especially females indicated that the risks in using the platform were more of confidentiality of data, especially with regards to contact details as some have had the experience of being stalked by drivers later on after requesting a drop off because drivers could have access to their contact details.

On the forms of adoption which have to do with how the platform is accessed, riders the findings point to some riders using the platform to substitute the means through which they find transportation. Whiles, for other riders, the platform complemented their means of finding taxi services.

IMPLICATIONS AND FUTURE RESEARCH DIRECTIONS

The significance of the study can be explored along three strands: implications to research, practice, and policy. These are presented below in the subsequent subsections.

Implication for Research

The study adds to the existing studies and knowledge regarding the gig economy, especially from a developing economy context. It further responds to the research gaps considering that not many scholarly studies have been done from a developing economy context.

Additionally, regarding the contribution of this research to knowledge, this research conceptualized a framework based on the UTAUT framework that has been widely applied in quantitative analyses within other studies. However, in this study, the UTAUT framework has been applied in the qualitative sense to identify the motivation and outcomes of participating in the gig economy. This research, therefore, provides a foundation for researchers to also explore the qualitative findings in this research with quantitative analyses of the factors identified for generalisation. Moreover, the framework adopted for the study was examined as the case where riders had already adopted the platform. A study could be explored as the case where riders are yet to adopt the platform.

Finally, as with all forms of peer-to-peer economy, there are three actors in the ecosystem; The riders(consumers), drivers (service providers) and the market aggregator (the digital platform). However, this study focuses on only one of the actors;(a) riders(consumers). Future studies could, therefore, explore the views of the drivers (service providers) and the market aggregator (the digital platform developers or initiator). Nevertheless, the author believes that the contribution that this study makes to the literature on the gig economy, especially from a developing economy context cannot be underplayed.

Implication for Policy

Concerning the implications of the research to policy, this research presents agencies responsible for employment and labour to have a practical overview of the nature of the gig economy in Ghana and what motivates people to join it. One area of interest in the gig economy has been about the filling of tax and income returns as most gig economy participants are not known to be keen payers of income tax. This research can, therefore, provide a fair idea to regulators on how the gig economy, especially in the transport sector operates so as to develop better measures to get them to file their tax returns and to widen the tax net for national development especially in developing economies.

Implication for Practice

Concerning the implications of the research to practice, this study unlocks the key motivating factors and outcomes for gig economy participants (riders) not only from literature but also by providing some form of evidence from the field. It further exploits its potentials in the provision and request for ride-hailing.

CONCLUSION

This chapter explored riders' perceptions of the use of digital platforms in the ride-hailing sector of the gig economy. The study focuses on riders who use the Uber ride-hailing application as a medium of accessing transportation, thereby assigning drivers the task of transporting them from one location to the other.

Findings from this empirical study suggest that Performance Expectancy, Social influence, Trust, Effort expectancy, and Facilitating conditions remain important factors that in riders' signing up and continuous use of the gig platform in question. The findings further suggest that riders found the platform to offer both personal and shared convenience, cost and time saving, as well as trustworthiness. The platform also substituted the means of finding transportation for some of the riders, whiles for other riders, it complemented their means of finding transportation.

Additionally, these factors lead to the Behavioural intention and Use behaviour of riders which further leads to some outcomes such as payments, risks, and forms of use of the platform where riders acknowledged that the platform was both complementary and substitutive in providing them with transportation services. This study is among the few articles that have sought to explore in detail user perceptions on gig platforms from a developing economy context and provides stimulating insights regarding the concept and how it is adopted add used in developing economies. A redefined conceptual framework based on findings is provided in *Appendix 1* of this chapter.

REFERENCES

Agrawal, T., Sao, A., Fernandes, K. J., Tiwari, M. K., & Kim, D. Y. (2013). A hybrid model of component sharing and platform modularity for optimal product family design. *International Journal of Production Research*, *51*(2), 614–625. doi:10.1080/00207543.2012.663106

Alhojailan, M. I. (2012). Thematic analysis: A critical review of its process and evaluation. *WestEast Journal of Social Sciences*, *1*(1), 39–47.

Aloisi, A. (2015). Commoditized workers: Case study research on labor law issues arising from a set of on-demand/gig economy platforms. *Comp. Lab. L. & Pol'y J.*, *37*, 653.

Alshehri, M., Drew, S., Alhussain, T., & Alghamdi, R. (2012). The impact of trust on e- government services acceptance: A study of users' perceptions by applying UTAUT model. *International Journal of Technology Diffusion*, *3*(2), 50–61. doi:10.4018/jtd.2012040105

Alwahaishi, S., & Snásel, V. (2013). Acceptance and use of information and communications technology: A UTAUT and flow based theoretical model. *Journal of Technology Management & Innovation*, *8*(2), 61–73. doi:10.4067/S0718-27242013000200005

Alzahrani, M. E., & Goodwin, R. D. (2012). Towards a UTAUT-based model for the study of E-Government citizen acceptance in Saudi Arabia. In *Proceedings of World Academy of Science, Engineering and Technology (No. 64)*. World Academy of Science, Engineering and Technology.

Baranowski, C. (2017). Freelance Isn't Free: The High Cost of New York City's Freelance Isn't Free Act on Hiring Parties. *Brook. J. Corp. Fin. & Com. L.*, *12*, 439.

Barnes, S. A., Green, A., & de Hoyos, M. (2015). Crowdsourcing and work: Individual factors and circumstances influencing employability. *New Technology, Work and Employment*, *30*(1), 16–31. doi:10.1111/ntwe.12043

Behrendt, C., & Nguyen, Q. A. (2018). Innovative approaches for ensuring universal social protection for the future of work. *Future of Work Research Paper Series*, (1).

Berg, J. (2015). Income security in the on-demand economy: Findings and policy lessons from a survey of crowdworkers. *Comp. Lab. L. & Pol'y J.*, *37*, 543.

Bergvall-Kåreborn, B., & Howcroft, D. (2014). A mazon Mechanical Turk and the commodification of labour. *New Technology, Work and Employment*, *29*(3), 213–223. doi:10.1111/ntwe.12038

Boateng, R. (2011). Mobile phones and micro-trading activities–conceptualizing the link. *Info, 13*(5), 48-62.

Brawley, A. M., & Pury, C. L. (2016). Work experiences on MTurk: Job satisfaction, turnover, and information sharing. *Computers in Human Behavior*, *54*, 531–546. doi:10.1016/j.chb.2015.08.031

Brinkley, I. (2016) In search of the Gig Economy. Lancaster: *The Work Foundation*. Retrieved June 30, from http://www. theworkfoundation. com/wp- content/uploads/2016/11/407_In-search- of-the- gig-economy _June2016. pdf

Broughton, A., Gloster, R., Marvell, R., Green, M., Langley, J., & Martin, A. (2018). *The Experiences of Individuals in the Gig Economy*, Department for Business, Energy & Industrial Strategy Burtch, G., Carnahan, S., & Greenwood, B. N. (2018). Can you gig it? An empirical examination of the gig economy and entrepreneurial activity. *Management Science*, *64*(12), 5497–5520. doi:10.1287/mnsc.2017.2916

Cardon, D., & Casilli, A. (2015). *What is the digital labor?* Ina.

Carson, N. (2012). *Before You Start Up, Practice in the Gig Economy*. Retrieved July 10, 2018 from http://upstart.bizjournals.com/resources/author/2012/09/06/before-you-start-up-get-practicegigs.html

Codagnone, C., Abadie, F., & Biagi, F. (2016). *The future of work in the 'sharing economy'. Market efficiency and equitable opportunities or unfair precarisation?* Institute for Prospective Technological Studies, Science for Policy report by the Joint Research Centre.

Crosby, A., & Rina, R. C. (2017). *The lure of the city, the possibilities of the village: crowdsourcing graphic designers in Indonesia*. Cumulus Open Design for E-very-thing.

Cutter, B., Litan, R., & Stangler, D. (2016). *The Good Economy*. Kansas City: Roosevelt Institute and Kauffman Foundation. Retrieved, July 10, 2018 from http://rooseveltinstitute.org/wp-content/uploads/2016/02/Good-Economy-Feb-29-2016.pdf

D'Cruz, P., & Noronha, E. (2016). Positives outweighing negatives: The experiences of Indian crowd-sourced workers. *Work Organisation, Labour & Globalisation*, *10*(1), 44–63. doi:10.13169/workorgalaboglob.10.1.0044

Davis, F. D. (1989). Perceived usefulness, perceived ease of use, and user acceptance of information technology. *Management Information Systems Quarterly*, *13*(3), 319–340. doi:10.2307/249008

De Stefano, V. (2015). The rise of the just-in-time workforce: On-demand work, crowdwork, and labor protection in the gig-economy. *Comp. Lab. L. & Pol'y J.*, *37*, 471.

Dokko, J., Mumford, M., & Schanzenbach, D. W. (2015). *Workers and the online gig economy*. The Hamilton Project.

Donovan, S. A., Bradley, D. H., & Shimabukuru, J. O. (2016). *What does the gig economy mean for workers?* Retrieved July 30, 2018, from https://digitalcommons.ilr.cornell.edu/cgi/viewcontent. cgi?referer=https://scholar.google.com/&httpsredir=1&article=2512&context=key_workplace

Dörnyei, Z. (2007). Creating a motivating classroom environment. In *International handbook of English language teaching* (pp. 719–731). Boston, MA: Springer. doi:10.1007/978-0-387-46301-8_47

Drahokoupil, J., & Fabo, B. (2016). The platform economy and the disruption of the employment relationship. *ETUI Research Paper-Policy Brief, 5*.

Farrell, D., & Greig, F. (2016). *Paychecks, paydays, and the online platform economy: Big data on income volatility*. JP Morgan Chase Institute.

Fidler, D. (n.d.). *Work, Interrupted*. Retrieved, September 20, 2018 from http://www.iftf.org/fileadmin/ user_upload/downloads/wfi/IFTF_Work- Interrupted_FullReport.pdf

Friedman, G. C. (2014). Workers without employers: Shadow corporations and the rise of the gig economy. *Review of Keynesian Economics*, *2*(2), 171–188. doi:10.4337/roke.2014.02.03

Fuad, A., & Hsu, C. Y. (2018). UTAUT for HSS: Initial framework to study health IT adoption in the developing countries. *F1000 Research*, 7. PMID:30109025

Graham, M., Hjorth, I., & Lehdonvirta, V. (2017). Digital labour and development: Impacts of global digital labour platforms and the gig economy on worker livelihoods. *Transfer: European Review of Labour and Research*, *23*(2), 135–162. doi:10.1177/1024258916687250 PMID:28781494

Graham, M., Ojanperä, S., Anwar, M. A., & Friederici, N. (2017). □Digital Connectivity and African Knowledge Economies□. *Questions de Communication*, (2), 345-360.□□□□□□□□□□□□□□□□□□□

Hamzat, S. A., & Mabawonku, I. (2018). *Influence of performance expectancy and facilitating conditions on use of digital library by engineering lecturers in universities in south-west*. Library Philosophy and Practice.

Heeks, R. (2017). *Decent Work and the Digital Gig Economy: A Developing Country Perspective on Employment Impacts and Standards in Online Outsourcing, Crowdwork, etc.* Global Development Institute. University of Manchester. https://www. gdi. manchester. ac. uk/research/publications/di/di-wp71

Kässi, O., & Lehdonvirta, V. (2018). Online labour index: Measuring the online gig economy for policy and research. *Technological Forecasting and Social Change*, *137*, 241–248. doi:10.1016/j.techfore.2018.07.056

Kenney, M., & Zysman, J. (2016). The rise of the platform economy. *Issues in Science and Technology*, *32*(3), 61.

Kessler, S. (2014). Pixel and dimed on (not) getting by in the gig economy. *Fast Company*. Retrieved September June 30, 2018 from http://www.fastcompany.com/3027355/pixel-and-dimedon-not-getting-by-in-the-gig-economy

Khanna, S., Ratan, A., Davis, J., & Thies, W. (2010, December). Evaluating and improving the usability of Mechanical Turk for low-income workers in India. In *Proceedings of the first ACM symposium on computing for development* (p. 12). ACM. 10.1145/1926180.1926195

Kooti, F., Grbovic, M., Aiello, L. M., Djuric, N., Radosavljevic, V., & Lerman, K. (2017, April). Analyzing Uber's ride-sharing economy. In *Proceedings of the 26th International Conference on World Wide Web Companion* (pp. 574-582). International World Wide Web Conferences Steering Committee. 10.1145/3041021.3054194

Kumar, V., Maheshwari, B., & Kumar, U. (2002). Enterprise resource planning systems adoption process: A survey of Canadian organizations. *International Journal of Production Research*, *40*(3), 509–523. doi:10.1080/00207540110092414

Lubrin, E., Lawrence, E., Zmijewska, A., Navarro, K. F., & Culjak, G. (2006, April). Exploring the benefits of using motes to monitor health: An acceptance survey. In *International Conference on Networking, International Conference on Systems and International Conference on Mobile Communications and Learning Technologies (ICNICONSMCL'06)* (pp. 208-208). IEEE. 10.1109/ICNICONSMCL.2006.94

Malik, F., Nicholson, B., & Heeks, R. (2017, May). Understanding the development implications of online outsourcing. In *International Conference on Social Implications of Computers in Developing Countries* (pp. 425-436). Springer. 10.1007/978-3-319-59111-7_35

Manyika, J., Lund, S., Robinson, K., Valentino, J., & Dobbs, R. (2015). A labor market that works: Connecting talent with opportunity in the digital age. June. *McKinsey Global Institute*. http://www.mckinsey.com/~/media/McKinsey/dotcom/Insights/Employment%20and%20growth/Connecting

Martin, C. J. (2016). The sharing economy: A pathway to sustainability or a nightmarish form of neoliberal capitalism? *Ecological Economics*, *121*, 149–159. doi:10.1016/j.ecolecon.2015.11.027

Martins, C., Oliveira, T., & Popovič, A. (2014). Understanding the Internet banking adoption: A unified theory of acceptance and use of technology and perceived risk application. *International Journal of Information Management*, *34*(1), 1–13. doi:10.1016/j.ijinfomgt.2013.06.002

Meelen, T., & Frenken, K. (2015). Stop saying Uber is part of the sharing economy. Fast Company, 14.

Miriri, D. (2017). Facebook offers tool to combat fake news in Kenya ahead of polls. *Reuters*, *4*, 2017.

O'Sullivan, A., & Shiffrin, S. M. (2003). *Economics: Principles in Action*. Pearson Prentice Hall.

Productivity Commission. (2016). *Digital Disruption: What do governments need to do*. Melbourne: Commonwealth of Australia.

Qorbani, D., Yamaguchi, Y., & Cosenz, F. (2017). *Analyzing Business Dynamics of Ride-Hailing Services*. In The International Conference Of The System Dynamics Society, Cambridge, MA.

Rienstra, S., Bakker, P., & Visser, J. (2015). *International comparison of taxi regulations and Uber.* KiM Netherlands Institute for Transport Policy.

Rilling, S. (2015). *Mobile banking acceptance among young consumers in Germany: an empirical analysis* (Doctoral dissertation).

Schmidt, F. A. (2017). *Digital labour markets in the platform economy mapping the political challenges of crowd work and gig work. Friedrich Ebert Stiftung.* Division for Economic and Social Policy.

Slavin, R. E. (1986). Best-evidence synthesis: An alternative to meta-analytic and traditional reviews. *Educational Researcher, 15*(9), 5–11. doi:10.3102/0013189X015009005

Smith, R., & Leberstein, S. (2015). *Rights on demand: Ensuring workplace standards and worker security in the on-demand economy.* National Employment Law Project.

Sørensen, A. T., & Shklovski, I. (2011). The Hugging Team: The Role of Technology in Business Networking Practices. In *ECSCW 2011: Proceedings of the 12th European Conference on Computer Supported Cooperative Work,* 24-28 September 2011, *Aarhus Denmark* (pp.333-352). Springer. 10.1007/978-0-85729-913-0_18

Srnicek, N. (2017). The challenges of platform capitalism: Understanding the logic of a new business model. *Juncture, 23*(4), 254–257. doi:10.1111/newe.12023

Stewart, A., & Stanford, J. (2017). Regulating work in the gig economy: What are the options? *TheEconomic and Labour Relations Review, 28*(3), 420–437. doi:10.1177/1035304617722461

Taiwo, A. A., Mahmood, A. K., & Downe, A. G. (2012, June). User acceptance of eGovernment: Integrating risk and trust dimensions with my husbandUTAUT model. In *2012 International Conference on Computer & Information Science (ICCIS)* (Vol. 1, pp. 109-113). IEEE. 10.1109/ICCISci.2012.6297222

Tarhini, A., El-Masri, M., Ali, M., & Serrano, A. (2016). Extending the UTAUT model to understand the customers' acceptance and use of internet banking in Lebanon: A structural equation modeling approach. *Information Technology & People, 29*(4), 830–849. doi:10.1108/ITP-02-2014-0034

Thomas, T., Singh, L., & Gaffar, K. (2013). The utility of the UTAUT model in explaining mobile learning adoption in higher education in Guyana. *International Journal of Education and Development Using ICT, 9*(3).

Torpey, E., & Hogan, A. (2016). *Working in a Gig Economy: Career Outlook: US Bureau of Labor Statistics.* United States Department of Labor: Bureau of Labor Statistics.

Venkatesh, V., Morris, M. G., Davis, G. B., & Davis, F. D. (2003). User acceptance of information technology: Toward a unified view. *Management Information Systems Quarterly, 27*(3), 425–478. doi:10.2307/30036540

Venkatesh, V., Thong, J. Y., & Xu, X. (2012). Consumer acceptance and use of information technology: Extending the unified theory of acceptance and use of technology. *Management Information Systems Quarterly, 36*(1), 157–178. doi:10.2307/41410412

Venkatesh, V., Thong, J. Y., & Xu, X. (2016). Unified theory of acceptance and use of technology: A synthesis and the road ahead. *Journal of the Association for Information Systems*, *17*(5), 328–376. doi:10.17705/1jais.00428

Venkatesh, V., & Zhang, X. (2010). Unified theory of acceptance and use of technology: US vs. China. *Journal of Global Information Technology Management*, *13*(1), 5–27. doi:10.1080/1097198X.2010.10856507

Zumbrun, J., & Sussman, A. L. (2016). Proof of a gig economy revolution is hard to find. *The Wall Street Journal*. Retrieved June 30, 2018 from http://www.wsj.com/articles/proof-ofa-gig-economy-revolution-is-hard-to-find-1437932539

ADDITIONAL READING

Economics, D. A. (2016). *Economic Effects of Ridesharing in Australia: Uber*. Deloitte Access Economics.

Hajkowicz, S. A., Reeson, A., Rudd, L., Bratanova, A., Hodgers, L., Mason, C., & Boughen, N. (2016). *Tomorrow's digitally enabled workforce: Megatrends and scenarios for jobs and employment in Australia over the coming twenty years*. Australian Policy Online.

Hunt, A., & Samman, E. (2019). Gender and the gig economy. Retrieved September 10, 2018 from https://www.odi.org/sites/odi.org.uk/files/resource-documents/12586.pdf

Stewart, A., & Stanford, J. (2017). Regulating work in the gig economy: What are the options? *Economic and Labour Relations Review*, *28*(3), 420–437. doi:10.1177/1035304617722461

KEY TERMS AND DEFINITIONS

Digital Platform: A technology that is usually in the form of a software or application that rides on the back of the internet and is used to perform one activity or the other.

Driver: A person who is assigned the task (through the Uber mobile application) of picking a rider up from one location to the other.

Gig: A short term job or task that is executed by a person for a reward.

Gig Economy: An employment space that is facilitated by technology (digital platforms) where employers offer short term tasks or jobs and workers deliver on the task or job by way of service for a reward.

Gig Employers: Persons who request a service or a task to be done for them via online platforms through the internet, which enables them to specify jobs or look for service providers.

Gig Workers: Providers of a gig service having been engaged based 'on-the-demand' of the service by the gig employer and receive payment for the job after its completion.

Mobile Money: A cashless and convenient way of transferring money and making payments for goods and services using a mobile phone.

Ride-Hailing: A form of transportation service delivered using platforms (usually through mobile applications) where riders connect with drivers.

Riders: Persons who use the Uber application to request transportation thereby assigning the driver the task of picking them from one location to another.

APPENDIX

Figure 2. Redefined Conceptual Framework based on Findings from Respondents

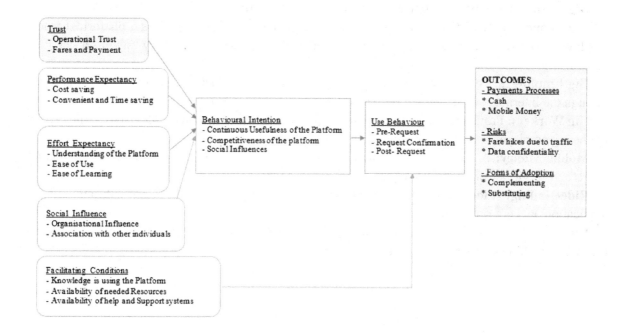

Chapter 13

Coming of Age?
Exploring the Role of Dynamic Capabilities in Social Commerce Firms – Evidence From a Ghanaian Enterprise

Edward Entee
Univeristy of Ghana, Ghana

Anthony Afful-Dadzie
Business School, University of Ghana, Ghana

ABSTRACT

Social networking sites such as Facebook have developed massive acceptance as commercial channels among users, and this is commonly known as social commerce. Despite the significance of social media sites for commercial purposes, entrepreneurs struggle with capability development as well as strategies to achieve benefits. To address this gap, this chapter presents a teaching case study that explores how a microentrepreneur used social media as a resource to create social commerce capabilities to achieve benefits. Lessons learnt are proposed in the case, and questions for reflections are proposed whilst a debate topic is also suggested.

INTRODUCTION

Heading to the mall with friends is usually a pleasurable and exciting experience. An occasion which sometimes leaves you with a good feeling about yourself and your new acquisitions without thinking about the effect in your income. That notwithstanding, being with your friends and getting their opinions on your choices is always a good time. In contrast, shopping online is an entirely different experience, it is easy and convenient, and sometimes you even receive free same-day delivery. Thus, with the increase in ownership of smartphones and social media usage, companies have found a way to combine e-commerce shopping experience with social media to birth social commerce. Social commerce is widely seen as

DOI: 10.4018/978-1-7998-2610-1.ch013

product discovery, and also a platform where shoppers connect while entrepreneurs and retailers try to transform the resultant community into sales.

Social commerce is flourishing as a result of the rapid development of Information technology globally, and its adoption by a lot of people, organizations and businesses. In a lot of these businesses, IT is operationalized in order to carry out business objectives, to help them interact with customers and also to promote their products. A study by Guo, Wang, and Leskovec (2011) propound that social network is the most prominent feature in predicting how customers choose their transaction partners. Therefore, with assistance from the internet and IT, a significant means of doing business using IT is through social commerce. Social commerce makes sense for most businesses considering the number of people on social network sites and the pervasive nature of the internet, and this is not limited to increasing the conversation surrounding a product or brand. For instance, companies can have informed choices about inventory management and product development through customer feedback on social network sites. Additionally, they can increase their market share and increase their customer base, and also personalize customer experience based on known preferences and tastes. There is also the added advantage of peer reviews and recommendations.

This teaching case depicts how an information technology entrepreneur leverages the power of social media and social networks to create a channel where customers can interact with the firm and also attract and create loyalty with customers. The case is based on data obtained from interviews with a micro-entrepreneur. The case uncovers the presence of informational and interactional social commerce capabilities. Overall, three lessons emerge from the case in developing capabilities; First, there is the need to combine both technical and non-technical resources. Second, personal social capital can be used in the development of social commerce capabilities, especially when it is being translated for commercial purposes. Third, the level of social commerce capabilities developed is contingent on the affordances of the social media platform in use.

SOCIAL COMMERCE AND SOCIAL MEDIA IN CONTEXT

The evolution of e-commerce and the widespread patronage of social media birthed social commerce (Han & Trimi, 2017), which is still in its infancy. Originated by Yahoo! in 2005 to describe a set of collaborative shopping tools such as user ratings, shared pick lists and user-generated content sharing recommendations and reviews. Social commerce also describes the convergence of social networks and e-commerce. In terms of purchasing decisions, the influence of social media is growing, thus affecting consumer behaviour. Examples of social commerce influencers and enablers include photo-sharing social networks such as Pinterest or Instagram. There is also those with niche services such as Airbnb, a social platform that provides short-term lodging.

Social media is an essential tool for firms – as of May 2016, Facebook adoption for marketing purpose was near-universal among professional marketers worldwide (Statista, 2018) closely followed by Twitter and LinkedIn. According to Matthews (2018), about 74 percent of consumers depend on social networks to help them make purchasing decisions which means that there is an excellent opportunity for brands to reach a wider audience and increase their profits. Recent figures by Statista (2018) suggests that social still ranks behind search, email and direct navigation in terms of average shopping value. Additionally, market leader Facebook ranks first in terms of e-commerce referral traffic. A study by Shopify shows that Instagram has the highest order value on average, while two-thirds of social media visits to Shopify can be traced back to Facebook. Statista again indicates that worldwide social commerce as at 2015 was $30 billion back in 2015 and goes on to indicate that online shopping order value via social as of Q3 2018 was 73.83USD and finally predicts that social commerce looks sets to reach $165.59 billion by 2021, giving a sizeable market share.

Social media is one of the most significant phenomena presently with worldwide accessibility to the internet. The number of global users of Social networking sites is predicted to reach 3.02 billion monthly active users by 2021 (Statista, 2018). Additionally, leading social networks sites such as Facebook has a high number of user accounts or active user engagements. For example, Facebook has surpassed the 1 billion monthly active user mark and as of the first quarter of 2017, has more than 2.2 billion monthly active users worldwide, as shown in Figure 1. Along with the popularity and commercial success of social networking sites and other forms of social media the term *social commerce* was conceived which presents an emerging phenomenon (Beisel, 2006; Rubel, 2006; Stephen & Toubia, 2010). For this teaching case, we define social commerce as a form of commerce that is mediated by social media and is converging both online and offline environments (Wang & Zhang, 2012).

Social commerce thus involves using social media which supports social interactions and user contributions to aid activities of buying and selling of products and services in the context of online and offline environments (Feng, Ye, & Collins, 2019; Liang, Ho, Li, & Turban, 2011; Wang & Zhang, 2012; Zhong, 2012). It also presents favourable circumstances for trade exchange through social media, which takes advantage of the interactive information technology infrastructure, social commerce is regarded as a new category of e-commerce, or the birth of a "referral economy" (Harkin, 2007).

The data from Figure 1 also points to a phenomenon which thrives on building a community which is a fertile ground to transact commerce. Will almost definitely increase repeat purchases and grow new customers through the creation of user experience (Doherty, 2019). Social media is a powerful tool and brands are leveraging its influence to drive conversions, traffic and revenues; this is called social commerce. Social commerce, therefore, in summary, is using social media as a medium to allow people to make purchases from their news feed.

DYNAMIC CAPABILITY AND SOCIAL COMMERCE

Dynamic capability enjoys a plurality of definitions in the literature (Barreto, 2010). Teece, Pisano, and Shuen (1997) for instance defined dynamic capabilities as "the firm's ability to integrate, build and reconfigure internal and external competences to address rapidly changing environment"(p. 516). Whiles Barreto (2010) defined DC as "the firm's potential to systematically solve problems, formed by its propensity to sense opportunities and threats, to make timely and market-oriented decisions, and to change its resource base" (p. 271). The focus in these definitions is on the dynamics that cause organizations to respond to changes in their environment using organizational resources. This focus allows the dynamic capability approach to steer clear of the criticisms levelled at the Resource-Based View (Easterby-Smith, Lyles, & Peteraf, 2009). To achieve competitive advantage, a firm needs to develop social media which is regarded as a technology resource. Its development goes through various stages. At the founding stage, a firm ascertains the need for social commerce adoption; use as interaction with customers or to facilitate product sales. At the developing stage, when the firm adopts the technology or agrees to adopt the technology, there is search and examination of viable alternatives to make the resource useful through rearranging existing resources, leveraging and integrating resources, and adjusting where

Figure 1. [Statistics from Statista 2018]

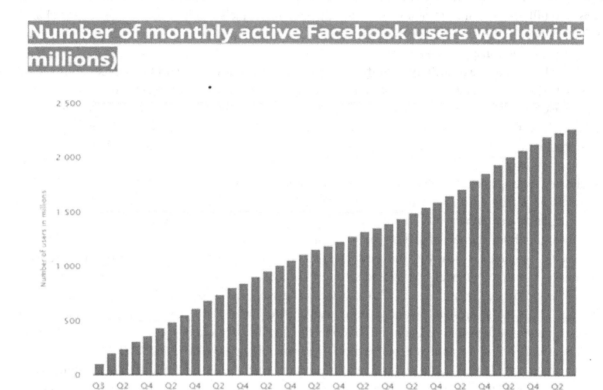

Number of monthly active Facebook users worldwide (millions)

necessary. At the maturity stage, the firm continues the use of social media such that it is fully integrated into the firm and thus grows into a new capability– social commerce capability.

This new capability may be evident in different ways. Thus, if the capability is informational, then a firm can use social commerce just for communication purposes only, for example, using Facebook to provide product information. If it is interactional, the firm can use social commerce to respond to queries or give instant and intelligent feedback, e.g. instant chat with customers or leads. If it is transactional, a firm can use social commerce to allow customer transactions, for example, selling products on Facebook Marketplace.

TURQUOISE MANAGEMENT CONSULT

Turquoise Management Consult is a Ghanaian owned sole proprietorship business which deals in catering services called Ara's Kitchen and general products. The business operates from a family apartment of the owner with no standard warehousing facilities. Some of the everyday items sold by Turquoise Management Consult are wristwatches, beads, towels, bed sheets, fabrics, bags, purses, wallets, shirts, dresses, sandals and food and catering services. The business started in 2015 with one person (the owner) who is a university graduate deciding to exploit the opportunities provided by social media. The idea of the business was birthed out of the fact that the owner's sisters were artists who designed various artefacts. In that regard, the owner who is senior among the three siblings requested to engage in the sales of the artefacts produced by the younger sisters. Since then the business has grown from just the sales of artefacts to the general merchandise. The remaining paragraphs outline the various strategies and the thinking behind those strategies to achieve a competitive edge in the field of this business 'operation.

The business runs two business models. The first model is the business-to-consumer (B2C) model, where Turquoise deals directly with individual customers. In this regard, the organization acquire products be it raw materials or processed items from upstream suppliers and sell them to available and "willing to buy" customers. In instances where there are stocked items or food orders, Turquoise engages in a direct advertisement to its customer base, and after getting offers for the particular products, it delivers. The second model is the business-to-business model where Turquoise yet again acts in its capacity as a business but in this instance supplies products to businesses at retail prices whom in-turn sell them to make a profit.

Concerning connecting with suppliers and customers, the business relies mostly on telephone, Facebook Messenger and WhatsApp channels. These channels, according to the owner of TMC, affords the effortless day-to-day operation of her business. She says;

The customers know I am available on WhatsApp 24/7 and Facebook. Of course, I have my off times, especially in the night, but I am active online with customers and suppliers.

Interestingly, the business has two social media platforms Facebook and WhatsApp. This revelation comes as a surprise as other businesses are leveraging on the combined powers of other social media platforms such as Facebook, Twitter, Instagram, and Snapchat to gain competitive advantage. The owner tells us that;

I do not believe in the mass usage of social media platforms. They are good, I see others making waves out there, but WhatsApp and Facebook work better for me. I may have no explanations for me not using the other platforms, but I believe WhatsApp and Facebook work fine. Maybe when we grow into a larger business and space, we will deploy other social media tools, but for now, it is just WhatsApp and Facebook.

With regards to how Turquois deploys the use of WhatsApp and Facebook in its operations, the owner has engaged the services of a graphic designer-friend who does attractive designs of promotions and available stocks. The image in Figure 2 is a sample design posted by Turquois to its customers, reminding them to start ordering for hampers for the festive season. The poster also details the individual items the business sells. As well as the WhatsApp number and the location of the organization. When asked why they kept the WhatsApp number on the e-poster, she responded that;

Others may want to repost the poster on other pages, so it is just prudent to keep the number there so in case someone else sees the poster somewhere he/she knows where to see me.

Apart from the e-posters that the business posts on WhatsApp and its Facebook page, they also post individual pictures of items that they need to push out to make way for new stock. For instance, Figure 6 presents a WhatsApp post from Turquois from the perspective of a customer which shows the individual advertisement of items not put in a design package but the real picture of the items an ex-

Figure 2. [Turquoise e-poster]

ample is depicted in Figure 3. The business also uses telephone follow-ups to complement the already existing social media tool she uses (i.e. WhatsApp and Facebook). This complement comes as a result of the owner willing to engage more with her clients and vice versa and also for delivery and payment purposes. Further, she asserts that;

Phone conversation comes handy when customers have specifications, especially when it comes to kitchen services.

Figure 3. [Food Advert]

Concerning the kitchen services which the business has branded *"Ara's Kitchen"* under the turquoise umbrella, the business posts attractive pictures of food items to prospective customers via their WhatsApp and Facebook platforms. These posts inform customers about the days on which foods are available and would be available at specific times.

For example, the Figure 3 above designates two food adverts from Ara's Kitchen with the inscription *"Your Saturday evening is about to change the best kelewele in town is loading"* obviously to incite the appetite of customers towards a new package they intend to introduce. This caption is then followed by Photo ads with the inscription *"kindly reply to this message to confirm your kelewele order(s) for tomorrow, Peace and Many Blessing."*

It must be noted that, Ara's kitchen posts ads on the nights before the designated day for respective foods as represented in Figure 4. This action is perceptibly to get customers to make up their minds before the day arrives as well as to help the business know the number of ingredients to acquire the following morning. In the words of the owner;

We like to post adverts on the day before the days of delivery. Also, we like to whet their appetite, so we let our able graphic designer do something for our customers to feel like the food is already available on their table.

We also do this because we want them to confirm so we know the amount of foodstuffs to buy the following day. Some of the ingredients are perishable, and we would run at a loss if we should assume many people will place orders and buy more just for us to come, and just a few orders come.

When asked whether the business searches for goods and services using social media tools, the owner responded saying;

oh no, we do not do a desperate search for people who have items that we would need. However, in our current dispensation, the people buzz at your door so do we even need to go searching, social media has become the second world.

This assertion is indicative of the fact that the business searches for people who are rendering services and dealing in goods that they require. In this instance the business does not necessarily *'go searching'* for people dealing in products of need instead, the owner tells us;

I see people advertise stuff on their WhatsApp statuses and Facebook pages…in cases that I find some interesting, I follow up with them and negotiate prices.

Concerning services, the owner avers that the only people she deals with the graphic designer who develops the concepts for her advertisements and the delivery service who delivers goods to customers.

Aside products, I do not meet in person with my graphic designer, he understands what we do so he does the designs and send them to me via WhatsApp where I also copy and broadcast to my client base. The only times we meet is on Sundays at church. However, we hardly talk about business when we meet in person.

SUPPLIER-CUSTOMER ENGAGEMENT

Customer engagement at Turquoise undergoes three main phases, first the owner posts e-posters of items for sale. These posts are done through her broadcast list of friends and potential customers on her list. Customers who express interest by asking of prices are then engaged by the owner and ensuing follow-ups in the subsequent days. The engagements are mostly held on WhatsApp.

Figure 4. [Turquoise ad]

Furthermore, when there is the need for a telephone conversation, in order to overcome the stress of having to express oneself by way of texting, she migrates the engagement to the telephone by calling the potential customer. Engagements of such nature usually occur when the nature of engagement has to be with food services. She avers that some people may be allergic to something and for that matter, would have to let us know what and what so that we would also know precisely how to serve. After the close of engagements, convinced customers proceed to place orders while unconvinced ones terminate the transaction. A single customer order can be a response to a message, as indicated in Figure 6.

When orders are confirmed, customers are then required to make payments via Mobile Money or make payment pay on delivery. It is worth noting that the organization does not send or receive electronic

Figure 5. [order, payment and delivery process]

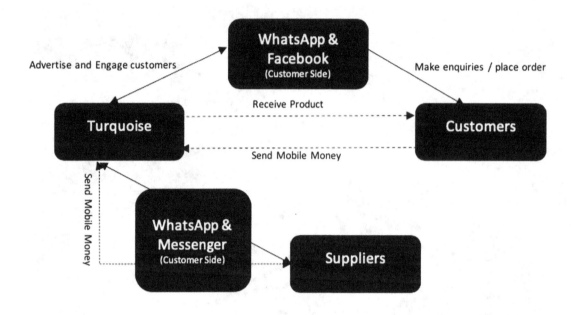

invoices from customers and suppliers. This method unsurprisingly is something they have not thought of; however, the owner claims that;

Most Ghanaians do not give regards to electronic invoices and receipts. I believe it is as a result of how we were brought up. From school to wherever we find ourselves, it is the paper systems we know.

Further, the business does not insist on electronic invoices; however, in cases where receipts are needed for bookkeeping reasons, the owner requests a snapshot of receipts she could not acquire instantly. In her words;

There are times I forget to take receipts for some of the things I buy from people, but for me to keep proper accounting records, I request they take pictures and send them to me via WhatsApp. Because I easily fall on the electronic copies and that helps a lot.

DELIVERY AND PAYMENT MECHANISMS

Compared to advanced jurisdictions, the organization sees Amazon as an institutional role model. In that regard, they strive to achieve the speed and customer focus of the model organization. For example, as soon as a customer begins to engage in a product, be it food or stocked products, a Turquoise worker is assigned to the respective customer. Who always checks up with the owner as to the status of the said

Figure 6. [Order Message]

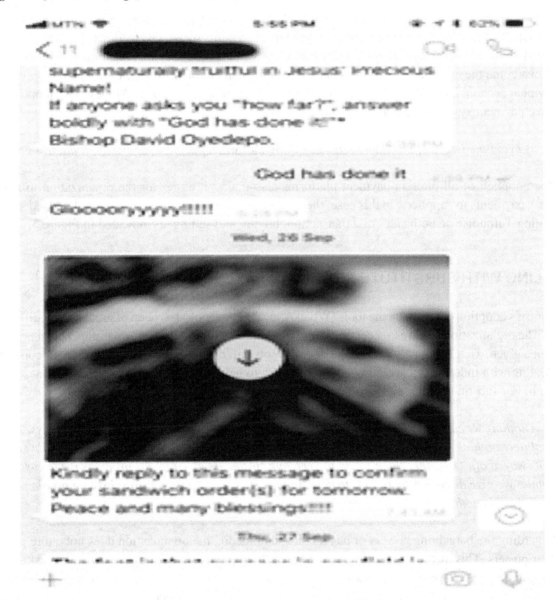

customer. Further, the organization sends frequent updates of the status of the order to the customer via WhatsApp, and in cases where images are needed, they promptly add them

This method of frequent updates can be likened to the tracking of products in advanced shopping environment;

We cannot afford to pay for an application to be built for us for this purpose in as much as we would want to do that; the means is not readily available; we are not there yet, so the manual system is our best shot.

Not far from the manual systems of operation comes with the question of whether the organization receives payments online or have other means of electronic payments. Evidence from field data designates to the fact that Turquoise does not have any online systems by which customers pay for products and food items. However, the adoption of mobile money platform by the organization helps them partially overcome the challenge of conventional electronic payment platforms. The business has all three m-payment accounts, i.e. *MTN Mobile Money*, *Vodafone Cash* and *AirtelTigo* Money. The adoption of all three payment systems she said;

Helps us avoid the issues of this interoperability thing that when people send money, it doesn't go.

The adoption of all three m-payment platforms also makes it easier for the organization to make cashless payments to suppliers. In this case, the essence of m-payment serves as a double-edged sword benefiting Turquoise on both sides of a transaction; buying and selling, as indicated in Figure 5.

DEALING WITH SUBSTITUTE PRODUCTS

Turquoise's adoption of social media tools (WhatsApp and Facebook) has been of great help in different ways. The organization believes success in overcoming threats in the business environment is a process and not a given. That is to say; social media does not solve all of the organizational challenges concerning dealing with industry threats; however, it is enough to help them in the avenues that they need and utilize it. For substitute products and services, the owner conjectures that;

There is nothing we can do about that one; there are substitutes for virtually everything nowadays. There is absolutely nothing we can do about it than to keep advertising what we have and hope our clients are not swayed off. One other thing we do to keep our customers glued to our products is the customer discounts. We give discounts to new customers, so they stick around, but as to substitute product competition, there is nothing we can do about it.

Regarding the bargaining powers of buyers on social media, the organization does not quote prices on their posters. This method is deliberate as the first thing interested customers of products ask is the prices. For example, *"the simplest messages I get apart from good morning is; how much"*. The business then sensing interest from a potential customer then quotes the prices appropriate to the product in question. In such an instance, they try as much as possible not to understate their prices in efforts to keep customers. On the other hand, she tells us;

We do not also push suppliers to state prices that will make them at a loss even though we would also want to buy products at lower prices.

Turquoise mode of reaching out to its customer base through the use of social commerce has improved its business operations. In effect, Turquoise can connect easily with customers via WhatsApp at a very minimal cost.

From the business model, it is clear that the introduction of social media marketing in TMC has brought a transformation in terms of customer base, product accessibility and demand, and revenue generation.

Turquoise management has been able to identify a simple social media tool like "WhatsApp" to support its activities. A tool widely used by the majority of people across the world with ease.

Questions for reflection are;

1. In your capacity as a retailer, what do you think is the future of social commerce?
2. From your standpoint, how willing are consumers to buy through social media?
3. Can you identify any three steps in implementing a social commerce strategy, and how can a retailer harness the power of social to effectively contribute to his/her bottom line?

Debate topic; Discuss the following statement in light of the above case.

Will social commerce at any time supplant e-commerce?

REFERENCES

Barreto, I. (2010). Dynamic Capabilities: A review of past research and an agenda for the future. *Journal of Management*, *36*(1), 256–280. doi:10.1177/0149206309350776

Beisel, D. (2006). *The Emerging Field of Social Commerce and Social Shopping*. Genuine VC.

Doherty, V. (2019). The Advancement Of Social Commerce: Should E-Commerce Brands Care? *Dynamic Capabilities : Current Debates and Future Directions*, *20*. doi:10.1111/j.1467-8551.2008.00609.x

Feng, B., Ye, Q., & Collins, B. J. (2019). A dynamic model of electric vehicle adoption: The role of social commerce in new transportation. *Information & Management*, *56*(2), 196–212. doi:10.1016/j.im.2018.05.004

Guo, S., Wang, M., & Leskovec, J. (2011). The Role of Social Networks in Online Shopping: Information Passing, Price of Trust, and Consumer Choice. In *Proceedings of the 12th ACM conference on Electronic commerce*. ACM. 10.1145/1993574.1993598

Han, H., & Trimi, S. (2017). Social Commerce Design : A Framework and Application. *Journal of Theoretical and Applied Electronic Commerce Research*, *12*(3), 50–68. doi:10.4067/S0718-18762017000300005

Harkin, F. (2007). *The Wisdom of Crowds*. Academic Press.

Liang, T.-P., Ho, Y.-T., Li, Y.-W., & Turban, E. (2011). What Drives Social Commerce: The Role of Social Support and Relationship Quality. *International Journal of Electronic Commerce*, *16*(2), 69–90. doi:10.2753/JEC1086-4415160204

Matthews, T. (2018). *What is social commerce? And Examples of campaigns*. Academic Press.

Rubel, S. (2006). *Trends to watch. Part II: social commerce--micro persuasion*. Academic Press.

Statista. (2018a). *Global Online shopping order value 2018, by traffic source*. Author.

Statista. (2018b). *Social commerce - statistics and facts*. Author.

Stephen, A. T., & Toubia, O. (2010). Deriving Value from Social Commerce Networks. *JMR, Journal of Marketing Research, 47*(2), 215–228. doi:10.1509/jmkr.47.2.215

Teece, D. D. J., Pisano, G., & Shuen, A. (1997). Dynamic capabilities and strategic management. *Strategic Management Journal, 18*(7), 509–533. doi:10.1002/(SICI)1097-0266(199708)18:7<509::AID-SMJ882>3.0.CO;2-Z

Wang, C., & Zhang, P. (2012). The Evolution of Social Commerce : The People, Management, Technology, and Information Dimensions. *Communications of the Association for Information Systems, 31*(1), 105–127.

Zhong, Y. (2012). Social Commerce: A New Electronic Commerce. *Whiceb*. Retrieved from http://aisel.aisnet.org/cgi/viewcontent.cgi?article=1051&context=whiceb2011

Chapter 14
Exploring Value Creation Through Application Programming Interfaces:
A Developing Economy Perspective

Joshua Ofoeda

(iD) https://orcid.org/0000-0001-7566-9989

University of Professional Studies, Accra, Ghana

ABSTRACT

Digital platforms continue to contribute to the global economy by enabling new forms of value creation. Whereas the Information Systems literature is dominated by digital platform research, less is said about Application Programming Interfaces (APIs), the engine behind digital platforms. More so, there is a dearth in the literature on how developing economy firms create value through API integration. To address these research gaps, the author conducted a case study on DigMob (Pseudonym), a digital firm that focuses on the sale of indigenous African music to understand how it created value through API integration. Based on Amit and Zott's value creation model, the findings suggest that DigMob's value creation occurs on a broader value network comprising suppliers (e.g., payment service providers) and customers. For instance, DigMob generated value through the API-enabled platform by ensuring that music lovers purchase their preferred songs at competitive prices. DigMob has also been able to increase their revenue and brand image. Similarly, musicians have been able to rake substantial amounts of money through the sales of their music on the platform.

INTRODUCTION

The ever-evolving business environment calls for stringent measures from businesses. The continues change in the environment is inevitable, and as such firms are continually thriving to explore numerous opportunities to transform their business, and also fulfil the varying needs of customers. Economic forces such as demand and supply are mostly responsible for some of these changes (Sturm, Pollard, & Craig,

DOI: 10.4018/978-1-7998-2610-1.ch014

2017). The fulfilment of customer needs is also necessitated mainly by the changing needs of customers, regulations, and competitors. Agility has, therefore, become an essential strategy for businesses today. As customers become agile through their changing needs, so are businesses also required to adapt to the changing demands of customers. Despite the myriad of challenges, organizations have to become more innovative, competitive, and remain relevant.

Additionally, firms must be able to create value to survive and succeed (Tantalo & Priem, 2016). Studies have shown that firms can create value through the adoption of various innovation and digital ecosystems (Oh, Chen, Wang, & Liu, 2015; Suseno, Laurell, & Sick, 2018). Moore (1993) contends that businesses that seek to be innovative cannot evolve in a vacuum. As such, they are encouraged to attract new resources, partners, suppliers to create networks (Moore, 1993). Accordingly, businesses are managing innovations through their ecosystems and have become platform leaders (Gawer & Cusumano, 2002). Others have developed a competitive advantage by leveraging their business ecosystems (Iansiti & Levien, 2004). Actors within the digital business ecosystem cooperate and compete at the same time (coopetition) to create new business products, coevolve capabilities, create value and satisfy the needs of customers (Pilinkienė & Mačiulis, 2014). In line with this, value creation has become an important area drawing attention from academics and practitioners (Ruivo, Oliveira, & Neto, 2015; Suseno, Laurell, & Sick, 2018; Gol, & Avital, 2019).

Digital platforms have become ideal technologies for firms that seek to be innovative. Consequently, digital platforms have found their way into the mainstream information systems literature (Tiwana, Konsynsky, & Bush, 2010; Ghazawneh & Henfridsson, 2013; Gawer, 2014; Reuver, Sørensen, & Basole, 2017). Notably, is the way they are transforming industries (Khan, Shafi, & Ahangar, 2018; Hinings, Gegenhuber, & Greenwood, 2018; Chanias, Myers, & Hess, 2019), enhancing value creation (Jonsson & Holmström, 2008; Lan, Ma, Zhu, Mangalagiu, & Thornton, 2017), and how they disrupt existing industries (Utesheva, Simpson, & Cecez-Kecmanovic, 2016; Chan, Teoh, A, & Pan, 2018). Digital platforms are conceptualized as technical, where the platform is as an extensible codebase, besides the ecosystem is made up of third-party modules supplementing the codebase (Reuver, Sørensen, & Basole, 2017). Another key feature of digital platforms is the interfaces and the ability for the various modules to interoperate (Tiwana, Konsynsky, & Bush, 2010; Ghazawneh & Henfridsson, 2013; Reuver, Sørensen, & Basole, 2017).

Multinational digital firms like Facebook have succeeded in transforming the way we connect with family and friends. Uber and Airbnb have reformed the sharing economy and hospitality industry, respectively (Reuver, Sørensen, & Basole, 2017). The emergence of Uber, for instance, is disrupting the existing taxi industry (Berger, Chen, & Frey, 2018). Regardless of the importance of digital platforms, digital transformation in some parts of the world Notably, Africa and other developing economies continue to face myriad challenges such as limited infrastructural development and poor Internet connectivity (Foster, Graham, Mann, Waema, & Friederici, 2018). Despite these challenges, developing countries such as Ghana are leveraging digital technologies as platforms for employment and growth (Lee, 2016). While digital platforms are receiving a majority of the hype, little is known about APIs (the underlying applications that enable digital platforms). The tissue that connects these digital platforms and the entire digital ecosystem are APIs (Iyengar, Khanna, Ramadath, & Stephens, 2017). Still unfortunately, there has been little research on APIs in the IS literature. While the success of most digital platforms is measured based on criteria such as profit hikes, increased adoption, among others, less is mentioned about APIs, especially in the mainstream IS literature.

Consequently, some firms place less value on APIs (Boulton, 2016). The likes of Amazon, Uber, eBay, Expedia, among others, who regard APIs as very important, are raking millions in revenue through opening their business using APIs. In 2013, for instance, Amazon featured over 2 million third-party sellers, which accounted for about 40% of the total sale (Benzell, Lagarda, & Alstyne, 2017).

Moreso, existing research on APIs has focused more on the technical dimensions such as API development (Diprose, Plimmer, MacDonald, & Hosking, 2014; Radevski, Hata, & Matsumoto, 2016; Santos, Prendi, Sousa, & Ribeiro, 2017; Scheller & Kühn, 2015; Santos & Myers, 2017) at the expense of other dimensions such as value creation; especially in developing economies. Hitherto, APIs were known and restricted to the IT departments in organizations since they were deemed to be mostly technical (Iyengar, Khanna, Ramadath, & Stephens, 2017). The narrative is no longer the same as managers are beginning to discuss the prospects of APIs at board meetings (Abigee, 2016). Recently, some authors Zachariadis and Ozcan (2017), Wulf and Blohm (2017) and Ofoeda and Boateng (2018) have introduced some social dimensions of APIs such as how APIs are transforming financial sectors, and how various institutions affect the API integration process. Besides, practitioner reports on APIs also abound (Abigee, 2016; Doerrfeld, Wood, Anthony, Sandoval, & Lauret, 2015-2016). Despite these developments, there is arguably no or limited literature on how firms create new value through open APIs. There seems to be a shortage of research on how developing economy firms create value through APIs. The object of this book chapter, therefore, is to empirically understand how a developing country firm creates value when it integrates open innovations such as APIs. To achieve the objective of this case study, the researcher chose a digital firm that relies heavily on APIs to bring change to the music industry in Ghana and Africa. The research question guarding this book chapter is; how do developing economy firms create value through API integration?

The rest of this book chapter is planned as follows. The next section provides literature on APIs and value creation, the two major concepts of this research. Section 3 explains the methodology for the study. The next section, after the methodology, explores the context of the study, thus DigMob. The subsequent section provides details of how DigMob provided an API-enable platform to respond to the challenges they were facing. Then, the outcome of the platform is also provided. The discussion, challenges, future research, and conclusions were also provided.

BACKGROUND

APIs and Value Creation

Software plays a critical part in our daily lives. Software is used almost across every facet of human endeavour. The software development field has grown massively over the last couple of years (Kroll, Richardson, Prikladnicki, & Audy, 2018). Businesses that quickly recognized software as an integral component of their business are now market leaders (Singh, 2019). In response to the essential nature of software to business survival, software developers are continuously discovering innovative ways to develop software to reduce the complex nature of software development (Park & Bae, 2011). APIs have become one of the significant innovations in the software development field (Ofoeda, Boateng, & Effah, 2019).

As mentioned in the introduction, APIs have become the indispensable tissue that securely connects digital platforms and ecosystems (Fatemi, 2019). Historically, APIs have been around for a while now, at least, since the advent of personal computers. Mainly, APIs; existed to support the exchange of information between multiple programs (IBM, 2016; Ofoeda, Boateng, & Effah, 2019). As technology advanced, however, there became popular on the web. Thus, there has been an exponential increase in the number of web APIs. Presently, there are more than 22,000 public APIs available on the Internet, which are helping organizations expand their operations (Santos, 2019), create new business value, and expand their capabilities (Anuff, 2017). Concerning their growth and the attention they have received over the years, several authors have sort to purpose various definitions of the term. For instance, some authors define APIs as they facilitate pragmatic reuse and improve the productivity of software development (Niu, Keivanloo, & Zou, 2016). Others, such as Qiu et al. (2016), explain APIs as the "sets of rules and specifications for software programs to interact with." Like Qiu et al. (2016), Willmott et al. (2016) also suggest that APIs details how software components should interrelate with each other, notably, how interconnectivity can enhance the sharing of resources.

APIs have several capabilities and brings countless benefits to organizations that rely on them for their business operations. The level of benefits derived from APIs, however, depends on how firms perceive APIs. For instance, according to programmableweb.com, firms need to have a comprehensive API strategy even though infrastructure is also vital. When considered as a strategy, APIs could bring millions of revenue to firms. Beyond that, they can also expand the customer base and add new streams of income (Hathaway, 2018). The popularity of APIs is generally measured in the number of calls made to an API.

Consequently, there is an increase in the revenue generation on API calls (Boulton, 2016). Some evidence in the form of reports suggests some values of APIs. Notably, are the return on investments. For instance, reports indicate that APIs do not only facilitate digital transactions but could also increase the net income of organizations to over $250,000. This amount could increase as firms continually exchange more data (Boulton, 2016). Multinational organizations such as Twilo, Stripe, Salesforce, Expedia, and eBay are making billions from APIs. Companies such as Twilo are cloud communication service providers, and they rely heavily on APIs to provide superior services to their customers. eBay, for instance, did not start as an API driven company but realized how beneficial APIs could be, hence, adopted it into their operations. Presently, more than 60% of eBay's revenue comes from APIs. Developers are, therefore, capitalizing on it to create almost a billion listings per quarter (Weaver, 2018).

Furthermore, studies have shown that even though APIs have the proclivity of adding some value to businesses, developing and integrating APIs is not enough. Critically, firms should accurately create, manage, and secure their APIs (Olavsrud, 2016). When firms adhere to the issues as mentioned above, they could achieve the value they so much desire. Without the management, monitoring, and security of APIs, firms could face severe consequences. Also, firms that adopt APIs are encouraged to have an API strategy. API strategies must be taught through carefully since they can have a considerable impact on the business (Fatemi, 2019). Most companies in the past have faced challenges because they have not done due diligence to their API strategies.

APIs also play a key role in digital disruption. The hospitality, entertainment, and transportation industries are few examples of businesses experiencing much disruption. Uber, Airbnb, Apple have successfully leverage APIs to build disruptive platforms. Uber, for instance, leverages the Google APIs to provide locations to customers who request their rides. The disruption guarantees more revenue generation for these digital firms and the creation of digital ecosystems (Boulton, 2016b). Several organizations are, therefore, relying on APIs to enhance the exchange of data both internally and externally. Whereas the internal transfer of data is useful, external information exchange has been touted as an integral component for business success; thus, organizations need to focus more on the external trade of information (Lyer & Subramaniam, 2015).

In today's highly connected world where there is much reliance on web services and mobile applications, APIs have become the backbone of digital ecosystems, and their role cannot be overemphasized. Most API developers are into social media APIs (Wendell, 2017), perhaps because of the increase in social media applications. More importantly is how APIs have ensured that companies do not only differentiate themselves but also evade getting disintermediated (McKendrick, 2019). Amazon, for instance, has succeeded in disintermediating companies by leveraging APIs to deliver products and services directly to consumers (McKendrick, 2019).

Generally, the existing empirical research on APIs seems to focus more on the technical issues such as the development, security, and usability of APIs (Shatnawi, Seriai, Sahraoui, & Alshara, 2016; Santos, Prendi, Sousa, & Ribeiro, 2016; Qiu, Li, & Leung, 2016; Niu, Keivanloo, & Zou, 2017; Wijayarathna & Arachchilage, 2019; Wijayarathna & Arachchilage, 2019b) at the neglect of other necessary dimensions such as value creation, performance, among others. Due to this trend of research, the concept of API and its integration was mostly a technical problem. However, lately, CEOs have become interested in APIs as it has become a tool for them to use to deliver more products and services to their clients (McKendrick, 2019). The managerial interest in APIs makes them a top priority in boardroom discussions (Deloitte, 2016). More so, geographically, API seems to be inclined towards the western and developed worlds at the neglect of the developing economies (Ofoeda & Boateng, 2018). Concerning the issues mentioned above, this book chapter seeks to explore how developing country firms create value through API integration.

Just like APIs, value creation has received a great deal of attention from researchers and practitioners from various disciplines (Vargo & Lusch, 2004; Adner & Kapoor, 2010; Grönroos & Voima, 2013). Value creation in the digital economy, however, is perceived as very complex since rivalry organizations can easily replicate a firm's resources or offerings (Amit and Zott, 2001; Suseno, Laurell, & Sick, 2018). The Internet, coupled with advancements in other technologies, is gradually compelling organizations to embrace various forms of open innovations and collaborate for new ideas (Rayna & Striukova, 2015; Suseno et al. 2018). In the wake of these innovative developments, every rational business seeks to create new value for their customers. Value creation among firms is, however, relative. It is worthy to note that what works for organization **A** might not work for organization **B**. Organizations must create value for their success and survival (Adner and Kapoor, 2010; Tantalo and Priem, 2016). The volatile and competitive market environment serves as a caution to organizations. Concerning this, organizations that are unable to create value through proper identification of the changing needs in customers and responding to those needs are left to struggle. Yoo, Henfridsson, & Lyytinen (2010) suggest that digital technologies create new values and contribute significantly to the economy.

Similar to biological ecosystems, different firms should engage each other to create new value to their customers (Peltoniemi, 2005), as it is better than what they can achieve alone (Pilinkienė & Mačiulis, 2014). Porter's (1985) value creation system describes value creation as a more elaborate set of activities that create and deliver value. Concerning this approach, value creation tends to focus on the network formed by businesses rather than the single organization (Jonsson, Westergren, & Holmström, 2008). The benefits that are derived are shared among the various partners in the network or ecosystem (Lavie, 2009; Bouncken, Fredrich, Kraus, & Ritala, 2019). Value creation, which is mostly synonymous with value systems, value networks, among others in the literature, refers to the ways organizations act to create value (Kothandaraman & Wilson, 2001; Jonsson, Westergren, & Holmström, 2008).

Evidence from the literature shows that value in most business ecosystems does not follow the linear or direct value creation process. Most of the members of the ecosystem are way outside the standard value chain (Iansiti and Levien, 2004; Clarysse, Wright, Bruneel, & Mahajan, 2014). This approach reemphasizes the horizontal relations that are formed from the networks that individual businesses form to create value. According to Kothandaraman and Wilson (2001), three key concepts characterize value creation in organizations: the organization's core capabilities, superior customer value, and the relationships it has with others. The skills that organizations possess, coupled with the connections, stimulate value creation Jonsson, Westergren, & Holmström, 2008). Based on Amit and Zott's (2001) value creation model, the critical concepts identified above are situated in the current case study.

In a whole, there is an immense literature on APIs, notably from a more technical dimension (E.g., Niu, Keivanloo, & Zou, 2017) and somewhat industry reports (E.g., Anuff, 2017; Fatemi, 2019). Also, there is enough literature on value creation (E.g., Clarysse, Wright, Bruneel, & Mahajan, 2014; Tantalo & Priem, 2016; Giesbrecht, Schwabe, & Schenk, 2017). However, when one approaches the problem from the perspective of value creation through API integration in general and particularly a developing economy perspective specifically, there seem to be arguably nonexistent empirical studies, hence the current study.

For clarity purposes, value creation is approached from the social dimension. The choice of the social aspect is first based on the research model used in the study; thus, Amit and Zott's (2001) value creation model. Second, the value creation, as studied in this study, transcends beyond the business to society (Dietz & Porter, 2012; Yamin et al., 2015). The concept of social value also includes capability development, finance, ethics, reputation, among others (Auerswald, 2009; Dietz & Porter, 2012).

METHODOLOGY

This case study forms part of a more extensive doctoral research which explores the sociotechnical issues surrounding API development and integration within developing economies. Aspects of this research have been published in various journals and conferences (E.g., Ofoeda & Boateng, 2018; Ofoeda, Boateng, & Effah, 2019). In line with the research question (refer to introduction), the researcher approaches the work from a Critical Realist perspective (Bhaskar, 1989) and a qualitative case study (Yin, 1994, 2003). This chapter adopted a critical realist philosophy because the researcher wanted to study the underlying mechanisms (identified as APIs) that enable digital platforms. Critically, the chapter gets beneath the surface of the much-touted digital platforms to understand the structures that shape those events (Mingers, 2004); thus, understanding how APIs contribute to value creation in a developing economy firm. Case studies are part of the methods that emphasize qualitative analysis (Yin, 1984). Techniques such as interviews, observations, are used to collect data from a small number of organizations. The case study approach also provides an excellent opportunity to understand the specific organizational problems; thus, by asking pungent questions to unravel the issues in organizations (Gable, 1994). One of the key advocates for qualitative methods, Benbasat et al. (1987), affirm that the use of case studies in IS research is vital because: first, it gives the researcher enough room to study an IS issue in its natural setting, thereby generating theories for practice. Second, case studies ensure that the researcher understands the nature and complexity of the organizational process. Third, the researcher can gain new insights into emerging areas. Yin (1984), another advocate of case studies, underscores the importance of using case studies. A notable one is that case studies are ideal for exploring underresearched subjects (in this case, APIs and value creation).

Based on these suggestions from previous research, the current chapter relies on case studies to understand how developing economies create value through APIs. The choice of qualitative research allows the meaning that people bring to phenomena and artefacts in their natural setting (Denzin & Lincoln, 2000). Through an in-depth investigation of a digital firm, the researcher also draws on the workers' experiences on API related matters. Typical with every qualitative case study research, data was collected from DigMob (a technology firm in Ghana) through in-depth interviews, company websites, official reports, and observations (Yin, 1989; Gable, 1994). These sources formed the empirical foundation for this study. The reason for selecting Ghana as a case site was the willingness of the respondents to cooperate and the availability of multiple sources of data (Peppard, 2001). Data was collected from multiple participants (12) in the case organization. By the time of the study, DigMob was on campaigns that sort to educate musicians on the benefits of using the platform, which gave the researcher the leeway to collect purposeful data through in-depth interviews. The qualitative data were collected between late 2017 to the early parts of 2019 at the premises of DigMob. The researcher and his assistant collected the research data. Respondents included the CEO, software developers, system administrators, among others. This study focused on workers at DigMob, and some few musicians who shared some insights into how DigMob has created value for them through their API-driven platform. For additional insights, interviews were conducted on artists and some music lovers (10) to solicit their views.

The collected data was analyzed based on the Miles & Huberman (1994) approach. Primarily, the procedure details the reading, summarization, reflection, and categorization of data into themes. Phase 1 of the analysis involved transcribing the interviews. The author, together with his assistant, compared notes to ascertain differences and similarities in the interviews in step 2 of the analysis. While reading, notes were taken, and the materials were summarized (Jonsson, Holmström, Holmström, 2008). Emergent themes and concepts were noted to ensure the theoretical flexibility of the research. The author also identified the themes that emerged out of the literature. Based on the data, it was evident that DigMob initiated an API-driven platform to solve an earlier challenge of delays in delivering music to its customers. Externally, customers needed an application that can help them purchase indigenous African music. In phase 3, Ami

Amit and Zott's (2001) value creation model was used to analyze value creation at DigMob. The data was then grouped into value creation for DigMob and value creation for the customers.

The empirical data was presented in the context of the identified problems. A copy of the result was sent to the respondents to improve the credibility, internal validity, and reliability of the data (Miles & Huberman,1994). The comments and suggestions from the respondents were incorporated into the final result (Jonsson et al., 2008). The study also presented some quotations from the interviews in the findings and discussions (Jonsson, Holmström, Holmström, 2008).

THE DIGMOB CONTEXT

Africa is gradually experiencing an increase in the number of digital entrepreneurs. The exponential growth is arguably attributable to the proliferation of digital technologies on the continent. There has been a higher diffusion of mobile and digital technologies in recent times (Ndung'u, 2017). Though entrepreneurs face multiple challenges, the zeal to succeed and make a difference is driving most young African entrepreneurs to survive amid the myriad of problems. Most young digital entrepreneurs are exploiting opportunities in the market despite the challenges they face. Like other developing economies such as Kenya, Ghana is becoming a gateway to innovation in the West African Sub Region. Having missed out on the Global Innovation Index in 2017, the country was back in 2018, arguably because of the many government interventions of making Ghana an economy driven by digital technologies. Several digital entrepreneurs have taken advantage of the digital space to deliver superior products and services to their customers. DigMob is one such company that is making a massive impact in Ghana. The CEO of DigMob, observing the developing country landscape, developed a digital platform to sell music online to music lovers.

The API-enabled platform was vital as a result of an earlier website they developed, which was problematic. Notable issues were delays in developing songs to customers. The delays came as a result of delivering music on CDs and DVDs. Most of DigMob's customers were not happy about this situation. Upon careful reflection, DigMob redesigned a new platform to enable the sale and delivery of digital music. After creating the platform, the next phase was to monetize the platform through customers' purchase of music. Concerning this, the entrepreneur decided to partner with the telecommunication service providers to integrate their APIs. The motivation for undertaking such an endeavour is to help musicians have a better life since most of them wallow in poverty after several years of being in the music business. Most musicians in Ghana especially are unable to receive economic value for their creative works and as such, depending on donations and charity when they retire from active work. Also, another inspiration is to help music lovers purchase music at affordable prices online.

According to the CEO, the platform was developed exclusively for African musicians and currently receiving stiff competition from the likes of iTunes. The platform, which is a subsidiary of the parent organization (TechG), can now boast of over 50,000 subscribers. As an artist-centred platform, DigMob seeks to ensure that artists benefit from their intellectual property. Since it established in 2015, the goal of the organization is to make the music industry profitable to musicians and provide an efficient platform for music lovers to buy songs. The CEO alluded to the fact that they recorded some Ghc128,000.00 and 2.3 million hits in Ghana and Africa diaspora in 2018. The gains made by the organization has attracted partnerships from giants as leading telecommunication service provider, MTN Ghana to give music lovers authentic music experience and allowing artists to make some good returns. The partnership also seeks to strengthen digital financial innovations in Ghana and the African continent. The partnership with MTN, for instance, allows music lovers to stream their favourite music for just GhC0.2 daily, GhC0.7 weekly, and GhC2.5 monthly.

DigMob is a typical technology company whose core business mandate is to provide high-quality technology solutions to clients. Initially, the organization started by selling advertising space for digital screens. These digital screens were located in taxis, and they had different advertising spaces which the company sold out to clients. Beyond the sale of digital displays, DigMob was also into the sales of online tickets for events and event organizers. The online ticket sales become part of the business module as a result of the many stampedes recorded at various event centres due to pressure in selling tickets at event centres. The online ticket sales were a perfect opportunity to increase the number of tickets sold besides providing efficiency to people who patronize events in Ghana. Though these two modules were profitable, online music sales became more prominent than the previous two modules.

As the years went by, the company, through its CEO, thought of coming up with another stream of income. Having analyzed the Ghanaian economy, the CEO and his employees, settled on online music sales. The music industry is reported to be a very lucrative one, besides Ghanaians are seen as music lovers. Nonetheless, most Ghanaians musicians are unable to make enough money for themselves despite the lucrative nature of the business. The CEO at DigMob reported that

Ghanaians are ardent music lovers. The sound of music characterizes most Ghanaian social gatherings. Ironically, those who create the music hardly see any good returns on their intellectual property. So, this is where we came in with our API-enabled platform.

DigMob, therefore, decided to mediate between the artists and music lovers. To do this, they needed to develop a new platform and also have a third-party that will be responsible for revenue generation. In a quest to develop the new platform, DigMob also needs to continue delivering products and services to their existing clients. There was, therefore, the need to rely on technologies that could allow them to work from home effectively. Initially, during the development and integration phases, they relied on google drive to transfer files between the development team. Google Drive was one of the imbued technologies adopted to enhance effective and efficient service delivery. As technology improves, the company now relies on Trelo for collaboration purposes. Trelo helps all developers to work on a project even from home. Team members are also kept up-to-date on the progress of the project. The contribution that each team member makes is also acknowledged.

Presently, DigMob is perceived by many as a competitor to giants like iTunes. It has carved a niche through its unique product development, which predominantly targets the African market. Before its current state, one of the interesting that happened was when the CEO decided to partner with other smaller firms. Despite the enormous investments made in the area of IT and other physical resources, a partnership was a critical factor that pushed the company to its current status. According to the CEO, it was becoming extremely tough to make it as a digital entrepreneur. Hence it became vital for them to partner with other companies to achieve their objective. Those partnered firms ended up becoming part of DigMob. The CEO noted the following:

As a very young startup company, it was very tough to go out there and make it due to the intense competition. I believe the best decision I ever made was to partner with another company that took care of marketing and branding our (API enabled) services. This company is now part of our term.

The success chalked by DigMob is as a result of the innovation taking place in the global music industry. It is not out of place to say that the global music industry is poised for greater heights. With music contributing to the GDP of most economies, it has become an industry where several investments are taking place. According to Rob Stringer (the CEO of Sony Music Entertainment), the music industry is *"the most fast-paced and innovative chapter business in decades. As such, the industry continues to grow the number of opportunities for artists to reach their audience..."*

PRESENTING AN API-ENABLED PLATFORM

Many organizations today are leveraging APIs to deliver superior services to their clients. DigMob creates APIs to expose its data for internal and external consumption. Internally, DigMob opens its data to be used by other departments in the organization. Externally, DigMob delivers APIs to expose their data to other partners and customers for consumption. DigMob continuously uses APIs to build both mobile and web applications. According to the CEO, the majority of the APIs that DigMob develops is consumed internally, even though external partners and customers consumed a good percentage. APIs help developers to integrate third-party services. In the case of DigMob, APIs are used to incorporate other back-office applications and incorporate third-party systems.

Consuming APIs developed by others is also common among organizations. Young digital entrepreneurs in Ghana are critical consumers of APIs from telecommunication companies. Primarily, telecommunication APIs support payment platforms with mobile money accounts. Mobile money has become one of the primary forms of payment in Ghana after the traditional cash payment. With an upsurge in the number of people using mobile phones, the percentage of people registered on mobile money has reached exponential levels. According to the Central Bank of Ghana, the number of active mobile money subscribers is close to 30 million (29,578,169; a 16.8% growth at the end of March 2019) (BoG, 2019). In addition to this, a recent World Bank report tips Ghana to be the fastest-growing mobile money market in Africa (Yire, 2019). The statistics prove a continuous increase in the use of mobile devices. Since APIs are predominantly used with mobile devices, digital firms a leveraging on this to deliver higher products and services. A participant in this study attests to how it will be difficult and financially unreasonable to develop their payment platforms. Concerning this, it became desirable to partner with telecommunication companies to provide their APIs.

Other firms already have what we want. As a result, we do not have to develop our payment platform at this time. We can consume the APIs of any of the telecommunication companies. Currently, we are consumers of APIs of the major telecommunication companies in Ghana. When we consume these APIs, it affords us a lot of convenience and business continuity.

With the digital revolution beckoning on us, every firm is striving to digitize their services. These individual firms can boast of their applications that they use to deliver products and services to their customers. For competition's sake, it is ideal for firms to form ecosystems since they are challenging to be re-engineered by competitors (Fisher, 2014). Firms that belong to the same ecosystem are likely to expose some of their data for consumption. According to Forbes, APIs act as the connective tissues that aids these firms to share their data securely (Fatemi, 2019).

Besides football, which is the nation's preferred sport, music is enjoyed by a more extensive section of Ghanaians. The power of music brings people of diverse backgrounds together. Though there are a variety of languages and cultures, music can transcend beyond those boundaries and unite people (IFPI, 2019). Ghanaian music such as highlife and hiplife are enjoyed in most parts of Africa and around the world. Nonetheless, most Ghanaian musicians are not living the life the populace expects of them. Most of them end up in poverty once they retire from active business. The reason is that most artists are unable to sell their music as they used to do in the past. The emergence of digital technologies makes it difficult for artists to make a profit because their songs are copied and distributed illegally. One participant who is an artist shared his experience with us:

There is no money in the business as people think. For artists who release single tracks or albums, you will realize that only a few people purchase their songs. Surprisingly, those who buy it distribute it to friends and families. Some even share it on free sharing sites like YouTube, WhatsApp groups, among others.

The challenges encountered by artists was one of the main driving forces behind the API enabled digital platform created by DigMob. Fundamentally, the platform is to allow music lovers to purchase their favourite genre of music online at affordable prices using various payment modes like mobile money. Under the mission of selling indigenous African music online, the CEO believed that a platform without payment would not achieve the needed benefits. There was, therefore, the need to embrace APIs to ensure that customers can buy music online. Besides downloads, streaming has become a significant source of profit-making for artists. Music lovers can pay subscription fees to help them stream their favourite music on the platform.

THE OUTCOME OF DIGITAL PLATFORM

The advances in technology make it tough to create a platform without APIs. Concerning this, having a digital platform that is powered by APIs has contributed positively to the success of our case organization. For instance, the company has drastically reduced the cost involved in developing applications from scratch, increased transparency in the music value chain, improve efficiency, increased return on investment, and increased reach to customers. As a digital firm, DigMob as expertise in developing applications for other clients. Connecting with third-party applications using APIs has reduced the costs and efforts in developing new forms of applications. One of the developers had this to share with us:

As a digital firm, we can develop our payment platform, but we thought there was no need. All we needed to do was to integrate the Telco's payment platform on our platform, and we are good to go.

Currently, DigMob has formed mutual relationships with numerous third-party applications that allow it to interface with them with ease. Notable are the major Telecommunication companies that provide payment platforms for their customers. With the increase in mobile money subscribers, customers can purchase songs through either the mobile money wallet or their airtime. The essence of such partnerships, which became successful from their relationships, ensured that all partners benefit from the collaboration. A media/marketing representative shared the following sentiments:

DigMob is not the only company that generates value through the process. Every entity that partners with DigMob have some value too. The Telcos that allow DigMob to interface with them also have an increase in customers just like the artists also make their money.

According to the CEO, the platform has increased transparency in the music value chain. Previously, musicians left the monitory aspects of the business in the hands of their managers. Some musicians in the past had to terminate contracts with their managers due to mistrust. The platform ensures that everything is transparent. For instance, the artists are involved in the contract signing and get to see the money they make at every point in time. Phil, a musician who posted his music on the platform, was happy with the amount earned in just a few months after putting his song on the platform.

I was able to put my song on DigMob, and without a manager, I have been able to get some good money. I hope to release my next latter this year, and I will put it on DigMob again. I think it gives me value for my money because it is not easy producing a song in Ghana.

The future for DigMob is boundless! The endless possibilities of the case organization are evident in the words of the CEO and some artists that believe they were making money from the platform.

Whereas most of the Ghanaian artists put their songs on DigMob, they also have their songs on iTunes. For some musicians and their managers, having their songs on iTunes and Google Play, among others, gives them international recognition and some good revenue, just like DigMob. Carl is a mushrooming manager and has this to say: *"We do not limit our songs to DigMob. DigMob is great, but when it comes to international appeal, DigMob is not at that level yet. It is good for my artist to have that international recognition".* Wizy, an ardent music lover, posits that *"sometimes you could buy a song on DigMob for as low as GHȻ1 (USD 0.09), but when you check on iTunes, the same song could cost like USD 1 (GHȻ5.4). For me, as a music lover, that is a good value".*

For instance, by consuming external APIs that support payment on their platform, they can increase returns on their investments. Internal consumption of APIs is quite prevalent in DigMob. However, external use forms a critical part of their operations. *"External consumption of APIs helps us to grow our ecosystem since we cannot survive alone in the digital space. External APIs also make sure we have a return on our investment through reaching markets we are unable to reach if we are alone and offering products and services that are unique and serves the needs of our numerous clients"* (CEO, DigMob).

DISCUSSION

DigMob and Value Creation

Most organizations adopt digital technologies to create value and offer significant benefits to the economy (Yoo, Henfridsson, & Lyytinen, 2010; Suseno, Laurell, & Sick, 2018). Digital innovations transcend beyond a single organization and its business model and affect other organizations in the ecosystem. Hence, the value that is created includes other partners and stakeholders (Loebbecke & Picot, 2015). As Fisher (2014) puts it, it is better to compete on ecosystems because they are difficult to replicate, and are also highly marketable. Having analyzed the operations and processes of DigMob, it is evident that the company created value in three (4) different ways of which are summarized below: First, music lovers get value when they purchase songs at competitive prices. Second, musicians also get rewarded for their creative works. Third, DigMob itself increased its stream of revenue and fourth, other third-party partners based on relationships also get new customers. From the findings of the case study, it became evident that the organization creates value.

Nevertheless, to understand DigMob creates value, we relied on the Amit and Zott's (2001) framework. The framework bifurcates value creation into four categories. The categories include complementarities, efficiency, novelty, and lock-in. Complementarities take place when a pack of products together gives a firm more value than the total cost of each distinct product. From the case study, it became clear that DigMob's partnerships and collaborations with third-party entities ensured that provided more value. Also, a large number of artists registered on the platform guaranteed cross-buying from the customers. With platform providing indigenous African music comprising all genres, customers can search and buy their preferred songs. Vertical complementarities, such as customer service are present at DigMob. The company provides 24/7 customer care support for clients. Horizontal complementarities (songs provided by DigMob, and payment platform provide by third-parties) are also evident from the case study. These complements generally increase the core value of the products. The importance of having complementary outputs is evident in previous literature (Brandenburger & Stuart, 1996). Kothandaraman and Wilson (2001) also portray complementarities in the form of relationship as critical drivers of value creation.

The second category of the framework is efficiency. A firm experiences efficiency when there is a reduction of costs involved in a particular transaction. For music lovers, they have the opportunity to buy music at very affordable prices. A music lover shared this experience: *"I do not know what happens behind the scenes, but I was able to purchase a song as low as GH0.5."*

For DigMob to achieve efficiency, there should be an increase in information symmetry between buyers and sellers by quickly updating the relevant information. Information symmetry ensures that all parties involved in the use of the platform benefit from rich online content that will enable them to make informed decisions. DigMob achieves this by continuously updating information on their platform. For instance, the amount an artist decides to sell a song is what is available for the customers. DigMob cannot resolve to sell a song at their preferred price. For that reason, every detail about a particular song is made available on DigMob's website.

The third category is a novelty, which concerns introducing new products and services and marketing products to intended consumers. For firms to maintain their customer base, it is imperative to add new products and services to customers. An application developer shared attest to this by saying: *"today's customers are very sophisticated. All of them have needs that they want you to meet. They can move to your competitor if they feel you are not providing them with the necessary services they need. For instance, our iPhone users are continuously on our necks to get the app on the iPhone store. Something we are determined to achieve."* Another issue identified at DigMob that relates to novelty is its ability to incorporate African symbols on its platform. The need for such symbols was based on feedback DigMob received from customers on what they want to see on the platform. In general, DigMob's initiative is mainly seen as a novelty since its product differs from that of its international competitors like iTunes, Spotify, and Google Play. Such novel developments have resulted in superior value creation at DigMob and have subsequently replaced the previous way of selling music to customers. The unique idea adopted by DigMob has also resulted in DigMob differentiating itself from its competitors. This finding seems to be consistent with previous research (Magretta, 2002; Morris, Schindehutte, & Allen, 2005; Zott, Amit, & Massa, 2011).

The final category is lock-in. Lock-in arises when consumers are keen on transacting business continually in the future. Once there is lock-in, it will be difficult for consumers to switch to transact business with their competitors. In the case of the current study, lock-in occurs when music artists subscribe to their services of DigMob, making it difficult for them to switch to other service provides. Though some artists still patronize the products from DigMob's competitors such as Spotify, they are locked in due to the subscription fees they are required to pay at DigMob on either daily, weekly, monthly, or yearly basis. Customers who opt for a one-year subscription, for instance, are locked-in. Another example of lock-in is when DigMob introduced promotion packages for artists in the form of loyalty programs. There are several instances where DigMob offers discounts for artists who place songs on their platform. Previous studies have shown that loyalty programs and special reward programs for customers can retain customers (Varian, 1999).

CHALLENGES IN THE TRANSFORMATION PROCESS

Like any other IS innovation, the integration of APIs and their related activities had some problems that are worthy of discussion. First, the digital divide in Ghana is a major huddle to the organization. With more than 2000 communities yet to receive mobile signals (Myjoyonline.com, 2018), DigMob believes

Figure 1: Sources of value creation (Amit & Zott,2001; p 504)

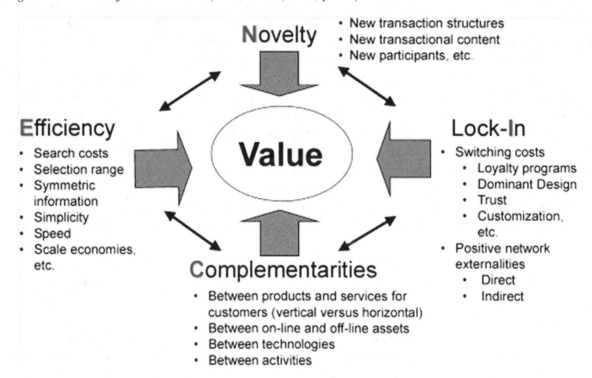

it is a great challenge to them, and hindering their objectives. One respondent (application developer) avers that

Our APIs are mostly mobile-driven, and it strives more on mobile devices. It is impossible to use a mobile device without a signal. So, for us, we hope the country will achieve 100% coverage very soon.

Another challenge DigMob faced at the time of this study was their inability to have their application on the iPhone store. The refusal to have the application on the iPhone store could emanate from the iPhone store trying to fight off competition. iTunes is a global brand and well known for selling music online. DigMob was, therefore, perceived as a competitor even though their focus was on African music. According to iTunes, they were unable to bring DigMob on board because there were some institutional issues that DigMob did not satisfy. *"In one of the correspondences with iTunes, they told us that we could not use their platform because we did not have the rights to sell music."* According to DigMob, it was a deliberate attempt to prevent their iPhone customers from using their platform. This single act by iTunes hindered their operations since they intended to capture both Android and iPhone users. The company was, however, focused on making sure that it has its application on the iPhone to expand its reach.

Furthermore, user acceptance was another major problem DigMob had to surmount. Before the development of the API-enabled platform, most musicians uploading their songs on global platforms like iTunes and Spotify. Similarly, music lovers were also comfortable with buying their songs on such global sellers. Concerning this, it was difficult for them to part way with the global brands, and deal with what they perceive as a local brand. It took some time for some of the musicians to be convinced and use the platform. Despite the acceptance, most musicians still had their songs on iTunes, Spotify, Google Play, among others.

FUTURE RESEARCH DIRECTIONS

The findings in this book chapter stir up questions that could guide future research, which could increase our knowledge in the area. First, this chapter only focused on a single case organization. Future research can investigate multiple organizations to broaden our understanding of the subject matter. Also, the study was undertaken from a developing economy perspective. For generalization purposes, the study advises that researchers conduct similar studies from other jurisdictions and industries. Third, most innovations end up disrupting existing institutions and processes. In the case of DigMob, one institution that is virtually facing extinction is the traditional music selling companies. Some of these traditional businesses are still operating despite the proliferation of digital platforms. A possible research area would be how these traditional businesses still create value.

CONCLUSION

The object of this book chapter is to explore how a developing economy firm creates value through API integration. As established in the introductory section, the normative IS literature is dominated by digital platform studies, at the expense of APIs. Based on a critical realist philosophy, and a qualitative case study methodology, the author reports that value creation is at the heart of every organization. Notably, the organization, third-party partners, and the users of the platform (artists and their fans) create value in various forms. Critically, the firm was able to increase return on its investment, reach a broader market, generate more revenue for musicians who are significant users of the platform and music lovers as well. In terms of contribution, this book chapter contributes to the IS literature in general. Specifically, it gives credence to an area that is less explored, thus APIs. Also, by observing digital platforms from a value creation perspective, this study contributes to the understanding of the body of knowledge on APIs with DigMob's operations and value chains, this area is unexplored in the literature. In terms of novelty, this research is perhaps the first to explore how APIs helps a developing economy firm create value, thus moving beyond the predominant technical analysis on APIs into some social dimensions such as value creation.

REFERENCES

Abigee. (2016). *The State of APIs:2016 Report on Impact of APIs on Digital Business.* Abigee.

Adner, R., & Kapoor, R. (2010). Value creation in innovation ecosystems: How the structure of technological interdependence affects firm performance in new technology. *Strategic Management Journal*, *31*(3), 306–333. doi:10.1002mj.821

Amit, R., & Zott, C. (2001). Value creation in e-business. *Strategic Management Journal*, *22*(6–7).

Anuff, E. (2017). *The API-First World.* Retrieved from Apigee.com: apigee.com/about/tags/ecosystems-0

Auerswald, P. (2009). Creating social value. *Stanford Social Innovation Review, 7*(2), 50–55.

Benbasat, I., Goldstein, D. K., & Mead, M. (1987). The case research strategy in studies of information systems. *Management Information Systems Quarterly, 11*(3), 369–386. doi:10.2307/248684

Benzell, S., Lagarda, G., & Alstyne, M. (2017). The Impact of APIs on Firm Performance. In *The Impact of APIs in Firm Performance.* Boston University Questrom School of Business Research Paper No. 2843326. Retrieved from Available at SSRN: https://ssrn.com/abstract=2843326

Berger, T., Chen, C., & Frey, C. B. (2018). Drivers of disruption? Estimating the Uber effect. *European Economic Review, 110,* 197–210. doi:10.1016/j.euroecorev.2018.05.006

Berman, S., & Marshall, A. (2014). The next digital transformation: From an individual-centred to an everyone-to-everyone economy. *Strategy and Leadership, 42*(5), 9‑17. doi:10.1108/SL-07-2014-0048

Bhaskar, R. (1989). *Reclaiming Reality.* London: Verso.

BoG. (2019). *Payment Systems.* Retrieved 04 25, 2019, from https://www.bog.gov.gh/: https://www.bog.gov.gh/payment-systems/payment-systems-statistics

Boulton, C. (2016, Nov 4). *How API adoption can boost annual profits.* Retrieved Jan 15, 2019, from https://www.cio.com/article/3138511/how-api-adoption-can-boosts-annual-profits.html

Boulton, C. (2016b, Oct 18). *CIOs move more dollars to digital transformation.* Retrieved 02 16, 2019, from https://www.cio.com/article/3131927/cios-move-more-dollars-to-digital-transformation.html

Bouncken, R., Fredrich, V., Kraus, S., & Ritala, P. (2019). (in press). Innovation alliances: Balancing value creation dynamics, competitive intensity, and market overlap. *Journal of Business Research, xxx–xxx.* doi:10.1016/j.jbusres.2019.10.004

Brandenburger, A., & Stuart, H. Jr. (1996). Value-based business strategy. *Journal of Economics & Management Strategy, 5*(1), 5–25. doi:10.1111/j.1430-9134.1996.00005.x

Chan, C., Teoh, S. A. Y., & Pan, G. (2018). Agility in responding to disruptive digital innovation: Case study of an SME. *Information Systems Journal, 29*(2), 436–455. doi:10.1111/isj.12215

Chanias, S., Myers, M., & Hess, T. (2019). Digital transformation strategy making in pre-digital organizations: The case of a financial services provider. *The Journal of Strategic Information Systems, 28*(1), 17–33. doi:10.1016/j.jsis.2018.11.003

Clarysse, B., Wright, M., Bruneel, J., & Mahajan, A. (2014). Creating value in ecosystems: Crossing the chasm between knowledge and business ecosystems. *Research Policy, 43*(7), 1164–1176. doi:10.1016/j.respol.2014.04.014

Deloitte. (2016, June 27). *APIs Help Drive Digital Transformation.* Retrieved 10 27, 2016, from http://deloitte.wsj.com/cio/2016/06/27/apis-help-drive-digital-transformation/

Dietz, A., & Porter, C. (2012). Making sense of social value creation: Three organizational case studies. *Emergence, 14*(3), 23–43.

Diprose, J., MacDonald, B., Hosking, J., & Plimmer, B. (2017). Designing an API at an appropriate abstraction level for programming. *Journal of Visual Languages and Computing*, *39*, 22–40. doi:10.1016/j.jvlc.2016.07.005

Diprose, J. P., Plimmer, B., MacDonald, B. A., & Hosking, J. G. (2014). A humancentric API for programming socially interactive robots. *Visual Languages and Human-Centric Computing (VL/HCC)*, *2014. IEEE Symposium*, 121-128.

Doerrfeld, B., Wood, C., Anthony, A., Sandoval, K., & Lauret, A. (2015-2016). *The API Economy: Disruption and the Business of APIs*. Nordic.

Fatemi, F. (2019, March 21). *How APIs Can Transform Your Company*. Retrieved 04 2, 2019, from https://www.forbes.com/sites/falonfatemi/2019/03/21/how-apis-can-transform-your-company/#2dddecfc668c

Fisher, R. (2014, Sept 25). *What Exactly is an API Platform? A Competitive Edge That is What!* Retrieved from https://nordicapis.com/what-exactly-is-an-api-platform-competitive-edge/

Foster, C., Graham, M., Mann, L., Waema, T., & Friederici, N. (2018). Digital Control in Value Chains: Challenges of Connectivity for East African Firms. *Economic Geography*, *94*(1), 68–86. doi:10.1080/00130095.2017.1350104

Gable, G. (1994). Integrating case study and survey research methods: An example in information systems. *European Journal of Information Systems*, *3*(2), 112–126. doi:10.1057/ejis.1994.12

Gawer, A., & Cusumano, M. (2002). *Platform Leadership: How Intel, Microsoft, and Cisco Drive Industry Innovation*. Harvard Business School Press.

Ghazawneh, A., & Henfridsson, O. (2013). Balancing Platform Control and External Contribution in Third-Party Development: The Boundary Resources Model. *Information Systems Journal*, *23*(2), 173–192. doi:10.1111/j.1365-2575.2012.00406.x

Giesbrecht, T., Schwabe, G., & Schenk, B. (2017). Service encounter thinklets: How to empower service agents to put value co-creation into practice. *Information Systems Journal*, *27*(2), 171–196. doi:10.1111/isj.12099

Gol, E. (2019). Crowd work platform governance toward organizational value creation. *The Journal of Strategic Information Systems*, *28*(2), 175–195. doi:10.1016/j.jsis.2019.01.001

Hathaway, A. (2018). *Tips On Monetizing APIs*. Retrieved 02 24, 2019, from https://nordicapis.com/tips-monetizing-apis/

Heikkilä, J.-P. (2013). An institutional theory perspective on e-HRM's strategic potential in MNC subsidiaries. *The Journal of Strategic Information Systems*, *22*(3), 238–251. doi:10.1016/j.jsis.2013.07.003

Hinings, B., Gegenhuber, T., & Greenwood, R. (2018). Digital innovation and transformation: An institutional perspective. *Information and Organization*, *28*(1), 52–61. doi:10.1016/j.infoandorg.2018.02.004

Iansiti, M., & Levien, R. (2004). *The Keystone Advantage: What the New Dynamics of Business Ecosystems Mean for Strategy, Innovation, and Sustainability*. Harvard Business School Press.

IBM. (2016). *Innovation in the API economy: Building winning experiences and new capabilities to compete*. IBM Executive report.

IFPI. (2019). *IFPI Global Music Report 2019: State of the music industry*. The Nielsen Company.

Iyengar, K., Khanna, S., Ramadath, S., & Stephens, D. (2017, September). *What it really takes to capture the value of APIs*. Retrieved January 2019, from https://www.mckinsey.com/: https://www.mckinsey.com/business-functions/mckinsey-digital/our-insights/what-it-really-takes-to-capture-the-value-of-apis

Jonsson, K., Westergren, U., & Holmström, J. (2008). Technologies for value creation: An exploration of remote diagnostics systems in the manufacturing industry. *Information Systems Journal, 18*(3), 227–245. doi:10.1111/j.1365-2575.2007.00267.x

Jonsson, K. W., & Holmström, J. (2008). Technologies for value creation: An exploration of remote diagnostics systems in the manufacturing industry. *Information Systems Journal, 18*(3), 227–245. doi:10.1111/j.1365-2575.2007.00267.x

Khan, N., Shafi, S., & Ahangar, H. (2018). Digitization of Cultural Heritage: Global Initiatives, Opportunities, and Challenges. *Journal of Cases on Information Technology, 20*(4), 1–16. doi:10.4018/JCIT.2018100101

Kothandaraman, P., & Wilson, D. (2001). The future of competition: Value-creating networks. *Industrial Marketing Management, 30*(4), 379–389. doi:10.1016/S0019-8501(00)00152-8

Kroll, J., Richardson, I., Prikladnicki, R., & Audy, J. (2018). Empirical evidence in follow the Sun software development: A systematic mapping study. *Information and Software Technology, 93*, 30–44. doi:10.1016/j.infsof.2017.08.011

Lan, J., Ma, Y., Zhu, D., Mangalagiu, D., & Thornton, T. (2017). Enabling value co-creation in the sharing economy: The case of Mobike. *Sustainability, 9*(9), 1–20. doi:10.3390u9091504

Lavie, D. (2009). Capturing value from alliance portfolios. *Organizational Dynamics, 38*(1), 26–36. doi:10.1016/j.orgdyn.2008.04.008

Loebbecke, C., & Picot, A. (2015). Reflections on societal and business model transformation arising from digitization and big data analytics: A research agenda. *The Journal of Strategic Information Systems, 24*(3), 149–157. doi:10.1016/j.jsis.2015.08.002

Lyer, B., & Subramaniam, M. (2015, January 7). The Strategic Value of APIs. *Harvard Business Review*. Retrieved from https://hbr.org/2015/01/the-strategic-value-of-aPIs

Magretta, J. (2002). Why business models matter. *Harvard Business Review, 80*, 3–8. PMID:12024761

McKendrick, J. (2019, July 30). *CEOs Are Talking About APIs, And Other Signs The World Is Turned Upside Down*. Retrieved November 9, 2019, from https://www.forbes.com: https://www.forbes.com/sites/joemckendrick/2019/07/30/ceos-are-talking-about-apis-and-other-signs-the-world-is-turned-upside-down/#39da06955750

Mingers, J. (2004). Re-establishing the Real: Critical Realism and Information Systems. In J. Mingers & L. Willcocks (Eds.), *Social Theory and Philosophy for Information Systems* (pp. 372–406). Chichester: Wiley.

Moore, J. (1993). Predators and prey: The new ecology of competition. *Harvard Business Review, 71*, 75–83. PMID:10126156

Morris, M., Schindehutte, M., & Allen, J. (2005). The entrepreneur's business model: Toward a unified perspective. *Journal of Business Research, 58*(6), 726–735. doi:10.1016/j.jbusres.2003.11.001

Myjoyonline.com. (2018, Sept 12). *Closing the digital divide crucial to Ghana's socio-economic development – Ursula.* Retrieved 02 1, 2019, from https://www.myjoyonline.com/: https://www.myjoyonline.com/news/2018/september-12th/closing-digital-divide-crucial-to-ghanas-socio-economic-devt-ursula.php

Ndung'u, N. (2017). New frontiers in Africa's digital potential. Harnessing Africa's Digital Potential: New tools for a new age.

Niu, H., Keivanloo, I., & Zou, Y. (2017). API usage pattern recommendation for software development. *Journal of Systems and Software*, 1–13.

Ofoeda, J., & Boateng, R. (2018). Institutional Effects on API Development and Integration in Developing Countries: Evidence from Ghana. *Twenty-Fourth Americas Conference on Information Systems*.

Ofoeda, J., Boateng, R., & Effah, J. (2019). Application Programming Interface (API) Research: A Review of the Past to Inform the Future. *International Journal of Enterprise Information Systems, 15*(3), 76–95. doi:10.4018/IJEIS.2019070105

Oh, E.-T., Chen, K.-M., Wang, L.-M., & Liu, R.-J. (2015). Value creation in regional innovation systems: The case of Taiwan's machine chine. *Technological Forecasting and Social Change, 100*(100), 118–129. doi:10.1016/j.techfore.2015.09.026

Olavsrud, T. (2016, April 19). *APIs abound, but challenges remain.* Retrieved 02 15, 2019, from https://www.cio.com/article/3058732/apis-abound-but-challenges-remain.html

Park, S., & Bae, D.-H. (2011). An approach to analyzing the software process change impact using process slicing and simulation. *Journal of Systems and Software, 84*(4), 528–543. doi:10.1016/j.jss.2010.11.919

Peltoniemi, M. (2005). Business ecosystem. A conceptual model of an organization population from the perspectives of complexity and evolution. *E-Business Research Center. Research Reports 18 Tampere.*

Peppard, J. (2001). Bridging the gap between the IS organization and the rest of the business: Plotting a route. *Information Systems Journal, 11*(3), 249–270. doi:10.1046/j.1365-2575.2001.00105.x

Pilinkienė, V., & Mačiulis, P. (2014). Comparison of different ecosystem analogies: The main economic determinants and levels of impact. *Procedia: Social and Behavioral Sciences, 156*, 365–370. doi:10.1016/j.sbspro.2014.11.204

Qiu, D., Li, B., & Leung, H. (2016). Understanding the API usage in Java. *Information and Software Technology, 73*, 81–100. doi:10.1016/j.infsof.2016.01.011

Radevski, S., Hata, H., & Matsumoto, K. (2016). Towards Building API Usage Example Metrics. *2016 IEEE 23rd International Conference on Software Analysis, Evolution, and Reengineering.*

Rayna, T., & Striukova, L. (2015). Open innovation 2.0: Is co-creation the ultimate challenge? *International Journal of Technology Management, 69*(1), 38–53. doi:10.1504/IJTM.2015.071030

Reuver, M., Sørensen, C., & Basole, R. (2017). The digital platform: A research agenda. *Journal of Information Technology.*

RogueWaveb, S. (2017). *Enterprise API management defined.* Rogue Wave Software, Inc.

Ruivo, P., Oliveira, T., & Neto, M. (2015). Using resource-based view theory to assess the value of ERP commercial-packages in SMEs. *Computers in Industry, 73,* 105–116. doi:10.1016/j.compind.2015.06.001

Sambamurthy, V., & Jarvenpaa, S. (2002). JSIS Editorial—Special Issue on "Trust in the Digital Economy.". *The Journal of Strategic Information Systems, 11*(3-4), 183–185. doi:10.1016/S0963-8687(02)00032-X

Santos, A., & Myers, B. (2017). Design annotations to improve API discoverability. *Journal of Systems and Software, 126,* 17–33. doi:10.1016/j.jss.2016.12.036

Santos, A., Prendi, G., Sousa, H., & Ribeiro, R. (2017). Stepwise API usage assistance using n-gram language models. *Journal of Systems and Software, 000,* 1–14.

Scheller, T., & Kühn, E. (2015). Automated measurement of API usability: The API Concepts Framework. *Information and Software Technology, 61,* 145–162. doi:10.1016/j.infsof.2015.01.009

Shatnawi, A., Seriai, A.-D., Sahraoui, H., & Alshara, Z. (2016). Reverse engineering reusable software components from object-oriented APIs. *Journal of Systems and Software,* 1–19.

Singh, T. (2019, August 29). *Software Ate The World; Now AI Is Eating Software.* Retrieved November 10, 2019, from https://www.forbes.com: https://www.forbes.com/sites/cognitiveworld/2019/08/29/software-ate-the-world-now-ai-is-eating-software/#2861882a5810

Spinellis, D., & Louridas, L. (2007). A framework for the static verification of API calls. *Journal of Systems and Software, 80*(7), 1156–1168. doi:10.1016/j.jss.2006.09.040

Sturm, R., Pollard, C., & Craig, J. (2017). *Application Performance Management (APM) in the Digital Enterprise Managing Applications for Cloud.* Elsevier Inc. doi:10.1016/B978-0-12-804018-8.00001-2

Suseno, Y., Laurell, C., & Sick, N. (2018). Assessing value creation in digital innovation ecosystems: A Social Media Analytics approach. *The Journal of Strategic Information Systems, 27*(4), 335–349. doi:10.1016/j.jsis.2018.09.004

Tantalo, C., & Priem, R. (2016). Value creation through stakeholder synergy. *Strategic Management Journal, 37*(2), 314–329. doi:10.1002mj.2337

Tiwana, A., Konsynsky, B., & Bush, A. (2010). Platform Evolution: Coevolution of Platform Architecture, Governance, and Environmental Dynamics. *Information Systems Research, 21*(4), 675–687. doi:10.1287/isre.1100.0323

Tsang, E. (2014). Case studies and generalization in information systems research: A critical realist perspective. *The Journal of Strategic Information Systems, 23*(2), 174–186. doi:10.1016/j.jsis.2013.09.002

Utesheva, A., Simpson, J., & Cecez-Kecmanovic, D. (2016). Identity metamorphoses in digital disruption: A relational theory of identity. *European Journal of Information Systems, 25*(4), 344–363. doi:10.1057/ejis.2015.19

Vargo, S., & Lusch, R. (2004). Evolving to a new dominant logic for marketing. *Journal of Marketing, 68*(1), 1–17. doi:10.1509/jmkg.68.1.1.24036

Varian, H. (1999, August). *Market structure in the network age.* Market Structure in the Network Age.

Weaver, H. (2018, Jul 17). *7 Cases of Extremely Successful API Adoption.* Retrieved 03 15, 2019, from https://nordicapis.com/7-cases-of-extremely-successful-api-adoption/

Wendell, S. (2017, March 17). *Social and Financial Among the Most Popular API Categories.* Retrieved from https://www.programmableweb.com/news/social-and-financial-among-most-popular-api-categories/research/2017/03/17

Wijayarathna, C., & Arachchilage, N. (2019). Why Johnny cannot develop a secure application? A usability analysis of Java Secure Socket Extension API. *Computers & Security, 80*, 54–73. doi:10.1016/j.cose.2018.09.007

Wijayarathna, C., & Arachchilage, N. (2019b). Using cognitive dimensions to evaluate the usability of security APIs: An empirical investigation. *Information and Software Technology, 115*, 5–19. doi:10.1016/j.infsof.2019.07.007

Willmott, S., Balas, G., & 3scale. (2016). *Winning in the API Economy: Using software and APIs to transform your business...* 3Scale. Retrieved from www.3scale.net

Yamin, M., Sinkovics, R., Sinkovics, N., Sinkovics, R., Hoque, S., & Czaban, L. (2015). A reconceptualisation of social value creation as social constraint alleviation. *Critical Perspectives on International Business, 11*(3/4), 340–363. doi:10.1108/cpoib-06-2014-0036

Yin, R. K. (1984). *Case Study Research: Design and Methods.* Academic Press.

Yin, R. K. (1993). Applications of case study research. London: Sage Publications.

Yin, R. K. (2003). *Case study research: Design and methods.* Newbury Park: Sage.

Yire, I. (2019, June 16). *Ghana tipped to be the fastest-growing mobile money market in Africa.* Retrieved June 16, 2019, from http://www.ghananewsagency.org/economics/ghana-tipped-to-be-the-fastest-growing-mobile-money-market-in-africa-151643

Yoo, Y., Henfridsson, O., & Lyytinen, K. (2010). The new organizing logic of digital innovation: An agenda for information systems research. *Information Systems Research, 21*(4), 724–735. doi:10.1287/isre.1100.0322

Zachariadis, M., & Ozcan, P. (2017). *The API Economy and Digital Transformation in Financial Services: The case of Open Banking.* Swift Institute Working Paper No 2016-001.

Zhong, H., Xie, T., Zhang, L., Pei, J., & Mei, H. (2009). MAPO: Mining and Recommending API Usage Patterns. *European Conference on Object-Oriented Programming*, 318-343. 10.1007/978-3-642-03013-0_15

Zibran, M., Eishita, F., & Roy, C. (2011). Useful, but usable factors affecting the usability of APIs. *18th Working Conf. on Reverse Engineering (WCRE)*, 151–155. 10.1109/WCRE.2011.26

Zott, C., Amit, R. H., & Massa, L. (2011). The Business Model: Recent Developments and Future Research. *Journal of Management*, *37*(4), 1019–1042. doi:10.1177/0149206311406265

Section 3
Information Systems and Socio-Economic Development

Chapter 15
Using a Qualitative Interpretive Approach in Educational Technology Implementation:
A Personal Experience From a Developing Country University

Ibrahim Osman Adam
University for Development Studies, Ghana

ABSTRACT

This chapter presents some methodological issues raised in the research process of an interpretive researcher in a maiden doctoral programme in a developing country. The chapter draws on a doctoral research experience which employed an interpretive case study approach as the methodology and a combined lens of activity and agency theories as to the theoretical foundation. The research relied on a single case study in a developing country context. The chapter offers an overview of some practicalities of carrying out a single case study research using an interpretive philosophy by presenting the different viewpoints using semi-structured interviews, documents and participant observation, and analysing the data through hermeneutics. The chapter presents some challenges and how interpretive research methods can be used as a clear methodological strategy, especially in an environment where many researchers are not familiar with this research approach. This reflective account provides lessons for others who wish to go through an interpretive process of researching an information systems phenomenon.

INTRODUCTION

The purpose of this chapter is to showcase the methodological issues an early career researcher encountered in a maiden PhD research programme. Being an interpretive researcher in a developing country context, the chapter is situated in a reflective sense showcasing the experience of the researcher in employing a combined lens of theories and using a single case study to offer an overview of some practicalities.

DOI: 10.4018/978-1-7998-2610-1.ch015

This reflective account is aimed at providing insight and practical lessons to early career researchers and postgraduate students embarking on a PhD and intending to using a qualitative methodology and an interpretive philosophy.

BACKGROUND

The nature of work and the workplace are rapidly changing, especially in our increasingly connected digital world, making some jobs and places of work obsolete. Today, work and the workplace are no longer tied to fixed locations. This change has led to some flexibility in terms of where, how and when people work (Lee, 2015). The three pillars have a co-shaping relationship and drive how work is conducted in recent times.

The Higher Education Institution (HEI) workplace is no exception to this change. HEIs are characterised by three main activities in their work environment: teaching, research, and administration. A work environment is a space in which work is performed (Bødker & Christiansen, 2002) and includes the surrounding conditions such as the physical office space or equipment and work processes. Over the years, work has been performed in work environments characterised by a physical office and physical workflows with employees sharing a common workspace and are not necessarily collaborating using communication and collaboration tools such as email and video conferencing (Schweitzer & Duxbury, 2010). Traditionally, teaching and administration in HEIs have been conducted in physically located settings. Teaching has been carried out in classrooms and offices with the use of physical tools such as chalk, marker, or chalkboard whilst administration has been conducted with physical tools such as office cabinets, paper-based mail and physical workflows with employees having to travel to the workplace.

Though globalisation and information technology have been key trends shaping this changing nature of the work environment, Information Systems (IS) research on HEIs systems over the years has focused more on e-learning and the virtual learning environment (VLE). As a result, less research attention has been given to virtualisation of work environment within HEIs. It is thus important that IS research on higher education information systems pays attention not only to the learning environment but also to the work environment since the work environment offers the necessary support for learning. Also, In recent years, the requirements of HEIs have changed because of the growing number of students, the data generated from their operations, and the need for information integration (Magal & Word, 2011; Pollock & Williams, 2008). As a result, HEIs in developing countries are migrating their physical work processes to the virtual

To address these, I embarked on a PhD journey to understand the contextual issues that could shape a developing country HEI's engagement of an external consultant to virtualise its work environments. In 2013, I started a PhD in Information Systems (IS) under the supervision of an interpretive researcher at the University of Ghana as one of the only two students to have started a PhD in IS in a Ghanaian University. My PhD explored the enablers and constraints that developing countries Higher Education Institutions (HEIs) could encounter in their attempt to migrate their physical work environments to a virtual work environment using an external consultant.

The PhD research was carried out in a Ghanaian University (Herein referred to as A-Uni). The theoretical foundation was a combined lens of activity and agency theories. The methodological approach was an interpretive case study to provide a rich insight into the HEI's engagement with the external consultant throughout the virtualisation process. The fieldwork for this study was conducted in a Ghanaian University (referred to here as 'A-Uni', a pseudonym). Ghana is a developing country in West Africa with a middle-income status and a constitutional democracy. A-Uni has made attempts in the past to virtualise its teaching and administrative work environment through the engagement of external consultants. The most recent is the attempt through the engagement of an external consultant to use open source technologies to virtualise both the teaching and administrative work environment.

A-Uni is one of the largest and oldest Universities in Ghana and embarked on a project with external funding facilitated by the Government of Ghana to implement an intranet portal and a content management system. The implementation of an intranet portal was a subproject of a bigger project and was to provide Enterprise Content Management and Intranet portal (ECMIP) to about 2000 staff of A-Uni. The main aim of the University was to digitalize its current paper/records of the University's Archives and automate their existing manual workflows around records/documents. This is the administrative work environment virtualisation case and was used as the first embedded case study.

The second case study was on the virtualisation of the teaching work environment. This involved a Teaching Management system (TMS). The TMS is a platform that provides a flexible and feature-rich environment for teaching, learning, research, and collaboration. As an open-source software suite developed by its adopter community, the TMS continually evolves in step with the needs of the students, faculty members and organisations it serves. The first case was denoted as case A and the second as case T, respectively.

COMBINED THEORETICAL LENS

Activity Theory is a theoretical framework for the analysis and understanding of human interaction and relationships through the use of tools and other influences within a social setting. The basis of the theory is the concept of activity. An activity involves different processes of doing something to accomplish an objective. An activity consists of a subject and an object which is mediated by a tool. Activity theory views the unit of analysis as the entire activity. Activities always take place within a context (Engestrom, 1987) which exist as a network of different elements that influence each other in what is called an activity system. An activity system consists of interacting components of the subject, object, rules, community, division of labour and mediating tools (Engestrom, 1987). In this study, therefore, I perceived the work environment virtualization process as an activity.

To address this limitation, I drew on agency theory which examines the relationship in which the principal delegates work to an agent (Jensen & Meckling, 1976). The relationships of subjects have not been widely discussed using activity theory and so the contradictions that may exist between the subjects as principal and agent are not explored. Activity does not consider the duality of actors (subjects) in principal-agent relationship and so though activity theory was selected because of its appropriateness to offer insight into the complex and sociotechnical nature of an HEI work environment virtualisation, it was limited in unearthing the enablers and constraints within the HEI and between the HEI (as a principal) and its agent (Consultant).

RESEARCH DESIGN

Research Paradigm

The assumptions made by different researchers inform how a phenomenon is understood (Becker & Niehaves, 2007). These assumptions inform and define the particular research paradigm that should be used for particular research. Myers and Avison (2002) consider paradigms as the fundamental philosophical assumptions which determine what can be considered as valid research and determine a researcher's ontological, epistemological and methodological stand (Guba & Lincoln, 1994). The ontology refers to the nature of reality. Simply it refers to what exists and is being studied. The epistemology is about the nature of the knowledge that can be learned about the reality being studied. Epistemological assumptions about a research issue under investigation concern the criteria by which valid knowledge about that phenomenon may be constructed (Chua, 1986). Lastly, the methodology is how knowledge about reality can be sought (Myers, 2013; Orlikowski & Baroudi, 1991b).

Choice of Interpretivism

The philosophical assumptions that underline this study were therefore drawn from the interpretive tradition (Walsham, 2006). The choice of the interpretive paradigm was based on the research questions largely and the philosophical background of the researcher. My research ontology was, therefore, to view work environment virtualisation as subjective reality based on the views of the several participants and myself. Epistemologically, I could also arrive at the subjective view of the work environment virtualisation based on an iterative and a reflexive process of understanding. Methodologically, I leaned towards a qualitative case study approach. It was as a result of this that interpretivism was found to be suitable in order to understand the reality of how a physical work environment is migrated to a virtual one through the social constructions and shared meanings of the people engaged in the context (Myers, 1997; Myers, 2013).

Interpretive Case Study

To investigate the virtualisation phenomenon within its real-life context of the HEI, an interpretive case study was used. Interpretive case studies do not recommend the use of hypotheses, and it is in reaction to this that Myers (2013, p. 78) sees case study as the use of empirical evidence from one or more organisations where an attempt is made to study the subject matter in context. Yin (2009) recommends the use of hypothesis and so I could not follow Yin's approach but rather an interpretive case study approach because, the study was seeking an in-depth understanding of how a physical work environment is migrated to a virtual one in the context of complex and broader social and organisational context (Walsham, 1993). Also, the use of the interpretive case study provided me with the opportunity to gather rich contextual data (Myers, 2013; Myers & Avison, 1997). Lastly, interpretive case study research was one clear way I could obtain a contextual understanding of the phenomenon in a dialogic and an inter-subjective manner between myself and the participants (Orlikowski & Baroudi, 1989; Orlikowski & Baroudi, 1991a).

I adopted a descriptive, single and embedded case study (Scholz & Tietje, 2002; Yin, 2010). A single case was used because the phenomenon being studied was within one organisation, and this ensured an in-depth study of the phenomenon. The case was embedded because it involved more than one unit of analysis. In the multiple units of analysis, a multiplicity of evidence was derived from the subunits, and this focused on different salient aspects of the case.

Researcher's Background and Role

In interpretive research, in-depth access to people, issues, and data is key to understanding subjective meanings that are attached to phenomena. To achieve this depth of my background, knowledge, and prejudices that shape the way things are perceived were critical (Walsham, 2006). Interpretive research requires an interaction between the researcher and the participants in order to understand the phenomenon under the study within a context in what is referred to as its dialogic nature. It is against this backdrop that my background is disclosed and also how I was involved in the research and how this involvement has influenced the research.

I am Ghanaian and have been a resident in Ghana for the most part of my life. I began searching for avenues for a teaching appointment in information systems as well as looking for avenues to start a PhD in Information Systems locally because of my interest and prior educational qualifications. Until I started the PhD my knowledge of research was positivist unbeknownst to me that there were alternative paradigms such as interpretive or critical. My orientation changed during the first-year coursework of my PhD and through my interactions with my supervisor.

The fieldwork for my PhD formed the fundamental basis of my interpretive study (Walsham, 2006). This is because it involved the choice of how to get involved, gaining access, collecting data and working in different contexts. As an interpretive researcher, I was a 'neutral observer' but not unbiased. Being neutral means that the participants do not see me as being aligned with a particular person or group within the organisation, have the motive of making money or have strong prior views of specific people, systems or processes within the organisation. My background was important in negotiating and gaining access to the organisation. Apart from this, gaining access to the participants and to documents within the organisation were all influenced by my background.

I established contacts during the requirements gathering process of one of the case study projects, implementation, and demonstrations as well as in meetings. My interaction with some potential participants during such meetings facilitated the data gathering when I later contacted them to be part of an interview. I had also met some of the participants during training sessions and introduced myself as a PhD student on the project and that I will be approaching them later in a year or two for interviews on their participation and use of the system.

Field Work and Selection of Case

The fieldwork for my PhD study was conducted in A-Uni in Ghana. The selection of the case was faced with several challenges raised by both some faculty and fellow doctoral students during seminar presentations of my doctoral research. Many faculty members strongly argued that a single case study was not enough for doctoral research. Whilst I had initial challenges in warding off and defending the use of the single case study for my PhD, two issues raised by Kuzel were particularly helpful. The selection of the cases was guided by the two issues of appropriateness and adequacy (Kuzel, 1992). In terms of appropriateness, I needed to demonstrate a fit for both the purpose of my research and the phenomenon of inquiry. In terms of adequacy which was concerned with how much is enough or how many cases (Kuzel, 1992; Miles & Huberman, 1994), the depth of the study to provide rich insight was used as a justification. To satisfy the appropriateness of the case study, purposeful sampling strategy was used (Patton, 1990, pp. 182-183) to choose the case as a single critical case for the study.

Also, I found that the two embedded subcases were appropriate because each represented the work environment in an HEI in a different way. The first case was concerned with the creation, maintenance and use of template-based virtual offices, virtual cabinets, folders and files and virtual workflows for the administrative work environment. The second case provides the platform for a flexible and feature-rich environment for collaboration in the teaching environment.

In terms of adequacy, this is satisfied in a trade-off between the breadth and depth of the case. In the single embedded case study, in-depth information is required while less depth is required as the number of cases increases (Patton, 1990) and this single embedded case provided in-depth information about the work environment in an HEI.

RESEARCH PRACTICALITIES

Ensuring Interpretivism in the Research

In my interpretive journey, Walsham's paper on interpretive case studies in IS research and how the contribution to knowledge can be attained as well as Klein and Myers paper on conducting and evaluating IS interpretive case studies (Klein & Myers, 1999) have been phenomenal in my understanding of interpretive research in IS. I tried in various ways to ensure that whilst I attempt to answer the research questions I must as well ensure that the findings are representative of the interpretive paradigm I have subscribed to. To ensure this, my use of the hermeneutic circle was key. This is a basic principle in interpretive studies. The principle means the whole of a text or a text analogue such as the phenomenon under study can only be understood by interpreting the 'whole' from its parts and vice versa (Gadamer, 1976b). Therefore, for me to understand what work environment virtualisation was in this study, the whole of the work environment virtualisation phenomenon was examined at two levels. First, the virtualisation activity at the HEI level and the virtualisation activity at the principal-agent level. The principal activity at the organisation level refers to the HEI's activity in virtualising its work environment while the second refers to the virtualisation activities at the principal-agent level. The hermeneutic circle was applied at these two different levels, and to understand each level required investigating various parts of the virtualisation activity system at the principal and the agent levels in terms of the tools, subject, rules, community, division of labour and objects as well as the actions and how this fed into the central activity.

This understanding of work environment virtualisation was achieved through an iterative process. This involved the understanding of the individual activities of the subjects as principal and agent and in terms of their collective activity. This meant that the individual activities and the collective activity were equally vital in shaping the virtualisation process. The only way I could relate the various aspects of the virtualisation activity to the virtualisation process was to view the HEIs virtualisation of its work environment with its social and historical context. It was only through this that the audience could understand how the situation being examined emerged.

To properly capture the context, the historical context of the HEI's work environment was examined to understand how its support or lack of support for the virtualisation process. In addition, each subcase started with an overview of the specific work context within which the virtualisation occurred. The cases also offered contextualised understanding by highlighting the interaction within actors in the case organisation and between actors in the organisation and that of the consultant organisations.

There was no way I could ensure this without interactions between me and the subjects. This ensured a critical reflection on how the data was socially constructed between me and the participants. This was necessary to ensure that I collaboratively worked with the participants to construct the data since I could not gather value-free data. This is important because as Geertz puts it, what I considered data was my own constructions of other people's constructions of what they are up to (Geertz, 1973, p. 9).

Much of the confusion regarding my research was my initial justification of how my findings could be generalized. Especially given the fact that I was using a single case study. Though I have argued in the past that though the case study was single, it, however, consisted of two embedded cases. Though the two cases could not suffice to satisfy the critique of the quantitatively biased faculty members who had never done any qualitative research of the sort I was engaged in. Their argument was that generalisations that follow sampling procedures cannot be made using interpretive studies. My resort to this persistent criticism was drawn from Myers that findings from interpretive studies can be used to draw general conclusions though such generalizations do not depend on the number of cases involved. Walsham (2006) supports this view that access to a limited number of organisations or even one organisation does not necessarily reduce the possibility of generalising from interpretive case studies. This was critical for me in drawing the validity of inferences from my one interpretive case study. This is because the validity of what I was going to draw did not depend on the representativeness of the cases in a statistical sense.

Even during my Viva, my research was criticized by a member of the audience for its lack of generalisability to population. In response, I made it clear that interpretive case studies can be used to make theoretical generalisations (Myers, 2013; Walsham, 1995) and the study, therefore, could generalise to theory by using a combination of existing theories to theorise the work environment virtualisation in a novel way.

This research went through a series of iterations. The research started with an initial focus on an HEI's use of intranet portals to manage content and ensure collaboration among administrative staff. Following this, my initial intention was to understand how HEIs deploy intranet technologies to facilitate virtual work. The initial research design and research questions were then based on concepts derived from the IS deployment literature. However, during the fieldwork, it became clearer to me that the HEI workplace, especially in the developing country context, were largely physical with individual HEIs attempting in various ways to move aspects or all of their work environments to virtual platforms. In view of this, the focus shifted from IS deployment of intranets in HEIs to the virtualisation of the work environment. This led to the modification of the research, and the questions were therefore updated accordingly.

The study also started with the normalisation process theory in mind. However, during the data analysis of the first round of fieldwork for the first embedded case study, it became necessary to draw on a theory to make sense of the complex data that was gathered and the apparent tensions between actors and some rules. Subsequently, activity theory was chosen as the theoretical lens. Several actors were involved in the virtualization process raising contradictions at different levels. The actors at some point were best described as principal and agent working collaboratively. This led to the study drawing on agency theory to explain the relationship. The data gathering and analysis were concurrent, but activity theory and agency theory still influenced the subsequent data gathering. This meant that an earlier emphasis on the HEI only was extended to include its agent.

The data analysis was conducted with the support of Nvivo as the qualitative data analysis software to manage the data. Nvivo was not completely used as the analytical tool because it was realised that the tool offered some structured approach for analysis that did not completely fit the iterative and inductive process of analysis required by an interpretive study. The software was therefore largely used for data management and transcription. To analyse the data, I continuously read and reflected on the gathered data as well as relying on feedback from participants for further clarifications and revisions. My experience was, therefore, consistent with the ontological and epistemological stance of interpretive philosophy that reality and knowledge are socially constructed between the researcher and the participants and not taken as given.

The study focused on different types of subjects. Especially on how different actors had different interpretations and how these reflected their particular interests. For instance, the management of the HEI saw the implementation of the virtual work environment as a solution to the challenging situation of physically managing documents and an opportunity for administrative staff and lecturers to work remotely. The management perceived the initiative as moving the HEI closer to its mission of attaining an international standard of a top HEI in Africa. Some administrative staff and some lecturers however expressed fear that though the system will support their work and ensure efficiency, it may eventually replace some staff and could lead to loss of jobs. This was consistent with the multiple-reality view of interpretive studies.

METHODS IN ACTION

Data Sources and Collection

Interviews

I used multiple sources of data and data gathering techniques (Myers, 2013). These included face-to-face interviews using semi-structured interviews, documentary evidence and participant observation. Due to the interpretive nature of the study interviews were the primary data source. This was because I realised that it was only through this method that I could best access the interpretations of participants regarding the actions and events taking place (Myers & Newman, 2007; Walsham, 1995). It also afforded me the opportunity to see things that are not ordinarily visible (Rubin & Rubin, 2011).

I prepared an interview guide using semi-structured questions, linked to the research questions and informed by constructs of both activity theory and agency theory. The interviews touched on the broad areas of the nature of the physical work environment, the involvement of the interviewees in the virtualisation process and their observation of any other phenomenon that affected the virtualisation process. In the process of the interviews, there was some fine-tuning to take care of emergent views and concepts. Each formal interview lasted between one hour and two hours and was audio-recorded following the participant's consent. The number of interviewees was not limited to a predefined number but involved project consultants, the local project team, users (administrative staff and lecturers), management and students identified through purposive sampling. The interviews continued until a number was arrived at heuristically (Guest, Bunce, & Johnson, 2006). This meant that I only stopped interviewing when nothing new was being gathered from the interviews. Some informal conversations were also struck with the head of directorates, institutes, centres, departments, units and other staff. These were not audio recorded but written up immediately after the conversation. Table 1 below provides a detailed breakdown of the interviews conducted and the participants at each unit of analysis.

Table 1. Breakdown of Interviews Conducted

Case	Participants/Interviewee	Interviews
A-Uni		Number
Sub-Units		
Case A: Administrative Work Environment Virtualisation	Project Consultants Project Manager(A-Uni) Task Team Leader Project Coordinator Project Officers Administrative Staff	4 1 1 1 4 22
Total Participants		**33**
Case T: Teaching Work Environment Virtualisation	Project Consultant A-Uni Management Staff Project Manager Project Officers Project Coordinators Administrative Staff Lecturers	4 5 1 4 2 6 10
Total Participants		**32**
OVERALL TOTAL OF PARTICIPANTS		**65**

Documents

I relied mainly on two main sources of documents to gain further insight. These were internally from the case organisation and from its website and externally from the Internet. The internal documents included the scope of work documents, requirements documents (business and software), project plans, minutes of meetings, correspondence including letters and emails between management and project consultants and contract documents. These secondary data helped me to learn about the key stakeholders, technical details and other organisational issues. It also helped me in exploring further issues during the interviews.

Participant Observation

I also did some personal observations by not only watching the research subjects from the outside but participating in the activities as well in order to gain an understanding from the inside (Myers, 1997). I participated in implementation meetings and briefing sessions as a researcher and a participant. After implementation, I observed the staff of the University using the systems in various ways. I participated in the use of the system during the user acceptance testing to gain better insight and understanding and to gather the appropriate data. There were also software demonstrations and walk-through sessions I participated in to understand the set-up of the virtual offices, virtual cabinets as well as the workflows. I was able to gather some additional data from the participants at various points through telephone and email exchanges both during and after the fieldwork. The end-point of my data gathering was not predetermined. I ended the data gathering when I reached a saturation point. After this end-point, I still conducted some follow-up data gathering through telephone, email and informal conversations. This was to clarify issues that were emerging after the formal interviews. In terms of the documents and staff of A-Uni, I had to ensure that the appropriate procedures for gaining access (Feldman, Bell, & Berger,

2004) were followed. I followed collaborative leads I had established with some units and individuals over the years. I also employed other strategies like endorsements and familiarity with staff.

DATA ANALYSIS

Both the data collection and the data analysis were concurrently conducted in this study (Myers, 2013). This is because the two belong to an iterative process and the results of one helped in guiding the other. The analysis was also inductive and this allowed themes to emerge from the data. The data collected was analysed using hermeneutics as the mode of analysis and activity theory and agency theory as the analytical lens. Though this process was non-linear and iterative, several stages could be discerned. The first stage in the data analysis was my immersion in the data (Green, Willis, Hughes, Small, Welch, Gibbs, & Daly, 2007). I listened to the recording of each interview especially after the interview when so much time had not elapsed, transcribing it, reading and re-reading the interview transcripts instead of waiting until the end of all interviews. This prevented me from wading through large amounts of data at one time if I had to wait until all the interviews are conducted. My immersion in the data involved both the documents collected and the audio recordings after each interview. For me, this was the only way a detailed examination of the documents and interviews could be conducted. The data immersion provided me clarity by providing me with the foundation to ensure that disjointed statements made during the interview or found in the documents were put in a clearer picture of the phenomenon under study.

The next thing I did was to transcribe the audio recordings and then code the transcripts and the documents. I examined each transcript and organised it by making judgments and tagging blocks of the transcripts. As part of the analysis, the work environment virtualisation activity was considered as the unit of analysis. A work environment virtualisation activity system was therefore modelled with several nodes representing the various elements of the activity. The nodes of the activity system were then used as the initial codes. I used the nodes as descriptive labels and applied them to segments of each transcript. The codes were created using Nvivo within which the audio recordings of the interviews had been imported and transcribed. The coding involved considering the context in which some statements in the interview data were made and labelling some single words, phrases, or whole paragraphs that contain information relating to each particular node in the activity system. Sometimes, in this process, a word, phrase or paragraph was attributed to more than one code. However, more information about the phenomenon was discovered as I worked through the transcripts, codes were added, and sometimes some old transcripts had to be revisited. This process involved moving back and forth through the transcripts. Using the codes, separate activity systems for the administrative work environment virtualisation and teaching work environment virtualisation were modelled.

At the next stage of the analysis, I created categories. To do this, I examined the way the codes could be linked in order to create coherent categories. In order to look for a 'good fit' between codes that share a relationship, each activity system was decomposed by breaking it down through an activity notation to provide a deeper analysis of each activity I went through above in an iterative manner and this enabled me to conduct a detailed investigation of the work environment virtualisation phenomenon. To make sense of what was happening within the activity systems, the data gathered was analysed by drawing on a concept from activity theory.

My reliance on the use of hermeneutics as an approach to analysing the qualitative data collected was key in the analysis. Hermeneutics provides a set of concepts to interpret and understand text (or multiple texts) and text-analogue (Myers, 2013). Text-analogues refers to things such as an organisation that can be represented by text. Hermeneutics is primarily concerned with making meaning of textual data and it provided me with the concepts to interpret and understand the meaning of transcripts and the documents collected. In hermeneutics, the understanding of a research phenomenon is derived through an iterative process between the understanding of the interdependent meaning of the parts and the whole (Cole & Avison, 2007; Myers, 2013).

There are several hermeneutics concepts. The hermeneutic circle which explains how a research phenomenon as a whole can become clear from the understanding of the individual parts and how the meaning of the individual parts can also only be clear from the understanding of the whole (Gadamer, 1976a). The text-analogue was A-Uni and the work environment virtualisation activity. I used this to understand how the elements of the activity systems shaped the understanding of the overall activity systems. It was through these that I was able to derive the meanings that are expected from the context of A-UNI's work environment virtualisation as a whole from the interpretations of the parts. I also realised that for me to understand the current nature of the work environment virtualisation, it is necessary to understand the historical context of the phenomena. To support my analysis of the historical context I used the hermeneutic concept of historicity. Historicity implied that the understanding of the phenomenon occurred in a historical context. This clarified the fact that the present virtualisation process was historically informed. This influenced my interpretations of the phenomenon because I had to take cognisance of the historical underpinnings that were influential to the present circumstances.

Finally, I conducted a cross-case analysis from the individual cases by comparing the findings from the individual cases to identify commonalities and differences as well as emerging patterns. This involved the repetitive reading of the individual case findings and comparing them. This generated some interesting themes.

PRACTICAL LESSONS LEARNED

During my first year of the PhD which was entirely a period of coursework, the philosophy of management research and advanced qualitative research methods were core courses. This period was an exciting but challenging one and a period of a steep learning curve on how different philosophical assumptions of a researcher can influence the choice of methods. I was fortunate that my supervisors were the lecturers in the philosophy of management research and advanced qualitative research and this afforded me the opportunity to make several follow-ups discussions with them to understand and clarify several paradigmatic issues in the philosophy of management research in general and the philosophy of information systems research in particular. My continuous interactions with my supervisors during this period and the three years following have been influential in shaping my thoughts on interpretive qualitative research.

I was challenged by my principal supervisor in several ways to ensure that the quality of my research meets the criteria for conducting and reporting the findings of interpretive research. Whilst pointing me to the relevance oftentimes, or challenging me to review current discourse in interpretive IS research, my principal supervisor's writings in interpretive research (Effah, 2011, 2014, 2015) as well as his views have tremendously shaped my views and challenged me to be a good interpretive researcher.

Interpretive research is not popularly applied in IS studies in developing countries such as Ghana. As a result, the approaches I took in my research was resisted on several fronts. This was very challenging especially as a novice researcher on my PhD. I remember my principal supervisor continuously telling me that this is not a straightforward way of doing research and that a lot of surprises could emerge from the iterative nature of the research. One thing, however, was clear. The interpretive case study research was a clear methodology and despite the numerous criticisms that what I was embarking on was not proper research, my principal supervisor once advised me that the best approach was to work harder and publish the findings of my research in acceptable journals and conferences. This worked wonders for me. Though my PhD was to produce a monograph thesis at the end of my study, I was able to have several conference papers accepted in renowned IS conference either as research in progress papers (Adam, Effah, & Boateng, 2016b) or complete research papers (Adam, Effah, & Boateng, 2016a). A journal paper was also published before I submitted my final thesis for examination (Adam, Effah, & Boateng, 2017). The reviews from these conferences and the journal paper were great feedback for me to improve my research. It also provided an avenue for many faculty members and other PhD colleagues to realise that interpretive research using a single case study was indeed a widely acceptable research route.

CONCLUSION

Interpretive research is not a straightforward research process. It can be likened to ants searching for food and following a pheromone trail. The process is iterative, challenging, and subjective. The challenge in gaining research access to organisations and research participants can be as challenging as interpreting the subjective meanings of text using hermeneutics. Therefore, from identifying data sources, through to data collection, data analysis to the reporting of findings, the iterative nature of research and the subjectivity never stops. However, these are guided by several principles that make interpretive research approach valuable and its findings credible and generalizable.

REFERENCES

Adam, I. O., Effah, J., & Boateng, R. (2016a). *Migrating from Physical to Virtual Administrative Work Environment: A Case Study of a Sub Saharan African Higher Education Institution* Paper presented at the Americas Conference on Information Systems, San Diego, CA.

Adam, I. O., Effah, J., & Boateng, R. (2016b). *Virtualisation of Administrative Work Environment in Developing Country Higher Education Institutions: An Activity Theory Perspective.* Paper presented at the European Conference on Information Systems, Instanbul, Turkey.

Adam, I. O., Effah, J., & Boateng, R. (2017). Virtualisation of an Administrative Work Environment in Higher Education: Managing Information in a Developing Country University. *Journal of Enterprise Information Management, 30*(5), 723–747. doi:10.1108/JEIM-06-2016-0119

Becker, J., & Niehaves, B. (2007). Epistemological perspectives on IS research: A framework for analysing and systematizing epistemological assumptions. *Information Systems Journal, 17*(2), 197–214. doi:10.1111/j.1365-2575.2007.00234.x

Bødker, S., & Christiansen, E. (2002). Lost and found in flexibility. *IRIS 2002.*

Chua, W. F. (1986). Radical developments in accounting thought. *The Accounting Review, 61*(4), 601–632.

Cole, M., & Avison, D. (2007). The potential of hermeneutics in information systems research. *European Journal of Information Systems*, *16*(6), 820–833. doi:10.1057/palgrave.ejis.3000725

Effah, J. (2011). *Tracing the emergence and formation of small dot-coms in an emerging digital economy: An actor-network theory approach*. Salford: University of Salford.

Effah, J. (2014). The rise and fall of a dot-com pioneer in a developing country. *Journal of Enterprise Information Management*, *27*(2), 228–239. doi:10.1108/JEIM-04-2012-0016

Effah, J. (2015). *Virtual Process Control Modelling in Organisational Semiotics: A Case of Higher Education Admission Information and Knowledge Management in Complex Systems* (pp. 51–59). Springer.

Engestrom, Y. (1987). *Learning by expanding*. Helsinki, Finland: Orienta-Konsultit.

Feldman, M. S., Bell, J., & Berger, M. T. (2004). *Gaining access: A practical and theoretical guide for qualitative researchers*. Rowman Altamira.

Gadamer, H.-G. (1976a). On the scope and function of hermeneutical reflection. *Philosophical Hermeneutics*, 18-44.

Gadamer, H.-G. (1976b). *Philosophical Hermeneutics*. University of California Press.

Geertz, C. (1973). *The Interpretation of Cultures*. New York: Basic Books.

Green, J., Willis, K., Hughes, E., Small, R., Welch, N., Gibbs, L., & Daly, J. (2007). Generating best evidence from qualitative research: The role of data analysis. *Australian and New Zealand Journal of Public Health*, *31*(6), 545–550. doi:10.1111/j.1753-6405.2007.00141.x PMID:18081575

Guba, E. G., & Lincoln, Y. S. (1994). Competing paradigms in qualitative research. Handbook of Qualitative Research, 2, 163-194.

Guest, G., Bunce, A., & Johnson, L. (2006). How many interviews are enough? An experiment with data saturation and variability. *Field Methods*, *18*(1), 59–82. doi:10.1177/1525822X05279903

Jensen, M. C., & Meckling, W. H. (1976). Theory of the firm: Managerial behavior, agency costs and ownership structure. *Journal of Financial Economics*, *3*(4), 305–360. doi:10.1016/0304-405X(76)90026-X

Klein, H. K., & Myers, M. D. (1999). A set of principles for conducting and evaluating interpretive field studies in information systems. *Management Information Systems Quarterly*, *23*(1), 67–93. doi:10.2307/249410

Kuzel, A. J. (1992). *Sampling in qualitative inquiry*. Academic Press.

Lee, J. (2015). *The Impact of ICT on Work*. Springer.

Magal, S. R., & Word, J. (2011). *Integrated business processes with ERP systems*. Wiley Publishing.

Miles, M. B., & Huberman, A. M. (1994). *Qualitative Data Analysis: An Expanded Sourcebook* (2nd ed.). Newbury Park, CA: Sage Publications.

Myers, M. D. (1997). Qualitative research in information systems. *Management Information Systems Quarterly*, *21*(2), 241–242. doi:10.2307/249422

Myers, M. D. (2013). Qualitative research in business and management. *Sage (Atlanta, Ga.)*.

Myers, M. D., & Avison, D. (1997). Qualitative research in information systems. *Management Information Systems Quarterly, 21*(2), 241–242. doi:10.2307/249422

Myers, M. D., & Avison, D. (2002). An introduction to qualitative research in information systems. *Qualitative Research in Information Systems, 4*, 3-12.

Myers, M. D., & Newman, M. (2007). The qualitative interview in IS research: Examining the craft. *Information and Organization, 17*(1), 2–26. doi:10.1016/j.infoandorg.2006.11.001

Orlikowski, W. J., & Baroudi, J. J. (1989). *IS research paradigms: method versus substance*. Academic Press.

Orlikowski, W. J., & Baroudi, J. J. (1991). Studying Information Technology in Organizations: Research Approaches and Assumptions. *Information Systems Research, 2*(1), 1–28. doi:10.1287/isre.2.1.1

Patton, M. Q. (1990). *Qualitative evaluation and research methods*. SAGE Publications, Inc.

Pollock, N., & Williams, R. (2008). *Software and organisations: The biography of the enterprise-wide system or how SAP conquered the world*. Routledge. doi:10.4324/9780203891940

Rubin, H. J., & Rubin, I. S. (2011). *Qualitative interviewing: The art of hearing data*. Sage Publications.

Scholz, R. W., & Tietje, O. (2002). Embedded case study methods. *Integrating Quantitative and Qualitative*.

Schweitzer, L., & Duxbury, L. (2010). Conceptualizing and measuring the virtuality of teams. *Information Systems Journal, 20*(3), 267–295. doi:10.1111/j.1365-2575.2009.00326.x

Walsham, G. (1993). *Interpreting information systems in organizations*. John Wiley & Sons, Inc.

Walsham, G. (1995). Interpretive case studies in IS research: Nature and method. *European Journal of Information Systems, 4*(2), 74–81. doi:10.1057/ejis.1995.9

Walsham, G. (2006). Doing interpretive research. *European Journal of Information Systems, 15*(3), 320–330. doi:10.1057/palgrave.ejis.3000589

Yin, R. K. (2009). *Case study research: Design and methods* (Vol. 5). Sage.

Yin, R. K. (2010). *Qualitative research from start to finish*. Guilford Press.

Chapter 16
Digitalising Healthcare in Developing Economies:
Challenges and Mitigating Strategies

Mansah Preko

Business School, University of Ghana, Ghana

Richard Osei-Boateng

37 Military Hospital, Ghana & Business School, University of Ghana, Ghana

Adekunle Ezekiel Durosinmi

Federal Medical Centre, Abeokuta, Nigeria

ABSTRACT

There is an increasing demand for the healthcare industry in developing economies to reform their existing fragmented paper-based systems to take advantage of the several opportunities that digitalisation brings. However, the existence of specific contextual factors constrains the process of digitalisation in most developing economies. Underpinned by the concepts of installed base and cultivation, this chapter adopts a qualitative multiple-case study approach to examine the contextual factors that influence the development, implementation, and adoption of digital health systems in the Ghanaian and Nigerian contexts. Results of this chapter reveal 13 key challenges and their corresponding mitigating strategies that were adopted in specific instances to facilitate digitalisation in both contexts. A comparison of findings for the two contexts is also discussed.

INTRODUCTION

There is an increased recognition that digital health systems and other health information technologies could better replace the traditional, fragmented paper-based health record systems in Developing Economies (DEs) (Mengiste, 2010). As a result, there has been an increasing demand by healthcare organisations to streamline their processes by adopting various kinds of digital innovations within the

DOI: 10.4018/978-1-7998-2610-1.ch016

health sectors of DEs. According to Fraser and Blaya (2010), some of the key factors that have accounted for the recent increase in adoption of these technologies include the availability of more robust, cheaper and lower power hardware/software; increased internet access and usage; and the emergence of several high-profile projects in most DEs. It is believed that the introduction of these digital innovations within the health sector could bring about significant cost reduction and improved efficiency and effectiveness, particularly, in the turnaround time for the delivery of healthcare services in DEs (Braa, Hanseth, Heywood, Mohammed, & Shaw, 2007). Other authors, including Kasemsap (2017), have even argued that the use of digital health systems in DEs has the potential to enhance healthcare performance and facilitate the achievement of strategic goals.

Despite the opportunities and benefits that digitalisation promises to the healthcare industry in DEs, its implementation is often fraught with context-sensitive challenges which inhibit its success (Mengiste, 2010). For instance, researchers (including Asare, Otoo-Arthur & Frimpong, 2017; O'Connor & O'Donoghue, 2015; Acheampong, 2012; etc.) have identified some of the underlying challenges that inhibit the successful digitalisation of healthcare services in DEs. Notable among them are the cultural, political, and cognitive factors (O'Connor & O'Donoghue, 2015), as well as other social factors which include the lack of commitment from staff, inadequate skills and knowledge at the local level to deploy new systems, and inconsistent power supplies (Adedeji, Irinoye, Ikono & Komolafe, 2018). Although some studies (e.g. Mengiste, 2010; Braa et al., 2007) have identified and proposed flexible strategies for mitigating IS implementation challenges within healthcare settings, we posit that research gaps still exist in specific localised contexts. In this chapter, we explore such challenges in the Ghanaian and Nigerian health sectors, which are both DEs with prospects of digitalising their health systems based on evidence observed in extant literature. Since context plays a role in Information Systems (IS) research (Hong, Chan, Thong, Chasalow & Dhillon, 2013), we argue that context-specific strategies would mitigate the underlying challenges, and facilitate digitalisation in these contexts, as well as other similar contexts.

This chapter, therefore, goes beyond mere factor lists of the challenges associated with digitalising the health sectors of DEs, to explore the different contextual challenges within localised settings, and the choices of actions that were adopted to mitigate such challenges. The chapter adopts the concepts of installed base and cultivation as its theoretical base to explore such factors within the Ghanaian and Nigerian contexts by addressing the main research questions: "What are the common and context-specific challenges that influence healthcare digitalisation in Developing Economies?" and "What context-specific strategies could be formulated and adopted to mitigate such challenges?". This chapter has both theoretical and practical implications for professionals, practitioners, and researchers on how specific strategies could be formulated to mitigate context-specific challenges that are associated with healthcare digitalisation in DEs.

The rest of the chapter is structured as follows: Section two presents a brief conceptualisation of digitalisation and its adoption within the health sectors of two DEs. Section three discusses the theoretical underpinning of the chapter. Section four presents the methodologies used. Section five presents the case descriptions and discussions of the chapter. Section six presents the implications of the study, as well as the conclusion and recommendations for future research.

LITERATURE REVIEW

Contextualising Digitalisation as a Socio-Technical Process

The sociotechnical concept is premised on the fact that all technologies are socially situated (Sawyer & Jarrahi, 2014). In Sawyer & Jarrahi's (2014) conceptualisation, they defined the sociotechnical concept as: "(1) the mutual constitution of people and technologies (and, specifically, digital technologies); (2) the contextual embeddedness of this mutuality; and, (3) the importance of their collective action". This conceptualisation posits that any Information System (IS) or IT artefact is embedded into a social context which both adapts to and helps to reshape social worlds through the course of their design, development, deployment and use. The materiality of such artefacts is therefore bound up with the historical and cultural aspects of their ongoing development and use; and these conditions, both material and cultural, cannot be ignored, abstracted, or assumed away. Hence, how people engage with various technological artefacts in the course of their work, communication, or in the process of educating themselves is a central theoretical concern in IS research (Orlikowski, 2000). However, adherents to this model of IS have paid relatively little attention to the environments of organisations and the temporal dimensions of technological innovations (Sawyer & Jarrahi, 2014).

In the context of IS healthcare research, several authors, have clarified the concept of digitalisation as a socio-technical process. For instance, Tilson, Lyytinen & Sorensen (2010) explained that, while 'digitisation' looks at the conversion of analogue data into digital data; digitalisation emphasises the change of socio-material structures such as new physical work arrangements, new work practices and routines, as well as new organisational and/or social structures. In another conceptualisation, Yoo, Lyytinen, Boland, & Berente (2010) clarified digitalisation as "the transformation of sociotechnical structures that were previously mediated by non-digital artefacts or relationships into ones that are mediated by digitised artefacts and relationships. Digitalisation, therefore, goes beyond a mere technical process of encoding diverse types of analogue information in digital format (i.e. digitisation), and involves organising new socio-technical structures with digitised artefacts, as well as the changes in the artefacts themselves". The foregoing conceptualisations clarify two main points: (1) the distinction between digitisation as a technical process, and digitalisation as a socio-technical process; (2) the concept of digitalisation which involves both material and social aspects. In this chapter, we adopt the conceptualisation of Mihailescu & Mihailescu (2018), which summarises digitisation as a technical requirement for digitalisation; and considers digitalisation as a form of technology-enabled social change.

Healthcare Digitalisation: The Ghanaian Context

Ghana is a developing economy with an estimated population of 27.41 million people as of 2015 (Gyamfi, Mensah, Oduro, Donkor & Mock, 2017). As an emerging economy, Ghana has demonstrated progress in getting most of its industries and sectors digitalised, including the healthcare industry. This is evidenced in how the country is developing routine Health Information Systems (HIS) in both government and district hospitals for collecting routine health information (Asare et al., 2017). Moreover, Ghana is consistently redesigning its healthcare system to include ICTs and its applications to improve care delivery and facilitate access to quality healthcare for its citizenry (Acquah-Swanzy, 2015).

The digitalisation of Ghana's healthcare services has often been guided by an eHealth strategy which was launched in 2010 by the Ministry of Health. Although the strategy was launched, the roll out was confronted with some challenges which made its implementation somewhat difficult. These challenges have been primarily attributed to the non-existence of policy guidelines for the implementation of Electronic Medical Record (EMR) systems and the sharing of data between hospitals and medical staff in Ghana (Acheampong, 2012). Besides, the country lacks regulatory bodies that monitor the progress and development of various e-health applications, which makes it even more difficult to achieve interoperability. The Ghanaian health sector, in general, suffers a shortage of skilled ICT personnel who can deliver large-scale e-health projects (Asare et al., 2017).

Despite the foregoing, however, Preko, Boateng & Effah (2019b) identified a number of factors that are shaping the healthcare industry in Ghana while supporting digitalisation. Notable among them is the introduction of electronic payment systems through visa platforms at various health facilities, and the use of mobile money wallets and transfers. The authors further identified the various collaborations between different state institutions including the Telecommunication, Banking, and Healthcare industries, which have enabled seamless transfers of funds within the respective institutions while providing a basis for digitalisation in the health sector. Again, the increasing use of smartphones and other digital technologies which support data and information sharing across various healthcare platforms were identified as shaping digitalisation in the health sector (Preko, et al., 2019b). Currently, the Ministry of Health (MOH) is piloting the use of drones for delivering healthcare in Ghana. These emerging and interesting developments in the Ghanaian context, amid the challenges, accounts for Ghana's inclusion in this study to present insights into the theme of the chapter.

Healthcare Digitalisation: The Nigerian Context

Nigeria is a developing economy with an estimated population of over 196 million people, constituting about 2.6% of the world's total population (National Population Commission, 2017). Despite several assertions of Nigeria's lack of a nationwide eHealth strategic framework for delivering effective healthcare (Adedeji et al., 2018), the country continues to witness the increasing advocacy by individuals and other state agencies to digitalise healthcare processes (Adeleke, Erinle, Ndana, Anamah, Ogundele & Aliyu, 2014). In view of that, the Nigerian government has taken steps to develop strategies over the years to provide effective National Health Management Information System (NHMIS) to be used as a decision-making tool at all levels, to improve patient care. Pursuant to the above, the Nigerian government also recognised the need for harmonising patients' health information through the use of Health Information Technologies (HIT). This harmonisation led to the review of the country's eHealth strategies, which included among others, HIT components of existing systems; proposals for strategies to establish interoperability standards; and capacity building within the health sector.

Despite attempts by the Nigerian government to digitalise healthcare services, Adedeji et al. (2018) noted that EMRs are being under-utilised in most tertiary healthcare institutions in Nigeria. In the authors' view, these systems and technologies have become 'status symbols' in some facilities due to the varying conflicting interests of the different stakeholders. Other authors, including Idowu, Cornford & Bastin (2008) have also identified specific factors that inhibit digitalisation of the Nigerian health sector. The factors, which were discovered through personal experiences and observations from the Nigerian context included: (1) The inconsistent power supply which causes damage to ICT equipment; (2) Government's attitude of not supporting the full use of ICT in healthcare delivery; (3) High cost of ICT peripherals in Nigeria; (4) Inadequate landline systems to support telephone and intranet connectivity within healthcare facilities; (5) High cost of fibre optics and internet bandwidth in Nigeria; (6) Resistance to new technologies on the part of hospital staff; and (7) Lack of maintenance culture on the part of individuals and state agencies. According to Idowu et al. (2008), these identified challenges had some sociotechnical underpinnings, which could be attributed to the people, the government and the ICT infrastructure. Other assessments by Adedeji et al. (2018) also revealed similar sociotechnical factors. The Nigerian context was, however, selected as one of the cases to represent DEs in this chapter because, despite the numerous challenges highlighted in literature, there are still efforts by the Nigerian government to digitalise its health sector. This usually represents the case for most DEs, and could, therefore, pass for using its findings to make some generalisations in other DE contexts.

THEORETICAL FRAMEWORK

This chapter adopts the concepts of installed base and cultivation, which emanated from the Information Infrastructure Theory (Hanseth, Monteiro & Hatling, 1996) as its theoretical base. The concepts of installed base and cultivation are used as a set of analytical tools for exploring socio-technical processes within different contexts, where large-scale and complex information systems are being introduced (Mengiste, 2010). Unlike traditional IS design approaches which treated system development as an activity that needed to be developed from scratch, contemporary IS approaches conceive it as dynamic events which change over time through on-going processes (Orlikowski, 1996). Hanseth et al. (1996) explain these contemporary design approaches, and change, as 'Information Infrastructure'.

The information infrastructure perspective, therefore, analyses systems as heterogenous inter-connected socio-technical networks (Hanseth and Monteiro, 1998). According to Mengiste (2010), the recent conceptualisation of viewing information systems as information infrastructure is as a result of the increasing complexities (from both social and technical perspectives) that are involved in the IS development and implementation processes. Considering these, some authors have explained the process of introducing new technologies and other standard work practices as an incremental process. For instance, Hanseth (2002) noted that:

The whole infrastructure cannot be changed instantly – the new has to be connected to the old. The new version of the infrastructure or artefact must be designed in a way making the old and the new linked together and interoperable in one way or another. In this way, the old, i.e. the installed base, heavily influence how the new can be designed (no page).

From the author's perspective, the processes involved in introducing change to large, and complex information systems require careful analysis and assessment of the installed base which encompasses all socio-technical entities (including work practices, standards, existing technologies, organisational commitment, etc.) (Hanseth, 2002). In the context of healthcare, for instance, Aanestad, Grisot, Hanseth & Vassilakopoulou (2017) emphasised that IT systems that are implemented in healthcare settings are usually complex projects that are intended to connect multiple sites. Hence, they usually consist of information infrastructure that may include multiple actors who have different needs and interests. In such instances, an information infrastructure may only work if some working resolutions are found between the multiple local interests and the over-arching interests of the network.

The Concept of Installed Base

The concept of the installed base refers to the existing (technical and non-technical) systems, which includes standards, work practices, routines, human resources, organisational structures, various software versions, physical and digital infrastructure, etc. (Mengiste, 2010). This concept, therefore, posits that any process in the development and implementation of an information infrastructure cannot be started from scratch; instead, the already existing systems, standards, processes, and procedures must be considered as new changes are introduced. Accordingly, projects for the creation of large-scale health information infrastructures are also shaped by the existing installed base, i.e., the organisational, institutional, regulatory, and sociotechnical arrangements that are already in place (Aanestad et al., 2017). In that way, the installed base shapes and influences the implementation of the new system (Hanseth, 2002). However, due to the degree of embeddedness of the installed base, change does not occur instantly, since the perceived change can heavily influence the design of the new information infrastructure (Hanseth & Monteiro, 1998). Thus, any changes to the installed base must be linked as extensions, revisions, or replacement.

The Concept of Cultivation

With the concept of cultivation, the design and implementation of an information infrastructure are considered as a long-term incremental strategy which extends and develops upon an existing installed base, rather than the radical change of the installed base itself (Hanseth &Monteiro, 1997). With the cultivation approach, an information infrastructure is never developed from scratch in principle. However, it draws much attention to the existing conditions and systems as part of the reality, which causes the cultivator, unlike the designer, to know when and how to intervene by changing existing systems, structures, and work practices (Mengiste, 2010). Thus, the cultivation approach also requires a prior analysis of the components of the installed base such as organisational, technological, social and political contexts.

METHODOLOGY

Research Approach and Methods

The chapter adopted a qualitative research approach which is based on the interpretative research tradition (Walsham, 1993). The approach was found to be more appropriate since it seeks to present an understanding of the complex social, technological and organisational issues that are related to the development, customisation, and implementation of information systems in different contexts (Mengiste, 2010). As noted by Walsham (1993), interpretative research is "aimed at producing an understanding of the context of the information system, and the process whereby the information system influences and is influenced by the context (Walsham 1993, pp. 4-5). In line with these, case studies were conducted in selected healthcare facilities within the Ghanaian and Nigerian contexts. The selections were based on facilities which had implemented digital health technologies to digitalise their healthcare processes. Again, multiple case studies were found to more appropriate for this study since it ensures in-depth exploration of a phenomenon (Yin, 2009). This chapter is, therefore, based on six hospitals in total (i.e., three from each context).

Data Collection

The empirical data presented here was collected over a period of two months. This included personal experiences from a hospital Chief Information Officer (CIO) who is also a co-author of this chapter. The CIO oversaw an EMR implementation project in a government hospital in Ghana, and also participated in conducting situational analysis, software customisation, and capacity building activities of the hospital since 2018. The other co-author from the Nigerian context has also been working in a healthcare facility in Abeokuta, Ogun State, over the past twelve years, and also doubles as a computer scientist. This co-author presented deep insights into the study by sharing his personal experiences over the period on similar digitalisation projects in Nigeria. Apart from the knowledge and experiences shared by the co-authors, who also happen to be practitioners in the health sector, other empirical data was used for this chapter. These were collected through interviews, observations, and field-generated documents (Easton, 2010). Semi-structured interviews with open-ended questions were conducted with managers of EMR systems, as well as development and implementation team members. A total of thirty-eight participants were interviewed from six major hospitals, with three from each context.

Data Analysis

The qualitative data was analysed based on an interpretive field research approach (Klein & Myers, 1999). This method of case study analysis allows for iteration between data collection and analysis while leveraging researchers' knowledge of existing relevant literature (Yin, 2009). The data analysis uncovered key themes, insights, and relationships to the underpinning theory, which also provided insights to further explain the phenomenon (Miles & Huberman, 1994; George & Kohnke, 2018). The analysis was conducted using the tools of interpretive case study analysis and the constant comparative method (Walsham, 1993). The key themes were grouped into "general" and "context-specific" challenges, as well as their corresponding mitigating strategies. The constant comparative method was subsequently employed to compare findings for the two contexts.

RESULTS AND DISCUSSION

Summary of Study Results

In this chapter, we identified thirteen key challenges that constrain healthcare digitalisation in DEs. Two major research questions: (1) "what are the common and context-specific challenges that influence healthcare digitalisation in developing economies?" and (2) "what context-specific strategies could be formulated and adopted to mitigate such challenges?" were asked to generate insights for the successful digitalisation of healthcare services in DEs. In answering the first research question, the data was juxtaposed against extant literature, to identify common challenges that are associated with healthcare digitalisation in general. This consequently presented an opportunity to identify challenges that were found to be context-specific. The tables below summarise the themes of common and context-specific challenges that were identified, as well as their corresponding mitigating strategies. The subsequent sections discuss these challenges in detail while emphasising the mitigating strategies that were adopted in each case.

Table 1: Common challenges and their corresponding mitigating strategies

Common Challenges	Mitigating Strategies
Funding – i.e. Initial cost of Purchase of EMR systems and the cost of maintenance (e.g. Mapesa, 2016; Mason et al., 2017; Gyamfi et al., 2017; Warren, 2017; Bedeley & Palvia, 2014; Brooks & Grotz, 2010; etc.)	• Negotiations with vendors to supply equipment on lease and make payments over time. • Competitive bidding through a tender process • Incremental delivery • Building partnerships through development partner support
Infrastructural challenges – including network connectivity and electricity instability (e.g. Gyamfi et al., 2017; Bedeley & Palvia, 2014; Mengiste, 2010, Mapesa, 2016; Idowu et al., 2008; Adedeji et al., 2018; etc.)	• Investment in appropriate network infrastructure (e.g. fibre optic cables and switches) to support equipment. • Procurement of generators to ensure constant electricity supply to servers and other IT infrastructure. • Investment in additional servers to work concurrently to reduce system downtimes. • Investment in healthcare facilities that are preped to receive future automation.
User acceptance/resistance (e.g. Mapesa, 2016; Warren, 2017; Idowu et al., 2008; etc.)	• Conscientisation • Motivation • Stakeholder involvement • Customisation • Incremental delivery through patches • Change management strategies
Change Management (e.g. Sidek & Martins, 2017; Warren, 2017; Mapesa, 2016; etc.)	• Conscientisation of staff • Consistent training and capacity building • Human Resource Policies
Product and Vendor Selection (e.g. Warren, 2017; Brooks & Grotz, 2010; Mapesa, 2016; etc.)	• Selection of products that are in line with the business processes of the respective facilities. • Tendering and bidding procedures which required product demonstrations. • Setting up implementation teams • Stakeholder involvement
Complexity of EMR systems (e.g. Mason et al., 2017; Brooks & Grotz, 2010; etc.)	• Vendor/product selection • Training • Stakeholder involvement • Customisation • Incremental delivery of patches
Systems and Strategy Alignment (e.g. Warren, 2017)	• Policy formulation
Security and Privacy Issues (e.g. Gyamfi et al., 2017; Mapesa, 2016; etc.)	• Conscientisation • Training • Password management • Policy formulation
Human Resource Constraints (e.g. Gyamfi et al., 2017; Mengiste, 2010; Bedeley & Palvia etc.)	• Recruitment of health IT professionals to help manage the EMR system • Capacity building

Detailed Discussion of Results: Major Challenges and Mitigating Strategies

Funding

"EMR implementations cost millions of dollars for large hospitals. The costs are not limited to hardware and software. One needs to plan for consulting, training, add-on software, and other related expenses" (Brooks and Grotz, 2010). These assertions were confirmed throughout the interview process. Responses gathered revealed that all the hospitals under study that sought to digitalise their processes were confronted

Table 2: Context-specific challenges and their corresponding mitigating strategies

Context-Specific Challenges	Mitigating Strategies
Data Migration issues	Reliance on vendors and other IT experts to help understand data and support a smooth migration
Computer literacy of staff (Technophobia)	• Consistent training • IT support
Lackadaisical attitude of staff - i.e. staff not getting interested because of past experiences of failed EMRs.	• Stakeholder involvement • Rolling out systems as planned and users getting interested with time
Browser Optimisation	System redesign by vendors to accommodate different browser platforms

with this initial challenge of huge costs of investments. Some respondents also revealed the high cost of maintenance, which included the development of other sub-systems to support their hospitals' operations. In their views, these separate expenditures had serious financial implications on their respective organisations. A CIO confirmed that:

Going digital is very expensive, it runs into millions of dollars. The hospital has to be really ready for such investments before they stick out their neck

Similar responses gathered from other participants also revealed how the initial cost of purchase and the cost of maintenance was such a big deal to the healthcare facilities.

Mitigating Strategies

To overcome this challenge, some of the hospitals had written agreements and negotiations with their respective vendors to supply the digital technologies on lease so they could make payments over time. This strategy seemed to be dominant among other strategies which sought to either select vendors based on the lowest price of a system or agreeing on the purchase of the initial system and then have vendors develop other systems to support it, in order to spread the payment. These principles were in line with the theoretical underpinning of this chapter since the concept of cultivation was applied in some sense. Other CIOs also adopted a strategy of agreeing with software vendors on an initial payment for development of the software and subsequently negotiated a good maintenance agreement after the full implementation. According to one CIO:

We made an initial payment to the vendor to aid the development of the software and its implementation, and also negotiated for a monthly maintenance agreement payment to the vendor after full implementation.

Infrastructural Challenges

Several studies (e.g. Bedeley & Palvia, 2014; Gyamfi et al., 2017; Mengiste, 2010, Mapesa, 2016; etc.) have revealed that infrastructural challenges constitute one of the major roadblocks for digitalisation in DEs. These assertions were confirmed in all the healthcare facilities under study as they indicated that the various infrastructure that were lacking impeded the smooth digitalisation process. Commonly named infrastructural barriers included internet and network connectivity, as well as inconsistent power supply. As indicated by Idowu et al. (2008), any country which has difficulty in providing Uninterrupted Power Supply (UPS) to its citizens will obviously have challenges in deploying ICTs. Other assertions on connectivity also confirmed Mapesa's (2016) study which suggested that network connectivity continues to remain a challenge in DEs because of the high costs of bandwidth. Some of the responses included:

Distribution Network Expansion Planning (DNEP) with Electronic Medical Records has some network reliability issues. With simultaneous switch placement and cables (CAT6 and Fibre), reliability issues in the planning stage were fundamental to guarantee suitable and sustainable performance from the viewpoint of system reliability.

Mitigating Strategies

In order to overcome this challenge, the various hospitals adapted various strategies to upgrade and expand their networks to all departments of their organisations. According to one CIO;

The fibre optic network, which is the backbone of the LAN infrastructure, needed to be upgraded and expanded to all departments. This was necessary in order to increase the speed of the network from 10/100Mbps to 100/1000Mbps.

In the case of inconsistent power supply, most of the facilities indicated that they had to invest in generators to ensure consistent power supply. Industrial UPSs have also been installed in some instances to keep the servers up constantly. Respondents also revealed their investments into backup servers, which were running simultaneously in the background to reduce system downtimes.

User Acceptance/Resistance

EMR systems are complex and inherently subject to sociological resistance to acceptance (Vessey & Ward, 2013). CIOs are, therefore, expected to understand both the internal and external issues that contribute to the opposition of new systems (Warren, 2017) before any changes to the installed base are made. The findings of this study revealed that user resistance was one of the significant barriers to EMR implementations. These findings were in line with the findings of other studies (e.g. Mapesa, 2016; Warren, 2017), which indicated similar reasons for user resistance in healthcare settings. Notable among these reasons included lack of computer literacy, fear of losing jobs, and fear of the unknown. Other staff were also not comfortable with the implementation of the EMRs due to their minimal knowledge on the information benefits that their organisations stood to gain with the new system. In the case of some caregivers (i.e. physicians and nurses) for instance, they felt the new system would cause delays in their workflows due to the time required in the data capturing process; which they consequently perceived as an added responsibility and an increase in workload. A medical officer said:

If I have to see all my patients on the system, then it is going to take forever for me to end my clinic, especially when the network may not be too reliable

Mitigating Strategies

In overcoming this challenge, the respective health facilities adapted various strategies which included conscientisation of staff on the potential information benefits that the hospitals stood to gain with the introduction of the new system. In some cases, staff were motivated to use the new system by allaying their fears and also making them realise the seamless information sharing capabilities that the new digital technologies have to offer. In other instances, user groups and implementation teams were set up from various departments to share views, challenges and opportunities of the new technologies. In most of the respondents' views, these groups were purposely created to give a sense of partnership among staff, nurses, and doctors. The user groups and implementation teams also assisted other staff members who needed assistance with the use of the system. In some instances, the teams helped the vendors in customising the systems to suit specific processes of the hospitals. In other instances, some modules which were needed for a smoother operation of the systems were developed based on stakeholders' recommendations and were integrated as patches to the central system. Finally, most of the respondents indicated that they had developed change management strategies for improving user acceptance of the system. This was done by identifying obstacles that could potentially inhibit users from accepting the new technologies which subsequently informed the development of various specific strategies, including the preceding to avert those challenges. In a user's view,

Various stakeholder engagements were arranged between the vendor, implementers and users to seek the views and opinions of users before full implementation. Lots of inputs were made by users, and the vendor used those inputs to redesign and customise the system.

Change Management

Change is one of the greatest fears of people, and therefore, requires patience and an open mind to implement change since it is not readily accepted (Brooks and Grotz, 2010). According to Hanseth & Monteiro (1998), change does not occur instantly in the design of new information infrastructure due to the degree of embeddedness of the installed base. Change management is, therefore, one of the critical factors to consider for the successful deployment of any new system due to the human components involved in the implementation and use of new technologies. Change management includes a set of activities, tools and techniques that are implemented to ensure that a new system achieves the required project outcomes (Sidek & Martins, 2017). Respondents admitted to such expectations of resistance to change and acceptance of the new technologies. Some respondents indicated that there were issues with users' reception of the new systems. For instance, one CIO noted that:

Due to the change from the manual processes to the automated EMR system, there were issues with users' reception of the system. Some employees feared to lose their jobs or feared being transferred. This called for extensive sensitisation about the benefits of the new system to the facility, the users and ultimately to their clientele.

Mitigating Strategies

Insights from the interviews revealed that participants from the different healthcare facilities identified various factors, which they considered particularly influential, in the design of change management interventions. These included the following: (1) Sensitisation of staff on the potential benefits of EMR systems to users, respective organisations and their clientele; (2) Awareness of the risks posed by technophobia; (3) Organisation of various training sessions and the setting up of various support teams to minimise the effects of technophobia; (4) Continuous improvements to the system through incremental delivery of patches, as well as other customised implementation strategies. Although some respondents admitted that no formalised plans were drawn with specified strategies for implementing change management in their respective facilities, they adopted these strategies independently to help them tackle both the human and organisational aspects of the system implementations.

Product and Vendor Selection

The integration of health information technologies usually requires thoughtful designs and careful structuring to facilitate a variety of uses as well as users (Silverman, 2013). However, the selection of an appropriate IT vendor continues to be one of the major challenges for most CIOs (Warren 2017). This is because, before the selection and adoption of an EMR technology, managers and CIOs have an obligation to consider a myriad of issues which may include interoperability, customer accessibility, financial requirements, internal business processes, as well as the means for training and learning, among others. Eastaugh (2013) however, cautions that, in considering the myriad of factors for the selection of a product/vendor, cost should not be the only basis for a final decision. Even though not all respondents alluded to the selection of product and vendor as one of the critical factors that could pose a challenge to the successful implementation of their EMRs, those who did actually believed that an appropriate choice of these two impacted the successful digitalisation of their facilities. For instance, some respondents indicated the following:

I had to look at different systems from different vendors before shortlisting a few to present to management and key stakeholders for a choice to be made, one CIO said.

Mitigating Strategies

In this study, we noted that most of the respondents admitted to the fact that the appropriate selection of products and vendors were one of the major decisions or strategies that aided the successful implementation of their EMRs. These assertions were attributed to the fact that the selected products were in line with the business processes of the respective healthcare facilities. This made it easier for them to quickly integrate the old processes with the new technologies. Again, most of the respondents indicated the combination of the product quality and cost were paramount in the selection of products and vendors. These were done through competitive bidding processes in each case, which also required product demonstrations and plans to support the respective facilities during and after system implementations. Most respondents, however, selected vendors based on product quality, ease of use, interoperability, organisational culture fit, etc. other than selection based on pricing alone. Some facilities also set up implementation teams at various levels to assist in the selection of an appropriate vendor since they had insights into what their business processes were. Some respondents indicated that stakeholder involvement in the product selection contributed a great deal to the success of their implementations.

Complexity of EMR Systems

Mason et al. (2017) noted that the emerging health information technologies have given rise to complexity, dynamism, uncertainty, and unpredictability. This assertion was evident in our study as most of the respondents alluded to the fact that they were not comfortable with the newly implemented technologies due to their level of complexity. In some facilities, for instance, this challenge was noted as a result of failure on the part of the respective facilities to follow the cultivation approach in implementing the new technologies. Thus, the radical change of their installed base caused some staff to develop impressions about the complexity of the implemented systems. This challenge also dovetailed into several other challenges, including user resistance, technology acceptance, and the lackadaisical attitude of staff, which needed to be dealt with.

Mitigating Strategies

As part of mitigating the challenge of system complexities, most of the respondents indicated that they adopted the strategy of stakeholder involvement during the selection of product and vendors for their respective facilities. Stakeholder engagement and involvement emerged as the dominant theme as all participants indicated that it was a critical success factor and a game changer in the whole implementation process. This included solution mapping, awareness and training, through to system selection and continued engagement during use (Warren, 2017). In addition to stakeholder engagements, training also played a significant role in diffusing the impressions of participants about the level of complexity of the implemented systems. According to Mapesa (2016), training provides an opportunity for individuals to first come into contact with any system and learn how to use it. Computer-aided training was therefore provided by vendors and their contractors in the respective facilities to allow participants to benefit from the EMR systems fully. Some facilities also resorted to the customisation of their systems in order to reduce the levels of complexities involved in accomplishing a task, while others adopted the concept of cultivation by building on the implemented systems with patches. For most respondents, the transition from the manual system to the digitised one was characterised by breaking down the complex processes to simpler ones to suit user preferences. Data was gathered from users on the complexity of the systems and what improvements or changes they required. These were acted on swiftly, and the system redesigned to suit user preferences. Some respondents indicated that:

A lot was gained after initial training of staff since most of them became very comfortable with the system after practising on it for the first time. Inputs were also made by users, making them feel a part of the systems' development.

Systems and Strategy Alignment

Vessy & Ward (2013) explained that both internal pressures of healthcare organisations such as financial and social acceptance of technology, and the external pressures from entities such as government, vendors, and competitors affect IT and strategic organisational alignment processes. This was confirmed by participants' responses, which revealed that the alignment of their organisational strategies and their EMR implementations were part of the challenges they needed to overcome to ensure successful digitalisation. Other respondents also identified the strategic alignment of systems, structure and culture with the design of the new digital technologies as one of their significant challenges. This is because every hospital is unique; in terms of size, areas of specialisation, organisational culture, structural designs, geographical location, etc. However, these attributes are expected to align with the newly implemented technologies in each case, since what works for one hospital may not necessarily work for the other (Warren, 2017). Some responses included:

We had to tweak the system to fit our needs, and this took a lot of time and effort since the military hospital does things differently from other hospitals.

Mitigating Strategies

Eastaugh (2013) emphasises the need for healthcare organisations to integrate their organisational strategy with information systems strategy as a way of achieving success with EMR implementations. Responses gathered confirmed this assertion and revealed that one of the mitigating strategies that were adopted by some of the healthcare facilities to achieve success was by developing strategies that integrated their IT infrastructure with the operational processes of the respective hospitals. Silvius & Stoop (2013) further explains that successful IT implementations are usually achieved through the cognitive ability to identify obstacles and develop strategies to avert resistance to acceptance. This assertion in literature was also confirmed in this study by respondents who indicated that the development of policies and the alignment of strategies enabled them to overcome the challenge of user resistance and technology acceptance in their respective facilities. In their views, these policies were formulated to pre-empt the anticipated challenges of user resistance to the technologies. Again, the alignment of systems was one of the common ways most CIOs adopted in dealing with their vendors' prototypes and proof of concepts. A CIO indicated that:

A policy document was developed over five months to help align EMR objectives to the hospital's strategy and also to ensure continuity and sustenance of the system.

Security and Privacy Issues

Brooks and Grotz (2010) noted that while medical privacy may be favourable for consumers of healthcare, it does not always allow for quick implementation of EMR systems. For instance, the authors confirmed how privacy laws are presenting themselves as bottlenecks for hospitals in their bid to exchange information beyond their organisational borders. This assertion was also confirmed by Gyamfi et al. (2017) in a Ghanaian context study which reveals that after the hospital under study expands beyond its organisational borders; the law would require that it goes to parliament for approval before data sharing across platforms would be approved and legalised. These legislative issues seemed to be a challenge to most of the respondents in this study since they indicated that there were no clear policy guidelines for data sharing in the health sector of the DEs under study. Apart from the legislative issues, it was further noted that the issue of confidentiality with regard to patient information also posed as one of the privacy challenges. This was because patients' information could be viewed and used remotely. Hence, the facilities had to ensure that the confidentiality of patients' records were preserved at all times. One respondent explained that:

In the face of rising medico-legal issues, privacy and confidentiality were key in the implementation of an EMR system. There is, therefore, the need to formulate policies that will safeguard the use and access to patient information on the electronic system.

Mitigating Strategies

From the privacy and security challenges identified by respondents, we noted that some mitigating strategies were adopted, nonetheless, to ensure successful digitalisation. For instance, some respondents indicated that although their country did not have clear legislative and policy guidelines for data transfer within the health sector, the hospital itself had some policies guiding the use and transfer of patient information. Other respondents indicated that their staff were sensitised extensively about the implications of privacy breaches in EMR systems. Some respondents also explained that they adopted training as part of their strategies to help sensitise staff on how to protect personal and patient information. This led to the adoption of password management for staff, which required them to change their passwords after a certain period automatically. A respondent indicated that:

A policy implementation committee was set up to develop standard operating procedures to guide the use of the EMR system and also to determine issues of access and protection of patients' information and usage and protection of passwords.

Human Resource Constraints

EMR implementations usually present opportunities for creating jobs which, in turn, has an overall positive impact on society. Brooks and Grotz (2010) note that the jobs created include healthcare workers turned into health information technology workers or IT workers trained to be knowledgeable in the medical field. These work adjustments, according to Brooks and Grotz (2010), usually affect implementation time for training, and in some cases, may lead to several mistakes than acceptable if proper training is not done. These assertions were confirmed in this study as participants attested to the changing work roles of some healthcare and IT professionals respectively to fill specific gaps in their facilities. These arrangements came about in some instances, as a result of a dual skill set that was required to fill certain gaps and positions in the healthcare facility. Other respondents also indicated the real need of ICT professionals who have the skill set to perform on the job and train others as well. In some instances, respondents emphasised on the lack of monitoring on the part of managers to ensure that the right things are done bearing in mind that change was a difficult process.

Mitigating Strategies

To mitigate the challenge of human resources, some facilities resorted to the recruitment of competent personnel in the various fields of specialisation, including healthcare and IT respectively, to increase staffing levels to support the new system. Other facilities also acknowledged the versatility of Health Informatics (HI) professionals. These respondents indicated that professionals from the HI field usually have a general understanding of both healthcare and IT domains. Hence, it was easier for them to fit into healthcare settings and perform various health IT roles. In the case of staff monitoring, line managers were actively involved at every stage of the implementation process to ensure that their staff were also involved and were doing the right thing. The active involvement of line managers also served as a form of motivation to some staff members to give off their best since a positive attitude towards the use of the system was a function of its success. Some responses included:

We chose a pharmacist with knowledge in IT to lead the implementation process since he understands the vendor language as well as the language of the users. This made for an easy and smooth implementation process.

Data Migration Issues

Data migration processes include all tasks related to the extraction from a source system, cleaning, transforming, validating, and loading data in a destination system. Most of the respondents revealed that moving data from the existing storage to the new system was fraught with various challenges such as data fragmentation, lack of knowledge of data source, differences in data types and fields, data integration problems, etc. These challenges constrained the ease of migrating data from their paper-based and legacy systems onto the new digital technologies.

Mitigating Strategies

To avert the challenges of data migration, most of the facilities had to depend on the expertise of vendors and other data experts to help with the migration process. In the respondents' views, this was necessary due to the high sensitivity of health records, which could not be compromised at any point during migration. Some respondents indicated that, although it called for extra expenditure, it was worth it since the hospital could not afford the consequences of distorted data. Some responses included:

The data was very complex, so we had to engage experts to help in understanding and migrating the data on to the new systems.

Computer Literacy of Staff: Technophobia

Technophobia, the fear or dislike of advanced technology or sophisticated devices, especially computer systems, was observed by most CIOs in their respective facilities. Some of the responses indicated that users who were not technology inclined were unwilling to receive the new system due to the fear of getting things done wrongly in the system or causing damage to it. The issue of technophobia was an essential factor to consider for a successful digitalisation since it was not only a barrier but a source of fear and apprehension which could consequently dovetail into user resistance and technology acceptance (Mapesa, 2016).

Mitigating Strategies

Phichitchaisopa & Naenna (2013) noted that allaying stakeholder fears is very critical to reducing user resistance and influencing user acceptance. In view of this, respondents revealed how this challenge called for extensive conscientization and education on how to perform basic computer tasks and how to use the EMR systems. In their views, the basic training was necessary because users' perceptions of the ease of use of the EMR was a significant factor for user acceptance and successful digitalisation. Some responses included:

We organised basic computer training for staff who had not used computers before to help allay their fears and make them comfortable to use the new systems.

Lackadaisical Attitudes of Staff

The study revealed that some of the medical facilities under study had users who did not seem to be interested in the ongoing implementation due to their past experiences with other failed EMR systems in the same facilities. According to the respondents of such facilities, the lackadaisical attitudes of users posed a severe threat to the successful implementation of their new system since these users sought to instigate other users not to get interested as well. One CIO noted that:

Such negative influence on others with the assumption that this new system will eventually fail was something that we really had to do deal with as a hospital.

Mitigating Strategies

The affected healthcare facilities adopted stakeholder involvement as one of their mitigating strategies. According to the respondents, bringing major stakeholders from the various levels on board from the vendor selection process, through implementation and training gives them a sense of appreciation of the new system. Other respondents also indicated that they had to roll out the systems as planned, and still followed the implementation schedule without relenting on anything. This got users interested with time when they realised the system was gaining grounds in terms of use. Some responses included:

Once the users realised that there was no turning back, they had to get involved before they could be rendered redundant.

Browser Optimisation

Respondents revealed that at the time of implementation, the existing browsers like Microsoft Edge, Internet Explorer and Firefox were not very compatible with the EMR system. Some features of the new system were not available with such browsers. However, MS Explorer was the only browser that worked best with the system, and that was with very limiting user options.

Mitigating Strategies

In mitigating this challenge, respondents of this unique challenge indicated that their vendors had to optimise the solution to accept other browsers like Firefox, Google Chrome, Safari etc. In some instances, Google Chrome had to be installed on all devices in the facility, which was both tedious and time-consuming. According to CIO of this facility;

The developer was urged to expand operability to other browser platforms, and this was done successfully.

Comparison of Findings for the Two Contexts

A comparison of findings for the two contexts was made based on the responses gathered through interviews, personal experiences of authors, and field generated data, using the constant comparative method by Walsham (1993). The comparison revealed several similarities in the challenges discussed above for both contexts. A few differences, however, emerged in responses relating to the infrastructural challenges in the respective contexts. The Nigerian context, for instance, revealed much emphasis on the infrastructural challenges as a result of the peculiar power problems in the country. This observation was not surprising to know since a number of similar studies (including Idowu et al., 2008; Adedeji et al., 2018) had identified "epileptic power supply" as the major underpinning challenge for ICT usage in Nigeria. Although some facilities reported similarly in the Ghanaian context, the emphasis on power, especially, was more from the Nigerian context than the Ghanaian context.

Further analysis revealed that the cost of ICT peripherals in Nigeria was also much higher than that of Ghana. This analysis was done by simply comparing prices of ICT peripherals against the standard of living among citizens in the respective countries. The analysis of the comparison confirmed the assertion of Adedeji et al. (2018), which revealed that the high costs of hardware and software in Nigeria, compared with the income of the average Nigerian, makes it difficult for most individuals and even government agencies to purchase ICTs. This same trend was observed in the general space of the Nigerian health sector, based on the responses gathered for this study.

In terms of human resource constraints, the Ghanaian context revealed some weaknesses in the area of human capacity in the health IT profession, compared to the Nigerian context. These observations were made based on the data gathered and the analysis thereof. Again, it was not surprising to note this weakness in the Ghanaian context because, Asare et al. (2017) had revealed similar findings in extant literature. Additionally, the challenge of browser optimisation was found to be a peculiar challenge in just one healthcare facility in the Ghanaian context, as no such responses were gathered from the rest of the facilities under study.

IMPLICATIONS OF THE STUDY FINDINGS

The findings of this chapter provide insights into the alternative strategies that could be adopted by information managers to achieve successful EMR implementations in DEs. These strategies, if adopted, could also lead to improved patient care and reduced healthcare costs. Additionally, the chapter contributes to social change by providing strategies and ideas for overcoming resistance to technological innovations. Further, the findings of this chapter may present a basis for changing the narrative in literature about the number of failed IS projects in DEs, and especially, in the health sector, by providing a potential for improving the overall percentage of successful EMR implementation across DEs.

Conclusion and Recommendation

This chapter sought to identify the challenges that are associated with digitalising healthcare in developing economies and the mitigating strategies that were adopted in each case to achieve success. Findings from this study reveal that multiple strategies can be adopted for each respective challenge, and at each phase of the digitalisation process. According to Hung, Chen, & Wang (2014), the healthcare setting is a very complex one; as such, CIOs within these contexts should be made to understand that successful digitalisation is mostly dependent on a number of factors including the organisational fit of the vendor, the technologies involved, as well as the end users of the system. Hence, focusing on just one factor, for instance, the technology, at the expense of the social system (i.e., users and the organisation) or vice versa could result in a total system failure. In view of this, it was observed from the findings of this study that, several sociotechnical strategies, including general and context-specific strategies, were adopted by the various healthcare facilities under study to mitigate those challenges.

One of the key findings of this study was that, although most of the participants knew what challenges to expect, and their anticipated mitigating strategies and ideas, most of them (representing their respective hospitals) had no formalised implementation plans for their systems. Hence, challenges were mitigated as and when they were identified and in some instances, without any formal plan to guide the process. This observation presents a basis for recommendations to be made to CIOs who wish to achieve the highest success wish EMR implementations. This chapter, therefore, concurs with Brooks & Grotz (2010) which concludes that "EMRs need to be implemented with common sense. Using common sense to implement an EMR system will conclude in success for the stakeholders of electronic medical records".

FUTURE RESEARCH

Due to the limitations of this chapter which did not allow the authors to capture evidence from all DE contexts, ongoing and future research is expected to carry out further investigations into other challenges that have not been identified and discussed in this chapter, especially, challenges that are peculiar to specific contexts within DEs. Doing so may present a broader perspective of the challenges that could be expected by CIOs and Health IT managers in DEs contexts when pursuing digitalisation in the health sector. Future research could also build on the foundations of this study to identify alternative strategies (including both social and technical solutions) that could be adopted by healthcare organisations to achieve successful digitalisation. Again, further studies could focus on juxtaposing the findings of this chapter with similar studies from the developed economies' perspective. This would present a holistic view of the challenges associated with the digitalisation of healthcare in general, and also present a basis for achieving successful implementations of IS in the healthcare industry.

REFERENCES

Aanestad, M., Grisot, M., Hanseth, O., & Vassilakopoulou, P. (2017). *Information Infrastructures Within European Health Care: Working with the Installed Base*. Cham, Switzerland: Springer. doi:10.1007/978-3-319-51020-0

Acheampong, E. K. (2012). The State of Information and Communication Technology Technology and Health Informatics in Ghana. *Online Journal of Public Health Informatics, 4*(2), 12–17. PMID:23569633

Acquah-Swanzy, M. (2015). *Evaluating Electronic Health Record Systems in Ghana: the Case of Effia Nkwanta Regional Hospital*. The Arctic University.

Adedeji, P., Irinoye, O., Ikono, R., & Komolafe, A. (2018). Factors Influencing the Use of Electronic Health Records Among Nurses in a Teaching Hospital in Nigeria. *Journal of Health Informatics in Developing Countries, 12*(2), 1–20.

Adeleke, I. T., Erinle, S. A., Ndana, A. M., Anamah, T. C., Ogundele, O. A., & Aliyu, D. (2014). Healht Information Technology in Nigeria: Stakeholders' Perpectives of Nationwide Implementations and Meaningful Use of the Emerging Technology in the Most Populous Black Nation. *American Journal of Health Research, 3*(1-1), 17-24.

Asare, S., Otoo-Arthur, D., & Frimpong, K. O. (2017). Assessing the Readiness of the Digitalization of Health Records: A Case of a Municipal Hospital in Ghana. *International Journal of Computer Science and Information Technology Research, 5*(4), 76–90.

Bedeley, R. T., & Palvia, P. (2014). A Study of the Issues of E-Health Care in Developing Countries: The Case of Ghana. *Twentieth Americas Conference on Information Systems,* 1-12.

Braa, J., Hanseth, O., Heywood, A., Mohammed, W., & Shaw, V. (2007). Developing Health Information Systems in Developing Countries: The Flexible Standards. *MIS Quarterly, 31,* 381–402.

Brooks, R., & Grotz, C. (2010). Implementation of Electronic Medical Records: How Healthcare Providers are Managing the Challenges of Going Digital. *Journal of Business & Economics Research, 8*(6), 73–84. doi:10.19030/jber.v8i6.736

Eastaugh, S. R. (2013). The total cost of EHR Ownership. *Healthcare Financial Management, 67*(2), 66–70. PMID:23413671

Easton, G. (2010). Critical Realism in Case Study Research. *Industrial Marketing Management, 39*(1), 118–128. doi:10.1016/j.indmarman.2008.06.004

Fraser, H. S., & Blaya, J. (2010). Implementing Medical Information Systems in Developing Countries, What Works and What Doesn't. *AMIA 2010 Symposium Proceedings,* 232-236.

George, J. F., & Kohnke, E. (2018). Personal Health Record Systems as Boundary Objects. *Communications of the Association for Information Systems, 42*(2), 21–50.

Gyamfi, A., Mensah, K. A., Oduro, G., Donkor, P., & Mock, C. N. (2017). Barriers and Facilitators to Electronic Medical Records in the Emergency Centre at Komfo Anokye Teaching Hospital, Kumasi-Ghana. *African Journal of Emergency Medicine,* 177–182. doi:10.1016/j.afjem.2017.05.002 PMID:30456135

Hanseth, O. (2002). *From Systems and Tolls to Networks and Infrastructures - From Design to Cultivation. Towards a Theory of ICT Solutions and its Design Methodology Implications.* Available at URL: http://heim.ifi.uio.no/~oleha/Publications/ib_ISR_3rd_resubm2.html

Hanseth, O., & Monteiro, E. (1997). *Understanding Information Infrastructure, Unpublished Manuscript.* Available at URL: http://heim.ifi.uio.no/~oleha/Publications/bok.pdf

Hanseth, O., & Monteiro, E. (1998). Changing Irreversible Networks: Institutionalisation and Infrastructure. *Proceedings of the 2oth edition of IRIS.*

Hanseth, O., Monteiro, E., & Hatling, M. (1996). Developing Information Infrastructure: The Tension Between Standardisation and Flexiblility. *Science, Technology & Human Values*, *21*(4), 407–426. doi:10.1177/016224399602100402

Hong, W., Chan, F. K., Thong, J. Y., Chasalow, L. C., & Dhillon, G. (2013). A Framework and Guidelines for Context-Specific Theorizing in Information Systems Research. *Information Systems Research*, *23*(2), 111–136.

Hung, S., Chen, C., & Wang, K. (2014). Critical Success Factors for the Implementation of Integrated Healthcare Information Systems Projects: An Organisational Fit Perspective. *Communications of the Association for Information Systems*, *34*, 775–796. doi:10.17705/1CAIS.03439

Idowu, P., Cornford, D., & Bastin, L. (2008). Health Informatics Deployment in Nigeria. *Journal of Health Informatics in Developing Countries*, *2*(1), 1–23.

Kasemsap, K. (2017). Telemedicine and electronic health: Issues and implications in developing countries. In *In Health information systems and the advancement of medical practice in developing countries* (pp. 149–167). IGI Global. doi:10.4018/978-1-5225-2262-1.ch009

Klein, H., & Myers, M. (1999). A Set of Principles for Conducting and Evaluating Intepretive Field Studies in Information Systems. *Management Information Systems Quarterly*, *23*(1), 67–93. doi:10.2307/249410

Mapesa, N. M. (2016). *Health Information Technology Implementation Strategies in Zimbabwe*. Walden University.

Mason, P., Mayer, R., Chien, W.-W., & Monestime, J. P. (2017). Overcoming Barriers to Implementing Electronic Health Records in Rural Primary Care Clinics. *Qualitative Report*, *22*(11), 2943–2955.

Mengiste, S. A. (2010). Analysing the Challenges of IS Implementation in Public Health Institutions of a Developing Country: The Need for Flexible Strategies. *Journal of Health Informatics in Developing Countries*, *4*(1), 1–17.

Mihailescu, M., & Mihailescu, D. (2018). The emergence of digitalisation in the context of health care. *51st Hawaii International Conference on System Sciences*, 3066-3071. 10.24251/HICSS.2018.387

Miles, M. B., & Huberman, A. M. (1994). *Qualitative Data Analysis* (2nd ed.). Thousand Oaks, CA: Sage Publications.

National Population Commission. (2007). National Population Commission and National Bureau of Statistics Estimates.

O'Connor, Y., & O'Donoghue, J. (2015). Contextual Barriers to Mobile Health Technology in African Countries: A Perspective Piece. *Journal MTM*, *4*(1), 31–34. doi:10.7309/jmtm.4.1.7

Orlikowski, W. J. (1996). Improvising Organisational Transformation over Time: A Situated Change Perspective. *Information Systems Research*, *7*(1), 63–92. doi:10.1287/isre.7.1.63

Orlikowski, W. J. (2000). Using Technology and Constituting Structures: A Practice Lens for Studying Technology in Organisations. *Organization Science*, *11*(4), 404–428. doi:10.1287/orsc.11.4.404.14600

Phichitchaisopa, N., & Naenna, T. (2013). Factors Affecting the adoption of Healthcare Information Technology. *EXCLI Journal*, *12*, 413–436. PMID:26417235

Preko, M., Boateng, R., & Effah, J. (2019b). Healthcare Digitalisation in Ghana: An Assessment Based on the Realist Social Theory. *25th Americas Conference on Information Systems*, 1-5.

Sawyer, S., & Jarrahi, M. H. (2014). Sociotechnical Approaches to the Study of Information Systems. In CRC Handbook of Computing. Chapman and Hall. doi:10.1201/b16768-7

Sidek, Y. H., & Martins, J. T. (2017). Perceived Critial Success Factors of Electronic Health Record System Implementation in a Dental Context: An Organisational Management Perspective. *International Journal of Medical Informatics*, *107*, 88–100. doi:10.1016/j.ijmedinf.2017.08.007 PMID:29029696

Silverman, R. D. (2013). EHRs, EMRs, and Health Information Technology: To Meaningful Use and Beyond. *Journal of Legal Medicine*, *34*(1), 1–6. doi:10.1080/01947648.2013.768134 PMID:23550980

Silvius, G. A., & Stoop, J. (2013). Relationship Between Strategic Information Systems Planning Situational Factors, Process Configuration and Success. *Journal of International Technology and Information Management*, *22*(1), 1–17.

Tilson, D., Lyytinen, K., & Sorensen, C. (2010). Digital Infrastructures: The Missing IS Research Agenda. *Information Systems Research, 21*(5).

Vessey, I., & Ward, K. (2013). The Dynamics of Sustainable IS alignment: The Case for IS Adaptivity. *Journal of the Association for Information Systems*, *14*(6), 283–311. doi:10.17705/1jais.00336

Walsham, G. (1993). *Interpreting Information Systems in Organizations*. Chichester: Wiley.

Warren, R. A. (2017). *Exploring Strategies for Successful Implementation of Electronic Health Records*. Walden University.

Yin, R. (2009). *Case Study Research: Design and Methods* (4th ed.). Thousand Oaks: Sage.

Yoo, Y., Lyytinen, K. J., Boland, R. J., & Berente, N. (2010a). *The Next Wave of Digital Innovation: Opportunities and Challenges*. A Report on the Research Workshop' Digital Challenges in Innovation Research.

Chapter 17
Mobile Technology Diffusion in a Developing Economy:
Adoption and Transformational Outcomes in a Higher Education Institution

Harriet Koshie Lamptey

University of Professional Studies, Accra, Ghana

ABSTRACT

This study is on the rising patronage of mobile data in a developing economy and changes that have ensued from its adoption by a higher education institution. Studies on the growing use of mobiles in higher education exist. This qualitative inquiry advances research on developing economies by providing evidence of transformational effects on a single case. Study participants were administrators who led the adoption process. Primary data was gathered from interviews while local and international reports delivered secondary facts on rising mobile data patronage. Findings indicate that mobile data patronage is influencing its pedagogical use. Adoption has resulted in institutional changes in the form of emerged roles and arrangements. If undisrupted by technological innovations or communal group behavior, the arrangements may gain legitimacy with time. From an institutional theory perspective, mobile technology appears to be playing an agential role on the landscape of the institution. The study cautions institutions to focus on pedagogical aims in their adoption of technology.

INTRODUCTION

Communication technology has permeated some aspects of organizational processes and has become the accepted channel for speedy processing and exchange amongst individuals and institutions. As a result, technology has been infused into some traditional processes to capitalize on the swift and accurate outcomes it generates. With the ease of use of portable devices and affordability of wireless connectivity media, anytime and anywhere communication has been made possible. The evolving characteristic of mobile technology grants it some transformational abilities that alter some actions within communities

DOI: 10.4018/978-1-7998-2610-1.ch017

in which it is used (Sumaili, Dlodlo & Osakwe, 2018)). With the current rise in the use of mobile data, the art of learning is being influenced (Meyer, 2010). Through the adoption of mobile Internet platforms, applications, communication tools, and media and the landscape of higher education is being transformed.

The objective of this study is to trail the growing popularity of mobiles in a developing economy (DE) and to uncover if its pedagogical pursuit has resulted in changes within a higher education institution (HEI). The first section begins with an account on the diffusion of mobile technology in DEs. A sub-section on the diffusion of mobiles in education in DEs is provided. Accessibility issues in the higher education sector of the selected DE are trailed. The guiding theory is stated and is followed by a brief description of the research methodology. Mobile telecommunication indicators within the selected DE are the first findings reported which are followed by reports on mobile data subscription trends. The state of mobile telecommunication infrastructure for education in the country is assessed. Reports on findings continue with a brief description of the technological infrastructure at the selected institution. The adoption process and emerging roles gathered from participant responses are stated. Changes that have resulted from the adoption process are discussed. Solutions and recommendations are given and the chapter concludes.

MOBILE TECHNOLOGY DIFFUSION IN DEVELOPING ECONOMIES

Mobile telephony and devices are reported to be more popular in many DEs compared to landline infra-structure (Statistics Global Mobile, 2014). Their popularity is based on their handiness and ease of use by both old and young generations. Affordability has increased the availability of mobile technology (Hasan et al, 2019). This may be influencing mobile acceptance and use. It was estimated that by the end of the year 2012, about ninety-six percent of the world's population will use mobile communication (Statistics Global Mobile, 2014), an indication of its worldwide pervasiveness.

Mobile devices are popular in DEs. For example, mobile phone penetration in Asia is higher than on any other continent because countries like China, Japan and Korea have the largest markets for penetration (Kathuria &Oh, 2018). In Malaysia, the diffusion rate of mobile phones had exceeded a hundred percent due to multiple subscriptions by customers (Ramli, Ismail & Idrus, 2010). Evidence shows that the growth and use of mobile devices in Africa are rising and reached a level of sixty-three and a half percent in 2012 (International Telecommunications Union ITU, 2013). Mobile technology is improving communication among underprivileged societies in the world. The privatization of the telecommunica-tion industry across Africa accounts for the extensive spread of mobile communication (Smith, 2018). In some DEs, marginalized groups that cannot obtain support from national governments are offered the opportunity from private investors. A perception exists that much more Web browsing is done on mobile devices by Africans than in any other region of the world as a result of its affordability. The per-vasiveness of mobile communication triggered researchers to consider their pedagogical use (Koszalka & Ntloedibe- Kuswani, 2010). The popularity and ease of use of mobile devices appears to be the reason why mobile-learning is ascending in DEs.

Mobile Technology in Education

Technology diffusion results in acceptance and use. Improvements in the processing capabilities and storage capacities of mobile devices have extended their primary function from communication and entertainment tools to educational aids (Duman, Orhon & Gedik, 2015). This suggests that their prior make as simple devices have changed into complex gadgets in response to changing user needs and trends. As a result, the usage scenarios of mobile devices have broadened, involving impulsive, casual, relative, handy, ubiquitous, prevalent and peculiar situations (Sharples et al, 2009). This diversity has paved a way for devices to be used as aids in educational environments including student retention, supporting different learning modes and a chance for persons who cannot afford regular forms of education (Paulins et al, 2015).

Currently, mobiles are getting reasonably priced and are becoming closely linked to education. The availability and simplicity of current developments appear to enhance ICTs preference in education. Whiles some researchers report on negative outcomes of learning with technology (Soyomi, Oloruntoba & Okafor, 2015), the account of others is favorable (Godwin-Jones, 2011). Social media and interactive tools that were considered unsettling have now become proficient and resourceful aids in educational settings. For example, collaborative Social-media (Facebook) and micro-blogging applications (Twitter) are reported to promote effective interaction for communities of learning (Dede, 2009). The application of mobile technology in education has connected formal and informal learning (Jaldemark, 2018). There is a perception that tertiary school completion in DEs will be dependent on mobile technology by 2020. Technology will change the prevailing methods of instructional delivery in HEIs (Isaias, 2018). Changes in existing procedures will necessitate new modes of operation. Therefore, a means of supporting programs' success should be followed because implementing novel procedures that are not maintainable is not beneficial (Bowen, 2014).

ICT and Mobile Technology Infrastructure for Education in Ghana

African countries are noted for economic hardships and challenged resources. Ghana as a nation has not fared poorly with regards to mobile technology acceptance. With initial Internet access via computers, some constraints such as the cost of devices, limited service providers and connectivity issues hindered availability and access. With cheaper mobiles and improved connectivity media, accessing On-line content is easier and more affordable (Kwakwa, 2012). Competition amongst service providers has created a vibrant industry with an active market that other sectors of the economy cannot do without. It appears that the terrain for mobile Internet is appreciably developed. Ghanaians seem to prefer handy devices for Web access. The patronage of mobile data is also on an ascent. Thus the environment needed to facilitate the use of mobiles in education appears to be in place.

Access Issues in Ghanaian Higher Education Institutions

There are reported challenges across different sectors of Ghana's national economy. A general national deficit with regards to public structures is reported (Badu, Edwards, Owusu- Manu & Brown, 2012). The three levels of education are constrained. Tertiary education is viewed as a pivot for nation-building since a capable human resource improves the living standards and global rankings of the state (Dzeto, 2014). Gradual improvements in living standards are increasing the number of potential entrants into tertiary institutions. Concerning higher education, the increasing demand for participation is a national issue since existing infrastructure cannot support the growing student numbers. Reports indicate that qualified applicants are denied access yearly (Abugre, 2017; Asabre & Enguah, 2012).

Various factors have been attributed to this setback. For example, with regards to the development of buildings, a construction audit report identifies improper planning, poor project management, design insufficiencies, compromised quality, corruption, and financial fraud as some of the issues hindering public and private construction works in Ghana (Bondinuba, Nansie, Dadzie, Djokoto & Sadique, 2017). Lack of a maintenance culture has led to the deterioration of facilities. The needed cost of maintenance creates a deficit between the demand and supply side of educational infrastructure (Sulemana, 2018). The combined effect of these factors is a hindrance to infrastructural expansion in educational institutions.

Quality challenges in Ghanaian Education

In traditional settings, spatial problems are reported to hinder quality educational development (MoE, 2011). Overcrowded lecture halls and low lecturers to student ratios are identified as the ripple effect of limited space. The value of training received at the tertiary level is challenged. The quality of tertiary training received is an indicator of the potential strategic benefits of a country (Oketch, 2016). Though the government provides support for infrastructural expansion for public institutions, the levels are described as inadequate (Arthur & Arthur, 2016). Alternative modes of funding infrastructure (Internally Generated Funds, Donor Agencies, Non- Governmental Institutions and Public-Private Partnerships) that were sought to augment national efforts have not solved the problem entirely (Badu, Kissi, Boateng & Antwi- Afari, 2018). Construction funding of educational facilities is of grave concern to both the public and private sectors. Newman & Duwiejua (2016) suggest the development of new guides that annul the limitations of existing mechanisms for fund allocation in the country, for better initiation and completion of building projects.

Pressures of Globalization

Social and national pressures that are a consequence of globalization are being experienced by people all over the world including Ghana (Banya, 2015; Nerad, 2015). Manual tasks that were hitherto handled by trained people have been eliminated through automation systems. This has resulted in job losses globally (Stone & Deadrick, 2015). The increasing use of technology has led to a highly competitive and professionally demanding work environment. The result has been a growing desire for academic and professional qualifications to enable persons to qualify for the competitively growing job-market (Attuahene & Owusu- Ansah, 2013). In Ghana, a growing number of working students in HEIs have been identified (Morley, 2012). Family obligations and financial difficulties compel them to work and school at the same time. Prevailing national and international pressures have altered the needs of tertiary students (Tumuheki, Zeelen, Openjuru, 2016; Lehman, 2014). The traditional model of learning is currently not suitable for all eligible students at the tertiary level of education. These identified issues necessitated the need for reforms in modes of delivery of tertiary education.

GUIDING THEORY

The Institutional Theory is believed to have evolved from established theories of the Political and Social Sciences and seeks to explain how plans, procedures, standards, and tasks are organized to shape social behavior. Though stability appears to be its main theme, advocates of the theory are inevitably exposed not only to conventionality but to transformation in social structures in some situations (Haunschild & Chandler, 2008). It also provides clarification on how social structures are created, accepted, used and discarded over time. From sociology, perspective institutionalism dwells on how shared actions and values influence the formation and sustenance of societal institutions whiles from an economics perspective institutionalism concerns the effect of beneficial results on institutions (Powell & Colyvas, 2008). The two views illustrate different outcomes that may result from studies guided by the theory. A new theory that adopts a multi-disciplinary approach has evolved from the old (Scott, 1987). This has resulted in variations and difficulties in understanding and use of the theory. Various constructs have been proposed for Institutional theory. The study adopts the three constructs of Scott (2008a). These are the regulative, normative and cultural-cognitive pillars. The regulative concerns carefully planned laws enacted to sustain institutions (Kondra & Hurst, 2009). The normative defines ethics and standards by which actor behavior and institutional forms can be related and evaluated and the cultural-cognitive concerns structures that shape meaning through collective ideas about communal truth (Scott, 2008a).

Institutional Theory and Information Systems (ISs)

Institutional theory is applied in the Information Systems (IS) discipline. Studies may be placed in two groups. One category is based on organizations exhibiting IS-related phenomena. These include studies on Human-Computer-Interactions within organizations. For example, Oostervink, Agterberg and Huysman (2016) in a study of an Enterprise Social Media (ESM) system at an IT Consultancy firm identified that professionals' collaborative experiences are based on dissimilar logics: job- role, firm nature and logics management. Others that emphasize the process of institutionalizing IT include a study on a Danish Home that demonstrated how theorization and translation (institutionalization) of mobile IT resulted in its legitimacy over ten years (Nielsen, Mathiassen and Newell, 2014). Other studies are on the debate surrounding the communal reasoning and legitimacy of IT institutionalization. This includes a study on IT innovation dispersion in a case involving computerized physician order entry systems (Kaganer, Pawlowski and Wiley-Patton, 2010). The study revealed several legitimized strategic patterns employed by vendors guided the development of a taxonomy of strategies for IT innovation validity.

The second category is on IS adoption, development, and implementation. These include studies on the adoption of Inter-Organizational Systems (Krell et al, 2016; Hsu et al, 2015). Another investigated the institutional constraints that arise with student involvement (as stakeholders) in the development and implementation of college-wide E-portfolios has been investigated (Silva, Delaney, Cochran, Jackson and Olivares, 2015). Findings indicate that in spite of requirements and policy constraints, student involvement is useful and can be incorporated at various stages of the process.

Institutional Theory and ISs in Education

Some research on ISs in education that applied Institutional theory are displayed in Table 1. Other prevalent studies are on entrepreneurship learning in organizations (Zhu, Rooney & Phillips, 2016; Philips & Tracey, 2007). Entrepreneurship is a significant part of neo-institutionalism is of interest to researchers. From another perspective, Chandler and Whang (2015) explored how organizations learn and identified knowledge-based strategies that shape adoption decisions and practices at the firm level. Again, to unearth adoption decisions of diverse educational environments, some comparative studies have been conducted. For example, Canhilal et al (2016) and Wilkins and Huisman (2012) have iden-

Table 1. Institutional theory and IS adoption in education

Authors	Main-Theme	Findings
Canhilal, Lepori & Seeber (2016)	Adoption of managerial and institutional logics by European universities	New Public Management pressures strongly influence managerial practices but shows no effect on academic logics
Li & Du (2016)	Higher education (HE) reforms in China	Two forces decentralization (endogenous) and globalization (exogenous) direct changes in HE administration and management
Vasudeva, Alexander & Jones (2015)	Role of diverse institutional logics on Inter-organizational learning with Inter Organizational Systems(IOS)	Dominant corporatist logics enhance IOS use whiles pluralistic logics cause decoupling of processes and affect IOSs
Wiseman & Chase-Mayoral (2013)	Examination of technology supported internationally comparative education	Infuse more micro institutional level studies to bridge micro and macro education levels for better comparative analysis
Pi-Tzong, Hsi-Peng & Tzu-Chuan (2012)	E-learning adoption and the role of social factors in promoting job training	Normative and mimetic pressures influence attitudes which affects e- learning adoption intention Coercive pressures show no effect on adoption intention
Wilkins & Huisman (2012)	Factors influencing motivation to adopt internationalization strategies in HE	Range of motivating factors influence adoption: legitimacy, status, risk ventures, risk avoidance, and new revenue sources

Source: (Author's construct)

tified pressures that motivate adoption decisions in educational institutions. In another comparative study, Wiseman, Astiz, and Baker (2013) investigated the improper application of institutional theory in comparative educational research.

Educational researches guided by institutional theory have two main perspectives: one on administration and management of institutions and the other on actual learning contexts. In the planning of educational institutions and the introduction of reforms, the roles of isomorphic pressures have been investigated by Denman and James (2016) and Li and Du (2016) respectively. Similarly, in real learning situations, the effect of drivers and barriers to blended learning adoption has been examined by Porter, Graham, Bodily and Sandberg (2016) whiles Zundans-Frazer and Bane (2016) explored the role of institutional practices on course design and evaluation. However, studies on the transformational role of technology in education appear limiting in institutional literature. This study aims to uncover the role of institutional elements on changes resulting from technological adoption in educational settings to contribute to the application and understanding of Institutional theory in IS studies.

METHODOLOGY

A two-staged process was followed in arriving at the inferences made in this chapter. The first stage involved an elicitation of both global and local secondary data on ICT development in the selected DE (Ghana). The global reports were analyzed and graphs extracted to display the improving trends in mobile technology diffusion. Some sub-continental and global comparisons were made on the county's rankings to show the pace of growth in technology development and use. Local reports on mobile data subscription trends were also examined to display its rising patronage.

The second stage involved primary data collection on a public higher education institution (HEI). Participants involved were six administrators of different ranks. The reason was to capture the varying perspectives of participants on the study purpose. Interview sessions were held in offices and recordings made with a smartphone. Data transcription was manually performed. Data were analyzed using Miles and Huberman's (1994) approach which involved a reduction of transcribed data, a grouping of data using identified relationships and preparation of a research report. The discussion was made in light of the new institutional theory.

FINDINGS

Mobile Telecommunication Indicators for Ghana

Fixed broadband was the initial mode of internet access. Patronage for this medium is gradually declining as simpler and affordable means have been made available through wireless technologies. Various ITU reports indicate that mobile cellular telephone subscription is the most patronized form of communication generally with active mobile broadband subscription increasing steadily. For example, a gradual rise occurred between 2007 and 2010 but between 2010 and 2016, the surge has been striking (ITU, 2016). This suggests a rising popularity and patronage of mobile data. Furthermore, present reports indicate that within the last five years, the growth rate of mobile data penetration has surpassed 20 percent yearly and is expected to reach 4.3 billion worldwide by the end of 2017 (ITU, 2017).

Eleven indicators, grouped into three sub-indices (access, use, and skills) are combined into a single standard called the ICT Development Index (IDI) which aids assessment and matches in ICT developments within member countries (ITU- Measuring the Information Society Report MISR, 2016). Globally, the IDI for Ghana in 2015 was 3.75 with a world ranking of 111 while in 2016, Ghana's IDI was 3.99 at a rank of 112. Internationally, the average increase in IDI between 2015 and 2016 was 0.2. The change in IDI for Ghana within the period is 0.25 which implies a fair position with regards to ICT development. For the location spread of IDI quartiles, Ghana is currently placed in the lower- middle category (ITU- MISR 2016). This indication on the world scale is not encouraging since it implies that ICT development in the country needs improvement.

At present, Ghana places sixth in IDI rankings in Africa. Eight countries (including Ghana) recorded improved IDI rankings between 2015 and 2016 as a result of mobile cellular and mobile broadband diffusion. Currently, Ghana's mobile broadband penetration ranks third in Africa which is led first by Cape Verde and secondly by Botswana (ITU- MISR, 2016).

Data Source: ITU MISR 2010-2016 (Figures unavailable for 2014)

Figure 1 is a line graph on IDIs in Ghana for over six years. Figures for the year 2014 are however unavailable. This may be due to the World Summit on Information Society that took place. The Access sub-index has shown an irregular pattern. A slight decrease occurred between the years 2010 and 2011 which was followed by a significant increase in 2012 and has only recorded slight increases in the years that followed. The skills sub-index which was initially high is gradually declining. Conversely, the use of sub-index which in the year 2010 was at a low value has been steadily improving. The IDI trend for

Figure 1. Line graph on IDI trends in Ghana between 2010 and 2016

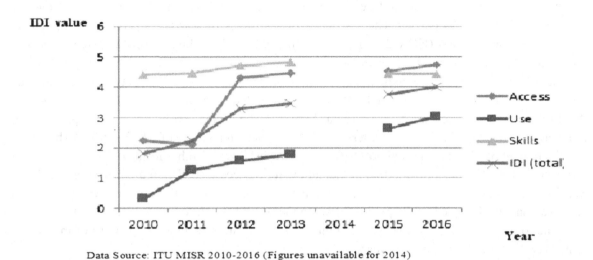

Data Source: ITU MISR 2010-2016 (Figures unavailable for 2014)

Ghana is growing though at a moderate pace. The economic environment requires revamping to support the use of technology, particularly the diffusion of ICTs in education and knowledge creation and sharing.

Mobile Data Subscription Trends in Ghana

Records indicate that in Sub Saharan Africa, mobile telecommunications were first introduced in Ghana in 1992. Similarly, the country is noted as one of the first few in Africa to have Internet access and Asymmetric Digital Subscriber Line (ADSL) broadband services (Sulzberger, 2001). With the current proliferation of mobile communication networks, mobile communication penetration is high above the African average. An ITU-MISR (2012) report states that mobile penetration in Ghana surged from 7 percent in 2010 to 23 percent in 2011. Subsequent improvements within the mobile communication industry resulted in the availability of mobile data. The rise of mobile devices and data led to Ghana's number one placement for mobile broadband penetration in Africa (ITU, 2012).

The National Communication Authority (NCA) reports that currently there are six telecom companies (Mobile Network Operators, MNOs) and four Broadband Wireless Access (BWA) operators in Ghana NCA-GH MNOs, 2017). Reports on mobile data transmissions between the years 2010 and 2012 are unavailable. From January 2013 to September 2017, telecommunication data is available to the public. Wireless technologies and handy devices are in vogue (Tanle & Abane, 2017). About 83 percent of the Ghanaian populace own mobile phones, with 14 percent of this figure possessing smartphones (NCA, 2017). Though used predominantly for communication, there are reports on changes in their use (Kwakwa, 2012). Mobile devices are getting popular in higher education and becoming an integral part of DL delivery in Ghana (Asunka, 2016; Asabre, 2012).

Each year the NCA releases to the general public, quarterly reports derived from data collected and analyzed monthly. Data released is to inform policy, academic and practitioner communities on the trends within the communication industry. In 2017, the NCA reported that mobile data subscription has been ascending between 2015 and 2017. Between the second and third quarters of 2017, subscription increased by 4.63 percent with an increase in the penetration rate of 0.28 percent within the period. The mobile data penetration rate at the end of the third quarter of 2016 was 69.22 percent and the 2017 figure reported was 79.94 percent. The year on year rate of increase was 10.72 percent for both prepaid and postpaid subscriptions (NCA, 2017). There is an increasingly mobile data patronage by users now, about voice data.

The NCA (2017) report also indicates that mobile data traffic is ascending. Between the second and third quarters of 2017, an increase of 16.95 percent was noted. The year- on year traffic expansion for the third quarter witnessed was 93.72 percent. Similarly, the average mobile data usage per subscription between the second and third quarters of 2017 recorded an increase of 12.83 percent. The year on year increment for the same period noted is 63.85 percent. Besides, other forms of internet access are decreasing. The NCA also reports that broadband wireless access (BWA) and penetration are falling. Specific reports indicate that the BWA penetration rate at the end of the third quarter was 3.33 percent. However, data traffic rose by 0.24 percent between the second and third quarters of 2017. Figures from this time to date are currently unavailable. Figure 6.6 is a chart that shows the pattern of mobile data transmission by MNOs within four years.

Figure 2. Chart on Ghanaian MNOs Mobile data subscription between 2013 and 2016

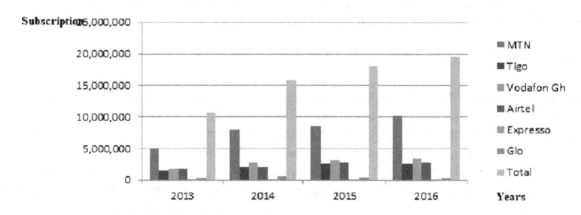

Data Source: NCA Historical Data Transmission Figures, 2013-2016

Data Source: NCA Historical Data Transmission Figures, 2013-2016

Figure 2 displays a four-year trend in mobile data transmission revealed by MNOs. Scancom Ghana (MTN) dominates with the performance of Vodafone Ghana (which is second in rankings) less than half of its penetration. Subscribers for Airtel and Milicom Ghana (Tigo) seem moderate but Expresso and Globacom Ghana appear not to be popular channels for data transmission. On average, steady growth in mobile data access is evident. Without facts from BWAs, subscription growths of 48.78 and 14.08 percent were reported for 2014 and 2015 respectively. With the inclusion of figures from three BWAs, a growth of 7.97 percent was recorded at the end of 2016.

For MNOs, the entire subscription for mobile data transmission as of April 2017 was 21,584,899. An increase in penetration rate from 70.9 to 76.22 percent occurred between January and April 2017 (NCA-GH MNOs, 2017). An ascent in data transmission through BWA is also reported. For instance, as of February 2017, the total involvement figure reported was 261,508. The penetration for Ultra Mobile Broadband (4G) Data transmission between December 2016 and April 2017 increased from 0.37 to 1.08 percent (NCA-GH 4GS, 2017). This figure, however, accounts for internet access via mobile and no- mobile devices.

Technological Infrastructure at the Selected HEI

With regular expansion in programs offered and the accompanying increase in student population, a public HEI introduced reforms in the management of academic work during the 2014/2015 academic year. The institution has a network infrastructure that was initially funded internally and has been undergoing expansion and improvement over the years through support from local telecommunications providers and a foreign donor. The network backbone which was initially Ethernet cabled is currently fiber- supported. A local area network hosts academic transactions, records, library catalogs, the electronic learning platform, and the university's Website. An online storage site named has also been set- up by the university. The storage site hosts internally conducted researches. There is an on-campus intranet that transmits faster than the Internet due to limitations in Internet transmission capacities.

To overcome Internet connectivity challenges a local telecommunications provider was outsourced to help improve connectivity. With foreign assistance in 2010, a Network Operations Center was set up to facilitate technology-supported learning. An earlier open-source Learning Management System (LMS) known as Knowledge Environment for Web-based Learning (KEWL) was introduced in 2004 but its acceptance and extent of use were very low. In the 2014/2015 academic year, another open-source LMS, SAKAI was introduced and it replaced the earlier package. The SAKAI, which runs on a dedicated server has received better acceptance.

Mobile Technology Adoption Process and Emerging Roles

In Ghana, a governmental rule signaled the adoption of technology into higher learning a decade ago. However, the growing popularity of mobile devices and student preference for the handy gadgets spurred institutional leaders to adopt mobile learning in addition to learning with computers. Leadership of the HEI initiates major adoption decisions as in the case of mobile technology espousal. Another responsibility leadership bears is to secure funding for development. Next technical experts offer suggestions on the types of systems needed and the development process to pursue. Infrastructural and systems development proceed afterward. Development, implementation and integration processes are handled by on-campus technical experts, with some external assistance, when technical hitches are encountered. A Course Development Unit (CDU) is responsible for the preparation of learning materials for the Online environment. Preparation by the CDU starts six months before a semester begins. This to ensure completion of the course development process to make digitized resources available to students. There is an educational technologist who supervises resource design and conversion into electronic formats. The unit supervisor revealed that:

Subject matter experts (lecturers) determine the structure and content of courses. To facilitate the process, a course is first re-structured. Upon completion of the structuring exercise, a training workshop is organized for the conversion of courses from print versions into digitized form. After standardization training into a format suitable for the LMS takes place. Video recordings are also made to provide bet-

ter replication of the traditional learning environment and improve comprehension. Where necessary other multimedia and tools are added to improve the learning set-up. In some situations, simulations are incorporated into content where appropriate. We aim to make mobiles enabled learning as efficient as possible.

On how user integration is achieved, another administrator revealed that:

At the start of each academic year, teams provide a week-long orientation and training for fresh students, before learning and tutoring begins. Teams are made up of various resource persons including academic advisors, program facilitators, career and counseling groups and student support services. The mix is to ensure that different inquiries by the student can be answered.

When questioned on what the teams do, the administrator clarified further that:

During orientation students are informed about the policies and procedures that govern the university and how to abide by making their quest for tertiary education successful. For integration with mobile learning, they are also trained to grasp navigation methods for resource access and the use of interactive tools on SAKAI. Demonstrations are performed to help students understand the methods and importance of participation in On-line collaborative activities as well.

At the HEI under investigation, mobiles for learning are through the blended model which involves both electronic and interactive teaching and learning. Interactive learning is a mode through which exchange between lecturers and students is ensured (Paladino, 2007). Interaction by physical contact during a face- to- face sessions is possible but some drawbacks (crowded lecture halls, shy students, etc.) are reported to reduce its effectiveness (Stowell, Oldham & Bennett, 2010). Measures of alleviating these issues are required for interaction benefits to be realized. In such situations, the use of technology to enhance interaction is encouraged (Domagk, Schwartz & Plass, 2010). When questioned on how the institution handles this challenge, a mobile-learning facilitator replied:

An out-sourced group of assistant lecturers in the various subject areas are responsible for On-line interaction with students. The reason is to alleviate the task of lecturers who are often saddled with multiple academic duties and as such may not relay much time for On-line interaction.

Data gathered also revealed that there is an established technical support team at an ICT Directorate made up of four units responsible for the use and maintenance of systems for the university. It is headed by a Webmaster who is supported by several systems and network administrators. They directly manage the Web-sites, mail servers and electronic resources of the university. There is a unit of hardware technicians who provide repair services for all university systems and students' computers at no cost. Another section, the training unit, offers literacy programs and user training workshops on newly acquired systems and applications as well as situations in which some changes occur on systems that affect the entire university community.

DISCUSSION

The institution adopted mobile learning based on a mimetic pressure arising from students' preference for mobiles (Pi-Tsong et al, 2012). After partnering with a major telecommunications provider for some time, the contract was abrogated and the university continued technological infrastructural development on its own. An external donor currently provides financial support for the expansion and maintenance of ICT infrastructure. With the advent of technology-enabled learning, there has been institutional re-designing as a result of the emergence of new structures and processes (Lehmann-Willenbrock, Beck, & Kauffeld, 2016). New structures imply the recruitment of new staff or the re-training of existing staff to take up new roles. Changes in recognized arrangements are the first signs of institutional transformation (Micelotta et al, 2017). Leadership often initiates changes but change acceptance by other actors is needed to develop legitimacy. Communal recognition of emerged roles becomes easier with individual and group involvement.

In the HEI investigated, the formation of new structures became necessary because technical expertise was required to handle technology-backed environments. Facilitating units, course development teams, mobile applications development teams, interaction monitoring groups, quality assurance directorates, etc. have been set up. Educational technologists for example, who are persons trained to play a key role in facilitating technology-supported learning, are now integral members of the institution's environment. They coordinate activities to make technology-backed learning a reality. Mobile application development staffs are responsible for content conversion into mobile formats and the modification of open-source interactive applications into forms that integrate well with institutional platforms. Interaction monitoring personnel are an outsourced group responsible for all On-line interaction sections with students.

The HEI is required to submit yearly records of staff strength and qualification, research output, student enrollment, etc. to a national monitoring agency. The introduction of new courses and technology adoption also required approval by certification. This is a reflection of the normative element that drives the moral of an institution and improves the image and self-worth of a university (Scott, 2008a). Highly-rated standards and rankings can generate positive outcomes on the institution. This is another source of institutional legitimacy. With recognition gaining, institutions acceptance by others improves resulting in affiliations that foster their well-being and development.

Institutions react to changes in their environment that affect their existence (Lipnicka & Verhoeven, 2014). The responses are not always submissive adjustments and may involve pragmatic efforts to withstand external pressures to attain stability (Ashworth, Boyne & Delbridge, 2009). In Ghana, the growing numbers of yearly applicants and the failure of existing physical infrastructure on campuses to support potentially qualified applicants necessitated a change in traditional modes of teaching and learning (Zhang et al, 2014). The situation triggered a state regulation for the use of ICTs in education in 2008. The regulation compelled public HEIs to develop the necessary technological infrastructure for teaching and learning. Thus the regulative pillar served as a driver that changed processes to either sustain or improve learning outcomes (Anderson & Chang, 2018). Adherence to the state policy is becoming an influential myth. Contemporary institutions tend to incorporate new ideas, forms, and processes as myths. Myths can affect internal arrangements to disrupt existing structures that lead to change, and besides necessitate the development of new forms of institutional structures (Gehman et al, 2016). A distinction should be made between the enabling technologies and new teaching and learning processes. By separating the technological artifact from the desired institutional activities (education), students' learning outcomes can be evaluated. In situations of unattained results, the HEI can identify hindrances to existing processes and adopt strategies to overcome challenges (Huther & Krucken, 2018).

SOLUTIONS AND RECOMMENDATIONS

The purpose of higher education is to train individuals to be equipped for the job market and national building. In light of the slow infrastructural development projects for physical expansion and inadequate funds that result in inaccessibility issues in DE HEIs, technology offers a means of alleviating the difficulties to pave opportunities for qualified entrants (Badu et al, 2018). Participation in tertiary level education is being improved through the incorporation of mobile devices and wireless technologies and processes that can sustain it are needed.

Internal and external factors influence organizations. The three pillars influence arrangements and processes in institutions. To prevent establishments from deteriorating, rules are set up to guide conduct and actions within the HEI. Rules can sometimes promote or hinder development. The standards that guide the setting up of an institution and its mode of operation influence what the institution regards as important (Abdelnour, Hasselbladh & Kallinikos 2017). Again, for institutions that uphold longstanding traditions and methods, change can be difficult. Likewise, the collective reasoning of an HEI influences what is deemed acceptable though this may not be obvious (Vasudeva et al, 2015). It directs individual and group perceptions which affect the stability and extent of change that can occur. Mobile technology adoption was undertaken to make mobile learning part of the methods of erudition. It was guided by regulations, standards and cultural beliefs of the institution. Pillars exhibit different roles in the institutional process. It is therefore advisable to study the effects of these pillars on mobile technology adoption to uncover issues that can hinder intended outcomes. Thus the HEI needs to be pedagogically focused on their technology adoption decisions.

FUTURE RESEARCH DIRECTIONS

With the growing diffusion of mobiles globally and its widespread adoption, studies on the nature of changes it can cause require investigation. This is to chart a path to find solutions to potentially detrimental changes that can arise.

CONCLUSION

Institutions interact with their environments. The environment induces changes in HEIs. For example, governmental regulations enforce restrictions on institutions that can result in changes through compliance with state directives. The emergence of new technology may alter existing processes through use such as resulted from the espousal of mobile technology for teaching and learning. Technology is playing the role of an agent in the transformation of the institution. Its introduction has led to the development of new arrangements and processes. The resultant changes include structural expansion, improved technological layouts, newly formed units, mobiles-facilitated operational processes to facilitate mobile-supported teaching and learning. HEIs are to produce quality education for the youth. The transformed landscape can be beneficial if the evolved structures and processes are well managed and sustained in light of the purposes of HEIs.

REFERENCES

Abdelnour, S., Hasselbladh, H., & Kallinikos, J. (2017). Agency and institutions in organization studies. *Organization Studies*, *38*(12), 1775–1792. doi:10.1177/0170840617708007

Abugre, J. B. (2017). Institutional governance and management systems in Sub-Saharan Africa higher education: Developments and challenges in a Ghanaian Research University. *Higher Education*, 1–17.

Anderson, G. L., & Chang, E. (2018). Competing Narratives of Leadership in Schools: The Institutional and Discursive Turns in Organizational Theory. The SAGE Handbook of School Organization, 84.

Arthur, P., & Arthur, E. (2016). Tertiary institutions and capacity building in Ghana: Challenges and the way forward. *Commonwealth and Comparative Politics*, *54*(3), 387–408. doi:10.1080/14662043.2016.1175690

Asabre, N. Y. (2012). Towards a perspective of Information Communication Technology in (ICT) learning: Migration from Electronic Learning (E-learning) to Mobile Learning (M- learning). *International Journal of Information and Communication Technology Research*, *2*(8), 646–649.

Asabere, N. Y., & Enguah, S. E. (2012). Integration of Expert Systems in Mobile Learning. *International Journal of Information and Communication Research*, *2*(1), 55–61.

Ashworth, R., Boyne, G., & Delbridge, R. (2007). Escape from the iron cage? Organizational change and isomorphic pressures in the public sector. *Journal of Public Administration: Research and Theory*, *19*(1), 165–187. doi:10.1093/jopart/mum038

Asunka, S. (2016). Instructor Perceptions and Intentions to Use a Tablet PC for Mobile Learning in a Ghanaian University: An Exploratory Case Study. In Handbook of Research on Mobile Devices and Applications in Higher Education Settings (pp. 495-517). IGI Global.

Attuahene, F., & Owusu-Ansah, A. (2013). A descriptive assessment of higher education access, participation, equity, and disparity in Ghana. *SAGE Open*, *3*(3). doi:10.1177/2158244013497725

Badu, E., Edwards, D. J., Owusu-Manu, D., & Brown, D. M. (2012). Barriers to the implementation of innovative financing (IF) of infrastructure. *Journal of Financial Management of Property and Construction*, *17*(3), 253–273. doi:10.1108/13664381211274362

Badu, E., Kissi, E., Boateng, E. B. & Antwi-Afari, M. F. (2018). Tertiary Educational Infrastructural Development in Ghana: Financing, Challenges, and Strategies. *Africa Education Review*, 1-17.

Banya, K. (2015). Globalization, policy directions, and higher education in Sub-Saharan Africa. In *Second International Handbook on Globalization, Education and Policy Research* (pp. 181–202). Dordrecht: Springer. doi:10.1007/978-94-017-9493-0_12

Bondinuba, F. K., Nansie, A., Dadzie, J., Djokoto, S. D., & Sadique, M. A. (2017). Construction Audits Practice in Ghana: A Review. *J. Civil Engineering and Architecture Research*, *4*(1), 1859–1872.

Bowen, W. G. (2014). Higher education in the digital age. *Croatian Economic Survey*, *16*(1), 161–185.

Canhilal, S. K., Lepori, B., & Seeber, M. (2016). Decision-Making Power and Institutional Logic in Higher Education Institutions: A Comparative Analysis of European Universities. In *Towards A Comparative Institutionalism: Forms, Dynamics and Logics across the Organizational Fields of Health Care and Higher Education*. Emerald Group Publishing Limited.

Chandler, D., & Whang, H. (2015). Learning from learning theory: A model of organizational adoption strategies at the micro-foundations of institutional theory. *Journal of Management*, *41*(5), 1446–1476.

Dede, C. (2009). Comments on Greenhow, Robelia, and Hughes: Technologies that facilitate generating knowledge and possibly wisdom. *Educational Researcher*, *38*(4), 260–263. doi:10.3102/0013189X09336672

Denman, B. D., & James, R. (2016). Cultural ecology and isomorphism applied to educational planning in China's Inner Mongolia: A new rubric. *International Journal of Comparative Education and Development*, *18*(1), 40–52. doi:10.1108/IJCED-10-2015-0003

Duman, G., Orhon, G., & Gedik, N. (2015). Research trends in mobile-assisted language learning from 2000 to 2012. *ReCALL*, *27*(02), 197–216. doi:10.1017/S0958344014000287

Dzeto, K. G. (2014). *Projecting Ghana into the real middle- income economy: The role of technical vocational education training*. Retrieved 22/02/2018 from http://library.fes.de/pdf-files/bueros/ghana/11300.pdf

Gehman, J., Lounsbury, M., & Greenwood, R. (2016). How institutions matter: From the micro-foundations of institutional impacts to the macro consequences of institutional arrangements. In *How Institutions Matter!* (pp. 1–34). Emerald Group Publishing Limited. doi:10.1108/S0733-558X201600048A002

Godwin Jones, R. (2011). Mobile apps for language learning. *Language Learning & Technology*, *15*(2), 2–11.

Hasan, A., Jha, K. N., Rameezdeen, R., Ahn, S., & Baroudi, B. (2019). Perceived Productivity Effects of Mobile ICT in Construction Projects. In *Advances in Informatics and Computing in Civil and Construction Engineering* (pp. 165–172). Cham: Springer. doi:10.1007/978-3-030-00220-6_20

Haunschild, P. R., & Chandler, D. (2008). Institutional- level learning: Learning as a source of institutional change. In The Sage Handbook of Organizational Institutionalism, (pp. 624-649). Thousand Oaks, CA: Sage.

Hsu, Y. C., Lin, Y. T., & Wang, T. (2015). A legitimacy challenge of a cross-cultural inters- organizational information system. *European Journal of Information Systems*, *24*(3), 278–294. doi:10.1057/ejis.2014.33

Hüther, O., & Krücken, G. (2018). Summarizing Reflections—Stability and Change in German Higher Education. In *Higher Education in Germany—Recent Developments in an International Perspective* (pp. 257–263). Cham: Springer. doi:10.1007/978-3-319-61479-3_8

International Telecommunications Union. (2017). *ICT Facts and Figures January to July 2017*. Retrieved 12/08/2017 from http://www.itu.int/en/mediacentre/Pages/2017-PR37.aspx

International Telecommunications Union. (2016). *ICT Facts and figures 2016*. Retrieved 15/08/2016 from http://www.itu.int/en/ITU D/Statistics/Documents/facts/ICTFactsFigures2016.pdf

International Telecommunications Union. (2016). *Measuring the Information Society Report*. Retrieved 18/08/2017 from https://www.itu.int/en/ITU D/Statistics/Documents/publications/misr2016/MISR2016-w4.pdf

International Telecommunications Union. (2013). *ICT Facts and Figures*. Retrieved from http://www.itu.int/en/ITU/Statistics/Documents/facts/ICTFactsFigures2013-e.pdf

International Telecommunications Union. (2012). *ICT Facts and figures 2012*. Retrieved 25/07/2017 from http://www.itu.int/en/ITU D/Statistics/Documents/facts/ICTFactsFigures2012.pdf

Isaias, P. (2018). Model for the enhancement of learning in higher education through the deployment of emerging technologies. *Journal of Information. Communication and Ethics in Society*, *16*(4), 401–412. doi:10.1108/JICES-04-2018-0036

Jaldemark, J. (2018). Contexts of learning and challenges of mobility: Designing for a blur between formal and informal learning. In *Mobile and Ubiquitous Learning* (pp. 141–155). Singapore: Springer. doi:10.1007/978-981-10-6144-8_9

Kaganer, E., Pawlowski, S. D., & Wiley-Patton, S. (2010). Building Legitimacy for IT Innovations: The Case of Computerized Physician Order Entry Systems. *Journal of the Association for Information Systems*, *11*(1), 1–33. doi:10.17705/1jais.00219

Kathuria, V., & Oh, K. Y. (2018). ICT access: Testing for convergence across countries. *The Information Society*, *34*(3), 166–182. doi:10.1080/01972243.2018.1438549

Kondra, A. Z., & Hurst, D. C. (2009). Institutional processes of organizational culture. *Culture and Organization*, *15*(1), 39–58. doi:10.1080/14759550802709541

Koszalka, T. A., & Ntloedibe-Kuswani, G. S. (2010). Literature on the safe and disruptive learning potential of mobile technologies. *Distance Education*, *31*(2), 139–157. doi:10.1080/01587919.2010.498082

Krell, K., Matook, S., & Rhode, F. (2016). The impact of legitimacy based motives on IS adoption success: An institutional theory perspective. *Information & Management*, *53*(6), 683–697. doi:10.1016/j.im.2016.02.006

Kwakwa, P. A. (2012). Mobile phone usage by micro and small scale enterprises in semi-rural Ghana. *International Review of Management and Marketing*, *2*(3), 156–164.

Lehmann-Willenbrock, N., Beck, S. J., & Kauffeld, S. (2016). Emergent team roles in organizational meetings: Identifying communication patterns via cluster analysis. *Communication Studies*, *67*(1), 37–57. doi:10.1080/10510974.2015.1074087

Li, J., & Du, J. (2016). Globalization and Decentralization Forces in China's Higher Education Administration and Management Reform (1953-2015): A Neo-institutional Analysis. *US-China Education Review*, *6*(1), 1–19.

Lipnicka, M., & Verhoeven, J. C. (2014). The application of New Institutionalism and the Resource Dependency theory for studying changes in universities within Europe. *Roczniki Nauk Spolecznych*, *42*(4), 7–30. doi:10.18290/rns.2017.45.3-12

Micelotta, E., Lounsbury, M., & Greenwood, R. (2017). Pathways of institutional change: An integrative review and research agenda. *Journal of Management*, *43*(6), 1885–1910. doi:10.1177/0149206317699522

Miles, M. B., & Huberman, A. M. (1994). Qualitative data analysis: An expanded sourcebook. Sage.

Ministry of Education. (2011). *Good infrastructure essential for quality education delivery*. Accra, Ghana: Author.

Morley, L. (2012). Experiencing higher education in Ghana and Tanzania: The symbolic power of being a student. In T. Hinton- Smith (Ed.), Widening Participation in higher education (pp. 245-266). Palgrave Macmillan.

National Communications Authority. (2017). *Quarterly statistical bulletin on communications in Ghana: Third quarter July to September*. Retrieved 15/02/2018 from https://nca.org.gh/assets/Uploads/stats-bulletin-Q3-2017.pdf

National Communication Authority. (2017). *4G Subscriptions January to April 2017*. Retrieved 5/02/2017 from https://nca.org.gh/assets/Uploads/4G-Subscription- Jan.-to-Apr.-2017.pdf

National Communication Authority. (2017). *MNOs Mobile Data Statistics 2017*. Retrieved from http://nca.org.gh/assets/Uploads/January-Reports-MNOs- Mobile-data-Statistics-2017.pdf

Nerad, M. (2015). From graduate student to world citizen in a global environment. *International Higher Education*, (40).

Newman, E. & Duwiejua, M. (2016). Models for innovative funding for higher education in Africa–The case of Ghana. *Towards Innovative Models for Funding Higher Education in Africa*, *1*, 1-19.

Nielsen, J. A., Mathiassen, L., & Newell, S. (2014). Theorization and translation in Information Technology Institutionalization: Evidence from Danish Homecare. *Management Information Systems Quarterly*, *38*(1), 165–186. doi:10.25300/MISQ/2014/38.1.08

Oostervink, N., Agterberg, M., & Huysman, M. (2016). Knowledge Sharing on Enterprise Social Media: Practices to Cope With Institutional Complexity. *Journal of Computer-Mediated Communication*, *21*(2), 156–176. doi:10.1111/jcc4.12153

Paulins, N., Balina, S., & Arhipova, I. (2015). Learning content development methodology for mobile devices. *Procedia Computer Science*, *43*, 147–153. doi:10.1016/j.procs.2014.12.020

Phillips, N., & Tracey, P. (2007). Opportunity recognition, entrepreneurial capabilities, and bricolage: Connecting institutional theory and entrepreneurship in strategic organization. *Strategic Organization*, *5*(3), 313–320. doi:10.1177/1476127007079956

Pi-Tzong, J. A. N., Hsi-Peng, L. U., & Tzu-Chuan, C. H. (2012). The adoption of e-learning: An institutional theory perspective. *The Turkish Online Journal of Educational Technology*, *11*(3), 326–343.

Porter, W. W., Graham, C. R., Bodily, R. G., & Sandberg, D. S. (2016). A qualitative analysis of institutional drivers and barriers to blended learning adoption in higher education. *The Internet and Higher Education*, *28*, 17–27. doi:10.1016/j.iheduc.2015.08.003

Ramli, A., Ismail, I. B., & Idrus, R. M. (2010). Mobile Learning Via SMS Among Distance Learners: Does Learning Transfer Occur? *International Journal of Interactive Mobile Technologies*, *4*(3), 30–35.

Powell, W. W., & Colyvas, J. A. (2008). Microfoundations of institutional theory. The Sage Handbook of Organizational Institutionalism, 276, 298.

Scott, W. R. (2008a). *Institutions and Organizations: Ideas and Interests* (3rd ed.). Thousand Oaks, CA: Sage.

Scott, W. R. (1987). The adolescence of institutional theory. *Administrative Science Quarterly*, *4*(4), 493–511. doi:10.2307/2392880

Sharples, M., Arnedillo-Sánchez, I., Milrad, M., & Vavoula, G. (2009). *Mobile learning*. Springer Netherlands.

Silva, M. L., Delaney, A. S., Cochran, J., Jackson, R., & Olivares, C. (2015). Institutional Assessment and the Integrative Core Curriculum: Involving students in the development of an e-Portfolio system. *International Journal of E-Portfolio*, *5*(2), 255–167.

Soyomi, J., Oloruntoba, S. A., & Okafor, B. (2015). Analysis of mobile phone impact on student academic performance in the tertiary institution. *International Journal of Emerging Technology and Advanced Engineering*, *5*(1), 361–367.

Statistics, G. M. (2014). *Part A: Mobile Subscribers worldwide*. Retrieved May 11th, 2014 from http://mobithinking.com/mobile-marketing-tools/lateste-mobile-stats/a#subscribers

Stone, D. L., & Deadrick, D. L. (2015). Challenges and opportunities affecting the future of human resource management. *Human Resource Management Review*, *25*(2), 139–145. doi:10.1016/j.hrmr.2015.01.003

Sulemana, M. (2018). The Provision of Educational Infrastructure and Academic Performance in Tertiary Institutions in Ghana: University of Developmental Studies (UDS), WA Campus as a Case Study. *Review of Higher Education in Africa*, *3*(1).

Sulzberger. (2001). *Internet Service Providers and communications solutions in Ghana*. Paper presented to the International Finance Corporation, World Bank.

Sumaili, A., Dlodlo, N., & Osakwe, J. (2018, October). Adopting Dynamic Capabilities of Mobile Information and Communication Technology in Namibian Small and Medium Enterprises. In 2018 Open Innovations Conference (OI) (pp. 213-222). IEEE. doi:10.1109/OI.2018.8535941

Tanle, A., & Abane, A. M. (2017). Mobile phone use and livelihoods: Qualitative evidence from some rural and urban areas in Ghana. *GeoJournal*, 1–11.

Tumuheki, P. B., Zeelen, J., & Openjuru, G. L. (2016). Towards a conceptual framework for developing capabilities of new types of students participating in higher education in Sub-Saharan Africa. *International Journal of Educational Development*, *47*, 54–62. doi:10.1016/j.ijedudev.2015.12.005

Vasudeva, G., Alexander, E. A., & Jones, S. L. (2015). Institutional logics and inter-organizational learning in technological arenas: Evidence from standard-setting organizations in the mobile handset industry. *Organization Science*, *26*(3), 830–846. doi:10.1287/orsc.2014.0940

Wilkins, S., & Huisman, J. (2012). The international branch campus as a transnational strategy in higher education. *Higher Education*, *64*(5), 627–645. doi:10.100710734-012-9516-5

Wiseman, A. W., Astiz, M. F. & Baker, D. P. (2013). Globalization and comparative education research: Misconceptions and applications of neo-institutional theory. *Journal of Supranational Policies of Education*, (1), 31-52.

Wiseman, A. W., & Chase-Mayoral, A. (2013). Shifting the Discourse on Neo-Institutional Theory in Comparative and International Education. *Annual Review of Comparative and International Education*, *20*, 99–126.

Zhu, Y., Rooney, D., & Phillips, N. (2016). Practice-based wisdom theory for integrating institutional logics: A new model for social entrepreneurship learning and education. *Academy of Management Learning & Education*, *15*(3), 607–625. doi:10.5465/amle.2013.0263

Zundans-Fraser, L., & Bain, A. (2016). How do institutional practices for course design and review address areas of need in Higher Education? *Higher Education Research & Development*, 1–13.

ADDITIONAL READING

Asongu, S. A., & Nwachukwu, J. C. (2018). Educational quality thresholds in the diffusion of knowledge with mobile phones for inclusive human development in sub-Saharan Africa. *Technological Forecasting and Social Change*, *129*, 164–172. doi:10.1016/j.techfore.2018.01.004

Crossan, A., McKelvey, N., & Curran, K. (2019). Mobile Technologies Impact on Economic Development in Sub-Saharan Africa. In Advanced Methodologies and Technologies in Network Architecture, Mobile Computing, and Data Analytics (pp. 1031-1039). IGI Global. doi:10.4018/978-1-5225-7598-6.ch075

Hamidi, H., & Chavoshi, A. (2018). Analysis of the essential factors for the adoption of mobile learning in higher education: A case study of students of the University of Technology. *Telematics and Informatics*, *35*(4), 1053–1070. doi:10.1016/j.tele.2017.09.016

Kruss, G., McGrath, S., Petersen, I. H., & Gastrow, M. (2015). Higher education and economic development: The importance of building technological capabilities. *International Journal of Educational Development*, *43*, 22–31. doi:10.1016/j.ijedudev.2015.04.011

Smith, M. A. (2018). *The 'Glocalization' of Mobile Telephony in West and Central Africa: Consumer Appropriation and Corporate Acculturation: A Cas*. Langaa RPCIG.

Traxler, J. M. (2018). Learning with mobiles in developing countries: Technology, language, and literacy. In Information and Technology Literacy: Concepts, Methodologies, Tools, and Applications (pp. 774-790). IGI Global.

Zapp, M., Marques, M., & Powell, J. J. (2018, November). European Educational Research (Re) Constructed: institutional change in Germany, the United Kingdom, Norway, and the European Union. *Symposium Books Ltd*. 10.15730/books.102

Zhang, G., Boyce, G., & Ahmed, K. (2014). Institutional changes in university accounting education in post-revolutionary China: From political orientation to internationalization. *Critical Perspectives on Accounting*, 25(8), 819–843. doi:10.1016/j.cpa.2013.10.007

Zhu, C. (2015). Organizational culture and technology-enhanced innovation in higher education. *Technology, Pedagogy and Education*, 24(1), 65–79. doi:10.1080/1475939X.2013.822414

KEY TERMS AND DEFINITIONS

Donor Agency: Foreign governments and firms that offer financial assistance to help fund programs in developing economies.

Internally Generated Funds: Monetary-yielding activities embarked on by governmental institutions to supplement government funds.

Mobile Learning: Mobile devices and technology-enabled learning.

Non-Governmental Institution: Non-profit making bodies that support various sectors of the economy in a country to improve development.

Public-Private Partnerships: Mutually beneficial associations formed between public and private institutions.

Technological Transformation: Form and process changes emanating from technology adoption and use within institutions.

Tertiary Institution: Institutions that offer post-secondary education.

Chapter 18
Development Impacts of Free Public Wi-Fi in Johannesburg

Judy Backhouse
https://orcid.org/0000-0002-6269-7910
United Nations University, Portugal

Hlelo Chauke
University of the Witwatersrand, South Africa

ABSTRACT

Information and communications technologies (ICTs) promise development gains, yet the complexity and opacity of the relationships between ICT initiative and development effect makes it difficult to identify these development gains or to theorize connections. This case study does both. First, it identifies the connections between the roll-out of free public Wi-Fi by the City of Johannesburg and changes that have resulted in city residents' lives. Second, it uses the choice framework to explain how these changes come about. This qualitative case study conducted interviews with users of the city's free public Wi-Fi service to understand how the service has changed the choices they have, leading to development in the sense of increased capabilities. Benefits identified included easier communications, savings in time and money, social and psychological benefits, as well as increased knowledge, business ideas, access to markets, access to job opportunities, and increased income. This study demonstrates how the linkages can be understood, albeit not in a linear fashion.

INTRODUCTION

With the promise to address a wide range of developmental challenges, the role of information and communications technology (ICT) is becoming widely accepted as an enabler to foster development for different countries and communities (Sein et al., 2016). ICT promises opportunities to address some of the Sustainable Development Goals, yet the complexity and opacity of the relationships between ICT initiative and development effect makes it difficult to understand the causal linkages and to design effective interventions.

DOI: 10.4018/978-1-7998-2610-1.ch018

Trying to connect the intuitive idea that ICT is good for development with the reality of many project failures (Heeks, 2002) has been the core work of ICT for Development (ICT4D) researchers in the past four decades (Walsham, 2017). This work has resulted in useful theoretical developments which are now being operationalized in ways that provide practitioners with deeper understandings as well as practical guides that can be followed to improve the chances of success.

This chapter examines how the linkages between ICT and development can be understood, using the case of the provision of free public Wi-Fi in Johannesburg, South Africa and its development effects. First, it examines understandings of development and the role of ICT, in particular the role of internet access for development. Second, it identifies the connections between the roll-out of free public Wi-Fi to residents of Johannesburg and the changes in resident's lives that have resulted. Third, it uses the Choice Framework (Kleine, 2010) to explain how these changes come about through increasing the choices available to residents. Finally, it reflects on lessons learned from this case that may be applicable to other ICT4D projects.

BACKGROUND

Understanding Development

Development is difficult to define and open to a range of interpretations. Sumner and Tribe (2008) identified three different meanings of development. In the first, development is understood as "a long-term process of structural societal transformation" that is concerned with socio-economic structural changes like the organisation of production, ownership, institutional structures, technology, and law. In the second, favoured by international development agencies, development is viewed as "a short-to-medium-term outcome of desirable targets" to be achieved based on agreed timelines. The third meaning is of development as "a discourse of Western modernity", that is as a social construct aligned with the idea of moving towards "modern" ways of living and being.

The concept of development is constantly being revised (Coelho et al., 2015). There has been a trend away from purely economic understandings of development in terms of increasing gross national product and per capita income (Hirschman, 1958), through various critiques, to a more nuanced form that includes social and ecological goals (Kleine, 2010). Development, as currently understood by ICT4D practitioners and researchers recognizes cultural and social differences and takes into account improvements in education, health, and quality of life (Andrade and Urquhart, 2010; Mthoko & Khene, 2018).

Starting in the 1980s, Sen developed a perspective on development as the freedom that an individual has to choose. Sen (1999) speaks of 'functionings' as the things that an individual wants to do or be and 'capability' as the different combinations of functionings that each individual can achieve. Clearly individuals may have a limited set of functionings available to them and may have to trade off one against the other when resources are limited. Development then happens when the capabilities of people increase, allowing bigger and more varied sets of functionings. Economic development brings bigger capability sets, but that is only part of the story. Increased freedom to choose those combinations of functionings that matter to the individual, may depend on broader social conditions or on personal agency.

Sen's work has been welcomed, but has proved difficult to operationalize. In particular, researchers have struggled to apply Sen's capability approach to development in specific contexts, while avoiding dictating specific development outcomes (Kleine, 2010). Sen insists that the capabilities to be developed should be chosen by the individual (Sen, 1997). What this means is that it is not possible to define intended development outcomes at the outset of any ICT4D intervention, given that such interventions often empower individuals to pursue development outcomes that they choose (Kleine, 2010). Such uncertainty in outcomes makes it difficult to design ICT4D interventions and requires a degree of open-mindedness towards the choices that people make as a result of the intervention.

Kleine (2010) went on to develop the Choice Framework as a means of operationalizing Sen's capability approach and understanding the connections between interventions that change structure and agency, the choices they facilitate and the development outcomes that result. This chapter adopts Sen's understanding of development and uses Kleine's Choice Framework to understand the case of the provision of free, public Wi-Fi in Johannesburg.

The Choice Framework

The Choice Framework (Figure 2) was developed by Kleine (2010) specifically for evaluating how ICTs contribute to development. The Choice Framework is based on Sen's capability approach, and operationalizes a model of how individuals make choices, taking into account the structural conditions and their own agency, towards self-defined development outcomes. Central to the Choice Framework are the choices that individuals make towards achieving the life they value and want to live. Whether and how these choices are made, depends on the agency of the individual and on the structures within which the individual is situated. Development can be observed when the freedom of choice for an individual expands, leading to a wider set of development outcomes.

Agency, for an individual, develops based on the set of resources that the individual has access to. Kleine identifies ten classes of resources that impact on the individual's sense of agency, including educational, psychological, information, financial, cultural, social, natural, material, geographical and health resources. The structural conditions that the individual is situated in, including the institutions, discourses, formal and informal rules, programmes, and ICT access also constrain or enable the choices that the individual can make, both directly, by influencing the dimensions of choice, and indirectly, by impacting on the set of resources that the individual is exposed to and hence their agency. Of course, agency can also impact on the structural conditions of the individual.

In terms of the Choice Framework, there are four dimensions of choice (Kleine, 2010). For individuals to be able to make choices, first there need to be a choice (existence of choice), secondly the individual needs to be aware of it (sense of choice), then they need to actually make the choice (use of choice) and finally, the outcomes need to match the choice expressed (achievement of choice). All four of these dimensions of choice need to be in place for an individual to make a choice and achieve a desired outcome.

The desired development outcome is primarily an expansion of the choices available to the individual (Sen, 1999). From there, the individual will be able to make choices to improve their life in terms of what they value. Changes that result from the choices made are thus secondary outcomes as a consequence of the primary development outcome of expanded choice.

The Importance of Internet Access

In the last decade, ICT has transformed several aspects of human everyday life. Scholars from different fields of study have acknowledged the pervasive effects that ICTs have had on different sectors of the

Figure 1. Kleine's Choice Framework
(Source: Adapted from Kleine, 2010)

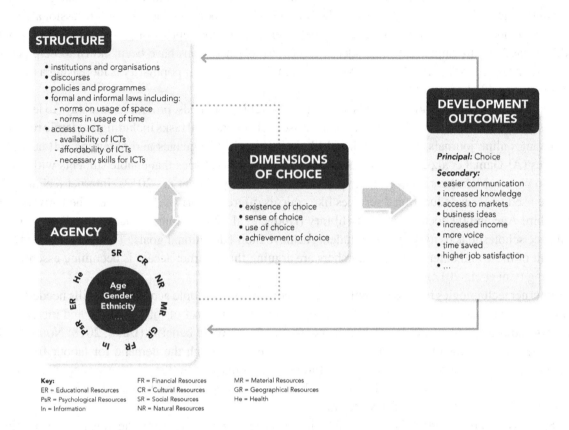

economy (Castellacci & Tveito, 2018). It is also now broadly accepted that ICT contributes to development beyond just economic aspects (Heeks & Kanashiro, 2009; Thapa et al., 2012; Zheng et al., 2018).

One of the key ICT advancements was the advent of the Internet which has become an important enabler for everyday life. Individuals are able to use the Internet to perform a wide range of activities that enable them to achieve their desired outcomes. This section argues for the importance of internet access in moving towards achieving sustainable development goals by looking at what past research has shown.

Internet access provides people with the ability to communicate with those in close proximity and further away, enabling individual connectedness. The challenges of remoteness have been studied in villages in a mountain region of Nepal (Thapa et al., 2012) and in mountainous Huancavelica, Peru (Heeks and Kanashiro, 2009). These studies show that internet access enables people to maintain social networks and gain access to information, reducing the isolation and feelings of exclusion of people in these areas. The Internet can be used to forge new social connections, enhance existing relationships and increase access to social resources (Alias, 2013; Islam et al., 2018; Nowland et al., 2017). The Internet is also a useful tool for reducing loneliness for those who struggle to connect in person, thus improving individual quality of life.

Internet connectivity has provided people with increased access to information about health and wellbeing (Castellacci & Tveito, 2018) making them more informed and better able to manage their health as well as participate in healthcare decision-making (Ben, 2016). Such information is widely accessed by people from teenagers to the elderly and studies show improvements in well-being as a result (Lifshitz et al., 2018; Utter et al., 2018). The Internet also supports the healthcare professional. There is strong evidence that therapist-guided internet interventions for depression are effective as a way to address the large treatment gap (Schröder et al., 2016). Medical apps have been shown to help people manage chronic illnesses like Diabetes Mellitus (Ben, 2016) and their popularity is increasing as a result of internet enabled devices (Klonoff, 2013).

The use of ICT in education changes learning and teaching methods, providing new ways to learn and access educational resources. The internet can be used for educational tasks including academic research, retrieving online journals, browsing virtual libraries, learning languages and obtaining full academic degrees (Al-Gamal et al., 2015) as well as virtual science laboratories that enable students without access to physical laboratories to conduct practical experiments (Cui et al., 2012). Internet technologies can be used to access educational services like courses offered by private companies, the University of the Third Age and the local community library (Hodge et al., 2017). Internet access has been found to enhance scholastic activities and help students achieve their educational goals (Tossell et al., 2015). As a result of these and other results, researchers are arguing that internet access is becoming essential for learning (Cui et al., 2012).

Internet technologies increases employment opportunities as people acquire ICT skills needed in the job market (Galperin and Viecens, 2017). They also reduce the cost of job searching and increase the opportunities available, resulting in higher incomes and economic benefits (Budu, 2018; Noor, 2018). The internet is claimed to have created new jobs "directly through the demand for labour from new technology-based enterprises and indirectly through the demand from the wider ecosystem" (Deloitte, 2014:15). For example, YouTube video makers have created their own employment by creating relevant, on-demand content, that attracts advertisers.

Studies have attempted to establish whether internet access plays a role in eradicating poverty however, the relationship is very complex and there have been calls for more studies to investigate it (Galperin & Viecens, 2017). Claims are that the internet helps to reduce poverty through increasing opportunities for economic activities and that access has a positive impact on standard of living through increased job and business opportunities, leading to higher income (Deloitte, 2014). Some of the literature seems to support this, showing that people develop new capabilities through education and better access to information while experiencing an increased sense of connection.

Access to the Internet has also been associated with negative outcomes such as social overload (Maier et al, 2015; Karwatzki et al., 2017), lack of privacy (Karwatzki et al., 2017) and aggressive behaviour (Rösner et al., 2016). While understanding these negative outcomes is important, they were not the subject of this study.

Internet Penetration in South Africa

Despite the development programmes that have been implemented in South Africa; the Reconstruction and Development Programme (RDP, 1994), Growth, Employment and Redistribution (GEAR, 1996), the Accelerated and Shared Growth Initiative for South Africa (ASGISA, 2005) and New Growth Path (GNP, 2010), South African internet penetration remains low compared to other countries. Internet World Stats (2017) and Statista (2017) estimate that the 5 countries in Africa with the most internet users are Nigeria, Egypt, Kenya, South Africa and Tanzania. Nigeria leads with 98.39 million internet users and

South Africa was estimated to have about 30.8 million internet users in 2017, an internet penetration rate of about 53.7% (Stats SA, 2018). This means that almost half of the South African population have no internet access. Making the internet available to all South Africans only gained traction with the National Development Plan (NDP) in 2012, a blueprint for eliminating poverty and reducing inequality in South Africa by 2030.

The problem of low internet penetration is multifaceted, but inappropriate policy frameworks and limited investment in infrastructure have contributed. It has also been attributed to high data costs. A study which compared the cheapest 1 gigabytes (GBs) of data in each African country ranked South Africa 35th of out of 49 countries with data costing seven times more in South Africa than in Egypt and nearly three times more than the same data in Ghana, Kenya and Nigeria (RAMP Index, 2018).

Recently there has been an increase in availability of Wi-Fi for internet access in public spaces (Hampton & Gupta, 2008). A number of cities have embarked on broadband infrastructure investments and projects to provide internet connectivity to residents (Mutula & Mostert, 2010). The City of Tshwane has rolled out over 780 free public Wi-Fi hotspots in townships such as Atteridgeville, Mamelodi and Soshanguve. The City of Ekurhuleni commenced a Wi-Fi project in January 2015 to provide Wi-Fi access to 695 buildings including libraries, clinics and other public buildings. The City of Cape Town rolled out free public Wi-Fi, starting in 2013, to make broadband internet accessible to households in under-served communities and has over 100 hotspots installed in public buildings across Cape Town (Geerdts et al., 2016).

This study looks at the free public Wi-Fi project offered by the City of Johannesburg, which is described below.

ABOUT THE STUDY

The Case of Free Public Wi-Fi in Johannesburg

As part of a Smart City strategy, the City of Johannesburg has been offering free public Wi-Fi to residents from city libraries, bus stops and other commonly used public spaces since 2015. The motivation for the project was to facilitate better communication with residents, to increase the information available to residents and to improve economic opportunities for residents (CoJ, 2018b).

The City of Johannesburg is one of five municipalities in the Gauteng province of South Africa, one of nine South African provinces. Gauteng is the smallest (in land area), but most populous province in South Africa with an estimated 14.7 million residents, more than a quarter of the population of the country (Stats SA, 2018). Despite its small size, Gauteng contributed 34% of the national GDP in 2017 (Stats SA, 2019b). Gauteng consists of three metropolitan municipalities, the City of Ekurhuleni, the City of Johannesburg and the City of Tshwane, as well as two district municipalities. The City of Johannesburg is the largest, with an estimated 4.9 million inhabitants, a population that is expected to double in the next 35 years (CoJ, 2018a). Seventy-two percent of the population of the City of Johannesburg are 'working age' (15-64 years old), however regional statistics show an overall unemployment rate in the province of 28.9% (Stats SA, 2019a).

The City of Johannesburg is divided into seven regions (Figure 2) with very different social and economic profiles including rural, township, suburban, industrial and dense commercial centres. Its borders extend from Midrand in the North-East, which houses the headquarters of large national and

Figure 2. City of Johannesburg Regions
(Source: City of Johannesburg)

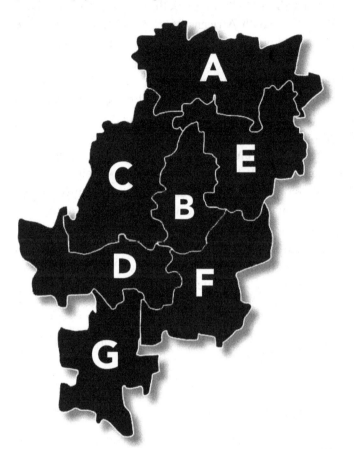

Region A	Dainfern, Diepsloot, Fourways, Ivory Park, Kya Sands, Lanseria, Midrand
Region B	Emmarentia, Greenside, Mayfair, Melville, Northcliff, Parktown, Randburg, Rosebank
Region C	Bram Fischerville, Constantia Kloof, Florida, Northgate, Roodepoort
Region D	Diepkloof, Dobsonville, Doornkop, Protea Glen, Soweto
Region E	Alexandra, Bruma, Houghton, Orange Grove, Sandton, Woodmead, Wynberg
Region F	Aeroton, Inner City, Johannesburg South, Southgate
Region G	Eldorado Park, Ennerdale, Lenasia, Orange Farm, Protea South, Weilers Farm

international companies, to the low-cost government housing and informal settlements of Orange Farm in the South, and the middle-class residential and commercial Roodepoort in the West. It includes the sprawling Soweto township and the high-tech centre of Sandton from where the country's sophisticated financial sector operates.

The City of Johannesburg has identified several socio-economic challenges to be prioritised, including over-population, poverty, inequality, a low human development index, a high unemployment rate, food security, HIV, and access to basic services (CoJ, 2018b). The City is committed to being responsive and to "pro-poor development" (CoJ, 2018a: p20-22). They also seek to "encourage innovation and efficiency through the smart city programme" (CoJ, 2018a: p22). The vision of the City's smart city strategy is that Johannesburg "makes decisions and governs through technologically enhanced engagement with its citizens who have universal access to services and information, where socio-economic development and efficient service delivery are at its core" (CoJ, 2018b: p45-46).

In support of this vision, the City of Johannesburg initiated the roll-out of free public Wi-Fi. By the end of 2016, the City had provided more than 1000 hotspots and they had been used by more than 400 000 residents. The City also set up a program of student assistants, the Johannesburg Digital Ambassadors, to raise awareness about the hotspots and to assist people to get connected and set up e-mail accounts. Each user is provided with 300 megabytes of data per day or 9 gigabytes per month, if used daily. There is also unlimited access to a set of services provided on the City's Maru a Jozi portal, http://maruajozi.joburg/.

While the number of people using the service is being monitored, it is more difficult to know what they are using it for and, more importantly, whether and how this increased access to the internet is benefitting the city residents. The research question that this study set out to answer was: How does the use of free public Wi-Fi impact the development of City of Johannesburg residents, as perceived by the residents?"

Research Methods

The paradigm for the study was interpretive, in keeping with the authors' understanding of people as social actors with multiple subjective meanings among them (Saunders et al., 2009). The intention was to gain deep insights into the complex processes of how development outcomes arise in the real-world context (Klein & Myers, 1999, Thirsk & Clark, 2017). Consequently, the study made use of qualitative methods in the natural settings of the respondents (Denzin & Lincoln, 1994). The authors conducted semi-structured face-to-face interviews using an interview guide.

This was a cross-sectional case study (Saunders et al., 2009) investigating what development impacts residents had experienced at a single point in time. The data was collected in October 2018, after the free public Wi-Fi had been available for around three years. This was judged a sufficiently long time for residents to have been able to see development impacts from the use of the service that might have unfolded over months or years.

The authors used purposive or judgmental sampling to select respondents (in this case Johannesburg residents who were using the free public Wi-Fi hotspots) best suited to answering the research questions (Saunders et al., 2009). The sampling was addressed in two stages. First, a selection of sites was made from all the sites where the city had installed free public Wi-Fi hotspots. Then, individual respondents were selected from the people present at each site on the day of data collection.

Although the free public Wi-Fi had been rolled out in several different kinds of public spaces, public libraries and community centres were selected for this study, because people were in these locations for some time, making interviews feasible. Previous experience of trying to conduct interviews at city bus stops found data collection difficult there because people spend less time at bus stops and interviews were interrupted by the arrival and departure of buses. Permission to conduct interviews at clinics could not be secured.

The next task was to select regions in which to look for libraries and community centres. The author's knowledge of context guided the selection (Thirsk & Clark, 2017). It seemed likely that residents in townships might use the free public Wi-Fi for tasks quite different to residents in the suburbs or business areas, so the authors selected Lenasia (region G) and Orlando East (region D) to compare with Sandton (region E) and Johannesburg (region F). Libraries and community centres within these regions were selected that (1) had been operating the free public Wi-Fi for at least a year, (2) were willing to allow data collection at the site and (3) were accessible to the interviewer.

Interviews were conducted by the second author who approached individuals in the sites who appeared to be above 18 years of age and were making use of the free public Wi-Fi at these sites. The research was explained to prospective participants and the age of participants was confirmed before inviting them to participate. Those who were willing, consented in writing to participate and to have the interview recorded.

Table 1. Distribution of respondents

Region	Site	Respondents
Region D, Soweto	Orlando East Public Library	2 respondents
Region D, Soweto	Orland East Community Centre	2 respondents
Region E, Sandton	Sandton Public Library	2 respondents
Region F, Johannesburg	Johannesburg Public Library	2 respondents
Region G, Johannesburg South	Lenasia Public Library	2 respondents
Region G, Johannesburg South	Lenasia Community Centre	2 respondents

In total twelve interviews were conducted as follows:

Nine of the respondents fell in the age-group 18-34 and three were aged 35 or older. Three of the respondents were women and nine were men. This selection was not intended to be representative, but rather to give a range of views that could be compared and contrasted to develop our understanding of the development impact (Thirsk & Clark, 2017).

Interview recordings were transcribed into text documents which were analysed using thematic analysis (Braun and Clarke, 2006). The authors made use of closed coding based on Kleine's (2010) Choice Framework. It became necessary to introduce additional codes for some benefits not identified in Kleine's framework. This is in keeping with the idea that development outcomes are the choices of individuals.

Benefits of Free Public Wi-Fi

All of the respondents interviewed felt that they had benefitted from the free public Wi-Fi and that it had improved their lives. The service saved them time and money. It made communication easier. In addition to facilitating formal learning, it increased their knowledge of other aspects of the world. They reported access to job opportunities, increased income, business ideas, access to markets and new opportunities. They also reported that coming to the library had enabled them to meet new people and made them feel more connected.

One respondent said that "it saves my time and it saves my energy because I need not to go to Johannesburg where there is a bigger library ... I don't have to go to the internet Café I just stay here and connect with my phone" (R1).

All respondents spoke about the financial benefit of using Wi-Fi, making comments like "I have managed to save money" (R7) and "I am saving money, because I am using MTN (cellular phone company); when other people are crying that MTN is eating their data, I know I can just come here" (R6). Respondents claimed savings even when they had to offset the cost of a taxi to come to the library, "I don't have to spend a lot of money in buying airtime, even though I am using a taxi; it is not a loss because the benefit outweighs the amount I spend to get here" (R4).

Most of the respondents recognised that access to free public Wi-Fi enabled them to communicate more easily. They spoke about using it to communicate with "friends and family" (R5) and "my family back in Limpopo" (R6). They also used it for business communication "to check if there is someone who inboxed me or someone has a question about an item or something" (R9) or in trying to secure jobs as Respondent 6 explains:

With employment agencies, they will say: 'We are going to send you an email now. Respond to the email and check what needs to be sent and then send it. So that we can call you to confirm the interview.' So, if you do not have data, you can just come and then check the email, get everything that you need, sort everything out and then they call you back for a job interview. Much convenient. (R6)

The service also gave respondents a wider choice of ways to communicate. Respondents 4, 8 and 10 spoke about the benefit of being able to communicate using video calls, "something you wouldn't do if you were using your own data" (R8). They also use "WhatsApp, Facebook and all the social media" (R6; also R1, R2, R3, R5, R10 and R12) and Skype "because the network is strong enough to do that" (R10).

Many of the respondents were engaged in formal learning and made use of the free public Wi-Fi to support their learning (R2, R3, R4, R7, R8, R9, R10 and R12). Respondent 3 used online tutorials when rewriting the national school leaving examination and Respondent 4 claimed that "it has boosted my marks", explaining that "I don't have as much books as the other students" but that "I get some textbooks on the Internet and … download them and study".

In addition to formal study, several of the respondents mentioned that the free public Wi-Fi expanded their general knowledge. For example, Respondent 8, who is studying engineering, has used the free public Wi-Fi to apply for internships and in the process has learned about the places that they might work in.

I actually get to see that these are the places where, most likely, I would be able to find internships or that job. So, I get to expand … ok, these are the place I might be working at beside being here, ekasi (in the township), I would have to go to Limpopo, I would have to go to Mpumalanga. I get to hear different places and see different places. (R8)

Respondents 1, 5, 6, 8, 9, 10 and 11 had used the free public Wi-Fi to apply for jobs. Respondents 1, 5, 6 and 9 stated clearly that it had increased their job opportunities. Respondent 5 said: "Well, I have been to a couple of interviews. I have had to cancel a couple of them because they were clashing, so it has improved the opportunities, dramatically actually." In addition to increasing the volume of opportunities, it had also increased the range of job opportunities available:

I use it normally for … doing job application. Ammm … they have changed! Unlike buying newspaper, unlike going to government offices to check on the papers that they put on the notice board, I can now check for jobs from private companies as well as government. Basically, that changed a lot, it has improved. (R6)

When asked whether the service had increased their income, all the respondents identified cost savings from not having to buy expensive data. Some indicated increased income from business activities (R4, R6 and R9) and one had found employment (R11). Many were using the service in the hope of improving their income in the future, by studying (R2, R3, R4, R7, R8, R9, R10 and R12), by applying for jobs (R5, R6, R8, R9, R11 and R12) or by increasing their work-related skills (R1, R3, R4, R6 and R11). Respondent 9 was doing courses "on how to grow your Instagram following" through Shopify Academy and Respondent 11 uses the Internet to "learn more about acting".

Seven of the twelve respondents indicated that they had used the free Wi-Fi access to come up with or to implement business ideas. These included doing school homework for payment (R4), online trading (R4, R5, R6 and R7), an online marketing company (R6), an online boutique (R9), a multimedia company (R10) and a property business (R12). Three of them (R4, R6 and R9) reported some degree of financial success with their businesses even if, "it's slow but, but at least now I am at breakeven point, so at least I don't have to cough money out of my pocket" (R9).

Respondent 3, an upcoming music producer, uses Facebook to access a bigger audience or fan base for their music, and is considering using YouTube to publish and sell "my beats". Respondent 9 uses the Wi-Fi hotspot to access social media to advertise an online shop as well as to access a bigger client base. The business uses social media to get online orders for clothing items from clients all over the country and ships the orders to clients using the postal service.

Respondents noted that they had more opportunities "like we learn for free, job seekers can look for jobs … they can apply for jobs and … they do everything like e-mailing CVs" (R4) and that they are able to take advantage of those opportunities. Respondent 6 explained "it is useless having opportunities and not having money … if you don't have money to buy data it means you are going to get those information late".

Baron and Gomez (2013) argued that public access computing enables users to build relationships and increase their sense of belonging and this was also observed in this study. Respondent 6 said "I have met new people" and although "I cannot say they are my friend; it is just people I usually see", there is a sense of connection, "I know I will find them here or they will find me". Respondent 11 says "I made friends here ... I met a lot of people though coming here" and Respondent 1 met someone who "is now my fiancé".

Most of the respondents (R1, R3, R4, R6, R7, R8, R9, R10 and R12) also mentioned using the service for leisure activities, saying "I just download some movies and download some games just for fun" (R4) and "I used to load some series from Netflix" (R9) or "I mostly download books, songs, motivational videos" (R12). Although not identified as benefits by respondents, who were quick to emphasise that they used the service for more serious tasks, clearly access to these forms of entertainment are also valued by them.

The evidence shows that the people using the free public Wi-Fi at the Johannesburg City libraries can identify several ways in which the service has improved their lives. They all saved money, and for one person, time. Communication had become easier with more ways to communicate for both social and business ends. The service facilitated formal learning by giving them access to resources that they would not otherwise have had, but it also provided resources for learning business skills and increasing their general knowledge of the world and staying informed about their individual interests. They had increased access to job opportunities, business ideas and markets which had resulted, for some, in increased income. They also reported social benefits and a greater sense of connection as well as access to leisure resources.

UNDERSTANDING HOW DEVELOPMENT HAPPENS

Recall that development is an increase in individual capabilities, or the different combinations of functionings that each individual can achieve (Sen, 1999). The Choice Framework (Klein, 2010) is valuable in understanding how development comes about. This section examines how the dynamics of this framework could be observed in the case study.

Structure

The interventions by the City of Johannesburg changed the structural conditions for residents. The programme introduced free Wi-Fi access into public locations. This increased access to ICTs by making internet access available and more affordable. By providing tutors to support people to connect and learn to use the internet, the program also addressed the structural issue of having the necessary ICT skills. The programme also changed norms, making internet access a service provided by the City where previously it had been the responsibility of the individual. For working people, who might have had access to the internet during office hours, there was now the option of accessing the internet after hours or at weekends and this is different because "there is no one watching me here like at the office" (R9).

On the other hand, there was evidence of structure still limiting the choices of individuals. The location of those venues where the service was installed was not always convenient. Several of the respondents walked (R1, R5, R6, R7, R8, R10, R11), some up to an hour each way (R1, R10) or paid taxi fares (R3, R4, R6, R9, R12) to get to the library. Respondent 6 said "Wi-Fi is a very good idea, but I would say they don't need to put it here only in Orlando, also in other locations like Pimville". Some locations had security measures, while others did not and this limited their use as people did not feel safe at certain times. The libraries had limited opening hours and this prevented one respondent from participating in online trading as the trading "starts at 12 and then the library closes at 1pm ... I only had 1 hour to place my trades" (R6).

A strong discourse was evident about the proper use of the facility, which was generally deemed to be for study or research. Respondents seemed reluctant to admit that they used the network for anything else, reassuring the interviewer that they prioritised more serious tasks, although it is not clear whether they were being entirely honest about this. Respondent 4 said, "Myself, when I am finished with my researches, I can download a movie", and Respondent 8 explained that their "first priority is to study" but then they use it for "everything". For those who were less susceptible to this discourse, the program expanded the use of libraries from primarily a place to study, to a social space, a place of entertainment, and a site of business.

In this case, changes in structure can be observed, that expand choices, but at the same time, structural influences that constrain the uses that residents can make of the service. These kinds of complex structural outcomes are inevitable in ICT4D projects and the framework forces researchers to pay attention to them and to think about how they are unfolding.

Resources and Agency

The free Wi-Fi programme brought a range of new or different resources to residents. By accessing the internet, people had access to new educational and information resources, and these then opened up financial resources as well. Respondents also found that they increased their geographic, psychological and social resources.

Respondents 2, 3, 4, 7, 8, 9, 10 and 12 were studying and made use of online learning resources. Respondent 3 explained that "I rewrote my matric (school leaving examination) in 2016. This Wi-Fi helped me a lot with tutorials ... I could now understand much better the subjects that I was rewriting." Respondent 7, a computer science student, uses MIT Open Courseware "for my modules like maths and computer science".

Access to the internet also increases more general information resources and respondents used it to learn more about their chosen field of work or hobbies or their areas of interest. Respondent 3 said "it improves me in the music production that I am working on; I can learn from other people's ideas and then put my own flavour." Respondent 5, a political science graduate, used it "to keep abreast with the current affairs" and gave as an example "there is a jobs summit to day, so I keep on checking what they are talking about right now". Respondent 11, a radio presenter, uses the Wi-Fi to access information on acting and to do research for his show.

As discussed above, all of the respondents reported that the free public Wi-Fi increased their financial resources by reducing their expenses. One reported having secured a job (R11) and three reported that they had attracted income from business activities (R4, R6, R9).

For some respondents, while the Wi-Fi had attracted them to use the library, being in this physical space gave them access to geographical, psychological or social resources. Respondent 9 explained that they used a particular library because it was close to shops, saying:

This one is convenient … if I go to the Savoy one I will have to bring lunch, I will have to bring in a lot of stuff because it is in the middle of a suburb, so there is no shops around … that is why I prefer this one so I am able to run errands in between. (R9)

Respondent 12 finds that being in the library improves focus, contributing to their psychological resources, "People are serious here, people are actually studying … you are like, yohh! I should be focused too." Respondent 4 has gained confidence, saying "I am confident … the more you use it, the more you understand." Respondents 1, 6 and 11 had met new people and made friends at the library, building their social resources. Respondent 1 explains how the service expands social and psychological resources in the community, saying:

Just before you got here, there was a man who came to ask to search for this other security company, he called the name. He asked me to connect and see where this place is in Krugersdorp, he need to go there tomorrow, they need people. It makes me happy because I was able to connect and got the place, the phone number and the address of that place and the street. And it is not only him, there are so many people who got assistance, I am also one of those people who got assistance using this Wi-Fi. (R1)

Material resources continue to constrain some of the respondents. Although Wi-Fi was now being provided, they still need devices to make use of it. There were some computers in the libraries, but not enough for everyone, so many relied on their own devices which were not always optimal. "This type of device I am using (displaying a Huawei smartphone), sometimes it can't connect to everything that I need, because it will say that the memory is full … I don't have better devices than this phone, I don't have a laptop or a tablet" (R1). Even if you have a laptop, you may be constrained to using a less optimal device by structural conditions. "I use my cell phone … because of safety, I cannot carry my laptop for 7 Kilometers" (R6).

The specific combination of resources that each person experiences can be understood as a measure of their individual agency (Alsop & Heinsohn, 2005) and these, combined with the prevailing structural conditions, result in individual empowerment in the form of individuals acting on their increased choices. Thus, we observe respondents acting to change their lives as a result of the increased resources they experience.

The Dimensions of Choice: Primary Outcome

The first way in which the free public Wi-Fi project increased choice was by offering respondents more choice in how they connect to the internet (existence of choice). All participants were aware that they could buy data and use their cellphones to connect to the internet but they pointed out that the free public Wi-Fi, although often inconvenient, and sometimes less safe, was cheaper. Other options that they had were to use the internet at work or use a private hotspot at home, but this project meant that they now had the additional choice of connecting for free in a public venue. In addition, there was a choice of hotspots. Respondent 6 said, "There is one at Park Station, the is one at Bree taxi rank as well as closer to Luthuli house." They chose where to use the Wi-Fi based on proximity, quality of the service and safety.

Secondly, the project increased awareness of choice through notices on the wall in the library (R5, R8) and through radio advertisements (R6). Some people learned about it through word-of-mouth, like Respondent 7 who "was told by my younger brother", while others became aware through observation "I saw a lot of people just sitting around the library, having their laptops and cellphones, then I asked 'What is happening there?'" (R6). People also found out about the Wi-Fi when looking for connections on their phones. They said "the phone would alert you that there is Wi-Fi" (R8) and "when I was checking if the Wi-Fi was available, I saw this one from the library" (R9).

Use of choice was supported by providing tutors to help those who needed guidance to connect. Respondent 1 said, "they were so helpful to connect us, to let us know about this Wi-Fi" and Respondent 3 echoed, "there were people that were training us, they helped us to register our accounts". Not all of the respondents needed this guidance. Respondents 5, 7, 9 and 12 indicated that their education enabled them to navigate the technology without assistance. With, or without assistance, all the respondents interviewed had succeeded in gaining access and were able to use the free public Wi-Fi.

Respondents reported that they had achieved their choice of accessing online services through the free public Wi-Fi, most of the time. Achievement of choice was, however, not consistent because the Wi-Fi didn't always work. People had no way to know whether it would be working or not and this created some frustration, especially for those who had to walk long distances or pay to get to the venue.

Well I was heartbroken. Considering the 35 minutes' walk to get here. I was heartbroken. If you consider the 35 minutes' walk to get here, and another 35 minutes to go back, and no one knows when it is going to be back up again. They are just telling us that they have reported it to the service provider, so we must just keep on checking. (R5)

Respondents who did experience interruptions in the Wi-Fi service felt that they had very little control over achievement of choice, perhaps because the service is free. They said, "We just say, 'Ok, it is not working' and leave; we don't even know who to complain to" (R6) and "What can we say? There is nothing I can say. It is free stuff, I can't complain" (R7).

There is evidence that respondents were able to navigate all four of the dimensions of choice, most of the time, with regards to their expanded choice of how to access the internet. In addition, the project also brought many more choices to the residents as a consequence of their greater access to the Internet. They had greater choice in how to use their financial resources; they had more options for communicating and greater choice in their leisure activities.

The Dimensions of Choice: Secondary Outcomes

The program resulted in more choices about how and what to learn. Several respondents used the internet to access formal studies (R2, R3, R4, R7, R8, R9, R10, R12), but they also about gaining access to alternative avenues for learning. Respondent 9, for example, takes courses in marketing through Shopify Academy in order to build their business because "when I built this e-commerce store, I realised I didn't know anything about marketing" and Respondent 6 has used it to learn about trading through webinars and videos. Some online resources are video based and hence costly to use so that "when I was using my own data, I would take like one module at a time or two at a time just to save data" (R9), but the free public Wi-Fi makes using these resources feasible. South Africa has a very limited tertiary education sector that serves only a small proportion of the population. Only 11,4% of South Africans older than 25 have completed a post-secondary course (Stats SA, 2019a) so this access to alternative sources of learning is invaluable.

Access to the internet also results in more choices of economic activities. Respondents used the internet to find jobs (R1, R5, R6, R8, R9, R10, R11), with the benefit of accessing a wider job market (R1, R5, R6, R9). Some of them had been able to participate in online trading (R4, R5, R6, R7). They also used it to get business ideas and to start businesses (R4, R5, R6, R7, R9, R10, R12) and to gain access to markets (R3, R9). Increasing the choices for economic activity is particularly important because South Africa has an unemployment rate of 27.6% and unemployment is as high as 55.2% for youth aged 15–24 (Stats SA, 2019a).

In exercising these choices, respondents had varying levels of success navigating the four dimensions of choice. Access to the internet increases the existence of choice in, for example, job or business opportunities, but awareness of choice depends to some extent on how individuals explore and find these opportunities. Use of choice was also variable, depending on the agency of the individual. Respondent 1 wants to be able to invest, but doesn't have money, so is learning more about investing for now. Use can also be hampered by structural issues such as the closing hours of the libraries, or safety concerns, or the 300MB limit which makes it "impossible" to study for "FAIS (Financial Advisory and Intermediary Services) credits" (R6). Respondent 7 explains that they can't trade because "the operating systems here are not compatible for my trading platform, Metatrader 4 [which needs] Ubuntu to be installed."

Achievement of choice is also unpredictable because of the many aspects that need to be in place, beyond internet access, for some of these choices to be realised. For example, Respondent 5 said that "it has disappointed me on a couple of occasions when I tried to apply for a master's program with Wits or UJ or with Unisa (local universities)". It is likely that the failure to submit an application in these cases lay with the University web sites, notorious for being unable to handle the volumes of applications they receive, and not with any failure on the part of the free, public Wi-Fi. However, such an experience can have a wider impact. When asked if he has tried to use the internet to make money, this respondent replies, "I thought, if it can't do such a simple transaction like online application, how can I make money out of it? I gave up. ... I got discouraged."

The free, public Wi-Fi project gave people in Johannesburg additional choices about how they could access the internet. Access to the information on the internet then brought a wealth of additional choices in terms of how they spent their money, how the communicated, and in their range of leisure activities. Residents had a wider selection of resources for learning and for economic activity. For people who had not previously had access to the internet, these choices would have been brought into existence by the program; for others, who were already aware of these choices, the program made it easier for them to use these choices. As they used and achieved these choices, the benefits that they identified materialised from the successful exercising of choice.

LESSONS LEARNED

This chapter has illustrated how Kleine's Choice Framework can be used to understand the dynamics of an ICT4D intervention; in this case showing how free, public Wi-Fi leads to development, where development is understood in terms of increased capabilities. We saw these increased capabilities reflected in the specific benefits that residents reported as a result of changed structures, improved agency and the successful exercise of choice.

The theoretical framing and the evidence point to ways in which ICT4D projects can be made more effective and this section discusses these lessons learned.

Human Systems are Complex and Dynamic

First it is necessary to understand that development is not a linear process with predictable outcomes. Human development can be viewed as a complex system and the presence in such systems of people, with the autonomy to make individual choices in pursuit of their personal goals, makes the outcomes unpredictable. While well-defined outcomes might be desired in motivating a project, they are best avoided. The most likely success will come from increasing the choices available to individuals in the system.

In this case, the focus of the project was simply on facilitating network access for residents, without any specific objectives in terms of what people might use that access for. This open-endedness allowed people to use the service (free Wi-Fi) in pursuit of a variety of personal goals and this is reflected in the benefits that they identified. Abuse of the system was limited by a daily cap per user, as well as by a discourse that favoured the use of the service for more 'serious' ends. Whether this discourse was designed into the intervention or not, it was an effective influence on how people used the service.

The dynamic nature of the system is also reflected in the interactions between structure, agency and choice. It is not possible to understand the process in a linear fashion (i.e. structural changes result in changes in agency, which lead to choice). Rather, there is a continual process of interaction between the elements of the system. This means that it is important to assess the systemic impacts in many directions, for example the impact that agency has on structure, the impact of choice on agency etc. An ongoing examination of all the interactions produces a rich understanding of the dynamics of the system.

Consider the Structural Context

In understanding the potential impact of an intervention, it is useful to think about the structural changes that are planned and that might result from the intervention. In this case a new programme was introduced with accompanying policies. New formal rules about the use were developed and informal rules emerged around who sat in which parts of the library and how to spend time using the service. Specific discourses grew up around the correct use of the service (for study and research), but also around the provision of the service and the role of the individuals in relation to a "free" service. The free, public Wi-Fi service increased access to ICT both in terms of infrastructure and the skills to use it.

It was not clear from the data to what extent the city had fostered the discourse around the proper use of the service or whether that emerged from the people using the service and a broader societal discourse about the need for education and information. However, this discourse did impact on the range of choices that individuals became aware of and made use of and hence on the secondary outcomes that were observed. There was little emphasis, for example, on the leisure benefits of the service.

Consider Individual Resources and Agency

Interventions that increase resources for the individual, and particularly those that increase resources in a number of different dimensions, are likely to have the most positive impacts on individual agency. In this case, increases in education, information and financial resources were observed, as well as changes in the geographical, psychological and social resources available to the participants. The impact of increased agency was observed in the decisions to exercise choice and the secondary outcomes that were achieved.

Agency depends not only on resources, but on other characteristics that position an individual in society. This study found relatively more men using the free, public Wi-Fi than women. This suggests that gender might have played a role in the extent to which people felt able to use the service. For example, navigating long distances to access the service could be riskier for women than for men, particularly in a society where violence against women is widespread and crime rates high. Thinking through the likely sources of agency brings to light such obstacles to who will use the service. Several respondents, for example, mentioned the need for security at the hotspots which may well increase the number of women benefitting from the service.

Address All Four Dimensions of Choice

In ensuring that interventions increase the choices available to individuals it is necessary to consider all four of the dimensions of choice. Firstly, the intervention must result in more options for the individual. In this case the free public Wi-Fi added internet access from one or more public libraries, to the existing options of no internet access, internet access from work or school, using data on a cell phone, using a private hotspot at home, or using free Wi-Fi at a coffee shop. Secondly the intervention needs to increase awareness of the choice. In this case the City of Johannesburg advertised the service, but people also found out from friends or just by being curious about the crowds around the library.

Thirdly, individuals need to exercise their choice. This decision is facilitated by many of the surrounding circumstances. So, for example, residents in this study were prepared to pay for taxis to get to a library or walk long distances, reflecting the value they placed on the service. However, this also highlights that other residents may not be able to access the service because of where it is located. Lack of security deterred some from using the service and the opening hours also constrained use. Identifying how such structural limitations might interact with individual resources and agency, will aid in identifying circumstances that limit the ability of people to use the increased choice.

Finally, people need to achieve the choice. In this case residents usually succeeded in accessing the internet, but some people found that the service was not working when they needed it, or that the information they sought was not available (something generally be outside of the control of the city). This makes it clear that, although some elements of the achievement of choice are beyond the control of the City, there are areas, where the City could facilitate the achievement of choice. Examples of these would be in ensuring uninterrupted electricity supply and efficient technical support for the libraries.

Plan Increased Choice, Observe Secondary Outcomes

The primary outcome that can be expected from a successful intervention is an increase in the choices that people experience. If there is no increase in choice then it is questionable whether any development has taken place, given the understanding of development that this research adopts. In this case we saw that Johannesburg residents spoke of increased choice in how they accessed online resources and that this access opened up greater choice in how they spent their money, how they communicated and in their range of leisure activities. They also had a wider choice of resources for learning and economic activities. They also expressed a sense of freedom that came with these choices, saying "Jah, *yona,* it is a good thing. It is up to you on what you chose to do with that good thing." (R8).

While Kleine's framework identifies some suggested outcomes for an ICT4D intervention, these are not intended to be prescriptive, but only illustrative. Secondary outcomes depend on the choices that people make and reflect what they value. Secondary outcomes that were observed included social and psychological benefits as well as economic benefits. In designing projects and in evaluating the outcomes, while certain benefits might be anticipated, it is important to allow the evidence to point to those that actually materialise, as identified by the people involved. Defining intended outcomes too narrowly might result in apparent failure if those expected outcomes do not result.

CONCLUSION

ICT4D lies at the intersection of ICT, development and the transformative process that connects the two (Sein et al., 2019). This chapter has made use of the Capability Approach (Sen 1999) to frame development as the freedom for people to live the lives that they have a reason to value. This study used Choice Theory (Kleine, 2010) to articulate the transformative process of how changes in the structural conditions, agency and elements of choice available to each individual, leads to an increase in the dimensions of choice and hence to individual development.

This case illustrates how the connections between interventions and outcomes can be understood in the context of a complex, dynamic system, although not in a linear fashion from action to outcome. It also illustrates how an analysis of the interactions of the parts of a system can lead to better understanding of the implementation and allow for modifications in order to improve the impacts.

ACKNOWLEDGMENT

The researchers are grateful for the support of the City of Johannesburg Library Services in carrying out this research.

REFERENCES

Al-Gamal, E., Alzayyat, A., & Ahmad, M. M. (2015). Prevalence of internet addiction and its association with psychological distress and coping strategies among university students in Jordan. *Perspectives in Psychiatric Care, 52*(1), 49–61. doi:10.1111/ppc.12102 PMID:25639746

Alias, N. A. (2013). *ICT development for social and rural connectedness*. New York, NY: Springer. doi:10.1007/978-1-4614-6901-8

Alsop, R., & Heinsohn, N. (2005). *Measuring empowerment in practice—structuring analysis and framing indicators*. Washington, DC: World Bank. doi:10.1596/1813-9450-3510

Andrade, A. D., & Urquhart, C. (2010). The affordances of actor network theory in ICT for development research. *Information Technology & People*, *23*(4), 352–374. doi:10.1108/09593841011087806

Ben, W. (2016). *Guidelines for mobile health applications adopted amongst adolescents* (Masters' dissertation). University of Johannesburg, Johannesburg, South Africa.

Braun, V., & Clarke, V. (2006). Using thematic analysis in psychology. *Qualitative Research in Psychology*, *3*(2), 77–101. doi:10.1191/1478088706qp063oa

Budu, J. (2018). Explaining online communities' contribution to socio-economic development. *GlobDev 2018, 9*. Retrieved from https://aisel.aisnet.org/globdev2018/9

Castellacci, F., & Tveito, V. (2018). Internet use and well-being: A survey and a theoretical framework. *Research Policy*, *47*(1), 308–325. doi:10.1016/j.respol.2017.11.007

City of Johannesburg. (2018a). *City of Johannesburg Annual Report 2016/17*. Retrieved from: https://joburg.org.za/documents_/Pages/Key%20Documents/Annual%20Report/201617%20Annual%20Report/Annual%20Report%20For%20Council.pdf

City of Johannesburg. (2018b). *City of Johannesburg Integrated Development Plan 2018/19 Review*. Retrieved from: https://www.joburg.org.za/documents_/Documents/Annexure%20A%20%202018-19%20IDP%20Review.pdf

Coelho, T. R., Segatto, A. P., & Frega, J. R. (2015). Analysing ICT and development from the perspective of the capabilities approach: A study in South Brazil. *The Electronic Journal on Information Systems in Developing Countries*, *67*(2), 1–14. doi:10.1002/j.1681-4835.2015.tb00480.x

Cui, L., Tso, F. P., Yao, D., & Jia, W. (2012). WeFiLab: A web-based Wi-Fi laboratory platform for wireless networking education. *IEEE Transactions on Learning Technologies*, *5*(4), 291–303. doi:10.1109/TLT.2012.6

Deloitte. (2014). *Value of connectivity. Economic and social benefits of expanding internet access*. Retrieved from: https://www2.deloitte.com/content/dam/Deloitte/ie/Documents/TechnologyMediaCommunications/2014_uk_tmt_value_of_connectivity_deloitte_ireland.pdf

Denzin, N. K., & Lincoln, Y. S. (1994). *The SAGE handbook of qualitative research*. Thousand Oaks, CA: Sage Publications.

Galperin, H., & Viecens, M. F. (2017). Connected for development? Theory and evidence about the impact of internet technologies on poverty alleviation. *Development Policy Review*, *35*(3), 1–2. doi:10.1111/dpr.12210

Geerdts, C., Gillwald, A., Calandro, E., Chair, E., Moyo, M., & Rademan, B. (2016). *Developing smart public Wi-Fi in South Africa*. Retrieved from: https://www.africaportal.org/publications/developing-smart-public-wi-fi-south-africa/

Hampton, K. N., & Gupta, N. (2008). Community and social interaction in the wireless city: Wi-Fi use in public and semi-public spaces. *New Media & Society, 10*(6), 831–850. doi:10.1177/1461444808096247

Heeks, R. (2002). Information systems and developing countries: Failure, success and local improvisations. *The Information Society, 18*(2), 101–112. doi:10.1080/01972240290075039

Heeks, R., & Kanashiro, L. L. (2009). Telecentres in mountain regions - A Peruvian case study of the impact of information and communication technologies on remoteness and exclusion. *Journal of Mountain Science, 6*(4), 320–330. doi:10.100711629-009-1070-y

Hirschman, A. O. (1958). *The strategy of economic development*. New Haven, CT: Yale University Press.

Hodge, H., Carson, D., Carson, C., Newman, L., & Garrett, J. (2017). Using Internet technologies in rural communities to access services: The views of older people and service providers. *Journal of Rural Studies, 54*, 469–478. doi:10.1016/j.jrurstud.2016.06.016

Index, R. A. M. P. (2018). *Cheapest prepaid mobile voice product by country (in USD)*. Retrieved from: https://researchictafrica.net/ramp_indices_portal/

Internet World Stats. (2017). *Internet users statistics for Africa (Africa internet usage, 2019 population stats and Facebook subscribers)*. Retrieved from: https://www.internetworldstats.com/stats1.htm

Islam, J. U., Rahman, Z., & Hollebeek, L. D. (2018). Consumer engagement in online brand communities: A solicitation of congruity theory. *Internet Research, 28*(1), 23–45. doi:10.1108/IntR-09-2016-0279

Karwatzki, S., Trenz, M., Tuunainen, V. K., & Veit, D. (2017). Adverse consequences of access to individuals' information: An analysis of perceptions and the scope of organisational influence. *European Journal of Information Systems, 26*(6), 688–715. doi:10.105741303-017-0064-z

Klein, H. K., & Myers, M. D. (1999). A set of principles for conducting and evaluating interpretive field studies in information systems. *Management Information Systems Quarterly, 23*(1), 67–93. doi:10.2307/249410

Kleine, D. (2010). ICT4What? Using the Choice Framework to operationalise the capability approach to development. *Journal of International Development, 22*(5), 674–692. doi:10.1002/jid.1719

Klonoff, D. C. (2013). The current status of mHealth for diabetes: Will it be the next big thing? *Journal of Diabetes Science and Technology, 7*(3), 749–758. doi:10.1177/193229681300700321 PMID:23759409

Lifshitz, R., Nimrod, G., & Bachner, Y. G. (2018). Internet use and well-being in later life: A functional approach. *Aging & Mental Health, 22*(1), 85–91. doi:10.1080/13607863.2016.1232370 PMID:27657190

Maier, C., Laumer, S., Eckhardt, A., & Weitzel, T. (2015). Giving too much social support: Social overload on social networking sites. *European Journal of Information Systems, 24*(5), 447–464. doi:10.1057/ejis.2014.3

Mthoko, H., & Khene, C. (2018). Building theory in ICT4D evaluation: A comprehensive approach to assessing outcome and impact. *Information Technology for Development*, *24*(1), 138–164. doi:10.108 0/02681102.2017.1315359

Mutula, M., & Mostert, J. (2010). Challenges and opportunities of e-government in South Africa. *The Electronic Library*, *28*(1), 38–53. doi:10.1108/02640471011023360

Noor, M. M. (2018). Rural Community Digital Technology Connectedness: Does ICT in Rural Area Contributes to Rural Development in Malaysia? *Social Sciences*, *13*(2), 316–322.

Nowland, R., Necka, E. A., & Caciopp, J. T. (2017). Loneliness and social internet use: Pathways to reconnection in a digital world? *Perspectives on Psychological Science*, *13*(1), 70–87. doi:10.1177/1745691617713052 PMID:28937910

Rösner, L., Winter, S., & Krämer, N. C. (2016). Dangerous minds? Effects of uncivil online comments on aggressive cognitions, emotions, and behavior. *Computers in Human Behavior*, *58*, 461–470. doi:10.1016/j.chb.2016.01.022

Saunders, M. N. K., Lewis, P., & Thornhill, A. (2009). *Research methods for business students* (5th ed.). Harlow, UK: Pearson Education.

Schröder, J., Berger, T., Westermann, S., Klein, J. P., & Moritz, S. (2016). Internet interventions for depression: New developments. *Dialogues in Clinical Neuroscience*, *18*(2), 203–212. PMID:27489460

Sein, M. K., Thapa, D., Hatakka, M., & Sæbø, Ø. (2016). What theories do we need to know to conduct ICT4D research? *Proceedings of SIG GlobDev Ninth Annual Workshop*.

Sein, M. K., Thapa, D., Hatakka, M., & Sæbø, Ø. (2019). A holistic perspective on the theoretical foundations for ICT4D research. *Information Technology for Development*, *25*(1), 7–25. doi:10.1080/0 2681102.2018.1503589

Sen, A. (1997). Maximisation and the act of choice. *Econometrica*, *65*(4), 745–779. doi:10.2307/2171939

Sen, A. (1999). *Development as freedom*. Oxford, UK: Oxford University Press.

Stats, S. A. (2018). Mid-year population estimates 2018. *Statistics South Africa media release*. Retrieved from http://www.statssa.gov.za/?p=11341

Stats, S. A. (2019a). Labour Force Survey of South Africa, Q1, 2019. *Statistics South Africa*. Retrieved from http://www.statssa.gov.za/?page_id=1854&PPN=P0211

Stats, S. A. (2019b). Four facts about our provincial economies. *Statistics South Africa*. Retrieved from http://www.statssa.gov.za/?p=12056

Sumner, A., & Tribe, M. (2008). *International Development Studies: Theories and Methods in Research and Practice*. London: Sage. doi:10.4135/9781446279397

Thapa, D., Sein, M. K., & Sæbø, Ø. (2012). Building collective capabilities through ICT in a mountain region of Nepal: Where social capital leads to collective action. *Information Technology for Development*, *18*(1), 5–22. doi:10.1080/02681102.2011.643205

Thirsk, L. M., & Clark, A. M. (2017). Using qualitative research for complex interventions: The contributions of hermeneutics. *International Journal of Qualitative Methods*, *16*(1), 1–10. doi:10.1177/1609406917721068

Tossell, C., Kortum, P., Shepard, C., Rahmati, A., & Zhong, L. (2015). Exploring smartphone addiction: Insights from long-term telemetric behavioural measures. *International Journal of Interactive Mobile Technologies*, *9*(2), 37–43. doi:10.3991/ijim.v9i2.4300

Utter, J., Lucassen, M., Denny, S., Fleming, T., Peiris-John, R., & Clark, T. (2018). Using the internet to access health-related information: Results from a nationally representative sample of New Zealand secondary school students. *International Journal of Adolescent Medicine and Health*. doi:10.1515/ijamh-2017-0096 PMID:29168960

Walsham, G. (2017). ICT4D research: Reflections on history and future agenda. *Information Technology for Development*, *23*(1), 18–41. doi:10.1080/02681102.2016.1246406

Zheng, Y., Hatakka, M., Sahay, S., & Andersson, A. (2018). Conceptualizing development in information and communication technology for development (ICT4D). *Information Technology for Development*, *24*(1), 1–14. doi:10.1080/02681102.2017.1396020

KEY TERMS AND DEFINITIONS

Agency: The sense and ability that an individual has to make choices and to act towards outcomes that they choose. Agency depends on the resources that individuals have access to.

Choice Framework: The framework put forward by Kleine to explain how changes in structure and agency interact and impact on the choices that people have, leading to development (Kleine, 2010).

Development: An increase in the freedom that individuals have to choose to lead their lives in ways that they value (based on Sen, 1999).

Dimensions of Choice: Four elements of choice that need to be achieved in order for a choice to be made. They include awareness of choice, sense of choice, use of choice and achievement of choice.

ICT4D: The study of how information and communications technologies might or might not impact development.

Internet Access: The ability to connect to the internet including having the use of a working device, a working network, the necessary skills, the confidence to use them and knowledge of what can be accessed on the internet.

Structure: The collection of institutions, rules, norms, discourses and technologies that frame, enable and constrain how an individual can and does act in a particular context.

Section 4
Future of Information Systems in Developing Economies

Chapter 19
Gamification Research:
Preliminary Insights Into Dominant Issues, Theories, Domains, and Methodologies

Kingsley Ofosu-Ampong
Business School, University of Ghana, Ghana

Thomas Anning-Dorson
Wits Business School, University of the Witwatersrand, South Africa

ABSTRACT

Despite advances in information technology, studies suggest that there is little knowledge of how developing countries are applying gamification in agriculture, education, business, health, and other domains. Thus, from a systematic review, this chapter examines the extent of gamification research in the developing country context. In this chapter, 56 articles were reviewed, and the search was done in the Scopus database. This chapter explains the idea of game design elements in information systems and provides real-world examples of gamified systems outcomes from developing countries. The authors conclude with directions for future research to extend our knowledge of gamification and advance the existing methodologies, domains, and theories.

INTRODUCTION

Gamified systems make tasks more engaging for learners, customers, or employees (Liu, Santhanam & Webster, 2017). In simple terms, *Gamification* is the use of game design elements in a non-game context. It can also be defined as "the use of game-based elements such as mechanics, aesthetics, and game thinking in non-game contexts aimed at engaging people, motivating action, enhancing learning, and solving problems" (Borges et al. 2014, p. 216). Areas in which gamification has been applied include education (Nah et al., 2014), health (Jones et al., 2014) sustainable energy (Lee et al., 2013; Oppong-Tawiah et al., 2018), crowdsourcing (Ipeirotis et al., 2014) enterprise resource planning (Alcivar & Abad, 2016), and tourism (Adukaite et al., 2017).

DOI: 10.4018/978-1-7998-2610-1.ch019

Gamified systems or applications have several benefits to organisations and users; most importantly, it helps make monotonous activities or work more enjoyable and can result in performance improvement (Theibes et al., 2014; Burke & Hilbrand, 2011). For example, Microsoft gamified its information systems to include *Ribbon Hero* to train users on Office Suite. By completing challenges and gaining experience points, users learn to use Word, PowerPoint, OneNote and, Excel; the design provides immediate feedback, track user progress with relevant tasks that reinforce user engagement and interest. Additionally, DirecTv added gamification tools such as points, leaderboards, and social recognition to change the mindset of its 1000-person IT department to eliminate finger-pointing and ensure no repetition of mistakes in their new tech policies and procedures.

The use of gamification and the integration of game design elements in various spheres of lives and non-work activities continue to attract attention in the literature (Koivisto & Hamari, 2019; Morschheuser et al., 2017; Osatuyi et al., 2017; Nah et al., 2014). For instance, Oppong-Tawiah et al. (2018) argue that developing a gamified mobile application has a tendency of changing behaviours, engaging learners (Suh et al.,2017), encouraging and promoting sustainable use of energy in offices. These practices have been manifested in Canada, Finland, the United States of America (UK) and among other developed regions (see also Osatuyi et al., 2017). Despite these advantages, there is a lack of knowledge on how gamification is utilised in developing country context to motivate and engage users (see Omotosho, Tyoden, Ayegba & Ayoola, 2019; Appiahene et al., 2017). Hence the main research question:

RQ: What is the extent of gamification research in the developing country context?

This study, therefore, explores the preliminary insight into research issues, theories, concepts, and methodologies employed in gamification studies in the developing country context. This study is structured into seven sections. Section one focused on the introductory section of the study; section two looked at conceptualisation gamification, while section three highlight the methodology and search criteria for the gamification review. Section four emphasised the dominant issues, conceptual and methodological approaches and dominant domains in gamification from DC context. The last section focused on research gaps for future gamification research.

CONCEPTUALISING GAMIFICATION

Nick Pelling in 2002 coined the term *gamification*; however, it became prominent in academic spheres in 2010. As stated earlier, the most popular and earliest definition is one coined by Deterding et al. (20011) as "the use of game design elements (means) in a non-game context (application context)." Other scholars have defined gamification to highlight the means and application contexts of game elements. For example, Zichermann and Cunningham (2011) defined it as "the process of game-thinking and game mechanics to engage users and solve problems." Fitz-Walter et al. (2011) also defined it as "adding game elements to an application to motivate use and enhance user experience" while Borges et al. defined gamification as "the use of game-based elements such as mechanics, aesthetics, and game thinking in non-game contexts aimed at engaging people, motivating action, enhancing learning, and solving problems." Moreover, it includes "the use of game design elements (such as points, badges, and leaderboards) in a non-game context to promote user engagement" (Mekler et al. 2013). The definitions postulate gamification to include user engagement, system motivation, and outcomes of game elements.

In developing countries, the definition has been in line with the application contexts, goals, and means of gamification. For example, Pilkington (2018) defined Gamification may be seen as "the explicit use of competition to promote student motivation, and the use of the motivational power of games does not seem unreasonable." Other definitions include "an educational approach which relies on activity played within the game" (Yassine et al. 2017), "the use of game-based mechanics, aesthetics, and game thinking to engage people, motivate action, promote learning, and solve problems" (Khaleel et al. 2016) and is "concerned with the use of video-game mechanics and elements in nongame contexts to encourage and engage users in the context by making sense of playfulness and fun" (Darejeh & Salim, 2016). The descriptions show that there is no clear definition of gamification but rather how game design elements are chosen to motivate and engage users is of paramount interest. In this regards, we define gamification as the *integration of game design elements into an existing system by achieving the target productivity of the system through fun or excitement while retaining the main routine functions of the system.* The definition provides an institutional value to the earlier definitions of gamification by incorporating unique features in the design of these applications and harnessing the current benefit of the system.

METHODOLOGY FOR REVIEW

Searches were done in the Scopus database. The study used Scopus because it indexes all the potentially relevant database which includes IEEE, AISel, ACM, and Springer. To increase the rigour and clarity of data collected – search by country, Scopus is preferred in conducting searches in various repositories (Pare et al., 2015). The search terms: TITLE-ABS-KEY (gamification, gamif*, gamification in Africa, gamification in developing countries) were used in the Scopus database. The study used journal articles published from 2010 (period gamification concept gained popularity in the academic environment) to 2019 (July).

Inclusion and Exclusion Criteria

The initial search resulted in 1978 hits *(search for gamification in developing countries, gamification and gamif*),* which were screened further (see figure 1). The papers retrieved were categorised per the publication type and the domain of study. The abstract, keywords and full text were screened for relevance, and duplicate articles were deleted. The overall process resulted in 180 reviews as full and empirical research papers. Empirical papers selected met the following criteria: 1. Some data collected 2. Reporting on data gathered 3. Analysis and results of the data obtained 4. The paper is from a developing country. Of the 182 studies in developing countries, 56 empirical studies were identified as studies from developing countries (see Appendix A for further inclusion criteria).

Dominant Issues in Gamification Research in Developing Countries

The review classified gamification into two themes – affordances and outcomes based on the previous reviews of Koivisto and Hamari (2019) to understand the current gamification trend across cultures and disciplines. Based on the development and new insight from this study, each of the two themes was further grouped into sub-themes as follows: Affordances – progress, social and immersion; Outcomes – psychological and behavioural. Traditionally, information systems discipline has been aligned to pro-

Figure 1. Screening Process in a Flow Diagram

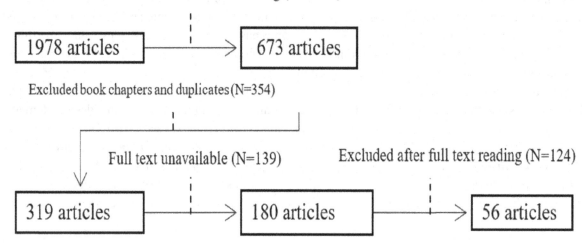

ductive and efficient use, and recently, the application of hedonic or non-utilitarian activities in systems (Koivisto & Hamari, 2019). To this end, the themes adopted in this review reflect a modification of previous works in gamification research.

Affordances theme relates to the perceived elements or properties that determine how the gamified application is used. Achievement, a sub-theme of affordances refers to the goal metrics that give feedback to the player (Zagal et al., 2005), social elements describe social networking features such as liking, commenting and status update (Kapp, 2013), immersion refers to the use of narratives, avatars, and stories (Eickhoff, Harris, de Vries, & Srinivasan, 2012). With the progress affordances, 25% of the papers were based on points and scores, 27% were leaderboards and levels, 12% were quizzes and timer, 20% were badges and trophies, 16% were progressed bars, achievements and status bars. Under social affordances, the most dominant game design elements were competition 36%, followed by teams 27%, social networking was 25%, and assistance - 12%. Storyline and narratives describe the story in the game or narrative (Nah, Zeng & Telaprolu, 2014) and are the dominantly (55%) used immersion affordances in the review. Though the virtual world (18%) is not a prominent element in the developing country context, Hakak et al. (2019) applied gamification in a cloud-assisted education, and learning found virtual awards as promising. However, they recommended more evaluation in terms of usability. Similarly, Avatars (27%), which represents a user within a gamified system and mostly in the form or rewards were less used (Azmi & Singh, 2015).

The outcome themes relate to psychological or behavioural features in the studies (Seaborn & Fels, 2015; Martí-Parreño et al. 2016; Majuri, Koivisto & Hamari, 2018). Psychological outcomes refer to the resultant effect on the use of gamification elements in the application, according to Adukaite et al. (2017), the teachers feel challenged with fun when accomplishing the task. There are three sub-themes under psychological outcomes: attitude towards gamification use, affective-social-cognitive, and challenges experienced. Users' attitudes towards gamification represent 30% of psychological outcomes and include perception of use, preference, and perception of game design elements. Challenges experienced by the users were 15% while affective-social-cognitive outcomes, which provides for a fun, social comparison, and flow experience (immersion in the game) were 55% of the psychological outcomes.

Similar to previous literature, gamified systems seek a desired outcome, which is the behavioural engagement of users in a learning task, assignment, or process (Kelders, Sommers-Spijkerman, & Goldberg, 2018). Thus, the review identified three sub-themes (behavioural outcomes): engagement, performance, and social interaction. Studies in behaviour outcomes examined whether the use of game elements increase or decrease engagement, performance, and social interaction. For instance, several researchers (Hakak et al. 2019; Omotosho et al., 2019; Kasinathan et al., 2018) embedded game elements into cloud-based and work activities found an increase in the engagement levels among the users. Besides, Ismail, Ahmad, Mohammad, Fakri, Nor, & Pa (2019) found that gamification led to performance increase, and it helps close the gap between current and desired performance for the user. Other studies describe fascinating ways gamification led to social interaction and influence in a community (Haruna et al., 2018). Based on our review, 29 papers (52%) were related to engagement, 21 articles (38%) were related to performance, and 6 papers (10%) were related to social interaction, e.g., being social influence and relatedness. For example, considering rice as Indonesia's most valuable commodity, Ardhito, Handayati, and Putranto (2019) gamified the supply chain to create a learning awareness for the smallholder farmers (90%) who are mainly in the rural areas. Using observation and interviews to solicit information from the rice producers, the researchers designed a suitable game for the farmers with the intent to enhance farming practices awareness, especially in the rice supply chain. These are the kind of innovations developing countries are using gamification to tackle everyday behavioural problems in their societies.

Dominant Conceptual Approaches in Gamification Research in Developing Countries

The review identified several papers that used theories, models, concepts, and frameworks. From Table 2, twenty-nine percent (29%) of the papers used no theories. The dearth of theories in gamification research has been acknowledged by Seaborn and Fels (2015) and hence the request for the application of theories to gamification away from the predominant ones. However, the "comprehensive and flexible sociocultural learning theory, Activity theory" (see Haruna et al., 2018) was used as a framework to design game-based learning and gamification instructional interventions to disseminate knowledge creation as a social practice among secondary school adolescents.

Additionally, Self-determination theory was used to predict the effectiveness of different game design elements to intrinsically motivate energy conservation behaviours among university students in Malaysia (see Wee & Choong, 2019). They identified the adolescents as the subjects, gamification teaching methods as the instrument and habits that curb imprudent sexual behaviour as the outcome. Ofosu-Ampong and Boateng also used the theory of gamified learning and flow theory to understand student's receptiveness of game design elements in learning management systems. Hakak et al. (2019) used the conceptual gamification model to investigate the applicability of gamification through cloud computing services.

Khaleel, Ashaari, and Wook (2019) used the ARCS (Attention, Relevance, Confidence, and Satisfaction) motivational model, to measure the effectiveness and motivation level of using game design elements on a website to learn programming language. However, other studies proposed a gamification model in various disciplines. Mgiba (2019) proposed the model of GM to aid the intervention of gamification in the success of marketing. The integrating model consists of attractiveness, congruence, reciprocity,

Table 1. Dominant Issues in Gamification Research in Developing Countries

Themes	Sub-themes	Elements	Number of papers	Percent
Affordances	Progress Affordances	Points, score	14	25%
		Leaderboard, levels	15	27%
		Quizzes, timer	7	12%
		Badges, trophies	11	20%
		Progress bars, achievements, status bars	9	16%
	Social Affordances	Teams	15	27%
		Competition	20	36%
		Social networking	14	25%
		Assistance	7	12%
	Immersion Affordances	Narratives, storyline	31	55%
		Avatars (visual representations of players within games)	15	27%
		Virtual world	10	18%
Outcomes	Psychological Outcomes	Attitude towards gamification use: e.g. Use experience, perception of gamification in education and learning, perception of organisational or classroom learning, satisfaction, subject to change	17	30%
		Challenges experience: e.g., Extra curriculum work, Constant online frustration, perceived difficulty, perceived ease of use, lack of training and know-how, cost of staying online, disengagement, anxiety, functionality of application	8	15%
		Affective/Social/Cognitive: e.g. Fun, immersion, flow experience, enjoyment, experience of emotions, perceived social interaction, social comparison, social influence, familiarity, motivation, perception of learning, involvement, perceived competition	31	55%
	Behavioural Outcomes	Engagement: e.g., System use, continuous use – complete task, quiz attendance, participation in discussions and the system, downloading and viewing course materials, physical activity	29	52%
		Performance: e.g., Position on leaderboards, learning, skills acquisition and progression, tracking points and badges, speed of completion, time, timely feedback and points, number of attempts to completion, course and exam grade, academic performance, stress release, physical activity	21	38%
		Social interaction: e.g., Social influence, cooperation, relatedness, number of colleagues, request for help to complete the task	6	10%

motivation, and customisation; and shows how the variables are related to motivating potential users to adopt gamification as a marketing tool.

Frameworks for gamification research include the MAKE (motivation, attitude, knowledge, and engagement) framework, which was used and developed by Haruna et al. (2018) to evaluate the effectiveness of three teaching methods (game-based learning, traditional and gamification). The MAKE framework represents the motivation, attitude, knowledge, and engagement of users towards a system. Many studies used frameworks, while others developed prototypes such as proof of concepts (the review found this as a standard practice with most studies). Azmi and Singh (2015) developed a gamified LMS in a Microsoft SharePoint based environment using a prototype (web-based software); the teachers monitored student's

Table 2. Dominant Conceptual Approaches – Research Frameworks in Gamification Research

Research Framework	Number of papers	Percent
No theory	16	29%
Gamified theory of learning	1	2%
Self-determination theory	6	11%
Gamifying process framework	1	2%
Conceptual	10	18%
ARCS motivational model	3	5%
ARCS+G model	1	2%
MAKE (motivation, attitude, knowledge, and engagement) framework	1	2%
Activity theory	1	2%
Model of GM	1	2%
Flow theory	3	5%
Treasure Hunt model	1	2%
Solo Taxonomy model	1	2%
intelligent Moodle (iMoodle)	1	2%
Gamification model (canvas)	2	3%
MDA framework	2	3%
MDE framework (mechanics, dynamics emotions	1	2%
Bloom Taxonomy model	1	2%
The user role model	1	2%
Cognitive evaluation theory	2	3%
Total	*56*	*100%*

performance through the analysis of test results. Using a framework, Ezezika et al. (2018) undertook a qualitative study to understand whether, and how, gamification of nutrition can have an impact on addressing the "problem of unhealthy eating among Nigerian adolescents." For example, to tackle the inability of gamification elements in inducing intrinsic motivation among students or gamified user, Hassan, Majeed, and Shoaib (2019) developed a framework that investigates the learning styles of users who interact with the gamified system. The framework identified the adaptive learning experiences of the students, and the results of the experiment revealed that learner motivation increased by 25% while the ratio of student drop-out reduced by 26%.

Rahman and Awang (2018) also proposed a framework using gamification techniques to improve information management in the resource as a service in Malaysia. Further, Kamunya, Maina, and Oboko (2019) identified the lack of rigour in the design of the evaluation of gamification frameworks. They found that 80% of gamification frameworks are without effective evaluations, and as observed by Nacke and Deterding (2017), *"this has hampered the growth and establishment of successful gamification implementation"* – due to the shortage of evidence for suitable designs.

Given this, the review argues that many studies on gamification utilise many frameworks, mostly developed to suit the context, organisation, or users. Thus, for a clear understanding of the phenomenon of gamification, frameworks, models, and conceptual papers are most considered. However, most studies lack theoretical backing to situate gamification as a new area of study in information systems. The disadvantage is a partial view of what exists in gamification and leads to the shortcoming of appropriate research design and method to explore gamification in the developing country context. Future research should continue developing frameworks to suit the context of users (requirement of gamification success) and also address the gaps in the theory. In total, 16 papers did not involve any theory, concept, or framework. Table 2 shows the research frameworks and the number of assigned papers.

Dominant Domains in Gamification Research in Developing Countries

Table 3 outlines the dominant domains of the research papers reviewed. However, some of the domains overlap, especially in the field of business. Out of the Fifty-six papers reviewed, the majority of the papers in gamification in DC were conducted in the domain of education. Interesting, Seaborn and Fels (2015) identified the domain of education and learning as the most dominant area in their review. Design and development of game design elements papers were the second-largest domain. The third-largest domain is the business sector, which includes banking, consumer behaviour, and marketing. Altogether,

Table 3. Dominant Domains in Gamification Research in Developing Countries

Domain	Forms of domain	Number of papers	Percent
Education	e-Learning applications, distant education, learner's personality, programming language	22	39%
Design and development of gamification	Medical education (e.g., Leptospirosis), exercise, stress management, sexual health education, family health app	13	23%
Business	Banking, consumer behaviour and marketing strategies, enterprise systems, management	12	21%
Transportation	Driving lessons	1	2%
Agriculture	Farming lessons, innovation, e-Agriculture	2	4%
Social networking	Sharing, information gathering, public education	3	5%
Energy conservation behaviour	Efficient electricity use, cost-effective, prevention strategies	1	2%
Nutrition	Knowledge of unhealthy eating – high salt, sugar, and saturated fat	2	4%
Total	56		*100%*

the three dominant areas comprised over 80% of the gamification domains in DC. The fourth and fifth dominant domains are social networking and agriculture/nutrition, respectively. The remained combined comprised 4% of the total dominant domains in gamification.

Methodological Approaches to Studying Gamification Research

In this section, the review identified 37 papers (66%) that were analyzed quantitatively – (descriptive 19 (51%), modeling 11 (30%) and comparison/association-based 7 (19%)); 7 papers (12.5%) were analyzed qualitatively, 7 design science papers (12.5%) and 5 papers (9%) used mixed method approach. Table 4 shows the methodological approaches in the existing studies.

Table 4. Methodological Approaches to the Study of Gamification

Methodological approaches	Number of papers	Percent
Quantitative	37	66%
Descriptive	*19*	*51%*
Modelling	*11*	*30%*
Comparison and association-based	*7*	*19%*
Qualitative	7	12.5%
Design science	7	12.5%
Mixed method	5	9%
Total	*56*	*100%*

Several papers used quantitative approach (Katule et al., 2016; Henning et al. 2017; Adukaite et al., 2017) to the study of gamification in DC, including those of Hamzah, Ali, Saman, Yusoff and Yacob (2015), who employed the motivational design model to study the influence of gamification on students' motivation (control and experiment group) in using e-learning applications. Further, Pilkington (2018), examined the behavioural change and student perception by adopting a playful approach to foster motivation in distance education in a computer programming course.

Studied that used design science approach include Yassine et al. (2017), who use the Solo Taxonomy to explore the pedagogical approaches and gameplay techniques involved in the development of serious games for teaching science courses in Morocco, and, El-Telbany and Elragal (2017), who developed a gamified process of the ERP lifecycle, to enhance its use and implementation process. However, Tlili et al. (2019) used a design methodology to model learner's personality and quantitatively tested the proposed approach (building an adaptive learning environment) for accuracy.

Some papers adopted a qualitative approach. For example, Ismail et al. (2019), explored the advantages of gamification through the use of Kahoot! application for formative assessment in medical education. Studies that used the mixed method approach include Khaleel, Ashaari, Wook and Ismail (2016), who identified the game design elements that can be gamified in a learning application and verified the elements multiple users (e.g., students, gamers and experts). Additionally, Haruna et al. (2018) investigate the extent (random control trial and experiments) to which game-based learning and gamification could improve sexual health education among students.

RESEARCH GAPS FOR FUTURE GAMIFICATION RESEARCH AND CONCLUSION

The identified gaps in literature align with two main themes: Adoption of gamified systems, and, theoretical and methodological agenda

Adoption of Gamified Systems

The review of existing literature on gamification shows that several factors must be considered when deploying gamification in DC, such as a proposed gamification framework (Ofosu-Ampong et al., 2019). Thus, future research framework should consider the motivational affordances, psychological, and behavioural outcomes (Deterding, 2015), and the need for the evaluation and cooperative approaches to the proposed framework. By cooperative strategies, Deci and Ryan (2000) advocate for a sense of relatedness to engage users towards a particular system as human beings are social elements. Additionally, while gamification has been a success in developed countries like Finland, the US, and Canada, the same cannot be said of developing countries. The cultural, political, economics, and social environment should be "prudently and sensibly considered" (Adukaite et al., 2017), not neglecting the influence of limited educational resources and outdated educational materials in DC (Hsu, 2015).

Moreover, to adopt and utilise gamification and innovation in DC, organisations and educational institutions would have to change their traditional and organisational ways of engaging employees, students, and customers (Agbatogun, 2010). Though the review has identified several gamification frameworks (mostly proposed but not evaluated frameworks) in the DC context, there is the need to adopt the successful, evaluated, and tested gamified frameworks from the developed countries; notwithstanding the cultural fit of such systems. Similarly, future research should integrate the contexts (e.g., culture, discipline, level of potential users, types of feedback, individual affordances - personalisation) in which gamification is implemented. The following are the proposed questions for future studies:

1. What techniques should organisations adapt and diversify to create gameful motivational affordances among potential users in developing countries?
2. What are the process and procedures (predeterminants of successful gamification) organisations should undertake while adopting gamification in developing countries?

Theoretical and Methodological Overview

While the substantial part of gamification literature has been applied to today's activities, applications, and systems to motivate and engage users, as well as making monotonous tasks more enjoyable. Some issues, however, hinder the development of the area. First, the methods and research models used in studying gamification research is scattered and mostly unclear (Koivisto & Hamari, 2019). For example, two studies examining exciting in gamified systems use different validated measurement instruments. Only a few studies have used similar validated measurements, and this poses a challenge when conducting a meta-analysis or comparing research results. Second, beyond optimistic expectations, there exists little empirical evidence to demonstrate that gamification satisfies user's intrinsic needs. Previous reviews suggest that there is lack of studies on gamification research that systematically investigate the effect of

Figure 2. Process involved in selecting articles for the review

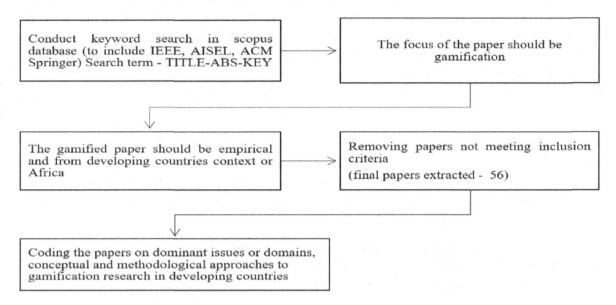

game design elements on user psychological and behavioural outcomes (Nacke & Deterding, 2017), the question this review poses for future studies is:

1. What are the theoretical explanations underlying the role of gamification in satisfying users' needs (intrinsic)?
2. What are the appropriate and consistent research models or measurement instruments to be followed?

Research could also explore areas of gamification research to concentrate on in developing countries of Africa.

CONCLUSION

The papers in this review show that research on gamification creates the avenue to bring together different perspectives from behavioural, psychological, design science, and developing countries cultures to develop knowledge in this widespread and growing field. The study concludes that educational institutions and businesses could complement their traditional learning and training with gamified information systems in developing countries, albeit in a fun, exciting and productive manner.

The review contributes to the limited dominant conceptual approaches and frameworks in the context of gamification in developing countries by emphasising the overarching role of game design elements in stimulating motivational affordances, psychological and behavioural outcomes towards user engagement. It further contributes to gamification frameworks and specific domains of gamification by revealing the complex consequences and exploring the pedagogical approaches and gameplay techniques involved in the development of serious games for training, teaching and learning.

In conclusion, this review responds to calls for more research on gamification in different contexts (Liu et al., 2017); and is aimed at triggering further exploration, discussion and understanding the development, adoption, application, use, and impact of gamification research in developing countries. Research in this field is also relevant because of the increasing importance of games permeating our work lives and non-work activities. Thus, this study encourages the discourse on the opportunities of gamification in impacting systems and various spheres of lives in developing countries.

REFERENCES

Adukaite, A., van Zyl, I., Er, Ş., & Cantoni, L. (2017). Teacher perceptions on the use of digital gamified learning in tourism education: The case of South African secondary schools. *Computers & Education*, *111*, 172–190. doi:10.1016/j.compedu.2017.04.008

Agbatogun, A. O. (2010). Self-concept, computer anxiety, gender and attitude towards interactive computer technologies: A predictive study among Nigerian teachers. *International Journal of Education and Development Using Information and Communication Technology*, *6*(2), 1-14.

Alcivar, I., & Abad, A. G. (2016). Design and evaluation of a gamified system for ERP training. *Computers in Human Behavior*, *58*, 109–118. doi:10.1016/j.chb.2015.12.018

Appiahene, P., Asante, G., Kesse-Yaw, B., & Acquah-Hayfron, J. (2017). Raising students programming skills using appiahene gamification model. In *ECGBL 2017 11th European Conference on Game-Based Learning* (pp. 14-21). Academic Conferences and Publishing Limited.

Ardhito, H. N., Handayati, Y., & Putranto, N. A. R. (2019). Enhancing the Awareness of Farmers' Towards Their Role Through Gamification. *The International Conference of Business and Banking Innovations (ICOBBI) Proceeding*, 17-27.

Azhari, N. N., Abdul Manaf, R., Ng, S. W., Bajunid, S. A., Bajunid, S. F., Gobil, M., ... Amin Nordin, S. (2019). Gamification, a Successful Method to Foster Leptospirosis Knowledge among University Students: A Pilot Study. *International Journal of Environmental Research and Public Health*, *16*(12), 2108. doi:10.3390/ijerph16122108 PMID:31207881

Azmi, M. A., & Singh, D. (2015). Schoolcube: Gamification for learning management system through microsoft sharepoint. *International Journal of Computer Games Technology*, *2015*, 9. doi:10.1155/2015/589180

Borges, S. S., Durelli, V. H. S., Reis, H. M., & Isotani, S. (2014). A Systematic Mapping on Gamification Applied to Education. *Proceedings of the 29th Annual ACM Symposium on Applied Computing*, 216-222. 10.1145/2554850.2554956

Burke, M., & Hiltbrand, T. (2011). How Gamification Will Change Business Intelligence. *Business Intelligence Journal*, *6*(2), 8–16.

Darejeh, A., & Salim, S. S. (2016). Gamification solutions to enhance software user engagement—A systematic review. *International Journal of Human-Computer Interaction*, *32*(8), 613–642. doi:10.1080/10447318.2016.1183330

Deci, E. L., & Ryan, R. M. (2000). The 'what' and 'why' of goal pursuits: Human needs and the self-determination of behaviour. *Psychological Inquiry, 11*(4), 227–268. doi:10.1207/S15327965PLI1104_01

Deterding, S. (2015). The lens of intrinsic skill atoms: A method for gameful design. *Human-Computer Interaction, 30*(3-4), 294–335. doi:10.1080/07370024.2014.993471

Deterding, S., Sicart, M., Nacke, L., O'Hara, K., & Dixon, D. (2011). Gamification using game-design elements in non-gaming contexts. In CHI'11 extended abstracts on human factors in computing systems (pp. 2425-2428). ACM. doi:10.1145/1979742.1979575

Eickhoff, C., Harris, C. G., de Vries, A. P., & Srinivasan, P. (2012). Quality through flow and immersion: gamifying crowdsourced relevance assessments. In *Proceedings of the 35th international ACM SIGIR conference on Research and development in information retrieval* (pp. 871-880). ACM. 10.1145/2348283.2348400

El-Telbany, O., & Elragal, A. (2017). Gamification of enterprise systems: A lifecycle approach. *Procedia Computer Science, 121*, 106–114. doi:10.1016/j.procs.2017.11.015

Ezezika, O., Oh, J., Edeagu, N., & Boyo, W. (2018). Gamification of nutrition: A preliminary study on the impact of gamification on nutrition knowledge, attitude, and behaviour of adolescents in Nigeria. *Nutrition and Health (Berkhamsted, Hertfordshire), 24*(3), 137–144. doi:10.1177/0260106018782211 PMID:29974803

Fitz-Walter, Z., Tjondronegoro, D., & Wyeth, P. (2011). Orientation Passport: Using Gamification to Engage University Students. *Proceedings of the 23rd Australian Computer-Human Interaction Conference*, 122-125. 10.1145/2071536.2071554

Hakak, S., Noor, N. F. M., Ayub, M. N., Affal, H., Hussin, N., & Imran, M. (2019). Cloud-assisted gamification for education and learning–Recent advances and challenges. *Computers & Electrical Engineering, 74*, 22–34. doi:10.1016/j.compeleceng.2019.01.002

Hamzah, W. M. A. F. W., Ali, N. H., Saman, M. Y. M., Yusoff, M. H., & Yacob, A. (2015). Influence of gamification on students' motivation in using e-learning applications based on the motivational design model. *International Journal of Emerging Technologies in Learning, 10*(2), 30–34. doi:10.3991/ijet.v10i2.4355

Haruna, H., Hu, X., Chu, S., Mellecker, R., Gabriel, G., & Ndekao, P. (2018). Improving sexual health education programs for adolescent students through game-based learning and Gamification. *International Journal of Environmental Research and Public Health, 15*(9), 2027. doi:10.3390/ijerph15092027 PMID:30227642

Hassan, M. A., Habiba, U., Majeed, F., & Shoaib, M. (2019). Adaptive gamification in e-learning based on students' learning styles. *Interactive Learning Environments*, 1–21. doi:10.1080/10494820.2019.1588745

Henning, M., Hagedorn-Hansen, D., & von Leipzig, K. H. (2017). Metacognitive learning: Skills development through gamification at the Stellenbosch learning factory as a case study. *South African Journal of Industrial Engineering, 28*(3), 105–112. doi:10.7166/28-3-1845

Hsu, H. C. C. (2015). Tourism and hospitality education in Asia. In D. Dredge, D. D. Airey, & M. J. Gross (Eds.), The routledge handbook of tourism and hospitality education (pp. 197–209). Academic Press.

Ipeirotis, P. G., & Gabrilovich, E. (2014, April). Quizz: targeted crowdsourcing with a billion (potential) users. In *Proceedings of the 23rd international conference on World wide web* (pp. 143-154). ACM. 10.1145/2566486.2567988

Ismail, M. A. A., Ahmad, A., Mohammad, J. A. M., Fakri, N. M. R. M., Nor, M. Z. M., & Pa, M. N. M. (2019). Using Kahoot! as a formative assessment tool in medical education: A phenomenological study. *BMC Medical Education*, *19*(1), 230. doi:10.118612909-019-1658-z PMID:31238926

Jones, B. A., Madden, G. J., & Wengreen, H. J. (2014). The FIT Game: Preliminary evaluation of a gamification approach to increasing fruit and vegetable consumption in school. *Preventive Medicine*, *68*, 76–79. doi:10.1016/j.ypmed.2014.04.015 PMID:24768916

Kamunya, S., Maina, E., & Oboko, R. (2019). A Gamification Model For E-Learning Platforms. In 2019 IST-Africa Week Conference (IST-Africa) (pp. 1-9). IEEE. doi:10.23919/ISTAFRICA.2019.8764879

Kapp, K. M. (2013). *The Gamification of Learning and Instruction Fieldbook: Ideas into Practice*. San Francisco: John Wiley & Sons.

Kasinathan, V., Mustapha, A., Fauzi, R., & Rani, M. F. C. A. (2018). Questionify: Gamification in Education. *International Journal of Integrated Engineering*, *10*(6). doi:10.30880/ijie.2018.10.06.019

Katule, N., Rivett, U., & Densmore, M. (2016, November). A family health app: Engaging children to manage wellness of adults. In *Proceedings of the 7th Annual Symposium on Computing for Development* (p. 7). ACM. 10.1145/3001913.3001920

Kelders, S. M., Sommers-Spijkerman, M., & Goldberg, J. (2018). Investigating the direct impact of a gamified versus nongamified well-being intervention: An exploratory experiment. *Journal of Medical Internet Research*, *20*(7), e247. doi:10.2196/jmir.9923 PMID:30049669

Kelders, S. M., Sommers-Spijkerman, M., & Goldberg, J. (2018). Investigating the direct impact of a gamified versus non-gamified well-being intervention: An exploratory experiment. *Journal of Medical Internet Research*, *20*(7), e247. doi:10.2196/jmir.9923 PMID:30049669

Khaleel, F. L., Ashaari, N. S., & Wook, T. S. M. T. (2019). An empirical study on gamification for learning programming language website. *Jurnal Teknologi, 81*(2).

Khaleel, F. L., Sahari, N., Wook, T. S. M. T., & Ismail, A. (2016). Gamification elements for learning applications. *International Journal on Advanced Science. Engineering and Information Technology*, *6*(6), 868–874.

Koivisto, J., & Hamari, J. (2019). The rise of motivational information systems: A review of gamification research. *International Journal of Information Management*, *45*, 191–210. doi:10.1016/j.ijinfomgt.2018.10.013

Lee, J. J., Ceyhan, P., Jordan-Cooley, W., & Sung, W. (2013). GREENIFY: A real world action game for climate change education. *Simulation & Gaming*, *44*(2–3), 349–365. doi:10.1177/1046878112470539

Liu, D., Santhanam, R., & Webster, J. (2017). Towards meaningful engagement: A framework for design and research on gamified information systems. *Management Information Systems Quarterly*, *41*(4), 1011–1034. doi:10.25300/MISQ/2017/41.4.01

Majuri, J., Koivisto, J., & Hamari, J. (2018). Gamification of education and learning: A review of empirical literature. In *Proceedings of the 2nd International GamiFIN Conference, GamiFIN 2018*. CEUR-WS.

Martí-Parreño, J., Seguí-Mas, D., & Seguí-Mas, E. (2016). Teachers' attitude towards and actual use of gamification. *Procedia: Social and Behavioral Sciences*, *228*, 682–688. doi:10.1016/j.sbspro.2016.07.104

Mekler, E. D. E., Brühlmann, F., Opwis, K., & Tuch, A. N. (2013). Disassembling Gamification: The Effects of Points and Meaning on User Motivation and Performance. In *CHI 2013 Extended Abstracts on Human Factors in Computing Systems* (pp. 1137–1142). New York: ACM Press. doi:10.1145/2468356.2468559

Mgiba, F. M. (2019). Integrating Five Theories in Pursuit of Marketing Success in Gamification Interventions: A Conceptual Paper. *International Review of Management and Marketing*, *9*(2), 45–53.

Morschheuser, B., Hamari, J., Koivisto, J., & Maedche, A. (2017). Gamified crowdsourcing: Conceptualization, literature review, and future agenda. *International Journal of Human-Computer Studies*, *106*, 26–43. doi:10.1016/j.ijhcs.2017.04.005

Nacke, L. E., & Deterding, C. S. (2017). The maturing of gamification research. *Computers in Human Behaviour*, 450-454.

Nah, F. F. H., Zeng, Q., Telaprolu, V. R., Ayyappa, A. P., & Eschenbrenner, B. (2014). Gamification of education: a review of literature. In *International conference on hci in business* (pp. 401-409). Springer. 10.1007/978-3-319-07293-7_39

Ofosu-Ampong, K., & Boateng, R. (2018). Gamifying Sakai: Understanding Game Elements for Learning. *Proceedings* of the *Twenty-fourth Americas Conference on Information Systems*. Retrieved from: https://aisel.aisnet.org/amcis2018/Education/Presentations/4

Ofosu-Ampong, K., Boateng, R., Anning-Dorson, T., & Kolog, E. A. (2019). Are we ready for Gamification? An exploratory analysis in a developing country. *Education and Information Technologies*, 1–20. doi:10.100710639-019-10057-7

Omotosho, A., Tyoden, T., Ayegba, P., & Ayoola, J. (2019). Gamified Approach to Improving Student's Participation in Farm Practice--A Case Study of Landmark University. *International Journal of Interactive Mobile Technologies*, *13*(5).

Oppong-Tawiah, D., Webster, J., Staples, S., Cameron, A. F., de Guinea, A. O., & Hung, T. Y. (2018). Developing a gamified mobile application to encourage sustainable energy use in the office. *Journal of Business Research*.

Osatuyi, B., Osatuyi, T., & De La Rosa, R. (2018). Systematic Review of Gamification Research in IS Education: A Multi-method Approach. *Communications of the Association for Information Systems*, *42*(1), 5.

Paré, G., Trudel, M. C., Jaana, M., & Kitsiou, S. (2015). Synthesizing information systems knowledge: A typology of literature reviews. *Information & Management*, *52*(2), 183–199. doi:10.1016/j.im.2014.08.008

Pilkington, C. (2018). A Playful Approach to Fostering Motivation in a Distance Education Computer Programming Course: Behaviour Change and Student Perceptions. *The International Review of Research in Open and Distributed Learning, 19*(3). doi:10.19173/irrodl.v19i3.3664

Rahman, M. N. A., Jaafar, J., Kadir, M. F. A., Shamsuddin, S. N., & Saany, S. I. A. (2018). Cloud-Based Gamification Model Canvas for School Information Management. *International Journal of Engineering & Technology, 7*(2.14), 28-31.

Seaborn, K., & Fels, D. I. (2015). Gamification in theory and action: A survey. *International Journal of Human-Computer Studies, 74*, 14–31. doi:10.1016/j.ijhcs.2014.09.006

Suh, A., Cheung, C. M. K., Ahuja, M., & Wagner, C. (2017). Gamification in the workplace: The central role of the aesthetic experience. *Journal of Management Information Systems, 34*(1), 268–305. doi:10.1080/07421222.2017.1297642

Thiebes, S., Lins, S., & Basten, D. (2014). Gamifying information systems - A synthesis of gamification mechanics and dynamics. *Proceedings of ECIS 2014 - The 22nd European Conference on Information Systems.*

Tlili, A., Denden, M., Essalmi, F., Jemni, M., Chang, M., Kinshuk, & Chen, N.-S. (2019). Automatic modelling learner's personality using learning analytics approach in an intelligent Moodle learning platform. *Interactive Learning Environments*, 1–15. doi:10.1080/10494820.2019.1636084

Wee, S. C., & Choong, W. W. (2019). Gamification: Predicting the effectiveness of variety game design elements to intrinsically motivate users' energy conservation behaviour. *Journal of Environmental Management, 233*, 97–106. doi:10.1016/j.jenvman.2018.11.127 PMID:30572268

Yassine, A., Chenouni, D., Berrada, M., & Tahiri, A. (2017). A Serious Game for Learning C Programming Language Concepts Using Solo Taxonomy. *International Journal of Emerging Technologies in Learning, 12*(3), 110. doi:10.3991/ijet.v12i03.6476

Zagal, J. P., Mateas, M., Fernandez-Vara, C., Hochhalter, B., & Lichti, N. (2005). Towards an ontological language for game analysis. *Proceedings of International DiGRA Conference: Changing Views - Worlds in Play*, 3-14.

Zichermann, G., & Cunningham, C. (2011). *Gamification by design: Implementing game mechanics in web and mobile apps*. O'Reilly Media, Inc.

Chapter 20
Exploring Factors Influencing Big Data and Analytics Adoption in Healthcare Management

Sampson Abeeku Edu
Cyprus International University, Cyprus

Divine Q. Agozie
Cyprus International University, Cyprus

ABSTRACT

Demand for improvement in healthcare management in the areas of quality, cost, and patient care has been on the upsurge because of technology. Incessant application and new technological development to manage healthcare data significantly led to leveraging on the use of big data and analytics (BDA). The application of the capabilities from BDA has provided healthcare institutions with the ability to make critical and timely decisions for patients and data management. Adopting BDA by healthcare institutions hinges on some factors necessitating its application. This study aims to identify and review what influences healthcare institutions towards the use of business intelligence and analytics. With the use of a systematic review of 25 articles, the study identified nine dominant factors driving healthcare institutions to BDA adoption. Factors such as patient management, quality decision making, disease management, data management, and promoting healthcare efficiencies were among the highly ranked factors influencing BDA adoption.

INTRODUCTION

Recent deliberations and developments on Big Data and Analytics and (BDA) have primarily resulted in many firms gaining leverage on data utilization due to availability of big data (Trieu, 2016; Popovic, Hackney, Coelho, & Jaklic, 2012; Visinescu, Jones, & Sidorova, 2017). Business Intelligence and Analytics capabilities have therefore provided a lot of opportunities for organizations operations and quality in decision making (Popovic, Hackney, Tassabehji, & Castelli, 2106; Wang & Hajli, 2017; Hagel,

DOI: 10.4018/978-1-7998-2610-1.ch020

2015; Agarwal & Dhar, 2014). For example, BI capabilities implementation results in creating business values (Wang & Hajli, 2017). Business values are, therefore, categorised into "organizational benefits, operational benefits, IT infrastructure benefits, managerial benefits and strategic benefits" (Wang & Hajli, 2017). Popovic, Hackney, Tassabehji and Castelli (2016) also indicated that application of BDA enhances business performance. Innovations in Business and Analytics through visual analytics have indeed improved how information is reported through dashboards and scorecards for quick decision making by managers (Turban, Ramesh, Delen, & King, 2011). Also, BDA tools like data mining have given organizations a lifeline to improve customer relationship and resolve intricate organization problems (Persson & Riyals, 2014).

The healthcare sector has also seen a tremendous growth of adopting BDA due to the enormous opportunities it offers (Chen, Chiang, & Storey, 2012; Denaxas & Morley, 2015; Wang & Hajli, 2017; Costa, 2014; Raghupathi & Raghupathi, 2014). Studies over the past decades have demonstrated that the integration of BDA with other health systems such as Electronic health (E-Health) systems, Telehealth systems and health care ecosystems, in general, improve healthcare (Luo, Wu, Gopukumar, & Zhao, 2016; Mehta & Pandit, 2018). Arguably, the healthcare sector is perceived to generate large volumes of data ranging from patient records, biomedical data and administrative records which are difficult to manage through traditional storage applications and analytical tools (Sakr & Elgammal, 2016). For example, data aggregation through BDA have enhanced healthcare data to be standardized (Shah & Pathak, 2014) and the agility to decision making (Wixcom, Yen, & Relich, 2013). Quality decision making in healthcare management is tremendously improved through the use of BDA (Chen et al., 2012). It is therefore essential to note that healthcare sectors efforts in the adoption of Big data and Business Intelligent provides business values (Wu, Li, Cheng, & Lin, 2016). Other studies revealed that the level of digitization of healthcare systems and continuous reliance of information technology to provide safe healthcare mostly contributed to BDA adoption (Agarwal, Gao, DesRoches, & Jha, 2010; Nicolini, Powell, Conville, & Matinez-Solano, 2008).

Albeit all the many successes BDA offers to the healthcare sector, it hinges on several factors or the intention of deployment and usage. These factors, when neglected, would lead to failure or undermine the sole purpose for BDA adoption in healthcare. The present study from IS literature posits several factors that regularly affect the benefits accrued to any new technology adopted by organizations. For example, Hung, Huang, Lin, Chen, and Tarn (2016) addressed specific factors influencing BDA adoption in no small extent. More importantly, healthcare preparedness and knowledge towards BDA implementation and application. Besides, there is lack of understanding of these factors from literature specifically attributed to BDA adoption for healthcare institutions (Murdoch & Detsky, 2013; Shah & Pathak, 2014; Watson, 2014) and evidence indicates that 60% failed in the quest (Deloitte Centre, 2015). Even though, these factors have resulted in some level of benefits firms could derive from new technology, Angeles (2013) emphasised a need for a clear direction for firm's technology to align to the new demands with innovations. Tornatzky and Fleischer (1990) have argued that firm's preparedness for new technology adoption is often by the level of technical abilities the firm has, characteristics of the organization and environmental context within which the firm operates. BDA adoption is, therefore, considered as new IS technological innovation that comes with its challenges and factors in its implementation, especially, for healthcare management (Safwan, Meredithand & Burst, 2016). There is, therefore, the need to explore further the factors leading to the success or failure of BDA adoption among healthcare institutions and more importantly, how developing countries can leverage from established healthcare institutions.

The motivation for this paper is to identify and report on empirical research findings on the factors influencing healthcare institutions decision to adopt BDA. Mainly, to provide insights from developed countries perspectives for such motivating factors and how healthcare institutions in developing economies could be aware of these findings for BDA adoptions as well. The study would also classify these critical factors for BDA adoption in healthcare management. The classification of these vital factors will enhance further discussions towards implication for practice and theory of BDA in Healthcare management. The study significantly used a systematic review of relevant literature on BDA adoption in healthcare.

This paper focused on:

1. Review of factors that influence Big Data and Analytics adoption in Healthcare.
2. Identifying dominant factors into classifications.
3. Rating factors mostly influencing Big Data and Analytics adoption in Healthcare.

The rest of the paper is organised into three sections: From E-Health to BDA application and implication in Healthcare, the methodology adopted for the study, Discussion of Literature findings and Conclusion of the study.

FROM E-HEALTH TO BIG DATA AND ANALYTICS ADOPTION

Increasingly, the drive to improve healthcare delivery has also seen technology applications such as BDA by healthcare institutions (Mehta & Pandit, 2018). From their review, Blayer, Fraser and Holt (2010) suggested how healthcare institutions are taking advantage of information communication and technology (ICT) in general, and related platforms to improve healthcare delivery. Over the last decade, significance reliance on ICT for healthcare delivery are ascribed to Electronic Health systems (e-health) (Edworthy, 2001; Alpay, Henkemans, Otten, Rovekamp, & Dumay, 2010; Christensen, Reynolds, & Griffiths, 2011). Primarily, e-health systems and applications are to promote health delivery services to improve patients care (Ramtohul, 2016). Ganesh (2004) pointed health policy, customer choices and technological capabilities as a driving force for e-health adoption. Other issues such as the characteristic of health institutions, that is, public, private or referral hospitals and peculiar needs also influence e-health adoption (Kesse-Tachi, Asmah, & Agbozo, 2019). The adoption of e-health is also due to responding to policy directions to effectively managed ambulatory care. For example, a study by Dunnebeil, Sunyaev, Blohm, Leimeister, and Krcmar (2012), revealed how healthcare policies towards telemedicine in Germany gradually influenced physicians to use e-health applications for ambulatory care. From a developing economies context, e-health adoption is also as a result of the need to meet both rural and urban health services. Miah, Hasan, and Gammack (2017) evaluated the success of e-health systems enabled through cloud platforms supporting medical doctors and healthcare workers to cure non-communicable infections in isolated communities in Bangladesh. In the case of Sub-Saharan countries, Adenuga, Iahad, and Miskon (2017) studied the motivating issues for telemedicine adoption in Nigeria by government hospitals. The study concluded on matters such as facilitating conditions, reinforcement issues and performance expectancy affecting clinicians' attitudes towards telemedicine adoptions. A survey conducted by Kesse-Tachi et al. (2019) further suggested that healthcare practitioners' characteristics have a significant influence on e-health adoption. Healthcare practitioners' characteristics such as educational level, age and gender, were among the influencing factors for e-health adoption.

Notably, from the views above, several decisions drive health institution towards e-health adoption. However, the nature of healthcare delivery services has changed significantly as a result of the large volumes of data generated through electronic medical systems, technology innovation, patients demands and real-time response for healthcare delivery services. The continuous implementations of e-health systems and other health platforms such as Mobile health have also contributed to an exponential amount of data generation. Consequently, these developments have potentially contributed to the adoption of BDA by healthcare institutions (Bates, Saria, Ohno-Machado, Shah, Escobar, 2014). The extraction, providing insights and knowledge creation through these large volumes of structured and unstructured data is complicated and therefore, the need for BDA adoption by healthcare. Accordingly, Sonnati, (2017), and Al-Qahtani and Al-Asem (2015) explored the prospects and usefulness health institutions derive through BDA adoption. A synthesis report by Gu, Li, Li and Liang (2017) further revealed a tremendous growth in BDA adoption in health informatics between 2003 to 2016 by healthcare institutions. Majority of these healthcare institutions were mainly from a developed country context, showing a lack of BDA adoption in developing countries.

Big data and analytics application have transcended beyond just a term which affects organizations' agility to decision making. The multiplicity that BDA applications offer has been described as the *"Game changer"* to improving an institution's efficiency and effectiveness (Wamba et al., 2016). Undeniably, the adoption and right attitude towards BDA implementation have provided a competitive advantage to most organizations. Liu (2014) proposed that, with BDA deployment and usage, differentiating high performing organizations from low performing organization is made easier through the level of revenues and cost of responding to customers.

Deploying Big data technologies has also introduced discussions towards Business Intelligent and applications. To some extent, it is just a "buzzwords" that describe the integration of analytical tools, architectures, applications, databases and methodologies towards transforming data to actionable results (Turban, Ramesh, Delen & King, 2011). The consequences for organizations adopting BDA & BI hinges on specific needs and factors that influence the decision towards embracing it. Some of these factors are prevailing market conditions, consumer demands, technology and societal pressure (Hung et al., 2016). The extent to which these factors influence organization decisions is categorized into several theoretical frameworks through empirical and exploratory studies in IS literature. Key among them is Technology Acceptance Model (TAM) (Davis, 1989; Davis, Bagozzi & Warshaw, 1989), Technology, Organization and Environmental framework (TOE) (Tornatzky & Fleischer, 1990), the Institutional theory (Dacin, Goodstein, & Scott, 2002) and the Diffusion of Innovation theory (Rogers, 2003). The effect of these factors on technology adoption differs from industry-specific depending on the exact need of the organization (Sun, Cegielski, Jia, & Hall, 2016).

To a large extent, these factors may not differ from the adoption of BDA application by Healthcare sectors. Implementation of BDA adoption has resulted in several prepositions from literature. Many studies have suggested its advantages or opportunities health institutions derive from its application (Denaxas & Morley, 2015; Sonnati, 2017). According to Wu et al. (2016), BDA capabilities have become the "promising future" for healthcare delivery. Consequently, this has influenced the level at which the healthcare sectors are adopting BDA to leverage healthcare delivery.

METHODOLOGY

Research Design

The research design is an exploratory approach that focused on describing findings from extant studies in the context of the study (Cresswell, 2014). In achieving this goal, the study adopted a systematic review approach to extract explicit academic journal in IS. Systematic review approach identified the step by step criteria in identifying journals to address the main aim of the study. The plan focused on the "inclusion and exclusion criteria" (Jesson, Matheson, & Lacey, 2011) to sort relevant articles identified. The search strategy was to identify related studies based on BDA adoption, appraise the quality of the journal and summarize evidence that distinguishes other articles. Academic Journals used for the search were from the following databases: Web of Science, Taylor and Francis, Elsevier, Scopus, IEEE, Emerald and Ebscohost.

Procedure and Sample selection

The search used keywords such as "big data", AND "business intelligent" AND "analytics" AND "critical factors OR influences", "adoption OR implementation", AND "healthcare OR hospitals". The keywords for the search revealed 952 articles. Some articles were dropped from the search due to duplication from other databases and also, a review of abstracts. The study adopted systematic and snowballing techniques to identify 150 articles which were selected because they met specific indicators for the study. A final sample of 25 articles was decided on using the inclusion and exclusion criteria approach through the systematic review concept in Table 1 below. These articles were critically considered based on the specific criteria adopted for this study.

Table 1. Inclusion and Exclusion Criteria

Criteria	Inclusion	Exclusion
Types of articles	Published Peer-reviewed journals	Articles not peer-reviewed
Literature Focus	BDA adoption in the health sector	Different sectors with BDA adoption
Language	Journal wrote in English	Non-English study
Year of study	2010 to 2017	Articles outside this study periods.

Results from Data Extraction and Literature

Articles extracted for the study categorised the name of the author, year of publication, the title of the article, name of journal and factors influencing adoption in Healthcare. Table 2 below shows the taxonomy of 25 articles systematically reviewed using the inclusion and exclusion criteria. According to Chawla and Davis (2013), Zhu and Cahan (2016), and Casselma, Onopa, and Khansa (2017), tracking and managing of patients' disease and care in real-time response based on data available through wearable devices are improving through BDA applications and tools. The literature review also revealed an improvement in healthcare efficiencies through the use of BDA in areas such as securing patient data and financial management (Sonnati, 2017), quality of care (Fosso, Anand, & Carter, 2013) and predicting specific patients for re-admission (Bates et al., 2012). In their review, Fosso et al. (2013) observed that the use of RFID applications provide enamours data to support the use of BDA to support healthcare services. Indeed, this has led to the use of BDA to personalized patients care in real-time (Chawla & Davis, 2013). Big data analytics and business intelligence applications have also harness data for precise decision-making to improve patients' outcomes (Ashrafi et al., 2014). Specifically, BDA adoption among healthcare institutions is mostly by factors such as quality decision making, managing patient data, and improving healthcare efficiency (Foshay & Kuziemsky, 2014). Identifying the promises and potential BDA offers, Raghupathi and Raghupathi (2014) indicated further insights such as data visualization BDA provides to healthcare practitioners. Ghosh and Scott (2011) also disclosed the "antecedent and catalysts for developing healthcare capability" and concluded that BDA capabilities are improving data visualization during surgical procedures. A systematic review by Thakur and Ramzan (2015), tracking disease pattern for specific treatment and patient care is through BDA and Hadoop applications. Findings from Bates et al. (2015) further revealed that BDA is becoming useful for monitoring, identifying and predicting high-risk patients for specific treatment among healthcare institutions. A review on BDA in "health informatics" by Kumar and Singh (2015) provided insight on how healthcare industries are adopting big data capabilities mainly for data management and quality decision- making. From the perspectives of telehealth in care management, Zhu and Cahan (2016) argue that wearable technologies have become the conduit for large data generation from patients. Big data analytics capabilities, therefore, leverage on telehealth and wearable technologies to manage and provide real-time analysis to respond to patients with a chronic illness before readmission. Casselma, Onopa, and Khansa (2107) pointed out that due to high demand for wearable technologies by patients, BDA applications have become essential for analysing, tracking and managing patients' diseases. Spriut, Vroon, and Batenburg (2014), on the other hand, emphasized BDA usefulness to improving patient's satisfaction through quality care and operational efficiency among health institutions in the Netherlands. Significantly, Ward, Marsolo and Froehle (2014), pointed out the continuous improvement of healthcare efficiency through the adoption of BDA in modern healthcare systems globally. Also, Zailani, Iranmanesh, Nikbin and Beng (2015) and Jee and Kim (2013) suggested recent healthcare operations, mostly from developed countries, are as a result of massive adoption of BDA. Big data and analytics are, therefore, are at the infant stages of approval or implementation in the developing countries. Finally, other studies show that the adoption of BDA has assisted in managing fraud in medical payments and reducing the cost of healthcare services (Sonnati, 2017).

From the above synthesis of the usefulness of BDA adoption from the 25 articles reviewed, Tables 2 to 5 further classified and conceptualised the various uses of BDA into nine (9) prevailing factors. As shown in Tables 2 to 5, these factors include Quality Decision Making, Patient Care Management, Medicine Tracking, Disease Tracking, Data Management, Data Visualization, Healthcare Efficiency, Securing Patient Data and Financial Management. Towards the aspect of improving the decision-making process, healthcare institutions, especially clinicians, rely on data generated from patients' medical records for real-time responses to emergency services. Also, BDA offers various visualization reports in a more user-friendly manner to support decision making by clinicians (Chan, Esteve, Fourniols, Escriba, & Campo, 2012). Other healthcare institutions were also leveraging on Data Visualization capabilities such as Dashboards and Scorecards in the surgical wards by Physicians and additional related financial or bill payment reporting. Data generated from wearable technologies also support medical carers with quick notification for real-time decision-making processes, especially for social health welfare (Wu, Li, Liu, & Zheng, 2017). Foshay and Kuziemsky (2014), Ashrafi, Kelleher and Kuilboer (2014), and Wang and Byrd (2017) also advocated that healthcare institutions and practitioners deploy BDA to generate insights from such data are critical to improving quick and concise diagnostics response to patients. For example, improving infant safety and health tracking through integrating wearable healthcare devices and big data platforms (Casselma et al., 2017). Another critical factor to BDA adoption in healthcare delivery is Patient management. From the review, healthcare institutions are harnessing the vast majority of data daily about the patient and eventually been used to manage and guarantee patient outcomes. Also, healthcare efficiency and improving productivity are driving the healthcare sector into BDA adoption. As a result, BDA is improving inventory management, financial management, quality healthcare at a low cost and confidence in decision making by healthcare practitioners.

Furthermore, the factors identified were ranked to indicate the most influencing factor(s) for BDA adoption by health institutions. Table 6 demonstrates that Patient care management is a critical factor for most healthcare institutions to monitor patients with exceptional cases such as diabetics patients, mental health cases and elderly care (Bellazsi, Dagliti, Sacchi, & Segani, 2015; Saravana, Eswari, Sampath & Lavanya, 2015). Big data and analytics re therefore used to respond to the critical needs of patients in real-time to prevent fatal occurrences. Disease management ranked as the second factor influencing healthcare sector decision to adopt BDA. With the aid of wearable devices or actuating devices which collect and share patient's health report in real-time, monitoring and tracking the level of infections for the physician for quick diagnostics at the early stages. The next factor influencing BDA adoption is decision making. A significant advantage of combining BDA and Hadoop tools is the high level of data processing without any human interaction, thereby reducing the level of errors in reports generated (Manikandan & Ravi, 2014). Ultimately, health practitioners depend on these reports to make a precise and quality decision. Most studies have also shown that the ultimate concerns for BDA adoption by healthcare institution is to improve efficiency in healthcare delivery. Accordingly, this factor is ranked fourth from the 25 literature articles reviewed which seek to promote the future of healthcare delivery at a low cost. Using BDA for data management is also rated to be important as an influencing factor from this study. As espoused by other studies, the healthcare sector is one of the most significant contributors of data and the adoption of BDA provides support and managing data accordingly. Factors such as Medicine tracking, Data visualization, securing patients data and financial management were the least factors for BDA adoption, as shown in Table 6.

The results from the systematic review also show that most of these factors identified are mainly due to changes in technological advancements and patients need. Thus, the motivation for most healthcare institutions to adopt BDA is through technological innovation to manage and monitor Patients care, quality healthcare and quality in decision making. The findings further identified the use of Radio Frequency Identification Device (RFID), Wearable devices and gesture-based technologies as the most common devices facilitating data gathering for BDA tools to provide critical information for quick decision-making processes.

CONCLUSION

The study presented a systematic review of existing studies in BDA adoption among health institutions. Significantly, this is as a result of the universal application of new technologies to enhance and improve

Table 2. Results from Literature Review

Name of Author	Year	Title of Article	Name of Journal	Use of BDA in Healthcare	Factors Conceptualization
Foshay and Kuziemsky	2014	Towards an implementation framework for business intelligence in healthcare	International Journal of Information Management	1. Impacts of information quality to the decision-making process. 2. Impact of Personnel issues. 3. Decision Timeliness 4. Decision Confidence	Quality Decision Making
Fosso et al.	2013	A literature review of RFID-enabled healthcare applications and issues	International Journal of Information Management	5. Identification of Blood bags for blood type Matching. 6. Medicine Tracking. 7. Detecting tampered Drugs. 8. Inventory Utilization. 9. Patience Management	Patient Management Medicine Tracking
Chawla and Davis	2013	Bringing Big Data to Personalized Healthcare: A Patient-Centred Framework	Journal of General Internal Medicine	10. Personalised healthcare by consumers through wearable devices.	Patient Management
Ashrafi et al.	2014	The impact of business intelligence on healthcare delivery in the USA	Interdisciplinary Journal of Information, Knowledge and Management	11. Harnessing data for precise decision-making to help improve patient outcomes, reduce costs, and ensure the future of the healthcare industry. 12. Streamline data and improve population health. 13. Instant guarantee to knowledge by Healthcare providers to deliver quality care at a low cost.	Quality Decision Making Data Management Healthcare Efficiency

healthcare delivery quality, efficiency and Patients monitors. With the level of extensive data generated from biomedical data, patient's data and health-related data, BDA has emerged as the frontier to provide insight to improve healthcare delivery. Generally, the paper sought to explore emerging issues advancing the adoption of BDA by healthcare institutions. Also, to classify these issues into prevailing factors and to provide an overview of the most common factor affecting BDA adoption. Relevant issues advancing BDA adoption ranges from improving patient's safety, securing patients records, monitoring and predicting. Other essential uses of BDA are specific for patients before readmission, using BDA to track disease patterns, harnessing data for precise decision making and an overall improvement in healthcare efficiency.

The issues identified from the review were classified into nine key factors influencing the level of BDA adoption. Among the nine discovered, patient care management revealed as the most recurring factor prompting healthcare institutions to deploy BDA to improve quality of care. Disease tracking management is the second factor affecting BDA adoption. Such arrangements are possible through RFIDs and wearable devices attached to patients' bodies for data collection. Respectively, quality decision making, improving healthcare efficiency, data management, data visualization, financial management, and securing patients data were among other factors promoting BDA adoption in healthcare. Through the systematic review, these factors provide clear strategies for healthcare institutions towards BDA to improve quality of healthcare more importantly for developing countries.

Interestingly, majority of the papers reviewed indicated that BDA adoption in healthcare is mostly from the developed economies which signify the continuous promotion of the study of BDA in emerging economies. In addition to further provide empirical research underpinning potentials for BDA deployment and usage in healthcare management, more importantly, to support patient's safety and cost-effectiveness. Finally, the study echoes the need for healthcare institutions to define a clear scope for BDA applications to maximise the value of its adoption.

Table 3. Results from Literature Review

Name of Author	Year	Title of Article	Name of Journal	Use of BDA in Healthcare	Factors Conceptualization
Zailani et al.	2015	"Determinants of RFID Adoption in Malaysia's Healthcare Industry: Occupational Level as a Moderator"	Journal of Medical Science	14. BI tools help to improve the security of data 15. BDA tools increase efficiency and productivity in healthcare and support staff delivery. 16. BDA tools in the Health Management Information System improve healthcare services offered to patients. 17. BDA tools are user-friendly for knowledge creation and reporting.	Securing Patient Data Healthcare Efficiency Data Visualization
Zhu and Cahan	2016	"Wearable technology and Telehealth in care management for chronic illness."	Health Information Management Systems	18. Notification of Health Emergency Services using wearable devices and BDA	Patient Management
Casselma et al.	2017	"Wearable Healthcare: Lessons from the past and a peek into the future."	Telematics and Informatics	19. Customer Demand for Wearable health device 20. For Infant safety and health tracking	Patient Management Disease Tracking
Amirian et al.	2017	"Using Big Data Analytics to extract disease surveillance information from the point of care diagnostics machines."	Pervasive and Mobile Computing	21. BDA supports d	Disease Tracking
Jee and Kim	2013	"Potentiality of Big Data in the Medical Sector: Focus on How to Reshape the Healthcare System"	Healthcare Informatics Research	22. For Healthcare Efficiency improvement 23. Disease Treatment	Healthcare Efficiency

Table 4. Results from Literature Review

Name of Author	Year	Title of Article	Name of Journal	Use of BDA in Healthcare	Factors Conceptualization
Chan et al.	2012	"Smart wearables systems: current status and future challenges."	Artificial Intelligence Medicine	24. For Real-time collection of healthcare data	Data Management
Lin, Brown, Yang, Li, and Lu	2011	"Data mining large-scale electronic health records for clinical support."	IEEE Intelligent System	25. To Identifying different diseases	Disease Tracking
Ward et al.	2014	"Application of business analytics in healthcare."	Business Horizons	26. For quality and efficient healthcare	Healthcare Efficiency
Wu et al.	2017	"Adoption of Big data and analytics in the mobile healthcare market: an economic perspective."	Electronic Commerce Research and Applications	27. For improving Social health welfare	Patient Management
Wang and Byrd	2017	"Business analytics-enabled decision-making effectiveness through knowledge absorptive capacity in healthcare."	Journal of Knowledge Management	28. For improving decision making effectiveness	Quality Decision Making
Ghosh and Scott	2011	"Antecedent and Catalysts for developing healthcare capability."	Communications of the Association for Information Systems	29. For Healthcare analytic capabilities 30. For visualization of surgical procedure	Data Visualization
Ferranti et al.	2010	"Bridging the gap: leveraging business intelligence tools in support of patient safety and financial effectiveness."	Journal of the American Medical Informatics Association	31. For improving patient's safety	Patient Management
Bardhan, Oh, Zheng and Kirksey	2014	"Predictive Analytics for Readmission of Patients with Congestive heart failure."	Information Systems Research	32. For monitoring a patient's readmission rate	Patient Management
Al-Qahtani and Al-Asem	2015	"Business Analytics in Healthcare: Opportunities and Challenges"	Information and Knowledge Management	33. For Diseases control 34. Tracking Patients healthier behaviours. 35. Mobile health for monitoring and treating patients timely	Disease Tracking Patient Management

Table 5. Results from Literature Review

Name of Author	Year	Title of Article	Name of Journal	Use of BDA in Healthcare	Factors Conceptualization
Sonnati	2017	"Improving Healthcare Using Big Data Analytics"	International Journal of Scientific and Technology Research	36. Detecting Fraud in Medical Payments. 37. Securing Patients Medical records. 38. Disease Management	Disease Tracking Data Management Financial Management
Bates et al.	2014	"Big Data in Healthcare: Using Analytics to Identify and Manage High-Risk and High-Cost Patients"	Health Affairs	39. Monitoring and predicting specific patients for readmission.	Disease Tracking Patient Care Management
Thakur and Ramzan	2015	"A Systematic Review on Cardiovascular disease using Big-Data by Hadoop."	Cloud system and big data engineering. IEEE	40. Tracking Disease pattern for appropriate treatment.	Disease Tracking
Raghupathi and Raghupathi	2014	"Big data Analytics in Healthcare: Promise and Potential."	Health Information Science and Systems	41. Gaining insight from Clinical Data.	Data Visualization
Tremblay, Hevner and Berndt	2012	"Design of an information Volatility measure for Healthcare decision making."	Decision Support Systems	42. Patient care and managing diseases	Patience Care Management
Spruit et al.	2014	"Towards Healthcare Business Intelligence in long-term care: an exploratory case study in the Netherlands."	Computer in Human Behaviour	43. Quality of care 44. Patient Satisfaction Healthcare improvement.	Disease Tracking Patient Management Healthcare Efficiency
Kumar and Singh	2017	"Review paper on Big Data in healthcare informatics."	International Research Journal of Engineering and Technology	45. Improvement in Patient Safety 46. Responding to Patients health needs	Data Management Disease Tracking Decision Making

Table 6. Rating of BDA Influencing Factors from 25 Articles

Factors	Frequency of Adoption	Ranking
Patient Management	12	1
Disease Tracking	8	2
Quality Decision Making	6	3
Medicine Tracking	1	7
Healthcare Efficiency	5	4
Financial Management	1	7
Data Management	4	5
Data Visualization	2	6
Securing Patient Data	1	7

REFERENCES

Adenuga, K. I., Iahad, N. A., & Miskon, S. (2017). Towards reinforcing telemedicine adoption amongst clinicians in Nigeria. *International Journal of Medical Informatics, 104,* 84–98. doi:10.1016/j.ijmedinf.2017.05.008 PMID:28599820

Agarwal, R., & Dhar, V. (2014). Editorial—big data, data science, and analytics: The opportunity and challenge of IS research. *Information Systems Research, 25*(3), 443–448. doi:10.1287/isre.2014.0546

Agarwal, R., Gao, G., DesRoches, C., & Jha, A. K. (2010). Research Commentary-The Digital Transformation of Healthcare: Current status and the Road Ahead. *Information Systems Research, 21*(4), 661–101. doi:10.1287/isre.1100.0327

Al-Qahtani, N., & Al-Asem, S. A. (2015). Business Analytics in Healthcare: Opportunities and Challenges. *Information and Knowledge Management, 5*(12).

Alpay, L., Henkemans, O. B., Otten, W., Rövekamp, T. A. J. M., & Dumay, A. C. M. (2010). E-health Applications and Services for Patient Empowerment: Directions for Best Practices in The Netherlands. *Telemedicine Journal and e-Health, 16*(7), 787–791. doi:10.1089/tmj.2009.0156 PMID:20815745

Angeles, R. (2013). Using the Technology-Organization-Environment framework and Zuboff's concepts for understanding environmental sustainability and RFID: Two case studies. *International Journal of Social, Management. Economics and Business Engineering, 7*(10), 1605–1613.

Ashrafi, N., Kelleher, L., & Kuilboer, J.-P. (2014). The Impact of Business Intelligence on Healthcare Delivery in the USA. *Interdisciplinary Journal of Information, Knowledge, and Management, 9.*

Bardhan, I., Oh, J., Zheng, Z., & Kirksey, K. (2014). Predictive Analytics for Readmission of Patients with Congestive heart failure. *Information Systems Research, 26*(1), 19–36. doi:10.1287/isre.2014.0553

Bates, D. W., Saria, S., Ohno-Machado, L., Shah, A., & Escoba, G. (2014). Big Data in Healthcare: Using Analytics to Identify and Manage High-Risk and High-Cost Patients. *Health Affairs, 33*(7), 1123–1131. doi:10.1377/hlthaff.2014.0041 PMID:25006137

Bellazsi, R., Dagliti, A., Sacchi, L., & Segani, D. (2015). Big Data Technologies: New Opportunities for Diabetes Management. *Journal of Diabetes Science and Technology, 9*(5), 1119-1125. . doi:10.1177/1932296815583505

Casselma, J., Onopa, N., & Khansa, L. (2017). Wearable Healthcare: Lessons from the past a peek into the future. *Telematics and Informatics, 34*(7), 1011–1023. doi:10.1016/j.tele.2017.04.011

Chan, M., Esteve, D., Fourniols, J. E., Escriba, C., & Campo, E. (2012). Smart wearable systems: Current status and future challenges. *Artificial Intelligence in Medicine, 56*(3), 137–156. doi:10.1016/j.artmed.2012.09.003 PMID:23122689

Chawla, N., & Davis, D. (2013). Bringing Big Data to Personalized Healthcare: A Patient-Centred. *Journal of General Internal Medicine, 28*(S3), 660–665. doi:10.100711606-013-2455-8

Chen, H., Chiang, R., & Storey, V. (2012). Business intelligence and analytics: From big data to big impact. *Management Information Systems Quarterly, 36*(4), 1165–1188. doi:10.2307/41703503

Christensen, H., Reynolds, J., & Griffiths, K., M. (2011). The use of e-health applications for anxiety and depression in young people: challenges and solutions. *Early Intervention in Psychiatry, 5*(1), 58-62. doi:10.1111/j.1751-7893.2010.00242

Costa, F. F. (2014). Big data in Biomedicine. *Drug Discovery Today, 17*(4), 433–440. doi:10.1016/j.drudis.2013.10.012 PMID:24183925

Cresswell, J. W. (2014). Research Design: qualitative, quantitative and mixed methods approach (4th ed.). Sage Publication Inc.

Dacin, M., Goodstein, J., & Scott, W. (2002). Institutional theory and institutional change: Introduction to the special research forum. *Academy of Management Journal, 45*(1), 45–56. doi:10.5465/amj.2002.6283388

Davis, F. (1989). Perceived usefulness, perceived ease of use and user acceptance of information technology. *Management Information Systems Quarterly, 13*(3), 318–339. doi:10.2307/249008

Davis, F., Bagozzi, R., & Warshaw, P. (1989). User acceptance of computer technology: A comparison of two theoretical models. *Management Science, 35*(8), 982–1003. doi:10.1287/mnsc.35.8.982

Deloitte Centre for Health Solution. (2015). *Health system analytics: The missing key to unlock value-based care*. Deloitte Development LCC.

Denaxas, S. C., & Morley, K. I. (2015). Big Biomedical data and Cardiovascular disease research: potentials and challenges. *European Heart Journal - Quality of Care and Clinical Outcomes, 1*(1), 9-16. doi:10.1093/ehjqcco/qcv005

Dunnebeil, S., Sunyaev, A., Blohm, I., Leimeister, J., & Krcmar, H. (2012). Determinants of physicians' technology acceptance for e-health in ambulatory care. *International Journal of Medical Informatics, 81*, 746-760. . doi:10.1016/jijmedinf.2012.02.002

Edworthy, S. M. (2001). Telemedicine in developing countries. *BMJ (Clinical Research Ed.), 323*(7312), 524–525. doi:10.1136/bmj.323.7312.524 PMID:11546681

Ferranti, J. M., Langman, K., Tanaka, D., McCall, J., & Ahmad, A. (2010). Bridging the gap: Leveraging business intelligence tools in support of patient safety and financial effectiveness. *Journal of the American Medical Informatics Association, 17*(2), 136–143. doi:10.1136/jamia.2009.002220 PMID:20190055

Foshay, N., & Kuziemsky, C. (2014). Towards an implementation framework for business intelligence in healthcare. *International Journal of Information Management, 34*(1), 20–27. doi:10.1016/j.ijinfomgt.2013.09.003

Fosso, S. W., Anand, A., & Carter, L. (2013). A literature review of RFID-enabled healthcare applications and issues. *Journal of International Management, 33*, 875–891. doi:10.1016/j.ijinfomgt.2013.07.005

Ghosh, B., & Scott, J. E. (2011). Antecedent and Catalysts for developing healthcare capability. *Communication of the Association for Information Systems*, 395-310.

Gu, D., Li, J., Li, X., & Liang, C. (2017). Visualizing the knowledge structure and evolution of big data research in healthcare informatics. *International Journal of Medical Informatics, 98*, 22–38. doi:10.1016/j.ijmedinf.2016.11.006 PMID:28034409

Hagel, J. (2015). Bringing analytics to life. *Journal of Accountancy, 219*, 24–25.

Hung, S. Y., Huang, Y. W., Lin, C. C., Chen, K. C., & Tarn, J. (2016). Factors Influencing Business Intelligence Systems Implementation Success in the Enterprises. Association for Information Systems.

Jee, K., & Kim, G.-K. (2013). The potentiality of Big Data in the Medical Sector: Focus on how to Reshape the Healthcare Sector. *Healthcare Informatics Research, 19*(2), 79–85. doi:10.4258/hir.2013.19.2.79 PMID:23882412

Jesson, J., Matheson, L., & Lacey, F. M. (2011). *Doing your Literature Review: Traditional and Systematic Techniques*. London: Sage Publications.

Kesse-Tachi, A., Asmah, A. E., & Agbozo, E. (2019). Factors influencing the adoption of eHealth technologies in Ghana. *Digital Health, 5*. doi:10.1177/2055207619871425

Lin, Y., Brown, R., Yang, H., Li, S., & Lu, H. (2011). Data mining large-scale electronic health records for clinical support. *IEEE Intelligent Systems, 23*, 87–90.

Liu, Y. (2014). Big data and predictive business analytics. *The Journal of Business Forecasting, 33*, 40–42.

Luo, J., Wu, M., Gopukumar, D., & Zhao, Y. (2016). Big Data Application in Biomedical Research and Healthcare: A Literature Review. *Biomedical Informatics Insights, 8*, 1-10. doi:10.4137/Bii.s31559

Manikandan, S. G., & Ravi, S. (2014). Big Data Analysis Using Apache Hadoop. *2014 International Conference on IT Convergence and Security (ICITCS)*, 1-4. 10.1109/ICITCS.2014.7021746

Mehta, N., & Pandit, A. (2017). Concurrence of big data analytics and healthcare: A systematic review. *International Journal of Medical Informatics, 114*, 57–65. doi:10.1016/j.ijmedinf.2018.03.013 PMID:29673604

Miah, S. J., Hassan, J., & Gammack, J. G. (2017). On-Cloud Healthcare Clinic: E-health consultancy approach for remote communities in a developing country. *Telematics and Informatics, 34*(1), 311–322. doi:10.1016/j.tele.2016.05.008

Murdoch, T., & Detsky, A. (2013). The inevitable application of big data to healthcare. *Journal of the American Medical Association, 309*(13), 1351–1352. doi:10.1001/jama.2013.393 PMID:23549579

Nicolini, D., Powell, J., Conville, P., & Matinez-Solano, L. (2008). Managing knowledge in the healthcare sector: A review. *International Journal of Management Reviews, 10*(3), 245-263. doi:10.1111/j.1468-2370.2007.00219

Persson, A., & Riyals, L. (2014). Making customer relationship decisions: Analytics v rules of thumb. *Journal of Business Research, 67*(8), 1725–1732. doi:10.1016/j.jbusres.2014.02.019

Popovic, A., Hackney, R., Coelho, P., & Jaklic, J. (2012). Towards Business Intelligence Systems Success: Effects of Maturity and Culture on Analytical Decision Making. *Decision Support Systems, 54*(1), 729–739. doi:10.1016/j.dss.2012.08.017

Popovic, A., Hackney, R., Tassabehji, R., & Castelli, M. (2106). The impact of big data analytics on firms' high-value business performance. *Information Systems Front*, 3-14. doi:10.100710796-016-9720-4

Raghupathi, W., & Raghupathi, V. (2014). Big data Analytics in Healthcare: Promise and Potential. *Health Information Science and Systems, 2*(3), 2–10. doi:10.1186/2047-2501-2-3 PMID:25825667

Ramtohul, I. (2016). Identifying the Adoption Process for Electronic Health Services: Qualitative Study. In H. Albach, H. Meffert, A. Pinkwart, R. Reichwald, & W. von Eiff (Eds.), *Boundaryless Hospital. Springer*. doi:10.1007/978-3-662-49012-9_15

Rogers, E. (2003). *Diffusions of Innovations*. New York: Free Press.

Safwan, E. R., Meredithand, R., & Burst, F. (2016). Business Intelligence (BI) system evolution: A case in a healthcare institution. *Journal of Decision Systems, 25*(1), 463–475. doi:10.1080/12460125.2016.1187384

Sakr, S., & Elgammal, A. (2016). Towards a Comprehensive Data Analytics Frameworks for Smart Healthcare Services. *Big Data Research., 4*, 44–58. doi:10.1016/j.bdr.2016.05.002

Saravana, K., N., M., Eswari, T., Sampath, P., & Lavanya, S. (2015). Predictive Methodology for Diabetic Data Analysis in Big Data. *Procedia Computer Science, 50*, 203-208. doi:10.1016/j.procs.2015.04.069

Shah, N., & Pathak, J. (2014). Why healthcare may finally be ready for big data. *Harvard Business Review*.

Sonnati, R. (2017). Improving Healthcare using Big Data Analytics. *International Journal of Scientific and Technology Research, 6*(3), 142–146.

Spruit, M., Vroon, R., & Batenburg, R. (2014). Towards Healthcare Business Intelligence in long-term care: An exploratory case study in the Netherlands. *Computers in Human Behavior, 30*, 698–707. doi:10.1016/j.chb.2013.07.038

Sun, S., Cegielski, C. G., Jia, L., & Hall, D. J. (2016). Understanding the Factors Affecting the Organizational Adoption of Big Data. *Journal of Computer Information Systems*. doi:10.1080/08874417.2016.1222891

Thakur, S., & Ramzan, M. (2015). A Systematic Review on Cardiovascular disease using Big-Data by Hadoop. Cloud system and big data engineering, IEEE, 351-355.

Tornatzky, L., & Fleischer, M. (1990). *The processes of technological innovation*. Lexington Books.

Tremblay, M., Hevner, A., & Berndt, D. (2012). Design of an information Volatility measure for Healthcare decision making. *Decision Support Systems*, *52*(2), 331–341. doi:10.1016/j.dss.2011.08.009

Trieu, V.-H. (2016). Getting value from Business Intelligence systems: A review and Agenda. *Decision Support System*, *93*(2017), 112-124. doi:10.1016/j.dss.2016.09.019

Turban, E., Ramesh, S., Delen, D., & King, D. (2011). Business Intelligence: A Managerial Approach (2nd ed.). Pearson Education, Inc.

Visinescu, L. L., Jones, M., & Sidorova, A. (2017). Improving Decision Quality: The Role of Business Intelligence. *Journal of Computer Information Systems*, *57*(1), 58–66. doi:10.1080/08874417.2016.1181494

Wamba, S. F., Anand, A., & Carter, L. (2013). A literature review of RFID-enabled healthcare applications and issues. *International Journal of Information Management*, *33*(5), 875–891. doi:10.1016/j.ijinfomgt.2013.07.005

Wamba, S. F., Gunasekaran, A., Akter, S., Ren, S., Dubey, R., & Childe, S. J. (2016). Big data analytics and firm performance: Effects of dynamic capabilities. *Journal of Business Research*, *70*(2017), 356-365. doi:10.1016/j.jbusres.2016.08.009

Wang, Y., & Byrd, T. A. (2017). Business analytics-enabled decision0making effectiveness through knowledge absorptive capacity in healthcare. *Journal of Knowledge Management*, *21*(3), 517–539. doi:10.1108/JKM-08-2015-0301

Wang, Y., & Hajli, N. (2017). Exploring the path to big data analytics success in healthcare. *Journal of Business Research*, *70*, 287–299. doi:10.1016/j.jbusres.2016.08.002

Ward, M., Marsolo, K., & Froehle, C. (n.d.). Application of business analytics in healthcare. *Business Horizon*, *57*(5), 571-582. doi:10.1016/j.bushor.2014.06.003

Watson, H. J. (2014). Tutorial: Big data analytics: Concepts, technologies, and applications. *Communications of the Association for Information Systems*, *34*(1), 1247–1268.

Wixcom, B., Yen, B., & Relich, M. (2013). Maximizing value from business analytics. *MIS Quarterly Executive*, *12*(2), 111–123.

Wu, J., Li, H., Liu, L., & Zheng, H. (2017). Adoption of Big data and analytics in the mobile healthcare market: An economic perspective. *Electronic Commerce Research and Applications*, *22*, 24-41. doi:10.1016/j.elerap.2017.02.002

Wu, J., Li, L., Cheng, S., & Lin, Z. (2016). The promising of healthcare services: When big data meet wearable technology. *Information & Management*, *53*, 1020–1033. doi:10.1016/j.im.2016.07.003

Zailani, S., Iranmanesh, M., Nikbin, D., & Beng, J. K. (2015). Determinants of RFID Adoption in Malaysia's Healthcare Industry: Occupational Level as a Moderator. *Journal of Medical Systems*, *39*(1), 172. doi:10.100710916-014-0172-4 PMID:25503418

Zhu, X., & Cahan, A. (2016). Wearable technologies and telehealth in care management for chronic illness. *Healthcare Information Management Systems*, 375-398.

Chapter 21
Information Systems Curriculum Research:
A Survey of Evidence

Kevor Mark-Oliver
Presbyterian University College, Ghana

ABSTRACT

While information system (IS) curriculum research has enjoyed recent attention from IS scholars, not many reviews exist. Those reviews are either outdated or focused on a particular strand of IS curriculum research which may not be comprehensive. In this chapter, the author presents a systematic review of information systems curriculum research published in information systems journals and selected conference proceedings in the past decade. The results point to many studies on identifying information systems competencies and their implications for curriculum design and delivery. Having observed that many of these issues are discussed at the undergraduate level and predominantly in the USA and UK, this chapter suggests, among others, future research at the graduate level and from other regions.

INTRODUCTION

The rapid technological change, the need to drive organizational innovation and competitiveness in an ever growing global knowledge economy, makes it imperative that people acquire the relevant 21st century employable skills and skills needed to fully participate in society (van Laar, van Deursen, van Dijk, & de Haan, 2017). Universities across the world have therefore been challenged, through the development of curricula, textbooks and relevant resources for training graduates, to respond to such disruptive environments in the labour market and for sustainable development (Picatoste, Pérez-Ortiz, & Ruesga-Benito, 2018).

Information Systems (IS) education research has gained recognition within the IS community and one prominent strand of research concerns developing and evaluating curriculum guidance for the IS discipline (Topi, 2019). As observed by Kruck et al. (2013), there is an increased awareness that educational issues in the IS discipline are important to both industry and academia. The relevance of the

DOI: 10.4018/978-1-7998-2610-1.ch021

content of IS curriculum and the quality of teaching may address the extant credibility crisis which characterises the IS discipline (Firth et al., 2011). It is therefore not surprising realising an increasing number of journals giving attention to computing and IS education (Kruck et al., 2013) and specific conference tracks on IS education being instituted. One dimension of IS education that is gaining popularity among scholars is IS curriculum research (Mills, Chudoba, & Olsen, 2016; Veltri et al., 2011). Despite its wide use in education and evidence of publications, there are not many comprehensive reviews of the literature on IS curriculum research. Similar literature review has been conducted by Longenecker et al. (2013). Whilst their work is valuable, it is focused on the trends of IS skills over a 50year period relevant to IS curriculum at the undergraduate level, identifying new and retired skills over the period, but does not review other relevant research issues, methodology and theoretical approaches to IS curriculum research. At the same time, it is important to review the literature over the past five years after the work of Longenecker et al. (2013).

The purpose of this paper is to review literature on IS curriculum research by identifying key issues, methodologies, conceptual approaches or theories and suggest relevant gaps for future research. A methodological review of extant literature, such us this, is a crucial endeavour for any academic research (Webster & Watson, 2002). The specific questions of focus in the study are:

1. What are the key research issues being studied by IS curriculum researchers?
2. What are the theoretical or conceptual approaches used in studying IS curriculum issues?
3. What methodological approaches are being used in studying IS curriculum issues?

The rest of the paper is structured as follows: Section two presents a way of classifying IS curriculum research. It is followed by a description of the methodology in Section three. The findings are presented in Section four with a discussion on the key research issues, theoretical/conceptual and methodological approaches presented in Section five. We conclude in Section six by identifying key research gaps and providing suggestions for future research.

CLASSIFYING IS CURRICULUM RESEARCH

This study is developed from the perspective of IS being a profession with employment-orientation. Consequently, the study views IS as a "field that prepares students to interface between non-technical organizational employees and managers and very technical IT professionals, with a focus on functions that are unlikely to be offshored" (Westfall, 2012).

In framing IS curriculum research, we start from the MIS curriculum studies dimensions proposed by Downey, McMurtrey and Zeltmann (2008) shown in Figure 1. The figure classifies IS curriculum studies depending on stakeholders, methodologies, and whether the research is focused on critical IS skills required or IS curricula or both. We extend these dimensions by an academic level categorization, theoretical/conceptual approaches. We also recognise adoption of or adherence to model curriculum by institutions implemented curriculum and outcome studies. Existing IS curriculum studies could be logically categorized based on these dimensions.

In this paper, studies that are categorised focused on organizational IS knowledge, skills and attitude and their implications for curricula development as "IS Competencies and IS Curricula" and those on IS curriculum design and delivery as "IS Curriculum change". We also identify studies that looks at the

Figure 1. MIS Curricula studies dimensions (Downey et al., 2008)

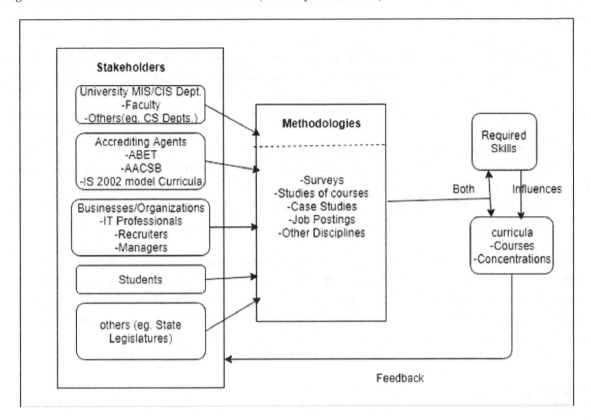

role of other stakeholders who are not directly involved in curriculum development and classified them as "stakeholder influence". Other categories drawn from the data included those on IS curriculum model "Adoption and Adherence", IS "Characterization" and IS curriculum "Outcomes".

METHODOLOGY

This paper adopts a Systematic Literature Review (SLR) approach to analyse the key research issues, conceptual/theoretical and methodological approaches in IS curriculum research. This was done by adopting the Preferred Reporting Items for Systematic Reviews and Meta-Analyses (PRISMA) approach (Moher et al., 2015).. The SLR, according to Moher et al (2009), uses systematic and explicit methods to identify, select, assess, collect and analyse data from studies selected for the review. We began with a search action conducted on ProQuest Central, Elsevier, ACM (Digital Library) and EBSCOhost, which are well accepted IS databases (Levy & Ellis, 2006, p. 186) using the Boolean search "(Information System OR IS) AND (Curriculum OR Skills OR competencies)". This was done for a period between 2008 and 2018. The selection of the papers was limited to peer-reviewed articles in journals published in English. High quality IS conferences such as the AIS Conferences (ICIS, AMCIS, ECIS, and PACIS) and its affiliate conferences like the HICSS were also searched using the same Boolean search criteria from 2013 to 2018. The result was practically screened using the following eligibility (Inclusion and exclusion) criteria:

1. The article must have been published in a peer reviewed journal or IS Conference of high repute.
2. Only empirical curriculum research papers were included from the Conferences. For instance, case descriptions were excluded.
3. The article must be focused on IS curriculum at the post-secondary level or institutions of higher learning (IHL).
4. The article must not only describe an IS curriculum.
5. Articles on curriculum of other disciplines with IS as a single or introductory course were excluded.
6. Articles on curriculum of other related disciplines either than IS were also excluded.
7. Instructional medium, pedagogy and other issues related to the broader IS education were also disregarded.

The eligibility was done through three steps. Firstly, by screening the titles of the articles and secondly, by the abstracts and finally by using the full paper with the eligibility criteria at each stage as a filter. The results were categorized by names of authors, year of publications, key research issues, journal/conference, level of analysis, educational level, methodology, theoretical/conceptual framework, Country and Region.

FINDINGS

The initial database search resulted in a total of 4,572 peer reviewed articles from scholarly journals and 172 conference papers from IS conferences. Applying publication restrictions to IS and Educational journals and removing duplications resulted into 934 articles. These were further screened using the title and abstracts to exclude 601 articles. The remaining 333 full text were read and assessed using the seven eligibility criteria. Eventually, the study included 140 journal articles and 22 Conferences that met the eligibility criteria. The flow chart in Figure 2 details the various stages.

Distribution of Articles per Journal and Conference Forums

The distribution of articles per journal is shown in Figure 3. It is observed that 77.86% of the articles studied are in recognized IS Journals, such as Communications of the AIS (CAIS), Journal of IS Education (JISE), Information Systems Education Journal (ISEDJ) and Journal of Computer Information Systems (JCIS). This result, though not different from some existing findings, is an indication of the commitment of the IS community to issues of IS curriculum and IS education in general. For example, in a review conducted by Kruck et al. (2013) of the scope and productivity of research in IS education, they found CAIS, JCIS and the JISE as the top three publishing journals in IS education.

At the same time, specific tracks in conference proceedings dedicated to IS education and/or IS curriculum were searched whilst general search was made for those without specific tracks. The distribution of articles per conference is shown in Figure 4. Of the 22 conference papers included, 81.82% were from AMCIS and the rest from ECIS and ICIS. The AMCIS and ICIS have dedicated tracks for discussing and publishing IS Education and IS Curriculum issues.

Figure 2. PRISMA Flowchart (adapted from van Laar et al., 2017)

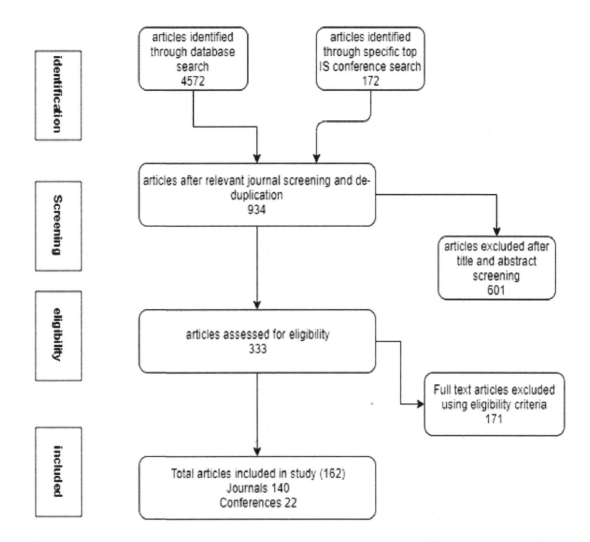

Distribution of Articles per Key Issues

We analyse the distribution of articles mapped to the key issues in the extended IS curricula study dimensions. The findings, as illustrated in Figure 5, indicate a concentration of focus on IS curriculum change. This is followed by research related to identifying critical IS competencies relevant to organizations and their implications for curricula development and delivery. Adoption and adherence and IS curricula outcome studies have also received some moderate attention whilst stakeholder influence and IS programme characterization studies receive less attention. Between 2008 and 2018, two IS curriculum models each, have been developed for undergraduate and graduate programmes. The specific issues being researched which answers our first research question are discussed in section four.

Figure 3. Distribution of IS curriculum articles by IS journal from 2008-2018 (Source: Authors)

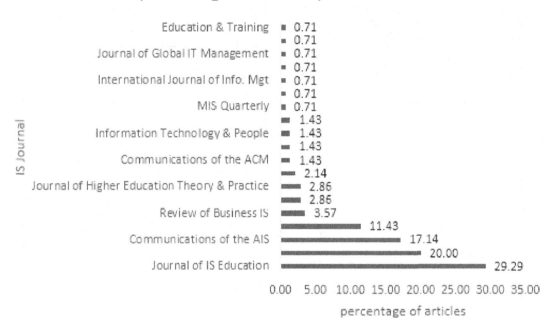

Figure 4. Distribution of IS curriculum articles by IS Conference from 2013-2018 (Source: Authors)

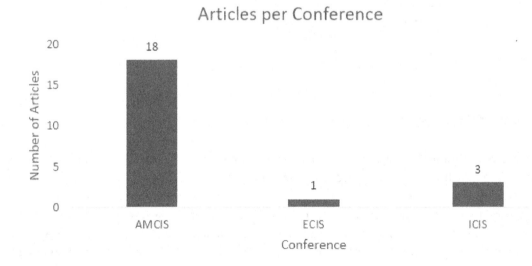

Figure 5. Distribution of IS curriculum articles among Key Issues from 2008-2018 (Source: Authors)

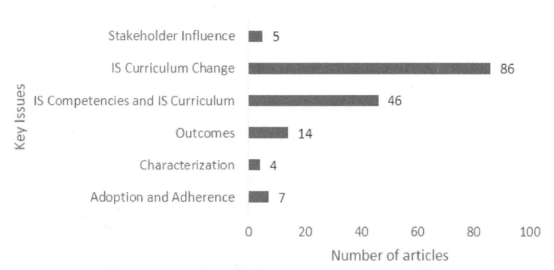

Distribution of IS Curriculum Research per Educational Level

Figure 6 shows the distribution of the articles among academic levels. Whilst there is much research on undergraduate IS curriculum (Benamati et al., 2010; Goncalves et al., 2016; Harris & Patten, 2015; Jones & Ceccucci, 2018; Jones & Liu, 2017; Longenecker et al., 2013; Zhang et al., 2014), IS curriculum research at the graduate level, despite a number of efforts (Chen et al., 2008; Schiller et al., 2015; Thouin et al., 2018; Topi et al., 2017), have been understudied. Similar observation of this gap has been made in the past (Gill & Hu, 1999; Jacobi et al. 2014; Kumar et al., 2017). This academic level categorization is relevant since IS competencies expected from an undergraduate level would be different from that of a graduate level. There are however research issues that are neither targeted at any of the specific levels nor both and are generic in nature which are classified under "General" (Gupta et al., 2015; Harris et al., 2012; Schirf & Serapiglia, 2017; Wang et al., 2016).

Geographical Distribution of IS Curriculum Research

The evidence, as indicated in Figure 7, shows a preponderance of IS curriculum studies in America, largely in the US or North America. This may be a reflection of the relative maturity of the IS discipline with strong professional associations in the region. Moreover, until the development of the IS 2010 and the MSIS 2016 IS model curricula that seemed to have some global characteristics, the preceding IS model curricula for both undergraduate and graduate schools had been developed in the North American region and around which researchers base their studies. However, Kaiser, Goles, Hawk, Simon, & Frampton (2011) suggest that different Regions value IS competencies differently and it would therefore be interesting to explore such North American dominance and the lack of IS curriculum research in other regions.

Figure 6. Distribution of IS curriculum research among Educational Levels from 2008-2018 (Source: Authors)

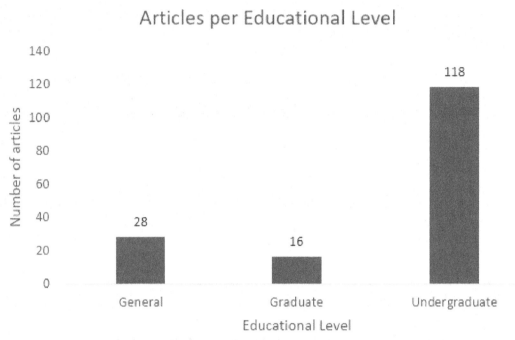

DISCUSSION

What are the Key Research Issues Being Studied by IS Curriculum Researchers?

We have already mapped out the key issues under the IS curriculum study dimensions. We will therefore consider specific issues being researched under each of these key issues.

Information Systems Programmes Characterization

The nature and character of IS academic programmes in universities continue to interest researchers due to its multidisciplinary nature. This is evident in the names of IS or similar programs and the resident host of these programs in academic institutions. Pierson, Kruck, & Teer (2008), for example, investigated the incidence of computer related majors in accredited business schools and examined their names. They found that information systems, management information systems, computer information systems, business information systems, and information technology are some of the names referring to the same or similar disciplines. The authors also suggested a periodic review of the names. This finding was relevant in examining IS Curricula. Similar result of different names was found by Apigian & Gambill (2010). Consequently, Brooks, Gambill, Clark and Clark (2016) like previous studies concluded, there was no move towards standardization.

Figure 7. Geographical distribution of IS Curriculum research from 2008 to 2018 (Source: Authors)

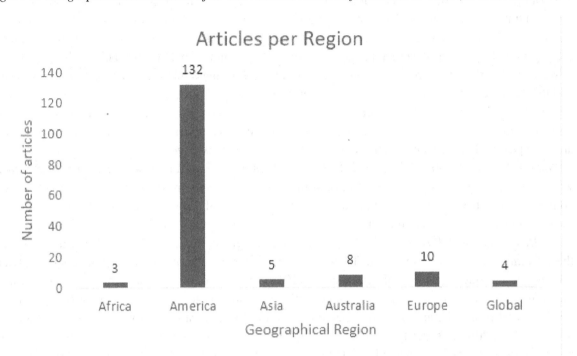

IS Competencies and IS Curriculum

This category of research looks at eliciting critical IS competencies relevant and needed by organizations and suggesting implications to IS curriculum or IS education in general. Such research is also relevant to organizational training and competency sourcing (Bullen, Abraham, Gallagher, Simon, & Zwieg, 2009; Ho & Frampton, 2010; Poston & Dhaliwal, 2015). There is almost a consensus that the goal of IS curriculum design and delivery is to aid in producing graduates with competencies that are required by organizations or industries (Benamati, Ozdemir, & Smith, 2010; Jarvenpaa, Ives, & Davis, 1991; Topi et al., 2017). These competencies are required for high organizational performance (Akman & Turhan, 2017). It is therefore not surprising, that IS curriculum research focused on change will often start with identifying relevant IS competencies or roles. This strand of research is critical due to the rapidly changing nature of technology, resulting in the retiring of some organizational roles and competencies, and demand for new IS competencies (Topi, 2019) in what some researchers have described as a *moving target* (Lee & Han, 2008). Over the period of this review, a number of IS curriculum research have been dedicated to identifying the required IS KSAs or competencies and IS roles in IT/IS workforce study (Agarwal & Ahmed, 2017; Akman & Turhan, 2017; Benamati et al., 2010; Henson & Kamal, 2010; Hwang & Soe, 2010; Jones et al., 2016; Lee & Han, 2008; Poston & Dhaliwal, 2015; Wang et al., 2016). For example, in their study of what skills were considered desirable for entry level IS positions, Jones et al. (2016) identified hard skills such as Microsoft Office, database/data warehouse/SQL, and knowledge of security, while the most important soft skills were willingness to learn, critical thinking, and attitude. This was in line with Benbasat et al. (1980) classification of IS employee skills as hard or soft. Peppard and Ward (2004) categorise IS KSAs as Business, Technical, Behaviour and Attitudinal. Havelka and

Merhout (2009) developed a theoretical model for Information technology competency and identified personal traits, professional skills, business knowledge and technical knowledge as a requirement for organizational IS competencies. Topi et al. (2008) in their development of an IS model curriculum grouped these personal traits and professional skills as individual foundational competencies. The researchers also argue that, the applicability of IS have moved beyond business into other domains, such as health, and that such domain knowledge is also relevant. It is therefore logical to use domain competency as a higher construct to include all applicable domains of which business is part. This is akin to Lee's et al. (2002) categorization of KSAs into IS core knowledge (technical), Organization and Society (domain), and interpersonal and personal traits (individual foundation knowledge).

Whilst the identification of required IS competencies may be useful, these competencies may overwhelm curriculum developers as a result of some constraints (Nunamaker et al., 1982). It is therefore common to identify researchers giving attention to examining the importance or value of each of the identified IS competencies to relevant stakeholders (See Kaiser et al., 2011; Lee & Mirchandani, 2010; Surendra & Denton, 2009) and for different geographic regions. For example, in a study to investigate the dynamics of the importance of IS/IT skills from the perspective of 70 IS/IT managers using latent growth curve modelling, Lee and Mirchandani (2010) found out among others that, wireless communications and applications, mobile commerce applications and protocols, IS security, web applications, services, and protocols, and data management were the top five rapidly growing skills. The authors also found out "that IS security, data management, project management and other business skills, web applications, services, and protocols, and wireless communications and applications are expected to be the most important five skills in the future" (Lee & Mirchandani, 2010, p.67). The researchers made recommendations for IS curriculum based on these findings. Also, organizations in low-wage regions value technical skills more than those in high-wage regions but places similar value on project management skills (Kaiser et al., 2011). Such a result has implications for outsourcing and curriculum design.

Another cluster of IS curriculum research is reviewing organizational IS KSAs or competencies and comparing them to an IS curriculum to identify gaps or the other way of reviewing IS curriculum and matching the learning outcomes to KSAs required by organizations to identify curriculum gaps.

These gaps, also known as discrepancies (Tesch et al., 2003) or deficiencies (Nelson, 1991), have been reported in extant literature (Agarwal & Ahmed, 2017; Apigian & Gambill, 2014; Henson & Kamal, 2010; Pauli et al., 2011; Poston & Dhaliwal, 2015; Schirf & Serapiglia, 2017; Stefanidis et al., 2013). These gaps arise out of varying perceptions of different stakeholders understanding or expectation of IS KSAs in industry and academia. It is recommended for a regular KSA needs assessment since the competency gaps is a moving target (Lee et al., 1995).

IS Curriculum Change

IS curriculum change is the dominant research area in IS curricula. This area of research reports the processes and experiences in the development of courses or curricula, revision of existing curricula, or integration of new courses into existing curricula to reflect current competencies required from graduates. The identified consensus competencies are drafted into learning outcomes (Topi et al., 2008). These processes are not to be seen as linear but complex activities that is receiving attention from IS curriculum researchers.

It is rational to expect a change in curriculum as a response to new innovation and technologies characterising the information systems field (Kesner, 2008; Topi et al., 2010; Topi et al., 2008). The adoption and use of information systems in new domains beyond business, such as health (Zhang et al., 2014) may trigger a change in the traditional IS curriculum or an IS model curriculum to cater for the specificities of the new domains. New IS roles have also served as a basis for curriculum change (Lee & Han, 2008). A number of strategies such as revision and integration may be used to improve an IS curriculum. For example, curriculum revision (Stevens et al., 2011; Veltri et al., 2011) results in a curriculum change by assessing the curriculum and deciding on removing less valued KSAs and including new important or valuable KSAs. The dominant strategy in IS curriculum change is integration (Fichman et al., 2014; Gupta et al., 2015; Jones & Liu, 2017; Martz et al, 2017; Mitri & Palocsay, 2015; Ramesh & Gerth, 2015; Sidorova, 2013; Wilson & Tulu, 2010).

Table 1 summarises key KSAs that have been integrated into IS curricula over the period of review. Though not defined, integration involves the inclusion of new KSAs into an existing IS curriculum. Integration of a number of technical, foundational and domain KSAs into an IS curriculum continue to be a subject of interest before and after the release of MSIS 2016 (Table 1). For example, a number of researchers continue to make a case for the integration of Big data and its related KSAs (Jafar et al., 2017; Parks et al., 2018) whilst others have looked at the integration of new foundational KSAs like creativity and problem solving (Martz et al., 2017), Service learning (Jones & Ceccucci, 2018) and intercultural communication (Mitchell & Benyon, 2018). It is interesting to note that, beyond the business domain, health is the other domain receiving attention from IS scholars (Lawler et al., 2016; Zhang et al., 2014; Zheng et al., 2014).

Curriculum Model Adoption and Adherence

The IS model curricula are recommendations that can be adopted or adapted and utilized by institutions. Reportage on situated adoption or adaptation and use of the IS model curriculum has empirical value to the IS community (see Bell et al., 2013; Fichman et al., 2014; Mills et al., 2012; Reynolds et al., 2016). These vary from assessing levels of adoption and utilization to narrating experiences of adoption. For example, Bell et al. (2013), after the publication of the IS 2010, evaluated the level of program adoption of the IS 2010 curriculum guidelines by collecting curriculum data from 127 AACSB-accredited undergraduate information systems programs across the United States. They found, among others, that IS programs exhibited a wide range of adherence to the IS 2010 core curriculum guidelines. This study is similar to Lifer et al. (2009) who mapped IS curriculum, implemented in US universities, to the IS 2002.

In a similar study, Mills et al. (2012), through a survey and a cluster analysis, categorised IS curriculum into Independent, Focused, Adoptive, and Flexible based on the levels of adherence to the IS 2010. Whilst these studies have been done for undergraduate IS model curricula, few of such studies have been done for graduate IS programs (Apigian & Gambill, 2014; Yang, 2012). On the other hand, Chatterjee et al. (2013) studied the challenges and barriers to the adoption of a health information systems curriculum by providing useful experiences. Factors such as contextual specificities (Larsson & Boateng, 2010), resources and local employment needs (Mills et al., 2012) may constrain the adoption of an IS model curriculum. In such a situation, adaptation becomes an implementation strategy. Issues of IS curriculum adaptation have been under researched. This may be because majority of IS curriculum research have been done in North America where the various IS model curricula are based and will logically capture the values and context of the region. Even in the American region, studies have shown less than 50% mean adherence to the IS model curricula (Mills et al., 2012; Bell et al., 2013). Mills et al. (2012) suggests such non-adherence may be deliberate to allow universities adapt to local employment needs or

Table 1. Summary of KSA Integration into IS Curriculum from 2008 to 2018 (Source: Authors)

KSA dimension	KSAs integrated	Study
Technical	Big Data, Data Analytics, Data Science	Sircar (2009), Sidorova (2013), Zheng et al. (2014), Aasheim et al. (2015), Davis & Woratschek (2015), Gupta et al. (2015), Mitri & Palocsay (2015), Molluzo & Lawler (2015), Mills et al. (2016), Mamonov & Misra (2015), Wymbs (2016), Lawler et al.(2016), Schwieger & Ladwig (2016), Jafar et al. (2017), Parks et al. (2018)
	ERP	Wang (2011), Scholtz et al (2012), Hepner & Dickson (2013)
	Cloud Computing	Lawler (2011), Chen et al (2012), Hwang et al. (2016),
	Information Security	Patten & Harris (2013), White et al. (2013), Sauls & Gudigantala (2013), Woodward et al. (2013), Harris & Patten (2015),
	IT Service Management	Cater-Steel et al (2010), Urbaczewski et al. (2011)
	Programming	Babb et al. (2014), Reynolds et al. (2017)
	HCI	Janicki et al. (2015)
	Green IT	Sendall & Shannon (2011)
	Entrepreneurship	Lang & Babb (2015), Jones & Liu (2017)
Foundational	Creativity and Problem Solving	Martz et al (2017)
	Ethics and Social Responsibility	Harris & Lang (2011), Cellucci et al. (2011)
	Service Learning	Jones & Ceccucci (2018)
	Inter Cultural Communication	Mitchel & Benvon (2018)
	Virtual Team Work	Chen et al (2008)
Domain		
	Health	Wilson & Tulu (2010), Celluci et al. (2011), Zhang et al (2014), Zheng et al (2014), Lawler et al.(2016)

may be due to genuine lack of resources to implement the required IS model curricula. Despite these arguments, no studies have explored the phenomenon of non-adherence.

Stakeholder Influence

The next strand of ISC change research focuses on stakeholders. There are a considerable number of stakeholders involved in curriculum development. They include IS professionals, Alumni, Faculty, students, managers, regulators and policy makers whose understanding and perceptions of IS competencies are valuable inputs to IS curriculum development. McCoy et al. (2015), using a web-based survey instrument, collected data from faculty members, recruiters, and students in the US about their perceived value of topics and subtopics in an IS curriculum. This is a typical multi-stakeholder IS curriculum studies. Others have studied from a single stakeholder perspective. Aasheim et al. (2009) investigated whether there is a disconnect between the importance of various skills and traits for entry-level IT workers as perceived by IT managers versus faculty teaching in IT-related fields. The researchers found out that there is no difference in importance of the broad categories of KSAs as perceived by these stakeholders. Such an exercise is valuable for curriculum revision.

In addition, there is a high concentration of micro-level IS curriculum research and analysis as compared to other levels of analysis (See Figure 8). The micro level in this case is where the focus of the analysis is on the individual stakeholders such as students, Alumni, Faculty, employees, IS professionals and employers, individual IS curriculum, and courses, individual universities or organizations and departments (Burns, Gao, Sherman, & Klein, 2018; Carlsson, Hedman, & Steen, 2010; Gupta, Goul, & Dinter, 2015; Henson & Kamal, 2010; Mitchell & Benyon, 2018; Parks, Ceccucci, & McCarthy, 2018; Sivakumar & Kwok, 2017). Meso-level analysis is however focused on IS competencies beyond a single organization or IS curriculum studies beyond a single university(Apigian & Gambill, 2010; Downey et al., 2008; Sonteya & Seymour, 2012; Stefanidis & Fitzgerald, 2010). What is lacking are Macro and Meta level studies. The Macro level is where the focus would be on the national level, investigating the role of institutions that deliver infrastructure, determine policy, and set rules and regulations. An example of such a study considers the role of professional, accrediting authorities and national context, in the design and delivery of IS Curricula (Knapp, Maurer, & Plachkinova, 2017; Landry, Daigle, Pardue, Colton, & Hunsinger, 2010; Saulnier & White, 2011; Tedre, Bangu, & Nyagava, 2009). The Meta level studies have a focus beyond one country, to a regional or sometimes global or cross-country level of analysis of IS curricula or IS competencies (Topi et al., 2010, 2017; Topi, Wright, & Kaiser, 2008).

Information Systems Curriculum Outcomes

This category of research considers issues related to the impact of IS curriculum implementation and adoption or what happens after an IS curriculum is developed. Currently, outcome studies on communicating IS curriculum, assessment, evaluation and IS enrolment were identified. Research issues around communicating and marketing an IS curriculum are scanty. May and Lending (2015) developed a conceptual model for communicating an IS curriculum and they demonstrated how the model could be useful to various stakeholders.

IS Curriculum Assessment is used to improve the quality of a course or programme (Gardiner, 1994). Assessment is different from curriculum evaluation in that, evaluation benchmarks the curriculum with some standards or model whilst assessment focuses on improving the programme (Merhout et al, 2008). Bacon and Stewart (2017) have criticized the current assessment approach as lacking the statistical power to make valid conclusions that can change the curriculum and called for new assessment approaches. At the same time, other studies consider expected outcomes or delivered outcomes (Anderson, 2017; Gill & Ritzhaupt, 2013; Karsten & Roth, 2015). Anderson (2017), for instance, studied how pedagogy influences learning outcomes of an IT curriculum. Chan et al. (2014) also looked at students' satisfactory factors from an IS curriculum whilst others evaluated an implemented curriculum with standardized models (Charland et al., 2015; Jacobson et al., 2011; McCoy et al., 2015).

Issues of IS enrolment, though not new, continues to receive renewed attention. There seem to be a deterministic notion that the solution to solving dwindling IS enrolment is through innovative curricula. It is therefore not surprising to find IS curriculum research paying attention to IS enrolment as outcomes

Figure 8. Distribution of IS curriculum articles per level of analysis from 2008-2018

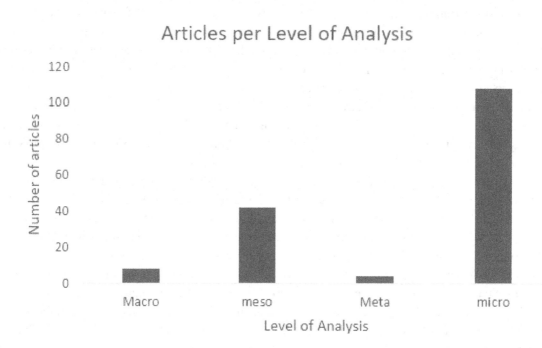

of a successful IS curriculum strategy (Kizior et al., 2010; Mills et al., 2017). Mills et al. (2017) studied empirically how curriculum-oriented and promotional interventions meet enrolment demands by introducing SQL into foundation information systems curricula. Others have studied factors that influences students' choice or selection of Information systems as a major (Akbulut-Bailey, 2012; Chen et al., 2016; Eom et al., 2015; Merhout et al., 2016).

What Are the Theoretical or Conceptual Approaches Used in Studying IS Curriculum Issues?

Information Systems Curriculum Models

Information Systems model curricula have been identified to be useful in meeting the changing IS environment (Couger et al., 1995). Gorgone et al. (2006) explains that "the model curriculum provides a standard against which individual colleges and universities can judge their own program" and that students and employers look for programs that are based on the models to understand what competencies a graduate should have. These curricula have been jointly developed by committees from different IS professional associations such as the ACM, the AIS, DPMA, and ICIS (example Ashenhurst, 1972; Couger et al., 1995; Topi et al., 2010; Topi et al., 2017) and by individual researchers (Ho & Frampton, 2010). These models have been developed for both graduate and undergraduate levels capturing improvements and the relevant IS competencies over time (Table 2). IS curriculum researchers have studied a number of issues mainly around these IS curriculum models and the dominant issues have been discussed in this review.

Table 2. A summary of some undergraduate and graduate IS Curriculum models

Undergraduate IS Curriculum models	Graduate IS Curriculum models
IS '95 (Davis et al., 1997)	MSIS 2000 (Gorgone et al., 2000)
IS 2002 (Gorgone et al., 2002)	MSIS 2006 (Gorgone et al., 2006)
IS 2010 (Topi et al., 2010)	MSIS 2016 (Topi et al., 2017)

Information Systems Curriculum Development Models

Tatnall and Davey (2002) provide three useful models of IS curriculum development based on the inter-action of various stakeholders. The researchers presented the negotiation model which recognises an IS curriculum as a product of negotiation of stakeholders with conflicting goals. The second is the *Actor Network approach* to curriculum development. This approach considers IS curriculum as an innovation created from the enrolment of powerful actors who have interest in the IS curriculum and the third approach, ecological model, borrows biological ecological concepts to explain the complex relationships between the various stakeholders in the development of the IS curriculum. Apart from Tatnall (2010) actor network account of how curriculum innovation occurs in an institution, there is lack of empirical evidence, within the period of study, of how these models have been used in explaining curriculum in-novation processes.

Other Behavioural Theories

The Theory of Reasoned Action has been used to study the factors that influences students' enrolment in IS programmes (Chen, 2014; Mills et al., 2017) by looking at attitude, behavior norms, and plans to enrol in an IS class in the future. Akbulut-Bailey (2012) and Chen et al. (2016) used the Social Cognitive Career Theory (SCCT) to study factors influencing students' selection of an IS programme.

In the study of the identification and ranking of IS competencies, the Resource Based View (RBV) of the firm have been useful (Hepner & Dickson, 2013; Swinarski, 2008). The baseball 'moneyball' theory has also been used to analyse the value of IS KSAs to different stakeholders (Surendra & Denton, 2009). In analysing IS KSA gaps, though new, the IT professional competency (ITPC) theory (Havelka & Merhout, 2009) seems promising but requires empirical evidence from different context to make it robust. Wymbs (2016) used the Innovation Process model to infuse business analytic courses into an undergraduate IS curriculum model.

Intercultural transformation theory has guided the design of an IS course (Sivakumar & Kwok, 2017). The Latent growth model was used in analysing trends in IS KSAs (Lee & Mirchandani, 2010). Wang et al. (2016) established that developers' intention to learn business skills is positively influenced by intrin-sic learning Motivation and both Absolute and Relative learning Self-efficacy (MARS). These theories have largely been applied at the individual and organizational levels with little emphasis on theories that considers the external environments of universities or IS departments which develop IS curriculum.

What Methodological Approaches Have Been Used in studying IS Curriculum Issues?

Considerable methodologies have been used to study the issues of IS curriculum (Figure 9) with a high number being case studies of experiences of IS curriculum development and implementation in the universities' "real life". For example, Ramesh and Gerth (2015) presents a case study describing how IS faculty, considering local requirements and guiding principles, designed a unique and innovative integrated core curriculum for a graduate IS program. Similarly, Wilson and Tulu (2010), using a case study, narrates how a health information system curriculum was developed. This is similar to other IS curriculum research case studies (Ho & Frampton, 2010; Chatterjee et al., 2013; Gupta et al., 2015; Mitri & Palocsay, 2015).

At the same time, surveys have been used to identify and rank IS competencies, study IS KSA gaps or IS curriculum gaps (Aasheim et al., 2009; Jones et al., 2016; Stefanadis, 2012; Stevens et al., 2011), IS curriculum adoption or adherence and course integration (Sendal et al., 2011; Mills et al., 2012; Clark, Clark et al., 2017) and IS enrolments choices and strategies (Mills et al., 2017). Other methodologies used include routine design where descriptive accounts of IS curricula design are given by putting together consensus competencies or learning outcomes (Topi et al., 2010; Topi et al., 2017) or a design science approach (Carlsson et al., 2010). IS curriculum recommendation and guidelines have been considered as a product or artifact of design science research (DSR) (Offermann et al., 2010). Alturki et al. (2012) differentiates design science and routine design based on the notion that the former develops new scientific knowledge whereas the latter apply scientific knowledge to solve problems. They also differentiate design science from action research (AR), though some authors either considers them as the same or the latter as a special instance of the former, "DSR has different research purposes, e.g. a new artifact invention; AR in the most cases, however, is to understand and change a complex reality". AR has been used in IS Curriculum research (Campbell, Pardue, & Campbell, 2015; Dunaway, 2017; Eom et al., 2015). Reports from academic panel or experts discussion on particular issues of IS curriculum activities have been useful and features in articles (Topi et al., 2011; Topi et al., 2008; Urbaczewski et al., 2011). Content analysis of job postings in popular newspapers or on websites over a period have been used to identify IS competencies required by organizations and dominant IS roles in organisations (Gardiner et al., 2017; Harris et al., 2012; Lee & Han, 2008; Murawski, 2017). Cater-Steel et al. (2010) also used a narrative enquiry method to describe how IT Service management was embedded in an undergraduate IS curriculum. We also found articles (Havelka & Merhout, 2009; Merhout et al., 2016) that used the Nominal Group Technique (NGT) for IS curriculum research.

The mixed method approach has also been used in IS curriculum research. This include the use of different methods within the same research (Chen et al., 2008; Helfert, 2011; Sivakumar & Kwok., 2017). The use of Games in IS competency assessments have been introduced. Charland et al. (2015) used an experimental Game to assess their ERP competencies after students have been exposed to an IS curriculum.With the forgoing evidence, we extend and re-categorize the IS curricula studies dimensions presented in Downey et al.(2008) in Figure 10.

Figure 9. Distribution of IS curriculum articles by research methods

CONCLUSION AND GAPS FOR FUTURE RESEARCH

This paper presents a systematic review of issues in IS curriculum research. Though not exhaustive, the attempt by this review to identify the key issues in IS curriculum research have unearthed a considerable number of gaps worth exploring in future research. There is the need for more knowledge in the design and delivery of IS curricula that enhances the competencies of graduates globally and in specific regions. From this review, an empirical, theoretical, methodological and contextual gaps are identified with a clear implication for future research. We present these gaps as follows:

Issue Gaps in IS Curriculum Research

Firstly, the IS curriculum issues studied in literature were largely from North America and Europe. There has been recommendation for studies in other regions since IS competencies are context sensitive (Kaiser et al., 2011; Osatuyi & Garza, 2014). Yang (2012), for example, recommends these studies in non-US universities and preferably in other regions of the world. So far, it is not clear whether the competencies identified in other regions are sufficient and relevant to organizations in other regions. Such a study will empirically and conceptually improve the global IS competency framework.

Secondly, there is, generally, little research on graduate IS curriculum compared to the undergraduate level. This is evident in this review and corroborated by previous work (Jacobi et al. 2014; Kumar et al., 2017). Thirdly, whilst there have been efforts to quantitatively measure the levels of adherence and adoption of implemented IS curricula to IS model curricula (Bell et al., 2013; Mills et al., 2012), it is

Figure 10. IS Curricula Studies Dimensions

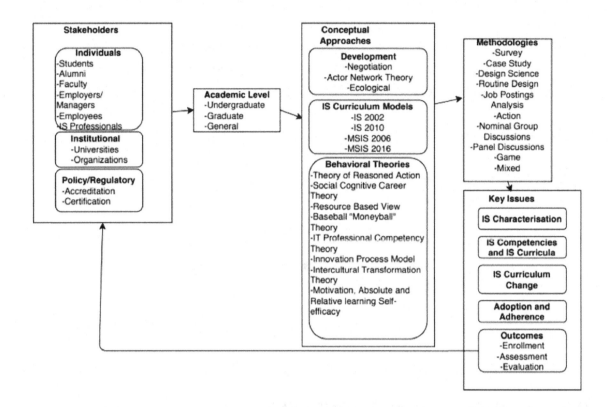

unknown the factors enabling or constraining IS curriculum model adherence. A study of such nature will guide universities to improve on their adoption or adherence and also provide a critical input to a future revision of the IS model curricula. The fourth issue of interest to IS curriculum research is with the level of analysis. There is predominantly micro-level research dealing with various stakeholders (IS professionals, managers, employers, employees, alumni, students, Faculty, Curriculum developers) with little known about meso-level factors such as the university policies, philosophy, culture etc. and how they influence the design and delivery of IS curricula. This could be expanded to macro factors such as the role of regulatory bodies such as Accreditation, government policies and legislation, and national culture on the IS curriculum innovation. The fifth suggestion for future research deals with a proper conceptualization of IS curriculum success that has been loosely used in the literature. There is the need for an understanding of what constitutes IS curriculum success and failure. With such an understanding, it is easier for researchers to share lessons learnt from successful or failed design or delivery of IS curricula.

Theory Gaps in IS Curriculum Research

There is a general lack of theory in IS curriculum studies. There is the need to develop theoretically grounded understanding of the issues in IS curriculum research. First of all, there is the need for increased empirical evidence of the use of Tatnall and Davey (2002) IS curriculum innovation and sociotechnical models to adequately ascertain its explanatory powers. Secondly, whilst the Resource Based View (Barney, 1991) has been used in identifying critical organizational competencies and roles, it would be interesting to combine it with other theories such as the baseball's "moneyball" theory (Surendra & Denton, 2009) that is used to explain how the competencies identified are valued by employers to have an integrated theory that identifies organizational IS competencies that are valuable to all stakeholders. Thirdly, how an IS model curriculum is accepted or adopted have not been theoretically explained (Osatuyi & Garza, 2014), notwithstanding few studies in behavioural intentions to integrate KSAs or courses or enrolment choices of students using the TRA or TPB.

At the same time, these few theories have focused on individual level analysis with little or no attention for theories that focuses on the external or macro factors and mechanisms that influence IS curriculum change in universities. Universities and IS departments are embedded in institutional fields and yet no research has looked at how these institutions influence IS curriculum design and delivery.

Methodological Gaps in IS Curriculum Research

Despite the preponderance of case study research on IS curriculum (Ramesh & Gerth, 2015; Ho & Frampton, 2010; Chatterjee et al., 2013; Gupta et al., 2015; Mitri & Palocsay, 2015), there is little evidence from other regions outside North America. Case studies of IS curriculum activities are therefore valuable in showcasing how the experiences in universities in these other regions compare with reported global case studies and lessons learnt could be shared or used to improve the global IS model curriculum. Furthermore, single case studies have been reported. Further studies could look at multiple case studies that compares the experiences of IS curriculum change in different universities and from different countries.

Again, a rigorous design science research seems to be the logical approach to IS curriculum design since the stages in a design science research almost logically maps to the stages of the design and delivery of an IS Curriculum yet little evidence of its use exists in extant literature. Future research could also consider DSR in the development of IS curricula. Finally, with such heterogonous stakeholders in the design and delivery of IS curriculum, the mixed method of case studies and surveys has the potential to provide deeper understanding of issues identified in this study.

REFERENCES

Aasheim, C. L., Li, L., & Williams, S. (2009). Knowledge and Skill Requirements for Entry-Level Information Technology Workers: A Comparison of Industry and Academia. *Journal of Information Systems Education, 20*(3), 349–357.

Aasheim, C. L., Williams, S., & Butler, E. S. (2009). Knowledge and Skill Requirements for IT Graduates. *Journal of Computer Information Systems, 49*(3), 48–53.

Aasheim, C. L., Williams, S., Rutner, P., & Gardiner, A. (2015). Data analytics vs. data science: A study of similarities and differences in undergraduate programs based on course descriptions. *Journal of Information Systems Education, 26*(2), 103–115.

Agarwal, N., & Ahmed, F. (2017). Developing collective learning extension for rapidly evolving information system courses. *Education and Information Technologies, 22*(1), 7–37. doi:10.100710639-015-9394-4

Akbulut-Bailey, A. (2012). Improving IS Enrolment Choices: The Role of Social Support. *Journal of Information Systems Education, 23*(3), 259–271.

Akman, I., & Turhan, C. (2017). Investigation of employers' performance expectations for new IT graduates in individual and team work settings for software development. *Information Technology & People*, *31*(1), 199–214. doi:10.1108/ITP-01-2017-0020

Alturki, A., Bandara, W., & Gable, G. (2012). Design Science Research and the Core of Information Systems. *Design Science Research in Information Systems. Advances in Theory and Practice*, *7286*, 309–327.

Anderson, D. L. (2017). Improving information technology curriculum learning outcomes. *Informing Science: The International Journal of an Emerging Transdiscipline*, *20*, 119–131. doi:10.28945/3746

Apigian, C. H., & Gambill, S. (2014). A Descriptive Study of Graduate Information Systems Curriculums. *The Review of Business Information Systems (Online)*, *18*(2), 47–52. doi:10.19030/rbis.v18i2.8978

Apigian, C. H., & Gambill, S. E. (2010). Are We Teaching the IS 2009 * Model Curriculum? *Journal of Information Systems*, *21*(4), 411–421.

Ashenhurst, R. L. (1972). Curriculum recommendations for graduate professional programs in information systems. *Communications of the ACM*, *15*(5), 363–398. doi:10.1145/355602.361320

Babb, J., Longenecker, H. E. J., Baugh, J., & Feinstein, D. (2014). Confronting the Issues of Programming In Information Systems Curricula: The Goal is Success. *Information Systems Education Journal*, *12*(1), 42–72.

Bacon, D. R., & Stewart, K. A. (2017). Why Assessment Will Never Work at Many Business Schools: A Call for Better Utilization of Pedagogical Research. *Journal of Management Education*, *41*(2), 181–200. doi:10.1177/1052562916645837

Barney, J. B. (1991). Firm resources and sustained competitive advantage. *Journal of Management*, *17*(1), 99–120. doi:10.1177/014920639101700108

Bell, C., Mills, R., & Fadel, K. (2013). An analysis of undergraduate information systems curricula: Adoption of the IS 2010 curriculum guidelines. *Communications of the Association for Information Systems*, *32*(1), 72–95.

Benamati, J. H., Ozdemir, Z. D., & Smith, H. J. (2010). Aligning undergraduate IS curricula with industry needs. *Communications of the ACM*, *53*(3), 152. doi:10.1145/1666420.1666458

Benbasat, I., Dexter, A. S., & Mantha, R. W. (1980). Impact of Organisational Maturity on Information Systems Skill Needs. *Management Information Systems Quarterly*, *4*(1), 21–34. doi:10.2307/248865

Brooks, S., Gambill, S., Clark, J., & Clark, C. (2016). What's in a Name? An Examination of Information System Degree Programs in AACSB International Accredited Schools. *Journal of Higher Education Theory and Practice*, *16*(6), 66–76.

Bullen, C. V., Abraham, T., Gallagher, K., Simon, J. C., & Zwieg, P. (2009). IT workforce trends: Implications for curriculum and hiring. *Communications of the Association for Information Systems*, *24*(1), 129–140.

Campbell, M., Pardue, J. H., & Campbell, A. A. (2015). Creating a Health Informatics Program : Is It Good For What Ails Us? *Twenty-first Americas Conference on Information Systems*, 1–8.

Carey, J., Galletta, D., Kim, J., Te'eni, D., Wildemuth, B., & Zhang, P. (2004). The Role of Human-Computer Interaction (HCI) in the Management Information Systems Curricula: A Call to Action. *Communications of the AIS, 13*.

Carlsson, S. A., Hedman, J., & Steen, O. (2010). Integrated Curriculum for a Bachelor of Science in Business Information Systems Design (BISD 2010). *Communications of AIS, 2010*(26), 525–546.

Cater-Steel, A., Hine, M. J., & Grant, G. (2010). Embedding IT service management in the academic curriculum: A cross-national comparison. *Journal of Global Information Technology Management, 13*(4), 64–92. doi:10.1080/1097198X.2010.10856526

Cellucci, L. W., Layman, E. J., Campbell, R., & Zeng, X. (2011). Integrating Healthcare Ethical Issues Into IS Education. *Journal of Information Systems Education, 22*(3), 215–224.

Chan, T., Rosemann, M., & Shiang-yen, T. (2014). Identifying Satisfaction Factors in Tertiary Education: The case of an Information Systems Program. *ICIS*, 1–17.

Charland, P., Léger, P., Cronan, T. P., & Robert, J. (2015). Developing and Assessing Erp Competencies : Basic and Complex Knowledge. *Journal of Computer Information Systems, 56*(1), 31–39. doi:10.1080/08874417.2015.11645798

Chatterjee, S., LeRouge, C. M., & Tremblay, M. C. (2013). Educating students in healthcare information technology: IS community barriers, challenges, and paths forward. *Communications of the Association for Information Systems, 33*(1), 1–14.

Chen, F., Sager, J., Corbitt, G., & Gardiner, S. C. (2008). Incorporating Virtual Teamwork Training into MIS Curricula. *Journal of Information Systems Education, 19*(1), 29–41.

Chen, L. (2014). Understanding IT Entrepreneurial Intention: An Information Systems View. *Journal of Computer Information Systems, 55*(1), 2–12. doi:10.1080/08874417.2014.11645736

Chen, L., Liu, Y., Gallagher, M., Pailthorpe, B., Sadiq, S., Shen, H. T., & Li, X. (2012). Introducing Cloud Computing Topics in Curricula. *Journal of Information Systems Education, 23*(3), 315–324.

Chen, L., Pratt, J. A., & Cole, C. B. (2016). Factors influencing students' major and career selection in systems development: An empirical study. *Journal of Computer Information Systems, 56*(4), 313–320. doi:10.1080/08874417.2016.1164005

Clark, J., Clark, C., Gambill, S., & Brooks, S. (2017). IS curriculum models, Course offerings, and Other Academic Myths/Hopes. *Journal of Higher Education Theory and Practice, 17*(9), 61–68.

Couger, J., Davis, G., Dologite, D., Feinstein, D., Gorgone, J., Jenkins, A., & Valacich, I. (1995). Guideline for undergraduate IS curriculum. *Management Information Systems Quarterly, 22*(3), 341–359. doi:10.2307/249599

Davis, G. A., & Woratschek, C. R. (2015). Evaluating Business Intelligence / Business Analytics Software for Use in the Information Systems Curriculum. *Information Systems Education Journal, 13*(1), 23–29.

Dunaway, M. M. (2017). Collaboration in a Data Analytics Curricula: An Active Learning Approach. *Proceedings of Americas Conference on Information Systems (AMCIS)*, 1–8.

Eom, M., Gudigantala, N., & Mitchell, G. (2015). Achieving success with a new design of hybrid information systems major: The case of University of ABC's Operations and Technology Management (OTM) program. *2015 Americas Conference on Information Systems, AMCIS 2015*, 1–12.

Fichman, R. G., Dos Santos, B. L., & Zheng, Z. (2014). Digital Innovation as a Fundamental and Powerful Concept in the IS Curriculum. *Management Information Systems Quarterly*, *38*(2), 329–353. doi:10.25300/MISQ/2014/38.2.01

Firth, D., King, J., Koch, H., Looney, C. A., Pavlou, P., & Trauth, E. M. (2011). Addressing the Credibility Crisis in IS. *Communications of the AIS*, *28*, 199–212.

Gardiner, A., Aasheim, C., Rutner, P., & Williams, S. (2017). Skill Requirements in Big Data: A Content Analysis of Job Advertisements. *Journal of Computer Information Systems*, *0*(0), 1–11.

Gardiner, L. (1994). *Redesigning Higher Education: Producing Dramatic Gains in Student Learning*. Washington, DC: George Washington University.

Gill, T. G., & Hu, Q. (1999). The evolving undergraduate information systems education: A survey of U.S. institutions. *Journal of Computer Information Systems*, *74*(5), 289–295.

Gill, T. G., & Ritzhaupt, A. D. (2013). Systematically Evaluating the Effectiveness of an Information Systems Capstone Course: Implications for Practice. *Journal of Information Technology Education: Research*, *12*, 69–94. doi:10.28945/1776

Goncalves, M. J. A., Rocha, Á., & Cota, M. P. (2016). Information management model for competencies and learning outcomes in an educational context. *Information Systems Frontiers*, *18*(6), 1051–1061. doi:10.100710796-016-9623-4

Gorgone, J. T. (2000). *Approaching MSIS 2000: A New-Fashioned Graduate Model*. Academic Press.

Gorgone, J. T., Davis, G. B., Valacich, J. S., Topi, H., Feinstein, D. L., & Longenecker, H. E. (2002). IS 2002 Model Curriculum and Guidelines for Undergraduate Degree Programs in Information Systems. *The Data Base for Advances in Information Systems*, *34*(1), 1–53.

Gorgone, J. T., Gray, P., Stohr, E. A., Valacich, J. S., & Wigand, R. T. (2006). MSIS 2006 : Model Curriculum and Guidelines for Graduate Degree Programs in Information Systems. *Communications of the Association for Information Systems*, *38*(2), 121–196.

Gupta, B., Goul, M., & Dinter, B. (2015). Business intelligence and big data in higher education: Status of a multi-year model curriculum development effort for business school undergraduates, MS graduates, and MBAs. *Communications of the Association for Information Systems*, *36*, 449–476. doi:10.17705/1CAIS.03623

Harris, A., & Lang, M. (2011). Incorporating Ethics and Social Responsibility in IS Education. *Journal of Information Systems Education*, *22*(3), 183–190.

Harris, A. H., Greer, T. H., Morris, S. A., Clark, W. J., & Greer, T. H. (2012). Information Systems Job Market Late 1970's-Early 2010's. *Journal of Computer Information Systems, 53*(1), 72–79.

Harris, M. A., & Patten, K. P. (2015). Using Bloom's and Webb's Taxonomies to Integrate Emerging Cybersecurity Topics into a Computing Curriculum. *Journal of Information Systems Education, 26*(3), 219–234.

Havelka, D., & Merhout, J. (2009). Toward a theory of information technology professional competence. *Journal of Computer Information Systems, 50*(2), 106–116.

Helfert, M. (2011). Characteristics of Information Systems and Business Informatics Study Programs. *Informatics in Education, 10*(1), 13–36.

Henson, K., & Kamal, M. (2010). Closing the Gap - Information Systems Curriculum And Changing Global Market. *American Journal of Business Education, 3*(5), 17–20. doi:10.19030/ajbe.v3i5.423

Hepner, M., & Dickson, W. (2013). The value of ERP curriculum integration: Perspectives from the research. *Journal of Information Systems Education, 24*(4), 309–326.

Ho, S. Y., & Frampton, K. (2010). A competency model for the information technology workforce: Implications for training and selection. *Communications of the Association for Information Systems, 27*(1), 63–80.

Hwang, D., Pike, R., & Manson, D. (2016). The Development of an Educational Cloud for IS Curriculum through a Student-Run Data Center. *Information Systems Education Journal, 14*(1), 62–70.

Hwang, D., & Soe, L. L. (2010). An Analysis of Career Tracks in the Design of IS Curricula in the US. *IS. Education Journal, 8*(13).

Jacobi, F., Jahn, S., Krawatzeck, R., Dinter, B., & Lorenz, A. (2014). Towards a Design Model for Interdisciplinary Information Systems Curriculum Development, as Exemplified by Big Data Analytics Education. *Proceedings of the European Conference on Information Systems (ECIS) 2014.*

Jacobson, C. M., Kasper, G. M., Mathieu, R. G., McFarland, D. J., & Meservy, R. D. (2011). AMCIS 2010 panel report: External benchmarks in information systems program assessment. *Communications of the Association for Information Systems, 29*(1), 367–378.

Jafar, M. J., Babb, J., & Abdullat, A. (2017). Emergence of Data Analytics in the Information Systems Curriculum Musa. *IS Education Journal, 15*(5).

Janicki, T. N., Cummings, J., & Healy, R. J. (2015). Incorporating a Human-Computer Interaction Course into Software Development Curriculums. *Information Systems Education Journal, 13*(3), 81–98.

Jarvenpaa, S. L., Ives, B., & Davis, G. B. (1991). Supply/Demand of IS Doctorates in the 1990s. *Communications of the ACM, 34*(1), 86–98. doi:10.1145/99977.99996

Jones, C. G., & Liu, D. (2017). Approaches to Incorporating IT Entrepreneurship into the Information Systems Curriculum. *Journal of Information Systems Education, 28*(November), 43–59.

Jones, K., & Ceccucci, W. (2018). International Service Learning in IS Programs: The Next Phase – An Implementation Experience. *IS Education Journal, 16*(4).

Jones, K., Leonard, L. N. K., & Lang, G. (2016). Desired Skills for Entry Level IS Positions: Identification and Assessment. *Journal of Computer Information Systems*, *0*(0), 1–7.

Kaiser, K. M., Goles, T., Hawk, S., Simon, J. C., & Frampton, K. (2011). Information Systems Skills Differences Between High-Wage and Low-Wage Regions : Implications for Global Sourcing. *Communications of the Association for Information Systems*, *29*(32), 605–626.

Karsten, R., & Roth, R. M. (2015). A Complementary Measure of MIS Program Outcomes: Useful Insights from a Student Perspective. *Journal of Information Systems Education*, *26*(2), 155–164.

Kesner, R. M. (2008). Business School Undergraduate Information Management Competencies: A Study of Employer Expectations and Associated Curricular Recommendations. *Communications of the Association for Information Systems*, *23*, 633–654. doi:10.17705/1CAIS.02335

Kizior, R. J., & Hidding, G. J. (2010). Emphasizing Business Analysis to Increase IS Enrollments. *IS Education Journal*, *8*(47), 3–8.

Kruck, S. E., Mathieu, R. G., & Mitri, M. (2013). Research in Information Systems Education: Scope and Productivity. *Journal of Computer Information Systems*, *54*(1), 34–41. doi:10.1080/08874417.2013.11645669

Kumar, A., Shah, V., & Smart, K. (2017). Moving Forward by Looking Backward : Using Backward Design to Develop an Innovative MSIS Program. In Twenty-third AMCIS (pp. 1–10). Academic Press.

Landry, J. P., Daigle, R. J., Pardue, J. H., Colton, D., & Hunsinger, S. (2010). IS 2002 and ABET Accreditation : Meeting the ABET Program Outcome Criteria Associate Editor. *Information Systems Education Journal*, *8*(67), 1–15.

Lang, G., & Babb, J. (2015). Addressing the 21st Century Paradox: Integrating Entrepreneurship in the Computer Information Systems Curriculum. *Information Systems Education Journal*, *13*(4), 81–91.

Larsson, U., & Boateng, R. (2010). Towards A Curriculum Adaptation Model for IS Undergraduate Education in Sub-Saharan Africa. In *Selected papers of the 32nd IRIS Seminar*. Tapir Academic Press.

Lawler, J., Joseph, A., & Howell-Barber, H. (2016). A Big Data Analytics Methodology Program in the Health Sector. *Information Systems Education Journal*, *14*(3), 63–75.

Lawler, J. P. (2011). Cloud Computing in the Curricula of Schools of Computer Science and Information Systems. *IS Education Journal*, *9*(2), 34–54.

Lee, C., & Han, H. (2008). Analysis of skills requirement for entry-level programmer/analysts in Fortune 500 corporations. *Journal of Information Systems Education*, *19*(1), 17–27.

Lee, D. M. S., Trauth, E. M., & Farwell, D. (1995). Critical Skills and Knowledge Requirements of IS Professionals: A Joint Academic/Industry Investigation. *Management Information Systems Quarterly*, *19*(3), 313–340. doi:10.2307/249598

Lee, K., & Mirchandani, D. (2010). Dynamics of the Importance of Is / It Skills. *Journal of Computer Information Systems*, *50*(4), 67–78.

Lee, S., Koh, S., Yen, D., & Tang, H. L. (2002). Perception gaps between IS academics and IS practitioners: An exploratory study. *Information & Management, 40*(1), 51–61. doi:10.1016/S0378-7206(01)00132-X

Levy, Y., & Ellis, T. J. (2006). A systems approach to conduct an effective literature review in support of information systems research. *Informing Science, 9,* 181–211. doi:10.28945/479

Lifer, J. D., Parsons, K., & Miller, R. E. (2009). A Comparison of Information Systems Programs at AACSB and ACBSP Schools in Relation to IS 2002 Model Curricula. *Journal of Information Systems Education, 20*(4), 469–476.

Longenecker, H. E. J., Feinstein, D., & Clark, J. D. (2013). Information Systems Curricula: A Fifty Year Journey. *Information Systems Education Journal, 11*(6), 71–95.

Mamonov, S., & Misra, R. (2015). Business Analytics in Practice and in Education: A Competency-based Perspective. *Information Systems Education Journal, 13*(1), 4–13.

Martz, B., Hughes, J., & Braun, F. (2017). Creativity and problem-solving: Closing the skills gap. *Journal of Computer Information Systems, 57*(1), 39–48. doi:10.1080/08874417.2016.1181492

May, J., & Lending, D. (2015). A conceptual model for communicating an integrated information systems curriculum. *Journal of Computer Information Systems, 55*(4), 20–27. doi:10.1080/08874417.2015.11645783

McCoy, S., Everard, A., & Jones, B. M. (2015). Foundations of information systems course content: A comparison of assigned value by faculty, recruiters, and students. *Communications of the Association for Information Systems, 36,* 697–705. doi:10.17705/1CAIS.03635

Merhout, J., Benamati, J., Rajkumar, T., Anderson, P., & Marado, D. (2008). Implementing direct and indirect assessment in the MIS curriculum. *Communications of the Association for Information Systems, 23*(24), 419–436.

Merhout, J., Havelka, D., & Rajkumar, T. M. (2016). Determining Factors that Lead Students to Study Information Systems using an Alumni Focus Group. *Twenty-Second Americas Conference on Information Systems,* 1–8.

Mills, R. J., Beaulieu, T. Y., & Johnson, J. J. (2017). Examining Micro-Level (SQL) Curriculum-Oriented and Promotional IS Enrollment Strategies. *Journal of Computer Information Systems, 57*(4), 299–308. doi:10.1080/08874417.2016.1180650

Mills, R. J., Chudoba, K. M., & Olsen, D. H. (2016). IS Programs Responding to Industry Demands for Data Scientists: A Comparison between 2011 - 2016. *Journal of Information Systems Education, 27*(2), 131–140.

Mills, R. J., Velasquez, N. F., Fadel, K. J., & Bell, C. C. (2012). Examining IS Curriculum Profiles and the IS 2010 Model Curriculum Guidelines in AACSB-Accredited Schools. *Journal of Information Systems Education, 23*(4), 417–428.

Mitchell, A., & Benyon, R. (2018). Adding intercultural communication to an IS curriculum. *Journal of Information Systems Education, 29*(1), 1–10.

Mitri, M., & Palocsay, S. (2015). The Emerging Business Intelligence and Analytics Discipline. Communications of the AIS, 37.

Moher, D., Liberati, A., Tetzlaff, J., & Altman, D. G. (2009). Preferred Reporting Items for Systematic Reviews and Meta-Analysis. The PRISMA statement. *Annals of Internal Medicine, 151*(4), 264–269. doi:10.7326/0003-4819-151-4-200908180-00135 PMID:19622511

Moher, D., Shamseer, L., Clarke, M., Ghersi, D., Liberati, A., Petticrew, M., ... Stewart, L. A. (2015). Preferred reporting items for systematic review and meta-analysis protocols (PRISMA-P) 2015 statement. *Systematic Reviews, 4*(1), 1–9. doi:10.1186/2046-4053-4-1 PMID:25554246

Molluzo, J. C., & Lawler, J. P. (2015). A Proposed Concentration Curriculum Design for Big Data Analytics for Information Systems Students. *Information Systems Education Journal, 13*(1), 45–57.

Murawski, M., & Bick, M. (2017). Demanded and Imparted Big Data Competences: Towards an Integrative Analysis. *Proceedings of the 25th European Conference on Information Systems (ECIS)*, 1375–1390.

Nelson, R. (1991). Educational needs as perceived by IS and End-User Personnel: A survey of knowledge and skill requirements. *Management Information Systems Quarterly, 15*(December), 503–525. doi:10.2307/249454

Nunamaker, J. F., Couger, J. D., & Davis, G. B. (1982). Information systems curriculum recommendations for the 80s: Undergraduate and graduate programs. *Communications of the ACM, 25*(11), 781–805. doi:10.1145/358690.358698

Offermann, P., Blom, S., Schönherr, M., & Bub, U. (2010). Artifact Types in Information Systems Design Science – A Literature Review. *Management Information Systems Quarterly, 6105*, 77–92.

Osatuyi, B., & Garza, M. (2014). IS 2010 curriculum model adoption in the United States. In *20th Americas Conference on Information Systems* (pp. 1–11). Academic Press.

Patten, K., & Harris, M. (2013). The Need to Address Mobile Device Security in the Higher Education IT Curriculum. *Journal of Information Systems Education, 24*(1), 41–53.

Pauli, W. E., Halverson, T., & Mckeown, J. (2011). The 2010 CIS Baccalaureate Degree Compared with IS 2010 Guidelines. *Journal of Higher Education Theory and Practice, 11*(2), 102–111.

Peppard, J., & Ward, J. (2004). Beyond strategic information systems: Towards an IS capability. *The Journal of Strategic Information Systems, 13*(2), 167–194. doi:10.1016/j.jsis.2004.02.002

Picatoste, J., Pérez-Ortiz, L., & Ruesga-Benito, S. M. (2018). A new educational pattern in response to new technologies and sustainable development. Enlightening ICT skills for youth employability in the European Union. *Telematics and Informatics, 35*(4), 1031–1038. doi:10.1016/j.tele.2017.09.014

Poston, R. S., & Dhaliwal, J. (2015). IS human capital: Assessing gaps to strengthen skill and competency sourcing. *Communications of the Association for Information Systems, 36*(34), 669–695.

Ramesh, V., & Gerth, A. B. (2015). Design of an integrated information systems master's core curriculum: A case study. *Communications of the Association for Information Systems, 36*, 301–316. doi:10.17705/1CAIS.03616

Reynolds, J. H., Adams, D. R., Ferguson, R. C., & Leidig, P. M. (2017). Programming in the IS Curriculum: Are Requirements Changing for the Right Reason? *Information Systems Education Journal*, *15*(1), 80–85.

Reynolds, J. H., Ferguson, R. C., & Leidig, P. M. (2016). A Tale of Two Curricula: The Case for Prerequisites in the IS Model Curriculum. *Information Systems Education Journal*, *14*(5), 17–24.

Saulnier, B., & White, B. (2011). IS 2010 and ABET Accreditation: An Analysis of ABET-Accredited Information Systems Programs. *Journal of Information Systems Education*, *22*(4), 347–354.

Sauls, J., & Gudigantala, N. (2013). Preparing Information Systems (IS) Graduates to Meet the Challenges of Global IT Security: Some Suggestions. *Journal of Information Systems Education*, *24*(1), 71–73.

Schiller, S., Goul, M., Iyer, L. S., Sharda, R., Schrader, D., & Asamoah, D. (2015). Build your dream (Not just big) analytics program. *Communications of the Association for Information Systems*, *37*(1), 811–826.

Scholtz, B., Cilliers, C., & Calitz, A. A. (2012). A Comprehensive, Competency-Based Education Framework Using Medium-Sized ERP Systems. *Journal of Information Systems Education*, *23*(4), 345.

Schwieger, D., & Ladwig, C. (2016). Protecting Privacy in Big Data: A Layered Approach for Curriculum Integration. *Information Systems Education Journal*, *14*(3), 45–54.

Sendall, P., & Shannon, L.-J. (2011). The Greening of the Information Systems Curriculum. *Information Systems Education Journal*, *9*(5), 27–45.

Sidorova, A. (2013). Business analysis as an opportunity for IS programs in business schools. *Communications of the Association for Information Systems*, *33*(1), 521–540.

Sircar, S. (2009). Business Intelligence in the Business Curriculum. *Communications of the Association for Information Systems*, *24*(24), 289–302.

Sivakumar, C., & Kwok, R. C. W. (2017). Course design based on enhanced intercultural transformation theory (EITT): Transforming information systems (IS) students into inventors during academic exchange. *Communications of the Association for Information Systems*, *40*(1), 402–419. doi:10.17705/1CAIS.04019

Stefanidis, A., & Fitzgerald, G. (2010). Mapping the Information Systems Curricula in UK Universities. *Journal of Information Systems*, *21*(4), 391–410.

Stefanidis, A., Fitzgerald, G., & Counsell, S. (2013). IS curriculum career tracks: A UK study. *Education + Training*, *55*(3), 220–233. doi:10.1108/00400911311309297

Stevens, D., Totaro, M., & Zhu, Z. (2011). Assessing It Critical Skills and Revising the MIS Curriculum. *Journal of Computer Information Systems*, *51*(3), 85–95.

Surendra, N. C., & Denton, J. W. (2009). Designing IS Curricula for Practical Relevance: Applying Baseball's "Moneyball" Theory. *Journal of Information Systems Education*, *20*(1), 77–85.

Swinarski, M. E. (2008, September). Focusing on IS Skills for the Middle and Senior Level Manager: A New Approach to the MBA Core IS Course. *Communications of the Association for Information Systems*, *23*, 163–178. doi:10.17705/1CAIS.02309

Tatnall, A., & Davey, B. (2002). Improving the chances of getting your IT curriculum innovation successfully adopted by the application of an ecological approach to innovation. *Informing Science*, 7, 87–103. doi:10.28945/504

Tatnall, A. D. (2010). Using actor-network theory to understand the process of information systems curriculum innovation. *Education and Information Technologies*, *15*(4), 239–254. doi:10.100710639-010-9137-5

Tedre, M., Bangu, N., & Nyagava, S. I. (2009). Contextualized IT Education in Tanzania: Beyond Standard IT Curricula. *Journal of Information Technology Education*, *8*, 101–124. doi:10.28945/162

Tesch, D., Jiang, J. J., & Klein, G. (2003). The impact of information system personnel skill discrepancies on stakeholder satisfaction. *Decision Sciences*, *34*(1), 107–129. doi:10.1111/1540-5915.02371

Thouin, M. F., Hefley, W. E., & Raghunathan, S. (2018). Student attitudes toward information systems graduate program design and delivery. *Journal of Information Systems Education*, *29*(1), 25–37.

Topi, H. (2016). IS Education: Using competency-based approach as foundation for information systems curricula. *ACM Inroads*, *7*(3), 27–28. doi:10.1145/2955099

Topi, H. (2019). Reflections on the Current State and Future of Information Systems Education. *Journal of Information Systems Education*, *30*(1), 1–9.

Topi, H., Helfert, M., Ramesh, V., Wigand, R. T., & Wright, R. T. (2011). Future of Master's Level Education in Information Systems. *Communications of AIS, 2011*(28), 437–452.

Topi, H., Karsten, H., Brown, S. A., Carvalho, J. A., Donnellan, B., Shen, J., Tan, B. C., & Thouin, M. F. (2017). *MSIS 2016 Global Competency Model for Graduate Degree Programs in Information Systems*. The Joint ACM/AIS MSIS Task Force.

Topi, H., Valacich, J. S., Wright, R. T., Kaiser, K. M., Nunamaker, J. F. Jr, Sipior, J. C., & de Vreede, G.-J. (2010). IS2010: Curriculum Guidelines for Undergraduate Degree Programs in Information Systems. *Communications of the Association for Information Systems*, *26*(1), 359–428.

Topi, H., Wright, R. T., & Kaiser, K. (2008). Revising Undergraduate IS Model Curriculum: New Outcome Expectations Revising Undergraduate IS Model Curriculum : New Outcome Expectations. *Communications of the Association for Information Systems*, *23*(December), 591–602.

Urbaczewski, A., Venkataraman, R., & Kontogiorgis, P. (2011). Panel discussion proposal: IT services management in the curriculum: Challenges, realizations, and lessons learned. *16th Americas Conference on Information Systems 2010, AMCIS 2010*, *28*(5), 1012–1015.

van Laar, E., van Deursen, A. J. A. M., van Dijk, J. A. G. M., & de Haan, J. (2017). The relation between 21st-century skills and digital skills: A systematic literature review. *Computers in Human Behavior*, *72*, 577–588. doi:10.1016/j.chb.2017.03.010

Veltri, N. F., Webb, H. W., Matveev, A. G., & Zapatero, E. G. (2011). Curriculum Mapping as a Tool for Continuous Improvement of IS Curriculum. *Journal of Information Systems Education*, *22*(1), 31–42.

von Konsky, B. R., Miller, C., & Jones, A. (2016). The Skills Framework for the Information Age: Engaging Stakeholders in Curriculum Design. *Journal of Information Systems Education, 27*(1), 37–50.

Wang, M. (2011). Integrating SAP to Information Systems Curriculum: Design and Delivery. *Information Systems Education Journal, 9*(5), 97–104.

Wang, Y.-Y., Lin, T.-C., & Tsay, C. H.-H. (2016). Encouraging IS developers to learn business skills: An examination of the MARS model. *Information Technology & People, 29*(2), 381–418. doi:10.1108/ITP-02-2014-0044

Webster, J., & Watson, R. T. (2002). Analysing The Past To Prepare For The Future: Writing A Literature Review. *Management Information Systems Quarterly, 26*(2), 13–23.

Westfall, R. D. (2012). An Employment-Oriented Definition of the Information Systems Field: An Educator's View. *Journal of Information Systems Education, 23*(1), 63–70.

White, G. L., Hewitt, B., & Kruck, S. E. (2013). Incorporating Global Information Security and Assurance in I.S. Education. *Journal of Information Systems Education, 24*(1), 11–17.

Wilson, E. V., & Tulu, B. (2010). The rise of a health-IT academic focus. *Communications of the ACM, 53*(5), 147. doi:10.1145/1735223.1735259

Woodward, B., Imboden, T., & Martin, N. L. (2013). An Undergraduate Information Security Program: More than a Curriculum. *Journal of Information Systems Education, 24*(1), 63–70.

Wymbs, C. (2016). Managing the Innovation Process: Infusing Data Analytics into the Undergraduate Business Curriculum (Lessons Learned and Next Steps). *Journal of Information Systems Education, 27*(1), 61–74.

Yang, S. C. (2012). The Master's Program in Information Systems (IS): A Survey of Core Curriculums of U.S. Institutions. *Journal of Education for Business, 87*(4), 206–213. doi:10.1080/08832323.2011.591847

Zhang, C., Reichgelt, H., Rutherfoord, R. H., & Wang, A. J. A. (2014). Developing Health Information Technology (HIT) Programs and HIT Curriculum: The Southern Polytechnic State University Experience. *Journal of Information Systems Education, 25*(4), 295–303.

Zheng, G., Zhang, C., & Li, L. (2014). Bringing Business Intelligence to Health Information Technology Curriculum. *Journal of Information Systems Education, 25*(4), 317–326.

Chapter 22

Resources and Value Co-Creation in Social Commerce:
Evidence From Business Models in a Developing Economy – A Viewpoint for Future Research

Edward Entee
Univeristy of Ghana, Ghana

ABSTRACT

Social media (SM) is fundamentally changing the way firms conduct business and, in the process, destroying existing business models (BM). Therefore, businesses need to have a BM adaptable to social commerce (SC), which is commerce utilizing social networking services. This viewpoint for future research has questions on the types of SC BM, the value co-created by these models, and the required resources. The study proposes a framework to explore potential BM associated with social media based on their requirements and evaluate the performance of these BM. On the tenets of the study, this viewpoint argues for the need to develop BM for SC and how value is co-created and the resources underpinning this co-creation.

INTRODUCTION

Recent developments in information and communication technology (ICT) has triggered new business models (Bharadwaj, El Sawy, Pavlou, & Venkatraman, 2013; Wang & Yu, 2017a) such as social commerce (SC). Similarly, the advancement of information and communication technology (ICT) is transforming the structure of social relationships in the space between the customers and firms through social technologies such as social media and social networking sites (Susarla, Oh, & Tan, 2012). Hence, these social technologies are fundamentally reshaping traditional business strategies that enable commerce to be done across boundaries of time, distance and functions (Banker, Bardhan, Chang, & Lin, 2006; Ettlie & Pavlou, 2006; Kohli & Grover, 2008; Rai, Pavlou, Im, & Du, 2012; Straub & Watson, 2001)

DOI: 10.4018/978-1-7998-2610-1.ch022

a significant forte of social commerce. Thus, social commerce is the use of social media to engage in commercial activities.

Social commerce enjoys a plurality of definitions. For instance, Wang and Zhang (2012) define social commerce as "a form of commerce that is mediated by social media and is converging both online and offline environments". While Yadav and Mahara (2018) refers to social commerce as "exchange-related activities that occur in, or are influenced by, an individual's social network in computer-mediated social environments, where the activities correspond to need recognition, pre-purchase, purchase, and post-purchase stages of a focal exchange". Similarly, in an earlier definition, Liang and Turban (2011) referred to social commerce as " online commerce applications that exploit social media and web 2.0 technologies. Lai (2010), on the other hand, defined social commerce as a phenomenon that combines three concepts (Social media, Web 2.0 Technologies and e-commerce). The various definitions highlight the presence of two essential components: social media and commerce. As noted by Liang, Ho, Li and Turban (2011) and Marsden (2009), the commerce component refers to exchange-related activities that include transactions. These transactions include pre, during and post transactional activities. The second component as espoused by Yadav, Valck, Hennig-thurau, Hoffman and Spann (2013) is the computer-mediated social environment (CMSEs).

Yahoo was the first to introduce the term social commerce in 2005 (Rubel, 2006), rapidly becoming a medium of value addition by mainstay e-commerce companies such as Amazon and eBay through customer engagement (Wang & Zhang, 2012). The first academic paper to use the term *social commerce* appeared in 2006 when *flowers.com* launched its first Facebook store in 2009 saw regular use of the term in practice (Busalim & Hussin, 2016) — since then, shopping on social media networks had increased exponentially. For example, social commerce adoption among retailers in North America moved from 17 percent in 2017 to 33 percent in 2018 (Clement, 2019). This growth trend provides a promising potential for companies to invest in social media to increase consumer engagement (Wang &Yu, 2017b).

Thus, global e-commerce pioneers like Amazon and eBay are now changing their market positions with the integration of social technologies like Facebook (Du & Wagner, 2007; Fagerstrøm & Ghinea, 2010; Kim & Srivastava, 2007; Ng, 2013).

SNSs are the bedrock of social commerce because they enhance the peculiarity of the relationship between sellers and their customers (Liang & Turban, 2011). Hence, scholars have argued that online shops using social media can result in value creation and co-creation for both customers and firms (Grange & Benbasat, 2013; Kohler, Fueller, Matzler, & Stieger, 2011; Kohler, Fueller, Stieger, & Matzler, 2011). Hence, social commerce has the potential for value co-creation (Hassan & Toland, 2013). As implied by the term, "co-creation involves a symbiotic relationship between a firm and its primary stakeholders" (Kohli & Grover, 2008), and suggest that value is co-created by integrating the available resources owned by collaborators (Vargo, Maglio, & Akaka, 2008). Hence, the objective of exchange in social commerce is to connect resources and value, in this case, the value created relies on the collaborators' particular contexts (Cai, Yuan, & Zhou, 2013).

There is an exponential growth of social commerce sites (Huang & Benyoucef, 2015) and as more of these sites are springing up potentially with different services and leaning towards various models, there is a tendency for traditional firms to enter the space to earn the benefits therein. Such a venture has the potential to change their existing business processes, hence the need to align to specific organizational goals and strategy carefully.

From those mentioned earlier, social commerce is essential. More importantly, it is creating a situation for firms to think about carefully. With this background as the backbone of this study, it has become necessary to understand the types of social commerce business models, and how value is co-created, and the resources which underpin this value co-creation process.

JUSTIFICATION FOR THIS RESEARCH

Previous research on social commerce has examined themes including social commerce definitions and conceptual models (Busalim & Hussin, 2016; Menon, Sigurdsson, Larsen, Fagerstrøm, & Foxall, 2016; Zhang & Benyoucef, 2016), adoption (Erdoğmuş & Tatar, 2015; Farivar, Yuan, & Turel, 2016; Yahia, Al-Neama, & Kerbache, 2018), risk (Farivar, Turel, & Yuan, 2017), trust and trust performance (Cheng, Gu, & Shen, 2019), biases (Samira Farivar, Yuan, & Turel, 2016) and factors that influence customer engagement (Busalim, Hussin, & Iahad, 2019; Wongkitrungrueng & Assarut, 2018).

These studies though valuable, also highlight several gaps for future research. First, there is an absence of agreement on the definition of social commerce. For example, Menon et al. (2016) and Yahia et al. (2018) defined social commerce as a combination of e-commerce and social interaction while Wang and Zhang (2012) defined social commerce as new or emerging phenomena, which is a subset of e-commerce which converges both online and offline environments. In contrast, social commerce has been defined as selling using social media sites such as Facebook (Ngai, Tao, & Moon, 2015). This plurality of social commerce definitions gives rise to different conceptualizations of the social commerce phenomena.

Comparably, studies on social e-commerce or use of social media in e-commerce tend to be more dominant (Hajli, Sims, Zadeh, & Richard, 2017; Huang & Benyoucef, 2013; Liang & Turban, 2011; Munawar, Hassanein, & Head, 2017) and there is a call for more research on social commerce, especially on the business models and how such firms operate. The dominance exists because e-commerce/e-business (and social e-commerce) predates social commerce (Hajli, 2015; Hajli & Sims, 2015; Kim & Park, 2013). In precis, authors need to focus more on social commerce, explore the business models which underpin social commerce activities – especially examining whether e-commerce models can also apply to social commerce or whether there are new business models which underpin these firms. However, even though studies indicate that firms are leveraging emerging social commerce platforms to build relationships and engage with customers, little empirical studies exist on the value generated by these firms or the business models of social commerce firms generate value. This research attempts to address these gaps.

Concerning social commerce business models and value generation, a review published by Communications of the Association for Information Systems (CAIS) (Parameswaran & Whinston, 2007) offers some directions. The review highlighted the need to explore current and potential business models associated with social networks concerning their requirements, identify feasible models and evaluate the performance of the business models. The review further, reiterates that research into these business models need to touch on themes such as how businesses can generate value through social networks. It is instructive to note that since the publication of the review in 2007, there seem to be no studies addressing the gaps highlighted in the study. A more recent review by (Wang & Zhang, 2012) calls for future research on social commerce to identify and develop business models. Also, the authors (Wang & Zhang, 2012) emphasize the need to explore how firms manage co-creating strategies as a result of an enormous amount of content from diverse channels and platforms. On the contrary, issues such as adoption (Friedrich, 2015; Hajli & Sims, 2015), designing social commerce platforms (Mikalef, Giannakos, & Pappas, 2017), sharing behaviour (Hsieh, Ya-Ting, & Leng-Heng, 2017), conflict and uncertainty (J. Cheng, Liu, & Du, 2017) consumer purchasing decision (Huang & Benyoucef, 2017), consumer purchase behaviour (Grange, Benbasat, & Burton-Jones, 2018), Value co-creation (Mikalef, Pappas, & Giannakos, 2017; Tajvidi, Wang, Hajli, & Love, 2017; Yu, Tsai, Wang, Lai, & Tajvidi, 2018) and Users' risk (Samira Farivar, Turel, & Yuan, 2018; Sharma & Crossler, 2014) have been studied.

Concerning theorization, another review of social commerce by Busalim and Hussin (2016) published by the International Journal of Information Management opines that the theoretical foundation of social commerce research is few and dispersed. The author of this research also, reiterate the arguments by Hajli (2014) and Wang and Zhang (2012) years earlier that development of grounded theories in this new area will be a challenge for both Information systems and strategic management researchers. A second review by Zhang and Benyoucef (2016) shows that several theories have been used to explain consumer behaviour on social networking sites. These theories used in the various studies were to test and develop explanatory models. There is the need, therefore, to consider theories that generate exploratory insights. The above assertions seem to agree with Boateng (2016), who used a strategic model to explain the complex interaction of resources as a firm seeks to integrate e-commerce capabilities with their strategic orientation.

This viewpoint further recommends the use of strategic theories to study firms in other industries and with the development of transactive and transformational capabilities. This study responds to these by adopting the Resource-Based View to explore how businesses can use resources to co-create value through social commerce.

Studies on social commerce have predominantly been from the developed, the Middle East and Asian economies perspectives (Leeraphong & Papasratorn, 2018; Qin, 2017; Vongsraluang & Bhatiasevi, 2017; Williams, 2018). Researchers in these contexts have studied issues such as articulating the drivers of social commerce (Sukrat, Mahatanankoon, & Papasratorn, 2018), factors that motivate users beyond their initial adoption to engage in post-adoption behaviors such as continuance use (Osatuyi & Qin, 2018) and social commerce acceptance among users and the factors affecting attitudes towards the phenomena (Gatautis & Medziausiene, 2014) in countries like China, Thailand, USA and Lithuania. There is also some research on social media in African countries (Jaunky, Roopchund, Ramesh, & Jaunky, 2018; Lekhanya, 2013). Despite these studies, research specifically focusing on social commerce in Africa are few (e.g. Lubua & Pretorius, 2018, 2019). These studies even though few have contributed to the use of social networks as income generation and the perceived relevance of social commerce in the African Context. However, these studies focus more on adoption and impact with little focus on strategy. Future research can draw on strategic issues to help understand further implications if we do not know successful social commerce, business models. Past e-commerce studies show evidence that firms in developing countries are always looking for technologies to become better and navigate around their constraints (Boateng, 2016). Therefore, it becomes essential that success stories of social commerce business models in Africa be studied, documented and analyzed to guide other firms.

OBJECTIVES TO BE ADDRESSED

Concerning the above research gaps, this chapter contends that future research should seek to develop a model that explains how firms create social commerce capabilities to achieve benefits. The model will offer a theoretical understanding of how social commerce firms develop, deploy and manage social media as a resource to create commercial benefits. This future research will be inspired by the theory of how firms develop, deploy and manage social media as a resource to create commercial benefits. This future research must also seek to understand how social commerce firms use social media technologies to overcome their constraints. This research will not merely incorporate relevant entrepreneurship and strategic management theories in order to enrich and extend IS research; it will also contribute to Dynamic Capabilities Model by conceptualizing the development, deployment and management of social media resources to achieve benefit in the context of a social commerce firm. This future research must particularly achieve the following objectives

1. To explore the dominant business models of social commerce Firms Developing Economies.
2. To understand the value co-created by social commerce-based firms
3. To explore the resources and capabilities that underpin the value generated by social commerce business models and how the resources are deployed.

The subsequent research questions are

1. What are the dominant business models of social commerce enterprises in Developing Countries?
2. How is value co-created by social commerce-based firms?
3. What resources and capabilities underpin the value generated by the business models and how they are deployed?

THEORETICAL JUSTIFICATION

The prevailing paradigm for how firms create value using available resources is the Resource-based View. For instance, Barua, Konana, Whinston and Yin (2004) use the RBV to address the processes through which value is created through internet-enabled value chain activities. The authors further argue that a firm's abilities to coordinate and exploit its resources create higher-order resource, which leads to improved operational and financial performance. However, another study (Ray, Muhanna, & Barney, 2005) investigates the differential effects of various Information Technology (IT) resources and capabilities on the performance of the customer service process. The findings of this study suggest that tacit, socially involved, firm-specific resources explain variation in process performance and that IT resources and capabilities without these attributes do not. A third study by Sarker, Sarker, Sahaym and Bjørn-Andersen (2012) explores the value co-creation in relationships between an ERP vendor and its partners. This study found that there are different mechanisms underlying value cocreation within B2B alliance. From the studies, we learn that first, the ability of the firm to effectively combine the set of specific resources to exploit market opportunities and be competitive is the focus of the RBV (Penrose, 1959). Second, resources are " stocks of available factors that are owned or controlled by the firm"(Amit & Schoemaker, 1993).

The Resource-Based View (Barney, 1991), a dominant theory in Strategic Management literature, therefore, is used as the underlying theoretical foundation for the following reasons. First, to study social commerce-based firms' abilities to manage and deploy technological resources (for example, social media) to co-create value. The RBV theory suggests that conventional technologies can be transformed into valuable resources when used in specific business processes (Dong, Xu, & Zhu, 2009). In addition, in previous IS studies the RBV has been used to study IT as a source of sustained competitive advantage (Mata, Fuerst, & Barney, 1995) and also to explain how IT value stems from the organizational use of IT than the technology itself (Clemons & Row, 1991; Markus & Soh, 1995). Second, the nature of resources required (for example, business processes) to co-create value. The RBV of the firm also stipulates that specific resources of the firm have the potential to generate sustained competitive, which will ultimately lead to superior organizational performance (Priem & Butler, 2001; Wernerfelt, 1995, 1984). These resources of the firm are categorized as tangible resources (human, physical, organizational and financial), and intangible resources (reputational, brand, trust, social and cultural) (Eisenhardt & Martin, 2000; Harrison, Hitt, Hoskisson, & Ireland, 2001). Third, how value co-creation is developed through external relationship management as cited by (Wade & Hulland, 2004), this is important because the main focus of social commerce-based firms is to exploit the use of the social technologies for value co-creation in interactions with their customers and other external partners.

The central theme of the RBV addresses the fundamental question of why firms are different and how they achieve and sustain competitive advantage by deploying their resources (Kostopoulos, Spanos, & Prastacos, 2002). Similarly, RBV has been used as a paradigm that combines different philosophies and frameworks from various disciplines (Mahoney & Pandian, 1992; Wade & Hulland, 2004). The RBV also posits that firms possess resources; a part of these resources enables the firms to achieve competitive advantage; another part of it leads to superior sustained performance (Barney,1991).

The author further reiterates that these resources, which are composed as heterogeneous resources, can create a competitive advantage if they have the following qualities:

Valuable: the resource can enable a firm to conceive or implement strategies that improve its efficiency or effectiveness;

Rare: a large number of competing firms should not possess the resources

Imperfectly Imitable: the resources should not be easily imitated due to unique historical conditions, causally ambiguous, or social complex;

Non-Substitutable: Other substitutes should not easily replace the resource.

However, advocates of RBV are unable to have a precise definition of what a resource is (Butler & Priem, 2001). This proliferation of definitions and classifications has raised complex issues in studies using RBV as it is unclear what these researchers mean the term "resources" (Butler & Priem, 2001).

CONCLUSION

The chapter has argued the need to identify and develop a model that explains how social commerce-based firms co-create value using available resources to achieve benefits. The significance of this research can be viewed from academic, practitioner and policy perspectives. In scholarship discourse, the development of social commerce research, like other fields of study, requires theorization and development of a conceptual framework.

From the research perspective, this research will reveal based on a theory the value that social commerce enterprises benefit from leveraging social media and web 2.0 technologies. This research cannot be overlooked because the research seeks to add to the existing body of knowledge regarding social commerce studies as well as to research gaps considering the paucity of studies on social commerce business models.

Regarding policy and practice, this research will inform practitioners about the resources needed to develop social commerce capabilities. This research will also provide adequate findings for Governments as well as other regulatory bodies to formulate policies and laws to govern the use of the internet and also use that as a means of job creation.

REFERENCES

Amit, R., & Schoemaker, P. J. H. (1993). Strategic Assets and Organizational Rent. *Strategic Management Journal*, *14*(1), 33–46. doi:10.1002/smj.4250140105

Banker, R. D., Bardhan, I. R., Chang, H., & Lin, S. (2006). Plant information systems, manufacturing capabilities, and plant performance. *Management Information Systems Quarterly*, *30*(2), 315–337. doi:10.2307/25148733

Barney, J. B. (1991). Firm Resources and Sustained Competitive Advantage. *Journal of Management*, *17*(1), 99–120. doi:10.1177/014920639101700108

Barua, A., Konana, P., Whinston, A. B., & Yin, F. (2004). An Empirical Investigation of Net-Enabled Business Value. MIS Quartely Quarterly, *28*(4), 585–620. Retrieved from https://www.jstor.org/stable/25148656

Bharadwaj, A., El Sawy, O. A., Pavlou, P. A., & Venkatraman, N. (2013). Digital business strategy: Toward a next generation of insights. *Management Information Systems Quarterly*, *37*(2), 471–482.

Boateng, R. (2016). Resources, Electronic-Commerce Capabilities and Electronic-Commerce Benefits: Conceptualizing the Links. *Information Technology for Development*, *22*(2), 242–264. doi:10.1080/02681102.2014.939606

Busalim, A. H., Che Hussin, A. R., & Iahad, N. A. (2019). Factors Influencing Customer Engagement in Social Commerce Websites: A Systematic Literature Review. *Journal of Theoretical and Applied Electronic Commerce Research*, *14*(2). doi:10.4067/S0718-18762019000200102

Busalim, A. H., & Hussin, A. R. C. (2016). Understanding social commerce: A systematic literature review and directions for further research. *International Journal of Information Management*, *36*(6), 1075–1088. doi:10.1016/j.ijinfomgt.2016.06.005

Butler, J. E., & Priem, R. L. (2001). Is the Resource-Based "View" a Useful Perspective for Strategic Management Research? doi:10.5465/AMR.2001.4011928

Cai, S., Yuan, Q., & Zhou, P. (2013). A resource mapping framework for value co-creation in social media. In *WHICEB 2013* (Vol. 14, p. 25). Proceedings; doi:10.1504/IJNVO.2014.065082

Cheng, J., Liu, R.-G., & Du, C. T. (2017). Exploring How Conflict and Uncertainty Affect Repurchase Intention in Social Commerce---The Mediating Effect of Perceived Deceptiveness. *International Conference on Electronic Business.*

Cheng, X., Gu, Y., & Shen, J. (2019). An integrated view of particularized trust in social commerce: An empirical investigation. *International Journal of Information Management, 45*, 1–12. doi:10.1016/j.ijinfomgt.2018.10.014

Clement, J. (2019). Social commerce adoption among retailers in North America from 2017 to 2018. Retrieved November 4, 2019, from https://www.statista.com/statistics/1017523/north-america-social-commerce-adoption-in-retail/

Clemons, E. K., & Row, M. C. (1991). Sustaining IT advantage: The role of structural differences. *Management Information Systems Quarterly, 15*(3), 275–292. doi:10.2307/249639

Dong, S., Xu, S. X., & Zhu, K. X. (2009). Research Note: Information technology in supply chains: The value of IT-enabled resources under competition. *Information Systems Research, 20*(1), 18–32. doi:10.1287/isre.1080.0195

Du, H. S., & Wagner, C. (2007). *The Role of Technology*. Content, and Context for the Success of Social Media.

Eisenhardt, K. M., & Martin, J. A. (2000). Dynamic Capabilities : What Are They? *Strategic Management Journal, 21*(10-11), 1105–1121. doi:10.1002/1097-0266(200010/11)21:10/11<1105::AID-SMJ133>3.0.CO;2-E

Erdoğmuş, İ. E., & Tatar, Ş. B. (2015). Drivers of Social Commerce through Brand Engagement. *Procedia: Social and Behavioral Sciences, 207*(212), 189–195. doi:10.1016/j.sbspro.2015.10.087

Ettlie, J. E., & Pavlou, P. A. (2006). Technology-based new product development partnerships. *Decision Sciences, 37*(2), 117–147. doi:10.1111/j.1540-5915.2006.00119.x

Fagerstrøm, A., & Ghinea, G. (2010). Web 2.0's Marketing Impact on Low-Involvement Consumers. *Journal of Interactive Advertising, 10*(2), 67–71. doi:10.1080/15252019.2010.10722171

Farivar, S. (2020). *Biases in Social Commerce Users ' Rational Risk Considerations*. ICIS.

Farivar, S., Turel, O., & Yuan, Y. (2017). A trust-risk perspective on social commerce use: An examination of the biasing role of habit. *Internet Research, 27*(3), 586–607. doi:10.1108/IntR-06-2016-0175

Farivar, S., Turel, O., & Yuan, Y. (2018). Skewing users' rational risk considerations in social commerce: An empirical examination of the role of social identification. *Information & Management, 55*(8), 1038–1048. doi:10.1016/j.im.2018.05.008

Farivar, S., Yuan, Y., & Turel, O. (2016). Understanding Social Commerce Acceptance: The Role of Trust, Perceived Risk, and Benefit. In Twenty-second Americas Conference on Information Systems (pp. 1–10). Retrieved from https://scholar.google.com/citations?view_op=view_citation&continue=/scholar%253Fhl%253Den%2526as_sdt%253D0,11%2526scilib%253D1&citilm=1&citation_for_view=iFHnt7IAAAAJ:8AbLer7MMksC&hl=en&oi=p

Friedrich, T. (2015). Analyzing the Factors that Influence Consumers ' Adoption of Social Commerce – A Literature Review Full Papers. *Twenty-First Americas Conference on Information Systems*, 1–16.

Gatautis, R., & Medziausiene, A. (2014). Factors Affecting Social Commerce Acceptance in Lithuania. Procedia - Social and Behavioral Sciences, 110(2013), 1235–1242. doi:10.1016/j.sbspro.2013.12.970

Grange, C., & Benbasat, I. (2013). The value of social shopping networks for product search and the moderating role of network scope. International Conference on Information Systems (ICIS 2013): Re-shaping Society Through Information Systems Design, 5, 4230–4241.

Grange, C., Benbasat, I., & Burton-Jones, A. (2018, March). A Network-Based Conceptualization of Social Commerce and Social Commerce Value. *Computers in Human Behavior*, •••, 1–14. doi:10.1016/j.chb.2018.12.033

Hajli, N. (2015). Social commerce constructs and consumer's intention to buy. *International Journal of Information Management, 35*(2), 183–191. doi:10.1016/j.ijinfomgt.2014.12.005

Hajli, N., & Sims, J. (2015). Social commerce: The transfer of power from sellers to buyers. *Technological Forecasting and Social Change, 94*, 350–358. doi:10.1016/j.techfore.2015.01.012

Hajli, N., Sims, J., Zadeh, A. H., & Richard, M.-O. (2017). A social commerce investigation of the role of trust in a social networking site on purchase intentions. *Journal of Business Research, 71*, 133–141. doi:10.1016/j.jbusres.2016.10.004

Hajli, N. M. (2014). The role of social support on relationship quality and social commerce. *Technological Forecasting and Social Change, 87*, 17–27. doi:10.1016/j.techfore.2014.05.012

Harrison, J. S., Hitt, M. A., Hoskisson, R. E., & Ireland, R. D. (2001). Resource complementarity in business combinations: Extending the logic to organizational alliances. *Journal of Management, 27*(6), 679–690. doi:10.1177/014920630102700605

Hassan, S., & Toland, J. (2013). A conceptual framework for value co-creation practices in C2C social commerce environment. *Proceedings of the 24th Australasian Conference on Information Systems.*

Hsieh, Y.-H., Ya-Ting, L., & Leng-Heng, C. (2017). The Influence of Customer's Sharing Behavior in Social Commerce. In *Twenty-third Americas Conference on Information Systems* (pp. 259–264). Academic Press.

Huang, Z., & Benyoucef, M. (2013). From e-commerce to social commerce: A close look at design features. *Electronic Commerce Research and Applications, 12*(4), 246–259. doi:10.1016/j.elerap.2012.12.003

Huang, Z., & Benyoucef, M. (2015). User preferences of social features on social commerce websites: An empirical study. *Technological Forecasting and Social Change, 95*, 57–72. doi:10.1016/j.techfore.2014.03.005

Huang, Z., & Benyoucef, M. (2017). The effects of social commerce design on consumer purchase decision-making: An empirical study. *Electronic Commerce Research and Applications, 25*, 40–58. doi:10.1016/j.elerap.2017.08.003

Jaunky, V. C., Roopchund, R., Ramesh, V., & Jaunky, V. (2018). Use of Social Media for Improving Student Engagement at Université des Mascareignes (UDM). *Proceedings of Fifth International Conference INDIA 2018.* 10.1007/978-981-13-3338-5_2

Kim, S., & Park, H. (2013). Effects of various characteristics of social commerce (s-commerce) on consumers' trust and trust performance. *International Journal of Information Management*, *33*(2), 318–332. doi:10.1016/j.ijinfomgt.2012.11.006

Kim, Y. A., & Srivastava, J. (2007). Impact of social influence in e-commerce decision making. Proceedings of the Ninth International Conference on Electronic Commerce - ICEC '07, 293. doi:10.1145/1282100.1282157

Kohler, T., Fueller, J., Matzler, K., Stieger, D., & Füller. (2011). CO-creation in virtual worlds: The design of the user experience. MIS Quarterly: Management Information Systems, 35(3), 773–788. doi:10.2307/23042808

Kohler, T., Fueller, J., Stieger, D., & Matzler, K. (2011). Avatar-based innovation: Consequences of the virtual co-creation experience. *Computers in Human Behavior*, *27*(1), 160–168. doi:10.1016/j.chb.2010.07.019

Kohli, R., & Grover, V. (2008). Business Value of IT: An Essay on Expanding Research Directions to Keep up with the Times. *Journal of the Association for Information Systems*, *9*(1), 23–39. doi:10.17705/1jais.00147

Kostopoulos, C. K., Spanos, Y. E., & Prastacos, G. P. (2002). The Rseource-Based View of the Firm and Innovation:Identification of Critical Linkages. In *The 2nd* (pp. 1–19). European Academy of Managemnt Conference; Retrieved from http://ecsocman.hse.ru/data/165/663/1219/rb_view.pdf

Leeraphong, A., & Papasratorn, B. (2018). S-Commerce Transactions and Business Models in Southeast Asia: A Case Study in Thailand. KnE Social Sciences, 3(1), 65. doi:10.18502/kss.v3i1.1397

Lekhanya, L. M. (2013). Cultural Influence On The Diffusion And Adoption Of Social Media Technologies By Entrepreneurs In Rural South Africa. International Business & Economics Research Journal, 12. Retrieved from https://openscholar.dut.ac.za/bitstream/10321/1123/1/lekhanya_ib_erj_2013.pdf

Liang, T., & Turban, E. (2011). Introduction to the Special Issue : Social Commerce : A Research Framework for Social Commerce. *International Journal of Electronic Commerce*, *16*(2), 2012. doi:10.2753/JEC1086-4415160201

Liang, T.-P., Ho, Y.-T., Li, Y.-W., & Turban, E. (2011). What Drives Social Commerce: The Role of Social Support and Relationship Quality. *International Journal of Electronic Commerce*, *16*(2), 69–90. doi:10.2753/JEC1086-4415160204

Lubua, E. W., & Pretorius, P. (2018). *The Impact of Demographic Factors to the Adoption of Social Commerce in Tanzania*. *In 2018 IST-Africa Week Conference (IST-Africa)* (pp. 1–12). IST-Africa Institute; Retrieved from www.IST-Africa.org/Conference2018

Lubua, E. W., & Pretorius, P. D. (2019). Factors determining the perceived relevance of social commerce in the African context. *South African Journal of Information Management*, *21*(1), 1–8. doi:10.4102/sajim.v21i1.959

Mahoney, J. T., & Pandian, J. R. (1992). The Resource-Based View Within the Conversation of Strategic Management. *Strategic Management Journal*, *13*(5), 363–380. doi:10.1002/smj.4250130505

Markus, M. L., & Soh, C. (1995). How IT creates business value: a process theory synthesis. ICIS 1995 Proceedings, 4.

Marsden, P. (2009). *The 6 dimensions of social commerce: rated and reviewed*. Social Commerce Today.

Mata, F. J., Fuerst, W. L., & Barney, J. B. (1995). Information technology and sustained competitive advantage: A Resourced-Based Analysis. *Management Information Systems Quarterly*, *19*(4), 487–505. doi:10.2307/249630

Mikalef, P., Giannakos, M., & Pappas, I. O. (2017). Designing social commerce platforms based on consumers' intentions. *Behaviour & Information Technology*, *36*(12), 1308–1327. doi:10.1080/01449 29X.2017.1386713

Mikalef, P., Pappas, I. O., & Giannakos, M. N. (2017). Value co-creation and purchase intention in social commerce:The enabling role of word- of-mouth and trust. In *Twenty-third Americas Conference on Information Systems* (pp. 1–10). Academic Press.

Munawar, M., Hassanein, K., & Head, M. (2017). Understanding the Role of Herd Behaviour and Homophily in Social Commerce. Special Interest Group on Human Computer Interaction, (SIGHCI 2017 Proceedings).

Ng, C. S. P. (2013). Intention to purchase on social commerce websites across cultures: A cross-regional study. *Information & Management*, *50*(8), 609–620. doi:10.1016/j.im.2013.08.002

Ngai, E. W. T., Tao, S. S. C., & Moon, K. K. L. (2015). Social media research: Theories, constructs, and conceptual frameworks. *International Journal of Information Management*, *35*(1), 33–44. doi:10.1016/j.ijinfomgt.2014.09.004

Osatuyi, B., & Qin, H. (2018). How vital is the role of affect on post-adoption behaviors? An examination of social commerce users. *International Journal of Information Management*, *40*(February), 175–185. doi:10.1016/j.ijinfomgt.2018.02.005

Parameswaran, M., & Whinston, A. (2007). Research Issues in Social computing. *Journal of the Association for Information Systems*, *8*(6), 336–350. doi:10.17705/1jais.00132

Penrose, E. (1959). *The theory of the firm*. John Wiley & Sons.

Priem, R. L., & Butler, J. E. (2001). Tautology in the resource-based view and the implications of externally determined resource value: Further comments. *Academy of Management Review*, *26*(1), 57–66. doi:10.5465/amr.2001.4011946

Qin, L. (2017). A Cross-Cultural Study of Interpersonal Trust in Social Commerce. *Journal of Computer Information Systems*, ***, 1–8. doi:10.1080/08874417.2017.1383865

Rai, A., Pavlou, P. A., Im, G., & Du, S. (2012). Interfirm IT Capability Profiles and Communications for Cocreating Relational Value: Evidence from the Logistics Industry. *Management Information Systems Quarterly*, *36*(1), 233–262. doi:10.2307/41410416

Ray, G., Muhanna, W. A., & Barney, J. B. (2005). Information Technology and the Performance of the Customer Service Process: A Resource Based Analysis. MIS Quarter, 29(4), 695–704. Retrieved from https://www.jstor.org/stable/25148703

Rubel, S. (2006). *Trends to watch. Part II: social commerce--micro persuasion*. Academic Press.

Sarker, S., Sarker, S., Sahaym, A., & Bjørn-Andersen, N. (2012). Exploring value cocreation in relationships betweenan ERP vendor and its partners : A revelatory case study. MIS Quarterly: Management. *Information Systems*, 36(1), 317–338. doi:10.2307/41410419

Sharma, S., & Crossler, R. E. (2014). Disclosing too much? Situational factors affecting information disclosure in social commerce environment. *Electronic Commerce Research and Applications*, 13(5), 305–319. doi:10.1016/j.elerap.2014.06.007

Straub, D. W., & Watson, R. T. (2001). Transformational Issues in Researching IS and Net-Enabled Organizations. *Information Systems Research*, 12(4), 337–345. doi:10.1287/isre.12.4.337.9706

Sukrat, S., Mahatanankoon, P., & Papasratorn, B. (2018). The Driving Forces of C2C Social Commerce in Thailand: A Developing Framework. KnE Social Sciences, 3(1), 108. doi:10.18502/kss.v3i1.1400

Susarla, A., Oh, J. H., & Tan, Y. (2012). Social networks and the diffusion of user-generated content: Evidence from youtube. *Information Systems Research*, 23(1), 23–41. doi:10.1287/isre.1100.0339

Tajvidi, M., Wang, Y., Hajli, N., & Love, P. E. D. (2017). Brand value Co-creation in social commerce: The role of interactivity, social support, and relationship quality. *Computers in Human Behavior*, •••, 1–8. doi:10.1016/j.chb.2017.11.006

Vargo, S. L., Maglio, P. P., & Akaka, M. A. (2008). On value and value co-creation: A service systems and service logic perspective. *European Management Journal*, 26(3), 145–152. doi:10.1016/j.emj.2008.04.003

Vishnu Menon, R. G., Sigurdsson, V., Larsen, N. M., Fagerstrøm, A., & Foxall, G. R. (2016). Consumer attention to price in social commerce: Eye tracking patterns in retail clothing ☆. *Journal of Business Research*, 69(11), 5008–5013. doi:10.1016/j.jbusres.2016.04.072

Vongsraluang, N., & Bhatiasevi, V. (2017). The determinants of social commerce system success for SMEs in Thailand. *Information Development*, 33(1), 80–96. doi:10.1177/0266666916639632

Wade, M., & Hulland, J. (2004). Review: The resource-based view and information systems research: Review, extension, and suggestions for future research. *Management Information Systems Quarterly*, 28(1), 107–142. doi:10.2307/25148626

Wang, C., & Zhang, P. (2012, November). The Evolution of Social Commerce : The People, Management, Technology, and Information Dimensions and Information Dimensions. *Communications of the Association for Information Systems*, 31, 105–127. doi:10.17705/1CAIS.03105

Wang, Y., & Yu, C. (2017a). Social interaction-based consumer decision-making model in social commerce: The role of word of mouth and observational learning. *International Journal of Information Management*, 37(3), 179–189. doi:10.1016/j.ijinfomgt.2015.11.005

Wang, Y., & Yu, C. (2017b). Social interaction-based consumer decision-making model in social commerce: The role of word of mouth and observational learning. *International Journal of Information Management*, *37*(3), 179–189. doi:10.1016/j.ijinfomgt.2015.11.005

Wernerfelt, B. (1984). A resource-based view of the firm. *Strategic Management Journal*, *5*(2), 171–180. doi:10.1002/smj.4250050207

Wernerfelt. (1995). A Resource-based view of the firm: tem years after. Strategic Management Journal, 16(2), 171–174.

Williams, M. D. (2018). Social commerce and the mobile platform: Payment and security perceptions of potential users. Computers in Human Behavior. doi:10.1016/j.chb.2018.06.005

Wongkitrungrueng, A., & Assarut, N. (2018, November). The role of live streaming in building consumer trust and engagement with social commerce sellers. *Journal of Business Research*. doi:10.1016/j.jbusres.2018.08.032

Yadav, M. S., De Valck, K., Hennig-thurau, T., Hoffman, D. L., & Spann, M. (2013). ScienceDirect Social Commerce : A Contingency Framework for Assessing Marketing Potential. *Journal of Interactive Marketing*, *27*(4), 311–323. doi:10.1016/j.intmar.2013.09.001

Ben Yahia, I., Al-Neama, N., & Kerbache, L. (2018). Investigating the drivers for social commerce in social media platforms: Importance of trust, social support and the platform perceived usage. *Journal of Retailing and Consumer Services*, *41*, 11–19. doi:10.1016/j.jretconser.2017.10.021

Yu, C.-H., Tsai, C.-C., Wang, Y., Lai, K.-K., & Tajvidi, M. (2018). Towards building a value co-creation circle in social commerce. Computers in Human Behavior, 105476. doi:10.1016/j.chb.2018.04.021

Zhang, K. Z., & Benyoucef, M. (2016). Consumer behavior in social commerce: A literature review. *Decision Support Systems*, *86*, 95–108. doi:10.1016/j.dss.2016.04.001

Chapter 23
Technology Addictions, Model Development, Measurement, and Effect on Performance From a Developing Country Context:
A Viewpoint for Future Research

Makafui Nyamadi
University of Ghana, Ghana

ABSTRACT

Technology addictions (TA) have become a global scourge in recent times, yet in information systems (IS) literature, while a lot of research is being done from developed countries and health-related disciplines, little attention is being paid to this menace by IS scholars from developing countries. To address this issue, this chapter provides a viewpoint on the future research that seeks to investigate from a multidisciplinary and stakeholder perspective what the nature of TA from developing country context is. It will also determine how the socio-technical interaction between human motivations and technology features result in TA, which is novel in IS literature.

INTRODUCTION

Technology Addiction (TA) has engaged the attention of Information Systems (IS) scholars in recent times (Nyamadi & Boateng, 2018; Tarafdar, Gupta, & Turel, 2015; Turel, Serenko, & Giles, 2011). This research from the researcher's perspective looks at addiction *as a state where one feels preoccupied with an uncoerced compulsion to repeat or continue the behavior that has severe negative consequences.* Griffiths defined TA as "non-chemical (behavioral) addictions which involve human-machine interaction" (Griffiths, 2005). He further stated that "technology addictions can be passive (e.g., television) or active (e.g., computer games) and usually contain inducing and reinforcing features which may contribute to the promotion of addictive tendencies" (Griffiths, 2005). Several forms of these TAs have engaged the

DOI: 10.4018/978-1-7998-2610-1.ch023

attention of researchers. For example; excessive microblogging (Li, Guo, & Sun, 2012), online games (Charlton & Danforth, 2007, Vinet & Zhedanov, 2010), internet (Akin & İskender, 2011), smartphones or mobile phones (Billieux, Maurage, Lopez-Fernandez, Kuss, & Griffiths, 2015), mobile email (Turel & Serenko, 2010), instant messaging (Huang & Leung, 2009), Social Network Site (SNS), and excessive usage (Andreassen, 2015). This paper will focus on three (3) different types of technology addictions, namely; online gaming addictions, smartphone addictions, and Social Networking Site (SNS) addictions.

The term Online Gaming Addiction (OGA) will be used synonymously with Internet Gaming Disorder (IGD) in this work. Section 3 of Diagnostics and Statistical Manual of Mental Disorders 5th ed. (DSM - 5) published by the American Psychiatric Association (APA) categorically mentioned Internet Gaming Disorder as the first TA that needs further research (APA, 2013). APA (2013) defined IGD as "persistent and recurrent use of the internet to engage in games, often with other players, leading to impairment or clinically significant distress." According to Jing and Hock (2012), the most popular game mode, which has one of the highest tendencies of being addictive, is Massively Multiplayer Online Role-Playing Games (MMORPGs). For example, World of Warcraft (WoW).

Smartphone addiction involves excessive interactions with a smartphone device, and mainly, the application functions it provides (Turel & Serenko, 2010). There is an emerging trend of compulsive and addictive usage of smartphones in recent times (Zhang et al., 2014). Smartphone users can also display psychological and behavioral maladaptive dependency, which may result in adverse problems (Zhang, Chongyang, & Matthew, 2014). These problematic uses of smartphones have resulted in harmful and disturbing outcomes (Wang, Lee, Yang, & Li, 2016).

SNS are virtual communities where users create individual public profiles, interact with real-life friends, and meet or make friends with other people based on shared interests (Kuss & Griffiths, 2011). There are three theoretical perspectives on the formation of SNS addictions. These are; the cognitive-behavioral model, the socio-cognitive model, and the social skills model (Turel & Serenko, 2012). The rapid rise in the time spent online by individuals is resulting in SNS addiction (Kuss & Griffiths, 2011). Examples of the social media platforms for promoting SNS activities are; Facebook, Twitter, WhatsApp, Instagram, LinkedIn, Snapchat, Google+, e.t.c.

The prevalence and insurgence of various forms of TAs have become significant concerns for stakeholders (Elhai, Dvorak, Levine, & Hall, 2017; Griffiths, 1995; Turel, Serenko, & Giles, 2011). It is, therefore, essential to engage multi-stakeholders in institutions of higher learning and other disciplines and backgrounds to know their diverse perspectives on what TA is and the different meanings they attribute to TA from developing country context.

Griffiths (2005) and West (2015) developed theories in health-related disciplines, but these theories did not account for IT Artifacts. In IS discipline, theories or models developed either focused on antecedents (causes) or consequences (outcomes) of technology addictions. For example; The leading TA publication in MISQ states that perceived ease of use, perceived usefulness (extrinsic), and perceived enjoyment (intrinsic) are the primary constructs that cause online auction addiction through behavioral usage intentions (Turel, Serenko, & Giles, 2011). Tarafdar, Gupta, & Turel (2013) suggested that to study TA, scholars should understand the antecedents and consequences.

Future research should focus on socio-technical interactions between human motivation systems (social) and technology characteristics or features of (SNS, Online Gaming, and Smartphones (technical) as the antecedents of TA. From a technological perspective, this research will consider the characteristics of technologies (King, Delfabbro, & Griffiths, 2010). The consequences of these technologies have behavioral effects (Griffiths, 1995; Turel, Serenko, & Giles, 2011; Turel & Serenko, 2012). Therefore, the technology addiction model (TADM) should cover the antecedents and consequences of TA. This future research should conductan integrative review of the three technology addictions platforms such as SNS addiction, online gaming addiction, and smartphone addictions. It will further translate antecedents, prevalence, and consequences into a nomological network. This nomological network will turn into a framework that will bring out the inconsistencies and omissions in literature. TAM Theory and UTAUT will be used to investigate the adoption and usage of technologies (Venkatesh & Bala, 2008; Venkatesh, Thong, & Xu, 2016).

PRIME Theory known in psychology as "Addiction Theory" and Flow Theory will be used to guide and differentiate the constructs from social and socio-technical perspectives, respectively (Csikszentmihalyi, 1975; West, 2015). This model will describe how the socio-technical interactions between human motivations and technology features lead to flow. A flow state can either develop into positive or negative outcomes. If the flow state has severe negative consequences on the user's life, then it results in addiction, as stated by Griffith, "activity cannot be described as an addiction if there are few (or no) negative consequences in the player's" (Griffiths, 2010).

RESEARCH PROBLEM

Technology Addiction is an emerging concern among stakeholders. As stated earlier, the American Psychiatric Association (APA) listed the first TA as Online Gaming Disorder and called for further research (APA, 2013). TA is researched extensively in clinical health-related disciplines such as nursing, psychiatry or mental health, psychology, neuroscience, e.t.c (Alcaro & Panksepp, 2011; Dong, Wang, Du, & Potenza, 2017; Gentile, 2009; Griffiths, 2005; Griffiths & Nuyens, 2017; Hyman, Malenka, & Nestler, 2006; Mak et al., 2017; Weinstein, Livny, & Weizman, 2017; Widyanto & Griffiths, 2006). However, in the Information Systems discipline, TA is relatively an under-researched area (Nyamadi & Boateng, 2018; Serenko & Turel, 2015; Turel, Serenko, & Giles, 2011; Vaghefi, Lapointe, & Boudreau-Pinsonneault, 2016). Extant literature on TA in IS has mainly focused on single platforms. Examples are; such as online gaming or internet game disorder (Jing & Hock, 2012), online auctioning (Turel, Serenko, & Giles, 2011), SNS (Polites, Serrano, & Thatcher, 2018), smartphone (Wang et al., 2016), and mobile email (Turel & Serenko, 2010). General literature, however, went beyond one platform to focus on two platforms. For example; social network sites and social media apps addiction (Eric, Hyunji, Sang, Han, & Oh, 2016), addiction to internet and online gaming (Ng & Wiemer-Hastings, 2005), internet and social media addiction (Brooks, Schneider, & Wang, 2016) problematic internet use and problematic online gambling (Yau et al., 2014). Since smartphone users are either addicted to SNS and online or mobile games (Jeong, Kim, Yum, & Hwang, 2016). It would, therefore, be useful and very significant to do an empirical study that would focus on three major platforms such as smartphones, online gaming, and SNS to conceptualize TA.

A literature review in Information System (IS) on TA has revealed that various theories of addictions either focus on antecedents (causes) or consequences (outcome). This model will encompass both the antecedents and consequences of TA. Also, theories developed in other disciplines do not consider the phenomenon around features of technologies that may have the tendencies of influencing users to engage with technologies and eventually become addicted. Technologies have some standard features that are addictive (Griffiths, 2005; King, Valença, & Nardi, 2010). It is, therefore, essential to find out the characteristics of technology features from a critical realist perspective and even further interrogate the socio-technical interactions between human motivations and technologies and how that eventually result in TA. Critical Realism will enable the researcher to "get beneath the surface to understand and explain why things are as they are, to hypothesize the structures and mechanisms that shape observable events" (Mingers, 2004, p.100).

Future research could, therefore, seek to provide or respond to this literature limitation by looking into what really motivates humans (technology users) to engage with technologies and eventually become addicted. Researchers can conduct an integrative review on SNS addiction, online gaming addiction, and smartphone addictions. It should focus on the well-known antecedents (pre-addictions), dimensions, and consequences (outcomes) that will integrate into nomological networks. These nomological networks may then translate into a framework that will bring out the inconsistencies and omissions in literature.

Scholars linked online gaming addiction to productivity and advocated for governments to develop regulations aimed at preventing it (Jing & Hock, 2012). Research showed that smartphone addiction has become prevalent in many nations (Walsh, White, Hyde, & Watson, 2008). For example, a report from China confirmed 48.9% of symptoms of smartphone addiction among users (Yen et al., 2009). Also, in Spain, about 8% of university students showed signs of problematic smartphone addiction (Beranuy, Oberst, Carbonell, & Chamarro, 2009; Jenaro, Flores, Gómez-Vela, González-Gil, & Caballo, 2007). An IPSO, a French company, reported that 18% of British citizens are dependent on the smartphone mobile device, and 53% recorded problematic behaviors smartphone (King, Valença, et al., 2010). SNSs addiction is dominant among young people who are mainly teenagers and students (Kuss & Griffiths, 2011). Surveys among 120 youth work managers and practitioners, reported SNS addiction as 23%, with its associated risks as cyberbullying (53%), disclosing personal information (35%), and sexual predators (22%).

RESEARCH PURPOSE

In reference to the above gaps, future research should seek to investigate technology addiction on academic performance among university students from developing country context. Such a study will build a model that describes how the sociotechnical interaction between human motivation (University Students) and characteristics of technologies (SNS, Online Gaming, and Smartphones) features results in the flow that eventually influence university students to become addicted to these technologies.

RESEARCH OBJECTIVES AND QUESTIONS

Research Objectives

1. To understand from multidisciplinary and stakeholders' perspective, the nature of TA from developing country context.
2. To describe how the sociotechnical interaction between human motivation (university students) and characteristics technology features (SNS, online gaming, and smartphones) results in TA.
3. To investigate the effect of TA on university students from developing country context.

Research Questions

1. What are the multidisciplinary and stakeholders' perspectives on the nature of TA from developing country context?
2. How does the sociotechnical interaction between human motivation (university students) and characteristics of technology (Internet, SNS, online gaming, and smartphones) features result in TA?
3. What is the effect of TA on university students from developing country context?

MANAGING TECHNOLOGY ADDICTIONS IN DEVELOPING COUNTRIES

This chapter argues for future research to examine the TA from policy, theory, practice, academic, and user perspectives. Research has, over the years, focused on developed countries, and a lot is being done from developed country context to mitigate the menace (Turel, Serenko, & Giles, 2011; Weinstein, Maraz, Griffiths, Lejoyeux, & Demetrovics, 2016). Again, using social media platforms such as Facebook, Twitter, WhatsApp, Instagram, LinkedIn, Snapchat, Google+, Hi5, and so on during productive times can be regulated as in some developed countries (Akdeniz, 2001; Jing & Hock, 2012; Lee, Kim, & Hong, 2017). From a policy perspective, the final work will help governments from developing countries to enact laws and regulate the various forms of TA, such as online gaming, online betting, and online gambling. From the practitioners' perspective, the final work will develop a model that explains and predict TA. This model will enable the IS community to develop design principles to block or mitigate TA. In academics, this future research will critically examine the antecedents (causes) and consequences (outcomes) of TA. It will also reveal the phenomenon behind the sociotechnical interactions between humans (social) and technologies (technical) and inform the research community of how that phenomenon results in addiction from developing country context. This future research will also help users to know when to discontinue or regulate themselves when using these technologies.

CONCLUSION

In conclusion, this chapter has put forward the need to research on TA in Information Systems from developing countries context. It has argued for the need to examine TA from developing country context by first investigating from multidisciplinary and stakeholders' perspective what the nature of TA is. It has also suggested the need to find out how the socio-technical interactions between human motivations (university students) and characteristics of technology (SNS, online gaming, and smartphones) features result in TA and the effect of TA on university students from developing country context. This chapter has provided a viewpoint that seeks to create a model to examine TAs through the lens of sociotechnical interactions between human motivation systems and the technology features, which is novel in IS literature. This model would provide the foundation for conducting future research on technology addictions. The model would be used to test different technologies and platforms. The overall purpose or goal is eventually to get a model that would describe and explain what technology addiction is from an IS perspective.

REFERENCES

Akdeniz, Y. (2001). Internet Content Regulation: UK Government and the control of internet content. *Computer Law & Security Review*, *17*(5), 303–317. doi:10.1016/S0267-3649(01)00505-2

Akin, A., & İskender, M. (2011). Internet addiction and depression, anxiety, and stress. *International Online Journal of Education Sciences*, *3*(1), 138–148.

Alcaro, A., & Panksepp, J. (2011). The SEEKING mind: Primal neuro-affective substrates for appetitive incentive states and their pathological dynamics in addictions and depression. *Neuroscience and Biobehavioral Reviews*, *35*(9), 1805–1820. doi:10.1016/j.neubiorev.2011.03.002 PMID:21396397

Andreassen, C. S. (2015). Online Social Network Site Addiction: A comprehensive review. *Current Addiction Reports*, *2*(2), 175–184. doi:10.100740429-015-0056-9

APA. (2013). *Diagnostic and Statistical Manual of Mental Disorders, 5*. APA.

Beranuy, M., Oberst, U., Carbonell, X., & Chamarro, A. (2009). Problematic Internet and Mobile Phone Use and Clinical Symptoms in College Students: The role of emotional intelligence. *Computers in Human Behavior*, *25*(5), 1182–1187. doi:10.1016/j.chb.2009.03.001

Billieux, J., Maurage, P., Lopez-Fernandez, O., Kuss, D. J., & Griffiths, M. D. (2015). Can Disordered Mobile Phone Use Be Considered a Behavioral Addiction? An update on current evidence and a comprehensive model for future research. *Current Addiction Reports*, *2*(2), 156–162. doi:10.100740429-015-0054-y

Brooks, S., Schneider, C., & Wang, X. A. (2016). Technology addictions and technostress: An examination of Hong Kong and the U.S. *Twenty-Second Americas Conference on Information Systems*, 1–10.

Charlton, J. P., & Danforth, I. D. W. (2007). Distinguishing addiction and high engagement in the context of online game playing. *Computers in Human Behavior*, *23*(3), 1531–1548. doi:10.1016/j.chb.2005.07.002

Csikszentmihalyi, M. (1975). Beyond boredom and anxiety. Jossey-Bass Publishers.

Davis, F. D. (1989). Perceived usefulness, perceived ease of use, and user acceptance of information technology. *MIS Quarterly: Management Information Systems*, *13*(3), 319–339. doi:10.2307/249008

Dong, G., Wang, L., Du, X., & Potenza, M. N. (2017). Gaming Increases Craving to Gaming-Related Stimuli in Individuals With Internet Gaming Disorder. *Biological Psychiatry: Cognitive Neuroscience and Neuroimaging*, *2*(5), 404–412. PMID:29560926

Elhai, J. D., Dvorak, R. D., Levine, J. C., & Hall, B. J. (2017). Problematic smartphone use: A conceptual overview and systematic review of relations with anxiety and depression psychopathology. *Journal of Affective Disorders*, *207*, 251–259. doi:10.1016/j.jad.2016.08.030 PMID:27736736

Eric, H., Hyunji, K., Sang, S., Han, P., & Oh, W. (2016). *Excessive Dependence on Mobile Social Apps : A Rational Excessive Dependence on Mobile Social Apps*. Academic Press.

Gentile, D. (2009). Pathological Video-Game Use Among Youth Ages 8 to 18. *Psychological Science*, *20*(5), 594–602. doi:10.1111/j.1467-9280.2009.02340.x PMID:19476590

Griffiths, M. (1995). Technological addictions. In Clinical psychology forum (p. 14). Academic Press.

Griffiths, M. (2010). Internet abuse and internet addiction in the workplace. *Journal of Workplace Learning*, *22*(7), 463–472. doi:10.1108/13665621011071127

Griffiths & Nuyens, F. (2017). An Overview of Structural Characteristics in Problematic Video Game Playing. *Current Addiction Reports*, 272–283. PMID:28845381

Griffiths. (2005). A components model of addiction within a biopsychosocial framework. *Journal of Substance Use, 10*(4), 191–197.

Huang, H. (2014). *Social Media Generation in Urban China*. Academic Press.

Huang, H., & Leung, L. (2009). Instant messaging addiction among teenagers in China: Shyness, alienation, and academic performance decrement. *Cyberpsychology & Behavior*, *12*(6), 675–679. doi:10.1089/cpb.2009.0060 PMID:19788380

Hyman, S. E., Malenka, R. C., & Nestler, E. J. (2006). Neural Mechanisms of Addiction: The Role of Reward-Related Learning and Memory. *Annual Review of Neuroscience*, *29*(1), 565–598. doi:10.1146/annurev.neuro.29.051605.113009 PMID:16776597

Jenaro, C., Flores, N., Gómez-Vela, M., González-Gil, F., & Caballo, C. (2007). Problematic internet and cell-phone use: Psychological, behavioral, and health correlates. *Addiction Research and Theory*, *15*(3), 309–320. doi:10.1080/16066350701350247

Jeong, S. H., Kim, H., Yum, J. Y., & Hwang, Y. (2016). What type of content are smartphone users addicted to?: SNS vs. games. *Computers in Human Behavior*, *54*, 10–17. doi:10.1016/j.chb.2015.07.035

Jia, R., & Jia, H. H. (2009). Factorial validity of problematic Internet use scales. *Computers in Human Behavior*, *25*(6), 1335–1342. doi:10.1016/j.chb.2009.06.004

Jing, D. Z., & Hock, C. C. (2012). Government Regulation of Online Game Addiction. *Communications of the Association for Information Systems*, *30*(13), 187–198.

King, D., Delfabbro, P., & Griffiths, M. (2010). Video game structural characteristics: A new psychological taxonomy. *International Journal of Mental Health and Addiction*, *8*(1), 90–106. doi:10.100711469-009-9206-4

King, V., Valença, A. M., & Nardi, A. E. (2010). Nomophobia: the mobile phone in panic disorder with agoraphobia: reducing phobias or worsening of dependence? *Cognitive and Behavioral Neurology*, *23*(1), 52–54. doi:10.1097/WNN.0b013e3181b7eabc PMID:20299865

Kuss, D. J., & Griffiths, M. D. (2011). Online social networking and addiction a review of the psychological literature. *International Journal of Environmental Research and Public Health*, *8*(9), 3528–3552. doi:10.3390/ijerph8093528 PMID:22016701

Lee, C., Kim, H., & Hong, A. (2017). Ex-post evaluation of illegalizing juvenile online game after midnight: A case of shutdown policy in South Korea. *Telematics and Informatics*, *34*(8), 1597–1606. doi:10.1016/j.tele.2017.07.006

Li, Q., Guo, X., & Sun, C. (2012). The Shadow of Microblogging Use: Relationship Between Usage Types and Addiction. *ICIS, 9*(2), 579–612.

Mak, K. K., Nam, J. E. K., Kim, D., Aum, N., Choi, J. S., Cheng, C., Watanabe, H. (2017). Cross-cultural adaptation and psychometric properties of the Korean Scale for Internet Addiction (K-Scale) in Japanese high school students. *Psychiatry Research, 249*, 343–348.

Mingers, J. (2004). Realizing information systems: Critical realism as an underpinning philosophy for information systems. *Information and Organization, 14*(2), 87–103. doi:10.1016/j.infoandorg.2003.06.001

Ng, B. D., & Wiemer-Hastings, P. (2005). Addiction to the internet and online gaming. *Cyberpsychology & Behavior, 8*(2), 110–113. doi:10.1089/cpb.2005.8.110 PMID:15938649

Nyamadi, M., & Boateng, R. (2018). The Influence of IT Artifacts on Players Leading to Internet Gaming Addiction among University Students in Africa. In *Americas Conference on Information Systems* (pp. 1–10). New Orleans, LA: Academic Press.

Polites, G. L., Serrano, C., & Thatcher, J. B. (2018). Understanding social networking site (SNS) identity from a dual systems perspective : An investigation of the dark side of SNS use. *European Journal of Information Systems, 9344*, 1–22.

Serenko, A., & Turel, O. (2015). *Integrating Technology Addiction and Use An Empirical Investigation of Facebook Users*. Conceptual Replication. doi:10.17705/1atrr.00002

Tarafdar, M., Gupta, A., & Turel, O. (2013). The dark side of information technology use. *Information Systems Journal, 23*(3), 269–275. doi:10.1111/isj.12015

Tarafdar, M., Gupta, A., & Turel, O. (2015). Introduction to the special issue on the 'dark side of information technology use' - part two. *Information Systems Journal, 25*(4), 315–317. doi:10.1111/isj.12076

Turel, O., & Serenko, A. (2010). Is mobile email addiction overlooked? *Communications of the ACM, 53*(5), 41. doi:10.1145/1735223.1735237

Turel, O., & Serenko, A. (2012). The benefits and dangers of enjoyment with social networking websites. *European Journal of Information Systems, 21*(5), 512–528. doi:10.1057/ejis.2012.1

Turel, O., Serenko, A., & Bontis, N. (2011). Family and work-related consequences of addiction to pervasive organizational technologies. *Information & Management, 48*(2–3), 88–95. doi:10.1016/j.im.2011.01.004

Turel, O., Serenko, A., & Giles, P. (2011a). Integrating Technology Addiction and Use An Empirical Investigation of Online Auction. *Management Information Systems Quarterly, 35*(4), 1043–1061. doi:10.2307/41409972

Vaghefi, I., Lapointe, L., & Boudreau-Pinsonneault, C. (2016). A typology of user liability to IT addiction. *Information Systems Journal, 27*(2), 125–169. doi:10.1111/isj.12098

Venkatesh, V., & Bala, H. (2008). Technology acceptance model 3 and a research agenda on interventions. *Decision Sciences, 39*(2), 273–315. doi:10.1111/j.1540-5915.2008.00192.x

Venkatesh, V., Thong, J., & Xu, X. (2016). A Unified Theory of Acceptance and Use of Technology: A synthesis and the road ahead. *Journal of the Association for Information Systems*, *17*(5), 328–376. doi:10.17705/1jais.00428

Vinet, L., & Zhedanov, A. (2010). A "missing" family of classical orthogonal polynomials. *Games and Culture*, *17*(2), 1–16.

Walsh, S. P., White, K. M., Hyde, M. K., & Watson, B. (2008). Dialing and driving: Factors influencing intentions to use a mobile phone while driving. *Accident; Analysis and Prevention*, *40*(6), 1893–1900. doi:10.1016/j.aap.2008.07.005 PMID:19068291

Wang, C., Lee, M. K. O., Yang, C., & Li, X. (2016). Understanding problematic smartphone use and its characteristics: A perspective on behavioral addiction. *Lecture Notes in Information Systems and Organisation*, *17*, 215–225. doi:10.1007/978-3-319-30133-4_15

Weinstein, A., Livny, A., & Weizman, A. (2017). New developments in brain research of internet and gaming disorder. *Neuroscience and Biobehavioral Reviews*, *75*, 314–330. doi:10.1016/j.neubio-rev.2017.01.040 PMID:28193454

Weinstein, A., Maraz, A., Griffiths, M. D., Lejoyeux, M., & Demetrovics, Z. (2016). *Compulsive Buying-Features and Characteristics of Addiction. In Neuropathology of Drug Addictions and Substance Misuse* (Vol. 3). Elsevier Inc.

West, R. (2015). *Prime theory of motivation*. Academic Press.

Widyanto, L., & Griffiths, M. (2006). Internet addiction: A critical review. *International Journal of Mental Health and Addiction*, *4*(1), 31–51. doi:10.100711469-006-9009-9

Yau, Y. H. C., Pilver, C. E., Steinberg, M. A., Rugle, L. J., Hoff, R. A., Krishnan-Sarin, S., & Potenza, M. N. (2014). Relationships between problematic Internet use and problem-gambling severity: Findings from a high-school survey. *Addictive Behaviors*, *39*(1), 13–21. doi:10.1016/j.addbeh.2013.09.003 PMID:24140304

Yen, C.-F., Tang, T.-C., Yen, J.-Y., Lin, H.-C., Huang, C.-F., Liu, S.-C., & Ko, C.-H. (2009). Symptoms of problematic cellular phone use, functional impairment, and its association with depression among adolescents in Southern Taiwan. *Journal of Adolescence*, *32*(4), 863–873. doi:10.1016/j.adolescence.2008.10.006 PMID:19027941

Zhang, K., Chen, C., Zhao, S., & Lee, M. (2014). Compulsive Smartphone Use: The Roles of Flow, Reinforcement Motives, and Convenience. *35th International Conference on Information Systems*.

Zhang, K., Chongyang, C., & Matthew, L. (2014). Understanding the Role of Motives in Smartphone Addiction. *PACIS 2014 Proceedings*.

Chapter 24
Cybercrime Research:
A Review of Research Themes, Frameworks, Methods, and Future Research Directions

Jonathan Nii Barnor

iD https://orcid.org/0000-0002-4937-5220

Business School, University of Ghana, Ghana

Alfred A. Patterson

Business School, University of Ghana, Ghana

ABSTRACT

Technological advancements have transformed the way people go about their daily lives. However, this development is not without unintended consequences, as cyber-criminals have also devised ways to gain leverage. The authors conducted a literature review on 106 articles across 40 journals to bring to fore cybercrime studies that have been conducted according to the research themes, methodological approaches, level of analysis, geographical focus, and publication outlets. Themes identified in the review were categorized under an existing typology of cybercrime: cyber-trespass, cyber-deception/theft, cyber-pornography and obscenity, and cyber-violence. This review suggested two main directions for future research in terms of socio-technical and theoretical approaches with five research questions. The originality of this review stems from the fact that it is arguably one of the first reviews that have reviewed cybercrime from a holistic perspective.

INTRODUCTION

Computers and computer-related technologies have become essential tools that have significantly affected various aspects of personal and social lives, ranging from education, business, to cultural and leisure activities (Moon, McCluskey, & McCluskey, 2010). However, as technology continues to develop and evolve, so do new opportunities for criminal and undesirable behaviours (Bryant, 2008). One of such is

DOI: 10.4018/978-1-7998-2610-1.ch024

cybercrime, which constitutes a spectrum of threats with increasingly significant impact on companies, individuals and public entities (Tapanainen & Lisein, 2017).

Issues of cybercrime have enjoyed a fair share of research conceivably because it is equally climbing into the categories of an ordinary day crime. Some of the scholarly works in this field include literature that underscores the need for laws, policies and regulatory frameworks to counter the cybercrime menace (Eboibi, 2017; Gerry & Moore, 2015; Hunton, 2011; Ju, Cho, Lee, & Ahn, 2016; Sun, Shih, & Hwang, 2015; Yilma, 2014), literature that highlight financial crimes and strategies to combatting these crimes. Such crimes may include, ICT aided banking crimes, digital currency crimes and credit card fraud (Bai & Koong, 2017; Bay, Cook, Grubisic, & Nikitkov, 2014; Bolimos & Choo, 2017; Hunton, 2012; Vahdati & Yasini, 2015). Some studies also place interest in stakeholders' engagement in the fight against cybercrime (Levi & Leighton Williams, 2013; Martin & Rice, 2011; Tehrani, Manap, & Taji, 2013) and security awareness and prevention (McGee & Byington, 2013; Singleton, 2013; Vlachos, Minou, Assimakopouos, & Toska, 2011). It is however worth noting that though these literature and others not cited above possess insights in cybercrime, there exist some knowledge gaps which call for the need to conduct an extensive review in cybercrime. One of such is the gap in the theories and frameworks used in studying cybercrime (Boateng, Olumide, Isabalija, & Budu, 2011; Holt & Bossler, 2014; Jaishankar, 2008).

Regardless of the rapid interest in literature, there seems to be a lack of concentration to cybercrime literature in information systems research. Cybercrime research in information systems therefore needs a systematic approach to classify the various contribution of scholars in the field. To fill this gap, this review provides a cumulative meta-analysis of cybercrime from 2010 to 2018. This is geared towards taking stock to provide an understanding of the theories, frameworks and models used over the period. This review is also to provide an understanding of the level of analysis of the papers analysed, methodologies employed, geographical focus as well as trends across the years specified. This study further seeks to contribute to building systematic reviews of cybercrime research in information systems.

With this standpoint, this review serves as a trigger for cybercrime reviews in information systems. The object of this review is to improve understanding of the phenomenon in information systems research and also to provide direction for policy formulation and practice. This review will also provide pointers for future research that will kindle interest in cybercrime studies. In this regard, this review answers the following research questions:

1) How has cybercrime been defined in literature?
2) Which cybercrime issues and themes have been examined in research?

This paper is organised into six sections. The first section projects a broad overview of the review and brings to the fore the research questions that the study seeks to answer. The second section presents a conceptualization of cybercrime. The third section outlines the methodology for the review, while section four presents the findings of the review. Discussion, conclusion and research gaps are respectively presented in the fifth and sixth sections.

CONCEPTUALISING CYBERCRIME

One challenge scholars encounter with cybercrime research arguably is the definition of the phenomenon. As indicated by Sarre, Lau and Chang (2018) there is still no precise and clear definition of cybercrime in academic parlance. Gordon and Ford (2006) for instance posit that even though the cybercrime phenomenon is not relatively new, there has been significant confusion amongst academics, computer security experts and users as to the extent of real cybercrime. A plausible reason for this could be attributed to that fact that the phenomenon occurs in several forms, and as such researchers study it from different perspectives. Also, the complexity involved in determining the scope of cybercrime depends on the scope of the phenomenon: while some authors may consider it from computer-related crimes (e.g. Bossler & Holt, 2009; Mohurle & Patil, 2017) others may consider it from the human-focused crime with the aid of computing devices. For example dating romance scam (Buchanan & Whitty, 2014; Whitty, 2013), identity theft (Acoca, 2008; Marcum, Higgins, Ricketts, & Wolfe, 2015), cyberbullying (Hoff & Mitchell, 2009; Vazsonyi, Machackova, Sevcikova, Smahel, & Cerna, 2012), credit card fraud (Mahmoudi & Duman, 2015; Zareapoor & Shamsolmoali, 2015).

Donn Parker, one of the first researchers in computer crime studies, defined the term as any intentional act in which one or more victims suffered or could have suffered a loss, and one or more perpetrators made or could have made a gain (Parker, 1976). It is however worth noting that, Parker (1976) did not use the term cybercrime; instead, the author used computer abuse. The use of abuse in the author's definition can largely be attributed to the fact that the study fused a number of computer crimes. These included vandalism, information and property fraud or theft, financial fraud and unauthorized use or sale of service. This stance has however been critiqued by succeeding researchers (Kling, 1980; Nycum, 1976). Kling (1980) cautions that the definition of computer abuse or crime becomes problematic when a computer is tangentially associated with victimization.

Cybercrime has been perceived in different perspectives in literature. That notwithstanding, Goodman (1997) proposes three general categories of cybercrime; computer targeted crimes, computer-mediated crimes and crimes where the computer is incidental. Computer targeted crimes involve situations where an innocent party's computer system is attacked by a criminal computer intruder (Goodman, 1997). Examples of this include hacking, malware circulation, denial of service attacks, eavesdropping (Marcum, Higgins, Ricketts, & Wolfe, 2014; Mohurle & Patil, 2017; Yan, Yu, Gong, & Li, 2016). Computer-mediated crimes consist of criminal activities that use computers as tools in the commission of internet crimes, for example, internet fraud, child pornography, cyberbullying (Bai & Koong, 2017; Jansen & Leukfeldt, 2015; Salu, 2005; Vazsonyi et al., 2012). Finally, a computer is incidental to the crime if the computer itself is not required for the crime, but is used in some way connected to the criminal activity. Examples include financial records on a drug dealer's machine, an inculpatory bomb recipe discovered on a computer hard drive after an explosion in the neighbouring town (Goodman, 1997). Such crimes may go unnoticed without forensic investigations and discovery.

The turn of the 21st century also came with its convention of the definition of cyber offences. This may primarily be linked to the diverse nature that cyber deviances are perpetrated. In this regard, scholars began to specify the various crimes which their definitions encompass. Adomi and Igun (2008) for instance, conceptualized cybercrime as any unlawful conduct carried out with the use of computers, electronic and ancillary devices. The details of their study suggested that their conceptualization of cybercrime included internet fraud, computer hacking and spreading of malicious codes. Similarly, Loader and Thomas (2013) who defined cybercrime as Computer-mediated activities which are either illegal or considered illicit by certain parties which can be conducted through global electronic networks included internet fraud, computer hacking, cyberpiracy and spreading of malicious codes in their study.

With this background, we conceptualise cybercrime as any unlawful conduct executed with the aid of any computing device or other forms of ICTs. These include all three categorisations identified by Goodman (1997); computer targeted, computer-mediated and crimes where computers are incidental.

METHODOLOGY FOR REVIEW

Identification and Collection of the Literature

In conducting this review, the researchers considered only peer-reviewed articles. Peer review, according to Solomon (2007) is generally seen as vital for the roles of forming an archive of knowledge and distributing rewards. Peer review also plays a crucial role in validating the quality of research in a field. In that regard, the authors employed two levels; first by searching for articles published in the Senior Scholars' Basket of Information Systems Journals and thence to high ranking journal databases. Details of the processes have been delineated in the ensuing sections.

Data Collection and Search Process

The articles considered for this review were articles publishing between 2010 and 2018. As earlier indicated, among the publications done on cybercrime within the period under consideration, only peer-reviewed articles were considered. The articles reviewed underwent two phases: first, the senior scholars' basket of information systems research was searched to cumulate cybercrime research journal articles from information systems. The returns indicated that very few studies had been done concerning cybercrime in information systems journals. The second set of downloads were done using JSTOR, Emerald, WILEY, Science Direct, and Taylor and Francis databases. These databases were selected as a result of the supply of prime journals they provide in information systems research.

In order to ensure relevance to the research questions, the authors examined each article regarding its title, abstract and where applicable the full text. After removing duplicate articles from the filtering, 109 articles remained for the review.

Inclusion and Exclusion Criteria

In searching for the articles, the descriptors used were *cybercrime, cyber crime, cyber fraud and internet fraud*. The downloaded articles were subjected to filtering in that, editorials and reports were eliminated because as earlier stated, the study set out to include only peer-reviewed articles in the review. Further, we only considered publications that had only full-body text in English. Studies which were deemed duplicates were also excluded. Finally, the downloaded articles were subjected to filtering in that editorials and reports were rejected.

3.3 Article Categorization

A total of 109 articles across 40 journals were analysed in this review. These articles were further categorised into themes, geographical area of focus, methodology, research framework and publication outlets. The classification in terms of methodology was done according to research methods employed by the researchers in conducting their studies; be it qualitative, quantitative, mixed methods and studies that did not explicitly state their methodologies. For instance, studies that emphasize objective measurements and statistical, mathematical, or numerical analysis of data collected through polls, questionnaires, and surveys, or by manipulating pre-existing statistical data using computational techniques were categorized under quantitative. The qualitative category on the other hand involved articles that made use of case study as a research method and with data collected through interviews and observations. The mixed-method category consolidated articles that combined both the quantitative and the qualitative methodologies. Finally, studies that did not make use of any of the methodologies mentioned above were grouped under the 'not mentioned' category.

With regards to categorising the literature under geographical focus, the selected articles were grouped under either of the seven continents; Asia, Africa, North America, South America, Antarctica, Europe and Australia. However, articles that focused on more than one country were placed under cross-country, while those without any country of focus were grouped under 'no region'.

There have been several calls for future studies to explore how social theories in criminology can assist in understanding the behaviour and intention of both the victim and perpetrators in cybercrime (Boateng, Olumide, Isabalija, & Budu, 2011; Holt & Bossler, 2014; Jaishankar, 2008). This therefore mandated the researchers not to overlook the essence of categorising the literature into theoretical approaches.

Articles were further classified under level of analysis. Four levels of analysis exist in information systems research. The micro-level studies related to articles which focused on individuals and organizations whiles meso level consolidated industry-level studies. Macro studies relate to studies that are nationally focused while meta-studies related to studies that go beyond the national level — for example, regional level or cross-country studies.

Finally, the review categorised the selected articles according to their publication outlets; journals.

PRESENTATION OF FINDINGS

Publication Outlets

As indicated, a total of 109 articles across 40 journals were considered for this review. Computer Law & Security Review published the highest number of articles in cybercrime studies (17). Journal of Financial Crime followed with a total of 11 and Journal of Money Laundering Control (10). Computers and security recorded 15 while Journal of Association of Information Systems consolidated 4 of the articles published during the period. Journal of Management Information Systems, International Journal of Law, Crime and Justice, Digital Investigation all recorded 3 each. Policing: An International Journal of Police Strategies & Management, Information Systems Research, Information Management & Computer Security and Digital Policy, Regulation and Governance all consolidated 2 each while Procedia Computer Science, Journal of Criminal Justice, Journal of Corporate Accounting & Finance, International Journal of Social Economics, Info Systems Journal and Information and Computer Security amassed

1 each. Third World Quarterly, The Journal of Risk Finance, The Electronic Library, The Comparative and International Law Journal of Southern Africa, Technological Forecasting & Social Change, Security and Communication Networks, Procedia Engineering, Procedia Economics and Finance, Perspectives in Science, Managerial and Decision Economics, Journal of Strategic Information Systems, Journal of Investment Compliance, International Review of Law, Computers & Technology, International Journal of Web Information Systems, International Journal of Accounting & Information Management, Information Security Journal: A Global Perspective Information & Communications Technology Law, Foresight, Computers and Human Behaviour, Computers & Security, Computer Networks, Advances in Autism, Accounting Perspectives also recorded 1 each.

Distribution of Articles by Methodology

Articles under this section were categorised into quantitative, qualitative, mixed methods, studies that did not make use of any specific method; not stated, and Simulation and Experiment. In that regard, quantitative studies recorded the highest number with 30 papers, followed by qualitative, 27 publications. Papers that made use of mixed-method amounted to 14 of the 109 papers reviewed while those that did not make use of any methodology accounted for 27 of the paper reviewed. Finally, Simulation and Experiment consolidated 7 articles.

Literature Classification by Geographical Focus

Articles considered for this study were further categorised under countries of focus. Evidence from the review suggested that studies that generally focussed on the issues of cybercrime without being country or regional specific accounted for 47 of the articles reviewed. The distribution of articles with regional specifications are as follows, North America 15, Cross-Country 15, Asia 12, Europe 8, Africa 7 and Australia 5.

Distribution of Articles by Years of Publication

The classification according to the years of publication of the articles indicated high rates in 2011 and 2017 both 13 in number. Even though there was a steady decline in the number of articles published between 2011 and 2014, the figure rose again in 2017. A plausible reason for the few articles recorded in 2018 can be attributed to the fact that it is the year under review and the figure thus can appreciate by the end of the year.

Level of Analysis

Concerning the level of analysis which considered whether articles published consisted mostly of individual-level analysis, organisational, national or international, it was observed that most papers did not mainly focus on any of the levels as mentioned above. In that, papers categorised under general recorded 41 of the papers reviewed. The Macro-level of analyses which consists of papers that were analysed on country level recorded 30 while cross-country focused papers recorded of 20. Individual and organisational level papers consolidated 10 and 8 respectively.

Table 1. Publication Outlets of Reviewed Articles

Journals	Publication
Computer Law & Security Review	17
Computers and security	15
Journal of Financial Crime	11
Journal of Money Laundering Control	10
Computers in Human Behaviour	4
Journal of Association of Information Systems	4
Digital Investigation	3
International Journal of Law, Crime and Justice	3
Journal of Management Information Systems	3
Digital Policy, Regulation and Governance	3
Information Management & Computer Security	3
Information Systems Research	3
Policing: An International Journal of Police Strategies & Management	3
InfoSystems Journal	2
Information & Computer Security	2
International Journal of Social Economics	2
Journal of Corporate Accounting & Finance	2
Journal of Criminal Justice	2
Procedia Computer Science	2
Accounting Perspectives	1
Advances in Autism	1
Computer Networks	1
Foresight	1
Information & Communications Technology Law	1
information Security journal: A Global Perspective	1
International Journal of Accounting & Information Management	1
International Journal of Web Information Systems	1
International Review of Law, Computers & Technology	1
Journal of Investment Compliance,	1
Journal of Strategic Information Systems	1
Managerial and Decision Economics	1
Perspectives in Science	1
Procedia Economics and Finance	1
Procedia Engineering	1
Security and Communication Networks	1
Technological Forecasting & Social Change	1
The Comparative and International Law Journal of Southern Africa	1
The Electronic Library	1
The Journal of Risk Finance	1
Third World Quarterly	1

Figure 1. Literature classification by Research Methodology.

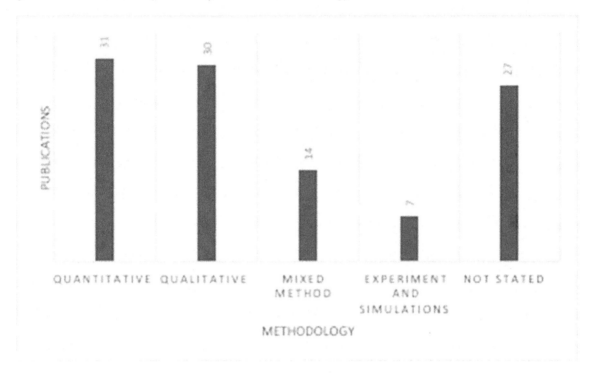

Figure 2. Literature Classification by Geographical Focus.

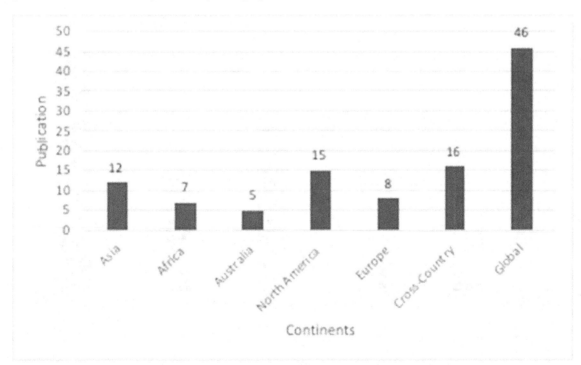

Figure 3. Literature classification by year of publication

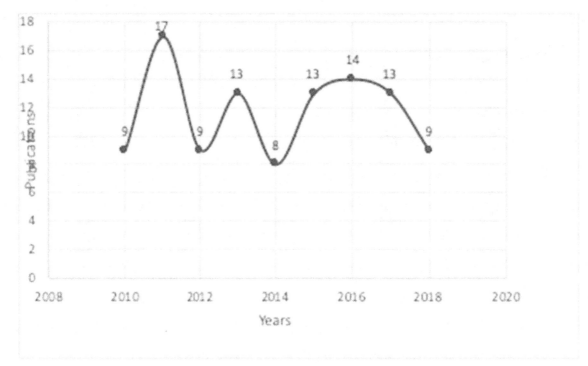

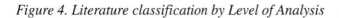

Figure 4. Literature classification by Level of Analysis

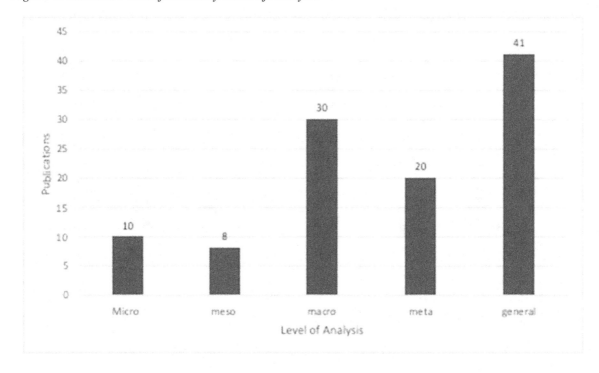

Theoretical/Conceptual Frameworks

Papers were also categorised under theories and research frameworks employed. Evidence from this respect indicated that most of the articles reviewed did not make use of theories. This category of categorisation unsurprisingly formed about 70% of the papers analysed (e.g. Arora, 2016; Lindsay, 2017; Menon & Guan Siew, 2012; Mueller, 2017). That notwithstanding, theories and frameworks used in the studies reviewed included Routine Activity Theory (e.g. Paek & Nalla, 2015; Prabowo, 2011; Reyns, 2015), Self-Control Theory (Bossler & Holt, 2010; Moon et al., 2010), General Theory of Crime (Donner, Marcum, Jennings, Higgins, & Banfield, 2014; Marcum et al., 2015). Other considerations of theory and frameworks include game theory, dynamic capabilities, integrated digital forensic process model, Technology Threat Avoidance Theory (TTAT).

Classification Framework

Cybercrime has been an issue of contention in recent times thereby attracting attention from different facets. It is against this backdrop that this review categorised the literature into themes and their subthemes. In that regard, the review categorised existing literature on various forms of technology-enabled crime using Wall (2003) four-category cybercrime typology: cyber-trespass, cyber-deception/theft, cyber-porn and obscenity, and cyber-violence. According to Holt and Bossler (2014) this is considered one of the most comprehensive frameworks to understand the incorporation of technology into various forms of offences.

The cyber-trespass category puts together studies that bordered on the crossing of invisible, yet salient boundaries of ownership on-line (Holt & Bossler, 2014). Such crimes include hacking, cracking, ransomware, botnets distribution of virus, among others (Bartholomae, 2018; Jeong, Kim, Kim, & So, 2011; Smith, 2015). The cyber-deception/theft categorisation recognises the different types of acquisitive harm that can take place within cyberspace (Wall, 2003). This category of crime reviewed included e-banking fraud, advance fee fraud, piracy, credit card fraud, consumer fraud.

The third typology is cyber-pornography and obscenity, which encompasses the range of sexual expression enabled by computer-mediated communications and the distribution of sexually explicit materials on-line (Holt & Bossler, 2014). Literature categorised under this section includes Cyber-pornography and child pornography (Hillman, Hooper, & Choo, 2014; Mthembu, 2012; Prichard, Watters, & Spiranovic, 2011; Verma, 2012). The cyber-violence category finally comprised of various ways that individuals can cause harm in real or virtual environments (Holt & Bossler, 2014). These crimes include cyber-terrorism, cyberbullying, cyberstalking and money laundering and terrorism financing.

DISCUSSION

This section presents the discussion on the findings presented in section 4 above. This section covers the publication outlets, years of publication, methodology, geographical focus, level of analysis, dominant research frameworks and finally the typologies of cybercrime studies.

Table 2. Cybercrime literature Classification framework

Theme	Sub-themes
Cyber-Trespass	Hacking, Cracking, Ransomware, Botnets Virus attacks
Cyber-deception/Theft	E-Banking Fraud, Advanced Fee Fraud, Piracy, Credit Card Fraud, Consumer Fraud
Cyber-Pornography and Obscenity	Cyber-pornography and child pornography.
Cyber-Violence	Cyber-terrorism, Cyberbullying, Cyber Stalking and money laundering and terrorism financing

Publication Outlets

As evident for from the findings provided in section 4.1, cybercrime literature cuts across most disciplines, thereby attracting interest from forty different journals from various disciplines. It is worth noting that literature reviewed from the Senior Scholars Basket cumulatively recorded 13.76% of the total papers reviewed. We believe these numbers will rise in the near future with calls for Cybercrime and Computer 'Digital' Forensics papers in the Journal of Information Systems (Apatas Technology and Society, 2018). Further, a plausible reason for this development could be as a result of the nature with which how cybercrime has been studied over a period of time. Thus, cybercrime has been studied socially focussed than the facilitating technologies that aid in the commission and mitigating cybercrime.

A critical look at the table of publication unsurprisingly revealed that Journal Computer Law & Security Review produced a chunk of studies conducted during the review period. This was predictable due to the myriad of discipline which publishes in this journal. (e.g. Intellectual Property, Information Technology, Telecommunications law, Data protection, software protection, IT contracts, Internet law, Electronic commerce, Computer Law).

Research Methodology

Observation realized from the review pointed to the fact that there were balances in the various methodologies employed in cybercrime studies. For instance, the review indicated that 31 out of the 109 papers made use of quantitative methods, while qualitative studies papers accumulated 30. This also translates into the various perspectives with which the topic is studied. For example, evidence from the root data points to the fact that papers that employed quantitative methods were mostly published in arguably positivism focused journals (e.g. Journal of Financial Crime, Journal of Money Laundering Control, Managerial and Decision Economics etc.). Considering the fact that some papers reviewed legal and regulatory frameworks and policies, a considerable amount of papers did not make use of any of the methodologies mentioned above. This again comes from the backdrop that different scholars view cybercrime from various perspectives.

Level of Analysis

The level of analysis categorization pools articles which were public with individual, organisational, national or cross-country focus. Evidence from the review points to the fact that most studies in cybercrime were general. Articles under the general category do not have specific research focus in that they seek to provide a general understanding of cybercrime. In spite of this, a significant amount of papers was published at the national-level examining the roles of institutions in the implementing policies and combating cybercrime. This direction gives credence to the fact that cybercrime needs to be tackled from the national level. It is further expected as presented in figure 4 that cross-country focus papers were also noteworthy. That notwithstanding, we believe further research focus on institutional and individual levels will be relevant at informing happenings on the ground as far as cybercrime is concerned.

Geographical Focus

This section describes the outcome of the categorization of literature according to their geographical focus. In this regard, we classified cybercrime literature under the respective continents, cross-continents and global perspectives. The outcome suggested that most of the studies conducted were globally focused. Such studies did not particularly use data source from any of the continents but discussed the issue of cybercrime generally. This finding corroborates with the finding under the level of analysis that cybercrime articles published between the period did not have specific geographical focus in that they seek to provide general understanding of cybercrime.

Nonetheless, the findings also pointed to the fact that studies in cybercrime did not nosedive the various continents. Thus, there were significant number of papers published with respect to Asia, Africa, Australia, North America and Europe. For instance, papers published with Africa in focus fixated on Nigeria, Ghana, Ethiopia and South Africa. Asian papers focused on Korea, Cambodia, Taiwan, Malaysia, India, Iran and the Kyrgyz Republic whereas papers with European focus zoomed on the United Kingdom, Greece, Cyprus and the Netherlands. As evident, most studies in cybercrime are not country-focused, it has become imperative therefore to conduct studies with data sources from individual countries. This will help in unveiling cybercriminal activities to the global communities on the perspectives of cybercriminal activities peculiar to the individual countries.

Year of Publication

Cybercrime has been given considerable attention in research over the years. Its evolutive nature therefore makes it not surprising that the publication trends do not experience numerical difference during the years of publication. Further, as technology evolves, we predict that cybercrime studies will keep evolving especially in relation to contemporary trend both in its commission and prevention. The publication trends are expected to rise in the coming years particular with the numerous calls for cybercrime research (e.g. Information Systems Journal, Crime Science, Information Technology & People etc.).

Dominant Research Frameworks in Cybercrime Studies

Theories and frameworks are essential in conducting research works. That being established, findings from the review was indicative of the fact that several theories were employed in the studies. Some of these theories and frameworks include Routine Activity Theory (Reyns, 2015; Yogi Prabowo, 2011), self-control theory (Bossler & Holt, 2010; Moon et al., 2010), Social learning theory (Marcum et al., 2015), general theory of crime (Donner et al., 2014; Marcum et al., 2015), Technology Threat Avoidance Theory (Liang & Xue, 2010).

Analysis of the findings further points to the fact that traditional cybercrime theories and frameworks employed by researchers over the period under review were relatively few. This comes to back the claim that cybercrime is multidisciplinary as such the perspectives of researchers matter in the study of the phenomenon. For example, Kraemer-Mbula, Tang and Rush (2013) used dynamic capabilities theory in conjunction with other models to study the cybercrime ecosystem. Their research examined cybercrime through an innovation lens, by examining how cybercriminals innovate, what the sources of innovation are and from where they emanate. They argued that by doing so, they contribute to the broad literature on cybercriminal activity, which is mainly populated by scholars in the fields of criminology, psychology, sociology, law and information technology.

In this regard, we link to the chorus for future studies to explore how social theories in criminal studies can help in understanding the behaviour and intention of both the victims and perpetrators in cybercrime.

Dominant Themes in Cybercrime Research

The classification scheme used for this review was adopted from Wall (2003) four-category cybercrime typology. In that regard, we identified four categories of crimes under which we classified the individual themes: cyber-trespass, cyber-deception/theft, cyber-porn and obscenity, and cyberviolence. This section will in essence explore each category in relation to the papers reviewed. The essence of this exercise is to establish relevant gaps in the and point out areas in cybercrime research that need expansion and clarification, thus pointers for future research.

Cyber-Trespass

Classification of literature under this category encompassed crime that edge on crossing boundaries into computer systems into spaces where rights of ownership or title have already been established. e.g. hacking, defacement, viruses (Ngo & Jaishankar, 2017; Wall, 2015). Sampled papers which bordered on this typology were indicative of the fact that hackers are motivated by several factors which may include perceived cost benefits and psychological benefits. Bartholomae (2018) for instance pointed out that there are three types of hackers; the good, the bad and the greedy. Ethical hackers have decent aims of making the world a better place by hacking systems to identify challenges and informing the owners of the systems about the loopholes. The main interest of bad hackers is fame among their communities. Such hackers may later transform into greedy hackers who aim to earn income from their activities. Such people hack into banking systems to steal credit card details which they sell at the credit card black market. Studies sampled under this category also identified that the hacking community could be broken into lone hackers and cyber gangs (organized) (Smith, 2015). Lone hackers have the least complex organizational structures; mostly one person in one geographical location. Literature recognizes that there are easy prosecutions of lone hackers due to the less sophistication of their attacks. This differs from that of the cybergangs as they implement a sophisticated level of operation. Governments mostly employ this group of cybercriminals in anticipation of cyber warfare. Smith (2015) surmises that in the future governments that do not have the resources or time to develop their cyber-attack centres, such as the Chinese or the USA, will hire these cyber gangs on a project-by-project basis.

Cyber-Deception/Theft

This section of classification dwelt on articles that discussed theft of material and also immaterial resources through piracy as well as credit card fraud via the Internet (Laue, 2011). Issues discussed in papers under this theme included advance fee fraud (Dobovšek, Lamberger, & Slak, 2013), banking fraud (Carminati, Caron, Maggi, Epifani, & Zanero, 2015; van der Meulen, 2013), credit card fraud (Li, Chen, & Nunamaker Jr, 2016; Papadopoulos & Brooks, 2011; Yogi Prabowo, 2011, 2012).

With regards to advanced fee fraud, papers analyzed point to the fact that advanced fee frauds are not declining in occurrence. Instead, they are continually developing and use both bulk sending and narrower targeting (Dobovšek et al., 2013). This form of crime however has the tendency of advancing into other forms of crimes (e.g. phishing, email spoofing and pilfering). Concerning credit card frauds, there were mixed concerns as to whether the phenomenon can be completely mitigated. For instance, Papadopoulos and Brooks (2011) suggest that a far more co-ordinated approach is needed to tackle credit card fraud with a lack of specialised knowledge of fraud a significant concern. Prabowo (2011) however established a common approach in preventing credit card fraud which the author believes is reducing offenders' opportunities to commit their offences, which often require a significant amount of resources and thus sound strategy needs to be properly formulated and executed. In that regard, Prabowo (2011) suggests that resources are mainly allocated to six key areas of fraud prevention: understanding of the real problems, fraud prevention policy, fraud awareness, technology-based protection, identity management and legal deterrence. These are supported in principle by four main groups in a payments system: user, institution, network and government and industry.

It is therefore worth noting that these types of frauds are global and no country is immune, nor can any country be excluded, from hosting the perpetrators (Dobovšek et al., 2013). We believe it has become a necessity to research on mitigating initiative on efforts in combatting credit card frauds.

Cyber-Porn and Obscenity

Categorization of papers for this typology saw two themes; cyber-pornography (Verma, 2012) and child pornography (Hillman et al., 2014; Mthembu, 2012; Prichard et al., 2011). Cyberspace facilitates access to child exploitation materials that were once difficult to locate, thereby providing instant access to children from all over the world or within a country (Choo, 2008). Cyber pornography is an increasingly visible problem in society today (Schell, Martin, Hung, & Rueda, 2007). Evidence from the literature reviewed indicates that although legislation and prosecutions are essential tools in the fight against online child exploitation, it is submitted that we also need to investigate alternative approaches to child exploitation.

Further other studies found that loopholes in legal and regulatory frameworks constitute the states and governments inability to deal with online child pornography adequately. In that regard, Mthembu (2012) suggest that an additional tool in combating online child pornography will be industry self-regulation, whereby industry codes of conduct and hotlines are developed and ISPs work collaboratively. ISPs are believed to be in a pivotal position to assist with combating, not just child pornography but other forms of internet crimes. Finally, focus on prevention and education is likely to go further towards protecting children from such exploitation either perpetrated by the offenders or the victims (e.g. sexting and in cases where victims were 'directed' by the offender to perform sexual acts on themselves in front of a webcam) (Simon & Choo, 2014).

Cyberviolence

The final typology borders on crimes include various ways that individuals can cause harm in real or virtual environments. Some of these crimes can be attributed to the high rate of smartphones and smart devices penetration and social media subscriptions. In that regard, unassuming people take on individual attitudes which translate into bullying online. Committed by an individual or a group of users, cyberbullying refers to the use of information and communication technology to harass others. Review of papers seems to acknowledge that cyberbullying has become a major problem along with the development of online communication and social media. Studies on cyber terrorism on the other hand have considered the subject from various perspective. E.g. economic impact (Hua & Bapna, 2013; Park, Levy, Son, Park, & Hwang, 2018), Behaviours of cyber-terrorists (Gross, Canetti, & Vashdi, 2016; Salleh, Selamat, Yusof, & Sahib, 2016) governance and mitigation (Mohamed, Jantan, & Abiodun, 2018) and Financing Cyberterrorism (Irwin, Slay, Raymond Choo, & Lui, 2014)

The studies acknowledge the internet has become a fertile ground for terrorists to obtain funds to support their operations by participating in activities ranging from credit card theft using phishing, hacking and keylogging attacks through to money laundering. As such, the studies advocated that organizations that comprise the critical national infrastructure need to invest more heavily in information security than other organizations. The studies also challenged governments to consider mitigating strategies such as subsidizing IS security investments, crafting "cyber terrorism intrusion compliance" policies, certifying such compliance, periodic IS security auditing of firms that comprise the critical national infrastructure and sharing lessons learned.

Research Gaps and Pointers for Future Research

Earlier discussions have touched on dominant issues and theoretical approaches in cybercrime studies. Based on the discussions, this section presents gaps found in the reviewed articles as well as present directions for future research. This will be done in two folds; sociotechnical approach to the study of cybercrime and secondly, theoretical approaches in cybercrime studies.

Cybercrime has been studied from various disciplines as such from various viewpoints. Notable among these perspectives is that research in the subject is either studied as purely technical or social (e.g. Ho, Lin, & Huang, 2012; Yilma, 2014, 2017). This development seems to tilt cybercrime studies towards one direction. Thus the social aspect of the phenomenon is mostly studied disregarding the roles played by the computers and systems that perpetrators employ or mediate the commission of crimes.

Evidence from reviews has identified that most cybercrime studies use components from traditional criminological theories particularly routine activity theory, social learning, and the general theory of crime (Holt & Bossler, 2014). The progressive adoption of internet and computer-related devices among people in developed and developing economies require that researchers find ways of merging traditional crime theories in studying contemporary crimes. These questions suggest directions for future research.

CONCLUSION

This study analyzed 109 studies in cybercrime. It further categorized the articles according to the year of publications, methodological approaches, level of analysis, geographical focus and publication outlets.

Table 3. Suggested questions for future research

Question	
Socio-Technical questions	• How are cybercrime perpetrators leveraging on emerging technological trends? • What are the technological determinants of cybercrime? • How does technology facilitate the commission of cybercriminal offences? • How do cybercrime perpetrators behave in cyberspace?
Theoretical Question	• How do social theories best address the contemporary issues of cybercrime?

Source: Authors' construct

Concerning the outlets of publications, it was revealed during analyses and the discussion that journals outside of the Senior Scholars' Basket of Information Systems Journals had more articles published than those that are particularly IS focused journals. A plausible reason was that cybercrime is interdisciplinary and as such, it was not surprising realizing that other journals have cumulatively published more than the those of IS orientation.

Geographically, it was evident that most cybercrime research had been conducted with no particular country in focus. This study therefore calls out that it has become imperative therefore to conduct studies with data sources from individual countries

Themes identified in the review were categorized under Wall, (2003) typology of cybercrime. This included Cyber-Trespass, Cyber-deception/Theft, Cyber-Pornography and Obscenity and Cyber-Violence. Finally, this review suggested two main directions for future research in terms of socio-technical and theoretical approaches with five research questions.

Table 4. Data Analysis

	2010	2011	2012	2013	2014	2015	2016	2017	2018	
Computer Law & Security Review	2	1	1	5	1	1		2	1	14
Computers and security		2	2	1	2	1	1	1	1	11
Journal of Financial Crime		2				4	1	2		9
Journal of Money Laundering Control		2	3	1	1	1				8
Computers in Human Behaviour					1	2	1	1		5
Journal of Association of Information Systems	1						1	1	2	5
Digital Investigation	2	1			1					4
International Journal of Law, Crime and Justice					1	2	1			4
Journal of Management Information Systems							2	2		4
Digital Policy, Regulation and Governance								3		3
Information Management & Computer Security		2		1						3
Information Systems Research	1	1	1							3
Policing: An International Journal of Police Strategies & Management			3							3
Info Systems Journal					2					2
Information & Computer Security							1		1	2
International Journal of Social Economics		2								2
Journal of Corporate Accounting & Finance				2						2
Journal of Criminal Justice	2									2
Procedia Computer Science									2	2
Accounting Perspectives				1						1
Advances in Autism						1				1
Computer Networks							1			1
Foresight								1		1
Information & Communications Technology Law		1								1
information Security journal: A Global Perspective							1			1
International Journal of Accounting & Information Management								1		1
International Journal of Web Information Systems		1								1
International Review of Law, Computers & Technology		1								1
Journal of Investment Compliance,							1			1
Journal of Strategic Information Systems				1						1
Managerial and Decision Economics								1		1
Perspectives in Science							1			1
Procedia Economics and Finance						1				1
Procedia Engineering			1							1
Security and Communication Networks							1			1
Technological Forecasting & Social Change				1						1
The Comparative and International Law Journal of Southern Africa		1								1
The Electronic Library		1								1
The Journal of Risk Finance							1			1
Third World Quarterly	1									1
	9	18	11	13	9	13	14	13	9	109

REFERENCES

Acoca, B. (2008). Online identity theft. *Organisation for Economic Cooperation and Development. The OECD Observer. Organisation for Economic Co-Operation and Development*, (268): 12.

Adomi, E. E., & Igun, S. E. (2008). Combating cyber crime in Nigeria. *The Electronic Library*, *26*(5), 716–725. doi:10.1108/02640470810910738

Apatas Technology and Society. (2018). *Information Systems Journal Special Issue on Cybercrime and Computer 'Digital' Forensics*. Retrieved from http://www.apatas.org/icccf-2018/isj/

Arora, B. (2016). Exploring and analyzing Internet crimes and their behaviours. *Perspectives on Science*, *8*, 540–542. doi:10.1016/j.pisc.2016.06.014

Bai, S., & Koong, K. S. (2017). Financial and other frauds in the United States: A panel analysis approach. *International Journal of Accounting & Information Management*, *25*(4), 413–433. doi:10.1108/IJAIM-03-2017-0033

Bartholomae, F. (2018). Cybercrime and cloud computing. A game theoretic network model. *Managerial and Decision Economics*, *39*(3), 297–305. doi:10.1002/mde.2904

Bay, D., Cook, G. L., Grubisic, J., & Nikitkov, A. (2014). Identifying fraud in online auctions: A case study. *Accounting Perspectives*, *13*(4), 283–299. doi:10.1111/1911-3838.12033

Boateng, R., Olumide, L., Isabalija, R. S., & Budu, J. (2011). Sakawa-cybercrime and criminality in Ghana. *Journal of Information Technology Impact*, *11*(2), 85–100.

Bolimos, I. A., & Choo, K.-K. R. (2017). Online fraud offending within an Australian jurisdiction. *Journal of Financial Crime*, *24*(2), 277–308. doi:10.1108/JFC-05-2016-0029

Bossler, A. M., & Holt, T. J. (2009). On-line activities, guardianship, and malware infection: An examination of routine activities theory. *International Journal of Cyber Criminology*, *3*(1).

Bossler, A. M., & Holt, T. J. (2010). The effect of self-control on victimization in the cyberworld. *Journal of Criminal Justice*, *38*(3), 227–236. doi:10.1016/j.jcrimjus.2010.03.001

Bryant, R. (2008). *Investigating digital crime*. John Wiley and Sons.

Buchanan, T., & Whitty, M. T. (2014). The online dating romance scam: Causes and consequences of victimhood. *Psychology, Crime & Law*, *20*(3), 261–283. doi:10.1080/1068316X.2013.772180

Carminati, M., Caron, R., Maggi, F., Epifani, I., & Zanero, S. (2015). BankSealer: A decision support system for online banking fraud analysis and investigation. *Computers & Security*, *53*, 175–186. doi:10.1016/j.cose.2015.04.002

Choo, K.-K. R. (2008). Organised crime groups in cyberspace: A typology. *Trends in Organized Crime*, *11*(3), 270–295. doi:10.100712117-008-9038-9

Dobovšek, B., Lamberger, I., & Slak, B. (2013). Advance fee frauds messages–non-declining trend. *Journal of Money Laundering Control*, *16*(3), 209–230. doi:10.1108/JMLC-04-2013-0012

Donner, C. M., Marcum, C. D., Jennings, W. G., Higgins, G. E., & Banfield, J. (2014). Low self-control and cybercrime: Exploring the utility of the general theory of crime beyond digital piracy. *Computers in Human Behavior, 34*, 165–172. doi:10.1016/j.chb.2014.01.040

Eboibi, F. E. (2017). A review of the legal and regulatory frameworks of Nigerian Cybercrimes Act 2015. *Computer Law & Security Review, 33*(5), 700–717. doi:10.1016/j.clsr.2017.03.020

Gerry, F. Q., & Moore, C. (2015). A slippery and inconsistent slope: How Cambodia's draft cybercrime law exposed the dangerous drift away from international human rights standards. *Computer Law & Security Review, 31*(5), 628–650. doi:10.1016/j.clsr.2015.05.008

Goodman, M. c D. (1997). Why the police don't care about computer crime. *Harvard Journal of Law & Technology, 10*, 466–494.

Gordon, S., & Ford, R. (2006). On the definition and classification of cybercrime. *Journal in Computer Virology, 2*(1), 13–20. doi:10.100711416-006-0015-z

Gross, M. L., Canetti, D., & Vashdi, D. R. (2016). The psychological effects of cyber terrorism. *Bulletin of the Atomic Scientists, 72*(5), 284–291. doi:10.1080/00963402.2016.1216502 PMID:28366962

Hillman, H., Hooper, C., & Choo, K.-K. R. (2014). Online child exploitation: Challenges and future research directions. *Computer Law & Security Review, 30*(6), 687–698. doi:10.1016/j.clsr.2014.09.007

Ho, L.-H., Lin, Y.-T., & Huang, C.-H. (2012). Influences of Online Lifestyle on Juvenile Cybercrime Behaviors in Taiwan. *Procedia Engineering, 29*, 2545–2550. doi:10.1016/j.proeng.2012.01.348

Hoff, D. L., & Mitchell, S. N. (2009). Cyberbullying: Causes, effects, and remedies. *Journal of Educational Administration, 47*(5), 652–665. doi:10.1108/09578230910981107

Holt, T. J., & Bossler, A. M. (2014). An assessment of the current state of cybercrime scholarship. *Deviant Behavior, 35*(1), 20–40. doi:10.1080/01639625.2013.822209

Hua, J., & Bapna, S. (2013). The economic impact of cyber terrorism. *The Journal of Strategic Information Systems, 22*(2), 175–186. doi:10.1016/j.jsis.2012.10.004

Hunton, P. (2011). A rigorous approach to formalising the technical investigation stages of cybercrime and criminality within a UK law enforcement environment. *Digital Investigation, 7*(3–4), 105–113. doi:10.1016/j.diin.2011.01.002

Hunton, P. (2012). Data attack of the cybercriminal: Investigating the digital currency of cybercrime. *Computer Law & Security Review, 28*(2), 201–207. doi:10.1016/j.clsr.2012.01.007

Irwin, S. M., Slay, A., Raymond, J., Choo, K.-K., & Lui, L. (2014). Money laundering and terrorism financing in virtual environments: A feasibility study. *Journal of Money Laundering Control, 17*(1), 50–75. doi:10.1108/JMLC-06-2013-0019

Jaishankar, K. (2008). Space transition theory of cyber crimes. *Crimes of the Internet*, 283–301.

Jansen, J., & Leukfeldt, R. (2015). How people help fraudsters steal their money: An analysis of 600 online banking fraud cases. In Socio-Technical Aspects in Security and Trust (STAST), 2015 Workshop On, (pp. 24–31). IEEE.

Jeong, O.-R., Kim, C., Kim, W., & So, J. (2011). Botnets: Threats and responses. *International Journal of Web Information Systems*, *7*(1), 6–17. doi:10.1108/17440081111125635

Ju, J., Cho, D., Lee, J. K., & Ahn, J.-H. (2016). *An Empirical Study on Anti-spam Legislation*. Academic Press.

Kling, R. (1980). Computer abuse and computer crime as organizational activities. *Computer/Law Journal*, *2*, 403.

Kraemer-Mbula, E., Tang, P., & Rush, H. (2013). The cybercrime ecosystem: Online innovation in the shadows? *Technological Forecasting and Social Change*, *80*(3), 541–555. doi:10.1016/j.techfore.2012.07.002

Laue, C. (2011). Crime potential of metaverses. In *Virtual Worlds and Criminality* (pp. 19–29). Springer. doi:10.1007/978-3-642-20823-2_2

Levi, M., & Leighton Williams, M. (2013). Multi-agency partnerships in cybercrime reduction: Mapping the UK information assurance network cooperation space. *Information Management & Computer Security*, *21*(5), 420–443. doi:10.1108/IMCS-04-2013-0027

Li, W., Chen, H., & Nunamaker, J. F. Jr. (2016). Identifying and profiling key sellers in cyber carding community: AZSecure text mining system. *Journal of Management Information Systems*, *33*(4), 1059–1086. doi:10.1080/07421222.2016.1267528

Liang, H., & Xue, Y. (2010). Understanding security behaviors in personal computer usage: A threat avoidance perspective. *Journal of the Association for Information Systems*, *11*(7), 394–413. doi:10.17705/1jais.00232

Lindsay, J. R. (2017). Restrained by design: The political economy of cybersecurity. *Digital Policy. Regulation & Governance*, *19*(6), 493–514. doi:10.1108/DPRG-05-2017-0023

Loader, B. D., & Thomas, D. (2013). *Cybercrime: Security and surveillance in the information age*. Routledge. doi:10.4324/9780203354643

Mahmoudi, N., & Duman, E. (2015). Detecting credit card fraud by modified Fisher discriminant analysis. *Expert Systems with Applications*, *42*(5), 2510–2516. doi:10.1016/j.eswa.2014.10.037

Marcum, C. D., Higgins, G. E., Ricketts, M. L., & Wolfe, S. E. (2014). Hacking in high school: Cybercrime perpetration by juveniles. *Deviant Behavior*, *35*(7), 581–591. doi:10.1080/01639625.2013.867721

Marcum, C. D., Higgins, G. E., Ricketts, M. L., & Wolfe, S. E. (2015). Becoming someone new: Identity theft behaviors by high school students. *Journal of Financial Crime*, *22*(3), 318–328. doi:10.1108/JFC-09-2013-0056

Martin, N., & Rice, J. (2011). Cybercrime: Understanding and addressing the concerns of stakeholders. *Computers & Security*, *30*(8), 803–814. doi:10.1016/j.cose.2011.07.003

McGee, J. A., & Byington, J. R. (2013). How to counter cybercrime intrusions. *Journal of Corporate Accounting & Finance*, *24*(5), 45–49. doi:10.1002/jcaf.21874

Menon, S., & Guan Siew, T. (2012). Key challenges in tackling economic and cyber crimes: Creating a multilateral platform for international co-operation. *Journal of Money Laundering Control, 15*(3), 243–256. doi:10.1108/13685201211238016

Mohamed, N. A., Jantan, A., & Abiodun, O. I. (2018). Protect Governments, and organizations Infrastructure against Cyber Terrorism (Mitigation and Stop of Server Message Block (SMB) Remote Code Execution Attack). *International Journal of Engineering, 11*(2), 261–272.

Mohurle, S., & Patil, M. (2017). A brief study of wannacry threat: Ransomware attack 2017. *International Journal of Advanced Research in Computer Science, 8*(5).

Moon, B., McCluskey, J. D., & McCluskey, C. P. (2010). A general theory of crime and computer crime: An empirical test. *Journal of Criminal Justice, 38*(4), 767–772. doi:10.1016/j.jcrimjus.2010.05.003

Mthembu, M. A. (2012). High road in regulating online child pornography in South Africa. *Computer Law & Security Review, 28*(4), 438–444. doi:10.1016/j.clsr.2012.05.010

Mueller, M. (2017). Is cybersecurity eating internet governance? Causes and consequences of alternative framings. *Digital Policy. Regulation & Governance, 19*(6), 415–428. doi:10.1108/DPRG-05-2017-0025

Ngo, F., & Jaishankar, K. (2017). Commemorating a Decade in Existence of the International Journal of Cyber Criminology: A Research Agenda to Advance the Scholarship on Cyber Crime. *International Journal of Cyber Criminology, 11*(1).

Nycum, S. (1976). The criminal law aspects of computer abuse: Part I–state penal laws. *RUTGERS J. COMPUTERS & L., 5*, 271–276.

Paek, S. Y., & Nalla, M. K. (2015). The relationship between receiving phishing attempt and identity theft victimization in South Korea. *International Journal of Law, Crime and Justice, 43*(4), 626–642. doi:10.1016/j.ijlcj.2015.02.003

Papadopoulos, A., & Brooks, G. (2011). The investigation of credit card fraud in Cyprus: Reviewing police "effectiveness.". *Journal of Financial Crime, 18*(3), 222–234. doi:10.1108/13590791111147442

Park, J., Levy, J., Son, M., Park, C., & Hwang, H. (2018). Advances in Cybersecurity Design: An Integrated Framework to Quantify the Economic Impacts of Cyber-Terrorist Behavior. In Security by Design (pp. 317–339). Springer.

Parker, D. B. (1976). Computer abuse perpetrators and vulnerabilities of computer systems. *Proceedings of the National Computer Conference and Exposition*, 65–73. 10.1145/1499799.1499810

Prabowo, H. Y. (2011). Building our defence against credit card fraud: A strategic view. *Journal of Money Laundering Control, 14*(4), 371–386. doi:10.1108/13685201111173848

Prichard, J., Watters, P. A., & Spiranovic, C. (2011). Internet subcultures and pathways to the use of child pornography. *Computer Law & Security Review, 27*(6), 585–600. doi:10.1016/j.clsr.2011.09.009

Reyns, B. W. (2015). A routine activity perspective on online victimisation: Results from the Canadian General Social Survey. *Journal of Financial Crime, 22*(4), 396–411. doi:10.1108/JFC-06-2014-0030

Salleh, N. M., Selamat, S. R., Yusof, R., & Sahib, S. (2016). Discovering Cyber Terrorism Using Trace Pattern. *International Journal of Network Security*, *18*(6), 1034–1040.

Salu, A. O. (2005). Online crimes and advance fee fraud in Nigeria-are available legal remedies adequate? *Journal of Money Laundering Control*, *8*(2), 159–167. doi:10.1108/13685200510621091

Sarre, R., Lau, L. Y.-C., & Chang, L. Y. C. (2018). *Responding to cybercrime: current trends*. Taylor & Francis.

Schell, B. H., Martin, M. V., Hung, P. C. K., & Rueda, L. (2007). Cyber child pornography: A review paper of the social and legal issues and remedies—and a proposed technological solution. *Aggression and Violent Behavior*, *12*(1), 45–63. doi:10.1016/j.avb.2006.03.003

Simon, M., & Choo, K.-K. R. (2014). *Digital forensics: challenges and future research directions*. Academic Press.

Singleton, T. (2013). Fighting the Cybercrime Plague. *Journal of Corporate Accounting & Finance*, *24*(5), 3–7. doi:10.1002/jcaf.21869

Smith, G. S. (2015). Management models for international cybercrime. *Journal of Financial Crime*, *22*(1), 104–125. doi:10.1108/JFC-09-2013-0051

Solomon, D. J. (2007). The role of peer review for scholarly journals in the information age. *The Journal of Electronic Publishing: JEP*, *10*(1). doi:10.3998/3336451.0010.107

Sun, J.-R., Shih, M.-L., & Hwang, M.-S. (2015). Cases study and analysis of the court judgement of cybercrimes in Taiwan. *International Journal of Law, Crime and Justice*, *43*(4), 412–423. doi:10.1016/j.ijlcj.2014.11.001

Tapanainen, T., & Lisein, O. (2017). *Mindfulness in Cyber-Security: The Case of a Government Agency*. Academic Press.

Tehrani, P. M., Manap, N. A., & Taji, H. (2013). Cyber terrorism challenges: The need for a global response to a multi-jurisdictional crime. *Computer Law & Security Review*, *29*(3), 207–215. doi:10.1016/j.clsr.2013.03.011

Vahdati, S., & Yasini, N. (2015). Factors affecting internet frauds in private sector: A case study in cyberspace surveillance and scam monitoring agency of Iran. *Computers in Human Behavior*, *51*, 180–187. doi:10.1016/j.chb.2015.04.058

van der Meulen, N. S. (2013). You've been warned: Consumer liability in Internet banking fraud. *Computer Law & Security Review*, *29*(6), 713–718. doi:10.1016/j.clsr.2013.09.007

Vazsonyi, A. T., Machackova, H., Sevcikova, A., Smahel, D., & Cerna, A. (2012). Cyberbullying in context: Direct and indirect effects by low self-control across 25 European countries. *European Journal of Developmental Psychology*, *9*(2), 210–227. doi:10.1080/17405629.2011.644919

Verma, A. (2012). Cyber pornography in India and its implication on cyber cafe operators. *Computer Law & Security Review*, *28*(1), 69–76. doi:10.1016/j.clsr.2011.11.003

Vlachos, V., Minou, M., Assimakopouos, V., & Toska, A. (2011). The landscape of cybercrime in Greece. *Information Management & Computer Security, 19*(2), 113–123. doi:10.1108/09685221111143051

Wall, D. (2003). *Crime and the Internet.* Routledge. doi:10.4324/9780203299180

Wall, D. S. (2015). The Internet as a conduit for criminal activity. In A. Pattavina (Ed.), *Information Technology and the Criminal Justice System* (pp. 77–98). Thousand Oaks, CA: Sage.

Whitty, M. T. (2013). The scammers persuasive techniques model: Development of a stage model to explain the online dating romance scam. *British Journal of Criminology, 53*(4), 665–684. doi:10.1093/bjc/azt009

Yan, Q., Yu, F. R., Gong, Q., & Li, J. (2016). Software-defined networking (SDN) and distributed denial of service (DDoS) attacks in cloud computing environments: A survey, some research issues, and challenges. *IEEE Communications Surveys and Tutorials, 18*(1), 602–622. doi:10.1109/COMST.2015.2487361

Yilma, K. M. (2014). Developments in cybercrime law and practice in Ethiopia. *Computer Law & Security Review, 30*(6), 720–735. doi:10.1016/j.clsr.2014.09.010

Yilma, K. M. (2017). Ethiopia's new cybercrime legislation: Some reflections. *Computer Law & Security Review, 33*(2), 250–255. doi:10.1016/j.clsr.2016.11.016

Yogi Prabowo, H. (2011). Building our defence against credit card fraud: A strategic view. *Journal of Money Laundering Control, 14*(4), 371–386. doi:10.1108/13685201111173848

Yogi Prabowo, H. (2012). A better credit card fraud prevention strategy for Indonesia. *Journal of Money Laundering Control, 15*(3), 267–293. doi:10.1108/13685201211238034

Zareapoor, M., & Shamsolmoali, P. (2015). Application of credit card fraud detection: Based on bagging ensemble classifier. *Procedia Computer Science, 48*, 679–685. doi:10.1016/j.procs.2015.04.201

Chapter 25
The Political Use of Social Networking Sites in Turkey:
A Systematic Literature Analysis

Burak Gökalp
https://orcid.org/0000-0002-0652-5903
Pamukkale University, Turkey

Naci Karkın
https://orcid.org/0000-0002-0321-1212
Pamukkale University, Turkey

Huseyin Serhan Calhan
https://orcid.org/0000-0002-5367-4020
Akdeniz University, Turkey

ABSTRACT

There are many developments affecting societal, cultural, and political relations. The ubiquitous spread of information and communication tools (ICTs) are among these developments. Studies in literature are not indifferent to the impacts brought about in politics by ICTs, particularly by social networking sites (SNSs). During the research, many studies were found that focus on changes and transformations induced by ICTs that unprecedentedly affect interactions and relationships in political life. SNSs, a part of ICTs, have transformative effects on elected and their voters. Though there are many papers that focus on SNSs and political use of SNSs, a void was observed in relevant literature focusing on synthesizing the literature on particular country cases. For this reason, a systematic literature analysis was performed. Findings of this chapter on the political use of SNSs in Turkey indicate that political actors do not fully take advantage of SNSs and their potentialities. The political use of SNSs presents a rhizomatic formation rather than being hierarchical.

DOI: 10.4018/978-1-7998-2610-1.ch025

INTRODUCTION

Developments in information and communications technologies (ICTs) have transformed many facets of society, including political and democratic relationships among citizens and representatives. What is previously seen difficult is regarded a routine of daily life lately with regard to access to information and political participation at the individual level. For example, paying bills using ICT tools, face to face communication through online means, appealing to administration through online means, even online voting in some countries are among these transformations. There is also a transformation with regard to ICTs use. The shift in web 1.0 to web 2.0 or web 3.0 also introduces new ways and potentialities to understand politics and to involve in political matters. Particularly, the growing rate of internet penetration in urban and rural fields supports a new media environment and political culture. In addition to the existence of actual life (offline), people also could have an existence in online platforms, mainly through social network sites (SNSs). It is arguable that the line between online and offline existence is being gradually ambiguous. Although there is an interaction between offline and online spheres, SNSs play a serious role to influence the offline sphere.

The digital behaviors of users is drawn attention in various disciplines such as marketing (Paquette, 2013; Alalwan, Rana, Dwivedi, & Algharabat, 2017), branding (Gancho, 2017; Alam & Khan, 2015), computer science (Thelwall, 2017), education (Tess, 2013; Hashim, Tan, & Rashid, 2015), health care (Merolli, Gray, & Martin-Sanchez, 2013), administration (Alryalat, Rana, Sahu, Dwivedi, & Tajvidi, 2017) and politics (Shirky, 2011). This chapter focuses on the political use of SNSs in a particular country by conducting a systematic literature analysis.

Technology through media serves well as a political mediator for various cases at different times. For instance, according to Benedict Anderson (1983), the emergence of nationalism is associated with the development of printing technologies (newspapers, books or any other printed outlets). Goebbels, notorious propaganda Minister of Germany at that time, used the radio in order to forge a legitimate basis for Nazi policies. Similarly, television (TV) is assessed as a political mediator in two aspects. Some scholars like Baudrillard (1981), criticized media in the context of the TV with regard to cultural formation and regeneration. Jhally and Livant (1986) pointed out the economy-politic relationship developed behind the TV screen. It is important to highlight that all studies and policies mentioned above are dominated through a top-down manner. That means neither printed materials nor radio/TV allow two-way communication. That is why media research mainly and mostly focuses on state formation, capitalism, or the critical cultural perspective aiming to reveal who the actual actors are that positioned behind.

It is worth note that the domination of the top-down manner is about to be replaced by communication technologies enabling two-way, or multi-way interaction. Shirky (2011, p. 29) remarks the change by giving examples of how short text messaging (SMS) contributed to collective action movements such as 2004 protests in Spain, and 2009 protests in Moldova.

Today relationships between media and politics are tackled in the context of social networking sites (SNSs). There are at least two reasons. First, social media does not present a one-way communication or information provision environment by public authorities but it is also interactively used by common people for many purposes, including political ones. People participate in online political discussions; use SNSs as a news source to feed in addition to employing them as a means of collective action. Secondly, political actors prefer SNSs to impel constituencies to move or search for ways to legitimate actions and discourses by dispersing them as wide as possible. For these very reasons, it is arguable that neither politicians nor the academicians are indifferent to ICTs (Sobaci & Karkin, 2013; Zhang, Johnson, Seltzer,

& Bichard, 2010), and their induced effects on politics. The effects of SNSs are remarkable particularly in getting interaction with young constituents (Baumgartner & Morris, 2010).

Induced by reality, SNSs are growing to form a research base, particularly of politics. This paper aims to contribute to SNSs research field by employing a systematic literature analysis on the extant literature on the political use of social media in Turkey, an emergent developing country.

This chapter has four sections. The first section presents a conceptual background for the political use of SNSs. Then the following section presents our review methodology with regard to conducting literature analysis. The methodology is followed by a section devoted to findings and discussion. The last section involves some conclusions.

BACKGROUND

This part is devoted to providing a conceptual background of SNSs, particularly its use of an interactive communication tool for campaigning purposes in politics. As is known, politicians are not indifferent to employ any communication tool (Sobaci & Karkin, 2013) to spread opinions, discourses and arguments to influence the respective constituents, if not all the voters. In addition to traditional communications tools (i.e. traditional media like newspapers, radio, television, and outlets), politicians also use ICTs and social media tools. As Kruikemeier, Gattermann and Vliegenthart (2018, p. 215) assert media coverage is crucial for political actors, particularly during campaigns and election times, to convey their political stance and viewpoints to the electorate. SNSs are particularly popular for having multi-way communication as opposed to one-way communication provided by traditional media (Arsono & Kusumawati, 2018) after "political communication and campaigning have been dominated by a top-down, asymmetrical pattern" for decades (Medina & Muñoz, 2014, p. 84) through traditional means.

As a new medium, one has to give some remarks on the political use of SNSs in general. For instance, due to its widespread use in Turkey, Twitter is concise and has an interactive nature presenting a functionality of reciprocity. Twitter also provides a medium for political discourses by broadening the public debates and facilitating social connectivity (Medina & Muñoz, 2014) and by constituting a novel arena as a mediation of public communication (Larsson & Moe, 2011).

Starting with the widespread use of the internet infrastructures, ICTs and SNSs have been densely employed in politics, particularly for campaigning purposes (Evans, Brown, & Wimberly, 2018). For example, Francia (2018) gives an example over Trump's candidacy that he successfully employed Twitter as unpaid or free media support for his campaign. Yet it is argued that we do not know the exact interaction between social media and democracy and how they have interacted since it is not fully open to researchers (Margetts, 2019, p. 107). However, changes and developments in technology have made an unprecedented transformation in how democracy and political system work as we know. There is a continuing discussion on whether, and if, how technology transforms the public sphere (Sun, 2018). Nonetheless, the experience that ICTs and social media tools already widens the political sphere to the engagement of ordinary citizens as both informants and contributors. Bay (2018) argues that political affection via manipulation and perception management of social media discussions is not just pertaining to the political sphere. They are also dispersed through popular culture by influencing the daily lives of ordinary people.

A meta-analysis made by Boulianne (2015) on social media use and participation clearly shows that there is a strong positive relationship between them found in the relevant literature. Margetts (2019) argues that social media tools have fuelled volatility and instability into politics that makes really hard to grasp what is going on and what to follow next, injecting unpredictability. If elections are in question, this should not be surprising because, as Bimber (2014, p. 130) argues "election campaigns are communications campaigns" in essence. Thus, politicians should follow up the challenges as brought by the technological developments, or any other determining and innovating factors. Bimber (2014) shows the campaigns of Obama in 2008, and a sophisticated one in 2012 among re-electing factors as how a politician should align his/her campaign adapting the changes induced by ICTs. Findings in the literature are not linear and aligned, mostly dependent on contextual factors. For example, Boulianne (2015, p. 524) argues that metadata derived from the regarded literature "suggest that social media use has minimal impact on participation in election campaigns" while Larsson and Moe (2013, p. 71) show some findings indicating "that while the bulk of the studied activity bares characteristics of a representative public sphere, traces of a participatory public sphere were also discerned". Despite a divergence about the Twitter effect on public participation, the literature significantly offers the role of Twitter as "a proxy for public opinion" to anticipate the results of elections (McKelvey, DiGrazia, & Rojas, 2014) since it has the potential to create performative power followed by the representational power through agenda-setting and framing during the presidential campaigns (Kreiss, 2016).

As main figures in the political arena, particularly at the discursive level, political candidates are expected to use various means, including information and communication technologies (ICTs) and new media tools, as such there lays strong feasibility to reach all the constituents. New media technologies also paved the way for those who are interested in information gathering for politics and political processes (Tewksburry, 2006). This is something concurrent with the inclination of personalization of politics in daily lives through ICTs and social media tools (Kim, 2012). It is also notable that growing rates of inclusion and participation in social media sites produce an impact to change the nature of mutual relations among peers, seemingly altering the very nature of political and public dialogue (Rodríguez, 2017). For this very reason, it is arguable that a growing number of scholars "have turned their attention to how socially mediated networks influence news consumption, political discourse, and political attitude formation" (de Zúñiga, Barnidge, & Diehl, 2018, p. 302). Among others, social media tools have the potentiality to impact the interactions between politicians and their respective constituents, including communications for various discourses during political campaigns. Contrary to traditional outlets, Sandberg and Öhberg (2017) argue that social media tools provide the political candidates with better control over self-images and discourses, potentially open to filtered interpretation. Yavuz, Karkin, Parlak, and Subay (2018) cite that Twitter, serving as a microblogging site with 280-character length postings commonly known as tweets, provides ordinary people with many options to use for peer communications, irrespective of any segment in society (Shi, Rui, & Whinston, 2014), including professional practices. SNSs use, in general, may range from having a social presence (Dunlap & Lowenthal 2009) and increasing online visibility/popularity (Vergeer, 2017) to spreading political messages (Guerrero-Solé, 2017) and interacting with voters (Graham, Broersma, Hazelhoff, & van 't Haar, 2013). Ikiz, Sobaci, Yavuz, and Karkin (2014) argue that Twitter, as an easy and diffusive SNS medium of communication with the public, is spectacularly functional to politicians to spread their arguments and opinions without any other mediating tools (Han & Kim, 2009). Twitter, as an SNS tool, is mainly employed as a mainstreaming medium of political interactions with all stakeholders during societal or political events (Hsu & Park, 2011). In this sense, SNSs are functional for personal and continuous dialogue (Enli & Skogerbø, 2013) with all the stakeholders including voters. For their importance and widespread use, academics are not indifferent to examine SNSs for political purposes. Thus there are papers that evaluate the impact of SNSs for political purposes (Hargittai & Litt, 2011; Hambrick, Simmons, Greenhalgh, & Greenwell, 2010; Aharony, 2012; Hughes, Rowe, Batey, & Lee, 2012).

SOCIAL MEDIA AS A POLITICAL TOOL

How Literature Pictures Political Use?

A systematic literature analysis is "a means of identifying, evaluating and interpreting all available research relevant to a particular research question, or topic area, or phenomenon of interest" (Budgen & Brereton, 2006, p. 1052). There are two ways to analyze the given literature as author-centric and concept-centric papers. Literature analysis is concept-centric by its nature. It is because the author-centric system fails to synthesize the literature (Webster & Watson, 2002, p. xvi). Performing a systematic literature analysis actually indicates that the level of accumulated knowledge and maturity of the field is sufficient to make use of some implications or deductions to shed light on future contributions. Thus, the systematic literature analysis is used to save cost and time to analyze and to synthesize the prior studies in the literature (Fisch & Block, 2018) while comprehending approaches, tendencies, and attitudes towards a specific field in a specific context. The analysis allows combining different answers to specific research questions and provides necessary data in order to explain consistencies as well as inconsistencies by arguing research mediators and findings (Roshental & DiMatteo, 2001, p. 61). There are a number of different reasons why a systematic literature review should be employed. Amongst all, Budgen and Brereton (2006, p. 1052) designate the common reasons as follows:

- To summarize existing literature.
- To designate places where the gaps in the literature are present.
- To help researchers about whether and how arguments are supported or not in previous studies.

The process of performing a systematic literature analysis begins with the formulation of a research question(s). The next step is collecting regarded studies within the particular frame of specific inclusion and exclusion criteria. After this stage, a comprehensive summary of the literature can be obtained by implementing the predetermined research questions to the arguments, findings, and conclusions (Crowther, Lim, & Crowther, 2010, pp. 3140-3141).

The reason for the selection of this methodology is because a systematic analysis of a diverse group of available studies may be beneficial to inform about the state of knowledge, to detect compatible methodologies and to focus on the political use of social media tools in Turkey.

For analysis, the following questions were formulated;

RQ1: What is the role of social media in the process of constructing a collective action movement in Turkey?
RQ2: What is the political actor's usage of social media in order to manipulate public opinion in Turkey?

The systematic analysis includes journal articles, book chapters, and conference papers. The research was conducted through the Google Scholar database by searching in two different languages, English and Turkish. To obtain results in English, "social media" and "Turkey" were employed as keywords as

Table 1. Distribution of the Studies

	Article	Book Chapter	Conference Papers	TOTAL
English	11	5	1	16
Turkish	3	-	-	3
TOTAL	14	5	1	19

together in the search engine. In order to attain a full range of studies in Turkish, "*Sosyal Medya*" and "*Türkiye*" were used as keywords together. The reason why two different languages were used is to reach a wider scope, thus to acquire more accurate conclusions. This concern was justified at the end of the elimination process. After elimination, the results showed that most of the studies in the extant literature were in English. In other words, if the conducting language were just the Turkish language, then it could have been culminated with inaccurate conclusions due to neglecting a huge part of the extant literature.

Regarding the studies in the English language, 110 papers were reached as of July 8, 2018. Also, 40 papers were found written in Turkish.

After collecting the papers, two folded elimination process was conducted in order to designate which study is compatible with the context of the research. The first phase of elimination was macro elimination in order to provide compatible articles with the research context. The second phase is micro elimination. The aim of micro elimination was finding compatible articles with the research questions (RQ1 and RQ2).

At first, macro elimination was run by removing the patents, quotations, and other studies like reviews and dissertations, in addition to non-academic sources such as reports or newspaper articles from the studies listed on Google Scholar. In the sequel of this elimination process, 48 English and 15 Turkish studies were found in total.

Following this step, micro elimination was posed in order to find compatible studies with the research questions. For this phase of elimination, all listed articles were read and the ones that directly relatable with the RQs were selected to proceed. The micro elimination criteria were as follows;

1. Is it relatable with RQ 1?
2. Is it relatable with RQ 2?

Finally, sixteen English and three Turkish, a total of nineteen articles were selected to analyze under the guidance of research questions and research context.

The data obtained from the analysis were primarily analyzed in connection with research questions (RQs). The articles selected to discuss the role of social media in the process of constructing a collective action movement and the political actor's usage of social media in order to manipulate public opinion in Turkey. A summary of the papers with regard to authors, methodology, core issue, scope/context of the paper, and a short conclusion was presented in Table 2.

The Function of Social Media to Enable Collective Action in Turkey

With regard to the RQ1, the topics of the papers are classified as a collective action. The analysis shows us two different manners inside of this classification, to control social media in order to avoid

Table 2. A Summary of Analyzed Papers

	Author(s)	Methodology	Core Issue	Scope/context of the study	Conclusion
1	Yolbulan Okan, Topcu, &Akyuz (2014)	Descriptive	Elections, Political Marketing, and Political Parties	Political marketing and the impact of social media usage on voters during March 30, 2014, local elections in Turkey.	The paper aims to examine the effects of political marketing, particularly aiming to present the effects of using social media on voters in the March 2014 local elections in Turkey.
2	Haciyakupoglu & Zhang (2015)	Qualitative	Collective Action	The role of Social Media played during Gezi Park Protests by focusing on how trust was constructed and maintained among protesters.	The most trusted information sources are visuals such as photos and videos. Although protesters put their trust videos and photos on Facebook, due to the low internet speed, they could not be able to use it extensively. Authors also stress that social media is not the reason of Gezi Park protests; it is only a preferable mediator in order to have information and get organized.
3	Demirhan (2014b)	Qualitative	Collective Action	Analysis of Twitter in order to reveal the role of Twitter during the Gezi Park protests by employing an analysis of the use of hashtags. The study focuses on how Twitter was used for collective gathering.	In Gezi Park, Twitter provides personal participation and compensate for mainstream/old media's deficiency with new media. On the other hand, social media is not independent of the offline world and offline politics. Twitter is a mediator to make digital "visible" to offline oppressed opinions and activities. In this case, interconnectedness reveals itself. Because even though social media is an "extension" of offline debates, social media also affects the opinions and activities in the offline world.
4	Çetinkaya, Şahin, & Kırık (2014)	Qualitative	Elections, Political Marketing, and Political Parties	The study focuses on information exchanges on social network sites and their political and social reflections.	The study shows that people tend to use social media for shopping, sports, and economic issues. After the Gezi Park protests, social media usage in order to collect domestic information increased. The research also reveals the fact that people do not trust social media in political and social unity sense. Participants state that social media has very little or no influence on politics. A few of them think social media can divide society into different ideological camps.
5	Balca (2015)	Qualitative	Collective Action	An analyze which examines new forms of protest in the digital sphere such as viral images, memes, and widely shared posts by protesters during Gezi Park demonstrations on social media.	The alternative media, namely new media, constitutes a basis for a new kind of collectivity. During the Gezi Park, people created a network society by liking, sharing and tweeting. Thus the traditional understanding of "collectivity" is altered by new media tools. Today the protesters are representing themselves as "being-with" which means they participate in the "action" but not everyone shares the same background, ideology or political tendency rather than the one-solid-body collectivity understanding. Gezi Park protests are an example of a new "being-with" kind of collective action.
6	Bayraktutan et al. (2013)	Mixed	Elections, Political Marketing, and Political Parties	The analysis argues that the role of social media usage and the content of messages. The authors analyzed the content of the messages to reveal how leaders and party members define democracy and democratic participation during the 2011 General Elections.	The article argues that the election-winning party is also the most twitter-user party. Secondly, the article claims that the ones that invested more in web 1.0 are also successful to use social media which are part of web 2.0 technologies.
7	Saka (2018)	Qualitative	Elections, Political Marketing, and Political Parties	The article focuses on the pro-government trolls in the context of shaping hegemony and counter-hegemony realms during Gezi Park Protests in 2013.	AKP is using social media officially and in unofficial ways. Aktrolls are the unofficial way. Aktrolls are using some methods in order to reshape public opinion such as; functioning as a form of social lynching, acquiring famous social media accounts using bot accounts, mobilizing non-Turkish languages and phishing of political purposes.
8	Hafdell (2014)	Qualitative	Collective Action	The study argues that social media is not just an alternative to mainstream media. It is also a complicated and new way to participate in politics.	Social Media is not only an alternative media tool, but it is also a sphere that counter-hegemonic representation can be materialized. The problematic relationships between political power, state, and the traditional media also reflect the same problems on social media. As a consequence, social media cannot come to life as an alternative media tool because of the self-censorship mechanism and pro-government staff (trolls) employed by the government.
9	Gündüz & Erdem-Kaya (2017)	Qualitative	Collective Action	The study mainly focuses on nationalist discourse in digital communities on social media sites. The authors also reveal the resistances and oppositions in the cultural and social sense.	Liking or sharing about "Turkish oriented content" is an indicator of "Turkishness" in the digital sphere. For instance, Facebook groups such as "Ataturk" or "Turkish Flag" constitute a basis in order to create a "Turkishness" feeling.
10	Güneyli, Ersoy, & Kıralp (2017)	Qualitative	Elections, Political Marketing, and Political Parties	The research focuses on the 2015 Election process in the context of approaches of terrorism of six political party leaders.	The study reveals that all six political actors have different approaches and definitions of "terrorism". Apart from this, the political actors use social media in order to target young citizens. Also, social media provide a suitable place for interactive political communication in which the actors are able to have the feedback instantly. Besides, the study points out those users are not just interested in domestic affairs but also interested in foreign affairs. Finally, social media is reflecting the agenda of the offline political sphere because the government desires the shape the society and one of the most influential tools to accomplish in social media.
11	Karataş & Saka (2017)	Qualitative	Collective Action	Analysis of Trolls after Gezi Park protests.	The Trolls are targeting opposition and accuse them of being a terrorist, traitors and so forth. They use a polarizing language based on religion and nationalism and labeling the "other" based on these.

continued on following page

Table 2. Continued

	Author(s)	Methodology	Core Issue	Scope/context of the study	Conclusion
12	Dursun (2013)	Qualitative	Collective Action	The study argues the control of political power on social media in Turkey, during the Gezi Park Resistance.	During the Gezi Park events, the government was successful to control the mainstream media. On the other hand, due to the international capital structure of Facebook and Twitter, the government is not successful to control social media sites. Because of these circumstances, the government employed pro-government staff assigned to generate pro-government content on social media and made some juridical amendments in order to overcome this difficulty.
13	Kurt & Karaduman (2012)	Qualitative	Elections, Political Marketing, and Political Parties	The study aims to examine the political usage of social media by parties that are represented in the parliament.	The social media awareness levels of Turkish politicians are not at an effective level.
14	Yüksel (2018)	Qualitative	Elections, Political Marketing, and Political Parties	The study analyzes policies of social media usage by the party in power in Turkey.	In the inner circle, the government is employing people (trolls) in order to create more powerful social media policies. In the outer circle, they make juridical amendments to provide a lawful base in order to make people less critical.
15	Demirhan (2014a)	Qualitative	Elections, Political Marketing, and Political Parties	The study analyzes the social media usage that is employed by political parties that a part of the members of the Grand National Assembly of Turkey after the 2011 elections.	The ruling and opposition parties do not use the whole capacity of social media. The study concludes that political parties are not targeting to develop interactive participation, particularly for the ruling party is engaging in creating public opinion via sharing messages to promote their goals.
16	Aydin & Guler (2016)	Qualitative	Collective Action	The article focuses on how the AKP implemented their policies on social media in order to create its own hegemony.	The government is using juridical amendments to enable them to block internet sites in order to construct their hegemony over Turkish society and state. People are oppressed by accusing "insulting the president", "violation family values" etc. Due to their social media activities.
17	Bayraktutan *et al.* (2014)	Mixed	Elections and Political Marketing, Political Parties	This study, analyzes social media, as an aspect of political communication, usage of political parties and leaders of political parties by using qualitative and quantitative methods. The aim of the study is to reveal how discursive political parties' practices of change on the basis of citizenship culture.	The study reveals that the party in power is also leading in terms of visibility. It is observed that political parties, that pay attention to web 1.0, are also represented in new media with the help of youth branches. However, it is claimed that parties and candidates, mostly, social media usage as a notice board and top-down transfer of discourses. On the other hand, political parties that cannot take place in mainstream media, use social media as a communication channel to become visible.
18	Şen & Kök (2017)	Qualitative	Collective Action	The study aimed to find out the potential of strengthening feminist activity through the example of three different feminist activist groups which created a democratic platform via Twitter. In this framework, with reference to online activism theories, the creative potential of the Internet, in the public sphere, for an activist group is discussed and it is focused on the nature of social network activities.	Online activist movements and groups which consist of those movements are not able to express themselves in the public sphere, thus, they use social media in order to affect public policy. Feminist groups not only organize online protests for challenges faced by women but also organize offline protests by online calls to action. It is also claimed that social media is important to develop resistance against hegemonic power structures and message transfer to the public. It is a fact that feminist activist groups are weak in policy determination for the problems of women. However social media contributes those groups for organizing, initiating a discussion, informing and liaising, meanwhile, it contributes to establishing an alternative public sphere and developing resistance against hegemonic power structures.
19	Darı (2018)	Qualitative	Elections, Political Marketing, and Political Parties	The aim is to assert usage of social media in politics as a communication tool, by examining SNS accounts of three political parties represented in TBMM and leaders of those three political parties,	Leaders and political parties use SNSs for reaching electors, information purposes and promotion. It is understood that political parties and leaders are not willing to use SNSs as a two-way communication tool.

counter-hegemonic discourses and anti-government actions within collective action. First is to block, or to limit the spread of the news through postings. The second is the generation, and the regeneration of pro-government content by employing trolls specifically assigned for boosting the government in online platforms.

In the first case, the government made some amendments which enabled the authorities to sue or detain people in question due to their postings through social media. Besides, amendments provide a legal basis in order to interfere in social media users' actions without a court order (Article 7, Article 11, Article 12, Article 14, and Article 16). The "amendments" were assessed in the category of collective action because the government has made an effort to push the opposition for self-censorship. According to the authors, the government intends to oppress opponents before their actions take place.

Secondly, the government uses social media itself to create a legitimate basis in order to manipulate society in the desired direction. The studies analyzed argue about allegations regarding the employment of

600 staff (trolls) to promote the government and their actions. In respect to their claims, the government employed a great number of people assigned to generate social media content to advocate government. This is, sometimes, by accusing the others to be traitor, sometimes by praising the government as heroes (Article 2, Article 7, Article 8, Article 11, Article 12, Article 14, and Article 15).

This case has two faces like mythological creature; Janus. One of its faces considers the collective action as the control over the public opinion by introduction legal and administrative regulations. The other side is fostering political marketing by employing pro-government trolls. It is argued that during the Gezi Park protest, both of the tools were operational in order to control the events. Shortly, the government mobilized political marketing tools (trolls) and legal and administrative measures together to overcome oppositional actions.

On the other hand, it seems that social media is a mediator for a new form of collective action. Specifically, Article 5 highlights that social media usage during a collective action forms a different kind of collectivity, namely connected action. The literature review shows that the authors tend to understand Gezi Park protests as a new kind of collective action, in the Turkish context, gathering the mass without questioning their backgrounds, perceived political views, or sexual identities. It means new collectivity does not consist of identical participants in contrast to the traditional collective actions, for example, labor or ethnic movements. In this case, social media forms a platform providing with non-identical people to gather for shared purposes.

The research question also reveals another topic. Social media does not provide the base source for collective action. Rather it provides necessary functional tools that facilitate them to occur. In other words, social media does not bear the sole credit for cases such as the Gezi Park, Arap Spring, and the Occupy Wall Street movements. What makes these events exclusive is the way they were organized. Articles 2, 3, 5, and 18 argue that social media is an organizational tool, as well as a basis for counter-hegemonic discourse. In this context, the literature does not just focus on the role of social media as an online reaction platform; on the contrary, it is also an offline reaction tool. Briefly, the offline agenda fills social media contents (Article 10, Article 3) that enables online and offline content-hegemonic discourse and action together.

Finally, the last issue related to RQ1, the analysis demonstrates that social media has proven as an alternative media venue. Article 8 and Article 5 emphasize that social media plays a role as an alternative information source due to the deficiency of traditional media. The articles lay weight on those people using social networking sites, particularly Twitter, as a novel source to collect information about what happened in Gezi Park because mainstream media neglected to give out.

Despite the general tendency in the collective action class, Article 4 constitutes a divergent approach to social media usage for political purposes. According to the interviews made by the author, people think that social media has no influence on politics and eventually divides society into different ideological camps.

The Use of Social Media by Political Actors to Manipulate Public Opinion

Concerning the second research question, there are four different topics addressed.

First of all, our analysis shows that political actors are incapable of understanding the "potentialities" of social media. The first indicator of this argument is the way how political actors use social media (or Web 2.0 in broader meaning) for electoral purposes. Articles 13, 15, 17, and 19 refer to the opinion that politicians using social media assume that they are as if web 1.0 tools. Politicians neglect the interactive features of social media tools enabling them to check the tendencies, or desires of voters. The related articles conclude that social media works like a giant billboard to announce and spread the news about the party or the candidate.

On the other hand, despite the failure of social media usage by political parties and other actors, the literature highlights the common feature of relative successful political usage of social media. Article 6 indicates that if a political party invests in web 1.0 technologies, for instance, SMS, it also reaches success in web 2.0 technologies such as Twitter, Facebook or YouTube.

SOLUTIONS AND RECOMMENDATIONS

Regarding RQ1 and RQ2, there are two different approaches found due to the nature of SNSs. These two approaches make a reference to the two-way communication function of SNSs. The first one indicates from-top-to-down communication function, namely "elections, political marketing, and political parties". The second one is the "collective action" which sheds light on the from-down-to-top relationships in the political use of SNSs.

The studies that are classified under the "collective actions" have also two different dispositions. The analysis showed that the studies analyzed are to indicate the presence of two policies adopted by the party in power in Turkey. The first one is the blockade placed before the political use of SNSs during social uprising or major societal events that were evaluated as threatening by the authorities. The second one is employing pro-government staff through SNSs. In the first case, the government seeks to oppress dissents by warning over the possibility of getting sued or getting under detention because of their actions/discourses posted through SNSs. In the second case, the government seeks to shape public opinion in order to reproduce its power.

In this context, the analysis reveals that the studies on the political use of SNSs in Turkey tend to claim that the field is regulated by administrative precautions taken the government rather than legislative regulations or court orders against the abuses via SNSs. This implies that the rule of law is violated arguing that separation of powers is not institutionalized yet. This finding draws attention to the constitutional rule in the context of check and balance mechanisms as well as freedom of speech or privacy.

The second disposition of collective action in the analysis shows the efforts to manipulate public opinion by using trolls. It is mostly argued through the studies that the government strives to support its legitimacy by employing trolls to promote themselves as well as blaming the opponents. This finding is consistent with the argument that the party in power in Turkey is a populist party (Özen, 2015, p. 16). Finchelstein (2017, p. 30) asserted that polarization is the logic of populism. Accordingly, the populist logic of the government reflected itself through the troll postings via the SNSs.

With regard to RQ 2, there are evaluations that political actors use social media mostly as one-way communication, or seeing the SNSs as an information and announcement board ignoring the potentiality of two-way communication. Thus political actors are supposed not to understand the potential of SNSs for the sake of multi-way interactions with the constituents. In this context, Picazo-Vela, Gutiérrez-Martínez and Luna-Reyes et al. (2012) take attraction to the risks related to the inability of public institutions to use the potentials of social media on losing control of dialogue with citizens on social media among others.

When analyzing studies conducted in Turkey, we have also noticed that there are no studies to understand the reasons behind this while it is mostly emphasized that the potentials of social media are not taken advantage of by the political actors. Spaiser, Chadefaux, Donna, Russman, and Helbing (2017), in their case study of Russian Protests in 2011-12, revealed that the Putin administration successfully used social media to suppress dissenting voices and manipulate the public between two elections. They argued that the Russian administration is blamed to pay a group of people for positive tweets on social media in such a way that dissent voices would be hard to speak up. In sum, it is found that the findings and arguments raised in studies focused on Turkey are parallel to the main inclinations found in the related literature.

LIMITATIONS AND FUTURE RESEARCH DIRECTIONS

This chapter has some limitations as well. First of all, we have conducted our qualitative analysis based on mainly journal articles, so the following reviews might include a various range of other academic papers like books, theses, official documents or newspaper columns. Second, the chapter has made a particular or narrow analysis, oncoming studies are recommended to have a wider focus in order to check the representability and validity of the findings based on a continent, rather than a specific country case in addition to performing a wider empirical analysis. Third, the chapter has a narrow focus, particularly political use of SNSs in a specific country case. The future papers could focus on a broad range of SNSs use in either a country case or on a comparative base. We strongly recommend the prospective papers to assess and to identify scholarly addressed motives of political use of SNSs, particularly before and after elections.

CONCLUSION

Development in information and communication technologies (ICTs) has a dramatic impact on many facets of society including the interactions between government and citizens. SNSs, as a part of ICTs, are no exclusion. Today what is called "media" is not just for some leisure activity, but also referring to a means of new forms of political participation. This presents a variety of forms of novel interactions, such as tweeting, liking, sharing, and commenting over public services by ordinary citizens, politically elected or appointed. In other words, digital forms of communication have become one of the primary components of self-expression and interaction with all the stakeholders due to the change from web 1.0 to web 2.0 or web 3.0 technologies.

In this context, social media is one of the new media platforms used all over the globe for a number of purposes from entertainment to politics. For this reason, SNSs have become a focal point for academicians and researchers. It is, therefore, possible to say that the field of researches on social media has expanded as parallel with the changing nature of social media preferences through user lenses. In the same manner, scholars in this field tend to focus on SNSs use with political purposes for expanding the extant literature on political communication. Accordingly, this study aims to contribute to this field by using a systematic literature analysis on the existing literature of the political use of SNSs in Turkey. For this very reason, this study analyzed 19 papers in total founded through the Google Scholar database. In this end, this literature review covers 19 studies in English and Turkish on the political use of social media based on two formulated research questions to evaluate what the features social media has brought to the political communication field in a particular country case which has been questioned for some time with regard to exerted limitations and control over use of SNSs.

While the first RQ is targeting the literature on the bottom-top use of social media, the second RQ is targeting the literature on the up-down use of social media in Turkey. Regarding the first RQ, the analysis put forward two different tendencies employed by official authorities. The first one is to control social media in order to avoid counter-hegemonic discourses and anti-government actions by blocking or to limit the circulation of news. The second is the generation, and the regeneration of pro-government content by employing trolls specifically assigned for fostering the support for the government in online platforms. Regarding the second one, the literature analysis shows that political actors are incapable of understanding the "potentialities" of social media. One might claim that how do some political actors approach social media limits themselves with one-way massage transmits although social media platforms provide two-way message transmission.

The literature analysis shows the consensus points as follows;

1. Social media usage for political purposes faces legal and administrative measures as well as employing trolls also.
2. Collective action has altered into the more rhizomatic formation rather than hierarchical formation.
3. Political actors are not capable to understand the potentialities of social media.

The contribution of this study to the literature is twofold. First, conceptually, we made a systematic literature analysis to fill a gap in the extant literature. Although Turkey is an important country case for the political use of SNSs, however, there is no such review with regard to Turkey. Thus, this paper descriptively contributes to the literature by investigating the motives behind the political use of SNSs. After the analysis, it is found that the political use of SNSs by citizens at large is worth noting and government control over political use of SNSs is clear. Second, it is identified how the government posed control over SNSs.

ACKNOWLEDGMENT

This research received no specific grant from any funding agency in the public, commercial, or not-for-profit sectors.

REFERENCES

Aharony, N. (2012). Twitter use by three political leaders: An exploratory analysis. *Online Information Review*, *36*(4), 587–603. doi:10.1108/14684521211254086

Alalwan, A. A., Rana, N. P., Dwivedi, Y. K., & Algharabat, R. (2017). Social media in marketing: A review and analysis of the existing literature. *Telematics and Informatics*, *34*(7), 1177–1190. doi:10.1016/j.tele.2017.05.008

Alam, M. S., & Khan, B. M. (2015). Impact of social media on Brand equity: A literature analysis. *AIMA Journal of Management & Research*, *9*(4), 1–12.

Alryalat, M. A. A., Rana, N. P., Sahu, G. P., Dwivedi, Y. K., & Tajvidi, M. (2017). Use of social media in citizen-centric electronic government services: A literature analysis. *International Journal of Electronic Government Research*, *13*(3), 55–79. doi:10.4018/IJEGR.2017070104

Anderson, B. (1983). *Imagined Communities*. London: Verso.

Arsono, D., & Kusumawati, D. (2018). Content Analysis Twitter Usage By Governor Candidates of West Java 2018. In *Proceedings of the 5th. International Conference on Social and Political Sciences (IcoSaPS 2018)* (pp. 183-188). Atlantis Press. 10.2991/icosaps-18.2018.41

Aydin, U. U., & Güler, C. (2016). From the construction of hegemony to state crisis political power and social media in Turkey. *Athens Journal of Mass Media and Communications*, *2*(2), 111–126. doi:10.30958/ajmmc.2.2.3

Balca, A. (2015). The construction of a new sociality through social media: The case of the Gezi uprising in Turkey. *Conjunctions: Transdisciplinary Journal of Cultural Participation*, *2*(1), 72–99. doi:10.7146/tjcp.v2i1.22271

Baudrillard, J. (1981). *Simulacra and Simulation* (S. Glaser, Trans.). Ann Arbor, MI: University of Michigan Press.

Baumgartner, J. C., & Morris, J. S. (2010). MyFaceTube Politics: Social Networking Web Sites and Political Engagement of Young Adults. *Social Science Computer Review*, *28*(1), 24–44. doi:10.1177/0894439309334325

Bay, M. (2018). Weaponizing the haters: *The Last Jedi* and the strategic politicization of pop culture through social media manipulation. *First Monday*, *23*(11). doi:10.5210/fm.v23i11.9388

Bayraktutan, G., Binark, M., Çom, T., Doğu, B., İslamoğlu, G., & Aydemir, A. T. (2013). The role of social media in political communication: Use of Twitter in the 2011 General Elections in Turkey. *Medianali*, *7*(13), 1–18.

Bayraktutan, G., Binark, M., Çom, T., Doğu, B., İslamoğlu, G., & Aydemir, A. T. (2014). Siyasal iletişim sürecinde sosyal medya ve Türkiye'de 2011 Genel Seçimlerinde Twitter kullanımı [Social media in process of political communication and Twitter use in 2011 General Elections in Turkey]. *Bilig*, *68*, 59–96. doi:10.12995/bilig.2014.6804

Bimber, B. (2014). Digital Media in the Obama Campaigns of 2008 and 2012: Adaptation to the Personalized Political Communication Environment. *Journal of Information Technology & Politics*, *11*(2), 130–150. doi:10.1080/19331681.2014.895691

Boulianne, S. (2015). Social media use and participation: A metaanalysis of current research. *Information Communication and Society*, *18*(5), 524–538. doi:10.1080/1369118X.2015.1008542

Budgen, D., & Brereton, P. (2006). Performing Systematic Literature Reviews in Software Engineering. In *Proceedings of the 28th international conference on Software engineering* (ICSE '06) (pp. 1051-1052). ACM. 10.1145/1134285.1134500

Çetinkaya, A., Şahin, Ö. E., & Kırık, A. M. (2014). A research on social and political use of social media in Turkey. *International Journal of Science Culture And Sport*, *2*(4), 49–60. doi:10.14486/IJSCS207

Crowther, M., Lim, W., & Crowther, M. A. (2010). Systematic Review and Meta-Analysis Methodology. *Blood, 116*(17), 3140–3146. doi:10.1182/blood-2010-05-280883 PMID:20656933

Darı, A. B. (2018). Sosyal medya ve siyaset: Türkiye'deki siyasi partilerin sosyal medya kullanımı [Social media and politics: Social media use by political parties in Turkey]. *Al-Farabi Uluslararası Sosyal Bilimler Dergisi, 1*(1), 1–11.

de Zúñiga, H. G., Barnidge, M., & Diehl, T. (2018). Political persuasion on social media: A moderated moderation model of political discussion disagreement and civil reasoning. *The Information Society, 34*(5), 302–315. doi:10.1080/01972243.2018.1497743

Demirhan, K. (2014a). Relationship between Social Media and Political Parties: The Case of Turkey. In A. Solo (Ed.), *Political Campaigning in the Information Age* (pp. 1–31). Hershey, PA: IGI Global. doi:10.4018/978-1-4666-6062-5.ch001

Demirhan, K. (2014b). Social Media Effects on the Gezi Park Movement in Turkey: Politics Under Hashtags. In B. Pătruţ & M. Pătruţ (Eds.), *Social Media in Politics: Case Studies on the Political Power of Social Media* (pp. 281–314). Cham, Switzerland: Springer. doi:10.1007/978-3-319-04666-2_16

Dunlap, J., & Lowenthal, P. (2009). Tweeting the Night Away: Using Twitter to Enhance Social Presence. *Journal of Information Systems Education, 20*(2), 129–136.

Dursun, O. (2013). Efforts of Control of Political Power over the Social Media in Turkey. In *Proceedings of the Fourth Annual Asian Conference on Media and Mass Communication* (pp. 1-13), Retrieved from http://papers.iafor.org/wp-content/uploads/conference-proceedings/MediAsia/MediAsia2013_proceedings.pdf

Enli, G. S., & Skogerbø, E. (2013). Personalized Campaigns in Party-Centred Politics. *Information Communication and Society, 16*(5), 757–774. doi:10.1080/1369118X.2013.782330

Evans, H. K., Brown, K. J., & Wimberly, T. (2018). "Delete Your Account": The 2016 Presidential Race on Twitter. *Social Science Computer Review, 36*(4), 500–508. doi:10.1177/0894439317728722

Finchelstein, F. (2017). *From fascism to populism in history*. Oakland, CA: University of California Press.

Fisch, C., & Block, J. (2018). Six tips for your (systematic) literature review in business and management research. *Management Review Quarterly, 68*(2), 103–106. doi:10.100711301-018-0142-x

Francia, P. L. (2018). Free Media and Twitter in the 2016 Presidential Election: The Unconventional Campaign of Donald Trump. *Social Science Computer Review, 36*(4), 440–455. doi:10.1177/0894439317730302

Gancho, S. P. M. (2017). Social Media: a literature review. *e-Revista LOGO, 6*(2), 1-20.

Graham, T., Broersma, M., Hazelhoff, K., & van 't Haar, G. (2013). Between Broadcasting Political Messages and Interacting with Voters. *Information Communication and Society, 16*(5), 692–716. doi: 10.1080/1369118X.2013.785581

Guerrero-Solé, F. (2017). Community Detection in Political Discussions on Twitter: An Application of the Retweet Overlap Network Method to the Catalan Process Toward Independence. *Social Science Computer Review, 35*(2), 244–261. doi:10.1177/0894439315617254

Gündüz, U., & Erdem, B. K. (2017). The concept of virtual nationalism in the digital age: Social media perspectives of Turkey. *Communication Today*, *8*(2), 18–29.

Güneyli, A., Ersoy, E., & Kıralp, S. (2017). Terrorism in the 2015 election period in Turkey content analysis of political leaders' social media activity. *Journal of Universal Computer Science*, *23*(3), 256–279.

Haciyakupoglu, G., & Zhang, W. (2015). Social media and trust during the Gezi protests in Turkey. *Journal of Computer-Mediated Communication*, *20*(4), 450–466. doi:10.1111/jcc4.12121

Hafdell, S. (2014). Social media and the "Menace to Society": Potential and limitations of alternative media in Turkey. *Glocal Times*, *21*, 1–14.

Hambrick, M. E., Simmons, J. M., Greenhalgh, G. P., & Greenwell, T. C. (2010). Understanding Professional Athletes' Use of Twitter: A Content Analysis of Athlete Tweets. *International Journal of Sport Communication*, *3*(4), 454–471. doi:10.1123/ijsc.3.4.454

Han, J., & Kim, Y. (2009). *Obama tweeting and twitted: Sotomayor's nomination and health care reform.* Paper presented at the annual meeting of the American Political Science Association, Toronto, Canada.

Hargittai, E., & Litt, E. (2011). The tweet smell of celebrity success: Explaining variation in Twitter adoption among a diverse group of young adults. *New Media & Society*, *13*(5), 824–842. doi:10.1177/1461444811405805

Hashim, K. F., Tan, F. B., & Rashid, A. (2015). Adult learners' intention to adopt mobile learning: A motivational perspective. *British Journal of Educational Technology*, *46*(2), 381–390. doi:10.1111/bjet.12148

Hsu, C., & Park, H. W. (2011). Sociology of hyperlink networks of Web 1.0, Web 2.0, and Twitter: A case study of South Korea. *Social Science Computer Review*, *29*(3), 354–368. doi:10.1177/0894439310382517

Hughes, D. J., Rowe, M., Batey, M., & Lee, A. (2012). A tale of two sites: Twitter vs. Facebook and the personality predictors of social media usage. *Computers in Human Behavior*, *28*(2), 561–569. doi:10.1016/j.chb.2011.11.001

Ikiz, O. O., Sobaci, M. Z., Yavuz, N., & Karkin, N. (2014). Political use of Twitter: the case of metropolitan mayor candidates in 2014 local elections in Turkey. In *Proceedings of the 8th International Conference on Theory and Practice of Electronic Governance* (pp. 41-50). New York, NY: ACM. 10.1145/2691195.2691219

Jhally, S., & Livant, B. (1986). Watching as working: The valorization of audience consciousness. *Journal of Communication*, *36*(3), 124–143. doi:10.1111/j.1460-2466.1986.tb01442.x

Karatas, D., & Saka, E. (2017). Online political trolling in the context of post-Gezi social media in Turkey. *International Journal of Digital Television*, *8*(3), 383–401. doi:10.1386/jdtv.8.3.383_1

Kim, Y. (2012). The Shifting Sands of Citizenship: Toward a Model of the Citizenry in Life Politics. *The Annals of the American Academy of Political and Social Science*, *644*(1), 147–158. doi:10.1177/0002716212456008

Kreiss, D. (2016). Seizing the moment: The presidential campaigns' use of Twitter during the 2012 electoral cycle. *New Media & Society, 18*(8), 1473–1490. doi:10.1177/1461444814562445

Kruikemeier, S., Gattermann, K., & Vliegenthart, R. (2018). Understanding the dynamics of politicians' visibility in traditional and social media. *The Information Society, 34*(4), 215–228. doi:10.1080/01972 243.2018.1463334

Kurt, H., & Karaduman, S. (2012). Usage of social media by political actors: An analysis on the usage of Twitter by leaders of political parties in Turkey. *Medianali, 6*(12), 1–15.

Larsson, A. O., & Moe, H. (2011). Studying political microblogging: Twitter users in the 2010 Swedish election campaign. *New Media & Society, 14*(5), 729–747. doi:10.1177/1461444811422894

Larsson, A. O., & Moe, H. (2013). Representation or Participation? Twitter Use During the 2011 Danish Election Campaign. *Javnost - The Public, 20*(1), 71-88. doi:10.1080/13183222.2013.11009109

Margetts, H. (2019). 9. Rethinking Democracy with Social Media. *The Political Quarterly, 90*(S1), 107-123. doi:10.1111/1467-923X.12574

McKelvey, K., DiGrazia, J., & Rojas, F. (2014). Twitter publics: How online political communities signaled electoral outcomes in the 2010 US house election. *Information Communication and Society, 17*(4), 436–450. doi:10.1080/1369118X.2014.892149

Medina, R. Z., & Muñoz, C. Z. (2014). Campaigning on Twitter: Towards the 'Personal Style' Campaign to Activate the Political Engagement During the 2011 Spanish General Elections. *Communication & Society / Comunicación y Sociedad, 27*(1), 83-106.

Merolli, M., Gray, K., & Martin-Sanchez, F. (2013). Health outcomes and related effects of using social media in chronic disease management: A literature review and analysis of affordances. *Journal of Biomedical Informatics, 46*(6), 957–969. doi:10.1016/j.jbi.2013.04.010 PMID:23702104

Özen, H. (2015). An Unfinished Grassroots Populism: The Gezi Park Protests in Turkey and Their Aftermath. *South European Society & Politics, 20*(4), 533–552. doi:10.1080/13608746.2015.1099258

Paquette, H. (2013). *Social media as a marketing tool: a literature review*. Major Papers by Master of Science Students. Paper 2. The University of Rhode Island, Retrieved from http://digitalcommons.uri.edu/tmd_major_papers/2

Picazo-Vela, S., Gutiérrez-Martínez, I., & Luna-Reyes, L. F. (2012). Understanding risks, benefits, and strategic alternatives of social media applications in the public sector. *Government Information Quarterly, 29*(4), 504–511. doi:10.1016/j.giq.2012.07.002

Rodríguez, M. P. (2017). Governance Models for the Delivery of Public Services through the Web 2.0 Technologies: A Political View in Large Spanish Municipalities. *Social Science Computer Review, 35*(2), 203–225. doi:10.1177/0894439315609919

Rosenthal, R., & DiMatteo, M. R. (2001). Meta-analysis: Recent Developments in Quantitative Methods for Literature Reviews. *Annual Review of Psychology, 52*(1), 59–82. doi:10.1146/annurev.psych.52.1.59 PMID:11148299

Saka, E. (2018). Social media in Turkey as a space for political battles: AKTrolls and other politically motivated trolling. *Middle East Critique*, *27*(2), 161–177. doi:10.1080/19436149.2018.1439271

Sandberg, L. A. C., & Öhberg, P. (2017). The role of gender in online campaigning: Swedish candidates' motives and use of social media during the European election 2014. *Journal of Information Technology & Politics*, *14*(4), 314–333. doi:10.1080/19331681.2017.1369918

Şen, A. F., & Kök, H. (2017). Sosyal medya ve feminist aktivizm: Türkiye'deki feminist grupların aktivizm biçimleri [Social media and feminist activism: Activism styles of feminist groups in Turkey]. *Atatürk İletişim Dergisi*, *13*, 73–86.

Shi, Z., Rui, H., & Whinston, A. (2014). Content Sharing in a Social Broadcasting Environment: Evidence from Twitter. *Management Information Systems Quarterly*, *38*(1), 123–142. doi:10.25300/MISQ/2014/38.1.06

Shirky, C. (2011). The political power of social media: Technology, the public sphere, and political change. *Foreign Affairs*, *90*(1), 28–41. Retrieved from http://www.jstor.org/stable/25800379

Sobaci, M. Z., & Karkin, N. (2013). The use of Twitter by mayors in Turkey: Tweets for better public services? *Government Information Quarterly*, *30*(4), 417–425. doi:10.1016/j.giq.2013.05.014

Spaiser, V., Chadefaux, T., Donna, K., Russman, F., & Helbing, D. (2017). Communication power struggles on social media: A case study of the 2011–12 Russian protests. *Journal of Information Technology & Politics*, *14*(2), 132–153. doi:10.1080/19331681.2017.1308288

Sun, W. (2018). A Critical Discourse Analysis of "Minority Women for Trump" Campaigns on Social Media. In N. Bilge & M. Marino (Eds.), *Reconceptualizing New Media and Intercultural Communication in a Networked Society* (pp. 303–327). Hershey, PA: IGI Global. doi:10.4018/978-1-5225-3784-7.ch012

Tess, P. A. (2013). The role of social media in higher education classes (real and virtual)–A literature review. *Computers in Human Behavior*, *29*(5), A60–A68. doi:10.1016/j.chb.2012.12.032

Tewksbury, D. (2006). Exposure to the Newer Media in a Presidential Primary Campaign. *Political Communication*, *23*(3), 313–332. doi:10.1080/10584600600808877

Thelwall, M. (2017). The Heart and Soul of the Web? Sentiment Strength Detection in the Social Web with SentiStrength. In J. Holyst (Ed.), *Cyberemotions: Collective Emotions in Cyberspace. Understanding Complex Systems* (pp. 119–134). Springer International Publishing. doi:10.1007/978-3-319-43639-5_7

Vergeer, M. (2017). Adopting, Networking, and Communicating on Twitter: A Cross-National Comparative Analysis. *Social Science Computer Review*, *35*(6), 698–712. doi:10.1177/0894439316672826

Webster, J., & Watson, R. T. (2002). Analyzing the Past to Prepare for the Future: Writing A Literature Review. *Management Information Systems Quarterly*, *26*(2), xiii–xxiii. Retrieved from http://www.jstor.org/stable/4132319

Yavuz, N., Karkın, N., Parlak, İ., & Subay, Ö. Ö. (2018). Political Discourse Strategies Used in Twitter during Gezi Park Protests: A Comparison of Two Rival Political Parties in Turkey. *International Journal of Public Administration in the Digital Age*, *5*(1), 82–96. doi:10.4018/IJPADA.2018010105

Yolbulan Okan, E., Topcu, A., & Akyuz, S. (2014). The role of social media in political marketing: 2014 Local Elections of Turkey. *European Journal of Business and Management, 6*(22), 131–140.

Yüksel, H. (2018). Social media strategies of political power: An analysis of the Ruling Party in Turkey. In F. Endong (Ed.), *Exploring the Role of Social Media in Transnational Advocacy* (pp. 153–178). Hershey, PA: IGI Global. doi:10.4018/978-1-5225-2854-8.ch008

Zhang, W., Johnson, T. J., Seltzer, T., & Bichard, S. L. (2010). The Revolution Will be Networked: The Influence of Social Networking Sites on Political Attitudes and Behavior. *Social Science Computer Review, 28*(1), 75–92. doi:10.1177/0894439309335162

ADDITIONAL READING

Effing, R., Van Hillegersberg, J., & Huibers, T. (2011). Social media and political participation: are Facebook, Twitter and YouTube democratizing our political systems? In R. Effing, J. van Hillegersberg, T. Huibers, E. Tambouris, A. Macintosh, & H. de Bruijn (Eds.), *Electronic Participation* (pp. 25–35). Berlin, Heidelberg: Springer; doi:10.1007/978-3-642-23333-3_3

Kelly Garrett, R. (2006). Protest in an information society: A review of literature on social movements and new ICTs. *Information Communication and Society, 9*(02), 202–224. doi:10.1080/13691180600630773

Kim, Y. (2011). The contribution of social network sites to exposure to political difference: The relationships among SNSs, online political messaging, and exposure to cross-cutting perspectives. *Computers in Human Behavior, 27*(2), 971–977. doi:10.1016/j.chb.2010.12.001

Sandoval-Almazan, R., & Gil-Garcia, J. R. (2014). Towards cyberactivism 2.0? Understanding the use of social media and other information technologies for political activism and social movements. *Government Information Quarterly, 31*(3), 365–378. doi:10.1016/j.giq.2013.10.016

Stieglitz, S., & Dang-Xuan, L. (2013). Social media and political communication: A social media analytics framework. *Social Network Analysis and Mining, 3*(4), 1277–1291. doi:10.100713278-012-0079-3

Tucker, J., Guess, A., Barberá, P., Vaccari, C., Siegel, A., Sanovich, S., ... Nyhan, B. (2018). *Social Media, Political Polarization, and Political Disinformation: A Review of the Scientific Literature*. Menlo Park, CA: William Flora Hewlett Foundation.

Zhang, W., & Chia, S. C. (2006). The effects of mass media use and social capital on civic and political participation. *Communication Studies, 57*(3), 277–297. doi:10.1080/10510970600666974

KEY TERMS AND DEFINITIONS

Information and Communication Technologies (ICT): Technologies that provide the flow of information through devices, internet, etc.

Politics: Activities that involve in the governance of a state or a region.

Social Media: Websites and mobile applications that users can produce and share contents with other users.

Social Network Sites (SNS): A social network site is an online platform that allows people to create a profile and interact with other users/profiles on the same website.

Chapter 26
Mutual Understanding in Interoperable/Integrated Financial Management Systems Implementation in the Public Sector:
A Viewpoint for Future Research

Bryan Acheampong
Business School, University of Ghana, Ghana

Ibrahim Bedi
Business School, University of Ghana, Ghana

ABSTRACT

While there has been some considerable investment in information systems implementation and usage in the public sector, success has often been limited. Attempts by researchers to address this situation has been diverse and often inconclusive. A publication by the MIS Quarterly journal offers some direction. The study, which focused on information systems development (ISD), highlighted the need to explore how mutual understanding among key stakeholders is created, or the extent to which they have a shared conception of the ISD project, and further how such mutual understanding is changing, develops, or deteriorates over time. On the tenets of the study, this chapter attempts to chart a path for future research in interoperable financial management systems implementation and usage in the public sector. It presents a viewpoint that establishes the need to explore the creation and sustenance of mutual understanding between stakeholders in the implementation and usage of interoperable or integrated financial management systems in the public sector.

DOI: 10.4018/978-1-7998-2610-1.ch026

INTRODUCTION

Interoperability is "the ability of two or more systems or elements to exchange information and to use the information that have been exchanged" (IEEE, 2000). It is also referred to as "the ability to share and exchange information using common syntax and semantics to meet an application-specific functional relationship through the use of a common interface" (ISO, 2002). Interoperable information systems tend to consist of two or more systems which are able the exchange and use information to facilitate the efficient running of diverse business processes and decision-making. Interoperability is becoming an emerging area and is of interest to both private and public sector institutions (Sharma & Panigrahi, 2015). For example, in the public sector,(which is the domain of this viewpoint) governments have a pressing need to develop interoperable information systems which integrate the public financial management processes such as budget preparation, budget execution, accounting and financial reporting, cash management, assets management, and human resource and payroll management (Alsharari & Youssef, 2017; World Bank, 2015; Hove & Wynne 2010; Rodin-Brown 2008). In this scenario, interoperability provides advantages such as lower costs and transparency in governance systems and processes thereby reducing opportunities for corruption, as well as redundant and repetitive processes (World Bank, 2015)).

Arguably, as government consist of diverse agencies, researchers have considered interoperability as one of the indicators for determining the maturity of the electronic government systems (Estermann, Riedl, & Neuroni, 2009). The interoperable information systems for coordinating public financial management processes often referred to in the public sector as Integrated financial management information systems (IFMIS), are deployed to replace all stand-alone, often legacy, financial management information systems used by the different public or government agencies across the public sector (Hendriks, 2013). IFMIS integrate all the financial management activities of government into a suite of applications that facilitate public financial management processes (Nuhu et al., 2018). In many developing economies, these systems are deployed as one of the core elements of public financial management (PFM) reform programs (World Bank, 2015). This is in response to the increasing pressure from institutions, including the International Monetary Fund, to improve fiscal management and reporting, and for governments to respond to the demand of better information disclosure (Alsharari & Youssef, 2017; World Bank, 2015).

For example, in South Africa, the integrated financial management information systems were deployed as part of a broader financial management reform in the public sector, which started in 1994 after democracy was attained. By a cabinet memo, the IFMIS was deployed to replace the different transversal systems, namely, Supply Chain Management, Human Resources, Finance and Business Intelligence with a single system (Hendriks, 2013); whereas in Ghana, the introduction of GIFMIS stemmed from a Public Financial Management Reform Program (PUFMARP) implemented from 1999-2008, to enhance monetary discipline and macro stability (Betley, Bird & Ghartey, 2012; Tanko, 2013; Nuhu et al., 2018). Per their primary objective, IFMIS consists of a number of interoperable modules which work together to ensure efficiency, transparency and accountability in all functional processes in fiscal management across all government agencies and departments. Evidence of the adoption of these systems has been well-documented with mixed results.

In a study on the impact of IFMIS in Somalia, Nor (2019) concluded that the revenue of federal government increased in the years 2013 to 2018 and thereby enhanced the confidence and relationship with international development agencies that public funds are being managed in a transparent, equitable and accountable manner. However, there was still the need to develop tax compliance rules to protect tax evasion and tax avoidance. Chalu (2019) also found evidence that IFMIS adoption had improved the quality of both the understandability and reliability in financial reporting in local governments in Tanzania. However, utilization capacity and internal audit effectiveness was critical to ensuring the reliability of financial reporting. Utilization capacity was constrained by weak IFMIS system policies, lack of knowledge and limited skills, limited management and technical support, limited understanding of IFMIS and resistance to change. These findings are consistent with other studies from Kenya and South Africa (Micheni, 2017; Gcora, & Chigona, 2019). For example, in South Africa, change management was not factored into the project during the IFMIS implementation in municipalities. The implementation focused primarily on the success of the IFMIS with little consideration of the needs of end-users. Hence user-resistance was encountered (Gcora, & Chigona, 2019). Besides, Micheni (2017) analysis of IFMIS adoption in selected Kenyan Counties concluded that change management should be handled better; this can be done through the provision of regular training and phased implementation (and testing) of IFMIS. Researchers and practitioners alike have also previously cautioned that limited results could be witnessed in the adoption of IFMIS in contexts where information technology infrastructure and skills are limited (Andrews 2013; Dorotinsky & Watkins 2013).

As a result, achieving interoperability or developing interoperable information systems is a complex phenomenon with constraints in various dimensions such as technology, organizational capabilities, syntactic and semantics (Scholl & Klischewski, 2007). The complexity is compounded by the fact that, for systems deployed in public sector, these constraints differ from the context in which they are deployed (for example, country to country) as they are dependent on the prevailing political, economic, social and technological conditions (Sharma & Panigrahi, 2015). For example, in Ghana and South Africa, it has been reported that the effective implementation of the government IFMIS is largely hinged on sustained political support and commitment, and change management amidst other technological, legal and social factors (Nuhu et al., 2018; Yeboah, 2015; Hendricks, 2013). The need for knowledge on how to sustain political support and commitment of different stakeholders and harmonize new and emerging interests of different government agencies to ensure continuous implementation and usage of IFMIS (and interoperable systems in general), has been therefore requested (Hendricks, 2013; Effah & Nuhu, 2017; Boateng, Acheampong & Bedi, 2019). A study that seeks to explore such knowledge is, therefore, a good step to the optimum achievement of the objectives of IFMIS and is a benefit to developing economies which have deployed such interoperable or integrated financial management information systems. That is the premise of this viewpoint.

RATIONALE FOR THIS RESEARCH

A review of extant research in interoperability classified the literature into four sub-themes: technical, syntactic, semantic and organizational interoperability (Boateng, Acheampong & Bedi, 2019). Technical interoperability refers to hardware or software components, systems, and platforms that enable machine-to-machine communication and are focused on communication protocols and the infrastructure required for those protocols to function (Rezaei et al., 2014; Van der Veer & Wiles, 2008). Syntactic interoperability refers to the ability of two systems or platforms to exchange data, and it is usually associated with message transfer by communication protocols as well as defined syntax and encoding (Rezaei et al., 2014; Van der Veer & Wiles, 2008). Semantic interoperability refers to the definition of content, and it deals with 'humans' rather than 'machines' interpretation of this content (Guijarro, 2009). Organizational interoperability refers to the capability of organisations to effectively communicate and transfer information across a diversity of information systems and various geographic regions and cultures (Kubicek & Cimander, 2009). The dominant research among these is organizational and semantic interoperability. These studies identified some concerns which can inform future research.

First, to adopt interoperable systems and take advantage of the standardization they offer, organisations will have to change their technical and organizational processes (Gogan, Williams, & Fedorowicz, 2007). Scholl et al. (2012) identify nine constraints on the implementation of interoperable platforms in government: constitutional or legal constraints, jurisdictional constraints, collaborative constraints, organizational constraints, informational constraints, managerial constraints, cost constraints, technological constraints and performance constraints. These create an environment that favors certain intergovernmental interactions but limits others at various levels. There is, a need to explore the techniques adopted by organisations and governmental institutions, especially those in developing countries in implementing interoperability (Boateng et al., 2019). Such studies can also explore the technological and non-technological (process, administrative and structural) changes that governmental institutions undergo in the process. Further, since interoperability or integrated systems like IFMIS, involve multiple stakeholders or intended users, it is important to understand how the differing interests of stakeholders are unified during the implementation of IFMIS and sustained during continuous use.

Second, there is largely a lack of theorization in interoperability studies (Boateng et al. 2019). The few studies which adopt some form of theorization used a theory, framework or model. The complex adaptive systems (CAS) theory (see Weichhart, 2015) was a theory used to conceptualize the dynamics of interoperable systems which learn and be functionally dependent (integrated with others) and independent (be changed without affecting others). Guijarro (2009) combined the eGovernment Interoperability Framework (eGIF), the Danish eGovernment Interoperability Framework (DIF) and the Le Cadre Commun d'Intéroperabilité (CCI) to survey how e-government agencies in Europe and the United States have developed tools such as interoperability frameworks and enterprise architectures. Specifically, the study proposes a two-phase interoperability roadmap of governments – enabler (interoperability framework) and alignment (enterprise architecture) phase. Enabler phase consists of providing the essential technical standards and policies to enable the seamless flow of information between different government agencies, and the alignment phase enables the alignment of administrative procedures with the technical systems.

Though these studies are valuable, there seems to be more focus on the technical dimensions of interoperability, which are key to ensuring data, process and communicative integration. Hence, the theoretical approaches tend to serve this focus of research. However, some studies, which use both technical and social theoretical approaches, tend to draw attention to the need to understand how the dynamics of interoperability impacts competing initiatives or interests of stakeholders. For example, Nayar and Beldona (2010) used the technology co-adoption model, inter-organizational systems standards and process innovations (IOS SPI (IOS SPI) model, and institutional theory to evaluate the strategic perspectives of key industry players regarding the potential of interoperability technology and examine the factors pertaining to their adoption. The study argued that different perspectives/interpretations of requisite industry standards and system functionalities by stakeholders can influence the nature of implementation of interoperability systems (Nayar & Beldona, 2010). This socio-technical perspective offers the opportunity for researchers to ask other questions, for example, the impact of mutual and competing interests, and contribute new knowledge in interoperability research.

A Case for Mutual Understanding in Interoperable Information Systems

This viewpoint argues for future research to address the outlined gaps. Concerning theorization, a longitudinal study published by MIS Quarterly (Jenkin et al., 2019) offers some direction. The study, which focused on information systems development (ISD), highlighted on the need to explore how mutual understanding (MU) among key stakeholders (business and IT managers, users, and developers) is created. It could also be seen as the extent to which they have a shared conception of the ISD project and further, how such mutual understanding changes, develops or deteriorates over time. This scenario is a likely characteristic in creating and sustaining or managing mutual interests and understanding in interoperable systems. Mutual, shared or congruent understanding refers to "the extent to which stakeholders have a shared conception of the project regarding, for example, its goals and processes, and stakeholder roles" (Gregory, Beck & Keil, 2013 cited in Jenkin et al., 2019). The literature on MU explains that MU is a focal cognitive outcome which stems from episodes of cognitive activities - sensegiving and sensemaking – during the ongoing dialogue among diverse stakeholders in a project (Gioia & Chittipeddi, 1991; Stigliani & Ravasi, 2012). Thus, during information systems development projects, the continuous dialogue between IT and business stakeholders involves episodes of sensegiving and sensemaking. Sense may be referred to as meaning or interpretation to a piece of information held by or known to an individual or a group concerning a phenomenon, artefact, situation, people or scenario. This sense can inform behavior or create an interest in an issue. IS projects often span a diversity of stakeholders with differing 'senses' or interests, those which conflict and those in concert.

These stakeholders if left unattended, may largely pursue individual 'senses' or interests. Sensemaking, therefore, refers to the frameworks through which individuals construct, interpret, update and reconstruct their meanings (Gioia & Chittipeddi, 1991). In organisations, sensemaking is a continuous interplay of sensemaking at the individual level, group level (unit, communities of practice, teams et cetera) and through conversations and artefacts (models, diagrams, reports et cetera) (Weick et al., 2005). After an individual makes 'sense', activities in a group or project may necessitate the individual to communicate their 'sense' to influence others' 'sense' or interpretation of a situation (sensemaking). Achieving that influence requires sensegiving. Thus, through sensegiviging, individuals influence the sensemaking of others or their 'senses' (Gioia & Chittipeddi, 1991). Sensegiving and sensemaking are arguably co-dependent on each other and in ISD projects. IT and business users have to provide sense through communication and artefacts.

The link between MU and project success is well-argued and established in MU literature (Lyytinen, 1987; Boateng & Hinson, 2009; Gregory et al., 2013). Jenkin et al. (2019) developed and tested a model which explores the relationships among project planning and control mechanisms; sensegiving and sensemaking activities by, and MU among, stakeholder groups; and project success. The use of this model in future studies has been emphasized.

Future research can draw on the model to explore the structures and mechanisms which underpin the creation and sustenance of mutual understanding in interoperable financial systems, particularly IFMIS, in developing economies. For example, in Ghana, there have been some studies on the GIFMIS. However, these studies have focused more on the implementation of the project and the impact of GIFMIS (Nuhu et al., 2018; Effah & Nuhu, 2017; Yeboah, 2015; Betley et al., 2012). However, from the information systems perspective, this viewpoint argues for the need to explore the theory of building and managing mutual understanding in ISD projects in a developing economy and how that mutual understanding and other factors shape project success. Nuhu et al. (2018) recommended that future studies should adopt non-deterministic theories and also focus on other government agencies to uncover unique institutional factors that have affected the implementation of GIFMIS in Ghana. In response, research that employs the theory of building and managing mutual understanding is a step towards the contribution of new knowledge.

Previous ISD studies link MU development to project planning (Wallace, Keil, & Rai, 2004) and control mechanisms (Gregory et al., 2013; Kirsch 2004), and cognitive activities (sensegiving and sensemaking) (Vlaar, van Fenema, Tiwari. 2008). However, the relationships among project management mechanisms, sensegiving, and sensemaking in interoperability systems have not been examined. The lack of knowledge is more pronounced when this gap is viewed from a developing economy perspective. In developing economies, public sector financial reforms have meta-level interests and influences (funding), which can also affect the development of MU and shape project management mechanisms. Addressing the above gaps from a developing economy perspective will, therefore, generate more valuable insights to follow-up the work of Jenkins et al. (2019).

OBJECTIVES TO BE ADDRESSED

In reference to the above research gaps, this chapter argues that future research should seek to develop a model that describes the creation and sustenance of mutual understanding between stakeholders in the implementation and usage of interoperable systems in a developing economy. This future research should draw on the theory of building and managing mutual understanding to explore the structures and mechanisms which underpin the creation and sustenance of mutual understanding in integrated financial management systems. Specifically, the future research should achieve the following objectives:

1. To understand how the differing interests of stakeholders are unified during implementation and sustained during continuous usage of integrated financial management systems; and
2. To understand how project management mechanisms (planning, control) affect cognitive activities (sensegiving, sensemaking) by key stakeholders, cognitive outcome (MU among key stakeholders), and project success of integrated financial management systems.

The ensuing research questions are

1. What are the interests of stakeholders involved in the implementation and continuous usage of integrated financial management systems?
2. How are the differing interests of stakeholders unified during implementation and sustained during continuous usage of integrated financial management systems?
3. How do project management mechanisms (planning, control) affect cognitive activities (sensegiving, sensemaking) by key stakeholders, cognitive outcome (MU among key stakeholders), and project success of integrated financial management systems?

SIGNIFICANCE AND CONCLUSION

This chapter has argued the need to develop a model that describes the creation and sustenance of mutual understanding between stakeholders in the implementation and usage of interoperable systems in a developing economy. The significance of carrying out this research can be viewed from academic, practitioner and policy perspectives. First, this future research will build on the work of Jenkins et al. (2019) which developed a model for exploring the relationships among project planning and control mechanisms; sensegiving and sensemaking activities by, and MU among, stakeholder groups; and project success in information systems development. The research, from a developing economy perspective, examines the application on this model in the implementation and continuous use of an integrated financial management system. The research will generate more valuable insights to follow-up the work of Jenkins et al. (2019) and also generate further understanding of the application of the theory of mutual understanding in information system development in a developing economy. The contextual influences, constraints, and dynamism of information system development and usage in developing economies have been demonstrated as an opportunity for contributing to theory (testing or building) (Boateng, 2016; Effah, 2011). This research will draw on this inspiration to develop a model that describes the creation and sustenance of mutual understanding between stakeholders in the implementation and usage of integrated financial management systems in a developing economy.

From a practitioner perspective, first, the proposed model will offer practitioners a guide to the creation and sustenance of mutual understanding between stakeholders in the implementation and usage of integrated financial management systems. This can inform future developments in IFMIS in developing economies. Second, practitioners can understand how project management activities affect cognitive activities (sensegiving, sensemaking) by key stakeholders, cognitive outcome (MU among key stakeholders), and project success. From a developing economy perspective, this knowledge has been elusive.

From a policy perspective, the research will help inform the development of policies and standards related to IFMIS and other integrated financial management systems for both governments and the private sector. It will also help in developing interoperable/integrated systems planning and control guidelines for both governments and the private sector.

REFERENCES

Alsharari, N. M., & Youssef, M. A. E. A. (2017). Management accounting change and the implementation of GFMIS: A Jordanian case study. *Asian Review of Accounting*, 25(2), 242–261. doi:10.1108/ARA-06-2016-0062

Andrews, M. (2013). The Limits of Institutional Reform in Development: Changing Rules for Realistic Solutions. New Delhi: Cambridge University Press. doi:10.1017/CBO9781139060974

Betley, M., Bird, A., & Ghartey, A. (2012). *Evaluation of Public Financial Management Reform in Ghana, 2001–2010*. Final Country Case Study Report.

Boateng, R. (2016). Resources, Electronic-Commerce Capabilities and Electronic-Commerce Benefits: Conceptualizing the Links. *Information Technology for Development*, 22(6), 1–23.

Boateng, R., Acheampong, B., & Bedi, I. (2019). Preliminary Insights into Dominant Issues, Theories and Methodologies in Platform Interoperability Research. In *Twenty-Fifth American Conference on Information Systems* (pp.1-10). Cancun, Mexico: Association for Information Systems Electronic Library.

Boateng, R., & Hinson, R. (2008). Information Systems Development: Where Does Knowledge Lie and How Does Learning Occur? *Development and Learning in Organizations*, *22*(3), 18–20. doi:10.1108/14777280810861785

Chalu, H. (2019). The effect of IFMIS adoption on financial reporting quality in Tanzanian local governments. *Business Management Review*, *22*(2), 1–31.

Dorotinsky, W., & Watkins, J. (2013). Government Financial Management Information Systems. In *The International Handbook of Public Financial Management* (pp. 797–816). London: Palgrave Macmillan. doi:10.1057/9781137315304_37

Effah, J., & Nuhu, H. (2017). Institutional barriers to digitalization of government budgeting in developing countries: A case study of Ghana. *The Electronic Journal on Information Systems in Developing Countries*, *82*(1), 1–17. doi:10.1002/j.1681-4835.2017.tb00605.x

Effah, P. (2011). A Ghanaian response to the study on 'widening participation in higher education in Ghana and Tanzania: Developing an equity scorecard'. *Research in Comparative and International Education*, *6*(4), 374–382. doi:10.2304/rcie.2011.6.4.374

Estermann, B., Riedl, R., & Neuroni, A. C. (2009, May). Integrated and transcendent e-Government: keys for analyzing organizational structure and governance. In *Proceedings of the 10th Annual International Conference on Digital Government Research: Social Networks: Making Connections between Citizens, Data and Government* (pp. 162-171). Digital Government Society of North America.

Gcora, N., & Chigona, W. (2019). Post-implementation evaluation and challenges of Integrated Financial Management Information Systems for municipalities in South Africa. *South African Journal of Information Management*, *21*(1), 1–12. doi:10.4102ajim.v21i1.1066

Gioia, D. A., & Chittipeddi, K. (1991). Sensemaking and sensegiving in strategic change initiation. *Strategic Management Journal*, *12*(6), 433–448. doi:10.1002mj.4250120604

Gogan, J. L., Williams, C. B., & Fedorowicz, J. (2007). RFID and interorganisational collaboration: political and administrative challenges. *Electronic Government, an International Journal*, *4*(4), 423-435.

Gregory, R. W., Beck, R., & Keil, M. (2013). Control balancing in information systems development offshoring projects. *Management Information Systems Quarterly*, *37*(4), 1211–1232. doi:10.25300/MISQ/2013/37.4.10

Guijarro, L. (2009). Semantic interoperability in eGovernment initiatives. *Computer Standards & Interfaces*, *31*(1), 174–180. doi:10.1016/j.csi.2007.11.011

Hendriks, C. J. (2013). Integrated Financial Management Information Systems: Guidelines for effective implementation by the public sector of South Africa. *South African Journal of Information Management*, *15*(1), 1–9.

IEEE. (2000). *The Authoritative Dictionary of IEEE Standards Terms* (7th ed.). IEEE Std.

ISO 16100. (2002). *Manufacturing Software Capability Profiling for interoperability, Part 1: Framework, TC 184/SC5/WG4*. Geneva, Switzerland: ICS 25.040.01, 2002.

Jenkin, T. A., Chan, Y. E., & Sabherwal, R. (2019). Mutual understanding in information systems development: Changes within and across projects. *Management Information Systems Quarterly*, *43*(2), 649–672. doi:10.25300/MISQ/2019/13980

Kirsch, L. J. (2004). Deploying Common Systems Globally: The Dynamics of Control. *Information Systems Research*, *4*(15), 374–395. doi:10.1287/isre.1040.0036

Kubicek, H., & Cimander, R. (2009). Three dimensions of organizational interoperability. *European Journal of ePractice, 6*, 1-12.

Lyytinen, K. (1987). Different Perspectives on Information Systems: Problems and Solutions. *ACM Computing Surveys*, *19*(1), 5–46. doi:10.1145/28865.28867

Micheni, E. M. (2017). Analysis of the Critical Success Factors of Integrated Financial Management Information Systems in Selected Kenyan Counties. *Journal of Finance and Accounting*, *5*(5), 185. doi:10.11648/j.jfa.20170505.12

Nayar, A., & Beldona, S. (2010). Interoperability and open travel alliance standards: Strategic perspectives. *International Journal of Contemporary Hospitality Management*, *22*(7), 1010–1032. doi:10.1108/09596111011066653

Nor, A. I. (2019). Increasing government revenue through integrated financial management system case of federal government of Somalia. *European Journal of Economic and Financial Research.*, *3*(5), 9–20.

Nuhu, H., Effah, J., & Van Belle, J. P. (2018). Implementing E-government Financial Systems in a Developing Country: An Institutional Perspective. *Development Informatics Association (IDIA 2018)*, 45.

Rezaei, R., Chiew, T. K., & Lee, S. P. (2014). A review on E-business Interoperability Frameworks. *Journal of Systems and Software*, *93*, 199–216. doi:10.1016/j.jss.2014.02.004

Scholl, H. J., & Klischewski, R. (2007). E-government integration and interoperability: Framing the research agenda. *International Journal of Public Administration*, *30*(8-9), 889–920. doi:10.1080/01900690701402668

Sharma, R., & Panigrahi, P. K. (2015). *Developing a roadmap for planning and implementation of interoperability capability in e-government. Transforming Government: People*, Process and Policy.

Stigliani, I., & Ravasi, D. (2012). Organizing thoughts and connecting brains: Material practices and the transition from individual to group-level prospective sensemaking. *Academy of Management Journal*, *55*(5), 1232–1259. doi:10.5465/amj.2010.0890

Tanko, S. (2013). *GIFMIS to manage public funds, Ghana News Agency*. Retrieved on 5 April 2019 from https://www.ghanaweb.com/GhanaHomePage/business/GIFMIS-to-manage-public-funds-273365#

van der Veer, H., & Wiles, A. (2008). Achieving technical interoperability. In *European telecommunications standards institute* (3rd ed.). ETSI White Paper No. 3.

Vlaar, P. W., van Fenema, P. C., & Tiwari, V. (2008). Cocreating understanding and value in distributed work: How members of onsite and offshore vendor teams give, make, demand, and break sense. *Management Information Systems Quarterly*, *32*(2), 227–255. doi:10.2307/25148839

Wallace, L., Keil, M., & Rai, A. (2003). How Software Project Risk Affects Project Performance: An Investigation of the Dimensions of Risk and an Exploratory Model. *Decision Sciences*, *2*(35), 289–321.

Weichhart, G. (2015). Supporting the evolution and interoperability of organisational models with e-learning technologies. *Annual Reviews in Control*, *39*, 118–127. doi:10.1016/j.arcontrol.2015.03.011

Weick, K. E., Sutcliffe, K. M., & Obstfeld, D. (2005). Organizing and the process of sensemaking. *Organization Science*, *16*(4), 409–421. doi:10.1287/orsc.1050.0133

World Bank. (2015). *Managing Change in PFM System Reforms: A Guide for Practitioners. Financial Management Information Systems Community of Practice*. World Bank Group. Retrieved on 12 June 2019 from http://bit.ly/2MtTrHy

Yeboah, S. K. (2015). *Public Sector Financial Management Reforms in Ghana: The Case of Ghana Integrated Financial Management Information System (GIFMIS)* (Masters Thesis). University of Ghana Business School. http://ugspace.ug.edu.gh

Chapter 27
Strategic Responses to Disruptive Digital Innovation and Their Effects in the News Media Industry:
A Viewpoint for Future Research

Vonbackustein Klaus Komla
Business School, University of Ghana, Ghana

ABSTRACT

Digital innovation (DI) drives the digitalisation of goods and services, which also destroys established business models while creating new value chains. This effect is known as disruptive digital innovation (DDI). Beyond transportation and lodging, the effect is also evident in the news media industry. DIs facilitate an ecosystem in which the distinction between service providers and users become blurred – social media is birthing microbloggers as alternatives to incumbent media networks. There are questions on how firms—both incumbent and startups—strategically respond to DDIs and their effects. For the news media in developing countries, the concern is more acute. First, there are fewer established news sources; second, internet and media regulations are often non-existent or nascent stages, so experimentation is easier for DDI-enabled firms and citizen journalists; and third, fake news is not healthy for contexts with a history of political instability or where people have limited avenues to verify news, be it online, radio, or print. The need for this research is now.

INTRODUCTION

Digital innovations have become a global phenomenon, but one with unintended and undesired effects. These digital innovations or technologies are creating digital disruption, rapidly digitizing businesses, breaking down industry barriers and creating new opportunities while destroying proven and successful business models (Weill & Woerner, 2015). Literature has established that digital innovations create a

DOI: 10.4018/978-1-7998-2610-1.ch027

hypercompetitive market environment that forces firms which desire to survive and remain competitive to become agile (Chan, Teoh, Yeow & Pan, 2019; Infosys, 2018). This effect is known as a Disruptive Digital Innovation (DDI) (Chan et al., 2019). It has also been expressed in other terminologies including Disruptive Information System Innovation (DISI) (Carlo, Lyytinen & Rose, 2011), Disruptive Innovation (DI) (Parry & Kawakami, 2017), or Disruptive Technology (DT) (Christensen, 1997).

Notably, research on digital disruption dates back to the theory of disruptive technologies of Christensen (1997) who described disruptive technology as a "technology that, when first introduced, delivers (1) inferior performance on key attributes valued by mainstream markets and (2) superior performance on alternative attributes valued by "fringe" customers" (Parry & Kawakami, 2017, p.141). Thereafter, over time, products developed through disruptive technologies may also deliver superior performance on the key attributes which are valued by the mainstream markets (Christensen, 1997). These products tend to outperform the dominant existing products on the key dimensions that drive customer choice (Sood & Tellis, 2011). Hence, incumbent firms which fail to respond to or invest in disruptive technologies tend to lose when the mainstream markets begin to value the products of disruptive technologies. The products of disruptive technologies are known as disruptive innovations or digital disruptive innovations. Digital disruptive innovations are products birthed from disruptive technologies that deliver superior performance on attributes that are valued by or become the choice of mainstream markets (Yu & Hand, 2010). Thus, incumbent firms may initially consider digital disruptive innovations as ''inferior' innovations, which may be cheaper, simpler, smaller, more convenient, more accessible or less commercially packaged and are only valued by niche customer segments (Christensen, 1997). However, over time, these 'inferior' innovations gradually improve and become good enough to serve the mainstream market as a cheaper or more accessible alternative (Kumaraswamy, Garud & Ansari, 2018; Tellis, 2006). In effect, incumbent firms who fail to unwed from their business model and long-standing offerings suffer declining performance (Kumaraswamy et al., 2018). Incumbents are, therefore, advised by Christensen to develop their disruption by setting up a separate business unit to manage DDIs (Christensen, 1997).

Despite these contributions by Christensen (1997), DDIs are continually emerging and the dynamics of this new emergence has raised a number of questions. Almost every industry or sector has experienced some form of disruption, which leads to change (Butler & Martin, 2016). Sectors in which technologies have been disruptive include transportation and ridesharing (Circella & Alemi, 2018) and healthcare (Kushins, Heard & Weber, 2017). These innovations serve as platforms which other companies embrace to build upon and therefore disrupt existing relationships in entire industries and ecosystems, instead of affecting specific incumbent firms (Kumaraswamy et al., 2018).

For example, Uber's ride-hailing platform establishes an ecosystem of ride-sharers which displaces or disrupts the traditional transport networks like taxicab services while blurring the boundaries between service providers and users (The Economist, 2015). This form of disruption is making it difficult for regulators to define the company in many countries, including those in Africa (Degadjor, 2018).

Another example is the rise of citizen journalism in the new media industry, which was birthed from the disruptive effects of social media and other Web 2.0 technologies. Wu (2017) notes that newsrooms' integration of social media and entrepreneurialism (entrepreneurial journalism) is blurring the line between reporters and editors. A hybrid model has been birthed; both reporters and editors take on promotional duties in addition to traditional journalistic roles. Further, professional journalists are now engaged in micro-blogging, moving from their traditional professional roles in a number of ways, including expressing personal opinions, sharing posts and offering background information on social media (Lasorsa, Lewis & Holton 2012).

These new and emerging disruptive technologies create products (DDIs) which are in themselves platforms for the creation of new products, services and disruptive business models. As a platform, they facilitate a space or an ecosystem that draws in both "fringe" customers and those from the mainstream market to participate in creating the disruption. Thus, the distinction between service providers and users of DDIs become blurred; they are now active participants of an ecosystem or platform which creates the disruption. In such scenarios, how can the performance of the DDI be defined since it is being co-created; it is not dependent only on the service provider, but users are now part of the disruptive process?

At this intersection of ecosystems and performativity, researchers can ask these questions. First, how are incumbent firms responding to DDIs which exist within an ecosystem or a platform which embraces collaboration, competition and temporal relationships? Second, in what ways, beyond cheaper, simpler, smaller, more convenient, and more accessible do such DDIs enable adopters/users outperform incumbent firms? Third, what are the broader ethical, social and political effects of the responses of incumbent firms as well as the strategies of the new entrant firms (enabled by the DDIs) (Kumaraswamy et al., 2018; Ozalp, Cennamo, & Gawer, 2018; Tellis, 2006). These questions form the premise of this viewpoint.

RATIONALE FOR THIS RESEARCH

Whereas most studies have focused on how larger firms, primarily in developed countries, get to be agile, there are few studies which focus on how small and medium-sized enterprises (SMEs) respond to DDI. A study in *Information Systems Journal* by Chan et al. (2019) attempted to address this imbalance. The study developed a framework on agility based on the processes of mitigating organizational rigidity, developing innovative capabilities, and balancing the tension of organizational ambidexterity (Chan et al., 2019). However, there is a need for more studies, especially in more dynamic and volatile industries like the news media industry, which has often been overlooked in previous industry reports on digital disruption (Infosys, 2018) but is gaining attention by researchers (Wu, 2017). The new media industry is being disrupted by DDIs that exist within an ecosystem or platform which embraces collaboration, competition and temporal relationships.

These DDIs enable the formation of start-ups which disrupt the traditional news media industry – creating opportunities for competition and collaboration and in some cases, interdependences. A study on how DDIs enable the formation and agility of start-ups in the news media industry in a developing economy is likely to generate fresh insights on the framework of Chan et al. (2018) whiles providing strategic guidelines on how incumbent and new firms in such contexts can respond to DDI while surviving and remaining competitive.

Then again, some research has suggested that large firms could adopt an acquisition strategy that targets younger firms to offset their lower and less radical innovation levels (Bertrand-Cloodt, Hagedoorn & Van Kranenburg, 2011). For example, in 2008, Google offered to buy the social news aggregator, Digg, for $200 million (Sherwin, 2012). These large firms may either wait for younger firms to experiment with and understand these technologies before acquiring them, or acquire them so the younger firms can experiment with DDI under the large firms' supervision (Zhang, Kettinger, Kolte & Yoo, 2018).

Research exploring this and related strategies can enhance the knowledge on how to strategically leverage DDI to become agile and achieve value. Other research could explore the reasons underpinning adopters' choices regarding the technologies they use as well as the extent to which adopters' choices are shaped by effective marketing of technologies (Al-Imarah & Shields, 2018). Further, extant studies describe the stages and characteristics of disruptive innovation that apply to both products and services in sectors such as the automobile and transport (Butler & Martin, 2016) and education (Al-Imarah & Shields, 2018) sectors. Future research can, therefore, explore contextual influences leading to the birth of disruptors or DDI firms in informal aspects of established industries like the news media industry. But, one may ask, why the news media industry?

A growing phenomenon in the news media industry birthed by DDIs is fake news or 'information disorder' - misinformation, disinformation, and mal-information. This has led to questions as to what news is trustworthy and the trustworthiness of the person – professional or 'citizen' journalist – who shares a story and the credibility of the news outlet reporting the story (Sterrett et al., 2019; Bakir & McStay, 2018). So the "new" news product could be considered inferior in that regard. Then again, research in Kenya, Nigeria and South Africa established that perceived exposure to disinformation is high, and that, trust in social and national media is low (Wasserman & Madrid-Morales, 2019). The authors also add that 'mis'- and disinformation campaigns in Africa have arguably been used to influence political agendas, and often countermeasures from governments tend to affect other democratic rights of actors who may not have been engaged in such campaigns. In a response to these undesirable effects of DDIs, a number of independent data-driven organisations are emerging to fact-check legacy news media as well as other news sources (Cheruiyot & Ferrer-Conill, 2018). Examples of such organisations include Open Up, Africa Check, and Code for Africa. A study by Cheruiyot and Ferrer-Conill (2018) on practitioners from these three organisations concluded that although such organisations may be considered as non-journalistic actors who work at the periphery of news media, their goals and activities are central to the journalistic discourse.

Thus, the birth of fake news from the unintended consequences of DDIs has led to such startups who are also leveraging related digital innovations to address information disorder and thereby bringing back order into the journalistic discourse. The goals and operations of these startups in the news media industry echo the recommendations of Chan et al. (2019). The authors recommend that information system researchers should direct more research into DDIs and make their contribution towards economic growth, employment creation, and a more inclusive world. DDIs which exist in ecosystems or create a platform that embraces new firms which make a positive impact on socio-economic development or reorder the undesirable effects of DDIs may be worth studying to explore these recommendations.

These gaps sum the premise of this viewpoint. The context of future research is proposed to be a developing economy. Previous studies on e-commerce in developing economies have alluded to how firms become dynamic and respond to the opportunities and threats of e-commerce (Boateng, 2016; Boateng, Molla, Heeks & Hinson, 2011). These studies focused on the use of resources to create dynamic capabilities and were silent on strategies to respond to DDI with agility. However, the upsurge of social media and other digital innovations in the media industry and its reported effects re-emphasises the need to understand of the impact of DDI and how firms in the news media industry can survive and be competitive (The Economist, 2015; Wu, 2017). The originality of this future research lies in the fact that this is perhaps one of the first studies which draw on DDI and agility in the news media industry from a developing economy perspective. Such knowledge has hitherto been scarce. The developing country perspective tends to matter for several reasons. First, there are fewer established news sources; second, internet and media regulations are often non-existent or nascent stages so experimentation is easier for DDI-enabled firms and citizen journalists; and third, fake news is not healthy for contexts with a history of political instability or where people have limited avenues to verify news, be it online, radio or print.

Hence, there are broader ethical, social and political consequences which need to be explored and addressed (Cheruiyot & Ferrer-Conill, 2018; Sterrett et al., 2019; Bakir & McStay, 2018).

OBJECTIVES TO BE ADDRESSED

In reference to the above research gaps, this chapter argues that future research should seek to provide a better understanding on what describes how firms achieve agility to respond to digital disruptive innovations in the news media industry in a developing economy. The research will offer a theoretical understanding of how incumbent firms respond to DDIs which exist within an ecosystem or a platform which embraces collaboration, competition and temporal relationships, and in what ways, beyond cheaper, simpler, smaller, more convenient, and more accessible, do such DDIs enable adopters/users outperform incumbent firms.

This research should draw on the theory of digital disruption (Christensen, 1997) and the framework for responding to disruptive digital innovation (Chan et al., 2019) to explore how firms achieve agility to respond to digital disruptive innovations in the news media industry in developing economies. Specifically, future research should achieve the following objectives:

1. To understand how incumbent firms in the news media industry in developing economies respond to DDIs which exist within an ecosystem or a platform which embraces collaboration, competition and temporal relationships; and
2. To understand the other ways, beyond cheaper, simpler, smaller, more convenient, and more accessible, that such DDIs enable adopters/users to outperform incumbent firms in the news media industry in developing economies.
3. To understand the broader ethical, social and political effects of the responses of incumbent firms as well as the strategies of the new entrant firms (enabled by the DDIs)

The ensuing research questions are

1. What are the forms of digital disruptions in the news media industry in developing economies?
2. How do incumbent firms in the news media industry in developing economies respond to DDIs which exist within an ecosystem or a platform which embraces collaboration, competition and temporal relationships?
3. What other ways, beyond cheaper, simpler, smaller, more convenient, and more accessible, do such DDIs enable adopters/users to outperform incumbent firms in the news media industry in developing economies?
4. What are the broader ethical, social and political effects of the responses of incumbent firms as well as the strategies of the new entrant firms (enabled by the DDIs)?

CONCLUSION

This chapter has argued the need to develop a model that describes how firms achieve agility to respond to digital disruptive innovations in the news media industry. The significance of carrying out this research can be viewed from academic, practitioner and policy perspectives. First, there have been calls to extend the theory of disruptive technology especially regarding disruption in platform-based ecosystems and new and emerging technologies (Kumaraswamy et al., 2018; Ozalp et al., 2018; Tellis, 2006). Extant research has argued that the idiosyncratic contextual influences of developing countries offer an opportunity to test or develop theory related to the adoption and use of digital innovations (Boateng, 2016; Boateng, Molla, & Heeks, 2009). This research, from a developing economy perspective, will respond to the gaps and thereby contribute to theory. The study will also generate more valuable insights to follow-up the work of Chan et al. (2019) and also generate further understanding of the application of the framework to studying firms responding to disruption in platform-based ecosystems.

From a practitioner perspective, the proposed model will offer practitioners in the news media industry the strategies to leverage, respond to and survive DDIs in a developing economy context. It would also provide insights on how DDIs enable news to perform better and also impact on socio-economic development. From a policy perspective, the research will also help inform the development of policies and standards related to managing DDIs for firms in the news media industry and also guide regulators in understanding the effects of digital innovations on the industry.

REFERENCES

Al-Imarah, A. A., & Shields, R. (2018). MOOCs, disruptive innovation and the future of higher education: A conceptual analysis. *Innovations in Education and Teaching International*, 1–12.

Bakir, V., & McStay, A. (2018). Fake news and the economy of emotions: Problems, causes, solutions. *Digital Journalism*, 6(2), 154–175. doi:10.1080/21670811.2017.1345645

Bertrand-Cloodt, D., Hagedoorn, J., & Van Kranenburg, H. (2011). The strength of R&D network ties in high-tech sectors–a multi-dimensional analysis of the effects of tie strength on innovation performance. *Technology Analysis and Strategic Management*, 23(10), 1015–1030. doi:10.1080/09537325.2011.621294

Boateng, R. (2016). Resources, Electronic-Commerce Capabilities and Electronic-Commerce Benefits: Conceptualizing the Links. *Information Technology for Development*, 22(6), 1–23.

Boateng, R., Heeks, R., Molla, A., & Hinson, R. (2011). Advancing e-commerce beyond readiness in a developing country: Experiences of Ghanaian firms. *Journal of Electronic Commerce in Organizations*, 9(1), 1–16. doi:10.4018/jeco.2011010101

Butler, F. C., & Martin, J. A. (2016). The auto industry: Adapt to disruptive innovations or risk extinction. *Strategic Direction*, 32(11), 31–34. doi:10.1108/SD-05-2016-0069

Carlo, J. L., Lyytinen, K., & Rose, G. M. (2011). Internet computing as a disruptive information technology innovation: The role of strong order effects1. *Information Systems Journal*, 21(1), 91–122. doi:10.1111/j.1365-2575.2009.00345.x

Chan, C. M. L., Teoh, S. Y., Yeow, A., & Pan, G. (2019). Agility in responding to disruptive digital innovation: Case study of an SME. *Information Systems Journal*, 29(2), 436–455. doi:10.1111/isj.12215

Cheruiyot, D., & Ferrer-Conill, R. (2018). Fact-Checking Africa. *Digital Journalism*, 6(8), 964–975. doi:10.1080/21670811.2018.1493940

Christensen, C. M. (1997). *The Innovator's Dilemma: When New Technologies Cause Great Firms to Fail*. Boston: Harvard Business School Press.

Circella, G., & Alemi, F. (2018). Transport policy in the era of ridehailing and other disruptive transportation technologies. In *Advances in Transport Policy and Planning* (Vol. 1, pp. 119–144). Academic Press.

Degadjor, M. (2018). UBER Branding Saga: Why Ghana's MoT and GPRTU got it wrong. *Daily Graphic*. Retrieved on 6 April 2019 https://www.graphic.com.gh/features/opinion/uber-branding-saga-why-ghana-mot-and-gprtu-got-it-wrong.html

Infosys. (2018). *How Enterprises are Steering through Digital Disruption*. Infosys Limited. Retrieved on 6 April 2019 from https://www.infosys.com/digital-outlook/Documents/exclusive-report-digital-outlook.pdf

Kumaraswamy, A., Garud, R., & Ansari, S. (2018). Perspectives on Disruptive Innovations. *Journal of Management Studies*, *55*(7), 1025–1042. doi:10.1111/joms.12399

Kushins, E. R., Heard, H., & Weber, J. M. (2017). Disruptive innovation in rural American healthcare: The physician assistant practice. *International Journal of Pharmaceutical and Healthcare Marketing*, *11*(2), 165–182. doi:10.1108/IJPHM-10-2016-0056

Ozalp, H., Cennamo, C., & Gawer, A. (2018). Disruption in platform-based ecosystems. *Journal of Management Studies*, *55*(7), 1203–1241. doi:10.1111/joms.12351

Parry, M. E., & Kawakami, T. (2017). The Encroachment Speed of Potentially Disruptive Innovations with Indirect Network Externalities: The Case of E-Readers. *Journal of Product Innovation Management*, *34*(2), 141–158. doi:10.1111/jpim.12333

Sherwin, A. (2012). Former darling of social media changes hands for a pittance as users move on to other attractions. *Independent*. Retrieved 10 July 2019, from https://www.independent.co.uk/life-style/gadgets-and-tech/news/in-2008-google-offered-200m-for-it-today-digg-was-sold-for-500000-7942217.html

Sood, A., & Tellis, G. J. (2011). Demystifying disruption: A new model for understanding and predicting disruptive technologies. *Marketing Science*, *30*(2), 339–354. doi:10.1287/mksc.1100.0617

Sterrett, D., Malato, D., Benz, J., Kantor, L., Tompson, T., Rosenstiel, T., ... Loker, K. (2019). Who Shared It?: Deciding What News to Trust on Social Media. *Digital Journalism*, *7*(6), 783–801. doi:10.1080/21670811.2019.1623702

Tellis, G. J. (2006). Disruptive technology or visionary leadership? *Journal of Product Innovation Management*, *23*(1), 34–38. doi:10.1111/j.1540-5885.2005.00179.x

The Economist. (2015). *Disrupting Mr. Disrupter*. Retrieved from 15 May 2018 from https://www.economist.com/business/2015/11/26/disrupting-mr-disrupter

Wasserman, H., & Madrid-Morales, D. (2019). *An Exploratory Study of "Fake News" and Media Trust in Kenya*. African Journalism Studies.

Weill, P., & Woerner, S. L. (2015). Thriving in an increasingly digital ecosystem. *Sloan Management Review*, *56*, 27–34.

Wu, Y. (2017). The Disruption of Social Media. *Digital Journalism*, *6*(6), 777–797. doi:10.1080/2167 0811.2017.1376590

Yu, D., & Hang, C. C. (2010). A Reflective Review of Disruptive Innovation Theory. *International Journal of Management Reviews*, *12*(4), 435–452. doi:10.1111/j.1468-2370.2009.00272.x

Zhang, C., Kettinger, W. J., Kolte, P., & Yoo, S. (2018). Established companies' strategic responses to sharing economy threats. *MIS Quarterly Executive*, *17*(1), 23–40.

Chapter 28
Digital Platforms and Value Creation:
A Viewpoint and Pointers for Future Research

Joseph Budu

🆔 https://orcid.org/0000-0002-0003-5807

*Department of Information Systems and Innovation, School of Technology, Ghana Institute of
Management and Public Administration, Ghana*

ABSTRACT

*Digital platforms bring together different goal-oriented actors to exchange value. This phenomenon
has attracted research to understand various aspects of it. These studies show sophisticated technologies
are likely to accompany advanced value creation strategies and higher performance gain, and
how organizational-level technology usage affects organizational value creation. Nonetheless, we still
lack a theoretical and practical understanding of how digital platforms in general, and those for music
specifically create value for industry stakeholders. Therefore, the purpose of this chapter is to make a
case for future research on digital platform value creation.*

INTRODUCTION

The music industry generates enormous economic value globally. For instance, in 2018, the total value
of the global music recording industry was US $19.1 billion (Moore, 2019). Unfortunately, developing
economies have not enjoyed much of this generated value. Thankfully, this disparity is reducing change
with the diffusion and use of Internet-based marketplaces known as digital platforms (Thies, Wessel,
& Benlian, 2018). On digital music platforms such as Spotify, Deezer, and Aftown, musicians sell their
music as digital singles, full albums, or streamed content (Koh, Hann, & Raghunathan, 2019). The benefits
the musicians accrue from such platforms are unclear. Therefore, we need to explain the value creation
mechanisms of digital music platforms in developing economies' music industry. Such explanations are
necessary to replicate successes and minimise unintended consequences. Unfortunately, explanations

DOI: 10.4018/978-1-7998-2610-1.ch028

of how digital music platforms create value are missing. Successive studies have attempted to explain aspects of value but still fall short of explaining the contributory mechanisms. Such attempts focus on the theoretical foundations of value creation in e-business (Amit & Zott, 2001); the value network concept and its value-creating logic (Peppard & Rylander, 2006); and how mobile ticketing technologies successfully enable revenue management (Li, Heck, & Vervest, 2009). Others also focus on the dynamic cycle of control points in creating value with digital business strategy (Pagani, 2013), creating and capturing value under moral hazard (Obloj & Zemsky, 2015), how the use of big data analytics affects value creation in supply chain management (Chen, Preston, & Swink, 2015), and a review of how the need to advance value capture theory (Gans & Ryall, 2017).

We find in these valuable studies that, in e-business new value can be created by how transactions are enabled, and that e-businesses' value creation potential hinges on efficiency, complementarities, lock-in, and novelty (Amit & Zott, 2001). Further, integrity and efficiency increase value creation and capture for all parties and are complements (Obloj & Zemsky, 2015). The studies also show that sophisticated technologies are more likely to accompany advanced value creation strategies and higher performance gain (Li et al., 2009). Moreover, organisational-level technology usage affects organisational value creation, a relationship moderated by environmental dynamism and technological factors (Chen et al., 2015). Nonetheless, we still lack a theoretical and practical understanding of how digital platforms in general, and those for music specifically, create value for industry stakeholders. These unexplained issues raise new questions that previous research has failed to answer. The purpose of this viewpoint article is to make a case for future research on digital platform value creation.

HIGHLIGHTS OF PREVIOUS DIGITAL PLATFORMS RESEARCH

Digital platforms related to value creation is quite scanty; research platform development issues dominate the area. The focal issues are in two groups; the first concerns the creation of digital platforms, while the other concerns the growth of digital platforms. On the one hand, studies that fall in the first group report on how some digital platform was created. Some researched platforms include those for robotics design (Keating & Oxman, 2013), software copy protection and digital rights management (Bahaa-eldin & Sobh, 2014), prescription of custom-made insoles (Mandolini, Brunzini, & Germani, 2016), personalised advertising (Athanasiadis & Mitropoulos, 2010), and a digital soil mapping (Jiang et al., 2016). A few studies have also sought to identify user requirements and system requirements and evaluation criteria for digital platforms. For instance, while user requirements, architecture and functionality were identified for a NeuroIS experimental platform called Brownie (Adam et al., 2017), an evaluation criterion for digital music service platforms has also been proposed (see Lin, Shih, Tzeng, & Yu, 2016).

On the other hand, those studies that fall in the second group, although fewer, have sought to explore the growth of digital platforms over time. These studies include an exploration of the role of information system capabilities in the development of digital platforms (see Tan et al., 2015), and how information technology enables market leadership through digital platforms (see Tan et al., 2016). This second group of research is related more to the business and organisational aspects of digital platforms and brings to the fore other related issues explored in extant research.

Digital platforms research studying aspects of value creation focus on competition. Competition is a focus of many digital platform studies, is not surprising considering that such platforms often seek to win an advantage over some existing traditional non-digital platform (Kim et al., 2016). Such competition further manifests in struggles between multiple digital service platforms due to different development paths (Ruutu, Casey, & Kotovirta, 2017), and among members who sell on platforms (Belleflamme & Toulemonde, 2016). Some of the causal factors identified include the risks posed by the number of developers used in developing a digital platform (Parker, Alstyne, & Jiang, 2017), and some features of digital platforms which give them market entry capabilities (Kazan & Damsgaard, 2016). Other value-related issues studied include how to innovate with digital platforms (Sedera, Lokuge, Grover, Sarker, & Sarker, 2016), and the fight for control over digital platform spaces (De Reuver & Ondrus, 2017).

Furthermore, the value-laden nature of digital platforms seems to have generated a lot of business model analysis studies. In this regard, while some papers only present descriptions and technical analysis of specific types of digital platforms like crowdfunding (e.g. Belleflamme, Omrani, & Peitz, 2015; Roskos, Brueck, & Lenhart, 2017), other papers have studied various business model issues including analysis and appraisals of platform models (e.g. Brown, Fishenden, Thompson, & Venters, 2017; Ranerup, Zinner, & Hedman, 2016; Tauscher & Laudien, 2017), platform revenue models (e.g. Chen, Fan, & Li, 2016), the configuration and redesign of platform business models (Parmentier & Gandia, 2017; Tauscher & Laudien, 2017), and classic business model analysis (Poel, Renda, & Ballon, 2007). Consumer issues on digital platforms are not missing from available research. There is research effort dedicated to understanding the adoption of digital platforms (e.g. Ruutu et al., 2017; Sanz & Crosbie, 2016), preference heterogeneity and consumer expectations in adopting digital platforms (Steiner, Wiegand, Eggert, & Backhaus, 2016), the factors that affect platform-based repurchases (Kim & Shin, 2017), and consumers' intentions for purchasing counterfeit goods on digital platforms (Thaichon & Quach, 2016).

The next section points some potential gaps for future research based on the previous digital platform research.

POINTERS FOR FUTURE RESEARCH

The existence of information systems and digital artefacts have had one form of impact or another. For instance, while social media has created opportunities for organisations to co-create and empower their customers (Dobele, Steel, & Cooper, 2015), digital platforms are creating new jobs (Graham, Hjorth, & Lehdonvirta, 2017), and causing structural transformation in the delivery of government services (Brown et al., 2017). Thus by extension, digital platforms could have an impact on their users as well even though this seems to be an under-researched issue. From an information communication technology for development (ICT4D) perspective, digital platforms could be a response to achieving poverty reduction in resource-poor contexts. However, future research about this issue needs to consider the context-dependence of the effect of information systems, especially when convincing arguments about IT-enabled socioeconomic development seem missing (Avgerou, 2010). The following research questions could be useful pointers.

1. How do digital platforms contribute to value creation in specific industries?
2. How do digital platforms impact on human capabilities?
3. How do digital platforms impact the environment?
4. What are the stakeholders' perceptions of impact created by digital platforms?

In the last decade, digitisation has dramatically affected most of the media industries, including that of music. As a result, consumers can now access a broader range of music files at a minimal cost, and through various devices like notebooks and smartphones. In contrast, music producers, especially in the developing world, may not be able to boast of the matching value. In light of this contradiction, there is a need for understanding the impact of digitisation on the music industry and to assess its effects on welfare (Aguiar & Martens, 2016, p. 27). Further, there is a lingering question about who benefits from music traded on digital platforms (Belleflamme & Toulemonde, 2016).

Further, value creation has been studied mostly from the business' perspective (Chen et al., 2015; Li et al., 2009; Obloj & Zemsky, 2015). Meanwhile, the leadership of information systems researchers have called for future research to extend beyond business management issues into issues of societal concern and benefit (Lee & Fedorowicz, 2018; Lee, 2016). Unfortunately, later value creation research perpetuates the focus on business management issues in information systems. For instance, a study published by the Journal of Management Information Systems (Grover, Chiang, Liang, & Zhang, 2018) focused on how businesses can create value using Big Data Analytics (BDA). The study highlighted on BDA's value proposition and how BDA's components create and release value for businesses. The study identifies two forms of organisational impact from BDA, namely, functional value (e.g., market share, financial performance) and symbolic value. Functional value refers to performance improvement directly resulting from adopting BDA. In contrast, symbolic value (e.g., positive brand image and reputation, mitigating environmental pressure) is mostly derived through the "signalling effect" of investment in BDA. Consequently, the study and its framework failed to theorise the value creation and its effect beyond the organisation.

Moreover, the gaps in prominent digital platform reviews (Asadullah, Faik, & Kankanhalli, 2018; De Reuver, Sørensen, & Basole, 2018; Rossotto et al., 2018) point that currently there is mostly a lack of theorisation in digital platform studies. Therefore, theorisation should underpin future digital platform research. Such research should, first, take into account digital platform's multiple dimensions – business model governance mode, ownership structure, and interaction mode when studying digital platforms or adopting them as a business strategy (Asadullah et al., 2018). Second, future research should advance conceptual clarity by providing explicit definitions that specify the sociotechnical nature of digital platforms; and define the proper scoping of digital platform concepts by studying platforms in different industry settings (De Reuver et al., 2018).

To address the new questions that digital music platforms generate, and the need to explain value creation beyond business management issues, future studies can draw on and extend Grover's et al. (2018) model to explore the structures and mechanisms which underpin value creation by digital music platforms. Such studies can explore the founding, acceptance, use and impact of a digital music platform developed to improve the revenues of musicians. Even though there have been some studies on digital music platforms (e.g. Koh et al., 2019), a study explaining value creation mechanisms should be unique in generating more valuable insights to follow-up the work of Grover et al. (2018). Such a study can pursue the following research questions:

1. What materiality of digital music platforms contributes to value creation;
2. How does the relationship between individual, organisational and societal actors with digital music platform materiality contribute to value creation?
3. How do digital music platforms create value for musicians and stakeholders in the music industry?
4. How do digital music platforms impact the music industry in developing countries?

CONCLUSION

This viewpoint has presented evidence for the need to develop theoretical explanations of how digital music platforms create value for musicians in a developing economy. Future research that will address the research gaps and questions outlined would be significant to academia, practice, and policy. First, such a study would build on the work of Grover et al. (2018), which developed a model to explain how to create value with Big Data Analytics in organisations. The research will conceptualise a model that explains value creation in digital music platforms. The research will generate more valuable insights to follow up Grover et al.'s (2019) and also generate further understanding of applying value creation theory in digital music platforms. The importance of context-specific theorising in information systems research has been cited as an essential endeavour (Hong, Chan, Thong, Chasalow, & Dhillon, 2014). Future studies based on this viewpoint's research gaps can draw on this motivation to develop a model that explains the creation of value for musicians. For the international audience, a model explaining the value creation mechanisms in digital music platforms can highlight contextual issues that affect value creation. For instance, such a study can foster understanding of when an indigenous platform is more valuable or beneficial in some contexts, and when an international digital platform would be more or less beneficial.

REFERENCES

Adam, M. T. P., Lux, E., Pfeiffer, J., Dorner, V., Muller, M. B., & Weinhardt, C. (2017). Brownie: A Platform for Conducting NeuroIS Experiments. *Journal of the Association for Information Systems*, *18*(4), 264–296. doi:10.17705/1jais.00457

Aguiar, L., & Martens, B. (2016). Digital music consumption on the Internet: Evidence from clickstream data. *Information Economics and Policy*, *34*, 27–43. doi:10.1016/j.infoecopol.2016.01.003

Amit, R., & Zott, C. (2001). Value creation in e-business. *Strategic Management Journal*, *22*(6-7), 493–520. doi:10.1002/smj.187

Asadullah, A., Faik, I., & Kankanhalli, A. (2018). Digital Platforms: A Review and Future Directions. *Twenty-second Pacific Asia Conference on Information Systems*. 10.1017/CCOL9780521862387.020

Athanasiadis, E., & Mitropoulos, S. (2010). A distributed platform for personalised advertising in digital interactive TV environments. *Journal of Systems and Software*, *83*(8), 1453–1469. doi:10.1016/j.jss.2010.02.040

Avgerou, C. (2010). Discourses on ICT and Development. *Information Technologies and International Development*, *6*(3), 1–18.

Bahaa-eldin, A. M., & Sobh, M. A. A. (2014). A comprehensive Software Copy Protection and Digital Rights Management platform. Ain Shams Engineering Journal, 5(3), 703–720. doi:10.1016/j.asej.2014.03.001

Belleflamme, P., Omrani, N., & Peitz, M. (2015). The economics of crowdfunding platforms. *Information Economics and Policy*, *33*, 11–28. doi:10.1016/j.infoecopol.2015.08.003

Belleflamme, P., & Toulemonde, E. (2016). Who benefits from increased competition among sellers on B2C platforms? *Research in Economics*, *70*(4), 741–751. doi:10.1016/j.rie.2016.08.006

Brown, A., Fishenden, J., Thompson, M., & Venters, W. (2017). Appraising the impact and role of platform models and Government as a Platform (GaaP) in UK Government public service reform: Towards a Platform Assessment Framework (PAF). *Government Information Quarterly*, *34*(2), 167–182. doi:10.1016/j.giq.2017.03.003

Chen, D. Q., Preston, D. S., & Swink, M. (2015). How the Use of Big Data Analytics Affects Value Creation in Supply Chain Management. *Journal of Management Information Systems*, *32*(4), 4–39. doi:10.1080/07421222.2015.1138364

Chen, J., Fan, M., & Li, M. (2016). Advertising versus brokerage model for online trading platforms. *Management Information Systems Quarterly*, *40*(3), 575–596. doi:10.25300/MISQ/2016/40.3.03

De Reuver, M., Sørensen, C., & Basole, R. C. (2018). The digital platform: A research agenda. *Journal of Information Technology*, *33*(2), 124–135. doi:10.1057/s41265-016-0033-3

Dobele, A., Steel, M., & Cooper, T. (2015). Sailing the seven C's of blog marketing: Understanding social media and business impact. *Marketing Intelligence & Planning*, *33*(7), 1087–1102. doi:10.1108/MIP-02-2015-0039

Gans, J., & Ryall, M. D. (2017). Value capture theory: A strategic management review. *Strategic Management Journal*, *38*(1), 17–41. doi:10.1002/smj.2592

Graham, M., Hjorth, I., & Lehdonvirta, V. (2017). Digital labour and development: Impacts of global digital labour platforms and the gig economy on worker livelihoods. *Transfer: European Review of Labour and Research*, *23*(2), 135–162. doi:10.1177/1024258916687250 PubMed

Grover, V., Chiang, R. H. L., Liang, T.-P., & Zhang, D. (2018). Creating Strategic Business Value from Big Data Analytics: A Research Framework. *Journal of Management Information Systems*, *35*(2), 388–423. doi:10.1080/07421222.2018.1451951

Hong, W., Chan, F. K. Y., Thong, J. Y. L., Chasalow, L. C., & Dhillon, G. (2014). A framework and guidelines for context-specific theorising in information systems research. *Information Systems Research*, *25*(1), 111–136. doi:10.1287/isre.2013.0501

Jiang, J., Zhu, A., Qin, C., Zhu, T., Liu, J., Du, F., ... An, Y. (2016). CyberSoLIM: A cyber platform for digital soil mapping. *Geoderma*, *263*, 234–243. doi:10.1016/j.geoderma.2015.04.018

Kazan, E., & Damsgaard, J. (2016). Towards a Market Entry Framework for Digital Payment Platforms. *Communications of the Association for Information Systems*, *38*, 761–783. doi:10.17705/1CAIS.03837

Keating, S., & Oxman, N. (2013). Compound fabrication: A multi-functional robotic platform for digital design and fabrication. *Robotics and Computer-integrated Manufacturing*, *29*(6), 439–448. doi:10.1016/j.rcim.2013.05.001

Kim, H., & Shin, D. (2017). The effects of platform as a technology standard on platform-based repurchases. doi:10.1108/DPRG-11-2016-0054

Kim, J., Kim, S., & Nam, C. (2016). Competitive dynamics in the Korean video platform market : Traditional pay TV platforms vs OTT platforms. *Telematics and Informatics*, *33*(2), 711–721. doi:10.1016/j.tele.2015.06.014

Koh, B., Hann, I.-H., & Raghunathan, S. (2019). Digitisation of music: Consumer adoption amidst piracy, unbundling, and rebundling. *Management Information Systems Quarterly*, *43*(1), 23–45. doi:10.25300/MISQ/2019/14812

Lee, J., & Fedorowicz, J. (2018). Identifying Issues for the Bright ICT Initiative: A Worldwide Delphi Study of IS Journal Editors and Scholars. *Communications of the Association for Information Systems*, *42*, 301–333. doi:10.17705/1CAIS.04211

Lee, J. K. (2016). Invited Commentary—Reflections on ICT-enabled Bright Society Research. *Information Systems Research*, *27*(1), 1–5. doi:10.1287/isre.2016.0627

Li, T., Heck, E. V., & Vervest, P. (2009). Information capability and value creation strategy: Advancing revenue management through mobile ticketing technologies. *European Journal of Information Systems*, *18*(1), 38–51. doi:10.1057/ejis.2009.1

Lin, C., Shih, Y., Tzeng, G., & Yu, H. (2016). A service selection model for digital music service platforms using a hybrid MCDM approach. *Applied Soft Computing*, *48*, 385–403. doi:10.1016/j.asoc.2016.05.035

Mandolini, M., Brunzini, A., & Germani, M. (2016). A collaborative web-based platform for the prescription of Custom-Made Insoles. *Advanced Engineering Informatics*.

Moore, F. (2019). Global recorded music sales totalled US $19.1 billion in 2018. Retrieved June 12, 2019, from https://www.ifpi.org/global-statistics.php

Obloj, T., & Zemsky, P. (2015). Value creation and value capture under moral hazard: Exploring the micro-foundations of buyer-supplier relationships. *Strategic Management Journal*, *36*(8), 1146–1163. doi:10.1002/smj.2271

Pagani, M. (2013). Digital business strategy and value creation: Framing the dynamic cycle of control points. *Management Information Systems Quarterly*, *37*(2), 617–632. doi:10.25300/MISQ/2013/37.2.13

Parker, G., Van Alstyne, M., & Jiang, X. (2017). Platform ecosystems: How developers invert the firm. *Management Information Systems Quarterly*, *41*(1), 255–266. doi:10.25300/MISQ/2017/41.1.13

Parmentier, G., & Gandia, R. (2017). Redesigning the business model: From one-sided to multi-sided. *The Journal of Business Strategy*, *38*(2), 52–61. doi:10.1108/JBS-09-2016-0097

Peppard, J., & Rylander, A. (2006). From Value Chain to Value Network : Insights for Mobile Operators. *European Management Journal*, *24*(2–3), 128–141. doi:10.1016/j.emj.2006.03.003

Poel, M., Renda, A., & Ballon, P. (2007). Business model analysis as a new tool for policy evaluation: Policies for digital content platforms. *Info*, *9*(5), 86–100. doi:10.1108/14636690710816471

Ranerup, A., Zinner, H., & Hedman, J. (2016). An analysis of business models in Public Service Platforms. *Government Information Quarterly*, *33*(1), 6–14. doi:10.1016/j.giq.2016.01.010

Reuver, M. D. (2017). When technological superiority is not enough: The struggle to impose the SIM card as the NFC Secure Element for mobile payment platforms. *Telecommunications Policy*, *41*(4), 253–262. doi:10.1016/j.telpol.2017.01.004

Roskos, K., Brueck, J., & Lenhart, L. (2017). An analysis of e-book learning platforms: Affordances, architecture, functionality and analytics. *International Journal of Child-Computer Interaction*, *12*, 37–45. doi:10.1016/j.ijcci.2017.01.003

Rossotto, C. M., Das, P. L., Ramos, E. G., Miranda, E. C., Farid Badran, M., Licetti, M. M., & Murciego, G. M. (2018). Digital platforms: A literature review and policy implications for development. *Competition and Regulation in Network Industries*, *19*(1–2), 1–17. doi:10.1177/1783591718809485

Ruutu, S., Casey, T., & Kotovirta, V. (2017). Development and competition of digital service platforms : A system dynamics approach. *Technological Forecasting and Social Change*, *117*, 119–130. doi:10.1016/j.techfore.2016.12.011

Sanz, E., & Crosbie, T. (2016). The meaning of digital platforms: Open and closed television infrastructure. *Poetics*, *55*, 76–89. doi:10.1016/j.poetic.2015.11.002

Sedera, D., Lokuge, S., Grover, V., Sarker, S., & Sarker, S. (2016). Innovating with enterprise systems and digital platforms: A contingent resource-based theory view. *Information & Management*, *53*(3), 366–379. doi:10.1016/j.im.2016.01.001

Steiner, M., Wiegand, N., Eggert, A., & Backhaus, K. (2016). Platform adoption in system markets: The roles of preference heterogeneity and consumer expectations. *International Journal of Research In Marketing Journal*, *33*(2), 276–296. doi:10.1016/j.ijresmar.2015.05.011

Tan, B., Lu, X., Pan, S. L., & Huang, L. (2015). The Role of IS Capabilities in the Development of Multi-Sided Platforms: The Digital Ecosystem Strategy of Alibaba.com. *Journal of the Association for Information Systems*, *16*(4), 248–280. doi:10.17705/1jais.00393

Tan, F. T. C., Tan, B., & Pan, S. (2016). Developing a Leading Digital Multi-sided Platform: Examining IT Affordances and Competitive. *Communications of the Association for Information Systems*, *38*, 738–760. doi:10.17705/1CAIS.03836

Tauscher, K., & Laudien, S. M. (2017). Understanding platform business models: A mixed methods study of marketplaces. *European Management Journal*, ▪▪▪, 1–11.

Thaichon, P., & Quach, S. (2016). Dark motives-counterfeit purchase framework : Internal and external motives behind counterfeit purchase via digital platforms. *Journal of Retailing and Consumer Services*, *33*, 82–91. doi:10.1016/j.jretconser.2016.08.003

Thies, F., Wessel, M., & Benlian, A. (2018). Network effects on crowdfunding platforms: Exploring the implications of relaxing input control. *Information Systems Journal*, *28*(6), 1239–1262. doi:10.1111/isj.12194

Chapter 29
Exploring the Scope of User Resistance:
A Bibliometric Review of 41 Years of Research

Sylvester Tetey Aseidu
Business School, University of Ghana, Ghana

Richard Boateng
https://orcid.org/0000-0002-9995-3340
Business School, University of Ghana, Ghana

ABSTRACT

Although innovation adoption has been given much attention in information systems (IS) literature, it has less to account for in user resistance. This chapter contributes to this ongoing debate through a bibliometric review of the user resistance research for the period 1978 to the first quarter of 2019 to provide a coherent overview of the recent research trends and theoretical cornerstones. The authors merged two approaches—co-citation analysis and bibliographic coupling—to (1) create a visualized network of articles that focus on 'user resistance' and (2) to create distinct yet related clusters of articles related thematically. In the findings, they illustrate via the co-citation analysis that user resistance research builds on four main theoretical cornerstones: status quo bias and equity implementation theories, organizational change, social influence and perceived usefulness, power and politics. In conclusion, more research is needed on this theme from a developing economy perspective as IS adoption and usage gains maturity.

INTRODUCTION

Introducing a new information system comes along with varied changes to how existing processes work. This equally affects how employees/users respond to such changes which are most often reflected in their work routines. These changes could be as small as installing a new feature or as big as making modifications to an existing system or as complex as deploying a new nationwide enterprise system

DOI: 10.4018/978-1-7998-2610-1.ch029

(Bin Taher, Krotov, & Silva, 2015). Users in each regard respond to such varied changes in different ways ranging from an upfront rejection to discontinued use over time, delayed use or partial use of the system, or positively embracing and wholeheartedly using the new system. Either of the former reactions can derail the objective for introducing an information system (IS) or render the entire project a failure (Gesulga, Berjame, Moquiala, & Galido, 2017).

Unlike other studies that have focused more on pre-adoption issues, not much has been done on post-adoption, with less to account for in the discussion of user resistance. From the ongoing discussions on user resistance, several arguments posit for the practical and theoretical relevance of more insightful reviews on user resistance (Bhattacherjee & Hikmet, 2007a; Lee & Joshi, 2017).

Firstly, the literature on user resistance, as fragmented as it is now, has barely been given the needed attention when compared to other IS literature like the adoption of innovation (Hsieh, 2015). Secondly, the literature on user resistance has been projected from different theoretical perspectives over the years (Laumer & Eckhardt, 2010). While it appears to remain a phenomenon in almost every project implementation, its understanding is now gaining more prominence in IS literature building on different theoretical insights from behavioral and organizational theories. Suggestions have been made on the need for a "school of thought" approach aimed at consolidating already existing theories and knowledge (Laumer & Eckhardt, 2012; Gauthier & Lagacé, 2015). Thirdly, evidence from the literature discussed in previous reviews (Laumer & Eckhardt, 2012) shows user resistance research is yet to deliver consistent and clear findings that inform best practice and offers coherent advice to managers so far.

Over the years, there have been other reviews done on user resistance in IS (Ali, Zhou, Miller, & Ieromonachou, 2016; Haddara & Moen, 2017; Laumer & Eckhardt, 2012). What sets this review apart from the previous reviews on user resistance are the different perspectives discussed and methods used (quantitative analysis using co-citation analysis and bibliometric coupling).

In complement to the findings of other reviews, this study seeks to avoid the bias associated with qualitative reviews. The review by Ali et al. (2016) for instance focuses on causes of user resistance without much focus on model suggestions nor the theories and methods used in the measure of user resistance as an IS phenomenon. Haddara and Moen (2017) provide a review focused mainly on user resistance in the domain of ERP based on 11 articles and not a review of user resistance as a general IS phenomenon that considers other domains. Their study did not consider the methodologies and theories as well as geographical distribution. Laumer and Eckhardt (2012) qualitatively reviewed the literature on models and theories used in explaining user resistance in IS research to which barely any other study has done a similar review since 2012. Their study focused on the theoretical orientations and the main result of the publications in their review but not the overall landscape of user resistance as a research phenomenon in IS literature. This review, however, takes into account the level of applicability concerning discussions at the individual, organizational (micro), sectoral (meso), national (macro), and/or global levels (meta). It also considers the respective stages of applicability with regards to user resistance at the implementation and use/impact stages as well as the distribution by geographical regions and research focus.

More specifically, there are ten reviews identified by Scopus that have been conducted on user resistance over the period. None of these studies used bibliometric methods in their review, making this study the first to use bibliometric coupling and co-citation analysis as a method of review in user resistance literature.

Bibliographic methods have proved quite useful and have been used extensively for a broad category of research (Kovács, Van Looy, & Cassiman, 2015; Fernandes Rodrigues Alves, Vasconcelos Ribeiro Galina, & Dobelin, 2018; van Oorschot, Hofman, & Halman, 2018). Bibliometric reviews are different from the most cited reviews in the IS domain (Adams, Berner, & Wyatt, 2004; Rivard & Lapointe, 2005; Saathoff, 2005). Comparing the conventional qualitative review to bibliometric methods, the latter can reduce the bias and subjectivity that are inherent in a reviewer's work (van Oorschot et al., 2018).

Unlike other highly cited and respected reviews, this review of user resistance is based on quantitative data, rather than qualitative interpretations which are subject to bias. This study presents a bibliometric review of user resistance for the period 1978 to the first quarter of 2019.

Thus, in particular, this study seeks to (1) identify the theoretical foundations of user resistance research, (2) highlight the current themes in user resistance research, and (3) present trends and potential future research directions. This review contributes extensively to IS literature by providing information on the current status of user resistance literature and a further provision of content relevant to researchers with insights, current trends and future direction for research. We consider this review as a guide to scholars in their future research endeavors.

We focus on two main questions with the first being: What are the theoretical cornerstones of user resistance? Secondly, what are the current trends in the field of user resistance research?

The rest of the chapter is organized as follows: in the next section, the methodology is discussed based on the scope of the literature search, the search strategy which highlights the inclusion and exclusion criteria of data used in the review. The third section discusses the theoretical cornerstones of user resistance research. The fourth section presents recent debates on user resistance research and lastly, a presentation of the key findings from the review which highlights gaps for future research.

DATA AND RESEARCH METHODS

Data Search

The Scope of Literature Search

The prime sources of data for this review are online journals specifically Scopus for the period 1978 to the first quarter of 2019. Scopus was selected because of its bibliographic coverage of a great number of the top IS databases. Acting as a multidisciplinary database, Scopus indexes articles that are published as full-texts in the respective databases such as ScienceDirect amongst others.

This review adopts a quantitative approach, specifically bibliometric analysis, which follows a series of processes. This approach aims to reduce the bias associated with literature reviews. Co-citation analysis and bibliographic coupling are used as techniques in this analysis. For the bibliometric analysis, this research adopts the four-step process as used by Kovács et al. (2015) which involved the; (a) development of search queries, (b) manual evaluation and filtering of search results using title, abstract and keywords to only include relevant articles, (c) analyzing the data from online journal using visualization of similarities (VOS) viewer software (software used in the construction and visualization of bibliometric networks), and finally (d) interpreting results of co-citation and bibliographic coupling. For interpretation, this review goes further to manually read all documents for subjective analysis and interpretation of results.

Search Strategy: Inclusion and Exclusion Criteria

The search for data for the bibliometric coupling and co-citation analysis was based solely on data derived from the Scopus database due to its bibliographic content. A search query was developed for the Scopus database using the "document search" option to search for the terms USER RESISTANCE first in "All Fields" but limited to the period "1978" to "Present". This produced a result of 158,268 articles (see Appendix One).

We then filtered this result using "title", "keywords", and "abstract" as filters in this manner [Abstract: user resistance] OR [Keywords: user resistance] OR [Title: user resistance]. This is to ensure that the articles used in this review are relevant to the user resistance research domain (see, for instance, Senyo, Addae, & Boateng, 2018). This review considered publications on user resistance that date between 1978 and 2019.

This period was chosen because preliminary analysis done on available reviews and meta-analysis of user resistance studies reflected that the date of the most cited publications is around twenty to thirty years back. Approximately 9,414 articles were found which reflected a default modification of search query by Scopus for "user" AND "resistance" reflecting lots of articles that do not in any way reflect the content this study is looking for. As a result, the search keywords were restricted with inverted commas to "user resistance" (treating it as one word) and the search repeated. The results were trimmed by the system from 9,414 to 270 relevant articles. This result was further filtered using the keywords INFORMATION SYSTEMS to exclude false-positive articles that discussed user resistance in contexts other than information systems, i.e. studies that fell within the category of search but has nothing to do the phenomenon under study (for instance user resistance to drugs/medication).

The result was reduced to a total of 232 articles that could be reviewed in greater depth. Since this result is a reflection of all document types at this stage of search and this review considered only peer-reviewed articles, this result was filtered to include only "articles" and "articles in press" excluding the other document category types such as reviews, conference papers, book chapters, editorials, reports, dissertations, etc. This further filter reduced the Scopus search result from 232 to 123 articles. The bibliometric review is based on the 123 articles even though insights are drawn from the other documents.

If the authors missed any article that does not relate to the focus of this study, these articles would appear on the periphery of a map generated by the VOS viewer software as a not so relevant article to the clusters with high density.

For the purpose of bibliometric analysis, we analyzed the remaining 123 data from Scopus using the VOS viewer software. We relied on this approach because as described by Van Eck and Waltman (2013), the VOS approach helps in the identification and visualization of thematic clusters based on the relatedness between publications (Eck & Waltman, 2013). As described by Kovacs et al. (2015), ... VOS is a unified approach that serves the purpose of creating maps and clusters of bibliometric networks to create and optimize algorithm amidst a clustered algorithm in one software package called the 'VOS-viewer' (Kovács et al., 2015). For the bibliometric review, this result of 123 articles was exported from Scopus as comma-separated values (CSV) tab-delimited output file. This file served as the raw input for the VOS viewer software.

The generated outputs were co-citation analysis of cited references and bibliographic coupling of the identified articles. The VOS viewer software identified all 123 articles suitable for the bibliographic coupling. This data had 5884 cited references of which 17 had a minimum of 6 citations for the co-citation analysis.

This minimum number of citations was manually chosen because of the limited number of data for this review. This is because a higher number of cited references reduce the number of articles and related clusters which would make it difficult to get a broader overview of the review. The statistical description of this dataset is presented in Figures 1 and 2.

At the final and fourth stage, the result of the bibliographic coupling and co-citation analysis is interpreted. For labelling and interpretation of each identified cluster, all articles were downloaded from Scopus following the links to the respective article sources. The derivation of the theoretical cornerstones of user resistance was based on the co-citation analysis of cited references (clusters 1, 2, 3, 4).

For the bibliographic coupling, the minimum citation of a document was limited to 20 of which 38 met the threshold out of the 123 documents. From this threshold, the VOSviewer software identified only 28 items as the largest set of connected items. We based our analysis on this set of connected items.

Methods

Co-Citation Analysis and Bibliometric Coupling

To overcome the bias associated with scientific literature reviews, many researchers emphasize the need for a process of a systematic review. The essence and principle of such systematic review lie in the replicability of the scientific process and transparency where bias and human error are minimized in the synthesis and mapping of fragmented studies (van Oorschot et al., 2018). Also, subjective bias from reviewers can be further reduced by the use of bibliometric analysis that is independent of the reviewer's preference or knowledge (Martínez-López, Merigó, Valenzuela-Fernández, & Nicolás, 2018; Merigó, Pedrycz, Weber, & de la Sotta, 2018). This review relies on bibliographic coupling and co-citation analysis as two bibliometric techniques thanks to the overlap between their patterns of reference.

Co-citation analysis links references together based on how they are cited together such that the higher the number of citations, the greater the influence of references and corresponding growth. In this sense, co-citation analysis is an ideal representation of the past vis-à-vis what was cited. Bibliographic coupling, on the other hand, connects articles based on how recent they are and references shared. In order words, these methods are opposite to each other making it ideal to use both in this study as a way of answering the research questions on what the theoretical trends are in user resistance literature and the directions of future research. To aid our interpretation, we carried out cluster analysis to group articles that are related, a way of presenting the subthemes of user resistance and objectively identifying the theoretical themes from the cited references (co-citation analysis). Also, this aided in identifying the trends and emerging perspectives of user resistance from the articles reviewed (bibliographic coupling).

This study used VOSviewer version 1.6.10. To use the VOS software, we opened the downloaded desktop version and from the map section at the file tab, we clicked on *create* to start our co-citation analysis process. We selected the option to read data from bibliographic database files, selected our Scopus CSV file and chose "Co-citation" as the type of analysis and "Cited references" as the unit of analysis using the default "Full Counting" as the counting method. For the minimum number of citations of a cited reference, we selected 6 as the value.

Of the 5884 cited references, 17 met the threshold. Leaving the number of cited references to be selected at 17, our co-citation analysis from the VOSviewer software produced the network visualization that is illustrated in Figure 3. This output produced 4 clusters that represent the articles that are most cited and with the most influence and growth within the user resistance literature. These clusters are discussed in the next section.

RESULTS

Demographic Representation of Articles

The classification of the geographical spectrum was done based on global, cross-continent, and continent basis. Since Scopus only allows for comparison of up to 15 countries, we exported the analyzed result as a CSV file into excel to generate a two-dimensional (2D) clustered column chart. This distribution is presented in Figure 1. The respective bars represent the number of publications that are related to the respective countries.

As revealed by the findings, three of the articles were not specific to the source of data. These were grouped as "undefined". Besides this, it can be deduced from the distribution that most of the identified research was focused on the developed economies context vis-à-vis USA and Europe, with the developing economies recording barely anything beyond an article each. This indicates that research on user resistance is more prevalent in developed economies than it is in developing economies. It is thus recommended that further studies be conducted in the developing economies context to provide a better understanding of the sociotechnical idiosyncrasies and contextual issues within these two digitally divided contexts. Since the economic development of any region or economy depends to a large extent on the success of its IS/IT adoption via successful IT project implementations and use, it is recommended that more research is conducted in the developing regions. With the higher rate of success in the adoption and use of IS/IT in the developed economies compared to developing economies, future research focused on developing economies could provide further insight that explains the gap between the technologically advanced economies and developing economies. Findings from such studies would explain and further reduce the digital divide gap if not close it completely.

Publication by Year

Similar to the publication by country, the search results were analyzed according to the years of publication as presented in Figure 2. It is evident from the findings that user resistance research has not gained much attention in general over the years in IS literature compared to other domains in the discussion of IT and innovation adoption. With the efforts of businesses and governments to digitalize their activities towards the digital economies global agenda, and the associated different success/failure rates of adoption of the different technology types, one would have expected to see evidence of more user resistance research interests. Instead, the findings show a slow increase in research interest from the '80s into the mid-2000s and a sudden drop after 2016. This suggests a shift in research attention to other areas in the IS domain instead of the continuous rise in research that one would expect. An indication that the user resistance domain is a grey area within the IS literature that needs more research.

Figure 1. Distribution according to countries of publication

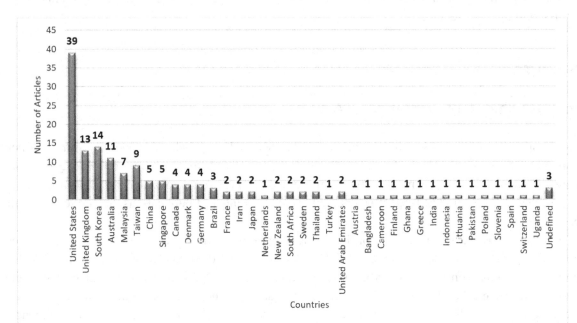

Figure 2. Distribution according to year(s) of publication

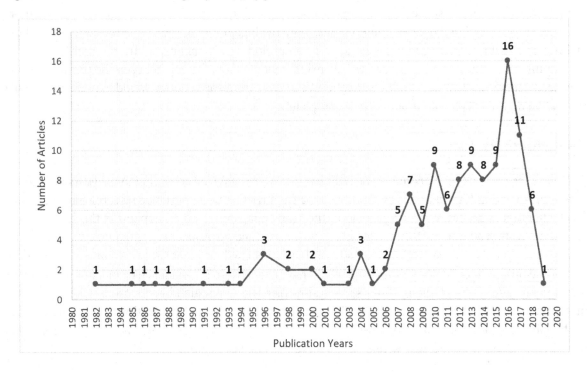

Co-citation Analysis: Theoretical Orientations/Foundations

This section presents the internal structures of user resistance and discusses the theoretical foundations discovered. These are represented by the clusters identified by the co-citation analysis. Figure 3 is a network map (a representation) of the identified clusters of cited references extracted from the VOS-viewer software.

Figure 3. Co-citation network of references cited by user resistance articles between 1978 and 2019

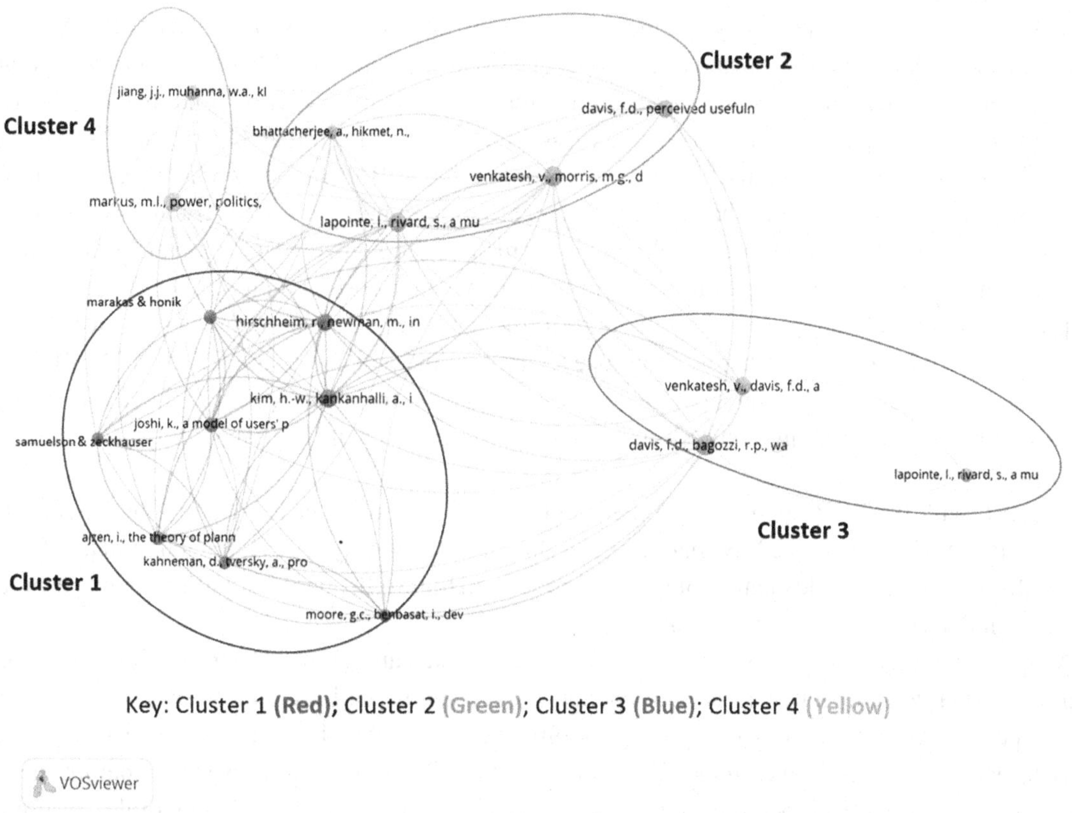

Key: Cluster 1 (Red); Cluster 2 (Green); Cluster 3 (Blue); Cluster 4 (Yellow)

Cluster 1 (8 articles): Status Quo Bias / Equity

The thematic orientation of this cluster can best be captured under the Status Quo Bias (SQB) and Equity Implementation perspectives or "school of thought". This is because the articles found under this category posit that user resistance can best be explained as an outcome of comparison of lose(s) to be suffered as against the gains to be made in switching to a new system (accepting change) and how a proposed change affects one's status in reflection of such lose(s) or gain(s). Most of these publications dwell on the SQB as their basis in explaining the preference of people to maintain their current situation/status or switch (Kim & Kankanhalli, 2009; Samuelson & Zeckhauser, 1988). Samuelson and Zeckhauser

(1988) described SQB in three main categories: psychological commitment, cognitive misperceptions, and rational decision making. They describe *rational decision making* to imply the assessment made before switching to an alternative concerning the net benefits of a change vis-à-vis the relative benefits and costs of the change.

When the costs are greater than the benefits, then there is a bias in the status quo. Uncertainty costs and transition costs are two types of costs identified in the rational decision making perspective. The cost suffered in adapting the new situation refers here to the transition cost. Further, the authors deduced subtypes of transition costs to include permanent costs and transient costs where the former is a result of the change and the latter occurs during the process of the change.

SQB can also be caused by uncertainty costs which are represented by the perception of risk or psychological uncertainty associated with the new alternative. When users are anxious and unsure of possible outcomes of a change, they can incur uncertainty costs with this switch to a new IS (Samuelson & Zeckhauser, 1988). Samuelson and Zeckhauser (1988) also explain SQB from a *cognitive misconception* perspective concerning loss aversion such that losses, irrespective of how small in changing from a current situation, are perceived far larger and most often overestimated than the actual loss in comparison to the gains in the perception of value. In explaining the SQB from the psychological commitment perspective, Samuelson and Zeckhauser (1988) posit that three main factors account for psychological commitment: the need to feel in control, social norms and sunk costs. The reluctance to switch to a new system because of previous commitment(s) explains sunk costs, where the actual costs here are the previous commitment(s). Social norms refer to the tendency of social contact – for instance, work colleague(s) – to influence another to either use (reinforce) or weaken (resist) a person's SQB. "Efforts to feel in control" draws more on a person's desire to control "their situation(s)". Since individuals do not lose control when making a switch to an unknown system or unfamiliar work pattern, this could result in SQB.

In synch with the SQB perspective, other publications from this cluster explain the antecedents of user resistance (Hirschheim & Newman, 1988; Kahneman & Tversky, 1979). Hirschheim and Newman (1988) discussed the complex nature of user resistance and highlight an individual's innate conservatism as the main determinant of user resistance.

Adapting the model of passive resistance misuse, Marakas and Honik (1996) posit that the rigidity of an individual towards a new system or change is exposed by the introduction of a new IT such that upon experiencing either fear or stress, such rigidity leads to reactive behaviours and resistance is most likely to occur. Kim and Kankanhalli (2009) also used the SQB to explain resistance before the adoption of a new IS and developed the user resistance construct as a resistance behavioral measure (Kim & Kankanhalli, 2009).

Corresponding to the net benefits in SQB theory, net inequity is suggested by previous research. Joshi (1991) developed the Equity-Implementation Model (EIM) upon examining resistance to change and the related issues that pertain to IS implementation from an equity theory perspective. The EIM posits that users assess their net equity concerning gains or losses using a three-level process. In assessing the overall net equity based on which resistance or acceptance occurs, users evaluate the changes in their inputs and outcomes. First, by assessing the net gain or loss in their efforts, in comparison to that of their colleagues and then with that of their employer(s) (Joshi, 1991).

Cluster 2 (4 Articles): Organizational Change and Levels of Resistance

This cluster mainly discusses user resistance at the firm level with most of the reference focused on levels of resistance with regards to groups as units and individuals in the context of organizational change (Davis, 1989; Venkatesh, Morris, Davis, & Davis, 2003; Lapointe & Rivard, 2005; Bhattacherjee & Hikmet, 2007). Bhattacherjee and Hikmet (2007) posit that researchers will better understand why individuals resist the use of technology if user resistance literature is incorporated into theoretical models of technology acceptance. They demonstrate this in their explanation of how physicians react to healthcare information systems by incorporating it into a model of IT usage, the antecedents of and the notion of resistance to change (Bhattacherjee & Hikmet, 2007b). Aspects of technology acceptance appear in this cluster (Davis, 1989; Venkatesh et al., 2003). Lapointe and Rivard (2005) posit that user resistance is as a result of mixed determinants which are mostly the interaction between system characteristics and initial conditions from both units of groups and individuals which influence the actual resistance behaviours or outcomes of resistance.

They argue that resistance behaviours come about as a result of threats that are perceived from the interaction of a given object, vis-à-vis an information system and initial conditions and based on this, proposed a model of resistance to IT implementation (Lapointe & Rivard, 2005b).

In brief, this cluster presents the explanation and measurement of user resistance from the perspective of organizational change. This is seen in the efforts to explain what accounts for resistance in the organization with an emphasis on the individual and group as a unit(s). This cluster also offers model proposals on how managers and decision-makers can assess the likelihood of success or failure of an organizational change at the introduction of an innovation or information system.

Cluster 3 (3 Articles): Perceived Usefulness and Social Influence

The focal discussion within this cluster is centered on the significance of the influence that perceived usefulness and subjective norms – as social influences - have in the prediction and explanation of user resistance with respect to intentions to use IT. From the perspective of perceived usefulness, the authors discuss the impact it has on technology resistance or acceptance (Davis, Bagozzi, & Warshaw, 1989; Venkatesh & Davis, 2000; Lapointe & Rivard, 2005). Venkatesh and Davis (2000) provide a detailed account of perceived usefulness as an important driver and determinant of the behavioral intentions to use technology (or not) in their study that extends the technology acceptance model (TAM2). On the side of social influence, Davis et al. (1989) and Venkatesh and Davis (2000) explain the impact of social influence on IT usage intentions and posit that such influence is more prevalent in mandatory settings than voluntary contexts (Davis et al., 1989).

Perceived usefulness is influenced by subjective norm via identification and internalization, where identification is when, by using a system, people seek to improve their work performance as well as their social status in their workgroup; and internalization is when people's perceptions on the usefulness of technology are influenced by the perceptions of others in their social network (Venkatesh & Davis, 2000).

Cluster 4 (2 Articles): Power / Politics

Articles in this cluster mostly discuss the relationship between social aspects of users of an innovation/IS and the perceived values in terms of net benefits associated with the switch. From the social perspective, authors here discuss the sociotechnical issues of a proposed change and the impact on their social status of affected stakeholders of such change. It can be said that deductions from this cluster are mostly based on the interaction theory or "school of thought". The interaction theory argues that the real reason(s) behind resistance behaviours are neither the people themselves nor the characteristics of the information system, but rather, has more to do with the interaction between both, and the impact that this has on the social life of the user after assessing this change in terms of a gain or loss. Markus (1983), explained resistance to refer to the outcome from the interaction between a system being implemented and the context within which such a system is used. This is such that if a user or group of users tend to have the perception that using a system would boost their social status and position of power, then they are more likely to embrace/accept the change and thus use the system. On the other hand, if users perceive that such a change would affect their social status and cause them to lose power, then they are more likely to resist such a system. Jiang et al. (2000) also highlight the perceived values placed on power and politics and the impact that high tendencies of loss of power and status have on resistance to the implementation of IS (Jiang, Muhanna, & Klein, 2000).

Bibliographic Coupling: Analysis of User Resistance Research

In this section, we use bibliographic coupling to study the longitudinal dataset and present the current trends in the user resistance literature. Figure 4 is an illustration of the bibliographic network of cited references with 5 clusters by the 123 articles on user resistance published between 1978 and 2019. Almost all the clusters seem distant from each other but connected indicating the different respective research interests. This can be inferred from how closely publications are tied to each other than others (van Oorschot et al., 2018). Central to these links is cluster D, which is at the centre of the periphery with connections/nodes to almost all the other clusters.

The identified clusters were labelled as:

Cluster A – "Change management in enterprise systems";
Cluster B – "User satisfaction over time";
Cluster C – "Comparison of pre and post usage of technology";
Cluster D – "The core of user resistance";
Cluster E – "Business process design and task change".

Table 1 presents an overview of research trends reflected in the bibliographic coupled clusters. Cluster A is a representation of publications that focus on enterprise systems with a keen interest in change management. It builds on Cluster 2 with IT-Conflict Resistance Theory (IT-CRT), Classical Management Theory being sample theories seen in this cluster. Cluster B focuses on user satisfaction over time and has publications that draw insight from theories like Affective Reward and Excitation Transfer theories. It builds on Cluster 1 in the co-citation analysis.

Cluster C builds on Clusters 1 & 3 and focuses on the use of technology both at the post and pre-implementation stages and has publications that leverage on theories like the Equity Implementation Model (EIM), Technology Acceptance Model (TAM) and IT Continuance Model. Cluster D focuses on the core of user resistance and does not build on any specific Cluster in the co-citation analysis but rather has a blend of almost all the other clusters of co-cited references. It has a representation of publications that leverage on the Status Quo Bias Theory and Dual Factor Theory.

Figure 4. Co-citation network of references cited by user resistance articles between 1978 and 2019

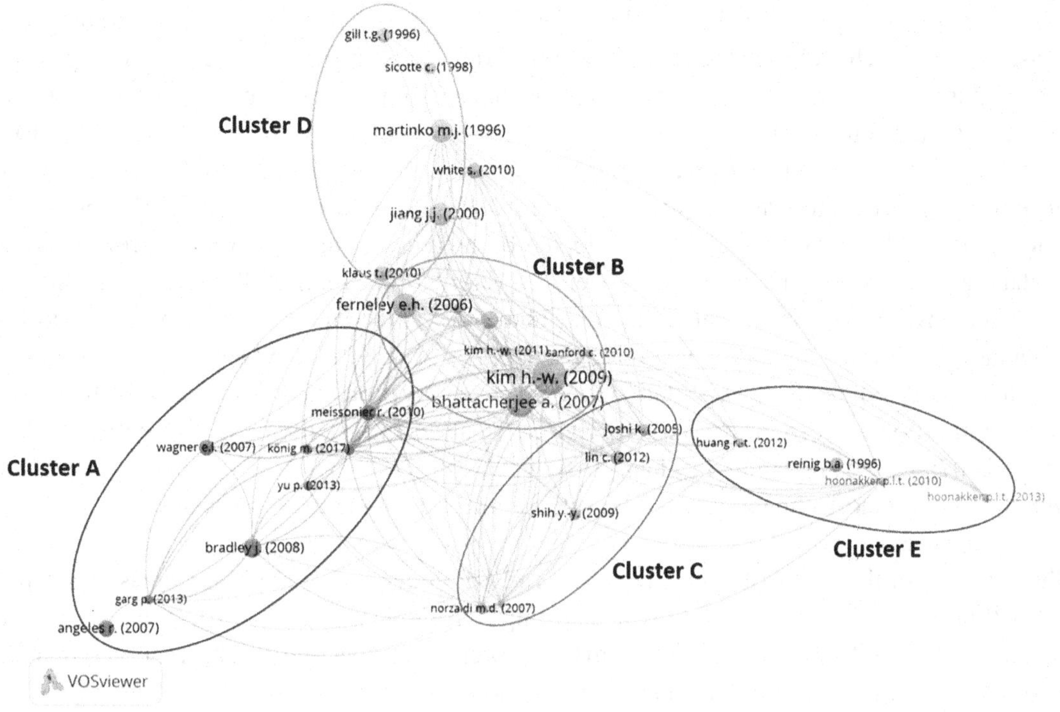

Key: Cluster A **(Red)**; Cluster B (Green); Cluster C **(Blue)**; Cluster D (Yellow); Cluster E **(Purple)**

Lastly, Cluster E builds on Cluster 2 with Attribution theory as an instance of theory seen here. It is represented by articles that focus on the business process design and task change. In the subsequent section, the five clusters are discussed in detail with a focus on the theoretical perspective and field of study.

Table 1: Overview of the Identified Bibliographic Coupled Clusters

Cluster	Builds upon cluster	Field under study	Theory/Model
A	2	Change Management in Enterprise Systems	IT-Conflict Resistance Theory (IT-CRT), Classical Management Theory
B	1	User satisfaction over time	Excitation Transfer Theory, Affective Reward
C	1 & 3	Comparison of pre & post usage of technology	EIM, IT Continuance, TAM
D	None in particular	The core of user resistance	EIM, SQB, Dual Factor Theory
E	2	Business process design and task change	Concourse Theory, Attribution Theory

Cluster A. Change Management in Enterprise Systems

This cluster comprised of eight articles and has the research trend labelled as "change management in enterprise systems". This cluster includes the contribution by König and Neumayr (2017) on radical innovation that discusses the concept of self-driving cars and introduces a number of articles that have addressed the varied dimensions over the period and its related technology acceptance or resistance issues involved. Further to this, it includes publications that mainly discuss the critical factors that influence the success or failure of enterprise resource planning (ERP) systems. Most of these publications address strategies of IS implementation that can be adopted by project managers and other project owners to ensure that value is created and captured (Angeles & Nath, 2007; Bradley, 2008; Garg & Garg, 2013; König & Neumayr, 2017). Specifically, the contributions of some authors focus on key aspects of IS implementation: pre-implementation involving the services of qualified and experienced resource personnel (Bradley, 2008); post-implementation where user motivation and participation is of concern as well as the impact on work routine, access to data/information and quality of service delivery (Wagner & Newell, 2007; Yu, Zhang, Gong, & Zhang, 2013).

Others address socio-technical issues with integration and standardization of systems, data, procedures, and policies.

Whereas most of the discussions broadly concern ERP in general, some of the areas of technology interest within this cluster include: automotive (König & Neumayr, 2017), e-procurement (Angeles & Nath, 2007) and e-health (Yu et al., 2013). From the theoretical perspective, an observation is that almost all the articles in this cluster employed qualitative methods such as cross-comparison case studies using situated learning and action research in their respective studies. Meissonier and Houzé (2010) through action research proposed the IT-Conflict Resistance Theory (IT-CRT) which posits that management should – where possible – enhance resistance as an approach aimed at anticipating and resolving "latent conflicts that are directly or indirectly related to the project" (Meissonier & Houzé, 2010).

Cluster B. User Satisfaction Over Time

This cluster includes four publications. The research trend it represents has been labelled as: "User satisfaction over time". It has been labelled as such because most of the publications in this cluster studied the innate characteristics of end-users that affect the long term use of a given technology. The objectives of these publications are focused on post-implementation vis-à-vis the initial desire to use a given technology in comparison to the actual usage and/or continued use of the technology. Why does the interest in using a technology reduce? Or subsequently, stop? More specifically, why does the interest in using a technology reduce even though the benefits of its use are largely agreed to far outweigh the consequences of not using it? In view of this, some of the publications base their measurement of user satisfaction with IS implementation on Provider Order Entry User Satisfaction and Usage Survey (POESUS) (Hoonakker, Carayon, & Walker, 2010; Hoonakker et al., 2013). This cluster focuses on the factors that stimulate or impede the sustained use of technology. Based on the density view, two themes were identified in the account for what stimulates or impedes such sustained use of technology. The intention to continue using a given technology at the individual level is addressed by the first theme whereas the second theme addresses such intention at the organizational group level. This cluster did not draw on established frameworks as found in the other clusters.

Even though this cluster does not directly build on any of the theoretical cornerstones in the previous section, it can be associated with cluster 1 as it aligns well with the equity or bias in the status quo associated with the use of technology. Some of the recurrent technologies of interest in this cluster include e-health, mobile technologies, e-learning, and group support systems.

Cluster C. Comparison of Pre and Post Usage of Technology

This cluster was made up of four articles and represented the research trend labelled in this study as: "comparison of pre & post usage of technology". This cluster deals with user groups as well as technologies that can be categorized as general-purpose technologies i.e. technologies that change the mode of operations and production and is relevant to a broad array of industries. The main concerns here are whether users perceive a sense of need or basis for using a given technology and the depth of usage i.e. whether users will continue to use the technology or usage will be reduced over time and/or eventually stopped (Joshi, 2005; Norzaidi, Salwani, Chong, & Rafidah, 2008; Shih & Huang, 2009; Lin & Rivera-Sánchez, 2012). This cluster builds upon clusters 1 and 3 which are theoretical cornerstones in the previous section. This cluster focuses chiefly on the extrinsic factors that determine the use or continued use of a given technology which reflects more of the characteristics discussed in cluster 3.

Some of the articles from this cluster made use of established frameworks within the user resistance and user acceptance of technology literature such as the Technology Acceptance Model (Shih & Huang, 2009), Equity Implementation Model (Joshi, 2005) and IT continuance Model (Lin & Rivera-Sánchez, 2012), Task-Technology-Fit (TTF) model (Daud Norzaidi, Choy Chong, Murali, & Intan Salwani, 2007).

Some of the authors based the rationale of their study solely on the models they adapted (e.g. EIM), whereas others borrowed factors from the TAM in a bid to develop a more integrated model. As a result, some of the factors studied in this cluster include top management support, perceived usefulness, usage and perceived ease of use.

Cluster D. The Core of User Resistance

This cluster comprised of eight articles and has the research trend labelled as "the core of user resistance". This is because, from the density view, this cluster can be found at the centre with links to almost all the other publications. It has more publications that address the challenges associated with the transitioning from old innovations to new ones at different levels of analysis. These publications proceed to make recommendations on the different mechanisms, tools and best practices that can be considered as measures of overcoming or mitigating the consequences of such challenges.

Besides the general discussion of ERP, some of the areas of technology interest in this cluster are electronic government, mobile technology (Sanford & Oh, 2010), electronic health (Bhattacherjee & Hikmet, 2007a), customer relationship management (CRM) (Selander & Henfridsson, 2012) and ERP (Kim & Kankanhalli, 2009; Kim, 2011). Publications in this cluster denote organizational change, procedure, policy making, organizational culture and user-centred design as the main relevant determinants of user resistance. The antecedents denoted in this cluster can be categorized into three well-established variables: environmental, technological and organizational antecedents. Cluster D builds on clusters 2 & 1 which were relevant theoretical cornerstones in the co-citation analysis.

However, cluster D focuses mainly on the impediments and contextual drivers that are predominant to IS adoption, while clusters 2 & 1 suggest models to explore the antecedents of innovation acceptance/resistance.

Methods used in this cluster are more qualitative than quantitative to which most are aimed towards theory proposal. This cluster recorded more articles that propose theories via development and extensions of other theories than the other clusters. Referring to "perceived threats" as key inhibitors to adoption of technology, and incorporating such inhibitors into technology acceptance model, Bhattacherjee and Hikmet (2007) proposed the dual-factor model in explaining, through an empirical study, what accounts for the rejection of hospital information technology (HIT) by physicians (Bhattacherjee & Hikmet, 2007a). Rivard and Lapointe (2012) developed a theoretical explanation of user resistance via set-theoretic and content analysis (which combines the advantages of large quantities of data analysis with the richness of case studies) in a Delphi study in explaining the patterns of influence that are exhibited by implementers when resistance occurs (Rivard & Lapointe, 2012).

By combining resistance and technology acceptance literature, Kim and Kankanhalli (2009) proposed the Status Quo Bias model as a measure of user resistance prior to the implementation of a new IS.

Cluster E. Business Process Design and Task Change

This cluster comprised of four articles and has the research trend labelled: "business process design and task change". The publications in this Cluster focus on the interaction between the social and the technical aspects of implementation and builds upon the theoretical assumptions discussed in cluster 2. In comparison to the other clusters, cluster E focuses more on a variety of enterprise systems that cut across different industries.

This cluster mainly posits that user resistance antecedents at the individual level are key to system implementation and use, but becomes more critical when dealing with more complex architectures such as enterprise systems implementation. In lieu of this, three main themes were identified in this cluster: people, system and the integration of both. Klaus et al. (2010) argue that if any IS implementation is to be successfully adopted and continuously used, then attention needs to be focused on the categories of users for whom a system is deployed.

In support of this argument, Jiang et al. (2000) posit that implementation ought to be carried out in a manner that takes cognizance of the respective modules or subsystems of an IS. Secondly, implemented features or new systems need to be treated as main systems whiles ensuring compatibility with other subsystems used by different stakeholders of a business entity. Mainly, this cluster discusses the impact of task and routine change on the motivation of users to adopting or resisting an innovation. Amongst some of the dimensions of adoption dynamics addressed in this cluster is the relevance of the clusters (bibliographic-coupled) over time.

The relative importance of the identified clusters is presented in table 1 above. From table 2, it can be deduced that cluster D had the highest number of citations per article compared to the other clusters. This is followed by cluster E, cluster A, cluster C, and cluster B respectively. That is, Cluster D on the "core of user resistance" has been cited the most over the years with Cluster A ("Change management in enterprise systems") having an average citation impact. This implies that there is currently a wide gap in user resistance research from the theoretical perspective where more calls are currently being made for a unified theoretical approach or "school of thought". Also, this implies there are calls for more mixed methods of study or at least more quantitative means that look at large sets of data in complex IS

Table 2. Indicators of Publication Output and Citation Impact per Thematic Cluster

Cluster	Cluster Label	Number of items	Average age of items	Total number of citations	Average number of citations per item	Average number of citations per year
A	Change Management in Enterprise Systems	8	8.375	417	3.383	54.125
B	User satisfaction over time	4	10.75	127	2.047	32.75
C	Comparison of pre & post usage of technology	4	10.5	151	1.888	30.2
D	The core of user resistance	8	9.375	1035	8.086	129.375
E	Business process design and task change	5	19	422	5.275	84.4
	Total	29	11.6	2178	4.136	66.17

implementations, for instance, government (public) IS implementations. This can be confirmed from Figure 5 which indicates the consistent increase in the number of citations since the year 2008. Also, from both Figure 5 and Table 2, it can be deduced that Cluster D has the highest number of articles along with other values even though publications were made after 2008 compared to the other clusters.

Figure 5. Number of citations per year per cluster

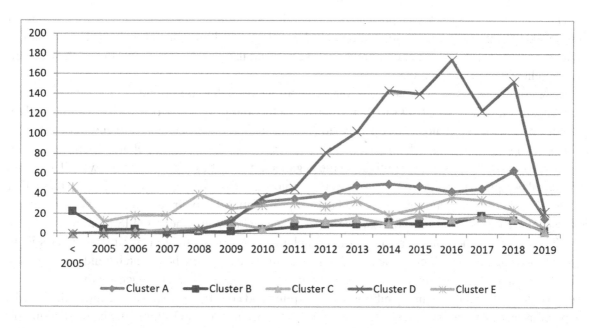

From the above analysis, one might inquire how this study differs or complements other reviews in the user resistance literature. In response to this concern, we compared our findings with previous reviews published within the period 1978 to 2019. Following our data inclusion and exclusion criteria presented

Table 3. Summary of previous reviews on User Resistance Deduced from Scopus

Author(s)	Focus of review	Type of review	Area of interest
Lapointe & Rivard (2005a)	Theories	Scoping review	Healthcare
Saathoff (2005)	Success factors to CPOE implementation	Conceptual review	Health CPOE
Ali et al. (2016)	Causes and strategies	Systematic review	General overview
Adams et al. (2004)	Antecedents and strategies	Scoping review	Healthcare
Sarris & Sawyer (1989)	Development of an IS in mental health	Overview	Healthcare
Ting, Kwok, Tsang, Lee, & Yee (2011)	Description of an architectural framework of an information system	Scoping review	Healthcare
Ramiller (2016)	General discussion	Overview	Human computer interaction
Salmon (2013)	General discussion	Overview	E-library

in the data gathering method, we identified 10 reviews from Scopus of which 2 were conference reviews as such were excluded. From the other 8 reviews, we identified 3 scoping reviews, 1 systematic review, 3 descriptive overviews, and 1 conceptual review. This distribution is presented in Table 3.

After carefully examining these 8 respective reviews, we made some observations. Our first observation is that 7 of the reviews offer a description of user resistance with a focus on the antecedents and mitigating strategies. Of these 7 reviews, 3 were reviews done as the basis of justification of research method and objectives and not articles entirely dedicated to exploring and presenting an exhaustive review as is the case with systematic reviews.

The other 4 of the 7 reviews presented a general discussion of characteristics of user resistance behaviours. Thirdly, in terms of search, appraisal, synthesis, and analysis, almost all the 8 identified reviews more or less fall short of comprehensive search and insightful assessments due to their general incomprehensive narrative nature.

Also, compared to the broader scope and in-depth analysis that are provided in systematic, meta-analytic, and other reviews (thanks to their rigorous methodologies), it was observed that almost all the previous reviews focused mostly on specific domains as includes health and library and were not broad enough with regards to research interest in user resistance over the years. Ali et al., (2016) focused on the antecedents and strategies for mitigating the negative impact of user resistance but was silent on the theoretical perspectives in each article reviewed. Lapointe and Rivard (2005a) focused on the theoretical perspectives in their scoping review as the basis of justification for their research, but not an in-depth analysis of the overall landscape of user resistance as a research phenomenon in IS literature.

What sets this review apart from – yet in complement of – previous user resistance reviews is the methods used in the data search and analysis and the distinction between the research trends and theoretical cornerstones in user resistance research. Explicitly connected yet distinct to each approach, this study used two distinct methods, namely bibliometric coupling and co-citation analysis to explore the broader scope of user resistance. Also, this bibliometric study contributes to the IS literature by confirming the findings of previous reviews on IS adoption and implementation.

Because of this, we consider this bibliometric review complementary and valuable in validating the interpretations of previous studies. Areas that have been researched and those that need attention have been presented in this study.

CONCLUSION

From the above sections, this study presents a comprehensive and systematic review of bibliographic literature in identifying the research trends and theoretical cornerstones of user resistance research. In acknowledgement and complement of other reviews, this study contributes to IS literature in various ways.

To begin with, it identifies that user resistance research is built mainly on four bibliographic clustering or theoretical cornerstones: (a) Status Quo Bias and Equity theory, (b) Organizational change and levels of resistance, (c) Perceived Usefulness and Social Influence, and (d) Power / Politics.

Secondly, by using bibliographic coupling, which is the first of such a method to be used in user resistance literature, this review assessed the current trends in user resistance literature. This technique identified five main research trends or clusters comprised of thematically related publications: (1) Change Management in Enterprise Systems, (2) User satisfaction over time, (3) Comparison of pre & post usage of technology, (4) The core of user resistance, and 5) Business process design and task change. Further comparative analysis of these trends suggests that the most cited clusters are those that focused on the core of user resistance and change management in enterprise systems. Thirdly, by integrating the research trends with the theoretical cornerstones, this study presents a coherent framework in assessing the relevance of user resistance research. Although reviews on user resistance have identified varying strands of user resistance research, this review extends the efforts of other reviews by quantifying the importance of clusters and exploring their related connections.

Significance of Research

This study provides a broader view of user resistance research over the years. It contributes to user resistance research by providing insights into trends on geographical focus, past, current and future research directions, methodology, trends on themes and research framework. This study highlights areas that need more research efforts as discussed in the future research directions. This includes the need for more research into the theoretical explanation of user resistance behavior, methodologies and contexts (and comparison of different contexts of study). Secondly, this study has provided insights into domain areas that have so far gotten the attention of IS researchers and those that are yet to. Most importantly, this study provides a basis to advance research toward a better understanding of user resistance. Lastly, it exposes practitioners to the implications of user resistance and thus provides the insight that can help inform the adoption of technology with regards to behaviors, techniques in the design of business processes and change which are critical to the success of an IS project.

Future Research Directions

This section presents areas of user resistance research that are worth considering in future studies. Firstly, irrespective of the maturity in the field of user resistance research, it appears organizational and psychological theories are yet to be exhausted in the exploration of their explanatory power. This is in the sense that resistance to the adoption and use of information systems (irrespective of the kind and nature of innovation) is a human behavioral outcome that requires critical cognitive processes that inform decision making. One would thus expect that such thought process, knowledge and subsequent decision making would be of prime focus in user resistance research. Per this, we suggest that future studies should take cognizance of the different categories of users while making use of other theoretical perspectives as used in, for instance, organization behaviour, marketing, and management research.

Most importantly, it was discovered from the review that there is high segregation in the literature on user resistance with regards to the absence of a holistic theoretical perspective of user resistance. The observation is that researchers – in their bid to explain user resistance – tend to limit their scope by conceptualizing along single streams of research and applying them to single contexts of specific innovations in most cases.

To establish a more holistic theoretical perspective, we recommend future research to consider the investigation of user resistance to innovation across different contexts as well as use more mixed methods in their studies.

Thirdly, studies on behavioral characteristics are claimed to rely mostly on qualitative research methods and case studies. To this, previous reviews have made calls for large-scale quantitative research to serve as complements to the existing case studies in user resistance research. Findings from this review confirm that for the past almost five decades, research in user resistance has been more skewed towards qualitative methods particularly case studies.

This review, however, also identified some quantitative studies most of which were found in "*user satisfaction over time*" and "*comparison of pre & post usage of technology*" clusters. This gives room to infer that the application of large-scale quantitative research might be more conducive to some thematic areas than others and are worth considering along with the recommendations above.

As can be deduced from this review, research on user resistance to technology adoption over the years is more skewed towards the health and health-related technologies domain. Since there are vast other areas that technology is being adopted and used across different societies, industries, and business domains, we strongly recommend that future research should consider research in other domain areas as well. It would be interesting to investigate user resistance in a mandatory and non-mandatory adoption setting across private and public sector environments, and more interestingly, a similar study that is comparative.

Limitations

While the method used in this review (bibliometric coupling and co-citation analysis) eliminates the bias associated with traditional reviews and expert surveys, it has its shortcomings. It is argued that bibliometric analysis (which we refer to as "mixed review method") cannot be considered a direct substitute to the extensive reading involved in other review methods.

Even though this review identified less than 150 suitable articles for this review for the period 1978 to 2019 as discussed in the data selection criteria, we discovered that there were other publications that did not fall within our search criteria yet were good fits to have considered but for the content of their abstracts, titles and keywords.

Because of this, we suggest that other studies that seek to replicate this review should consider these other publications that could not make it to our review, as including them might yield different results. That aside, we suggest that future studies should consider structuring their abstracts, titles and keywords well enough to reflect the focus of their studies.

Also, limiting our threshold to a minimum of 6 citations of cited references implies that we may have missed some articles that have probably been published recently but are yet to receive the citations needed (6 citations for this study) to fit them into this review.

Lastly, concerning impact factor and number of citations, although the core collection of Scopus meets the highest standards, we recommend a comparison of the data used in this study with that of Web of Science (WoS) or related bibliographic database. This is because WoS equally has high content standards with a strong coverage of bibliographic and citation data that's dates back to 1900 (Mascarenhas, Ferreira, & Marques, 2018). We recommend this because subsequent studies that consider our recommendation might further evaluate the robustness of their bibliometric review with a comparison of data from two or more bibliographic databases.

REFERENCES

Adams, B., Berner, E. S., & Wyatt, J. R. (2004). Applying Strategies to Overcome User Resistance in a Group of Clinical Managers to a Business Software Application: A Case Study. *Journal of Organizational and End User Computing, 16*(4), 55–64. doi:10.4018/joeuc.2004100104

Ali, M., Zhou, L., Miller, L., & Ieromonachou, P. (2016). User resistance in IT : A literature review. *International Journal of Information Management, 36*(1), 35–43. doi:10.1016/j.ijinfomgt.2015.09.007

Angeles, R., & Nath, R. (2007). Business-to-business e-procurement: Success factors and challenges to implementation. *Supply Chain Management, 12*(2), 104–115. doi:10.1108/13598540710737299

Bhattacherjee, A., & Hikmet, N. (2007a). Physician's resistance toward healthcare information technology: A theoretical model and empirical test. *European Journal of Information Systems, 16*(January), 725–737. doi:10.1057/palgrave.ejis.3000717

Bhattacherjee, A., & Hikmet, N. (2007b). Physicians' resistance toward healthcare information technologies: A dual-factor model. Proceedings of the Annual Hawaii International Conference on System Sciences, 1–10. doi:10.1109/HICSS.2007.437

Bin Taher, N. A., Krotov, V., & Silva, L. (2015). A framework for leading change in the UAE public sector. *The International Journal of Organizational Analysis, 23*(3), 348–363. doi:10.1108/IJOA-10-2014-0809

Bradley, J. (2008). Management based critical success factors in the implementation of Enterprise Resource Planning systems. *International Journal of Accounting Information Systems, 9*(3), 175–200. doi:10.1016/j.accinf.2008.04.001

Daud Norzaidi, M., Choy Chong, S., Murali, R., & Intan Salwani, M. (2007). Intranet usage and managers' performance in the port industry. *Industrial Management & Data Systems, 107*(8), 1227–1250. doi:10.1108/02635570710822831

Davis, F. D. (1989). Perceived Usefulness, Perceived Ease of Use, and User Acceptance of Information Technology. *Management Information Systems Research Center, 13*(3), 319–340. doi:10.1155/2013/591796

Davis, F. D., Bagozzi, R. P., & Warshaw, P. R. (1989). User Acceptance of Computer Technology: A Comparison of Two Theoretical Models. *Management Science, 35*(8), 982–1003. doi:10.1287/mnsc.35.8.982

Eck, N. J. Van, & Waltman, L. (2013). VOSviewer Manual. doi:10.3402/jac.v8.30072

Fernandes Rodrigues Alves, M., Vasconcelos Ribeiro Galina, S., & Dobelin, S. (2018). *Literature on organizational innovation: past and future.* Innovation & Management Review; doi:10.1108/INMR-01-2018-001

Garg, P., & Garg, A. (2013). An empirical study on critical failure factors for enterprise resource planning implementation in Indian retail sector. *Business Process Management Journal, 19*(3), 496–514. doi:10.1108/14637151311319923

Gauthier, F., & Lagacé, D. (2015). Critical Success Factors in the Development and Implementation of Special Purpose Industrial Tools: An Ergonomic Perspective. Procedia Manufacturing, 3(Ahfe), 5639–5646. doi:10.1016/j.promfg.2015.07.773

Gesulga, J. M., Berjame, A., Moquiala, K. S., & Galido, A. (2017). Barriers to Electronic Health Record System Implementation and Information Systems Resources: A Structured Review. *Procedia Computer Science, 124*, 544–551. doi:10.1016/j.procs.2017.12.188

Haddara, M., & Moen, H. (2017). User resistance in ERP implementations: A literature review. *Procedia Computer Science, 121*, 859–865. doi:10.1016/j.procs.2017.11.111

Hirschheim, R., & Newman, M. (1988). Information systems and user resistance: Theory and practice. *The Computer Journal, 31*(5), 398–408. doi:10.1093/comjnl/31.5.398

Hoonakker, P. L. T., Carayon, P., Brown, R. L., Cartmill, R. S., Wetterneck, T. B., & Walker, J. M. (2013). Changes in end-user satisfaction with computerized provider order entry over time among nurses and providers in intensive care units. *Journal of the American Medical Informatics Association, 20*(2), 252–259. doi:10.1136/amiajnl-2012-001114 PubMed

Hoonakker, P. L. T., Carayon, P., & Walker, J. M. (2010). Measurement of CPOE end-user satisfaction among ICU physicians and nurses. *Applied Clinical Informatics, 1*(3), 268–285. doi:10.4338/ACI-2010-03-RA-0020 PubMed

Hsieh, P. J. (2015). Healthcare professionals' use of health clouds: Integrating technology acceptance and status quo bias perspectives. *International Journal of Medical Informatics, 84*(7), 512–523. doi:10.1016/j.ijmedinf.2015.03.004 PubMed

Jiang, J. J., Muhanna, W. A., & Klein, G. (2000). User resistance and strategies for promoting acceptance across system types. *Information & Management, 37*(1), 25–36. doi:10.1016/S0378-7206(99)00032-4

Joshi, K. (1991). A Model of Users' Perspective on Change: The Case of Information Systems Technology Implementation. *Management Information Systems Quarterly, 15*(2), 229. doi:10.2307/249384

Joshi, K. (2005). Understanding User Resistance and Acceptance during the Implementation of an Order Management System: A Case Study Using the Equity Implementation Model. *Journal of Information Technology Case and Application Research, 7*(1), 6–20. doi:10.1080/15228053.2005.10856057

Kahneman, D., & Tversky, A. (1979). Prospect Theory: An Analysis of Decision under Risk. *Econometrica, 47*(2), 263–292. doi:10.2307/1914185

Kim, H. W. (2011). The effects of switching costs on user resistance to enterprise systems implementation. *IEEE Transactions on Engineering Management, 58*(3), 471–482. doi:10.1109/TEM.2010.2089630

Kim, H.-W., & Kankanhalli, A. (2009). Investigating User Resistance to Information Systems Implementation: A Status Quo Bias Perspective. *Management Information Systems Quarterly, 33*(3), 567. doi:10.2307/20650309

König, M., & Neumayr, L. (2017). Users' resistance towards radical innovations: The case of the self-driving car. *Transportation Research Part F: Traffic Psychology and Behaviour, 44*, 42–52. doi:10.1016/j.trf.2016.10.013

Kovács, A., Van Looy, B., & Cassiman, B. (2015). Exploring the scope of open innovation: A bibliometric review of a decade of research. *Scientometrics, 104*(3), 951–983. doi:10.1007/s11192-015-1628-0

Lapointe, L., & Rivard, S. (2005a). A multilevel model of resistance to information technology implementation. *Management Information Systems Quarterly, 29*(3), 2005. doi:10.2307/25148692

Lapointe, L., & Rivard, S. (2005b). A Multilevel Model of Resistance to Information Technology Implementation. *Management Information Systems Quarterly, 29*(3), 461–491. doi:10.2307/25148692

Laumer, S., & Eckhardt, A. (2010). Why do People Reject Technologies? - Towards an Understanding of Resistance to IT-induced Organizational Change. *Thirty First International Conference on Information Systems.*

Laumer, S., & Eckhardt, A. (2012). Why Do People Reject Technologies: A Review of User Resistance Theories. In Information Systems Theory (Vol. 29, pp. 63–86). doi:10.1007/978-1-4419-6108-2_4

Lee, K., & Joshi, K. (2017). Examining the use of status quo bias perspective in IS research: Need for re-conceptualizing and incorporating biases. *Information Systems Journal, 27*(6), 733–752. doi:10.1111/isj.12118

Lin, J., & Rivera-Sánchez, M. (2012). Testing the Information Technology Continuance Model on a Mandatory SMS-Based Student Response System Testing the Information Technology Continuance Model on a Mandatory SMS-Based Student Response System. *Communication Education, 61*(2), 89–110. doi:10.1080/03634523.2011.654231

Martínez-López, F. J., Merigó, J. M., Valenzuela-Fernández, L., & Nicolás, C. (2018). Fifty years of the European Journal of Marketing : A bibliometric analysis. *European Journal of Marketing, 52*(1/2), 439–468. doi:10.1108/EJM-11-2017-0853

Mascarenhas, C., Ferreira, J. J., & Marques, C. (2018, February). University–industry cooperation: A systematic literature review and research agenda. *Science & Public Policy,* ▪▪▪, 1–11. doi:10.1093cipolcy003

Meissonier, R., & Houzé, E. (2010). Toward an IT conflict-resistance theory: Action research during IT pre-implementation. *European Journal of Information Systems, 19*(5), 540–561. doi:10.1057/ejis.2010.35

Merigó, J. M., Pedrycz, W., Weber, R., & de la Sotta, C. (2018). Fifty years of Information Sciences: A bibliometric overview. *Information Sciences, 432*, 245–268. doi:10.1016/j.ins.2017.11.054

Norzaidi, M. D., Salwani, M. I., Chong, S. C., & Rafidah, K. (2008). A study of intranet usage and resistance in Malaysia's port industry. *Journal of Computer Information Systems, 49*(1), 37–47. doi:10.1080/08874417.2008.11645304

Ramiller, N. (2016). New Technology and the Post-human Self: Rethinking Appropriation and Resistance. ACM SIGMIS Database. *The Data Base for Advances in Information Systems, 47*(4), 23–33. doi:10.1145/3025099.3025102

Rivard, S., & Lapointe, L. (2005). A multilevel model of resistance to information technology implementation. *Management Information Systems Quarterly, 29*(3), 2005. doi:10.2307/25148692

Rivard, S., & Lapointe, L. (2012). Information Technology Implementers' Responses to User Resistance: Nature and Effects. *Management Information Systems Quarterly, 36*(3), 897–920. doi:10.2307/41703485

Saathoff, A. (2005). Human factors considerations relevant to CPOE implementations. *Journal of Healthcare Information Management, 19*(3), 71–78. Retrieved from http://www.ncbi.nlm.nih.gov/pubmed/16045087 PubMed

Samuelson, W., & Zeckhauser, R. (1988). Status quo bias in decision making. *Journal of Risk and Uncertainty, 1*(1), 7–59. doi:10.1007/BF00055564

Sanford, C., & Oh, H. (2010). The Role of User Resistance in the Adoption of a Mobile Data Service. *Cyberpsychology, Behavior, and Social Networking, 13*(6), 663–672. doi:10.1089/cyber.2009.0377 PubMed

Sarris, A., & Sawyer, M. G. (1989). Automated information systems in mental health services: A review. *International Journal of Mental Health, 18*(4), 18–30. doi:10.1080/00207411.1989.11449141

Selander, L., & Henfridsson, O. (2012). Cynicism as user resistance in IT implementation. *Information Systems Journal, 22*(4), 289–312. doi:10.1111/j.1365-2575.2011.00386.x

Senyo, P. K., Addae, E., & Boateng, R. (2018). Cloud computing research: A review of research themes, frameworks, methods and future research directions. *International Journal of Information Management, 38*(1), 128–139. doi:10.1016/j.ijinfomgt.2017.07.007

Shih, Y., & Huang, S.-S. (2009). The Actual Usage of ERP Systems : An Extended. *Journal of Research and Practice in Information Technology, 41*(3), 263–276.

Ting, S. L., Kwok, S. K., Tsang, A. H. C., Lee, W. B., & Yee, K. F. (2011). Experiences sharing of implementing template-based electronic medical record system (TEMRS) in a Hong Kong medical organization. *Journal of Medical Systems, 35*(6), 1605–1615. doi:10.1007/s10916-010-9436-9 PubMed

van Oorschot, J. A. W. H., Hofman, E., & Halman, J. I. M. (2018). A bibliometric review of the innovation adoption literature. *Technological Forecasting and Social Change, 134*(June), 1–21. doi:10.1016/j.techfore.2018.04.032

Venkatesh, M. Morris., Davis., & Davis. (2003). User Acceptance of Information Technology: Toward a Unified View. Management Information Systems Quarterly, 27(3), 425–478. doi:10.2307/30036540

Venkatesh, V., & Davis, F. D. (2000). A Theoretical Extension of the Technology Acceptance Model: Four Longitudinal Field Studies. *Management Science, 46*(2), 186–204. doi:10.1287/mnsc.46.2.186.11926

Wagner, E. L., & Newell, S. (2007). Exploring the importance of participation in the post-implementation period of an ES project: A neglected area. *Journal of the Association for Information, 8*(10), 508–524. doi:10.17705/1jais.00142

Yu, P., Zhang, Y., Gong, Y., & Zhang, J. (2013). Unintended adverse consequences of introducing electronic health records in residential aged care homes. *International Journal of Medical Informatics*, *82*(9), 772–788. doi:10.1016/j.ijmedinf.2013.05.008 PubMed

APPENDIX: ARTICLE SEARCH PROCESS AND RESULTS

Figure 6. Article search process and results

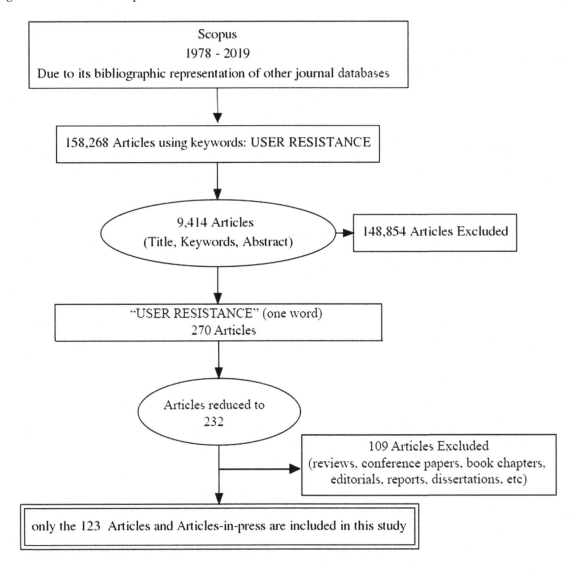

Compilation of References

8.

Aanestad, M., Grisot, M., Hanseth, O., & Vassilakopoulou, P. (2017). *Information Infrastructures Within European Health Care: Working with the Installed Base*. Cham, Switzerland: Springer. doi:10.1007/978-3-319-51020-0

Aasheim, C. L., Li, L., & Williams, S. (2009). Knowledge and Skill Requirements for Entry-Level Information Technology Workers: A Comparison of Industry and Academia. *Journal of Information Systems Education*, 20(3), 349–357.

Aasheim, C. L., Williams, S., & Butler, E. S. (2009). Knowledge and Skill Requirements for IT Graduates. *Journal of Computer Information Systems*, 49(3), 48–53.

Aasheim, C. L., Williams, S., Rutner, P., & Gardiner, A. (2015). Data analytics vs. data science: A study of similarities and differences in undergraduate programs based on course descriptions. *Journal of Information Systems Education*, 26(2), 103–115.

Aasi, P., Rusu, L., & Han, S. (2016). The Influence of Organizational Culture on IT Governance Performance: Case of The IT Department in a Large Swedish Company. doi:10.1109/HICSS.2016.638

Abdelnour, S., Hasselbladh, H., & Kallinikos, J. (2017). Agency and institutions in organization studies. *Organization Studies*, 38(12), 1775–1792. doi:10.1177/0170840617708007

Abe, R. (2019). Introducing autonomous buses and taxis : Quantifying the potential benefits in Japanese transportation systems. *Transportation Research Part A, Policy and Practice*, 126(1), 94–113. doi:10.1016/j.tra.2019.06.003

Abhishek, & Hemchand, S. (2016). Adoption of sensor-based communication for mobile marketing in India. Journal of Indian Business Research, 8(1), 65-76.

Abid, M., & Abbasi, M. (2014). *Antecedents and Outcomes of Consumer Buying Attitude: The Case of Pakistani Counterfeit Market*. Academic Press.

Abigee. (2016). *The State of APIs:2016 Report on Impact of APIs on Digital Business*. Abigee.

Aboelmaged, M. G. (2010). Predicting e-procurement adoption in a developing country: An empirical integration of technology acceptance model and theory of planned behaviour. *Industrial Management & Data Systems*, 110(3), 392–414. doi:10.1108/02635571011030042

Abrahão, R., Moriguchi, S. N., & Andrade, D. F. (2016). Intention of adoption of mobile payment: An analysis in the light of the Unified Theory of Acceptance and Use of Technology (UTAUT). RAI Revista de Administração e Inovação, 13(3), 221–230. doi:10.1016/j.rai.2016.06.003

Abubakar, A. D., Bass, J. M., & Allison, I. (2014). Cloud computing: Adoption issues for sub-Saharan African SMEs. *The Electronic Journal on Information Systems in Developing Countries*, 62(1), 1–17. doi:10.1002/j.1681-4835.2014. tb00439.x

Abugre, J. B. (2017). Institutional governance and management systems in Sub-Saharan Africa higher education: Developments and challenges in a Ghanaian Research University. *Higher Education*, 1–17.

Accenture Consulting. (2015). North America consumer digital payments survey. Retrieved from https://www.accenture.com/t20151021T165757__w__/us-en/_acnmedia/Accenture/next-gen/na-payment-survey/pdfs/Accenture-Digital-Payments-Survey-North-America-Accenture-Executive-Summary.pdf

Acheampong, E. K. (2012). The State of Information and Communication Technology Technology and Health Informatics in Ghana. *Online Journal of Public Health Informatics*, 4(2), 12–17. PMID:23569633

Acheampong, O., & Moyaid, S. A. (2016). An integrated model for determining business intelligence systems adoption and post-adoption benefits in banking sector. *Journal of Administrative and Business Studies*, 2(2), 84–100. doi:10.20474/jabs-2.2.4

Achinstein, P. (2010). The War on Induction : Whewell Takes On Newton and Mill (Norton Takes On Everyone). *Philosophy of Science*, 77(December), 728–739. doi:10.1086/656540

Acılar, A. (2011). Exploring the aspects of digital divide in a developing country. *Issues in Informing Science and Information Technology*, 8, 231–244. doi:10.28945/1415

Acoca, B. (2008). Online identity theft. *Organisation for Economic Cooperation and Development. The OECD Observer. Organisation for Economic Co-Operation and Development*, (268): 12.

Acquah-Swanzy, M. (2015). *Evaluating Electronic Health Record Systems in Ghana: the Case of Effia Nkwanta Regional Hospital*. The Arctic University.

Adam, I. O., Effah, J., & Boateng, R. (2016a). *Migrating from Physical to Virtual Administrative Work Environment: A Case Study of a Sub Saharan African Higher Education Institution* Paper presented at the Americas Conference on Information Systems, San Diego, CA.

Adam, I. O., Effah, J., & Boateng, R. (2016b). *Virtualisation of Administrative Work Environment in Developing Country Higher Education Institutions: An Activity Theory Perspective.* Paper presented at the European Conference on Information Systems, Instanbul, Turkey.

Adam, I. O., Effah, J., & Boateng, R. (2017). Virtualisation of an Administrative Work Environment in Higher Education: Managing Information in a Developing Country University. *Journal of Enterprise Information Management*, 30(5), 723–747. doi:10.1108/JEIM-06-2016-0119

Adam, I. O., & Musah, A. (2015). Small and medium enterprises (SMEs) in the cloud in developing countries: A synthesis of the literature and future research directions. *Journal of Management and Sustainability*, 5(1), 115. doi:10.5539/jms.v5n1p115

Adam, M. T. P., Lux, E., Pfeiffer, J., Dorner, V., Muller, M. B., & Weinhardt, C. (2017). Brownie: A Platform for Conducting NeuroIS Experiments. *Journal of the Association for Information Systems*, 18(4), 264–296. doi:10.17705/1jais.00457

Adams, B., Berner, E. S., & Wyatt, J. R. (2004). Applying Strategies to Overcome User Resistance in a Group of Clinical Managers to a Business Software Application: A Case Study. *Journal of Organizational and End User Computing*, 16(4), 55–64. doi:10.4018/joeuc.2004100104

Adedeji, P., Irinoye, O., Ikono, R., & Komolafe, A. (2018). Factors Influencing the Use of Electronic Health Records Among Nurses in a Teaching Hospital in Nigeria. *Journal of Health Informatics in Developing Countries*, *12*(2), 1–20.

Adeleke, I. T., Erinle, S. A., Ndana, A. M., Anamah, T. C., Ogundele, O. A., & Aliyu, D. (2014). Healht Information Technology in Nigeria: Stakeholders' Perpectives of Nationwide Implementations and Meaningful Use of the Emerging Technology in the Most Populous Black Nation. *American Journal of Health Research, 3*(1-1), 17-24.

Adenuga, K. I., Iahad, N. A., & Miskon, S. (2017). Towards reinforcing telemedicine adoption amongst clinicians in Nigeria. *International Journal of Medical Informatics*, *104*, 84–98. doi:10.1016/j.ijmedinf.2017.05.008 PMID:28599820

Adewumi, A., Odunjo, V., & Misra, S. (2015). Developing a mobile application for a taxi service company in Nigeria. In *2015 International Conference on Computing, Communication and Security (ICCCS)* (pp. 1-5). IEEE. 10.1109/CCCS.2015.7374204

Adner, R., & Kapoor, R. (2010). Value creation in innovation ecosystems: How the structure of technological interdependence affects firm performance in new technology. *Strategic Management Journal*, *31*(3), 306–333. doi:10.1002mj.821

Adomavicius, G., Bockstedt, Gupta, & Kauffman. (2008). Making Sense of Technology Trends in the Information Technology Landscape : A Design Science Approach. *Management Information Systems Quarterly*, *32*(4), 779–809. doi:10.2307/25148872

Adomi, E. E., & Igun, S. E. (2008). Combating cyber crime in Nigeria. *The Electronic Library*, *26*(5), 716–725. doi:10.1108/02640470810910738

Adukaite, A., van Zyl, I., Er, Ş., & Cantoni, L. (2017). Teacher perceptions on the use of digital gamified learning in tourism education: The case of South African secondary schools. *Computers & Education*, *111*, 172–190. doi:10.1016/j.compedu.2017.04.008

Afzal, W., Roland, D., & Al-Squri, M. N. (2009). Information asymmetry and product valuation: An exploratory study. *Journal of Information Science*, *35*(2), 192–203. doi:10.1177/0165551508097091

Agag, G. M., & El-Masry, A. A. (2016). Why do consumers trust online travel websites? Drivers and outcomes of consumer trust toward online travel websites. *Journal of Travel Research*. doi:10.1177/0047287516643185

Agarwal, N., & Ahmed, F. (2017). Developing collective learning extension for rapidly evolving information system courses. *Education and Information Technologies*, *22*(1), 7–37. doi:10.100710639-015-9394-4

Agarwal, R., & Dhar, V. (2014). Editorial—big data, data science, and analytics: The opportunity and challenge of IS research. *Information Systems Research*, *25*(3), 443–448. doi:10.1287/isre.2014.0546

Agarwal, R., Gao, G., DesRoches, C., & Jha, A. K. (2010). Research Commentary-The Digital Transformation of Healthcare: Current status and the Road Ahead. *Information Systems Research*, *21*(4), 661–101. doi:10.1287/isre.1100.0327

Agarwal, R., & Prasad, J. (1998). A conceptual and operational definition of personal innovativeness in the domain of information technology. *Information Systems Research*, *9*(2), 204–215. doi:10.1287/isre.9.2.204

Agarwal, S., Khapra, M., Menezes, B., & Uchat, N. (2007). *Security issues in mobile payment systems*. Indian Institute of Technology Bombay India.

Agbatogun, A. O. (2010). Self-concept, computer anxiety, gender and attitude towards interactive computer technologies: A predictive study among Nigerian teachers. *International Journal of Education and Development Using Information and Communication Technology*, *6*(2), 1-14.

Agrawal, T., Sao, A., Fernandes, K. J., Tiwari, M. K., & Kim, D. Y. (2013). A hybrid model of component sharing and platform modularity for optimal product family design. *International Journal of Production Research*, *51*(2), 614–625. doi:10.1080/00207543.2012.663106

Aguiar, L., & Martens, B. (2016). Digital music consumption on the Internet: Evidence from clickstream data. *Information Economics and Policy*, *34*, 27–43. doi:10.1016/j.infoecopol.2016.01.003

Aharony, N. (2012). Twitter use by three political leaders: An exploratory analysis. *Online Information Review*, *36*(4), 587–603. doi:10.1108/14684521211254086

Ahmed, A. A. G. E. (2019). Benefits and Challenges of Internet of Things for Telecommunication Networks. In Telecommunication Networks-Trends and Developments. IntechOpen.

Ajzen, I. (1991). The theory of planned behaviour. *Organizational Behavior and Human Decision Processes*, *50*(2), 179–211. doi:10.1016/0749-5978(91)90020-T

Ajzen, I., & Fishbein, M. (1980). *Understanding attitudes and predicting social behaviour*. Englewood Cliffs, NJ: Prentice-Hall.

Akbulut-Bailey, A. (2012). Improving IS Enrolment Choices: The Role of Social Support. *Journal of Information Systems Education*, *23*(3), 259–271.

Akdeniz, Y. (2001). Internet Content Regulation: UK Government and the control of internet content. *Computer Law & Security Review*, *17*(5), 303–317. doi:10.1016/S0267-3649(01)00505-2

Aker, J. C., & Mbiti, I. M. (2010). Mobile phones and economic development in Africa. *The Journal of Economic Perspectives*, *24*(3), 207–232. doi:10.1257/jep.24.3.207

Akin, A., & İskender, M. (2011). Internet addiction and depression, anxiety, and stress. *International Online Journal of Education Sciences*, *3*(1), 138–148.

Akman, I., & Turhan, C. (2017). Investigation of employers' performance expectations for new IT graduates in individual and team work settings for software development. *Information Technology & People*, *31*(1), 199–214. doi:10.1108/ITP-01-2017-0020

Akomea-Frimpong, I., Andoh, C., Akomea-Frimpong, A., & Dwomoh-Okudzeto, Y. (2019). Control of Fraud on Mobile Money Services in Ghana: an exploratory study. Journal of Money Laundering Control, 300-317.

Al-aboud, F. N. (2011). Strategic Information Systems Planning : A Brief Review. *International Journal of Computer Science and Network Security*, *11*(5), 179–183.

Alain, Y. C., Lacka, E., Li, B., & Chan, H. K. (2018). The role of social media in enhancing Guanxi and perceived effectiveness of e-commerce institutional mechanism in the online marketplace. *Information & Management*, *55*(5), 621–632. doi:10.1016/j.im.2018.01.003

Al-Alawi, A. I., & Al-Ali, F. M. (2015). Factors affecting e-commerce adoption in SMEs in the GCC: An empirical study of Kuwait. *Research Journal of Information Technology*, *7*(1), 1–21. doi:10.3923/rjit.2015.1.21

Alalwan, A. A., Rana, N. P., Dwivedi, Y. K., & Algharabat, R. (2017). Social media in marketing: A review and analysis of the existing literature. *Telematics and Informatics*, *34*(7), 1177–1190. doi:10.1016/j.tele.2017.05.008

Alam, M. S., & Khan, B. M. (2015). Impact of social media on Brand equity: A literature analysis. *AIMA Journal of Management & Research*, *9*(4), 1–12.

Alamri, S., Almutiri, N., Ballahmar, H., & Zafar, A. (2016). Strategic information system planning: A case study of a service delivery company. *Iarjset, 3*(5), 78–84. doi:10.17148/IARJSET.2016.3518

Alam, S. S., Ali, M. Y., & Jani, M. F. M. (2011). An empirical study of factors affecting electronic commerce adoption among SMEs in Malaysia. *Journal of Business Economics and Management, 12*(2), 375–399. doi:10.3846/16111699.2011.576749

Alam, S. S., Khatibi, A., Ahmad, M. I. S., & Ismail, H. B. (2008). Factors affecting e-commerce adoption in the electronic manufacturing companies in Malaysia. *International Journal of Commerce and Management, 17*(1/2), 125–139. doi:10.1108/10569210710776503

Alarcón-Del-Amo, M. D. C., Lorenzo-Romero, C., & Gómez-Borja, M.-A. (2012). Analysis of acceptance of social networking sites. *African Journal of Business Management, 6*(29), 8609–8619. doi:10.5897/AJBM11.2664

Al-Bakri, A. A., & Katsioloudes, M. I. (2015). The factors affecting e-commerce adoption by Jordanian SMEs. *Management Research Review, 38*(7), 726–749. doi:10.1108/MRR-12-2013-0291

Alcaro, A., & Panksepp, J. (2011). The SEEKING mind: Primal neuro-affective substrates for appetitive incentive states and their pathological dynamics in addictions and depression. *Neuroscience and Biobehavioral Reviews, 35*(9), 1805–1820. doi:10.1016/j.neubiorev.2011.03.002 PMID:21396397

Alcivar, I., & Abad, A. G. (2016). Design and evaluation of a gamified system for ERP training. *Computers in Human Behavior, 58*, 109–118. doi:10.1016/j.chb.2015.12.018

Aldrich, R. S. (2018). *Resilience (Library Futures Series, Book 2)* (Vol. 2). American Library Association.

Alfahl, H., Houghton, L., & Sanzogni, L. (2017). Mobile Commerce Adoption in Saudi Organizations: A Qualitative Study. *International Journal of Enterprise Information Systems, 13*(4), 31–57. doi:10.4018/IJEIS.2017100103

Al-Gahtani, S. S. (2016). Empirical investigation of e-learning acceptance and assimilation: A structural equation model. Applied Computing and Informatics, 12(1), 27–50. doi:10.1016/j.aci.2014.09.001

Al-Gamal, E., Alzayyat, A., & Ahmad, M. M. (2015). Prevalence of internet addiction and its association with psychological distress and coping strategies among university students in Jordan. *Perspectives in Psychiatric Care, 52*(1), 49–61. doi:10.1111/ppc.12102 PMID:25639746

Algharabat, R., Alalwan, A. A., Rana, N. P., & Dwivedi, Y. K. (2017). Three-dimensional product presentation quality antecedents and their consequences for online retailers: The moderating role of virtual product experience. *Journal of Retailing and Consumer Services, 36*, 203–217. doi:10.1016/j.jretconser.2017.02.007

Alhojailan, M. I. (2012). Thematic analysis: A critical review of its process and evaluation. *WestEast Journal of Social Sciences, 1*(1), 39–47.

Alias, N. A. (2013). *ICT development for social and rural connectedness*. New York, NY: Springer. doi:10.1007/978-1-4614-6901-8

Ali, M., Zhou, L., Miller, L., & Ieromonachou, P. (2016). User resistance in IT : A literature review. *International Journal of Information Management, 36*(1), 35–43. doi:10.1016/j.ijinfomgt.2015.09.007

Al-Imarah, A. A., & Shields, R. (2018). MOOCs, disruptive innovation and the future of higher education: A conceptual analysis. *Innovations in Education and Teaching International*, 1–12.

Ali, R. H. R. M., Mohamad, R., Talib, Y. Y. A., & Abdullah, A. (2017). Strategic IS Planning Practices : A Case of Medium Manufacturing Company in Malaysia. In *SHS Web of Conferences* (Vol. 02006, pp. 1–6). 10.1051hsconf/20173402006

Alkhalisi, Z. (2019). Uber is buying its Middle East rival Careem for $3.1 billion. *CNN Business*. Retrieved from https://edition.cnn.com/2019/03/26/tech/uber-careem-acquisition/index.html

Alkhunaizan, A., & Love, S. (2012). Predicting consumer decisions to adopt mobile commerce in Saudi Arabia. *Proceedings from 19th Americas Conference on Information Systems*, 1 – 9

Almeida, F., Silva, P., & Leite, J. (2017). Proposal of a carsharing system to improve urban mobility. *Theoretical and Empirical Researches in Urban Management*, *12*(3), 32–44.

Aloisi, A. (2015). Commoditized workers: Case study research on labor law issues arising from a set of on-demand/gig economy platforms. *Comp. Lab. L. & Pol'y J.*, *37*, 653.

Alonso, B., Barreda, R., Olio, L., & Ibeas, A. (2018). Modelling user perception of taxi service quality. *Transport Policy*, *63*(1), 157–164. doi:10.1016/j.tranpol.2017.12.011

Alpay, L., Henkemans, O. B., Otten, W., Rövekamp, T. A. J. M., & Dumay, A. C. M. (2010). E-health Applications and Services for Patient Empowerment: Directions for Best Practices in The Netherlands. *Telemedicine Journal and e-Health*, *16*(7), 787–791. doi:10.1089/tmj.2009.0156 PMID:20815745

Al-Qahtani, N., & Al-Asem, S. A. (2015). Business Analytics in Healthcare: Opportunities and Challenges. *Information and Knowledge Management, 5*(12).

Alqatan, S., Noor, N. M. M., Man, M., & Mohemad, R. (2017). A theoretical discussion of factors affecting the acceptance of m-commerce among SMTEs by integrating TTF with TAM. *International Journal of Business Information Systems*, *26*(1), 66–111. doi:10.1504/IJBIS.2017.086057

Alrousan, M. K., & Jones, E. (2016). A conceptual model of factors affecting e-commerce adoption by SME owner/managers in Jordan. *International Journal of Business Information Systems*, *21*(3), 269–308. doi:10.1504/IJBIS.2016.074762

Alryalat, M. A. A., Rana, N. P., Sahu, G. P., Dwivedi, Y. K., & Tajvidi, M. (2017). Use of social media in citizen-centric electronic government services: A literature analysis. *International Journal of Electronic Government Research*, *13*(3), 55–79. doi:10.4018/IJEGR.2017070104

Alsharari, N. M., & Youssef, M. A. E. A. (2017). Management accounting change and the implementation of GFMIS: A Jordanian case study. *Asian Review of Accounting*, *25*(2), 242–261. doi:10.1108/ARA-06-2016-0062

Alshare, K. A., & Lane, P. L. (2011). Predicting student-perceived learning outcomes and satisfaction in ERP courses: An empirical investigation. *Communications of the Association for Information Systems*, *28*(1), 571–584.

Alshehri, M., Drew, S., Alhussain, T., & Alghamdi, R. (2012). The impact of trust on e- government services acceptance: A study of users' perceptions by applying UTAUT model. *International Journal of Technology Diffusion*, *3*(2), 50–61. doi:10.4018/jtd.2012040105

Alshubaily, N. F., & Altameem, A. A. (2017). The Role of Strategic Information Systems (SIS) in Supporting and Achieving the Competitive Advantages (CA): An Empirical Study on Saudi Banking Sector. *International Journal of Advanced Computer Science and Applications*, *8*, 128–139.

Alsop, R., & Heinsohn, N. (2005). *Measuring empowerment in practice—structuring analysis and framing indicators*. Washington, DC: World Bank. doi:10.1596/1813-9450-3510

Altameem, A. A., Aldrees, A. I., & Alsaeed, N. A. (2014). Strategic Information Systems Planning (SISP). In *Proceedings of the World Congress on Engineering and Computer Science* (Vol. I, pp. 22–24). San Francisco: WCECS.

Alter, S. (2006). Work Systems and IT Artifacts - Does the Definition Matter? *Communications of the Association for Information Systems, 17*(14), 299–313.

Alturki, A., Bandara, W., & Gable, G. (2012). Design Science Research and the Core of Information Systems. *Design Science Research in Information Systems. Advances in Theory and Practice, 7286*, 309–327.

Alwahaishi, S., & Snásel, V. (2013). Acceptance and use of information and communications technology: A UTAUT and flow based theoretical model. *Journal of Technology Management & Innovation, 8*(2), 61–73. doi:10.4067/S0718-27242013000200005

Alwan, A. A., Dwivedi, Y. K., Nripendra, P. R., & Algharabat, R. (2018). Examining factors influencing Jordanian customers' intentions and adoption of internet banking: Extending UTAUT2 with risk. *Journal of Retailing and Consumer Services, 40*, 125–138. doi:10.1016/j.jretconser.2017.08.026

Alwan, A. A., Dwivedi, Y. K., Rana, N. P., Lal, B., & Williams, M. D. (2015). Consumer adoption of Internet banking in Jordan: Examining the role of hedonic motivation, habit, self-efficacy and trust. *Journal of Financial Services Marketing, 20*(2), 145–157. doi:10.1057/fsm.2015.5

Alzahrani, M. E., & Goodwin, R. D. (2012). Towards a UTAUT-based model for the study of E-Government citizen acceptance in Saudi Arabia. In *Proceedings of World Academy of Science, Engineering and Technology (No. 64)*. World Academy of Science, Engineering and Technology.

Ambrosini, V., & Bowman, C. (2009). What are dynamic capabilities and are they a useful construct in strategic management? *International Journal of Management Reviews, 11*(1), 29–49. doi:10.1111/j.1468-2370.2008.00251.x

Amegbe, H., Hanu, C., & Nuwasiima, A. (2017). Small-scale individual entrepreneurs and the usage of mobile money and mobile commerce in facilitating business growth in Ghana. *Management Science Letters, 7*(8), 373–384. doi:10.5267/j.msl.2017.5.004

Amit, R., & Schoemaker, P. J. H. (1993). Strategic Assets and Organizational Rent. *Strategic Management Journal, 14*(1), 33–46. doi:10.1002/smj.4250140105

Amit, R., & Zott, C. (2001). Value creation in e-business. *Strategic Management Journal, 22*(6–7).

Amrollahi, A., Ghapanchi, A. H., & Talaei-Khoei, A. (2013). A Systematic Literature Review on Strategic Information Systems Planning : Insights from the Past Decade. *Pacific Asia Journal of the Association for Information Systems, 5*(2), 39–66. doi:10.17705/1pais.05203

Anderson, G. L., & Chang, E. (2018). Competing Narratives of Leadership in Schools: The Institutional and Discursive Turns in Organizational Theory. The SAGE Handbook of School Organization, 84.

Anderson, B. (1983). *Imagined Communities*. London: Verso.

Anderson, D. L. (2017). Improving information technology curriculum learning outcomes. *Informing Science: The International Journal of an Emerging Transdiscipline, 20*, 119–131. doi:10.28945/3746

Andrade, A. D., & Urquhart, C. (2010). The affordances of actor network theory in ICT for development research. *Information Technology & People, 23*(4), 352–374. doi:10.1108/09593841011087806

Andreassen, C. S. (2015). Online Social Network Site Addiction: A comprehensive review. *Current Addiction Reports, 2*(2), 175–184. doi:10.100740429-015-0056-9

Andrés, A. R., & Asongu, S. A. (2013). Fighting Software Piracy: Which Governance Tools Matter in Africa? *Journal of Business Ethics, 118*(3), 667–682. doi:10.100710551-013-1620-7

Andrews, M. (2013). The Limits of Institutional Reform in Development: Changing Rules for Realistic Solutions. New Delhi: Cambridge University Press. doi:10.1017/CBO9781139060974

Angeles, R. (2013). Using the Technology-Organization-Environment framework and Zuboff's concepts for understanding environmental sustainability and RFID: Two case studies. *International Journal of Social, Management. Economics and Business Engineering*, *7*(10), 1605–1613.

Angeles, R., & Nath, R. (2007). Business-to-business e-procurement: Success factors and challenges to implementation. *Supply Chain Management*, *12*(2), 104–115. doi:10.1108/13598540710737299

Ankrah, E. (2016). Strategic Issues in Information Systems Planning from the Ghanaian Perspective. *International Review of Management and Marketing*, *6*(4), 1055–1065.

Ansong, E., & Boateng, R. (2017). Organisational adoption of telecommuting: Evidence from a developing country. *The Electronic Journal on Information Systems in Developing Countries*, *12008*. doi:10.1002/isd2.12008

Ansong, E., & Boateng, R. (2019). Surviving in the digital era–business models of digital enterprises in a developing economy. Digital Policy. *Regulation & Governance*, *21*(2), 164–178. doi:10.1108/DPRG-08-2018-0046

Antonova, A. (2015). Emerging technologies and organizational transformation. In Technology, Innovation, and Enterprise Transformation (pp. 20-34). IGI Global. doi:10.4018/978-1-4666-6473-9.ch002

Anuff, E. (2017). *The API-First World*. Retrieved from Apigee.com: apigee.com/about/tags/ecosystems-0

APA. (2013). *Diagnostic and Statistical Manual of Mental Disorders, 5*. APA.

Apatas Technology and Society. (2018). *Information Systems Journal Special Issue on Cybercrime and Computer 'Digital' Forensics*. Retrieved from http://www.apatas.org/icccf-2018/isj/

Apigian, C. H., & Gambill, S. (2014). A Descriptive Study of Graduate Information Systems Curriculums. *The Review of Business Information Systems (Online)*, *18*(2), 47–52. doi:10.19030/rbis.v18i2.8978

Apigian, C. H., & Gambill, S. E. (2010). Are We Teaching the IS 2009 * Model Curriculum? *Journal of Information Systems*, *21*(4), 411–421.

Appiahene, P., Asante, G., Kesse-Yaw, B., & Acquah-Hayfron, J. (2017). Raising students programming skills using appiahene gamification model. In *ECGBL 2017 11th European Conference on Game-Based Learning* (pp. 14-21). Academic Conferences and Publishing Limited.

Apte, C., Liu, B., Pednault, E. P., & Smyth, P. (2002). Business Applications of Data Mining. *Communications of the ACM*, *45*(8), 49–53. doi:10.1145/545151.545178

Apulu, I., & Latham, A. (2011). Drivers for information and communication technology adoption: A case study of Nigerian small and medium-sized enterprises. *International Journal of Business and Management*, *6*(5), 51–60. doi:10.5539/ijbm.v6n5p51

Aral, S., & Weill, P. (2007). IT assets, organizational capabilities, and firm performance: How resource allocations and organizational differences explain performance variation. *Organization Science*, *18*(5), 763–780. doi:10.1287/orsc.1070.0306

Archibugi, D., & Michie, J. (1997). Technological globalization and national systems of innovation: an introduction. *Technology, globalization and economic performance*, 1-23.

Ardhito, H. N., Handayati, Y., & Putranto, N. A. R. (2019). Enhancing the Awareness of Farmers' Towards Their Role Through Gamification. *The International Conference of Business and Banking Innovations (ICOBBI) Proceeding*, 17-27.

Arli, D., Tjiptono, F., & Porto, R. (2015). The impact of moral equity, relativism and attitude on individuals' digital piracy behaviour in a developing country. *Marketing Intelligence & Planning*, *33*(3), 348–365. doi:10.1108/MIP-09-2013-0149

Arora, B. (2016). Exploring and analyzing Internet crimes and their behaviours. *Perspectives on Science*, *8*, 540–542. doi:10.1016/j.pisc.2016.06.014

Arpaci, I. (2015). A comparative study of the effects of cultural differences on the adoption of mobile learning. *British Journal of Educational Technology*, *46*(4), 699–712. doi:10.1111/bjet.12160

Arsono, D., & Kusumawati, D. (2018). Content Analysis Twitter Usage By Governor Candidates of West Java 2018. In *Proceedings of the 5th. International Conference on Social and Political Sciences (IcoSaPS 2018)* (pp. 183-188). Atlantis Press. 10.2991/icosaps-18.2018.41

Arthur, P., & Arthur, E. (2016). Tertiary institutions and capacity building in Ghana: Challenges and the way forward. *Commonwealth and Comparative Politics*, *54*(3), 387–408. doi:10.1080/14662043.2016.1175690

Asabere, N. Y., & Enguah, S. E. (2012). Integration of Expert Systems in Mobile Learning. *International Journal of Information and Communication Research*, *2*(1), 55–61.

Asabre, N. Y. (2012). Towards a perspective of Information Communication Technology in (ICT) learning: Migration from Electronic Learning (E-learning) to Mobile Learning (M- learning). *International Journal of Information and Communication Technology Research*, *2*(8), 646–649.

Asadullah, A., Faik, I., & Kankanhalli, A. (2018). Digital Platforms: A Review and Future Directions. *Twenty-second Pacific Asia Conference on Information Systems*. 10.1017/CCOL9780521862387.020

Asare, S., Otoo-Arthur, D., & Frimpong, K. O. (2017). Assessing the Readiness of the Digitalization of Health Records: A Case of a Municipal Hospital in Ghana. *International Journal of Computer Science and Information Technology Research*, *5*(4), 76–90.

Aseidu-Addo, S. (2019, November 11). Cyber fraud: Ghanaians lose $200m in 3 years. Retrieved from https://www.graphic.com.gh/business/business-news/ghana-news-momo-fraud-threatens-emerging-payment-technologies.html

Ashenhurst, R. L. (1972). Curriculum recommendations for graduate professional programs in information systems. *Communications of the ACM*, *15*(5), 363–398. doi:10.1145/355602.361320

Ashrafi, N., Kelleher, L., & Kuilboer, J.-P. (2014). The Impact of Business Intelligence on Healthcare Delivery in the USA. *Interdisciplinary Journal of Information, Knowledge, and Management, 9*.

Ashworth, R., Boyne, G., & Delbridge, R. (2007). Escape from the iron cage? Organizational change and isomorphic pressures in the public sector. *Journal of Public Administration: Research and Theory*, *19*(1), 165–187. doi:10.1093/jopart/mum038

Asia-Pacific Economic Cooperation. (2018). *Small and Medium Enterprises Working Group*. Retrieved from https://www.apec.org/Groups/SOM-Steering-Committee-on-Economic-and-Technical-Cooperation/Working-Groups/Small-and-Medium-Enterprises

Asongu, S. A. (2013). Harmonizing IPRs on software piracy: Empirics of trajectories in Africa. *Journal of Business Ethics*, *118*(1), 45–60. doi:10.100710551-012-1552-7

Asongu, S. A., Nwachukwu, J. C., & Orim, S. M. I. (2018). Mobile phones, institutional quality and entrepreneurship in Sub-Saharan Africa. *Technological Forecasting and Social Change*, *131*, 183–203. doi:10.1016/j.techfore.2017.08.007

Asongu, S., & Boateng, A. (2018). Introduction to Special Issue : Mobile Technologies and Inclusive Development in Africa Introduction to Special Issue : Mobile Technologies and. *Journal of African Business*, *19*(3), 297–301. doi:10.1 080/15228916.2018.1481307

Asongu, S., & Boateng, A. (2018). *Introduction to special issue: mobile technologies and inclusive development in Africa*. Academic Press.

Asunka, S. (2016). Instructor Perceptions and Intentions to Use a Tablet PC for Mobile Learning in a Ghanaian University: An Exploratory Case Study. In Handbook of Research on Mobile Devices and Applications in Higher Education Settings (pp. 495-517). IGI Global.

Athanasiadis, E., & Mitropoulos, S. (2010). A distributed platform for personalised advertising in digital interactive TV environments. *Journal of Systems and Software*, *83*(8), 1453–1469. doi:10.1016/j.jss.2010.02.040

Attaran, M. (2017). The rise of 3-D printing: The advantages of additive manufacturing over traditional manufacturing. *Business Horizons*, *60*(5), 677–688. doi:10.1016/j.bushor.2017.05.011

Attuahene, F., & Owusu-Ansah, A. (2013). A descriptive assessment of higher education access, participation, equity, and disparity in Ghana. *SAGE Open*, *3*(3). doi:10.1177/2158244013497725

Aubert, B. A., Houde, J. F., Rivard, S., & Patry, M. (2017). Determinants of contract completeness for information technology outsourcing. *Information Technology Management*, *18*(4), 277–292. doi:10.1007/s10799-016-0265-5

Auerswald, P. (2009). Creating social value. *Stanford Social Innovation Review*, *7*(2), 50–55.

Au, Y. A., & Kauffman, R. J. (2008). The economics of mobile payments: Understanding stakeholder issues for an emerging financial technology application. *Electronic Commerce Research and Applications*, *7*(2), 141–164. doi:10.1016/j. elerap.2006.12.004

Avgerou, C. (2001). The significance of context in information systems and organizational change. *Information Systems Journal*, *11*(1), 43–63. doi:10.1046/j.1365-2575.2001.00095.x

Avgerou, C. (2008). Information systems in developing countries : A critical research review. *Journal of Information Technology*, *23*(3), 133–146. doi:10.1057/palgrave.jit.2000136

Avgerou, C. (2010). Discourses on ICT and Development. *Information Technologies and International Development*, *6*(3), 1–18.

Avram, M. G. (2014). Advantages and challenges of adopting cloud computing from an enterprise perspective. *Procedia Technology*, *12*, 529–534. doi:10.1016/j.protcy.2013.12.525

Awa, H. O., Ukoha, O., & Emecheta, B. C. (2016). Using TOE theoretical framework to study the adoption of ERP solution. *Cogent Business & Management*, *3*(1), 1–23. doi:10.1080/23311975.2016.1196571

Awiagah, R., Kang, J., & Lim, J. I. (2016). Factors affecting e-commerce adoption among SMEs in Ghana. *Information Development*, *32*(4), 815–836. doi:10.1177/0266666915571427

Aydin, U. U., & Güler, C. (2016). From the construction of hegemony to state crisis political power and social media in Turkey. *Athens Journal of Mass Media and Communications*, *2*(2), 111–126. doi:10.30958/ajmmc.2.2.3

Ayyagari, M., Beck, T., & Kunt, A. D. (2007). Small and medium enterprises across the globe. *Small Business Economics*, *29*(4), 415–434. doi:10.100711187-006-9002-5

Azemi, Y., & Ozuem, W. (2015). Social media and SMEs in transition countries. In *Computer-mediated marketing strategies: Social media and online brand communities* (pp. 114–133). IGI Global. doi:10.4018/978-1-4666-6595-8.ch005

Azhari, N. N., Abdul Manaf, R., Ng, S. W., Bajunid, S. A., Bajunid, S. F., Gobil, M., ... Amin Nordin, S. (2019). Gamification, a Successful Method to Foster Leptospirosis Knowledge among University Students: A Pilot Study. *International Journal of Environmental Research and Public Health*, *16*(12), 2108. doi:10.3390/ijerph16122108 PMID:31207881

Azmi, M. A., & Singh, D. (2015). Schoolcube: Gamification for learning management system through microsoft sharepoint. *International Journal of Computer Games Technology*, *2015*, 9. doi:10.1155/2015/589180

Azogu, I., Norta, A., Papper, I., Longo, J., & Draheim, D. (2019). A Framework for the Adoption of Blockchain Technology in Healthcare Information Management Systems: A Case Study of Nigeria. In *Proceedings of the 12th International Conference on Theory and Practice of Electronic Governance* (pp. 310-316). ACM. 10.1145/3326365.3326405

Babb, J., Longenecker, H. E. J., Baugh, J., & Feinstein, D. (2014). Confronting the Issues of Programming In Information Systems Curricula: The Goal is Success. *Information Systems Education Journal*, *12*(1), 42–72.

Bacon, D. R., & Stewart, K. A. (2017). Why Assessment Will Never Work at Many Business Schools: A Call for Better Utilization of Pedagogical Research. *Journal of Management Education*, *41*(2), 181–200. doi:10.1177/1052562916645837

Bada, O. (2013). *The Emerging Role of Fashion Tourism and The Need for A Development Strategy in Lagos, Nigeria.* Case Study: Lagos Fashion and Design Week.

Badu, E., Kissi, E., Boateng, E. B. & Antwi-Afari, M. F. (2018). Tertiary Educational Infrastructural Development in Ghana: Financing, Challenges, and Strategies. *Africa Education Review*, 1-17.

Badu, E., Edwards, D. J., Owusu-Manu, D., & Brown, D. M. (2012). Barriers to the implementation of innovative financing (IF) of infrastructure. *Journal of Financial Management of Property and Construction*, *17*(3), 253–273. doi:10.1108/13664381211274362

Baethge, C., Klier, J., & Klier, M. (2016). Social commerce—State-of-the-art and future research directions. *Electronic Markets*, *26*(3), 269–290. doi:10.100712525-016-0225-2

Bahaa-eldin, A. M., & Sobh, M. A. A. (2014). A comprehensive Software Copy Protection and Digital Rights Management platform. Ain Shams Engineering Journal, 5(3), 703–720. doi:10.1016/j.asej.2014.03.001

Bain, J. S. (1956). Barriers to new competition (Vol. 3). Harvard University Press. doi:10.4159/harvard.9780674188037

Bai, S., & Koong, K. S. (2017). Financial and other frauds in the United States: A panel analysis approach. *International Journal of Accounting & Information Management*, *25*(4), 413–433. doi:10.1108/IJAIM-03-2017-0033

Baker, A. (2013). The gradual transformation? The incremental dynamics of macroprudential regulation. *Regulation & Governance*, *7*(4), 417–434. doi:10.1111/rego.12022

Baker, J. (2012). The technology–organization–environment framework. In *Information Systems Theory* (pp. 231–245). New York: Springer. doi:10.1007/978-1-4419-6108-2_12

Bakir, V., & McStay, A. (2018). Fake news and the economy of emotions: Problems, causes, solutions. *Digital Journalism*, *6*(2), 154–175. doi:10.1080/21670811.2017.1345645

Bakke, S., & Henry, R. M. (2015). Unraveling the Mystery of New Technology Use: An Investigation into the Interplay of Desire for Control, Computer Self-efficacy, and Personal Innovativeness. *AIS Transactions on Human-Computer Interaction*, *7*(4), 270–293. doi:10.17705/1thci.00075

Baktha, K. (2017). Mobile Application Development: All the Steps and Guidelines for Successful Creation of Mobile App: Case Study. *International Journal of Computer Science and Mobile Computing*, *6*(9), 15–20.

Balca, A. (2015). The construction of a new sociality through social media: The case of the Gezi uprising in Turkey. *Conjunctions: Transdisciplinary Journal of Cultural Participation*, 2(1), 72–99. doi:10.7146/tjcp.v2i1.22271

Bandyopadhyay, K., & Barnes, C. (2012). An analysis of factors affecting user acceptance of ERP Systems in the United States. *International Journal of Human Capital and Information Technology Professionals*, 3(1), 1–14. doi:10.4018/jhcitp.2012010101

Banker, R. D., Bardhan, I. R., Chang, H., & Lin, S. (2006). Plant information systems, manufacturing capabilities, and plant performance. *Management Information Systems Quarterly*, 30(2), 315–337. doi:10.2307/25148733

Banya, K. (2015). Globalization, policy directions, and higher education in Sub-Saharan Africa. In *Second International Handbook on Globalization, Education and Policy Research* (pp. 181–202). Dordrecht: Springer. doi:10.1007/978-94-017-9493-0_12

Bao, J., & Sun, X. (2010). *A conceptual model of factors affecting e-Commerce adoption by SMEs in China.* Paper presented at the Fourth International Conference on Management of e-Commerce and e-Government, Chengdu, Sichuan, China. 10.1109/ICMeCG.2010.43

Baranowski, C. (2017). Freelance Isn't Free: The High Cost of New York City's Freelance Isn't Free Act on Hiring Parties. *Brook. J. Corp. Fin. & Com. L.*, 12, 439.

Bardhan, I., Oh, J., Zheng, Z., & Kirksey, K. (2014). Predictive Analytics for Readmission of Patients with Congestive heart failure. *Information Systems Research*, 26(1), 19–36. doi:10.1287/isre.2014.0553

Barnes, S. A., Green, A., & de Hoyos, M. (2015). Crowdsourcing and work: Individual factors and circumstances influencing employability. *New Technology, Work and Employment*, 30(1), 16–31. doi:10.1111/ntwe.12043

Barney, J. (2001). Is the resource-based "view" a useful perspective for strategic management research? Yes. *Academy of Management Review*, 26(1), 41–56.

Barney, J. B. (1991). Firm resources and sustained competitive advantage. *Journal of Management*, 17(1), 99–120. doi:10.1177/014920639101700108

Barney, J. B. (1991). Firm Resources and Sustained Competitive Advantage. *Journal of Management*, 17(1), 99–120. doi:10.1177/014920639101700108

Baron, J., & Spulber, D. F. (2017). *The Effect of Technological Change on Firm Survival and Growth-Evidence from Technology Standards.* Chicago: NorthWest University.

Barreda, A. A., Bilgihan, A., Nusair, K., & Okumus, F. (2015). Generating brand awareness in Online Social Networks. *Computers in Human Behavior*, 50, 600–609. doi:10.1016/j.chb.2015.03.023

Barreto, I. (2010). Dynamic Capabilities: A review of past research and an agenda for the future. *Journal of Management*, 36(1), 256–280. doi:10.1177/0149206309350776

Bartholomae, F. (2018). Cybercrime and cloud computing. A game theoretic network model. *Managerial and Decision Economics*, 39(3), 297–305. doi:10.1002/mde.2904

Barua, A., Konana, P., Whinston, A. B., & Yin, F. (2004). An Empirical Investigation of Net-Enabled Business Value. MIS Quartely Quarterly, 28(4), 585–620. Retrieved from https://www.jstor.org/stable/25148656

Baškarada, S. (2014). Qualitative Case Study Guidelines. *Qualitative Report*, 19(24), 1–18.

Bateman, M. J., & Ludwig, T. D. (2003). Managing distribution quality through an adapted incentive program with tiered goals and feedback. *Journal of Organizational Behavior Management*, 23(1), 33–55. doi:10.1300/J075v23n01_03

Bates, D. W., Saria, S., Ohno-Machado, L., Shah, A., & Escoba, G. (2014). Big Data in Healthcare: Using Analytics to Identify and Manage High-Risk and High-Cost Patients. *Health Affairs*, *33*(7), 1123–1131. doi:10.1377/hlthaff.2014.0041 PMID:25006137

Baudrillard, J. (1981). *Simulacra and Simulation* (S. Glaser, Trans.). Ann Arbor, MI: University of Michigan Press.

Baumgartner, J. C., & Morris, J. S. (2010). MyFaceTube Politics: Social Networking Web Sites and Political Engagement of Young Adults. *Social Science Computer Review*, *28*(1), 24–44. doi:10.1177/0894439309334325

Bay, D., Cook, G. L., Grubisic, J., & Nikitkov, A. (2014). Identifying fraud in online auctions: A case study. *Accounting Perspectives*, *13*(4), 283–299. doi:10.1111/1911-3838.12033

Bay, M. (2018). Weaponizing the haters: *The Last Jedi* and the strategic politicization of pop culture through social media manipulation. *First Monday*, *23*(11). doi:10.5210/fm.v23i11.9388

Bayraktutan, G., Binark, M., Çom, T., Doğu, B., İslamoğlu, G., & Aydemir, A. T. (2013). The role of social media in political communication: Use of Twitter in the 2011 General Elections in Turkey. *Medianali*, *7*(13), 1–18.

Bayraktutan, G., Binark, M., Çom, T., Doğu, B., İslamoğlu, G., & Aydemir, A. T. (2014). Siyasal iletişim sürecinde sosyal medya ve Türkiye'de 2011 Genel Seçimlerinde Twitter kullanımı [Social media in process of political communication and Twitter use in 2011 General Elections in Turkey]. *Bilig*, *68*, 59–96. doi:10.12995/bilig.2014.6804

Beatty, R. C., Shim, J. P., & Jones, M. C. (2001). Factors influencing corporate web site adoption: A time-based assessment. *Information & Management*, *38*(6), 337–354. doi:10.1016/S0378-7206(00)00064-1

Beaudry, A., & Pinsonneault, A. (2005). Understanding User Responses to Information Technology: A Coping Model of User Adaptation. *Management Information Systems Quarterly*, *29*(3), 493–524. doi:10.2307/25148693

Becker, J. U., Clement, M., & Schaedel, U. (2010). The Impact of Network Size and Financial Incentives on Adoption and Participation in New Online Communities. *Journal of Media Economics*, *23*(3), 165–179. doi:10.1080/08997764 .2010.502515

Becker, J., & Niehaves, B. (2007). Epistemological perspectives on IS research: A framework for analysing and systematizing epistemological assumptions. *Information Systems Journal*, *17*(2), 197–214. doi:10.1111/j.1365-2575.2007.00234.x

Bedeley, R. T., & Palvia, P. (2014). A Study of the Issues of E-Health Care in Developing Countries: The Case of Ghana. *Twentieth Americas Conference on Information Systems*, 1-12.

Beheshti, H. M., & Bures, A. L. (2000). Information technology's critical role in corporate downsizing. *Industrial Management & Data Systems*, *100*(1), 31–35. doi:10.1108/02635570010310575

Behrendt, C., & Nguyen, Q. A. (2018). Innovative approaches for ensuring universal social protection for the future of work. *Future of Work Research Paper Series*, (1).

Beisel, D. (2006). *The Emerging Field of Social Commerce and Social Shopping*. Genuine VC.

Bellazsi, R., Dagliti, A., Sacchi, L., & Segani, D. (2015). Big Data Technologies: New Opportunities for Diabetes Management. *Journal of Diabetes Science and Technology*, *9*(5), 1119-1125. . doi:10.1177/1932296815583505

Bell, C., Mills, R., & Fadel, K. (2013). An analysis of undergraduate information systems curricula: Adoption of the IS 2010 curriculum guidelines. *Communications of the Association for Information Systems*, *32*(1), 72–95.

Belleflamme, P., Omrani, N., & Peitz, M. (2015). The economics of crowdfunding platforms. *Information Economics and Policy*, *33*, 11–28. doi:10.1016/j.infoecopol.2015.08.003

Belleflamme, P., & Toulemonde, E. (2016). Who benefits from increased competition among sellers on B2C platforms? *Research in Economics*, *70*(4), 741–751. doi:10.1016/j.rie.2016.08.006

Ben Yahia, I., Al-Neama, N., & Kerbache, L. (2018). Investigating the drivers for social commerce in social media platforms: Importance of trust, social support and the platform perceived usage. *Journal of Retailing and Consumer Services*, *41*, 11–19. doi:10.1016/j.jretconser.2017.10.021

Ben, W. (2016). *Guidelines for mobile health applications adopted amongst adolescents* (Masters' dissertation). University of Johannesburg, Johannesburg, South Africa.

Benamati, J. H., Ozdemir, Z. D., & Smith, H. J. (2010). Aligning undergraduate IS curricula with industry needs. *Communications of the ACM*, *53*(3), 152. doi:10.1145/1666420.1666458

Benbasat, I., Dexter, A. S., & Mantha, R. W. (1980). Impact of Organisational Maturity on Information Systems Skill Needs. *Management Information Systems Quarterly*, *4*(1), 21–34. doi:10.2307/248865

Benbasat, I., Goldstein, D. K., & Mead, M. (1987). The case research strategy in studies of information systems. *Management Information Systems Quarterly*, *11*(3), 369–386. doi:10.2307/248684

Benzell, S., Lagarda, G., & Alstyne, M. (2017). The Impact of APIs on Firm Performance. In *The Impact of APIs in Firm Performance*. Boston University Questrom School of Business Research Paper No. 2843326. Retrieved from Available at SSRN: https://ssrn.com/abstract=2843326

Beranuy, M., Oberst, U., Carbonell, X., & Chamarro, A. (2009). Problematic Internet and Mobile Phone Use and Clinical Symptoms in College Students: The role of emotional intelligence. *Computers in Human Behavior*, *25*(5), 1182–1187. doi:10.1016/j.chb.2009.03.001

Berger, T., Chen, C., & Frey, C. B. (2018). Drivers of disruption? Estimating the Uber effect. *European Economic Review*, *110*, 197–210. doi:10.1016/j.euroecorev.2018.05.006

Berg, J. (2015). Income security in the on-demand economy: Findings and policy lessons from a survey of crowdworkers. *Comp. Lab. L. & Pol'y J.*, *37*, 543.

Bergvall-Kåreborn, B., & Howcroft, D. (2014). A mazon Mechanical Turk and the commodification of labour. *New Technology, Work and Employment*, *29*(3), 213–223. doi:10.1111/ntwe.12038

Berman, S., & Marshall, A. (2014). The next digital transformation: From an individual-centred to an everyone-to-everyone economy. *Strategy and Leadership*, *42*(5), 9–17. doi:10.1108/SL-07-2014-0048

Bertrand-Cloodt, D., Hagedoorn, J., & Van Kranenburg, H. (2011). The strength of R&D network ties in high-tech sectors–a multi-dimensional analysis of the effects of tie strength on innovation performance. *Technology Analysis and Strategic Management*, *23*(10), 1015–1030. doi:10.1080/09537325.2011.621294

Betley, M., Bird, A., & Ghartey, A. (2012). *Evaluation of Public Financial Management Reform in Ghana, 2001–2010.* Final Country Case Study Report.

Bharadwaj, A., El Sawy, O. A., Pavlou, P. A., & Venkatraman, N. V. (2013). Digital business strategy: Toward a next generation of insights. *Management Information Systems Quarterly*, *37*(2), 471–482. doi:10.25300/MISQ/2013/37:2.3

Bhaskar, R. (1989). *Reclaiming Reality*. London: Verso.

Bhatia, V. (2018). Examining consumers' attitude towards the purchase of counterfeit fashion products. *Journal of Indian Business Research*, *10*(2), 193–207. doi:10.1108/JIBR-10-2017-0177

Bhattacherjee, A., & Hikmet, N. (2007b). Physicians' resistance toward healthcare information technologies: A dual-factor model. Proceedings of the Annual Hawaii International Conference on System Sciences, 1–10. doi:10.1109/HICSS.2007.437

Bhattacherjee, A., & Hikmet, N. (2007a). Physician's resistance toward healthcare information technology: A theoretical model and empirical test. *European Journal of Information Systems*, *16*(January), 725–737. doi:10.1057/palgrave.ejis.3000717

Bian, X., & Veloutsou, C. (2017). Consumers' attitudes regarding non-deceptive counterfeit brands in the UK and China. In Advances in Chinese Brand Management (pp. 331-350). Palgrave Macmillan.

Billhardt, H., Fernández, A., Ossowski, S., Palanca, J., & Bajo, J. (2019). Taxi dispatching strategies with compensations. *Expert Systems with Applications*, *122*(1), 173–182. doi:10.1016/j.eswa.2019.01.001

Billieux, J., Maurage, P., Lopez-Fernandez, O., Kuss, D. J., & Griffiths, M. D. (2015). Can Disordered Mobile Phone Use Be Considered a Behavioral Addiction? An update on current evidence and a comprehensive model for future research. *Current Addiction Reports*, *2*(2), 156–162. doi:10.100740429-015-0054-y

Bimber, B. (2014). Digital Media in the Obama Campaigns of 2008 and 2012: Adaptation to the Personalized Political Communication Environment. *Journal of Information Technology & Politics*, *11*(2), 130–150. doi:10.1080/19331681.2014.895691

Bin Taher, N. A., Krotov, V., & Silva, L. (2015). A framework for leading change in the UAE public sector. *The International Journal of Organizational Analysis*, *23*(3), 348–363. doi:10.1108/IJOA-10-2014-0809

Birkinshaw, J., & Goddard, J. (2009). The management spectrum. *Business Strategy Review*, *20*(4), 30–35. doi:10.1111/j.1467-8616.2009.00627.x

Birtchnell, T., & Hoyle, W. (2014). *3D printing for development in the global south: The 3D4D challenge.* Springer. doi:10.1057/9781137365668

Blay, A. (2019). Creating jobs using the digital economy. Retrieved July 28, 2019, from http://www.ghanaweb.com/GhanaHomePage/NewsArchive/Creating-jobs-using-the-digital-economy-448958

Boadi, R. A., Boateng, R., Hinson, R., & Opoku, R. A. (2007). Preliminary insights into m-commerce adoption in Ghana. *Information Development*, *23*(4), 253–265. doi:10.1177/0266666907084761

Boateng, R. (2011). Mobile phones and micro-trading activities–conceptualizing the link. *Info, 13*(5), 48-62.

Boateng, R., Acheampong, B., & Bedi, I. (2019). Preliminary Insights into Dominant Issues, Theories and Methodologies in Platform Interoperability Research. In *Twenty-Fifth American Conference on Information Systems* (pp.1-10). Cancun, Mexico: Association for Information Systems Electronic Library.

Boateng, R. (2011). Mobile phones and micro-trading activities–conceptualizing the link. *Info, 13*(5), 48–62.

Boateng, R. (2016). *Research made easy.* CreateSpace Independent Publishing Platform.

Boateng, R. (2016). Resources, Electronic-Commerce Capabilities and Electronic-Commerce Benefits: Conceptualizing the Links. *Information Technology for Development*, *22*(2), 242–264. doi:10.1080/02681102.2014.939606

Boateng, R. (2016). Resources, Electronic-Commerce Capabilities and Electronic-Commerce Benefits: Conceptualizing the Links. *Information Technology for Development*, *22*(6), 1–23.

Boateng, R. (2017). *Information Technology Policy and Strategy: The Workbook Edition (The Workbook).* Accra: CreateSpace Independent Publishing Platform.

Boateng, R., Heeks, R., Molla, A., & Hinson, R. (2011). Advancing E-Commerce Beyond Readiness in a Developing Country. *Journal of Electronic Commerce in Organizations*, *9*(1), 1–16. doi:10.4018/jeco.2011010101

Boateng, R., & Hinson, R. (2008). Information Systems Development: Where Does Knowledge Lie and How Does Learning Occur? *Development and Learning in Organizations*, *22*(3), 18–20. doi:10.1108/14777280810861785

Boateng, R., Molla, A., & Heeks, R. (2009). E-commerce in Developing Economies: A Review of Theoretical Frameworks and Approaches. In K. Rouibah, O. Khalil, & H. Ella (Eds.), *Emerging Markets, and E-commerce in Developing Economies*. Hershey, PA: IGI Publishing. doi:10.4018/978-1-60566-100-1.ch001

Boateng, R., Olumide, L., Isabalija, R. S., & Budu, J. (2011). Sakawa-cybercrime and criminality in Ghana. *Journal of Information Technology Impact*, *11*(2), 85–100.

Bødker, S., & Christiansen, E. (2002). Lost and found in flexibility. *IRIS 2002*.

Boell, S. K., & Cecez-Kecmanovic, D. (2014). A Hermeneutic Approach for Conducting Literature Reviews and Literature Searches. *Communications of the Association for Information Systems*, *34*(12), 257–286.

BoG. (2019). *Payment Systems*. Retrieved 04 25, 2019, from https://www.bog.gov.gh/: https://www.bog.gov.gh/payment-systems/payment-systems-statistics

Bolimos, I. A., & Choo, K.-K. R. (2017). Online fraud offending within an Australian jurisdiction. *Journal of Financial Crime*, *24*(2), 277–308. doi:10.1108/JFC-05-2016-0029

Bolton, R. N., Parasuraman, A., Hoefnagels, A., Migchels, N., Kabadayi, S., Gruber, T., ... Solnet, D. (2013). Understanding Generation Y and their use of social media: A review and research agenda. *Journal of Service Management*, *24*(3), 245–267. doi:10.1108/09564231311326987

Bond, E. W. (1982). A direct test of the" lemons" model: The market for used pickup trucks. *The American Economic Review*, *72*(4), 836–840.

Bondinuba, F. K., Nansie, A., Dadzie, J., Djokoto, S. D., & Sadique, M. A. (2017). Construction Audits Practice in Ghana: A Review. *J. Civil Engineering and Architecture Research*, *4*(1), 1859–1872.

Bonilla, S., Silva, H., Terra da Silva, M., Franco Gonçalves, R., & Sacomano, J. (2018). Industry 4.0 and sustainability implications: A scenario-based analysis of the impacts and challenges. *Sustainability*, *10*(10), 3740. doi:10.3390u10103740

Boone, J. (2000). Technological progress, downsizing and unemployment. *Economic Journal (London)*, *110*(465), 581–600. doi:10.1111/1468-0297.00555

Boonsiritomachai, W., & Pitchayadejanant, K. (2017). Determinants affecting mobile banking adoption by generation Y based on the Unified Theory of Acceptance and Use of Technology Model modified by the Technology AcceptanceModel concept. Kasetsart Journal of Social Sciences. doi:10.1016/j.kjss.2017.10.005

Borges, S. S., Durelli, V. H. S., Reis, H. M., & Isotani, S. (2014). A Systematic Mapping on Gamification Applied to Education. *Proceedings of the 29th Annual ACM Symposium on Applied Computing*, 216-222. 10.1145/2554850.2554956

Bossler, A. M., & Holt, T. J. (2009). On-line activities, guardianship, and malware infection: An examination of routine activities theory. *International Journal of Cyber Criminology*, *3*(1).

Bossler, A. M., & Holt, T. J. (2010). The effect of self-control on victimization in the cyberworld. *Journal of Criminal Justice*, *38*(3), 227–236. doi:10.1016/j.jcrimjus.2010.03.001

Boulianne, S. (2015). Social media use and participation: A metaanalysis of current research. *Information Communication and Society*, *18*(5), 524–538. doi:10.1080/1369118X.2015.1008542

Boulton, C. (2016, Nov 4). *How API adoption can boost annual profits*. Retrieved Jan 15, 2019, from https://www.cio.com/article/3138511/how-api-adoption-can-boosts-annual-profits.html

Boulton, C. (2016b, Oct 18). *CIOs move more dollars to digital transformation*. Retrieved 02 16, 2019, from https://www.cio.com/article/3131927/cios-move-more-dollars-to-digital-transformation.html

Bouncken, R., Fredrich, V., Kraus, S., & Ritala, P. (2019). (in press). Innovation alliances: Balancing value creation dynamics, competitive intensity, and market overlap. *Journal of Business Research, xxx–xxx*. doi:10.1016/j.jbusres.2019.10.004

Bourreau, M., & Verdier, M. (2010). *Cooperation for innovation in payment systems: The case of mobile payments*. Academic Press.

Bowen, W. G. (2014). Higher education in the digital age. *Croatian Economic Survey, 16*(1), 161–185.

Bowser, A., Sloan, M., Michelucci, P., & Pauwels, E. (2017). *Artificial Intelligence: A Policy-Oriented Introduction*. Academic Press.

Braa, J., Hanseth, O., Heywood, A., Mohammed, W., & Shaw, V. (2007). Developing Health Information Systems in Developing Countries: The Flexible Standards. *MIS Quarterly, 31*, 381–402.

Bradley, J. (2008). Management based critical success factors in the implementation of Enterprise Resource Planning systems. *International Journal of Accounting Information Systems, 9*(3), 175–200. doi:10.1016/j.accinf.2008.04.001

Brandenburger, A., & Stuart, H. Jr. (1996). Value-based business strategy. *Journal of Economics & Management Strategy, 5*(1), 5–25. doi:10.1111/j.1430-9134.1996.00005.x

Braun, V., Clarke, V., & Terry, G. (2014). Thematic analysis. Qual Res Clin Health Psychol, (24), 95-114.

Braun, V., & Clarke, V. (2006). Using thematic analysis in psychology. *Qualitative Research in Psychology, 3*(2), 77–101. doi:10.1191/1478088706qp063oa

Brawley, A. M., & Pury, C. L. (2016). Work experiences on MTurk: Job satisfaction, turnover, and information sharing. *Computers in Human Behavior, 54*, 531–546. doi:10.1016/j.chb.2015.08.031

Brinkley, I. (2016) In search of the Gig Economy. Lancaster: *The Work Foundation*. Retrieved June 30, from http://www.theworkfoundation. com/wp- content/uploads/2016/11/407_In-search- of-the- gig-economy _June2016. pdf

Brooks, R., & Grotz, C. (2010). Implementation of Electronic Medical Records: How Healthcare Providers are Managing the Challenges of Going Digital. *Journal of Business & Economics Research, 8*(6), 73–84. doi:10.19030/jber.v8i6.736

Brooks, S., Gambill, S., Clark, J., & Clark, C. (2016). What's in a Name? An Examination of Information System Degree Programs in AACSB International Accredited Schools. *Journal of Higher Education Theory and Practice, 16*(6), 66–76.

Brooks, S., Schneider, C., & Wang, X. A. (2016). Technology addictions and technostress: An examination of Hong Kong and the U.S. *Twenty-Second Americas Conference on Information Systems*, 1–10.

Broséus, J., Rhumorbarbe, D., Morelato, M., Staehli, L., & Rossy, Q. (2017). A geographical analysis of trafficking on a popular darknet market. *Forensic Science International, 277*, 88–102. doi:10.1016/j.forsciint.2017.05.021 PMID:28624673

Broughton, A., Gloster, R., Marvell, R., Green, M., Langley, J., & Martin, A. (2018). *The Experiences of Individuals in the Gig Economy,* Department for Business, Energy & Industrial Strategy Burtch, G., Carnahan, S., & Greenwood, B. N. (2018). Can you gig it? An empirical examination of the gig economy and entrepreneurial activity. *Management Science, 64*(12), 5497–5520. doi:10.1287/mnsc.2017.2916

Brown, A., Fishenden, J., Thompson, M., & Venters, W. (2017). Appraising the impact and role of platform models and Government as a Platform (GaaP) in UK Government public service reform: Towards a Platform Assessment Framework (PAF). *Government Information Quarterly*, *34*(2), 167–182. doi:10.1016/j.giq.2017.03.003

Brown, C. V. (2003). The IT organization of the future. In J. N. Luftman (Ed.), *Competing in the Information Age: Align in the Sand* (pp. 191–207). New York, NY: Oxford University Press; doi:10.1093/0195159535.003.0009

Bryant, R. (2008). *Investigating digital crime*. John Wiley and Sons.

Brynjolfsson, E., & McAfee, A. (2011). *Race against the machine: How the digital revolution is accelerating innovation, driving productivity, and irreversibly transforming employment and the economy*. Brynjolfsson and McAfee.

Bryson, J. M. (2011). *Strategic planning for public and nonprofit organizations: A guide to strengthening and sustaining organizational achievement* (Vol. 1). San Francisco, CA: Jossey-Bass.

Buchanan, T., & Whitty, M. T. (2014). The online dating romance scam: Causes and consequences of victimhood. *Psychology, Crime & Law*, *20*(3), 261–283. doi:10.1080/1068316X.2013.772180

Budgen, D., & Brereton, P. (2006). Performing Systematic Literature Reviews in Software Engineering. In *Proceedings of the 28th international conference on Software engineering* (ICSE '06) (pp. 1051-1052). ACM. 10.1145/1134285.1134500

Budu, J. (2018). Explaining online communities' contribution to socio-economic development. *GlobDev 2018, 9*. Retrieved from https://aisel.aisnet.org/globdev2018/9

Bukht, R., & Heeks, R. (2017). Defining, Conceptualising and Measuring the Digital Economy (No. 68). Retrieved from http://www.gdi.manchester.ac.uk/research/publications/working-papers/di/

Bullen, C. V., Abraham, T., Gallagher, K., Simon, J. C., & Zwieg, P. (2009). IT workforce trends: Implications for curriculum and hiring. *Communications of the Association for Information Systems*, *24*(1), 129–140.

Burgelman, R. A., & Grove, A. (2007). Cross-Boundary Disruptors: Powerful Inter-Industry Entrepreneurial Change Agents. *Strategic Entrepreneurship Journal*, *1*(3–4), 315–327. doi:10.1002/sej.27

Burke, M., & Hiltbrand, T. (2011). How Gamification Will Change Business Intelligence. *Business Intelligence Journal*, *6*(2), 8–16.

Burns, E., & Laskowski, N. (2018). *A machine learning and AI guide for enterprises in the cloud*. Retrieved from https://searchenterpriseai.techtarget.com/definition/AI-Artificial-Intelligence

Busalim, A. H., Che Hussin, A. R., & Iahad, N. A. (2019). Factors Influencing Customer Engagement in Social Commerce Websites: A Systematic Literature Review. *Journal of Theoretical and Applied Electronic Commerce Research*, *14*(2). doi:10.4067/S0718-18762019000200102

Busalim, A. H., & Hussin, A. R. C. (2016). Understanding social commerce: A systematic literature review and directions for further research. *International Journal of Information Management*, *36*(6), 1075–1088. doi:10.1016/j.ijinfomgt.2016.06.005

Business Insides. (2011). *The Development of Small and Medium Enterprise in Vietnam*. Retrieved from http://businessinsides.com/development-vietnam-small-medium-enterprises.html

Buterin, V. (2015). *On Public and Private Blockchains*. Retrieved from https://blog.ethereum.org/2015/08/07/on-public-and-private-Blockchains/

Butler, J. E., & Priem, R. L. (2001). Is the Resource-Based "View" a Useful Perspective for Strategic Management Research? doi:10.5465/AMR.2001.4011928

Butler, F. C., & Martin, J. A. (2016). The auto industry: Adapt to disruptive innovations or risk extinction. *Strategic Direction*, *32*(11), 31–34. doi:10.1108/SD-05-2016-0069

Buying, M. (2016). Facebook and Twitter will take 33per cent share of US digital display market by 2017. http://www.emarketer.com/Article/Facebook-Twitter

Byrd, T. A., Lewis, B. R., & Bradley, R. V. (2006). Is Infrastructure : The Influence of Senior it Leadership and Strategic Information Systems Planning IS Infrastructure : The Influence Of Senior It Leadership And Strategic Information Systems Planning. *Journal of Computer Information Systems ISSN*, *47*(1), 101–113.

Cai, S., Yuan, Q., & Zhou, P. (2013). A resource mapping framework for value co-creation in social media. In *WHICEB 2013* (Vol. 14, p. 25). Proceedings; doi:10.1504/IJNVO.2014.065082

Camilleri, J., & Neuhofer, B. (2017). Value co-creation and co-destruction in the Airbnb sharing economy. *International Journal of Contemporary Hospitality Management*, *29*(9), 2322–2340. doi:10.1108/IJCHM-09-2016-0492

Campbell, M., Pardue, J. H., & Campbell, A. A. (2015). Creating a Health Informatics Program : Is It Good For What Ails Us? *Twenty-first Americas Conference on Information Systems*, 1–8.

Canhilal, S. K., Lepori, B., & Seeber, M. (2016). Decision-Making Power and Institutional Logic in Higher Education Institutions: A Comparative Analysis of European Universities. In *Towards A Comparative Institutionalism: Forms, Dynamics and Logics across the Organizational Fields of Health Care and Higher Education*. Emerald Group Publishing Limited.

Cardon, D., & Casilli, A. (2015). *What is the digital labor?* Ina.

Carey, J., Galletta, D., Kim, J., Te'eni, D., Wildemuth, B., & Zhang, P. (2004). The Role of Human-Computer Interaction (HCI) in the Management Information Systems Curricula: A Call to Action. *Communications of the AIS, 13*.

Carlo, J. L., Lyytinen, K., & Rose, G. M. (2009). Internet computing as a disruptive information technology innovation: The role of strong order effects. *Information Systems Journal*, 1–36. doi:10.1111/j.1365-2575.2009.00345.x

Carlsson, C., Carlsson, J., Hyvonen, K., Puhakainen, J., & Walden, P. (2006, January). Adoption of mobile devices/services-searching for answers with the UTAUT. In Proceedings of the 39th annual Hawaii international conference on system sciences (HICSS'06) (Vol. 6, pp. 132a-132a). IEEE. doi:10.1109/HICSS.2006.38

Carlsson, S. A., Hedman, J., & Steen, O. (2010). Integrated Curriculum for a Bachelor of Science in Business Information Systems Design (BISD 2010). *Communications of AIS, 2010*(26), 525–546.

Carlsson, Õ. U., & Wadensten, B. (2018). Professional practice-related training and organizational readiness for change facilitate implementation of projects on the national core value system in care of older people. *Nursing Open*, *5*(4), 593–600. doi:10.1002/nop2.185 PMID:30338105

Carminati, M., Caron, R., Maggi, F., Epifani, I., & Zanero, S. (2015). BankSealer: A decision support system for online banking fraud analysis and investigation. *Computers & Security*, *53*, 175–186. doi:10.1016/j.cose.2015.04.002

Carr, D. J., Barnidge, M., Lee, B. G., & Tsang, S. J. (2014). Cynics and sceptics: Evaluating the credibility of mainstream and citizen journalism. *Journalism & Mass Communication Quarterly*, *91*(3), 452–470. doi:10.1177/1077699014538828

Carson, N. (2012). *Before You Start Up, Practice in the Gig Economy*. Retrieved July 10, 2018 from http://upstart.bizjournals.com/resources/author/2012/09/06/before-you-start-up-get-practicegigs.html

Casselma, J., Onopa, N., & Khansa, L. (2017). Wearable Healthcare: Lessons from the past a peek into the future. *Telematics and Informatics*, *34*(7), 1011–1023. doi:10.1016/j.tele.2017.04.011

Castellacci, F., & Tveito, V. (2018). Internet use and well-being: A survey and a theoretical framework. *Research Policy, 47*(1), 308–325. doi:10.1016/j.respol.2017.11.007

Cater-Steel, A., Hine, M. J., & Grant, G. (2010). Embedding IT service management in the academic curriculum: A cross-national comparison. *Journal of Global Information Technology Management, 13*(4), 64–92. doi:10.1080/10971 98X.2010.10856526

Cavaye, A. L. (1996). Case study research: A multi-faceted research approach for IS. *Information Systems Journal, 6*(3), 227–242. doi:10.1111/j.1365-2575.1996.tb00015.x

Cellucci, L. W., Layman, E. J., Campbell, R., & Zeng, X. (2011). Integrating Healthcare Ethical Issues Into IS Education. *Journal of Information Systems Education, 22*(3), 215–224.

Cepal, N. (2018). *Emerging challenges and shifting paradigms: New perspectives on international cooperation for development.* Academic Press.

Çetinkaya, A., Şahin, Ö. E., & Kırık, A. M. (2014). A research on social and political use of social media in Turkey. *International Journal of Science Culture And Sport, 2*(4), 49–60. doi:10.14486/IJSCS207

Cetin, T., & Deakin, E. (2019). Regulation of taxis and the rise of ridesharing. *Transport Policy, 76*(1), 149–158. doi:10.1016/j.tranpol.2017.09.002

Chalu, H. (2019). The effect of IFMIS adoption on financial reporting quality in Tanzanian local governments. *Business Management Review, 22*(2), 1–31.

Chan, T., Rosemann, M., & Shiang-yen, T. (2014). Identifying Satisfaction Factors in Tertiary Education: The case of an Information Systems Program. *ICIS*, 1–17.

Chan, C., Teoh, S. A. Y., & Pan, G. (2018). Agility in responding to disruptive digital innovation: Case study of an SME. *Information Systems Journal, 29*(2), 436–455. doi:10.1111/isj.12215

Chandler, D., & Whang, H. (2015). Learning from learning theory: A model of organizational adoption strategies at the micro-foundations of institutional theory. *Journal of Management, 41*(5), 1446–1476.

Chandra, S., Srivastava, S. C., & Theng, Y. L. (2010). Evaluating the role of trust in consumer adoption of mobile payment systems: An empirical analysis. CAIS, 27(29), 27.

Chanias, S., Myers, M., & Hess, T. (2019). Digital transformation strategy making in pre-digital organizations: The case of a financial services provider. *The Journal of Strategic Information Systems, 28*(1), 17–33. doi:10.1016/j.jsis.2018.11.003

Chan, M., Esteve, D., Fourniols, J. E., Escriba, C., & Campo, E. (2012). Smart wearable systems: Current status and future challenges. *Artificial Intelligence in Medicine, 56*(3), 137–156. doi:10.1016/j.artmed.2012.09.003 PMID:23122689

Chan, Y. E., & Reich, B. H. (2007). IT Alignment: What Have We Learned? *Journal of Information Technology, 22*(4), 297–315. doi:10.1057/palgrave.jit.2000109

Charland, P., Léger, P., Cronan, T. P., & Robert, J. (2015). Developing and Assessing Erp Competencies : Basic and Complex Knowledge. *Journal of Computer Information Systems, 56*(1), 31–39. doi:10.1080/08874417.2015.11645798

Charlton, J. P., & Danforth, I. D. W. (2007). Distinguishing addiction and high engagement in the context of online game playing. *Computers in Human Behavior, 23*(3), 1531–1548. doi:10.1016/j.chb.2005.07.002

Chatain, P., McDowell, J., Cedric, M., Schott, P., & Willebois, E. (2011). *Preventing Money Laundering and Terrorist Financing: A Practical Guide for Bank Supervisors.* Washington, DC: World Bank.

Chatterjee, S., LeRouge, C. M., & Tremblay, M. C. (2013). Educating students in healthcare information technology: IS community barriers, challenges, and paths forward. *Communications of the Association for Information Systems*, *33*(1), 1–14.

Chatterjee, S., Sarker, S., & Siponen, M. (2017). How Do Mobile ICTs Enable Organizational Fluidity : Toward a Theoretical Framework. *Information & Management*, *54*(1), 1–13. doi:10.1016/j.im.2016.03.007

Chau, N. T., & Deng, H. (2018b). *Critical Determinants for Mobile Commerce Adoption in Vietnamese SMEs: A Preliminary Study.* Paper presented at the 29th Australasian Conference on Information Systems, Sydney, Australia. 10.5130/acis2018.am

Chaudhry, P., & Zimmerman, A. (2013). The global growth of counterfeiting trade. In *Protecting Your Intellectual Rights*. New York, NY: Springer. doi:10.1007/978-1-4614-5568-4_2

Chau, N. T., & Deng, H. (2018a). Critical Determinants for Mobile Commerce Adoption in Vietnamese SMEs: A Conceptual Framework. *Procedia Computer Science*, *138*, 433–440. doi:10.1016/j.procs.2018.10.061

Chau, P. Y., & Tam, K. Y. (1997). Factors affecting the adoption of open systems: An exploratory study. *Management Information Systems Quarterly*, *21*(1), 1–24. doi:10.2307/249740

Chawla, N., & Davis, D. (2013). Bringing Big Data to Personalized Healthcare: A Patient-Centred. *Journal of General Internal Medicine*, *28*(S3), 660–665. doi:10.100711606-013-2455-8

Chen, C. (2017). Modelling Passengers ' Reaction to Dynamic Prices in Ride-on-demand Services : A Search for the Best Fare. In *Proceedings of the ACM on Interactive, Mobile, Wearable and Ubiquitous Technologies* (Vol. 1, pp. 1–23). ACM.

Chen, D. Q., Preston, D. S., & Swink, M. (2015). How the Use of Big Data Analytics Affects Value Creation in Supply Chain Management. *Journal of Management Information Systems*, *32*(4), 4–39. doi:10.1080/07421222.2015.1138364

Chen, F., Sager, J., Corbitt, G., & Gardiner, S. C. (2008). Incorporating Virtual Teamwork Training into MIS Curricula. *Journal of Information Systems Education*, *19*(1), 29–41.

Chen, G., Xu, B., Lu, M., & Chen, N. S. (2018). Exploring blockchain technology and its potential applications for education. *Smart Learning Environments*, *5*(1), 1. doi:10.118640561-017-0050-x

Cheng, J., Liu, R.-G., & Du, C. T. (2017). Exploring How Conflict and Uncertainty Affect Repurchase Intention in Social Commerce---The Mediating Effect of Perceived Deceptiveness. *International Conference on Electronic Business*.

Cheng, T. E., Lam, D. Y., & Yeung, A. C. (2006). Adoption of internet banking: An empirical study in Hong Kong. *Decision Support Systems*, *42*(3), 1558–1572. doi:10.1016/j.dss.2006.01.002

Cheng, X., Gu, Y., & Shen, J. (2019). An integrated view of particularized trust in social commerce: An empirical investigation. *International Journal of Information Management*, *45*, 1–12. doi:10.1016/j.ijinfomgt.2018.10.014

Cheng, Y., Huang, L., Ramlogan, R., & Li, X. (2017). Forecasting of potential impacts of disruptive technology in promising technological areas: Elaborating the SIRS epidemic model in RFID technology. *Technological Forecasting and Social Change*, *117*, 170–183. doi:10.1016/j.techfore.2016.12.003

Chen, H., Chiang, R., & Storey, V. (2012). Business intelligence and analytics: From big data to big impact. *Management Information Systems Quarterly*, *36*(4), 1165–1188. doi:10.2307/41703503

Chen, J., Fan, M., & Li, M. (2016). Advertising versus brokerage model for online trading platforms. *Management Information Systems Quarterly*, *40*(3), 575–596. doi:10.25300/MISQ/2016/40.3.03

Chen, L. (2014). Understanding IT Entrepreneurial Intention: An Information Systems View. *Journal of Computer Information Systems*, 55(1), 2–12. doi:10.1080/08874417.2014.11645736

Chen, L., Liu, Y., Gallagher, M., Pailthorpe, B., Sadiq, S., Shen, H. T., & Li, X. (2012). Introducing Cloud Computing Topics in Curricula. *Journal of Information Systems Education*, 23(3), 315–324.

Chen, L., Pratt, J. A., & Cole, C. B. (2016). Factors influencing students' major and career selection in systems development: An empirical study. *Journal of Computer Information Systems*, 56(4), 313–320. doi:10.1080/08874417.2016.1164005

Chen, Y., Wang, Y., Nevo, S., Jin, J., Wang, L., & Chow, W. S. (2014). IT capability and organizational performance: The roles of business process agility and environmental factors. *European Journal of Information Systems*, 23(3), 326–342. doi:10.1057/ejis.2013.4

Chen, Y., & Zahedi, F. M. (2016). Individuals' internet security perception and behaviour: Polycontextual contrast between the United States and China. *Management Information Systems Quarterly*, 40(1), 205–222. doi:10.25300/MISQ/2016/40.1.09

Cheruiyot, D., & Ferrer-Conill, R. (2018). Fact-Checking Africa. *Digital Journalism*, 6(8), 964–975. doi:10.1080/216 70811.2018.1493940

Cheung, R., & Vogel, D. (2013). Predicting user acceptance of collaborative technologies: An extension of the technology acceptance model for e-learning. *Computers & Education*, 63(2), 160–175. doi:10.1016/j.compedu.2012.12.003

Choi, B., Raghu, T. S., Vinzé, A., & Dooley, K. J. (2017). Effectiveness of standards consortia: Social network perspectives. *Information Systems Frontiers*, ▪▪▪, 1–12.

Choi, H., Park, J., & Jung, Y. (2018). The role of privacy fatigue in online privacy behaviour. *Computers in Human Behavior*, 81, 42–51. doi:10.1016/j.chb.2017.12.001

Chong, A. Y. L. (2013). Predicting m-commerce adoption determinants: A neural network approach. *Expert Systems with Applications*, 40(2), 523–530. doi:10.1016/j.eswa.2012.07.068

Choo, K.-K. R. (2008). Organised crime groups in cyberspace: A typology. *Trends in Organized Crime*, 11(3), 270–295. doi:10.100712117-008-9038-9

Cho, S. H., Fang, X., & Tayur, S. (2015). Combating Strategic Counterfeiters in Licit and Illicit Supply Chains. *Manufacturing & Service Operations Management: M & SOM*, 17(3), 273–289. doi:10.1287/msom.2015.0524

Christensen, C. M. (1997). The Innovator's Dilemma: When New Technologies Cause Great Firms to Fail. Boston, MA: Harvard Business School Press.

Christensen, H., Reynolds, J., & Griffiths, K., M. (2011). The use of e-health applications for anxiety and depression in young people: challenges and solutions. *Early Intervention in Psychiatry*, 5(1), 58-62. doi:10.1111/j.1751-7893.2010.00242

Christensen, C. (1997). *The innovator's dilemma: when new technologies cause great firms to fail*. Boston, MA: Harvard Business Review.

Christensen, C. M. (1997). *The Innovator's Dilemma: When New Technologies Cause Great Firms to Fail*. Boston: Harvard Business School Press.

Christensen, C. M. (2006). The ongoing process of building a theory of disruption. *Journal of Product Innovation Management*, 23(1), 39–55. doi:10.1111/j.1540-5885.2005.00180.x

Christozov, D., Chukova, S., & Mateev, P. (2009). On two types of warranties: Warranty of malfunctioning and warranty of misinforming. *Asia-Pacific Journal of Operational Research*, 36(3), 399–420. doi:10.1142/S0217595909002274

Chuang, T. T., Nakatani, K., Chen, J. C. H., & Huang, I. L. (2007). Examining the impact of organizational and owner's characteristics on the extent of e-commerce adoption in SMEs. *International Journal of Business and Systems Research*, *1*(1), 61–80. doi:10.1504/IJBSR.2007.014770

Chua, W. F. (1986). Radical developments in accounting thought. *The Accounting Review*, *61*(4), 601–632.

Chu, T. H., & Chen, Y. Y. (2016). With good, we become good: Understanding e-learning adoption by the theory of planned behaviour and group influences. *Computers & Education*, *92*(1), 37–52. doi:10.1016/j.compedu.2015.09.013

Chwelos, P., Benbasat, I., & Dexter, A. S. (2001). Empirical test of an EDI adoption model. *Information Systems Research*, *12*(3), 304–321. doi:10.1287/isre.12.3.304.9708

Čiarnienė, R., & Vienažindienė, M. (2014). Management of the contemporary fashion industry: Characteristics and challenges. *Procedia: Social and Behavioral Sciences*, *156*, 63–68. doi:10.1016/j.sbspro.2014.11.120

Circella, G., & Alemi, F. (2018). Transport policy in the era of ridehailing and other disruptive transportation technologies. In *Advances in Transport Policy and Planning* (Vol. 1, pp. 119–144). Academic Press.

City of Johannesburg. (2018a). *City of Johannesburg Annual Report 2016/17*. Retrieved from: https://joburg.org.za/documents_/Pages/Key%20Documents/Annual%20Report/201617%20Annual%20Report/Annual%20Report%20For%20Council.pdf

City of Johannesburg. (2018b). *City of Johannesburg Integrated Development Plan 2018/19 Review*. Retrieved from: https://www.joburg.org.za/documents_/Documents/Annexure%20A%20%202018-19%20IDP%20Review.pdf

Ciuriak, D., & Ptashkina, M. (2019). *Leveraging the Digital Transformation for Development: A Global South Strategy for the Data-Driven Economy. Policy Brief*. Centre for International Governance Innovation.

Clarke, I. III. (2008). Emerging value propositions for m-commerce. *The Journal of Business Strategy*, *25*(2), 41–57.

Clark, J., Clark, C., Gambill, S., & Brooks, S. (2017). IS curriculum models, Course offerings, and Other Academic Myths/Hopes. *Journal of Higher Education Theory and Practice*, *17*(9), 61–68.

Clarysse, B., Wright, M., Bruneel, J., & Mahajan, A. (2014). Creating value in ecosystems: Crossing the chasm between knowledge and business ecosystems. *Research Policy*, *43*(7), 1164–1176. doi:10.1016/j.respol.2014.04.014

Clement, J. (2019). Social commerce adoption among retailers in North America from 2017 to 2018. Retrieved November 4, 2019, from https://www.statista.com/statistics/1017523/north-america-social-commerce-adoption-in-retail/

Clemons, E. K., & Row, M. C. (1991). Sustaining IT advantage: The role of structural differences. *Management Information Systems Quarterly*, *15*(3), 275–292. doi:10.2307/249639

Codagnone, C., Abadie, F., & Biagi, F. (2016). *The future of work in the 'sharing economy'. Market efficiency and equitable opportunities or unfair precarisation?* Institute for Prospective Technological Studies, Science for Policy report by the Joint Research Centre.

Coelho, T. R., Segatto, A. P., & Frega, J. R. (2015). Analysing ICT and development from the perspective of the capabilities approach: A study in South Brazil. *The Electronic Journal on Information Systems in Developing Countries*, *67*(2), 1–14. doi:10.1002/j.1681-4835.2015.tb00480.x

Cole, M., & Avison, D. (2007). The potential of hermeneutics in information systems research. *European Journal of Information Systems*, *16*(6), 820–833. doi:10.1057/palgrave.ejis.3000725

Coleman, S. (2012). Believing the news: From sinking trust to atrophied efficacy. *European Journal of Communication*, *27*(1), 35–45. doi:10.1177/0267323112438806

Collins, A. (2017). *Four reasons to question the hype around Blockchain.* https://www. weforum. org/agenda/2017/07/four-reasons-to-question-the-hype-around-blockchain

Connolly, A., & Kick, A. (2015). *What Differentiates Early Organization Adopters of Bitcoin From Non-Adopters?* Academic Press.

Connolly, L. Y., & Wall, D. S. (2019). The rise of crypto-ransomware in a changing cybercrime landscape: Taxonomising countermeasures. *Computers & Security, 87,* 101568. doi:10.1016/j.cose.2019.101568

Constantiou, I. D., Damsgaard, J., & Knutsen, L. (2006). Exploring perceptions and use of mobile services: User differences in an advancing market. *International Journal of Mobile Communications, 4*(3), 231–247. doi:10.1504/IJMC.2006.008940

Cooper, R. B., & Zmud, R. W. (1990). Information technology implementation research: A technological diffusion approach. *Management Science, 36*(2), 123–139. doi:10.1287/mnsc.36.2.123

Coovert, M. D., & Thompson, L. F. (2013). Toward a synergistic relationship between psychology and technology. In *The psychology of workplace technology* (pp. 25–42). Routledge. doi:10.4324/9780203735565

Costa, F. F. (2014). Big data in Biomedicine. *Drug Discovery Today, 17*(4), 433–440. doi:10.1016/j.drudis.2013.10.012 PMID:24183925

Couger, J., Davis, G., Dologite, D., Feinstein, D., Gorgone, J., Jenkins, A., & Valacich, I. (1995). Guideline for undergraduate IS curriculum. *Management Information Systems Quarterly, 22*(3), 341–359. doi:10.2307/249599

Coursaris, C., Hassanein, K., & Head, M. (2008). Mobile Technologies and the Value Chain: Participants, activities and value creation. *International Journal of Business Science and Applied Management, 3*(3), 14–30.

Cousins, K., & Robey, D. (2015). Managing work-life boundaries with mobile technologies: An interpretive study of mobile work practices. *Information Technology & People, 28*(1), 34–71. doi:10.1108/ITP-08-2013-0155

Cresswell, J. W. (2014). Research Design: qualitative, quantitative and mixed methods approach (4th ed.). Sage Publication Inc.

Creswell, J. W. (2014). Research Design: Qualitative, Quantitative, and Mixed Methods Approaches. Retrieved from https://books.google.com.gh/books?id=PViMtOnJ1LcC

Crosby, A., & Rina, R. C. (2017). *The lure of the city, the possibilities of the village: crowdsourcing graphic designers in Indonesia.* Cumulus Open Design for E-very-thing.

Crowther, M., Lim, W., & Crowther, M. A. (2010). Systematic Review and Meta-Analysis Methodology. *Blood, 116*(17), 3140–3146. doi:10.1182/blood-2010-05-280883 PMID:20656933

Csikszentmihalyi, M. (1975). Beyond boredom and anxiety. Jossey-Bass Publishers.

Cudjoe, A. G., Anim, P. A., & Nyanyofio, J. G. N. T. (2015). Determinants of mobile banking adoption in the Ghanaian banking industry: A case of access bank Ghana limited. *Journal of Computer and Communications, 3*(02), 1–19. doi:10.4236/jcc.2015.32001

Cui, L., Tso, F. P., Yao, D., & Jia, W. (2012). WeFiLab: A web-based Wi-Fi laboratory platform for wireless networking education. *IEEE Transactions on Learning Technologies, 5*(4), 291–303. doi:10.1109/TLT.2012.6

Cutter, B., Litan, R., & Stangler, D. (2016). *The Good Economy.* Kansas City: Roosevelt Institute and Kauffman Foundation. Retrieved, July 10, 2018 from http://rooseveltinstitute.org/wp-content/uploads/2016/02/Good-Economy-Feb-29-2016.pdf

Cybersecurity Ventures. (2019). *Cyberattacks are the fastest growing crime and predicted to cost the world $6 trillion annually by 202.* Available at: https://www.prnewswire.com/news-releases/cyberattacks-are-the-fastest-growing-crime-and-predicted-to-cost-the-world-6-trillion-annually-by-2021-300765090.html

D'Cruz, P., & Noronha, E. (2016). Positives outweighing negatives: The experiences of Indian crowdsourced workers. *Work Organisation, Labour & Globalisation, 10*(1), 44–63. doi:10.13169/workorgalaboglob.10.1.0044

Dacin, M., Goodstein, J., & Scott, W. (2002). Institutional theory and institutional change: Introduction to the special research forum. *Academy of Management Journal, 45*(1), 45–56. doi:10.5465/amj.2002.6283388

Dahlberg, T., Guo, J., & Ondrus, J. (2015). A critical review of mobile payment research. *Electronic Commerce Research and Applications, 14*(5), 265–284. doi:10.1016/j.elerap.2015.07.006

Dahlberg, T., Mallat, N., Ondrus, J., & Zmijewska, A. (2008). Past, present and future of mobile payments research: A literature review. *Electronic Commerce Research and Applications, 7*(2), 165–181. doi:10.1016/j.elerap.2007.02.001

Dahlman, C., Mealy, S., & Wermelinger, M. (2016). *Harnessing the Digital Economy for Developing Countries.* Paris: OECD.

Dang, L. M., Piran, M., Han, D., Min, K., & Moon, H. (2019). A Survey on Internet of Things and Cloud Computing for Healthcare. *Electronics (Basel), 8*(7), 768. doi:10.3390/electronics8070768

Darejeh, A., & Salim, S. S. (2016). Gamification solutions to enhance software user engagement—A systematic review. *International Journal of Human-Computer Interaction, 32*(8), 613–642. doi:10.1080/10447318.2016.1183330

Darı, A. B. (2018). Sosyal medya ve siyaset: Türkiye'deki siyasi partilerin sosyal medya kullanımı [Social media and politics: Social media use by political parties in Turkey]. *Al-Farabi Uluslararası Sosyal Bilimler Dergisi, 1*(1), 1–11.

Daskalaki, S., Avouris, N., Goudara, M., & Avouris, N. (2003). Data mining for decision support on customer insolvency in telecommunications business. *European Journal of Operational Research, 2217*(2), 239–255. doi:10.1016/S0377-2217(02)00532-5

Daud Norzaidi, M., Choy Chong, S., Murali, R., & Intan Salwani, M. (2007). Intranet usage and managers' performance in the port industry. *Industrial Management & Data Systems, 107*(8), 1227–1250. doi:10.1108/02635570710822831

Dauda, S. Y., & Lee, J. (2015). Technology adoption: A conjoint analysis of consumers' preference on future online banking services. *Information Systems, 53*, 1–15. doi:10.1016/j.is.2015.04.006

Davis, F. D. (1989). Perceived usefulness, perceived ease of use, and user acceptance of information technology. *Management Information Systems Quarterly, 13*(3), 319–340. doi:10.2307/249008

Davis, F. D. (1989). Perceived usefulness, perceived ease of use, and user acceptance of information technology. *Management Information Systems Quarterly, 13*(3), 319–340. doi:10.2307/249008

Davis, F. D. (1989). Perceived Usefulness, Perceived Ease of Use, and User Acceptance of Information Technology. *Management Information Systems Research Center, 13*(3), 319–340. doi:10.1155/2013/591796

Davis, F. D., Bagozzi, R. P., & Warshaw, P. R. (1989). User Acceptance of Computer Technology: A Comparison of Two Theoretical Models. *Management Science, 35*(8), 982–1003. doi:10.1287/mnsc.35.8.982

Davis, F. D., Bagozzi, R. P., & Warshaw, P. R. (1992). Extrinsic and intrinsic motivation to use computers in the workplace. *Journal of Applied Social Psychology, 22*(14), 1111–1132. doi:10.1111/j.1559-1816.1992.tb00945.x

Davis, F., Bagozzi, R., & Warshaw, P. (1989). User acceptance of computer technology: A comparison of two theoretical models. *Management Science, 35*(8), 982–1003. doi:10.1287/mnsc.35.8.982

Davis, G. A., & Woratschek, C. R. (2015). Evaluating Business Intelligence / Business Analytics Software for Use in the Information Systems Curriculum. *Information Systems Education Journal, 13*(1), 23–29.

de Albuquerque, J. P., Diniz, E. H., & Cernev, A. K. (2016). Mobile payments: A scoping study of the literature and issues for future research. *Information Development, 32*(3), 527–553. doi:10.1177/0266666914557338

De Haes, S., & Van Grembergen, W. (2004). IT governance and its mechanisms. *Information Systems Control Journal, 1*, 27–33.

De Kerviler, G., Demoulin, N. T., & Zidda, P. (2016). Adoption of in-store mobile payment: Are perceived risk and convenience the only drivers. *Journal of Retailing and Consumer Services, 31*, 334–344. doi:10.1016/j.jretconser.2016.04.011

de Luna, I. R., Liébana-Cabanillas, F., Sánchez-Fernández, J., & Muñoz-Leiva, F. (2019). Mobile payment is not all the same: The adoption of mobile payment systems depending on the technology applied. *Technological Forecasting and Social Change, 146*, 931–944. doi:10.1016/j.techfore.2018.09.018

de Reuver, M., Verschuur, E., Nikayin, F., Cerpa, N., & Bouwman, H. (2015). Collective action for mobile payment platforms: A case study on collaboration issues between banks and telecom operators. *Electronic Commerce Research and Applications, 14*(5), 331–344. doi:10.1016/j.elerap.2014.08.004

De Stefano, V. (2015). The rise of the just-in-time workforce: On-demand work, crowdwork, and labor protection in the gig-economy. *Comp. Lab. L. & Pol'y J., 37*, 471.

de Zúñiga, H. G., Barnidge, M., & Diehl, T. (2018). Political persuasion on social media: A moderated moderation model of political discussion disagreement and civil reasoning. *The Information Society, 34*(5), 302–315. doi:10.1080/01972243.2018.1497743

Deci, E. L., & Ryan, R. M. (2000). The 'what' and 'why' of goal pursuits: Human needs and the self-determination of behaviour. *Psychological Inquiry, 11*(4), 227–268. doi:10.1207/S15327965PLI1104_01

Dede, C. (2009). Comments on Greenhow, Robelia, and Hughes: Technologies that facilitate generating knowledge and possibly wisdom. *Educational Researcher, 38*(4), 260–263. doi:10.3102/0013189X09336672

Degadjor, M. (2018). UBER Branding Saga: Why Ghana's MoT and GPRTU got it wrong. *Daily Graphic*. Retrieved on 6 April 2019 https://www.graphic.com.gh/features/opinion/uber-branding-saga-why-ghana-mot-and-gprtu-got-it-wrong.html

Delbufalo, E. (2015). The influence of supply network structure on firm's multiple innovation capabilities: A longitudinal study in the fashion industry. *Management Decision, 53*(10), 2457–2476. doi:10.1108/MD-07-2014-0431

Deloitte Centre for Health Solution. (2015). *Health system analytics: The missing key to unlock value-based care*. Deloitte Development LCC.

Deloitte. (2014). *Value of connectivity. Economic and social benefits of expanding internet access*. Retrieved from: https://www2.deloitte.com/content/dam/Deloitte/ie/Documents/TechnologyMediaCommunications/2014_uk_tmt_value_of_connectivity_deloitte_ireland.pdf

Deloitte. (2016, June 27). *APIs Help Drive Digital Transformation*. Retrieved 10 27, 2016, from http://deloitte.wsj.com/cio/2016/06/27/apis-help-drive-digital-transformation/

DeLone, W. H., & McLean, E. R. (1992). Information systems success: The quest for the dependent variable. *Information Systems Research, 3*(1), 60–95. doi:10.1287/isre.3.1.60

DeLone, W. H., & McLean, E. R. (2003). The DeLone and McLean Model of Information Systems Success: A Ten-Year Update. *Journal of Management Information Systems, 19*(4), 9–30. doi:10.1080/07421222.2003.11045748

Demirhan, K. (2014a). Relationship between Social Media and Political Parties: The Case of Turkey. In A. Solo (Ed.), *Political Campaigning in the Information Age* (pp. 1–31). Hershey, PA: IGI Global. doi:10.4018/978-1-4666-6062-5.ch001

Demirhan, K. (2014b). Social Media Effects on the Gezi Park Movement in Turkey: Politics Under Hashtags. In B. Pătruţ & M. Pătruţ (Eds.), *Social Media in Politics: Case Studies on the Political Power of Social Media* (pp. 281–314). Cham, Switzerland: Springer. doi:10.1007/978-3-319-04666-2_16

Demorouti, E., Mostert, K., & Bakker, A. B. (2010). Burnout and work engagement: A thorough investigation of the independency of both constructs. *Journal of Occupational Health Psychology*, *15*(3), 209–222. doi:10.1037/a0019408 PubMed

Denaxas, S. C., & Morley, K. I. (2015). Big Biomedical data and Cardiovascular disease research: potentials and challenges. *European Heart Journal - Quality of Care and Clinical Outcomes, 1*(1), 9-16. doi:10.1093/ehjqcco/qcv005

Denman, B. D., & James, R. (2016). Cultural ecology and isomorphism applied to educational planning in China's Inner Mongolia: A new rubric. *International Journal of Comparative Education and Development*, *18*(1), 40–52. doi:10.1108/IJCED-10-2015-0003

Denzin, N. K., & Lincoln, Y. S. (1994). *The SAGE handbook of qualitative research*. Thousand Oaks, CA: Sage Publications.

Denzin, N. K., & Lincoln, Y. S. (2005). Introduction: The discipline and practice of qualitative research. In N. K. Denzin & S. Lincoln (Eds.), *The Sage handbook of qualitative research* (pp. 1–32). Thousand Oaks, CA: Sage.

Denzin, N. K., & Lincoln, Y. S. (2008). *The landscape of qualitative research*. Los Angeles, CA: SAGE Publications.

Deterding, S., Sicart, M., Nacke, L., O'Hara, K., & Dixon, D. (2011). Gamification using game-design elements in non-gaming contexts. In CHI'11 extended abstracts on human factors in computing systems (pp. 2425-2428). ACM. doi:10.1145/1979742.1979575

Deterding, S. (2015). The lens of intrinsic skill atoms: A method for gameful design. *Human-Computer Interaction*, *30*(3-4), 294–335. doi:10.1080/07370024.2014.993471

Devos, J., Van Landeghem, H., & Deschoolmeester, D. (2012). The theory of the lemon markets in IS research. *Information Systems Theory*, 213-229.

Dewan, S. G., & Chen, L. D. (2005). Mobile payment adoption in the US: A cross-industry, cross platform solution. *Journal of Information Privacy and Security*, *1*(2), 4–28. doi:10.1080/15536548.2005.10855765

Dewan, S., & Hsu, V. (2004). Adverse selection in electronic markets: Evidence from online stamp auctions. *The Journal of Industrial Economics*, *52*(4), 497–516. doi:10.1111/j.0022-1821.2004.00237.x

Dhillon, G., Coss, D., & Hackney, R. (2001). Interpreting the role of disruptive technologies in e-businesses. *Logistics Information Management*, *14*(1/2), 163–171. doi:10.1108/09576050110363167

Dienlin, T., & Trepte, S. (2015). Is the privacy paradox a relic of the past? An in-depth analysis of privacy attitudes and privacy behaviours. *European Journal of Social Psychology*, *45*(3), 285–297. doi:10.1002/ejsp.2049

Dietz, A., & Porter, C. (2012). Making sense of social value creation: Three organizational case studies. *Emergence*, *14*(3), 23–43.

Dimitrov, M., & Osman, I. (2012). *The Impact of Cloud Computing on Organizations in Regard to Cost and Security* (Unpublished Master's Thesis). Umea University, Umea, Sweden.

Diprose, J. P., Plimmer, B., MacDonald, B. A., & Hosking, J. G. (2014). A humancentric API for programming socially interactive robots. *Visual Languages and Human-Centric Computing (VL/HCC), 2014. IEEE Symposium*, 121-128.

Diprose, J., MacDonald, B., Hosking, J., & Plimmer, B. (2017). Designing an API at an appropriate abstraction level for programming. *Journal of Visual Languages and Computing, 39*, 22–40. doi:10.1016/j.jvlc.2016.07.005

Dobele, A., Steel, M., & Cooper, T. (2015). Sailing the seven C's of blog marketing: Understanding social media and business impact. *Marketing Intelligence & Planning, 33*(7), 1087–1102. doi:10.1108/MIP-02-2015-0039

Dobovšek, B., Lamberger, I., & Slak, B. (2013). Advance fee frauds messages–non-declining trend. *Journal of Money Laundering Control, 16*(3), 209–230. doi:10.1108/JMLC-04-2013-0012

Doe, J., van de Wetering, R., Honyenuga, B., Versendaal, J., & Boateng, R. (2018). *Delphi Panel Discussion of F-TAM: Industry Experts and Academic Perspectives*. Academic Press.

Doerrfeld, B., Wood, C., Anthony, A., Sandoval, K., & Lauret, A. (2015-2016). *The API Economy: Disruption and the Business of APIs*. Nordic.

Doherty, V. (2019). The Advancement Of Social Commerce: Should E-Commerce Brands Care? *Dynamic Capabilities : Current Debates and Future Directions, 20*. doi:10.1111/j.1467-8551.2008.00609.x

Dokko, J., Mumford, M., & Schanzenbach, D. W. (2015). *Workers and the online gig economy*. The Hamilton Project.

Dong, G., Wang, L., Du, X., & Potenza, M. N. (2017). Gaming Increases Craving to Gaming-Related Stimuli in Individuals With Internet Gaming Disorder. *Biological Psychiatry: Cognitive Neuroscience and Neuroimaging, 2*(5), 404–412. PMID:29560926

Dong, S., Xu, S. X., & Zhu, K. X. (2009). Research Note: Information technology in supply chains: The value of IT-enabled resources under competition. *Information Systems Research, 20*(1), 18–32. doi:10.1287/isre.1080.0195

Donner, C. M., Marcum, C. D., Jennings, W. G., Higgins, G. E., & Banfield, J. (2014). Low self-control and cybercrime: Exploring the utility of the general theory of crime beyond digital piracy. *Computers in Human Behavior, 34*, 165–172. doi:10.1016/j.chb.2014.01.040

Donovan, S. A., Bradley, D. H., & Shimabukuru, J. O. (2016). *What does the gig economy mean for workers?* Retrieved July 30, 2018, from https://digitalcommons.ilr.cornell.edu/cgi/viewcontent.cgi?referer=https://scholar.google.com/&httpsredir=1&article=2512&context=key_workplace

Dörnyei, Z. (2007). Creating a motivating classroom environment. In *International handbook of English language teaching* (pp. 719–731). Boston, MA: Springer. doi:10.1007/978-0-387-46301-8_47

Dorotinsky, W., & Watkins, J. (2013). Government Financial Management Information Systems. In *The International Handbook of Public Financial Management* (pp. 797–816). London: Palgrave Macmillan. doi:10.1057/9781137315304_37

Drahokoupil, J., & Fabo, B. (2016). The platform economy and the disruption of the employment relationship. *ETUI Research Paper-Policy Brief, 5*.

Drnevich, P. L., & Croson, D. C. (2013). Information Technology and business-level strategy: Toward an integrated theoretical perspective. *Management Information Systems Quarterly, 37*(2), 483–509. doi:10.25300/MISQ/2013/37.2.08

Duane, A., O'Reilly, P., & Andreev, P. (2014). Realising M-Payments: Modelling consumers' willingness to M-pay using Smart Phones. *Behaviour & Information Technology, 33*(4), 318–334. doi:10.1080/0144929X.2012.745608

Duan, X., Deng, H., & Corbitt, B. (2012). Evaluating the critical determinants for adopting e-market in Australian small and medium-sized enterprises. *Management Research Review, 35*(3), 289–308. doi:10.1108/01409171211210172

Duan, X., Deng, H., & Luo, F. (2019). An integrated approach for identifying the efficiency-oriented drivers of electronic markets in electronic business. *Journal of Enterprise Information Management, 32*(1), 60–74. doi:10.1108/JEIM-05-2018-0090

Duarte, P., Silva, S. C., & Ferreira, M. B. (2018). How convenient is it? Delivering online shopping convenience to enhance customer satisfaction and encourage e-WOM. *Journal of Retailing and Consumer Services, 44*, 161–169. doi:10.1016/j.jretconser.2018.06.007

Duffett, R. G. (2015c). The influence of Facebook advertising on cognitive attitudes amid Generation Y. *Electronic Commerce Research, 15*(2), 243–267. doi:10.1007/s10660-015-9177-4

Duffett, R. G. (2017). Influence of social media marketing communications on young consumers' attitudes. *Young Consumers, 18*(1), 19–39. doi:10.1108/YC-07-2016-00622

Du, H. S., & Wagner, C. (2007). *The Role of Technology*. Content, and Context for the Success of Social Media.

Duman, G., Orhon, G., & Gedik, N. (2015). Research trends in mobile-assisted language learning from 2000 to 2012. *ReCALL, 27*(02), 197–216. doi:10.1017/S0958344014000287

Dunaway, M. M. (2017). Collaboration in a Data Analytics Curricula: An Active Learning Approach. *Proceedings of Americas Conference on Information Systems (AMCIS)*, 1–8.

Dunlap, J., & Lowenthal, P. (2009). Tweeting the Night Away: Using Twitter to Enhance Social Presence. *Journal of Information Systems Education, 20*(2), 129–136.

Dunnebeil, S., Sunyaev, A., Blohm, I., Leimeister, J., & Krcmar, H. (2012). Determinants of physicians' technology acceptance for e-health in ambulatory care. *International Journal of Medical Informatics, 81*, 746-760. . doi:10.1016/jijmedinf.2012.02.002

Duranti, L., & Rogers, C. (2012). Trust in digital records: An increasingly cloudy legal area. *Computer Law & Security Report, 28*(5), 522–531. doi:10.1016/j.clsr.2012.07.009

Durkin, M., Mulholland, G., & Mccartan, A. (2015). A socio-technical perspective on social media adoption : A case from retail banking. *International Journal of Bank Marketing, 33*(7), 944–962. doi:10.1108/IJBM-01-2015-0014

Dursun, O. (2013). Efforts of Control of Political Power over the Social Media in Turkey. In *Proceedings of the Fourth Annual Asian Conference on Media and Mass Communication* (pp. 1-13), Retrieved from http://papers.iafor.org/wp-content/uploads/conference-proceedings/MediAsia/MediAsia2013_proceedings.pdf

Dutton, W. H. (2013). *Internet studies: The foundations of a transformative field*. Oxford University Press. doi:10.1093/oxfordhb/9780199589074.013.0001

Dwivedi, Y. K., Rana, N. P., Jeyaraj, A., Clement, M., & Williams, M. D. (2017). Re-examining the Unified Theory of Acceptance and Use of Technology (UTAUT): Towards a Revised Theoretical Model. doi:10.100710796-017-9774-y

Dwivedi, M., Yadav, A., & Venkatesh, U. (2011). Use of social media by national tourism organizations: A preliminary analysis. *Information Technology & Tourism, 13*(2), 93–103. doi:10.3727/109830512X13258778487353

Dyer, J. H., & Singh, H. (1998). The relational view: Cooperative strategy and sources of inter-organizational competitive advantage. *Academy of Management Review, 23*(4), 660–679. doi:10.5465/amr.1998.1255632

Dzeto, K. G. (2014). *Projecting Ghana into the real middle- income economy: The role of technical vocational education training*. Retrieved 22/02/2018 from http://library.fes.de/pdf-files/bueros/ghana/11300.pdf

Earl, M. J. (1990). Approaches To Strategic Information Systems Planning Experience In Twenty-One United Kingdom Companies. In ICIS 1990 Proceedings (pp. 271–277). Academic Press.

Earl, M. J. (1989). *Management strategies for information technology.* Prentice-Hall, Inc.

Earl, M. J. (1990). Approaches in Information Systems Planning. In R. D. Galliers & D. E. Leidner (Eds.), *Strategic information management: Challenges and strategies in managing information systems* (3rd ed., pp. 181–215). Butterworth-Heinemann.

Earl, M. J. (1993). Experiences in Strategic Information Systems Planning. *Management Information Systems Quarterly, 17*(March), 1–25. doi:10.2307/249507

Eastaugh, S. R. (2013). The total cost of EHR Ownership. *Healthcare Financial Management, 67*(2), 66–70. PMID:23413671

Easton, G. (2010). Critical Realism in Case Study Research. *Industrial Marketing Management, 39*(1), 118–128. doi:10.1016/j.indmarman.2008.06.004

Eboibi, F. E. (2017). A review of the legal and regulatory frameworks of Nigerian Cybercrimes Act 2015. *Computer Law & Security Review, 33*(5), 700–717. doi:10.1016/j.clsr.2017.03.020

Eck, N. J. Van, & Waltman, L. (2013). VOSviewer Manual. doi:10.3402/jac.v8.30072

Edworthy, S. M. (2001). Telemedicine in developing countries. *BMJ (Clinical Research Ed.), 323*(7312), 524–525. doi:10.1136/bmj.323.7312.524 PMID:11546681

Effah, J. (2011). *Tracing the emergence and formation of small dot-coms in an emerging digital economy: An actor-network theory approach.* Salford: University of Salford.

Effah, J. (2014). The rise and fall of a dot-com pioneer in a developing country. *Journal of Enterprise Information Management, 27*(2), 228–239. doi:10.1108/JEIM-04-2012-0016

Effah, J. (2015). *Virtual Process Control Modelling in Organisational Semiotics: A Case of Higher Education Admission Information and Knowledge Management in Complex Systems* (pp. 51–59). Springer.

Effah, J., & Nuhu, H. (2017). Institutional barriers to digitalization of government budgeting in developing countries: A case study of Ghana. *The Electronic Journal on Information Systems in Developing Countries, 82*(1), 1–17. doi:10.1002/j.1681-4835.2017.tb00605.x

Effah, P. (2011). A Ghanaian response to the study on 'widening participation in higher education in Ghana and Tanzania: Developing an equity scorecard'. *Research in Comparative and International Education, 6*(4), 374–382. doi:10.2304/rcie.2011.6.4.374

Eickhoff, C., Harris, C. G., de Vries, A. P., & Srinivasan, P. (2012). Quality through flow and immersion: gamifying crowdsourced relevance assessments. In *Proceedings of the 35th international ACM SIGIR conference on Research and development in information retrieval* (pp. 871-880). ACM. 10.1145/2348283.2348400

Eisenhardt, K. M. (1989). Building theories from case study research. *Academy of Management Review, 14*(4), 532–550. doi:10.5465/amr.1989.4308385

Eisenhardt, K. M., & Martin, J. A. (2000). Dynamic Capabilities : What Are They? *Strategic Management Journal, 21*(10-11), 1105–1121. doi:10.1002/1097-0266(200010/11)21:10/11<1105::AID-SMJ133>3.0.CO;2-E

Eisenhardt, K., & Martin, J. (2000). Dynamic capabilities: What are they? *Strategic Management Journal, 21*(10–11), 1105–1121. doi:10.1002/1097-0266(200010/11)21:10/11<1105::AID-SMJ133>3.0.CO;2-E

El Sawy, O. A., & Pereira, F. (2013). Digital business models: review and synthesis. In *Business Modelling in the Dynamic Digital Space* (pp. 13–20). Springer; doi:10.1007/978-3-642-31765-1_2.

Elbanna, A., & Newman, M. (2016). Disrupt the Disruptor : Rethinking 'Disruption' in Digital Innovation. In *10th Mediterranean Conference on Information Systems* (p. pp.58-71). Paphos, Cyprus: Academic Press.

Elhai, J. D., Dvorak, R. D., Levine, J. C., & Hall, B. J. (2017). Problematic smartphone use: A conceptual overview and systematic review of relations with anxiety and depression psychopathology. *Journal of Affective Disorders, 207,* 251–259. doi:10.1016/j.jad.2016.08.030 PMID:27736736

El-Telbany, O., & Elragal, A. (2017). Gamification of enterprise systems: A lifecycle approach. *Procedia Computer Science, 121,* 106–114. doi:10.1016/j.procs.2017.11.015

eMarketer. (2018). *Worldwide Retail and Ecommerce Sales: eMarketer's Updated Forecast and New M-commerce Estimates for 2016-2021.* Retrieved from https://www.emarketer.com/Report/Worldwide-Retail-Ecommerce-Sales-eMarketers-Updated-Forecast-New-Mcommerce-Estimates-20162021/2002182

Engestrom, Y. (1987). *Learning by expanding.* Helsinki, Finland: Orienta-Konsultit.

Enli, G. S., & Skogerbø, E. (2013). Personalized Campaigns in Party-Centred Politics. *Information Communication and Society, 16*(5), 757–774. doi:10.1080/1369118X.2013.782330

Eom, M., Gudigantala, N., & Mitchell, G. (2015). Achieving success with a new design of hybrid information systems major: The case of University of ABC's Operations and Technology Management (OTM) program. *2015 Americas Conference on Information Systems, AMCIS 2015,* 1–12.

Erdoğmuş, İ. E., & Tatar, Ş. B. (2015). Drivers of Social Commerce through Brand Engagement. *Procedia: Social and Behavioral Sciences, 207*(212), 189–195. doi:10.1016/j.sbspro.2015.10.087

Erevelles, S., Fukawa, N., & Swayne, L. (2016). Big Data consumer analytics and the transformation of marketing. *Journal of Business Research, 69*(2), 897–904. doi:10.1016/j.jbusres.2015.07.001

Eric, H., Hyunji, K., Sang, S., Han, P., & Oh, W. (2016). *Excessive Dependence on Mobile Social Apps : A Rational Excessive Dependence on Mobile Social Apps.* Academic Press.

Estermann, B., Riedl, R., & Neuroni, A. C. (2009, May). Integrated and transcendent e-Government: keys for analyzing organizational structure and governance. In *Proceedings of the 10th Annual International Conference on Digital Government Research: Social Networks: Making Connections between Citizens, Data and Government* (pp. 162-171). Digital Government Society of North America.

Ettlie, J. E., & Pavlou, P. A. (2006). Technology-based new product development partnerships. *Decision Sciences, 37*(2), 117–147. doi:10.1111/j.1540-5915.2006.00119.x

European Commission. (2018). *User guide to the SME definition.* Retrieved from http://ec.europa.eu/regional_policy/sources/conferences/state-aid/sme/smedefinitionguide_en.pdf

Evans, H. K., Brown, K. J., & Wimberly, T. (2018). "Delete Your Account": The 2016 Presidential Race on Twitter. *Social Science Computer Review, 36*(4), 500–508. doi:10.1177/0894439317728722

Evans, J. S. B. T., & Over, D. E. (2013). Reasoning to and from belief : Deduction and induction are still distinct. *Thinking & Reasoning, 19*(3), 267–283. doi:10.1080/13546783.2012.745450

Evans, N., Ralston, B., & Broderick, A. (2009). Strategic thinking about disruptive technologies. *Strategy and Leadership, 37*(1), 23–30. doi:10.1108/10878570910926034

Ezezika, O., Oh, J., Edeagu, N., & Boyo, W. (2018). Gamification of nutrition: A preliminary study on the impact of gamification on nutrition knowledge, attitude, and behaviour of adolescents in Nigeria. *Nutrition and Health (Berkhamsted, Hertfordshire), 24*(3), 137–144. doi:10.1177/0260106018782211 PMID:29974803

Fabian, P., & Wolfgang, S. (2018). How to measure generalized trust in news media? An adaptation and test of scales. *Communication Methods and Measures.* doi:10.1080/19312458.2018.1506021

Fagerstrøm, A., & Ghinea, G. (2010). Web 2.0's Marketing Impact on Low-Involvement Consumers. *Journal of Interactive Advertising, 10*(2), 67–71. doi:10.1080/15252019.2010.10722171

Farivar, S., Yuan, Y., & Turel, O. (2016). Understanding Social Commerce Acceptance: The Role of Trust, Perceived Risk, and Benefit. In Twenty-second Americas Conference on Information Systems (pp. 1–10). Retrieved from https://scholar.google.com/citations?view_op=view_citation&continue=/scholar%253Fhl%253Den%2526as_sdt%253D0,11%2526scilib%253D1&citilm=1&citation_for_view=iFHnt7IAAAAJ:8AbLer7MMksC&hl=en&oi=p

Farivar, S. (2020). *Biases in Social Commerce Users' Rational Risk Considerations.* ICIS.

Farivar, S., Turel, O., & Yuan, Y. (2017). A trust-risk perspective on social commerce use: An examination of the biasing role of habit. *Internet Research, 27*(3), 586–607. doi:10.1108/IntR-06-2016-0175

Farivar, S., Turel, O., & Yuan, Y. (2018). Skewing users' rational risk considerations in social commerce: An empirical examination of the role of social identification. *Information & Management, 55*(8), 1038–1048. doi:10.1016/j.im.2018.05.008

Farrell, D., & Greig, F. (2016). *Paychecks, paydays, and the online platform economy: Big data on income volatility.* JP Morgan Chase Institute.

Fatemi, F. (2019, March 21). *How APIs Can Transform Your Company.* Retrieved 04 2, 2019, from https://www.forbes.com/sites/falonfatemi/2019/03/21/how-apis-can-transform-your-company/#2dddecfc668c

Feigin, B. (2008). *Mobile Application Development.* A presentation for Android Mobile Development.

Feldman, M. S., Bell, J., & Berger, M. T. (2004). *Gaining access: A practical and theoretical guide for qualitative researchers.* Rowman Altamira.

Femina, B. T., & M., S. E. (2015). An Efficient CRM-Data Mining Framework for the Prediction of Customer Behaviour. In Procedia - Procedia Computer Science (pp. Vol. 46, pp. 725–731). Elsevier Masson SAS. . doi:10.1016/j.procs.2015

Feng, B., Ye, Q., & Collins, B. J. (2019). A dynamic model of electric vehicle adoption: The role of social commerce in new transportation. *Information & Management, 56*(2), 196–212. doi:10.1016/j.im.2018.05.004

Fernandes Rodrigues Alves, M., Vasconcelos Ribeiro Galina, S., & Dobelin, S. (2018). *Literature on organizational innovation: past and future.* Innovation & Management Review; doi:10.1108/INMR-01-2018-001

Fernandes, C. (2013). Analysis of counterfeit fashion purchase behaviour in UAE, Journal of Fashion Marketing and Management. *International Journal (Toronto, Ont.), 17*(1), 85–97.

Ferranti, J. M., Langman, K., Tanaka, D., McCall, J., & Ahmad, A. (2010). Bridging the gap: Leveraging business intelligence tools in support of patient safety and financial effectiveness. *Journal of the American Medical Informatics Association, 17*(2), 136–143. doi:10.1136/jamia.2009.002220 PMID:20190055

Fichman, R. G., Dos Santos, B. L., & Zheng, Z. (2014). Digital Innovation as a Fundamental and Powerful Concept in the IS Curriculum. *Management Information Systems Quarterly, 38*(2), 329–353. doi:10.25300/MISQ/2014/38.2.01

Fidler, D. (n.d.). *Work, Interrupted.* Retrieved, September 20, 2018 from http://www.iftf.org/fileadmin/user_upload/downloads/wfi/IFTF_Work- Interrupted_FullReport.pdf

Finchelstein, F. (2017). *From fascism to populism in history.* Oakland, CA: University of California Press.

Firth, D., King, J., Koch, H., Looney, C. A., Pavlou, P., & Trauth, E. M. (2011). Addressing the Credibility Crisis in IS. *Communications of the AIS, 28*, 199–212.

Fisch, C., & Block, J. (2018). Six tips for your (systematic) literature review in business and management research. *Management Review Quarterly, 68*(2), 103–106. doi:10.100711301-018-0142-x

Fishbein, M., & Ajzen, I. (1975). *Belief, attitude, intention, and behavior: An introduction to theory and research.* Addison-Wesley.

Fisher, R. (2014, Sept 25). *What Exactly is an API Platform? A Competitive Edge That is What!* Retrieved from https://nordicapis.com/what-exactly-is-an-api-platform-competitive-edge/

Fitz-Walter, Z., Tjondronegoro, D., & Wyeth, P. (2011). Orientation Passport: Using Gamification to Engage University Students. *Proceedings of the 23rd Australian Computer-Human Interaction Conference*, 122-125. 10.1145/2071536.2071554

Fletcher, R., & Park, S. (2017). The impact of trust in the news media on online news consumption and participation. Digital Journalism, 1–19. Doi:10.1080/21670811.2017.1279979

Foerster-Metz, U. S., Marquardt, K., Golowko, N., Kompalla, A., & Hell, C. (2018). Digital Transformation and its Implications on Organizational Behavior. *Journal of EU Research in Business.*

Foshay, N., & Kuziemsky, C. (2014). Towards an implementation framework for business intelligence in healthcare. *International Journal of Information Management, 34*(1), 20–27. doi:10.1016/j.ijinfomgt.2013.09.003

Fosso, S. W., Anand, A., & Carter, L. (2013). A literature review of RFID-enabled healthcare applications and issues. *Journal of International Management, 33*, 875–891. doi:10.1016/j.ijinfomgt.2013.07.005

Foster, C., Graham, M., Mann, L., Waema, T., & Friederici, N. (2018). Digital Control in Value Chains: Challenges of Connectivity for East African Firms. *Economic Geography, 94*(1), 68–86. doi:10.1080/00130095.2017.1350104

Francia, P. L. (2018). Free Media and Twitter in the 2016 Presidential Election: The Unconventional Campaign of Donald Trump. *Social Science Computer Review, 36*(4), 440–455. doi:10.1177/0894439317730302

Francisconi, M. (2017). *An explorative study on blockchain technology in application to port logistics.* Academic Press.

Fraser, H. S., & Blaya, J. (2010). Implementing Medical Information Systems in Developing Countries, What Works and What Doesn't. *AMIA 2010 Symposium Proceedings*, 232-236.

Frederick, D. E. (2016). Ebooks as a disruptive technology. Managing Ebook Metadata in Academic Libraries, 11–24. doi:10.1016/B978-0-08-100151-6.00002-0

French, A. M. (2016). The Digital Revolution: Internet of Things, 5G, and Beyond. *Communications of AIS, 38*(May), 840–850.

Friedman, G. C. (2014). Workers without employers: Shadow corporations and the rise of the gig economy. *Review of Keynesian Economics, 2*(2), 171–188. doi:10.4337/roke.2014.02.03

Friedrich, T. (2015). Analyzing the Factors that Influence Consumers ' Adoption of Social Commerce – A Literature Review Full Papers. *Twenty-First Americas Conference on Information Systems*, 1–16.

Fuad, A., & Hsu, C. Y. (2018). UTAUT for HSS: Initial framework to study health IT adoption in the developing countries. *F1000 Research*, 7. PMID:30109025

Gable, G. (1994). Integrating case study and survey research methods: An example in information systems. *European Journal of Information Systems*, *3*(2), 112–126. doi:10.1057/ejis.1994.12

Gadamer, H.-G. (1976a). On the scope and function of hermeneutical reflection. *Philosophical Hermeneutics*, 18-44.

Gadamer, H.-G. (1976b). *Philosophical Hermeneutics*. University of California Press.

Galinec, D., Možnik, D., & Guberina, B. (2017). Cybersecurity and cyber defense: national level strategic approach. *Automatika: časopis za automatiku, mjerenje, elektroniku, računarstvo i komunikacije, 58*(3), 273-286.

Galliers, R. D., & Leidner, D. E. (2014). *Strategic information management: challenges and strategies in managing information systems*. Routledge. doi:10.4324/9781315880884

Gallup. (2016). Americans' trust in mass media sinks to new low. Retrieved from http://www.gallup.com/poll/195542/Americans-trust-mass-media-sinks-new-low.aspx

Galperin, H., & Viecens, M. F. (2017). Connected for development? Theory and evidence about the impact of internet technologies on poverty alleviation. *Development Policy Review*, *35*(3), 1–2. doi:10.1111/dpr.12210

Gancho, S. P. M. (2017). Social Media: a literature review. *e-Revista LOGO, 6*(2), 1-20.

Gangwar, H., Date, H., & Raoot, A. D. (2014). Review on IT adoption : Insights from recent technologies. *Journal of Enterprise Information Management*, *27*(4), 488–502. doi:10.1108/JEIM-08-2012-0047

Gans, J., & Ryall, M. D. (2017). Value capture theory: A strategic management review. *Strategic Management Journal*, *38*(1), 17–41. doi:10.1002/smj.2592

Garbers, Y., & Konradt, U. (2014). The effect of financial incentives on performance : A quantitative review of individual and team-based financial incentives. *Journal of Occupational and Organizational Psychology*, *87*(1), 102–137. doi:10.1111/joop.12039

Garcia-murillo, M., Macinnes, I., & Bauer, J. M. (2018). Techno-unemployment : A framework for assessing the effects of information and communication technologies on work. *Telematics and Informatics*, *35*(1), 1863–1876. doi:10.1016/j.tele.2018.05.013

Gardiner, A., Aasheim, C., Rutner, P., & Williams, S. (2017). Skill Requirements in Big Data: A Content Analysis of Job Advertisements. *Journal of Computer Information Systems*, *0*(0), 1–11.

Gardiner, L. (1994). *Redesigning Higher Education: Producing Dramatic Gains in Student Learning*. Washington, DC: George Washington University.

Garg, P., & Garg, A. (2013). An empirical study on critical failure factors for enterprise resource planning implementation in Indian retail sector. *Business Process Management Journal*, *19*(3), 496–514. doi:10.1108/14637151311319923

Gartner. (2019, July 22nd). Data Mining. Retrieved from https://www.gartner.com/it-glossary/data-mining

Gatautis, R., & Medziausiene, A. (2014). Factors Affecting Social Commerce Acceptance in Lithuania. Procedia - Social and Behavioral Sciences, 110(2013), 1235–1242. doi:10.1016/j.sbspro.2013.12.970

Gauthier, F., & Lagacé, D. (2015). Critical Success Factors in the Development and Implementation of Special Purpose Industrial Tools: An Ergonomic Perspective. Procedia Manufacturing, 3(Ahfe), 5639–5646. doi:10.1016/j.promfg.2015.07.773

Gawer, A., & Cusumano, M. (2002). *Platform Leadership: How Intel, Microsoft, and CiscoDrive Industry Innovation*. Harvard Business School Press.

Gcora, N., & Chigona, W. (2019). Post-implementation evaluation and challenges of Integrated Financial Management Information Systems for municipalities in South Africa. *South African Journal of Information Management*, *21*(1), 1–12. doi:10.4102ajim.v21i1.1066

Gecchelin, T., & Webb, J. (2019). Modular dynamic ride-sharing transport systems. *Economic Analysis and Policy*, *61*(1), 111–117. doi:10.1016/j.eap.2018.12.003

Geerdts, C., Gillwald, A., Calandro, E., Chair, E., Moyo, M., & Rademan, B. (2016). *Developing smart public Wi-Fi in South Africa*. Retrieved from: https://www.africaportal.org/publications/developing-smart-public-wi-fi-south-africa/

Geertz, C. (1973). *The Interpretation of Cultures*. New York: Basic Books.

Gehman, J., Lounsbury, M., & Greenwood, R. (2016). How institutions matter: From the micro-foundations of institutional impacts to the macro consequences of institutional arrangements. In *How Institutions Matter!* (pp. 1–34). Emerald Group Publishing Limited. doi:10.1108/S0733-558X201600048A002

General Statistics Office of Vietnam. (2017). *Small and medium enterprises are getting smaller*. Retrieved from gso.gov.vn

General Statistics Office of Vietnam. (2019a). *The Socio-Economic Situation in 2018*. Retrieved from https://www.gso.gov.vn/default.aspx?tabid=621&ItemID=19037

General Statistics Office of Vietnam. (2019b). *Statistical Yearbook of Vietnam 2018*. Retrieved from https://www.gso.gov.vn/default_en.aspx?tabid=515&idmid=5&ItemID=19299

Gentile, D. (2009). Pathological Video-Game Use Among Youth Ages 8 to 18. *Psychological Science*, *20*(5), 594–602. doi:10.1111/j.1467-9280.2009.02340.x PMID:19476590

George, J. F., & Kohnke, E. (2018). Personal Health Record Systems as Boundary Objects. *Communications of the Association for Information Systems*, *42*(2), 21–50.

Gerry, F. Q., & Moore, C. (2015). A slippery and inconsistent slope: How Cambodia's draft cybercrime law exposed the dangerous drift away from international human rights standards. *Computer Law & Security Review*, *31*(5), 628–650. doi:10.1016/j.clsr.2015.05.008

Gesulga, J. M., Berjame, A., Moquiala, K. S., & Galido, A. (2017). Barriers to Electronic Health Record System Implementation and Information Systems Resources: A Structured Review. *Procedia Computer Science*, *124*, 544–551. doi:10.1016/j.procs.2017.12.188

Ge, Y., Jabbari, P., Mackenzie, D., & Tao, J. (2017). Effects of a Public Real-Time Multi-Modal Transportation Information Display on Travel Behavior and Attitudes. *Journal of Public Transportation*, *20*(2), 40–65. doi:10.5038/2375-0901.20.2.3

Ghanaweb. (2019). Retrieved from MoMo fraud: How scammers steal your money: https://www.ghanaweb.com/GhanaHomePage/NewsArchive/Momo-fraud-How-scammers-steal-your-money-791051

Ghazawneh, A., & Henfridsson, O. (2013). Balancing Platform Control and External Contribution in Third-Party Development: The Boundary Resources Model. *Information Systems Journal*, *23*(2), 173–192. doi:10.1111/j.1365-2575.2012.00406.x

Ghobakhloo, M., & Tang, S. H. (2013). The role of owner/manager in adoption of electronic commerce in small businesses: The case of developing countries. *Journal of Small Business and Enterprise Development*, *20*(4), 754–787. doi:10.1108/JSBED-12-2011-0037

Ghosh, B., & Scott, J. E. (2011). Antecedent and Catalysts for developing healthcare capability. *Communication of the Association for Information Systems*, 395-310.

Giesbrecht, T., Schwabe, G., & Schenk, B. (2017). Service encounter thinklets: How to empower service agents to put value co-creation into practice. *Information Systems Journal, 27*(2), 171–196. doi:10.1111/isj.12099

Gill, T. G., & Hu, Q. (1999). The evolving undergraduate information systems education: A survey of U.S. institutions. *Journal of Computer Information Systems, 74*(5), 289–295.

Gill, T. G., & Ritzhaupt, A. D. (2013). Systematically Evaluating the Effectiveness of an Information Systems Capstone Course: Implications for Practice. *Journal of Information Technology Education: Research, 12*, 69–94. doi:10.28945/1776

Gillwald, A., Moyo, M., Odufuwa, F., Frempong, G., & Kamoun, F. (2014). *The cloud over Africa*. Cape Town, South Africa: Research ICT Africa.

Gioia, D. A., & Chittipeddi, K. (1991). Sensemaking and sensegiving in strategic change initiation. *Strategic Management Journal, 12*(6), 433–448. doi:10.1002mj.4250120604

Gitau, L., & Nzuki, D. (2014). Analysis of Determinants of M-commerce Adoption by Online consumers. *Journal of Theoretical and Applied E-commerce Research, 4*, 88–94.

Godwin Jones, R. (2011). Mobile apps for language learning. *Language Learning & Technology, 15*(2), 2–11.

Goerzig, D., & Bauernhansl, T. (2018). Enterprise architectures for the digital transformation in small and medium-sized enterprises. *Procedia CIRP, 67*, 540–545. doi:10.1016/j.procir.2017.12.257

Gogan, J. L., Williams, C. B., & Fedorowicz, J. (2007). RFID and interorganisational collaboration: political and administrative challenges. *Electronic Government, an International Journal, 4*(4), 423-435.

Gol, E. (2019). Crowd work platform governance toward organizational value creation. *The Journal of Strategic Information Systems, 28*(2), 175–195. doi:10.1016/j.jsis.2019.01.001

Golshan, B. (2018). *Digital Capability and Business Model Reconfiguration: a co-evolutionary perspective* (Doctoral dissertation). Linnaeus University Press.

Goncalves, M. J. A., Rocha, Á., & Cota, M. P. (2016). Information management model for competencies and learning outcomes in an educational context. *Information Systems Frontiers, 18*(6), 1051–1061. doi:10.100710796-016-9623-4

Gonzalez, A., Schlautmann, A., Casahuga, G., & Romero, M. (2017) Digital transformation in developing countries. *Public services, Technology & innovation management, Arthur D Little*. Retrieved from https://www.adlittle.se/sites/default/files/viewpoints/adl_digital_in_emerging_markets.pdf

Goode, L. (2011) *Worth It? An App to Get a Cab, Wall Street Journal (Blog)*. Available at: http://blogs.wsj.com/digits/2011/06/17/worth-it-an-app-to-get-a-cab/.

Goodhue, D. L., & Thompson, R. L. (1995). Task-technology fit and individual performance. *Management Information Systems Quarterly, 19*(2), 213–236. doi:10.2307/249689

Goodier, R. (2016). Sensors ring the changes. *Appropriate Technology, 43*(3), 50.

Goodman, M. c D. (1997). Why the police don't care about computer crime. *Harvard Journal of Law & Technology, 10*, 466–494.

Goomas, D. T., & Ludwig, T. D. (2007). Enhancing incentive programs with proximal goals and immediate feedback. *Journal of Organizational Behavior Management, 27*(1), 33–68. doi:10.1300/J075v27n01_02

Gordon, S., & Ford, R. (2006). On the definition and classification of cybercrime. *Journal in Computer Virology, 2*(1), 13–20. doi:10.100711416-006-0015-z

Gorgone, J. T. (2000). *Approaching MSIS 2000: A New-Fashioned Graduate Model.* Academic Press.

Gorgone, J. T., Davis, G. B., Valacich, J. S., Topi, H., Feinstein, D. L., & Longenecker, H. E. (2002). IS 2002 Model Curriculum and Guidelines for Undergraduate Degree Programs in Information Systems. *The Data Base for Advances in Information Systems, 34*(1), 1–53.

Gorgone, J. T., Gray, P., Stohr, E. A., Valacich, J. S., & Wigand, R. T. (2006). MSIS 2006 : Model Curriculum and Guidelines for Graduate Degree Programs in Information Systems. *Communications of the Association for Information Systems, 38*(2), 121–196.

Goswami, A., & Dutta, D. (2016). E-Commerce Adoption by Women Entrepreneurs in India: An Application of the UTAUT Model. 8TH IEEE International Conference on Control System, Computing and Engineering. DOI:10.5296/ber.v6i2.10560

Govindarajulu, N., & Daily, B. F. (2004). Motivating employees for environmental improvement Motivating employees for environmental improvement. *Industrial Management & Data Systems, 104*(4), 364–372. doi:10.1108/02635570410530775

Goyal, M., & Vohra, R. (2012). Applications of Data Mining in Higher Education. *International Journal of Computational Science, 9*(2), 113–120.

Graham, M., Ojanperä, S., Anwar, M. A., & Friederici, N. (2017). ⬜Digital Connectivity and African Knowledge Economies⬜. *Questions de Communication,* (2), 345-360. ⬜⬜⬜⬜⬜⬜⬜⬜⬜⬜⬜⬜⬜⬜⬜⬜⬜⬜⬜

Graham, M., Hjorth, I., & Lehdonvirta, V. (2017). Digital labour and development: Impacts of global digital labour platforms and the gig economy on worker livelihoods. *Transfer: European Review of Labour and Research, 23*(2), 135–162. doi:10.1177/1024258916687250 PMID:28781494

Graham, T., Broersma, M., Hazelhoff, K., & van 't Haar, G. (2013). Between Broadcasting Political Messages and Interacting with Voters. *Information Communication and Society, 16*(5), 692–716. doi:10.1080/1369118X.2013.785581

Grandhi, S., & Wibowo, S. (2016). Mobile Commerce Adoption in North American Organizations: An Empirical Study of Organizational Factors. *Communications of the IBIMA, 2016,* 1–17. doi:10.5171/2016.682007

Grange, C., & Benbasat, I. (2013). The value of social shopping networks for product search and the moderating role of network scope. International Conference on Information Systems (ICIS 2013): Reshaping Society Through Information Systems Design, 5, 4230–4241.

Grange, C., Benbasat, I., & Burton-Jones, A. (2018, March). A Network-Based Conceptualization of Social Commerce and Social Commerce Value. *Computers in Human Behavior,* •••, 1–14. doi:10.1016/j.chb.2018.12.033

Grant, R. M. (1999). The resource-based theory of competitive advantage: implications for strategy formulation. In *Knowledge and strategy* (pp. 3–23). Elsevier; doi:10.1016/B978-0-7506-7088-3.50004-8.

Gräther, W., Kolvenbach, S., Ruland, R., Schütte, J., Torres, C., & Wendland, F. (2018). Blockchain for Education: Lifelong Learning Passport. In W. Prinz & P. Hoschka (Eds.), *Proceedings of the 1st ERCIM Blockchain Workshop 2018, Reports of the European Society for Socially Embedded Technologies.* Doi:10.18420/blockchain2018_07

Grech, A., & Camilleri, A. F. (2017). *Blockchain in education.* Academic Press.

Green, J., Willis, K., Hughes, E., Small, R., Welch, N., Gibbs, L., & Daly, J. (2007). Generating best evidence from qualitative research: The role of data analysis. *Australian and New Zealand Journal of Public Health, 31*(6), 545–550. doi:10.1111/j.1753-6405.2007.00141.x PMID:18081575

Greenwood, B. N., & Wattal, S. (2017). Show Me the Way to Go Home: An Empirical Investigation of Ride-Sharing and Alcohol Related Motor Vehicle Fatalities. *Management Information Systems Quarterly, 41*(1), 163–187. doi:10.25300/MISQ/2017/41.1.08

Gregory, R. W., Beck, R., & Keil, M. (2013). Control balancing in information systems development offshoring projects. *Management Information Systems Quarterly, 37*(4), 1211–1232. doi:10.25300/MISQ/2013/37.4.10

Grewal, D., Roggeveen, A. L., & Nordfält, J. (2017). The future of retailing. *Journal of Retailing, 93*(1), 1–6. doi:10.1016/j.jretai.2016.12.008

Griffiths & Nuyens, F. (2017). An Overview of Structural Characteristics in Problematic Video Game Playing. *Current Addiction Reports*, 272–283. PMID:28845381

Griffiths, M. (1995). Technological addictions. In Clinical psychology forum (p. 14). Academic Press.

Griffiths, P. (2016). Bolstering Urbanization Efforts: Africa's Approach to the New Urban Agenda. Academic Press.

Griffiths. (2005). A components model of addiction within a biopsychosocial framework. *Journal of Substance Use, 10*(4), 191–197.

Griffiths, M. (2010). Internet abuse and internet addiction in the workplace. *Journal of Workplace Learning, 22*(7), 463–472. doi:10.1108/13665621011071127

Gross, M. L., Canetti, D., & Vashdi, D. R. (2016). The psychological effects of cyber terrorism. *Bulletin of the Atomic Scientists, 72*(5), 284–291. doi:10.1080/00963402.2016.1216502 PMID:28366962

Grover, V., Chiang, R. H. L., Liang, T.-P., & Zhang, D. (2018). Creating Strategic Business Value from Big Data Analytics: A Research Framework. *Journal of Management Information Systems, 35*(2), 388–423. doi:10.1080/07421222.2018.1451951

Guba, E. G., & Lincoln, Y. S. (1994). Competing paradigms in qualitative research. Handbook of Qualitative Research, 2, 163-194.

Gu, D., Li, J., Li, X., & Liang, C. (2017). Visualizing the knowledge structure and evolution of big data research in healthcare informatics. *International Journal of Medical Informatics, 98*, 22–38. doi:10.1016/j.ijmedinf.2016.11.006 PMID:28034409

Guerrero-Solé, F. (2017). Community Detection in Political Discussions on Twitter: An Application of the Retweet Overlap Network Method to the Catalan Process Toward Independence. *Social Science Computer Review, 35*(2), 244–261. doi:10.1177/0894439315617254

Guest, G., Bunce, A., & Johnson, L. (2006). How many interviews are enough? An experiment with data saturation and variability. *Field Methods, 18*(1), 59–82. doi:10.1177/1525822X05279903

Guijarro, L. (2009). Semantic interoperability in eGovernment initiatives. *Computer Standards & Interfaces, 31*(1), 174–180. doi:10.1016/j.csi.2007.11.011

Guin, U., DiMase, D., & Tehranipoor, M. (2014). Counterfeit integrated circuits: Detection, avoidance, and the challenges ahead. *Journal of Electronic Testing, 30*(1), 9–23. doi:10.100710836-013-5430-8

Gündüz, U., & Erdem, B. K. (2017). The concept of virtual nationalism in the digital age: Social media perspectives of Turkey. *Communication Today, 8*(2), 18–29.

Güneyli, A., Ersoy, E., & Kıralp, S. (2017). Terrorism in the 2015 election period in Turkey content analysis of political leaders' social media activity. *Journal of Universal Computer Science, 23*(3), 256–279.

Guo, J., Nikou, S., & Bouwman, H. (2015). Business model for mobile payment in China. *International Journal of Systems and Service-Oriented Engineering, 5*(2), 20–43. doi:10.4018/IJSSOE.2015040102

Guo, S., Wang, M., & Leskovec, J. (2011). The Role of Social Networks in Online Shopping: Information Passing, Price of Trust, and Consumer Choice. In *Proceedings of the 12th ACM conference on Electronic commerce.* ACM. 10.1145/1993574.1993598

Gupta, B., Goul, M., & Dinter, B. (2015). Business intelligence and big data in higher education: Status of a multi-year model curriculum development effort for business school undergraduates, MS graduates, and MBAs. *Communications of the Association for Information Systems, 36*, 449–476. doi:10.17705/1CAIS.03623

Gupta, V. (2017). A brief history of blockchain. *Harvard Business Review, 28.*

Gurumurthy, K. M., & Kockelman, K. M. (2018). Analyzing the dynamic ride-sharing potential for shared autonomous vehicle fleets using cellphone data from Orlando, Florida. *Computers, Environment and Urban Systems, 71*(1), 177–185. doi:10.1016/j.compenvurbsys.2018.05.008

Gyamfi, A., Mensah, K. A., Oduro, G., Donkor, P., & Mock, C. N. (2017). Barriers and Facilitators to Electronic Medical Records in the Emergency Centre at Komfo Anokye Teaching Hospital, Kumasi-Ghana. *African Journal of Emergency Medicine*, 177–182. doi:10.1016/j.afjem.2017.05.002 PMID:30456135

Haciyakupoglu, G., & Zhang, W. (2015). Social media and trust during the Gezi protests in Turkey. *Journal of Computer-Mediated Communication, 20*(4), 450–466. doi:10.1111/jcc4.12121

Haddara, M., & Moen, H. (2017). User resistance in ERP implementations: A literature review. *Procedia Computer Science, 121*, 859–865. doi:10.1016/j.procs.2017.11.111

Hafdell, S. (2014). Social media and the "Menace to Society": Potential and limitations of alternative media in Turkey. *Glocal Times, 21*, 1–14.

Hagel, J. (2015). Bringing analytics to life. *Journal of Accountancy, 219*, 24–25.

Hair, J. F., Black, W. C., Babin, B. J., Anderson, R. E., & Tatham, R. L. (2010). *Multivariate data analysis* (7th ed.). Upper Saddle River, NJ: Pearson Prentice Hall.

Hajli, N. (2015). Social commerce constructs and consumer's intention to buy. *International Journal of Information Management, 35*(2), 183–191. doi:10.1016/j.ijinfomgt.2014.12.005

Hajli, N. M. (2014). The role of social support on relationship quality and social commerce. *Technological Forecasting and Social Change, 87*, 17–27. doi:10.1016/j.techfore.2014.05.012

Hajli, N., & Sims, J. (2015). Social commerce: The transfer of power from sellers to buyers. *Technological Forecasting and Social Change, 94*, 350–358. doi:10.1016/j.techfore.2015.01.012

Hajli, N., Sims, J., Zadeh, A. H., & Richard, M. O. (2017). A social commerce investigation of the role of trust in a social networking site on purchase intentions. *Journal of Business Research, 71*, 133–141. doi:10.1016/j.jbusres.2016.10.004

Hakak, S., Noor, N. F. M., Ayub, M. N., Affal, H., Hussin, N., & Imran, M. (2019). Cloud-assisted gamification for education and learning–Recent advances and challenges. *Computers & Electrical Engineering, 74*, 22–34. doi:10.1016/j.compeleceng.2019.01.002

Hambrick, M. E., Simmons, J. M., Greenhalgh, G. P., & Greenwell, T. C. (2010). Understanding Professional Athletes' Use of Twitter: A Content Analysis of Athlete Tweets. *International Journal of Sport Communication, 3*(4), 454–471. doi:10.1123/ijsc.3.4.454

Hamdan, A. R., Yahaya, J. H., Deraman, A., & Jusoh, Y. Y. (2016). The success factors and barriers of information technology implementation in small and medium enterprises: An empirical study in Malaysia. *International Journal of Business Information Systems*, *21*(4), 477–494. doi:10.1504/IJBIS.2016.075257

Hamelin, N., Nwankwo, S., & El Hadouchi, R. (2013). 'Faking brands': Consumer responses to counterfeiting. *Journal of Consumer Behaviour*, *12*(3), 159–170. doi:10.1002/cb.1406

Hamka, F., Bouwman, H., De Reuver, M., & Kroesen, M. (2014). Mobile customer segmentation based on smartphone measurement. *Telematics and Informatics*, *31*(2), 220–227. doi:10.1016/j.tele.2013.08.006

Hampton, K. N., & Gupta, N. (2008). Community and social interaction in the wireless city: Wi-Fi use in public and semi-public spaces. *New Media & Society*, *10*(6), 831–850. doi:10.1177/1461444808096247

Hamzah, H. H. B., Keattch, O., Covill, D., & Patel, B. A. (2018). The effects of printing orientation on the electrochemical behaviour of 3D printed acrylonitrile butadiene styrene (ABS)/carbon black electrodes. *Scientific Reports*, *8*(1), 9135. doi:10.103841598-018-27188-5 PMID:29904165

Hamzah, W. M. A. F. W., Ali, N. H., Saman, M. Y. M., Yusoff, M. H., & Yacob, A. (2015). Influence of gamification on students' motivation in using e-learning applications based on the motivational design model. *International Journal of Emerging Technologies in Learning*, *10*(2), 30–34. doi:10.3991/ijet.v10i2.4355

Hamzat, S. A., & Mabawonku, I. (2018). *Influence of performance expectancy and facilitating conditions on use of digital library by engineering lecturers in universities in south-west.* Library Philosophy and Practice.

Han, J., & Kim, Y. (2009). *Obama tweeting and twitted: Sotomayor's nomination and health care reform.* Paper presented at the annual meeting of the American Political Science Association, Toronto, Canada.

Han, L., Xin, R. L., & Zhang, H. X. (2017). Resolving the privacy paradox: Toward a cognitive appraisal and emotion approach to online privacy behaviours. Information & Management Journal, *54*(8), 1012–1022. doi:10.1016/j.im.2017.02.005

Hand, D. (1998). Data Mining : Statistics and More? *The American Statistician*, *52*(2), 112–118.

Han, H., & Trimi, S. (2017). Social commerce design: A framework and application. *Journal of Theoretical and Applied Electronic Commerce Research*, *12*(3), 50–68. doi:10.4067/S0718-18762017000300005

Hanitzsch, T., Van-Dalen, A., & Steindl, N. (2017). Caught in the nexus: A comparative and longitudinal analysis of public trust in the press. *The International Journal of Press/Politics*, *20*(2), 1–21. doi:10.1177/1940161217740695

Han, J., Kamber, M., & Pei, J. (2011). *Data Mining: Concepts and Techniques.* Elsevier.

Hanseth, O. (2002). *From Systems and Tolls to Networks and Infrastructures - From Design to Cultivation. Towards a Theory of ICT Solutions and its Design Methodology Implications.* Available at URL: http://heim.ifi.uio.no/~oleha/Publications/ib_ISR_3rd_resubm2.html

Hanseth, O., & Monteiro, E. (1997). *Understanding Information Infrastructure, Unpublished Manuscript.* Available at URL: http://heim.ifi.uio.no/~oleha/Publications/bok.pdf

Hanseth, O., & Monteiro, E. (1998). Changing Irreversible Networks: Institutionalisation and Infrastructure. *Proceedings of the 2oth edition of IRIS.*

Hanseth, O., Monteiro, E., & Hatling, M. (1996). Developing Information Infrastructure: The Tension Between Standardisation and Flexiblility. *Science, Technology & Human Values*, *21*(4), 407–426. doi:10.1177/016224399602100402

Hargittai, E., & Litt, E. (2011). The tweet smell of celebrity success: Explaining variation in Twitter adoption among a diverse group of young adults. *New Media & Society*, *13*(5), 824–842. doi:10.1177/1461444811405805

Harkin, F. (2007). *The Wisdom of Crowds*. Academic Press.

Harpool, R. (2017). *Perceptions of Distributed Ledger Technology by Financial Professionals With Fiduciary Responsibilities at Select institutions of Higher Education*. ProQuest LLC.

Harrigan, P., Evers, U., Miles, M., & Daly, T. (2017). Customer engagement with tourism social media brands. *Tourism Management, 59*, 597–609. doi:10.1016/j.tourman.2016.09.015

Harris, A. H., Greer, T. H., Morris, S. A., Clark, W. J., & Greer, T. H. (2012). Information Systems Job Market Late 1970's-Early 2010's. *Journal of Computer Information Systems, 53*(1), 72–79.

Harris, A., & Lang, M. (2011). Incorporating Ethics and Social Responsibility in IS Education. *Journal of Information Systems Education, 22*(3), 183–190.

Harris, M. A., & Patten, K. P. (2015). Using Bloom's and Webb's Taxonomies to Integrate Emerging Cybersecurity Topics into a Computing Curriculum. *Journal of Information Systems Education, 26*(3), 219–234.

Harrison, J. S., Hitt, M. A., Hoskisson, R. E., & Ireland, R. D. (2001). Resource complementarity in business combinations: Extending the logic to organizational alliances. *Journal of Management, 27*(6), 679–690. doi:10.1177/014920630102700605

Harry, B., Vos, H. D., & Haaker, T. (2008). Mobile service innovation and business models. Springer.

Haruna, H., Hu, X., Chu, S., Mellecker, R., Gabriel, G., & Ndekao, P. (2018). Improving sexual health education programs for adolescent students through game-based learning and Gamification. *International Journal of Environmental Research and Public Health, 15*(9), 2027. doi:10.3390/ijerph15092027 PMID:30227642

Harun, H., & Hashim, M. K. (2017). Strategic Information Systems Planning : A Review Of Its Concept, Definitions And Stages Of Development. In *Proceedings of 3rd International Conference on Information Technology and Computer Science Held* (pp. 133–141). Bangkok: Academic Press.

Harvey, M. G. (1987). Industrial product counterfeiting: Problems and proposed solutions. *Journal of Business and Industrial Marketing, 2*(4), 5–13. doi:10.1108/eb006038

Hasan, A., Jha, K. N., Rameezdeen, R., Ahn, S., & Baroudi, B. (2019). Perceived Productivity Effects of Mobile ICT in Construction Projects. In *Advances in Informatics and Computing in Civil and Construction Engineering* (pp. 165–172). Cham: Springer. doi:10.1007/978-3-030-00220-6_20

Hashim, J. (2007). Information and communication technology adoption among SME owner in Malaysia. *International Journal of Business and Information, 2*(2), 221–240.

Hashim, K. F., Tan, F. B., & Rashid, A. (2015). Adult learners' intention to adopt mobile learning: A motivational perspective. *British Journal of Educational Technology, 46*(2), 381–390. doi:10.1111/bjet.12148

Hassan, M. A., Habiba, U., Majeed, F., & Shoaib, M. (2019). Adaptive gamification in e-learning based on students' learning styles. *Interactive Learning Environments*, 1–21. doi:10.1080/10494820.2019.1588745

Hassan, S., & Toland, J. (2013). A conceptual framework for value co-creation practices in C2C social commerce environment. *Proceedings of the 24th Australasian Conference on Information Systems.*

Hathaway, A. (2018). *Tips On Monetizing APIs*. Retrieved 02 24, 2019, from https://nordicapis.com/tips-monetizing-apis/

Haunschild, P. R., & Chandler, D. (2008). Institutional- level learning: Learning as a source of institutional change. In The Sage Handbook of Organizational Institutionalism, (pp. 624-649). Thousand Oaks, CA: Sage.

Havelka, D., & Merhout, J. (2009). Toward a theory of information technology professional competence. *Journal of Computer Information Systems*, *50*(2), 106–116.

Hayashi, F. (2012). Mobile payments: What's in it for consumers. Economic Review-Federal Reserve Bank of Kansas City, 35.

Hayes, J. (2018). *The theory and practice of change management*. Palgrave. doi:10.1057/978-1-352-00132-7

Heeks, R. (2016). Examining "Digital Development" (No. 64). Retrieved from http://www.gdi.manchester.ac.uk/research/publications/di/

Heeks, R. (2017). *Decent Work and the Digital Gig Economy: A Developing Country Perspective on Employment Impacts and Standards in Online Outsourcing, Crowdwork, etc.* Global Development Institute. University of Manchester. https://www. gdi. manchester. ac. uk/research/publications/di/di-wp71

Heeks, R. (2002). i-development, not e-development: Special issue on ICTs and development. Journal of International Development. *The Journal of the Development Studies Association*, *14*(1), 1–11.

Heeks, R. (2002). Information systems and developing countries: Failure, success and local improvisations. *The Information Society*, *18*(2), 101–112. doi:10.1080/01972240290075039

Heeks, R. (2017). *Information and Communication Technology for Development*. Abingdon, UK: Routledge; doi:10.4324/9781315652603.

Heeks, R., & Kanashiro, L. L. (2009). Telecentres in mountain regions - A Peruvian case study of the impact of information and communication technologies on remoteness and exclusion. *Journal of Mountain Science*, *6*(4), 320–330. doi:10.100711629-009-1070-y

Heikkilä, J.-P. (2013). An institutional theory perspective on e-HRM's strategic potential in MNC subsidiaries. *The Journal of Strategic Information Systems*, *22*(3), 238–251. doi:10.1016/j.jsis.2013.07.003

Helfat, C. E., Finkelstein, S., Mitchell, W., Peteraf, M., Singh, H., Teece, D. J., & Winter, S. G. (2007). *Dynamic Capabilities- Understanding Strategic Change in Organizations*. Oxford: Blackwell Publishing.

Helfert, M. (2011). Characteristics of Information Systems and Business Informatics Study Programs. *Informatics in Education*, *10*(1), 13–36.

Henama, U. S., & Sifolo, P. P. S. (2017). Uber: The South Africa experience. *African Journal of Hospitality, Tourism and Leisure*, *6*(2), 1–10.

Henderson, J. C., & Venkatraman, N. (1993). Strategic Alignment: Leveraging Information Technology for Transforming Organizations. *IBM Systems Journal*, *32*(1), 4–16. doi:10.1147/sj.382.0472

Hendricks, D. (2015). The Trouble with the Internet of Things. London Datastore. *Greater London Authority*. Retrieved from https://data.london.gov.uk/blog/the-trouble-with-the-internet-of-things/

Hendriks, C. J. (2013). Integrated Financial Management Information Systems: Guidelines for effective implementation by the public sector of South Africa. *South African Journal of Information Management*, *15*(1), 1–9.

Henning, M., Hagedorn-Hansen, D., & von Leipzig, K. H. (2017). Metacognitive learning: Skills development through gamification at the Stellenbosch learning factory as a case study. *South African Journal of Industrial Engineering*, *28*(3), 105–112. doi:10.7166/28-3-1845

Henseler, J., & Chin, W. W. (2010). A comparison of approaches for the analysis of interaction effects between latent variables using partial least squares path modeling. *Structural Equation Modeling*, *17*(1), 82–109. doi:10.1080/10705510903439003

Henson, K., & Kamal, M. (2010). Closing the Gap - Information Systems Curriculum And Changing Global Market. *American Journal of Business Education*, *3*(5), 17–20. doi:10.19030/ajbe.v3i5.423

Henten, A. H., & Windekilde, I. M. (2016). Transaction costs and the sharing economy. *Info*, *18*(1), 1–15. doi:10.1108/info-09-2015-0044

Hepner, M., & Dickson, W. (2013). The value of ERP curriculum integration: Perspectives from the research. *Journal of Information Systems Education*, *24*(4), 309–326.

Herstein, R., Drori, N., Berger, R., & Barnes, B. R. (2015). Anti-counterfeiting strategies and their influence on attitudes of different counterfeit consumer types. *Psychology and Marketing*, *32*(8), 842–859. doi:10.1002/mar.20822

Highfield, T., Harrington, S., & Bruns, A. (2013). Twitter, as a technology for audience and fandom. *Information Communication and Society*, *16*(3), 16–33. doi:10.1080/1369118X.2012.756053

Hileman, G. (2016). *State of Blockchain Q1 2016: Blockchain Funding Overtakes Bitcoin – CoinDesk*. Retrieved from https://www.coindesk.com/state-of-Blockchain-q1-2016/

Hill, C. (2019). *The Future of British Foreign Policy: Security and Diplomacy in a World After Brexit*. John Wiley & Sons.

Hillman, H., Hooper, C., & Choo, K.-K. R. (2014). Online child exploitation: Challenges and future research directions. *Computer Law & Security Review*, *30*(6), 687–698. doi:10.1016/j.clsr.2014.09.007

Hinings, B., Gegenhuber, T., & Greenwood, R. (2018). Digital innovation and transformation: An institutional perspective. *Information and Organization*, *28*(1), 52–61. doi:10.1016/j.infoandorg.2018.02.004

Hirschheim, R., & Newman, M. (1988). Information systems and user resistance: Theory and practice. *The Computer Journal*, *31*(5), 398–408. doi:10.1093/comjnl/31.5.398

Hirschman, A. O. (1958). *The strategy of economic development*. New Haven, CT: Yale University Press.

Hodge, H., Carson, D., Carson, C., Newman, L., & Garrett, J. (2017). Using Internet technologies in rural communities to access services: The views of older people and service providers. *Journal of Rural Studies*, *54*, 469–478. doi:10.1016/j.jrurstud.2016.06.016

Hoecht, A., & Trott, P. (2014). How should firms deal with counterfeiting? A review of the success conditions of anti-counterfeiting strategies. *International Journal of Emerging Markets*, *9*(1), 98–119. doi:10.1108/IJOEM-02-2011-0014

Hoe, L., Hogg, G., & Hart, S. (2003). Faking it: Counterfeiting and consumer contradictions. *European Advances in Consumer Behaviour*, *6*, 60–67.

Hoff, D. L., & Mitchell, S. N. (2009). Cyberbullying: Causes, effects, and remedies. *Journal of Educational Administration*, *47*(5), 652–665. doi:10.1108/09578230910981107

Hofstede, G. (1980). *Culture's consequences: Comparing values, behaviours, institutions and organizations across nations*. Thousand Oaks, CA: Sage Publications.

Ho, L.-H., Lin, Y.-T., & Huang, C.-H. (2012). Influences of Online Lifestyle on Juvenile Cybercrime Behaviors in Taiwan. *Procedia Engineering*, *29*, 2545–2550. doi:10.1016/j.proeng.2012.01.348

Hollenstein, H. (2002). *Determinants of the adoption of information and communication technologies (ICT): An empirical analysis based on firm-level data for the Swiss business sector*. KOF Working Papers, No. 60. ETH Zurich, KOF Swiss Economic Institute.

Holt, T. J., & Bossler, A. M. (2014). An assessment of the current state of cybercrime scholarship. *Deviant Behavior*, *35*(1), 20–40. doi:10.1080/01639625.2013.822209

Hong, H. G. (2015). Success Factors of Mobile-Commerce System. *Indian Journal of Science and Technology*, *8*(7), 630–637. doi:10.17485/ijst/2015/v8iS7/70451

Hong, W., Chan, F. K. Y., Thong, J. Y. L., Chasalow, L. C., & Dhillon, G. (2014). A framework and guidelines for context-specific theorising in information systems research. *Information Systems Research*, *25*(1), 111–136. doi:10.1287/isre.2013.0501

Hong, W., Chan, F. K., Thong, J. Y., Chasalow, L. C., & Dhillon, G. (2013). A Framework and Guidelines for Context-Specific Theorizing in Information Systems Research. *Information Systems Research*, *23*(2), 111–136.

Hoonakker, P. L. T., Carayon, P., Brown, R. L., Cartmill, R. S., Wetterneck, T. B., & Walker, J. M. (2013). Changes in end-user satisfaction with computerized provider order entry over time among nurses and providers in intensive care units. *Journal of the American Medical Informatics Association*, *20*(2), 252–259. doi:10.1136/amiajnl-2012-001114 PubMed

Hoonakker, P. L. T., Carayon, P., & Walker, J. M. (2010). Measurement of CPOE end-user satisfaction among ICU physicians and nurses. *Applied Clinical Informatics*, *1*(3), 268–285. doi:10.4338/ACI-2010-03-RA-0020 PubMed

Hoque, R. M., Hossin, E. M., & Khan, W. (2016). Strategic Information Systems Planning (SISP) Practices In Health Care Sectors Of Bangladesh. *European Scientific Journal*, *12*(6), 307–321. doi:10.19044/esj.2016.v12n6p307

Ho, S. Y., & Frampton, K. (2010). A competency model for the information technology workforce: Implications for training and selection. *Communications of the Association for Information Systems*, *27*(1), 63–80.

Hovelja, T., Rožanec, A., & Rupnik, R. (2010). Measuring The Success Of The Strategic Information Systems Planning. *Management*, *15*(2), 25–46.

Hovelja, T., Vasilecas, O., & Rupnik, R. (2013). A Model Of Influences Of Environmental Stakeholders On Strategic Information Systems Planning Success In And Enterprise. *Technological and Economic Development of Economy*, *19*(3), 465–488. doi:10.3846/20294913.2013.818591

Hsieh, P. J. (2015). Healthcare professionals' use of health clouds: Integrating technology acceptance and status quo bias perspectives. *International Journal of Medical Informatics*, *84*(7), 512–523. doi:10.1016/j.ijmedinf.2015.03.004 PubMed

Hsieh, Y.-H., Ya-Ting, L., & Leng-Heng, C. (2017). The Influence of Customer's Sharing Behavior in Social Commerce. In *Twenty-third Americas Conference on Information Systems* (pp. 259–264). Academic Press.

Hsu, H. C. C. (2015). Tourism and hospitality education in Asia. In D. Dredge, D. D. Airey, & M. J. Gross (Eds.), The routledge handbook of tourism and hospitality education (pp. 197–209). Academic Press.

Hsu, C. L., & Lin, J. C. C. (2016). Factors affecting the adoption of cloud services in enterprises. *Information Systems and e-Business Management*, *14*(4), 791–822. doi:10.100710257-015-0300-9

Hsu, C., & Park, H. W. (2011). Sociology of hyperlink networks of Web 1.0, Web 2.0, and Twitter: A case study of South Korea. *Social Science Computer Review*, *29*(3), 354–368. doi:10.1177/0894439310382517

Hsu, Y. C., Lin, Y. T., & Wang, T. (2015). A legitimacy challenge of a cross-cultural inters- organizational information system. *European Journal of Information Systems*, *24*(3), 278–294. doi:10.1057/ejis.2014.33

Hua, J., & Bapna, S. (2013). The economic impact of cyber terrorism. *The Journal of Strategic Information Systems*, *22*(2), 175–186. doi:10.1016/j.jsis.2012.10.004

Huang, H. (2014). *Social Media Generation in Urban China*. Academic Press.

Huang, H., & Leung, L. (2009). Instant messaging addiction among teenagers in China: Shyness, alienation, and academic performance decrement. *Cyberpsychology & Behavior*, *12*(6), 675–679. doi:10.1089/cpb.2009.0060 PMID:19788380

Huang, Z., & Benyoucef, M. (2013). From e-commerce to social commerce: A close look at design features. *Electronic Commerce Research and Applications*, *12*(4), 246–259. doi:10.1016/j.elerap.2012.12.003

Huang, Z., & Benyoucef, M. (2015). User preferences of social features on social commerce websites: An empirical study. *Technological Forecasting and Social Change*, *95*, 57–72. doi:10.1016/j.techfore.2014.03.005

Huang, Z., & Benyoucef, M. (2017). The effects of social commerce design on consumer purchase decision-making: An empirical study. *Electronic Commerce Research and Applications*, *25*, 40–58. doi:10.1016/j.elerap.2017.08.003

Hughes, D. J., Rowe, M., Batey, M., & Lee, A. (2012). A tale of two sites: Twitter vs. Facebook and the personality predictors of social media usage. *Computers in Human Behavior*, *28*(2), 561–569. doi:10.1016/j.chb.2011.11.001

Humbani, M., & Wiese, M. (2018). A cashless society for all: Determining consumers' readiness to adopt mobile payment services. *Journal of African Business*, *19*(3), 409–429. doi:10.1080/15228916.2017.1396792

Hung, S. Y., Huang, Y. W., Lin, C. C., Chen, K. C., & Tarn, J. (2016). Factors Influencing Business Intelligence Systems Implementation Success in the Enterprises. Association for Information Systems.

Hung, S., Chen, C., & Wang, K. (2014). Critical Success Factors for the Implementation of Integrated Healthcare Information Systems Projects: An Organisational Fit Perspective. *Communications of the Association for Information Systems*, *34*, 775–796. doi:10.17705/1CAIS.03439

Hung, S., Yen, D. C., & Wang, H. (2006). Applying data mining to telecom churn management. *Expert Systems with Applications*, *31*(3), 515–524. doi:10.1016/j.eswa.2005.09.080

Hunton, P. (2011). A rigorous approach to formalising the technical investigation stages of cybercrime and criminality within a UK law enforcement environment. *Digital Investigation*, *7*(3–4), 105–113. doi:10.1016/j.diin.2011.01.002

Hunton, P. (2012). Data attack of the cybercriminal: Investigating the digital currency of cybercrime. *Computer Law & Security Review*, *28*(2), 201–207. doi:10.1016/j.clsr.2012.01.007

Hussin, H., & Noor, R. M. (2005). *Innovating business through e-commerce: Exploring the willingness of Malaysian SMEs.* Paper presented at the Second International Conference on Innovation in IT, Dubai, UAE.

Hüther, O., & Krücken, G. (2018). Summarizing Reflections—Stability and Change in German Higher Education. In *Higher Education in Germany—Recent Developments in an International Perspective* (pp. 257–263). Cham: Springer. doi:10.1007/978-3-319-61479-3_8

Huy, L. V., Rowe, F., Truex, D., & Huynh, M. Q. (2012). An empirical study of determinants of e-commerce adoption in SMEs in Vietnam: An economy in transition. *Journal of Global Information Management*, *20*(3), 23–54. doi:10.4018/jgim.2012070102

Hwang, D., Pike, R., & Manson, D. (2016). The Development of an Educational Cloud for IS Curriculum through a Student-Run Data Center. *Information Systems Education Journal*, *14*(1), 62–70.

Hwang, D., & Soe, L. L. (2010). An Analysis of Career Tracks in the Design of IS Curricula in the US. *IS. Education Journal*, *8*(13).

Hyman, S. E., Malenka, R. C., & Nestler, E. J. (2006). Neural Mechanisms of Addiction: The Role of Reward-Related Learning and Memory. *Annual Review of Neuroscience*, *29*(1), 565–598. doi:10.1146/annurev.neuro.29.051605.113009 PMID:16776597

Iacovou, C. L., Benbasat, I., & Dexter, A. S. (1995). Electronic data interchange and small organizations: Adoption and impact of technology. *Management Information Systems Quarterly, 19*(4), 465–485. doi:10.2307/249629

Iansiti, M., & Levien, R. (2004). *The Keystone Advantage: What the New Dynamics of Business Ecosystems Mean for Strategy, Innovation, and Sustainability*. Harvard Business School Press.

IBM. (2016). *Innovation in the API economy: Building winning experiences and new capabilities to compete*. IBM Executive report.

Ibrahim, A. M., Jose, R. R., Rabie, A. N., Gerstle, T. L., Lee, B. T., & Lin, S. J. (2015). Three-dimensional printing in developing countries. *Plastic and Reconstructive Surgery. Global Open, 3*(7), e443. doi:10.1097/GOX.0000000000000298 PMID:26301132

Idowu, P., Cornford, D., & Bastin, L. (2008). Health Informatics Deployment in Nigeria. *Journal of Health Informatics in Developing Countries, 2*(1), 1–23.

IEEE. (2000). *The Authoritative Dictionary of IEEE Standards Terms* (7th ed.). IEEE Std.

Ifinedo, P. (2011). Internet/e-business technologies acceptance in Canada's SMEs: An exploratory investigation. *Internet Research, 21*(3), 255–281. doi:10.1108/10662241111139309

IFPI. (2019). *IFPI Global Music Report 2019: State of the music industry*. The Nielsen Company.

Ikiz, O. O., Sobaci, M. Z., Yavuz, N., & Karkin, N. (2014). Political use of Twitter: the case of metropolitan mayor candidates in 2014 local elections in Turkey. In *Proceedings of the 8th International Conference on Theory and Practice of Electronic Governance* (pp. 41-50). New York, NY: ACM. 10.1145/2691195.2691219

Ilin, V., Ivetic, J., & Simic, D. (2017). Understanding the determinants of e-business adoption in ERP-enabled firms and non-ERP-enabled firms: A case study of the Western Balkan Peninsula. *Technological Forecasting and Social Change, 125*, 206–223. doi:10.1016/j.techfore.2017.07.025

Iman, N. (2018). Is mobile payment still relevant in the fintech era. *Electronic Commerce Research and Applications, 30*, 72–82. doi:10.1016/j.elerap.2018.05.009

Inamdar, P. (2015). "PVO"-a solution to brand piracy. *The Business & Management Review, 5*(4), 62.

Index, R. A. M. P. (2018). *Cheapest prepaid mobile voice product by country (in USD)*. Retrieved from: https://researchictafrica.net/ramp_indices_portal/

Indiatsy, C. M., Mwangi, M. S., Mandere, E. N., Bichanga, J. M., & George, G. E. (2014). The application of Porter's five forces model on organization performance: A case of cooperative bank of Kenya Ltd. *European Journal of Business and Management, 6*(16), 75–85.

Infosys. (2018). *How Enterprises are Steering through Digital Disruption*. Infosys Limited. Retrieved on 6 April 2019 from https://www.infosys.com/digital-outlook/Documents/exclusive-report-digital-outlook.pdf

International Telecommunications Union. (2012). *ICT Facts and figures 2012*. Retrieved 25/07/2017 from http://www.itu.int/en/ITU D/Statistics/Documents/facts/ICTFactsFigures2012.pdf

International Telecommunications Union. (2013). *ICT Facts and Figures*. Retrieved from http://www.itu.int/en/ITU/Statistics/Documents/facts/ICTFactsFigures2013-e.pdf

International Telecommunications Union. (2016). *ICT Facts and figures 2016*. Retrieved 15/08/2016 from http://www.itu.int/en/ITU D/Statistics/Documents/facts/ICTFactsFigures2016.pdf

International Telecommunications Union. (2016). *Measuring the Information Society Report.* Retrieved 18/08/2017 from https://www.itu.int/en/ITU D/Statistics/Documents/publications/misr2016/MISR2016-w4.pdf

International Telecommunications Union. (2017). *ICT Facts and Figures January to July 2017.* Retrieved 12/08/2017 from http://www.itu.int/en/mediacentre/Pages/2017-PR37.aspx

Internet World State. (2019). *Internet penetration in Africa March 31, 2019.* Retrieved July 3, 2019, from, https://www.internetworldstats.com/stats1.htm

Internet World Stats. (2017). *Internet users statistics for Africa (Africa internet usage, 2019 population stats and Facebook subscribers).* Retrieved from: https://www.internetworldstats.com/stats1.htm

Inukollu, V. N., Keshamoni, D. D., Kang, T., & Inukollu, M. (2014). *Factors influencing quality of mobile apps: Role of mobile app development life cycle.* arXiv preprint arXiv:1410.4537

Ipeirotis, P. G., & Gabrilovich, E. (2014, April). Quizz: targeted crowdsourcing with a billion (potential) users. In *Proceedings of the 23rd international conference on World wide web* (pp. 143-154). ACM. 10.1145/2566486.2567988

Iqbal, J. (2018). Role of Data Mining in Managerial Decisions. International Journal of Scientific Research in Computer Science. *Engineering and Information Technology*, *4*(1), 262–267.

Irfan, M., Putra, S. J., Alam, C. N., Subiyakto, A., & Wahana, A. (2017). Readiness factors for information system strategic planning among universities in developing countries : a systematic review. In *2nd International Conference on Computing and Applied Informatics* (pp. 1–7). IOP Publishing.

Irwin, S. M., Slay, A., Raymond, J., Choo, K.-K., & Lui, L. (2014). Money laundering and terrorism financing in virtual environments: A feasibility study. *Journal of Money Laundering Control*, *17*(1), 50–75. doi:10.1108/JMLC-06-2013-0019

Isaias, P. (2018). Model for the enhancement of learning in higher education through the deployment of emerging technologies. *Journal of Information. Communication and Ethics in Society*, *16*(4), 401–412. doi:10.1108/JICES-04-2018-0036

Islam, J. U., Rahman, Z., & Hollebeek, L. D. (2018). Consumer engagement in online brand communities: A solicitation of congruity theory. *Internet Research*, *28*(1), 23–45. doi:10.1108/IntR-09-2016-0279

Islam, R., Islam, R., & Mazumder, T. (2010). Mobile application and its global impact. *IACSIT International Journal of Engineering and Technology*, *10*(6), 72–78.

Ismail, M. H., Khater, M., & Zaki, M. (2017). *Digital Business Transformation and Strategy: What Do We Know So Far.* Cambridge Service Alliance.

Ismail, N. (2017). The importance of data mining. Retrieved from https://www.information-age.com/importance-data-mining-123469819/

Ismail, M. A. A., Ahmad, A., Mohammad, J. A. M., Fakri, N. M. R. M., Nor, M. Z. M., & Pa, M. N. M. (2019). Using Kahoot! as a formative assessment tool in medical education: A phenomenological study. *BMC Medical Education*, *19*(1), 230. doi:10.118612909-019-1658-z PMID:31238926

ISO 16100. (2002). *Manufacturing Software Capability Profiling for interoperability, Part 1: Framework, TC 184/SC5/WG4.* Geneva, Switzerland: ICS 25.040.01, 2002.

Iyengar, K., Khanna, S., Ramadath, S., & Stephens, D. (2017, September). *What it really takes to capture the value of APIs.* Retrieved January 2019, from https://www.mckinsey.com/: https://www.mckinsey.com/business-functions/mckinsey-digital/our-insights/what-it-really-takes-to-capture-the-value-of-apis

Jackson, T. (2017, May). Uber's Africa Push Hits Roadblocks. Fortune, 14.

Jackson, J. D., Mun, Y. Y., & Park, J. S. (2013). An empirical test of three mediation models for the relationship between personal innovativeness and user acceptance of technology. *Information & Management, 50*(4), 154–161. doi:10.1016/j.im.2013.02.006

Jacobi, F., Jahn, S., Krawatzeck, R., Dinter, B., & Lorenz, A. (2014). Towards a Design Model for Interdisciplinary Information Systems Curriculum Development, as Exemplified by Big Data Analytics Education. *Proceedings of the European Conference on Information Systems (ECIS) 2014.*

Jacobson, C. M., Kasper, G. M., Mathieu, R. G., McFarland, D. J., & Meservy, R. D. (2011). AMCIS 2010 panel report: External benchmarks in information systems program assessment. *Communications of the Association for Information Systems, 29*(1), 367–378.

Jafar, M. J., Babb, J., & Abdullat, A. (2017). Emergence of Data Analytics in the Information Systems Curriculum Musa. *IS Education Journal, 15*(5).

Jain, M., Le, A. N. H., Lin, J. Y. C., & Cheng, J. M. S. (2011). Exploring the factors favoring m-commerce adoption among Indian MSMEs: A TOE perspective. *Tunghai Management Review, 13*(1), 147–188.

Jaishankar, K. (2008). Space transition theory of cyber crimes. *Crimes of the Internet*, 283–301.

Jaldemark, J. (2018). Contexts of learning and challenges of mobility: Designing for a blur between formal and informal learning. In *Mobile and Ubiquitous Learning* (pp. 141–155). Singapore: Springer. doi:10.1007/978-981-10-6144-8_9

Jamsrandorj, U. (2017). *Decentralized access control using blockchain* (Master's thesis, University of Saskatchewan, Saskatoon). Retrieved from https://ecommons.usask.ca/bitstream/handle/10388/8087/JAMSRANDORJ-THESIS 2017.pdf?sequence=1

Janicki, T. N., Cummings, J., & Healy, R. J. (2015). Incorporating a Human-Computer Interaction Course into Software Development Curriculums. *Information Systems Education Journal, 13*(3), 81–98.

Jansen, J., & Leukfeldt, R. (2015). How people help fraudsters steal their money: An analysis of 600 online banking fraud cases. In Socio-Technical Aspects in Security and Trust (STAST), 2015 Workshop On, (pp. 24–31). IEEE.

Jarvenpaa, S. L., Ives, B., & Davis, G. B. (1991). Supply/Demand of IS Doctorates in the 1990s. *Communications of the ACM, 34*(1), 86–98. doi:10.1145/99977.99996

Jarvenpaa, S. L., & Lang, K. R. (2005). Managing the paradoxes of mobile technology. *Information Systems Management, 22*(4), 7–23. doi:10.1201/1078.10580530/45520.22.4.20050901/90026.2

Jaunky, V. C., Roopchund, R., Ramesh, V., & Jaunky, V. (2018). Use of Social Media for Improving Student Engagement at Université des Mascareignes (UDM). *Proceedings of Fifth International Conference INDIA 2018.* 10.1007/978-981-13-3338-5_2

Jee, K., & Kim, G.-K. (2013). The potentiality of Big Data in the Medical Sector: Focus on how to Reshape the Healthcare Sector. *Healthcare Informatics Research, 19*(2), 79–85. doi:10.4258/hir.2013.19.2.79 PMID:23882412

Jenaro, C., Flores, N., Gómez-Vela, M., González-Gil, F., & Caballo, C. (2007). Problematic internet and cell-phone use: Psychological, behavioral, and health correlates. *Addiction Research and Theory, 15*(3), 309–320. doi:10.1080/16066350701350247

Jenkin, T. A., Chan, Y. E., & Sabherwal, R. (2019). Mutual understanding in information systems development: Changes within and across projects. *Management Information Systems Quarterly, 43*(2), 649–672. doi:10.25300/MISQ/2019/13980

Jennings, H., & Ude, I. (2011). *New African Fashion*. New York: Prestel.

Jensen-Haxel, P. (2015). A New Framework for a Novel Lattice: 3D Printers, DNA Fabricators, and the Perils in Regulating the Raw Materials of the Next Era of Revolution, Renaissance, and Research. *Wake Forest JL & Poly, 5*, 231.

Jensen, M. C., & Meckling, W. H. (1976). Theory of the firm: Managerial behavior, agency costs and ownership structure. *Journal of Financial Economics, 3*(4), 305–360. doi:10.1016/0304-405X(76)90026-X

Jeon, B. N., Han, K. S., & Lee, M. J. (2006). Determining factors for the adoption of e-business: The case of SMEs in Korea. *Applied Economics, 38*(16), 1905–1916. doi:10.1080/00036840500427262

Jeong, O.-R., Kim, C., Kim, W., & So, J. (2011). Botnets: Threats and responses. *International Journal of Web Information Systems, 7*(1), 6–17. doi:10.1108/17440081111125635

Jeong, S. H., Kim, H., Yum, J. Y., & Hwang, Y. (2016). What type of content are smartphone users addicted to?: SNS vs. games. *Computers in Human Behavior, 54*, 10–17. doi:10.1016/j.chb.2015.07.035

Jesson, J., Matheson, L., & Lacey, F. M. (2011). *Doing your Literature Review: Traditional and Systematic Techniques.* London: Sage Publications.

Jhally, S., & Livant, B. (1986). Watching as working: The valorization of audience consciousness. *Journal of Communication, 36*(3), 124–143. doi:10.1111/j.1460-2466.1986.tb01442.x

Jiang, J. J., Muhanna, W. A., & Klein, G. (2000). User resistance and strategies for promoting acceptance across system types. *Information & Management, 37*(1), 25–36. doi:10.1016/S0378-7206(99)00032-4

Jiang, J., Zhu, A., Qin, C., Zhu, T., Liu, J., Du, F., ... An, Y. (2016). CyberSoLIM: A cyber platform for digital soil mapping. *Geoderma, 263*, 234–243. doi:10.1016/j.geoderma.2015.04.018

Jia, R., & Jia, H. H. (2009). Factorial validity of problematic Internet use scales. *Computers in Human Behavior, 25*(6), 1335–1342. doi:10.1016/j.chb.2009.06.004

Jiménez, M., Romero, L., Domínguez, I. A., Espinosa, M. D. M., & Domínguez, M. (2019). Additive Manufacturing Technologies: An Overview about 3D Printing Methods and Future Prospects. *Complexity.*

Jin, X., Zheng, H., Jin, R., & Li, Y. (2017). Understanding Consumers' trust in third-party Online Payment. In PACIS (p. 175). Academic Press.

Jing, D. Z., & Hock, C. C. (2012). Government Regulation of Online Game Addiction. *Communications of the Association for Information Systems, 30*(13), 187–198.

Jin, H., Park, S. T., & Li, G. (2015). Factors influencing customer participation in mobile SNS: Focusing on Wechat in China. *Indian Journal of Science and Technology, 8*(26), 1–8. doi:10.17485/ijst/2015/v8i26/80714

Johnson, T. J., & Kaye, B. K. (2015). Reasons to believe: Influence of credibility on motivations for using social networks. *Computers in Human Behavior, 50*, 544–555. doi:10.1016/j.chb.2015.04.002

Joinson, A. N., Reips, U. D., Buchanan, T., & Paine Schofield, C. B. (2010). Privacy, trust, and self-disclosure online. *Human-Computer Interaction, 25*(1), 1–24. doi:10.1080/07370020903586662

Jones, K., & Ceccucci, W. (2018). International Service Learning in IS Programs: The Next Phase – An Implementation Experience. *IS Education Journal, 16*(4).

Jones, B. A., Madden, G. J., & Wengreen, H. J. (2014). The FIT Game: Preliminary evaluation of a gamification approach to increasing fruit and vegetable consumption in school. *Preventive Medicine, 68*, 76–79. doi:10.1016/j.ypmed.2014.04.015 PMID:24768916

Jones, C. G., & Liu, D. (2017). Approaches to Incorporating IT Entrepreneurship into the Information Systems Curriculum. *Journal of Information Systems Education, 28*(November), 43–59.

Jones, K., Leonard, L. N. K., & Lang, G. (2016). Desired Skills for Entry Level IS Positions: Identification and Assessment. *Journal of Computer Information Systems, 0*(0), 1–7.

Jones, S., Irani, Z., Sivarajah, U., & Love, P. E. (2017). Risks and rewards of cloud computing in the UK public sector: A reflection on three Organizational case studies. *Information Systems Frontiers*, 1–24.

Jonsson, K., Westergren, U., & Holmström, J. (2008). Technologies for value creation: An exploration of remote diagnostics systems in the manufacturing industry. *Information Systems Journal, 18*(3), 227–245. doi:10.1111/j.1365-2575.2007.00267.x

Joshi, K. (1991). A Model of Users' Perspective on Change: The Case of Information Systems Technology Implementation. *Management Information Systems Quarterly, 15*(2), 229. doi:10.2307/249384

Joshi, K. (2005). Understanding User Resistance and Acceptance during the Implementation of an Order Management System: A Case Study Using the Equity Implementation Model. *Journal of Information Technology Case and Application Research, 7*(1), 6–20. doi:10.1080/15228053.2005.10856057

Ju, J., Cho, D., Lee, J. K., & Ahn, J.-H. (2016). *An Empirical Study on Anti-spam Legislation*. Academic Press.

Junglas, I., & Watson, R. T. (2006). The U-Constructs : Four Information Drives. *Communications of the Association for Information Systems, 17*(26), 569–592.

Kaaria, S. K., & Njuguna, R. (2019). Organizational Attributes and Implementation of Enterprise Resource Planning: A Case of Kenya Medical Research Institute, Kilifi County. *International Journal of Current Aspects, 3*(II), 231–242. doi:10.35942/ijcab.v3iII.20

Kabanda, S., & Brown, I. (2017). A structuration analysis of Small and Medium Enterprise (SME) adoption of E-Commerce: The case of Tanzania. *Telematics and Informatics, 34*(4), 118–132. doi:10.1016/j.tele.2017.01.002

Kaganer, E., Pawlowski, S. D., & Wiley-Patton, S. (2010). Building Legitimacy for IT Innovations: The Case of Computerized Physician Order Entry Systems. *Journal of the Association for Information Systems, 11*(1), 1–33. doi:10.17705/1jais.00219

Kahneman, D., & Tversky, A. (1979). Prospect Theory: An Analysis of Decision under Risk. *Econometrica, 47*(2), 263–292. doi:10.2307/1914185

Kaiser, K. M., Goles, T., Hawk, S., Simon, J. C., & Frampton, K. (2011). Information Systems Skills Differences Between High-Wage and Low-Wage Regions : Implications for Global Sourcing. *Communications of the Association for Information Systems, 29*(32), 605–626.

Kamariotou, M., & Kitsios, F. (2015). Information Systems Phases and Firm Performance: A conceptual Framework. Paper presented at 1st International Conference on Business Informatics and Modelling.

Kamariotou, M., & Kitsios, F. (2015). Innovating with Strategic Information Systems Strategy. Paper presented at International Conference on Applied Innovation, Arta, Greece.

Kamariotou, M., & Kitsios, F. (2018). An Empirical Evaluation of Strategic Information Systems Planning Phases in SMEs : Determinants of Effectiveness. In Proceedings of 6th International Symposium and 28th National Conference on Operational Research (pp. 67–72). Retrieved from http://eeee2017.uom.gr/HELORS_2017_Book_of_Proceedings.pdf

Kamunya, S., Maina, E., & Oboko, R. (2019). A Gamification Model For E-Learning Platforms. In 2019 IST-Africa Week Conference (IST-Africa) (pp. 1-9). IEEE. doi:10.23919/ISTAFRICA.2019.8764879

Kane, G. C., Palmer, D., Phillips, A. N., Kiron, D., & Buckley, N. (2015). Strategy, not technology, drives digital transformation. *MIT Sloan Management Review and Deloitte University Press, 14*, 1–25.

Kapoor, K. K., Tamilmani, K., Rana, N. P., Patil, P., Dwivedi, Y. K., & Nerur, S. (2018). Advances in social media research: Past, present and future. *Information Systems Frontiers, 20*(3).

Kapp, K. M. (2013). *The Gamification of Learning and Instruction Fieldbook: Ideas into Practice*. San Francisco: John Wiley & Sons.

Karatas, D., & Saka, E. (2017). Online political trolling in the context of post-Gezi social media in Turkey. *International Journal of Digital Television, 8*(3), 383–401. doi:10.1386/jdtv.8.3.383_1

Karimi, J. (2017). *Effects of Enterprise Resource Planning Implementation on Organizational Performance in the Transport Industry in Kenya* (Doctoral dissertation). United States International University-Africa.

Karsten, R., & Roth, R. M. (2015). A Complementary Measure of MIS Program Outcomes: Useful Insights from a Student Perspective. *Journal of Information Systems Education, 26*(2), 155–164.

Karwatzki, S., Trenz, M., Tuunainen, V. K., & Veit, D. (2017). Adverse consequences of access to individuals' information: An analysis of perceptions and the scope of organisational influence. *European Journal of Information Systems, 26*(6), 688–715. doi:10.105741303-017-0064-z

Kasemsap, K. (2017). Telemedicine and electronic health: Issues and implications in developing countries. In *In Health information systems and the advancement of medical practice in developing countries* (pp. 149–167). IGI Global. doi:10.4018/978-1-5225-2262-1.ch009

Kasinathan, V., Mustapha, A., Fauzi, R., & Rani, M. F. C. A. (2018). Questionify: Gamification in Education. *International Journal of Integrated Engineering, 10*(6). doi:10.30880/ijie.2018.10.06.019

Kässi, O., & Lehdonvirta, V. (2018). Online labour index: Measuring the online gig economy for policy and research. *Technological Forecasting and Social Change, 137*, 241–248. doi:10.1016/j.techfore.2018.07.056

Kathuria, V., & Oh, K. Y. (2018). ICT access: Testing for convergence across countries. *The Information Society, 34*(3), 166–182. doi:10.1080/01972243.2018.1438549

Katule, N., Rivett, U., & Densmore, M. (2016, November). A family health app: Engaging children to manage wellness of adults. In *Proceedings of the 7th Annual Symposium on Computing for Development* (p. 7). ACM. 10.1145/3001913.3001920

Katz, R. (2017). Social and economic impact of digital transformation on the economy. *International Telecommunication Union (ITU)*. Retrieved from https://www.itu.int/en/ITU-D/Conferences/GSR/Documents/GSR2017/Soc_Eco_impact_Digital_transformation_finalGSR.pdf

Kaufman, I., & Horton, C. (2015, Dec.). Digital transformation: leveraging digital technology with core values to achieve sustainable business goals. *Eur. Financ. Rev.*, 63-67.

Kaur, B. P., & Aggrawal, H. (2013). Exploration of Success Factors of Information System. *International Journal of Computer Science Issues, 10*(1), 226–235.

Kavadias, S., Ladas, K., & Loch, C. (2016). The transformative business model. *Harvard Business Review, 94*(10), 91–98.

Kayser, V., Nehrke, B., & Zubovic, D. (2018). Data science as an innovation challenge: from big data to value proposition. *Technology Innovation Management Review, 8*(3).

Kazan, E., & Damsgaard, J. (2016). Towards a Market Entry Framework for Digital Payment Platforms. CAIS, 38, 37.

Kazan, E., & Damsgaard, J. (2016). Towards a Market Entry Framework for Digital Payment Platforms. *Communications of the Association for Information Systems, 38*, 761–783. doi:10.17705/1CAIS.03837

Keating, S., & Oxman, N. (2013). Compound fabrication: A multi-functional robotic platform for digital design and fabrication. *Robotics and Computer-integrated Manufacturing, 29*(6), 439–448. doi:10.1016/j.rcim.2013.05.001

Keen, P., & Williams, R. (2013). Value architectures for digital business: Beyond the business model. *Management Information Systems Quarterly, 37*(2), 643–648.

Kelders, S. M., Sommers-Spijkerman, M., & Goldberg, J. (2018). Investigating the direct impact of a gamified versus nongamified well-being intervention: An exploratory experiment. *Journal of Medical Internet Research, 20*(7), e247. doi:10.2196/jmir.9923 PMID:30049669

Kelley, P. G., Cranor, L. F., & Sadeh, N. (2013). Privacy as part of the app decision-making process. *CHI, 2013*, 1–11.

Kennedy, J. P., Wilson, J., & Labrecque, R. (2017). Towards a more proactive approach to brand protection: Development of the Organisational Risk Assessment for Product Counterfeiting (ORAPC). *Global Crime, 18*(4), 329–352. doi:10.1080/17440572.2017.1313733

Kenney, M., & Zysman, J. (2016). The rise of the platform economy. *Issues in Science and Technology, 32*(3), 61.

Kesner, R. M. (2008). Business School Undergraduate Information Management Competencies: A Study of Employer Expectations and Associated Curricular Recommendations. *Communications of the Association for Information Systems, 23*, 633–654. doi:10.17705/1CAIS.02335

Kesse-Tachi, A., Asmah, A. E., & Agbozo, E. (2019). Factors influencing the adoption of eHealth technologies in Ghana. *Digital Health, 5*. doi:10.1177/2055207619871425

Kessler, S. (2014). Pixel and dimed on (not) getting by in the gig economy. *Fast Company*. Retrieved September June 30, 2018 from http://www.fastcompany.com/3027355/pixel-and-dimedon-not-getting-by-in-the-gig-economy

Keyton, J. (2017). Communication in organizations. *Annual Review of Organizational Psychology and Organizational Behavior, 4*(1), 501–526. doi:10.1146/annurev-orgpsych-032516-113341

Khaleel, F. L., Ashaari, N. S., & Wook, T. S. M. T. (2019). An empirical study on gamification for learning programming language website. *Jurnal Teknologi, 81*(2).

Khaleel, F. L., Sahari, N., Wook, T. S. M. T., & Ismail, A. (2016). Gamification elements for learning applications. *International Journal on Advanced Science. Engineering and Information Technology, 6*(6), 868–874.

Khalifa, M., Cheng, S. K. N., & Shen, K. N. (2012). Adoption of mobile commerce: A confidence model. *Journal of Computer Information Systems, 53*(1), 14–22.

Khan, N., Shafi, S., & Ahangar, H. (2018). Digitization of Cultural Heritage: Global Initiatives, Opportunities, and Challenges. *Journal of Cases on Information Technology, 20*(4), 1–16. doi:10.4018/JCIT.2018100101

Khanna, S., Ratan, A., Davis, J., & Thies, W. (2010, December). Evaluating and improving the usability of Mechanical Turk for low-income workers in India. In *Proceedings of the first ACM symposium on computing for development* (p. 12). ACM. 10.1145/1926180.1926195

Khudnev, E. (2017). *Blockchain: Foundational technology to change the world* (Master's thesis, Lapland University of Applied Sciences). Retrieved from https://www.theseus.fi/bitstream/handle/10024/138043/Evgenii_Khudnev_Thesis.pdf?sequence=1

Kim, H., & Shin, D. (2017). The effects of platform as a technology standard on platform-based repurchases. doi:10.1108/DPRG-11-2016-0054

Kim, Y. A., & Srivastava, J. (2007). Impact of social influence in e-commerce decision making. Proceedings of the Ninth International Conference on Electronic Commerce - ICEC '07, 293. doi:10.1145/1282100.1282157

Kim, C., Ko, E., & Koh, J. (2016). Consumer attitudes and purchase intentions toward fashion counterfeits: Moderating the effects of types of counterfeit goods and consumer characteristics. *Journal of Global Fashion Marketing*, 7(1), 15–29. doi:10.1080/20932685.2015.1105109

Kim, D., Park, K., Park, Y., & Ahn, J. H. (2019). Willingness to provide personal information: Perspective of privacy calculus in IoT services. *Computers in Human Behavior*, 92, 273–281. doi:10.1016/j.chb.2018.11.022

Kim, G. S., Park, S. B., & Oh, J. (2008). An examination of factors influencing consumer adoption of short message service (SMS). *Psychology and Marketing*, 25(8), 769–786. doi:10.1002/mar.20238

Kim, H. W. (2011). The effects of switching costs on user resistance to enterprise systems implementation. *IEEE Transactions on Engineering Management*, 58(3), 471–482. doi:10.1109/TEM.2010.2089630

Kim, H., & Karpova, E. (2010). Consumer attitudes toward fashion counterfeits: Application of the theory of planned behaviour. *Clothing & Textiles Research Journal*, 28(2), 79–94. doi:10.1177/0887302X09332513

Kim, H.-W., & Kankanhalli, A. (2009). Investigating User Resistance to Information Systems Implementation: A Status Quo Bias Perspective. *Management Information Systems Quarterly*, 33(3), 567. doi:10.2307/20650309

Kim, J. E., & Johnson, K. P. (2014). Shame or pride? The moderating role of self-construal on moral judgments concerning fashion counterfeits. *European Journal of Marketing*, 48(7/8), 1431–1450. doi:10.1108/EJM-02-2013-0110

Kim, J., Kim, S., & Nam, C. (2016). Competitive dynamics in the Korean video platform market : Traditional pay TV platforms vs OTT platforms. *Telematics and Informatics*, 33(2), 711–721. doi:10.1016/j.tele.2015.06.014

Kim, S., & Hyun, T. (2018). Examining the antecedents and consequences of mobile app engagement. *Telematics and Informatics*, 35(1), 148–158. doi:10.1016/j.tele.2017.10.008

Kim, S., & Park, H. (2013). Effects of various characteristics of social commerce (s-commerce) on consumers' trust and trust performance. *International Journal of Information Management*, 33(2), 318–332. doi:10.1016/j.ijinfomgt.2012.11.006

Kim, T. T., Suh, Y. K., Lee, G., & Choi, B. G. (2010). Modelling roles of task-technology fit and self-efficacy in hotel employees' usage behaviour of hotel information systems. *International Journal of Tourism Research*, 12(6), 709–725. doi:10.1002/jtr.787

Kim, Y. (2012). The Shifting Sands of Citizenship: Toward a Model of the Citizenry in Life Politics. *The Annals of the American Academy of Political and Social Science*, 644(1), 147–158. doi:10.1177/0002716212456008

Kind, T. (2015). Professional guidelines for social media use a starting point. *AMA Journal of Ethics*, 17(5), 441–447. doi:10.1001/journalofethics.2015.17.5.nlit1-1505 PubMed

King, D., Delfabbro, P., & Griffiths, M. (2010). Video game structural characteristics: A new psychological taxonomy. *International Journal of Mental Health and Addiction*, 8(1), 90–106. doi:10.100711469-009-9206-4

King, V., Valença, A. M., & Nardi, A. E. (2010). Nomophobia: the mobile phone in panic disorder with agoraphobia: reducing phobias or worsening of dependence? *Cognitive and Behavioral Neurology*, 23(1), 52–54. doi:10.1097/WNN.0b013e3181b7eabc PMID:20299865

King, W. R. (1988). How Effective is Your Information Systems Planning? *Long Range Planning*, *21*(5), 103–112. doi:10.1016/0024-6301(88)90111-2

Kirsch, L. J. (2004). Deploying Common Systems Globally: The Dynamics of Control. *Information Systems Research*, *4*(15), 374–395. doi:10.1287/isre.1040.0036

Kiruthika, K., & Sivakumar, S. (2017). Analysis of Students' behaviour and learning using classification of Data mining methods. *International Journal of Computational and Applied Mathematics*, *12*(1).

Kitsios, F., & Kamariotou, M. (2016). Decision Support Systems and Business Strategy : A conceptual framework for Strategic Information Systems Planning. 2016 6th International Conference on IT Convergence and Security (ICITCS), 1–5. 10.1109/ICITCS.2016.7740323

Kiunguyu, K. (2019). Ghana: Google Opens Its First Artificial Intelligence Lab on the Continent. *All Africa*. Retrieved from https://allafrica.com/stories/201904180055.html

Kizior, R. J., & Hidding, G. J. (2010). Emphasizing Business Analysis to Increase IS Enrollments. *IS Education Journal*, *8*(47), 3–8.

Kleine, D. (2010). ICT4What? Using the Choice Framework to operationalise the capability approach to development. *Journal of International Development*, *22*(5), 674–692. doi:10.1002/jid.1719

Klein, H. K., & Myers, M. D. (1999). A set of principles for conducting and evaluating interpretive field studies. *Management Information Systems Quarterly*, *23*(1), 67–94. doi:10.2307/249410

Kline, R. B. (2011). *Principles and practice of structural equation modelling*. New York, NY: The Guilford Press.

Kling, R. (1980). Computer abuse and computer crime as organizational activities. *Computer/Law Journal*, *2*, 403.

Klonoff, D. C. (2013). The current status of mHealth for diabetes: Will it be the next big thing? *Journal of Diabetes Science and Technology*, *7*(3), 749–758. doi:10.1177/193229681300700321 PMID:23759409

Klouwenberg, M. K., Koot, W. J. D., & Van Schaik, J. A. M. (1995). Establishing business strategy with information technology. *Information Management & Computer Security*, *3*(5), 8–20. doi:10.1108/09685229510104945

Knorr, E., & Gruman, G. (2008). What cloud computing really means. *InfoWorld*, *7*, 20–20.

Koh, B., Hann, I.-H., & Raghunathan, S. (2019). Digitisation of music: Consumer adoption amidst piracy, unbundling, and rebundling. *Management Information Systems Quarterly*, *43*(1), 23–45. doi:10.25300/MISQ/2019/14812

Koh, C. E., Prybutok, V. R., Ryan, S. D., & Wu, Y. A. (2010). A model for mandatory use of software technologies: An integrative approach by applying multiple levels of abstraction of informing science. Informing Science. *The International Journal of an Emerging Trans Discipline*, *13*, 177–203.

Kohler, T., Fueller, J., Matzler, K., Stieger, D., & Füller. (2011). CO-creation in virtual worlds: The design of the user experience. MIS Quarterly: Management Information Systems, 35(3), 773–788. doi:10.2307/23042808

Kohler, T., Fueller, J., Stieger, D., & Matzler, K. (2011). Avatar-based innovation: Consequences of the virtual co-creation experience. *Computers in Human Behavior*, *27*(1), 160–168. doi:10.1016/j.chb.2010.07.019

Kohli, R., & Grover, V. (2008). Business Value of IT: An Essay on Expanding Research Directions to Keep up with the Times. *Journal of the Association for Information Systems*, *9*(1), 23–39. doi:10.17705/1jais.00147

Kohli, R., & Johnson, S. (2011). Digital Transformation in Latecomer Industries: CIO and CEO Leadership Lessons from Encana Oil & Gas (USA) Inc. *MIS Quarterly Executive*, *10*(4).

Koivisto, J., & Hamari, J. (2019). The rise of motivational information systems: A review of gamification research. *International Journal of Information Management, 45*, 191–210. doi:10.1016/j.ijinfomgt.2018.10.013

Kok, J. N., Boers, E. J., Kosters, W. A., Van der Putten, P., & Poel, M. (2009). Artificial intelligence: Definition, trends, techniques, and cases. *Artificial Intelligence*, 1.

Kokolakis, S. (2017). Privacy attitudes and privacy behaviour: A review of current research on the privacy paradox phenomenon. *Computers & Security, 64*, 122–134. doi:10.1016/j.cose.2015.07.002

Kolog, E. C.S., M., & T., T. (2018). Using Machine Learning for Sentiment and Social Influence Analysis in Text. In Proceedings of the International Conference on Information Technology & Systems, (pp. 1-14). Ecudor. doi:10.1007/978-3-319-73450-7_43

Kolog, E. A., & Montero, C. S. (2018). Towards automated e-counselling system based on counsellors emotion perception. *Education and Information Technologies, 23*(2), 1–23. doi:10.1007/s10639-017-9643-9

Kolog, E., Montero, S. C., & Sutinen, E. (2016). Annotation Agreement of Emotions in Text: The Influence of Counselors' Emotional State on their Emotion Perception. In *Proceeding of International Conference on Advanced Learning Technologies (ICALT)* (pp. 357-359). IEEE.

Kondra, A. Z., & Hurst, D. C. (2009). Institutional processes of organizational culture. *Culture and Organization, 15*(1), 39–58. doi:10.1080/14759550802709541

König, M., & Neumayr, L. (2017). Users' resistance towards radical innovations: The case of the self-driving car. *Transportation Research Part F: Traffic Psychology and Behaviour, 44*, 42–52. doi:10.1016/j.trf.2016.10.013

Kooti, F., Grbovic, M., Aiello, L. M., Djuric, N., Radosavljevic, V., & Lerman, K. (2017, April). Analyzing Uber's ridesharing economy. In *Proceedings of the 26th International Conference on World Wide Web Companion* (pp. 574-582). International World Wide Web Conferences Steering Committee. 10.1145/3041021.3054194

Kostopoulos, C. K., Spanos, Y. E., & Prastacos, G. P. (2002). The Rseource-Based View of the Firm and Innovation:Identification of Critical Linkages. In *The 2nd* (pp. 1–19). European Academy of Managemnt Conference; Retrieved from http://ecsocman.hse.ru/data/165/663/1219/rb_view.pdf

Koszalka, T. A., & Ntloedibe-Kuswani, G. S. (2010). Literature on the safe and disruptive learning potential of mobile technologies. *Distance Education, 31*(2), 139–157. doi:10.1080/01587919.2010.498082

Kotabe, M., & Kothari, T. (2016). Emerging market multinational companies' evolutionary paths to building a competitive advantage from emerging markets to developed countries. *Journal of World Business, 51*(5), 729–743. doi:10.1016/j.jwb.2016.07.010

Kothandaraman, P., & Wilson, D. (2001). The future of competition: Value-creating networks. *Industrial Marketing Management, 30*(4), 379–389. doi:10.1016/S0019-8501(00)00152-8

Kothman, I., & Faber, N. (2016). How 3D printing technology changes the rules of the game: Insights from the construction sector. *Journal of Manufacturing Technology Management, 27*(7), 932–943. doi:10.1108/JMTM-01-2016-0010

Kovács, A., Van Looy, B., & Cassiman, B. (2015). Exploring the scope of open innovation: A bibliometric review of a decade of research. *Scientometrics, 104*(3), 951–983. doi:10.1007/s11192-015-1628-0

Kovacs, G., & Spens, K. M. (2005). Abductive reasoning in logistics. *International Journal of Physical Distribution & Logistics Management, 35*(2), 132–144. doi:10.1108/09600030510590318

Kraemer-Mbula, E., Tang, P., & Rush, H. (2013). The cybercrime ecosystem: Online innovation in the shadows? *Technological Forecasting and Social Change, 80*(3), 541–555. doi:10.1016/j.techfore.2012.07.002

Krantz, J. (2001). Dilemmas of organizational change: A systems psychodynamic perspective. *The systems psychodynamics of organizations: Integrating the group relations approach, psychoanalytic, and open systems perspectives*, 133-156.

Kreiss, D. (2016). Seizing the moment: The presidential campaigns' use of Twitter during the 2012 electoral cycle. *New Media & Society, 18*(8), 1473–1490. doi:10.1177/1461444814562445

Krell, K., Matook, S., & Rhode, F. (2016). The impact of legitimacy based motives on IS adoption success: An institutional theory perspective. *Information & Management, 53*(6), 683–697. doi:10.1016/j.im.2016.02.006

Kroll, J., Richardson, I., Prikladnicki, R., & Audy, J. (2018). Empirical evidence in follow the Sun software development: A systematic mapping study. *Information and Software Technology, 93*, 30–44. doi:10.1016/j.infsof.2017.08.011

Kruck, S. E., Mathieu, R. G., & Mitri, M. (2013). Research in Information Systems Education: Scope and Productivity. *Journal of Computer Information Systems, 54*(1), 34–41. doi:10.1080/08874417.2013.11645669

Kruikemeier, S., Gattermann, K., & Vliegenthart, R. (2018). Understanding the dynamics of politicians' visibility in traditional and social media. *The Information Society, 34*(4), 215–228. doi:10.1080/01972243.2018.1463334

Kuan, K. K. Y., & Chau, P. Y. K. (2001). A Perception-based Model for EDI Adoption in Small Business Using a Technology-Organization-environment Framework. *Information & Management, 38*(8), 507–512. doi:10.1016/S0378-7206(01)00073-8

Kubicek, H., & Cimander, R. (2009). Three dimensions of organizational interoperability. *European Journal of ePractice, 6*, 1-12.

Kuhn, T. S. (1962). The structure of scientific revolutions. *Journal of the History of the Behavioral Sciences, 2*, 274–276.

Kumar, A., Shah, V., & Smart, K. (2017). Moving Forward by Looking Backward : Using Backward Design to Develop an Innovative MSIS Program. In Twenty-third AMCIS (pp. 1–10). Academic Press.

Kumaraswamy, A., Garud, R., & Ansari, S. (2018). Perspectives on Disruptive Innovations. *Journal of Management Studies, 55*(7), 1025–1042. doi:10.1111/joms.12399

Kumar, V., Maheshwari, B., & Kumar, U. (2002). Enterprise resource planning systems adoption process: A survey of Canadian organizations. *International Journal of Production Research, 40*(3), 509–523. doi:10.1080/00207540110092414

Kurnia, S., Karnali, R. J., & Rahim, M. M. (2015). A qualitative study of business-to-business electronic commerce adoption within the Indonesian grocery industry: A multi-theory perspective. *Information & Management, 52*(4), 518–536. doi:10.1016/j.im.2015.03.003

Kurnia, S., Smith, S. P., & Lee, H. (2014). Consumer's perception of mobile internet in Australia. *E-Business Review, 5*(1), 19–32.

Kurt, H., & Karaduman, S. (2012). Usage of social media by political actors: An analysis on the usage of Twitter by leaders of political parties in Turkey. *Medianali, 6*(12), 1–15.

Kushins, E. R., Heard, H., & Weber, J. M. (2017). Disruptive innovation in rural American healthcare: The physician assistant practice. *International Journal of Pharmaceutical and Healthcare Marketing, 11*(2), 165–182. doi:10.1108/IJPHM-10-2016-0056

Kuss, D. J., & Griffiths, M. D. (2011). Online social networking and addiction a review of the psychological literature. *International Journal of Environmental Research and Public Health*, 8(9), 3528–3552. doi:10.3390/ijerph8093528 PMID:22016701

Kuzel, A. J. (1992). *Sampling in qualitative inquiry*. Academic Press.

Kwakwa, P. A. (2012). Mobile phone usage by micro and small scale enterprises in semi-rural Ghana. *International Review of Management and Marketing*, 2(3), 156–164.

Lai, P. M., & Chuah, K. B. (2010, October). Developing an analytical framework for mobile payments adoption in retailing: A supply-side perspective. In 2010 Fourth International Conference on Management of e-Commerce and e-Government (ICMeCG) (pp. 356–361). IEEE doi:10.1109/ICMeCG.2010.79

Lai, K. K. Y., & Zaichkowsky, J. L. (1999). Brand imitation: Do the Chinese have different views? *Asia Pacific Journal of Management*, 16(2), 179–192. doi:10.1023/A:1015482707900

Lakhal, S., & Khechine, H. (2017). Relating personality (Big Five) to the core constructs of the unified theory of acceptance and use of technology. *Journal of Computers in Education*, 4(3), 251–282. doi:10.1007/s40692-017-0086-5

Lakhal, S., Khechine, H., & Pascot, D. (2013). Student behavioural intention to use desktop video conferencing in a distance course: Integration of autonomy to the UTAUT model. *Journal of Computing in Higher Education*, 25(2), 93–121. doi:10.1007/s12528-013-9069-3

Lamberton, C., & Stephen, A. T. (2016). A Thematic Exploration of Digital, Social Media, and Mobile Marketing: Research Evolution from 2000 to 2015 and an Agenda for Future Inquiry. *Journal of Marketing*, 80(6), 146–172. doi:10.1509/jm.15.0415

Landis, J. R., & Koch, G. G. (1977). The measurement of observer agreement for categorical data. *Biometrics*, 33(1), 159–174. doi:10.2307/2529310 PubMed

Landry, J. P., Daigle, R. J., Pardue, J. H., Colton, D., & Hunsinger, S. (2010). IS 2002 and ABET Accreditation : Meeting the ABET Program Outcome Criteria Associate Editor. *Information Systems Education Journal*, 8(67), 1–15.

Lang, G., & Babb, J. (2015). Addressing the 21st Century Paradox: Integrating Entrepreneurship in the Computer Information Systems Curriculum. *Information Systems Education Journal*, 13(4), 81–91.

Lan, J., Ma, Y., Zhu, D., Mangalagiu, D., & Thornton, T. (2017). Enabling value co-creation in the sharing economy: The case of Mobike. *Sustainability*, 9(9), 1–20. doi:10.3390u9091504

Lapointe, L., & Rivard, S. (2005a). A multilevel model of resistance to information technology implementation. *Management Information Systems Quarterly*, 29(3), 2005. doi:10.2307/25148692

Lapointe, L., & Rivard, S. (2005b). A Multilevel Model of Resistance to Information Technology Implementation. *Management Information Systems Quarterly*, 29(3), 461–491. doi:10.2307/25148692

Larsson, A. O., & Moe, H. (2013). Representation or Participation? Twitter Use During the 2011 Danish Election Campaign. *Javnost - The Public*, 20(1), 71-88. doi:10.1080/13183222.2013.11009109

Larsson, U., & Boateng, R. (2010). Towards A Curriculum Adaptation Model for IS Undergraduate Education in Sub-Saharan Africa. In *Selected papers of the 32nd IRIS Seminar*. Tapir Academic Press.

Larsson, A. O., & Moe, H. (2011). Studying political microblogging: Twitter users in the 2010 Swedish election campaign. *New Media & Society*, 14(5), 729–747. doi:10.1177/1461444811422894

Lashinsky, A. (2017) *What could take down Uber, Fortune.com*. Available at: http://fortune.com/2017/05/18/uber-travis-kalanick-woes/

Laue, C. (2011). Crime potential of metaverses. In *Virtual Worlds and Criminality* (pp. 19–29). Springer. doi:10.1007/978-3-642-20823-2_2

Laukkanen, T., & Lauronen, J. (2005). Consumer value creation in mobile banking services. *International Journal of Mobile Communications*, *3*(4), 325–338. doi:10.1504/IJMC.2005.007021

Laumer, S., & Eckhardt, A. (2012). Why Do People Reject Technologies: A Review of User Resistance Theories. In Information Systems Theory (Vol. 29, pp. 63–86). doi:10.1007/978-1-4419-6108-2_4

Laumer, S., & Eckhardt, A. (2010). Why do People Reject Technologies? - Towards an Understanding of Resistance to IT-induced Organizational Change. *Thirty First International Conference on Information Systems*.

Laurell, C. (2016). Fashion spheres – from a systemic to a stereological perspective of fashion. *Journal of Fashion Marketing and Management: An International Journal*, *20*(4), 520–530. doi:10.1108/JFMM-04-2016-0033

Lausch, A., Schmidt, A., & Tischendorf, L. (2015). Data mining and linked open data – New perspectives for data analysis in environmental research. *Ecological Modelling*, *295*, 5–17. doi:10.1016/j.ecolmodel.2014.09.018

Lavie, D. (2009). Capturing value from alliance portfolios. *Organizational Dynamics*, *38*(1), 26–36. doi:10.1016/j.orgdyn.2008.04.008

Lawler, J. P. (2011). Cloud Computing in the Curricula of Schools of Computer Science and Information Systems. *IS Education Journal*, *9*(2), 34–54.

Lawler, J., Joseph, A., & Howell-Barber, H. (2016). A Big Data Analytics Methodology Program in the Health Sector. *Information Systems Education Journal*, *14*(3), 63–75.

Leclercq-Vandelanoitte, A., & Plé, L. (2016). *How do Customers-Employees interactions influence Organizational Change? A Theoretical Framework*. Retrieved from https://pdfs.semanticscholar.org/b01b/79404a40663ac7a9ab626b933b5c8b56a7ad.pdf

Lederer, A. L. (2013). The Information Systems Planning Process Meeting the challenges of information systems planning. Strategic Information Management, 216.

Lederer, A. L., & Sethi, V. (1991). Critical dimensions of strategic information systems planning. *Decision Sciences*, *22*(1), 104–119. doi:10.1111/j.1540-5915.1991.tb01265.x

Lederer, A. L., & Sethi, V. (1991). Guidelines for strategic information planning. [PubMed]. *The Journal of Business Strategy*, *12*(6), 38–43. doi:10.1108/eb039454

Lederer, A. L., & Sethi, V. (1992a). Meeting the Challenges of Information Systems Planning. [PubMed]. *Long Range Planning*, *25*(2), 69–80. doi:10.1016/0024-6301(92)90194-7

Lederer, A. L., & Sethi, V. (1992b). Root Causes of Strategic Information Systems Planning Implementation Problems. *Journal of Management Information Systems*, *9*(1), 25–45. doi:10.1080/07421222.1992.11517946

Lederer, A. L., & Sethi, V. (1998). The Implementation of Strategic Information Systems Planning Methodologies. *Management Information Systems Quarterly*, *12*(3), 445–461. doi:10.2307/249212

Lee, A. R., Son, S. M., & Kim, K. K. (2016). Information and communication technology overload and social networking service fatigue: A stress perspective. *Computers in Human Behavior*, *55*, 51–61. doi:10.1016/j.chb.2015.08.011

Lee, A. S., & Baskerville, R. L. (2003). Generalizing Generalizability in Information Systems Research. *Information Systems Research*, *14*(3), 221–243. doi:10.1287/isre.14.3.221.16560

Lee, C., & Han, H. (2008). Analysis of skills requirement for entry-level programmer/analysts in Fortune 500 corporations. *Journal of Information Systems Education*, *19*(1), 17–27.

Lee, C., Kim, H., & Hong, A. (2017). Ex-post evaluation of illegalizing juvenile online game after midnight: A case of shutdown policy in South Korea. *Telematics and Informatics*, *34*(8), 1597–1606. doi:10.1016/j.tele.2017.07.006

Lee, D. M. S., Trauth, E. M., & Farwell, D. (1995). Critical Skills and Knowledge Requirements of IS Professionals: A Joint Academic/Industry Investigation. *Management Information Systems Quarterly*, *19*(3), 313–340. doi:10.2307/249598

Lee, J. (2015). *The Impact of ICT on Work*. Springer.

Lee, J. J., Ceyhan, P., Jordan-Cooley, W., & Sung, W. (2013). GREENIFY: A real world action game for climate change education. *Simulation & Gaming*, *44*(2–3), 349–365. doi:10.1177/1046878112470539

Lee, J. K. (2016). Invited Commentary—Reflections on ICT-enabled Bright Society Research. *Information Systems Research*, *27*(1), 1–5. doi:10.1287/isre.2016.0627

Lee, J., & Fedorowicz, J. (2018). Identifying Issues for the Bright ICT Initiative: A Worldwide Delphi Study of IS Journal Editors and Scholars. *Communications of the Association for Information Systems*, *42*, 301–333. doi:10.17705/1CAIS.04211

Lee, K., & Joshi, K. (2017). Examining the use of status quo bias perspective in IS research: Need for re-conceptualizing and incorporating biases. *Information Systems Journal*, *27*(6), 733–752. doi:10.1111/isj.12118

Lee, K., & Mirchandani, D. (2010). Dynamics of the Importance of Is / It Skills. *Journal of Computer Information Systems*, *50*(4), 67–78.

Lee, M. K. O., & Cheung, C. M. K. (2004). Internet retailing adoption by small-to-medium sized enterprises: A multiple-case study. *Information Systems Frontiers*, *6*(4), 385–397. doi:10.1023/B:ISFI.0000046379.58029.54

Lee, P. M. (2013). Use Of Data Mining In Business Analytics To Support Business Competitiveness. *Review of Business Information System*, *17*(2), 53–58. doi:10.19030/rbis.v17i2.7843

Leeraphong, A., & Papasratorn, B. (2018). S-Commerce Transactions and Business Models in Southeast Asia: A Case Study in Thailand. KnE Social Sciences, 3(1), 65. doi:10.18502/kss.v3i1.1397

Lee, S., Koh, S., Yen, D., & Tang, H. L. (2002). Perception gaps between IS academics and IS practitioners: An exploratory study. *Information & Management*, *40*(1), 51–61. doi:10.1016/S0378-7206(01)00132-X

Lee, S., Lee, B., & Kim, H. (2019). Decisional factors leading to the reuse of an on-demand ride service. *Information & Management*, *56*(4), 493–506. doi:10.1016/j.im.2018.09.010

Lee, Y. H., Hsiao, C., & Purnomo, S. H. (2014). An empirical examination of individual and system characteristics on enhancing e-learning acceptance. *Australasian Journal of Educational Technology*, *30*(5), 561–579. doi:10.14742/ajet.381

Lee, Y. H., Hsieh, Y. C., & Hsu, C. N. (2011). Adding innovation diffusion theory to the technology acceptance model: Supporting employees' intentions to use e-learning systems. *Journal of Educational Technology & Society*, *14*(4), 124–137.

Lehmann-Willenbrock, N., Beck, S. J., & Kauffeld, S. (2016). Emergent team roles in organizational meetings: Identifying communication patterns via cluster analysis. *Communication Studies*, *67*(1), 37–57. doi:10.1080/10510974.2015.1074087

Lehrer, C., Wieneke, A., vom Brocke, J., Jung, R., & Seidel, S. (2018). How big data analytics enables service innovation: Materiality, affordance, and the individualization of service. *Journal of Management Information Systems*, *35*(2), 424–460. doi:10.1080/07421222.2018.1451953

Leiner, B. M., Cerf, V. G., Clark, D. D., Kahn, R. E., Kleinrock, L., Lynch, D. C., ... Wolff, S. (2009). A brief history of the Internet. *Computer Communication Review*, *39*(5), 22–31. doi:10.1145/1629607.1629613

Lekhanya, L. M. (2013). Cultural Influence On The Diffusion And Adoption Of Social Media Technologies By Entrepreneurs In Rural South Africa. International Business & Economics Research Journal, 12. Retrieved from https://openscholar.dut.ac.za/bitstream/10321/1123/1/lekhanya_ib_erj_2013.pdf

Lemieux, V. L. (2016). Trusting records: Is Blockchain technology the answer? *Records Management Journal*, *26*(2), 110–139. doi:10.1108/RMJ-12-2015-0042

Leong, L. Y., Hew, T. S., Tan, G. W. H., & Ooi, K. B. (2013). Predicting the determinants of the NFC-enabled mobile credit card acceptance: A neural networks approach. *Expert Systems with Applications*, *40*(14), 5604–5620. doi:10.1016/j.eswa.2013.04.018

Levi, M., & Leighton Williams, M. (2013). Multi-agency partnerships in cybercrime reduction: Mapping the UK information assurance network cooperation space. *Information Management & Computer Security*, *21*(5), 420–443. doi:10.1108/IMCS-04-2013-0027

Levy, Y., & Ellis, T. J. (2006). A systems approach to conduct an effective literature review in support of information systems research. *Informing Science*, *9*, 181–211. doi:10.28945/479

Liang, H., Saraf, N., Hu, Q., & Xue, Y. (2007). Assimilation of enterprise systems: The effect of institutional pressures and the mediating role of top management. *Management Information Systems Quarterly*, *31*(1), 59–87. doi:10.2307/25148781

Liang, H., & Xue, Y. (2010). Understanding security behaviors in personal computer usage: A threat avoidance perspective. *Journal of the Association for Information Systems*, *11*(7), 394–413. doi:10.17705/1jais.00232

Liang, T.-P., Ho, Y.-T., Li, Y.-W., & Turban, E. (2011). What Drives Social Commerce: The Role of Social Support and Relationship Quality. *International Journal of Electronic Commerce*, *16*(2), 69–90. doi:10.2753/JEC1086-4415160204

Liang, T., & Turban, E. (2011). Introduction to the Special Issue : Social Commerce : A Research Framework for Social Commerce. *International Journal of Electronic Commerce*, *16*(2), 2012. doi:10.2753/JEC1086-4415160201

Li, B., & Szeto, W. Y. (2019). Taxi service area design : Formulation and analysis. *Transportation Research Part E, Logistics and Transportation Review*, *125*(1), 308–333. doi:10.1016/j.tre.2019.03.004

Liberati, A., Altman, D. G., Tetzlaff, J., Mulrow, C., Gøtzsche, P. C., Ioannidis, J. P., ... Moher, D. (2009). The PRISMA statement for reporting systematic reviews and meta-analyses of studies that evaluate health care interventions: Explanation and elaboration. *PLoS Medicine*, *6*(7), e1000100. doi:10.1371/journal.pmed.1000100 PMID:19621070

Liébana-Cabanillas, F., Marinkovic, V., de Luna, I. R., & Kalinic, Z. (2018). Predicting the determinants of mobile payment acceptance: A hybrid SEM-neural network approach. *Technological Forecasting and Social Change*, *129*, 117–130. doi:10.1016/j.techfore.2017.12.015

Liébana-Cabanillas, F., Ramos de Luna, I., & Montoro-Ríos, F. (2017). Intention to use new mobile payment systems: A comparative analysis of SMS and NFC payments. *Economic Research Journal*, *30*(1), 892–910.

Liébana-Cabanillas, F., Ramos de Luna, I., & Montoro-Ríos, F. J. (2015). User behaviour in QR mobile payment system: The QR Payment Acceptance Model. *Technology Analysis and Strategic Management*, *27*(9), 1031–1049. doi:10.1080/09537325.2015.1047757

Liébana-Cabanillas, F., Sánchez-Fernández, J., & Muñoz-Leiva, F. (2014). Antecedents of the adoption of the new mobile payment systems: The moderating effect of age. *Computers in Human Behavior*, *35*, 464–478. doi:10.1016/j.chb.2014.03.022

Liew, B. T., Kang, M., Yoo, E., & You, J. (2013). Investigating the determinants of mobile learning acceptance in Korea. In J. Herrington, A. Couros, & V. Irvine (Eds.), Proceedings of EdMedia 2013 – world conference on educational media and technology (pp. 1424 – 1430). Academic Press.

Li, F., & Yi, Z. (2017). Counterfeiting and piracy in supply chain management: Theoretical studies. *Journal of Business and Industrial Marketing*, *32*(1), 98–10. doi:10.1108/JBIM-09-2015-0171

Lifer, J. D., Parsons, K., & Miller, R. E. (2009). A Comparison of Information Systems Programs at AACSB and ACBSP Schools in Relation to IS 2002 Model Curricula. *Journal of Information Systems Education*, *20*(4), 469–476.

Lifshitz, R., Nimrod, G., & Bachner, Y. G. (2018). Internet use and well-being in later life: A functional approach. *Aging & Mental Health*, *22*(1), 85–91. doi:10.1080/13607863.2016.1232370 PMID:27657190

Li, J., & Du, J. (2016). Globalization and Decentralization Forces in China's Higher Education Administration and Management Reform (1953-2015): A Neo-institutional Analysis. *US-China Education Review*, *6*(1), 1–19.

Li, J., & Hou, L. (2019). A reflection on the taxi reform in China: Innovation vs. Tradition. *Computer Law & Security Review*, *35*(1), 251–262. doi:10.1016/j.clsr.2019.02.005

Li, L. (2013). Technology designed to combat fakes in the global supply chain. *Business Horizons*, *56*(2), 167–177. doi:10.1016/j.bushor.2012.11.010

Li, L., & Wang, X. (2018). M-Commerce Adoption in SMEs of China: The Effect of Institutional Pressures and the Mediating Role of Top Management. *Journal of Electronic Commerce in Organizations*, *16*(2), 48–63. doi:10.4018/JECO.2018040103

Lim, S. C., Baharudin, A. S., & Low, R. Q. (2016). E-commerce adoption in Peninsular Malaysia: Perceived strategic value as moderator in the relationship between perceived barriers, organizational readiness and competitor pressure. *Journal of Theoretical & Applied Information Technology*, *91*(2), 228–237.

Lin, C. S., Tzeng, G. H., Chin, Y. C., & Chang, C. C. (2010). Recommendation sources on the intention to use e-books in academic digital libraries. *The Electronic Library*, *28*(6), 844–857. doi:10.1108/02640471011093534

Lin, C., Shih, Y., Tzeng, G., & Yu, H. (2016). A service selection model for digital music service platforms using a hybrid MCDM approach. *Applied Soft Computing*, *48*, 385–403. doi:10.1016/j.asoc.2016.05.035

Lincoln, Y. S., & Denzin, N. K. (2000). *The handbook of qualitative research*. Los Angeles, CA: SAGE Publications.

Lindsay, J. R. (2017). Restrained by design: The political economy of cybersecurity. *Digital Policy. Regulation & Governance*, *19*(6), 493–514. doi:10.1108/DPRG-05-2017-0023

Lin, H. F. (2014). Understanding the determinants of electronic supply chain management system adoption: Using the technology–organization–environment framework. *Technological Forecasting and Social Change*, *86*, 80–92. doi:10.1016/j.techfore.2013.09.001

Lin, H. M., Chen, W. J., & Nien, S. F. (2014a). The study of achievement and motivation by e-learning: A case study. *International Journal of Information and Education Technology (IJIET)*, *4*(5), 421–425. doi:10.7763/IJIET.2014.V4.442

Lin, J., & Rivera-Sánchez, M. (2012). Testing the Information Technology Continuance Model on a Mandatory SMS-Based Student Response System Testing the Information Technology Continuance Model on a Mandatory SMS-Based Student Response System. *Communication Education*, *61*(2), 89–110. doi:10.1080/03634523.2011.654231

Lin, Y., Brown, R., Yang, H., Li, S., & Lu, H. (2011). Data mining large-scale electronic health records for clinical support. *IEEE Intelligent Systems*, *23*, 87–90.

Lipnicka, M., & Verhoeven, J. C. (2014). The application of New Institutionalism and the Resource Dependency theory for studying changes in universities within Europe. *Roczniki Nauk Spolecznych*, *42*(4), 7–30. doi:10.18290/rns.2017.45.3-12

Lippert, S. K., & Govindarajulu, C. (2006). Technological, organizational, and environmental antecedents to web services adoption. *Communications of the IIMA*, *6*(1), 146–160.

Li, Q., Guo, X., & Sun, C. (2012). The Shadow of Microblogging Use: Relationship Between Usage Types and Addiction. *ICIS*, *9*(2), 579–612.

Li, T. Y., & Ho, B. C. T. (2015). Factors influencing the Technology Adoption of Mobile Commerce in Taiwan by Using the Revised UTAUT Model. *The Asian Conference on Psychology and Behavioural Sciences*, 1-17.

Li, T., Heck, E. V., & Vervest, P. (2009). Information capability and value creation strategy: Advancing revenue management through mobile ticketing technologies. *European Journal of Information Systems*, *18*(1), 38–51. doi:10.1057/ejis.2009.1

Liu, D., Santhanam, R., & Webster, J. (2017). Towards meaningful engagement: A framework for design and research on gamified information systems. *Management Information Systems Quarterly*, *41*(4), 1011–1034. doi:10.25300/MISQ/2017/41.4.01

Liu, F., Zhao, X., Chau, P. Y. K., & Tang, Q. (2015). Roles of perceived value and individual differences in the acceptance of mobile coupon applications. *Internet Research*, *25*(3), 471–495. doi:10.1108/IntR-02-2014-0053

Liu, J., Kauffman, R. J., & Ma, D. (2015). Competition, cooperation, and regulation: Understanding the evolution of the mobile payments technology ecosystem. *Electronic Commerce Research and Applications*, *14*(5), 372–391. doi:10.1016/j.elerap.2015.03.003

Liu, Y. (2014). Big data and predictive business analytics. *The Journal of Business Forecasting*, *33*, 40–42.

Li, W., Chen, H., & Nunamaker, J. F. Jr. (2016). Identifying and profiling key sellers in cyber carding community: AZSecure text mining system. *Journal of Management Information Systems*, *33*(4), 1059–1086. doi:10.1080/07421222.2016.1267528

Li, Y. (2018). *The Strategic Decision on Mobile Payment: A Study on Merchants Adoption*. Academic Press.

Loader, B. D., & Thomas, D. (2013). *Cybercrime: Security and surveillance in the information age*. Routledge. doi:10.4324/9780203354643

Loebbecke, C., & Picot, A. (2015). Reflections on societal and business model transformation arising from digitization and big data analytics: A research agenda. *The Journal of Strategic Information Systems*, *24*(3), 149–157. doi:10.1016/j.jsis.2015.08.002

Lokuge, S., Sedera, D., Grover, V., & Xu, D. (2019). Organizational readiness for digital innovation : Development and empirical calibration of a construct. *Information & Management Journal*, *56*(3), 445–461. doi:10.1016/j.im.2018.09.001

Longenecker, H. E. J., Feinstein, D., & Clark, J. D. (2013). Information Systems Curricula: A Fifty Year Journey. *Information Systems Education Journal*, *11*(6), 71–95.

Łopaciuk, A., & Łoboda, M. (2013). Global beauty industry trend in the 21st century. *Management, knowledge and learning international conference,* 19-21.

Lubrin, E., Lawrence, E., Zmijewska, A., Navarro, K. F., & Culjak, G. (2006, April). Exploring the benefits of using motes to monitor health: An acceptance survey. In *International Conference on Networking, International Conference on Systems and International Conference on Mobile Communications and Learning Technologies (ICNICONSMCL'06)* (pp. 208-208). IEEE. 10.1109/ICNICONSMCL.2006.94

Lubua, E. W., & Pretorius, P. (2018). *The Impact of Demographic Factors to the Adoption of Social Commerce in Tanzania. In 2018 IST-Africa Week Conference (IST-Africa)* (pp. 1–12). IST-Africa Institute; Retrieved from www.IST-Africa.org/Conference2018

Lubua, E. W., & Pretorius, P. D. (2019). Factors determining the perceived relevance of social commerce in the African context. *South African Journal of Information Management, 21*(1), 1–8. doi:10.4102/sajim.v21i1.959

Lu, M. T., Hu, S. K., Huang, L. H., & Tzeng, G. H. (2015). Evaluating the implementation of business-to-business m-commerce by SMEs based on a new hybrid MADM model. *Management Decision, 53*(2), 290–317. doi:10.1108/MD-01-2014-0012

Luna, D. R., Mayan, J. C., García, M. J., Almerares, A. A., & Househ, M. (2014). Challenges and potential solutions for big data implementations in developing countries. *Yearbook of Medical Informatics, 23*(01), 36–41. doi:10.15265/IY-2014-0012 PMID:25123719

Luo, J., Wu, M., Gopukumar, D., & Zhao, Y. (2016). Big Data Application in Biomedical Research and Healthcare: A Literature Review. *Biomedical Informatics Insights, 8,* 1-10. doi:10.4137/Bii.s31559

Lu, Y., Yang, S., Chau, P. Y., & Cao, Y. (2011). Dynamics between the trust transfer process and intention to use mobile payment services: A cross-environment perspective. *Information & Management, 48*(8), 393–403.

Lyer, B., & Subramaniam, M. (2015, January 7). The Strategic Value of APIs. *Harvard Business Review.* Retrieved from https://hbr.org/2015/01/the-strategic-value-of-aPIs

Lyytinen, K. (1987). Different Perspectives on Information Systems: Problems and Solutions. *ACM Computing Surveys, 19*(1), 5–46. doi:10.1145/28865.28867

Lyytinen, K., & Rose, G. M. (2003). The Disruptive nature of Information Technology innovations: The case of Internet computing in systems development in organisations. *Management Information Systems Quarterly, 27*(4), 557–596. doi:10.2307/30036549

MacGregor, R. C., Bunker, D., & Kartiwi, M. (2010). The perception of barriers to e-commerce adoption by SMEs: A comparison of three countries. In *Global perspectives on small and medium enterprises and strategic information systems: International approaches* (pp. 145–168). Hershey, PA: IGI Global. doi:10.4018/978-1-61520-627-8.ch008

Madan, K., & Yadav, R. (2016). Behavioural intention to adopt mobile wallet: A developing country perspective. *Journal of Indian Business Research, 8*(3), 227–244. doi:10.1108/JIBR-10-2015-0112

Magal, S. R., & Word, J. (2011). *Integrated business processes with ERP systems.* Wiley Publishing.

Magazzino, C., & Michela, M. (2014). Counterfeiting in Italian regions: An empirical analysis based on new data. *Journal of Financial Crime, 21*(4), 400–410. doi:10.1108/JFC-01-2014-0001

Magretta, J. (2002). Why business models matter. *Harvard Business Review, 80,* 3–8. PMID:12024761

Mahadevan, B., & Venkatesh, N. S. (2000, November). Building On-line Trust for Business to Business E-Commerce. *IT Asia Millennium Conference.*

Mahmoudi, N., & Duman, E. (2015). Detecting credit card fraud by modified Fisher discriminant analysis. *Expert Systems with Applications, 42*(5), 2510–2516. doi:10.1016/j.eswa.2014.10.037

Mahoney, J. T., & Pandian, J. R. (1992). The Resource-Based View Within the Conversation of Strategic Management. *Strategic Management Journal, 13*(5), 363–380. doi:10.1002/smj.4250130505

Mahroeian, H. (2012). A study on the effect of different factors on e-Commerce adoption among SMEs of Malaysia. *Management Science Letters, 2*(7), 2679–2688. doi:10.5267/j.msl.2012.08.021

Maier, C., Laumer, S., Eckhardt, A., & Weitzel, T. (2015). Giving too much social support: Social overload on social networking sites. *European Journal of Information Systems, 24*(5), 447–464. doi:10.1057/ejis.2014.3

Mai, J. E. (2016). No TitleBig data privacy: The datafication of personal information. *The Information Society, 32*(3), 192–199. doi:10.1080/01972243.2016.1153010

Majuri, J., Koivisto, J., & Hamari, J. (2018). Gamification of education and learning: A review of empirical literature. In *Proceedings of the 2nd International GamiFIN Conference, GamiFIN 2018.* CEUR-WS.

Mak, K. K., Nam, J. E. K., Kim, D., Aum, N., Choi, J. S., Cheng, C., Watanabe, H. (2017). Cross-cultural adaptation and psychometric properties of the Korean Scale for Internet Addiction (K-Scale) in Japanese high school students. *Psychiatry Research, 249*, 343–348.

Malhotra, A., & Van Alstyne, M. (2014). The dark side of the sharing economy... and how to lighten it. *Communications of the ACM, 57*(11), 24–28. doi:10.1145/2668893

Malik, F., Nicholson, B., & Heeks, R. (2017, May). Understanding the development implications of online outsourcing. In *International Conference on Social Implications of Computers in Developing Countries* (pp. 425-436). Springer. 10.1007/978-3-319-59111-7_35

Mallat, N., & Tuunainen, V. K. (2008). Exploring merchant adoption of mobile payment systems: An empirical study. e-Service Journal, 6(2), 24–57. doi:10.2979/esj.2008.6.2.24

Mallat, N., Rossi, M., Tuunainen, V. K., & Oorni, A. (2006, January). The impact of use situation and mobility on the acceptance of mobile ticketing services. In Proceedings of the 39th Annual Hawaii International Conference on System Sciences (HICSS'06) (Vol. 2, pp. 42b-42b). IEEE. doi:10.1109/HICSS.2006.472

Mallat, N. (2007). Exploring consumer adoption of mobile payments - A qualitative study. *The Journal of Strategic Information Systems, 16*(4), 413–432. doi:10.1016/j.jsis.2007.08.001

Mallat, N., Rossi, M., Tuunainen, V. K., & Öörni, A. (2009). The impact of use context on mobile services acceptance: The case of mobile ticketing. *Information & Management, 46*(3), 190–195. doi:10.1016/j.im.2008.11.008

Mamonov, S., & Misra, R. (2015). Business Analytics in Practice and in Education: A Competency-based Perspective. *Information Systems Education Journal, 13*(1), 4–13.

Mandolini, M., Brunzini, A., & Germani, M. (2016). A collaborative web-based platform for the prescription of Custom-Made Insoles. *Advanced Engineering Informatics.*

Manikandan, S. G., & Ravi, S. (2014). Big Data Analysis Using Apache Hadoop. *2014 International Conference on IT Convergence and Security (ICITCS)*, 1-4. 10.1109/ICITCS.2014.7021746

Manyika, J., Lund, S., Robinson, K., Valentino, J., & Dobbs, R. (2015). A labor market that works: Connecting talent with opportunity in the digital age. June. *McKinsey Global Institute*. http://www.mckinsey.com/~/media/McKinsey/dotcom/Insights/Employment%20and%20growth/Connecting

Manyika, J., Lund, S., Chui, M., Bughin, J., Woetzel, J., Batra, P., & Sanghvi, S. (2017). *Jobs lost; jobs gained: Workforce transitions in a time of automation*. McKinsey Global Institute.

Mapesa, N. M. (2016). *Health Information Technology Implementation Strategies in Zimbabwe*. Walden University.

Marcum, C. D., Higgins, G. E., Ricketts, M. L., & Wolfe, S. E. (2014). Hacking in high school: Cybercrime perpetration by juveniles. *Deviant Behavior*, *35*(7), 581–591. doi:10.1080/01639625.2013.867721

Marcum, C. D., Higgins, G. E., Ricketts, M. L., & Wolfe, S. E. (2015). Becoming someone new: Identity theft behaviors by high school students. *Journal of Financial Crime*, *22*(3), 318–328. doi:10.1108/JFC-09-2013-0056

Margetts, H. (2019). 9. Rethinking Democracy with Social Media. *The Political Quarterly, 90*(SI), 107-123. doi:10.1111/1467-923X.12574

Markus, M. L., & Soh, C. (1995). How IT creates business value: a process theory synthesis. ICIS 1995 Proceedings, 4.

Marr, B. (2018). 7 Amazing Real-World Examples Of 3D Printing In 2018. *Forbes*. Retrieved from https://www.forbes.com/sites/bernardmarr/2018/08/22/7-amazing-real-world-examples-of-3d-printing-in-2018/#73d2cca06585

Marsden, P. (2009). *The 6 dimensions of social commerce: rated and reviewed*. Social Commerce Today.

Martin, C. J. (2016). The sharing economy: A pathway to sustainability or a nightmarish form of neoliberal capitalism? *Ecological Economics*, *121*, 149–159. doi:10.1016/j.ecolecon.2015.11.027

Martínez-López, F. J., Merigó, J. M., Valenzuela-Fernández, L., & Nicolás, C. (2018). Fifty years of the European Journal of Marketing : A bibliometric analysis. *European Journal of Marketing*, *52*(1/2), 439–468. doi:10.1108/EJM-11-2017-0853

Martin, N., & Rice, J. (2011). Cybercrime: Understanding and addressing the concerns of stakeholders. *Computers & Security*, *30*(8), 803–814. doi:10.1016/j.cose.2011.07.003

Martin, S. S., Catalan, B. L., & Jeronimo, M. A. R. (2012). Factors determining firms' perceived performance of mobile commerce. *Industrial Management & Data Systems*, *112*(6), 946–963. doi:10.1108/02635571211238536

Martin, S. S., & Jimenez, N. (2015). A Typology of Firms Regarding M-Commerce Adoption. *International Journal of Information System Modeling and Design*, *6*(4), 42–56. doi:10.4018/IJISMD.2015100103

Martins, C., Oliveira, T., & Popovič, A. (2014). Understanding the Internet banking adoption: A unified theory of acceptance and use of technology and perceived risk application. *International Journal of Information Management*, *34*(1), 1–13. doi:10.1016/j.ijinfomgt.2013.06.002

Martins, J. T., & Nunes, M. B. (2016). 'Academics ' e-learning adoption in higher education institutions : A matter of trust adoption'. *The Learning Organization*, *23*(5), 299–331. doi:10.1108/TLO-05-2015-0034

Martí-Parreño, J., Seguí-Mas, D., & Seguí-Mas, E. (2016). Teachers' attitude towards and actual use of gamification. *Procedia: Social and Behavioral Sciences*, *228*, 682–688. doi:10.1016/j.sbspro.2016.07.104

Martz, B., Hughes, J., & Braun, F. (2017). Creativity and problem-solving: Closing the skills gap. *Journal of Computer Information Systems*, *57*(1), 39–48. doi:10.1080/08874417.2016.1181492

Mascarenhas, C., Ferreira, J. J., & Marques, C. (2018, February). University–industry cooperation: A systematic literature review and research agenda. *Science & Public Policy*, •••, 1–11. doi:10.1093cipolcy003

Mashagba, F. F. A., Mashagba, E. F. A., & Nassar, M. O. (2013). Exploring Technological Factors Affecting the Adoption of M-Commerce in Jordan. *Australian Journal of Basic and Applied Sciences, 7*(6), 395–400.

Mason, P., Mayer, R., Chien, W.-W., & Monestime, J. P. (2017). Overcoming Barriers to Implementing Electronic Health Records in Rural Primary Care Clinics. *Qualitative Report, 22*(11), 2943–2955.

Mata, F. J., Fuerst, W. L., & Barney, J. B. (1995). Information technology and sustained competitive advantage: A Resourced-Based Analysis. *Management Information Systems Quarterly, 19*(4), 487–505. doi:10.2307/249630

Mata, F., Fuerst, W., & Barney, J. (1995). Information Technology and Sustained Competitive Advantage: A Resource-Based Analysis. *Management Information Systems Quarterly, 19*(4), 487–505. doi:10.2307/249630

Matthews, T. (2018). *What is social commerce? And Examples of campaigns.* Academic Press.

Mayer, R. C., Davis, J. H., & Schoorman, D. F. (1995). An integrative model of organizational trust. *Academy of Management Review, 20*(3), 709–734. doi:10.5465/amr.1995.9508080335

May, J., & Lending, D. (2015). A conceptual model for communicating an integrated information systems curriculum. *Journal of Computer Information Systems, 55*(4), 20–27. doi:10.1080/08874417.2015.11645783

McCoy, S., Everard, A., & Jones, B. M. (2015). Foundations of information systems course content: A comparison of assigned value by faculty, recruiters, and students. *Communications of the Association for Information Systems, 36*, 697–705. doi:10.17705/1CAIS.03635

McFarlan, F. W., & McKenny, J. (1983). *Corporate Information Management: the issues facing senior management.* DOW-Jones-Irein.

McGee, J. A., & Byington, J. R. (2013). How to counter cybercrime intrusions. *Journal of Corporate Accounting & Finance, 24*(5), 45–49. doi:10.1002/jcaf.21874

McKelvey, K., DiGrazia, J., & Rojas, F. (2014). Twitter publics: How online political communities signaled electoral outcomes in the 2010 US house election. *Information Communication and Society, 17*(4), 436–450. doi:10.1080/1369 118X.2014.892149

McKendrick, J. (2019, July 30). *CEOs Are Talking About APIs, And Other Signs The World Is Turned Upside Down.* Retrieved November 9, 2019, from https://www.forbes.com: https://www.forbes.com/sites/joemckendrick/2019/07/30/ceos-are-talking-about-apis-and-other-signs-the-world-is-turned-upside-down/#39da06955750

McKeown, I., & Philip, G. (2003). Business transformation, information technology and competitive strategies: Learning to fly. *International Journal of Information Management, 23*(1), 3–24. doi:10.1016/S0268-4012(02)00065-8

Medanta. (2018). *Life-Saving Creativity- 3D Printed Titanium Spine.* Retrieved from https://www.medanta.org/life-saving-creativity-3d-printed-titanium-spine/

Medina, R. Z., & Muñoz, C. Z. (2014). Campaigning on Twitter: Towards the 'Personal Style' Campaign to Activate the Political Engagement During the 2011 Spanish General Elections. *Communication & Society / Comunicación y Sociedad, 27*(1), 83-106.

Meelen, T., & Frenken, K. (2015). Stop saying Uber is part of the sharing economy. Fast Company, 14.

Mehta, N., & Pandit, A. (2017). Concurrence of big data analytics and healthcare: A systematic review. *International Journal of Medical Informatics, 114*, 57–65. doi:10.1016/j.ijmedinf.2018.03.013 PMID:29673604

Meijer, D.B. (2017). *Consequences of the implementation of blockchain technology.* Academic Press.

Meissonier, R., & Houzé, E. (2010). Toward an IT conflict-resistance theory: Action research during IT pre-implementation. *European Journal of Information Systems*, *19*(5), 540–561. doi:10.1057/ejis.2010.35

Mekler, E. D. E., Brühlmann, F., Opwis, K., & Tuch, A. N. (2013). Disassembling Gamification: The Effects of Points and Meaning on User Motivation and Performance. In *CHI 2013 Extended Abstracts on Human Factors in Computing Systems* (pp. 1137–1142). New York: ACM Press. doi:10.1145/2468356.2468559

Mengiste, S. A. (2010). Analysing the Challenges of IS Implementation in Public Health Institutions of a Developing Country: The Need for Flexible Strategies. *Journal of Health Informatics in Developing Countries*, *4*(1), 1–17.

Menon, S., & Guan Siew, T. (2012). Key challenges in tackling economic and cyber crimes: Creating a multilateral platform for international co-operation. *Journal of Money Laundering Control*, *15*(3), 243–256. doi:10.1108/13685201211238016

Mentzas, G. (1997). Implementing an IS Strategy -A Team Approach. *Long Range Planning*, *30*(1), 84–95. doi:10.1016/S0024-6301(96)00099-4

Merali, Y., Papadopoulos, T., & Nadkarni, T. (2012). Information systems strategy: Past, present, future? *The Journal of Strategic Information Systems*, *21*(2), 125–153.

Meraviglia, L. (2015). Counterfeiting, fashion and the civil society. *Journal of Fashion Marketing and Management*, *19*(3), 230–248. doi:10.1108/JFMM-06-2013-0084

Merhi, M. I. (2015). Factors influencing higher education students to adopt podcast: An empirical study. *Computers & Education*, *83*(2), 32–43. doi:10.1016/j.compedu.2014.12.014

Merhout, J., Benamati, J., Rajkumar, T., Anderson, P., & Marado, D. (2008). Implementing direct and indirect assessment in the MIS curriculum. *Communications of the Association for Information Systems*, *23*(24), 419–436.

Merhout, J., Havelka, D., & Rajkumar, T. M. (2016). Determining Factors that Lead Students to Study Information Systems using an Alumni Focus Group. *Twenty-Second Americas Conference on Information Systems*, 1–8.

Merigó, J. M., Pedrycz, W., Weber, R., & de la Sotta, C. (2018). Fifty years of Information Sciences: A bibliometric overview. *Information Sciences*, *432*, 245–268. doi:10.1016/j.ins.2017.11.054

Merolli, M., Gray, K., & Martin-Sanchez, F. (2013). Health outcomes and related effects of using social media in chronic disease management: A literature review and analysis of affordances. *Journal of Biomedical Informatics*, *46*(6), 957–969. doi:10.1016/j.jbi.2013.04.010 PMID:23702104

Metzger, M. J., & Flanagin, A. J. (2017). Psychological approaches to credibility assessment online. In S. S. Sundar (Ed.), *The handbook of the psychology of communication technology* (pp. 445–466). Chichester, UK: Wiley.

Mgiba, F. M. (2019). Integrating Five Theories in Pursuit of Marketing Success in Gamification Interventions: A Conceptual Paper. *International Review of Management and Marketing*, *9*(2), 45–53.

Miah, S. J., Hassan, J., & Gammack, J. G. (2017). On-Cloud Healthcare Clinic: E-health consultancy approach for remote communities in a developing country. *Telematics and Informatics*, *34*(1), 311–322. doi:10.1016/j.tele.2016.05.008

Miailhe, N., & Hodes, C. (2017). The Third Age of Artificial Intelligence. *Field Actions Science Reports. The Journal of Field Actions*, (17), 6-11.

Miao, J. J., & Tran, Q. D. (2018). Study on E-Commerce Adoption in SMEs Under the Institutional Perspective: The Case of Saudi Arabia. *International Journal of E-Adoption*, *10*(1), 53–72. doi:10.4018/IJEA.2018010104

Miao, M., & Jayakar, K. (2016). Mobile payments in Japan, South Korea and China: Cross-border convergence or divergence of business models? *Telecommunications Policy*, *40*(2-3), 182–196. doi:10.1016/j.telpol.2015.11.011

Miazi, M. N. S., Erasmus, Z., Razzaque, M. A., Zennaro, M., & Bagula, A. (2016). Enabling the Internet of Things in developing countries: Opportunities and challenges. In *2016 5th International Conference on Informatics, Electronics and Vision (ICIEV)* (pp. 564-569). IEEE.

Micelotta, E., Lounsbury, M., & Greenwood, R. (2017). Pathways of institutional change: An integrative review and research agenda. *Journal of Management, 43*(6), 1885–1910. doi:10.1177/0149206317699522

Micheni, E. M. (2017). Analysis of the Critical Success Factors of Integrated Financial Management Information Systems in Selected Kenyan Counties. *Journal of Finance and Accounting, 5*(5), 185. doi:10.11648/j.jfa.20170505.12

Mihailescu, M., & Mihailescu, D. (2018). The emergence of digitalisation in the context of health care. *51st Hawaii International Conference on System Sciences*, 3066-3071. 10.24251/HICSS.2018.387

Mikalef, P., Giannakos, M., & Pappas, I. O. (2017). Designing social commerce platforms based on consumers ' intentions. *Behaviour & Information Technology, 36*(12), 1308–1327. doi:10.1080/0144929X.2017.1386713

Mikalef, P., Pappas, I. O., & Giannakos, M. N. (2017). Value co-creation and purchase intention in social commerce:The enabling role of word- of-mouth and trust. In *Twenty-third Americas Conference on Information Systems* (pp. 1–10). Academic Press.

Mikalef, P., Pappas, I. O., Krogstie, J., & Giannakos, M. (2018). Big data analytics capabilities: A systematic literature review and research agenda. *Information Systems and e-Business Management, 16*(3), 547–578. doi:10.100710257-017-0362-y

Miles, M. B., & Huberman, A. M. (1994). Qualitative data analysis: An expanded sourcebook. Sage.

Miles, M. B., & Huberman, A. M. (1994). *Qualitative Data Analysis* (2nd ed.). Thousand Oaks, CA: Sage Publications.

Miles, M. B., & Huberman, A. M. (1994). *Qualitative Data Analysis: An Expanded Sourcebook* (2nd ed.). Newbury Park, CA: Sage Publications.

Miller, D. (2003). An Asymmetry-Based View of Advantage: Towards an Attainable Sustainability. *Strategic Management Journal, 24*(10), 961–976. doi:10.1002/smj.316

Mills, R. J., Beaulieu, T. Y., & Johnson, J. J. (2017). Examining Micro-Level (SQL) Curriculum-Oriented and Promotional IS Enrollment Strategies. *Journal of Computer Information Systems, 57*(4), 299–308. doi:10.1080/08874417.2016.1180650

Mills, R. J., Chudoba, K. M., & Olsen, D. H. (2016). IS Programs Responding to Industry Demands for Data Scientists: A Comparison between 2011 - 2016. *Journal of Information Systems Education, 27*(2), 131–140.

Mills, R. J., Velasquez, N. F., Fadel, K. J., & Bell, C. C. (2012). Examining IS Curriculum Profiles and the IS 2010 Model Curriculum Guidelines in AACSB-Accredited Schools. *Journal of Information Systems Education, 23*(4), 417–428.

Milovic, B., & Milovic, M. (2012). Prediction and Decision Making in Health Care using Data Mining. *International Journal of Public Health Science, 1*(2), 69–76. doi:10.11591/ijphs.v1i2.1380

Mingers, J. (2004). Realizing information systems: Critical realism as an underpinning philosophy for information systems. *Information and Organization, 14*(2), 87–103. doi:10.1016/j.infoandorg.2003.06.001

Mingers, J. (2004). Re-establishing the Real: Critical Realism and Information Systems. In J. Mingers & L. Willcocks (Eds.), *Social Theory and Philosophy for Information Systems* (pp. 372–406). Chichester: Wiley.

Ministry of Education. (2011). *Good infrastructure essential for quality education delivery*. Accra, Ghana: Author.

Miriri, D. (2017). Facebook offers tool to combat fake news in Kenya ahead of polls. *Reuters, 4*, 2017.

Mishra, T., Kumar, D., & Gupta, S. (2014). Mining Students' Data for Performance Prediction. In *Fourth International Conference on Advanced Computing & Communication Technologies* (pp. 255–262). 10.1109/ACCT.2014.105

Mital, M., Chang, V., Choudhary, P., Papa, A., & Pani, A. K. (2018). Adoption of Internet of Things in India: A test of competing models using a structured equation modeling approach. *Technological Forecasting and Social Change, 136,* 339–346. doi:10.1016/j.techfore.2017.03.001

Mitchell, A., & Benyon, R. (2018). Adding intercultural communication to an IS curriculum. *Journal of Information Systems Education, 29*(1), 1–10.

Mitri, M., & Palocsay, S. (2015). The Emerging Business Intelligence and Analytics Discipline. Communications of the AIS, 37.

Mohamed, N. A., Jantan, A., & Abiodun, O. I. (2018). Protect Governments, and organizations Infrastructure against Cyber Terrorism (Mitigation and Stop of Server Message Block (SMB) Remote Code Execution Attack). *International Journal of Engineering, 11*(2), 261–272.

Mohammed, N., Ismail, A. G., & Muhammad, J. (2015). Evidence on market concentration in Malaysian dual banking system. *Procedia: Social and Behavioral Sciences, 172,* 169–176. doi:10.1016/j.sbspro.2015.01.351

Moher, D., Liberati, A., Tetzlaff, J., & Altman, D. G. (2009). Preferred Reporting Items for Systematic Reviews and Meta-Analysis. The PRISMA statement. *Annals of Internal Medicine, 151*(4), 264–269. doi:10.7326/0003-4819-151-4-200908180-00135 PMID:19622511

Moher, D., Shamseer, L., Clarke, M., Ghersi, D., Liberati, A., Petticrew, M., ... Stewart, L. A. (2015). Preferred reporting items for systematic review and meta-analysis protocols (PRISMA-P) 2015 statement. *Systematic Reviews, 4*(1), 1–9. doi:10.1186/2046-4053-4-1 PMID:25554246

Mohr, I. (2013). The impact of social media on the fashion industry. *Journal of Applied Business and Economics., 15*(2), 17–22.

Mohurle, S., & Patil, M. (2017). A brief study of wannacry threat: Ransomware attack 2017. *International Journal of Advanced Research in Computer Science, 8*(5).

Molla, A., & Licker, P. S. (2005). eCommerce adoption in developing countries: A model and instrument. *Information & Management, 42*(6), 877–899. doi:10.1016/j.im.2004.09.002

Molla, A., & Licker, P. S. (2014). Perceived E-Readiness Factors in E-Commerce Adoption. *An Empirical Investigation in a Developing Country Perceived E-Readiness Factors in E-Commerce Adoption : An Empirical Investigation in a, 4415.* doi:10.1080/10864415.2005.11043963

Molluzo, J. C., & Lawler, J. P. (2015). A Proposed Concentration Curriculum Design for Big Data Analytics for Information Systems Students. *Information Systems Education Journal, 13*(1), 45–57.

Momeni, A., & Rost, K. (2016). Identification and monitoring of possible disruptive technologies by patent-development paths and topic modelling. *Technological Forecasting and Social Change, 104,* 16–29. doi:10.1016/j.techfore.2015.12.003

Moncrief, W. C., Marshall, G. W., & Rudd, J. M. (2015). Social media and related technology: Drivers of change in managing the contemporary sales force. *Business Horizons, 58*(1), 45–55. doi:10.1016/j.bushor.2014.09.009

Moon, B., McCluskey, J. D., & McCluskey, C. P. (2010). A general theory of crime and computer crime: An empirical test. *Journal of Criminal Justice, 38*(4), 767–772. doi:10.1016/j.jcrimjus.2010.05.003

Moore, F. (2019). Global recorded music sales totalled US $19.1 billion in 2018. Retrieved June 12, 2019, from https://www.ifpi.org/global-statistics.php

Moore, G. C., & Benbasat, I. (1991). Development of an instrument to measure the perceptions of adopting an information technology innovation. *Information Systems Research, 2*(3), 192–222. doi:10.1287/isre.2.3.192

Moore, J. (1993). Predators and prey: The new ecology of competition. *Harvard Business Review, 71*, 75–83. PMID:10126156

Moore, M. (2017). *Turning Personality Into Data. The Chemistry of Conversation.* Mattersight.

Morgan, R. E., & Page, K. (2008). Managing business transformation to deliver strategic agility. *Strategic Change, 17*(5-6), 155–168. doi:10.1002/jsc.823

Morley, L. (2012). Experiencing higher education in Ghana and Tanzania: The symbolic power of being a student. In T. Hinton- Smith (Ed.), Widening Participation in higher education (pp. 245-266). Palgrave Macmillan.

Morris, M., Schindehutte, M., & Allen, J. (2005). The entrepreneur's business model: Toward a unified perspective. *Journal of Business Research, 58*(6), 726–735. doi:10.1016/j.jbusres.2003.11.001

Morschheuser, B., Hamari, J., Koivisto, J., & Maedche, A. (2017). Gamified crowdsourcing: Conceptualization, literature review, and future agenda. *International Journal of Human-Computer Studies, 106*, 26–43. doi:10.1016/j.ijhcs.2017.04.005

Mosley, R. C. Jr. (2012). Social Media Analytics : Data Mining Applied to Insurance Twitter Posts. *Casualty Actuarial Society, 2*, 1–36.

Mothobi, O., & Grzybowski, L. (2017). Infrastructure deficiencies and adoption of mobile money in Sub-Saharan Africa. *Information Economics and Policy, 40*, 71–79. doi:10.1016/j.infoecopol.2017.05.003

Mounce, R., & Nelson, J. D. (2019). On the potential for one-way electric vehicle car-sharing in future mobility systems. *Transportation Research Part A, Policy and Practice, 120*(1), 17–30. doi:10.1016/j.tra.2018.12.003

Mthembu, M. A. (2012). High road in regulating online child pornography in South Africa. *Computer Law & Security Review, 28*(4), 438–444. doi:10.1016/j.clsr.2012.05.010

Mthoko, H., & Khene, C. (2018). Building theory in ICT4D evaluation: A comprehensive approach to assessing outcome and impact. *Information Technology for Development, 24*(1), 138–164. doi:10.1080/02681102.2017.1315359

Mueller, M. (2017). Is cybersecurity eating internet governance? Causes and consequences of alternative framings. *Digital Policy. Regulation & Governance, 19*(6), 415–428. doi:10.1108/DPRG-05-2017-0025

Muhammed, K., Zaharaddeen, I., Rumana, K., & Turaki, A. M. (2015). Cloud computing adoption in Nigeria: Challenges and benefits. *International Journal of Scientific and Research Publications, 5*(7), 2250–3153.

Mullakara, R. (2017). A Perspective on Artificial Intelligence and Machine Learning. IEEE India Infomation, 12(4), 33-36. http://sites.ieee.org/indiacouncil/files/2018/01/p33-p35.pdf

Mulligan, C. (2017). *Blockchain and Digital Transformation.* Retrieved from Imperial College London website: https://www.imperial.ac.uk/media/imperial-college/research-and-innovation/thinkspace/public/1000_Catherine-Mulligan.pdf

Munawar, M., Hassanein, K., & Head, M. (2017). Understanding the Role of Herd Behaviour and Homophily in Social Commerce. Special Interest Group on Human Computer Interaction, (SIGHCI 2017 Proceedings).

Murawski, M., & Bick, M. (2017). Demanded and Imparted Big Data Competences: Towards an Integrative Analysis. *Proceedings of the 25th European Conference on Information Systems (ECIS)*, 1375–1390.

Murdoch, T., & Detsky, A. (2013). The inevitable application of big data to healthcare. *Journal of the American Medical Association, 309*(13), 1351–1352. doi:10.1001/jama.2013.393 PMID:23549579

Murphy, J. T., & Carmody, P. (2017). Africa's information revolution : Technical regimes and produc- tion networks in South Africa and Tanzania. *Journal of Economic Geography, 17*, 265–266. doi:10.1093/jeg/lbw038

Musa, A., Khan, H. U., & AlShare, K. A. (2015). Factors influence consumers' adoption of mobile payment devices in Qatar. *International Journal of Mobile Communications, 13*(6), 670–689. doi:10.1504/IJMC.2015.072100

Musangu, L. M., & Kekwaletswe, R. M. (2011). Strategic Information Systems Planning And Environmental Uncertainty : *The Case Of South African Small Micro And Medium Enterprises. In IADIS International Conference Information Systems* (pp. 70–78). Academic Press.

Mutula, S. M., & Mostert, J. (2010). Challenges and opportunities of e-government in South Africa. *The Electronic Library, 28*(1), 38–53. doi:10.1108/02640471011023360

Myers, M. D., & Avison, D. (2002). An introduction to qualitative research in information systems. *Qualitative Research in Information Systems, 4*, 3-12.

Myers, M. (2009). Qualitative research in business and management. *Sage (Atlanta, Ga.).*

Myers, M. D. (1997). Qualitative research in information systems. *Management Information Systems Quarterly, 21*(2), 241–242. doi:10.2307/249422

Myers, M. D. (1999). Investigating information systems with ethnographic research. *Communications of the Association for Information Systems, 2*(1), 23.

Myers, M. D. (2013). *Qualitative Research in Business & Management* (N. S. Kirsty Smy, Ed.). 2nd ed.). Sage Publications.

Myers, M. D. (2013). Qualitative research in business and management. *Sage (Atlanta, Ga.).*

Myers, M. D., & Newman, M. (2007). The qualitative interview in IS research: Examining the craft. *Information and Organization, 17*(1), 2–26. doi:10.1016/j.infoandorg.2006.11.001

Myjoyonline.com. (2018, Sept 12). *Closing the digital divide crucial to Ghana's socio-economic development – Ursula.* Retrieved 02 1, 2019, from https://www.myjoyonline.com/: https://www.myjoyonline.com/news/2018/september-12th/closing-digital-divide-crucial-to-ghanas-socio-economic-devt-ursula.php

Nacke, L. E., & Deterding, C. S. (2017). The maturing of gamification research. *Computers in Human Behaviour,* 450-454.

Nafea, I., & Younas, M. (2014). *Improving the performance and reliability of mobile commerce in developing countries.* Paper presented at the International Conference on Mobile Web and Information Systems, Barcelona, Spain. 10.1007/978-3-319-10359-4_9

Nagy, D., Schuessler, J., & Dubinsky, A. (2016). Defining and identifying disruptive innovations. *Industrial Marketing Management, 57*, 119–126. doi:10.1016/j.indmarman.2015.11.017

Nah, F. F. H., Zeng, Q., Telaprolu, V. R., Ayyappa, A. P., & Eschenbrenner, B. (2014). Gamification of education: a review of literature. In *International conference on hci in business* (pp. 401-409). Springer. 10.1007/978-3-319-07293-7_39

Nakamoto, S. (2008). *Bitcoin: A Peer-to-Peer Electronic Cash System.* Academic Press.

National Communication Authority. (2017). *4G Subscriptions January to April 2017.* Retrieved 5/02/2017 from https://nca.org.gh/assets/Uploads/4G-Subscription- Jan.-to-Apr.-2017.pdf

National Communication Authority. (2017). *MNOs Mobile Data Statistics 2017*. Retrieved from http://nca.org.gh/assets/Uploads/January-Reports-MNOs- Mobile-data-Statistics-2017.pdf

National Communications Authority. (2017). *Quarterly statistical bulletin on communications in Ghana: Third quarter July to September*. Retrieved 15/02/2018 from https://nca.org.gh/assets/Uploads/stats-bulletin-Q3-2017.pdf

National Population Commission. (2007). National Population Commission and National Bureau of Statistics Estimates.

Nayar, A., & Beldona, S. (2010). Interoperability and open travel alliance standards: Strategic perspectives. *International Journal of Contemporary Hospitality Management, 22*(7), 1010–1032. doi:10.1108/09596111011066653

Ndung'u, N. (2017). New frontiers in Africa's digital potential. Harnessing Africa's Digital Potential: New tools for a new age.

Nelson, R. (1991). Educational needs as perceived by IS and End-User Personnel: A survey of knowledge and skill requirements. *Management Information Systems Quarterly, 15*(December), 503–525. doi:10.2307/249454

Nerad, M. (2015). From graduate student to world citizen in a global environment. *International Higher Education,* (40).

Nevo, S., & Wade, M. R. (2010). The formation and value of IT-enabled resources: Antecedents and consequences of synergistic relationships. *Management Information Systems Quarterly, 34*(1), 163–183. doi:10.2307/20721419

Newkirk, H. E., Lederer, A. L., & Srinivasan, C. (2003). Strategic information systems planning : Too little or too much? *The Journal of Strategic Information Systems, 12*(3), 201–228. doi:10.1016/j.jsis.2003.09.001

Newman, E. & Duwiejua, M. (2016). Models for innovative funding for higher education in Africa–The case of Ghana. *Towards Innovative Models for Funding Higher Education in Africa, 1*, 1-19.

Nezakati, H., Harati, A., & Elahi, R. (2014). Effective Attributes of Successful Strategic Information Systems Planning for Public Organizations in Middle East - Preliminary Study. *Journal of Applied Statistics, 14*(15), 1701–1710.

Ngai, E. W. T., Tao, S. S. C., & Moon, K. K. L. (2015). Social media research: Theories, constructs, and conceptual frameworks. *International Journal of Information Management, 35*(1), 33–44. doi:10.1016/j.ijinfomgt.2014.09.004

Ng, B. D., & Wiemer-Hastings, P. (2005). Addiction to the internet and online gaming. *Cyberpsychology & Behavior, 8*(2), 110–113. doi:10.1089/cpb.2005.8.110 PMID:15938649

Ng, C. S. P. (2013). Intention to purchase on social commerce websites across cultures: A cross-regional study. *Information & Management, 50*(8), 609–620. doi:10.1016/j.im.2013.08.002

Ngo, F., & Jaishankar, K. (2017). Commemorating a Decade in Existence of the International Journal of Cyber Criminology: A Research Agenda to Advance the Scholarship on Cyber Crime. *International Journal of Cyber Criminology, 11*(1).

Nicolini, D., Powell, J., Conville, P., & Matinez-Solano, L. (2008). Managing knowledge in the healthcare sector: A review. *International Journal of Management Reviews, 10*(3), 245-263. doi:10.1111/j.1468-2370.2007.00219

Nielsen, J. A., Mathiassen, L., & Newell, S. (2014). Theorization and translation in Information Technology Institutionalization: Evidence from Danish Homecare. *Management Information Systems Quarterly, 38*(1), 165–186. doi:10.25300/MISQ/2014/38.1.08

Nigania, J. (2019, July 23rd). Understanding The Term Data Mining And Its Impact On Business. Retrieved from https://www.houseofbots.com/news-detail/4545-1-understanding-the-term-data-mining-and-its-impact-on-business

Nikou, S., Bouwman, H., & de Reuver, M. (2014). A Consumer Perspective on Mobile Service Platforms: A Conjoint Analysis Approach. CAIS, 34, 82.

Nisar, T. M., & Whitehead, C. (2016). *Brand interactions and social media: Enhancing user loyalty through social networking sites.* Computers in Human Behaviour.

Niu, H., Keivanloo, I., & Zou, Y. (2017). API usage pattern recommendation for software development. *Journal of Systems and Software*, 1–13.

Njenga, A. K., Litondo, K., & Omwansa, T. (2016). A Theoretical Review of Mobile Commerce Success Determinants. *Journal of Information Engineering and Applications*, *6*(5), 13–23.

Nkohkwo, Q. N. A., & Islam, M. S. (2013). Challenges to the Successful Implementation of e-Government Initiatives in Sub-Saharan Africa: A Literature Review. Electronic. *Journal of E-Government*, *11*(1).

Nolan, R., & McFarlan, F. W. (2005). Information technology and the board of directors. [PubMed]. *Harvard Business Review*, *83*(10), 96.

Noor, M. M. (2018). Rural Community Digital Technology Connectedness: Does ICT in Rural Area Contributes to Rural Development in Malaysia? *Social Sciences*, *13*(2), 316–322.

Nor, A. I. (2019). Increasing government revenue through integrated financial management system case of federal government of Somalia. *European Journal of Economic and Financial Research.*, *3*(5), 9–20.

Noris, J. (2019). *Machine Learning with the Raspberry Pi: Experiments with Data and Computer ViSION.* Academic Press.

Norzaidi, M. D., Salwani, M. I., Chong, S. C., & Rafidah, K. (2008). A study of intranet usage and resistance in Malaysia's port industry. *Journal of Computer Information Systems*, *49*(1), 37–47. doi:10.1080/08874417.2008.11645304

Nowland, R., Necka, E. A., & Caciopp, J. T. (2017). Loneliness and social internet use: Pathways to reconnection in a digital world? *Perspectives on Psychological Science*, *13*(1), 70–87. doi:10.1177/1745691617713052 PMID:28937910

Nsengimana, J. P. (2017). Reflections upon periclitations in privacy: Perspectives from Rwanda's digital transformation. *Health and Technology*, *7*(4), 377–388. doi:10.100712553-017-0196-0

Nuhu, H., Effah, J., & Van Belle, J. P. (2018). Implementing E-government Financial Systems in a Developing Country: An Institutional Perspective. *Development Informatics Association (IDIA 2018)*, 45.

Nunamaker, J. F., Couger, J. D., & Davis, G. B. (1982). Information systems curriculum recommendations for the 80s: Undergraduate and graduate programs. *Communications of the ACM*, *25*(11), 781–805. doi:10.1145/358690.358698

Nyamadi, M., & Boateng, R. (2018). The Influence of IT Artifacts on Players Leading to Internet Gaming Addiction among University Students in Africa. In *Americas Conference on Information Systems* (pp. 1–10). New Orleans, LA: Academic Press.

Nycum, S. (1976). The criminal law aspects of computer abuse: Part I–state penal laws. *RUTGERS J. COMPUTERS & L.*, *5*, 271–276.

Nylén, D., & Holmström, J. (2015). Digital innovation strategy: A framework for diagnosing and improving digital product and service innovation. *Business Horizons*, *58*(1), 57–67. doi:10.1016/j.bushor.2014.09.001

O'Connor, Y., & O'Donoghue, J. (2015). Contextual Barriers to Mobile Health Technology in African Countries: A Perspective Piece. *Journal MTM*, *4*(1), 31–34. doi:10.7309/jmtm.4.1.7

O'Sullivan, A., & Shiffrin, S. M. (2003). *Economics: Principles in Action.* Pearson Prentice Hall.

Obal, M. (2017). What drives post-adoption usage? Investigating the negative and positive antecedents of disruptive technology adoption intentions. *Industrial Marketing Management*, *63*, 42–52. doi:10.1016/j.indmarman.2017.01.003

Obar, J. A., & Wildman, S. S. (2015). Social media definition and the governance challenge: An introduction to the special issue. *Telecommunications Policy*, *39*(9), 745–750. doi:10.1016/j.telpol.2015.07.014

Obloj, T., & Zemsky, P. (2015). Value creation and value capture under moral hazard: Exploring the micro-foundations of buyer-supplier relationships. *Strategic Management Journal*, *36*(8), 1146–1163. doi:10.1002/smj.2271

Obradovic, D. (2016). The role innovation on strategic orientations and competitiveness of enterprises. Ecoforum Journal, 5(1).

Ochara, N. M. (2013). Linking Reasoning to Theoretical Argument in Information Systems Research. *Proceedings of the Nineteenth Americas Conference on Information Systems*, 1–11.

Odoom, R., Anning-Dorson, T., & Acheampong, G. (2017). Antecedents of social media usage and performance benefits in small and medium-sized enterprises (SMEs). *Journal of Enterprise Information Management*, *30*(3), 383–399. doi:10.1108/JEIM-04-2016-0088

Offermann, P., Blom, S., Schönherr, M., & Bub, U. (2010). Artifact Types in Information Systems Design Science – A Literature Review. *Management Information Systems Quarterly*, *6105*, 77–92.

Ofoeda, J., & Boateng, R. (2018). Institutional Effects on API Development and Integration in Developing Countries: Evidence from Ghana. *Twenty-Fourth Americas Conference on Information Systems*.

Ofoeda, J., Boateng, R., & Effah, J. (2019). Application Programming Interface (API) Research: A Review of the Past to Inform the Future. *International Journal of Enterprise Information Systems*, *15*(3), 76–95. doi:10.4018/IJEIS.2019070105

Ofosu-Ampong, K., & Boateng, R. (2018). Gamifying Sakai: Understanding Game Elements for Learning. *Proceedings of the Twenty-fourth Americas Conference on Information Systems*. Retrieved from: https://aisel.aisnet.org/amcis2018/Education/Presentations/4

Ofosu-Ampong, K., Boateng, R., Anning-Dorson, T., & Kolog, E. A. (2019). Are we ready for Gamification? An exploratory analysis in a developing country. *Education and Information Technologies*, 1–20. doi:10.100710639-019-10057-7

Oh, E.-T., Chen, K.-M., Wang, L.-M., & Liu, R.-J. (2015). Value creation in regional innovation systems: The case of Taiwan's machine chine. *Technological Forecasting and Social Change*, *100*(100), 118–129. doi:10.1016/j.techfore.2015.09.026

Olavsrud, T. (2016, April 19). *APIs abound, but challenges remain*. Retrieved 02 15, 2019, from https://www.cio.com/article/3058732/apis-abound-but-challenges-remain.html

Oliveira, T., & Martins, M. F. (2010). Understanding e-business adoption across industries in European countries. *Industrial Management & Data Systems*, *110*(9), 1337–1354. doi:10.1108/02635571011087428

Oliveira, T., & Martins, M. F. (2011). Literature review of information technology adoption models at firm level. *The Electronic Journal Information Systems Evaluation*, *14*(1), 110–121.

Oliveira, T., Thomas, M., Baptista, G., & Campos, F. (2016). Mobile payment: Understanding the determinants of customer adoption and intention to recommend the technology. *Computers in Human Behavior*, *61*, 404–414. doi:10.1016/j.chb.2016.03.030

Omotosho, A., Tyoden, T., Ayegba, P., & Ayoola, J. (2019). Gamified Approach to Improving Student's Participation in Farm Practice--A Case Study of Landmark University. *International Journal of Interactive Mobile Technologies*, *13*(5).

Ondego, B., & Moturi, C. (2016). Evaluation of the Implementation of the e-Citizen in Kenya. *Evaluation*, *10*(4).

Ondrus, J., & Pigneur, Y. (2009). Near field communication: An assessment for future payment systems. *Information Systems and e-Business Management, 7*(3), 347–361. doi:10.1007/s10257-008-0093-1

Ong, D. L. T., Chiang, T. T. S., & Pung, A. X. Y. (2015). To Buy or To Lie: Determinants of Purchase Intention of Counterfeit Fashion in Malaysia. *International Conference on Marketing and Business Development Journal*, (1), 49-56.

Oomen, I., & Leenes, I. (2008). Privacy risk perceptions and privacy protection strategies. In E. de Leeuw, S. Fischer-Hübner, J. Tseng, & J. Borking (Eds.), *Policies and Research in Identity Management* (pp. 121–138). Boston: Springer Verlag; doi:10.1007/978-0-387-77996-6_10.

Oostervink, N., Agterberg, M., & Huysman, M. (2016). Knowledge Sharing on Enterprise Social Media: Practices to Cope With Institutional Complexity. *Journal of Computer-Mediated Communication, 21*(2), 156–176. doi:10.1111/jcc4.12153

Oppenheimer, J., Spicer, M., Trejos, A., Zille, P., Benjamin, J., Cavallo, D., & Leo, B. (2011). Putting young Africans to work: Addressing Africa's youth unemployment crisis. *The Brenthurst Foundation, Discussion Paper, 8*.

Oppong-Tawiah, D., Webster, J., Staples, S., Cameron, A. F., de Guinea, A. O., & Hung, T. Y. (2018). Developing a gamified mobile application to encourage sustainable energy use in the office. *Journal of Business Research*.

Organisation for Economic Co-operation and Development. (2015). OECD Digital Economy Outlook. Retrieved from http://www.oecd.org/sti/oecd-digital-economy-outlook-2015-9789264232440-en.html

Orlikowski, W. J., & Baroudi, J. J. (1989). *IS research paradigms: method versus substance*. Academic Press.

Orlikowski, W. (2009). The Sociomateriality of Organisational Life: Considering Technology in Management Research. *Cambridge Journal of Economics, 34*(1), 125–141. doi:10.1093/cje/bep058

Orlikowski, W. J. (1996). Improvising Organisational Transformation over Time: A Situated Change Perspective. *Information Systems Research, 7*(1), 63–92. doi:10.1287/isre.7.1.63

Orlikowski, W. J. (2000). Using Technology and Constituting Structures: A Practice Lens for Studying Technology in Organisations. *Organization Science, 11*(4), 404–428. doi:10.1287/orsc.11.4.404.14600

Orlikowski, W. J., & Baroudi, J. J. (1991). Studying Information Technology in Organizations: Research Approaches and Assumptions. *Information Systems Research, 2*(1), 1–28. doi:10.1287/isre.2.1.1

Ortutay, B. (2012). *Beyond Facebook: A look at social network history*. Academic Press.

Osatuyi, B., & Garza, M. (2014). IS 2010 curriculum model adoption in the United States. In *20th Americas Conference on Information Systems* (pp. 1–11). Academic Press.

Osatuyi, B., Osatuyi, T., & De La Rosa, R. (2018). Systematic Review of Gamification Research in IS Education: A Multi-method Approach. *Communications of the Association for Information Systems, 42*(1), 5.

Osatuyi, B., & Qin, H. (2018). How vital is the role of affect on post-adoption behaviors? An examination of social commerce users. *International Journal of Information Management, 40*(February), 175–185. doi:10.1016/j.ijinfomgt.2018.02.005

Otieno, E. O., & Kahonge, A. M. (2014). Adoption of Mobile Payments in Kenyan Businesses: A Case Study of Small and Medium Enterprises in Kenya. *International Journal of Computers and Applications, 107*(7), 5–12. doi:10.5120/18761-0041

Ott, L., & Theunissen, P. (2015). Reputations at risk: Engagement during social media crises. *Public Relations Review, 41*(1), 97–102. doi:10.1016/j.pubrev.2014.10.015

Owusu, A., Agbemabiese, G. C., Abdurrahman, D. T., & Soladoye, B. A. (2017). Determinants Of Business Intelligence Systems Adoption In Developing Countries : An Empirical Analysis From Ghanaian Banks. *Journal of Internet Banking and Commerce, 22*(S8), 1–25.

Owusu, A., Ghanbari-baghestan, A., & Kalantari, A. (2017). Investigating the Factors Affecting Business Intelligence Systems Adoption : A Case Study of Private Universities in Malaysia. *International Journal of Technology Diffusion, 8*(2), 1–25. doi:10.4018/IJTD.2017040101

Ozalp, H., Cennamo, C., & Gawer, A. (2018). Disruption in platform-based ecosystems. *Journal of Management Studies, 55*(7), 1203–1241. doi:10.1111/joms.12351

Özen, H. (2015). An Unfinished Grassroots Populism: The Gezi Park Protests in Turkey and Their Aftermath. *South European Society & Politics, 20*(4), 533–552. doi:10.1080/13608746.2015.1099258

Ozili, P. K. (2018). Impact of digital finance on financial inclusion and stability. *Borsa Istanbul Review, 18*(4), 329–340. doi:10.1016/j.bir.2017.12.003

Ozyirmidokuza, K. E., Uyar, K., & Ozyirmidokuza, H. M. (2015). *A Data Mining Based Approach to a Firm's Marketing Channel. In 22nd International Economic Conference* (pp. 1–10). Economic Prospects in the Context of Growing Global and Regional Interdep; doi:10.1016/S2212-5671(15)00975-2.

Paek, S. Y., & Nalla, M. K. (2015). The relationship between receiving phishing attempt and identity theft victimization in South Korea. *International Journal of Law, Crime and Justice, 43*(4), 626–642. doi:10.1016/j.ijlcj.2015.02.003

Pagani, M. (2013). Digital business strategy and value creation: Framing the dynamic cycle of control points. *Management Information Systems Quarterly, 37*(2), 617–632. doi:10.25300/MISQ/2013/37.2.13

Pan, Y. (2015). How to counteract negative effect of adverse selection in Chinese e-commerce market? *Comparative analysis on credit scoring system and guarantee system of TAOBAO.*

Papadopoulos, A., & Brooks, G. (2011). The investigation of credit card fraud in Cyprus: Reviewing police "effectiveness.". *Journal of Financial Crime, 18*(3), 222–234. doi:10.1108/13590791111147442

Pappas, I. O., Giannakos, M. N., & Mikalef, P. (2017). Investigating students' use and adoption of with-video assignments: Lessons learnt for video-based open educational resources. *Journal of Computing in Higher Education, 29*(1), 160–177. doi:10.1007/s12528-017-9132-6

Paquette, H. (2013). *Social media as a marketing tool: a literature review*. Major Papers by Master of Science Students. Paper 2. The University of Rhode Island, Retrieved from http://digitalcommons.uri.edu/tmd_major_papers/2

Parameswaran, M., & Whinston, A. (2007). Research Issues in Social computing. *Journal of the Association for Information Systems, 8*(6), 336–350. doi:10.17705/1jais.00132

Paré, G., & Kitsiou, S. (2017). Methods for Literature Reviews. In *Handbook of eHealth Evaluation: An Evidence-based Approach*. University of Victoria.

Paré, G., Trudel, M. C., Jaana, M., & Kitsiou, S. (2015). Synthesizing information systems knowledge: A typology of literature reviews. *Information & Management, 52*(2), 183–199. doi:10.1016/j.im.2014.08.008

Parida, V., Sjödin, D., & Reim, W. (2019). *Reviewing literature on digitalization, business model innovation, and sustainable industry: Past achievements and future promises*. Academic Press.

Park, J., Levy, J., Son, M., Park, C., & Hwang, H. (2018). Advances in Cybersecurity Design: An Integrated Framework to Quantify the Economic Impacts of Cyber-Terrorist Behavior. In Security by Design (pp. 317–339). Springer.

Parker, C. M., & Castleman, T. (2009). Small firm e-business adoption: A critical analysis of theory. *Journal of Enterprise Information Management, 22*(1/2), 167–182. doi:10.1108/17410390910932812

Parker, D. B. (1976). Computer abuse perpetrators and vulnerabilities of computer systems. *Proceedings of the National Computer Conference and Exposition,* 65–73. 10.1145/1499799.1499810

Parker, G., Van Alstyne, M., & Jiang, X. (2017). Platform ecosystems: How developers invert the firm. *Management Information Systems Quarterly, 41*(1), 255–266. doi:10.25300/MISQ/2017/41.1.13

Park, S., & Bae, D.-H. (2011). An approach to analyzing the software process change impact using process slicing and simulation. *Journal of Systems and Software, 84*(4), 528–543. doi:10.1016/j.jss.2010.11.919

Park, Y., Ju, J., & Ahn, J. H. (2015). Are People really concerned about their privacy? Privacy paradox in a mobile environment. *The Fifteenth International Conference on Electronic Business,* 123-128.

Parmentier, G., & Gandia, R. (2017). Redesigning the business model: From one-sided to multi-sided. *The Journal of Business Strategy, 38*(2), 52–61. doi:10.1108/JBS-09-2016-0097

Parry, M. E., & Kawakami, T. (2017). The Encroachment Speed of Potentially Disruptive Innovations with Indirect Network Externalities: The Case of E-Readers. *Journal of Product Innovation Management, 34*(2), 141–158. doi:10.1111/jpim.12333

Parviainen, P., Tihinen, M., Kääriäinen, J., & Teppola, S. (2017). Tackling the digitalization challenge: How to benefit from digitalization in practice. *International Journal of Information Systems and Project Management, 5*(1), 63-77.

Patten, K., & Harris, M. (2013). The Need to Address Mobile Device Security in the Higher Education IT Curriculum. *Journal of Information Systems Education, 24*(1), 41–53.

Patton, M. Q. (1990). *Qualitative evaluation and research methods.* SAGE Publications, Inc.

Paulins, N., Balina, S., & Arhipova, I. (2015). Learning content development methodology for mobile devices. *Procedia Computer Science, 43,* 147–153. doi:10.1016/j.procs.2014.12.020

Pauli, W. E., Halverson, T., & Mckeown, J. (2011). The 2010 CIS Baccalaureate Degree Compared with IS 2010 Guidelines. *Journal of Higher Education Theory and Practice, 11*(2), 102–111.

Pavlou, P. A., & Dimoka, A. (2006). The nature and role of feedback text comments in online marketplaces: Implications for trust building, price premiums, and seller differentiation. *Information Systems Research, 17*(4), 392–414. doi:10.1287/isre.1060.0106

Pavlou, P. A., & El Sawy, O. A. (2010). The 'Third Hand': IT-Enabled Competitive Advantage in Turbulence through Improvisational Capabilities. *Information Systems Research, 21*(3), 443–471. doi:10.1287/isre.1100.0280

Pavlou, P. A., Liang, H., & Xue, Y. (2007). Understanding and mitigating uncertainty in online exchange relationships: A principal-agent perspective. *Management Information Systems Quarterly, 31*(1), 105–136. doi:10.2307/25148783

Peltoniemi, M. (2005). Business ecosystem. A conceptual model of an organization population from the perspectives of complexity and evolution. *E-Business Research Center. Research Reports 18 Tampere.*

Penrose, E. (1959). *The theory of the firm.* John Wiley & Sons.

Penrose, E. G. (1959). *The Theory of the Growth of the Firm.* New York: Wiley.

Peppard, J. (2001). Bridging the gap between the IS organization and the rest of the business: Plotting a route. *Information Systems Journal, 11*(3), 249–270. doi:10.1046/j.1365-2575.2001.00105.x

Peppard, J., & Rylander, A. (2006). From Value Chain to Value Network : Insights for Mobile Operators. *European Management Journal, 24*(2–3), 128–141. doi:10.1016/j.emj.2006.03.003

Peppard, J., & Ward, J. (2004). Beyond strategic information systems: Towards an IS capability. *The Journal of Strategic Information Systems, 13*(2), 167–194. doi:10.1016/j.jsis.2004.02.002

Pereira, G. M. de C., & Pereira, S. C. F. (2011). A quantitative analysis applying Agency theory to Purchasing Department. POMS 23rd Annual Conference, 25–85.

Perez, L., & Paulino, V. D. S. (2017). Taking advantage of disruptive innovation through changes in value networks : Insights. *Supply Chain Management, 22*(2), 97–106. doi:10.1108/SCM-01-2017-0017

Perez, M. P., Martnez, S. A., Carnicer, P. L., & Jimenez, M. J. V. (2004). A technology acceptance model of innovation adoption: The case of teleworking. *European Journal of Innovation Management, 7*(4), 280–291. doi:10.1108/14601060410565038

Persson, A., & Riyals, L. (2014). Making customer relationship decisions: Analytics v rules of thumb. *Journal of Business Research, 67*(8), 1725–1732. doi:10.1016/j.jbusres.2014.02.019

Peter, A. (2018, July 23). Data Mining And Its Relevance To Business. Retrieved from https://analyticstraining.com/data-mining-and-its-relevance-to-business/

Petrenkoa, V. V. (2015). Fashion: The Game of Social Meaning as the Cynical Strategy of Consumption. *Procedia: Social and Behavioral Sciences, 200*, 506–513.

Petre, R. (2013). Data mining solutions for the business environment. *Database Systems Journal, 4*(4), 21–29.

Petronio, S. (2015). Communication privacy management theory. *The international encyclopedia of interpersonal communication*, 1-9.

Pettenati, M. C., & Cigognini, M. E. (2007). Social networking theories and tools to support connectivist learning activities. *International Journal of Web-Based Learning and Teaching Technologies, 2*(3), 42–60. doi:10.4018/jwltt.2007070103

Phau, I., & Teah, M. (2009). Devil wears (counterfeit) Prada: A study of antecedents and outcomes of attitudes towards counterfeits of luxury brands. *Journal of Consumer Marketing, 26*(1), 15–27. doi:10.1108/07363760910927019

Phichitchaisopa, N., & Naenna, T. (2013). Factors Affecting the adoption of Healthcare Information Technology. *EXCLI Journal, 12*, 413–436. PMID:26417235

Phillips, N., & Tracey, P. (2007). Opportunity recognition, entrepreneurial capabilities, and bricolage: Connecting institutional theory and entrepreneurship in strategic organization. *Strategic Organization, 5*(3), 313–320. doi:10.1177/1476127007079956

Picatoste, J., Pérez-Ortiz, L., & Ruesga-Benito, S. M. (2018). A new educational pattern in response to new technologies and sustainable development. Enlightening ICT skills for youth employability in the European Union. *Telematics and Informatics, 35*(4), 1031–1038. doi:10.1016/j.tele.2017.09.014

Picazo-Vela, S., Gutiérrez-Martínez, I., & Luna-Reyes, L. F. (2012). Understanding risks, benefits, and strategic alternatives of social media applications in the public sector. *Government Information Quarterly, 29*(4), 504–511. doi:10.1016/j.giq.2012.07.002

Picoto, W. N., Belanger, F., & Palma-dos-Reis, A. (2014). An organizational perspective on m-business: Usage factors and value determination. *European Journal of Information Systems, 23*(5), 571–592. doi:10.1057/ejis.2014.15

Pilinkienė, V., & Mačiulis, P. (2014). Comparison of different ecosystem analogies: The main economic determinants and levels of impact. *Procedia: Social and Behavioral Sciences, 156*, 365–370. doi:10.1016/j.sbspro.2014.11.204

Pilkington, C. (2018). A Playful Approach to Fostering Motivation in a Distance Education Computer Programming Course: Behaviour Change and Student Perceptions. *The International Review of Research in Open and Distributed Learning, 19*(3). doi:10.19173/irrodl.v19i3.3664

Pines, E. (2016, Dec.). Uber's bold move. *Forbes*, 58–74.

Pinto, M. B., & Yagnik, A. (2016). Fit for Life : A content analysis of fitness tracker brands use of Facebook in social media marketing. *Journal of Brand Management, 24*(1), 49–67. doi:10.1057/s41262-016-0014-4

Pipitwanichakarn, T., & Wongtada, N. (2019). Mobile commerce adoption among the bottom of the pyramid: A case of street vendors in Thailand. *Journal of Science and Technology Policy Management, 10*(1), 193–213. doi:10.1108/JSTPM-12-2017-0074

Pitchford, N. J., Chigeda, A., & Hubber, P. J. (2019). Interactive apps prevent gender discrepancies in early grade mathematics in a low-income country in Sub-Sahara Africa. *Developmental Science*, 12864. doi:10.1111/desc.12864 PMID:31120168

Pi-Tzong, J. A. N., Hsi-Peng, L. U., & Tzu-Chuan, C. H. (2012). The adoption of e-learning: An institutional theory perspective. *The Turkish Online Journal of Educational Technology, 11*(3), 326–343.

Poel, M., Renda, A., & Ballon, P. (2007). Business model analysis as a new tool for policy evaluation: Policies for digital content platforms. *Info, 9*(5), 86–100. doi:10.1108/14636690710816471

Polites, G. L., Serrano, C., & Thatcher, J. B. (2018). Understanding social networking site (SNS) identity from a dual systems perspective : An investigation of the dark side of SNS use. *European Journal of Information Systems, 9344*, 1–22.

Pollack, T. A. (2010). Strategic Information Systems Planning. In 2010 ASCUE Proceedings (pp. 47–58). Academic Press.

Pollock, N., & Williams, R. (2008). *Software and organisations: The biography of the enterprise-wide system or how SAP conquered the world*. Routledge. doi:10.4324/9780203891940

Ponelis, S. R. (2015). Using interpretive qualitative case studies for exploratory research in doctoral studies: A case of Information Systems research in small and medium enterprises. *International Journal of Doctoral Studies, 10*(1), 535–550. doi:10.28945/2339

Popovic, A., Hackney, R., Tassabehji, R., & Castelli, M. (2106). The impact of big data analytics on firms' high-value business performance. *Information Systems Front*, 3-14. doi:10.100710796-016-9720-4

Popovic, A., Hackney, R., Coelho, P., & Jaklic, J. (2012). Towards Business Intelligence Systems Success: Effects of Maturity and Culture on Analytical Decision Making. *Decision Support Systems, 54*(1), 729–739. doi:10.1016/j.dss.2012.08.017

Porter, M. E. (1985). *The Competitive Advantage: Creating and Sustaining Superior Performance*. Free Press.

Porter, M. E. (2008). *Competitive strategy: Techniques for analyzing industries and competitors*. Simon and Schuster.

Porter, M. E., & Millar, V. E. (1985). How information gives you competitive advantage. *Harvard Business Review, 63*(4), 149–174.

Porter, W. W., Graham, C. R., Bodily, R. G., & Sandberg, D. S. (2016). A qualitative analysis of institutional drivers and barriers to blended learning adoption in higher education. *The Internet and Higher Education, 28*, 17–27. doi:10.1016/j.iheduc.2015.08.003

Poston, R. S., & Dhaliwal, J. (2015). IS human capital: Assessing gaps to strengthen skill and competency sourcing. *Communications of the Association for Information Systems, 36*(34), 669–695.

Pötzsch, S. (2009). Privacy awareness: a means to solve the privacy paradox? In The Future of Identity in the Information Society. Springer-Verlag. doi:10.1007/978-3-642-03315-5_17

Pousttchi, K. (2008). A modeling approach and reference models for the analysis of mobile payment use cases. *Electronic Commerce Research and Applications, 7*(2), 182–201. doi:10.1016/j.elerap.2007.07.001

Powell, W. W., & Colyvas, J. A. (2008). Microfoundations of institutional theory. The Sage Handbook of Organizational Institutionalism, 276, 298.

Prabowo, H. Y. (2011). Building our defence against credit card fraud: A strategic view. *Journal of Money Laundering Control, 14*(4), 371–386. doi:10.1108/13685201111173848

Prasarry, Y. V., Astuti, E. S., & Suyadi, I. (2015). Factor Affecting the Adoption of Mobile Commerce (A study on SMEs in Malang). *European Journal of Business and Management,* ▪▪▪, 30–35.

Preko, M., Boateng, R., & Effah, J. (2019b). Healthcare Digitalisation in Ghana: An Assessment Based on the Realist Social Theory. *25th Americas Conference on Information Systems*, 1-5.

Premkumar, G. (2003). A meta-analysis of research on information technology implementation in small business. *Journal of Organizational Computing and Electronic Commerce, 13*(2), 91–121. doi:10.1207/S15327744JOCE1302_2

Premkumar, G., & King, W. R. (1991). Assessing Strategic Information Systems Planning. *Long Range Planning, 24*(5), 41–58. doi:10.1016/0024-6301(91)90251-I

Premkumar, G., Ramamurthy, K., & Nilakanta, S. (1994). Implementation of electronic data interchange: An innovation diffusion perspective. *Journal of Management Information Systems, 11*(2), 157–186. doi:10.1080/07421222.1994.11518044

Prichard, J., Watters, P. A., & Spiranovic, C. (2011). Internet subcultures and pathways to the use of child pornography. *Computer Law & Security Review, 27*(6), 585–600. doi:10.1016/j.clsr.2011.09.009

Priem, R. L., & Butler, J. E. (2001). Tautology in the resource-based view and the implications of externally determined resource value: Further comments. *Academy of Management Review, 26*(1), 57–66. doi:10.5465/amr.2001.4011946

Productivity Commission. (2016). *Digital Disruption: What do governments need to do.* Melbourne: Commonwealth of Australia.

Qin, L. (2017). A Cross-Cultural Study of Interpersonal Trust in Social Commerce. *Journal of Computer Information Systems,* ▪▪▪, 1–8. doi:10.1080/08874417.2017.1383865

Qiu, D., Li, B., & Leung, H. (2016). Understanding the API usage in Java. *Information and Software Technology, 73*, 81–100. doi:10.1016/j.infsof.2016.01.011

Qorbani, D., Yamaguchi, Y., & Cosenz, F. (2017). *Analyzing Business Dynamics of Ride-Hailing Services.* In The International Conference Of The System Dynamics Society, Cambridge, MA.

Queiroz, M. (2017). Mixed results in strategic IT alignment research: A synthesis and empirical study. *European Journal of Information Systems, 26*(1), 21–36.

Queiroz, M., Tallon, P. P., Sharma, R., & Coltman, T. (2018). The role of IT application orchestration capability in improving agility and performance. *The Journal of Strategic Information Systems, 27*(1), 4–21. doi:10.1016/j.jsis.2017.10.002

Quoquab, F., Pahlevan, S., Mohammad, J., & Thurasamy, R. (2017). Factors affecting consumers' intention to purchase counterfeit product: Empirical study in the Malaysian market. *Asia Pacific Journal of Marketing and Logistics, 29*(4), 837–853. doi:10.1108/APJML-09-2016-0169

Rachapila, T., & Jansirisak, S. (2013). Using Porter's Five Forces Model for analysing the competitive environment of Thailand's sweet corn industry. *International Journal of Business and Social Research*, *3*(3), 174–184.

Rachinger, M., Rauter, R., Müller, C., Vorraber, W., & Schirgi, E. (2018). Digitalization and its influence on business model innovation. *Journal of Manufacturing Technology Management*.

Rackoff, N., Wiseman, C., & Ullrich, W. A. (1985). Information Systems for Competitive Advantage : Implementation of a Planning Process. *Management Information Systems Quarterly*, *9*(4), 285–294. doi:10.2307/249229

Radevski, S., Hata, H., & Matsumoto, K. (2016). Towards Building API Usage Example Metrics. *2016 IEEE 23rd International Conference on Software Analysis, Evolution, and Reengineering.*

Raghupathi, W., & Raghupathi, V. (2014). Big data Analytics in Healthcare: Promise and Potential. *Health Information Science and Systems*, *2*(3), 2–10. doi:10.1186/2047-2501-2-3 PMID:25825667

Rahayu, R., & Day, J. (2015). Determinant factors of e-commerce adoption by SMEs in developing country: Evidence from Indonesia. *Procedia: Social and Behavioral Sciences*, *195*, 142–150. doi:10.1016/j.sbspro.2015.06.423

Rahman, A., & Airini. (2017). Emerging Technologies with Disruptive Effects: A Review. PERINTIS eJournal, 7(2).

Rahman, M. N. A., Jaafar, J., Kadir, M. F. A., Shamsuddin, S. N., & Saany, S. I. A. (2018). Cloud-Based Gamification Model Canvas for School Information Management. *International Journal of Engineering & Technology, 7*(2.14), 28-31.

Rai, A., Pavlou, P. A., Im, G., & Du, S. (2012). Interfirm IT Capability Profiles and Communications for Cocreating Relational Value: Evidence from the Logistics Industry. *Management Information Systems Quarterly*, *36*(1), 233–262. doi:10.2307/41410416

Rainer, R. K., Cegielski, C. G., & Prince, B. (2010). *Introduction to information systems: Supporting and transforming business* (3rd ed.). John Wiley & Sons.

Rainie, L. (2018). Americans' complicated feelings about social media in an era of privacy concerns (White paper). Fact Tank News.

Ramadan, R., & Aita, J. (2018). A model of mobile payment usage among Arab consumers. *International Journal of Bank Marketing*, *36*(7), 1213–1234. doi:10.1108/IJBM-05-2017-0080

Raman, K. (2015). Machine Learning From Human Preferences And Choices. PhD thesis at Cornell University: https://ecommons.cornell.edu/handle/1813/40961

Ramdani, B., Kawalek, P., & Lorenzo, O. (2009). Predicting SMEs' adoption of enterprise systems. *Journal of Enterprise Information Management*, *22*(1), 10–24. doi:10.1108/17410390910922796

Ramesh, V., & Gerth, A. B. (2015). Design of an integrated information systems master's core curriculum: A case study. *Communications of the Association for Information Systems*, *36*, 301–316. doi:10.17705/1CAIS.03616

Ramiller, N. (2016). New Technology and the Post-human Self: Rethinking Appropriation and Resistance. ACM SIGMIS Database. *The Data Base for Advances in Information Systems*, *47*(4), 23–33. doi:10.1145/3025099.3025102

Ramli, A., Ismail, I. B., & Idrus, R. M. (2010). Mobile Learning Via SMS Among Distance Learners: Does Learning Transfer Occur? *International Journal of Interactive Mobile Technologies*, *4*(3), 30–35.

Ramos-de-Luna, I., Montoro-Ríos, F., & Liébana-Cabanillas, F. (2016). Determinants of the intention to use NFC technology as a payment system: An acceptance model approach. *Information Systems and e-Business Management*, *14*(2), 293–314. doi:10.1007/s10257-015-0284-5

Ramtohul, I. (2016). Identifying the Adoption Process for Electronic Health Services: Qualitative Study. In H. Albach, H. Meffert, A. Pinkwart, R. Reichwald, & W. von Eiff (Eds.), *Boundaryless Hospital. Springer.* doi:10.1007/978-3-662-49012-9_15

Rana, N. P., Barnard, D. J., Baabdullah, A. M., Rees, D., & Roderick, S. (2019). Exploring barriers of m-commerce adoption in SMEs in the UK: Developing a framework using ISM. *International Journal of Information Management, 44,* 141–153. doi:10.1016/j.ijinfomgt.2018.10.009

Rana, N. P., Dwivedi, Y. K., Lal, B., Williams, M. D., & Clement, M. (2017). Citizens' adoption of an electronic government system: Towards a Unified View. *Information Systems Frontiers, 19*(3), 549–568. doi:10.1007/s10796-015-9613-y

Ranerup, A., Zinner, H., & Hedman, J. (2016). An analysis of business models in Public Service Platforms. *Government Information Quarterly, 33*(1), 6–14. doi:10.1016/j.giq.2016.01.010

Rangga, A. A., Setyohadi, D. B., & Santoso, A. J. (2017). Strategic Planning of Information System (Case Study: Ministry of Religious Affairs in Southwest Sumba). *International Journal of Computer Engineering and Information Technology, 9*(7), 143–149.

Rao, U. H., & Nayak, U. (2014). *Malicious software and anti-virus software. In The InfoSec Handbook* (pp. 141–161). Berkeley, CA: Apress.

Rasmussen, D., & Eliasmith, C. (2011). A Neural Model of Rule Generation in Inductive Reasoning. *Topics in Cognitive Science, 3*(1), 140–153. doi:10.1111/j.1756-8765.2010.01127.x PMID:25164178

Rauniar, R., Rawski, G., Yang, J., & Johnson, B. (2014). Technology acceptance model (TAM) and social media usage: An empirical study on Facebook. *Journal of Enterprise Information Management, 27*(1), 6–30. doi:10.1108/JEIM-04-2012-0011

Ray, G., Muhanna, W. A., & Barney, J. B. (2005). Information Technology and the Performance of the Customer Service Process: A Resource Based Analysis. MIS Quarter, 29(4), 695–704. Retrieved from https://www.jstor.org/stable/25148703

Rayle, L., Shaheen, S., Chan, N., Dai, D., & Cervero, R. (2014). App-Based, On-Demand Ride Services: Comparing Taxi and Ridesourcing Trips and User Characteristics in San Francisco. University of California Transportation Center.

Rayna, T., & Striukova, L. (2015). Open innovation 2.0: Is co-creation the ultimate challenge? *International Journal of Technology Management, 69*(1), 38–53. doi:10.1504/IJTM.2015.071030

Razzaq, A., Ayub, A., Arzu, F., & Aslam, M. S. (2013). The nexus between technological learning, downsizing, employee commitment, and organizational performance. *Business Management Dynamics, 2*(10), 74.

Reijers, W., & Coeckelbergh, M. (2016). The Blockchain as a Narrative Technology: Investigating the Social Ontology and Normative Configurations of Cryptocurrencies. *Philosophy & Technology,* 1–28.

Rejeb, A. (2018). Blockchain Potential in Tilapia Supply Chain in Ghana. *Acta Technica Jaurinensis, 11*(2), 104–118. doi:10.14513/actatechjaur.v11.n2.462

Report, U. (2018). Technology and Innovation development. Switzerland: *United Nations Conference on Trade and Development.*

Reuver, M. D. (2017). When technological superiority is not enough: The struggle to impose the SIM card as the NFC Secure Element for mobile payment platforms. *Telecommunications Policy, 41*(4), 253–262. doi:10.1016/j.telpol.2017.01.004

Reuver, M., Sørensen, C., & Basole, R. (2017). The digital platform: A research agenda. *Journal of Information Technology.*

Reynolds, J. H., Adams, D. R., Ferguson, R. C., & Leidig, P. M. (2017). Programming in the IS Curriculum: Are Requirements Changing for the Right Reason? *Information Systems Education Journal, 15*(1), 80–85.

Reynolds, J. H., Ferguson, R. C., & Leidig, P. M. (2016). A Tale of Two Curricula: The Case for Pre-requisites in the IS Model Curriculum. *Information Systems Education Journal, 14*(5), 17–24.

Reyns, B. W. (2015). A routine activity perspective on online victimisation: Results from the Canadian General Social Survey. *Journal of Financial Crime, 22*(4), 396–411. doi:10.1108/JFC-06-2014-0030

Rezaei, R., Chiew, T. K., & Lee, S. P. (2014). A review on E-business Interoperability Frameworks. *Journal of Systems and Software, 93*, 199–216. doi:10.1016/j.jss.2014.02.004

Ricardo, & Barbosa. (2019, July 23). Importance Of Data Mining In Today's Business World. Retrieved from https://www.ricardo-barbosa.com/importance-of-data-mining-in-todays-business-world/

Rienstra, S., Bakker, P., & Visser, J. (2015). *International comparison of taxi regulations and Uber*. KiM Netherlands Institute for Transport Policy.

Rilling, S. (2015). *Mobile banking acceptance among young consumers in Germany: an empirical analysis* (Doctoral dissertation).

Rishi, B. J., & Goyal, D. P. (2008). Article information. *Journal of Advances in Management Research, 5*(1), 46–55.

Rivard, S., & Lapointe, L. (2012). Information Technology Implementers' Responses to User Resistance: Nature and Effects. *Management Information Systems Quarterly, 36*(3), 897–920. doi:10.2307/41703485

Roberts, N., & Grover, V. (2012). Leveraging information technology infrastructure to facilitate a firm's customer agility and competitive activity: An empirical investigation. *Journal of Management Information Systems, 28*(4), 231–270. doi:10.2753/MIS0742-1222280409

Rockart, J. F. (1979). Chief executives define their own data needs. [PubMed]. *Harvard Business Review, 57*(2), 81–93.

Rodríguez, M. P. (2017). Governance Models for the Delivery of Public Services through the Web 2.0 Technologies: A Political View in Large Spanish Municipalities. *Social Science Computer Review, 35*(2), 203–225. doi:10.1177/0894439315609919

Rogers, B. (2016). The Social Costs of Uber. *University of Chicago Law Review Dialogue, 82*(85), 85–102.

Rogers, E. (2003). *Diffusions of Innovations*. New York: Free Press.

Rogers, E. M. (1995). *Diffusion of Innovations*. New York, NY: The Free Press.

Rogers, E. M. (1995). Lessons for guidelines from the diffusion of innovations. *Joint Commission Journal on Quality and Patient Safety, 21*(7), 324–328. PubMed

RogueWaveb, S. (2017). *Enterprise API management defined*. Rogue Wave Software, Inc.

Rondan-Cataluña, J. F., Arenas-Gaitán, J., & Ramírez-Correa, P. (2015). A comparison of the different versions of popular technology acceptance models A non-linear perspective. *Kybernetes, 44*(5), 788–805. doi:10.1108/K-09-2014-0184

Rooksby, J., & Dimitrov, K. (2017). Trustless education? A blockchain system for university grades. In *New Value Transactions*. Understanding and Designing for Distributed Autonomous Organisations, Workshop at DIS.

Rosenthal, R., & DiMatteo, M. R. (2001). Meta-analysis: Recent Developments in Quantitative Methods for Literature Reviews. *Annual Review of Psychology, 52*(1), 59–82. doi:10.1146/annurev.psych.52.1.59 PMID:11148299

Roskos, K., Brueck, J., & Lenhart, L. (2017). An analysis of e-book learning platforms: Affordances, architecture, functionality and analytics. *International Journal of Child-Computer Interaction, 12*, 37–45. doi:10.1016/j.ijcci.2017.01.003

Rösner, L., Winter, S., & Krämer, N. C. (2016). Dangerous minds? Effects of uncivil online comments on aggressive cognitions, emotions, and behavior. *Computers in Human Behavior, 58*, 461–470. doi:10.1016/j.chb.2016.01.022

Rossotto, C. M., Das, P. L., Ramos, E. G., Miranda, E. C., Farid Badran, M., Licetti, M. M., & Murciego, G. M. (2018). Digital platforms: A literature review and policy implications for development. *Competition and Regulation in Network Industries, 19*(1–2), 1–17. doi:10.1177/1783591718809485

Rouse, M. (2011). Digital Enterprise. Retrieved May 3, 2018, from https://searchcio.techtarget.com/definition/Digital-enterprise

Rouse, M. (2018, July 23rd). Disruptive technology. Retrieved from https://whatis.techtarget.com/definition/disruptive-technology

Rousseeuw, P. (1987). Silhouettes: A Graphical Aid to the Interpretation and Validation of Cluster Analysis. *Computational & Applied Mathematics, 20*, 53–65. doi:10.1016/0377-0427(87)90125-7

Rubel, S. (2006). *Trends to watch. Part II: social commerce--micro persuasion.* Academic Press.

Rubel, S. (2006). *Trends to watch. Part II: social commerce--micro persuasion.* Academic Press.

Rubin, H. J., & Rubin, I. S. (2011). *Qualitative interviewing: The art of hearing data.* Sage Publications.

Ruivo, P., Oliveira, T., & Neto, M. (2015). Using resource-based view theory to assess the value of ERP commercial-packages in SMEs. *Computers in Industry, 73*, 105–116. doi:10.1016/j.compind.2015.06.001

Russell, S. J., & Norvig, P. (2016). *Artificial intelligence: a modern approach.* Malaysia: Pearson Education Limited.

Ruutu, S., Casey, T., & Kotovirta, V. (2017). Development and competition of digital service platforms : A system dynamics approach. *Technological Forecasting and Social Change, 117*, 119–130. doi:10.1016/j.techfore.2016.12.011

Saathoff, A. (2005). Human factors considerations relevant to CPOE implementations. *Journal of Healthcare Information Management, 19*(3), 71–78. Retrieved from http://www.ncbi.nlm.nih.gov/pubmed/16045087 PubMed

Sadeh, N. (2003). *M-commerce: Technologies, services, and business models.* John Wiley & Sons.

Safwan, E. R., Meredithand, R., & Burst, F. (2016). Business Intelligence (BI) system evolution: A case in a healthcare institution. *Journal of Decision Systems, 25*(1), 463–475. doi:10.1080/12460125.2016.1187384

Saka, E. (2018). Social media in Turkey as a space for political battles: AKTrolls and other politically motivated trolling. *Middle East Critique, 27*(2), 161–177. doi:10.1080/19436149.2018.1439271

Sakr, G. E., Elhajj, I. H., & Mitri, G. (2011). Efficient forest fire occurrence prediction for developing countries using two weather parameters. *Engineering Applications of Artificial Intelligence, 24*(5), 888–894. doi:10.1016/j.engappai.2011.02.017

Sakr, S., & Elgammal, A. (2016). Towards a Comprehensive Data Analytics Frameworks for Smart Healthcare Services. *Big Data Research., 4*, 44–58. doi:10.1016/j.bdr.2016.05.002

Salah, K. (2013). *E-commerce and small and medium enterprises in least developed countries: The case of Tanzania (PhD).* University of Cape Town.

Salanovaa, J. M., Estrada, M., Aifadopoulou, G., & Mitsakis, E. (2011). A review of the modeling of taxi services. *Procedia: Social and Behavioral Sciences, 20*(1), 150–161. doi:10.1016/j.sbspro.2011.08.020

Salisbury, W., Pearson, R., Pearson, A., & Miller, D. (2001). Identifying barriers that keep shoppers off the world wide web: Developing a scale of perceived web security. *Industrial Management & Data Systems, 101*(4), 165–176.

Salleh, N. M., Selamat, S. R., Yusof, R., & Sahib, S. (2016). Discovering Cyber Terrorism Using Trace Pattern. *International Journal of Network Security, 18*(6), 1034–1040.

Salu, A. O. (2005). Online crimes and advance fee fraud in Nigeria-are available legal remedies adequate? *Journal of Money Laundering Control, 8*(2), 159–167. doi:10.1108/13685200510621091

Salwani, I. M., Marthandan, G., Norzaidi, M. D., & Chong, S. C. (2009). E-commerce usage and business performance in the Malaysian tourism sector: Empirical analysis. *Information Management & Computer Security, 17*(2), 166–185. doi:10.1108/09685220910964027

Samaha, K., & Dahawy, K. (2010). Information System Strategy Development and Implementation in the Egyptian Small and Medium Construction Enterprises. In E-Strategies for Technological Diffusion and Adoption: National ICT Approaches for Socioeconomic Development (pp. 88–121). IGI Global. doi:10.4018/978-1-60566-388-3.ch005

Sambamurthy, V., & Jarvenpaa, S. (2002). JSIS Editorial—Special Issue on "Trust in the Digital Economy.". *The Journal of Strategic Information Systems, 11*(3-4), 183–185. doi:10.1016/S0963-8687(02)00032-X

Samuelson, W., & Zeckhauser, R. (1988). Status quo bias in decision making. *Journal of Risk and Uncertainty, 1*(1), 7–59. doi:10.1007/BF00055564

Sandberg, L. A. C., & Öhberg, P. (2017). The role of gender in online campaigning: Swedish candidates' motives and use of social media during the European election 2014. *Journal of Information Technology & Politics, 14*(4), 314–333. doi:10.1080/19331681.2017.1369918

Sanford, C., & Oh, H. (2010). The Role of User Resistance in the Adoption of a Mobile Data Service. *Cyberpsychology, Behavior, and Social Networking, 13*(6), 663–672. doi:10.1089/cyber.2009.0377 PubMed

Santos, A., & Myers, B. (2017). Design annotations to improve API discoverability. *Journal of Systems and Software, 126*, 17–33. doi:10.1016/j.jss.2016.12.036

Santos, A., Prendi, G., Sousa, H., & Ribeiro, R. (2017). Stepwise API usage assistance using n-gram language models. *Journal of Systems and Software, 000*, 1–14.

Sanz, E., & Crosbie, T. (2016). The meaning of digital platforms: Open and closed television infrastructure. *Poetics, 55*, 76–89. doi:10.1016/j.poetic.2015.11.002

Saprikis, V., & Vlachopoulou, M. (2012). Determinants of suppliers' level of use of B2B e-marketplaces. *Industrial Management & Data Systems, 112*(4), 619–643. doi:10.1108/02635571211225512

Saravana, K., N., M., Eswari, T., Sampath, P., & Lavanya, S. (2015). Predictive Methodology for Diabetic Data Analysis in Big Data. *Procedia Computer Science, 50*, 203-208. doi:10.1016/j.procs.2015.04.069

Sarker, S., Sarker, S., Sahaym, A., & Bjørn-Andersen, N. (2012). Exploring value cocreation in relationships betweenan ERP vendor and its partners : A revelatory case study. MIS Quarterly: Management. *Information Systems, 36*(1), 317–338. doi:10.2307/41410419

Sarpong, G. D., Howard, E. K., & Osei-Ntiri, K. (2011). Globalization of the fashion industry and its effects on Ghanaian independent fashion designers. *Journal of Science and Technology, 31*(3), 97–106.

Sarre, R., Lau, L. Y.-C., & Chang, L. Y. C. (2018). *Responding to cybercrime: current trends.* Taylor & Francis.

Sarris, A., & Sawyer, M. G. (1989). Automated information systems in mental health services: A review. *International Journal of Mental Health*, *18*(4), 18–30. doi:10.1080/00207411.1989.11449141

Saulnier, B., & White, B. (2011). IS 2010 and ABET Accreditation: An Analysis of ABET-Accredited Information Systems Programs. *Journal of Information Systems Education*, *22*(4), 347–354.

Sauls, J., & Gudigantala, N. (2013). Preparing Information Systems (IS) Graduates to Meet the Challenges of Global IT Security: Some Suggestions. *Journal of Information Systems Education*, *24*(1), 71–73.

Saunders, M., Lewis, P., & Thornhill, A. (2009). *Research methods for business students*. Pearson education.

Sawyer, S., & Jarrahi, M. H. (2014). Sociotechnical Approaches to the Study of Information Systems. In CRC Handbook of Computing. Chapman and Hall. doi:10.1201/b16768-7

Schell, B. H., Martin, M. V., Hung, P. C. K., & Rueda, L. (2007). Cyber child pornography: A review paper of the social and legal issues and remedies—and a proposed technological solution. *Aggression and Violent Behavior*, *12*(1), 45–63. doi:10.1016/j.avb.2006.03.003

Scheller, T., & Kühn, E. (2015). Automated measurement of API usability: The API Concepts Framework. *Information and Software Technology*, *61*, 145–162. doi:10.1016/j.infsof.2015.01.009

Scherer, F. M. (1980). *Industrial market structure and economic performance*. Boston: Houghton Mifflin.

Schermann, M., Hemsen, H., Buchmüller, C., Bitter, T., Krcmar, H., Markl, V., & Hoeren, T. (2014). Big data: An interdisciplinary opportunity for information systems research. *Business & Information Systems Engineering*, *5*(5), 261–266. doi:10.100712599-014-0345-1

Schermer, B. W., Custer, B., & van der Hof, S. (2014). The crisis of content: How stronger legal protection may lead to weaker consent in data protection. *Ethics and Information Technology*, *16*(2), 171–182.

Schiavi, G. S., & Behr, A. (2018). Emerging technologies and new business models: A review of disruptive business models. *Innovation & Management Review*, *15*(4), 338–355. doi:10.1108/INMR-03-2018-0013

Schiller, S., Goul, M., Iyer, L. S., Sharda, R., Schrader, D., & Asamoah, D. (2015). Build your dream (Not just big) analytics program. *Communications of the Association for Information Systems*, *37*(1), 811–826.

Schiro, J. B., & Baker, R. L. (2009). Downsizing and organizational change survivors and victims: Mental health issues. *International Journal of Applied Management and Technology*, *7*(1), 3.

Schmidt, F. A. (2017). *Digital labour markets in the platform economy mapping the political challenges of crowd work and gig work. Friedrich Ebert Stiftung*. Division for Economic and Social Policy.

Scholl, H. J., & Klischewski, R. (2007). E-government integration and interoperability: Framing the research agenda. *International Journal of Public Administration*, *30*(8-9), 889–920. doi:10.1080/01900690701402668

Scholtz, B., Cilliers, C., & Calitz, A. A. (2012). A Comprehensive, Competency-Based Education Framework Using Medium-Sized ERP Systems. *Journal of Information Systems Education*, *23*(4), 345.

Scholz, R. W., & Tietje, O. (2002). Embedded case study methods. *Integrating Quantitative and Qualitative*.

Schreffler, E. N. (2018). Better Integrating Travel Choices into Future Urban Mobility Systems : The Day the Highways Stood Still. *Journal of Public Transportation*, *21*(1), 82–91. doi:10.5038/2375-0901.21.1.9

Schröder, J., Berger, T., Westermann, S., Klein, J. P., & Moritz, S. (2016). Internet interventions for depression: New developments. *Dialogues in Clinical Neuroscience*, *18*(2), 203–212. PMID:27489460

Schweitzer, L., & Duxbury, L. (2010). Conceptualizing and measuring the virtuality of teams. *Information Systems Journal, 20*(3), 267–295. doi:10.1111/j.1365-2575.2009.00326.x

Schwieger, D., & Ladwig, C. (2016). Protecting Privacy in Big Data: A Layered Approach for Curriculum Integration. *Information Systems Education Journal, 14*(3), 45–54.

Scott, W. R. (1987). The adolescence of institutional theory. *Administrative Science Quarterly, 4*(4), 493–511. doi:10.2307/2392880

Scott, W. R. (2008a). *Institutions and Organizations: Ideas and Interests* (3rd ed.). Thousand Oaks, CA: Sage.

Seaborn, K., & Fels, D. I. (2015). Gamification in theory and action: A survey. *International Journal of Human-Computer Studies, 74,* 14–31. doi:10.1016/j.ijhcs.2014.09.006

Sedera, D., Lokuge, S., Grover, V., Sarker, S., & Sarker, S. (2016). Innovating with enterprise systems and digital platforms: A contingent resource-based theory view. *Information & Management, 53*(3), 366–379. doi:10.1016/j.im.2016.01.001

Sedmak, A. (2016). The Innovator's Dilemma: When New Technologies Cause Great Firms to Fail. *Defense AR Journal, 23*(4), 414.

Sein, M. K., Thapa, D., Hatakka, M., & Sæbø, Ø. (2016). What theories do we need to know to conduct ICT4D research? *Proceedings of SIG GlobDev Ninth Annual Workshop.*

Sein, M. K., Thapa, D., Hatakka, M., & Sæbø, Ø. (2019). A holistic perspective on the theoretical foundations for ICT4D research. *Information Technology for Development, 25*(1), 7–25. doi:10.1080/02681102.2018.1503589

Selander, L., & Henfridsson, O. (2012). Cynicism as user resistance in IT implementation. *Information Systems Journal, 22*(4), 289–312. doi:10.1111/j.1365-2575.2011.00386.x

Sen, A. (1997). Maximisation and the act of choice. *Econometrica, 65*(4), 745–779. doi:10.2307/2171939

Sen, A. (1999). *Development as freedom.* Oxford, UK: Oxford University Press.

Şen, A. F., & Kök, H. (2017). Sosyal medya ve feminist aktivizm: Türkiye'deki feminist grupların aktivizm biçimleri [Social media and feminist activism: Activism styles of feminist groups in Turkey]. *Atatürk İletişim Dergisi, 13,* 73–86.

Sendall, P., & Shannon, L.-J. (2011). The Greening of the Information Systems Curriculum. *Information Systems Education Journal, 9*(5), 27–45.

Senyo, P. K., Addae, E., & Boateng, R. (2018). Cloud computing research: A review of research themes, frameworks, methods and future research directions. *International Journal of Information Management, 38*(1), 128–139. doi:10.1016/j.ijinfomgt.2017.07.007

Serenko, A., & Turel, O. (2015). *Integrating Technology Addiction and Use An Empirical Investigation of Facebook Users.* Conceptual Replication. doi:10.17705/1atrr.00002

Seyal, A. H., & Rahman, M. N. A. (2003). A preliminary investigation of e-commerce adoption in small & medium enterprises in Brunei. *Journal of Global Information Technology Management, 6*(2), 6–26. doi:10.1080/1097198X.2003.10856347

Seyal, A. H., Rahman, M. N. A., & Mohammad, H. A. Y. (2007). A quantitative analysis of factors contributing electronic data interchange adoption among Bruneian SMEs: A pilot study. *Business Process Management Journal, 13*(5), 728–746. doi:10.1108/14637150710823183

Shah, N., & Pathak, J. (2014). Why healthcare may finally be ready for big data. *Harvard Business Review.*

Sharma, K., Shrivastava, G., & Kumar, V. (2011). Web Mining : *Today and Tomorrow. International Conference on Electronics Computer Technology* (pp. 399–403). IEEE.

Sharma, R., & Panigrahi, P. K. (2015). *Developing a roadmap for planning and implementation of interoperability capability in e-government. Transforming Government: People*, Process and Policy.

Sharma, S., & Crossler, R. E. (2014). Disclosing too much? Situational factors affecting information disclosure in social commerce environment. *Electronic Commerce Research and Applications, 13*(5), 305–319. doi:10.1016/j.elerap.2014.06.007

Sharples, M., Arnedillo-Sánchez, I., Milrad, M., & Vavoula, G. (2009). *Mobile learning.* Springer Netherlands.

Sharples, M., & Domingue, J. (2016, September). The blockchain and kudos: A distributed system for educational record, reputation, and reward. In *European Conference on Technology Enhanced Learning* (pp. 490-496). Springer. 10.1007/978-3-319-45153-4_48

Shatnawi, A., Seriai, A.-D., Sahraoui, H., & Alshara, Z. (2016). Reverse engineering reusable software components from object-oriented APIs. *Journal of Systems and Software*, 1–19.

Shen, Y. C., Huang, C. Y., Chu, C. H., & Hsu, C. T. (2010). A benefit–cost perspective of the consumer adoption of the mobile banking system. *Behaviour & Information Technology, 29*(5), 497–511. doi:10.1080/01449290903490658

Sherif, K., Zmud, R. W., & Browne, G. J. (2006). Managing Peer-to-Peer Conflicts in Disruptive Information Technology Innovations: The Case of Software Reuse. *Management Information Systems Quarterly, 30*(2), 339–356. doi:10.2307/25148734

Sherwin, A. (2012). Former darling of social media changes hands for a pittance as users move on to other attractions. *Independent.* Retrieved 10 July 2019, from https://www.independent.co.uk/life-style/gadgets-and-tech/news/in-2008-google-offered-200m-for-it-today-digg-was-sold-for-500000-7942217.html

Shih, Y. Y., Chen, C. Y., Wu, C. H., Huang, T., & Shiu, S. H. (2010). *Adopted intention of mobile commerce from TAM perspective: An empirical study of real estate industry.* Paper presented at the Portland International Center for Management of Engineering and Technology Conference, Phuket, Thailand.

Shih, Y., & Huang, S.-S. (2009). The Actual Usage of ERP Systems : An Extended. *Journal of Research and Practice in Information Technology, 41*(3), 263–276.

Shirky, C. (2011). The political power of social media: Technology, the public sphere, and political change. *Foreign Affairs, 90*(1), 28–41. Retrieved from http://www.jstor.org/stable/25800379

Shi, Z., Rui, H., & Whinston, A. (2014). Content Sharing in a Social Broadcasting Environment: Evidence from Twitter. *Management Information Systems Quarterly, 38*(1), 123–142. doi:10.25300/MISQ/2014/38.1.06

Shklovski, I., Mainwaring, S. D., Skúladóttir, H. H., & Borgthorsson, H. (2014). Leakiness and creepiness in-app space: Perceptions of privacy and mobile app use. CHI 2014, 2347-2356. doi:10.1145/2556288.2557421

Siamagka, N. T., Christodoulides, G., Michaelidou, N., & Valvi, A. (2015). Determinants of social media adoption by B2B organizations. *Industrial Marketing Management, 51*, 89–99. doi:10.1016/j.indmarman.2015.05.005

Sia, S. K., Soh, C., & Weill, P. (2013). How DBS Bank Pursued a Digital Business Strategy. *Management Information Systems Quarterly, 27*(2), 471–662.

Siau, K., Sheng, H., Nah, F., & Davis, S. (2004). A qualitative investigation on consumer trust in mobile commerce. *International Journal of Electronic Business, 2*(3), 283–300. doi:10.1504/IJEB.2004.005143

Sidek, Y. H., & Martins, J. T. (2017). Perceived Critial Success Factors of Electronic Health Record System Implementation in a Dental Context: An Organisational Management Perspective. *International Journal of Medical Informatics*, *107*, 88–100. doi:10.1016/j.ijmedinf.2017.08.007 PMID:29029696

Sidorova, A. (2013). Business analysis as an opportunity for IS programs in business schools. *Communications of the Association for Information Systems*, *33*(1), 521–540.

Silbert, S. (2015). *How mobile payments will grow in 2016*. Academic Press.

Silva, M. L., Delaney, A. S., Cochran, J., Jackson, R., & Olivares, C. (2015). Institutional Assessment and the Integrative Core Curriculum: Involving students in the development of an e-Portfolio system. *International Journal of E-Portfolio*, *5*(2), 255–167.

Silverman, R. D. (2013). EHRs, EMRs, and Health Information Technology: To Meaningful Use and Beyond. *Journal of Legal Medicine*, *34*(1), 1–6. doi:10.1080/01947648.2013.768134 PMID:23550980

Silvius, G. A., & Stoop, J. (2013). Relationship Between Strategic Information Systems Planning Situational Factors, Process Configuration and Success. *Journal of International Technology and Information Management*, *22*(1), 1–17.

Simmel, G. (2009). *Sociology: Inquiries into the construction of social forms*. Leiden: Brill; doi:10.1163/ej.9789004173217.i-698.

Simmons, R., Effah, J., & Boateng, R. (2019). Digital Innovation and Taxi Services : The Case of Uru in Ghana. In *Twenty-fifth Americas Conference on Information Systems* (pp. 1–10). Cancun: AIS.

Simmons, R. O. (2018). Disruptive Digital Technology Services: The Case of Uber Car Ridesharing in Ghana. In *Twenty-fourth Americas Conference on Information Systems, AMCIS 16-18 August*. New Orleans, LA: AIS.

Simon, M., & Choo, K.-K. R. (2014). *Digital forensics: challenges and future research directions*. Academic Press.

Singh, A. (2016). The future of mobile wallets in India. The Hindu Business Line, 10.

Singh, S., & Srivastava, S. (2018). Moderating effect of product type on online shopping behaviour and purchase intention: An Indian perspective. Cogent Arts & Humanities, 5(1), 1495043. doi:10.1080/23311983.2018.1495043

Singh, T. (2019, August 29). *Software Ate The World; Now AI Is Eating Software*. Retrieved November 10, 2019, from https://www.forbes.com: https://www.forbes.com/sites/cognitiveworld/2019/08/29/software-ate-the-world-now-ai-is-eating-software/#2861882a5810

Singleton, T. (2013). Fighting the Cybercrime Plague. *Journal of Corporate Accounting & Finance*, *24*(5), 3–7. doi:10.1002/jcaf.21869

Sircar, S. (2009). Business Intelligence in the Business Curriculum. *Communications of the Association for Information Systems*, *24*(24), 289–302.

Sivakumar, C., & Kwok, R. C. W. (2017). Course design based on enhanced intercultural transformation theory (EITT): Transforming information systems (IS) students into inventors during academic exchange. *Communications of the Association for Information Systems*, *40*(1), 402–419. doi:10.17705/1CAIS.04019

Slade, E. L., Dwivedi, Y. K., Piercy, N. C., & Williams, M. D. (2015). Modeling consumers' adoption intentions of remote mobile payments in the United Kingdom: Extending UTAUT with innovativeness, risk, and trust. *Psychology and Marketing*, *32*(8), 860–873. doi:10.1002/mar.20823

Slade, E. L., Williams, M. D., & Dwivedi, Y. K. (2013). Mobile payment adoption: Classification and review of the extant literature. *The Marketing Review*, *13*(2), 167–190. doi:10.1362/146934713X13699019904687

Slade, E., Dwivedi, Y., Williams, M., & Piercy, N. (2016). An empirical investigation of remote mobile payment adoption. In *Let's Get Engaged! Crossing the Threshold of Marketing's Engagement Era* (pp. 441–442). Cham: Springer; doi:10.1007/978-3-319-11815-4_122.

Slavin, R. E. (1986). Best-evidence synthesis: An alternative to meta-analytic and traditional reviews. *Educational Researcher*, *15*(9), 5–11. doi:10.3102/0013189X015009005

Sledgianowski, D., Luftman, J., & Reilly, R. R. (2006). Development and Validation of an Instrument to Measure Maturity of IT Business Strategic Alignment Mechanisms. Information Resources Management, 13(6), 18–33. doi:10.4018/irmj.2006070102

Smith, E. J., & Kollars, N. A. (2015). QR panopticism: User behaviour triangulation and barcode-scanning applications. Inf. Secure. J. Global Perspect, 24(4–6), 157–163. doi:10.1080/19393555.2015.1085113

Smith, R., & Leberstein, S. (2015). *Rights on demand: Ensuring workplace standards and worker security in the on-demand economy.* National Employment Law Project.

Smith, G. S. (2015). Management models for international cybercrime. *Journal of Financial Crime*, *22*(1), 104–125. doi:10.1108/JFC-09-2013-0051

Smith, H. J., Dinev, T., & Xu, H. (2011). Information privacy research: An interdisciplinary review. *Management Information Systems Quarterly*, *35*(4), 989–1015. doi:10.2307/41409970

Smith, J. W. (2016). The Uber-all economy of the future. *Independent Review*, *20*(3), 383–390.

Smith, R. (2007). The disruptive potential of game technologies. *Research Technology Management*, *50*(2), 57–64. doi:10.1080/08956308.2007.11657431

Sobaci, M. Z., & Karkin, N. (2013). The use of Twitter by mayors in Turkey: Tweets for better public services? *Government Information Quarterly*, *30*(4), 417–425. doi:10.1016/j.giq.2013.05.014

Solomon, D. J. (2007). The role of peer review for scholarly journals in the information age. *The Journal of Electronic Publishing: JEP*, *10*(1). doi:10.3998/3336451.0010.107

Sonnati, R. (2017). Improving Healthcare using Big Data Analytics. *International Journal of Scientific and Technology Research*, *6*(3), 142–146.

Sood, A., & Tellis, G. J. (2011). Demystifying disruption: A new model for understanding and predicting disruptive technologies. *Marketing Science*, *30*(2), 339–354. doi:10.1287/mksc.1100.0617

Sørensen, A. T., & Shklovski, I. (2011). The Hugging Team: The Role of Technology in Business Networking Practices. In *ECSCW 2011: Proceedings of the 12th European Conference on Computer Supported Cooperative Work*, 24-28 September 2011, *Aarhus Denmark* (pp.333-352). Springer. 10.1007/978-0-85729-913-0_18

Sovani, A., & Jayawardena, C. (2017). How should Canadian tourism embrace the disruption caused by the sharing economy? *Worldwide Hospitality and Tourism Themes*, *5*. doi:10.1108/WHATT-05-2017-0023

Soyomi, J., Oloruntoba, S. A., & Okafor, B. (2015). Analysis of mobile phone impact on student academic performance in the tertiary institution. *International Journal of Emerging Technology and Advanced Engineering*, *5*(1), 361–367.

Spaiser, V., Chadefaux, T., Donna, K., Russman, F., & Helbing, D. (2017). Communication power struggles on social media: A case study of the 2011–12 Russian protests. *Journal of Information Technology & Politics*, *14*(2), 132–153. doi:10.1080/19331681.2017.1308288

Spinellis, D., & Louridas, L. (2007). A framework for the static verification of API calls. *Journal of Systems and Software*, *80*(7), 1156–1168. doi:10.1016/j.jss.2006.09.040

Spremić, M., & Šimunic, A. (2018). Cyber Security Challenges in Digital Economy. In *Proceedings of the World Congress on Engineering* (*Vol. 1*). Academic Press.

Spruit, M., Vroon, R., & Batenburg, R. (2014). Towards Healthcare Business Intelligence in long-term care: An exploratory case study in the Netherlands. *Computers in Human Behavior*, *30*, 698–707. doi:10.1016/j.chb.2013.07.038

Srnicek, N. (2017). The challenges of platform capitalism: Understanding the logic of a new business model. *Juncture*, *23*(4), 254–257. doi:10.1111/newe.12023

Stake, R. E. (1995). *The art of case study research*. Los Angeles, CA: SAGE Publications.

Statista. (2018a). *Global Online shopping order value 2018, by traffic source*. Author.

Statista. (2018b). *Social commerce - statistics and facts*. Author.

Statista. (2019a). *Smartphone penetration rate as share of the population in Vietnam from 2017 to 2023*. Retrieved from https://www.statista.com/statistics/625458/smartphone-user-penetration-in-vietnam/

Statista. (2019b). *Vietnam - Statistics & Facts*. Retrieved from https://www.statista.com/topics/4598/vietnam/

Statistics, G. M. (2014). *Part A: Mobile Subscribers worldwide*. Retrieved May 11th, 2014 from http://mobithinking.com/mobile-marketing-tools/lateste-mobile-stats/a#subscribers

Stats, S. A. (2018). Mid-year population estimates 2018. *Statistics South Africa media release*. Retrieved from http://www.statssa.gov.za/?p=11341

Stats, S. A. (2019a). Labour Force Survey of South Africa, Q1, 2019. *Statistics South Africa*. Retrieved from http://www.statssa.gov.za/?page_id=1854&PPN=P0211

Stats, S. A. (2019b). Four facts about our provincial economies. *Statistics South Africa*. Retrieved from http://www.statssa.gov.za/?p=12056

Stefanidis, A., & Fitzgerald, G. (2010). Mapping the Information Systems Curricula in UK Universities. *Journal of Information Systems*, *21*(4), 391–410.

Stefanidis, A., Fitzgerald, G., & Counsell, S. (2013). IS curriculum career tracks: A UK study. *Education + Training*, *55*(3), 220–233. doi:10.1108/00400911311309297

Steiner, M., Wiegand, N., Eggert, A., & Backhaus, K. (2016). Platform adoption in system markets: The roles of preference heterogeneity and consumer expectations. *International Journal of Research In Marketing Journal*, *33*(2), 276–296. doi:10.1016/j.ijresmar.2015.05.011

Steinmetz, K., & Vella, M. (2017, June). Chaos at the world's most valuable venture-backed company is forcing to question its values. *Time*, 23–28.

Stephen, A. T., & Toubia, O. (2010). Deriving Value from Social Commerce Networks. *JMR, Journal of Marketing Research*, *47*(2), 215–228. doi:10.1509/jmkr.47.2.215

Sterrett, D., Malato, D., Benz, J., Kantor, L., Tompson, T., Rosenstiel, T., ... Loker, K. (2019). Who Shared It?: Deciding What News to Trust on Social Media. *Digital Journalism*, *7*(6), 783–801. doi:10.1080/21670811.2019.1623702

Stevens, D., Totaro, M., & Zhu, Z. (2011). Assessing It Critical Skills and Revising the MIS Curriculum. *Journal of Computer Information Systems*, *51*(3), 85–95.

Stewart, A., & Stanford, J. (2017). Regulating work in the gig economy: What are the options? *TheEconomic and Labour Relations Review, 28*(3), 420–437. doi:10.1177/1035304617722461

Stigliani, I., & Ravasi, D. (2012). Organizing thoughts and connecting brains: Material practices and the transition from individual to group-level prospective sensemaking. *Academy of Management Journal, 55*(5), 1232–1259. doi:10.5465/amj.2010.0890

Stockdale, R., & Standing, C. (2004). Benefits and barriers of electronic marketplace participation: An SME perspective. *Journal of Enterprise Information Management, 17*(4), 301–311. doi:10.1108/17410390410548715

Stone, D. L., & Deadrick, D. L. (2015). Challenges and opportunities affecting the future of human resource management. *Human Resource Management Review, 25*(2), 139–145. doi:10.1016/j.hrmr.2015.01.003

Stouthuysen, K., Teunis, I., Reusen, E., & Slabbinck, H. (2018). Initial trust and intentions to buy: The effect of vendor-specific guarantees, customer reviews and the role of online shopping experience. *Electronic Commerce Research and Applications, 27*, 23–38. doi:10.1016/j.elerap.2017.11.002

Straub, D. W., & Watson, R. T. (2001). Transformational Issues in Researching IS and Net-Enabled Organizations. *Information Systems Research, 12*(4), 337–345. doi:10.1287/isre.12.4.337.9706

Straub, D., Boudreau, M. C., & Gefen, D. (2004). Validation guidelines for IS positivist research. *Communications of the Association for Information Systems, 13*(1), 379–427.

Strauß, S. (2015). Datafication and the Seductive Power of Uncertainty—A Critical Exploration of Big Data Enthusiasm. Information-an International Interdisciplinary Journal, 6(4), 836–847. Retrieved from http://mdpi.com/2078-2489/6/4/836

Stroppa, A., di Stefano, D., & Parrella, B. (2016). *Social media and luxury goods counterfeit: a growing concern for government, industry and consumers worldwide.* Academic Press.

Sturm, U., Gold, M., Luna, S., Schade, S., Ceccaroni, L., Kyba, C. C. M., . . . Piera, J. (2018). *Defining principles for mobile apps and platforms development in citizen science.* Retrieved from https://nhm.openrepository.com/bitstream/handle/10141/622315/Defining+principles+for+mobile+apps+and+platformsdevelopment+in+citizen+science.pdf?sequence=1

Sturm, R., Pollard, C., & Craig, J. (2017). *Application Performance Management (APM) in the Digital Enterprise Managing Applications for Cloud.* Elsevier Inc. doi:10.1016/B978-0-12-804018-8.00001-2

Suh, A., Cheung, C. M. K., Ahuja, M., & Wagner, C. (2017). Gamification in the workplace: The central role of the aesthetic experience. *Journal of Management Information Systems, 34*(1), 268–305. doi:10.1080/07421222.2017.1297642

Sukrat, S., Mahatanankoon, P., & Papasratorn, B. (2018). The Driving Forces of C2C Social Commerce in Thailand: A Developing Framework. KnE Social Sciences, 3(1), 108. doi:10.18502/kss.v3i1.1400

Sulemana, M. (2018). The Provision of Educational Infrastructure and Academic Performance in Tertiary Institutions in Ghana: University of Developmental Studies (UDS), WA Campus as a Case Study. *Review of Higher Education in Africa, 3*(1).

Sulzberger. (2001). *Internet Service Providers and communications solutions in Ghana.* Paper presented to the International Finance Corporation, World Bank.

Sumaili, A., Dlodlo, N., & Osakwe, J. (2018, October). Adopting Dynamic Capabilities of Mobile Information and Communication Technology in Namibian Small and Medium Enterprises. In 2018 Open Innovations Conference (OI) (pp. 213-222). IEEE. doi:10.1109/OI.2018.8535941

Sumner, A., & Tribe, M. (2008). *International Development Studies: Theories and Methods in Research and Practice.* London: Sage. doi:10.4135/9781446279397

Sundar, S. S., Kang, H., Wu, M., Go, E., & Zhang, B. (2013). Unlocking the privacy paradox: Do cognitive heuristics hold the key? Proceedings of CHI'13 Extended Abstracts on Human Factors in Computing Systems, 811–816. doi:10.1145/2468356.2468501

Sun, J., & Chi, T. (2018). Key factors influencing the adoption of apparel mobile commerce: An empirical study of Chinese consumers. *Journal of the Textile Institute, 109*(6), 785–797. doi:10.1080/00405000.2017.1371828

Sun, J.-R., Shih, M.-L., & Hwang, M.-S. (2015). Cases study and analysis of the court judgement of cybercrimes in Taiwan. *International Journal of Law, Crime and Justice, 43*(4), 412–423. doi:10.1016/j.ijlcj.2014.11.001

Sun, S., Cegielski, C. G., Jia, L., & Hall, D. J. (2016). Understanding the Factors Affecting the Organizational Adoption of Big Data. *Journal of Computer Information Systems.* doi:10.1080/08874417.2016.1222891

Sun, W. (2018). A Critical Discourse Analysis of "Minority Women for Trump" Campaigns on Social Media. In N. Bilge & M. Marino (Eds.), *Reconceptualizing New Media and Intercultural Communication in a Networked Society* (pp. 303–327). Hershey, PA: IGI Global. doi:10.4018/978-1-5225-3784-7.ch012

Surendra, N. C., & Denton, J. W. (2009). Designing IS Curricula for Practical Relevance: Applying Baseball's "Moneyball" Theory. *Journal of Information Systems Education, 20*(1), 77–85.

Susanne, B., & Menno, D. T. (2017). The privacy paradox – Investigating discrepancies between expressed privacy concerns and actual online behaviour – A systematic literature review. *Telematics and Informatics, 34*(7), 1038–1058. doi:10.1016/j.tele.2017.04.013

Susarla, A., Oh, J. H., & Tan, Y. (2012). Social networks and the diffusion of user-generated content: Evidence from youtube. *Information Systems Research, 23*(1), 23–41. doi:10.1287/isre.1100.0339

Susarla, A., Oh, J.-H., & Tan, Y. (2012). Social Networks and the Diffusion of User-Generated Content: Evidence from YouTube. *Information Systems Research, 23*(1), 123–141. doi:10.1287/isre.1100.0339

Suseno, Y., Laurell, C., & Sick, N. (2018). Assessing value creation in digital innovation ecosystems: A Social Media Analytics approach. *The Journal of Strategic Information Systems, 27*(4), 335–349. doi:10.1016/j.jsis.2018.09.004

Swinarski, M. E. (2008, September). Focusing on IS Skills for the Middle and Senior Level Manager: A New Approach to the MBA Core IS Course. *Communications of the Association for Information Systems, 23,* 163–178. doi:10.17705/1CAIS.02309

Synnott, W. R., & Gruber, W. H. (1982). *Information resource management: Opportunities and strategies for the 1980s.* John Wiley & Sons, Inc.

Tabachnick, B. G., & Fidell, L. S. (2013). *Using multivariate statistics.* Boston: Allyn and Bacon.

Taiwo, A. A., Mahmood, A. K., & Downe, A. G. (2012, June). User acceptance of eGovernment: Integrating risk and trust dimensions with my husbandUTAUT model. In *2012 International Conference on Computer & Information Science (ICCIS)* (Vol. 1, pp. 109-113). IEEE. 10.1109/ICCISci.2012.6297222

Tajvidi, M., Wang, Y., Hajli, N., & Love, P. E. D. (2017). Brand value Co-creation in social commerce: The role of interactivity, social support, and relationship quality. *Computers in Human Behavior, •••,* 1–8. doi:10.1016/j.chb.2017.11.006

Tan, B., Lu, X., Pan, S. L., & Huang, L. (2015). The Role of IS Capabilities in the Development of Multi-Sided Platforms: The Digital Ecosystem Strategy of Alibaba.com. *Journal of the Association for Information Systems, 16*(4), 248–280. doi:10.17705/1jais.00393

Tan, F. C., Tan, B., Lu, A., & Land, L. (2017). Delivering Disruption in an Emergent Access Economy : A Case Study of an E-hailing Platform. *Communications of the Association for Information Systems, 41*(22), 497–516. doi:10.17705/1CAIS.04122

Tan, F. T. C., Tan, B., & Pan, S. (2016). Developing a Leading Digital Multi-sided Platform: Examining IT Affordances and Competitive. *Communications of the Association for Information Systems, 38*, 738–760. doi:10.17705/1CAIS.03836

Tan, G. W. H., Ooi, K. B., Chong, S. C., & Hew, T. S. (2014). NFC mobile credit card: The next frontier of mobile payment? *Telematics and Informatics, 31*(2), 292–307. doi:10.1016/j.tele.2013.06.002

Tang, F., Tian, V. I., & Zaichkowsky, J. (2014). Understanding counterfeit consumption. *Asia Pacific Journal of Marketing and Logistics, 26*(1), 4–20. doi:10.1108/APJML-11-2012-0121

Tan, K. S., Chong, S. C., Lin, B., & Eze, U. C. (2009). Internet-based ICT adoption: Evidence from Malaysian SMEs. *Industrial Management & Data Systems, 109*(2), 224–244. doi:10.1108/02635570910930118

Tanko, S. (2013). *GIFMIS to manage public funds, Ghana News Agency.* Retrieved on 5 April 2019 from https://www.ghanaweb.com/GhanaHomePage/business/GIFMIS-to-manage-public-funds-273365#

Tanle, A., & Abane, A. M. (2017). Mobile phone use and livelihoods: Qualitative evidence from some rural and urban areas in Ghana. *GeoJournal*, 1–11.

Tan, M., & Teo, T. S. (2000). Factors influencing the adoption of Internet banking. *Journal of the Association for Information Systems, 1*(1), 5. doi:10.17705/1jais.00005

Tan, P. J. B. (2013). Applying the UTAUT to understand factors affecting the use of English E-Learning websites in Taiwan. *SAGE Open, 3*(4), 1–12. doi:10.1177/2158244013503837

Tantalo, C., & Priem, R. (2016). Value creation through stakeholder synergy. *Strategic Management Journal, 37*(2), 314–329. doi:10.1002mj.2337

Tapanainen, T., & Lisein, O. (2017). *Mindfulness in Cyber-Security: The Case of a Government Agency.* Academic Press.

Tarafdar, M., Gupta, A., & Turel, O. (2013). The dark side of information technology use. *Information Systems Journal, 23*(3), 269–275. doi:10.1111/isj.12015

Tarafdar, M., Gupta, A., & Turel, O. (2015). Introduction to the special issue on the 'dark side of information technology use' - part two. *Information Systems Journal, 25*(4), 315–317. doi:10.1111/isj.12076

Tarhini, A., El-Masri, M., Ali, M., & Serrano, A. (2016). Extending the UTAUT model to understand the customers' acceptance and use of internet banking in Lebanon: A structural equation modeling approach. *Information Technology & People, 29*(4), 830–849. doi:10.1108/ITP-02-2014-0034

Tarhini, A., El-Masri, M., Ali, M., & Serrano, A. (2016a). Extending the UTAUT model to understand the customers' acceptance and use of internet banking in Lebanon: A structural equation modelling approach. *Information Technology & People, 29*(4), 783–801. doi:10.1108/ITP-02-2014-0034

Tarhini, A., Hone, K., Liu, X., & Tarhini, T. (2016b). Examining the moderating effect of individual-level cultural values on users' acceptance of E-learning in developing countries: A structural equation modelling of an extended technology acceptance model. *Interactive Learning Environments.* doi:10.1080/10494820.2015.1122635

Tatnall, A. D. (2010). Using actor-network theory to understand the process of information systems curriculum innovation. *Education and Information Technologies*, *15*(4), 239–254. doi:10.100710639-010-9137-5

Tatnall, A., & Davey, B. (2002). Improving the chances of getting your IT curriculum innovation successfully adopted by the application of an ecological approach to innovation. *Informing Science*, *7*, 87–103. doi:10.28945/504

Taufik, M., & Jain, P. K. (2013). Role of build orientation in layered manufacturing: A review. *International Journal of Manufacturing Technology and Management*, *27*(1-3), 47–73. doi:10.1504/IJMTM.2013.058637

Tauscher, K., & Laudien, S. M. (2017). Understanding platform business models: A mixed methods study of marketplaces. *European Management Journal*, ▪▪▪, 1–11.

Taylor, E. (2016). Mobile payment technologies in retail: A review of potential benefits and risks. *International Journal of Retail & Distribution Management*, *44*(2), 159–177. doi:10.1108/IJRDM-05-2015-0065

Taylor, S., & Todd, P. A. (1995b). Understanding information technology usage: A test of competing models. *Information Systems Research*, *6*(4), 144–176. doi:10.1287/isre.6.2.144

Tedre, M., Bangu, N., & Nyagava, S. I. (2009). Contextualized IT Education in Tanzania: Beyond Standard IT Curricula. *Journal of Information Technology Education*, *8*, 101–124. doi:10.28945/162

Teece, D. D. J., Pisano, G., & Shuen, A. (1997). Dynamic capabilities and strategic management. *Strategic Management Journal*, *18*(7), 509–533. doi:10.1002/(SICI)1097-0266(199708)18:7<509::AID-SMJ882>3.0.CO;2-Z

Teece, D., Pisano, G., & Shuen, A. (1997). Dynamic Capabilities and Strategic Management. *Strategic Management Journal*, *18*(7), 509–533. doi:10.1002/(SICI)1097-0266(199708)18:7<509::AID-SMJ882>3.0.CO;2-Z

Tehrani, P. M., Manap, N. A., & Taji, H. (2013). Cyber terrorism challenges: The need for a global response to a multi-jurisdictional crime. *Computer Law & Security Review*, *29*(3), 207–215. doi:10.1016/j.clsr.2013.03.011

Tehubijuluw, F. K. (2017). The Digital Technology and the Threat of Downsizing into Indonesia's Banking Industry Performance. *International Journal of Trade, Economics and Finance*, *8*(4).

Tellis, G. J. (2006). Disruptive technology or visionary leadership? *Journal of Product Innovation Management*, *23*(1), 34–38. doi:10.1111/j.1540-5885.2005.00179.x

Tembhurne, D. S., Adhikari, P. J., & Babu, P. R. (2019). A Review study on Application of Data Mining Techniques in CRM of Pharmaceutical Industry. *IJSRST International Journal of Scientific Research in Science and Technology*, *6*(2), 1–7.

Templier, M., & Paré, G. (2015). A framework for guiding and evaluating literature reviews. *Communications of the Association for Information Systems*, *37*(1), 6.

Teo, E., Fraunholz, B., & Unnithan, C. (2005, July). Inhibitors and facilitators for mobile payment adoption in Australia: A preliminary study. In ICMB 2005. International Conference on Mobile Business, 2005 (pp. 663–666). IEEE. doi:10.1109/ICMB.2005.47

Teo, T. S. H., & Ang, J. S. K. (1999). Critical success factors in the alignment of IS plans with business plans. *International Journal of Information Management*, *19*(2), 173–185. doi:10.1016/S0268-4012(99)00007-9

Teo, T. S. H., & Ang, J. S. K. (2001). An examination of major IS planning problems. *International Journal of Information Management*, *21*(6), 457–470. doi:10.1016/S0268-4012(01)00036-6

Teo, T. S., & Pok, S. H. (2003). Adoption of WAP-enabled mobile phones among Internet users. *Omega*, *31*(6), 483–498. doi:10.1016/j.omega.2003.08.005

Tesch, D., Jiang, J. J., & Klein, G. (2003). The impact of information system personnel skill discrepancies on stakeholder satisfaction. *Decision Sciences*, *34*(1), 107–129. doi:10.1111/1540-5915.02371

Tess, P. A. (2013). The role of social media in higher education classes (real and virtual)–A literature review. *Computers in Human Behavior*, *29*(5), A60–A68. doi:10.1016/j.chb.2012.12.032

Teubner, T., & Flath, C. M. (2015). The Economics of Multi-Hop Ride Sharing Creating New Mobility Networks Through IS. *Business & Information Systems Engineering*, *57*(5), 311–324. doi:10.100712599-015-0396-y

Tewksbury, D. (2006). Exposure to the Newer Media in a Presidential Primary Campaign. *Political Communication*, *23*(3), 313–332. doi:10.1080/10584600600808877

Thaichon, P., & Quach, S. (2016). Dark motives-counterfeit purchase framework : Internal and external motives behind counterfeit purchase via digital platforms. *Journal of Retailing and Consumer Services*, *33*, 82–91. doi:10.1016/j.jretconser.2016.08.003

Thakur, S., & Ramzan, M. (2015). A Systematic Review on Cardiovascular disease using Big-Data by Hadoop. Cloud system and big data engineering, IEEE, 351-355.

Thapa, D., Sein, M. K., & Sæbø, Ø. (2012). Building collective capabilities through ICT in a mountain region of Nepal: Where social capital leads to collective action. *Information Technology for Development*, *18*(1), 5–22. doi:10.1080/02681102.2011.643205

The Economist. (2015). *Disrupting Mr. Disrupter*. Retrieved from 15 May 2018 from https://www.economist.com/business/2015/11/26/disrupting-mr-disrupter

Thelwall, M. (2017). The Heart and Soul of the Web? Sentiment Strength Detection in the Social Web with SentiStrength. In J. Holyst (Ed.), *Cyberemotions: Collective Emotions in Cyberspace. Understanding Complex Systems* (pp. 119–134). Springer International Publishing. doi:10.1007/978-3-319-43639-5_7

Thelwell, R. (2019). 5 real life applications of Data Mining and Business Intelligence. Retrieved from https://www.matillion.com/insights/5-real-life-applications-of-data-mining-and-business-intelligence/

Thiebes, S., Lins, S., & Basten, D. (2014). Gamifying information systems - A synthesis of gamification mechanics and dynamics. *Proceedings of ECIS 2014 - The 22nd European Conference on Information Systems*.

Thies, F., Wessel, M., & Benlian, A. (2018). Network effects on crowdfunding platforms: Exploring the implications of relaxing input control. *Information Systems Journal*, *28*(6), 1239–1262. doi:10.1111/isj.12194

Thirsk, L. M., & Clark, A. M. (2017). Using qualitative research for complex interventions: The contributions of hermeneutics. *International Journal of Qualitative Methods*, *16*(1), 1–10. doi:10.1177/1609406917721068

Thomas, T., Singh, L., & Gaffar, K. (2013). The utility of the UTAUT model in explaining mobile learning adoption in higher education in Guyana. *International Journal of Education and Development Using ICT, 9*(3).

Thomas, D. (2016). Costs, benefits, and adoption of additive manufacturing: A supply chain perspective. *International Journal of Advanced Manufacturing Technology*, *85*(5-8), 1857–1876. doi:10.100700170-015-7973-6 PMID:28747809

Thomas, D. S., & Gilbert, S. W. (2014). Costs and cost-effectiveness of additive manufacturing. *NIST Special Publication*, *1176*, 12.

Thomas, G. (2011). A typology for the case study in social science following a review of definition, discourse, and structure. *Qualitative Inquiry*, *17*(6), 511–521. doi:10.1177/1077800411409884

Thouin, M. F., Hefley, W. E., & Raghunathan, S. (2018). Student attitudes toward information systems graduate program design and delivery. *Journal of Information Systems Education*, *29*(1), 25–37.

Tidd, J., & Bessant, J. R. (2018). *Managing innovation: integrating technological, market and organizational change.* John Wiley & Sons.

Tilson, D., Lyytinen, K., & Sorensen, C. (2010). Digital Infrastructures: The Missing IS Research Agenda. *Information Systems Research, 21*(5).

Ting, S. L., & Ip, W. H. (2015). Combating the counterfeits with web portal technology. *Enterprise Information Systems*, *9*(7), 661–680. doi:10.1080/17517575.2012.755713

Ting, S. L., Kwok, S. K., Tsang, A. H. C., Lee, W. B., & Yee, K. F. (2011). Experiences sharing of implementing template-based electronic medical record system (TEMRS) in a Hong Kong medical organization. *Journal of Medical Systems*, *35*(6), 1605–1615. doi:10.1007/s10916-010-9436-9 PubMed

Tiwana, A., Konsynsky, B., & Bush, A. (2010). Platform Evolution: Coevolution of Platform Architecture, Governance, and Environmental Dynamics. *Information Systems Research*, *21*(4), 675–687. doi:10.1287/isre.1100.0323

Tlili, A., Denden, M., Essalmi, F., Jemni, M., Chang, M., Kinshuk, & Chen, N.-S. (2019). Automatic modelling learner's personality using learning analytics approach in an intelligent Moodle learning platform. *Interactive Learning Environments*, 1–15. doi:10.1080/10494820.2019.1636084

Tobbin, P., & Kuwornu, J. K. (2011). Adoption of mobile money transfer technology: Structural equation modeling approach. *European Journal of Business and Management*, *3*(7), 59–77.

Topi, H., Helfert, M., Ramesh, V., Wigand, R. T., & Wright, R. T. (2011). Future of Master's Level Education in Information Systems. *Communications of AIS, 2011*(28), 437–452.

Topi, H., Karsten, H., Brown, S. A., Carvalho, J. A., Donnellan, B., Shen, J., Tan, B. C., & Thouin, M. F. (2017). *MSIS 2016 Global Competency Model for Graduate Degree Programs in Information Systems.* The Joint ACM/AIS MSIS Task Force.

Topi, H. (2016). IS Education: Using competency-based approach as foundation for information systems curricula. *ACM Inroads*, *7*(3), 27–28. doi:10.1145/2955099

Topi, H. (2019). Reflections on the Current State and Future of Information Systems Education. *Journal of Information Systems Education*, *30*(1), 1–9.

Topi, H., Valacich, J. S., Wright, R. T., Kaiser, K. M., Nunamaker, J. F. Jr, Sipior, J. C., & de Vreede, G.-J. (2010). IS2010: Curriculum Guidelines for Undergraduate Degree Programs in Information Systems. *Communications of the Association for Information Systems*, *26*(1), 359–428.

Topi, H., Wright, R. T., & Kaiser, K. (2008). Revising Undergraduate IS Model Curriculum: New Outcome Expectations Revising Undergraduate IS Model Curriculum : New Outcome Expectations. *Communications of the Association for Information Systems*, *23*(December), 591–602.

Tornatzky, L. G., & Fleischer, M. (1990). *The Processes of Technological Innovation.* Lexington, MA: Lexington Books.

Tornatzky, L. G., & Klein, K. J. (1982). Innovation characteristics and innovation adoption-implementation: A meta-analysis of findings. *IEEE Transactions on Engineering Management*, *EM-29*(1), 28–45. doi:10.1109/TEM.1982.6447463

Tornatzky, L., & Fleischer, M. (1990). *The processes of technological innovation.* Lexington Books.

Torpey, E., & Hogan, A. (2016). *Working in a Gig Economy: Career Outlook: US Bureau of Labor Statistics.* United States Department of Labor: Bureau of Labor Statistics.

Tossell, C., Kortum, P., Shepard, C., Rahmati, A., & Zhong, L. (2015). Exploring smartphone addiction: Insights from long-term telemetric behavioural measures. *International Journal of Interactive Mobile Technologies, 9*(2), 37–43. doi:10.3991/ijim.v9i2.4300

Tremblay, M., Hevner, A., & Berndt, D. (2012). Design of an information Volatility measure for Healthcare decision making. *Decision Support Systems, 52*(2), 331–341. doi:10.1016/j.dss.2011.08.009

Tribunella, T., & Tribunella, H. (2016, May). Twenty questions on the Sharing economy and mobile accounting apps. *The CPA Journal.*

Trieu, V.-H. (2016). Getting value from Business Intelligence systems: A review and Agenda. *Decision Support System, 93*(2017), 112-124. doi:10.1016/j.dss.2016.09.019

Trivedi, H. (2013). *Cloud computing adoption model for governments and large enterprises* (Doctoral dissertation, Massachusetts Institute of Technology). Retrieved from https://dspace.mit.edu/bitstream/handle/1721.1/80675/857768311-MIT.pdf?sequence=2&isAllowed=y

Tsai, H. S., & Gururajan, R. (2007). Motivations and challenges for M-business transformation: A multiple-case study. *Journal of Theoretical and Applied Electronic Commerce Research, 2*(2), 19–33.

Tsang, E. (2014). Case studies and generalization in information systems research: A critical realist perspective. *The Journal of Strategic Information Systems, 23*(2), 174–186. doi:10.1016/j.jsis.2013.09.002

Tsfati, Y., & Ariely, G. (2014). Individual and contextual correlates of trust in media across 44 countries. *Communication Research, 41*(6), 760–782. doi:10.1177/0093650213485972

Tumuheki, P. B., Zeelen, J., & Openjuru, G. L. (2016). Towards a conceptual framework for developing capabilities of new types of students participating in higher education in Sub-Saharan Africa. *International Journal of Educational Development, 47*, 54–62. doi:10.1016/j.ijedudev.2015.12.005

Turban, E., Ramesh, S., Delen, D., & King, D. (2011). Business Intelligence: A Managerial Approach (2nd ed.). Pearson Education, Inc.

Turel, O., & Serenko, A. (2010). Is mobile email addiction overlooked? *Communications of the ACM, 53*(5), 41. doi:10.1145/1735223.1735237

Turel, O., & Serenko, A. (2012). The benefits and dangers of enjoyment with social networking websites. *European Journal of Information Systems, 21*(5), 512–528. doi:10.1057/ejis.2012.1

Turel, O., Serenko, A., & Bontis, N. (2011). Family and work-related consequences of addiction to pervasive organizational technologies. *Information & Management, 48*(2–3), 88–95. doi:10.1016/j.im.2011.01.004

Turel, O., Serenko, A., & Giles, P. (2011a). Integrating Technology Addiction and Use An Empirical Investigation of Online Auction. *Management Information Systems Quarterly, 35*(4), 1043–1061. doi:10.2307/41409972

Turkyilmaz, C. A., & Uslu, A. (2014). The role of individual characteristics on consumers counterfeit purchasing intentions: Research in fashion industry. *Journal of Management Marketing and Logistics, 1*(3), 259–275.

Turk, Ž., & Klinc, R. (2017). Potentials of blockchain technology for construction management. *Procedia Engineering, 196*, 638–645. doi:10.1016/j.proeng.2017.08.052

Uber. (2017). *Driver requirements: how to drive with Uber, Uber website.* Available at: https://www.uber.com/en-GH/drive/requirements/

Ullah, A., & Lai, R. (2013). A systematic review of business and information technology alignment. *ACM Transactions on Management Information Systems, 4*(1), 1–30. doi:10.1145/2445560.2445564

Umezurike, S. A. & Olusola, O. (2017). South Africa's 'Africa Renaissance' Project: Between Rhetoric and Practice. *The Scientific Journal for Theory and Practice of Socio-Economic Development 2016, 5*(10), 263-278

Underwood, S. (2016). Blockchain Beyond Bitcoin. *Communications of the ACM, 59*(11), 15–17. doi:10.1145/2994581

UNDP. (2017). *IBM launches "digital"- nation Africa": invests $70 to bring digital skills to Africa with Free, Watson-powered skills platform for 25 million people.* United Nations Development Program. Retrieved from, http://www.za.undp.org/content/south_africa/en/home/presscenter/pressreleases/2017/02/08/ibm-launches-digital-nation-africa-invests-70-million-to-bring-digital-skills-to-africa-with-free-watson-powered-skills-platform-for-25-million-people.html

Uotila, J., Keil, T., & Maula, M. (2017). Supply-side network effects and the development of information technology standards. *Management Information Systems Quarterly, 41*(4), 1207–1226. doi:10.25300/MISQ/2017/41.4.09

Upadhyay, P., & Chattopadhyay, M. (2015). Examining mobile based payment services adoption issues. *Journal of Enterprise Information Management, 28*(4), 490–507. doi:10.1108/JEIM-04-2014-0046

Urbaczewski, A., Venkataraman, R., & Kontogiorgis, P. (2011). Panel discussion proposal: IT services management in the curriculum: Challenges, realizations, and lessons learned. *16th Americas Conference on Information Systems 2010, AMCIS 2010, 28*(5), 1012–1015.

Utesheva, A., Simpson, J., & Cecez-Kecmanovic, D. (2016). Identity metamorphoses in digital disruption: A relational theory of identity. *European Journal of Information Systems, 25*(4), 344–363. doi:10.1057/ejis.2015.19

Utter, J., Lucassen, M., Denny, S., Fleming, T., Peiris-John, R., & Clark, T. (2018). Using the internet to access health-related information: Results from a nationally representative sample of New Zealand secondary school students. *International Journal of Adolescent Medicine and Health.* doi:10.1515/ijamh-2017-0096 PMID:29168960

Vaghefi, I., Lapointe, L., & Boudreau-Pinsonneault, C. (2016). A typology of user liability to IT addiction. *Information Systems Journal, 27*(2), 125–169. doi:10.1111/isj.12098

Vahdati, S., & Yasini, N. (2015). Factors affecting internet frauds in private sector: A case study in cyberspace surveillance and scam monitoring agency of Iran. *Computers in Human Behavior, 51*, 180–187. doi:10.1016/j.chb.2015.04.058

Van der Boor, P., Oliveira, P., & Veloso, F. (2014). Users as innovators in developing countries: The global sources of innovation and diffusion in mobile banking services. *Research Policy, 43*(9), 1594–1607. doi:10.1016/j.respol.2014.05.003

van der Meulen, N. S. (2013). You've been warned: Consumer liability in Internet banking fraud. *Computer Law & Security Review, 29*(6), 713–718. doi:10.1016/j.clsr.2013.09.007

van der Veer, H., & Wiles, A. (2008). Achieving technical interoperability. In *European telecommunications standards institute* (3rd ed.). ETSI White Paper No. 3.

Van Doorn, J., Mende, M., Noble, S. M., Hulland, J., Ostrom, A. L., Grewal, D., & Petersen, J. A. (2017). Domo arigato Mr Roboto: Emergence of automated social presence in organizational frontlines and customers' service experiences. *Journal of Service Research, 20*(1), 43–58. doi:10.1177/1094670516679272 van Laar, E., van Deursen, A. J. A. M., van Dijk, J. A. G. M., & de Haan, J. (2017). The relation between 21st-century skills and digital skills: A systematic literature review. *Computers in Human Behavior*, *72*, 577–588. doi:10.1016/j.chb.2017.03.010

van Oorschot, J. A. W. H., Hofman, E., & Halman, J. I. M. (2018). A bibliometric review of the innovation adoption literature. *Technological Forecasting and Social Change*, *134*(June), 1–21. doi:10.1016/j.techfore.2018.04.032

Vargo, S. L., Maglio, P. P., & Akaka, M. A. (2008). On value and value co-creation: A service systems and service logic perspective. *European Management Journal*, *26*(3), 145–152. doi:10.1016/j.emj.2008.04.003

Vargo, S., & Lusch, R. (2004). Evolving to a new dominant logic for marketing. *Journal of Marketing*, *68*(1), 1–17. doi:10.1509/jmkg.68.1.1.24036

Varian, H. (1999, August). *Market structure in the network age*. Market Structure in the Network Age.

Vasquez, M. (2015). Embracing 3D Printing. *Mechanical Engineering Magazine Select Articles*, *137*(08), 42–45.

Vasudeva, G., Alexander, E. A., & Jones, S. L. (2015). Institutional logics and inter organizational learning in technological arenas: Evidence from standard-setting organizations in the mobile handset industry. *Organization Science*, *26*(3), 830–846. doi:10.1287/orsc.2014.0940

Vazsonyi, A. T., Machackova, H., Sevcikova, A., Smahel, D., & Cerna, A. (2012). Cyberbullying in context: Direct and indirect effects by low self-control across 25 European countries. *European Journal of Developmental Psychology*, *9*(2), 210–227. doi:10.1080/17405629.2011.644919

VCCI. (2016). *Digital technologies: Opportunities for Vietnamese SMEs*. Retrieved from http://www.nhandan.com.vn/hangthang/van-hoa/item/29999102-co-hoi-cho-cac-doanh-nghiep-nho-va-vua-viet-nam.html

Vecchiato, R. (2017). Disruptive innovation, managerial cognition, and technology competition outcomes. *Technological Forecasting and Social Change*, *116*, 116–12. doi:10.1016/j.techfore.2016.10.068

VECITA. (2017). *Only 20% of small and medium-sized enterprises have been ready for electronic commerce*. Retrieved from https://tintuc.inet.vn/chi-20-doanh-nghiep-vua-va-nho-tiep-can-thuong-mai-dien-tu.html

Veit, D., Clemons, E., Benlian, A., Buxmann, P., Hess, T., Kundisch, D., & Spann, M. (2014). Business models. *Business & Information Systems Engineering*, *6*(1), 45–53. doi:10.1007/s12599-013-0308-y

Veltri, N. F., Webb, H. W., Matveev, A. G., & Zapatero, E. G. (2011). Curriculum Mapping as a Tool for Continuous Improvement of IS Curriculum. *Journal of Information Systems Education*, *22*(1), 31–42.

Venkatesh, M. Morris., Davis., & Davis. (2003). User Acceptance of Information Technology: Toward a Unified View. *Management Information Systems Quarterly*, *27*(3), 425–478. doi:10.2307/30036540

Venkatesh, V. (2006). Where To Go From Here? Thoughts on Future Directions for Research on Individual-Level Technology Adoption with a Focus on Decision Making. *Decision Sciences*, *37*(4), 497–519. doi:10.1111/j.1540-5414.2006.00136.x

Venkatesh, V., & Bala, H. (2008). Technology acceptance model 3 and a research agenda on interventions. *Decision Sciences*, *39*(2), 273–315. doi:10.1111/j.1540-5915.2008.00192.x

Venkatesh, V., & Davis, F. D. (2000). A theoretical extension of the technology acceptance model: Four longitudinal field studies. *Management Science*, *46*(2), 186–204. doi:10.1287/mnsc.46.2.186.11926

Venkatesh, V., & Davis, F. D. (2000). A Theoretical Extension of the Technology Acceptance Model: Four Longitudinal Field Studies. *Management Science*, *46*(2), 186–204. doi:10.1287/mnsc.46.2.186.11926

Venkatesh, V., Morris, M. G., Davis, G. B., & Davis, F. D. (2003). User acceptance of information technology: Toward a unified view. *Management Information Systems Quarterly, 27*(3), 425–478. doi:10.2307/30036540

Venkatesh, V., Morris, M. G., Davis, G. B., & Davis, F. D. (2003). User acceptance of information technology: Toward a unified view. *Management Information Systems Quarterly, 27*(3), 425–478. doi:10.2307/30036540

Venkatesh, V., Thong, J. Y. L., & Xu, X. (2012). Consumer Acceptance and Use of Information Technology: Extending the Unified Theory of Acceptance and Use of Technology. *Management Information Systems Quarterly, 36*(1), 157–178. doi:10.2307/41410412

Venkatesh, V., Thong, J. Y. L., & Xu, X. (2016). Unified Theory of Acceptance and Use of Technology: A synthesis and the road ahead. *Journal of the Association for Information Systems, 17*(5), 328–376. doi:10.17705/1jais.00428

Venkatesh, V., Thong, J., & Xu, X. (2012). Consumer acceptance and use of information technology: Extending the unified theory of acceptance and use of technology. *Management Information Systems Quarterly, 36*(1), 157–178. doi:10.2307/41410412

Venkatesh, V., & Zhang, X. (2010). Unified theory of acceptance and use of technology: US vs. China. *Journal of Global Information Technology Management, 13*(1), 5–27. doi:10.1080/1097198X.2010.10856507

Venkatesh, V., & Zhang, X. (2010). Unified theory of acceptance and use of technology: uS vs. China. *Journal of Global Information Technology Management, 13*(1), 5–27. doi:10.1080/1097198X.2010.10856507

Ventola, C. L. (2014). Medical applications for 3D printing: Current and projected uses. *P&T, 39*(10), 704. PMID:25336867

Vergeer, M. (2017). Adopting, Networking, and Communicating on Twitter: A Cross-National Comparative Analysis. *Social Science Computer Review, 35*(6), 698–712. doi:10.1177/0894439316672826

Verma, A. (2012). Cyber pornography in India and its implication on cyber cafe operators. *Computer Law & Security Review, 28*(1), 69–76. doi:10.1016/j.clsr.2011.11.003

Vernon, W. (2009). The Delphi technique: A review. *International Journal of Therapy and Rehabilitation, 16*(2), 69–76. doi:10.12968/ijtr.2009.16.2.38892

Vessey, I., & Ward, K. (2013). The Dynamics of Sustainable IS alignment: The Case for IS Adaptivity. *Journal of the Association for Information Systems, 14*(6), 283–311. doi:10.17705/1jais.00336

Vietnam eCommerce and Digital Economy Agency. (2018). *Vietnam E-commerce White Paper 2018.* Retrieved from http://www.idea.gov.vn/?page=document

Vinet, L., & Zhedanov, A. (2010). A "missing" family of classical orthogonal polynomials. *Games and Culture, 17*(2), 1–16.

Vishnu Menon, R. G., Sigurdsson, V., Larsen, N. M., Fagerstrøm, A., & Foxall, G. R. (2016). Consumer attention to price in social commerce: Eye tracking patterns in retail clothing ☆. *Journal of Business Research, 69*(11), 5008–5013. doi:10.1016/j.jbusres.2016.04.072

Visinescu, L. L., Jones, M., & Sidorova, A. (2017). Improving Decision Quality: The Role of Business Intelligence. *Journal of Computer Information Systems, 57*(1), 58–66. doi:10.1080/08874417.2016.1181494

Vlaar, P. W., van Fenema, P. C., & Tiwari, V. (2008). Cocreating understanding and value in distributed work: How members of onsite and offshore vendor teams give, make, demand, and break sense. *Management Information Systems Quarterly, 32*(2), 227–255. doi:10.2307/25148839

Vlachos, V., Minou, M., Assimakopouos, V., & Toska, A. (2011). The landscape of cybercrime in Greece. *Information Management & Computer Security, 19*(2), 113–123. doi:10.1108/09685221111143051 von Konsky, B. R., Miller, C., & Jones, A. (2016). The Skills Framework for the Information Age: Engaging Stakeholders in Curriculum Design. *Journal of Information Systems Education, 27*(1), 37–50.

Vongsraluang, N., & Bhatiasevi, V. (2017). The determinants of social commerce system success for SMEs in Thailand. *Information Development, 33*(1), 80–96. doi:10.1177/0266666916639632

Wade, M., & Hulland, J. (2004). Review: The resource-based view and information systems research: Review, extension, and suggestions for future research. *Management Information Systems Quarterly, 28*(1), 107–142. doi:10.2307/25148626

Wagner, E. L., & Newell, S. (2007). Exploring the importance of participation in the post-implementation period of an ES project: A neglected area. *Journal of the Association for Information, 8*(10), 508–524. doi:10.17705/1jais.00142

Wallace, L., Keil, M., & Rai, A. (2003). How Software Project Risk Affects Project Performance: An Investigation of the Dimensions of Risk and an Exploratory Model. *Decision Sciences, 2*(35), 289–321.

Wall, D. (2003). *Crime and the Internet*. Routledge. doi:10.4324/9780203299180

Wall, D. S. (2015). The Internet as a conduit for criminal activity. In Λ. Pattavina (Ed.), *Information Technology and the Criminal Justice System* (pp. 77–98). Thousand Oaks, CA: Sage.

Walsham, G. (1993). *Interpreting Information Systems in Organizations*. Chichester: Wiley.

Walsham, G. (1993). *Interpreting information systems in organizations*. John Wiley & Sons, Inc.

Walsham, G. (1995). Interpretive case studies in IS research : Nature and method. *European Journal of Information Systems, 4*(2), 74–81. doi:10.1057/ejis.1995.9

Walsham, G. (1995). The emergence of interpretivism in IS research. *Information Systems Research, 6*(4), 376–394. doi:10.1287/isre.6.4.376

Walsham, G. (2006). Doing interpretive research. *European Journal of Information Systems, 15*(3), 320–330. doi:10.1057/palgrave.ejis.3000589

Walsham, G. (2017). ICT4D research: Reflections on history and future agenda. *Information Technology for Development, 23*(1), 18–41. doi:10.1080/02681102.2016.1246406

Walsh, S. P., White, K. M., Hyde, M. K., & Watson, B. (2008). Dialing and driving: Factors influencing intentions to use a mobile phone while driving. *Accident; Analysis and Prevention, 40*(6), 1893–1900. doi:10.1016/j.aap.2008.07.005 PMID:19068291

Wamba, S. F., & Carter, L. (2013). *Twitter adoption and use by SMEs: An empirical study*. Paper presented at the 46th Hawaii International Conference on System Sciences. 10.1109/HICSS.2013.577

Wamba, S. F., Gunasekaran, A., Akter, S., Ren, S., Dubey, R., & Childe, S. J. (2016). Big data analytics and firm performance: Effects of dynamic capabilities. *Journal of Business Research, 70*(2017), 356-365. doi:10.1016/j.jbusres.2016.08.009

Wang, X., Ardakani, H. M., & Schneider, H. (2017). Does Ride Sharing have Social Benefits? In *Twenty-third Americas Conference on Information Systems* (pp. 1–8). Boston: Academic Press.

Wang, C., Lee, M. K. O., Yang, C., & Li, X. (2016). Understanding problematic smartphone use and its characteristics: A perspective on behavioral addiction. *Lecture Notes in Information Systems and Organisation, 17*, 215–225. doi:10.1007/978-3-319-30133-4_15

Wang, C., & Zhang, P. (2012). The Evolution of Social Commerce : The People, Management, Technology, and Information Dimensions. *Communications of the Association for Information Systems, 31*(1), 105–127.

Wang, C., & Zhang, P. (2012, November). The Evolution of Social Commerce : The People, Management, Technology, and Information Dimensions and Information Dimensions. *Communications of the Association for Information Systems*, *31*, 105–127. doi:10.17705/1CAIS.03105

Wang, H., He, W., & Wang, F. K. (2012). Enterprise cloud service architectures. *Information Technology Management*, *13*(4), 445–454. doi:10.100710799-012-0139-4

Wang, H., & Wang, S. (2008). A knowledge management approach to data mining process for business intelligence. *Industrial Management & Data Systems*, *108*(5), 622–634. doi:10.1108/02635570810876750

Wang, M. (2011). Integrating SAP to Information Systems Curriculum: Design and Delivery. *Information Systems Education Journal*, *9*(5), 97–104.

Wang, S., & Cheung, W. (2004). E-business adoption by travel agencies: Prime candidates for mobile e-business. *International Journal of Electronic Commerce*, *8*(3), 43–63. doi:10.1080/10864415.2004.11044298

Wang, Y. S., Li, H. T., Li, C. R., & Zhang, D. Z. (2016). Factors affecting hotels' adoption of mobile reservation systems: A technology-organization-environment framework. *Tourism Management*, *53*, 163–172. doi:10.1016/j.tourman.2015.09.021

Wang, Y., & Byrd, T. A. (2017). Business analytics-enabled decision0making effectiveness through knowledge absorptive capacity in healthcare. *Journal of Knowledge Management*, *21*(3), 517–539. doi:10.1108/JKM-08-2015-0301

Wang, Y., & Hajli, N. (2017). Exploring the path to big data analytics success in healthcare. *Journal of Business Research*, *70*, 287–299. doi:10.1016/j.jbusres.2016.08.002

Wang, Y.-Y., Lin, T.-C., & Tsay, C. H.-H. (2016). Encouraging IS developers to learn business skills: An examination of the MARS model. *Information Technology & People*, *29*(2), 381–418. doi:10.1108/ITP-02-2014-0044

Wang, Y., & Yu, C. (2017a). Social interaction-based consumer decision-making model in social commerce: The role of word of mouth and observational learning. *International Journal of Information Management*, *37*(3), 179–189. doi:10.1016/j.ijinfomgt.2015.11.005

Ward, M., Marsolo, K., & Froehle, C. (n.d.). Application of business analytics in healthcare. *Business Horizon, 57*(5), 571-582. doi:10.1016/j.bushor.2014.06.003

Ward, J., & Peppard, J. (2002). *AM Strategic Planning for Information Systems*. Academic Press.

Wardlow, G. (1989). Alternative Modes of Inquiry for Agricultural Education. *Journal of Agricultural Education*, *30*(4), 2–7. doi:10.5032/jae.1989.04002

Warren, R. A. (2017). *Exploring Strategies for Successful Implementation of Electronic Health Records*. Walden University.

Wasserman, H., & Madrid-Morales, D. (2019). *An Exploratory Study of "Fake News" and Media Trust in Kenya*. African Journalism Studies.

Watson, H. J. (2014). Tutorial: Big data analytics: Concepts, technologies, and applications. *Communications of the Association for Information Systems*, *34*(1), 1247–1268.

Weaver, H. (2018, Jul 17). *7 Cases of Extremely Successful API Adoption*. Retrieved 03 15, 2019, from https://nordicapis.com/7-cases-of-extremely-successful-api-adoption/

Webb, N. (2013). Vodafone puts mobility at the heart of business strategy: Transformation improves performance of employees and organization as a whole. *Human Resource Management International Digest*, *21*(1), 5–8. doi:10.1108/09670731311296410

Webster, J., & Watson, R. T. (2002). Analysing The Past To Prepare For The Future: Writing A Literature Review. *Management Information Systems Quarterly*, *26*(2), 13–23.

Webster, J., & Watson, R. T. (2002). Analyzing the Past to Prepare for the Future: Writing A Literature Review. *Management Information Systems Quarterly*, *26*(2), xiii–xxiii. Retrieved from http://www.jstor.org/stable/4132319

Wee, S. C., & Choong, W. W. (2019). Gamification: Predicting the effectiveness of variety game design elements to intrinsically motivate users' energy conservation behaviour. *Journal of Environmental Management*, *233*, 97–106. doi:10.1016/j.jenvman.2018.11.127 PMID:30572268

Weichhart, G. (2015). Supporting the evolution and interoperability of organisational models with e-learning technologies. *Annual Reviews in Control*, *39*, 118–127. doi:10.1016/j.arcontrol.2015.03.011

Weick, K. E., Sutcliffe, K. M., & Obstfeld, D. (2005). Organizing and the process of sensemaking. *Organization Science*, *16*(4), 409–421. doi:10.1287/orsc.1050.0133

Weill, P., & Woerner, S. (2015). Thriving in an increasingly digital ecosystem. *MIT Sloan Management Review*, *56*(4), 27–34.

Weill, P., & Woerner, S. L. (2015). Thriving in an increasingly digital ecosystem. *Sloan Management Review*, *56*, 27–34.

Weinman, J. (2016). The Internet of Things for Developing Economies. *CIO*. Available at: https://www.cio.com/article/3027989/the-internet-of-things-for-developing-economies.html

Weinstein, A., Livny, A., & Weizman, A. (2017). New developments in brain research of internet and gaming disorder. *Neuroscience and Biobehavioral Reviews*, *75*, 314–330. doi:10.1016/j.neubiorev.2017.01.040 PMID:28193454

Weinstein, A., Maraz, A., Griffiths, M. D., Lejoyeux, M., & Demetrovics, Z. (2016). *Compulsive Buying-Features and Characteristics of Addiction. In Neuropathology of Drug Addictions and Substance Misuse* (Vol. 3). Elsevier Inc.

Weiss, S. M., & Indurkhya, N. (1998). *Predictive data mining: a practical guide*. Esevier.

Wendell, S. (2017, March 17). *Social and Financial Among the Most Popular API Categories*. Retrieved from https://www.programmableweb.com/news/social-and-financial-among-most-popular-api-categories/research/2017/03/17

Wernerfelt. (1995). A Resource-based view of the firm: tem years after. Strategic Management Journal, 16(2), 171–174.

Wernerfelt, B. (1984). A resource-based view of the firm. *Strategic Management Journal*, *5*(2), 171–180. doi:10.1002/smj.4250050207

West, R. (2015). *Prime theory of motivation*. Academic Press.

West, D. M. (2015). *What happens if robots take the jobs? The impact of emerging technologies on employment and public policy*. Washington, DC: Centre for Technology Innovation at Brookings.

Westerman, G., Bonnet, D., & McAfee, A. (2014). The nine elements of digital transformation. *MIT Sloan Management Review*, *55*(3), 1–6.

Westfall, B. (2019, July 23rd). Can you dig it: what is data mining and how can it help your small business. Retrieved from https://lab.getapp.com/what-is-data-mining-small-business/

Westfall, R. D. (2012). An Employment-Oriented Definition of the Information Systems Field: An Educator's View. *Journal of Information Systems Education*, *23*(1), 63–70.

White, G. L., Hewitt, B., & Kruck, S. E. (2013). Incorporating Global Information Security and Assurance in I.S. Education. *Journal of Information Systems Education*, *24*(1), 11–17.

Whitman, N.I. (1990). The committee meeting alternative: Using the Delphi technique. *Journal of Advanced Nursing, 20*(7-8), 30-36.

Whitty, M. T. (2013). The scammers persuasive techniques model: Development of a stage model to explain the online dating romance scam. *British Journal of Criminology, 53*(4), 665–684. doi:10.1093/bjc/azt009

Widjajaa, A. E. Jengchung V. C., Sukococ, B. M., & Quang-An, H. (2019). Understanding users' willingness to put their personal information on the personal cloud-based storage applications: An empirical study. Computers in Human Behavior Journal, 167-185.

Widyanto, L., & Griffiths, M. (2006). Internet addiction: A critical review. *International Journal of Mental Health and Addiction, 4*(1), 31–51. doi:10.100711469-006-9009-9

Wijayarathna, C., & Arachchilage, N. (2019). Why Johnny cannot develop a secure application? A usability analysis of Java Secure Socket Extension API. *Computers & Security, 80*, 54–73. doi:10.1016/j.cose.2018.09.007

Wijayarathna, C., & Arachchilage, N. (2019b). Using cognitive dimensions to evaluate the usability of security APIs: An empirical investigation. *Information and Software Technology, 115*, 5–19. doi:10.1016/j.infsof.2019.07.007

Wiles, M. A., Jain, S. P., Mishra, S., & Lindsey, C. (2010). Stock market response to regulatory reports of deceptive advertising: The moderating effect of omission bias and firm reputation. *Marketing Science, 29*(5), 828–845. doi:10.1287/mksc.1100.0562

Wilkins, S., & Huisman, J. (2012). The international branch campus as a transnational strategy in higher education. *Higher Education, 64*(5), 627–645. doi:10.100710734-012-9516-5

Williams, M. D. (2018). Social commerce and the mobile platform: Payment and security perceptions of potential users. Computers in Human Behavior. doi:10.1016/j.chb.2018.06.005

Williams, M. D., Roderick, S., Davies, G. H., & Clement, M. (2017). *Risk, trust, and compatibility as antecedents of mobile payment adoption.* Academic Press.

Williamson, O. E. (1991). Strategizing, Economizing, and Economic Organization. Strategic Management Journal, 12(Winter Special Issue), 75–94.

Williams, P. A., & Woodward, A. J. (2015). Cybersecurity vulnerabilities in medical devices: A complex environment and multifaceted problem. *Medical Devices (Auckland, N.Z.), 8*, 305. doi:10.2147/MDER.S50048 PMID:26229513

Willmott, S., Balas, G., & 3scale. (2016). *Winning in the API Economy: Using software and APIs to transform your business...* 3Scale. Retrieved from www.3scale.net

Wilson, B. J., & Zillante, A. (2010). More information, more ripoffs: Experiments with public and private information in markets with asymmetric information. *Review of Industrial Organization, 36*(1), 1–16. doi:10.100711151-010-9240-1

Wilson, E. V., & Tulu, B. (2010). The rise of a health-IT academic focus. *Communications of the ACM, 53*(5), 147. doi:10.1145/1735223.1735259

Wingreen, S. C., Mazey, N. C. H. L., Baglione, S. L., & Storholm, G. R. (2018). Transfer of electronic commerce trust between physical and virtual environments: Experimental effects of structural assurance and situational normality. *Electronic Commerce Research.* doi:10.100710660-018-9305

Wiredu, G. O. (2007). User appropriation of mobile technologies: Motives, conditions and design properties. *Information and Organization, 17*(2), 110–129. doi:10.1016/j.infoandorg.2007.03.002

Wiseman, A. W., Astiz, M. F. & Baker, D. P. (2013). Globalization and comparative education research: Misconceptions and applications of neo-institutional theory. *Journal of Supranational Policies of Education,* (1), 31-52.

Wiseman, A. W., & Chase-Mayoral, A. (2013). Shifting the Discourse on Neo-Institutional Theory in Comparative and International Education. *Annual Review of Comparative and International Education, 20,* 99–126.

Wixcom, B., Yen, B., & Relich, M. (2013). Maximizing value from business analytics. *MIS Quarterly Executive, 12*(2), 111–123.

Wongkitrungrueng, A., & Assarut, N. (2018, November). The role of live streaming in building consumer trust and engagement with social commerce sellers. *Journal of Business Research.* doi:10.1016/j.jbusres.2018.08.032

Woodward, B., Imboden, T., & Martin, N. L. (2013). An Undergraduate Information Security Program: More than a Curriculum. *Journal of Information Systems Education, 24*(1), 63–70.

World Bank. (2015). *Managing Change in PFM System Reforms: A Guide for Practitioners. Financial Management Information Systems Community of Practice.* World Bank Group. Retrieved on 12 June 2019 from http://bit.ly/2MtTrHy

World Economic Forum. (2015). The Global Competitiveness Report 2015. Retrieved August 4, 2018, from The Global Competitive Report website: http://www.weforum.org/reports/global-competitiveness-report-2015

Wu, J., Li, H., Liu, L., & Zheng, H. (2017). Adoption of Big data and analytics in the mobile healthcare market: An economic perspective. *Electronic Commerce Research and Applications, 22,* 24-41. doi:10.1016/j.elerap.2017.02.002

Wu, B., & Zhang, C. (2014). Empirical study on continuance intentions towards E-learning 2.0 systems. *Behaviour & Information Technology, 33*(10), 1027–1038. doi:10.1080/0144929X.2014.934291

Wu, J. H., & Wang, S. C. (2005). What drives mobile commerce: An empirical evaluation of the revised technology acceptance model. *Information & Management, 42*(5), 719–729. doi:10.1016/j.im.2004.07.001

Wu, J., Li, L., Cheng, S., & Lin, Z. (2016). The promising of healthcare services: When big data meet wearable technology. *Information & Management, 53,* 1020–1033. doi:10.1016/j.im.2016.07.003

Wu, X., Kumar, V., Quinlan, J. R., Ghosh, J., Yang, Q., Motoda, H., & Dan, J. H. (2008). Top 10 algorithms in data mining. *Knowledge and Information Systems, 14*(1), 1–37. doi:10.1007/s10115-007-0114-2

Wu, Y. (2017). The Disruption of Social Media. *Digital Journalism, 6*(6), 777–797. doi:10.1080/21670811.2017.1376590

Wyman, K. M. (2017). Taxi Regulation in the Age of Uber. *New York University Journal of Legislation and Public Policy, 20*(1), 2–51.

Wymbs, C. (2016). Managing the Innovation Process: Infusing Data Analytics into the Undergraduate Business Curriculum (Lessons Learned and Next Steps). *Journal of Information Systems Education, 27*(1), 61–74.

Wymer, S. A., & Regan, E. A. (2005). Factors influencing e-commerce adoption and use by small and medium businesses. *Electronic Markets, 15*(4), 438–453. doi:10.1080/10196780500303151

Yablonski, S.A. (2016). Multi-sided search platforms: global and local. Doi:10.1504/IJTMKT.2016.077394

Yadav, M. S., De Valck, K., Hennig-thurau, T., Hoffman, D. L., & Spann, M. (2013). ScienceDirect Social Commerce : A Contingency Framework for Assessing Marketing Potential. *Journal of Interactive Marketing, 27*(4), 311–323. doi:10.1016/j.intmar.2013.09.001

Yaeger, K., Martini, M., Rasouli, J., & Costa, A. (2019). Emerging Blockchain Technology Solutions for Modern Healthcare Infrastructure. *Journal of Scientific Innovation in Medicine, 2*(1), 1. doi:10.29024/jsim.7

Yale, R. N., Jensen, J. D., Carcioppolo, N., Sun, Y., & Liu, M. (2015). Examining first- and second-order factor structures for news credibility. *Communication Methods and Measures, 9*(3), 152–169. doi:10.1080/19312458.2015.1061652

Yamin, M., Sinkovics, R., Sinkovics, N., Sinkovics, R., Hoque, S., & Czaban, L. (2015). A reconceptualisation of social value creation as social constraint alleviation. *Critical Perspectives on International Business, 11*(3/4), 340–363. doi:10.1108/cpoib-06-2014-0036

Yanchar, S. C., South, Æ. J. B., Williams, Æ. D. D., Allen, S., & Wilson, Æ. B. G. (2010). Struggling with theory? A qualitative investigation of conceptual tool use in instructional design. *Educational Technology Research and Development, 58*(1), 39–60. doi:10.100711423-009-9129-6

Yang, S. C. (2012). The Master's Program in Information Systems (IS): A Survey of Core Curriculums of U.S. Institutions. *Journal of Education for Business, 87*(4), 206–213. doi:10.1080/08832323.2011.591847

Yan, Q., Yu, F. R., Gong, Q., & Li, J. (2016). Software-defined networking (SDN) and distributed denial of service (DDoS) attacks in cloud computing environments: A survey, some research issues, and challenges. *IEEE Communications Surveys and Tutorials, 18*(1), 602–622. doi:10.1109/COMST.2015.2487361

Yao, J. T. (2015). The impact of counterfeit-purchase penalties on anti-counterfeiting under deceptive counterfeiting. *Journal of Economics and Business, 80*, 51–61. doi:10.1016/j.jeconbus.2015.04.002

Yassine, A., Chenouni, D., Berrada, M., & Tahiri, A. (2017). A Serious Game for Learning C Programming Language Concepts Using Solo Taxonomy. *International Journal of Emerging Technologies in Learning, 12*(3), 110. doi:10.3991/ijet.v12i03.6476

Yau, Y. H. C., Pilver, C. E., Steinberg, M. A., Rugle, L. J., Hoff, R. A., Krishnan-Sarin, S., & Potenza, M. N. (2014). Relationships between problematic Internet use and problem-gambling severity: Findings from a high-school survey. *Addictive Behaviors, 39*(1), 13–21. doi:10.1016/j.addbeh.2013.09.003 PMID:24140304

Yavuz, N., Karkın, N., Parlak, İ., & Subay, Ö. Ö. (2018). Political Discourse Strategies Used in Twitter during Gezi Park Protests: A Comparison of Two Rival Political Parties in Turkey. *International Journal of Public Administration in the Digital Age, 5*(1), 82–96. doi:10.4018/IJPADA.2018010105

Yeboah, S. K. (2015). *Public Sector Financial Management Reforms in Ghana: The Case of Ghana Integrated Financial Management Information System (GIFMIS)* (Masters Thesis). University of Ghana Business School. http://ugspace.ug.edu.gh

Yen, C.-F., Tang, T.-C., Yen, J.-Y., Lin, H.-C., Huang, C.-F., Liu, S.-C., & Ko, C.-H. (2009). Symptoms of problematic cellular phone use, functional impairment, and its association with depression among adolescents in Southern Taiwan. *Journal of Adolescence, 32*(4), 863–873. doi:10.1016/j.adolescence.2008.10.006 PMID:19027941

Yilma, K. M. (2014). Developments in cybercrime law and practice in Ethiopia. *Computer Law & Security Review, 30*(6), 720–735. doi:10.1016/j.clsr.2014.09.010

Yilma, K. M. (2017). Ethiopia's new cybercrime legislation: Some reflections. *Computer Law & Security Review, 33*(2), 250–255. doi:10.1016/j.clsr.2016.11.016

Yılmaz, H. E., Sirel, A., & Esen, M. F. (2019). The Impact of Internet of Things Self-Security on Daily Business and Business Continuity. In *Handbook of Research on Cloud Computing and Big Data Applications in IoT* (pp. 481–498). IGI Global. doi:10.4018/978-1-5225-8407-0.ch021

Yin, R. K. (1984). *Case Study Research: Design and Methods*. Academic Press.

Yin, R. K. (2009). *Case study research: Design and methods* (Vol. 5). Sage.

Yin, R. (2009). *Case Study Research: Design and Methods* (4th ed.). Thousand Oaks: Sage.

Yin, R. K. (1993). Applications of case study research. London: Sage Publications.

Yin, R. K. (1994). Discovering the future of the case study. Method in evaluation research. *Evaluation Practice, 15*(3), 283–290. doi:10.1016/0886-1633(94)90023-X

Yin, R. K. (1994). Discovering the future of the case study: Method in evaluation research. *Evaluation Practice, 15*(3), 283–290. doi:10.1016/0886-1633(94)90023-X

Yin, R. K. (2003). *Case study research: Design and methods.* Newbury Park: Sage.

Yin, R. K. (2009). *Case study research, design and methods* (3rd ed.). Newbury Park, CA: Sage.

Yin, R. K. (2010). *Qualitative research from start to finish.* Guilford Press.

Yire, I. (2019, June 16). *Ghana tipped to be the fastest-growing mobile money market in Africa.* Retrieved June 16, 2019, from http://www.ghananewsagency.org/economics/ghana-tipped-to-be-the-fastest-growing-mobile-money-market-in-africa-151643

Yli-Huumo, J., Ko, D., Choi, S., Park, S., & Smolander, K. (2016). Where is current research on blockchain technology?—A systematic review. *PLoS One, 11*(10), e0163477. doi:10.1371/journal.pone.0163477 PMID:27695049

Yogi Prabowo, H. (2012). A better credit card fraud prevention strategy for Indonesia. *Journal of Money Laundering Control, 15*(3), 267–293. doi:10.1108/13685201211238034

Yolbulan Okan, E., Topcu, A., & Akyuz, S. (2014). The role of social media in political marketing: 2014 Local Elections of Turkey. *European Journal of Business and Management, 6*(22), 131–140.

Yoo, Y., Lyytinen, K. J., Boland, R. J., & Berente, N. (2010a). *The Next Wave of Digital Innovation: Opportunities and Challenges.* A Report on the Research Workshop' Digital Challenges in Innovation Research.

Yoon, C., & Kim, H. (2013). Understanding computer security behavioral intention in the workplace: An empirical study of Korean firms. *Information Technology & People, 26*(4), 401–419. doi:10.1108/ITP-12-2012-0147

Yoo, Y., Henfridsson, O., & Lyytinen, K. (2010). The new organizing logic of digital innovation: An agenda for information systems research. *Information Systems Research, 21*(4), 724–735. doi:10.1287/isre.1100.0322

Young, A. L., & Quan-Haase, A. (2013). Privacy protection strategies on Facebook. *Information Communication and Society, 16*(4), 479–500. doi:10.1080/1369118X.2013.777757

Young, M., & Farber, S. (2019). The who, why, and when of Uber and other ride-hailing trips : An examination of a large sample household travel survey. *Transportation Research Part A, Policy and Practice, 119*(1), 383–392. doi:10.1016/j.tra.2018.11.018

Yu, C.-H., Tsai, C.-C., Wang, Y., Lai, K.-K., & Tajvidi, M. (2018). Towards building a value co-creation circle in social commerce. Computers in Human Behavior, 105476. doi:10.1016/j.chb.2018.04.021

Yu, D., & Hang, C. C. (2010). A Reflective Review of Disruptive Innovation Theory. *International Journal of Management Reviews, 12*(4), 435–452. doi:10.1111/j.1468-2370.2009.00272.x

Yüksel, H. (2018). Social media strategies of political power: An analysis of the Ruling Party in Turkey. In F. Endong (Ed.), *Exploring the Role of Social Media in Transnational Advocacy* (pp. 153–178). Hershey, PA: IGI Global. doi:10.4018/978-1-5225-2854-8.ch008

Yumna, H., Khan, M. M., Ikram, M., & Ilyas, S. (2019, April). Use of Blockchain in Education: A Systematic Literature Review. In *Asian Conference on Intelligent Information and Database Systems* (pp. 191-202). Springer. 10.1007/978-3-030-14802-7_17

Yu, P., Zhang, Y., Gong, Y., & Zhang, J. (2013). Unintended adverse consequences of introducing electronic health records in residential aged care homes. *International Journal of Medical Informatics, 82*(9), 772–788. doi:10.1016/j.ijmedinf.2013.05.008 PubMed

Yu, S., & Ibtasam, S. (2018, June). A qualitative exploration of Mobile money in Ghana. In *Proceedings of the 1st ACM SIGCAS Conference on Computing and Sustainable Societies* (p. 21). ACM; doi:10.1145/3209811.3209863.

Yusoff. (2015). A Review on Critical Success Factors of SISP Nor Hanani binti Mohd Yusoff. The Journal of Management and Science, 1(2), 1–6.

Zachariadis, M., & Ozcan, P. (2017). *The API Economy and Digital Transformation in Financial Services: The case of Open Banking.* Swift Institute Working Paper No 2016-001.

Zafeiropoulou, A. M., Millard, D. E., Webber, C., & O'Hara, K. (2013). Unpicking the privacy paradox: Can structuration theory helps to explain location-based privacy decisions? WebSci '13 Proceedings of the 5th Annual ACM Web Science Conference, 463–472.

Zagal, J. P., Mateas, M., Fernandez-Vara, C., Hochhalter, B., & Lichti, N. (2005). Towards an ontological language for game analysis. *Proceedings of International DiGRA Conference: Changing Views - Worlds in Play,* 3-14.

Zailani, S., Iranmanesh, M., Nikbin, D., & Beng, J. K. (2015). Determinants of RFID Adoption in Malaysia's Healthcare Industry: Occupational Level as a Moderator. *Journal of Medical Systems, 39*(1), 172. doi:10.100710916-014-0172-4 PMID:25503418

Zareapoor, M., & Shamsolmoali, P. (2015). Application of credit card fraud detection: Based on bagging ensemble classifier. *Procedia Computer Science, 48,* 679–685. doi:10.1016/j.procs.2015.04.201

Zhang, K., Chongyang, C., & Matthew, L. (2014). Understanding the Role of Motives in Smartphone Addiction. *PACIS 2014 Proceedings.*

Zhang, W., Kang, L., Jiang, Q., & Bian, Y. (2018). More than the Tone: The Impact of Social Media Opinions on Innovation Investments. In *The 26th European Conference on Information Systems (ECIS) 2018. European Conference on Information Systems.*

Zhang, B., Wu, M., Kang, H., Go, E., & Sundar, S. S. (2014). Effects of security warnings and instant gratification cues on attitudes toward mobile websites. *Telematics and Informatics, 34,* 1038–1058. doi:10.1145/2556288.2557347

Zhang, C., Kettinger, W. J., Kolte, P., & Yoo, S. (2018). Established companies' strategic responses to sharing economy threats. *MIS Quarterly Executive, 17*(1), 23–40.

Zhang, C., Reichgelt, H., Rutherfoord, R. H., & Wang, A. J. A. (2014). Developing Health Information Technology (HIT) Programs and HIT Curriculum: The Southern Polytechnic State University Experience. *Journal of Information Systems Education, 25*(4), 295–303.

Zhang, K. Z., & Benyoucef, M. (2016). Consumer behavior in social commerce: A literature review. *Decision Support Systems, 86,* 95–108. doi:10.1016/j.dss.2016.04.001

Zhang, K., Chen, C., Zhao, S., & Lee, M. (2014). Compulsive Smartphone Use: The Roles of Flow, Reinforcement Motives, and Convenience. *35th International Conference on Information Systems.*

Zhang, M., Guo, L., Hu, M., & Liu, W. (2017). Influence of customer engagement with company social networks on stickiness : Mediating effect of customer value creation. *International Journal of Information Management, 37*(3), 229–240. doi:10.1016/j.ijinfomgt.2016.04.010

Zhang, W., Johnson, T. J., Seltzer, T., & Bichard, S. L. (2010). The Revolution Will be Networked: The Influence of Social Networking Sites on Political Attitudes and Behavior. *Social Science Computer Review, 28*(1), 75–92. doi:10.1177/0894439309335162

Zhang, Y., & Lin, Z. (2018). Predicting the helpfulness of online product reviews: A multilingual approach. *Electronic Commerce Research and Applications, 27*, 1–10. doi:10.1016/j.elerap.2017.10.008

Zhao, Y., & Kurnia, S. (2014). *Exploring Mobile Payment Adoption in China.* PACIS.

Zheng, G., Zhang, C., & Li, L. (2014). Bringing Business Intelligence to Health Information Technology Curriculum. *Journal of Information Systems Education, 25*(4), 317–326.

Zheng, Y., Hatakka, M., Sahay, S., & Andersson, A. (2018). Conceptualizing development in information and communication technology for development (ICT4D). *Information Technology for Development, 24*(1), 1–14. doi:10.1080/02681102.2017.1396020

Zhiping, W. (2009). *Chinese customer's attitude and adopt intention on mobile commerce.* Paper presented at the 6th International Conference on Service Systems and Service Management, Xiamen, China. 10.1109/ICSSSM.2009.5174977

Zhong, Y. (2012). Social Commerce: A New Electronic Commerce. *Whiceb.* Retrieved from http://aisel.aisnet.org/cgi/viewcontent.cgi?article=1051&context=whiceb2011

Zhong, H., Xie, T., Zhang, L., Pei, J., & Mei, H. (2009). MAPO: Mining and Recommending API Usage Patterns. *European Conference on Object-Oriented Programming*, 318-343. 10.1007/978-3-642-03013-0_15

Zhong, J. (2009). *A comparison of mobile payment procedures in Finnish and Chinese markets.* BLED.

Zhou, N., Zhang, S., Chen, J. E., & Han, X. (2017). The role of information technologies (ITs) in firms' resource orchestration process: A case analysis of China's "Huangshan 168.". *International Journal of Information Management, 37*(6), 713–715. doi:10.1016/j.ijinfomgt.2017.05.002

Zhou, T. (2013). An empirical examination of continuance intention of mobile payment services. *Decision Support Systems, 54*(2), 1085–1091. doi:10.1016/j.dss.2012.10.034

Zhou, Z., Dou, W., Jia, G., Hu, C., Xu, X., Wu, X., & Pan, J. (2016). A method for real-time trajectory monitoring to improve taxi service using GPS big data. *Information & Management, 53*(8), 964–977. doi:10.1016/j.im.2016.04.004

Zhu, X., & Cahan, A. (2016). Wearable technologies and telehealth in care management for chronic illness. *Healthcare Information Management Systems*, 375-398.

Zhu, Y. (2017). *Cloud computing: current and future impact on organizations* (Unpublished Master's Thesis). Western Oregon University.

Zhu, G., So, K. K. F., & Hudson, S. (2016). Inside the sharing economy: Understanding consumer motivations behind the adoption of mobile applications. *International Journal of Contemporary Hospitality Management, 9*, 1–56. doi:10.1108/IJCHM-09-2016-0496

Zhu, K., Dong, S., Xu, S. X., & Kraemer, K. L. (2006). Innovation diffusion in global contexts: Determinants of post-adoption digital transformation of European companies. *European Journal of Information Systems, 15*(6), 601–616. doi:10.1057/palgrave.ejis.3000650

Zhu, K., Kraemer, K. L., & Xu, S. (2006). The process of innovation assimilation by firms in different countries: A technology diffusion perspective on e-business. *Management Science, 52*(10), 1557–1576. doi:10.1287/mnsc.1050.0487

Zhu, Y., Rooney, D., & Phillips, N. (2016). Practice-based wisdom theory for integrating institutional logics: A new model for social entrepreneurship learning and education. *Academy of Management Learning & Education, 15*(3), 607–625. doi:10.5465/amle.2013.0263

Zibran, M., Eishita, F., & Roy, C. (2011). Useful, but usable factors affecting the usability of APIs. *18th Working Conf. on Reverse Engineering (WCRE)*, 151–155. 10.1109/WCRE.2011.26

Zichermann, G., & Cunningham, C. (2011). *Gamification by design: Implementing game mechanics in web and mobile apps*. O'Reilly Media, Inc.

Zollo, M., & Winter, S. G. (2002). Deliberate learning and the evolution of dynamic capabilities. *Organization Science, 13*(3), 339–351. doi:10.1287/orsc.13.3.339.2780

Zott, C., Amit, R. H., & Massa, L. (2011). The Business Model: Recent Developments and Future Research. *Journal of Management, 37*(4), 1019–1042. doi:10.1177/0149206311406265

Zubovic, A., Pita, Z., & Khan, S. (2014). A Framework For Investigating The Impact Of Information Systems Capability On Strategic Information Systems Planning. In *PACIS 2014* (p. 317). Proceedings; Retrieved from http://aisel.aisnet.org/pacis2014

Zumbrun, J., & Sussman, A. L. (2016). Proof of a gig economy revolution is hard to find. *The Wall Street Journal*. Retrieved June 30, 2018 from http://www.wsj.com/articles/proof-ofa-gig-economy-revolution-is-hard-to-find-1437932539

Zundans-Fraser, L., & Bain, A. (2016). How do institutional practices for course design and review address areas of need in Higher Education? *Higher Education Research & Development*, 1–13.

About the Contributors

Richard Boateng is an Associate Professor of Information Systems at the University of Ghana Business School. Richard's research experience covers digital economy, e-business, internet banking and social media. His papers have been published in or are forthcoming in the International Journal of Information Management, Internet Research, Qualitative Market Research: An International Journal, and many others.

* * *

Bryan Acheampong is an information systems doctoral researcher at the University of Ghana Business School. His research interests including digital platforms, interoperable systems, e-government applications, financial management systems, and systems development in the public sector. He has over ten years of experience in developing and managing financial management systems in developing economies. His recent publication on a review of interoperable systems was published in the proceedings of the 2019 Americas Conference of Information Systems.

Ibrahim Osman Adam is a senior lecturer and holds a PhD in Information Systems from the University of Ghana Business School. Ibrahim holds a first class bachelor's degree in Business Administration (Accounting Option) from the University of Ghana, an MSc in Development Management from the London School of Economics and Political Science (LSE) (UK), and another MSc in Applied Informatics from the Henley Business School, University of Reading (UK). Ibrahim Osman is a Chartered Accountant and a member of the Institute of Chartered Accountants (Ghana). He teaches management information systems, accounting information systems and computer applications in management both at the undergraduate and postgraduate levels at the School of Business and Law, University for Development Studies, Wa Ghana. His research interest are information systems in higher education, cloud computing and ICT4D.

Anthony Afful-Dadzie Anthony Afful-Dadzie is a senior lecturer at the Operations and Management Information Systems department at the University of Ghana Business School. He employs operations research and decision analysis techniques in various research areas including healthcare, energy planning, and information systems.

Divine Quasie Agozie holds MPhil in Operations Management from the University of Ghana, Legon. He is a PhD candidate in Management Information System and a Research assistant in the School of

Applied Sciences at Cyprus International University. His research interest is in Data mining, natural language and online privacy.

Samuel Anim-Yeboah is a Doctoral Researcher at the University of Ghana Business School. He is also a lecturer and consultant in informatics, management information systems and entrepreneurship. Samuel is interested in digital technology and enterprise research, focusing on Digital Entrepreneurship, Digital Transformation and Enterprise Systems.

Thomas Anning-Dorson is a Senior Lecturer at Wits Business School, University of the Witwatersrand, Johannesburg, South Africa and a Research Associate at the School of Consumer Intelligence and Information Systems, University of Johannesburg. Thomas is a Research Fellow at McGill University, Montreal, Canada through the Queen Elizabeth Scholars Program. Dr. Anning-Dorson's research interests are in Digital Business, Innovation, Services Management, Competitive Strategies, and Emerging Markets.

Eric Ansong is a Doctoral Researcher in Information Systems at the University of Ghana. He is also an adjunct lecturer of Management Information Systems at the School of Research and Graduate Studies of the Wisconsin International University College, Accra. His research interests include technology adoption, innovations in education, Digital business strategies and ICT4D. He is currently researching on the Digital business strategy of enterprises in Africa. Eric Ansong has published a number of research articles in peer-reviewed academic journals and has presented papers in international conferences which include the Hawaii International Conference on System Sciences (HICSS). He has had the opportunity to work in a number of research projects such as the Microsoft in collaboration with Research ICT Africa Network project on Cloud computing in the public sector, Building Stronger Universities (BSU) e-learning and Problem Based Learning (PBL) in University of Ghana, the Council for the Development of Social Science Research in Africa (CODESRIA) project on technology-mediated faculty-student interactions, among others.

Sylvester T. Asiedu is a Doctoral Researcher at the Operations and Management Information Systems Department of the University of Ghana Business School. From 2013 to present, he has been an Adjunct Lecturer at the School of Technology with the Ghana Institute of Management and Public Administration, GIMPA. During 2009 to 2015, he was a Tutor with the University of Ghana distant education program. He is the founder of Eudemonia International Foundation, an NGO focused on quality community healthcare advocacy through research, preventive, and educational initiatives and where possible, curative interventions. He is a dedicated, resourceful and goal-driven professional leader and educator interested in sustainable initiatives driven by business needs and social impact. Sylvester's research interest covers E-governance and management of IT, e-learning, social media, entrepreneurship, ICTD, E-health, gender and ICT, machine learning, and data analytics at global, national, industrial, organizational and community levels.

Judy Backhouse has experience as both an academic scholar and an information and communications technologies (ICT) practitioner. She is currently a Senior Academic Fellow at the United Nations University, after eight years as an Associate professor at the University of the Witwatersrand in Johannesburg. Her recent research has been into the role of information systems in implementing smart city agendas in the African context. She has researched ICT for development as well as aspects of e-government. Dr

Backhouse has worked in the private and public sectors. In the private sector she worked in technical and management roles over a twelve-year career which began with designing and programming systems and ended with the strategic management of ICT within organisations. She spent two years at the South African Council on Higher Education where she was responsible for monitoring the Higher Education Sector in South Africa and advising the Minister of Higher Education. She also has experience as an entrepreneur, having launched (and closed) a co-working business in Johannesburg.

Nii Barnor Jonathan Barnor is doctoral researcher in the University of Ghana Business School. He has a masters degree in management information systems and a bachelors degree in linguistics and music. His research interests are cybercrime, information systems security, information systems adoption, ICT for development, digital mobile maps and digital technologies.

Ibrahim Bedi is a chartered accountant and a Senior Lecturer at the Department of Accounting, University of Ghana Business School. He is a fellow, the Association of Certified Chartered Accountants (UK); member, the Institute of Chartered Accountants, Ghana; member, American Accounting Association; treasurer, African Accounting and Finance Association; and member, International Association of Accounting Educators and Researchers. He is the Internal Auditor of the University of Ghana Business School. His research areas cover International Financial Reporting Standards (IFRS), the IFRS for SMEs, International Standards on Auditing, International Internal Audit Standards, and tax audit on tax compliance.

Frederick Edem Broni Jr. is an MPhil candidate in Management Information Systems and also a Graduate Research Assistant at the Operations and Management Information Systems Department (OMIS), University of Ghana Business School (UGBS). His background is in Computer Science and Management. His research interests are in Blockchain, Cryptocurrencies, Cloud Computing, Online Security and Privacy, and E-learning.

Joseph Budu is a lecturer at Ghana Institute of Management and Public Administration. He is a hybrid researcher who is interested in understanding how information systems could be used to achieve strategic goals in business and education. Recently, these interests have been extended to providing information on www.researchcoa.ch to help today's youth excel in their academic and social lives.

Ngoc Tuan Chau is a faculty member at the Faculty of Statistics and Informatics, University of Economics – The University of Danang, Vietnam. He holds the first bachelor degree in Mathematics & Informatics, the second bachelor degree in Business Administration, and master degree in Database Professional. He is currently a PhD student in Business Information Systems at RMIT University, Melbourne, Australia. His research interests are in the areas of business information systems, business innovation, and business analytics.

Hlelo Chauke holds a Masters of Commerce in Information Systems from the University of the Witwatersrand. A Business Analyst by profession in the South African Financial Services industry specialising in Business Intelligence & Client Analytics. His research interest includes technology adoption and information & communications technology for development (ICT4D), with a specific focus on the impact of information & communications technology on societies.

Hepu Deng is a professor in information systems at the school of Business Information Technology and Logistics, RMIT University, Melbourne, Australia. His research interests are in the areas of decision analysis, intelligent systems, digital business, knowledge management, e-government, e-learning, and their applications in business. The multidisciplinary nature of his research and the emphasis on both theoretical and applied research are exemplified by numerous refereed publications in top refereed international journals and at major refereed international conferences including Journal of Operational Research Society, European Journal of Operational Research, Computers and Operations Research, International Journal of Approximate Reasoning, IEEE Transactions on Systems, man, and Cybernetics, Government Information Quarterly, Expert Systems with Applications, Computers and Mathematics with Applications, International Journal of E-Government Research, Journal of Systems and Information Technology, and Management Research Review, etc.

Samuel Nii Odoi Devine is a researcher and member of faculty in the Department of Information and Communication Technology in the Presbyterian University College, Ghana. He holds an M.Sc. in IT and B.Sc. in ICT. He has his research interests in the areas of knowledge management, machine learning applications, natural language processing, and information security awareness. He is also a prolific writer and avid speaker with a strong affinity for computers, and has been involved in several projects as a consultant in the integration of information systems into the operations of a number of organizations.

Adekunle Durosinmi is a Postgraduate Student at the Caleb University, Lagos, Nigeria, offering MSc in Computer Science. His main research interest is in the area of Computer Security. Adekunle has also co-authored a number of research publications in the area of Information and Communication Technology (ICT). He doubles as an ICT staff at the Federal Medical Centre, Abeokuta, Ogun State, Nigeria, and a member of the Computer Professional Registration Council of Nigeria (CPN).

Sampson Abeeku Edu holds MPhil in Operations Management from the University of Ghana, Legon. He is a research assistant in the School of Applied Sciences at Cyprus International University. He is a PhD candidate in Management Information Systems at Cyprus International University with key research focus in Digital innovations deployment, Data Analytics, Information Security and Business Process Modelling for operational excellence.

Edward Entee is a Doctoral Researcher in information systems at the Department of Operations and Management Information Systems of the University of Ghana Business School. Edward's research interest is multidisciplinary which spans in the areas of information and communication technologies (ICT) for development, electronic governance, social media, electronic business, and social commerce.

Emmanuel Awuni Kolog is a Lecturer at the Department of Operations and Management Information Systems of the University of Ghana Business School. Emmanuel's research interest is multidisciplinary which spans in the areas of Human language technologies (Affect detection), Text-based machine learning applications, business intelligence and Information systems.

Vonbackustein Klaus Komla is an information systems doctoral researcher at the University of Ghana Business School. His research interests include digital innovation, digital disruption, the interplay between technology and media, and social media and journalism. He has over ten years of experience in developing and managing information and digital innovations in the news media industry in developing economies.

Harriet Koshie Lamptey is a lecturer in information systems at the University of Professional Studies Ghana. She holds a doctoral degree in information systems from University of Ghana. Her research interests cover information systems and education, mobile learning, institutional theory and critical realism.

Kevor Mark-Oliver is a lecturer of information systems at Presbyterian University College in Ghana. He is currently pursuing his PhD in Information systems at University of Ghana. He holds a Master of science degree in Information Technology and has been active in research for the past five years. His research interests include IS curriculum, Information system security and Information Technology Institutional theory and Startegic responses to Institutional responses.

Muesser Cemal Nat is an Associate Professor at the Cyprus International University. Her area of research is digital learning, educational technology, social media, management information systems. She is also the head of MIS department and e-learning coordinator at Cyprus International University.

Makafui Nyamadi is a Doctoral Researcher in Information Systems at the University of Ghana Business School. Makafui is currently a Lecturer at Ho Technical University, Ghana. His research interests include technology addictions, digital platforms, cybersecurity and theory development. His research has been published in International Conference on Information Systems (ICIS), American Conference on Information Systems (AMCIS) and Hawaii International Conference on Systems Sciences (HICSS). He is also a HICSS Doctoral Fellow. He participated in Doctoral Consortium at AMCIS 2018, and IFIP 8.6 2019. He has 6 publications to his credit.

Joshua Ofoeda received his Master of Philosophy (MPhil) in Management Information Systems from the University of Ghana Business School in 2015. He was hired as an assistant lecturer by the University of Professional Studies, Accra in the year 2016. He is currently a lecturer at the same school where he lectures in courses such as E-commerce, Management Information Systems, Introduction to Information Technology, among others. He has authored five research articles on various issues such as e-banking, e-government, Application Programming Interfaces, Digital Platforms, among others. Joshua is currently pursuing a PhD programme in Information Systems at the University of Ghana Business School.

Joshua Ofori-Amanfo is a lecturer at the Department of Operations and Management Information systems, University of Ghana Business School.

Kingsley Ofosu-Ampong is a doctoral student in Information Systems at the University of Ghana Business School. He holds a BA and MBA degree in Management Information Systems from Ghana. His research investigates the impact of motivational technologies in learning, and issues in human-computer interactions. Kingsley's current research focuses on gamification, technology-enhanced learning, and motivational affordances.

Richard Osei-Boateng is the Officer in Charge of the Health Information Systems at the 37 Military Hospital. He is a second-year PhD Candidate at the University of Ghana Business School with a specialisation in Health Policy and Management. Richard's research interest is in the area of health finance, Electronic Medical Record (EMR) systems and Contemporary Issues in the New Public Health. He was very instrumental in the setting up of the EMR systems at the 37 Military hospital, Accra, Ghana.

Acheampong Owusu is a Lecturer at the Operations and Management Information Systems (OMIS) Department at the University of Ghana Business School and holds a PhD from Limkokwing University of Creative Technology, Cyberjaya, Malaysia. His research interests include Business Intelligence (BI) Systems and Analytics, Technology Diffusion and its impact on organizations, Cloud Computing, and Ecommerce. Acheampong has published several research articles in peer-reviewed journals.

Alfred Patterson is an MPhil Student of the University of Ghana Business School at the Department of Operation and Management of Information Systems. Alfred's research areas include cybercrime studies and the application of information systems in justice delivery.

Obed Kwame Adzaku Penu holds an MPhil in Management Information Systems from the University of Ghana. He is currently a Teaching and Research Assistant at the Operations and Management Information Systems Department (OMIS), University of Ghana Business School (UGBS). He has also worked with a Ghanaian software development firm on a number of software engineering projects as a software tester and documentation writer. His research interests lies in Digital Innovations and Platforms, Digitalisation (enterprise IS/IT implementation and Usage), e-Learning, e & s -Commerce and Artificial Intelligence, Internet of Things (IoT) and Information Systems Security.

Mansah Preko is a PhD candidate in Information Systems at the University of Ghana Business School. She holds a Bachelor's degree in Information and Communication Technology, and a Master's degree in Management Information Systems. Mansah's research interest remains in the area of Digital Health Technologies, with emphasis on its applications within healthcare settings of developing economies. Mansah has previously researched into how healthcare technologies can be used to mitigate brain drain in developing economies, using the Ghanaian health sector as a case. She has also conducted other preliminary studies to assess the extent of digitalisation in the Ghanaian health sector using the Critical Realist's approach. Mansah's PhD thesis is built on the foundations of these studies to explore the impact of healthcare digitalisation on service delivery from a multi-stakeholder perspective in Ghana.

Robert Ohene-Bonsu Simmons is a Ph.D. candidate in Information Systems at the University of Ghana Business School.

Yaa Amponsah Twumasi is an Information System doctoral researcher from the University of Ghana Business School. Ms. Twumasi's research interest is on the role information system plays in counterfeiting and piracy in the fashion and beauty industry. Her previous research was the Adoption and the use of Social Media in Manufacturing Firms. In 2016-2017, she worked as a Research/Teaching Assistant with the Department of Marketing and Entrepreneurship, University of Ghana Business School. Ms. Twumasi in 2000 established Veyat Enterprise Limited, a fashion and beauty consultancy.

Eunice Yeboah Afeti is PhD researcher at the University of Ghana Business School.

690

Index

A

Access 34, 45, 49, 71-73, 77, 84-85, 97, 104, 116-117, 146, 148, 151, 157, 168-171, 175, 182-183, 185-186, 190-191, 193, 197, 210, 216-217, 219, 228, 230, 232, 239-240, 244, 252, 254-255, 259-260, 263, 270-271, 278, 322, 324-326, 329-330, 333-334, 346, 356, 360-364, 367, 369, 374-393, 395, 493, 504, 543, 560

Adinkra 218, 220, 226

Administrator Perspectives 354

Adoption 2-3, 9, 14-15, 17-22, 25-26, 28-29, 39, 44-45, 51-54, 56, 58, 62-69, 74-75, 83-90, 98, 109, 114-117, 119-121, 123-127, 129, 131-142, 161-165, 169-176, 182, 190-191, 194, 196, 198-199, 204, 206, 227-235, 237-251, 256-258, 263, 269-271, 275-277, 282-283, 292-293, 296, 310, 315, 332-333, 343, 346, 353-355, 358-359, 363, 365-366, 368-373, 406, 408, 413-420, 423, 425-427, 430-431, 433, 439, 441, 444-446, 448, 454, 459-461, 465, 467, 473, 494, 517, 523-525, 529, 537, 542, 546-549, 553, 556, 562, 564-566, 570

Agency 97, 103, 111-112, 115, 142, 164, 231, 318-320, 324-325, 327, 330, 365, 367, 373-376, 385-386, 388-391, 395, 501, 514, 530

Analytics 2, 32-34, 47, 94, 97, 182, 185, 188, 197, 200, 203-204, 312, 314, 372, 412-419, 423-427, 447, 449-455, 457, 520, 541, 543-545, 547

Anti-Counterfeiting Technologies 217-218, 226

Application Programming Interface (API) 295, 297-301, 303-304, 309-316

B

Benefits 3, 12, 22, 51, 62, 71, 115, 117-118, 123-124, 132, 134, 141, 150, 155, 157-158, 161-162, 169, 171-173, 176, 178-183, 191-192, 198, 204-206, 228, 230, 233, 249, 252, 255, 261, 276, 281, 298-299, 301, 305-306, 333, 341-343, 357, 364, 374, 378, 382, 384, 389-392, 398, 414, 459, 461, 463-464, 478, 492, 518, 528, 537, 540, 543, 545, 556-557, 560

Bibliographic coupling 548, 550-552, 558, 565

Bibliometric analysis 548, 550-552, 566, 569

Big Data 2, 30-31, 49, 51, 54, 68, 72, 94, 97, 112, 158, 182, 185, 188, 191, 197, 200, 202-204, 207, 275, 312, 413-419, 423-427, 439, 450-452, 454-455, 541, 543-545

Bitcoin 162, 166-168, 174-177

Blockchain 2, 160-177, 182, 207

Business decisions 28-30, 44-45, 148

Business Systems Planning (BSP) 4, 11, 27

Business-Led 4, 11, 15, 27

C

Case Study 11, 22, 25-27, 90, 93, 100, 112-114, 136, 138, 140, 143-144, 146, 153, 155, 157-158, 174, 199, 223, 226-227, 234, 236, 244-245, 250, 273, 281, 295, 297, 300-301, 306, 309-311, 315, 318-324, 329, 331, 338, 351, 353, 367, 371-372, 374, 381, 384, 393, 409, 411, 426, 444, 447, 454, 467, 469, 484, 497, 501, 513, 517, 519, 528-529, 537, 567-568

Choice Framework 374-377, 382, 384, 389, 393, 395

Classification 9, 28-29, 32-36, 42-43, 45, 47, 49, 249, 415, 437, 484-485, 487-490, 492-493, 498, 508, 553

Clustering 28-29, 33-34, 36-37, 42, 45, 49, 208, 565

Co-Citation analysis 548-552, 555, 558, 561, 564, 566

D

E

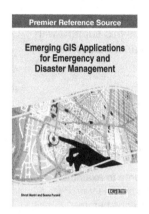
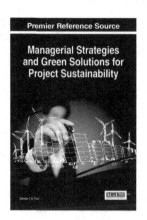

Printed in the United States
By Bookmasters